July 9-12, 2017
Bratislava, Slovakia

I0047353

Association for Computing Machinery

Advancing Computing as a Science & Profession

UMAP'17

Proceedings of the 25th Conference on
User Modeling, Adaptation and Personalization

Sponsored by:
ACM SIGCHI & ACM SIGWEB

Supported by:
User Modeling Inc., National Science Foundation, Microsoft, & Springer

**Association for
Computing Machinery**

Advancing Computing as a Science & Profession

The Association for Computing Machinery
2 Penn Plaza, Suite 701
New York, New York 10121-0701

Notice to Past Authors of ACM-Published Articles
ACM intends to create a complete electronic archive of all articles and/or other material previously published by ACM. If you have written a work that has been previously published by ACM in any journal or conference proceedings prior to 1978, or any SIG Newsletter at any time, and you do NOT want this work to appear in the ACM Digital Library, please inform permissions@acm.org, stating the title of the work, the author(s), and where and when published.

ISBN: 978-1-4503-4635-1 (Digital)

ISBN: 978-1-4503-5610-7 (Print)

Additional copies may be ordered prepaid from:

ACM Order Department
PO Box 30777
New York, NY 10087-0777, USA

Phone: 1-800-342-6626 (USA and Canada)
+1-212-626-0500 (Global)
Fax: +1-212-944-1318
E-mail: acmhelp@acm.org
Hours of Operation: 8:30 am – 4:30 pm ET

Printed in the USA

UMAP 2017 Chairs' Welcome

UMAP 2017, the 25th ACM International Conference on User Modeling, Adaptation, and Personalization was hosted in Bratislava, Slovakia, from July 9 to 12, 2017. UMAP is the premier international conference for researchers and practitioners working on systems that adapt to individual users or to groups of users. UMAP is the successor of the biennial User Modeling (UM) and Adaptive Hypermedia and Adaptive Web-based Systems (AH) conferences that were merged in 2009. It has traditionally been organized under the auspices of User Modeling Inc. Since 2016, UMAP is an ACM conference, sponsored by ACM SIGCHI and SIGWEB.

The conference spans a wide scope of topics related to user modeling, adaptation, and personalization. UMAP 2017 is focused on bringing together cutting-edge research from user interaction and modeling, adaptive technologies, and delivery platforms. It includes high-quality peer-reviewed papers featuring substantive new research in one of five research tracks, each chaired by leaders in the field

- Intelligent User interfaces (track chair: Nava Tintarev)

- Recommender Systems (track chairs: Bamshad Mobasher and Jonathan Gemmel)

- Technology-Enhanced Adaptive Learning (track chair: Milos Kravic)

- Personalized Social Web (track chairs: Luca Maria Aiello)

- Adaptive Hypermedia, Adaptive Web (track chair: Peter Brusilovsky)

The conference received a total of 130 submissions. Each submission was carefully reviewed by members of the Program Committee (PC), while the Track Chairs (TCs) coordinated the reviews and provided recommendations to the Program Chairs. The international Program Committee (PC) consisted of 132 members who were assisted by 43 subreviewers. These were leading researchers as well as highly promising young researchers.

Submissions were assigned to 1 TC member and received at least 3 reviews. After the initial reviews were submitted, the designated TC facilitated discussion amongst reviewers in order to resolve differences and correct misunderstandings. The TC then provided a recommendation to the Program Chairs. The final decisions were based on these recommendations, the meta-reviews, and reviewer scores.

A total of 131 submissions were reviewed. Out of 80 regular paper submissions, 29 were accepted (36% acceptance rate); out of 51 short paper submissions, 11 were accepted (22% acceptance rate). This year, we did not invite regular papers to be published as short papers, but instead invited them to either be included in the main proceedings as extended abstracts, or be published in the adjunct proceedings Late Breaking Results track (LBR). Six of them were published in the LBR track, and a total of 27 extended abstracts are published in the main proceedings.

Review and acceptance statistics are as follows:

UMAP Venue	Reviewed	Accepted	Acceptance rate
Full Papers	80	29	36.2%
Short Papers	51	11	21.5%
Full + Short Papers	131	40	30.5%

The program also features 3 demos, 3 theory, opinion and reflection papers and 14 late breaking results papers presented in UMAP poster session, which collectively showcase the wide spectrum of novel ideas and latest results in user modeling, adaptation and personalization.

We also invited three distinguished keynote speakers, each illustrating significant issues and prospective directions for the field.

Pearl Pu, School of Computer and Communication Sciences at EPFL, describes in her talk the various challenges related to understanding, detecting, and visualizing emotions in large text datasets.

Jennifer Golbeck, University of Maryland, focuses on how to consider issues of privacy and consent when users cannot explicitly state their preferences, The Creepy Factor, and how to balance users concerns with the benefits personalized technology can offer.

Paul De Bra, Eindhoven University of Technology, discusses in his talk "After twenty-five years of user modeling and adaptation what makes us UMAP?" how the field evolved, insights into where the field is headed, and the hottest topics for exploration.

The conference includes a doctoral consortium that provides an opportunity for doctoral students to explore and develop their research interests under the guidance of distinguished scholars. This track received 15 submissions, of which seven were accepted as full papers and six as posters.

A set of 8 workshops rounded off the program:

- *EdRecSys: Educational Recommender Systems* organized by Kurt Driessens (University of Maastricht, The Netherlands), Irena Koprinska (University of Sydney, Australia), Olga C. Santos (Spanish National University for Distance Education, Spain), Evgueni Smirnov (University of Maastricht, The Netherlands), Kalina Yacef (University of Sydney, Australia), Osmar Zaiane (University of Alberta, Canada)

- *EvalUMAP: Towards Comparative Evaluation in User Modeling, Adaptation and Personalization* organized by Owen Conlan, Liadh Kelly, Kevin Koidl, Seamus Lawless, Athanasios Staikopoulos (Trinity College Dublin, Ireland)

- *HAAPIE: Human Aspects in Adaptive and Personalized Interactive Environments* organized by Panagiotis Germanakos (SAP SE, Germany), Styliani Kleanthous-Loizou (University of Cyprus, Cyprus), George Samaras (Department of Computer Science, University of Cyprus), Vania Dimitrova (University of Leeds, UK), Ben Steichen (Santa Clara University, USA)

- *PALE: Personalization Approaches in Learning Environments* organized by Milos Kravcik (RWTH Aachen University, Germany), Olga C. Santos (UNED,Spain), Jesus G. Boticario (UNED, Spain), Maria Bielikova (FIIT STUBA,Slovakia), Tomas Horvath (Eotvos Lorand University, Budapest, Hungary)

- *PATCH: Personalized Access to Cultural Heritage* organized by Liliana Ardissono (University of Torino, Italy), Cristina Gena (University of Torino, Italy), Tsvi Kuflik, (University of Haifa, Israel)

- *SOAP: Surprise, Opposition, and Obstruction in Adaptive and Personalized Systems* organized by Peter Knees (Johannes Kepler University Linz, Austria), Kristina Andersen (Studio for Electro Instrumental Music, Amsterdam, the Netherlands), Alan Said (Recorded Future, Gothenburg, Sweden), and Marko Tkalcic (Free University of Bozen-Bolzano, Italy)

- *THUM: Temporal and Holistic User Modeling* organized by Cataldo Musto (University of Bari Aldo Moro, Italy), Amon Rapp (University of Torino, Italy), Federica Cena (University of Torino, Italy), Frank Hopfgartner (University of Glasgow), Judy Kay (University of Sidney, Australia), Giovanni Semeraro (University of Bari Aldo Moro, Italy) Veronika Bogina (University of Haifa, Israel), David Konopnicki (IBM Research, Haifa, Israel), Tsvi Kuflik (University of Haifa, Israel), Bamshad Mobasher (DePaul University, Chicago, USA)

- *WPPG: Fifty Shades of Personalization, Workshop on Personalization in Serious and Persuasive Games and Gameful Interactions* organized by Elke Mattheiss (Austrian Institute of Technology), Marc Busch (Austrian Institute of Technology), Rita Orji (University of Waterloo, Canada), Gustavo F. Tondello (University of Waterloo, Canada), Andrzej Marczewski (Motivait, UK), Wolfgang Hochleitner (University of Applied Sciences Upper Austria), Michael Lankes (University of Applied Sciences Upper Austria), Manfred Tscheligi (University of Salzburg, Austria).

Finally, UMAP hosted two tutorials:

- *Semantics-Aware Techniques for Social Media Analysis, User Modeling, and Recommender Systems* (half-day) by Pasquale Lops and Cataldo Musto(University of Bari Aldo Moro, Italy)

- *Designing cross-space learning analytics and personalised support* (half-day) by Roberto Martinez-Maldonado (University of Technology Sydney, Australia), Abelardo Pardo (University of Sydney, Australia) and Davinia Hernandez-Leo (Universitat Pompeu Fabra, Spain).

Maria Bielikova
General Chair
Slovak University of
Technology in Bratislava

Eelco Herder
General Chair
L3S Research Center, Hannover,
Radboud Universiteit Nijmegen

Federica Cena
Programme Chair
University of Torino

Michel Desmarais
Programme Chair
Polytechnique Montreal

Table of Contents

UMAP 2017 Keynote Addresses

UMAP 2017 Long Papers

UMAP 2017 Short Papers

UMAP 2017 Doctoral Consortium Papers

UMAP 2017 Extended Abstracts

UMAP 2017 Conference Organization

General Chairs: Maria Bielikova *(Slovak University of Technology in Bratislava, Slovakia)*
Eelco Herder *(L3S Research Center, Germany and Radboud Universiteit Nijmegen, The Netherlands)*

Program Chairs: Federica Cena *(University of Torino, Italy)*
Michel Desmarais *(Polytechnique University, Montreal, Canada)*

Track Chairs: **Personalized Recommender Systems**
Jonathan Gemmell *(DePaul University, USA)*
Bamshad Mobasher *(DePaul University, USA)*

Adaptive Hypermedia and the Semantic Web
Peter Brusilovsky *(University of Pittsburgh, USA)*

Intelligent User Interfaces
Nava Tintarev *(Delft University of Technology, the Netherlands)*

Technology-Enhanced Adaptive Learning
Milos Kravcik *(German Research Center for Artificial Intelligence, Germany)*

Personalized Social Web
Luca Maria Aiello *(Bell Labs Cambridge, UK)*

Late-Breaking Results, Theory, Opinion & Reflection and Demo Chairs: Dhaval Thakker *(University of Leeds, UK)*
Marko Tkalcic *(Free University of Bolzano, Italy)*

Doctoral Consortium Chairs: Panagiotis Germanakos *(University of Cyprus, Cyprus & SAP SE, Germany)*
Kalina Yacef *(University of Sydney, Australia)*

Workshop and Tutorials Chairs: Cecile Paris *(CSIRO ICT Centre, Australia)*
Olga Santos *(Spanish National University for Distance Education, Spain)*

Student Support Chairs: David Chin *(University of Hawaii, USA)*
Michal Kompan *(Slovak University of Technology in Bratislava, Slovakia)*

Publicity Chairs: Rikki Prince *(University of Southampton, UK)*
Cataldo Musto *(University of Bari, Italy)*

Proceedings Chair: Kirsten A. Smith *(University of Southampton, UK)*

Local Arrangements Chair: Jakub Simko *(Slovak University of Technology in Bratislava, Slovakia)*

Registration Chair: Milena Zeithamlova *(Action M Agency, Prague, Czech Republic)*

Web Master: Patrik Hlavac *(Slovak University of Technology in Bratislava, Slovakia)*

Program Committee: Luca Maria Aiello *(Bell Labs Cambridge, UK)*
Kenro Aihara *(National Institute of Informatics, Japan)*
Esma Aimeur *(University of Montreal, Canada)*
Liliana Ardissono *(University of Torino, Italy)*
Ivon Arroyo *(Worcester Polytechnic Institute, USA)*
Martin Atzmueller *(University of Kassel, Germany)*
Nilufar Baghaei *(UNITEC, New Zealand)*
Ryan Baker *(Teachers College, Columbia University, USA)*
Mathias Bauer *(mineway GmbH, Germany)*
Shlomo Berkovsky *(CSIRO, Australia)*
Nadia Berthouze *(University College London, UK)*
Gautam Biswas *(Vanderbilt University, USA)*
Kristy Elizabeth Boyer *(University of Florida, USA)*
Derek Bridge *(University College Cork, Ireland)*
Paul Brna *(University of Leeds, UK)*
Gregoire Burel *(The Open University, UK)*
Robin Burke *(DePaul University, USA)*
Iván Cantador *(Universidad Autónoma de Madrid, Spain)*
Giuseppe Carenini *(University of British Columbia, Canada)*
Rosa M. Carro *(Universidad Autonoma de Madrid, Spain)*
Eva Cerezo *(Universidad de Zaragoza, Spain)*
Li Chen *(Hong Kong Baptist University, Hong Kong)*
Min Chi *(North Carolina State University, USA)*
David Chin *(University of Hawaii, USA)*
Cristina Conati *(University of British Columbia, Canada)*
Paolo Cremonesi *(Politecnico di Milano, Italy)*
Alexandra Cristea *(University of Warwick, UK)*
Sidney D'Mello *(University of Notre Dame, USA)*
Elizabeth M. Daly *(IBM Research, Ireland)*
Paul De Bra *(Eindhoven University of Technology, the Netherlands)*
Munmun De Choudhury *(Georgia Institute of Technology, USA)*
Marco De Gemmis *(University of Bari, Italy)*
Pasquale De Meo *(Università degli Studi di Messina, Italy)*
Ernesto Diaz-Aviles *(IBM Research, Ireland)*
Vania Dimitrova *(School of Computing, University of Leeds, UK)*
Peter Dolog *(Aalborg University, Denmark)*
Benedict Du Boulay *(Informatics Department, University of Sussex, UK)*
Casey Dugan *(IBM T.J. Watson Research, USA)*
Miriam Fernandez *(Knowledge Media Institute, UK)*
Bruce Ferwerda *(Johannes Kepler University, Austria)*
Davide Fossati *(Emory University, USA)*
Ujwal Gadiraju *(L3S Research Center, Germany)*
Fabio Gasparetti *(ROMA TRE University, Italy)*
Mouzhi Ge *(Universitaet der Bundeswehr Munich, Germany)*

Program Committee (continued): Cristina Gena *((University of Torino, Italy)*

Rosella Gennari *(Free University of Bozen-Bolzano, Italy)*

Panagiotis Germanakos *(University of Cyprus, Cyprus)*

Werner Geyer *(IBM T.J. Watson Research, USA)*

Bradley Goodman *(The MITRE Corporation, USA)*

Ido Guy *(Yahoo Research, Israel)*

Conor Hayes *(Insight Centre for Data Analytics, NUI Galway, Ireland)*

Jesse Hoey *(University of Waterloo, Canada)*

Tobias Hossfeld *(University of Duisburg-Essen, Germany)*

Andreas Hotho *(University of Wuerzburg, Germany)*

Geert-Jan Houben *(TU Delft, the Netherlands)*

Eva Hudlicka *(Psychometrix Associates, USA)*

Isabelle Hupont *(Institut des Systèmes Intelligents et de Robotique, France)*

Dietmar Jannach *(TU Dortmund, Germany)*

Robert Jäschke *(L3S Research Center, Germany)*

W. Lewis Johnson *(Alelo Inc., USA)*

Alexandros Karatzoglou *(Telefonica Research, Spain)*

Styliani Kleanthous Loizou *(University of Nicosia, Cyprus)*

Bart Knijnenburg *(Clemson University, USA)*

Alfred Kobsa *(University of California, Irvine, USA)*

Kenneth Koedinger *(Carnegie Mellon University, USA)*

Irena Koprinska *(University of Sydney, Australia)*

Joseph Konstan *(University of Minnesota, USA)*

Milos Kravcik *(German Research Center for Artificial Intelligence, Germany)*

Antonio Krueger *(DFKI, Germany)*

Tsvi Kuflik *(The University of Haifa, Israel)*

Bob Kummerfeld *(University of Sydney, Australia)*

Neal Lathia *(Skyscanner, UK)*

Séamus Lawless *(Trinity College Dublin, Ireland)*

James Lester *(North Carolina State University, USA)*

Pasquale Lops *(University of Bari, Italy)*

Bernd Ludwig *(University Regensburg, Germany)*

Roberto Martinez-Maldonado *(University of Technology Sydney, Australia)*

Judith Masthoff *(University of Aberdeen, UK)*

Gordon McCalla *(University of Saskatchewan, Canada)*

Alessandro Micarelli *(Roma Tre University, Italy)*

Tanja Mitrovic *(University of Canterbury, UK)*

Riichiro Mizoguchi *(Japan Advanced Institute of Science & Technology, Japan)*

Kasia Muldner *(Carleton University, Canada)*

Cataldo Musto *(Dipartimento di Informatica – University of Bari, Italy)*

Wolfgang Nejdl *(L3S and University of Hannover, Germany)*

Roger Nkambou *(Université du Québec À Montréal, Canada)*

John O'Donovan *(University of California Santa Barbara, USA)*

Program Committee (continued): Georgios Paliouras *(Institute of Informatics & Telecommunications, NCSR "Demokritos", Greece)*

Alexandros Paramythis *(Contexity AG, Switzerland)*

Cécile Paris *(CSIRO ICT Centre, Australia)*

Christopher Peters *(KTH Royal Institute of Technology, Sweden)*

Luiz Pizzato *(Commonwealth Bank of Australia, Australia)*

Kaska Porayska-Pomsta *(UCL Knowledge Lab, UK)*

Rikki Prince *(University of Southampton, UK)*

Francesco Ricci *(Free University of Bozen-Bolzano, Italy)*

Ma. Mercedes T. Rodrigo *(Ateneo de Manila University, Philippines)*

Domenico Rosaci *(University Mediterranea of Reggio Calabria, Italy)*

Alan Said *(University of Skövde, Sweden)*

George Samaras *(University of Cyprus, Cyprus)*

Olga C. Santos *(aDeNu Research Group, UNED, Spain)*

Markus Schedl *(Johannes Kepler University, Austria)*

Giovanni Semeraro *(University of Bari, Italy)*

Bracha Shapira *(Ben-Gurion University, Israel)*

Elena Simperl *(University of Southampton, UK)*

Barry Smyth *(University College Dublin, Ireland)*

Mohammad Soleymani *(University of Geneva, Switzerland)*

Marcus Specht *(Open University of the Nethderlands, The Netherlands)*

Ben Steichen *(Santa Clara University, USA)*

Markus Strohmaier *(University of Koblenz-Landau, Germany)*

Andrea Tagarelli *(University of Calabria, Italy)*

Dhavalkumar Thakker *(University of Bradford, UK)*

Marko Tkalcic *(Free University of Bolzano, Italy)*

Ilaria Torre *(University of Genoa, Italy)*

Christoph Trattner *(KMI, TU-Graz, Austria)*

Raphaël Troncy *(EURECOM, France)*

Khiet Truong *(University of Twente, the Netherlands)*

Giovanna Varni *(University Pierre and Marie Curie, France)*

Julita Vassileva *(University of Saskatchewan, Canada)*

Amali Weerasinghe *(The University of Adelaide, Australia)*

Martijn Willemsen *(Eindhoven University of Technology, the Netherlands)*

Kalina Yacef *(The University of Sydney, Australia)*

Massimo Zancanaro *(FBK-cit, Italy)*

Markus Zanker *(Free University of Bozen-Bolzano, Italy)*

Diego Zapata-Rivera *(Educational Testing Service, USA)*

Jie Zhang *(Nanyang Technological University, Singapore)*

Yong Zheng *(Illinois Institute of Technology, USA)*

Additional reviewers:

Marwan Al-Tawil
Muhammad Anwar
Sandra Baldassarri
Christine Bauer
Marios Belk
Praveen Chandar
Devendra Chaplot
Nicholas Diana
Mark Graus
Giannis Haralabopoulos
Matthias Hirth
Georgios Katsimpras
Mohammad Khalil
Sébastien Lallé
Chen Lin
Pasquale Lops
Ling Luo
Ye Mao

Florian Metzger
Fedelucio Narducci
Enrico Palumbo
Chris Phethean
Dimitris Pierrakos
Amon Rapp
Steffen Schnitzer
Shitian Shen
Chun-Hua Tsai
Andreu Vall
Dimitrios Vogiatzis
Feng Wang
Stephan Weibelzahl
Daniel Weidele
Wen Wu
Albin Zehe
Daniel Zoller

UMAP 2017 Sponsors & Supporters

Sponsors:

Supporters:

After Twenty-Five Years of User Modeling and Adaptation...What Makes us UMAP?

Paul De Bra
Eindhoven University of Technology
Eindhoven, the Netherlands
debra@tue.nl

ABSTRACT

ACM UMAP 2017 is the 25th conference on User Modeling, on Adaptive Hypermedia, or on both together (since 2009). The research has actually been going on for more than 25 years as initially there was a conference only every two years. This keynote offers both reflection on the past and outlook into the future, with the burning question: What makes us UMAP? We perform research on modeling users (individuals as well as groups), not just for fun but to use these models for recommendations and for adaptation. That's not unique to us. In recommender systems analyzing user behavior is needed in order to give better and better recommendations, and likewise an area like educational data mining analyzes how learners study in order to best guide them to new learning material or followup courses. With analysis of social networks and website adaptation we step into the same research area that is covered by the hypertext community. If all of this is "us" but "not just us", where is our identity?

One key characteristic of User Modeling is our quest to come up with *understandable* user models, or *scrutable* as Judy Kay coins them. The same is true for the adaptation: we strive to understand why certain adaptation happens or why a certain recommendation is given. UMAP research is not complete if we cannot understand the chain that leads from user action to (a perhaps much later) system reaction.

As we move from *expert-driven adaptation* towards *data-driven adaptation* the problem of understanding the user-modeling-to-adaptation process is becoming harder and harder. But we need this understanding to ensure that adaptation continues to adapt in the right way under continuously changing circumstances (both in what we adapt and in the users and context we adapt to). We need the understanding also to prevent continuous adaptation from creating filter bubbles and to avoid creating the illusion that the recommendations will always be "right" because of the "wisdom of the crowd" principle.

One key element has always been missing from UMAP, and this keynote will fill that void: we need to practice what we preach. Therefore, the conference proceedings will only contain this abstract, but there will be a real paper to go with this abstract. That paper cannot be printed because it is *adaptive*. The URL of the keynote paper is http://gale.win.tue.nl/keynote/.

ACM Reference format:
Paul De Bra. 2017. After Twenty-Five Years of User Modeling and Adaptation...What Makes us UMAP?. In *Proceedings of UMAP '17, July 09-12, 2017, Bratislava, Slovakia*, , 1 pages.
DOI: http://dx.doi.org/10.1145/3079628.3079662

I'll be Watching You: Policing the Line betweem Personalization and Privacy

Keynote

Jennifer Golbeck

College of Information Studies, University of Maryland, College Park

USA

jgolbeck@umd.edu

ABSTRACT

Personalization, recommendations, and user modeling can be powerful tools to improve people's experiences with technology and to help them f i n d information. However, we also know that people   underestimate how much of their personal information is used by our technology and they generally do not understand how much   algorithms can discover about them. Both privacy and ethical techa nology have issues of consent at their heart. This talk will look at how to consider issues of privacy and consent when users cannot   explicitly state their preferences, The Creepy Factor, and how to balance users' concerns with the benefits personalized technology can offer.

KEYWORDS

Personalization, Privacy

ACM Reference   format:
Jennifer Golbeck. 2017. I'll be watching you: policing the line between   personalization and privacy. In Proceedings of the 2017 Conference on User Modeling, Adaptation and Personalization, Bratislava, Slovakia, July 2017
(UMAP'17), 1 pages.   DOI:

BIO

Jennifer Golbeck is Director of the Social Intelligence Lab and an Associate Professor in the College of Information Studies at the University of Maryland, College Park.

Her research focuses on analyzing and computing with social media, focused on predicting user attributes, and using the results to design and build systems that improve the way people interact   with information online.

UMAP'17, July 9--12, 2017, Bratislava, Slovakia
© 2017 Copyright held by the owner/author(s).
ACM ISBN 978-1-4503-4635-1/17/07.
DOI: http://dx.doi.org/10.1145/3079628.3079661

Emotion Analysis in Natural Language

Pearl Pu
Ecole Polytechnique Fédérale de Lausanne (EPFL)
Lausanne
Switzerland
pearl.pu@epfl.ch

ABSTRACT

What is human emotion? It turns out there are more than 90 definitions. Among the most recent well-accepted ones, emotion is understood as our reaction to external and internal events such as a loud noise (external, surprise), being told we passed the college entrance exam (external, joy), or a thought that triggered the memory of a bygone love (internal, sad). We care about emotions because they **motivate** us to take actions, **influence** the quality of our decisions, and **enhance** our ability to empathize and communicate.

In this talk, I will describe the various challenges related to understanding, detecting, and visualizing emotions in large text datasets. To show you the research methodology we have explored and developed, I will demonstrate concrete steps and systems for eliciting emotion annotations from crowd workers, motivating and incentivizing them, building domain-specific lexicons, processing modifiers such as negations and intensifiers, and detecting emotions in human dialogs such as those found in TV series and movies.

The talk will end with some suggestions for future work in this area including building emotion-aware dialog systems.

KEYWORDS

Emotion; Natural Language; HCI

1 BIO

Dr. Pearl Pu leads the Human Computer Interaction Group in the School of Computer and Communication Sciences at EPFL. Her research is multi-disciplinary and focuses on issues in the intersection of human computer interaction, artificial intelligence, and behavioral science. Over her long career, she has worked on decision support and recommender systems, user preference elicitation, emotion analysis in social media, and information visualization.

She serves on several editorial positions: the AI Magazine, the ACM Transactions on Interactive Intelligent Systems, the User Modeling and User Adapted Interaction, and IEEE Multimedia (past). She is a member of the steering committee of the ACM International Conference on Recommender Systems.

She holds a Ph.D. in Computer and Information Sciences from the University of Pennsylvania in the United States and was a recipient of the research initiation award (now research career award) from the US National Science Foundation, as well as 13 Research Awards from the Swiss National Science Foundation, and 3 Technology Innovation Awards. Her team won the Worldwide Innovation Challenge in recognition of her scientific and entrepreneurial contribution in emotion recognition in social media.

UMAP '17, July 09-12, 2017, Bratislava, Slovakia

DOI: http://dx.doi.org/10.1145/3079628.3079660

Nudge your Workforce: A Study on the Effectiveness of Task Notification Strategies in Enterprise Mobile Crowdsourcing

Sarah Bashirieh, Sepideh Mesbah, Judith Redi
and Alessandro Bozzon
Delft University of Technology
Mekelweg 4
Delft, The Netherlands
sara.bashiri@gmail.com,s.mesbah@tudelft.nl
J.A.Redi@tudelft.nl,a.bozzon@tudelft.nl

Zoltán Szlávik and Robert-Jan Sips
IBM Benelux, Centre for Advanced Studies.
Johan Huizingalaan 765
Amsterdam, The Netherlands
zoltan.szlavik@ibm.nl.com
robert-jan.sips@ibm.nl.com

ABSTRACT

As crowdsourcing gains popularity, organisations seek ways to systematically and reliably involve their workforce with data processing pipelines. Mobile crowdsourcing allows for opportunistic task executions and thus, potentially, for higher throughput. However, how to engage and to retain employees in enterprise crowdsourcing campaigns is still an open research topic. This paper discusses the results of a study performed in IBM Benelux. We surveyed 93 employees to discover the factors that might affect engagement in mobile enterprise crowdsourcing. The survey informed the design of an experiment that aimed at investigating the effectiveness of different task notification strategies. We studied how factors such as time and context of notification can affect the participation and retention of employees. Results show that break times are the most suitable for crowd work, and that "aggressive" notification strategies act as deterrent for participation, while moderate yet regular nudges are the most likely to retain contributors.

CCS CONCEPTS

•**Information systems** →**Incentive schemes;** •**General and reference** →*Evaluation;* •**Applied computing** →*Enterprise information systems;*

KEYWORDS

Crowdsourcing; Notification; Enterprise; Workplace; Location-Aware Computing

1 INTRODUCTION

Enterprise crowdsourcing – i.e. the use of crowdsourcing approaches that harness the collective intelligence of an industrial firm's employees – is often seen as a way to systematically access the rich (and often tacit) knowledge and skills of a workforce across business divisions and hierarchical structures. Concrete examples of application domains for enterprise crowdsourcing include collaborative design and innovation, customers support, workplace awareness, and knowledge creation [7, 9, 16, 29, 34, 35].

The main advantage of enterprise crowdsourcing lies in the availability of a crowd of performers that are trusted, and operating in the context of an already retributed employment. Employees operate under contracts signed in order to commit to corporate norms and values, including, for instance, intellectual property rights [35]. The commitment from employees to employers helps decreasing malicious behaviours during task execution, and, arguably, makes employees always available for contribution, possibly in an opportunistic manner. To this end, mobile (or situated) crowdsourcing represent an interesting alternative w.r.t. traditional desktop crowdsourcing [19]. By exploiting the common availability of powerful mobile devices (e.g. smartphone), and considering that many people almost always have their devices with them, it is now possible to push tasks anywhere and anytime. Given the lack of agreed-upon regulations for the use of crowdsourcing within an organisation [5, 12], current crowd work models within enterprises must address delicate trade-offs, such as the one between an employee's primary work and the crowd work, or the one between the promotion of wide employee participation and management oversight and control over the workforce's activities [3].

With this work, we aimed at furthering the understanding on how enterprise mobile crowdsourcing (EMC) could be sustainably adopted in a traditional work environment. We investigated which factors might affect the engagement, participation, and retention of employees with EMC campaigns. The investigation took place in the multinational enterprise environment of *IBM Netherlands*, where we sought answer to the following research questions:

RQ1 : When and how would employees be willing to perform mobile crowdsourcing tasks in an enterprise environment?

The goal is to understand when employees are more likely to interact with their mobile devices, and which type of crowd work would they be willing to perform. Driven by previous literature, we created and advertised a survey that ultimately involved 93 participants.

We discovered that: 1) employees are generally willing to perform crowdsourcing tasks during some (but not all) of their break times. 2) Task duration is an important participation condition: results show that employees prefer to devote short attention spans to crowd work. 3) Personal motivations are preferential reasons for

Robert-Jan Sips is currently affiliated with *myTomorrows*. His current e-mail address is robert-jan.sips@mytomorrows.com.

participation. For instance employees are willing to contribute if they sense the opportunity to learn, or to improve their workplace conditions.

To better understand how EMC could be sustainably adopted in an enterprise environment, we incorporated the results from the survey into the design of a mobile crowdsourcing experiment. The goal was to assess the effectiveness of alternative task notification strategies for enterprise crowdsourcing, thus, seeking answer to the following research question:

RQ2 How can notification (nudging) strategies affect the participation, retention and task commitment in enterprise mobile crowdsourcing?

We created a novel enterprise mobile crowdsourcing platform (*E-Crowd*) that allows employees to download and execute arbitrarily complex tasks directly onto their smartphone. The platform includes a mobile application with activity-awareness capabilities, to infer, for instance, whether a person is walking or not. Mechanisms devoted to the dynamic allocation of tasks, and push-based notifications, allowed us to experiment with time-aware and activity-aware notification strategies, while providing employees with a selection of different tasks to perform. Our findings suggest that task commitment (i.e. the amount of time devoted to EMC) is not affected by the selected notification strategy, while participation (i.e. the frequency of participation in EMC campaigns) and retention (i.e. the likelihood of an employee not to abandon the platform) are favoured by moderate yet regular nudges.

Enterprises are complex socio-technical systems. The role that enterprise crowdsourcing could play in traditional organisations is yet to be fully understood, let alone exploited. Our work contributes new insights on how and when employees can be engaged to contribute with crowd work. This additional knowledge can be used to promote the acceptance of this useful work paradigm within companies, and inform the design of a next generation of EMC systems that are efficient yet respectful of pre-existing work norms and dynamics.

2 RELATED WORK

Enterprise crowdsourcing. In enterprise crowdsourcing, organisations can benefit from the knowledge, intelligence and expertise of their employees to solve problems that cannot (or are not economical to) be completely outsourced to external workforces. Enterprise crowdsourcing can target workers external to the organisation [28] or a mix of external and internal populations [7]. The focus of this study is on enterprise crowdsourcing performed by a company's own workforce. Enterprise crowdsourcing proved applicable in a variety of domains, including collaborative design and innovation, customers support, workplace awareness, and knowledge creation [7, 10, 16, 29, 34, 35]. Yet, the theory and practice of Enterprise crowdsourcing currently lacks a clear understanding of how employees could be systematically engaged, and durably retained, in crowdsourcing campaigns. MCNet [26] addressed the crowdsourcing of WLAN measurements within an office environment, adducing as incentive for participation the increase of WLAN quality for employees. "Games for Crowds" [20] studies the effectiveness of a game-centred approach to Enterprise crowdsourcing,

where users could play, create, and share simple games that harness the collective intelligence of employees within the enterprise. Stanculescu et al. [30] discuss the effectiveness of gamification techniques as engagement strategies for employees' participation in enterprise learning and social awareness tasks. MET [4] addressed the problem of providing the right incentives for Enterprise crowdsourcing participation, while preserving management oversight and control with monetary reward. To the best of our knowledge, our work is the first that studies how notification strategies can play a role in the success of enterprise crowdsourcing initiatives. We contribute an experiment based on a rigorous experimental design, and supported by a robust application-independent mobile crowdsourcing platform designed for the enterprise context.

Mobile Crowdsourcing in The Enterprise. Mobile phones provide flexibility in crowdsourcing task execution. Workers are able to ubiquitously contribute to crowdsourcing tasks using their mobile data connection, or local WiFi networks [2]. A key characteristic of mobile crowdsourcing relates to its opportunistic or participatory nature [15, 27]. Rather than sitting at a desk, workers can engage with a crowd work platform in a variety of different contexts and environments. This creates opportunities for more efficient execution of crowd work campaigns, but also provides a different set of challenges [21] (e.g. battery limitations, screen size, and lack of effective input devices). Several studies show that one of the main obstacles for large adoption is the presence of proper participation incentives [8, 27, 31, 36]. Commercial mobile crowdsourcing platforms provide monetary rewards, while academic and volunteer-based platforms rely on non-monetary incentives such as social rewards [17]. Few studies investigate the relationship between notification time, a user's location, and the likelihood and quality of users' responses. [23] show that user response probability to information notification is higher before and after a location change event. A recent work [22] investigates the issues of task notification design, to assess when, where, and to whom tasks should be suggested in on-the-go crowdsourcing. Results suggest that small changes in notification radius and timing can have a significant effect on individual participation and actions.

Novelty. In this paper, we combine qualitative and quantitative analysis to understand when and how employees would be willing to perform EMC tasks, and which notification strategies are the most effective in eliciting workers' contributions. We investigate a set of aspects relevant to enterprise mobile crowdsourcing (participation, retention and task commitment), that are only partially covered related work. No previous work investigating interruption and notification strategies [1, 6, 14, 25, 32], enterprise crowdsourcing [4, 30, 35], or mobile crowdsourcing [31] performed a survey, a longitudinal experiment, and post-experiment interviews in an enterprise environment. This is an important difference, as the demographics and motivation of participants are completely different, e.g. from those of a crowd of students.

3 INCENTIVES AND OPPORTUNITIES FOR EMPLOYEES' PARTICIPATION IN EMC CAMPAIGNS

The first part of our work investigates the likelihood of employees participating in enterprise mobile crowdsourcing (EMC) campaigns using their mobile phones (**RQ1**). At the same time, we seek insights into when employees are more likely to interact with their mobile phones – to check the presence of notifications from one or more installed applications. The assumption is that employees are normally busy with their business-related activities (e.g. meetings), and that unsolicited activities on their mobile devices can only happen opportunistically, or at pre-defined times of the day.

We created a survey[1], aimed at complementing results from previous work in terms of: 1) understanding of employees' motivations for (enterprise) crowd work; 2) knowledge of the amount of crowd work employees would be willing to execute; and 3) identification of the best times and context for effective notifications (nudging). The survey has been advertised using email invitations across departments, and the company's internal social network. An introductory page provided employees with information about the goals and scope of the survey, together with some explanation about crowdsourcing and its applications. The survey could be filled anonymously.

We targeted employees that used their smart phones as part of their daily activities. 93 employees participated in the survey; 20% of which were female, a ratio that reasonably approximates the company's gender distribution worldwide. 53% of the employees owned an iOS device, while 47% and Android device. The majority of participants (41%) were in the 46 to 55 year old range; 29% between 36 and 45; 19.2% between 26 and 35; 8.4% between 55 and 65; and 2.4% in the 18 to 25 year range. 42% of the participants worked in the engineering department, 41% in sales, and the rest from the other departments. 5% of the participants were managers.

3.1 How much crowd work would employees be willing to perform during a normal working day?

With this question, we aim at understanding how much crowd work (i.e. number of tasks) employees would be willing to execute each day during office hours. We rely on employees' self-assessment as it is not trivial to estimate an optimal number in an empirical manner, at least in a non-intrusive way [23]. As the duration of tasks can affect user voluntary participation, we also asked employees to express preferences about the preferred temporal length of execution. Table 1 reports the distribution of answers in the surveyed population. Numbers in bold highlight that the dominating factor is the **total** amount of daily time to be allocated (**from 5 to 10 minutes**), rather than the duration of single tasks, or the total amount of tasks. Employees indicated preference for short tasks, with length up to *2 minutes*. For instance 47% and 58% indicated the willingness to respectively perform work for up to 5 minutes (1 minute per task), or 10 minutes (2 minutes per task).

# Daily Tasks	Duration		
	1 min	2 min	5 min
1 task	5.2%	17.1%	**54%**
2 to 5 tasks	**47%**	**58%**	30.2%
5 to 10 tasks	**26%**	17%	8%
10 to 15 tasks	12%	5.2%	0%
15 to 20 tasks	5.2%	0%	0%
More than 20	4%	2.6%	2.6%
No task	0%	0%	5.2%

Table 1: Preferred amount and duration of EMC tasks.

3.2 Which type of crowdsourcing tasks would incentivise employee participation?

Monetary incentives are often not suitable for enterprise crowdsourcing, both for managerial and legal reasons. We therefore investigate which non-monetary motivators explored in previous work (e.g. improving quality of work [26], improving the well-being of the workforce [29], or learning [30]) are the most popular among employees. *Learning Something New* was identified as the most popular motivation for participation (with 32% of preferences), followed by *Improving Work Conditions and Quality of Work* (24%) and *Having Fun* (18%). Interestingly, the *Improvement of the Company's performance* (14%) was perceived as more important than the improvement of one's *Performance Appraisal* (10%). No employee mentioned social relationships as the most motivating factor.

3.3 When do employees check the notifications on their smart phones?

Finally, we asked employees for information about their most likely availability during working time. Previous work [23] shows that employees are not responsive to the notifications on their phone at home and during meetings. By answering this question, we aim at pinpointing one or more time intervals, during a normal working day, when employees are more likely to check notifications.

We asked employees about whether they check notifications on their smartphones during coffee breaks, lunch breaks, during walking to the coffee machine, lunch room and meeting rooms. Results show that employees mostly check notifications on their smart phones *during standard breaks – excluding lunch time –* and *while walking* to coffee machines, lunch room and meeting rooms. This is an interesting outcome suggesting that: 1) break times have the potential to be good moments to solicit activities that are not related with employees' regular assignments; and 2) notification checking is more likely to happen while *walking* from one place to another (e.g. from the desk to the coffee machine) than when standing (e.g. at the coffee machine). The result also suggests that employees value their break times, possibly as a space for socialisation, and are therefore less willing to sacrifice it; therefore, the few minutes before and after the break are potentially more suitable for extemporary activity.

4 THE EFFECT OF NOTIFICATION STRATEGIES ON EMC PARTICIPATION, RETENTION AND TASK COMMITMENT

The second part of the work investigates how different notification strategies can affect the participation, retention and task commitment in enterprise mobile crowdsourcing (**RQ2**).

---

[1]The survey adopted in this work, as well as the complete set of results are available to readers at https://sites.google.com/site/enterprisemobilecrowd

We designed and created an enterprise mobile crowdsourcing platform called *E-Crowd*, presented in Section 4.1. Inspired by the survey results reported in the previous section, we focused on two dimensions of study (independent variables), namely: 1) the *temporal distribution* of notifications; and 2) the *activity context* (i.e. walking) of employees. To reduce the space of experimental conditions, the type of available tasks were not considered as independent variables, but designed and implemented a fixed set of mobile crowdsourcing tasks.

Using a between-subject 2*2 factorial design, we created four distinct notification (nudging) strategies. The experimental design is discussed in the homonymous subsection. We made use of several metrics to assess (and compare) employees' *participation, retention* and *commitment* to the task; these metrics are described Section 4.2, while Section 4.3 presents the results of the experiment.

4.1 The E-Crowd platform

The platform consists of a back-end component and a front-end component. The back-end component (developed in *node.js*) includes functionality related to:1) registration and authentication of participants; 2) registration and allocation of crowdsourcing tasks; 3) integration and execution of custom notification strategies; 4) balanced allocation of participants to different experimental configurations; and 5) logging of participants activities. The front-end consists of an iOS application[2], implemented in *Swift 2*. Users can authenticate using their device Identifier (automatically retrieved from the phone metadata), so to allow anonymous participation and unique identification.

The application also includes activity-awareness capabilities, based on the *Core Motion* framework offered by the iOS environment. The motion activity is detected by the device hardware, specifically, the accelerometer and the gyroscope. The *Core Motion* framework provides an estimation of the current activity of the user, as inferred from the device.[3] To avoid battery draining (and, therefore, discourage employees' participation), motion activity is probed only at specific time spans (during break times) using the silent notification mechanism of iOS. [4]

Upon opening of the *E-Crowd* application, participants receive 5 tasks (Figure 1). To prevent bias in the results due to the order of task presentation, each participant is assigned a task list composed by a set of random tasks drawn from type-specific pools.

To minimise learning bias, executed tasks are never reassigned to users. By choosing a task, participants are provided with a brief description of the task's purpose, and with instructions for execution. Users can either "Start" o"Pass" a task (Figure 2). Starting a task allows users to execute the assigned activity and submit the results (Figure 3). When passing a task, participants are requested to provide a reason for rejection (e.g. *I don't like this task, The task is complicated, User Interface is not friendly* – see Figure 4). The logging functionality keeps track of several usage statistics, including task opening, task starting and passing, and task submission. The system also logs when the application is opened directly from

---

[2]Due to technical constraints, this experiment includes only participants operating an iOS device.
[3]Examples of detected activities are walking, running, driving, or stationary. http://developer.apple.com/library/ios/documentation/EventHandling
[4]http://developer.apple.com/library/ios/documentation/NetworkingInternet

the notification message. The application also checked at regular intervals if the participant decided to block notifications from the *E-Crowd* application.

4.2 Experimental design

The goal of the experiment was to measure how participation, retention, and task commitment (dependent variables) vary as a function of different notification configurations.

Independent Variables. The *Temporal Distribution* variable defines the time slots (during the working day) when the *E-Crowd* back-end pushes notifications to a given employee. The variable can assume two values, defined according to the survey results: 1) "Popular Break Time" (**PB**), which dispatches a single notification in each of the two time slots 10:00AM - 11.00AM (morning coffee break) and 12:00AM - 1.00PM (lunch break); and 2) "All Break Times" (**AB**), which includes also the time slots 9:00AM - 10.00AM (start of the day), 2:00PM - 3.00PM and 3:00PM - 4.00PM (afternoon coffee break) and 5:00PM - 6:00PM(end of the day).

The *Activity Context* variable could assume two values: 1) "Fixed Activities" (**FA**), indicating that a notification will be sent to the participants exactly at the begin of break times (**AB** or **PB**); and 2) "Walking Activities" (**WA**), which send a notifications only after the detection of the *first* walking activity during the targeted time slot. Lack of motion detection, due, for instance, to the employee not moving from the desk (or not carrying the phone along) results in no emitted notification. Regardless the configuration, a welcome notification was delivered at the start of working days (8.50AM), to remind employees of the ongoing experiment.

	Group 1	Group 2	Group 3	Group 4
Popular Breaks	X		X	
All Breaks		X		X
Fixed Activities	X	X		
Walking Activities			X	X

Table 2: The four experimental treatment groups.

The resulting four treatment groups were organised as in Table 2. In *Group 1*, employees received notifications at popular break times; employees in *Group 2* received notifications at all break times, including the start and the end of a working day; in *Group 3*, employees received notifications at popular break times only if a walking activity is detected; finally, employees in *Group 4* received notification at all break times, but only when walking.

Our running hypothesis is that both the frequency of notification and the activity awareness would affect the likelihood of employees to: 1) react to notifications (thus opening the app); 2) execute crowd work; and 3) persist with their crowd work activities over time.

The between-subjects design was adopted to limit the effect of learning biases, but presents two main drawbacks: 1) it requires a large number of participants; and 2) it introduces variability due to the distribution of individual characteristics of the participants. The first issue has been tackled by deploying and advertising the tool with the company's internal network, which hosts a large potential number of employees, and resulted in a good participation. To minimise the chances of bias due to subjects' variability, at signup participants were randomly assigned to a treatment group.

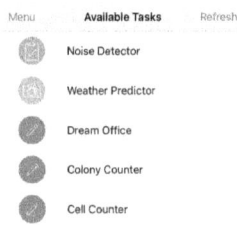

Figure 1: *E-Crowd*: Home Screen with Task List

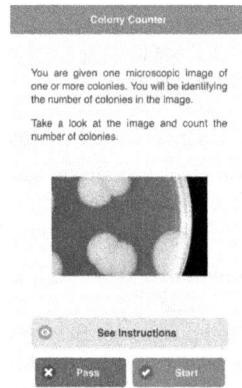

Figure 2: *E-Crowd*: Cell Annotation Task Instructions

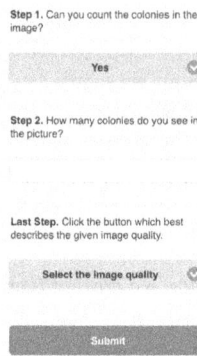

Figure 3: *E-Crowd*: Task Execution Interface

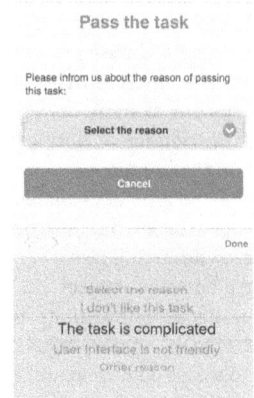

Figure 4: *E-Crowd*: Task Rejection Form

Dependent Variables. *Participation, retention* and *commitment* were quantitatively measured by analysing the logs produced by the *E-Crowd* application.

Participation is defined as the degree of involvement with the smartphone application; it is measured in terms of number of access to the application, and in terms of number of executed tasks. The average amount of application access and task execution falls into the category of *online behaviour metrics*, and are a good indicative of user participation, normalising for the sign up time.

To measure *retention*, i.e. the likelihood of an employee not to abandon the application, we compute at the proportion of participants who opened the mobile application more than once, and the frequency of their executed tasks. These numbers are captured in a *employee retention curve*, defined by the proportion of users who revisited *E-Crowd* and the frequency of their interactions [24]. The steepness of the slope indicates the level of engagement with the application. A steep slope implies that many employees interacted with the application only a few times; a flatter slope indicates that only a few employees abandoned the application after interacting with it just few times, while many employees had frequent interactions. Within each treatment group, we compute the number of access and executed task by all users and display a regression plot of the data.

Task commitment measures the amount of time dedicated to task execution; we consider it indication of employees' interest in the offered tasks, and a proxy for trustworthy execution. The time is measured as the amount of seconds between pressing the "Start" button, and successful task execution

Tasks Design. The survey highlighted a number of classes of tasks that are perceived by employees as motivating for participation. We included three types of tasks.

T1 – Content Creation (*Weather Predictor*) requires employees to take a picture of the outside weather in their current location. T2 – Image Annotation (*Colony Counter* and *Cell Counter*) requires employees to tap on their screen to *annotate* microscopic images of colonies or cells.

T1 and T2 tasks have direct benefit for the company (i.e. *improving the enterprise output*), as they are related to ongoing and advertised research endeavours.

T3 – Survey (*Dream Office* and *Noise Detector*) tasks are related to the *improvement of the quality of work*. They request employees to provide subjective assessments of environmental properties of the workplace, such as the experienced noise level, or the perceived office temperature and office lightning.

Tasks types were selected so to match both the preference of workers (from survey, *Dream Office* and *Noise Detector*) and the real world industrial needs of the company – specifically, the need to train the IBM Watson technology for application in the medical (*Colony Counter, Cell Counter*) and weather prediction domains. The selection of task types was also driven by the need to minimise the chances of confounding effects due to unbalance in task types, or due to individual task preferences.

All tasks were designed for optimal visualisation on a mobile phone screen. The amount work demanded by each task was tailored to fit a 1 minute execution time. To make ensure that employees were properly aware of the purpose of each task, the selection of a task from the list triggered a modal window containing a small explanation, always available in the task description page (see Figure 2). The time required to read the instructions of the task is considered a one-time penalty, and therefore negligible w.r.t. task execution time.

4.3 Experimental Results

The experiment has been conducted in the company's regional headquarter. Recruitment has been performed on a voluntary base, through advertisement. We sent emails in the corporate mailing list, advertised the experiment in the enterprise social network, and placed banners in strategic places (e.g. the cafeteria and bathrooms).

Participants interacted with the *E-Crowd* platform and mobile application for a number of days, depending on the signup date. The experiment ran for 2 months, between April 1st 2016 and June 1st 2016. During the observation interval, 83 employees installed the app. As employees could install the app at any time in this period, we considered the activities of each participant only during their first month of participation, regardless of their moment of enrolment. Notably, we logged no occurrence of employees disabling the notification functionality of the *E-Crowd* application.

4.3.1 General Participation Statistics. Participants differed per roles in the organisation, age groups and treatment groups. Figures are reported in Table 3–4. Most of the employees belonged to the *Engineering* and *Sales* department: this distribution reflects the actual allocation of employees within the company's headquarter. Other departments (e.g. legal) were also represented, but with fewer employees. We therefore aggregated them in a single category. Overall, managers accounted for 5% of the overall population. The distribution of employees across age groups also resembles the actual one of the company.

The amount of executed tasks is evenly distributed across departments. The differences across role groups and age groups are not significant (respectively $p > 0.19$ and $p > 0.28$). Participants in the 26--35 cohort are on average the most active. A consistent amount of participants (14%) were passive (i.e. inactive). 33% of them were managers. Due to technical limitations, we could not verify if these passive users uninstalled the application, or simply ignored all the incoming notifications.

We observed a considerable amount of activity during weekends, and outside official office hours (when participants did not receive notifications). As we are primarily interested in the direct effect of notification strategies, next sections will only report results based on activities and tasks completed during weekdays and office hours.

Dept.	#Em	#Ex	#Ex_{WH}	%EX_{OH}	μ_{ex}	$\mu_{ex_{WH}}$	%pas
Engin.	24	304	239	21.3	2.6	9.96	12.5
Sales	32	370	191	48.3	11.5	5.97	15.6
Other	27	401	313	22	13.8	11.59	14.8

Table 3: Distribution of executed tasks across departments. *#Em*: number of participants. *#Ex*: number of executions including, off-time and weekends. *#Ex_{WH}*: number of executions performed during working hours. *%EX_{OH}* is the percentage of task executions performed outside working hours. *μ_{ex}*: average amount of executions per users. *$\mu_{ex_{WH}}$*: average amount of executions per users during working hours. *%pas* indicates the percentage of passive users.

Age	#Em	#Ex	#Ex_{WH}	%EX_{OH}	μ_{ex}	$\mu_{ex_{WH}}$	%pas
18–25	5	25	21	16	5	4.2	20
26–35	13	268	200	25.3	20.6	15.38	7.6
36–45	21	259	181	30	12.3	8.62	9.5
46–55	33	435	261	40	13	7.91	21.2
56–65	11	88	80	9	8	7.27	9

Table 4: Number of executed tasks in different age groups. Columns are the same as in Table 3.

Table 5 shows general participation statistics across the four treatment groups. Differences in the number of times the application has been opened are significant ($p < 0.004$), thus suggesting an effect due different treatment groups. **Group 1 (PB, FA)** features the highest number of application opening *and* successful task executions, while **Group 3 (PB, WA)** has the lowest.

	Group 1	Group 2	Group 3	Group 4
Participation Statistics				
# Open	319	102	85	149
# Pass	40	3	0	3
# Submit	259	188	114	136
Participation Statistics per Task Type				
T1 % pass	0.3%	0.5%	0%	0%
T1 % submit	6%	5.8%	6.1%	7.9%
T2 % pass	13%	0.5%	0%	2.2%
T2 % submit	53.2%	49.7%	59.6%	54.7%
T3 % pass	0%	0.5%	0%	0%
T3 % submit	27.5%	43%	34.5%	35.2%

Table 5: Participation statistics per treatment groups and task type. *#Open*: Number of time that users open the app and receive a list of tasks. *#Pass*: Number of rejected tasks. *#Submit*: Number of executed tasks.

We observe no statistically significant difference between groups in terms of amount of successfully submitted tasks ($p > 0.496$). Therefore, we cannot prove a relevant effect of the treatment groups on the number of successful executions. The distribution of submitted tasks also does not vary is a statistically significant manner across task types (see bottom of Table 5). Interestingly, the popularity of task types is aligned with previous findings in crowdsourcing literature (*Annotation > Survey > Content Creation*) [18]. To understand if the usability of the user interface could have been a motivating factor for inactivity or abandonment, we ran a parallel experiment where we asked participants to complete a Standard Usability Survey (SUS) [11]. The participants of this parallel experiment were drawn from the same population, but none was enrolled in the main experiment. The average SUS score for *E-Crowd* was found to be 72.5 (between "good" and "excellent"). The result shows that the application user interface did not suffer from usability problems that would significantly affect results.

4.3.2 How do temporal distribution and activity awareness of notifications affect the participation in EMC campaigns? We first investigate the effect that the amount of notifications might have on participation. Based on previous work [23], we hypothesise a negative effect on both the interaction with the app, and with the amount of executed tasks. To test the hypothesis, we compare these figures averaging across users assigned to the PB, AB, FA, and WA configurations. Table 6 and Table 7 show the results. Users assigned to a **PB** configuration opened the app, on average, 1.6 times more than **AB** users. A Mann-Whitney test ($U = 514$, $p = 0.21$) shows that it is not possible to account this difference to varying temporal distributions. Users without activity awareness (**FA**) opened the application more often, but the average difference is not statistically significant (Mann-Whitney $U = 471.5, p = 0.11$). Differences in terms of number of executed tasks are minimal (Table 7) and not statistically significant across temporal distributions (**PB** vs. **AB**: Mann-Whitney, $U = 583.5, p = 0.16$). Such differences are instead greater (and statistically significant) across activity awareness configurations (**FA** vs. **WA**: Mann-Whitney U-test, $U = 662.5, p = 0.02$).

	#Open	#Em	μ_{op}	σ_{op}	Med_{op}
PB	397	35	11.34	26.09	4
AB	243	33	7.36	14.77	4
FA	419	38	11.02	25.12	4.5
WA	221	30	7.96	15.32	4

Table 6: App opening statistics. #*Open*: number of app opening. #*Em*: number of participants. μ_{op}, σ_{op}, Med_{op}: average, std.deviation, and median # of app opening per user.

	#Submit	#Em	μ_{ex}	σ_{ex}	Med_{ex}
PB	373	33	11.30	13.69	8
AB	324	31	10.45	12.66	6
FA	447	34	13.14	15.40	8
WA	250	30	8.33	9.50	5.5

Table 7: Task execution statistics . #*Submit*: number of submitted tasks. #*Em*: number of participants. μ_{op}, σ_{op}, Med_{op}: average, std.dev., and median # of app opening per user.

While we can't provide strong statistical evidence for our initial hypothesis, the result suggests that higher frequency of notifications (during planned break times) might be beneficial in terms of interaction with the applications, but not in terms of the amount of executed crowd work, which tends to be reduced. On the other hand, a reduction on the number of notifications due to activity awareness has negative effects on both interaction with the application and with the number of executed tasks.

4.3.3 How do temporal distribution and activity awareness of notifications affect user retention in EMC campaigns? We measure user retention curve by calculating the amount of users who executed exactly x (frequency of their executed tasks) tasks in total [24]. The steepness of the slope is an indicator of the level of user retention. In the light of the results obtained with user participation, we hypothesise that an excessive amount of notification might have a detrimental effect on users, which tend to abandon the application after just executing a few tasks.

Figure 5 shows the user retention curves across experimental configurations. In terms of number of interactions with the application, the rate of change of the **AB** configuration is double with respect to the **PB** configuration (**PB** $coeff = -0.079$, $intercept = 3.281$, **AB** $coeff = -0.18$, $intercept = 4.606$). The difference is even more pronounced when considering activity awareness (**FA** $coeff = -0.092$, $intercept = 3.282$, **WA** $coeff = -0.233$, $intercept = 4.75$). In terms of number of submitted tasks, the rate of change of the **AB** configuration is approximately 20% larger than the one of the **PB** configuration (**PB** $coeff = -0.027$, $intercept = 2.48$, **AB** $coeff = -0.35$, $intercept = 2.47$). The rate of the **WA** is, in absolute terms, the larger (**FA** $coeff = -0.022$, $intercept = 2.00$, **AB** $coeff = -0.41$, $intercept = 2.62$). The **AB** and **WA** configurations feature steeper slopes.

These trends are consistent with the results from the user participation analysis. The results supports our previous conclusion: a wrong amount of notifications (respectively, too many in the **AB** configuration, or too few in the **WA** configuration) can lead to a more "enthusiastic" initial participation, but could also cause a quicker *crowd out* effect.

4.3.4 How do temporal distribution and activity awareness of notifications affect task commitment in EMC campaigns? Task commitment is measured in terms of the amount of time dedicated to complete the execution of a task. Considering the previous results, we hypothesis commitment to also be affected by variations in notifications configuration. Table 8 shows the average task duration time. Results contradict our hypothesis, as that task commitment is not affected by the temporal distribution of notifications (**PB** vs. **AB**: Mann-Whitney U-test, $U = 492$, $p = 0.399$) nor by the presence of activity awareness functionalities. (**FA** vs. **WA**: Mann-Whitney U-test, $U = 437$, $p = 0.164$).

	μ	σ	$Median$
PB	50.45	24.05	40.33
AB	47.80	27.64	43.6
FA	48.44	29.62	39.7
WA	50.00	20.8	45.66

Table 8: Mean, standard deviation and median of response time (seconds) to complete tasks.

5 DISCUSSION

The survey (**RQ1**) provided a number of relevant insights. Results show that employees are not bothered by smartphone notifications, at least during popular breaks. Employees already have non-work related interactions with their smartphone during coffee breaks, while walking to lunch, walking to coffee breaks and while walking to a meeting room. Note that all these activities include walking. These results suggest that all these moments could be potentially suitable for crowd work execution, especially if the tasks to be executed are of short duration: employees declared a preference for short tasks, with the duration of up to two minutes. The nature of the task is also of importance: *learning*, *purpose*, and *well-being* appear to be the most compelling reason for participation.

Answering **RQ1** informed the design of an experiment that accounted for the preferences of the targeted population. We studied notification strategies on mobile phones as a mean to pro-actively invite employees at strategic times (**RQ2**). The strategies addressed in this work had no significant effect in terms of commitment (i.e. average amount of time spent executing each task), thus providing additional evidences of the general positive attitude of employees towards the crowd work, once engaged with it. Strategies were instead influential for participation and retention: frequent notifications lead to lower retention and task executions. The result suggests that, in EMC, an excessive amount of notification can facility the feared "crowd-out" effect.

The presence of activity-awareness functionalities resulted in significantly lower participation and retention. This is an interesting result, that contrasts with the outcome of the survey. It is possible to hypothesise that the presence of notifications on the mobile device (e.g. after returning from a break, if the device has been left on the desk) is more important than their real-time detection. The hypothesis is consistent with recent findings [22] that show how (in the context of situational crowdsourcing) small changes in notification timing can have a significant effect on individual participation and actions. The verification of this hypothesis in the context of EMC is left to future work.

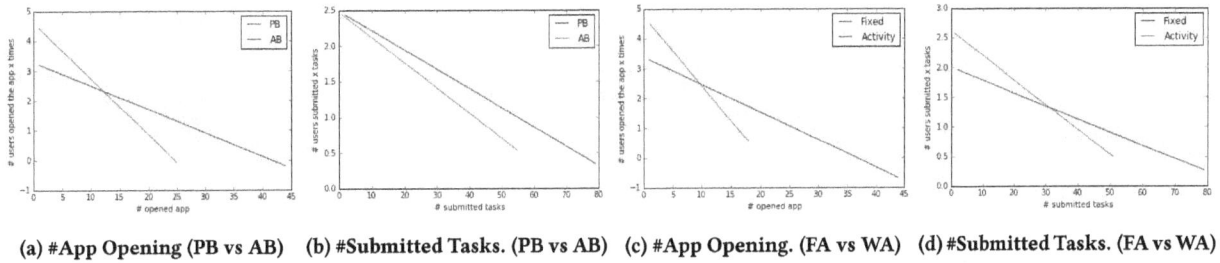

(a) #App Opening (PB vs AB)   (b) #Submitted Tasks. (PB vs AB)   (c) #App Opening. (FA vs WA)   (d) #Submitted Tasks. (FA vs WA)

Figure 5: User retention curves for number of app openings and number of submitted tasks.

Regardless of treatment groups and strategies, a larger number of tasks were executed between 9:00AM to 10:59AM comparing to other time slots. This shows that users are more willing to execute tasks in the morning. This result is in line with the survey results. The experimental observation interval had a duration of 4 weeks, i.e. 22 working days. Considering all active users, the average amount of execution per user is 10.4 during 22 days, meaning 0.47 task per day. This average result can be considered satisfactory, given the adopted advertisement and recruitment strategy. However, it is not in line with the outcome of the survey. Due to the anonymity of participants, we cannot exclude that external factors (e.g. pressing deadlines) could have affected participation.

Despite notifications being blocked outside office hours, 30% of all executions were performed during time slots that could be considered as belonging to employees' "free" time. This is an interesting result, that we further investigated with informal interviews conducted (at the end of the experimental period) with employees that decided to disclose their identity. These participants revealed that they were indeed interested in contributing to the objectives of the tasks offered by *E-Crowd*, but that they only had time to use the app during weekends, and outside office hours. These interviews provide evidence that, when properly motivated, EMC can connect employees with relevant tasks also during their free time.

Threats to validity. To minimise internal validity threats, we considered issues such as *history, selection, instrumentation* and *maturation* [13]. The *history* effect is concerned with the possibility that participants discuss the tasks among themselves, or find out about their special treatment group. Such an effect cannot be ruled out, but its impact is minimised as all treatment groups were similarly affected. *Selection* threat was addressed by randomly assigning participants to treatment groups. Moreover, the demographic distribution of participants in both the survey and the experiment resembled the one of the company. The limitation to participants operating an iOS device could have introduced a selection bias that we cannot rule out. The *instrumentation* threat was addressed by using the same procedure to measure the dependent variables for all the treatment groups. By relying on activity awareness functionalities that are built-in iOS devices, we minimised the likelihood of measurement errors due to implementation issues. To account for the *maturation* threat, we randomly created task lists for each participants, and considered only the first month of the contributions for all treatment groups.

Based on the above discussion, we believe the results provided in this work to be valid contributions.

6 CONCLUSION

Our research aims at better understanding the opportunities and limitations with the application of a mobile crowdsourcing paradigm in the enterprise environment. In this paper, we have presented the results of a survey and an experiment conducted in *IBM Netherlands*. Being the first experiment of this kind performed in an enterprise environment, the results are intrinsically important and novel.

The survey provided novel insights about: 1) the time slots (e.g. breaks) and context (e.g. while walking) when employees are more likely to interact with their mobile devices and perform crowd work; and 2) the type of crowd work that employees would be willing to perform during a working day. The results of our survey confirm the result of other exploratory studies performed in other environments and companies, but give additional insights on the types and duration of tasks preferred by employees.

A novel enterprise mobile crowdsourcing platform (E-Crowd) enabled the implementation of notification strategies with varying temporal distribution and activity awareness. The platform allowed for the execution of an experiment that involved 83 employees. We found that timely notifications can foster participation and retention. We found significant differences among treatment groups in terms of participation and retention. The outcome of the experiment is in contrast with the survey results, as activity awareness lead to lower participation and retention.

Future Work. This work provides plenty of inspirations for future research directions. We plan to further investigate the potential benefit that *learning* tasks could provide in terms of user engagement and retainment. Applications such as DuoLingo [33] clearly demonstrated that significant crowdsourcing results can be obtained when the incentives of the user and the one of the company align.

As 30% of all executions were voluntarily performed outside office hours, we are interested in understanding the potential for EMC when employees are not at work. The research will necessarily address ethical concerns about whether organisations should be allowed to enable EMC outside working hours, thus invading employees' private time. It will be interesting to assess the benefits, in terms of amount and quality of work, of EMC tasks performed outside office hours. Other relevant directions include the development and testing of personalised task notification strategies, and the potential benefits deriving from the adoption of incentive schemes based on gamification techniques.

REFERENCES

[1] Piotr D. Adamczyk and Brian P. Bailey. 2004. If Not Now, when?: The Effects of Interruption at Different Moments Within Task Execution. In *Proceedings of the SIGCHI Conference on Human Factors in Computing Systems (CHI '04)*. ACM, New York, NY, USA, 271–278. DOI:http://dx.doi.org/10.1145/985692.985727

[2] Florian Alt, Alireza Sahami Shirazi, Albrecht Schmidt, Urs Kramer, and Zahid Nawaz. 2010. Location-based crowdsourcing: extending crowdsourcing to the real world. In *Proceedings of the 6th Nordic Conference on Human-Computer Interaction: Extending Boundaries*. ACM, 13–22.

[3] Anupriya Ankolekar, Filippo Balestrieri, and Sitaram Asur. 2016. MET: An Enterprise Market for Tasks. In *Proceedings of the 19th ACM Conference on Computer Supported Cooperative Work and Social Computing Companion (CSCW '16 Companion)*. ACM, New York, NY, USA, 225–228. DOI:http://dx.doi.org/10.1145/2818052.2869113

[4] Anupriya Ankolekar, Filippo Balestrieri, and Sitaram Asur. 2016. MET: An Enterprise Market for Tasks. In *Proceedings of the 19th ACM Conference on Computer Supported Cooperative Work and Social Computing Companion*. ACM, 225–228.

[5] Obinna Anya. 2015. Bridge the Gap!: What Can Work Design in Crowdwork Learn from Work Design Theories?. In *Proceedings of the 18th ACM Conference on Computer Supported Cooperative Work & Social Computing (CSCW '15)*. ACM, New York, NY, USA, 612–627. DOI:http://dx.doi.org/10.1145/2675133.2675227

[6] Brian P Bailey and Joseph A Konstan. 2006. On the need for attention-aware systems: Measuring effects of interruption on task performance, error rate, and affective state. *Computers in human behavior* 22, 4 (2006), 685–708.

[7] Osvald M Bjelland and Robert Chapman Wood. 2008. An inside view of IBM's' Innovation Jam'. *MIT Sloan management review* 50, 1 (2008), 32.

[8] Alessandro Bozzon, Marco Brambilla, Stefano Ceri, Andrea Mauri, and Riccardo Volonterio. 2014. *Pattern-Based Specification of Crowdsourcing Applications*. Springer International Publishing, Cham, 218–235. DOI:http://dx.doi.org/10.1007/978-3-319-08245-5_13

[9] Alessandro Bozzon, Ilio Catallo, Eleonora Ciceri, Piero Fraternali, Davide Martinenghi, and Marco Tagliasacchi. 2012. A Framework for Crowdsourced Multimedia Processing and Querying. In *CrowdSearch 2012 workshop at WWW 2012*, ceur ws (Ed.), Vol. 842. 42–47. http://ceur-ws.org/Vol-842/crowdsearch-bozzon.pdf

[10] Alessandro Bozzon, Piero Fraternali, Luca Galli, and Roula Karam. 2014. Modeling crowdsourcing scenarios in socially-enabled human computation applications. *Journal on Data Semantics* 3, 3 (2014), 169–188. http://dx.doi.org/10.1007/s13740-013-0032-2

[11] John Brooke and others. 1996. SUS-A quick and dirty usability scale. *Usability evaluation in industry* 189, 194 (1996), 4–7.

[12] Melissa Cefkin, Obinna Anya, Steve Dill, Robert Moore, Susan Stucky, and Osariemo Omokaro. 2014. Back to the Future of Organizational Work: Crowdsourcing and Digital Work Marketplaces. In *Proceedings of the Companion Publication of the 17th ACM Conference on Computer Supported Cooperative Work & Social Computing (CSCW Companion '14)*. ACM, New York, NY, USA, 313–316. DOI:http://dx.doi.org/10.1145/2556420.2558858

[13] Thomas D Cook, Donald Thomas Campbell, and Arles Day. 1979. *Quasi-experimentation: Design & analysis issues for field settings*. Vol. 351. Houghton Mifflin Boston.

[14] Mary Czerwinski, Ed Cutrell, and Eric Horvitz. 2000. Instant Messaging: Effects of Relevance and Timing. In *People and Computers XIV: Proceedings of HCI 2000*, Vol. 2. 71–76. https://www.microsoft.com/en-us/research/publication/instant-messaging-effects-of-relevance-and-timing/

[15] Vincenzo Della Mea, Eddy Maddalena, and Stefano Mizzaro. 2015. Mobile crowdsourcing: four experiments on platforms and tasks. *Distributed and Parallel Databases* 33, 1 (2015), 123–141. DOI:http://dx.doi.org/10.1007/s10619-014-7162-x

[16] Stephen Dill, Robert Kern, Erika Flint, and Melissa Cefkin. 2013. The Work Exchange: Peer-to-Peer Enterprise Crowdsourcing.. In *HCOMP (Works in Progress / Demos) (AAAI Workshops)*, Vol. WS-13-18. AAAI. http://dblp.uni-trier.de/db/conf/hcomp/hcomp2013w.html#DillKFC13a

[17] Johann Füller, Katja Hutter, and Mirijam Fries. 2012. Crowdsourcing for Goodness Sake: Impact of Incentive Preference on Contribution Behavior for Social Innovation. *Adv Int Market* 23 (2012), 137–159.

[18] Ujwal Gadiraju, Ricardo Kawase, and Stefan Dietze. 2014. A Taxonomy of Microtasks on the Web. In *Proceedings of the 25th ACM Conference on Hypertext and Social Media (HT '14)*. ACM, New York, NY, USA, 218–223. DOI:http://dx.doi.org/10.1145/2631775.2631819

[19] Jorge Goncalves, Simo Hosio, Vassilis Kostakos, Maja Vukovic, and Shin'ichi Konomi. 2015. Workshop on Mobile and Situated Crowdsourcing. In *Adjunct Proceedings of the 2015 ACM International Joint Conference on Pervasive and Ubiquitous Computing and Proceedings of the 2015 ACM International Symposium on Wearable Computers (UbiComp/ISWC'15 Adjunct)*. ACM, New York, NY, USA, 1339–1342. DOI:http://dx.doi.org/10.1145/2800835.2800966

[20] Ido Guy, Anat Hashavit, and Yaniv Corem. 2015. Games for crowds: A crowdsourcing game platform for the enterprise. In *Proceedings of the 18th ACM Conference on Computer Supported Cooperative Work & Social Computing*. ACM, 1860–1871.

[21] Jiyin He, Kai Kunze, Christoph Lofi, SanjayK. Madria, and Stephan Sigg. 2014. Towards Mobile Sensor-Aware Crowdsourcing: Architecture, Opportunities and Challenges. In *Database Systems for Advanced Applications*, Wook-Shin Han, Mong Li Lee, Agus Muliantara, Ngurah Agus Sanjaya, Bernhard Thalheim, and Shuigeng Zhou (Eds.). Lecture Notes in Computer Science, Vol. 8505. Springer Berlin Heidelberg, 403–412. DOI:http://dx.doi.org/10.1007/978-3-662-43984-5_31

[22] Yongsung Kim, Emily Harburg, Shana Azria, Aaron Shaw, Elizabeth Gerber, Darren Gergle, and Haoqi Zhang. 2016. Studying the Effects of Task Notification Policies on Participation and Outcomes in On-the-go Crowdsourcing. In *Proceedings of the Fourth AAAI Conference on Human Computation and Crowdsourcing, HCOMP 2016*.

[23] Vlaho Kostov, Takashi Tajima, Eiichi Naito, and Jun Ozawa. 2006. Analysis of appropriate timing for information notification based on indoor user's location transition. In *Pervasive Computing and Communications, 2006. PerCom 2006. Fourth Annual IEEE International Conference on*. IEEE, 6–pp.

[24] Edith Law and Luis Von Ahn. 2009. Input-agreement: a new mechanism for collecting data using human computation games. In *Proceedings of the SIGCHI Conference on Human Factors in Computing Systems*. ACM, 1197–1206.

[25] Tadashi Okoshi, Julian Ramos, Hiroki Nozaki, Jin Nakazawa, Anind K. Dey, and Hideyuki Tokuda. 2015. Reducing Users' Perceived Mental Effort Due to Interruptive Notifications in Multi-device Mobile Environments. In *Proceedings of the 2015 ACM International Joint Conference on Pervasive and Ubiquitous Computing (UbiComp '15)*. ACM, New York, NY, USA, 475–486. DOI:http://dx.doi.org/10.1145/2750858.2807517

[26] S. Rosen, Sung-Ju Lee, Jeongkeun Lee, P. Congdon, Z.M. Mao, and K. Burden. 2014. MCNet: Crowdsourcing wireless performance measurements through the eyes of mobile devices. *Communications Magazine, IEEE* 52, 10 (October 2014), 86–91. DOI:http://dx.doi.org/10.1109/MCOM.2014.6917407

[27] John P Rula, Vishnu Navda, Fabián E Bustamante, Ranjita Bhagwan, and Saikat Guha. 2014. No one-size fits all: Towards a principled approach for incentives in mobile crowdsourcing. In *Proceedings of the 15th Workshop on Mobile Computing Systems and Applications*. ACM, 3.

[28] Ada Scupola and Hanne Westh Nicolajsen. 2014. The impact of enterprise crowdsourcing on company innovation culture: The case of an engineering consultancy. In *Nordic Contributions in IS Research*. Springer, 105–120.

[29] Robert-Jan Sips, Alessandro Bozzon, Gerard Smit, and Geert-Jan Houben. 2015. *Engineering the Web in the Big Data Era: 15th International Conference, ICWE 2015, Rotterdam, The Netherlands, June 23-26, 2015, Proceedings*. Springer International Publishing, Cham, Chapter The Inclusive Enterprise: Vision and Roadmap, 621–624. DOI:http://dx.doi.org/10.1007/978-3-319-19890-3_43

[30] Laurentiu Catalin Stanculescu, Alessandro Bozzon, Robert-Jan Sips, and Geert-Jan Houben. 2016. Work and Play: An Experiment in Enterprise Gamification. In *Proceedings of the 19th ACM Conference on Computer-Supported Cooperative Work & Social Computing, CSCW 2016, San Francisco, CA, USA, February 27 - March 2, 2016*. 345–357. DOI:http://dx.doi.org/10.1145/2818048.2820061

[31] Rannie Teodoro, Pinar Ozturk, Mor Naaman, Winter Mason, and Janne Lindqvist. 2014. The Motivations and Experiences of the On-demand Mobile Workforce. In *Proceedings of the 17th ACM Conference on Computer Supported Cooperative Work & Social Computing (CSCW '14)*. ACM, New York, NY, USA, 236–247. DOI:http://dx.doi.org/10.1145/2531602.2531680

[32] Liam D. Turner, Stuart M. Allen, and Roger M. Whitaker. 2015. Interruptibility Prediction for Ubiquitous Systems: Conventions and New Directions from a Growing Field. In *Proceedings of the 2015 ACM International Joint Conference on Pervasive and Ubiquitous Computing (UbiComp '15)*. ACM, New York, NY, USA, 801–812. DOI:http://dx.doi.org/10.1145/2750858.2807514

[33] Luis von Ahn. 2013. Duolingo: Learn a Language for Free While Helping to Translate the Web. In *Proceedings of the 2013 International Conference on Intelligent User Interfaces (IUI '13)*. ACM, New York, NY, USA, 1–2. DOI:http://dx.doi.org/10.1145/2449396.2449398

[34] M. Vukovic. 2009. Crowdsourcing for Enterprises. In *2009 Congress on Services - I*. 686–692. DOI:http://dx.doi.org/10.1109/SERVICES-I.2009.56

[35] Maja Vukovic and Claudio Bartolini. 2010. Towards a research agenda for enterprise crowdsourcing. In *Proceedings of the 4th International Conference on Leveraging Applications of Formal Methods, Verification, and Validation - Volume Part I (ISoLA'10)*. Springer, Berlin, Heidelberg, 425–434. http://dl.acm.org/citation.cfm?id=1939281.1939323

[36] Jie Yang, Alessandro Bozzon, and Geert-Jan Houben. 2015. Harnessing Engagement for Knowledge Creation Acceleration in Collaborative Q&A Systems. In *User Modeling, Adaptation and Personalization: 23rd International Conference, UMAP 2015, Dublin, Ireland, June 29 – July 3, 2015. Proceedings*, Francesco Ricci, Kalina Bontcheva, Owen Conlan, and Séamus Lawless (Eds.). Springer International Publishing, Cham, 315–327. DOI:http://dx.doi.org/10.1007/978-3-319-20267-9_26

Long and Short-Term Recommendations with Recurrent Neural Networks

Robin Devooght
IRIDIA, Université Libre de Bruxelles
1050, Brussels, Belgium
robin.devooght@ulb.ac.be

Hugues Bersini
IRIDIA, Université Libre de Bruxelles
1050, Brussels, Belgium
bersini@ulb.ac.be

ABSTRACT

Recurrent neural networks have recently been successfully applied to the session-based recommendation problem, and is part of a growing interest for collaborative filtering based on sequence prediction. This new approach to recommendations reveals an aspect that was previously overlooked: the difference between short-term and long-term recommendations. In this work we characterize the full short-term/long-term profile of many collaborative filtering methods, and we show how recurrent neural networks can be steered towards better short or long-term predictions. We also show that RNNs are not only adapted to session-based collaborative filtering, but are perfectly suited for collaborative filtering on dense datasets where it outperforms traditional item recommendation algorithms.

KEYWORDS

Collaborative Filtering; Recommender Systems; Recurrent Neural Network; Sequence Prediction

1 INTRODUCTION

Collaborative filtering methods most often consider the user as a static entity whose interests are fixed in time. Matrix factorization for example uses all the ratings (or implicit feedback) of a user to build a representation of its general tastes, oblivious to the possible evolution of taste or fading interests of the user. Some, like time-SVD++, incorporate the timestamp of ratings in order to improve ratings prediction [12], but the use of the sequential nature of interactions between users and items has been poorly studied.

Recently however some methods have started to frame the item recommendation problem of collaborative filtering as a sequence prediction problem [8, 9, 20]: given that the user consumed this item, then this one, etc. which item will he consume next ? The motivation for those works comes from the nature of the data: they either tackle datasets with a

very large number of users but extremely sparse information about those users [8] or session-based dataset where users are only identified for the time of a session, and recommendations must therefore be based only on the last few clicks of the user[9, 20]. In both cases it is not realistic to build a model for every users, and they instead take the approach of directly recommending items based on the few past interactions of the user. The use of sequence information allowed to compensate for the scarcity of recorded interactions between users and items.

In the first part of our paper we show that methods based on sequence prediction (and especially recurrent neural networks) are similarly powerful on dense datasets. The sequence of actions of the user holds indeed a lot of information: it can reveal the evolution of a user's taste, it might help to identify which items became irrelevant with regards to the current user's interests, or which items make part of a vanishing interest.

This paper then highlights an aspect of recommender systems that was previously overlooked but is revealed by the sequence prediction approach: the difference between short-term and long-term predictions. Long term predictions aim to identify which items the user will consume *eventually*, without regards for when exactly he will consume them, while short-term predictions should accurately predict the immediate behavior of the user: what he will consume *soon*, and in the extreme case, what he will consume *next*. In the static setting, this distinction does not make sense because the order of items is ignored (both during training and testing), but in the sequence-based approach this distinction is evident because sequence prediction algorithms are specifically design to predict *the next* item, which make them especially good at short-term predictions, sometimes at the cost of worse long-term predictions.

Some applications are more oriented towards short-term predictions while others aim to make good long-term predictions (e.g. recommending the next song in a playlist versus recommending a book based on everything that the user has read). We study in details this short-term/long-term aspect of recommendation systems and make the following contributions:

- We introduce a practical visualization of the short-term/long-term profile of any recommender system and use it to compare several algorithms.
- We show how to modify the RNN to find a good trade-off between long and short-term predictions.

- We explore the relationship between short-term predictions and diversity.

Our code is available at https://github.com/rdevooght/ sequence-based-recommendations, and our data, with the precise training/validation/test splits used in the experiments, is available at http://iridia.ulb.ac.be/~rdevooght/rnn_cf_ data.zip.

2 RELATED WORK

Some early works have framed collaborative filtering as a sequence prediction problem and used simple Markov chain methods to solve it. In the early 2000s, Zimdars et al. tested a Markov model for web-page recommendation[21]. Mobasher et al. adopted a similar approach, using sequential pattern mining[15]. Both showed the superiority of methods based on sequence over nearest-neighbors approaches. In [2, 18], Brafman et al. defended the view of recommendation systems as a Markov decision process, and although the predictive model was not their main focus, they did present in [18] a Markov chain approach, improved by some heuristics such as skipping and clustering.

The community then has gradually lost interest in the sequence prediction approach, with the only major work in many years being FPMC[17], which combines the matrix factorization of the user-item matrix with Markov chains, and is still considered to be the state-of-the-art in sequence-based recommendations.

Recently however, several papers have explored sequence-based recommendation, mostly motivated by the need to produce recommendations without building a user model[8, 9, 20]. Hidasi et al. has applied gated RNN to session based collaborative filtering using two objective functions, BPR (from [16]) and the newly formulated TOP1[9]. Tan et al. then improved on those results through data manipulation and variation in the training methods[20].

It is also worth noting that Spotify might have been using it as far back as 2014 [1] to build playlists. They however do not seem to be using gated RNN, and they are using a hierachical softmax output in order to deal with the very large number of items (they have much more songs than netflix or movielens have movies).

He and McAuley took another approach with Fossil[8], an algorithm similar in spirit to FPMC, but instead of factorizing the user-item matrix, they take inspiration from the item-similarity based approaches[11] and factorize the item-item matrix.

Guàrdia-Sebaoun et al. used word2vec (a well-known unsupervised word embedding algorithm [14]) to build a representation of the item based on sequences[7]. They then model the users as a transition vector between item representations and used it to predict the next items in the sequence[1].

---

[1]We tried it on our datasets but the results were very poor. Our implementation of the method is available with the rest of our code.

Table 1: Dataset descriptions. For Movielens and Netflix each sequence represents a user, while in RSC15 they represent sessions.

Dataset	#sequences	#items	#interactions
Movielens	6040	3706	1,000,209
Netflix	480,189	17,770	100,480,507
RSC15	7,981,581	37,486	31,708,505

3 COLLABORATIVE FILTERING WITH RNN

The idea of using recurrent neural networks for collaborative filtering is a recent one, and they have not yet been thoroughly tested on dense datasets. In the following we compare the RNN with multiple state-of-the-art collaborative filtering algorithm and show that they perform well on dense and sparse datasets.

We use n and m to represent the number of users and items in the dataset. $\mathcal{S}_u$ represents the sequence of items with which user u interacted.

3.1 Datasets

We use three datasets whose characteristics are shown in Table 1. **Movielens** and **Netflix** are well-known datasets recording the ratings of users on a catalog of movies. Because the timestamp of each rating is available, it is possible to construct for each user the sequence of movies he rated. It is worth precising that we do not use the values of the ratings in any way, we are only trying to predict which movie a user will rate, based on what he rated before.

The **RecSys'15 Challenge** (RSC15) dataset is a collection of navigation sessions on an e-commerce website and it differs from the two movie datasets in many ways. First of all, its sequential nature is much more evident and concerns much shorter time scales. The sequences do not represent users, but only short navigation sessions, which means that long sequences are much less frequent (the median length of a sequence is 3 in RSC15 against 96 in Movielens). The much larger number of sequences and their relative shortness makes it less practical and less pertinent to use methods based matrix factorization, that would need to build a representation for each session.

Each set is divided into training, validation and test subsets: N randomly chosen users and all their ratings to constitute the test set, N others to constitute the validation set and all the remaining users for the training set. We used $N = 500$ for Movielens 1M, $N = 1000$ for Netflix and $N = 10k$ for RSC15.

In Movielens and Netflix, any item can appear only once in the rating history of any user, and we helped all the methods on those datasets by forcing them to recommend items that the user had not yet seen.

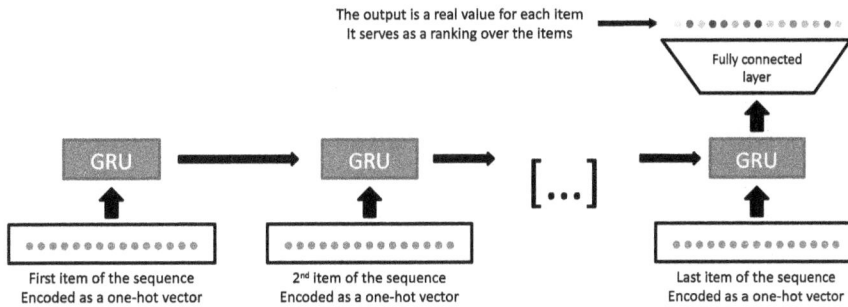

Figure 1: Schematic representation of the RNN.

3.2 Recurrent neural networks

Recurrent neural networks (RNN) are commonly used for language modeling, where they are trained to learn sequences of words [13]. We take a similar approach by considering each item as a word, the catalog of items as the full vocabulary, and the history of each user as a sample sequence. The RNN runs through the sequence of items consumed by a user, item by item, as depicted in Figure 1. At each time step, the input is the one-hot encoding of the current item, and the final output is a fully-connect layer with a neuron for each item in the catalog. The k items whose neurons are activated the most are used as the k recommendations.

The state-of-the-art in recurrent neural networks is what are called "gated" RNNs, where the internal state of the RNN is controlled by one or more small neural networks called gates, with the most common architectures being the LSTM[10] and the GRU[3]. In the following we used the GRU for easier comparison with other works[9, 20], but the LSTM works just as well.

A major aspect of the RNN is the choice of an appropriate objective function. In the following experiments we compare two different objective functions[2].

Categorical cross-entropy (CCE), the most common loss in language modeling. It is defined as $\text{CCE}(\mathbf{o}, i) = \log(\text{softmax}(\mathbf{o})_i)$ where $\mathbf{o}$ is the output vector of the RNN and i is the correct item. A major problem of CCE is that its complexity is linear in the number of items (because of the computation of the softmax) which can be very expensive in application with large catalog.

Hinge is an objective function that is based on the objective function of SVMs. Unlike CCE, it does not depend on the comparison of outputs between items, but on the independent comparison of the output of each item against a fixed threshold. We define it as follows: $\text{Hinge}(\mathbf{o}, i) = \sum_{j \in \mathcal{C}} \max(0, 1 - o_j) - \gamma \sum_{j \in \mathcal{F}} \max(0, o_j)$, where $\mathcal{C}$ is the set of good recommendations, $\mathcal{F}$ is the set of bad recommendations and γ is a factor used to balance the influence of the error on the correct item and the error on the much more numerous incorrect items. In the following, $\mathcal{C}$ contains only

the next item in the sequence, and $\mathcal{F}$ contains all the other items. Because γ is difficult to choose intuitively, we use instead $\beta = \gamma |\mathcal{F}| / |\mathcal{C}|$. β is easier to interpret: $\beta = 1$ means that correct and incorrect items have the same weight on the objective function, $\beta = 2$ means that the incorrect items weight twice as much, etc. The Hinge objective function is as expensive to compute as the CCE, but its interest relies in the fact that it can be used to define several items as being correct (see Section 5.3).

3.2.1 Training Procedure. We used the standard mini-batch stochastic gradient descent method (see e.g. [6, Section 8.1.3]). A training instance is produced by randomly cutting the sequence of a user's interactions into two parts; the first part is fed to the RNN, and the first item of the second part is used as the correct item in the computation of the objective function. The training consists of looping over the users, and for each user generating b training instances (or less if the length of the sequence is less than b) that are used as a mini-batch. We used $b = 16$ in our experiments.

3.2.2 Parameters. In the following experiments we arbitrarily set the size of the GRU cell to $k = 50$. We used the Adagrad learning scheduler[4]. The learning rate (l), the β parameter of Hinge are tuned on the validation set of Movielens. RNNs are usually trained on sequences up to a certain length, and the maximum length (M_l) is a difficult parameter to choose: longer length means potentially more informed prediction, but it also significantly increases the training time. We arbitrarily set $M_l = 30$ after observing its influence on training time and recommendation quality on the Movielens validation set. Our implementation is based on the Lasagne framework for Theano[3], and parameters that were not mentioned are kept to Lasagne defaults.

3.3 Competing Methods

We compare the RNN with two static methods of top-N recommendation: one based on nearest neighbors and one on matrix factorization. We also compare the RNN with a simple Markov chain that can be seen as a baseline for the sequence prediction approach, and with FPMC [17] and Fossil [8], the state-of-the-art for recommendations based on

---

[2]Objective functions are often paired with a specific choice of non-linearity on the last layer, like softmax and CCE. We chose to consider the last layer without non-linearity and to incorporate the non-linearity in the definition of the objective function.

[3]See http://lasagne.readthedocs.io and http://www.deeplearning.net/software/theano/

sequences. Finally, POP is the baseline that always rank items according to their frequency in the training set.

3.3.1 User-Based Nearest Neighbors.
User-based nearest neighbors or user KNN is one of the oldest method of collaborative filtering, yet still a strong baseline for top-N recommendation. A score s_{ij} is computed between a user i and an item j:

$$s_{ij} = \sum_{u \in \mathcal{N}_k(i)} c_{iu} \mathbb{1}(j \in \mathcal{S}_u) \qquad (1)$$

Where c_{iu} is the similarity between users i and u, $\mathcal{N}_k(i)$ is the set k users closest to i according to the similarity measure c, and $\mathbb{1}(j \in \mathcal{S}_u)$ is the indicator function that evaluates to 1 if item j belongs to the sequence of items of user u, or else evaluates to 0. We used the cosine similarity measure, which is usually preferred for item recommendation:

$$c_{iu} = |\mathcal{S}_i \cap \mathcal{S}_u| / \sqrt{|\mathcal{S}_i||\mathcal{S}_u|} \qquad (2)$$

The size of the neighborhood (k) was tuned on the Movielens validation set.

3.3.2 BPR-MF.
BPR-MF is a state-of-the-art matrix factorization method for top-N recommendation devised by [16] and based on the BPR ranking loss. We used the original implementation of BPR-MF, available in the MyMediaLite framework [5]. BPR-MF has many parameters; we tuned the number of features (k) ourselves and kept the default values of MyMediaLite for the others.

3.3.3 Markov Chain.
In this simple method, the users' behavior is modeled by a Markov chain whose states are the different items. The transition probabilities between items are inferred from the transition frequencies observed in the training set. At any time the state of a user corresponds to the last item that he consumed, and the recommendations for that user will be the k items with the highest transition probabilities from that state. In other words, if the last item consumed by a user is the item j, the k first recommendations of the Markov model will be the k items that followed most often the item j in the sequences coming from other users. This is equivalent to a bigram model in language modeling in which the words become the items.

3.3.4 FPMC.
FPMC combines traditional factorization method and factorized Markov chains[17]. Factorized Markov chains are a way to estimate transition probabilities from sparse data by factorizing the transition matrix (i.e. the matrix whose element i, j is the transition probability between items i and j). FPMC factorizes two matrices simultaneously: the user-item matrix and the transition matrix, using a BPR-like loss. For a given user and a given item, the predictions are simply made by summing the similarity based on the user-item matrix factorization and based on the transition matrix factorization.

The main parameters of FPMC are the rank k of the factorizations (in principle one could use a different rank for the user-item and transition matrix factorization, but we use the same), the initial learning rate l, the learning rate decay

Table 2: Parameters values used in the experiments. We tuned each method on the validation set of Movielens, then used the same parameters in all the experiments (except if specified otherwise). See methods description for the meaning of the parameters.

Method	parameters
RNN-CCE	$k = 50$, $l = 0.1$, $M_l = 30$
RNN-Hinge	$k = 50$, $l = 0.1$, $M_l = 30$, $\beta = 6$
UserKNN	$k = 80$
BPRMF	$k = 200$ for Movielens, $k = 100$ for Netflix
FPMC	$k = 100$, $l = 0.016$, $\alpha = 0.99$, $\lambda = 0.003$
Fossil	$k = 100$, $l = 0.02$, $\alpha = 0.97$, $\lambda = 0.0025$, $\beta = 0.5$

factor α (which multiplies the learning rate after each epoch) and the regularization λ.

3.3.5 Fossil.
Fossil[8] is inspired by FPMC and by FISM[11]: instead of factorizing the user-item matrix, it factorizes the item-item matrix. The predicted score of an item i, for a user u is:

$$s_{ui} = b_i + \frac{1}{|\mathcal{S}_u|^\beta} \sum_{j \in \mathcal{S}_u} <\mathbf{v}_j, \mathbf{h}_i> +(\eta + \eta_u) <\mathbf{v}_{\text{last}(\mathcal{S}_u)}, \mathbf{h}_i>$$
$$(3)$$

Where the vector of bias $\mathbf{b}$, the $m \times k$ matrices $\mathbf{V}$ and $\mathbf{H}$, the trade-off vector η and the trade-off bias η are the parameters learned by the model, β is an hyper-parameters, and last($\mathcal{S}_u$) is the last item with which the user interacted.

The trading procedure is similar to the one of FPMC, and the parameters are the same (k, l, α, and λ), with the addition of the β parameter.

3.4 Testing Procedure

For each user of the test set, the method can base its recommendations on the first half of the user's ratings and on the model previously built on the training set (or on the training set directly, in the case of the nearest neighbors methods). Those recommendations are evaluated against the second half of the user's rating, using the metrics described in Section 3.5. The metrics are then averaged over all test users. We use $\mathcal{S}_u^T$ to represent the second half of the ratings of user u.

BPR-MF, Fossil and FPMC can only produce recommendations to user that were in the training set (as they need to built a model for each user). For that reason, those methods are trained on a larger training set than the other methods, that includes the first half of the ratings of each of the test users. This is an unfair but unfortunately unavoidable advantage for those methods.

Since BPR-MF, FPMC, Fossil and RNNs produce stochastic models, table 3 gives the average and the standard deviation of the results over ten models.

3.5 Metrics

We compare the different methods through a range of metrics designed to capture various qualities of the recommendation systems. In the following metrics an item i is a "correct recommendation" for user u if and only if $i \in \mathcal{S}_u^t$.

- **Recall.** The usual metrics for top-N recommendation, defined as the number of correct recommendations divided by the number of unique items in $\mathcal{S}_u^t$.
- **sps.** The Short-term Prediction Success captures the ability of the method to predict the next item in the sequence. It is 1 if the next item (i.e. the first item of $\mathcal{S}_u^t$) is present in the recommendations, 0 else.
- **User coverage.** The fraction of users who received at least one correct recommendation. The average recall (and precision) hides the distribution of success among users. A high recall could still mean that many users do not receive any good recommendation. This metrics captures the generality of the method.
- **Item coverage.** The number of distinct items that were correctly recommended. It captures the capacity of the method to make diverse, successful, recommendations.
- **Blockbusters share.** The percentage of correct recommendations that are about items among the 1% most popular items in the dataset. This metric should be read knowing that the 1% most popular items constitute 8.8% of the interactions in Movielens, 22.4% in Netflix and 28.6% in RSC15.

All those metrics are computed "at 10", i.e. in a setting where the recommendation systems produces ten recommendations for each user.

3.6 Analysis

The results are shown in Table 3. The methods using the sequence information are impressively much better than the others in terms of sps. It is worth underlying the quality of those results: given ten trials (i.e. ten recommendations), the RNN-CCE is able to predict the next movie seen by 33% of the users of Movielens and 41% of the users of Netflix, while methods not based on the sequence are below 15%.

Interestingly, the methods with a high sps generally have a larger item coverage and recommend less often the most frequent items. This link between diversity of recommendation and short-term predictions will be explored in Section 6. In particular, the item coverage of the RNN-CCE is more than twice the one of the User KNN.

As a global observation, the RNN proves to be a very promising method for all considered metrics, not only on session-based datasets where it was tested by [9, 20], but also on dense datasets. It dominates the other methods in every aspects on the Movielens dataset and is only beaten in terms of recall by BPR-MF and User KNN on Netflix, where both methods rely heavily on the skewed distribution of the items frequency.

4 SHORT-TERM / LONG-TERM PROFILE

The experiments show that some methods can be good on short-term prediction (according to the sps) but bad on long-term predictions (according to the recall) and vice-versa. We

believe that this is an important characteristic to consider when adopting an algorithm for a real application. For example, online shops or music radio should probably favors short-term predictions as they need to capture the temporary interest of the user, while information websites and books recommender systems might be more interested in building deep understanding of their users' long term preferences. A finer representation of the short-term/long-term profile of recommendation methods is therefore useful.

Each recommendation method is producing a ranking over all the items in the catalog. Our approach is to measure the average rank of the N next items in the user sequence. As N increases, the average rank changes smoothly from a measure of short-term predictions to a measure of long-term predictions. For example, consider a user who interacted with $2q$ items in the following order: $x_1, x_2, \ldots, x_{2q}$. We use the algorithm of interest to produce a ranking $\mathbf{r}$ over all the items, based on the first half of the sequence (from x_1 to x_q), where r_i is the rank of item i (smaller rank being better). We then compute the average rank at N as: av-r@$N = \sum_{i=1}^{N} r_{x_{q+i}}/N$ for all $N \in 1, \ldots, q$. When av-r@N is average over all users in the test set, it offers a useful representation of the quality of an algorithm on the complete short-term/long-term spectrum[4].

Figure 2 shows the short-term/long-term profile of the different CF algorithms. The only method that performs evenly on short and long term is POP, which does not build a user model at all. As expected, the three methods based on sequence prediction (MC, RNN and FPMC) are much better on short-term prediction than on long-term ones, with this tendency being marked the most for RNN. Interestingly, User KNN is also better on short-term predictions than long-term ones. This reveals that the taste and interests of users do change over time, and that it is hard to predict the interest of a user in the far future.

User KNN is still better than RNN and FPMC for long-term prediction, and Figure 2 suggests that, on Movielens at least, it becomes an interesting option when it is important to make good predictions about actions more than 20 steps in the future. Although not shown here, the choice of the objective function of the RNN with Hinge loss as a similar short-term / long-term profile than RNN-CCE.

5 IMPROVING RNNS ON LONG-TERM PREDICTIONS

As we saw, RNNs are trained specifically to perform short-term predictions and can be outperformed by other methods in terms of long-term prediction. In this section we explore three ways to increase the performances of RNNs on long-term predictions, two based on manipulating the training set and one on changing the objective function. These approaches offer a practical tuning mechanism to trade some short-term

---

[4]It is important to notice the difference between this use of the "@N" notation from its more common usage in section 3: here N refers to the number of items that form the ground truth, while it generally refers to the number of recommendations that the algorithm is allowed to make.

Table 3: Comparison of top-N recommendation methods on Movielens 1M, Netflix and RSC15

| | Method | Metrics (@10) | | | | |
		sps (%)	Item coverage	User coverage (%)	rec (%)	Blockbusters share (%)
Movielens	POP	5.0	50	65.6	3.62	97.73
	BPR-MF	12.44 ± 1.26	388.50 ± 14.32	82.94 ± 1.27	5.58 ± 0.12	44.08 ± 1.43
	User KNN	14.40	277	80.8	6.31	50.36
	MC	29.20	518	77.0	4.90	16.47
	FPMC	28.10 ± 0.71	614.00 ± 10.32	82.94 ± 1.45	5.70 ± 0.13	14.26 ± 0.71
	Fossil	22.46 ± 1.67	556.40 ± 39.81	83.04 ± 0.61	6.32 ± 0.14	11.22 ± 1.98
	RNN-CCE	33.45 ± 1.17	669.75 ± 15.58	87.73 ± 0.98	7.52 ± 0.14	13.91 ± 0.28
	RNN-Hinge	30.91 ± 2.15	611.56 ± 45.52	88.40 ± 0.82	7.72 ± 0.17	16.40 ± 1.92
Netflix	POP	5.92	54	68.2	4.65	100
	BPR-MF	9.93 ± 0.70	591.60 ± 16.36	79.19 ± 0.71	6.88 ± 0.09	73.84 ± 1.32
	User KNN	13.04	383	80.84	8.49	79.86
	MC	32.50	594	64.50	3.17	53.02
	FPMC	26.38 ± 0.80	542.56 ± 6.87	70.98 ± 0.46	3.75 ± 0.08	64.53 ± 0.51
	Fossil	24.26 ± 0.64	852.78 ± 28.32	76.93 ± 0.77	5.17 ± 0.12	40.07 ± 1.78
	RNN-CCE	41.00 ± 0.99	845.88 ± 26.00	82.43 ± 0.48	6.37 ± 0.16	53.15 ± 1.39
	RNN-Hinge	32.28 ± 0.87	935.20 ± 38.23	78.92 ± 0.65	5.76 ± 0.24	39.29 ± 0.43
RSC15	POP	1.24	11	2.24	1.2	100
	MC	39.50	2945	46.55	32.76	33.33
	RNN-CCE	52.78 ± 0.08	3536.67 ± 4.99	59.34 ± 0.10	44.52 ± 0.06	33.14 ± 0.17
	RNN-Hinge	35.12 ± 0.27	2374.33 ± 21.93	43.18 ± 0.16	30.24 ± 0.23	33.76 ± 0.30

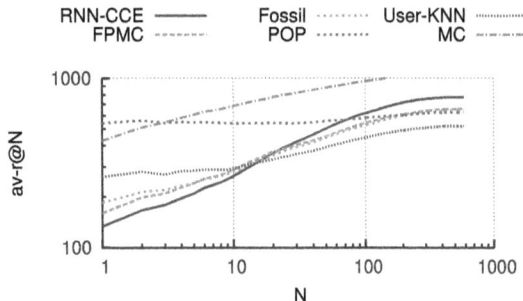

Figure 2: Short-term/long-term profile of RNN-CCE, User KNN, FPMC, Fossil, MC and POP on Movielens.

accuracy for more long-term accuracy, making the RNN a more versatile solution for collaborative filtering.

The three approaches explored in the following are to randomly alter the training sequences with either a dropout or a shuffling mechanism, or to train the RNN to predict the n next items (rather the *the* next one).

5.1 Dropout

The dropout mechanism is well known in deep learning. It consists in randomly deactivating some neurons during training in order to improve the robustness of the model [19]. Our concept of dropout is slightly different, and consists in randomly removing some items from a training sequence, before using it to train the RNN. More precisely, each time a user is drawn from the dataset, each of the items in its sequence of interactions is deleted with a probability p, and

that altered sequence is used to train the RNN. This means that the RNN is often trained to predict not the next item in the sequence, but actually the second or third next item.

Figure 3a shows the influence of the dropout probability on the sps and recall. As expected, when the dropout probability increases the long-term predictions improve while the short-term ones decline. It is nevertheless impressive that the recall still increases with very high (80%) dropout.

Interestingly, the models seem to be overall improved with small dropout probabilities, with both the sps and recall increasing, which suggest that, as observed in many other deep learning methods, a little bit of dropout is always helpful.

5.2 Shuffle Sequences

Our second approach is similar to dropout in spirit: the introduction of noise into the training sequences can affect short patterns more than long-term ones, and the resulting model will therefore be more attuned to those long-term patterns. Instead of dropout, the noise we use here is a slight shuffling of the training sequences. The difficulty is to shuffle in a way that will destroy very short patterns without completely loosing the sequential aspect of the data. Our solution is that each item in the sequence can be swapped with another item with a probability p, and it is swapped with the item in position $i + r$ in the sequence, where i is the position of the current item and r is a normally distributed offset: $r \sim round(N(0, \sigma))$.

Figure 3b shows the influence of the shuffle probability on the sps and recall, with $\sigma = 3$. The impact is smaller than with dropout, but nonetheless clear. With a shuffle

(a) Dropout

(b) Shuffling

(c) Multi-targets, hinge loss

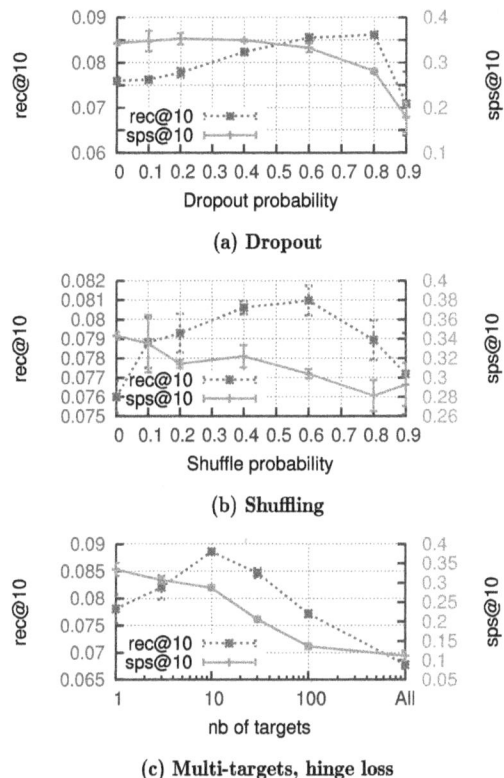

Figure 3: Influence of dropout, shuffle and multiple targets on short and long-term predictions on Movielens.

Figure 4: Impact of the different strategies to improve long-term recommendations on the short-term/long-term profile of RNNs on Netflix

Figure 3c shows the influence of t on the sps and recall on Movielens. When t increases, the sps decreases as expected, and the recall increases at first and then decreases. The fact that the recall decreases when the number of targets becomes too large might be due to the inability of the RNN to master an increasingly difficult problem. Indeed, the set of possible solutions dramatically increases when you go from predicting one item to predicting a hundred, and the training set might be too small to learn a good model.

5.4 Comparison of the Three Approaches

We compare the three strategies for improving long-term recommendations on Netflix. We fixed the dropout probability and the shuffle probability to 0.6 based on Figure 3a and 3b. We also tested the combination of dropout and shuffling. Table 4 shows the impact of the different strategies in terms of the metrics described in Section 3.5, and Figure 4 shows how those strategies affect the short-term/long-term profile of the methods.

Each strategy significantly improves the recall, with the combination of dropout and shuffling working the best. Although the User KNN still has a higher recall, the quality of its recommendations is questionable, as they are much less diverse than those of the RNNs. Interestingly, RNN-Hinge with 10 targets is much more diverse than the other methods (in terms of item coverage and blockbusters share), and although it is worse than RNN-CCE in terms of sps and recall, its high diversity might make it the preferred method.

6 SEQUENCE PREDICTION FAVORS DIVERSITY IN RECOMMENDATIONS

As observed in Section 3, methods with a high sps tend to also have more diverse recommendations (in terms of item coverage). We argue that this is because it is possible to produce high recall using only very frequent items, but reaching a high sps requires to use less frequent items. In other words, optimizing short-term predictions puts more pressure on the capacity of the model to produce diverse recommendations.

The reasoning is the following: the correct predictions in terms of sps are a subset of the correct predictions in terms

probability between 0.2 and 0.6 the recall is improved without decreasing much the sps.

5.3 Multiple Targets

The objective functions of RNNs are designed to build models good at short-term predictions. Indeed, CCE is comparing the output value of the true next item to other items, and pushing the model to give to the true next item a higher value than to the others. The hinge loss on the other hand does not work by comparing items between themselves, but by comparing the output value of each item against a fixed threshold. With the hinge loss, the recommendation problem is treated as m binary classification problem (one for each item) where the question is whether or not it should be recommended to the user. This allows to select multiple items as positive targets, as they are all treated independently, and it can be used to produce a loss function that favors long-term rather than short term predictions.

Many ways can be imagined to select which items should be positive or negative targets. In the following we used the t next items in the sequence as the positive items. If $t = 1$ it is equivalent to the experiments in Section 3, if $t = 10$ the RNN is trained to produce an output value higher than 1 for the 10 next items in the sequence, and lower than 0 for the other items.

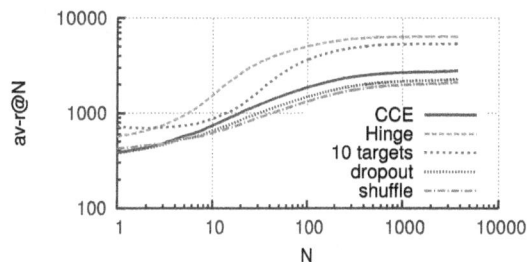

Table 4: Performances on Netflix of the RNN trained with dropout, shuffling or multiple targets. The results of the User KNN, RNN-CCE and RNN-Hinge where copied from Table 3 for easier comparison.

Method	Metrics (@10)				
	sps (%)	Item coverage	User coverage (%)	rec (%)	Blockbusters share (%)
User KNN	13.04	383	80.84	8.49	79.86
RNN-Hinge	32.28 ± 0.87	935.20 ± 38.23	78.92 ± 0.65	5.76 ± 0.24	39.29 ± 0.43
RNN-Hinge 10 targets	11.51 ± 0.48	1013.00 ± 7.07	83.05 ± 0.45	6.63 ± 0.05	24.57 ± 0.25
RNN-CCE	41.00 ± 0.99	845.88 ± 26.00	82.43 ± 0.48	6.37 ± 0.16	53.15 ± 1.39
RNN-CCE + dropout	38.01 ± 0.77	868.75 ± 6.94	83.38 ± 0.76	6.82 ± 0.09	52.29 ± 0.36
RNN-CCE + shuffle	33.77 ± 0.58	851.00 ± 13.06	85.19 ± 0.13	6.96 ± 0.12	54.58 ± 0.54
RNN-CCE + dropout & shuffle	32.76 ± 0.61	866.67 ± 8.01	85.02 ± 0.41	7.25 ± 0.05	53.32 ± 0.56

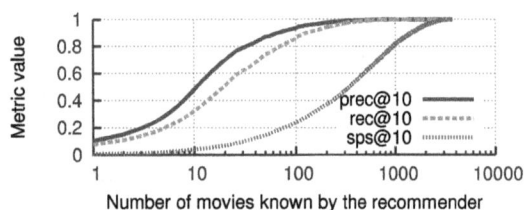

(a) Movielens 1M

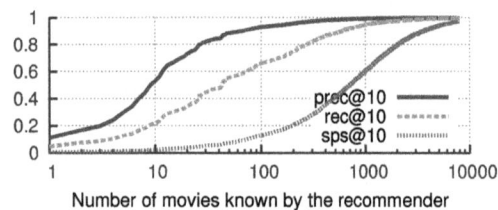

(b) Netflix

Figure 5: Evolution of the rec@10, prec@10 and sps@10 for a recommendation that can only recommend the top t most popular items. The maximum value of the rec@10 is actually much smaller than 1 but we normalized the recall here by dividing it by its maximum value to make the graph more readable.

of recall; because of that, any given item will be a correct prediction for more users in terms of long term predictions than in terms of short term predictions; the result is that it takes fewer items to make correct long term predictions for a given percentage of users than it takes to make correct short term predictions.

We illustrate that with a simple experiment. Consider an oracle (i.e. a perfect recommendation system) that can only recommend items within the t most popular ones; Figure 5 shows how the rec@10, prec@10 and sps@10 increase as t increases on two real datasets[5]. The rec@10 and prec@10 converge very fast, they reach 80% of their maximum value with a small fraction of the items, and each new item brings

---

[5]prec@10 stands for "precision at 10" which is defined as the fraction of correct recommendations in the first 10 recommendations made by the algorithm.

only a marginal improvement. The sps@10 on the other hand has a much slower convergence and requires therefore a higher diversity of recommendation to reach 80% of its maximum value; we therefore expect that training a recommendation system to optimize the sps rather than the recall or precision will force it to produce more diverse recommendations.

7 CONCLUSION

Our results show that recurrent neural networks are a powerful tool for collaborative filtering, even outside of the sparse session-based settings where it was first introduced. We achieved the best results using the categorical cross-entropy objective function.

RNNs performed especially well on short-term recommendations, but we also observed that adding noise to the training sequence (such as dropout and shuffling) improves its success on long-term recommendations. Moreover, the recommendations produced by the RNN are more diverse and depends less on the most frequent items than those of factorization-based and neighborhood-based approaches. Interestingly, producing diverse recommendations might be linked to the performances in short-term predictions, making the methods based on sequence predictions inherently more diverse.

Acknowledgments. R. Devooght is supported by the Belgian Fonds pour la Recherche dans l'Industrie et l'Agriculture (FRIA, 1.E041.14). Some of the results were obtained using a Tesla K40 donated by the NVIDIA Corporation.

REFERENCES

[1] E. Bernhardsson. Recurrent neural networks for collaborative filtering, 2014. [Online; accessed 20-Mai-2016].

[2] R. I. Brafman, D. Heckerman, and G. Shani. Recommendation as a stochastic sequential decision problem. In *ICAPS*, pages 164–173, 2003.

[3] K. Cho, B. Van Merriënboer, D. Bahdanau, and Y. Bengio. On the properties of neural machine translation: Encoder-decoder approaches. *arXiv preprint arXiv:1409.1259*, 2014.

[4] J. Duchi, E. Hazan, and Y. Singer. Adaptive subgradient methods for online learning and stochastic optimization. *Journal of Machine Learning Research*, 12(Jul):2121–2159, 2011.

[5] Z. Gantner, S. Rendle, C. Freudenthaler, and L. Schmidt-Thieme. MyMediaLite: A free recommender system library. In *Proceedings of the 5th ACM Conference on Recommender Systems (RecSys 2011)*, 2011.

[6] I. Goodfellow, Y. Bengio, and A. Courville. *Deep Learning*. The MIT Press, 2016. http://www.deeplearningbook.org.

[7] E. Guàrdia-Sebaoun, V. Guigue, and P. Gallinari. Latent trajectory modeling: A light and efficient way to introduce time in recommender systems. In *Proceedings of the 9th ACM Conference on Recommender Systems*, pages 281–284. ACM, 2015.

[8] R. He and J. McAuley. Fusing similarity models with markov chains for sparse sequential recommendation. In *Proceedings of ICDM'16*, 2016.

[9] B. Hidasi, A. Karatzoglou, L. Baltrunas, and D. Tikk. Session-based recommendations with recurrent neural networks. In *Proceedings of ICLR'16*, 2016.

[10] S. Hochreiter and J. Schmidhuber. Long short-term memory. *Neural computation*, 9(8):1735–1780, 1997.

[11] S. Kabbur, X. Ning, and G. Karypis. Fism: factored item similarity models for top-n recommender systems. In *Proceedings of the 19th ACM SIGKDD international conference on Knowledge discovery and data mining*, pages 659–667. ACM, 2013.

[12] Y. Koren. Collaborative filtering with temporal dynamics. *Communications of the ACM*, 53(4):89–97, 2010.

[13] T. Mikolov, M. Karafiát, L. Burget, J. Cernocký, and S. Khudanpur. Recurrent neural network based language model. In *INTERSPEECH*, volume 2, page 3, 2010.

[14] T. Mikolov, I. Sutskever, K. Chen, G. S. Corrado, and J. Dean. Distributed representations of words and phrases and their compositionality. In *Advances in Neural Information Processing Systems (NIPS)*, pages 3111–3119, 2013.

[15] B. Mobasher, H. Dai, T. Luo, and M. Nakagawa. Using sequential and non-sequential patterns in predictive web usage mining tasks. In *Data Mining, 2002. ICDM 2003. Proceedings. 2002 IEEE International Conference on*, pages 669–672. IEEE, 2002.

[16] S. Rendle, C. Freudenthaler, Z. Gantner, and L. Schmidt-Thieme. Bpr: Bayesian personalized ranking from implicit feedback. In *Proceedings of the twenty-fifth conference on uncertainty in artificial intelligence*, pages 452–461. AUAI Press, 2009.

[17] S. Rendle, C. Freudenthaler, and L. Schmidt-Thieme. Factorizing personalized markov chains for next-basket recommendation. In *Proceedings of the 19th international conference on World wide web*, pages 811–820. ACM, 2010.

[18] G. Shani, R. I. Brafman, and D. Heckerman. An mdp-based recommender system. In *Proceedings of the Eighteenth conference on Uncertainty in artificial intelligence*, pages 453–460. Morgan Kaufmann Publishers Inc., 2002.

[19] N. Srivastava, G. E. Hinton, A. Krizhevsky, I. Sutskever, and R. Salakhutdinov. Dropout: a simple way to prevent neural networks from overfitting. *Journal of Machine Learning Research*, 15(1):1929–1958, 2014.

[20] Y. K. Tan, X. Xu, and Y. Liu. Improved recurrent neural networks for session-based recommendations. In *Proceedings of the 1st Workshop on Deep Learning for Recommender Systems*, pages 17–22. ACM, 2016.

[21] A. Zimdars, D. M. Chickering, and C. Meek. Using temporal data for making recommendations. In *Proceedings of the Seventeenth conference on Uncertainty in artificial intelligence*, pages 580–588. Morgan Kaufmann Publishers Inc., 2001.

Using Learning Analytics to Devise Interactive Personalised Nudges for Active Video Watching

Vania Dimitrova
University of Leeds, UK
v.g.dimitrova@leeds.ac.uk

Antonija Mitrovic
University of Canterbury, NZ
tanja.mitrovic@canterbury.ac.nz

Alicja Piotrkowicz
University of Leeds, UK
scap @leeds.ac.uk

Lydia Lau
University of Leeds, UK
l.m.s.lau@leeds.ac.uk

Amali Weerasinghe
University of Adelaide, Australia
amali.weerasinghe@adelaide.edu.au

ABSTRACT

Videos can be a powerful medium for acquiring soft skills, where learning requires contextualisation in personal experience and ability to see different perspectives. However, to learn effectively while watching videos, students need to actively engage with video content. We implemented interactive notetaking during video watching in an active video watching system (AVW) as a means to encourage engagement. This paper proposes a systematic approach to utilise learning analytics for the introduction of adaptive intervention - a choice architecture for personalised nudges in the AVW to extend learning. A user study was conducted and used as an illustration. By characterising clusters derived from user profiles, we identify different styles of engagement, such as parochial learning, habitual video watching, and self-regulated learning (which is the target ideal behaviour). To find opportunities for interventions, interaction traces in the AVW were used to identify video intervals with high user interest and relevant behaviour patterns that indicate when nudges may be triggered. A prediction model was developed to identify comments that are likely to have high social value, and can be used as examples in nudges. A framework for interactive personalised nudges was then conceptualised for the case study.

CCS Concepts

• **Applied Computing** → **Education** → **Interactive learning environments**

Keywords

Video-based learning; soft-skills; personalised nudges, analytics.

1. INTRODUCTION

Video-based learning [49] is widely used in both formal education and informal learning in a variety of contexts, such as MOOCs [18,47], flipped classroom [27] and problem-based learning [21]. The plethora of video content that is shared in social media platforms provides easily accessible materials for learning and teaching. Video sharing site usage has increased more than double from 2006 to 2013 [39]. On YouTube alone, 300 hours of video is uploaded every minute and almost 5 billion videos are watched

UMAP '17, July 09-12, 2017, Bratislava, Slovakia.
© 2017 Copyright is held by the owner/author(s).
ACM ISBN 978-1-4503-4635-1/17/07.
http://dx.doi.org/10.1145/3079628.3079683

every day (*statisticbrain.com/youtube-statistics*). This creates enormous opportunities for using videos for learning in a broad range of domains. Using videos is especially powerful for soft skills learning [12, 13], where contextualization in personal experience and ability to see different perspectives are crucial (e.g. communicating, negotiating, collaborating). Moreover, video-based learning is seen as one of the main strategies to provide engaging learning environments for the millennials [2] who are a major target cohort for soft skills learning.

However, watching videos is inherently a passive form of learning. Numerous studies have shown that students have to actively engage with video content to learn effectively [10-13,25,38,49]. Embedding interactive activities, e.g. quizzes or assessment problems, in the videos have proven successful for engagement [17,24,26,48], but these require substantial effort from the teacher and are hard to reuse. Collaborative annotation and interactive note taking [10] provide alternatives to engage learners, which require less effort from the educators and enable reuse of content.

Our research adopts interactive note-taking in video watching for soft skill learning. Previous studies found that the approach is effective only when the students actively engage with video content [34] and requirements are gathered for interactive personalised nudges to promote desired learning behaviour [35]: assist students noticing important points in videos, linking video snippets to aspects related to soft skill learning (e.g. recognise key skill elements, contextualise in past and future experience) and broadening soft skill learning portfolio (e.g. notice a variety of skill elements and use various reflection triggers when making notes).

The research presented here aims at *developing a systematic approach to design interactive personalised nudges for active video watching* - a novel approach that utilises analytics to derive personalisation features for extending a video-based learning environment. Both explicit user profiles (from questionnaires) and interaction traces (from system logs) are used to: (i) characterise student engagement in video-based learning, (ii) identify when interventions can be made, and (iii) predict what comments by other people may be useful as examples in the nudges. The outcome will feed into a unique choice-architecture-driven framework for the design of interactive personalised nudges.

1.1 Active Video Watching Approach

The active video watching approach taps into students' experiences with social media sites for video sharing (e.g. YouTube) and integrates interactive notetaking during video watching to facilitate student engagement and reflective learning. The approach is illustrated with the **Active Video Watching (AVW) system** [34]. In AVW, the teacher selects a set of videos for a class and defines aspects to serve as mini-scaffolds for learning. Aspects aim to draw the student's attention to specific points related to the target soft skill and to trigger reflective experiential learning. This paper uses an AVW instantiation for pitch presentations, which includes four YouTube video tutorials on giving presentations and four examples of pitch presentations. The following aspects are provided to stimulate recall and reflection on students' own experiences - in tutorials: "*I am rather good at this*", "*I did/saw this in the past*", "*I didn't realize I wasn't doing it*" and "*I like this point*"; in example videos, the aspects provided correspond to concepts covered in the tutorials: "*Delivery*", "*Speech*", "*Structure*" and "*Visual aids*".

Initially students watch and comment on videos individually in the **PersonalSpace**, using the aspects to tag their comments (Fig. 1). To enter a comment, student stops the video, types in their thoughts and selects an aspect. The system records the comment and the time elapsed from the start of the video. Once the teacher approves comments for sharing, anonymised comments are available for browsing in the **SocialSpace**. A second level of mini-scaffolds is provided where the students are encouraged to rate the comments. The ratings, which are designed to further promote reflection, are: "*This is useful for me*", "*I hadn't thought of this*", "*I didn't notice this*", "*I don't agree with this*", and "*I like this point*".

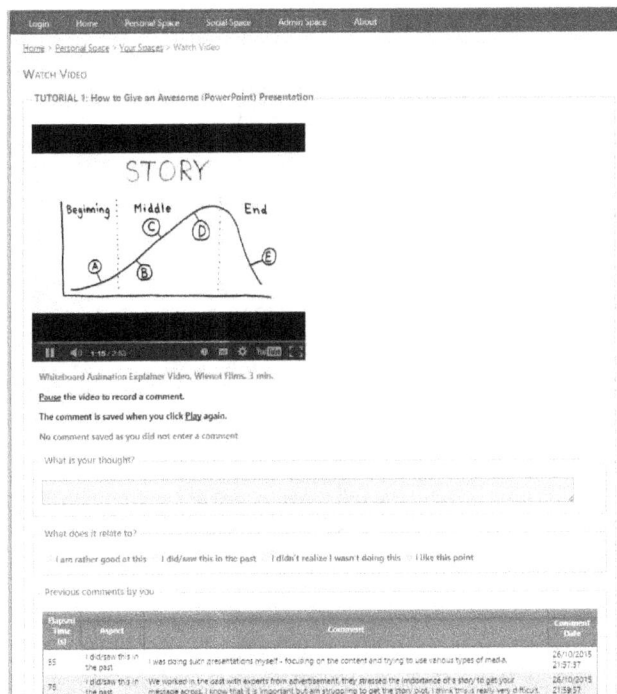

Figure 1: AVW PersonalSpace - watching a tutorial.

Two AVW studies were conducted in March and July 2016 with postgraduates and undergraduates respectively, focusing on pitch presentations [34, 35]. The studies examined whether learning was happening and what kind of interactions contributed to learning. The findings showed that participants who engaged in constructive learning (i.e. wrote comments in the PersonalSpace and rated comments in the SocialSpace) improved their conceptual understanding of presentation skills, while minimal improvement for those who did not. Hence, further extension of AVW with appropriate interventions to encourage effective engagement with videos is needed. This is the aim of the research presented here.

1.2 Nudges and Choice Architecture

To promote engagement with videos that leads to better learning, while at the same time preserving the learners' freedom to interact with videos in a way they prefer (as common in social media platforms), we propose the use of intelligent nudges.

Nudges were introduced in decision support [46] as a form of interventions which influence people's behaviour to make choices that lead to better lives (paternalism) but in an unobtrusive and non-compulsory manner (libertarian). Behaviour change is complex and so are the corresponding interventions. **Choice architecture**, which defines the ways to select and present choices that can lead to better behaviour, is the core when designing nudges [36,46].

To design a choice architecture for AVW nudges, we follow the development process proposed in Münscher et al. [36] and utilise learning analytics. The key principles of behaviour change [33] are noted: (i) maximise *capability* to regulate own behaviour; (ii) increase/reduce *motivation* to engage /discontinue in the desired/undesired behaviour; (iii) maximise *opportunity* to support self-regulation. These principles are adopted for the AVW choice architecture in the following way:

- *capability*: take into account both the learner's self-regulation capabilities and their knowledge /experience of the soft skill;
- *motivation*: aim to increase the learner's motivation to engage in active video watching and to improve their knowledge;
- *opportunity*: automatically identify opportunities to support engagement in active video watching to improve learning.

1.3 Structure of Paper

Section 2 positions the work in relevant literature. Section 3 outlines the AVW study that collected the data for analytics. Sections 4 to 6 illustrate an implementation of the proposed approach: the use of clustering techniques to understand engagement behaviours – problems/targets (S.4); a crowdwisdom-inspired method for identifying opportunities for intervention: video comments are analysed to identify the timing to trigger interventions and suitable example comments for sharing (S.5); a framework for designing interactive personalised nudges (S.6). The paper concludes with the main contribution and future work.

2. RELATED WORK

Nudges have been used in social science for interventions in lifestyle and to influence choice [46]. While sharing many features with persuasion [31], nudge is more about behaviour changes while persuasion focuses on changing beliefs. Nudge is also adopted in educational systems, including both signposting and interactive interventions. Although not explicitly called nudges, open student models can act as signposting nudges to promote reflection and self-awareness [7,27,29], with open social student models promote social comparisons [6]. These are static intervention approaches which focus on the design of effective visualisations, and rely on the students' abilities to interpret such visualisations. On the other hand, interactive intervention approaches rely on the system automatically triggers short dialogue scripts to nudge the learners to the desired behaviour. Interactive nudges can be simple reminders of college tasks [8], prompts for goal setting and reflection [27] or for navigation support [45], and dialogue games for reflection [15] or for articulation of thoughts [41]. Our approach uses interactive scripts combined with social comparison inspired by open social student modelling. We provide a unique choice-architecture-driven framework to guide the provision of suitable personalised nudges to promote video engagement for learning. Choice architecture has recently been suggested as foundational for the design of personalised interactive systems [22], though primarily used in recommender systems such as e-commerce or tourism [5]. This work is the first attempt to devise choice architecture for personalised nudges to improve learning.

Our approach uses learning analytics to inform the design of personalization nudges in this case by exploiting machine learning methods for clustering and classification. Clustering algorithms are commonly used to design user-adaptive systems by identifying stereotypes of users [16,19,32,37]. In educational settings where a range of individual differences and interaction parameters have to be considered, stereotyping require a large corpus of data. Instead, we adopt a stereotype-inspired approach that uses clusters and statistical analysis to identify problem behaviour, target behaviour and bottlenecks for not achieving the target behavior. This is combined with the analysis of interaction behaviour by other users (as in open social student models) to identify areas in a video when interactive interventions may be appropriate.

We use classification methods to predict whether comments can attract people's attention and can be used as examples to trigger learning. This builds on considerable research in using text (and features extracted from text) to predict the popularity of content [3, 4, 30, 43]. The target measures to predict differ from number of comments [44] to page views or social media reactions [1]. Predictions are useful to identify items of 'good' quality content that can be used in recommendations, e.g. to automatically select the most interesting social media messages to show to a reader of a news article [42]. Similarly, we use features extracted from text and the user profile to predict 'good' quality comments. Our prediction model infers whether a given comment is of high social value, i.e. can trigger reflective learning or can induce opinion. The feature engineering and the findings of the prediction offer useful insights for researchers willing to exploit social content to enhance learning.

3. EXPERIMENTAL SET UP

An AVW user study was conducted in March 2016 to inform the design of personalised nudges. The goal was to investigate whether AVW was effective in supporting engagement and reflection, as well as to identify problem behaviours and what support may be provided. The participants were postgraduate students recruited through invitation sent to several mailing lists. Participation was on a voluntarily basis, including a prize draw for $100 vouchers.

Method. The study had two phases, each one week long.

Phase 1: (PersonalSpace) After informed consent, the participants completed Survey I (collecting user profiles such as demographic information, background experiences, motivation and attitudes, and their conceptual knowledge /key concepts related to pitch presentation). The participants then received instructions on the use of AVW PersonalSpace, and advice on watching tutorials before examples. There were no further instructions as we aimed to provide an ecologically valid data collection approach which mimicked closely informal learning through video watching in YouTube. At the end of Phase 1, we administered Survey II to re-test conceptual knowledge; to identify cognitive load using NASA-TLX [20]; and to check the perceived usefulness of the PersonalSpace using Technology Acceptance Model (TAM) [14].

Phase 2: (SocialSpace) The participants used the AVW SocialSpace to explore and rate the comments made by the others. At the end of week 2, we administered Survey III which was the same as Survey II but applied to the AVW SocialSpace.

Data logging. AVW logged the temporal data on user interactions. In this paper, we primarily use the interaction logs in the PersonalSpace and the data collected with Surveys I and II.

User ratings provided in the SocialSpace are used for identifying comments which are valuable to other learners.

Participants. 48 participants completed the profile survey. Survey II was completed by 41 participants, some of whom did not make any comments in the PersonalSpace. Since the goal of this paper is to investigate participants' engagement, we report here the **38 participants** (26 females and 12 males) who made comments in Phase 1 and completed Surveys I and II. 17 participants were younger than 30, with the biggest group (14 participants) being aged 24-29. 6 participants were 48 or older. English was the first language for 23 participants, while the first languages of the remaining 15 participants included various Asian and European languages. 28 participants were PhD students. No difference between males and females, or between younger and more mature students, for prior training received on presentation skills, but there was a significant difference between native (2,48, sd = .99) and non-native English speakers (1.67, sd = .62) (U = 210.5, p = .014). There were no significant differences on how much experience the participants had on giving presentations, how often they watched YouTube videos, or used YouTube for learning for any categories.

Table 1: Summary of the MSLQ questions

	All (38)	Female (26)	Male (12)
Academic Control	3.91 (.46)	3.96 (.46)	3.79 (.45)
Self Efficacy	3.72 (.56)	3.65 (.57)	3.89 (.51)
Task Value	4.49 (.38)	4.58 (.33)	4.31 (.44)
Intrinsic Motivation	4.05 (.52)	4.1 (.51)	3.96 (.56)
Extrinsic Motivation	3.37 (.83)	3.28 (.74)	3.58 (1)
Effort	2.93 (.44)	2.9 (.46)	2.98 (.39)
Elaboration	4.13 (.54)	4.15 (.57)	4.08 (.5)
Rehearsal	3.4 (.8)	3.29 (.79)	3.66 (.81)
Organisation	3.84 (.94)	3.94 (.99)	3.63 (.8)
Self-regulation	3.61 (.39)	3.52 (.36)	3.8 (.38)

Survey I also contained the questions from the Motivated Strategies for Learning Questionnaire (MSLQ) [40]. There were 46 questions, with the Likert scale of 1 (*Not at all true of me*) to 5 (*Very true of me*). The responses to MSLQ questions are summarized into ten dimensions in Table 1. The participants scored in the upper half of the scale on all dimensions, which is not surprising given that our participants were postgraduate students. The only marginally significant difference between male/female students is for Task Value (U = 98, p = .07), in which female scores higher.

AVW interaction overview. An initial statistical analysis of the collected data shows that the participants made 744 comments in the PersonalSpace, with the average of 19.58 comments per video (sd = 13.19). There was no significant difference between the number of comments on tutorials and examples across different demographic categories (gender, age, native/non-native speaker). Table 2 presents the distribution of comments over various aspects. The participants could make a comment without selecting an aspect, and that happened more often for tutorials (TA5) than for examples (EA5). For the four examples, comments are almost equally distributed over the given aspects, showing that the participants were watching the videos with those aspects in mind.

Survey II contained TAM questions, the replies to which were on the Likert scale from 1 (extremely likely) to 7 (extremely unlikely). The average score for usefulness of PersonalSpace (based on five questions) was 2.46 (sd=1.09), showing acceptable use. The participants answered the NASA-TLX questions on the cognitive workload imposed by the PersonalSpace using the Likert scale from 1 (Low) to 20 (High). The participants found: (i) commenting on the videos moderately demanding (mean = 9.89, sd=4.87); (ii) watching and commenting on videos relatively challenging, with the average score 8.55 (sd=4.21), and there was strong positive correlation between Demand and Effort (r = .539, p < .001); (iii) regarding whether they felt discouraged, irritated, stressed or annoyed when watching and commenting on the videos, the average score was 5.79 (sd=4.48); (iv) the self-perceived performance in identifying useful points about presentation skills has the mean score of 12.76 (sd=4.48). The distribution of scores for Performance was significantly different (U = 229, p = .02) for female and male participants, with male participants reporting higher values; no other significant differences between categories.

Table 2: Distribution of comments over aspects (TA – tutorial aspect, EA – example aspect)

Aspects	Comments	Ratings
TA1: I like this point	171	639
TA2: I didn't realize I wasn't doing this	50	166
TA3: I am rather good at this	33	128
TA4: I did/saw this in the past	52	249
TA5: No aspect selected	103	382
EA1: Delivery	81	224
EA2: Speech	67	194
EA3: Structure	68	218
EA4: Visual aids	61	176
EA5: No aspect selected	58	202

Conceptual knowledge of presentation skills. The change in conceptual knowledge between surveys was used as an indicator of learning. Each participant had one minute per question in the survey to write phrases they associated with (i) structure, (ii) delivery and speech, and (iii) visual aids. We developed an ontology of presentations, consisting of three taxonomies related to these areas. The answers were marked by three independent markers, indicating the number of ontology entities found with each response. The inter-rater reliability was high: the Krippendorff's alpha was 0.894. The final scores were finalised by a fourth marker using the majority vote, or if impossible, extra marking.

The average score for conceptual knowledge from Survey I (CK1) was 12.89 (sd=6.44); Survey II (CK2) was 13.74 (6.46); Survey III (CK3) was 15.86 (6.18). Repeated measures ANOVA on the conceptual knowledge scores for the study revealed a significant effect overall ($F_{(2,68)}$ = 6.18, p = .003) with the partial eta squared of 0.15 (medium effect). The pairwise comparison shows there was a significant increase from Survey 1 to Survey 3 (p = .01).

In summary, we found evidence of learning, but *have not found significant differences* on previous experience, motivation for learning, or engagement levels between various categories of participants (e.g. age, gender). A possible explanation may be that this is a homogeneous group. However, closer examination of the data shows that there are individual differences between students on how many comments they made, and the social value of their comments. Hence, we investigate if a combination of factors can be used to discover behavioural patterns.

4. CHARACTERISING BEHAVIOUR

The first step in designing the choice architecture for video engagement in AVW is to identify **problem behaviour** and **target behaviour**. We do this by using unsupervised machine learning to derive clusters for characterising engagement behaviour.

We generated clusters using the k-means algorithm in SPSS, starting with 15 standardized variables from Survey I. In each run

of the algorithm, variables that were not significant were removed, resulting in the final three clusters using the following variables: experience with giving presentations (*Exp*), using YouTube for learning (*Y4L*), initial conceptual knowledge (*CK1*), six MSLQ variables – self-efficacy (*SE*), academic control (*AC*), extrinsic motivation (*EM*), rehearsal (*Reh*), self-regulation (*SR*) and organization (*Org*). Fig. 2 illustrates the cluster centers, while Table 3 reports the significant differences between the clusters (using the 2-sided Kruskal-Wallis test). We report pairs of clusters with a significant difference on a particular variable in the last column, with a Bonferroni correction.

Cluster C1 has higher numbers for comments/ratings in comparison to C2, but the differences are not significant. C1 is lowest on experience overall, and lower than C2 on the use of YouTube for learning. C1 has the lowest scores for self-efficacy, extrinsic motivation, rehearsal, self-regulation and organization. Generally, this group is comparatively closed-minded and we refer C1 as *Parochial Learners*. Surprisingly, they find AVW the most useful, yet they did not benefit that much as there was no significant improvement of their conceptual knowledge.

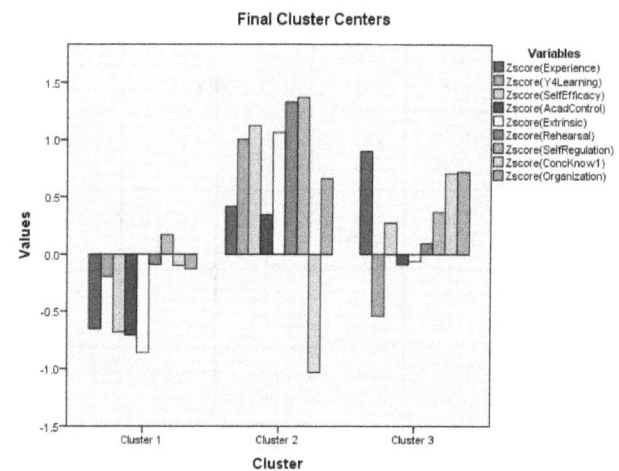

Figure 2: Cluster centres from Survey 1

The C2 participants are confident, self-regulated students but were significantly less engaged than those in cluster C3. They scored higher on extrinsic motivation, rehearsal and self-regulation. At the same time, their conceptual knowledge at the start of the study was the lowest. A possible explanation of their behaviour is that they are used to watching videos in a passive way so did not engage sufficiently. There was a marginally significant improvement on conceptual knowledge for this cluster ($\chi2(2)$ = 5.407, p = .067). The pairwise Wilcoxon Signed-rank test revealed a significant difference between CK1 and CK2 (z = 2.003, p = .045) and also between CK1 and CK3 (z = 2.2, p = .028). We refer to C2 as *Habitual Video Watchers*.

Cluster C3 is the "ideal" cluster illustrating the target user behaviour with AVW. The participants in this cluster were actively engaged while watching the videos, making the highest number of comments and receiving the highest number of ratings on their comments (significantly higher in comparison to C1 and C2). This cluster is highest on previous experience and conceptual knowledge on the pretest (CK1), and lowest on using YouTube for learning. The Friedman test revealed a significant improvement ($\chi2(2)$ = 6.11, p = .047) on conceptual knowledge scores from Survey I to Survey III. The pairwise Wilcoxon Signed-rank test revealed a significant difference between CK1 and CK3 (z = 2.16, p = .03). We refer to C3 as *Engaged Self-regulated Learners*.

Table 3: Means (sd) for all participants and 3 clusters (C – comments, R – Ratings, U – TAM Usefulness). ** and * denote significance at the 0.01/0.05 level respectively

	All (38)	C1 (14)	C2 (7)	C3 (17)	Diff
Exp**	2.87 (.78)	2.21 (.58)	3 (.58)	3.35 (.61)	C1-C2 * C1-C3 **
Y4L**	2.71 (1.01)	2.64 (1.01)	3.86 (.9)	2.29 (.69)	C1-C2 * C2-C3 **
SE**	3.73 (.56)	3.29 (.45)	4.31 (.4)	3.83 (.41)	C1-C2 ** C1-C3 *
EM**	3.37 (.83)	2.84 (.59)	4.29 (.34)	3.44 (.81)	C1-C2 ** C2-C3 *
Reh**	3.4 (.8)	3.11 (.49)	4.32 (.49)	3.27 (.85)	C1-C2 ** C2-C3 *
SR**	3.61 (.39)	3.45 (.31)	4.08 (.32)	3.55 (.33)	C1-C2 ** C2-C3 *
Org*	3.84 (.94)	3.25 (.99)	4.14 (.75)	4.21 (.73)	C1-C3 *
CK1**	12.89 (6.43)	11.86 (5.16)	6.71 (5.22)	16.29 (5.83)	C2-C3 **
CK2*	13.74 (6.46)	12.71 (6.37)	9.14 (3.93)	16.47 (6.31)	C2-C3 *
CK3*	15.86 (6.18)	14.46 (6.36)	12 (5.89)	18.87 (4.93)	C2-C3 *
C*	19.58 (13.19)	18.71 (14.38)	10 (7.26)	24.24 (12.27)	C2-C3 *
R*	68.08 (49.36)	63.79 (45.64)	32.29 (19.31)	86.35 (53.59)	C2-C3 *
U**	3.91 (.38)	3.65 (.34)	4.24 (.37)	3.99 (.27)	C1-C2 ** C1-C3 *
VTA*	2.39 (1. 29)	2.21 (1.05)	1.29 (1.25)	3 (1.17)	C2-C3 *
VEA*	2.63 (1.72)	3.07 (1.39)	1 (1.73)	2.94 (1.64)	C1-C2 * C2-C3 *
RC**	3.5 (4.21)	2.29 (2.7)	.71 (1.25)	5.65 (4.99)	C2-C3 **
PropR**	.28 (.22)	.21 (.17)	.1 (.19)	.41 (.21)	C1-C3 * C2-C3 **

We further analysed the comments made by each cluster in terms of aspects. In Table 3, the Variety of Tutorial Aspects (VTA) and Variety for Example Aspects (VEA) are reported. The average number of distinct aspects used by the whole population for tutorials is 2.39. There was a significant difference on the average VTA scores of the three clusters (H = 9.25, p = .01), with C3 being

significantly higher than C2 (p = .01). Fig. 3 shows the average number of comments per tutorial aspects for the three clusters, as well as for reflective aspects (RA, which includes TA2, TA3 and TA4). There was a significant difference on the average number of reflective comments (RC in Table 3) (H = 11.87, p = .003), with C3 making significantly more reflective comments in comparison to C2 (p = .01). There was also a significant difference on the proportional use of reflective aspects (PropR) (H = 11.78, p = .003), with C3 having a significantly higher proportion in comparison to C1 (p = .04) and C2 (p = .005). Most of the comments the C2 participants made used TA1 or no aspect. There was also a significant difference between the average numbers of aspects for comments on examples (H = 7.59, p = .022), with a significant pairwise difference between C1 and C2 (p = .04), and also between C2 and C3 (p = .03).

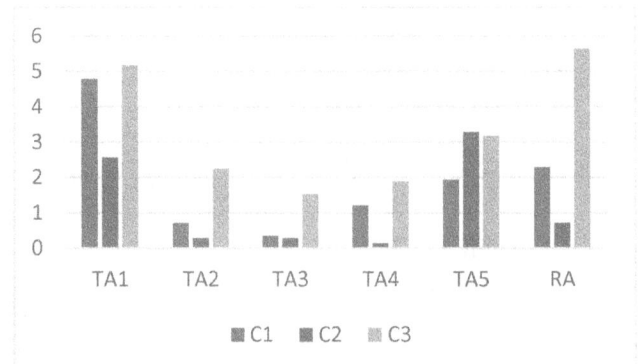

Figure 3: Average number of comments per tutorial aspect

To summarise the findings above, two main patterns of problem behaviours were identified - C1: *Parochial Learners* and C2: *Habitual Video Watchers*; with the target behaviour being C3: *Engaged Self-regulated Learners*. Participants in C3 had their conceptual knowledge improved significantly during the study. They made the most comments, which had the highest social value, and used reflective aspects significantly more often in comparison to C1 and C2. The participants in cluster C1, who did not improve their conceptual knowledge during the study, had low experience, and lacked self-regulation and learning skills. Although they commented on videos, their comments had low social value. Their SR and learning skill need to be improved. The participants in cluster C2 had strong SR and learning skills, but had lowest prior conceptual knowledge and the lowest engagement level. They need to acquire more conceptual understanding in order to recognise opportunities for commenting/rating, to be able to engage at a higher level and use a greater variety of aspects when commenting.

5. IDENTIFYING OPPORTUNITIES FOR INTERVENTION

To design nudges, we need to identify opportunities for intervention, i.e. to decide **when** there may be a suitable time for an intervention, and **what** to include in a nudge. For this, we propose the use of interaction traces generated by learners in the user study. We look for video intervals worthy for attention and investigate ways to identify comments for examples in the nudges.

5.1 Attention Intervals

An attention interval I is defined as a continuous stretch of video consisting of a set of comments C. The granularity of continuity is determined by how big time gap θ is allowed between adjacent comments. We define an aggregation predicate $A(C)$, which aggregates comments from a given set C, as follows:

$$A(C) \equiv \forall(c_i \in C) \; \exists(c_j \in C) \; [(c_i \neq c_j) \wedge distance(c_i, c_j) \leq \theta]$$

This allows us to aggregate comments in attention intervals that indicate areas in a video where users have noted something. Table 4 summarises the output of interval aggregation for the eight videos used in the study. The time distance parameter θ was set to 4" for tutorials and 6" for examples, and was selected as the maximum number that gives a reasonable interval partitioning (larger values of θ will aggregate almost all comments in one interval).

Table 4: Summary of the interval aggregation for each video.

Video	Length	# of Comments	# of Intervals	Avg.Int. Length	# Int. with Length>10"
T1	2.54'	89	10	9"(13)	2
T2	7.37'	110	20	6"(7)	2
T3	6.55'	120	23	6"(4)	4
T4	6.22'	90	15	6"(3)	3
E1	3.23'	79	9	11"(7)	4
E2	8.28'	93	19	7"(4)	7
E3	6.48'	100	20	9"(6)	8
E4	3.25'	63	7	15"(11)	5

Because the intervals vary in length, number of comments, representation of clusters and aspects, we look at ways to extract those that are useful to encourage engagement. Taking into account that the intervals can be used to direct a user to a place in the video and that he/she would have to have adequate time to absorb the point made, the interval length can be used as a filter to get useful attention intervals. For example, if we put a filter of length greater than 10", the number of attention intervals reduces noticeably, as shown in Table 4. Other ways to filter could be applied, e.g. take the k longest intervals for each video.

Further processing of the comments in an interval allows us to identify useful patterns for the timing of interventions. Considering that the problem behaviour for AVW nudges is related mainly to clusters C1 and C2 and the target behaviour is related to cluster C3 (as identified in Section 3), we further analyse the behaviour of clusters with these intervals. Five patterns were identified (see illustrations in Fig. 4). When cluster C1 was the only one engaged (pattern **P4**), the comments referred to unimportant aspects (e.g. a comment noting that power point should be used). In such cases, the learner may be encouraged to continue to look at aspects in other intervals, such as those where many people commented and used diverse aspects (pattern **P1**). We noted intervals when a cluster did not engage, while the others did (patterns **P2** and **P5**). When learners from a disengaged cluster approach such intervals, existing comments can be shown as examples of other people's opinions to direct attention to important aspects and to stimulate interaction. There were intervals where only cluster C3 (our target behaviour) engaged (pattern **P3**), and this indicate learning points that only people with experience in the soft skill may notice. It may be hard to stimulate learners from clusters C1 and C2 to notice these points when they lack experience; instead, once the learner is at such an interval, s/he can be encouraged to pause and read comments from more experienced people for reflection.

5.2 Comments with Social Value

While attention intervals and patterns can indicate when to make a nudge, comments from others can provide examples that can be used in a nudge to stimulate engagement. Not every comment will be stimulating. As a proxy for the social value of a comment, i.e. whether the comment will be of interest to others, the ratings received in the SocialSpace will be used.

Table 5 summarises the rating metrics - ratings R1-R3 *Trigger Learning*, as they indicate that people notice something new,

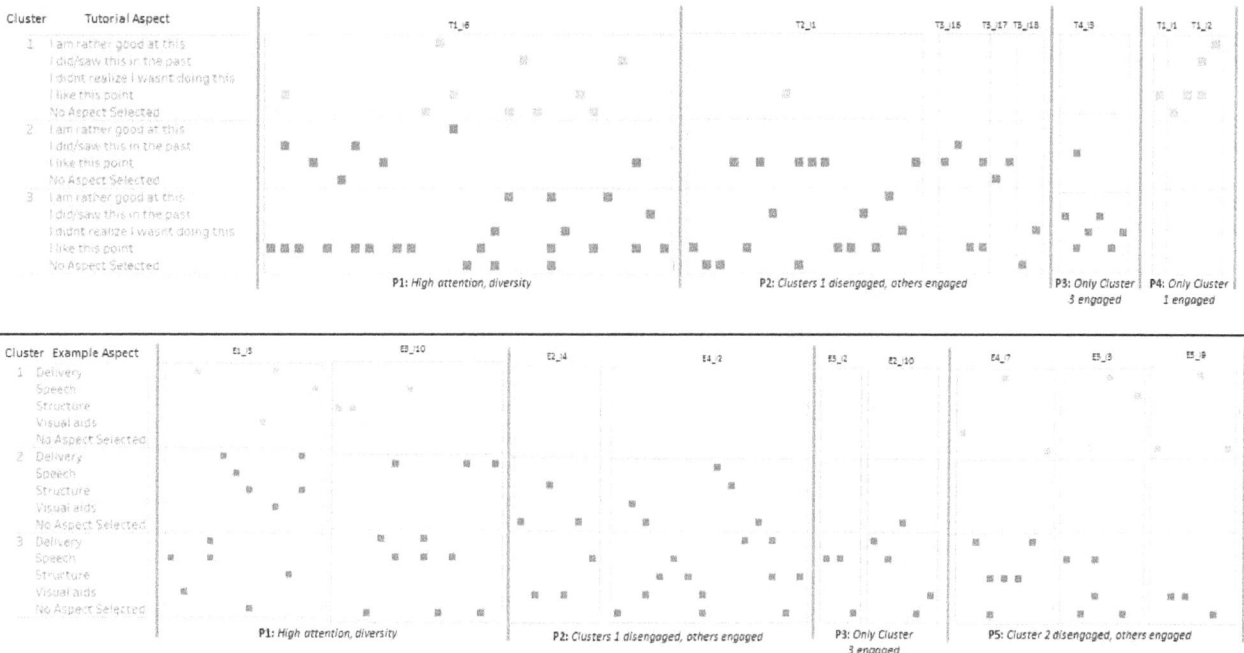

Figure 4: Interval patterns that indicate situations when interventions can be triggered. Top- intervals from tutorial videos (*Ti_Ij* indicates interval *j* in tutorial *i*). Bottom- intervals from example videos (*Ei_Ij* indicates interval *j* in example *i*).

unnoticed in their own comments; while R4-R5 *Induce Opinion*, as people state that they disagree or that they like the point.

Table 5: Summary of the ratings on comments in SocialSpace.

Class	Rating category	# Ratings
Trigger Learning	R1: This is useful for me	349
	R2: I hadn't thought of this	260
	R3: I didn't notice this	241
Induce Opinion	R4: I do not agree with this	213
	R5: I like this point	1643

We present a method to identify high social value comments, using linguistic and user profile features of comments, and employ natural language processing and machine learning techniques. The data set used includes 742 comments, which range in length from 1 to 97 tokens (median=10) and follow a Zipfian distribution. For calculating correlations and in the prediction model, the ratings were normalised by the total number of ratings on a given video.

Feature Engineering. In order to find high social value comments, we consider three feature groups: the comments' linguistic content, domain-specific keywords, and comment metadata (including the user profile and aspects).

Linguistic features. We used the Linguistic Inquiry and Word Count (LIWC) tool (https://liwc.wpengine.com) which analyses texts and returns the percentages of words from its topical dictionaries. These dictionaries include grammar, affect, cognitive processes, formality, and punctuation. Since comments do not always follow proper grammar, the approach using keyword counts as employed by LIWC is more appropriate than full parsing and discourse analysis. LIWC output consists of 93 features.

Domain-specific keywords. Since experience in the relevant domain could lead to writing higher social value comments, we created a lexicon of keywords that relate to various aspects of making presentations (delivery/speech, structure, visual aids). The lexicon consists of 380 single words (e.g. *articulate*, *outline*) and 61 phrases (e.g. *easy to understand*). We implement two features: the proportion of domain-specific keywords to all tokens in the comment text, and the conceptual knowledge terms provided by the learners in the study pre-test in Survey I (as described in Section 3).

Metadata. Comment metadata (26 features) were implemented as binary features. The metadata relates to the user profile: gender, English as native language (both implemented as binary features), self-reported experience level in this domain, engagement with the system (# comments made, # videos watched), user cluster (from Section 4), and results from the MSLQ (Survey I).

Notable correlations. We calculated correlations between feature values and the three target measures for example and tutorial videos separately. Kendall's tau was used for numeric features and point-biserial correlation for binary features (we report: * p<.05, **p<.01, *** p<.001). We found approximately a third of them to have a significant correlation with at least one target measure. Significant correlations fall across all feature groups highlighting the need to consider different aspects of comments in order to predict their social value.

In general, there were noticeably more significant correlations between linguistic features and target measures for example videos, whereas for tutorial videos user profile features were significantly correlated more often. Comments made by users with a higher pre-existing knowledge of the domain were more likely to trigger learning (.08* for tutorials, .11** for examples). For tutorials,

comments from users who are intrinsically motivated (.09*) and have good organization skills (.11**) were more likely to trigger learning. Similarly, comments from users who engaged more by commenting on tutorials were more likely to induce opinions (.08*). In terms of linguistic features comments with higher proportions of personal pronouns (especially 'we') are more likely to induce opinions in example videos (personal pronouns: .11**, 'we': .1*). Also in example videos, there is a negative correlation between learning ratings and using words relating to negative emotion (e.g. *hurt*, -.16***), anger (e.g. *annoy*, -.1*) and risk (e.g. *doubt*, -.12*), and a positive correlation between opinion ratings and using words relating to causation (e.g. *because*, .1*), certainty (e.g. *always*, .1*), and future (e.g. *soon*, .14**). For tutorial videos comments with longer sentences (words per sentence: .09**) and with more words relating to space (e.g. *down*, .1**) are more likely to get opinion ratings, while a higher proportion of words relating to the body (e.g. *hands*, -.09*) is negatively correlated with learning ratings. Comments with the aspect "*I didn't realize I wasn't doing it*" are more likely to trigger learning on tutorial videos (.12*).

Prediction Model. Our aim is to identify comments with high social value. A high social value comment is one which has a number of ratings in the top quartile for the dataset. Thus each comment is denoted as a 'Good' or 'Not Good', making this a binary classification task. In order to address the class imbalance (only approx. 22% of the comments belong to the 'Good' class), we utilise a method called SMOTE [9], which undersamples the majority class and synthetically oversamples the minority class. Furthermore, we remove any features which have zero or near-zero variance. We tested a number of algorithms. Random Forest yielded the best results (it has been shown to work well on datasets with a mix of numeric and binary features).

Evaluation. We run a 10-fold cross-validation and report accuracy (percentage of correctly classified instances), precision and recall. Results are reported in Table 6. Majority class baseline achieves .77 accuracy and zero precision and recall. The prediction model achieves very good performance of at least 90% accuracy for all measures, with at least .83 precision and .92 recall. This means

Table 6: Classification results.

All Ratings			Trigger Learning			Induce Opinion		
Acc.	Prec.	Rec.	Acc.	Prec.	Rec.	Acc.	Prec.	Rec.
.90	.84	.93	.90	.83	.92	.91	.85	.93

that we can accurately identify comments with high social value.

Table 7: Example comments with predicted class/actual class.

(1) *Important to have faith in yourself and believe that your message is important* (Tutorial, Good/Good)
(2) *A lot to remember, but good tips* (Tutorial, Not Good/Not Good)
(3) *Clear ending, the audience leaves remembering the main idea.* (Example, Good/Good)
(4) *confusing visual* (Example, Not Good/Not Good)
(5) *Speaks very quickly, comes across as passionate, but some pauses would be better* (Example, Good/Not Good)
(6) *speaking quickly* (Example, Not Good/Good)

Overall, the output of the prediction model indicates that it is possible to identify comments with high social value. Examples (1)-(4) in Table 7 show that the model makes correct prediction across video types. Examples (5) and (6) highlight the challenging nature of our task. They address a similar point and even use some similar words, however (6) attracted more ratings. These similarities between comments in different classes leads to some confusion in the model. Hence, we propose that it will be more appropriate to use the 'Good' class probability as a measure for ranking comments, and this will allow to select from a pool of comments those which are of the best quality within the given set.

6. FRAMEWORK FOR INTERACTIVE PERSONALISED NUDGES

This section utilises the analytics presented in sections 4 and 5 to instantiate a choice-architecture-driven framework for specifying interactive personalised nudges to improve active video watching (illustrated in AVW). Following [15], we present each nudge as a **dialogue game** $N=<G,P,T,O>$, where G defines the goal of the game (i.e. the problem behaviour that we want to change with the nudge), P defines the conditions when the game will be triggered (i.e. situation(s) when the intervention will be generated), T defines the interaction template (canned text which is instantiated according to the context), and O defines the expected outcome (elements of target behaviour we want to achieve with the nudge).

Context model. To enable adaptation, we propose a context model $C=<U_{YT}, U_K, U_{MSLQ}, U_L, V_I, V_C>$ that includes information about both the user and the video. Explicit profiling obtained before interaction with AVW (Section 3) includes U_{YT} (the user's experience in using YouTube videos for learning), U_K (the user's knowledge and previous experience in the target skill), and U_{MSLQ} (the MSLQ scales used for generating the clusters: self-efficacy, extrinsic motivation, rehearsal, self-regulation, and organization). Implicit profiling from interaction logs U_L includes the number of comments and frequencies of video aspect usage (Section 4). The video information aggregates the interaction traces by others (Section 5), including V_I (the set of high attention intervals with detected interaction patterns) and V_C (for each comment, the probability that the comment belongs to class 'Good' social value).

Nudge categories. Münscher et al. [36] aggregate the empirically tested choice architecture interventions into three nudge categories, which can be used to guide the design of AVW nudges:

Decision information nudges facilitate the perceptual processes of problem representation, formulation, or framing to help people process the available information that can affect their behavior. In AVW, this includes nudges that provide information before interacting with AVW or before entering intervals when making comments would be beneficial for learning.

Decision structure nudges facilitate assessment and selection of alternatives when a decision is to be made, including range/composition of options and default options. In AVW, this refers to nudges that help identify the appropriate aspect for a comment or show comments made by others. These nudges are made when the learner is within an attention interval and there is a learning point to be noticed and associated to an aspect.

Decision assistance nudges foster deliberate commitment and remind people of behavioral options. In AVW, this refers to nudges that provide feedback on engagement and 'reward' positive engagement behaviour. They can be triggered after an attention interval is passed or after a video has been watched.

In addition to the intervention techniques for each nudge category suggested in [36], tips for teacher interventions informed by MSLQ categories [23] are also used to devise nudges with pedagogical goals. Table 8 illustrates the three nudge types, with corresponding techniques: provide social reference point, use prompted choice, and facilitate commitment. There can be nudges with the same goal which can be triggered in different preconditions and can be implemented with different nudging techniques.

Table 8: Example dialogue games for AVW nudges.

N1: [Decision information: provide social reference point]
G: Direct the attention of a Parochial Learner.
P: U_K is low, U_{MSLQ} values are lower than collective mean, # of comments in U_L is around the video average. The learner is approaching an attention interval with pattern *P3* (only Cluster 3 engaged), it has at least one 'Good' social value comment.
T: *'You are about to watch a part where other students made comments, for example* [show 'Good' social value comment].'
O: The learner makes a relevant comment.
N2: [Decision structure: use prompted choice]
G: Promote engagement of a Habitual Video Watcher.
P: U_{YT} is high, U_K is low, U_{MSLQ} values are higher than the collective mean, variety of used video aspects as indicated by the aspect frequency in U_L is low, the learner is in an attention interval with pattern *P1* (high attention high diversity).
T: *'Have you thought about* [unused aspect]. *For example, somebody else has said* [show 'Good' social value comment].'
O: The learner starts to relate comments to more video aspects.
N3: [Decision assistance: facilitate commitment]
G: Reward positive behaviour.
P: The learner has made a comment that has a high probability to belong to 'Good' social value class.
T: *'You made a very good comment that can be useful to others* [show user comment].
O: The learner's motivation and knowledge increase.

7. CONCLUSIONS

The work presented here contributes to an emerging research stream that exploits the synergy between the areas of learning analytics and user-adaptive systems. We pioneer a data-driven approach where insights from analytics are used to inform the provision of user-adaptive interventions in an existing system. This is illustrated with a case study that used AVW to learn about pitch presentation. Our main contribution is a systematic methodology to (i) populate a context model for learning through active video watching, which includes information about both the learner (explicit and implicit profiling) and the video (aggregating traces of user interaction with videos) and (ii) devise the choice architecture for active video watching nudges, by identifying from the analytics (a) problem behaviours and a target behaviour, (b) appropriate attention intervals and patterns for triggering nudges, and (c) comments that can be used as examples in the nudges to trigger reflective learning or to induce opinion.

Our future work will examine the effectiveness of the nudges in AVW with an experimental study, and *how* to provide the nudges in addition to the *when* and *what*. Transferability to other population and systems will need to be investigated.

Acknowledgements. This research was supported by the EU-FP7-ICT-257184 ImREAL grant, an EPSRC Doctoral Training Grant, a teaching development grant from the University of Canterbury, and an Ako Aotearoa grant.

REFERENCES

[1] I. Arapakis, B. B. Cambazoglu, and M. Lalmas. 2014. On the feasibility of predicting news popularity at cold start. In *International Conference on Social Informatics*. Springer International Publishing. 290-299.

[2] E. Arelando 2013. The Millennials Are Coming! Proven Engagement Strategies. *Learning Solutions Magazine*.

[3] V. G. Ashok, S. Feng, and Y. Choi. 2013. Success with style: Using writing style to predict the success of novels. *Poetry*, *580*(9), 70.

[4] R. Bandari, S. Asur, and B.A. Huberman. 2012. The Pulse of News in Social Media: Forecasting Popularity. In *ICWSM*.

[5] E. Bothos, D. Apostolou, and G. Mentzas. 2015. Recommender systems for nudging commuters towards eco-friendly decisions. *Intelligent Decision Technologies*, *9*(3), 295-306.

[6] P. Brusilovsky, S. Somyürek, J. Guerra, R. Hosseini, and V. Zadorozhny. 2015. The value of social: Comparing open student modeling and open social student modeling. *Proc. Int. Conf. User Modeling, Adaptation, and Personalization*. Springer International Publishing. 44-55.

[7] S. Bull, and J. Kay. 2016. SMILI☺: a framework for interfaces to learning data in Open Learner Models, learning analytics and related fields. *Artificial Intelligence in Education*, *26*(1), 293-331.

[8] B. L. Castleman, and L. C. Page. 2013. Summer nudging: Can text messages and peer mentor outreach increase college going among low-income high school graduates. In *Soc. for Research on Educational Effectiveness Spring Conf., DC*.

[9] N. V. Chawla, K. W. Bowyer, L. O. Hall, and W. P. Kegelmeyer. 2002. SMOTE: synthetic minority over-sampling technique. *Journal of artificial intelligence research*, 16, 321-357.

[10] M. A. Chatti, M. Marinov, O. Sabov, et al. (2016). Video annotation and analytics in Course-Mapper. *Smart Learning Environments*, 3(1), 10.

[11] M. T. Chi, and R. Wylie. 2014. The ICAP framework: Linking cognitive engagement to active learning outcomes. *Educational Psychologist*, 49(4), 219-243.

[12] C. A. Conkey, C. Bowers, J. Cannon Bowers, and A. Sanchez. 2013. Machinima and Video- Based Soft-Skills Training for Frontline Healthcare Workers. *Games for health*, 2(1), 39-43.

[13] M. W. Cronin, and K. A. Cronin. 1992. Recent empirical studies of the pedagogical effects of interactive video instruction in "soft skill" areas. *Computing in Higher Education*, 3(2), 53.

[14] F. D. Davis. 1989. Perceived usefulness, perceived ease of use, and user acceptance of information technology. *MIS quarterly*, 319-340.

[15] V. Dimitrova, and P. Brna. 2016. From Interactive Open Learner Modelling to Intelligent Mentoring: STyLE-OLM and Beyond. *Artificial Intelligence in Education*, 26(1), 332-349.

[16] E. Frias-Martinez, S. Y. Chen, R. D. Macredie, and X. Liu. 2007. The role of human factors in stereotyping behavior and perception of digital library users: a robust clustering approach. *User Modeling and User-Adapted Interaction*, 17(3), 305-337.

[17] M. Giannakos, D. Sampson, and Ł. Kidziński, 2016. Introduction to smart learning analytics: foundations and developments in video-based learning. *Smart Learning Environments*, 3(1), 1-9.

[18] P. J. Guo, J. Kim, and R. Rubin. 2014. How Video Production Affects Student Engagement: An Empirical Study of MOOC Videos. *Proc. 1st ACM Conf. Learning at Scale*. 41-50.

[19] Y. Hara, Y. Tomomune, and M. Shigemori. 2004. Categorization of Japanese TV viewers based on program genres they watch. *User Modeling and User-Adapted Interaction*, 14, 87-117.

[20] S. G. Hart. 2006. NASA-task load index (NASA-TLX); 20 years later. *Proc. the Human Factors and Ergonomics Society annual meeting*, 50(9), Sage Publications. 904-908.

[21] H. U. Hoppe, M. Müller, A. Alissandrakis, M. Milrad, C. Schneegass, and N. Malzahn. 2016. "VC/DC"-Video versus Domain Concepts in Comments to Learner-generated Science Videos. In *24th Int. Conf. on Computers in Education*. Asia-Pacific Society for Computers in Education. *172-181.*

[22] A. Jameson, B. Berendt, S. Gabrielli, F. Cena, C. Gena, F. Vernero, and K. Reinecke. 2014. Choice architecture for human-computer interaction. *Foundations and Trends® in Human–Computer Interaction*, 7(1–2), 1-235.

[23] G. R. Johnson. 1991. Teaching Tips for Users of the Motivated Strategies for Learning Questionnaire (MSLQ).

[24] A. Kleftodimos and G. Evangelidis. 2016. Using open source technologies and open internet resources for building an interactive video based learning environment that supports learning analytics. *Smart Learning Environments*, 3(1), 1-23.

[25] K. R. Koedinger, J. Kim, J. Z. Jia, E. A. McLaughlin, and N. L. Bier. 2015. Learning is not a spectator sport: Doing is better than watching for learning from a MOOC. *Proc. 2nd ACM Conference on Learning@ Scale*. ACM. 111-120.

[26] G. Kovacs. 2016. Effects of in-video quizzes on MOOC lecture viewing, *Proc. 3rd Learning @ Scale*, 31-40.

[27] M. Kravčík, and R. Klamma. 2011. On psychological aspects of learning environments design. In *European Conference on Technology Enhanced Learning*. Springer. 436-441.

[28] G. Kurtz, A. Tsimerman, and O. Steiner-Lavi. 2014. The Flipped-Classroom Approach: The Answer to Future Learning? *European J. of Open, Distance and E-learning*, 17(2), 172-182.

[29] Y. Long and V. Aleven. 2017. Enhancing learning outcomes through self-regulated learning support with an Open Learner Model. *User Modeling and User-Adapted Interaction*, 1-34.

[30] A. Louis and A. Nenkova. 2013. What Makes Writing Great? First Experiments on Article Quality Prediction in the Science Journalism Domain. *Transactions of the Association for Computational Linguistics*, 1, 341-352.

[31] J. Masthoff and J. Vassileva. 2015. Tutorial on Personalization for Behaviour Change. In *Proceedings of the 20th International Conference on Intelligent User Interfaces (IUI '15)*. ACM. 439-442.

[32] L. N. Michaud, and K. F. McCoy. 2004. Empirical derivation of a sequence of user stereotypes for language learning. *User modeling and user-adapted interaction*, 14(4), 317-350.

[33] S. Michie, M. M. van Stralen, and R. West. 2011. The behaviour change wheel: a new method for characterising and

designing behaviour change interventions. *Implementation science*, 6(1), 42.

[34] A. Mitrovic, V. Dimitrova, A. Weerasinghe, and L. Lau. 2016. Reflexive experiential learning using active video watching for soft skills training. *Proc. 24th Int. Conf. Computers in Education*. APSCE. 192-201.

[35] A. Mitrovic, V. Dimitrova, L. Lau, A. Weerasinghe, and M. Mathews. 2017. Supporting constructive video-based learning: requirements elicitation from exploratory studies. (*accepted for 19th Int. Conf. on Artificial Intelligence in Education -AIED 2017*).

[36] R. Münscher, M. Vetter, and T. Scheuerle. 2015. A review and taxonomy of choice architecture techniques. *Journal of Behavioral Decision Making*, 29, 511-524.

[37] G. Paliouras, V. Karkaletsis, C. Papatheodorou, and C. D. Spyropoulos. 1999. Exploiting learning techniques for the acquisition of user stereotypes and communities. In *UM99 User Modeling*. Springer Vienna. 169-178.

[38] A. Pardo, N. Mirriahi, S. Dawson, Y. Zhao, A. Zhao, and D. Gaševic. 2015. Identifying learning strategies associated with active use of video annotation software. *Proc. 5th Int. Conf. Learning Analytics and Knowledge*. ACM. 255-259.

[39] Pew Research Centre. 2015. 5 facts about online video, for YouTube's 10th birthday, Report, January 2015.

[40] P. R. Pintrich, and E. V. De Groot. 1990. Motivational and self-regulated learning components of classroom academic performance. *Journal of educational psychology*, 82(1), 33.

[41] R. A. Sottilare, A. Graesser, X. Hu, and B. Goldberg. (Eds.). 2014. *Design Recommendations for Intelligent Tutoring Systems: Volume 2-Instructional Management* (Vol. 2). US Army Research Laboratory.

[42] T. Stajner, B. Thomee, A.M.Popescu, M.Pennacchiotti, and A. Jaimes. 2013. Automatic selection of social media responses to news. *Proc. 19th ACM SIGKDD international conference on Knowledge discovery and data mining*. ACM. 50-58

[43] C. Tan, L. Lee, and B. Pang. 2014. The effect of wording on message propagation: Topic- and author-controlled natural experiments on Twitter. *Proc. ACL 2014*.

[44] A. Tatar, P. Antoniadis, M. D. De Amorim, and S. Fdida. 2014. From popularity prediction to ranking online news. *Social Network Analysis and Mining*, 4(1), 1-12.

[45] D. Thakker, D. Despotakis, V. Dimitrova, L. Lau, and P. Brna. 2012. Taming digital traces for informal learning: a semantic-driven approach. In *European Conf. Technology Enhanced Learning*. Springer. 348-362.

[46] R. H. Thaler, and C. R. Sunstein. 2008. *Nudge: Improving Decisions about Health, Wealth, and Happiness*. Yale University Press, New Haven.

[47] I. Vieira, A. P. Lopes, and F. Soares. 2014. The potential benefits of using videos in higher education. *Proc. EDULEARN14 Conf.* (pp. 0750-0756). IATED Publications.

[48] J. Wachtler, M. Hubmann, H. Zöhrer, and M. Ebner. 2016. An analysis of the use and effect of questions in interactive learning-videos. *Smart Learning Environments*, 3(1), 13.

[49] A. M. F. Yousef, M. A. Chatti, and U. Schroeder. 2014. The state of video-based learning: A review and future perspectives. *Int. J. Adv. Life Sci*, 6(3/4), 122-135.

A Multi-Armed Bandit Model Selection for Cold-Start User Recommendation

Crícia Z. Felício
Instituto Federal do Triângulo Mineiro
Uberlândia, MG, Brazil
cricia@iftm.edu.br

Klérisson V. R. Paixão
Universidade Federal de Uberlândia
Uberlândia, MG, Brazil
klerisson@ufu.br

Celia A. Z. Barcelos
Universidade Federal de Uberlândia
Uberlândia, MG, Brazil
celiazb@ufu.br

Philippe Preux
Université de Lille & CRIStAL
Villeneuve D'ascq, France
philippe.preux@inria.fr

ABSTRACT

How can we effectively recommend items to a user about whom we have no information? This is the problem we focus on in this paper, known as the cold-start problem. In most existing works, the cold-start problem is handled through the use of many kinds of information available about the user. However, what happens if we do not have any information? Recommender systems usually keep a substantial amount of prediction models that are available for analysis. Moreover, recommendations to new users yield uncertain returns. Assuming that a number of alternative prediction models is available to select items to recommend to a cold user, this paper introduces a *multi-armed bandit* based model selection, named PdMS. In comparison with three baselines, PdMS improves the performance as measured by the *nDCG*. These improvements are demonstrated on real, public datasets.

CCS CONCEPTS

•**Information systems** → **Recommender systems**; *Retrieval effectiveness;* Personalization;

KEYWORDS

Recommender system; Cold-start problem; Model selection; Multi-armed bandits

1 INTRODUCTION

Given a cold user, such as a new Netflix' client, how can we effectively recommend movies to him? In most existing works, a typical recommender system will request initial ratings [11, 49] and/or it will harvest the World Wide Web looking for the user's tastes [22, 44] to bootstrap the system. But apart from that, what happens if we do not have the right information to build the user's profile? So, how can we estimate the tastes of a new user without

UMAP'17, July 9–12, 2017, Bratislava, Slovakia
© 2017 ACM. 978-1-4503-4635-1/17/07...$15.00
DOI: http://dx.doi.org/10.1145/3079628.3079681

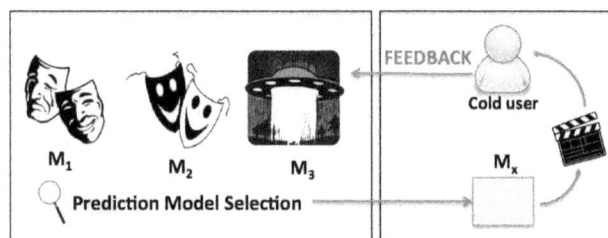

Figure 1: PdMS relies on feedback to learn how to appropriately select a consensual prediction model to deliver more accurate recommendations to cold users.

prior side information? The focus of this paper is on offering better recommendations for such cold users.

Different prediction models are used to deal with distinct stages of a user experience. For example, a particular model works better in earlier stages when the recommender system does not know much about the user. Then, as the number of interactions increases, another model may become more effective, and therefore, the recommendation system switches to the more powerful model. Switching methods [9] were designed to handle the cold-start problem. The idea is to switch from one model to an other once the system has enough data about the user, so that the user is no longer cold.

While the concept of switching models [6] is not new, the availability of several cold-start methods provides enriched resources to *model selection*. Applied to the cold-start stage, a model selection method may be seen as a framework to alternate among prediction models to find the most suitable one at each time, as the user warms-up. Few works have sought to empirically assess the efficacy of a model selection, specifically at the cold-start stage [8, 55].

In this paper, we propose PdMS (Figure 1), an effective *Prediction Model Selection* method to deal with cold users. Many proposed solutions to deal with this problem use side information, which may be of different kinds, such as social information [2, 13], user click behavior [37, 53], location-based information [12, 41], user's visual perception [16, 17], and, more broadly speaking, contextual information [1]. Particularly, we delve into user feedback, but without prior information about the user.

The first insight is to explore how a model selection can be useful at all to provide better recommendations to cold users. The reason we choose to select prediction models instead of building new ones is that these models have been tuned based on users already encountered by the recommender system: these models have already captured a lot of information about the users of the system so that it is *a priori* a good idea to try to frame any new user into an already known category; so, a cold user might be best served by one already tuned model available in the system [20].

The second insight is to consider our goal as a multi-armed bandit (MAB) problem [3]. Recommender systems dealing with a new user repeatedly propose items yielding uncertain returns. In this situation, we face a problem of sequential decision-making under uncertainty: an action amounts to selecting a particular model to serve a particular user; actions have to be selected to find a suitable prediction model for the user at hand, and to investigate other ones (explore vs. exploit). The idea is to be benefit from the relative performance of various prediction models [14], an idea also reminiscent of ensemble methods. Therefore, a model selection that maximizes the recommendation gain might be more precise.

Our primary contributions are:

- We show how to formalize the model selection problem faced by the recommendation system as a multi-armed bandit problem.
- We introduce PdMS, an effective approach to deal with cold users, *i.e.* users for whom no prior side information is available.
- We empirically put PdMS to the test on four real, public datasets.

This paper is organized as follows. First, we further motivate the need for a new cold-start method and its main concept (Section 2). Next, we present the approach and how it works (Section 3). Section 4 describes our experimental settings. Section 5 discusses the results of the experiments. Then, Section 6 discusses related work, and Section 7 concludes the paper.

2 BACKGROUND

As a motivating example, let us consider the domain of movie recommendations. Based on the ratings already collected we can apply a recommendation algorithm and make predictions for the movies not already rated using the personalized preferences from each user. User's preferences might indicate a preferred movie genre, director, actors, etc, and be represented by a prediction model.

Now, let us assume a new (cold) user u is looking for movies he would like to watch. A common situation is that the new user has not yet given any rating and no other information is available about him. However, he is admitted into the system, without providing any profile information. The new user probably has similar tastes to some other users in the system. Then for the initial recommendations, one way to recommend to him can be use a prediction model which is dealing correctly with other users.

Assume that for each recommended movie the cold user gives a feedback that will be used to make the next recommendation. So, the recommender system will first explore the different prediction models and then use feedback to select the most appropriate

model for this user, at his current stage of interaction with the recommender system.

Before going any further, we introduce some terminology and notations on recommender systems, and on multi-armed bandits.

Let U be a set of m users and I be a set of n items. We assume that each user $u \in U$ and each item $i \in I$ has a unique identifier. The user-item rating matrix is $R = [r_{u,i}]_{m \times n}$, where each entry $r_{u,i}$ is either the rating given by user u on item i, or unknown. In a live system, as new ratings are entered by users, the rating matrix R depends on time t, so that the notation should be R_t; in the paper, we often drop this t index as long as the meaning of sentences is not in jeopardy. The recommendation task is based on the prediction of the missing values of the user-item rating matrix. Then, prediction models are used to rank items and recommend the k top-ranked.

A Multi-Armed Bandit problem is a sequential decision problem where an algorithm continually chooses among a set of possible actions (arms) which we assume to be finite in this paper. At each time step t, an arm a is selected and pulled which leads to a reward $X_a(t)$. This reward is distributed according to a certain unknown law. Here, we consider that the goal is to learn, as fast as possible, through repeated arm pulls, the arm that returns the maximum expected reward.

In this work, we assume a set of prediction models as the arms from Multi-Armed Bandit problem. Then, a bandit algorithm is sequentially applied to choose among the prediction models either the best performing one at the moment (exploitation), or an other model to better estimate its performance (exploration). We rely on the $UCB1$ algorithm [3] and ϵ-Greedy algorithm [54] to implement our model selection. $UCB1$ maintains the mean reward of each arm (prediction model) a, denoted by $\bar{X}_a$. Each time arm a is played, the mean reward $\bar{X}_a$ is updated. The number of pulls of arm a is denoted by n_a. In both notations, t is implicit.

In UCB1, each arm is initially pulled a couple of times to estimate its mean reward. Then, at turn t, UCB1 selects arm $a(t)$ according to Equation (1).

$$a(t) = \arg \max_{s=1...k} \left(\bar{X}_{a_s} + \sqrt{\frac{2 \ln t}{n_{a_s}}} \right) \qquad (1)$$

The chosen arm is the one maximizing the sum of the mean reward $\bar{X}_a$, and a confidence term $ba(t) := \sqrt{\frac{2 \ln t}{n_a}}$. At each t, the arm to be played is selected as the one maximizing the balance between immediate profit and the gathering of useful information.

UCB1 is particularly appealing because of its theoretical guarantees: as the number of pulls increases, we know that the number of sub-optimal arms being pulled grows as the logarithm of the number of pulls, that is very slowly; we also know that it can not grow slower than that.

UCB1 with tunned constant is a variant of UCB1 where the confidence term is represented as $\sqrt{\frac{C \ln t}{n_a}}$, where C is the exploration constant to tune.

ϵ-Greedy also maintains the mean reward of each arm (prediction model) a, denoted by $\bar{X}_a$. At each round, the ϵ-Greedy algorithm selects the arm with the highest mean reward with probability $1 - \epsilon$, and selects an arm uniformly at random with probability ϵ.

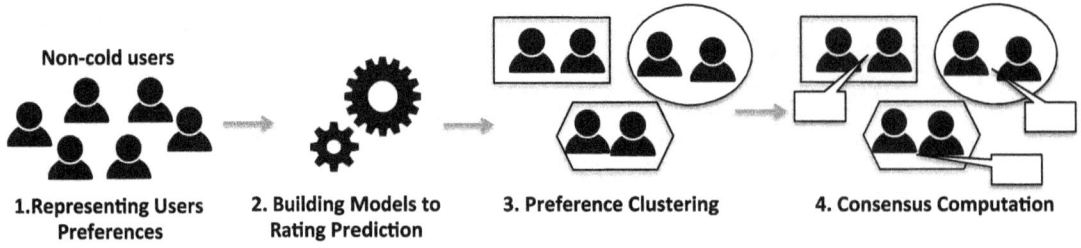

Figure 2: Overview of PdMS model building illustration.

The ϵ-decreasing greedy variant consists in slowly decreasing ϵ along time. Hence, the algorithm moves from purely random ($\epsilon = 1$) to purely greedy ($\epsilon = 0$). The theoretical guarantees of this selection strategy are not as good as for UCB1. However, it is known to often perform very-well in practice.

3   PdMS APPROACH

To exemplify the problem, let us consider a toy example: a user-item matrix is represented in Table 1a. We apply a matrix factorization algorithm to complete it, namely the BiasedMF[1] algorithm [32]: this step is detailed in section 3.1. We obtain the predicted ratings as shown in Table 1b.

At this point, we depart from the standard approach. Keeping in mind that this is just a toy example given for the sake of explaining our approach, we consider that each row of Table 1b is a prediction model.

When a new user comes into the system, we can choose one of the 5 prediction models to make recommendations for him. However this is not reasonable in a real-world recommendation system, where we have millions of users. Then, our first challenge is to reduce the number of prediction models available to the switch process. Considering the rows of the rating matrix, it is possible to cluster them: each cluster is made of users that basically assign the same ratings to the same items. It is a common assumption in matrix factorization that the rows of rating matrices can be clustered (that's actually the reason why rating matrices have low rank).

According to this intuition, we define PdMS as an algorithm made of two phases: (i) computing and updating prediction models and (ii) recommendation. Phase (i) is presented in the next section; it is based on our prior work [20]. Phase (ii) is then presented in the subsequent section.

3.1   Model Computing and Updating

To define the set of prediction models, we apply three steps: Rating prediction, Preference clustering, and Consensus computation. We illustrate this process in Figure 2, where the first step consists in obtain the user-item rating matrix of non-cold users and step 2, 3, and 4 are explained as follows.

Rating prediction. From the user-item rating matrix, composed only for non-cold users, we use a matrix factorization technique to get a matrix of predicted ratings R'. R' is expressed as a product of latent factors, $R' = PQ^T$, where P is the user latent factor matrix,

---

and Q is the item latent factor matrix. The predicted rating of the item i_k by user u_j is $R'_{u_j, i_k} = predict(u_j, i_k, P, Q)$, the details of this function depending on the completion method being used.

As an example, Table 1b shows the predicted rating matrix R' obtained from the user-item matrix of Table 1a, as completed using the BiasedMF algorithm. With BiasedMF, the prediction function is $predict(u_j, i_k, P, Q) = \mu + b_{u_j} + b_{i_k} + P_{u_j} Q^T_{i_k}$, where μ is the overall average rating, b_{u_j} is the deviation from μ of user u_j ratings, b_{i_k} is the deviation from μ of item i_k ratings, P_{u_j} is the u_j^{th} row of matrix P which are the latent factors for user u_j, and $Q_{i_k}^{\text{th}}$ row of matrix Q which are the latent factors for item i_k. Finally, given the predicted rating matrix R', the preference vector for a user u_j is defined as the predicted ratings for user u_j, $\theta_j = R'_{u_j}$.

Preference clustering. Given a predicted rating matrix R', we can cluster users according to their preference vectors, that are the rows of R'. A distance function and a clustering algorithm C are used. After clustering, we have a set of clusters $C = \{C_s\}$, where each cluster C_s contains a set of users with similar preferences.

Consensus computation. For each cluster C_s, we apply a consensus operator $\mathcal{A}$ to get the consensual preference vector $\hat{\theta}_s$ of cluster C_s. In this paper, the consensus operator is the average, that is $\hat{\theta}_{s,k}$ is the average predicted rating for item k, the average being computed on the subset of users belonging to cluster C_s. We obtain $M = \{M_1 = (C_1, \hat{\theta}_1), \dots, M_K = (C_K, \hat{\theta}_K)\}$, the set of prediction models where each M_s is composed of a cluster of users C_s and its consensual preference vector $\hat{\theta}_s$. Table 1c shows the result of clustering the predicted rating matrix rows (Table 1b) in 2 clusters and presents their consensual preference vectors $\hat{\theta}_1$ and $\hat{\theta}_2$.

Model Update. In a live recommendation system, due to the computational cost, the predicted rating matrix R' is computed from times to times only. At any time, R' is computed using a rating matrix R_{t_p} available at some earlier time $t_p \leq t$. As new ratings are entered into the system, these new ratings may be compared to those that have been predicted; so we compare the known entries of R_t at the current time t with the corresponding predictions available in R_{t_p}; when the divergence between the observed ratings and the predicted ratings becomes too large, it is time to update the model. To be more specific, let $diff(t) = \sum_{(u,i) \text{known at time } t} |r_{u,i} - r'_{u,i}|$ After each update on R at any time $t > t_p$, it is straightforward to update $diff(t)$ incrementally. Then, we decide on updating M once $diff(t)$ reaches a certain threshold.

---

[1]The name BiasedMF comes from the LibRec library.

Table 1: (a) Example of a user-item rating matrix R. "-" means that the user has not rated the item. (b) Predicted rating matrix R'. (c) Consensual preference vector.

(a)								(b)								(c)						
	i_1	i_2	i_3	i_4	i_5	i_6	i_7		i_1	i_2	i_3	i_4	i_5	i_6	i_7		i_1	i_2	i_3	i_4	i_5	i_6	i_7
u_1	5	2	4	-	5	1	-	u_1	4.6	2.09	4.23	4.24	4.84	1.07	1.0	u_1	4.6	2.09	4.23	4.24	4.84	1.07	1.0
u_2	4	-	5	-	5	-	1	u_2	4.2	3.8	4.42	5.0	4.86	2.28	1.2	u_2	4.2	3.8	4.42	5.0	4.86	2.28	1.2
u_3	2	5	3	5	-	-	-	u_3	1.97	4.84	3.22	4.87	2.68	2.68	1.61	$\hat{\theta}_1$	4.4	2.94	4.32	4.62	4.85	1.67	1.1
u_4	1	-	2	-	2	-	-	u_4	1.19	3.24	2.17	3.56	1.92	1.23	1.0	u_3	1.97	4.84	3.22	4.87	2.68	2.68	1.61
u_5	-	-	3	4	1	-	-	u_5	1.77	3.16	2.81	4.07	1.14	1.6	1.56	u_4	1.19	3.24	2.17	3.56	1.92	1.23	1.0
																u_5	1.77	3.16	2.81	4.07	1.14	1.6	1.56
																$\hat{\theta}_2$	1.64	3.74	2.73	4.16	1.91	1.83	1.39

3.2 Recommendation

From the previous steps, the recommendation system has a predicted rating for each item for the current user to recommend to. Now, it has to decide which items will be recommended.

For that purpose, we propose PdMS as a method to select a prediction model and determine the items to recommend to a user. PdMS applies a multi-armed bandit algorithm to that end.

PdMS: After getting the prediction models, we sort the consensual preference vectors according to their ratings. So, for each $\hat{\theta}_s$ we have a $\hat{\theta}'_s$ that represents the consensual preference vector in a sorted order. The idea is to recommend first the items with the highest ratings in each model. We hypothesize that this strategy can contribute to learn users preference faster. For instance, the correspondent $\hat{\theta}'_1$ to $\hat{\theta}_1$ in Table 1c will have the sorted list of items equal to $\{i_5, i_4, i_1, i_3, i_2, i_6, i_7\}$, while for $\hat{\theta}'_2$ we will have $\{i_4, i_2, i_3, i_5, i_6, i_1, i_7\}$. At each time t a recommendation for a user u is made according to a bandit algorithm $\mathcal{B}$ as follows:

(1) Select a prediction model M_s using the bandit algorithm $\mathcal{B}$;
(2) Select i^* from $\hat{\theta}'_s$ the next top-rated item not yet recommended to u;
(3) Recommend item i^* to user u;
(4) Receive a feedback from u;
(5) Compute the reward;
(6) Update the prediction model statistics of $\mathcal{B}$.

Note that we consider that PdMS approach will be applied to make recommendations to users that are initially new users who remain cold until they have provided a certain amount of preferences/feedback on recommended items. The threshold to determine when a user is not cold anymore can be different for distinct systems. Arguably, a user quickly loses the interest of a recommender system if he is compelled to provide many ratings [15, 22, 38]. Experiments have demonstrated that several state-of-art systems are able to provide recommendations with reasonable quality after getting 15 ratings from the cold user [11, 50]. In this paper we measure the method performance after 5, 10, 15 and 20 recommendations using the *nDCG* metric. As soon as the user is not cold anymore the system can switch to a personalized prediction model.

Computing the Reward. The goal of step 5 in PdMS is to compute the reward using the feedback of the recommendation. It is computed applying the following method:

Feedback-based reward: We define the reward measure in Equation (2) based on the feedback of the recommendation. In this way, when a user gives a higher feedback for a recommended item, we will have a high reward. This method is easily adapted to implicit feedback, such as a clicks, views, purchases, *etc.*

$$X_{M_s}(t) = \frac{r_{u,i}}{r_{max}} \quad (2)$$

Where r_{max} represents the largest rating in the dataset and $r_{u,i}$ is the feedback of user u for the recommended item i according to the selected model M_s. For a implicit feedback we can consider that the value of $r_{u,i}$ is binary. For example, in a music recommender system we will have $r_{u,i} = 1$ if the user listens to a recommended song and $r_{u,i} = 0$ otherwise.

Example: Consider that the system will offer recommendations for two cold users, user u_a and u_b based on the consensual prediction models in 1c. Using PdMS UCB1 approach, it will initially make a random selection of prediction models. Suppose that for u_a the system first recommends the item i_5, according to $\hat{\theta}'_1$ and receives a feedback equal to 4. If $r_{max} = 5$, we will have a reward equal to 0.8 for prediction model $\hat{\theta}'_1$.

In the next recommendation using $\hat{\theta}'_2$ the item i_4 is recommended and receives a feedback equal to 1, then the reward to $\hat{\theta}'_2$ will be 0.2. At this point, for u_a we have a mean reward of 0.8 to $\hat{\theta}'_1$ and 0.2 to $\hat{\theta}'_2$ with one trial to each prediction model. Applying Equation (1), the next u_a recommendation will be i_1 using $\hat{\theta}'_1$ that represents the arm with the highest mean reward at that moment.

For the second user u_b, suppose the system will first select $\hat{\theta}'_2$ and recommend item i_4 receiving a feedback of 5, and then recommend item i_5 receiving a feedback of 2. The mean reward for user u_b is 0.4 to $\hat{\theta}'_1$ and 1 to $\hat{\theta}'_2$. In this case, the item i_2 will be the next recommendation of user u_b using $\hat{\theta}'_2$.

Considering a scenario where users are not logged-in or that we cannot identify the users, the PdMS system will see them like cold users. The first recommendation will be offered with the random selection of prediction models. Then, we rely on the user feedback to make the trade-off between exploitation/exploration. So that, even not logged user can take advantage of tunned prediction models already in the system.

With this running example, it is reasonable to assume that a new user can be framed into already known categories, which might foster the initial experience of the new user.

4 EXPERIMENTS

In this section, we give an overview of the datasets used in the experiments. Then, we describe the evaluation protocol used, and the other methods that we compare to ours.

4.1 Datasets

We evaluate PdMS on 4 real movies datasets. Table 2 summarizes their main features.

Table 2: Dataset features.

Dataset	Users	Items	Ratings	Sparsity (%)
Facebook	498	169	49,729	40.9
FilmTrust	1,508	2,071	35,494	98.86
Movielens	943	1,682	100,000	93.7
Flixster	1,323	1,175	811,726	47.78

Facebook Dataset [19] a survey from Facebook's users requested to rate a list of movies. Ratings range from 1 to 5.

Filmtrust Dataset [26] is about rate and sharing movies. Ratings range from 0.5 (min) to 4 (max).

Movielens Dataset [28] collected by the GroupLens Research Project contains movies ratings from users that rated at least 20 movies in a 1 to 5 range.

Flixster Dataset [29] collected from a social movie site, contains movies ratings in a 0.5 to 5 range.

4.2 Evaluation Criteria

As we focus on cold users, we adopt the leave-one-out protocol [52]: at each round, we train on all users but one which is used as a test user. As we do not use any information about the test user, it is a cold user. We call this protocol a **0-rating protocol**.

Ranking quality is measured computing the Normalized Discounted Cumulative Gain (nDCG) metric, see Equation (3). $DCG(u)$ is the discounted cumulative gain of predicted ranking for a target user u, $DCG^*(u)$ is the ground truth and N is the number of users in the result set. $DCG^*(u)$ is defined by equation (4). In that equation, $r_{u,1}$ is the rating (according to the user feedback) of the item first recommended for user u, t is the recommendation time, $r_{u,t}$ is the user feedback for the item recommended in turn t and T is the size of the ranked list.

$$NDCG = \frac{1}{N} \sum_u \frac{DCG(u)}{DCG^*(u)} \qquad (3)$$

$$DCG(u) = r_{u,1} + \sum_{t=2}^{T} \frac{r_{u,t}}{\log_2 t} \qquad (4)$$

4.3 Comparison Methods

To assess the effectiveness of our PdMS model, we compare it to the following baselines:

Global Average: A standard "popular" baseline, which recommends using the global average rate for an item.

Most Popular: Another standard baseline that rank the items based on the number of ratings received and recommend the top-ranked.

Random-MS: The Random-MS is a baseline we proposed that selects at random a prediction model. It receives as input the set of prediction models M and makes a recommendation for a user u at each time t according to the steps:

(1) Randomly select a prediction model M_s;
(2) Randomly select an item i not recommended yet from $\hat{\theta}_s$;
(3) Recommend item i to user u;
(4) Receive a feedback from u.

Parameter Settings. We use LibRec [24], which provides an implementation of Global Average. The implementation of Random-MS and PdMS are built on top of BiasedMF algorithm in LibRec library. We cluster BiasedMF prediction models and in the recommendation process we include the implementation of Random-MS, PdMS UCB1, PdMS UCB1 with tuned constant, PdMS ϵ-Greedy and PdMS ϵ-decreasing Greedy algorithm.

Experiments were executed with 10 latent factors and 100 iterations. We executed Random-MS 5 times and get the average result. With PdMS, we also experimentally test several cluster size. Then we set the optimal number of clusters to 4 clusters for FilmTrust, 3 clusters for Facebook , Movielens and Flixster. Beside this, we apply K-means (using the Euclidean distance measure) as the clustering algorithm.

For PdMS ϵ-Greedy we test ϵ in $\{0.1, 0.2, 0.3, 0.4, 0.5\}$. The optimal ϵ value is 0.3 for Facebook dataset and 0.2 for Filmtrust, Movielens and Flixster dataset. PdMS ϵ-Decreasing greedy start with $\epsilon = 0.9$ and we use the function $\frac{0.5\epsilon}{t}$ to decrease ϵ value at each new recommendation.

For PdMS UCB1 with tunned constant we test different values to C where C in $\{0.05, 0.1, 0.2, 0.5, 0.8, 1, ..., 16\}$ and obtained $C = 0.05$ as the optimal value in all datasets.

5 RESULTS AND DISCUSSION

This section reports our results and further discussions. We aim to answer the following questions:

Q1: How effective is PdMS to offer initial recommendations to cold users?

Q2: Are the PdMS results reliable, or random and noisy?

Table 3 presents the $nDCG$ at rank size of 5, 10, 15, and 20 per method. Note that PdMS has two variants, UCB1 and ϵ-Greedy.

5.1 Recommendation Effectiveness (Q1)

Comparing the results of PdMS to Global Average, we note the following improvements regarding $nDCG@5$: 13.1% on Facebook, 5.9% on Filmtrust, 12.4% on Movielens and 11.6% on Flixster. The

Table 3: We compute the *nDCG* of three baseline approaches and four PdMS variants across four datasets. The four last rows represents the results of PdMS.

(a) Facebook

	Method	@5	@10	@15	@20
		Rank size			
	Global Average	0.728	0.734	0.740	0.749
	Most Popular	0.813	0.808	0.813	0.814
	Random-MS	0.714	0.719	0.725	0.732
PdMS	ϵ-Greedy	0.858	0.851	0.849	0.849
	ϵ-decreasing greedy	0.858	0.852	0.851	0.849
	UCB1	0.858	0.851	0.849	0.848
	UCB1 tuned constant	0.859	0.854	0.851	0.850

(b) Filmtrust

	Method	@5	@10	@15	@20
		Rank size			
	Global Average	0.800	0.808	0.814	0.821
	Most Popular	0.819	0.824	0.832	0.839
	Random-MS	0.805	0.811	0.815	0.818
PdMS	ϵ-Greedy	0.859	0.858	0.861	0.862
	ϵ-decreasing greedy	0.859	0.859	0.860	0.861
	UCB1	0.859	0.857	0.860	0.861
	UCB1 tuned constant	0.858	0.859	0.860	0.861

(c) Movielens

	Method	@5	@10	@15	@20
		Rank size			
	Global Average	0.735	0.749	0.765	0.780
	Most Popular	0.786	0.795	0.807	0.822
	Random-MS	0.729	0.739	0.755	0.772
PdMS	ϵ-Greedy	0.858	0.859	0.865	0.874
	ϵ-decreasing greedy	0.859	0.859	0.866	0.874
	UCB1	0.857	0.858	0.865	0.874
	UCB1 tuned constant	0.858	0.859	0.866	0.875

(d) Flixster

	Method	@5	@10	@15	@20
		Rank size			
	Global Average	0.708	0.718	0.721	0.724
	Most Popular	0.766	0.767	0.769	0.769
	Random-MS	0.706	0.704	0.705	0.707
PdMS	ϵ-Greedy	0.824	0.821	0.820	0.819
	ϵ-decreasing greedy	0.823	0.822	0.821	0.821
	UCB1	0.822	0.821	0.819	0.817
	UCB1 tuned constant	0.823	0.822	0.821	0.820

comparison against Random-MS is similar with the following improvements: 14.5% on Facebook, 5.4% on Filmtrust, 13% on Movielens and 11.8% on Flixster. Most Popular presents better results than the others two baselines and compared with this method our approach achieves the following *nDCG*@5 improvements: 4.6% on Facebook, 4% on Filmtrust, 7,3% on Movielens and 5.8% on Flixster.

From Table 3, we first observe that PdMS consistently outperforms all baselines in all four datasets. Note that on Filmtrust, PdMS gain is smaller when compared to Global Average. That might be so because of the rating distribution. 68.14% of Filmtrust ratings are greater or equal to 3, see Figure 3b. On the other hand, a smaller gain of PdMS in all datasets when compared with Most Popular, mainly to Facebook and Filmtrust dataset, indicates that in general the most popular items receive the greater ratings.

In particular, the difference between PdMS variants are small, and we now assess their significance.

5.2 Randomness Analysis (Q2)

We examine whether the recommendations generated by PdMS are significantly better than those made by baseline methods and its variants on the different datasets by performing a null hypothesis test. We express *H0* as: Recommendations offered from Global Average, Random-MS, Most Popular and PdMS (ϵ-Greedy, UCB1, ϵ-Greedy Decreasing and UCB1 with tunned constant) are distributed identically on all 4 datasets.

We checked the normality of the results with a Shapiro-Wilk test, and their homogeneity of the results (*nDCG*) using a Bartlett test.

The tests reject both assumptions of normality, and homogeneity. Then, to check whether the null hypothesis holds, we run Kruskal-Wallis tests on the *nDCG* results, using the 95% confidence level, (*i.e.*, p-value < 0.05). The Kruskal-Wallis test is a non-parametric test to assess whether samples originate from the same distribution.

Between two baselines, Global Average and Random-MS there is no statistically significant difference. However, Most Popular outperforms both. The difference between PdMS and all baselines are significant, the p-value of Kruskal-Wallis test is less than $2.2 10^{-16}$, therefore we reject the null hypothesis *H0*. In conclusion, PdMS performs significantly better than the 3 other baselines, but the four PdMS variants have similar results.

5.3 Limitations and Future Work

PdMS design decisions suggest a set of limitations, many of which we hope to address in future work.

First, we considered only one type of collaborative filtering algorithm, the Matrix Factorization. It is not clear whether conclusions generalize beyond this setting. Future work could compare it to state of the art systems. However, the approaches that are compared are all based on the same completed matrix, so that they should all suffer in the same way from the result of the matrix factorization. Second, we compare the two exploration model, ϵ-Greedy and UCB1, and their variants ϵ-decreasing greedy and UCB1 with tuned constant. However, we did not experiment optimization of bandit algorithms. Future work could also perform experiments with optimized methods.

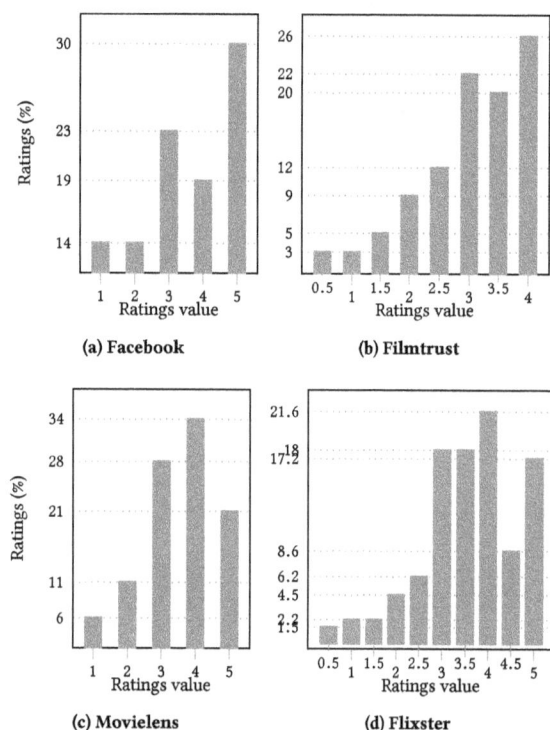

Figure 3: Rating distribution per dataset.

Another threat arises from the evaluation criteria. We rely on *nDCG* score to access our approach, mainly because we were investigating the recommendation quality. Overall it presents high accuracy levels, but we might check other metrics to ensure a fair evaluation [31]. For example, user coverage study would be required to reveal whether our approach can offer recommendation to a large audience; and likewise, catalog coverage [51].

We also intend to work in a mechanism to identify when a user is not cold anymore. The idea is to harness the available models in the systems as much as possible, without sooner resort to typical recommendation models.

6 RELATED WORK

This section reviews prior works on user cold-start problem. Additionally, concerning the goal of the paper, we distinguish between two threads of related work. First, we elaborate on approaches that are coping with model selection for recommendation. Second, we survey approaches focusing on applications of Bandits in recommender systems.

User Cold-Start Recommendation

The history of cold-start problem in academia and industry to recommender systems is long [30]. A number of studies have proposed methods to improve certain aspects of the cold user problem.

One trend of these studies has been towards the application of multiple matrix factorization techniques for cold-start problems. The challenge is to predict the rating of deliberated held out

cells in the user-item matrix. Then, a myriad of machine learning techniques have been applied such as clustering [39], classification [27], regression [45], or singular value decomposition [48]. Barjasteh et al. proposed a two-stage algorithm to factorize the rating matrix and then factorizes user similarity matrix and item similarity matrix [4, 5]. However, for massive scale of users, computing the similarity matrix might be prohibitive due to the computational resource power demanded and real-time constraints.

Even achieving high accuracy, the matrix completion task has shown to be insufficient to make the best recommendations. Other works cope with cold-start problems by the design of user interactions, basically, a survey given during the recommender system sign-up process. The idea is to ask new members to rate set of movies, instead of one movie at a time [11, 23].

Another trend of research has been towards designing new prediction models. The typical approach is to use side information to build a prediction model [1], specially using social information. For instance, the work of Ma et al. is matrix factorization based approach that incorporates contextual social information into prediction models [40]. In the same direction, Pereira and Hruschka proposed a hybrid system to recommend for users without ratings, but they rely on demographic information [47]. Social recommenders are often expensive due to the need of model computation whenever new user ratings arrive. Zhao et al. explored the combination of user-item relationship with item content to learning the preferences of user in more scalable way [57]. Wongchokprasitti et al. studied the possibility to use user models built by one system to another to address the cold start problem [56]. Peng et al. present a method to better weight the impact of user's attributes, preferences and item's popularity in multi-level regression model [46]. Guo et al. focused on both user modeling and trust modeling [25]. They proposed an improved recommender model based on trusted neighbors. Meo et al. found that centrality metrics are the most reliable way to spot reputable users in trust networks [43].

Herein, we advocate that the growing amount of prediction models opens an important problem of model selection. Specifically, we investigate how to handle a cold user without prior side information. Moreover, our approach exploits models already built in the system.

Model Selection in Recommender System

Cold user eventually warms up (or leaves the system). From that perspective, model selection methods have been applied to recommender systems as a switching mechanism between stages of a user experience [9].

Our work is inspired by techniques for selecting models, however, we are interested in selecting better models within the cold-start stage. There are some common themes between our approach and the work of Billsus and Pazzani [6]. They proposed a news recommender system that leverages explicit feedback from the user to build and update the user model. We also rely on user's feedback. However we use feedback to analyze which model among a set of consensual ones might be the best one.

Our approach builds on the same understand from Ekstrand and Riedl [14], different prediction models unveil distinct results for the same user. While their focus is on switch hybrids systems, we proposed a solution to switch among consensual prediction models existing in the same system. Specially within cold-start stage, Braunhofer et al. also proposed a switching mechanism, but dependent on contextual information [8].

Bandits in Recommender System

In the following, we review approaches which applied Bandits algorithms in recommender systems.

Li et al. reported on personalized recommendation of news articles as a contextual bandit problem [35]. They propose LɪɴUCB, an extension to the UCB algorithm. It selects the news based on mean and standard deviation. It also has a factor α to control the exploration/exploitation trade-off. Moreover, Caron and Bhagat incorporate social components into bandit algorithms to tackle the cold-start problem [10]. They designed an improved bandit strategy to model the user's preference using multi-armed bandits. Several works model the recommendation problem using a MAB setting in which the items to be recommended are the arms [7, 21, 42]. In a different way, Lacerda et al. model users as arms to recommend daily-deals [33, 34]. They consider strategies for splitting users into exploration and exploitation. Li et al. proposed to double cluster users and items using bandits. We also rely on clustering users, but to reach a consensual model that could be leverage by our model selection strategy [36].

In our prior work [18], we presented a research proposal with the goal of analyzing existing prediction models taken from recommender systems to better understand their nature. Our study reported here, relies on and extends our previous study design. The goal of PdMS is the selection of existing prediction models that might offer better recommendations for cold users. Our MAB setting is also different, since the arms are consensual prediction models. Besides that, our approach requires no prior effort from the user.

7 CONCLUSIONS

In this paper, we showed how a careful model selection can provide better recommendations to full cold-start user. Furthermore, our approach, PdMS, performed reasonably well even with no prior side information, but exploring feedback to frame new users into known categories. It achieves 85% accuracy levels of $nDCG@5$. To sum-up, our contributions are:

- A formalization of the model selection as a multi-armed bandit problem (Sections 2 and 3).
- PdMS, which is an effective approach to recommend for users without prior side information (Section 3).
- An empirical evaluation of PdMS against four real, public datasets (Section 4 and 5).

Looking forward, PdMS envisions recommender systems in which substantial amount of prediction models is available for analysis, making possible a new wave of intelligent recommender systems.

Acknowledgments

We would like to thank the Brazilian research agencies CAPES, CNPq and FAPEMIG. K.V.R. Paixão is sponsored by a scholarship from CAPES. Ph. Preux' research is funded by Contrat de Plan État Région Data, French Ministry of Higher Education and Research, and CNRS; he also thanks the support of Inria, and SequeL.

REFERENCES

[1] Gediminas Adomavicius and Alexander Tuzhilin. 2011. Context-Aware Recommender Systems. In *Recommender Systems Handbook*, Francesco Ricci, Lior Rokach, Bracha Shapira, and Paul B. Kantor (Eds.). Springer US, Boston, MA, 217–253.

[2] D. H. Alahmadi and X. J. Zeng. 2015. Twitter-Based Recommender System to Address Cold-Start: A Genetic Algorithm Based Trust Modelling and Probabilistic Sentiment Analysis. In *IEEE 27th International Conference on Tools with Artificial Intelligence (ICTAI'15)*. 1045–1052.

[3] Peter Auer, Nicolò Cesa-Bianchi, and Paul Fischer. 2002. Finite-time Analysis of the Multiarmed Bandit Problem. *Machine Learning* 47, 2 (2002), 235–256.

[4] Iman Barjasteh, Rana Forsati, Farzan Masrour, Abdol-Hossein Esfahanian, and Hayder Radha. 2015. Cold-Start Item and User Recommendation with Decoupled Completion and Transduction. In *Proceedings of the 9th ACM Conference on Recommender Systems (RecSys '15)*. ACM, New York, NY, USA, 91–98.

[5] Iman Barjasteh, Rana Forsati, Dennis Ross, Abdol-Hossein Esfahanian, and Hayder Radha. 2016. Cold-Start Recommendation with Provable Guarantees: A Decoupled Approach. *IEEE Trans. on Knowl. and Data Eng.* 28, 6 (June 2016), 1462–1474.

[6] Daniel Billsus and Michael J. Pazzani. 2000. User Modeling for Adaptive News Access. *User Modeling and User-Adapted Interaction* 10, 2-3 (Feb. 2000), 147–180.

[7] Djallel Bouneffouf, Amel Bouzeghoub, and Alda Lopes Gançarski. 2012. A Contextual-Bandit Algorithm for Mobile Context-Aware Recommender System. In *Proceedings of the 19th International Conference Neural Information Processing, Doha, Qatar, November 12-15, Part III (ICONIP '12)*. Springer Berlin Heidelberg, Berlin, Heidelberg, 324–331.

[8] Matthias Braunhofer, Victor Codina, and Francesco Ricci. 2014. Switching Hybrid for Cold-starting Context-aware Recommender Systems. In *Proceedings of the 8th ACM Conference on Recommender Systems (RecSys '14)*. ACM, New York, NY, USA, 349–352.

[9] Robin Burke. 2002. Hybrid Recommender Systems: Survey and Experiments. *User Modeling and User-Adapted Interaction* 12, 4 (Nov. 2002), 331–370.

[10] Stéphane Caron and Smriti Bhagat. 2013. Mixing Bandits: A Recipe for Improved Cold-start Recommendations in a Social Network. In *Proceedings of the 7th Workshop on Social Network Mining and Analysis (SNAKDD '13)*. ACM, New York, NY, USA, Article 11, 9 pages.

[11] Shuo Chang, F. Maxwell Harper, and Loren Terveen. 2015. Using Groups of Items for Preference Elicitation in Recommender Systems. In *Proceedings of the 18th ACM Conference on Computer Supported Cooperative Work & Social Computing (CSCW '15)*. ACM, New York, NY, USA, 1258–1269.

[12] Chen Cheng, Haiqin Yang, Irwin King, and Michael R. Lyu. 2012. Fused Matrix Factorization with Geographical and Social Influence in Location-based Social Networks. In *Proceedings of the Twenty-Sixth AAAI Conference on Artificial Intelligence (AAAI'12)*. AAAI Press, 17–23.

[13] Julien Delporte, Alexandros Karatzoglou, Tomasz Matuszczyk, and Stéphane Canu. 2013. Socially Enabled Preference Learning from Implicit Feedback Data. In *Machine Learning and Knowledge Discovery in Databases: European Conference, Prague, Czech Republic, Proceedings, Part II*, Hendrik Blockeel, Kristian Kersting, Siegfried Nijssen, and Filip Železný (Eds.). Springer Berlin Heidelberg, Berlin, Heidelberg, 145–160.

[14] Michael Ekstrand and John Riedl. 2012. When Recommenders Fail: Predicting Recommender Failure for Algorithm Selection and Combination. In *Proceedings of the Sixth ACM Conference on Recommender Systems (RecSys '12)*. ACM, New York, NY, USA, 233–236.

[15] Mehdi Elahi, Francesco Ricci, and Neil Rubens. 2014. Active Learning Strategies for Rating Elicitation in Collaborative Filtering: A System-wide Perspective. *ACM Trans. Intell. Syst. Technol.* 5, 1, Article 13 (Jan. 2014), 33 pages.

[16] Crícia Z. Felício, Claudianne M. M. de Almeida, Guilherme Alves, Fabíola S. F. Pereira, Klérisson V. R. Paixão, and Sandra de Amo. 2016. Visual Perception Similarities to Improve the Quality of User Cold Start Recommendation. In *Advances in Artificial Intelligence: 29th Canadian Conference on Artificial Intelligence, Proceedings*, Richard Khoury and Christopher Drummond (Eds.). Springer International Publishing, Cham, 96–101.

[17] Crícia Z. Felício, Claudianne M. M. de Almeida, Guilherme Alves, Fabíola S. F. Pereira, Klérisson V. R. Paixão, Sandra de Amo, and Celia A. Z. Barcelos. 2016. VP-Rec: A Hybrid Image Recommender Using Visual Perception Network. In *IEEE 28th International Conference on Tools with Artificial Intelligence (ICTAI'16)*. 70–77.

[18] Crícia Z. Felício, Klérisson V. R. Paixão, Celia A. Z. Barcelos, and Philippe Preux. 2016. Multi-Armed Bandits to Recommend for Cold-Start User. In *Proceedings of the 4rd Symposium on Knowledge Discovery, Mining and Learning*. 182–185.

[19] Crícia Zilda Felício, Klérisson Vinícius Ribeiro Paixão, Guilherme Alves, Sandra de Amo, and Philippe Preux. 2016. Exploiting social information in pairwise preference recommender system. *Journal of Information and Data Management (JIDM)* 7, 2 (2016), 99–115.

[20] Crícia Zilda Felício, Klérisson Vinícius Ribeiro Paixão, Celia Aparecida Zorzo Barcelos, and Philippe Preux. 2016. Preference-Like Score to Cope with Cold-Start User in Recommender Systems. In *IEEE 28th International Conference on Tools with Artificial Intelligence (ICTAI'16)*. 62–69.

[21] Sertan Girgin, Jérémie Mary, Philippe Preux, and Olivier Nicol. 2012. Managing advertising campaigns — an approximate planning approach. *Frontiers of Computer Science* 6, 2 (2012), 209–229.

[22] Nadav Golbandi, Yehuda Koren, and Ronny Lempel. 2010. On Bootstrapping Recommender Systems. In *Proceedings of the 19th ACM International Conference on Information and Knowledge Management (CIKM '10)*. ACM, New York, NY, USA, 1805–1808.

[23] Carlos A. Gomez-Uribe and Neil Hunt. 2015. The Netflix Recommender System: Algorithms, Business Value, and Innovation. *ACM Trans. Manage. Inf. Syst.* 6, 4, Article 13 (Dec. 2015), 19 pages.

[24] Guibing Guo, Jie Zhang, Zhu Sun, and Neil Yorke-Smith. 2015. LibRec: A Java Library for Recommender Systems. In *Posters, Demos, Late-breaking Results and Workshop Proceedings of the 23rd Conference on User Modeling, Adaptation, and Personalization (UMAP 2015), Dublin, Ireland, June 29 - July 3, 2015*.

[25] Guibing Guo, Jie Zhang, and Daniel Thalmann. 2012. A Simple but Effective Method to Incorporate Trusted Neighbors in Recommender Systems. In *Proceedings of the 20th International Conference on User Modeling, Adaptation, and Personalization (UMAP'12)*. Springer-Verlag, Berlin, Heidelberg, 114–125.

[26] Guibing Guo, Jie Zhang, and Neil Yorke-Smith. 2013. A Novel Bayesian Similarity Measure for Recommender Systems. In *Proceedings of the Twenty-Third International Joint Conference on Artificial Intelligence (IJCAI '13)*. AAAI Press, 2619–2625.

[27] Guibing Guo, Jie Zhang, and Neil Yorke-Smith. 2016. A Novel Evidence-Based Bayesian Similarity Measure for Recommender Systems. *ACM Trans. Web* 10, 2, Article 8 (May 2016), 30 pages.

[28] F. Maxwell Harper and Joseph A. Konstan. 2015. The MovieLens Datasets: History and Context. *ACM Trans. Interact. Intell. Syst.* 5, 4, Article 19 (Dec. 2015), 19 pages.

[29] Mohsen Jamali and Martin Ester. 2010. A Matrix Factorization Technique with Trust Propagation for Recommendation in Social Networks. In *Proceedings of the Fourth ACM Conference on Recommender Systems (RecSys '10)*. ACM, New York, NY, USA, 135–142.

[30] Dietmar Jannach, Paul Resnick, Alexander Tuzhilin, and Markus Zanker. 2016. Recommender Systems — Beyond Matrix Completion. *Commun. ACM* 59, 11 (Oct. 2016), 94–102.

[31] Daniel Kluver and Joseph A. Konstan. 2014. Evaluating Recommender Behavior for New Users. In *Proceedings of the 8th ACM Conference on Recommender Systems (RecSys '14)*. ACM, New York, NY, USA, 121–128.

[32] Yehuda Koren. 2008. Factorization Meets the Neighborhood: A Multifaceted Collaborative Filtering Model. In *Proceedings of the 14th ACM SIGKDD International Conference on Knowledge Discovery and Data Mining (KDD '08)*. ACM, New York, NY, USA, 426–434.

[33] Anisio Lacerda, Rodrygo L. Santos, Adriano Veloso, and Nivio Ziviani. 2015. Improving Daily Deals Recommendation Using Explore-then-exploit Strategies. *Inf. Retr.* 18, 2 (April 2015), 95–122.

[34] Anisio Lacerda, Adriano Veloso, and Nivio Ziviani. 2013. Exploratory and Interactive Daily Deals Recommendation. In *Proceedings of the 7th ACM Conference on Recommender Systems (RecSys '13)*. ACM, New York, NY, USA, 439–442.

[35] Lihong Li, Wei Chu, John Langford, and Robert E. Schapire. 2010. A Contextual-bandit Approach to Personalized News Article Recommendation. In *Proceedings of the 19th International Conference on World Wide Web (WWW '10)*. ACM, New York, NY, USA, 661–670.

[36] Shuai Li, Alexandros Karatzoglou, and Claudio Gentile. 2016. Collaborative Filtering Bandits. In *Proceedings of the 39th International ACM SIGIR Conference on Research and Development in Information Retrieval (SIGIR '16)*. ACM, New York, NY, USA, 539–548.

[37] Jiahui Liu, Peter Dolan, and Elin Rønby Pedersen. 2010. Personalized News Recommendation Based on Click Behavior. In *Proceedings of the 15th International Conference on Intelligent User Interfaces (IUI '10)*. ACM, New York, NY, USA, 31–40.

[38] Benedikt Loepp, Tim Hussein, and Jüergen Ziegler. 2014. Choice-based Preference Elicitation for Collaborative Filtering Recommender Systems. In *Proceedings of the 32Nd Annual ACM Conference on Human Factors in Computing Systems (CHI '14)*. ACM, New York, NY, USA, 3085–3094.

[39] Meilian Lu, Zhen Qin, Yiming Cao, Zhichao Liu, and Mengxing Wang. 2014. Scalable News Recommendation Using Multi-dimensional Similarity and Jaccard-Kmeans Clustering. *J. Syst. Softw.* 95 (Sept. 2014), 242–251.

[40] Hao Ma, Tom Chao Zhou, Michael R. Lyu, and Irwin King. 2011. Improving Recommender Systems by Incorporating Social Contextual Information. *ACM Trans. Inf. Syst.* 29, 2, Article 9 (April 2011), 23 pages.

[41] Augusto Q. Macedo, Leandro B. Marinho, and Rodrygo L.T. Santos. 2015. Context-Aware Event Recommendation in Event-based Social Networks. In *Proceedings of the 9th ACM Conference on Recommender Systems (RecSys '15)*. ACM, New York, NY, USA, 123–130.

[42] Jérémie Mary, Romaric Gaudel, and Philippe Preux. 2015. Bandits and Recommender Systems. In *Revised Selected Papers of the First International Workshop on Machine Learning, Optimization, and Big Data. Vol. 9432*. Springer-Verlag, Inc., New York, NY, USA, 325–336.

[43] Pasquale De Meo, Katarzyna Musial-Gabrys, Domenico Rosaci, Giuseppe M. L. Sarnè, and Lora Aroyo. 2017. Using Centrality Measures to Predict Helpfulness-Based Reputation in Trust Networks. *ACM Trans. Internet Technol.* 17, 1, Article 8 (Feb. 2017), 20 pages.

[44] Alan Mislove, Bimal Viswanath, Krishna P. Gummadi, and Peter Druschel. 2010. You Are Who You Know: Inferring User Profiles in Online Social Networks. In *Proceedings of the Third ACM International Conference on Web Search and Data Mining (WSDM '10)*. ACM, New York, NY, USA, 251–260.

[45] Seung-Taek Park and Wei Chu. 2009. Pairwise Preference Regression for Cold-start Recommendation. In *Proceedings of the Third ACM Conference on Recommender Systems (RecSys '09)*. ACM, New York, NY, USA, 21–28.

[46] Furong Peng, Xuan Lu, Chao Ma, Yuhua Qian, Jianfeng Lu, and Jingyu Yang. 2017. Multi-level preference regression for cold-start recommendations. *International Journal of Machine Learning and Cybernetics* (2017), 1–14.

[47] Andre Luiz Vizine Pereira and Eduardo Raul Hruschka. 2015. Simultaneous co-clustering and learning to address the cold start problem in recommender systems. *Knowledge-Based Systems* 82 (2015), 11 – 19.

[48] Huseyin Polat and Wenliang Du. 2005. SVD-based Collaborative Filtering with Privacy. In *Proceedings of the 2005 ACM Symposium on Applied Computing (SAC '05)*. ACM, New York, NY, USA, 791–795.

[49] Al Mamunur Rashid, George Karypis, and John Riedl. 2008. Learning Preferences of New Users in Recommender Systems: An Information Theoretic Approach. *SIGKDD Explor. Newsl.* 10, 2 (Dec. 2008), 90–100.

[50] Al Mamunur Rashid, George Karypis, and John Riedl. 2008. Learning Preferences of New Users in Recommender Systems: An Information Theoretic Approach. *SIGKDD Explor. Newsl.* 10, 2 (Dec. 2008), 90–100.

[51] Alan Said and Alejandro Bellogín. 2014. Comparative Recommender System Evaluation: Benchmarking Recommendation Frameworks. In *Proceedings of the 8th ACM Conference on Recommender Systems (RecSys '14)*. ACM, New York, NY, USA, 129–136.

[52] Claude Sammut and Geoffrey I. Webb (Eds.). 2010. *Leave-One-Out Cross-Validation*. Springer US, Boston, MA, 600–601.

[53] L. Song, C. Tekin, and M. van der Schaar. 2016. Online Learning in Large-Scale Contextual Recommender Systems. *IEEE Transactions on Services Computing* 9, 3 (May 2016), 433–445.

[54] Richard S Sutton and Andrew G Barto. 1998. *Reinforcement learning: An introduction*. MIT press Cambridge.

[55] Liang Tang, Yexi Jiang, Lei Li, and Tao Li. 2014. Ensemble Contextual Bandits for Personalized Recommendation. In *Proceedings of the 8th ACM Conference on Recommender Systems (RecSys '14)*. ACM, New York, NY, USA, 73–80.

[56] Chirayu Wongchokprasitti, Jaakko Peltonen, Tuukka Ruotsalo, Payel Bandyopadhyay, Giulio Jacucci, and Peter Brusilovsky. 2015. User Model in a Box: Cross-System User Model Transfer for Resolving Cold Start Problems. In *Proceedings of the 23rd International Conference on User Modeling, Adaptation and Personalization (UMAP'15)*. Springer International Publishing, Cham, 289–301.

[57] Z. Zhao, H. Lu, D. Cai, X. He, and Y. Zhuang. 2016. User Preference Learning for Online Social Recommendation. *IEEE Transactions on Knowledge and Data Engineering* 28, 9 (Sept 2016), 2522–2534.

Fine-Grained Open Learner Models: Complexity Versus Support

Julio Guerra-Hollstein
Instituto de Informática, Universidad
Austral de Chile
jguerra@inf.uach.cl

Jordan Barria-Pineda
School of Information Sciences,
University of Pittsburgh
jab464@pitt.edu

Christian D. Schunn
Learning Research and Development
Center, University of Pittsburgh
schunn@pitt.edu

Susan Bull
Institute of Education, University
College London

Peter Brusilovsky
School of Information Sciences,
University of Pittsburgh
peterb@pitt.edu

ABSTRACT

Open Learner Models (OLM) show the learner model to users to assist their self-regulated learning by, for example, helping prompt reflection, facilitating planning and supporting navigation. OLMs can show different levels of detail of the underlying learner model, and can also structure the information differently. As a result, a trade-off may exist between the potential for better support for learning and the complexity of the information shown. This paper investigates students' perceptions about whether offering more and richer information in an OLM will result in more effective support for their self-regulated learning. In a first study, questionnaire responses relating to designs for six visualisations of varying complexity led to the implementation of three variations on one of the designs. A second controlled study involved students interacting with these variations. The study revealed that the most useful variation for searching for suitable learning material was a visualisation combining a basic coloured grid, an extended bar chart-like visualisation indicating related concepts, and a learning gauge.

KEYWORDS

Open learner model; navigation support; user study

1 INTRODUCTION

Learner models about student knowledge or skills are typically kept hidden in adaptive educational systems. Opening these models to students could improve transparency and open a channel for student feedback about the model, as well as to enable the student to better understand the state of their knowledge, reason about their knowledge, and use this understanding to better plan his or her learning [6]. A question that has not yet been well-explored is how much information about one's own knowledge the student should be exposed to, to achieve these benefits. Student knowledge has been modelled using knowledge components of different granularity levels from coarse grain course topics to fine-grain skills and concepts (e.g. [1]). Finer-grain models can clearly offer students more information to support their understanding, reasoning, and planning, but finer-grain visualisations might overwhelm students. If information overload is a concern, how might this be usefully addressed? How much information is enough?

This paper presents our exploration of a finer-grain OLM for the domain of learning to program. This area provides natural support for multi-level domain and learner modeling. On the one hand, programming knowledge for a language like *Java* could be considered at the level of broad topics such as variables, conditions, loops, etc. This is the way in which topics are presented in textbooks and courses (with a chapter or a lecture usually devoted to one such topic). On the other hand, knowledge analysis reveals many dozens of small domain concepts such as a specific operators, data types, etc., for which students can have different levels of knowledge. In our past work, we extensively explored personalization and OLM at the larger topic level [31]. We demonstrated that topic-level OLMs could guide students to the most appropriate topics, improve learning outcomes, and increase their engagement. We also demonstrated that open social learner models, an extension of OLM with social comparison on relative performance at the topic-level, further increases the value of OLMs [2, 17]. However, we also observed several limitations of topic-level modeling. For example, averaging knowledge over relatively large topics, topic-level OLMs might hide treacherous knowledge "holes" – missing concepts within otherwise reasonably learned topics. It also offers little support for guiding students to the most appropriate learning content within a topic. Indeed, in a topic-level learner model, all problems associated with a topic may contribute equally to the topic - while finer-level modeling permits the distinction of problems that can help fill the knowledge "holes" from those that push the student to practice already well-learned concepts.

In this work, we augment topic-level OLMs with a more fine-grained concept-level extension and evaluate whether the finer-grained model offers better support for activities that rely on OLM, such as next problem selection. We started with a user study (Study 1) that engaged students in comparing several designs of concept-level OLM in three contexts. The visualisation that was considered most favorably by students was then implemented and evaluated in the second study (Study 2). This study focused on a context for which an OLM could be especially useful: selecting appropriate problems to practice. To understand whether our fine-grained

UMAP '17, Bratislava, Slovakia
© 2017 Copyright held by the owner/author(s). Publication rights licensed to ACM. 978-1-4503-4635-1/17/07...$15.00
DOI: http://dx.doi.org/10.1145/3079628.3079682

model visualisation offers too much or too little information in this context, we contrasted our basic design with two other extensions. One extension offered additional information, while another, instead, offered support for interpreting the information already available. In this paper we present both studies and discuss the results obtained. We believe that these results offer guidance for the future work on fine-grained OLM visualisations.

2 RELATED WORK

Open Learner Models have been implemented in multiple contexts and with different levels of interactivity and complexity [6]. In the context of this paper, the most relevant work is that on the presentation and understandability of OLM visualisations. It has been recognized that, as a representation of a learner model (which is a complex system running in the background), an OLM has to be designed to be understandable and interpretable in order to provide pedagogical support [3, 21]. While some studies have found that simple indicators like *skillometers* are preferred by students [11], other studies support more complex representations such as concept maps [25], for example, as tools to represent and refine assessment claims on learners' knowledge [33]. Moreover, some researcher have proposed offering multiple OLM views, from simple to detailed to structured, giving options that satisfy different students' preferences [5, 8, 11, 24]. More recent work has taken the issue of complexity and interpretability by extending the OLM with more elaborate features such as indicators of effort, progress, or working style [28]. Our previous work on a questionnaire study of a wide variety of visualisations from different systems found that students expected structured visualisations such as visualizations of Prerequisites and of a Hierarchical Tree (from [24]) to best support the task of identifying what to work on next [4]. However, it was unclear why students might prefer these representations over other structured views such as concept maps. These findings motivate our present work.

3 MASTERY GRIDS FRAMEWORK

The starting point of our exploration of fine-grained OLMs is the Mastery Grids (MG) interface, which is a combination of an OLM visualisation with social comparison and a personalized interface for accessing learning content [2, 15, 22]. The original MG interface uses a coarse-grained OLM that aggregates and visualizes the learner's knowledge level of topics (relatively coarse grained units of domain knowledge). Figure 1 shows Mastery Grids with the social comparison feature activated. The first row of cells represents the learner's knowledge for each course topic using different intensities of green (darker green corresponding to more knowledge). The third row represents the average topic-by-topic knowledge of the peer group (i.e., the rest of the class) using different intensities of blue. The second row offers an easy comparison using a differential color: it becomes green when the learner is ahead, or blue if the class is ahead. By clicking in a topic cell, the content activities within the topic are displayed as cells linked to the activities, making the MG an interactive navigational tool. MG is a domain-independent framework and so far, we have developed MG-based courses for Java, Python, and SQL programming. These courses were used as research platforms to evaluate the effects of the MG-based OLM

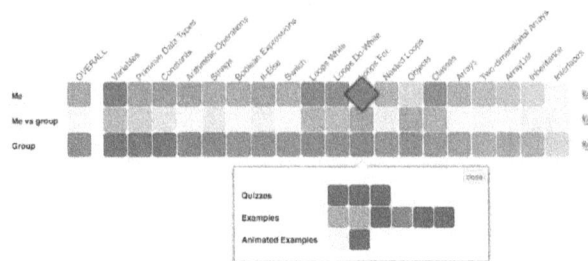

Figure 1: Mastery Grids interface for Java programming

with and without social comparison on learning and engagement [2, 15].

In the context of this paper, it is important that the MG interface is built on top of a learner modeling and personalization framework that includes a two-level domain model, a learner model, and a content model. Since we use the same framework to implement the finer-grained OLM on top of the MG, we introduce the most essential components of this framework below.

- The *Fine-Grained Domain Model* is composed of a set of Knowledge Components (KCs) that represent elementary units of knowledge such as skills or concepts. For the Java domain, we use 114 KCs from an ontology developed by our group. Examples of KCs are *int data type, addition, variable initialization, String concatenation, for loop, constructor,* and *inherited method.*

- The *Coarse-Grained Domain Model* is composed of a list of topics that represent relatively large fragments of domain knowledge. While the KC-level model is defined by the structure of the domain, the list of topics reflects a pedagogical approach to teaching the domain. Our infrastructure allows different instructors to introduce their preferred sequence of topics for the domain. Structurally, each topic could be mapped into a subset of KCs. Taken together, topic and KCs define a two-level hierarchical domain model.

- *Activities-KC mapping* is used to connect learning activities (examples, problems, animations) to a set of KCs by allow to be practiced in the activities. This mapping can be established manually or automatically. For the Java domain, this mapping is done automatically by the content parser presented in [16], with optional expert refinement (see [19]). In this domain, content activities have between 2 and 70 associated KCs.

- *Activity-Topic mapping* associates each course activity with one of the course topics. This mapping, which essentially defines the structure of a course, is usually done manually by course instructors who adopt a specific sequence of topics. In the Java domain, the structure of activities was assembled with the help of instructors of programming courses. The organization of the course influences the decomposition of topics into KCs: an activity only contains KCs of the topic in which it belongs or from topics covered previously.

- The *Learner Model* represents an estimation of learner knowledge for each component of the domain model. The sources for this knowledge estimation are activity traces produced by the learner's work with different leaning activities. The Learner Model uses these activity traces and the mapping between activities and domain model components (topics or KCs) to update the learner's knowledge level for each topic or concept related to

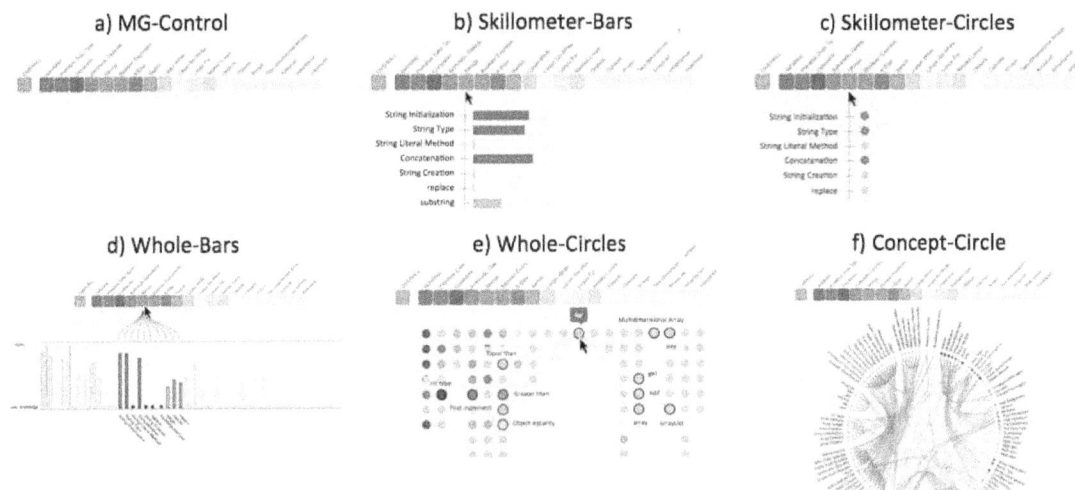

Figure 2: The 6 visualizations prototyped for Study 1.

the activity performed. For example, when the learner solves a problem that contains the KC *for-loop*, the LM will consider this as evidence of knowing the KC and will update its estimation. Note that the knowledge level for domain topics visualized by the MG interface can be modelled independently or calculated as an aggregation of knowledge of concepts included into the topic. In past studies of the MG interface, we explored both approaches. Details of the current Learner Model implementation can be found in [18, 19].

4   DEVELOPING THE RICH-OLM

A coarse-grain topic-level OLM provides limited support for some important aspects of Self-Regulated learning (SRL) such as the ability to recognize knowledge gaps and next problem selection. To offer better support for SRL, we designed and implemented a fine-grained OLM visualization that fully reflects the information maintained by the Learner Model in our infrastructure described in the previous section. Our goal was to find a visualization approach that complements the current topic-based MG interface and maintains a compromise between complexity and the potential support that it offers to learners. In this paper we refer to a combination of the original topic-based OLM (Mastery Grids) and fine-grain OLM as the *Rich-OLM*.

4.1   Study 1: Comparing Design Options for a Fine-Grained OLM

To understand how to effectively visualize the knowledge-component (KC) space and how much information is needed, we designed a controlled user study that we call *Study 1*. We designed five different visualizations with different levels of information about the concept space and its relationships. All visualizations include the topic level visualization (Mastery Grids). We excluded the social comparison features in order to focus on the complexity issues of the fine-grained level. These designs, together with a control version (Mastery Grids alone) are presented in Figure 2. Visualization options varied in terms of the amount of information displayed (show KCs only within the topic, show all KCs at the same time, show connections between KCs), and the visual element used for

representing each KC (bars or circles). Knowledge in each KC is represented with shades of green as in Mastery Grids, and in the case of using bars to represent KCs, we represent such information with both color and size. This decision was motivated to avoid possible biases caused by the use or non-use of color. The designed visualisations were inspired by a wide range of common visual representations previously used in OLM such as *skillometers* (e.g. [7, 9, 23, 27, 32]), *bar charts* or *histograms* (e.g.[26, 30]), and *concept maps* (e.g.[11, 24, 29]). Although the prototypes were presented as paper mock-ups to subjects, we described them to subjects as functional prototypes with some interactivity features (e.g. how they react when a concept is *mouseovered*).

- *Skillometer-Bars*: Shows the list of KC associated to a specific topic as it is pointed to. Each KC is represented with its name and a bar indicating the estimated knowledge.
- *Skillometer-Circles*: Similar to Skillometer-Bars, but KCs are here represented with colored circles.
- *Whole-Bars*: Shows all KCs in the course (114) with bar chart parallel to the coarse-grained visualization. The idea is that when topics are pointed to, the related concepts are highlighted.
- *Whole-Circles*: KCs are positioned under the topic to which they belong and represented with a colored circles. When a concept is pointed to, the name is shown and the connections to other concepts are also shown with the names of the related concepts. These connections are Skill-Combinations [19] and represent pairs of concepts that should be practised together.
- *Concept-Circle*: Another view of the whole space where names and connections are shown all at the same time. KC are represented with small colored circles. Pointing to a KC will highlight its connected KCs. Pointing to a topic will highlight the group of related concepts in the circle.

Subjects were offered a presentation of the Learner Model, including all the information described above, and a description of the visualizations shown in Figure 2. We provided several mock-ups for each of them to describe interactivity. Clarifications were given to subjects to ensure that the features of the more complex representations were understood. Subject were selected among students who had previous experience using Mastery Grids in a course.

Then subjects received a survey with three parts, each setting a different context or *scenario* in order to collect a broader subjective evaluation. Part 1 involves a general scenario. Part 2 involves a scenario of preparing for a hypothetical quiz on a specific topic. Part 3 presents the scenario of a midterm exam covering a number of topics. In each part, questions were phrased to match the specific scenario. For example, in the case of part 2, questions explicitly ask the subject to think on the support of the visualization to prepare for the specific topic of the quiz. The questions covered different aspects (the examples in parenthesis are the questions as phrased for Part 1): *preparation checking* ("The visualization helps me to check whether I am doing well enough in the course"), *knowledge reflection* ("The visualization makes me think about my knowledge in the course"), *strength and weaknesses identification* (2 questions: "The visualization helps me to identify the strengths (weaknesses) in my knowledge of the course contents"), *motivation to explore* ("The visualization motivates me to look for further material to learn more about the course contents"), *easy understand* ("The visualization is easy to understand"), and *topic awareness* ("The visualization helps me to have a better idea of the content involved in each of the topics of the course'). Each part of the survey was presented as a matrix, with the rows containing the questions and the columns containing the 6 visualizations to facilitate comparative answers. In Parts 2 and 3, where the overall stated goal is to prepare for a quiz or midterm exam, we included two additional items: *plan next* ("The visualization helps me to plan what to do next in order to prepare for the quiz"), and *quantify work* ("The visualization helps me to quantify how much work I should do to prepare for the quiz"). At the end of the session, subjects were asked to indicate the best and the worst visualization, and provide an explanation of their choices.

Forty two subjects (Information Sciences Master students and Computer Science undergraduate students at the University of Pittsburgh) completed the study. Each received US $20 for participating and signed an informed consent. Multilevel linear regression analysis was performed for each of the aspects measured (dependent variables). Random effect of subject in the repeated measures was specified, and models were built using a Maximum Likelihood method. We use the software *R* and the function *lme* to run these analyses (see Chapter 13 of [13] for details of this type of analyses). For space constraints, and since we are not looking for detailed differences but rather are seeking to inform design decisions, we report only general trends observed.

A first run of the analysis contrasted the perception of the visualizations, averaging the answers per visualization across different scenarios. The patterns of preferences show a preference for *Whole-Bars* that is similar across items of the survey with only slight differences. Post-hoc comparisons were performed using a Tukey contrast between the visualization options. Results show a clear advantage of all visualizations over both the control version (*MG-control*) and the *Skillometer-Circles* for all dependent variables, except for *easy understand*, where *MG-control* is, not surprisingly, generally better evaluated. While generally evaluated higher, *Whole-Bars* did not show clear difference compared to *Skillometer-Bars*. These two

Table 1: Study 1, the visualizations that were most often chosen as the best and the worst.

Visualization	Best	Worst
Whole-Bars	14	1
Concept-Circle	14	13

visualizations using bars were evaluated higher than visualizations that use circles to represent KCs.

A second run of analysis was performed for each survey item separately by scenario. Results showed lower scores in the *quiz* scenario, especially for the aspects *strengths and weaknesses identification*, *knowledge reflexion*, *motivation to explore*, and *topic awareness*, which suggest that there is room to improve the system to support more specific tasks.

Interestingly, overall preferences (best and worst) divide opinions between complex representations. Table 1 shows that while the same amount of participants choose *Whole-Bars* and *Concept-Circle*, this last visualization is chosen as the last preferred visualization because of "overwhelming" complexity.

From Study 1, we learned that students prefer bars than circles to represent their knowledge of concepts. They also think that bars are easier to understand. These findings are consistent with preferences for skillometers found in previous research [11], but also suggest that the preference might be due to the visual element used (the bar) and not necessarily the level of complexity offered (no difference between *Whole-Bars* and *Skillometer-Bars*). Visualizations with connections, which were evaluated as more complex, were not judged as more helpful in any of the aspects. However, preferences for *Concept-Circle* were extremely divided (best and worst). Multiple preferences have been recognized in the literature and addressed presenting alternative visualizations [8, 11]. We also learned that visualizations might bring different levels of support depending on the scenario. These scenarios involve different goals students have while using the system. A "take away" is that the current alternatives do not seem to support the *quiz* scenario well, and other features might be needed to improve this. The evidenced differences between scenarios also suggest that it is important for evaluations to specify well defined tasks. Although evaluation for *Whole-Bars* and *Skillometer-Bars* are similar in the questionnaire, subjects stated that for tasks like preparing for a midterm, they will prefer to use a visualization that shows the whole concept space. This was a strong reason to select a visualization that includes both global and local context. We conclude that the "sweet spot" is the *Whole-Bars* visualization, though there is an interesting research idea in exploring *Concept-Circle* as an alternative visualization.

4.2 The Rich-OLM

Attending to the results of Study 1, we implemented a Rich-OLM based on the *Whole-Bars* prototype. It shows the topics with their progress and all the concepts of the course in parallel. When a topic is pointed, related concepts are highlighted (the rest are shaded out). When the learner clicks a topic, the activities contained are shown, and the concepts related to this topic are highlighted, with their names at the bottom of each bar. Figure 3 shows a screenshot when entering the topic *Arithmetic Operations* (Java programming course). The full interface includes social comparison at the levels

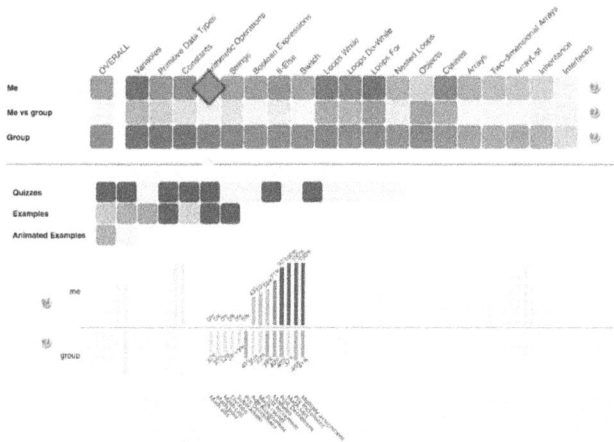

Figure 3: Full Rich-OLM interface. The user has entered a topic and the concept bar chart has shaded out and highlighted only the concepts related.

of topics and concepts, the latter represented as blue bars growing down from the x-axis of the concept bar chart. The visualization was completely built using the javascript library *d3* (www.d3js.org).

While evaluating Rich-OLM will require different aspects aligned to different purposes of use and self-regulated learning tasks to be included, we here prioritize the evaluation of the support that the system brings when students are focused in a specific topic and searching for the best activity to engage with. We then designed and performed a second controlled user study to inform this, which is described in the following section.

5 STUDY 2 DESIGN

To evaluate the Rich-OLM, we designed a controlled user experiment contrasting three versions of the visualization for a specific task: find the piece of content that best helps the student to increase their level of mastery in a specific topic.

The first version of the visualization is shown in Figure 4 and is simply called *KC*. It includes the basic features of the visualization of concepts (or KCs) without social comparison.

The second version (*KCG* (KC + Gauge)) in Figure 5 adds a visual aid specifically designed to direct the interpretation of the information displayed by the KC visualization towards a sense of the relevance of each of the activities within a topic. Gauges are popular to represent single values and at the same time setting meaningful boundaries, and have also been used in learning analytics visualizations [10, 12, 14, 20]. We then designed the *estimated learning gauge*, or simply, *gauge*. The *Gauge* does not add extra information, as the social comparison feature does, but instead presents an interpretative view of the information shown in the concept bar chart: when the learner is inside a topic and points to a content activity, the gauge counts the number of related KCs that are already known, familiar (or partially known) and not known (or new) to the learner based on predefined thresholds. To position the needle, the estimation of learning (which can also be considered as a measure of *difficulty*) is computed using Equation 1.

$$learning_{estimated} = \frac{0.5 * kcs_{familiar} + kcs_{new}}{kcs_{known} + kcs_{familiar} + kcs_{new}} \quad (1)$$

The third version of the visualization in the study, *KCS* (KC + Social Comparison), is shown in Figure 6. This visualization provides all the information of the full Rich-OLM interface, including the social comparison features, but does not include the *Gauge*.

We use a version of the Java course with 12 topics (Variables and Types, Arithmetic Operations, Strings, Decisions, etc). Each topic has between 13 and 29 content activities of different types (see Section 3). Multiple topics allow us to ask subjects to repeat the task using different visualizations, implementing a within-subject design. To carry out Study 2, we developed a simple interface with which subjects can follow the steps of the study at their own pace.

Before starting the tasks, subjects completed a *pretest* consisting of 24 problems covering the 12 topics (2 problems from each topic). The goals were: (a) to have a measure of the previous knowledge of the subjects, that will be used in the analyses, and (b) to feed the Learner Model to be shown in tasks. Following the pretest, subjects viewed a short video explaining the basic KC visualization and its interactive features.

Tasks were presented in groups of 4 for each visualization. Visualizations were introduced to subjects in different orders following a Latin-Square design. Each visualization was first presented with a short tutorial explaining its features, a training step where subjects were free to try the visualization, and an interactive self-assessment test to corroborate that subjects understood the features (if failed, subjects were asked to call the study coordinator for clarifications). Then the tasks for the visualization were introduced one by one, and each task involved one specific topic. The instructions were: "*Focus in the topic marked with the orange dot. Select the best activity (to maximize your mastery of the target topic) by right-clicking in its cell. Just pick the activity, avoid solving quizzes or going through examples.*" Each topic is inspected only once (12 topics = 1 topic per task, 4 tasks for each visualization, 3 visualizations) and topics were assigned randomly to avoid bias due to the variability of the topics.

After every two tasks, the subjects were asked to fill out a *task survey* about their experience performing the previous two tasks. It covers the usefulness of the visualization, and its influence in making them reflect on their knowledge. Table 2 shows the items of the survey. Answers options are on a 7-point Likert scale (1:Strongly disagree - 7:Strongly agree). Some items were reversed (*R*). To facilitate the analyses in the next section, questions were given an identifier, which is shown in the first column of Table 2. Additionally, we included four questions from the *NASA-TLX*[1] survey (see Table 3). These questions are presented with sliders running from 0 to 1.

Finally, after the series of 12 tasks were completed, subjects were asked to fill out a *final survey* in which were asked to (1) rank the three interfaces according their own preference and explain their ranking, and (2) rate the ease of understanding and ease of use of each visualization using a 7-point Likert scale (1:Extremely easy - 7: Extremely difficult).

Twenty nine subjects completed Study 2, with all of them completing all steps and surveys. However, some subjects did not explicitly select an activity at the end of the tasks: one subject missed the activity selection in all 12 tasks, two missed this in 10

---

[1]NASA Task Load Index: https://humansystems.arc.nasa.gov/groups/tlx/

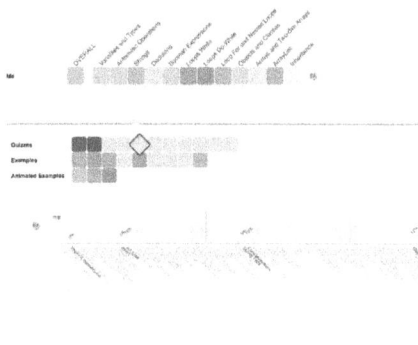

Figure 4: KC basic visualization.   Figure 5: KCG (KCs+Gauge).   Figure 6: KCS (KCs+social comparison)

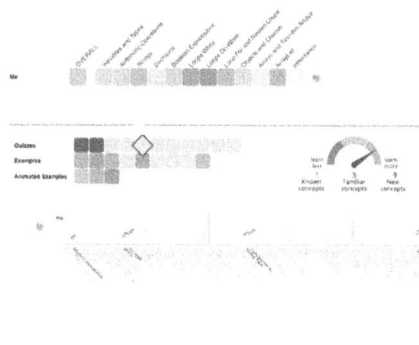

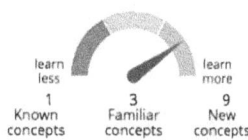

Figure 7: Detail of the Gauge visual aid.

Table 2: Usefulness and self-reflection *task survey*.

Item	Statement
confidence	I am confident that I selected a good activity for the tasks
usefulChoose	The visualization was useful to decide which activity to choose
ledUseless (R)	The visualization at times led me to less useful activities
findLearn	The visualization helped me to find activities where I think I can learn something new
thinkKnowledge	The visualization made me think about my own knowledge in programming concepts
notHelpful (R)	The visualization did not help me much while searching for a good activity for the target topic
avoidEasier	The visualization helped me to avoid choosing activities which I think are too easy for me
avoidHarder	The visualization helped me to avoid choosing activities which I think are too hard for me
criticalEfficacy	Without the visualization I will probably fail to select a good activity for the target topic
criticalEfficiency	Without the visualization I will probably spend more time selecting an activity for the target topic

tasks, four missed it in two tasks, and one subject missed it in 1 task. Analysis involving selected activities does not include these missing cases. Subjects spent roughly between half an hour and an hour and a half completing the *Study 2* (median = 40 minutes, mean = 50 minutes).

6 RESULTS

Table 4 shows the basic statistics for each of the questions in the task survey. Recall that responses were measured on a Likert scale from 1 to 7. NASA TLX survey items 1, 4, 5 and 6 were measured with a continuous scale from 0 to 1. The results of the pretest revealed that subjects had a relative high level of experience (*Median* = .79).

Table 3: NASA-TLX survey.

Item	Statement
TLX1	Mental Demand: How mentally demanding was the task? (0:Very low - 1:Very high)
TLX4	Performance: How successful were you in accomplishing what you were asked to do? (0:Perfect - 1:Failure)
TLX5	Effort: How hard did you have to work to accomplish your level of performance? (0:Very low - 1:Very high)
TLX6	Frustration: How insecure, discouraged, irritated, stressed, and annoyed were you? (0:Very low - 1:Very high)

Table 4: Summary statistics of task surveys.

Question	Mean	SD	Question	Mean	SD
confidence	5.97	0.98	avoidHarder	4.83	1.83
usefulChoose	5.80	1.05	criticalEfficacy	5.18	1.46
ledUselessR	3.53	1.81	criticalEfficiency	5.7	1.14
findLearn	6.13	0.90	TLX1	0.29	0.27
thinkKnowledge	6.14	0.92	TLX4	0.20	0.22
notHelpfulR	2.92	1.52	TLX5	0.27	0.24
avoidEasier	5.63	1.23	TLX6	0.15	0.18

Only one subject scored less than 50%. We further classified the subjects into a *pretest group*: low or high. We grouped using the median as a compromise to avoid having very small groups in the statistical analyses.

6.1 Survey differences among visualizations

Averages of survey responses show a general tendency to evaluate the treatment *KCG* as higher, although significant differences were not found. Since correlations were significant and high for many pairs of questions in the survey, and before advancing with more elaborated analyses, we performed a Factor Analysis using Varimax rotation. Three factors were discovered. The first factor groups together the items *confidence, usefulChoose, findLearn* and *avoidEasier*. Since *confidence* is conceptually a different aspect, we create the score *USEFUL* only averaging *usefulChoose, findLearn* and *avoidEasier*. The second factor discovered contains *criticalEfficacy, criticalEfficiency* and *thinkKnowledge*. Again, this last item is conceptually different, so we computed the score *CRITICAL* by

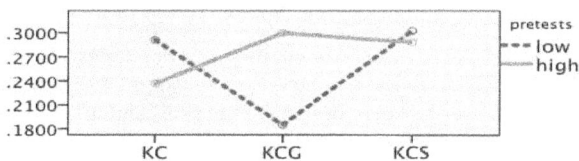

Figure 8: Interaction between treatment and pretest group for the measure of Effort (TLX5).

averaging *criticalEfficacy* and *criticalEfficiency*. The third factor groups the reversed questions, *ledUselessand* and *notHelpful*, which we averaged in the score *UNHELPFUL*.

To uncover differences among treatments (visualizations), we performed repeated-measures ANOVA methods on the scores *USEFUL*, *CRITICAL* and *UNHELPFUL* by treatment. Pretest-group (high, low) was added as a between-subjects factor. A significant effect of treatment was found for the score *USEFUL*, $F(1.4, 37.7) = 3.961$, $p = .041$, partial $\eta^2 = .128$. The sphericity assumption was violated in this analysis, so the Greenhouse-Geiser correction was applied. No significant difference was found for the other two variables *CRITICAL* and *UNHELPFUL*. Also, no significant effect of pretest group, nor interaction between pretest group and treatment were found. Simple contrast (comparing *KCG* against *KC* and *KCS*) showed a marginally significant difference between *KCG* and *KCS*, $F(1, 27) = 4.134$, $p = .052$, partial $\eta^2 = .133$, indicating higher evaluation of *Gauge*. However, more elaborated pairwise comparison using Bonferroni correction only found a marginal difference between treatments *KC* and *KCS* ($p = .074$). Subjects tended to judge the *USEFUL* of the visualization lower in *KCS* (Mean = 5.604) than in *KC* (Mean = 5.953) for the task defined in the study.

Similar analyses were run for TLX items (*mental demand, performance, effort* and *frustration*). No main effect of treatment was found for any of them, nor main effect of pretest groups. Nevertheless, a marginally significant interaction of the treatment and pretest groups was found for the perception of *effort* (TLX 5), $F(2, 54) = 2.936$, $p = .062$, partial $\eta^2 = .098$. Figure 8 shows this interaction: lower pretest group (which in fact represents subjects with a medium level of knowledge) expressed less *effort* when using the interface containing the *Gauge*. We note that similar patterns, although not resulting in significant effects or interactions, were observed for the other TLX scores.

6.2 Behavior differences among treatments

Click activity collected while performing a task is summarized in the following variables:

- *countSelectActs*: number of activities selected in the task (subjects might have thought twice before going to the next task).
- *lastSelectedActDifficulty*: difficulty value of the last activity selected in the task which correspond to the computed *estimated learning* (see Equation 1 in Section 5) .
- *lastSelectedActRelativeRanking*: if we rank all the activities that the user has mouseovered by their difficulty score, this is the position of the last selected activity divided by the number of activities mouseovered. The value ranges between 0 and 1, 0 being the higher ranking.
- *countMouseoverActivities, timeMouseoverActivities*: number and sum of time spent in mouseovering activities. We only counted

Table 5: Log activity summary.

Variable	Mean	SD
countSelectActs	0.98	0.62
lastSelectedActDifficulty	0.75	0.13
lastSelectedActRelativeRanking	0.37	0.30
countMouseoverActivities	3.76	5.33
countMouseoverConcepts	0.67	1.63
timeMouseoverActivities	13.62	24.07
timeMouseoverConcepts	3.49	13.75
countActivityOpened	1.75	2.98

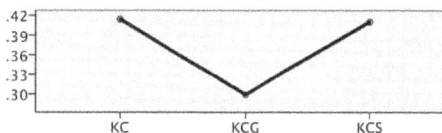

Figure 9: Ranking of difficulty (relative) of the selected activity. Lower value means higher ranking.

mouseover actions that lasted for 1 second or more to reduce noise of involuntary actions.

- *countMouseoverConcepts, timeMouseoverConcepts*: number and sum of time spent in mouseovering concepts (KCs). Similar to before, only mouse over actions of more than 1 second are counted.
- *countActivityOpened*: although we advised subjects not to open activities, in some situations they did so.

Table 5 reports mean and standard deviation (SD) of the variables computed. Note that subjects rarely pointed to concepts. The difficulty of the last activity selected is close to the overall mean of difficulty (*Mean = .75, SD = .12*). Very high correlations were found between *countMouseoverActivities* and *timeMouseoverActivities* ($r = .89$) and between *countMouseoverConcepts* and *timeMouseoverConcepts* ($r = .84$), thus we discarded the time variables and keep the counts in the following analyses.

To analyse differences of behavior among treatments, we aggregated the log data variables grouping tasks within each treatment (4 tasks in each treatment) and performed repeated-measures ANOVA on log activity variables by treatment. Pretest group was added as a between subject factor. Subjects who did not select activities in tasks were removed from these analyses. The normality (Shapiro-Wilk) assumption holds only for the variable *lastSelectedActRelativeRanking*. Sphericity (Mauchly's test) holds for variables *lastSelectedActRelativeRanking* and *countMouseoverActivities*.

Results of the analysis found a significant effect of treatment only on *lastSelectedActRelativeRanking*, $F(2, 46) = 4.700$, $p = .014$, partial $\eta^2 = .170$. Pairwise comparisons with a Bonferroni correction showed a marginally significant difference between treatments *KCG* and *KC* ($p = .083$), and between *KCG* and *KCS* ($p = .053$). Subjects selected more difficult activities (relative to the difficulty of the activities inspected) when using *KCG* (Mean = .299, SE = .038), compared to when using *KC* (Mean = .414, SE = .046) or when using the *KCS* (Mean = .410, SE = .033). Figure 9 shows the pattern of this effect.

No significant interaction between treatment and pretest group was found for any of the log variables. However, a significant

Table 6: Survey 2 summary. Count of rank preferences (rank 1 is top preference), and statistics on the ease of understanding and ease of use expressed by subjects.

	Ranking of Visualizations					Understand		Use	
	Rank1	Rank2	Rank3	Mean	SD	Mean	SD	Mean	SD
KC	0	13	15	2.54	0.51	2.48	1.43	2.38	1.42
KCG	20	6	2	1.36	0.62	2.21	1.50	1.90	1.23
KCS	8	9	11	2.11	0.83	2.52	1.50	2.48	1.43

effect of pretest group was found for countMouseoverActivities, $F(1, 23) = 8.709$, $p = .007$, partial $\eta^2 = .275$, and countActivityOpened, $F(1, 23) = 6.477$, $p = .018$, partial $\eta^2 = .220$. High pretest subjects did less mouse-over activities, but they opened activities more, regardless of the visualization.

6.3 Relations between survey and log variables

To better understand the subjective evaluation (survey), we now consider the relations with the log data (objective measures). Since log variables were collected by task and there was one survey for every two tasks, we aggregated log variables across tasks for each survey: Counting variables were added, whereas difficulty of the last activity selected and its ranking were averaged. Correlations (using Spearman) between task survey items and log variables revealed some interesting associations. In general, when subjects did more mouse over activities (which we can consider as more work) they lowered their perception of confidence in the task (confidence countMouseoverActivities, $r_s = -.222$, $p = .003$), they thought the system was less helpful to avoid harder activities (avoidHarder countMouseoverActivities, $r_s = -.281$, $p < .001$), but also declared lower frustration (TLX6 countMouseoverActivities, $r_s = -.210$, $p = .006$). Variable lastSelectedActDifficulty was negatively correlated to both reversed measures ledUseless ($r_s = -.343$, $p < .001$) and notHelpful ($r_s = -.273$, $p = .001$), which suggests that positive perception of the support given by the system followed the selection of more difficult activities. Similar correlations were found for countSelectedActs, and this variable also shows a negative correlation to frustration ($r_s = -.239$, $p = .001$), which indicated less frustration when subjects did not complete the task in one shot. Finally, countActivityOpened was negatively correlated to TLX4 (performance), which means that lower levels of failure were perceived after opening more activities.

6.4 Overall perception of the visualizations

At the end of the study session, subjects provided an overall evaluation of their experience. Table 6 summarizes the ranking that subjects gave to the three visualizations and the mean and standard deviation of the responses to questions about ease of understanding and ease of use. We can see in this table the tendency of KCG as easier to understand and use, but differences were not significant. With reference to ranking, the KCG was considered the best by 20 subjects and the worst only for 2 subjects, with a Friedman test shows is a significant difference, $\chi^2(2) = 19.929$, $p < .001$. Free text explanation of the rankings were requested. Ten subjects explicitly referred to the advantages of using the gauge. For example, one subject said "the Gauge provides a summary/overview of the knowledge both the student have mastered and haven't learned, which saves a great bunch of time for comparing between different

concepts and keeping a clear track of all processes". Five subjects expressed the value of social comparison features, for example "in the social comparison I have a direct and obvious guide as to where others skills are and therefore where my skills should probably be". Four subjects valued comparison as motivating: "comparison motivates us to perform better and improve our knowledge in the programming concepts". However, 7 subjects expressed a negative perception of these features: "i am not concerned about the progress of the class and how much I have completed when compared to them". Three subjects expressed concern about the gauge and how it works: "the gauge is somewhat distracting because some exercise covers concepts under other topics, and the number in the gauge always seduce me choose the one that can cover more new topics".

7 CONCLUSIONS

In this work we show the design and evaluation process we followed to develop a Rich-OLM, an OLM system combining coarse-grained and fine-grained pieces of the underlying learner model. Since more detailed information adds complexity to the visualisation that makes it harder to understand by learners, our challenge was to balance the amount of information displayed and the potential support offered. To find and assess a design for the fine-grained OLM, we performed two user studies. The first study evaluates different alternative visualizations with different levels of information. We found that learners prefer a bar chart form of knowledge visualization: they found these easier to understand, even when they present a detailed complete view of the whole concept space. Based on the results of this study, we developed Rich-OLM, which uses a bar chart to represent a learner's concept-level knowledge.

In the second study we evaluated the developed Rich-OLM in the context of problem selection. To determine whether our Rich-OLM offers the right amount of information to support this task, we compared three versions of the Rich-OLM interface: a basic Rich-OLM, a version with a support tool to help the user in comprehending the OLM data (a gauge summarizing learner information on concepts related to content activities) and a version that offers additional information on the top of the basic version data (social comparison in both topic and concept level). Evaluation also focused on a clearly defined task: to find activities to increase students' mastery of specific topics. Results showed the positive effect of the gauge, especially in reducing the effort that less-prepared learners needed to complete the task, along with a very clear preference declared by subjects when comparing to other visualizations. These results support the idea that to allow effective support while using a learning system, a fine-grained OLM can be enhanced with visual elements helping to interpret the data shown (which could in many cases be of high complexity) [28].

REFERENCES

[1] Peter Brusilovsky and Eva Milln. 2007. User models for adaptive hypermedia and adaptive educational systems. (2007).
[2] Peter Brusilovsky, Sibel Somyurek, Julio Guerra, Roya Hosseini, Vladimir Zadorozhny, and Paula Durlach. 2016. Open Social Student Modeling for Personalized Learning. IEEE Transactions on Emerging Topics in Computing 4, 3 (2016), 450–461. http://doi.ieeecomputersociety.org/10.1109/TETC.2015.2501243
[3] Susan Bull. 2012. Preferred features of open learner models for university students. In International Conference on Intelligent Tutoring Systems. Springer, 411–421.
[4] Susan Bull, Peter Brusilovsky, Rafael Araujo, and Julio Guerra. 2016. Individual and Peer Comparison Open Learner Model Visualisations to Identify What to

Work On Next. In *24th Conference on User Modeling, Adaptation and Personalization*. CEUR.

[5] Susan Bull, Inderdip Gakhal, Daniel Grundy, Matthew Johnson, Andrew Mabbott, and Jing Xu. 2010. Preferences in multiple-view open learner models. In *European Conference on Technology Enhanced Learning*. Springer, 476–481.

[6] Susan Bull and Judy Kay. 2010. Open learner models. In *Advances in intelligent tutoring systems*. Springer, 301–322.

[7] Susan Bull and Andrew Mabbott. 2006. 20000 inspections of a domain-independent open learner model with individual and comparison views. In *International Conference on Intelligent Tutoring Systems*. Springer, 422–432.

[8] Ricardo Conejo, Monica Trella, Ivan Cruces, and Rafael Garcia. 2011. INGRID: A web service tool for hierarchical open learner model visualization. In *International Conference on User Modeling, Adaptation, and Personalization*. Springer, 406–409.

[9] Albert T Corbett and Akshat Bhatnagar. 1997. Student modeling in the ACT programming tutor: Adjusting a procedural learning model with declarative knowledge. In *User modeling*. Springer, 243–254.

[10] Luis de la Fuente Valentín and Daniel Burgos Solans. 2014. Am I doing well? A4Learning as a self-awareness tool to integrate in Learning Management Systems. *Campus Virtuales* 3, 1 (2014), 32–40.

[11] Dandi Duan, Antonija Mitrovic, and Neville Churcher. 2010. Evaluating the effectiveness of multiple open student models in EER-Tutor. (2010).

[12] Mohammad Hassan Falakmasir, I-Han Hsiao, Luca Mazzola, Nancy Grant, and Peter Brusilovsky. 2012. The impact of social performance visualization on students. In *Advanced Learning Technologies (ICALT), 2012 IEEE 12th International Conference on*. IEEE, 565–569.

[13] Andy Field. 2012. *Discovering Statistics Using R*. Sage.

[14] Giovanni Fulantelli, Davide Taibi, and Marco Arrigo. 2013. A semantic approach to mobile learning analytics. In *Proceedings of the First International Conference on Technological Ecosystem for Enhancing Multiculturality*. ACM, 287–292.

[15] Julio Guerra, Roya Hosseini, Sibel Somyürek, and Peter Brusilovsky. 2016. An Intelligent Interface for Learning Content: Combining an Open Learner Model and Social Comparison to Support Self-Regulated Learning and Engagement. IUI.

[16] Roya Hosseini and Peter Brusilovsky. 2013. Javaparser: A fine-grain concept indexing tool for java problems. In *The First Workshop on AI-supported Education for Computer Science (AIEDCS 2013)*. University of Pittsburgh, 60–63.

[17] I. Han Hsiao, Fedor Bakalov, Peter Brusilovsky, and Birgitta Knig-Ries. 2013. Progressor: social navigation support through open social student modeling. *New Review of Hypermedia and Multimedia* 19, 2 (2013), 112–131. DOI:http://dx.doi.org/citeulike-article-id:12534194doi:10.1080/13614568.2013.806960

[18] Yun Huang, J Guerra, and Peter Brusilovsky. A data-driven framework of modeling skill combinations for deeper knowledge tracing. In *Proc. of the 9th Intl. Conf. on Educational Data Mining*.

[19] Yun Huang, J Guerra, and Peter Brusilovsky. 2016. Modeling skill combination patterns for deeper knowledge tracing. In *Proceedings of the 6th Workshop on Personalization Approaches in Learning Environments (PALE 2016)*. 24th conference on User Modeling, Adaptation, and Personalization (UMAP 2016), CEUR workshop proceedings, this volume.

[20] Imran Khan and Abelardo Pardo. 2016. Data2U: scalable real time student feedback in active learning environments. In *Proceedings of the Sixth International Conference on Learning Analytics & Knowledge*. ACM, 249–253.

[21] Check Yee Law, John Grundy, Andrew Cain, and Rajesh Vasa. 2015. A preliminary study of open learner model representation formats to support formative assessment. In *Computer Software and Applications Conference (COMPSAC), 2015 IEEE 39th Annual*, Vol. 2. IEEE, 887–892.

[22] Tomasz D Loboda, Julio Guerra, Roya Hosseini, and Peter Brusilovsky. 2014. Mastery Grids: An Open Source Social Educational Progress Visualization. In *Open Learning and Teaching in Educational Communities*. Springer, 235–248.

[23] Yanjin Long and Vincent Aleven. 2013. Supporting studentsfi self-regulated learning with an open learner model in a linear equation tutor. In *International Conference on Artificial Intelligence in Education*. Springer, 219–228.

[24] Andrew Mabbott and Susan Bull. 2006. Student preferences for editing, persuading, and negotiating the open learner model. In *International Conference on Intelligent Tutoring Systems*. Springer, 481–490.

[25] Adrian Maries and Amruth Kumar. 2008. The effect of student model on learning. In *Advanced Learning Technologies, 2008. ICALT'08. Eighth IEEE International Conference on*. IEEE, 877–881.

[26] Luca Mazzola and Riccardo Mazza. 2010. GVIS: a facility for adaptively mashing up and representing open learner models. In *European Conference on Technology Enhanced Learning*. Springer, 554–559.

[27] Antonija Mitrovic and Brent Martin. 2007. Evaluating the effect of open student models on self-assessment. *International Journal of Artificial Intelligence in Education* 17, 2 (2007), 121–144.

[28] Kyparisia A Papanikolaou. 2015. Constructing interpretative views of learnersfi interaction behavior in an open learner model. *IEEE Transactions on Learning Technologies* 8, 2 (2015), 201–214.

[29] Diana Pérez-Marín, Enrique Alfonseca, Pilar Rodríguez, and I Pascual-Neito. 2007. A study on the possibility of automatically estimating the confidence value of studentsfi knowledge in generated conceptual models. *Journal of Computers* 2, 5 (2007), 17–26.

[30] Lei Shi and Alexandra I Cristea. 2016. Learners Thrive Using Multifaceted Open Social Learner Modeling. *IEEE MultiMedia* 23, 1 (2016), 36–47.

[31] Sergey Sosnovsky and Peter Brusilovsky. 2015. Evaluation of Topic-based Adaptation and Student Modeling in QuizGuide. *User Modeling and User-Adapted Interaction* 25, 4 (2015), 371–424. DOI:http://dx.doi.org/10.1007/s11257-015-9164-4

[32] Gerhard Weber and Peter Brusilovsky. 2001. ELM-ART: An adaptive versatile system for Web-based instruction. *International Journal of Artificial Intelligence in Education (IJAIED)* 12 (2001), 351–384.

[33] Diego Zapata-Rivera, Eric Hansen, Valerie J Shute, Jody S Underwood, and Malcolm Bauer. 2007. Evidence-based approach to interacting with open student models. *International Journal of Artificial Intelligence in Education* 17, 3 (2007), 273–303.

Where To Go Next?
Exploiting Behavioral User Models in Smart Environments

Seyyed Hadi Hashemi
University of Amsterdam
Amsterdam, The Netherlands
hashemi@uva.nl

Jaap Kamps
University of Amsterdam
Amsterdam, The Netherlands
kamps@uva.nl

ABSTRACT

There is a growing interest in using the Internet of Things (IoT) to create smart environments, which hold the promise to provide personalized experience based on the trail of user interactions with smart devices. We experiment with behavioral user models based on interactions with smart devices in a museum, and investigate the personalized recommendation of what to see after visiting an initial set of Point of Interests (POIs), a key problem in personalizing museum visits or tour guides. We have logged users' onsite physical information interactions of visits in a museum. Moreover, to have a better understanding of users' information interaction behaviors and their preferences, we have collected and studied query logs of a search engine of the same collection, and we have found similarities between users' online digital and onsite physical information interaction behaviors. We exploit user modeling based on users' different information interaction behaviors and experiment with a novel approach to a critical one-shot POI recommendation using deep neural multilayer perceptron based on explicitly given users' contextual information, and set-based extracted features using users' physical information interaction behaviors and similar users' digital information interaction behaviors. Experimental results indicates that our proposed behavioral user modeling, using both physical and digital user information interaction behaviors, improves the onsite POI recommendation baselines' performances in all common Information Retrieval evaluation metrics. Our proposed approach provides an effective way to achieve a high precision at rank 1 in onsite critical one-shot POI recommendation problem.

KEYWORDS

Human information interaction; Onsite logs; Behavioral user models; POI recommendation; Internet of things

ACM Reference format:
Seyyed Hadi Hashemi and Jaap Kamps. 2017. Where To Go Next? Exploiting Behavioral User Models in Smart Environments. In *Proceedings of UMAP'17, July 9-12, 2017, Bratislava, Slovakia, , 9 pages.*
DOI: http://dx.doi.org/10.1145/3079628.3079687

Figure 1: Interactive POIs in a museum physical space

1 INTRODUCTION

The last decade witnessed a tremendous interests in implementation of Internet of Things (IoT) in different applications[2, 3, 10, 16–18, 25], such as smart shopping malls and smart museums, which provides the infrastructure for understanding users' physical interaction behavior and consequently their preferences in interacting with smart environments. This prompts the question:

How tracking people in their real-life and understanding their interaction behaviors would be helpful? Is it possible to give effective suggestions to users by user tracking using IoT but without getting any explicit information about their preferences like ratings?

Imagine you are at a huge museum like the Louvre Museum in Paris and you want to explore the museum. Usually, it is impossible to visit the whole objects of some big museums like the Louvre Museum in one day. Moreover, museum free roaming is more desirable in comparison to the traditional fixed walking route designed in a non-personalized way. Providing personalized experiences for users is so valuable in this context and will help them to visit all interesting objects of the museum according to their preferences. In this case, how amazing would it be if the contextual recommender system can tell you accurately what to visit without using any history or explicit feedback from you?

Emergence of the above applications leads to rise interests in logging users' onsite physical information interactions, which creates a new potentially exponentially growing data like search engine query logs. Although understanding users' search behavior and their information needs based on query logs is well-studied [7, 29], to the best of our knowledge, there is not any study on how to understand users' behaviors and their information needs based on similarities between users' onsite physical and online digital information interaction behaviors. Addressing this research problem by

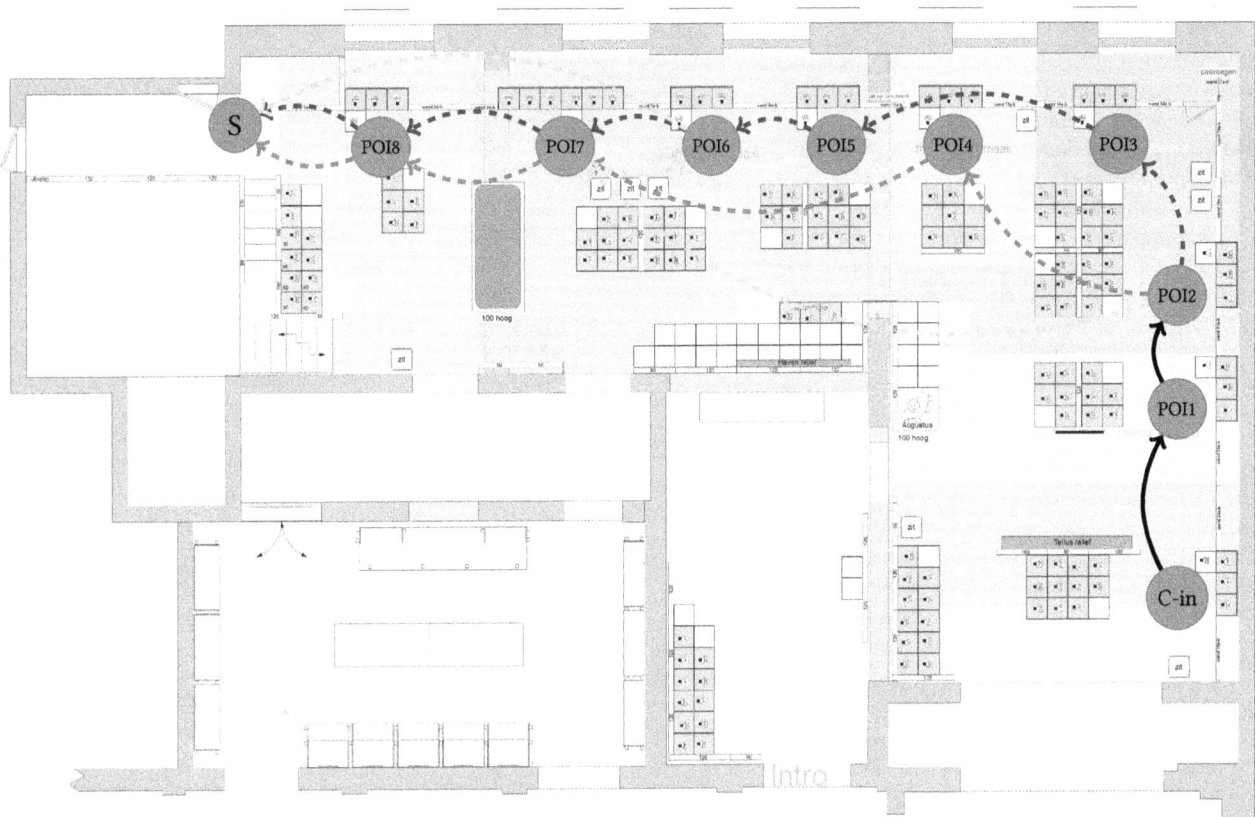

Figure 2: Variance in onsite users' behavior after visiting a set of POIs. The figure indicates variance of three visitors' preferences in visiting POIs. Each of them shown by a different color, and the black edges are the ones walked by all the three visitors. *C-in* is the check-in station and the *S* is the check-out station.

learning a behavioral user model using both onsite physical and online digital user behaviors is our main contribution in this paper.

To this aim, users' onsite physical interactions of visits in a museum and users' online query logs of a search engine of the same collection are logged. Onsite physical information interactions are based on unlocking contents of an installed iPod at each POI using RFID tags. Figure 1 shows an example of the museum space with the mentioned installation. In this way, we log users' interactions with POIs and track users' visits in the museum.

As it is shown in Figure 2, users behave differently after visiting a set of POIs. Figure 2 plots walk-through graph of 3 real users after checking in at POI1 and POI2. The blue and red paths show walk-through behaviors of two users tend to check-in at POIs one after the other but with different preferences. The green path shows a user who behaves completely different from the other two and does not check-in at POIs one after the other. This figure shows an example of how different are users onsite physical behaviors, which indicates understanding and prediction of users' onsite physical behaviors are challenging and difficult.

In this paper, our main aim is to study the question: *How to model users' information interaction behavior with IoT having an aim of providing a personalized onsite POI recommendation?* Specifically, we answer the following research questions:

(1) *How to understand users' onsite physical behavior and create a behavioral user model that is able to effectively predict relevant unseen POIs?*
(2) *How strong are different users' interaction behaviors with IoT in understanding users' preferences?*
  (a) *Are online digital behaviors similar to onsite physical behaviors? Does understanding online digital users' information interaction behaviors have a positive effect in learning a model to predict unseen relevant POIs and complete users' personalized onsite visits?*
  (b) *What are the relative importance of each feature extracted based on different users' interaction behaviors in effectiveness of POI recommendation systems?*
(3) *How effective is behavioral POI recommendation system in one-shot POI recommendation problem?*

The rest of the paper is organized as follows. In Section 2, we review some related work on context aware recommendation and POI recommendation systems. Section 3 is devoted to stating the problem and discussing baselines. Our proposed onsite POI recommendation approach is detailed in Section 4. The experimental setup and results are discussed in Section 5 and 6. Finally, we present the conclusions and future work in Section 7.

2   RELATED WORK

In this section, we discuss related work on context aware recommendation systems, POI recommendation systems, and recommendation systems in museums.

Traditionally, recommendation systems deal with applications having just two types of entities, users and items. However, creation of more complex and realistic applications leads to interests in a new line of research about how to incorporate contextual information as an extra dimension to the recommendation systems. There are 3 ways of incorporating context in the recommender systems: contextual pre-filtering, contextual post-filtering, and contextual modeling [1]. As the later approach is closer to our study in this paper, we will discuss some of the related research in the contextual modeling.

In order to contextually model the context aware recommendation system, Karatzoglou et al. proposed a multiverse recommendation method based on tensor factorization [21], which integrate contextual information by modeling data as User-Item-Context N-dimensional tensor instead of traditional 2-dimensional User-Item matrix. One problem of this method is the data sparseness, which is proportional to the number of defined context in their method. Liu et al. [22] proposed to partition the User-Item matrix by grouping ratings of similar context, which could be helpful to decrease the data sparseness. The other problem of the multiverse recommendation method is that it only works for categorical features. To overcome this problem, Rendle et al. [26] proposed to use factorization machines to model contextual information. The above studies are done to model contextual information, however none of them are really scalable and effective for the recent exponentially growing data.

There have also been lots of studies to solve the POI recommendation problem in both academia and industry [14, 38]. They generally try to adapt traditional recommendation algorithms to the POI recommendation problem. One line of research includes collaborative filtering and matrix factorization approaches in location-based social networks (LBSNs). Berjani et al. in [5] proposed regularized matrix factorization, in which they apply personalized collaborative filtering on dimensionally reduced user-POI matrices to minimize the squared regularized error. In addition to the geographical aspects, they are some researches in POI recommendation that in addition to the geographical dimension, tried to include temporal dimension in the matrix factorization framework [11, 13].

Within the POI recommendation literature, there are some studies that are related to ours in the sense that they studied users' check-in behavior [24, 27, 30-34, 36, 37]. As three interesting examples of these related works, Zheng et al. proposed collaborative location activity filtering [35]. Particularly, they used collective factorization to recommend locations or activities to users. To this aim, they used comments having GPS data in a web-based GPS management system as a data source. Moreover, Ye et al. in [31] proposed a collaborative POI recommendation algorithm based on geographical influence. To this aim, they used users check in activities in LBSNs. At last, Scholz et al. [27] studied talk attendance prediction in an academic conference using a link prediction approach. To this aim, they logged talk attendance behavior using RFID tags. However, none of the above studies used both the actual users' onsite physical information interaction behaviors and users' online digital click-through behaviors.

As another line of related research, there are several researches that study recommender systems for museum visitors. Grieser et al. [12] studied next exhibition recommendation problem in the museum space using visitors history. They applied Naive Bayes learning model using textual description, geospatial proximity and popularity of exhibitions. In their study, popularity baseline, which is one of our defined baseline in this paper, was reported as the most successful next exhibition recommendation model.

Bohnert et al. [6] studied unseen exhibition recommendation using nearest-neighbor content-based filtering approach by taking visitors explicit ratings of exhibitions as inputs. They did the study using 41 museum visitors as participants. Moreover, in a recent work of Bartolini et al. [4], they study recommendation of diverse multimedia data across several web repositories, and arrangement of them in visiting paths. They consider location, number of persons and weather condition as context in their contextual pre-filtering system, and they did the study based on 90 users as participants.

Apart from different recommendation methods being used in the above studies in the museum domain, they are very limited in term of number of participants. In addition, none of them log and study users' onsite physical information interactions behaviors. In this paper, we log more than 21,000 users' visits of a museum in a 5 months period, and our proposed model is based on users' both online digital and onsite physical information interaction behaviors.

Closest in spirit to our work is [17], in which users' onsite physical behaviors in the existence of a crowd of users have been studied. They studied skip or stay behavior prediction in checking in different POIs as a classification problem. Their study is different from ours as they do not investigate on similarities between users' physical and digital behaviors. Moreover, we study a POI ranking problem in this paper but they did research on onsite physical interaction behavior classification problem.

3   BACKGROUND AND PRELIMINARIES

In this section, we state the behavioral unseen POI recommendation problem and the best baselines comparable with our proposed model.

3.1   Problem Statement

Let $\mathbf{u} = \{u_1, u_2, ..., u_i\} \subset U^i$ be a subset of users visited a smart environment, $\mathbf{c}_{seen} = \{c_1, c_2, ..., c_j\} \subset C^j{}_{seen}$ a subset of seen or occurred contexts, and $\mathbf{p}_{seen} = \{p_1, p_2, ..., p_k\} \subset P^k{}_{seen}$ a subset of seen POIs. Then, let $\mathbf{R}_{seen} \in \mathbb{R}^{i \times j \times k}_{seen}$ be a user-context-POI matrix containing i users, j seen contexts and k seen POIs. Value $r_{i,j,k} \in \mathbf{R}_{seen}$ refers to the visit frequency of user i, in context j to the POI k. In this paper, due to the fact that museum visitors rarely check in to a POI more than once, we have used binary seen or unseen values rather than considering the frequency.

Having above information about users, given a subset of unseen contexts (i.e., $\mathbf{c}_{unseen} = \{c_1, c_2, ..., c_m\} \subset C^m{}_{unseen}$), and a subset of unseen POIs (i.e., $\mathbf{p}_{unseen} = \{p_1, p_2, ..., p_n\} \subset P^n{}_{unseen}$), the behavioral unseen POI recommendation problem is estimation of $r_{i,m,n} \in \mathbf{R}_{unseen}$ based on users interaction behaviors with the seen POIs, in which $\mathbf{R}_{unseen} \in \mathbb{R}_{unseen}^{i \times m \times n}$ is a user-context-POI matrix containing i users, m unseen contexts and n unseen POIs.

3.2 Baselines

In this section, baselines created for the evaluation purposes are detailed.

3.2.1 Popularity. The popularity based recommendation ranks POIs candidates according to their popularity scores. The popularity is computed as the number of users who checked in at each POI. The popularity baseline is usually used in evaluation of personalized recommendation systems and it is informed as a very challenging and hard-to-beat baseline [23].

3.2.2 Bias-Based Filtering. As Hashemi et.al. discussed in [16], there are some biases in onsite user information interaction logs. They introduces the walk-through position-bias that shows users tend to visit POIs one after the other from check-in to check-out stations. They also observed time-rank bias that indicates users tend to spend less time at the end of exhibitions. Considering these two biases, the probability of checking in at a POI is proportional to the distance from the Check-out station. Therefore, Bias-based baseline ranks POIs based on their distance from the check-out station.

3.2.3 Content-Based Filtering. As descriptions of POIs in museums are well curated, they are very informative source of information that makes the content-based filtering as a very effective baseline in this domain. In this study, each POI contains 3 museum objects with reach descriptions. In order to build a content-based filtering model, we build a profile of each user after visiting a set of POIs using Language Modeling framework. Each profile's language model is based on all seen objects of $\mathbf{p}_{seen}$.

Since we have profiles of users at each context, KL-Divergence of each unseen POI's language model and the profile is considered as content-based filtering scores for ranking unseen POIs.

4 POI RECOMMENDATION USING USERS' BEHAVIORS

This section studies how to predict relevant POIs to the given user and context based on users' interaction behaviors, aiming to answer our first research question: *How to understand users' onsite physical behavior and create a behavioral user model that is able to effectively predict relevant unseen POIs?*

In order to model the set-based contextual POI recommendation, we cast the context-aware recommendation problem to a binary classification problem, in which relevant POIs are labeled 1 and irrelevant ones labeled 0. In this way, we try to learn a behavioral model to predict relevant unseen POIs to the given user and context based on the user's interaction behaviors in the context. Then, relevance probability of POIs to the user and context pairs will be used to rank the unseen POIs. To this aim, a set of features that represent users' interaction behaviors in given contexts is defined.

4.1 Feature Set

In order to learn an effective model to rank POIs, we have extracted 18 different features. As it is shown in Table 1, we have classified features to 3 sets, namely, explicit context, onsite and online.

Explicit context refers to information explicitly given by users about the context. In our study, we collected users' gender, their preferred language, their age range and their chosen perspective of the narratives at the exhibition. Previous study on these explicit contexts [16] shows that users behave differently in these different contexts. For example, as it is discussed in [16], children tends to spend less time in front of the POI about the death. Therefore, it seems a reasonable set of features to consider as explicit contexts.

The second group of features is the one gathered onsite without asking users to give any information about their preferences. These features extracted based on users walk-through data. f_5 is the number of seen POIs, which can be considered as a confidence indicator of some other features' scores like f_6. f_6 is the content-based filtering score of POI candidate based on the profile built using the seen POIs. This content-based filtering score is calculated based on the onsite POI descriptions and users' onsite interactions. That is why it is considered as one of the onsite features in our feature classification.

In addition to f_5 and f_6, we build users' walk-through graph using their onsite interactions with POIs based on the train set onsite information interaction logs, and calculate f_7, f_8, f_9, f_{10}, f_{11} and f_{12} features. Details of these features are available in Table 1.

The third group of features is defined based on an onsite selected POIs using the onsite users' interactions logs. However, the feature calculation is based on online click-through graph of the museum search engine. Therefore, we classified them as online features. The online click-through graph is filtered to the objects available at onsite POIs. In this study, each onsite POI contains 3 different museum objects. We merge all the objects related to each POI as one node, and the click-through graph's edges are aggregated from all the edges of POIs' objects. As a result, same as onsite walk-through graph, the online click-through graph has onsite POIs as nodes. Details of these features are available in Table 1.

4.2 Learning Model

In order to learn a set-based behavioral POI recommendation model, we have implemented a logistic regression classifier and a deep neural multilayer perceptron with dropouts to estimate relevance of each POI to the given user after visiting a set of POIs. The logistic regression classifier and the deep multilayer perceptron have been trained separately based on each group of features extracted using different users' information interaction behaviors to study which user information interaction behavior is more effective in understanding users' preferences in their interactions with the IoT in smart environment. In the rest of this section, we will detail the logistic regression and the deep multilayer perceptron implemented for the set-based behavioral POI recommendation.

4.2.1 Logistic Regression. Logistic regression classifier is a linear classifier that transparently helps to understand contribution of each feature in estimation of POIs relevancy. In fact, we would like to know which trained logistic classifier performs better and why. To this aim, we train different logistic regression classifiers based on different feature sets using different users' interaction behaviors.

In order to learn a logistic classifier, we use variable $c \in \{0, 1\}$ to show relevance of a POI to a user in a context. Specifically, $P_\theta(c = 1 | u, c, p)$ is the relevance score of the POI p to the user u

Table 1: Defined features to predict relevant unseen POIs to users after visiting a set of POIs.

Feature	Category	Description
f_1	Explicit Context	Gender (e.g., Female)
f_2	Explicit Context	Language (e.g., English)
f_3	Explicit Context	Visitor age range (e.g., Adults)
f_4	Explicit Context	Chosen perspective (e.g., Roman)
f_5	Onsite	Seen POIs set size
f_6	Onsite	Content-based relevance score of a POI candidate to a profile created using seen POIs' content that was shown onsite
f_7	Onsite	Unseen POI's PageRank in onsite visits walk-through weighted graph built based on a train set
f_8	Onsite	Unseen POI's PageRank in onsite visits walk-through unweighted graph built based on a train set
f_9	Onsite	Unseen POI's centrality in onsite visits walk-through graph built based on a train set
f_{10}	Onsite	Minimum distance of the seen set of POIs to the POI candidate in the onsite visits walk-through graph built based on a train set
f_{11}	Onsite	Median distance of the seen set of POIs to the POI candidate in the onsite visits walk-through graph built based on a train set
f_{12}	Onsite	Mean distance of the seen set of POIs to the POI candidate in the onsite visits walk-through graph built based on a train set
f_{13}	Online	Unseen POI's PageRank in Online click-through weighted graph built based on a train set
f_{14}	Online	Unseen POI's PageRank in Online click-through unweighted graph built based on a train set
f_{15}	Online	Unseen POI's Centrality in Online click-through graph built based on a train set
f_{16}	Online	Minimum distance of the seen set of POIs to the POI candidate in the Online click-through graph built based on a train set
f_{17}	Online	Median distance of the seen set of POIs to the POI candidate in the Online click-through graph built based on a train set
f_{18}	Online	Mean distance of the seen set of POIs to the POI candidate in the Online click-through graph built based on a train set

and the context c, in which θ is unknown parameters learned using maximum likelihood estimation (MLE) based on the train set. Given the relevance judgments r of each POI p_k to a user u_i and context c_j in the train set, the likelihood L of the train set is as follows:

$$L = \prod_{i=1}^{|U|} \prod_{j=1}^{|C|} \prod_{k=1}^{|P_{seen}|} P_\theta(c = 1|u_i, c_j, p_k)^r P_\theta(c = 0|u_i, c_j, p_k)^{1-r},$$

in which we assume relevance judgments r are generated independently. We model $P_\theta(c = 1|u_i, c_j, p_k)$ by logistic function on a linear combination of features created based on each specific group of users' information interaction behaviors. Then, we optimize the unknown parameters θ by maximizing the following log likelihood function:

$$\theta^* = argmax_\theta \sum_{i=1}^{|U|} \sum_{j=1}^{|C|} \sum_{k=1}^{|P_{seen}|} rlogP_\theta(c = 1|u_i, c_j, p_k)$$
$$+ (1 - r) logP_\theta(c = 0|u_i, c_j, p_k).$$

In order to turn the logistic classifier scores to probabilities, we have used the softmax function:

$$S(y_i) = \frac{e^{y_i}}{\sum_j e^{y_j}},$$

in which y_i is the logistic classifier score, and $S(y_i)$ is the output relevance probability of our behavioral POI recommendation model.

At last, we rank unseen POIs based on the logistic classifier output probability of POIs' relevancy being estimated based on features created using interaction behaviors of a given user in a context.

4.2.2 Deep Neural Multilayer Perceptron. In this subsection, we investigate on a deep neural multilayer perceptron by an aim of improving effectiveness of the POI recommendation to be used in critical one-shot POI recommendation applications. The motivation behind the critical one-shot POI recommendation is that an irrelevant recommendation sometimes has a very negative effect in users' experience in a way that they might be incorrectly guided to an uninteresting department of a museum that leads to a dissatisfied experience. In this model, for each user in a context, our main goal is to recommend a POI which is highly relevant to them. In the one-shot POI recommendation, we do not care about relevant POIs retrieved after rank 1. In the rest of this section, we detail our deep multilayer perceptron with an aim of improving effectiveness of POI recommendation to be used for the critical one-shot POI recommendation problem.

In order to learn a set based behavioral POI recommendation and learn users' onsite complicated physical behaviors, we have used a deep neural network with 3 hidden layers having 326 units. To learn an effective model and overcome overfitting problem, we have used a dropout feedforward neural network. Let $l \in \{1, 2, 3\}$ be the index of the hidden layers of the network. Let $z^{(l)}$ be the vector of input to layer l and $y^{(l)}$ be the vector of outputs from layer l. The dropout neural network is modelled as follows for any hidden unit i and $l \in \{0, 1, 2\}$[19, 28]:

$$r^{(l)} \sim Bernoulli(p),$$
$$\tilde{y}^{(l)} = r^{(l)} * y^{(l)},$$
$$z_i^{(l+1)} = w_i^{(l+1)} \tilde{y}^{(l)} + b_i^{(l+1)},$$
$$y_i^{(l+1)} = f(z_i^{(l+1)}),$$

where $r^{(l)}$ denotes a vector of independent Bernoulli random variables having probability p of being 1, $\tilde{y}^{(l)}$ is thinned outputs created by multiplying a sample of $r^{(l)}$ vector by outputs of layer l (i.e., $y^{(l)}$) and used as input for the next layer $l + 1$, $w^{(l)}$ and $b^{(l)}$ are weights and biases at layer l, and f is an activation function, which is rectified linear units (ReLUs) in our setup. This process is done at each layer.

Following many researches in neural network domain, we have used $p = 0.5$ in our dropout network. This value is reported as a close to optimal value for a wide range of networks in different applications [28].

In the learning phase, the derivatives of the loss function are back-propagated through the dropout network. The dropout network is trained using the stochastic gradient descent (SGD) algorithm with mini batches, which is widely used algorithm for training neural networks. The learning rates are adjusted based on adaptive gradient algorithm (AdaGrad) [8]. In the test phase, the sub-network is used without dropout, but the weights are scaled as $W_{test}^{(l)} = pW^{(l)}$.

For the classification purpose and having probabilities as outputs, we have used Logistic classifier in the last layer. The logistic classifier in the last layer is trained same as the logistic regression classifier being discussed in previous subsection. The only difference is that, in the logistic classifier being used in the last layer, we model $P_\theta(c = 1|u_i, c_j, p_k)$ by logistic function on a linear combination of inputs from the last hidden layer units' outputs. At last, the final relevance probability of $P_\theta(c = 1|u_i, c_j, p_k)$ is used to rank unseen POIs based on features created using interaction behaviors of a given user in a context.

5 EXPERIMENTAL SETUP

In this section, we describe our experimental setup. We first describe the data set used in this paper, and second detail the evaluation methodology used in this study.

5.1 Dataset

The dataset of this study is based on onsite and online interaction logs collected at an archeological museum. In this archeological museum, RFID tags are provided as a key to access some additional information about objects being shown in the museum. Users can enter their preferences at the beginning of the museum exhibition in order to personalize the content being shown in all of the POIs. These preferences are perspectives of the narratives, language, gender and the user's age range.

After checking in, users are free to put their tags on RFID readers of POIs to unlock contents being shown about objects at the POIs. Each POI contains 3 different archeological objects. Users are free

Table 2: An example of records created for the test collection using a user session. The judgments are based on seen POI set-size 2 and 3.

Context	Query Seen POI set	Candidate	Relevance
c_1	<POI1,POI2>	POI3	0
c_1	<POI1,POI2>	POI4	1
c_1	<POI1,POI2>	POI5	0
c_1	<POI1,POI2>	POI6	0
c_1	<POI1,POI2>	POI7	1
c_1	<POI1,POI2>	POI8	0
c_1	<POI1,POI2,POI4>	POI3	0
c_1	<POI1,POI2,POI4>	POI5	0
c_1	<POI1,POI2,POI4>	POI6	0
c_1	<POI1,POI2,POI4>	POI7	1
c_1	<POI1,POI2,POI4>	POI8	0

to interact with POIs in any order. They can watch short movies, interact with 3D photos of POIs' objects, or read contents about objects being shown at POIs. At last, users might check out in a summary station, in which they might leave their name, birth date and email. In this paper, 5 months onsite logs of the museum with more than 21,000 sessions is used, which leads to 3,925 high-quality onsite sessions to be used for evaluation purposes.

In addition to the users' onsite information interaction logs, we also collected query logs of the museum search engine. The online features, detailed in Table 1, have been extracted based on 18,001 high-quality sessions created by filtering bot sessions.

5.2 Evaluation Methodology

In our collected onsite information interaction logs, about 16,000 out of 21,000 sessions either did not have any interactions with POIs or they did not check out at the summary station, and about 1,000 of them had interactions with all the POIs. In order to avoid bias over users who are interested in visiting all or none of the POIs at the museum, we exclude all sessions have checked in at all or none of the POIs at the exhibition. As a result of this preprocessing step, 3,925 out of 21,000 high-quality onsite information interaction sessions remains for creating the test collection.

Considering the walk-through graph, for each user in a session and at each checked in POI during their visit, we created a test collection using the seen set of POIs, the user and the explicit contexts as the query and the unseen POIs as the candidates, for which we have judgments based on the user's session. Basically, we know which POI candidates are visited by the user and consider them as relevant POIs. The rest of the POIs are considered as irrelevant POIs.

Doing the above procedure in building the test collection leads to create a contextual set-based POI recommendation test collection having 1,083,623 judgments. Table 2 shows an example of records created using a user session. To test our proposed model, in order to avoid overfitting, we have done 5-fold cross-validation, in which for each fold as a test set, 3 out of the 4 remained folds randomly sampled and used as a train set, and the remained fold used as a validation set. We repeat the process for all the five folds and report the average of the evaluation metrics.

5.3 Evaluation Metrics

For the evaluation of the defined set-based behavioral POI recommendation task, we cast the problem to a ranking task and use mean reciprocal-rank (*MRR*), mean average precision (*MAP*) and R-precision (*R-Prec*) as metrics that are effective to evaluate proposed models. Moreover, in order to evaluate the one-shot POI recommendation systems, we use precision at rank 1 (*P@1*) as an evaluation metric.

The *MRR* is the average of the reciprocal ranks of the first relevant result for a set of queries Q as $MRR = \frac{1}{|Q|} \sum_{i=1}^{|Q|} \frac{1}{rank_i}$. For a single query, *AP* is defined as the average of the $p@n$ values (i.e., p@n = $\frac{\# \ relevant \ POIs \ in \ top \ n \ results}{n}$) for all relevant POIs as $AP = \frac{\sum_{n=1}^{N} p@n \times rel(n)}{R}$, in which n is the rank, N is the number of retrieved POIs candidates, and $rel(n)$ is a binary function indicating the relevance of a given rank. *MAP* is the mean value of the *APs* computed for all queries. *R-Prec* is precision at rank R where R is the number of relevant candidates for the given query. At last, $p@1$ is the precision at rank 1.

6 EXPERIMENTAL RESULTS

In this section, we provide answer to the research questions stated in the introduction section.

6.1 POI Recommendation Using Users' Information Interaction Behaviors

This section answer our second research question: *How strong are different users' interaction behaviors with IoT in understanding users' preferences?*

To this aim, we have used each of the three groups of features extracted based on each information interaction behaviors to train a POI recommendation system. Specifically, we have trained three different logistic regression classifiers, which are trained based on: 1) the explicit context features (i.e., Logistic Regression-Explicit Context) 2) the onsite features (i.e., Logistic Regression-Onsite) and 3) the online features (i.e., Logistic Regression-Online).

In the rest of this subsection, we first investigate whether users' online digital interaction behaviors are similar to the users' onsite physical behavior. Then, we detail relative importance of each feature extracted based on features' weights being learned by logistic regression classifiers using each type of users' interaction behaviors with an aim of understanding users' behaviors.

6.1.1 Onsite Physical Behavior vs. Online Digital Behavior. We first look at the question: *Are online digital behaviors similar to onsite physical behaviors? Does understanding online digital users' information interaction behaviors have a positive effect in learning a model to predict unseen relevant POIs and complete users' personalized onsite visits?*

In order to answer this research question, we compare POI recommendation systems trained based on each type of interaction behavior. As it is shown in Figure 3, the POI recommendation system trained based on users' online digital interaction behavior is not only as good as the other POI recommendation systems being

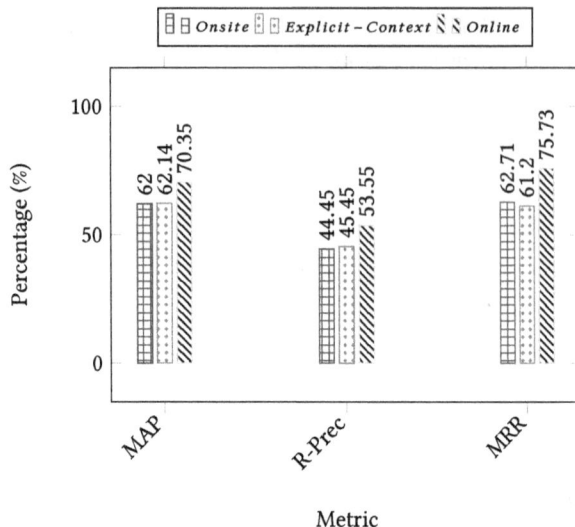

Figure 3: Effectiveness of different types of users' interaction behavior in understanding their onsite preferences.

trained based on either explicit context or onsite interaction behaviors, but also is performing better than them in terms of all common tested information retrieval metrics. This experiment indicates that availability of the considerable amount of online interaction logs in comparison to onsite interaction logs leads to training an effective onsite POI recommendation system based on users' online digital interaction behaviors. As we achieve an effective onsite POI recommendation system based on users' online digital interaction behaviors, we conclude that there is a similarity between onsite physical and online digital information interaction behaviors.

6.1.2 Features Relative Importance in Understanding Users' Interaction Behaviors. We now look at the question: *What are the relative importance of each feature extracted based on different users' interaction behaviors in effectiveness of POI recommendation systems?*

To this aim, we normalize features' weights being learned in each logistic regression classifier trained for each group of features separately. Then, average of the normalized features' weights over the 5-fold cross-validation are reported and compared in Figure 4.

As it is shown in Figure 4, among the explicit context interaction, the chosen language (i.e., f_2) at the start of museum visits is relatively more important in comparison to other explicit context based features. Moreover, mean distance of the seen POIs to a POI candidate in the onsite visits' walk-through graph (i.e., f_{12}) has relatively more importance in comparison to other onsite interaction behavior based features. Regarding the online interaction behaviors, median distance of the seen set of POIs to the given candidate in the online click-through graph (i.e., f_{17}) is relatively more important than other online features in the effectiveness of the POI recommendation systems.

6.2 One-Shot POI Recommendation Using Users' Interaction Behaviors

This section answer our third research question: *How effective is behavioral POI recommendation system in one-shot POI recommendation problem?* To this aim, we study effectiveness of the

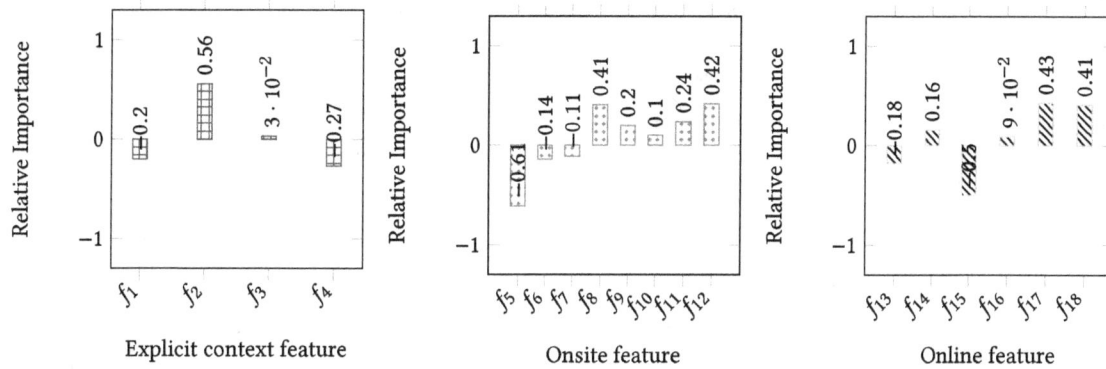

Figure 4: Features' relative importance in POI recommendation trained based on each group of users' information interaction behaviors.

Table 3: Set-based one-shot POI recommendation effectiveness comparison between the *Deep MLP-Online* and baselines. * indicates the improvement is statistically significant ($\rho < 0.05$).

Run	P@1	MRR
Content-based Filtering	57.45	75.68
Popularity	60.86	77.67
Bias-Based Filtering	61.57	77.71
Logistic Regression-Online	56.97	75.73
Deep MLP-Online	**75.81 (23.12%*)**	**86.39 (11.17%*)**

implemented deep multilayer perceptron in one-shot onsite POI recommendation problem in comparison to the discussed baselines as well as the logistic regression POI recommendation system. In addition to baselines' effectiveness, Table 3 shows performance of the best deep multilayer perceptron (i.e., Deep MLP) and logistic regression classifiers, trained based on online digital interaction behaviors, in terms of $p@1$ and *MRR*.

As it is shown in Table 3, the deep MLP significantly improves the best hard-to-beat baseline (i.e., Bias-Based Filtering) in one-shot POI recommendation. In particular, the deep MLP has 23.12% improvement over the bias-based filtering baseline in term of $p@1$, which is the only used metric that measure one-shot POI recommendation performance. This experimental result shows that our proposed deep MLP one-shot POI recommendation system is very effective, and can lead to an interesting personalized experience in such a critical application.

7 DISCUSSION AND CONCLUSIONS

The main focus of this paper is the study of how to build a behavioral user model for the set-based POI recommendation problem using users' both onsite and online information interaction behaviors. A study on the strength of using each type of users' interaction behaviors with IoT in understanding users' onsite information interaction preferences shows that POI recommendation systems trained using features extracted from a combination of both onsite physical and online digital information interaction behaviors (i.e.,

online features) performs better than the ones trained by explicitly given context or onsite information interaction behavior. Therefore, we conclude that there is a similarity between onsite physical and online digital interaction preferences that causes an improvement on the onsite POI recommendation effectiveness. Moreover, we have studied the critical one-shot POI recommendation problem. According to our analysis, the learned models based on just basic explicit given contexts or onsite users' behaviors do not improve the hard-to-beat defined baselines (i.e., popularity and bias-based filtering). However, using a deep multilayer perceptron based on features extracted by online interaction behaviors leads to a significant improvement over the best baseline in all the defined evaluation metrics. Specifically, it has a statistically significant improvement over all baselines with 23% improvement in term of $p@1$ and 11% improvement in term of *MRR*. Therefore, our proposed approach is very effective in critical one-shot POI recommendation. The proposed behavioral user model is very general and can be widely used in any environment with an integrated Internet of Things (IoT) infrastructure. Specifically, in the Cultural Heritage domain, the implemented technology being used in this study and implemented within the European meSch project [1], is listed in [9, 20] as one of the implemented technologies in museums that provides a more interactive and multisensory experiences for visitors. This is one of the technologies mentioned in museum edition of the NMC Horizon 2015 and 2016 reports as a technology being integrated in museums in four to five years time-to-adoption horizon. As a future work, we are going to increase number of POIs in the museum and see how effective is the proposed behavioral set-based POI recommendation model for the bigger datasets. Moreover, in addition to the evaluation detailed in this paper based on a high volume of real users, we are eager to do a user study to test our proposed behavioral user model. As another line of future work, we will investigate on using recursive neural network to improve our proposed behavioral user models to be used in contextual suggestion problem [15].

ACKNOWLEDGMENTS

This research is funded in part by the European Community's FP7 (project meSch, grant # 600851).

---

[1] http://www.mesch-project.eu/

REFERENCES

[1] Gediminas Adomavicius and Alexander Tuzhilin. 2011. Context-aware recommender systems. In *Recommender systems handbook*. Springer, 217–253.

[2] Luigi Atzori, Antonio Iera, and Giacomo Morabito. 2010. The internet of things: A survey. *Computer networks* 54, 15 (2010), 2787–2805.

[3] Payam Barnaghi, Wei Wang, Cory Henson, and Kerry Taylor. 2012. Semantics for the Internet of Things: early progress and back to the future. *International Journal on Semantic Web and Information Systems (IJSWIS)* 8, 1 (2012), 1–21.

[4] Ilaria Bartolini, Vincenzo Moscato, Ruggero G Pensa, Antonio Penta, Antonio Picariello, Carlo Sansone, and Maria Luisa Sapino. 2016. Recommending multimedia visiting paths in cultural heritage applications. *Multimedia Tools and Applications* 75, 7 (2016), 3813–3842.

[5] Betim Berjani and Thorsten Strufe. 2011. A Recommendation System for Spots in Location-based Online Social Networks. In *Proceedings of the 4th Workshop on Social Network Systems (SNS '11)*. ACM, 4:1–4:6.

[6] Fabian Bohnert, Ingrid Zukerman, and Junaidy Laures. 2012. GECKOmmender: Personalised theme and tour recommendations for museums. In *International Conference on User Modeling, Adaptation, and Personalization*. Springer, 26–37.

[7] Aleksandr Chuklin, Ilya Markov, and Maarten de Rijke. 2015. Click Models for Web Search. *Synthesis Lectures on Information Concepts, Retrieval, and Services* 7, 3 (2015), 1–115.

[8] John Duchi, Elad Hazan, and Yoram Singer. 2011. Adaptive subgradient methods for online learning and stochastic optimization. *Journal of Machine Learning Research* 12, Jul (2011), 2121–2159.

[9] A Freeman, S Adams Becker, M Cummins, E McKelroy, C Giesinger, and B Yuhnke. 2016. NMC horizon report: 2016: Museum edition. *The New Media Consortium, Austin, Texas2016* (2016).

[10] Peter Friess. 2013. *Internet of things: converging technologies for smart environments and integrated ecosystems*. River Publishers.

[11] Huiji Gao, Jiliang Tang, Xia Hu, and Huan Liu. 2013. Exploring Temporal Effects for Location Recommendation on Location-based Social Networks. In *Proceedings of the 7th ACM Conference on Recommender Systems (RecSys '13)*. ACM, 93–100.

[12] Karl Grieser, Timothy Baldwin, and Steven Bird. 2007. Dynamic path prediction and recommendation in a museum environment. In *Proc. of the Workshop on Language Technology for Cultural Heritage Data (LaT-eCH 2007)*. 49–56.

[13] Jean-Benoit Griesner, Talel Abdessalem, and Hubert Naacke. 2015. POI Recommendation: Towards Fused Matrix Factorization with Geographical and Temporal Influences. In *Proceedings of the 9th ACM Conference on Recommender Systems (RecSys '15)*. ACM, 301–304.

[14] Ido Guy. 2015. The Role of User Location in Personalized Search and Recommendation. In *Proceedings of the 9th ACM Conference on Recommender Systems (RecSys '15)*. ACM, 236–236.

[15] Seyyed Hadi Hashemi, Charles L. A. Clarke, Jaap Kamps, Julia Kiseleva, and Ellen M. Voorhees. 2016. Overview of the TREC 2016 Contextual Suggestion Track. In *Proceeding of Text REtrieval Conference (TREC)*.

[16] Seyyed Hadi Hashemi, Wim Hupperetz, Jaap Kamps, and Merel van der Vaart. 2016. Effects of Position and Time Bias on Understanding Onsite Users' Behavior. In *Proceedings of the 2016 ACM on Conference on Human Information Interaction and Retrieval (CHIIR '16)*. ACM, 277–280.

[17] Seyyed Hadi Hashemi and Jaap Kamps. 2017. Skip or Stay: Users' Behavior in Dealing with Onsite Information Interaction Crowd-Bias. In *Proceedings of the 2017 ACM on Conference on Human Information Interaction and Retrieval (CHIIR '17)*. ACM.

[18] José M Hernández-Muñoz, Jesús Bernat Vercher, Luis Muñoz, José A Galache, Mirko Presser, Luis A Hernández Gómez, and Jan Pettersson. 2011. Smart cities at the forefront of the future internet. In *The Future Internet Assembly*. Springer, 447–462.

[19] Geoffrey E. Hinton, Nitish Srivastava, Alex Krizhevsky, Ilya Sutskever, and Ruslan Salakhutdinov. 2012. Improving neural networks by preventing co-adaptation of feature detectors. *CoRR* abs/1207.0580 (2012).

[20] Larry Johnson, Samantha Adams Becker, Victoria Estrada, and Alex Freeman. 2015. *The NMC Horizon Report: 2015 Museum Edition*. ERIC.

[21] Alexandros Karatzoglou, Xavier Amatriain, Linas Baltrunas, and Nuria Oliver. 2010. Multiverse Recommendation: N-dimensional Tensor Factorization for Context-aware Collaborative Filtering. In *Proceedings of the Fourth ACM Conference on Recommender Systems (RecSys '10)*. ACM, 79–86.

[22] Xin Liu and Karl Aberer. 2013. SoCo: A Social Network Aided Context-aware Recommender System. In *Proceedings of the 22Nd International Conference on World Wide Web (WWW '13)*. ACM, 781–802.

[23] Claudio Lucchese, Raffaele Perego, Fabrizio Silvestri, Hossein Vahabi, and Rossano Venturini. 2012. How Random Walks Can Help Tourism. In *Proceedings of Advances in Information Retrieval: 34th European Conference on IR Research, ECIR 2012*.

[24] Moon-Hee Park, Jin-Hyuk Hong, and Sung-Bae Cho. 2007. Location-based recommendation system using bayesian user's preference model in mobile devices. In *International Conference on Ubiquitous Intelligence and Computing*. Springer, 1130–1139.

[25] Charith Perera, Arkady Zaslavsky, Peter Christen, and Dimitrios Georgakopoulos. 2014. Context aware computing for the internet of things: A survey. *IEEE Communications Surveys & Tutorials* 16, 1 (2014), 414–454.

[26] Steffen Rendle, Zeno Gantner, Christoph Freudenthaler, and Lars Schmidt-Thieme. 2011. Fast Context-aware Recommendations with Factorization Machines. In *Proceedings of the 34th International ACM SIGIR Conference on Research and Development in Information Retrieval (SIGIR '11)*. ACM, 635–644.

[27] Christoph Scholz, Jens Illig, Martin Atzmueller, and Gerd Stumme. 2014. On the Predictability of Talk Attendance at Academic Conferences. In *Proceedings of the 25th ACM Conference on Hypertext and Social Media*. ACM, 279–284.

[28] Nitish Srivastava, Geoffrey E Hinton, Alex Krizhevsky, Ilya Sutskever, and Ruslan Salakhutdinov. 2014. Dropout: a simple way to prevent neural networks from overfitting. *Journal of Machine Learning Research* 15, 1 (2014), 1929–1958.

[29] Gang Wang, Xinyi Zhang, Shiliang Tang, Haitao Zheng, and Ben Y. Zhao. 2016. Unsupervised Clickstream Clustering for User Behavior Analysis. In *Proceedings of the 2016 CHI Conference on Human Factors in Computing Systems (CHI '16)*. ACM, 225–236.

[30] Xiangye Xiao, Yu Zheng, Qiong Luo, and Xing Xie. 2010. Finding Similar Users Using Category-based Location History. In *Proceedings of the 18th SIGSPATIAL International Conference on Advances in Geographic Information Systems (GIS '10)*. ACM, 442–445.

[31] Mao Ye, Peifeng Yin, Wang-Chien Lee, and Dik-Lun Lee. 2011. Exploiting Geographical Influence for Collaborative Point-of-interest Recommendation. In *Proceedings of the 34th International ACM SIGIR Conference on Research and Development in Information Retrieval (SIGIR '11)*. ACM, 325–334.

[32] Josh Jia-Ching Ying, Eric Hsueh-Chan Lu, Wen-Ning Kuo, and Vincent S. Tseng. 2012. Urban Point-of-interest Recommendation by Mining User Check-in Behaviors. In *Proceedings of the ACM SIGKDD International Workshop on Urban Computing (UrbComp '12)*. ACM, 63–70.

[33] Vincent W. Zheng, Bin Cao, Yu Zheng, Xing Xie, and Qiang Yang. 2010. Collaborative Filtering Meets Mobile Recommendation: A User-centered Approach. In *Proceedings of the Twenty-Fourth AAAI Conference on Artificial Intelligence (AAAI'10)*. AAAI Press, 236–241.

[34] Vincent W. Zheng, Yu Zheng, Xing Xie, and Qiang Yang. 2010. Collaborative Location and Activity Recommendations with GPS History Data. In *Proceedings of the 19th International Conference on World Wide Web (WWW '10)*. ACM, 1029–1038.

[35] Vincent W. Zheng, Yu Zheng, Xing Xie, and Qiang Yang. 2010. Collaborative Location and Activity Recommendations with GPS History Data. In *Proceedings of the 19th International Conference on World Wide Web (WWW '10)*. ACM, 1029–1038.

[36] Yu Zheng, Lizhu Zhang, Xing Xie, and Wei-Ying Ma. 2009. Mining Interesting Locations and Travel Sequences from GPS Trajectories. In *Proceedings of the 18th International Conference on World Wide Web (WWW '09)*. ACM, 791–800.

[37] Jinfeng Zhuang, Tao Mei, Steven C.H. Hoi, Ying-Qing Xu, and Shipeng Li. 2011. When Recommendation Meets Mobile: Contextual and Personalized Recommendation on the Go. In *Proceedings of the 13th International Conference on Ubiquitous Computing (UbiComp '11)*. ACM, 153–162.

[38] Onno Zoeter. 2015. Recommendations in Travel. In *Proceedings of the 9th ACM Conference on Recommender Systems (RecSys '15)*. ACM, 234–234.

A New Statistical Density Clustering Algorithm based on Mutual Vote and Subjective Logic Applied to Recommender Systems*

Charif Haydar
Sailendra
2 Rue Jacques Villermaux
Nancy, France 54000
charif.haydar@sailendra.fr

Anne Boyer
University of Lorraine
P.O. Box 1212
Nancy, France 54000
anne.boyer@loria.fr

ABSTRACT

Data clustering is an important topic in data science in general, but also in user modeling and recommendation systems. Some clustering algorithms like K-means require the adjustment of many parameters, and force the clustering without considering the clusterability of the dataset. Others, like DBSCAN, are adjusted to a fixed density threshold, so can't detect clusters with different densities. In this paper we propose a new clustering algorithm based on the mutual vote, which adjusts itself automatically to the dataset, demands a minimum of parameterizing, and is able to detect clusters with different densities in the same dataset. We test our algorithm and compare it to other clustering algorithms for clustering users, and predict their purchases in the context of recommendation systems.

KEYWORDS

Density based clustering; Recommender systems; Subjective logic

1 INTRODUCTION

Data clustering is an important issue for many computer science applications [16]. Such as machine learning, image processing, pattern recognition, user modeling and recommendation systems (RS) [10, 18].

Recommendation systems are deeply dependent on the user-item rating matrix, which is usually very sparse. In clustering, users are represented by vectors generated from the rating matrix. Obviously, users' vectors are very sparse too, which makes computing distances between them a complicated issue, and generates irregular shaped clusters with high variant densities.

K-means [9, 17] figures as the most used algorithm for clustering applications. It is easy to use, rapid, and gives good results in most cases. It was also widely applied for RS [7, 14, 19]. Its main drawbacks reside in the difficulty of finding the optimal k (number of clusters), the acute sensitivity of the algorithm to the initialization parameters and that it can only detect well separated clusters, and has difficulty detecting non-spherical shapes or widely different sizes or densities [16].

Another family of clustering algorithms is the density based clustering family, which a main quality the ability to detect different shapes of clusters [16]. The most well-known algorithms from this family are DBSCAN [6] and shared Nearest Neighbor (SNN) [15]. They are still very sensitive to their parameters, and do not perform well in high variant density environments.

In this paper, we propose a density based clustering algorithm called mutual vote (MV) that uses a statistical model to adapt itself to each vector's perception of its neighborhood, and aggregate the perception of neighboring vectors. This allows the vectors to mutually decide to fit in the same cluster or not. MV requires less parametrizing, and adapt automatically to variant density zones.

We demonstrate the effectiveness of our algorithm by applying it to a real taken from the sales of J.Milliet, a company that sells various types of drinks. We compare the performance of our algorithm to that of other clustering algorithms in terms of labeling clusters and prediction users' purchases. Our results show the advantages of our algorithm, especially in terms of prediction.

This paper is organized as follows: in the next section we present a general framework explaining how each clustering method works. In the third section we present our algorithm. Then we describe our experiments and evaluation strategies. The last section contains the conclusions and the perspectives for future work.

2 GENERAL FRAMEWORK

Clustering has contributed to improve recommendation system's performance in many ways; such as scalability [14], cold start [19] (when RS can't recommend items to a new user), and to simply identify a group of users having a specific behavior [7, 10].

In the recommendation context, the users are represented as multidimensional vectors, where each item (product) represents a dimension. Values of vectors refer to the rating values attributed by users to the items.

In real applications as most users rate a limited number of items, most vectors' values are unknown.

Clustering algorithm tries to regroup similar vectors in the same cluster, so as to maximize vectors' similarity within the cluster, and maximize it with vectors from other clusters. To achieve this, the algorithm has to overcome some challenges such as determining when two vectors are close enough to be in the same cluster, or to determine how many clusters exist in a given dataset.

Computing distances in sparse vectors is a complicated task. We illustrate that by the example in table 1. The table contains the purchases records of four users and 11 items, where 1 represents that the user has purchased the item, and (−) means that the user did not purchase the item.

---

*Produces the permission block, and copyright information

	i_1	i_2	i_3	i_4	i_5	i_6	i_7	i_8	i_9	i_{10}	i_{11}
A	1	1	1	1	-	1	-	-	-	-	-
B	1	-	1	-	1	1	1	1	1	-	-
C	-	1	-	1	-	-	-	-	-	1	1
D	-	-	-	-	1	-	1	1	1	-	-

Table 1: Distances interpretation exemple

It is rational to say that any distance measure will consider that the more two users have common purchase, the more they are close to each other.

Let's consider the distances form the vector A perspectives: B is the nearest vector to A, because they share 3 items, C comes in the second place with 2 common items, and D is in the last place with no items in common. Obviously, A would likely be in the same cluster with B, probably with C, but not with D.

B and C share no items, so they would not be in the same cluster with each other. A choice should be made to associate A to only one of them, as B is the closer to A, it sounds more reasonable to say that B is the better choice to A.

On the side of B, it is true that he has 3 common items with A, but he also has 4 items with D. As A and D has no shared items between them, it is more reasonable to prefer to associate B to D because it is closer. By consequence, B would ignore the "invitation" to join A, to the favor of joining D.

Following the same logic, D also would prefer to be associated to B, because he is the closest vector to it, which will lead to form a cluster of B and D.

The choices for A are now updated, he would be either associated to B and D together; so being with D in the same cluster without any common purchase between them, which will decrease the similarity inside the cluster. Or be associated to C which is farther from him than B, and so increases the similarity with items outside the cluster.

According to this example, it is obvious that each vector has its own conception to other vectors configuration around it, which can be contradictory with other vectors' conceptions. We are convinced that a clustering algorithm working in RS's domain must be adapted to deal with situations of sparse vectors. Our algorithm belongs to the density based algorithms family, it uses aggregation functions a mutual votes between vector to come over the problem of sparse vectors. We compare it to two algorithms from the same family (DBSCAN and SNN), and to K-means as this latter is the most used in RS domain. In the following section we give an idea about each of the three algorithms.

2.1 Kmeans

Kmeans is the most widespread clustering algorithm. K is the desired number of clusters. To initialize the algorithm we choose k vectors as centers of clusters randomly or according to a model [1], then each vector in the dataset is attributed to the nearest center to it, at the end of this operation we recompute the centers of clusters, and we reattribute vectors to the new centers. This operation is repeated until centers are stabilized or predefined maximum number of iterations is reached. Many works were done to automatize the compute of k [8].

K-means has difficulty in detecting the âĂIJnaturalâĂİ clusters, when clusters have non-spherical shapes or widely different sizes or densities[16].

2.2 DBSCAN

DBSCAN is the most known density based clustering algorithm. It depends on the parameter *Eps*. Eps-neighborhood of a point p is the set of points whose distance of p is less than a threshold *Eps*.

$$N_{Eps}(p) = \{q \in D | dist(p, q) \leq Eps\}$$

DBSCAN algorithm labels all points with one of three labels.

- Core point: points whose N_{Eps} size is larger than a threshold *MinPts*. i.e. p has a minimal number of neighbors
- Border point: a border point is one which is not core point itself, but it falls in the neighborhood of at least one core point.
- Noise point: a noisy point is a point which is neither core point nor border point.

Noise points are eliminated (these points can't be clustered by DBSCAN). All core points that exists in the neighborhood of each others are added to the same cluster. Border points are then added to the clusters of their associated core points.

DBSCAN is capable to Discover clusters of arbitrary shapes [3], but it can have trouble in detection clusters in datasets where the densities of clusters vary widely. It has another drawback when used in high dimensional data because density is more difficult to define for such context [16].

2.3 Shared Nearest Neighbors (SNN)

SNN algorithm was firstly proposed by [11], and then used by many others [2, 12].

The algorithm starts by finding the nearest n neighbor for each vector, then computes the number of shared neighbors between each couple of vectors, this number shows the strength of the link between them. It then represents the dataset as a graph, deletes all links that are weaker than a threshold T where $T < n$. The resulting clusters correspond to the connected vectors in the shared nearest neighbor graph after sparsifying it using the threshold T [15].

This algorithm is very sensitive to the chosen thresholds, so small changes in thresholds can lead to brutal changes in resulting clusters.

3 OUR PROPOSED ALGORITHM (MUTUAL VOTES)

The idea of our algorithm is to give vectors the possibility to exchange invitations between them, so decide mutually if they would rather end up in the same cluster.

In the literature another usage of negotiation between vectors was proposed in [5, 13], where agents in multi-agents system negotiation to improve their respective ontologies. Semantic similarity is extracted from agents negotiations, and used to cluster them by K-means. In our method where no explicit negotiations between vectors exists, similarity is computed using classical metrics (Jaccard in our case), and then negotiation (in form of mutual votes) are used to fit each vector to a cluster.

Our algorithm constructs a directed graph of users' neighborhood. It computes the distances between each couple of users. It then extracts for each user his list of distances, composed by all his distances from other users. For each user, it normalizes distances list by computing the z-scores and removes all users whom distances are larger that mean distance minus one standard deviation. It calls the remaining list the neighbors list. This step allow us to keep only users who are significantly close according the user, so without having a global threshold for all users.

It then transforms neighbors list to candidates list. The candidate list contains users whom the current users want to invite to join his cluster. Each candidate is associated to a score equals to willingness of the current user to invite him to his cluster. The transformation of neighbors list to candidates list consists in computing these scores according to the equation:

$$c(u_n) = 1 - \frac{d_{un} - d_{min}}{\tau - d_{min}} \tag{1}$$

Where: d_{un} is the distance between the candidate and the current user. d_{min} is the distance between the current user and the closest user to him. τ is the threshold (mean minus one standard deviation).

It is obvious that scores in candidates list are always within the range $[0, 1]$, where the score of the closest neighbor is 1.

The idea now is that each user will -implicitly- send a request to the user in the top of his candidates list, asking him to join his cluster. The receiver of the request, will accept if the sender is in the top of the list, if not, then he will reject the request. In case of acceptance, both users become members of the same cluster, and their candidates lists will be merged using an aggregation function.

Aggregation function is a key tool in the algorithm, it decides the sizes and the form of the clusters. It determines how much the clusters will be welcoming or hostile to new users. We have tried many types of aggregation functions, the most adapted was the aggregation function of subjective logic (SL). This leads us to dedicate the following subsection to explain main components of SL, before illustrating our version of the algorithm in the next subsection.

3.1 Subjective logic

Subjective is an extension of probabilistic logic that associate each probability to an owner, and model it as an opinion. The symbol ω_o^v refers to the opinion of the owner v on the object o. The simplest form of SL opinion is called binomial opinion. A binomial opinions is a quadruple $\omega_o^v = (b, d, u, a)$; where b represents the mass of belief, d the mass of disbelief, and u the mass of uncertainty, and a is the base rate (the priori probabilty in case of absence of information). The sum of the three masses is always 1.

The three masses are calculated via positive interactions counter r, negative interactions counter s, and non-informative prior weight w. using the following equations:

$$b = \frac{r}{r + s + w} \tag{2}$$

$$d = \frac{s}{r + s + w} \tag{3}$$

$$u = \frac{w}{r + s + w} \tag{4}$$

Binomial opinion is based on statistical beta distribution, the non-informative w is initialized to 0.5 which ensures that the prior (i.e. when r = s = 0) Beta pdf with default base rate a = 0.5 is a uniform pdf. Table 2 shows the initial case of the binomial opinion and its changes by new interactions:

state	r	s	w	b	d	u
Initial state	0	0	2	0	0	1
New positive interaction	1	0	2	1/3	0	2/3
New negative interaction	1	1	2	1/4	1/4	2/4

Table 2: Binomial opinion

Finally, binomial opinion is reduced to a numeric probability expressed by the expected value:

$$Ex = b + a \times u \tag{5}$$

In the original case w is a fixed value. We are trying to model the opinion of a cluster X about another cluster Y. In our model, when a user $x_n \in X$ wants to invite a user $y_m \in Y$ to his cluster, a positive interaction is added to the opinion of X on Y. As the willingness of x_n is related to the score of y_m in his candidates list, then the interaction is not always completely positive. We consider that the interaction is completely positive only when y_m is on the top of the candidates list of x_n, because only in this case x_n is fully willing that y_m joins his cluster. Otherwise, the interaction comprises a mass of uncertainty beside the mass of willingness, in this case we consider that the mass of willingness corresponds to the $score(x_n, y_m)$, and the mass of uncertainty corresponds to $(1 - score(x_n, y_m))$. By consequence, we update both r and w as follow:

$$\begin{aligned} &= r + score(x_n, y_m) \\ w &= w + (1 - score(x_n, y_m)) \end{aligned} \tag{6}$$

In the other case; when y_m is not in the candidates list of x_n, we consider that x_n is hostile to be in the same cluster with y_n. As we have no score to evaluate the hostility of x_n. we update our variables as follow:

$$\begin{aligned} &= s + \alpha \\ w &= w + (1 - \alpha) \end{aligned} \tag{7}$$

Where $\alpha \in [0, 1]$ represents a hostility barometer.

We suppose the base rate as $a = 0.5$, and $\alpha = 0.5$, which corresponds to an average behavior of vectors (neither welcoming nor hostile to other vectors). Finally, as the expected value is a probability and we want our system to express positive and negative opinions, we shift it to form a score in the range $[-1, +1]$.

3.2 Current version of the algorithm

In the current version of the algorithm, we start by computing the candidates list of each user. Then we consider each user as a cluster. We also consider that each cluster has a binomial opinion of one interaction on each cluster in the candidate list of the former user. We collect opinions in a coupling list of type (key, value), where the key is formed of two clusters, and the value is formed of their respective opinions on each other, in addition to the average of both expected values Ex of both opinions. The following formula illustrates an element of the list, where A and B are vectors.

$$\overbrace{(\{Cl[A], Cl[B]\}}^{Key}, \overbrace{\{\omega_B^A, \omega_A^B, AVG(Ex_{\omega_B^A}, Ex_{\omega_A^B})\})}^{Value}$$

In the case when only one opinion exists (B is in the candidates list of A but A is not in the candidates list of B), we add one opinion ω_A^B formed with one negative interaction (equation 7) to express that B is hostile to A.

We order the coupling list by the descending value of the last field (the average of both opinions).

The next step consists on merging clusters of the couple on the top of the list, then updating all other elements containing one cluster of the merged couple, before proceeding to merging a new couple according to the new list.

The following example illustrated how merging is done: Suppose we have the following list:

($\{[A], [B]\}, \{1.0, 1.0, 1.0\}$)
($\{[B], [D]\}, \{0.9, 0.7, 0.8\}$)
($\{[A], [C]\}, \{0.8, 0.6, 0.7\}$)
($\{[B], [C]\}, \{0.5, 0.7, 0.6\}$)

Where in the first line we have the clusters A, B in the first two columns, the values $score([A], [B])$ and $score([B], [A])$ in the third and forth column, and the average score in the last column.

$[A]$ and $[B]$ are merged first, and the list will be transformed as follow:

($\{[A, B], [C]\}, \{0.425, 0.325, 0.375\}$)
($\{[A, B], [D]\}, \{0.100, 0.050, 0.075\}$)

The value of $score([A, B], [C])$ is an opinion where:

$r = r + score([A], [C]) + score([B], [C]) = 0.0 + 0.8 + 0.9 = 1.7$
$s = 0$
$w = w + (1 - score([A], [C])) + (1 - score([B], [C])) = 2.0 + 0.2 + 0.1 = 2.3$

So:
$b = 1.7/4 = 0.425$
$d = 0/4 = 0.0$
$u = 2.3/4 = 0.575$

and finally the expected value is:
$Ex = 0.425 + 0.5 * 0.575 = 0.7125$

We shift the value to be within the range $[-1, +1]$:
$score([A, B], [C]) = 0.425$

Whereas concerning the $score([A, B], [D])$:
$r = r + score([B], [D]) = 0.0 + 0.9 = 0.9$
$s = s + \alpha = 0 + 0.5 = 0.5$
$w = w + (1 - score([B], [D])) + (1 - \alpha) = 2.0 + 0.1 + 0.5 = 2.6$

Using the same steps as in $score([A, B], [C])$:
$score([A, B], [D]) = 0.1$

In the same way we compute $score([C], [A, B])$ and $score([D], [A, B])$.

Even thought basically $[D]$ had a strong relationship with $[B]$, the relationship is weakened when B joins $[A]$, because D has no relationship with $[A]$. The new cluster $[A, B]$ will prefer adding $[C]$ rather than $[D]$. Nevertheless, the new cluster still has a positive opinion about $[D]$, so he still can join them in a later time. The relationship is eliminated from the list only when the strength of the link becomes negative. We keep on merging cluster as elements exist in the relationship list.

The pseudo code of the algorithm:

Algorithm 1 Mutual votes

1: Initilize list $ClMessages \leftarrow (A, B, \omega_B^A, \omega_A^B, Avg(\omega_B^A, \omega_A^B))$
2: **for each** $d_1 \in \mathcal{D}ata$ **do**
3:     Initialize list $Dists(d_1) \leftarrow$ distances between d_1 and all other data points
4:     $Z_{d_1} \leftarrow Avg(Dists_{d_1}) - StdDev(Dists_{d_1})$
5:     Initialize list $NBRS(d_1) \leftarrow$ members of $Dists_{d_1}$ whose z-score is smaller than Z_{d_1}
6:     Initialize list $C(d_1) \leftarrow$ applying equation (1)
7:     UpdateClMessages($C(d_1)$)
8: **end for**
9: **repeat**
10:     Merge($ClMessages(0)(0), ClMessages(0)(1)$)
11:     Delete($ClMessages(0)$)
12:     OrderByAvg($ClMessages$)
13: **until** $ClMessages(0)(4) < 0$

---

4 EXPERIMENTS AND EVALUATION

Our experiments aim to validate our proposed algorithm by comparing its performance to that of K-means, DBSCAN, and SNN in a recommendation task. As purchases are binary values we use Jaccard distance [4] in all our distance computations.

Experiments are done in three steps; (1) we use each algorithm to cluster the training part of the dataset. (2) We extract up to 20 labels by cluster. In this perspective, each item is represented as a set of keywords form its descriptions (title, category, sub-category, ...). For each user purchasing an item, the keywords set of the item is add to the cluster of the user. The cluster, then, is represented as a large set of keywords. We use Chi-square test to compute if the presence of a given keyword is significantly high compared to its presence in the rest of the clusters. We keep keywords with highest Chi-square test scores as labels of the cluster. (3) In this step, will try to predict the items that users will purchase (in the test part of the dataset). A list of predicted items by user is calculated, the size of the list equals twice the size of the test items list of the user, in the perspective that we wanted to give the algorithm two chances to predict a purchase (this rule can be modified but the main issue is that it would be applied in the same way to all algorithms. To compute the prediction list for a user v from the cluster C, we calculate the Jaccard similarity between each item in the dataset and the labels of C, we subtract items that have already been purchased by v in the training part, we then formulate the prediction list by keeping only a list of $2 \times N$ items with the highest Jaccard similarity to C (N is the number of items that v purchased in the test part). In this strategy recommendations are completely dependent on the clustering algorithm, the only personalization done is filtering out items that have already been purchased.

Steps (2) and (3) are independent of the clustering method. The algorithms are evaluated by the number of users to whom they can generate recommendation (coverage), and the percentage of test items they succeed to predict (precision). We aggregate both metrics in the F-metric. We avoided using statistical metrics like Squared Errors' Sum because they are adapted only to spherical-clusters which will give benefits to K-means.

In this application, labels are important for human inspection, detecting typical behaviors, adjusting marketing strategies, and to generate the recommendations. To the best of our knowledge, no objective metrics exist to evaluate labels quality, this is usually done by human experts or semantic ontologies. Nevertheless, we propose three indicators as a trial to evaluate the quality of labels, the indicators are based on remarks taken from human experts who evaluated subjectively our labels.

In the following, we start by explaining the used dataset, then we discuss the impact of the clustering on the recommendations performance, and the quality of the labels.

4.1 Dataset

J.Milliet is a french company of drinks distribution to bars and restaurants. Its products belong to many categories (liquors, beers, fruits juices, sodas, and water). The challenge here is to be able to propose to a client v relevant products depending on similar clients to him, and also to identify typical behaviors and domains of interest of different categories of clients, in order to adjust the marketing strategies. The dataset contains about 2400 clients profile, 5329 products, and two months of sales records. Clients are very heterogeneous. They have very diverse purchasing behaviors, depending on a long list of factors such as: being a bar or a restaurant, having a license to sell alcohol or not, having conventions with some producers so being obliged to purchase only their products in their category.

Practically, we divide the dataset into five divisions, each division contains a fifth of user sales, we then proceed to a cross validation by using four divisions for training and one for test, and we repeat the operation five times by changing the test division.

4.2 Clustering and recommendation performance

In this section, we illustrate the results of clustering of the four used algorithms:

4.2.1 K-means. We tried many k values (following the Fibonacci sequence) in order to obtain the optimal number in term of recommendation precision. We used the version of the machine learning library (mllib) of Apache spark:

K	clusters	precision	coverage	F
5	3	35.34%	100%	0.52
8	5	40.45%	100%	0.58
13	6	39.47%	100%	0.57
21	9	39.23%	100%	0.56
34	11	40.98%	100%	0.58
55	15	39.85%	100%	0.57
89	17	41.02%	100%	0.58
144	**24**	**41.42%**	**100%**	**0.59**
233	30	40.40%	100%	0.57

Table 3: Kmeans clustering and recommendation precision

In table 3 clusters count does not correspond to k because we decided to eliminate clusters containing less than 5 users, and to redistribute these users to the closest cluster.

K-means arrives rapidly to an acceptable level of prediction, and then it improves slightly with larger k, it shows certain stability towards different k, so even though $k = 144$ gives the best performance, other values are close to it.

4.2.2 DBSCAN. Table 4 illustrates DBSCAN results with different parameters values. The best performance is obtained with a maximal distance $MaxD = 0.8$ and $Eps = 5$. Even in its best performance, DBSCAN still has a very low precision 24%, and an insufficient coverage (only 56% of users have been attributed to clusters).

We suppose that the explanation of this low performance reside in the variance of the density of clusters. DBSCAN can't detect clusters of different densities. Table 4 reveals a very fluctuated performance, which make us think that each configuration allow the detection only a different subset of clusters.

Eps	MaxD	clusters	precision	coverage	F
5	0.7	4	04.20%	20.5%	0.07
5	**0.8**	**5**	**24.06%**	**56.26%**	**0.34**
8	0.7	4	3.81%	18.22%	0.06
8	0.8	2	21.53%	53.06%	0.31
13	0.7	3	3.07%	13.02%	0.05
13	0.8	2	19.69%	49.47%	0.28
21	0.7	2	2.5%	21.50%	0.04
21	0.8	2	16.06%	45.46%	0.24
34	0.8	2	12.79%	39.94%	0.19

Table 4: DBSCAN clustering and recommendation

4.2.3 SNN. SNN also shows high fluctuation in its results. Even though this method is more adapted to different clusters density, results in table 5 show that it is difficult to find a unique threshold for all users. This is because of the that vectors contains a high number of empty values.

4.2.4 Mutual Vote (MV). We chose to Adjust the hostility barometer to the middle ($\alpha = 0.5$), this makes vectors neutral towards each others (neither welcoming nor hostile).

Table 6 regroups the performance of MV with the best performances of each of the precedent algorithms.

It is obvious that MV outdoes the three algorithms. The high flexibility of the algorithm allows it to fit to the data space topology. Normalizing distances and keeping only meaningful ones according to the local zone of multidimensional space, gives the algorithm a high capacity to fit to different types of zones in the space. Furthermore, giving each vector the capacity to decide in function of his own opinion, and trying to find the compromise with others' opinions, gives the algorithm the capacity to work in a dataset marked by the lack of values.

n	t	clusters	precision	coverage	F
5	2	9	35.32%	88.58%	0.50
5	3	37	17.94%	34.78%	0.24
8	**3**	**11**	**39.81%**	**82.58%**	**0.54**
8	5	18	11.36%	18.89%	0.14
13	5	13	31.5%	74.76%	0.44
13	8	14	10.1%	17.7%	0.13
21	8	10	30.79%	75.8%	0.44
21	13	13	10.21%	17.2%	0.13
34	13	7	33.21%	79.39%	0.47
34	21	15	10.63%	20.84%	0.14
55	21	5	35.14%	84.7%	0.50
55	34	13	12.89%	25.26%	0.17
89	55	11	21.13%	35.56%	0.27
144	89	6	32.37%	50.59%	0.39

Table 5: SNN clustering and recommendation

Method	clusters	precision	coverage	F
DBSCAN	5	24.06%	56.26%	0.34
SNN	11	39.81%	82.58%	0.54
K-means	24	41.42%	100%	0.59
MV	53	47.38%	100%	0.64

Table 6: Best methods performances clustering and recommendation

4.3 Labels

Performance results show that k-means has the closest performance to MV, that is why in this part we are only interested by labels generated by these two algorithms.

Usually, labels evaluation relies either on ontologies and semantics, or on human experts. In our case, we asked several persons working in computer science and in commercial domains to evaluate our sets of labels. Basically, they attested to the coherence and usability of labels sets of both algorithms, with a hesitant preference to MV. As this judgment still subjective, we tried to understand some of the factors on which they relied in their decisions, and worked on modeling them into indicators of labels' quality that we propose in this section.

We consider that a good clustering method, results clusters that represent a unique type of clients' behavior each. A unique behavior in our context corresponds to a specific set of domains of interest. Domains of interest of a cluster can be deduced from its labels, that is why sharing less labels with other clusters, icreases the capacity of a cluster to represent an identified unique type of clients behavior.

Nevertheless, Our labeling method tolerates the attribution of the same label to different clusters. Because practically some clusters can share limited parts of their domains of interest. Even though the more clusters share domains of interest the more they are similar, which challenges the decision of separating them.

4.3.1 Unique labels. A unique label is a label that has been attributed to only one cluster. We consider that the more unique labels are present in clustering the better it is. Because this confirm

that the cluster represents a particular separated behavior of a subset of clients, which is the main objective of the clustering.

Figure 1 illustrates the percentage of labels frequencies among clusters. 49.5% of labels attributed by our method were unique labels versus 50.9% in K-means. 19.4% were attributed to two clusters versus 17.4% in K-means, and so on.

Percentage are similar, even though the number of clusters in MV is nearly twice the number of clusters in K-means, which normally should increase the probability of attributing the same label twice.

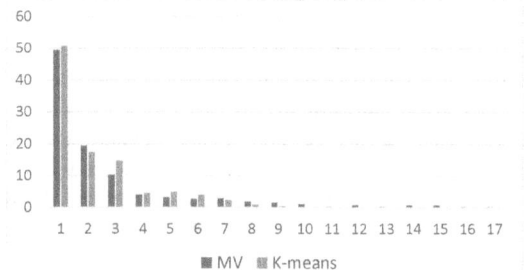

Figure 1: Percentage of label frequency among clusters

Considering this probability and the number of clusters generated by MV, we can deduce from figure 1 that the percentage of unique clusters in MV is competitive to it in K-means.

4.3.2 Clusters labels' overlapping. Labels overlapping concern the average number of labels shared by two clusters. As we said before, it is normal that some clusters share parts of their domains of interest. Such as having a cluster of clients who are interested in french wine, and another one of those who are interested in Italian wine. Both clusters would share the terms "wine" and "10-15° of alcohol". After all, labels overlapping should have a high value in order to keep the independence of each cluster. To the best of our knowledge, no studies in the literature exist to determine a threshold of overlapping, but we assume that it should be brought the lowest possible level.

According to our results, the maximum number of shared labels between two clusters in MV is 14. Median is 1, average 1.98 and standard deviation is 2.8 As for K-means; the maximum number of shared labels between two clusters is 18. Median is 1, average 2.13 and standard deviation is 3.47.

This indicator shows a slight advantage to MV that tends to make less labels overlapping.

4.3.3 Large clusters robustness. A robust cluster must has coherent labels that speak for its global tenor. Large clusters are more likely to contain several tenors inside them. In this indicator somehow a subjective one, we try here to deduce a title for each cluster throughout its labels. As it is impossible to list all the clusters of the two algorithms, we limit our analysis to the largest five clusters of each algorithm.

MV. MV's clusters' labels are listed in table 7. Note that the symbol (◦) refers to the percentage of alcohol (so 5-10° means drinks having between 5% and 10% of alcohol, and 20°+ refers to drinks with more than 20% of alcohol).

We note that labels are homogenous by cluster, and that they allow identifying a specific domain of interest by cluster. In table 7, we can easily identify the domains of interest; they are in order: (1) beer, (2) fruit juice (3) beer drums, (4) spirituous, (5) soda and water. However, in certain clusters we can find one or two outsider labels, that do not belong to the same domain as the rest of the labels, but there is still some logic in putting them together; like whiskey with fruit juices (to make some cocktails). Finally, we refer to the case of clusters (1) and (3), even both clusters' domains are about beer, but labels represent different format and brands, this is because some clients have convention with certain producers, so they purchase only their products.

Size	Labels
168	package multi-taste beers bottles, Beer, Beer St Feuillien, Beer Lindemans, 5-10°, Beer Carolus, Kriek beer, Beers large form
81	Granini juices, fruit juice small size bottle, fruit juice, Tomintoul Whiskey, sodas, dormant tomintoul, Marie Brizard, syrup, abricot, orange, fritz, ananas, rogue
78	Beer drums, Drum, St Stefanus beer, Amber beer, loic Raison beer, 5-10°, Grolsch beer, ciders, Kriek beer
75	spirituous, 20°+, fruit juice in jar, Monin, syrups, 70cl, Rhum, Liqueurs and creams,cafe, Tequila
74	Soda nomadic bottle, box, sodas, Fanta, Coca, Oasis, Maid, Seven up, Water nomadic bottle, orange, coke, life, Sprite

Table 7: MV Large clusters' labels

K-means. In table 8 we observe the labels of the largest five clusters of the k-means clustering. The first cluster contains about 30% of the entire population (compared to 7% in the case of MV), its labels show a high interest in beer in addition to some wine. It is normal that in big clusters it is difficult to find a unique common domain of interest. The second cluster describes an interest in sodas, water, sparkling water, and beer drums, and it is very similar to the fifth one (even concerning the brands), whereas the forth one shows interest in the same domain, but with different category of non-alcoholic drinks, which can be caused by different conventions mentioned sooner, and make it stand out from them. As for the third cluster it demonstrate a total interest in spirituous drinks.

We note that large clusters in MV are slightly more robust and thematic than it in K-means in term of labels representativeness, because mutual vote labels represent more unanimous behavior inside the cluster, and more difference from other clusters than it in K-means.

However, evaluating labels objectively is still a confusing issue, especially in the absence of standard metrics. Even though, We propose three indicators that might tell us something about the quality of labels. The global conclusion is that the quality of labels might be slightly better in Mutual vote. The two algorithms have

Size	Labels
581	Beers, package multi-taste beers bottles, 5-10°, Drums, Wine, 75cl, −5°, special beer drums, red wine, Dupont, bio, Beer mini drum
258	Cola, sodas, Coca, water, zero, drums, light, Vittel, Perrier, Pellegrino
142	spirituous, 20°+, 70cl, 15-20°, Liqueurs and creams, Briottet, cream, Martini, Porto, Bianco
128	Soda nomadic bottle, Coca, sodas, water nomadic bottle, Maid, box, life, 33cl, Cola, zero, water, Oasis, x30, spure
128	water, Evian, Pellegrino, cola, Badoit, sodas, Coca, zero

Table 8: K-means Large clusters' labels

similar distributions of labels over the clusters. On the other hand, Mutual vote records less labels overlapping, and slightly more coherent labels by cluster. We refer to fact that MV has tendency to generate smaller clusters compared to K-means, the small size of cluster make it easier to find a common domain of interest of the user. Our results encouraging but need more experimental work to be confirmed.

5 CONCLUSIONS AND PERSPECTIVES

In this paper we presented new clustering algorithm based on density and mutual votes. We applied the algorithm on a real dataset with the objective of clustering users for a recommendation system, then labeling the clusters, before using the labels to compute recommendations to users. Our proposed algorithm is tested for the clustering task in the recommendation application and compared to many existing clustering algorithms.

We showed that our algorithm adjust itself automatically to the typology of the dataset in high dimensional space, and needs no parametring. We proved empirically that our algorithm surpasses the other algorithms in terms of prediction precision and coverage. In addition, it is capable to attribute good quality labels to the resulting clusters.

The current results are encouraging to test the algorithm on other types of data, especially larger datasets to test its scalability. As the algorithm depends on the normal statistical distribution, it can be possible in larger data to test comparing each user to a random sample of users, which will accelerate the computing of distances matrix, but will result a less complete graph. Our perspective is test the capacity of the algorithm to perform good clustering using such incomplete graph.

REFERENCES

[1] M Emre Celebi, Hassan A Kingravi, and Patricio A Vela. 2013. A comparative study of efficient initialization methods for the k-means clustering algorithm. *Expert Systems with Applications* 40, 1 (2013), 200–210.
[2] Levent Ertoz, Michael Steinbach, and Vipin Kumar. 2002. A new shared nearest neighbor clustering algorithm and its applications. In *Workshop on Clustering High Dimensional Data and its Applications at 2nd SIAM International Conference on Data Mining*. 105–115.
[3] Martin Ester, Hans-Peter Kriegel, Jörg Sander, Xiaowei Xu, and others. 1996. A density-based algorithm for discovering clusters in large spatial databases with noise.. In *Kdd*, Vol. 96. 226–231.
[4] Raihana Ferdous and others. 2009. An efficient k-means algorithm integrated with Jaccard distance measure for document clustering. In *Internet, 2009. AH-ICI 2009. First Asian Himalayas International Conference on.* IEEE, 1–6.

[5] Salvatore Garruzzo and Domenico Rosaci. 2008. Agent clustering based on semantic negotiation. *ACM Transactions on Autonomous and Adaptive Systems (TAAS)* 3, 2 (2008), 7.

[6] ZHOU Shui Geng, ZHOU Ao Ying, and CAO Jing. 2000. A Data-partitioning-based DBSCAN Algorithm. *Journal of computer research and development* 10 (2000), 000.

[7] Mustansar Ali Ghazanfar and Adam Prügel-Bennett. 2014. Leveraging clustering approaches to solve the gray-sheep users problem in recommender systems. *Expert Systems with Applications* 41, 7 (2014), 3261–3275.

[8] Greg Hamerly, Charles Elkan, and others. 2003. Learning the k in k-means. In *NIPS*, Vol. 3. 281–288.

[9] John A Hartigan and Manchek A Wong. 1979. Algorithm AS 136: A k-means clustering algorithm. *Journal of the Royal Statistical Society. Series C (Applied Statistics)* 28, 1 (1979), 100–108.

[10] Charif Haydar, Azim Roussanaly, and Anne Boyer. 2012. Clustering users to explain recommender systems' performance fluctuation. In *International Symposium on Methodologies for Intelligent Systems*. Springer, 357–366.

[11] Raymond Austin Jarvis and Edward A Patrick. 1973. Clustering using a similarity measure based on shared near neighbors. *IEEE Transactions on computers* 100, 11 (1973), 1025–1034.

[12] Sonal Kumari, Saurabh Maurya, Poonam Goyal, Sundar S Balasubramaniam, and Navneet Goyal. 2016. Scalable Parallel Algorithms for Shared Nearest Neighbor Clustering. In *High Performance Computing (HiPC), 2016 IEEE 23rd International Conference on*. IEEE, 72–81.

[13] Domenico Rosaci. 2015. Finding semantic associations in hierarchically structured groups of Web data. *Formal Aspects of Computing* 27, 5-6 (2015), 867–884.

[14] Badrul M Sarwar, George Karypis, Joseph Konstan, and John Riedl. 2002. Recommender systems for large-scale e-commerce: Scalable neighborhood formation using clustering. In *Proceedings of the fifth international conference on computer and information technology*, Vol. 1.

[15] Michael Steinbach, Levent Ertöz, and Vipin Kumar. 2004. The challenges of clustering high dimensional data. In *New Directions in Statistical Physics*. Springer, 273–309.

[16] Pang-Ning Tan, Michael Steinbach, and Vipin Kumar. 2013. Data mining cluster analysis: basic concepts and algorithms. *Introduction to data mining* (2013).

[17] Grigorios Tzortzis and Aristidis Likas. 2014. The MinMax k-Means clustering algorithm. *Pattern Recognition* 47, 7 (2014), 2505–2516.

[18] Chu-Xu Zhang, Zi-Ke Zhang, Lu Yu, Chuang Liu, Hao Liu, and Xiao-Yong Yan. 2014. Information filtering via collaborative user clustering modeling. *Physica A: Statistical Mechanics and its Applications* 396 (2014), 195–203.

[19] Daqiang Zhang, Ching-Hsien Hsu, Min Chen, Quan Chen, Naixue Xiong, and Jaime Lloret. 2014. Cold-start recommendation using bi-clustering and fusion for large-scale social recommender systems. *IEEE Transactions on Emerging Topics in Computing* 2, 2 (2014), 239–250.

RouteMe: A Mobile Recommender System for Personalized, Multi-Modal Route Planning

Daniel Herzog
Department of Informatics
Technical University of Munich
Boltzmannstr. 3
85748 Garching bei München,
Germany
herzogd@in.tum.de

Hesham Massoud
Department of Informatics
Technical University of Munich
Boltzmannstr. 3
85748 Garching bei München,
Germany
hesham.massoud@tum.de

Wolfgang Wörndl
Department of Informatics
Technical University of Munich
Boltzmannstr. 3
85748 Garching bei München,
Germany
woerndl@in.tum.de

ABSTRACT

Route planner systems support commuters and city visitors in finding the best route between two arbitrary points. More advanced route planners integrate different transportation modes such as private transport, public transport, car- and bicycle sharing or walking and are able combine these to multi-modal routes. Nevertheless, state-of-the-art planner systems usually do not consider the users' personal preferences or the wisdom of the crowd when suggesting multi-modal routes. Including the knowledge and experience of locals who are familiar with local transport allows identification of alternative routes which are, for example, less crowded during peak hours. Collaborative filtering (CF) is a technique that allows recommending items such as multi-modal routes based on the ratings of users with similar preferences. In this paper, we introduce RouteMe, a mobile recommender system for personalized, multi-modal routes which combines CF with knowledge-based recommendations to increase the quality of route recommendations. We present our hybrid algorithm in detail and show how we integrate it in a working prototype. The results of a user study show that our prototype combining CF, knowledge-based and popular route recommendations outperforms state-of-the-art route planners.

CCS CONCEPTS

•**Information systems →Recommender systems;**

KEYWORDS

Recommender System, Multi-Modal Route Planning, Collaborative Filtering, Knowledge-based Recommendation, Mobile Application

1 INTRODUCTION

A popular scenario in the everyday life of many people is choosing the optimal way to travel from one point to another. A large number of tools exist for this purpose. Route planners are systems that offer users assistance in finding the best route to reach destinations. Multi-modal route planners combine different transportation modes

such as private and public transport, car- and bicycle sharing or walking in one journey [2]. For example, a commuter can use park and ride facilities to switch from a private car to public transport and use a bicycle sharing system to reach her or his workplace after leaving the subway.

State-of-the-art route planning systems such as Google Maps or Apple Maps suggest fastest or shortest routes between two arbitrary locations but usually do not consider the users' personal preferences or the wisdom of the crowd when suggesting multi-modal routes. This is important because route planning should not be understood as a traditional shortest path problem. Instead, route planners should adapt the route suggestions more to the users' needs [10]. Including the opinion of others in the route generation process could help to identify routes maximizing the user's satisfaction in a given situation. Locals using public transport regularly have a better understanding of which routes to use to reach a destination. This is especially helpful during peak hours when streets and public transport are crowded. Having access to such knowledge allows commuters to identify alternatives to crowded routes and means of transport.

Integrating recommender systems (RSs) in route planners is a promising way to overcome the presented drawbacks of state-of-the-art route planners. RSs are software tools and techniques that identify items such as movies or restaurants that are most likely of interest to the user, hence they are a valuable solution to the information overload problem [14]. One of the most used techniques of RSs is collaborative filtering (CF), which recommends items to users based on similarities to other users. CF is domain free because the recommendations rely solely on the similarity of users regarding their feedback on items and interaction with the system. We argue that CF should be used in route planners to recommend multi-modal routes as this technique is a powerful tool for taking into account the opinions and experience of other users.

In this work, we introduce RouteMe, a novel, mobile RS for personalized, multi-modal routes. The recommended items in RouteMe are complete routes between two arbitrary locations. We show that CF can be used to increase the quality of the route recommendations through using the wisdom of the crowd. In addition, we explain how to extend this approach using a knowledge-based component to overcome the cold start problem of pure CF recommendations. We present the combination of both techniques to a hybrid route recommendation algorithm in detail and show how we integrate the algorithm in a working prototype. The quality of the recommendations and the usability of our mobile application are evaluated in

UMAP'17, July 9–12, 2017, Bratislava, Slovakia
© 2017 ACM. 978-1-4503-4635-1/17/07...$15.00
DOI: http://dx.doi.org/10.1145/3079628.3079680

a user study. We will present the setup of the study, its outcome and discuss the results. This paper terminates with a conclusion and an outlook on future work.

2 RELATED WORK

A lot of research in the field of route planning examines route recommendations for tourists. Such tourist trip RSs often tackle the Orienteering Problem (OP) and its variants which try to combine multiple points of interest (POIs) such as restaurants, museums and monuments along enjoyable routes to maximize the entertainment for the user [21]. Some of the recent OP variants allow the integration of public transport into the route generation process [8]. Some researchers integrated their work in practical tourist trip applications. The City Trip Planner is a web application that recommends multi-day tourist trips while respecting certain constraints such as the user's budget or opening hours of POIs [20]. Xie et al. [23] developed CompRecTrip for recommending sets or sequences of POIs. Another similar web and mobile application called DailyTRIP is presented by Gavalas et al [9].

Compared to route planners for tourists, only a few applications exist that personalize public transport or multi-modal transportation between two arbitrary locations to recommend routes to commuters, for example. Qixxit[1] is an example of such a mobile application integrating taxis, carsharing or rental bikes into the multi-modal routes. The application can search for fast or cheap routes and the user can include or exclude single means of transport. Tiramisu[2] provides real-time arrival information for buses and allows users to share information on the fullness of buses and to report transport-related problems. Hence, the crowd supports users in finding out which bus to take but the system does not integrate other means of transport into the route planning.

Over the past years, some research has been done to improve and personalize recommendations of best routes between two arbitrary locations. Tumas and Ricci [18] introduced the personalized mobile city transport advisory system PECITAS which recommends multi-modal routes in the city of Bolzano. Compared to our work, it is based on a pure knowledge-based RS and does not take the opinion of other users into account. Quercia et al. [13] developed a system that suggests routes that are not only short but also pleasant. Their evaluation shows that their approach is able to suggest routes that are perceived to be more beautiful, quiet and happy. However, it suggest only walking routes and does not integrate public transport. Codina et al. [5] developed a route planner that recommends routes based on a content-based and context-aware RS but does not integrate CF. Their system suggests routes composed of one or more of the following modalities: walk, bike, public and private transport. They proposed the contextual factors to be either user-specific factors, for example the purpose of the journey, or environmental-based factors, for example, the time of day or temperature. Experiments showed that the context-aware strategies they developed outperform the context-free baseline approach. Another context-aware RS for multi-modal route planning is suggested by Samsel et al. [15]. Recommendations are adapted according to the user's personal preferences, contextual information such as

the weather and also the opinions of others. In a user study with 101 participants, the authors showed that the users prefer a personalized, context aware itinerary selection over the traditional departure-time based sorting of suggested routes. Their first Android prototype uses a text based interface only and is not yet available for download.

In this work, we present a novel approach to recommend multi-modal routes. We show how to use CF to recommend any kind of multi-modal route between two arbitrary points. Our RS accesses a large number of different routes but in practice, no or only very little feedback is available for the majority of all routes in the system. We present a solution to handle this sparsity in the user-route rating matrix and to deal with the cold start problem in a CF system by extending our approach with knowledge-based recommendations. Besides respecting the user's preferences and the wisdom of the crowd, our RS is also able to highlight popular routes. We implement our hybrid approach in a fully working, mobile prototype providing a graphical user interface which is well-known from state-of-the art route planner applications. This prototype is evaluated in a user study with regards to the quality of the recommendations and the user experience of the mobile application. The development of the RS and its evaluation were introduced in [11].

3 A HYBRID RECOMMENDATION ALGORITHM FOR MULTI-MODAL ROUTES

As explained, CF promises to identify routes that increase the user's satisfaction even if this route means making a detour. In this work, the recommended items are complete routes from an arbitrary origin to a destination. Itineraries from the same origin to the same destination using the same transportation modes and passing through the same stops are considered to be the same route. The departure time is not taken into account in this work; this means that the exact same itinerary at two different departure times is considered to be the same route. This allows us to reduce the number of potential recommendations. As many of the items in a RS using CF lack feedback, especially when the number of users is still low, the RS has to deal with a sparse user-item matrix making it difficult to recommend routes [1]. Sparsity and the cold start problem are the reason why we introduce a hybrid technique combining CF and knowledge-based recommendations in RouteMe. This approach enables three different kinds of route recommendations: routes recommended because of other users with similar preferences, routes based solely on the user's personal preferences and popular routes. In the following, we present our approach in detail.

3.1 Collaborative Filtering Recommendations

CF algorithms can be differentiated into model-based and memory-based approaches. Memory-based methods utilize the entire user-item dataset to compute the neighborhood set of users or items based on a similarity measure. Based on this neighborhood, the system produces recommendations using the arithmetic mean of ratings or another similar algorithm. Using the entire dataset leads to a high recommendation accuracy but is costly in computation. On the other hand, the model-based approach uses feedback information about the items and the users to precompute a model offline. The precomputed model can then be used to generate the

---

[1]https://www.qixxit.de/
[2]http://www.tiramisutransit.com/

recommendations instead of using the whole dataset every time a recommendation is requested. This reduces the run-time complexity of the recommendation generation. [3]

The Correlated Cross-Occurrence (CCO) is a CF algorithm based on the open source, scalable machine-learning libraries Apache Mahout[3] and Apache Spark[4] [7]. It exhibits advantages of both the model-based and memory-based approaches [16]. In addition, the algorithm takes into account any kind of user behavior, implicit or explicit, to precompute a prediction model. This solves the problem of sparsity of the user-item matrix, which could be caused due to the rareness of explicit feedback. Using this information, the algorithm builds three kinds of matrices for each feedback:

- History matrix: records all the user's interaction history in a user-item matrix.
- Co-occurrence matrix: transforms the history matrix into an item-item matrix, recording which items co-occurred together in user histories for the current interaction.
- Indicator matrix: keeps only the interesting co-occurrences that will be used in the computation of item recommendation scores. For example, an item that is purchased or viewed by everyone is probably not a good indicator for taste. The algorithm removes the uninteresting co-occurrences using a Log Likelihood Ratio (LLR) test to determine which co-occurrences are anomalous enough to be indicators.

All the previous modeling is precomputed before a recommendation is requested. When calculating a recommendation score for a user, the user's history vector is multiplied by the indicator matrix:

$$r = (L^T P)h_P, \tag{1}$$

where $L^T P$ is the indicator matrix and h_P is the user's history vector.

In our scenario, different user interactions and feedback can be used to recommend multi-modal routes to a user. The algorithm should not treat all of these actions equally, for a example, liking a specific route should be weighted more than just viewing the route. Therefore, the algorithm treats only one action as the primary indicator of preference and the rest of the indicators are tested for correlation to this action using an LLR test as well. The matrices for each of the indicators contribute to the final recommendation score:

$$r = (L^T P)h_P + (L^T S)h_S + (L^T T)h_T + ..., \tag{2}$$

where $(L^T P)h_P$ is the recommendation score of the primary action. $(L^T S)h_S$, $(L^T T)h_T$, ... are the recommendation scores for routes based on other actions. In this work, we treat the explicit feedback of liking an event as the primary action indicating user preferences. Viewing a route is an implicit feedback, which is another action indicating route taste. In addition, the last viewed routes are another indicator as this route is often the one the user decides to take before closing the app.

The precomputed training part of the presented algorithm scales linearly. When the user-item base increases in size, the computation

[3] http://mahout.apache.org/
[4] http://spark.apache.org/

can be parallelized by simply adding more nodes to a distributed cluster [16].

3.2 Knowledge-based Recommendations

Significant drawbacks of CF are the cold start problem and a sparse user-item rating matrix [1]. Knowledge-based RSs provide a solution to these problems because they do not require any item ratings or feedback from the users [6]. However, before generating a recommendation, the users' preferences have to be elicited in an explicit manner.

The main idea of the knowledge-based RS in our multi-modal route planer is to recommend items to the users based on a predefined preference set of the user. Our prototype differentiates between travel mode and route type preferences. Travel mode preferences describe the means of transport the users prefer in the form of an ordered list of travel modes. The travel modes that RouteMe offers are:

- Bus
- Bicycling
- Driving
- S-Bahn (Commuter train)
- Tram
- U-Bahn (Subway)
- Walking

Route type preferences describe which types of routes the user prefers. In our work, route types can be either routes with the least overall time or routes with the least number of transportation mode changes.

In order to rank the potential recommendations according to the user preferences, a utility scheme based on the Multi-Attribute Utility Theory (MAUT) can be declared [6]. As von Neumann and Morgenstern explained, if the possible combinations of factors in a list are finite, then a von Neumann-Morgenstern utility function (VNM-utility function) can be formulated for each item [12]. Using the result of such a function for each item, a final ranking can be composed for the whole recommendation result space.

The knowledge-based filter ranks the routes based on a MAUT utility function we devised. The strict utility we used is the travel mode preference. For each route there are two factors affecting the utility to the user: the travel modes and the uniformity of the route. For example, if a user likes to use buses over trams, he will most likely prefer a route containing only buses than a mixture of both. So we define the uniformity of a route as the inverse of the number of distinct travel modes in a route. For example, if a route contains only one travel mode, we consider it 100% uniform. If it contains two distinct travel modes, we consider it 50% uniform. We then assign a score to each travel mode from 6 (most preferred travel mode) to 0 (least preferred travel mode) for each user. We then multiply this uniformity coefficient to the sum of travel mode scores in a route to come up with our utility function:

$$r = \frac{1}{n} \sum_{t=1}^{n} R_t, \tag{3}$$

where R is a tuple of travel mode scores for the route, R_t is the travel mode score at position t in the tuple, n is the number of distinct travel modes in the route and $\frac{1}{n}$ is the uniformity coefficient.

For instance, if the user's first preference is bus travel and the second preference is tram travel, the system would give the bus a score of 6 and the tram a score 5. If there is a route X that consists only of a bus, the output of our utility function is 6. If there is a route Y that consists of a bus and tram, the score is $\frac{1}{2}(6 + 5) = 5.5$. Therefore, route X will be ranked higher than route Y in the recommendation list.

Finally, the knowledge-based recommender ranks the routes in a descending order of the aforementioned utility function. In case of ties, the route type preference of the user and the popularity of routes resolves the tie. If a route is popular among other users, we boost the utility of knowledge-based recommendations so that the route is ranked higher than a non-popular route with the same user preferences. For this we propose to extend the utility function of Formula 3 for knowledge-based recommendations by boosting the popular routes' scores by 1:

$$u(R) = \begin{cases} \frac{1}{n}(\sum_{t=1}^{n} R_t + 1) & \text{if popular} \\ \frac{1}{n}(\sum_{t=1}^{n} R_t) & \text{otherwise} \end{cases} \quad (4)$$

3.3 Hybrid Recommendations

Several techniques to hybridize recommendation methods exist. We decided to implement a cascade hybrid system. The idea of a cascade hybrid system is to give one technique a strict priority, while the lower priority recommender breaks ties in the scoring of the higher one. This selection was suitable for our solution given the fact that we considered CF as the main source of recommendations for routes and knowledge-based recommendations as a secondary technique to eliminate the cold start problem and to break ties of the collaborative technique. [4]

To sum up the hybridization, we first rank the routes according to their CF scores from the recommendation engine. Then we apply the modified knowledge-based utility function of Formula 4 on the routes with no or tied CF scores to rank the routes according to user preference and popularity. With this design, we ensure that the cold start problem is completely eliminated by providing the user with personalized CF, knowledge-based and popularity-based route recommendations.

4 IMPLEMENTATION OF THE MOBILE PROTOTYPE

Our prototype is composed of the following parts: the RouteMe API, a database, Google Maps APIs, our recommendation engine and the RouteMe mobile application.

The RouteMe API is a web service implemented using Java with the Spring framework and running on an Apache Tomcat Server. It receives queries from the mobile application and communicates with the recommendation engine to receive route recommendations for each query. Relevant user data such as transportation mode preferences are stored in an NoSQL MongoDB database.

We decided to use Google Maps as the data source for our RS as it supports different transportation modes such as public transit, bicycling and walking. In addition, Google Maps has exclusive access to the transit data of the city of Munich where the evaluation of the RS took place. This was a key criterion for us as at least some of the participants of a user study should be familiar with the local public transport to simulate commuters. We used the Directions API[5] to fetch the routes that our RS recommends to users based on origin-destination search queries. In addition, the Google Places API[6] is used for the autocomplete feature when searching for destinations.

We used PredictionIO[7], an open source machine learning server, for deploying the universal recommender[8] which implements the CCO CF algorithm. The engine not only generates CF recommendations, but also popularity-based recommendations based on the amount of usage events.

The mobile application was implemented to run on the iPhone Operating System (iOS) using Apple's programming language Swift. Figure 1 shows the main screens of the mobile application. Screenshot (a) illustrates the search result with routes recommended by the CF component. A hint explains that the multi-modal routes are recommended because of other users with similar preferences. Screenshot (b) shows knowledge-based route recommendations solving the cold start problem. In this example, the first two routes are ranked higher than the third route because they turned out to be popular. The third screenshot (c) shows the detail view of a route recommendation. The user has the option to like the route to provide feedback to the RS. In our first prototype, users like a route to share their overall impression of a route. In future, feedback should be multifaceted, e.g., the duration, price or crowdedness of a route should be rated by the users.

5 USER STUDY

We conducted a user study to find out if the recommendations of our approach offer a significant added value compared to state-of-the-art route planning systems.

5.1 Goals

Our user study had the following four objectives:

- Quantitative evaluation of the recommendation algorithm accuracy.
- Quantitative comparison between selected properties of the prototype against those of a state-of-the-art baseline. The properties are listed in Table 2.
- Quantitative evaluation of the user experience of the prototype.
- Qualitative evaluation of prototype through the participant's feedback.

In order to achieve these goals, we conducted a user study with 17 participants (4 females and 13 males). We tried to find participants with different backgrounds and levels of experience to reflect potential future users in the study.

Almost all of the commercially available multi-modal route planners currently require that the users choose the mode of transportation before searching for routes. However, we wanted to find a baseline that can recommend routes without this requirement in order to be similar to our prototype in that regard. We chose

---

[5] https://developers.google.com/maps/documentation/directions/
[6] https://developers.google.com/places/
[7] http://prediction.incubator.apache.org/
[8] https://github.com/actionml/template-scala-parallel-universal-recommendation

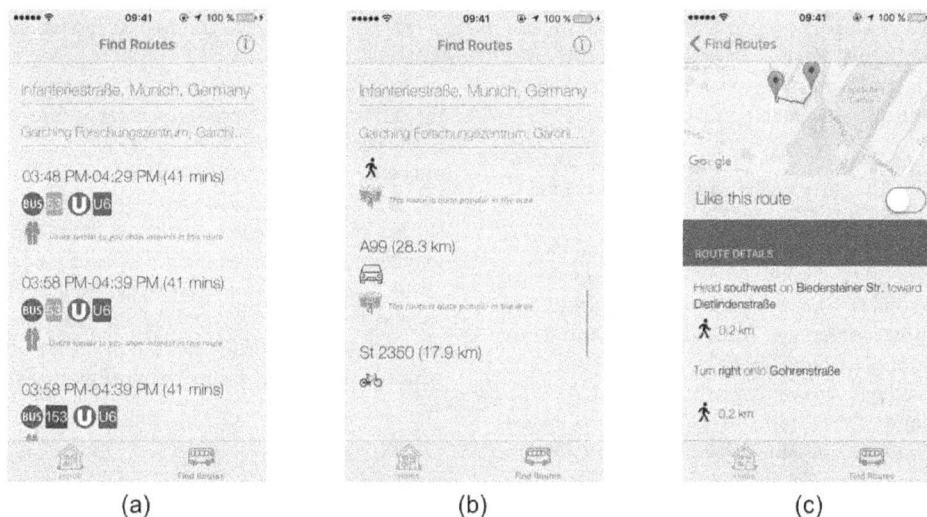

Figure 1: Screenshots of the mobile application

Google Maps[9] as the baseline application for the user study as it uses the same data source of route planning as our prototype. The web version of Google Maps has a *Recommended travel mode* tab that recommends routes to users regardless of a specific transportation mode. This feature is not available on the mobile app version of Google Maps. The recommendations can be seen as a pure knowledge-based RS without our CF extensions making Google Maps a valuable baseline application for our user study.

As explained, CF requires user ratings to generate recommendations. As there were no users in our system before the study took place, we created some mock users and limited the user study to a selected list of origin-destination pairs. This approach allowed us to have enough ratings in the user-item rating matrix to test all types of recommendations provided by RouteMe.

5.2 Setup and Results

The user study was conducted as a lab study. The main task of the participants was to interact with the RouteMe application and the baseline application to solve a list of predefined tasks. The evaluation of the applications was composed of three phases: At first, the participants had to decide which recommended route in each application they liked most. The ranking of this route in the recommendation lists was used to calculate the accuracy of the recommendations. Then, the participants had to complete two questionnaires to share their opinion on the general idea of the prototype and on different properties of RouteMe and the baseline application. Finally, the participants completed another questionnaire to evaluate the user experience. In addition, the Concurrent Think Aloud (CTA) technique was used to collect and understand the participants's thoughts while they were interacting with the prototype [19].

In the following, we present the setup of each phase of the user study and the results in detail.

5.2.1 Ranking Accuracy. In the first phase of the user study, the participants were asked to interact with RouteMe and Google Maps in parallel. They were asked to solve four different tasks presented in the form of scenarios such as: *"Some of your friends are telling you about using a new app called RouteMe that can recommend routes to you based on your preferences and preferences of the users with route tastes similar to yours. You have decided to use the app to find a route to go home from Marienplatz."*

For each task, a list of route results are given to the participant both in RouteMe and Google Maps. The participants are asked to write down the ranking of the route most relevant to them given the circumstances of the task. The information retrieval metric Mean Reciprocal Rank (MRR) was used to measure the accuracy of the recommendation list based on the ranking. The MRR is computed as follows [22]:

$$MRR = \frac{1}{|Q|} \sum_{i=1}^{|Q|} \frac{1}{rank_i}, \tag{5}$$

where Q is a sample of queries and $rank_i$ refers to the rank position of the first relevant document for the *i-th* query. It was simple to compute this metric for RouteMe after the participants had written down the rank of the most relevant route after each task. It was not as simple, however, for Google Maps since the routes are displayed on several tabs. We determine the ranking of a Google Maps route as follows: At most three recommend routes can be displayed in the *Recommended travel mode* tab. In some situations, a route that is relevant to the user might not be included in the recommendation making it necessary for the user to switch tabs. In this case, the ranking of the selected route is the rank of this route in its specific tab added to the number of routes in the *Recommended travel mode* tab, which is always 3.

The MRR was calculated for each participant after solving the four tasks. RouteMe had a mean MRR of 0.8241 while Google Maps had a mean of 0.5139. A two-tailed paired t-test with a significance level of 0.05 was executed to test if the difference between the

⁹https://www.google.de/maps

computed MRR values of all participants on both RouteMe and Google Maps was significant. Results show a P value of 0.0003 on a 95% confidence interval indicating a statistically significant difference between RouteMe and Google Maps.

5.2.2 Questionnaires about the general idea and different properties of the application.
The participants were asked to complete two questionnaires comprised of 5-point Likert scale statements that asked the participants for their opinion on the general idea of the solution and on properties of both RouteMe and Google Maps. For all the Likert statements the answers where evaluated with the value 2 for the most positive response (strongly agree) and -2 for the most negative response (strongly disagree).

Table 1 summarizes the results of the participant rating of the general idea of the solution. The majority of the participants agreed or strongly agreed that every possible type of recommendation (personalized recommendation, CF recommendation, popular route recommendation) provided by RouteMe was useful.

Table 2 lists seven different statements used to evaluate relevant properties of RouteMe and Google Maps such as satisfaction, persuasiveness and trust. Two-tailed paired t-tests were used to determine if RouteMe is superior to Google Maps with regard to each of the properties tested. Results showed that RouteMe is superior to Google Maps with regard to all properties except trust. We believe this result is not surprising because RouteMe and Google Maps require similar user data to recommend routes.

5.2.3 User Experience Questionnaire.
At the conclusion of the study, the participants were asked to fill out the User Experience Questionnaire (UEQ)[10] used to evaluate the user experience of the prototype and to compare this experience to a benchmark dataset. The UEQ uses 26 Likert scale-formatted questions to asses properties of user experience and groups responses into six user experience scales:

- Attractiveness: Measures the general impression about RouteMe.
- Perspicuity: Measures whether RouteMe was simple to use and easy to understand.
- Efficiency: Measures whether RouteMe helped the users accomplish their tasks without performing unneeded effort.
- Dependability: Measures the level of control users felt while interacting with RouteMe.
- Stimulation: Measures whether the participants were excited and motivated to use RouteMe.
- Novelty: Measures the level of interest users felt about RouteMe and whether they felt it was an innovative product.

The black dots in Figure 2 show how RouteMe performs in each of the six categories. The UEQ tool offers another computation that provides a better picture of the quality of the product under test. This computation compares the measured user experience of the product to a benchmark dataset containing data from 246 product evaluations (with a total of 9905 participants in all the evaluations). The benchmark classifies the six user experience scales of the product under test into five categories: excellent, good, above

average, below average and bad, in comparison to the benchmark dataset.

Figure 2 illustrates that participants rated RouteMe as excellent in the categories attractiveness, perspicuity and efficiency. Compared to the benchmark products, RouteMe lays in the range of the 10% of best results in regards to these three scales. It can also be seen that it scores good for stimulation and novelty because only 10% of the benchmark results received a higher score. Finally, according to our results, the dependability scale of RouteMe is above average. The dependability scale aggregates four user experience properties such as *Predictable vs Unpredictable*. On average, the participants were neutral about the predicability of the RouteMe application which explains why RouteMe scores worse on the dependability scale.

5.2.4 Interaction Feedback.
The notes that were taken while the participants were using the app showed that most of them were very happy to receive personalized recommendations when searching for routes. They also made their decisions about which route to take more quickly and confidently when using RouteMe than when using Google Maps. Most participants were also pleasantly surprised by unexpected route results, which shows that the recommendations are serendipitous. The route selections made by the majority of the participants also showed that they trusted the route recommendations from similar users over the routes they personally preferred. The prototype also proved to be quite simple, intuitive and easy to use given the fact that the participants required little or no help or assistance while performing the tasks.

The participants identified those features that could be improved or extended and those they did not care for. For example:

- Some participants wanted to know more details about why users are similar to each other. Their claim was that the recommendations were not convincing enough without having more details.
- Some mentioned it would help in the decision making process to know how many similar users show interest in a certain recommended route.
- Some participants thought the idea of having friends on the app and getting route recommendations from friends would be beneficial.
- Some said it would be crucial to have a function to remove an undesired travel preference completely from their preference, instead of only assigning it a low rank.
- Some participants thought that the preferences to set explicitly on the app are insufficient.
- Some participants wanted to see more information for non-transit routes, such as the duration.
- One participant mentioned the fact that turn-by-turn navigation would be a valuable feature

There were also some recurring usability hurdles faced by the participants that we noticed during the lab usability test. These include unclear or missing buttons, confusion with the 12-hour clock format and problems with the map, seen in Figure 1 (c), which appears to be too small for some users.

---

[10]http://www.ueq-online.org/

Table 1: Questionnaire about the general idea of the application and its results.

#	Statement	-2 (Strongly disagree)	-1	0	+1	+2 (Strongly agree)
1	I find getting personalized route recommendations in route planning services useful.	0		0	2	10	5
2	I find getting route recommendations in route planning services, based on similar users to me and my usage history, useful.	0		0	4	7	6
3	I find getting popular route recommendations in route planning services useful.	0		1	3	8	5

Table 2: Questionnaire about different properties of the application and its results.

#	Property	Statement	∅ RouteMe	∅ Google Maps	P value	Significant?
1	Ranking Accuracy	The ranking of routes for my search queries fitted my preferences.	1.06	-0.06	0.0008	Yes
2	Satisfaction	I was satisfied with the route the app helped me take.	1.18	0.41	0.0030	Yes
3	Persuasiveness	The app helped me take a route that I could have missed if I weren't using it.	0.65	-0.41	0.0004	Yes
4	Transparency	The app explained to me clearly why the route results were sorted that way.	0.41	-0.65	0.0316	Yes
5	Decision Effort	The app helped me make my decision about which route to take easily.	0.71	0.06	0.0112	Yes
6	Trust	I trusted using the app and didn't find it invading my privacy.	1.29	1.00	0.3690	No
7	Intention to Return	I would use this app again to find routes to my destinations.	1.35	0.94	0.0144	Yes

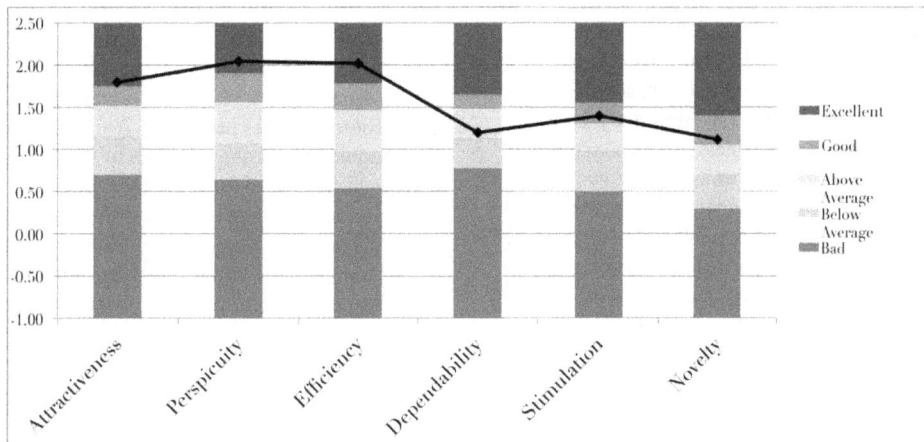

Figure 2: UEQ results and comparison with a benchmark dataset

5.3 Summary and Discussion

The results of our user study show that personalized recommendations lead to an improvement the quality of route planning systems. The participants were satisfied with all kinds of recommendations provided by RouteMe: CF, knowledge-based and popular route recommendations. Compared with a state-of-the-art route planning system, RouteMe proved to deliver more accurate recommendations, users were more satisfied with the experience and routes were found more easily. This is an interesting finding because

Google Maps and RouteMe use the same route database. However, RouteMe is able to identify alternative routes that seem to be less obvious to take but are actually a better choice for some people. In our study, collaborative recommendations were mainly generated based on the ratings we created prior to the user study but the participants were able to improve the recommendations by liking routes while interacting with the application. Furthermore, the users rated the user experience of the RouteMe application very favorably. Even though these results are promising, Google Maps as a baseline posed some potential experimental errors that have to be mentioned. First, the different route results display mechanism previously discussed. In contrast to RouteMe which is a mobile app, Google Maps is a web application: we were unable to control or fix several variables not under study related to this difference. For example, having to use a mouse for Google Maps whereas touch gestures are used on the phone for RouteMe. For more accurate results, RouteMe should be compared to a similar, mobile application that does not yet implement our algorithm.

Most RSs recommend single items such as consumer goods, movies or restaurants. Applications that already recommend some kind of route, such as tourist trip planner, recommend a set of POIs and combine them along fast or enjoyable routes. In this work, we tried a different approach. Instead of recommending single locations or a set of locations, a complete, multi-modal route represents the item recommended to the user. Compared to state-of-the-art route planners, RouteMe recommends not only the fastest and shortest routes or routes with selected means of transport but also uses the wisdom of the crowd to identify alternative routes that might not satisfy the criteria of current route planners but are possibly a better choice for users. The feedback we collected during the user study confirms our hypothesis that CF should be used for route recommendations to receive results that are better adapted to the user's preferences in a given situation.

The main goal of our work is to not only support commuters that know a city very well but also to support people not familiar with public transport in a given city such as tourists. When talking to our participants and listening to their feedback, some concrete scenarios where our system would be really helpful were revealed. Some thought it would be extremely important in a country with inaccurate traffic or transit information. Some participants even related some real life situations they faced in the past where they thought RouteMe would have saved them. One situation mentioned involved traveling to the airport. Usually most people taking routes to the airport carry luggage with them. However, some routes lack facilities, such as elevators or escalators, that help in transferring luggage from one transportation vehicle to another, but alternative routes might have such facilities. The participant mentioned that RouteMe would have saved them from taking a route without facilities since our app includes recommendations from other travelers who might have provided information on alternative routes that make luggage transfer easier.

Another interesting feedback we received is the desire to receive route recommendations from friends. In our first prototype, we implemented CCO as a CF algorithm to identify routes recommended by other users in the system. The results of the user study show that our implementation is able to generate accurate results. Nevertheless, it has been shown that the users' trust in recommendations can be increased when the recommendations are made by friends [17]. Instead of considering all rating of all users in the system, only those of relevant persons such as friends should be taken into account to improve our system. This might be an important step to increase the trust in our system, the only property where RouteMe does not perform significantly better than state-of-the-art route planners.

6 CONCLUSION AND FUTURE WORK

In this work, we presented a novel approach for recommending multi-modal travel routes. We evaluated the quality of our hybrid algorithm as well as the user experience of the application in a user study with 17 participants. Results show that the combination of CF, knowledge-based and popular route recommendations outperforms state-of-the-art route planner software. In addition, the users liked the developed iOS prototype application and could conceivably imagine using such a route planner system in future.

Our application provides seven travel modes offered by the Google Maps API. Further travel modes such as taxis, carsharing or rental bikes should be included in future versions of our route planner to generate more sophisticated, multi-modal route recommendations.

In our solution we used the *Like* event as the strongest indicator of route preferences. However, users might, subconsciously, prefer the routes they have actually taken in contrast to the ones they have explicitly liked on the system. Furthermore, the implemented prototype could be vulnerable to attacks, for example, when a user makes false interactions intentionally, such as liking routes she or he actually does not like. This could cause misleading or inaccurate predictive models. Nevertheless, the system could be enhanced to handle false likes by integrating a turn-by-turn navigation feature that could detect if the users have actually taken a route. Such implicit feedback promises another solution for the sparsity problem RouteMe has to deal with similar to other CF RSs with large item databases.

Several previous works made multi-modal transport recommendations context-aware [5] [15]. Our RS does not yet take contextual information such as the weather into account. This is an important part of a route RS as a user might want to avoid walking or bicycling in case of bad weather and prefer a less popular route instead if this route provides protection from rain, wind or snow. Future work should extend our approach to a context-aware RS to use the wisdom of the crowd for route recommendations while still being flexible enough to adapt to the current context.

Finally, a larger user study with more participants should be conducted to collect more meaningful user feedback. Our study was designed as a lab study to collect a first feedback rapidly. We mocked other users and user feedback in the system and limited the user study to a selected list of origin-destination pairs. A field study with real users using RouteMe in real scenarios (for example when searching for a route from to home to work) is necessary to better understand how well our approach works.

ACKNOWLEDGMENTS

This work is part of the TUM Living Lab Connected Mobility (TUM LLCM) project and has been funded by the Bavarian Ministry of Economic Affairs and Media, Energy and Technology (StMWi) through the Center Digitisation.Bavaria, an initiative of the Bavarian State Government.

REFERENCES

[1] Gediminas Adomavicius and Alexander Tuzhilin. 2005. Toward the Next Generation of Recommender Systems: A Survey of the State-of-the-Art and Possible Extensions. *IEEE Trans. on Knowl. and Data Eng.* 17, 6 (June 2005), 734–749. DOI: http://dx.doi.org/10.1109/TKDE.2005.99

[2] Hannah Bast, Daniel Delling, Andrew Goldberg, Matthias Müller-Hannemann, Thomas Pajor, Peter Sanders, Dorothea Wagner, and Renato F. Werneck. 2016. Route Planning in Transportation Networks. In *Algorithm Engineering: Selected Results and Surveys*, Lasse Kliemann and Peter Sanders (Eds.). Springer International Publishing, Cham, 19–80. DOI: http://dx.doi.org/10.1007/978-3-319-49487-6_2

[3] John S. Breese, David Heckerman, and Carl Kadie. 1998. Empirical Analysis of Predictive Algorithms for Collaborative Filtering. In *Proceedings of the Fourteenth Conference on Uncertainty in Artificial Intelligence (UAI'98)*. Morgan Kaufmann Publishers Inc., San Francisco, CA, USA, 43–52. http://dl.acm.org/citation.cfm?id=2074094.2074100

[4] Robin Burke. 2002. Hybrid Recommender Systems: Survey and Experiments. *User Modeling and User-Adapted Interaction* 12, 4 (Nov. 2002), 331–370. DOI: http://dx.doi.org/10.1023/A:1021240730564

[5] Victor Codina, Jose Mena, and Luis Oliva. 2015. *Context-Aware User Modeling Strategies for Journey Plan Recommendation.* Springer International Publishing, Cham, 68–79. DOI: http://dx.doi.org/10.1007/978-3-319-20267-9_6

[6] Alexander Felfernig, Michael Jeran, Gerald Ninaus, Florian Reinfrank, Stefan Reiterer, and Martin Stettinger. 2014. Basic Approaches in Recommendation Systems. In *Recommendation Systems in Software Engineering*, Martin P. Robillard, Walid Maalej, Robert J. Walker, and Thomas Zimmermann (Eds.). Springer Berlin Heidelberg, Berlin, Heidelberg, 15–37. DOI: http://dx.doi.org/10.1007/978-3-642-45135-5_2

[7] Pat Ferrel. 2016. Correlated Cross-Occurrence (CCO): How to make data behave as we want. (January 2016). Retrieved February 8, 2017 from http://actionml.com/blog/cco.

[8] Ander Garcia, Olatz Arbelaitz, Maria Teresa Linaza, Pieter Vansteenwegen, and Wouter Souffriau. 2010. Personalized Tourist Route Generation. In *Proceedings of the 10th International Conference on Current Trends in Web Engineering (ICWE'10)*. Springer-Verlag, Berlin, Heidelberg, 486–497. http://dl.acm.org/citation.cfm?id=1927229.1927285

[9] Damianos Gavalas, Michael Kenteris, Charalampos Konstantopoulos, and Grammati Pantziou. 2012. Web application for recommending personalised mobile tourist routes. *Software, IET* 6, 4 (2012), 313–322.

[10] Bing Liu. 1995. Using Knowledge to Isolate Search in Route Finding. In *Proceedings of the 14th International Joint Conference on Artificial Intelligence - Volume 1 (IJCAI'95)*. Morgan Kaufmann Publishers Inc., San Francisco, CA, USA, 119–124.

[11] Hesham Massoud. 2016. *Collaborative and Knowledge-based Filtering for Multimodal Route Recommendations.* Master's thesis. Department of Informatics, Technical University of Munich (TUM), Germany.

[12] Oskar Morgenstern and John Von Neumann. 1944. *Theory of Games and Economic Behavior* (3 ed.). Princeton University Press.

[13] Daniele Quercia, Rossano Schifanella, and Luca Maria Aiello. 2014. The Shortest Path to Happiness: Recommending Beautiful, Quiet, and Happy Routes in the City. In *Proceedings of the 25th ACM Conference on Hypertext and Social Media (HT '14)*. ACM, New York, NY, USA, 116–125. DOI: http://dx.doi.org/10.1145/2631775.2631799

[14] Francesco Ricci, Lior Rokach, and Bracha Shapira. 2015. Recommender Systems: Introduction and Challenges. In *Recommender Systems Handbook*, Francesco Ricci, Lior Rokach, and Bracha Shapira (Eds.). Springer US, Boston, MA, 1–34. DOI: http://dx.doi.org/10.1007/978-1-4899-7637-6_1

[15] Christian Samsel, Karl-Heinz Krempels, and Gerrit Garbereder. 2016. Personalized, Context-aware Intermodal Travel Information. In *Proceedings of the 12th International Conference on Web Information Systems and Technologies, WEBIST 2016, Rome, Italy, April 23-25, 2016*, Vol. 2. SCITEPRESS, 148–155. DOI: http://dx.doi.org/10.5220/0005855501480155

[16] Sebastian Schelter, Christoph Boden, and Volker Markl. 2012. Scalable Similarity-based Neighborhood Methods with MapReduce. In *Proceedings of the Sixth ACM Conference on Recommender Systems (RecSys '12)*. ACM, New York, NY, USA, 163–170. DOI: http://dx.doi.org/10.1145/2365952.2365984

[17] Rashmi Sinha, , Rashmi Sinha, and Kirsten Swearingen. 2001. Comparing Recommendations Made by Online Systems and Friends. In *In Proceedings of the DELOS-NSF Workshop on Personalization and Recommender Systems in Digital Libraries*.

[18] Gytis Tumas and Francesco Ricci. 2009. Personalized Mobile City Transport Advisory System. In *Information and Communication Technologies in Tourism 2009: Proceedings of the International Conference in Amsterdam, The Netherlands, 2009*, Wolfram Höpken, Ulrike Gretzel, and Rob Law (Eds.). Springer Vienna, Vienna, 173–183. DOI: http://dx.doi.org/10.1007/978-3-211-93971-0_15

[19] M. J. van den Haak and M. D. T. de Jong. 2003. Exploring two methods of usability testing: concurrent versus retrospective think-aloud protocols. In *IEEE International Professional Communication Conference, 2003. IPCC 2003. Proceedings.* 3 pp.–. DOI: http://dx.doi.org/10.1109/IPCC.2003.1245501

[20] Pieter Vansteenwegen, Wouter Souffriau, Greet Vanden Berghe, and Dirk Van Oudheusden. 2011. The City Trip Planner. *Expert Syst. Appl.* 38, 6 (June 2011), 6540–6546. DOI: http://dx.doi.org/10.1016/j.eswa.2010.11.085

[21] Pieter Vansteenwegen and Dirk Van Oudheusden. 2007. The mobile tourist guide: an OR opportunity. *OR Insight* 20, 3 (2007), 21–27.

[22] Ellen M. Voorhees. 1999. The TREC-8 Question Answering Track Report.. In *Trec*, Vol. 99. 77–82.

[23] M. Xie, L. V. S. Lakshmanan, and P. T. Wood. 2011. CompRec-Trip: A composite recommendation system for travel planning. In *2011 IEEE 27th International Conference on Data Engineering.* 1352–1355. DOI: http://dx.doi.org/10.1109/ICDE.2011.5767954

Stereotype Modeling for Problem-Solving Performance Predictions in MOOCs and Traditional Courses

Roya Hosseini, Peter Brusilovsky
University of Pittsburgh
Pittsburgh, USA
{roh38,peterb}@pitt.edu

Michael Yudelson
Carnegie Mellon University
Pittsburgh, USA
yudelson@andrew.cmu.edu

Arto Hellas
University of Helsinki
Helsinki, Finland
arto.hellas@helsinki.fi

ABSTRACT

Stereotypes are frequently used in real life to classify students according to their performance in class. In literature, we can find many references to *weaker students*, *fast learners*, *struggling students*, etc. Given the lack of detailed data about students, these or other kinds of stereotypes could be potentially used for user modeling and personalization in the educational context. Recent research in MOOC context demonstrated that data-driven learner stereotypes could work well for detecting and preventing student dropouts. In this paper, we are exploring the application of stereotype-based modeling to a more challenging task – predicting student problem-solving and learning in two programming courses and two MOOCs. We explore traditional stereotypes based on readily available factors like gender or education level as well as some advanced data-driven approaches to group students based on their problem-solving behavior. Each of the approaches to form student stereotype cohorts is validated by comparing models of student learning: do students in different groups learn differently? In the search for the stereotypes that could be used for adaptation, the paper examines ten approaches. We compare the performance of these approaches and draw conclusions for future research.

KEYWORDS

Individual differences, Java, MOOC, Student modeling

1 INTRODUCTION

In the field of user modeling, it is common to distinguish stereotype user models and feature-based user models from one another [4]. Stereotypical user models attempt to cluster the multitude of users of an adaptive system into several groups (called stereotypes) that are considered to have similar needs in the sense of adaptation. The adaptation mechanisms treat all users who belong to the same stereotype in the same way. In contrast, feature-based models attempt to model specific features of individual users such as knowledge, interests, and goals. During the user's work with the system, these features may change, so the goal of feature-based models is to track and represent an up-to-date state for modeled features and use it for adaptation. Stereotypical user modeling is

one of the oldest approaches to user modeling. It was originally developed by Elaine Rich [21] and was extensively used in many early user-adaptive systems [14]. However, over the years, feature-based user modeling approaches became dominant in almost all types of adaptive systems. With their better ability to represent individual users, feature-based models empowered many advanced personalization approaches. For example, in the area of adaptive educational systems, it has become common to represent domains to be learned as a set of knowledge components (KCs) and to independently model a learner's knowledge of each of these KCs. This leads to sophisticated knowledge modeling approaches, such as Bayesian knowledge tracing [6] that, in turn, has enabled high-quality prediction of student problem-solving performance and various personalization approaches.

Surprisingly, once online learning was scaled up to thousands of learners in modern massive open online courses (MOOCs), stereotype-based modeling was brought back to the forefront. We can cite many recent papers that mine MOOC log data in search of stereotypes that group users with the same behavior [1, 15, 23, 26, 27]. This work follows the same expectations as the early work on stereotypes in user modeling field: to make MOOCs adaptive, all users that belong to the same stereotype are expected to receive the same treatment from the system. So far, the work on stereotypes in these MOOC contexts has demonstrated some good results in predicting MOOC dropouts and failures. It does show that stereotypes could be useful for detection and possible prevention of these key MOOC problems. Could we deduce that further research on MOOCs will herald a major comeback for stereotype-based modeling? On one hand, the remarkable scale of MOOC data and new approaches to mining these data might open a way to more reliable stereotype construction that differs considerably from expert-defined stereotypes employed in the early days of user modeling. These stereotypes could potentially work much better by competing (or even winning) against feature-based models. On the other hand, current work on stereotypes and prediction in MOOCs has predominately focused on predicting coarse-grained (course-level) behavior, such as failure or dropout. It is not evident that stereotypes could be useful for predicting finer-grained problem-solving behavior, given that each course can feature many dozens of problems or exercises to solve.

In this paper, we have attempted to explore the prospects of stereotypes in MOOCs "beyond dropouts" – for predicting student performance at the problem level. We used data from a programming MOOC that included a large share of problem-solving activities and provided fine-grained data about user problem-solving behavior. Our goal was to find stereotypes that could be useful (or actionable) for predicting a user's success at solving problems. In

UMAP '17, July 09–12, 2017, Bratislava, Slovakia
© 2017 ACM. 978-1-4503-4635-1/17/07...$15.00
DOI: http://dx.doi.org/10.1145/3079628.3079672

this context, "useful" means that problem-solving performance predictions would be different enough between stereotypes to enable personalized guidance to direct users to the most useful learning content. If useful stereotype-level models are found, then it is possible to use stereotypes for problem-level personalization; i.e., to predict problem-solving performance independently for each stereotype and use it to offer different interventions for different stereotypes. For example, all students within a given stereotype could be switched to a new topic once a chance to solve problems correctly for the current topic becomes high, or remedial material could be offered if the chance to solve a problem is too low.

The paper presents our attempts to find actionable stereotypes. Section 2 presents the context of our work. Section 3 explains our dataset, followed by Section 4, which elaborates on our assessment methodology. Section 5 reports our attempts to use simple demographic stereotypes, while Sections 6–7 present our search for more reliable behavior-based stereotypes. Sections 8–9 explain our findings on the behavior-based stereotypes. Surprisingly, despite our intermediate success in finding interesting behavior-based stereotypes, none of the stereotypes explored in this paper appeared to be truly "useful". Section 10 summarizes our results and discusses outcomes. We believe that our data points to a need to use finer-grained feature-based user models to support performance prediction and personalization for individual problems.

2 RELATED WORK

2.1 Student Behavior Analysis in MOOCs

Due to a large volume of available data and a surprisingly low completion rate, the analysis of student behavior in MOOCs emerged as an important topic just a few years ago. Perhaps one of the very first studies on MOOCs and behavior was the work in [3] that focused on the amount of time that students spent on various activities, as well as on demographic information about the students. In a more recent attempt [1], a taxonomy of individual learner behaviors was developed to examine the different behavior patterns of high- and low-achieving students. Another attempt was the work of [26], which adopted a content analysis approach to analyze students' cognitively relevant behaviors in a MOOC discussion forum and explored the relationship between the quantity and quality of that participation with their learning gains. In a similar attempt, [23] presented a hierarchy to categorize MOOC students into different engagement groups, based on their styles of engagement.

Overall, past studies have generally focused on resource usages, such as viewing course lectures, quizzes, assignments, and discussion forum activities to find the behavior of different groups of students and attempt to relate those behaviors with high and low levels of learning. However, there is some evidence from past work that demonstrates that focusing solely on resource usage might not lead to a reliable method to separate weak and strong students [5].

Unlike the past studies, the current work analyzes student behaviors by finding micro-patterns in student problem-solving activities, rather than by examining resource usage. Two similarly-minded attempts can be found in [24], which focused on the search for problem-solving strategies, and [27], which defined study habits by mining student navigation. However, neither of them explored behaviors by closely examining how students solved problems.

2.2 Assessment Data Analysis in Programming

Analyzing student solutions to programming assignments has received much attention during the past years. Recent work has used submission data to reveal multiple correct and incorrect ways to solve the same problem [9, 13], build an intelligent scaffolding system [22], model student knowledge in a program development context [20, 29], predict student grade [16], and understand student coding behavior through conceptual analysis [12].

The current paper contributes to the existing body of literature on analysis of assessment data by using compilation and submission data collected from students' problem-solving activities in a Java MOOC to understand (1) individual patterns of problem-solving (coding) behavior; (2) the impact of discovered behaviors on student performance in the programming course; and (3) any implications of the behaviors for accurately modeling student knowledge.

3 DATA

The data for the study comes from four introductory programming courses and MOOCs offered at a research-oriented University in Europe in 2014 and 2015. A single iteration of the programming course lasted for seven weeks and used Java as the programming language. Each week, students worked on tens of programming assignments with varying complexity. Less complex assignments were given when a new topic or construct (e.g., loops) was introduced, and as students created a number of smaller programs with those constructs, they moved to larger assignments that required the use of multiple constructs. The students worked on the assignments in the NetBeans environment. The assignments were downloaded into the programming environment through the Test My Code-plugin [25], which was used to assess the students' code automatically, as well as to collect data from the programming process of those students who consented to the use of their data for research purposes.

The collected data included key-presses with time, assignment information, and student id, and was aggregated to describe meaningful events in the students' programming process. The events used for this study were *running the program*, *running the tests for the program*, and *submitting the program for grading*; also, the first five generic events (inserting or removing text) were included for each assignment to make it possible to analyze transitions to meaningful events. For each event, information on program compilation and correctness were extracted for the data in a posthoc analysis using JUnit test sets, and finally, *programming concepts* for each problem-solving state were extracted using JavaParser [11].

Students were given a demographic questionnaire that solicited their age, gender, programming background, and the highest level of education attained. Out of 2739 students that started the courses, 1788 students were included in the initial sample (the cutoff was 2500 recorded events, which corresponds to roughly a 33rd percentile of the first week of the course workload). Out of those, 798 students answered the questionnaire and were included in the final analysis sample. Table 1 shows key statistics for all participants.

4 THE ASSESSMENT APPROACH

In this work, we attempted to determine whether separating students into various cohorts for the group-based adaptation would be useful. In particular, we are interested whether we could find

| Course | Student sample | | Age | Gender | Programming background | Prior education |
	Initial	Final	min / mean / max	M / F / NA	None / Some / More	Pri.&Sec. / College / Grad
MOOC 2014	1286	90	16 / 32.3 / 65	90% / 9% / 1%	4% / 81% / 15%	63% / 12% / 25%
Traditional 2014	263	192	18 / 23.2 / 44	62% / 38% / 0%	59% / 38% / 3%	78% / 3% / 19%
MOOC 2015	984	372	15 / 30.8 / 66	77% / 22% / 1%	30% / 60% / 10%	58% / 13% / 29%
Traditional 2015	206	144	19 / 24.3 / 45	63% / 35% / 2%	56% / 39% / 5%	74% / 3% / 23%

Table 1: Background information on the students that took the courses.

groups of students that are so distinct that their members learn differently. As a criterion to judge whether we were able to obtain the desired split between groups when looking at multiple ways to group students, we used differences between *models of student learning* in each group. Our rule of thumb is that if groups are truly different in how their members learn, the group models would demonstrate different performance in a cross-prediction task.

Before turning to the innovative approaches to separate students by their programming behavior, we demonstrate our evaluation approach by assessing simpler ways of grouping. These simpler groupings would include those known *a priori* (e.g., demographics, prior achievements) and those known *a posteriori* (e.g., overall course performance). By comparing innovative approaches to the simpler ones, we also monitor whether our behavior-based approach differs enough from existing approaches. Naturally, we would prefer behavior clustering results that do not align with simpler groupings. After evaluating existing simpler approaches to student grouping, we will examine student clustering using programming behavior mining. All approaches will be validated using groups/clusters models of learning and predicting across group/cluster boundaries.

4.1 Modeling Student Learning

To model student learning, we used an approach called performance factors analysis [18] that is based on logistic regression. PFA represents student abilities as a random factor θ_i, concept difficulties as fixed-factor intercepts β_k, and concept learning rates from correct and incorrect submissions as γ_k and ρ_k, respectively. Equation (1) shows the canonical form of the PFA. Here, σ is the inverse logistic function, while s_{ik} and f_{ik} are the counts of the prior student's successful and failed attempts to apply concepts.

$$P\left(Y_i = 1 | \theta, \beta, \gamma, \rho\right) = \sigma\left(\theta_i + \sum_k \left(\beta_k + \gamma_k s_{ik} + \rho_k f_{ik}\right)\right) \quad (1)$$

Our choice of model was based on the compensatory nature of the PFA – multiple concepts used in student's submissions, together, form a cumulative signal that results in the observed outcome. The other candidate modeling approach – Bayesian knowledge tracing [6] – is not intended for multi-concept student transaction data.

We have made two modifications to the PFA, both of which improved the overall fit. First, we have switched from concepts defined across problems to within-problem concepts. Second, we $log(x+1)$-transformed the concept opportunity count. Both of these modifications proved to be useful in the work by Yudelson et al. [29], which considered data from the same source. The modifications only changed the scope of concepts and the way opportunity counting is done, while the canonical form of PFA remained the same.

In contrast to [29], we pre-processed the data differently. First, every snapshot of the student code was treated as an atomic unit of data. It was deemed successful if all tests passed; otherwise, the problem attempt was unsuccessful. Second, we only considered snapshots where students were testing, running, or submitting their code – i.e., purposefully checking it for correctness. Intermediate snapshots were not considered for student modeling. Consecutive testing, running, or submitting the code without modifications in between was treated as one attempt. Third, we considered all concepts that were used in student's code. Only considering changes in concepts with or without special treatment for removals (as in [29]) led to model performance degradation under our data pre-processing setup. Finally, we considered only students for whom we had background information (798 out of 1788 students).

Due to our modifications, the upper boundary for the number of PFA concept parameters went from 143*3-1 = 428 to 143*240*3-1 = 102,959. However, because of the problem-concept matrix sparsity, the actual number of parameters was 13542*3-1 = 40,625. Also, given the size of the data (about 392,000 student submissions), it was not possible to use conventional statistical packages. We used a modified LIBLINEAR tool [7]. The modification[1] was in the form of an additional solver that allowed grouped L^2-penalties to approximate random factors. The modified LIBLINEAR retained the ability of the original version to tackle large datasets successfully.

4.2 Comparing Student Models across Groups

The primary goal of this work was to find at least two groups of students in our sample that have *different models of learning*. Following the approach piloted in [28], given the breakdown of a student sample into n groups/clusters, we sub-sampled each group 20 times to extract 80 students as a training set and 20 students as a test set. Sub-sample models were built from each of the 80-student training set. We then used each of the $n * 20$ models to predict n corresponding sub-samples: one sample matched the group that the model was built on, while the rest were from the other group(s). Finally, we plotted n^2 model accuracies (means and standard errors), n of which represented model performance within the group, while the rest were between the groups.

Our criterion for students in different groups *learning differently* was that within-group model performance would be visibly better than between-group model performance. In the case where $n > 2$, that should be true for at least two groups out of n. An example of the *ideal* separation is shown in red in Figure 1. Here, a model built on group A is superior to the model built on group B when predicting test data from group A. At the same time, when predicting test data of group B, model B wins on *its own ground*. Thus, we say that

---

[1]https://github.com/IEDMS/liblinear-mixed-models

models *A* and *B* are sufficiently different since they prevail on the student strata they were built on and forfeit on other student strata. An *expected* case is marked in blue. We previously discovered this phenomenon in [28]. In this case, there is a domination of one model over the others, irrespective of the origin of the sub-sample. Such cases are marked in blue (model *B* vs. model *C*). Finally, a *sub-optimal* case of model *A* vs. model *C* (marked in green) occurs when one model wins on *its own ground* (here, *A*) but does not have an edge over or loses to the other model (here, *C*).

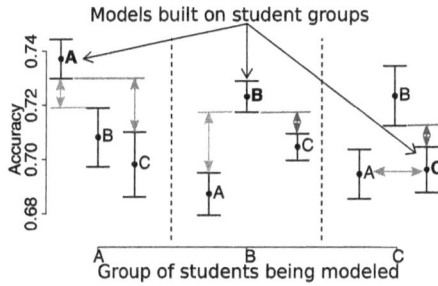

Figure 1: Between-group student model prediction accuracy differences (means and standard errors). Red arrows mark an *ideal* case, blue – *expected* case, green – *sub-optimal* case.

5   SIMPLE STUDENT GROUPING

As an example of our assessment approach, we first examined simpler demographic- and course performance-based approaches to student grouping. For the demographic data, we used gender and education level reported in the background information. Performance data were extracted from the course statistics available at the end. These groupings are summarized in the top five rows of Table 2.

Gender. Students were split by gender. The majority of students were males (about 71%).

Education level. Students were split into three groups. There were 524 students that had primary and secondary education, 154 students who attended college, and 120 students in graduate school.

Number of transactions. Students were split into three equal percentile groups – low, medium, and high – by the total number of problem attempts. When we employed a similar approach to investigate student groupings in [28], a subset of students that yielded more data produced a globally superior model as well. This grouping serves as our check for that phenomenon.

Problems Solved. This grouping was produced by an agglomerative clustering of four course-level counts: problems solved (at least one submission 100% correct), problems partially solved (at least one submission > 0% correct), problems attempted but not solved (at least one submission of 0% correct), and problems not attempted. The clustering yielded three groups: low (mostly not attempting problems), high (mostly solving problems), and medium (everyone else). This grouping is an overall student performance measure.

Percent Correct. This grouping was a split with three percentile groups with low, medium, and high values of overall percentage correct of the times students purposefully tested, ran, or submitted their code. This grouping separates students by their diligence.

Approach (no. features)	Cluster sizes	Prediction diff.	
		Score	Cluster to note
Gender† *(1)*	570, **228**	0.33	Female
Edu.‡ *(1)*	524, 154, 120	0.00	
#Trans.‡ *(1)*	266, 266, **266**	0.67	High
P.Solv.‡ *(4)*	218, 316, 264	0.00	
%Corr.‡ *(1)*	266, 266, 266	0.00	
C1 (45)	**383**, 415	0.67	1
C2 (245)	**416**, 382	0.67	1
C3 (245)	258, **158**, 382	0.67	2
C4 (245)	**295**, 503	0.67	1
C5 (245)	389, **272**, 137	0.67	2

† Male and Female; ‡ These groupings have 3 levels: Low, Medium, and High

Table 2: Approaches to clustering students. Top rows indicate simpler groupings while bottom rows (C1-C5) indicate advanced behavior-based clustering approaches.

Our preference for the cross-prediction group separation is in the order mentioned in Section 4.2: *ideal*, *expected*, and *suboptimal*. For simplicity's sake, we scored both group and cluster separations. A score of 1.0 would mean that the separation is *ideal*, a score of 0.67 would mean that the separation is *expected*, a score of 0.33 would mean that the separation is *suboptimal*, and otherwise score is 0.00. Cross-prediction differences between simpler groupings are addressed in the top five rows of the "Prediction diff." columns of Table 2. Out of the five simpler grouping approaches, only two had a non-zero score. In the case of gender contrasts, a model of female students had the edge over the model of male students when predicting the test data of female students. When predicting test data of male students, both models performed the same. Concerning the total number of student transactions grouping, the model of students contributing the most data had an edge. In fact, it was better than others, no matter what the test data predicted.

6   BEHAVIOR MINING

The key idea behind our behavior mining approach is to characterize student problem-solving behavior on the level of micro-patterns that define how the student progresses to the correct solution through several incorrect solutions, and how his or her knowledge grows from assignment to assignment. To build the micro-patterns, we started by processing student intermediate programming steps that classified the programming behavior at each step (section 6.1). Then, we applied sequential pattern mining to extract sequential micro-patterns (section 6.2). Next, the most frequent micro-patterns were used to build a profile vector (we call it a genome) that represented student problem-solving behavior. The stability of the behavior vector built from micro-patterns was checked to ensure the validity of our approach to mining problem-solving behaviors (section 6.3). Each of these parts is explained in more detail below.

6.1   Processing Intermediate Steps

To determine student problem-solving behavior, we started by looking into how students progressed in coding their problem solutions. We used *snapshots*, intermediate programming steps that were captured from student coding activities. Each snapshot recorded the submitted code and its correctness on a suite of tests designed for each problem. As in [12], to mine programming behavior, we first examined conceptual differences between consecutive snapshots – i.e., we observed which concepts were added or removed on each step, and inspected how these changes were associated with improving or decreasing the correctness of the program. For simplicity, the conceptual difference was approximated as the numerical difference between the number of concepts in two snapshots. The procedure for mining the behaviors included two main steps: (a) labeling sequence of students' snapshots in each problem, and (b) mining micro-patterns of frequent behaviors (we call them genes), by conducting sequence mining on all of the labeled snapshots.

To label the sequence of student snapshots in a particular problem, the snapshots that were captured for the student in that problem (including generic, test, run, and submit snapshots) were collected and ordered by time. Each snapshot in the sequence was labeled based on the change in the *programming concepts* and *correctness* from the previous snapshot. The previous snapshot for the first snapshot in the sequence was defined as snapshot $\emptyset$, where the code has no concepts and passes no tests. Table 3 lists the labels that we used during labeling snapshots. The zero correctness value is to distinguish the snapshots where no tests were passed.

Correctness	Concepts		
	Increase	*Decrease*	*Same*
Increase	a	b	c
Same	d	e	f
Decrease	g	h	i
Zero	j	k	l

Table 3: Labels for encoding behavior in a snapshot.

As an illustration, assume that we have two snapshots for a student. The first snapshot has 10 concepts and passes half of the tests, while the second has 20 concepts and passes all of the tests. To label the first snapshot, we compare its number of concepts and correctness to the snapshot $\emptyset$ that has zero concepts and correctness. Since both the number of concepts and the ratio of passed tests increased in the first snapshot, it would be labeled as "a". The label for the second snapshot would be "a" too because the student added more concepts and increased the ratio of passed tests to one. As a result, the sequence of student snapshots would be labeled as "_aa_" – obtained by concatenating the labels of each individual snapshot. The "_" symbol marks the start and the end of the sequence.

Additionally, to distinguish between short and long steps (which is an important aspect of problem-solving behavior), another dimension could be added to each label to convey the extent of time that was spent on a snapshot. Since different students might have different speeds at programming, it is reasonable to use individualized thresholds for classifying the time spent on a step as short or long. This way, a snapshot would be labeled as short or long, depending on the time being shorter or greater than the median of time distribution for each student. In our coding, lowercase letters (a–l) represent *short* steps, and uppercase letters (A–L) represent *long* steps. For example, assuming that the median of time distribution for the student in the aforementioned example is 10 minutes, and that the student spent 15 minutes to develop the code in the first snapshot and another 2 minutes to make the minor change in the second snapshot, then the sequence of her snapshots would be labeled as "_Aa_".

We labeled 137,504 sequences of snapshots that were contributed by 1788 students solving 241 problems. The length of sequences ranged from 1 to 475, with an average of 5.3; 92,549 sequences had more than one step, 64,328 had more than two steps, 48,195 had more than three steps, and 38,768 had more than four steps.

6.2 Mining Problem-Solving Micro-Patterns

We mined frequent sequential patterns in students problem-solving sequences using an implementation of the SPAM algorithm [2] offered by the SPMF Library [8]. The input data to the SPAM consisted of 9254 sequences with at least two steps in them. SPAM discovers all frequent sequential patterns that occur in more than *minsup* of students' sequences. In this work, we chose a small *minsup* (e.g., 1% and 5%) to capture the patterns that are less frequent and may occur only in small groups of students. Also, no gap was allowed in SPAM to force the discovered patterns to have steps that appear consecutively in students' sequences. Finally, the length of the patterns was limited to two or more, as we were interested in observing how students progressed in their code in consecutive steps. SPAM discovered 245 frequent programming patterns occurring in more than 1% of students' sequences that were labeled with respect to change of concept, correctness, and time spent on a snapshot[2]. The top 20 common patterns and their frequency of occurrence are provided in Table 4.

Patterns 1–5	Patterns 6–10	Patterns 11–15	Pattern 16–20
AA (19.78%)	DD (8.53%)	Ac (6.24%)	Jc (6.04%)
AD (13.75%)	aA (8.31%)	DA (6.22%)	_Af (6.01%)
_AA (12.17%)	Ad (8.26%)	_AD (6.18%)	dD (5.61%)
Aa (9.75%)	Af (8.15%)	Dd (6.15%)	DE (5.57%)
AA_ (8.69%)	JJ (7.22%)	JA (6.13%)	Jj (5.45%)

Table 4: Top 20 frequent programming patterns occurring in more than 1% of students' problem-solving sequences. The numbers in parenthesis are the occurrence frequencies.

6.3 Using Micro-Patterns to Model Behavior

We used the micro-patterns discovered by sequential pattern mining to build individual behavior profiles as frequency vectors that showed how frequently each micro-pattern from a discovered set of 245 appeared in a given student's problem-solving behavior. The frequency vectors were normalized to add up to 1 in each vector. This approach was first introduced in [10], where it was used to find problem-solving behaviors in parameterized exercises. Following this paper, we also call the micro-pattern-based student profile the *problem-solving genome*.

To ensure that the vector of micro-patterns frequencies can capture stable characteristics of the student (i.e., it is as stable as a real

---

[2]Assuming that all sequences have an average length of 5, the maximum number of patterns that could be found has an order of magnitude of 8: There are 24^5 possible sequences that could be obtained from 24 labels (a–l, A–L), and the number of possible substrings in a 5-character sequence is $5 \times (5 + 1)/2 = 15$. Thus, the total number of patterns that could be found from sequences with a length of 5 is $24^5 \times 15 = 119,439,360$.

genome), [10] suggested to check the stability of the vector by splitting student sequences into two "halves" and to build the student's behavior vector from each of the two halves. If the two half-vectors (i.e., profiles built separately from each half of split data) of the same student were closer to each other than to half-vectors of other students, then we have strong evidence to claim that the behavior profile vector (genome) is stable. Following this suggestion, we split student sequences in two ways: once by randomizing sequences and dividing them into halves (random-split), and once by ordering sequences by time and dividing them into early and late halves (temporal-split). Then, we built behavior vectors for each half and calculated pairwise distances between the first and second half-vector of the same student (self-distance), and first/second half-vector of the student with first/second half-vectors of other students (others-distance). The distance between half-vectors was calculated using Jensen-Shannon (JS), as it is a common measure used for computing distance between frequency distributions.

We performed a paired Wilcoxon signed rank test to compare values of "self-distance" calculated from the first and second half-vectors of the same student to values of "others-distance" calculated from the first/second half-vector of the student with first/second half-vectors of other students. We found the random-split self-distance ($Mean = 0.349, SE = 0.003$) to be significantly lower than others-distance ($Mean = 0.659, SE = 0.001$), $p < 0.001$. Similar results were obtained with the temporal-split, while the self-distance in the temporally split half-vectors ($Mean = 0.425, SE = 0.002$) was larger than randomly split half-vectors, it was still significantly smaller than the others-distance ($Mean = 0.653, SE = 0.001$), $p < 0.001$. These observations supported the stability of using micro-pattern frequencies to represent student's problem-solving behavior. Also, the behavior profiles obtained with the proposed approach uniquely characterized student's problem-solving behavior and set them apart from the others.

Once we established stable vector-based profiles of student behavior, our next step was to use the micro-pattern representation of problem-solving behavior to group students based on their problem-solving styles. The next two sections explain the behavior groups that we found and their impact on student performance.

7 BEHAVIOR-BASED GROUPS

7.1 Clustering Students into Behavior Groups

To identify similar problem-solving behavior groups, we built behavior vectors of micro-patterns frequencies for each student and clustered students by using these vectors. To build the behavior vector, we used the problem-solving sequences of each student, obtained from all of the problems that they attempted to solve during the course. Each sequence represented consecutive snapshots that were captured while students were developing the program as a solution for a problem. We tried five different settings for clustering students behavior (see Table 5), changing the clustering method (hierarchical, spectral), and the number of clusters (2,3). We made sure that cluster labels in the advanced student groupings (C1-C5) did not have a significant overlap with the simpler groupings of students (discussed in Section 5) or between each other. C2-C5 labeled the snapshots based on concepts, correctness, and amount

of time that a student spent on the snapshot, while C1 did not consider time. Also, the number of micro-patterns used in the labeling process differed: 45 patterns that were used in building behavior vectors in the first setting were obtained by setting SPAM *minsup* to 5%. The number of patterns in the rest of the settings was 245, which were obtained by setting SPAM *minsup* to 1%.

Approach	#Patterns (Minsup)	Clustering Method (#Clusters)	Time
C1	45 (5%)	Hierarchical (2)	
C2	245 (1%)	Hierarchical (2)	✓
C3	245 (1%)	Hierarchical (3)	✓
C4	245 (1%)	Spectral (2)	✓
C5	245 (1%)	Spectral (3)	✓

Table 5: Settings of the advanced clustering approaches.

7.2 Interpreting Discovered Clusters

In this section, we examine the nature of behavior-based grouping in greater detail. To make the differences clearer, we use settings with two clusters. As the clustering demonstrated, all three two-cluster settings separated students into two similar groups: one group with more constructive building steps, and one group who often massaged the code (i.e., added/reduced concepts without increasing the code correctness), and/or struggled in consecutive steps with no success. The settings with three clusters yielded a similar grouping for students as well, except that it separated a third group who had mixed behaviors as being closer to other two clusters in a subset of micro-patterns. As an example, Figure 2 illustrates the behavior groups that we obtained by spectral clustering with two clusters (Table 5, row 4). The Y-axis shows the ratio of occurrence of the top 20 micro-patterns for the two clusters. These patterns are re-ordered by the absolute difference between the two clusters.

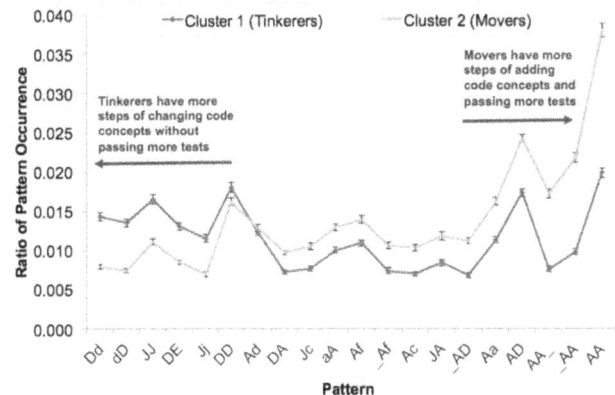

Figure 2: Top 20 programming patterns and their ratio of occurrence in each cluster from clustering approach C4. Patterns are ordered by the absolute difference of ratios between Cluster 1 (tinkerers) and Cluster 2 (movers). Error bars show standard error of the mean. The lines are added to distinguish the points that belong to different clusters.

As the figure shows, the groups differ by the frequency of micro-patterns on the extreme sides of the plot. As the left side shows, students in Cluster 1 have a higher frequency of "tinkering" patterns

(*Dd*, *dD*, *JJ*, *DE*, *Jj*), while the right side shows that the students in Cluster 2 demonstrate a much higher frequency of careful building patterns (*Aa*, *AD*, *AA_*, *_AA*, *AA*). More specifically, students in Cluster 1 frequently increased the conceptual content of their programs in consecutive steps with a long amount of time spent on at least one of those steps (*Dd*, *dD*), spent a long time for increasing concepts in one steps and then took another long step decreasing concepts of their program (*DE*), or spent a long time at least on one step to increase conceptual content of their programs and not only failed in increasing the level of correctness, but also jumped back to the point where no test was passed (*JJ*, *Jj*). On the other hand, students in Cluster 2 did considerably less "tinkering" while focusing on large incremental building steps, in which they often spent a long time building their program. They often had long steps in which they added more concepts to the code and successfully increased its correctness (or at least did not degrade code correctness) (*AD*). They had these building steps more frequently when they started developing their program (*_AA*), while they were on mid-stages of code development (*AA*, *Aa*, *AD*), and also at the time they ended development (*AA_*).

We think that the behavior-based split separated the students into the groups that Perkins et al. (1986) called *tinkerers* and *movers* [19]. Movers gradually add concepts to the solution while increasing the correctness of the solution in each step. On the other hand, tinkerers try to solve a programming problem by writing some code and then making changes in the hopes of getting it to work.

8 BEHAVIOR-BASED CLUSTERS VALIDATION

The bottom five rows under the header "Prediction diff." in Table 2 describe between-cluster model prediction differences, in terms of both the scores and the noteworthy clusters. None of the behavioral clustering approaches were scored as *ideal*, as we have not found at least two clusters that were voted as sufficiently different by the cluster models of student learning. However, all of the clustering approaches received an *expected* score: there was one cluster in each approach that dominated at least one other cluster.

Figure 3 graphically illustrates some of these results. The accuracy of each cluster's model cross-prediction for behavior-based clustering C4 is shown in Figure 3(a). There, we see that the Cluster 1 model wins when predicting test data from both clusters. Figure 3(b) is an illustration of cross-prediction accuracy differences in the case of Behavior-based clustering C5. Cluster 2, here, has superior prediction accuracy over Cluster 1 in both cases. In both of these figures, we see an *expected* case of one cluster model domination (as defined in Figure 1). We chose to visualize these particular clustering results since they represent two typical cases: C4 with two clusters only; and C4 with three clusters, where we only check two out of three prediction tasks to contrast Clusters 1 and 2.

9 ANALYSIS OF CLUSTER DIFFERENCES

The results of cross-prediction using behavior-based cluster models demonstrated that the discovered clusters (tinkerers, movers) were not performance-based stereotypes. In other words, the two clusters that we found did not differ sufficiently to form stereotypes that could better predict student performance and serve as a basis for personalization. While the clusters failed to separate students into

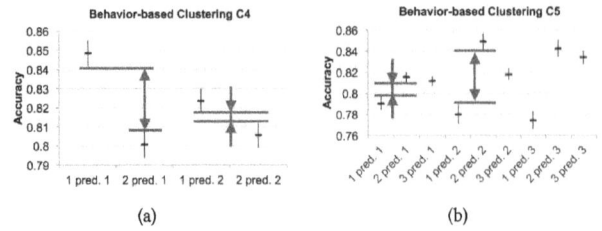

Figure 3: Between-cluster student group model prediction accuracy differences for Behavior-based clustering approaches (a) C4 and (b) C5.

classic performance-based stereotypes (such as weak or strong), we observed that they separated students into distinctive groups with stable but different behaviors. Given the belief of some programming instructors that tinkering is not an ideal problem-solving behavior, we wanted to perform a deeper performance-focused analysis of our discovered behavior-based clusters. In this section, we inspect cluster performance in more detail.

Tinkerers Are Less Efficient and Have Lower Grades. To gain an insight into how the two behavior groups differed in terms of their performance, we looked into a set of performance measures that included: 1) the number of attempted problems; 2) the number of solved problems; 3) the average steps taken to solve the problem, where steps were only test, run, and submit snapshots; 4) the average time (in seconds) spent on solving the problem; 5) the effectiveness score; and 6) the final course grade. Effectiveness score is a measure of instructional efficiency and represents student performance on the problems that a student solved, as well as the mental effort that a student spent on solving those problems. Here, we chose the time on problem-solving as an approximate measure of student mental effort and compute an effectiveness score, as introduced in [17].

Table 6 presents performance statistics for each of the aforementioned measures among students in Cluster 1 (tinkerers) and students in Cluster 2 (movers) (note that these clusters were plotted in Figure 2). A Wilcoxon ranked sum test was performed to measure the difference on each performance measure in Cluster 1 and Cluster 2. As the table shows, there is a significant difference between the two clusters in several cases. On average, students in Cluster 2 took fewer steps to solve the problem ($M_2 = 3.4, M_1 = 5.9$), were faster at solving the problems ($M_2 = 630.0, M_1 = 998.1$), and as a result, were also more efficient in solving the problems ($M_2 = 0.4, M_1 = -0.3$). Furthermore, the average student grade was also higher in Cluster 2 than in Cluster 1 ($M_2 = 3.4, M_1 = 2.9$). While all parameters commonly used as signs of good performance point to Cluster 2, we should be careful when interpreting this result as a clear sign of the superior problem-solving abilities of students in Cluster 2. Making fewer larger steps is the very essence of problem-solving approach of Cluster 2, and it is no surprise that students from this cluster looked more efficient. On the other hand, there was no significant difference between clusters in respect of the number of solved problems, although students in Cluster 2 attempted more problems and solved more problems, on average, as compared to those in Cluster 1.

Performance Measure	Cluster 1	Cluster 2	Wilcoxon Test
#Attmpted Probs.	81.3 (1.7)	82.8 (1.3)	73,456
#Solved Probs.	68.1 (1.4)	70.9 (1.0)	68,860
Avg. Attempts to Solve	5.9 (0.2)	3.4 (0.1)	123,790***
Avg. Time to Solve	998.1 (27.5)	630.0 (16.7)	111,950***
Effectiveness Score	-0.3 (0.1)	0.4 (0.0)	7253*
Course Grade	2.9 (0.2)	3.4 (0.1)	43,068***

* : $p < .05$; *** : $p < .001$

Table 6: Performance statistics (Mean,SE) for Cluster 1 ($N = 295$), and Cluster 2 ($N = 503$). Wilcoxon rank sum was performed to compare performance of Clusters 1 and 2.

Patterns Tend to Distinguish Low vs. High Performers. From what we observed, we know that one group was thinking in a constructive manner; that is, students in Cluster 2 often thought for a long time, added concepts, and increased code correctness (patterns _AA, AA, AA_ in Figure 2). On the other hand, students in Cluster 1 seem to be weaker because they had more unsuccessful steps, they added concepts with no test being passed, or they changed (added/removed) concepts that did not influence the code's correctness (see patterns *Dd, dD, DE* in Figure 2). Apparently, Cluster 1 represents students who are less efficient in their problem-solving – evaluated by performance measures like effectiveness score, and average attempts for solving the problem. As a result, it seems likely that weaker students would be in this group.

When we investigated the relationship between the micro-patterns in each group and the performance measures further, we found that certain patterns are positively or negatively associated with performance[3]. In particular, some patterns that represent mostly tinkering behavior were negatively related to both the number of problems that student solved and their effectiveness score (_jj, JjJ, ic_, _JJJ, jJJ, JJk, _JK, FF). On the other hand, we found an instance of a constructive building pattern (_AAD) to be positively associated with both of these measures. Additionally, we observed that a pattern could have a different impact on different measures. In our case, pattern *bA* was positively related to the number of solved problems and was negatively related to effectiveness score.

Both Groups Include a Mixture of Strong and Weak Students. Why the tendency toward low- and high- performance among tinkerers and movers did not result in a grouping that accurately reflects performance-based stereotypes? This can be explained by elaborating on how weak and strong students were distributed across the two groups. There were both strong and weak students who exhibited similar problem-solving behavior. To check this hypothesis, we compared the overlap between the clustering that resulted in two groups of tinkerers and movers (i.e., clustering C4) and the two performance-based clustering (i.e., *Problem Solved*, and *Percent Correct*). We found little overlap between group labels that were found by these clustering approaches. This is sufficient evidence to let us conclude that there were both weak and strong students among movers and tinkerers.

It appeared that strong and weak students were dispersed within each behavior group. We observed that a large number of students

in Cluster 1 (tinkerers) were strong students. These students performed well, but they exhibited the same problem-solving behavior as poor students. This clarifies that behavior-based clusters represented different behaviors in solving problems, rather than the classic weak/strong performance groups.

10 DISCUSSION AND FUTURE WORK

We have set out to find at least two groups of students that could be considered to learn differently, as captured by the models of their learning. Just like in [28], where the domain is K-12 math, we found that, across all of the grouping/clustering approaches that we have considered, there is always a sub-sample of students who can effectively be used to build a model of learning for the whole population. While this is not the result we hoped for, it conveys an important message. This means that finding a useful learning-focused stereotype, like *good students* or *slow students*, is not trivial. There might be students who approach learning differently, but the distinction between these approaches are orthogonal to the conventional dimensions that we apply to quantify learning.

A set of simpler, as well as more advanced, behavior-based student grouping approaches that we tried did not result in discernible differences in cross-prediction accuracies. There is always one sub-population of students that contributes to a model that could be universally used for all. Our hypothesis is that adapting student models by swapping alternative parameterizations based on student stereotypes is not the correct approach. Although classic stereotype models have demonstrated their new value in the educational context as a basis for behavior prediction and personalized intervention, they seem to be failing as alternative models of student learning.

To date, the basis for our conclusion is limited: We looked at data from traditional courses and MOOCs in one field that originated from one University in Finland. The education system there might be different from the rest of the world and the sample of students could have influenced the behavior grouping and the performance of our models. In future work, we would like to obtain a larger, more representative sample of student data and re-run our analysis to validate and reconfirm our findings. Furthermore, we performed clustering separately on student demographic and performance data, and also on the genome data. In future work, it would be interesting to explore the clustering and student modeling using a combination of these sources. Finally, although the discovered clusters of tinkerers and movers were not useful for modeling student learning, they could be beneficial to researchers for other kinds of personalization. In particular, future work should investigate whether we can recognize a student as a tinkerer or mover sufficiently early and whether this early classification can be used to reduce less productive tinkering behavior using proper scaffolding.

ACKNOWLEDGMENTS

This work used the Extreme Science and Engineering Discovery Environment (XSEDE), which is supported by NSF award OCI-1053575. Specifically, it used the Bridges system, which is supported by NSF award ACI-1445606, at the Pittsburgh Supercomputing Center.

---

[3]Generalized linear model was used to model the performance measure of interest. Dependent variables were micro-patterns that had little correlation, if any.

REFERENCES

[1] Ashton Anderson, Daniel Huttenlocher, Jon Kleinberg, and Jure Leskovec. 2014. Engaging with massive online courses. In *World Wide Web Conf.* 687–698.

[2] Jay Ayres, Jason Flannick, Johannes Gehrke, and Tomi Yiu. 2002. Sequential pattern mining using a bitmap representation. In *Knowledge Discovery and Data Mining Conf.* 429–435.

[3] Lori Breslow, David E Pritchard, Jennifer DeBoer, Glenda S Stump, Andrew D Ho, and Daniel T Seaton. 2013. Studying learning in the worldwide classroom: Research into edX's first MOOC. *Research & Practice in Assessment* 8 (2013), 13–25.

[4] Peter Brusilovsky and Eva Millán. 2007. User models for adaptive hypermedia and adaptive educational systems. In *The Adaptive Web: Methods and Strategies of Web Personalization*, Peter Brusilovsky, Alfred Kobsa, and Wolfgang Neidl (Eds.). Lecture Notes in Computer Science, Vol. 4321. Springer-Verlag, Berlin Heidelberg New York, 3–53.

[5] John Champaign, Kimberly F Colvin, Alwina Liu, Colin Fredericks, Daniel Seaton, and David E Pritchard. 2014. Correlating skill and improvement in 2 MOOCs with a student's time on tasks. In *Learning@scale Conf.* 11–20.

[6] Albert T. Corbett and John R. Anderson. 1995. Knowledge tracing: Modeling the acquisition of procedural knowledge. *User Modeling and User-Adapted Interaction* 4, 4 (1995), 253–278.

[7] Rong-En Fan, Kai-Wei Chang, Cho-Jui Hsieh, Xiang-Rui Wang, and Chih-Jen Lin. 2008. LIBLINEAR: A library for large linear classification. *Journal of machine learning research* 9 (2008), 1871–1874.

[8] Philippe Fournier-Viger, Jerry Chun-Wei Lin, Antonio Gomariz, Ted Gueniche, Azadeh Soltani, Zhihong Deng, and Hoang Thanh Lam. 2016. The SPMF Open-Source Data Mining Library Version 2. In *Joint European Conf. on Machine Learning and Knowledge Discovery in Databases.* 36–40.

[9] Elena L Glassman, Jeremy Scott, Rishabh Singh, Philip J Guo, and Robert C Miller. 2015. OverCode: Visualizing variation in student solutions to programming problems at scale. *Computer-Human Interaction Transaction* 22, 2 (2015), 7.

[10] Julio Guerra, Shaghayegh Sahebi, Yu-Ru Lin, and Peter Brusilovsky. 2014. The problem solving genome: Analyzing sequential patterns of student work with parameterized exercises. In *Educational Data Mining Conf.* 153–160.

[11] Roya Hosseini and Peter Brusilovsky. 2013. JavaParser: A Fine-Grained Concept Indexing Tool for Java Problems. In *AI-supported Education for Computer Science Workshop.* 60–63.

[12] Roya Hosseini, Arto Vihavainen, and Peter Brusilovsky. 2014. Exploring Problem Solving Paths in a Java Programming Course. In *Psychology of Programming Interest Group Conf.* 65–76.

[13] Jonathan Huang, Chris Piech, Andy Nguyen, and Leonidas Guibas. 2013. Syntactic and functional variability of a million code submissions in a machine learning mooc. In *AIED 2013 Workshops Proceedings Volume.* 25–32.

[14] Judy Kay. 1994. Lies, damned lies and stereotypes: pragmatic approximations of users. In *Fourth International Conference on User Modeling*, Alfred Kobsa and Diane Litman (Eds.). MITRE, 175–184.

[15] René F Kizilcec, Chris Piech, and Emily Schneider. 2013. Deconstructing disengagement: analyzing learner subpopulations in massive open online courses. In *Proceedings of the third international conference on learning analytics and knowledge.* ACM, 170–179.

[16] Christian Murphy, Gail Kaiser, Kristin Loveland, and Sahar Hasan. 2009. Retina: helping students and instructors based on observed programming activities. *ACM SIGCSE Bulletin* 41, 1 (2009), 178–182.

[17] Fred GWC Paas and Jeroen JG Van Merriënboer. 1993. The efficiency of instructional conditions: An approach to combine mental effort and performance measures. *Human Factors: The Journal of the Human Factors and Ergonomics Society* 35, 4 (1993), 737–743.

[18] Philip I Pavlik Jr, Hao Cen, and Kenneth R Koedinger. 2009. Performance Factors Analysis – A New Alternative to Knowledge Tracing. In *Artificial Intelligence in Education Conf.* 121–130.

[19] David N. Perkins, Chris Hancock, Renee Hobbs, Fay Martin, and Rebecca Simmons. 1986. Conditions of learning in novice programmers. *Journal of Educational Computing Research* 2, 1 (1986), 37–55.

[20] Chris Piech, Mehran Sahami, Daphne Koller, Steve Cooper, and Paulo Blikstein. 2012. Modeling how students learn to program. In *ACM Technical Symposium on Computer Science Education.* 153–160.

[21] Elaine A. Rich. 1983. Users are individuals: individualizing user models. *International Journal on the Man-Machine Studies* 18 (1983), 199–214.

[22] Kelly Rivers and Kenneth R Koedinger. 2013. Automatic generation of programming feedback: A data-driven approach. In *AI-supported Education for Computer Science Workshop*, Vol. 50–59.

[23] Kshitij Sharma, Patrick Jermann, and Pierre Dillenbourg. 2015. Identifying Styles and Paths toward Success in MOOCs. In *Educational Data Mining Conf.* 408–411.

[24] Krisztina Tóth, Heiko Rölke, Samuel Greiff, and Sascha Wüstenberg. 2014. Discovering Students' Complex Problem Solving Strategies in Educational Assessment. In *Educational Data Mining Conf.* 225–228.

[25] Arto Vihavainen, Thomas Vikberg, Matti Luukkainen, and Martin Pärtel. 2013. Scaffolding Students' Learning Using Test My Code. In *Innovation and Technology in Computer Science Education.* 117–122.

[26] Xu Wang, Diyi Yang, Miaomiao Wen, Kenneth Koedinger, and Carolyn P Rosé. 2015. Investigating How Student's Cognitive Behavior in MOOC Discussion Forums Affect Learning Gains.. In *Educational Data Mining Conf.* 226–233.

[27] Miaomiao Wen and Carolyn Penstein Rosé. 2014. Identifying latent study habits by mining learner behavior patterns in massive open online courses. In *Conf. on Information and Knowledge Management.* 1983–1986.

[28] Michael Yudelson, Steve Fancsali, Steve Ritter, Susan Berman, Tristan Nixon, and Ambarish Joshi. 2014. Better Data Beats Big Data. In *Educational Data Mining Conf.* 205–208.

[29] Michael Yudelson, Roya Hosseini, Arto Vihavainen, and Peter Brusilovsky. 2014. Investigating automated student modeling in a Java MOOC. In *Educational Data Mining Conf.* 261–264.

Learner Modeling for Integration Skills

Yun Huang
Intelligent Systems Program, University of Pittsburgh
Pittsburgh, PA, USA
yuh43@pitt.edu

Julio Guerra-Hollstein
Instituto de Informática & School of Information Sciences,
Universidad Austral de Chile & University of Pittsburgh
Valdivia, Chile
jguerra@inf.uach.cl

Jordan Barria-Pineda
School of Information Sciences, University of Pittsburgh
Pittsburgh, PA, USA
jab464@pitt.edu

Peter Brusilovsky
School of Information Sciences & Intelligent Systems
Program, University of Pittsburgh
Pittsburgh, PA, USA
peterb@pitt.edu

ABSTRACT

Complex skill mastery requires not only acquiring individual basic component skills, but also practicing integrating such basic skills. However, traditional approaches to knowledge modeling, such as Bayesian knowledge tracing, only trace knowledge of each decomposed basic component skill. This risks early assertion of mastery or ineffective remediation failing to address skill integration. We introduce a novel integration-level approach to model learners' knowledge and provide fine-grained diagnosis: a Bayesian network based on a new kind of knowledge graph with progressive integration skills. We assess the value of such a model from multifaceted aspects: performance prediction, parameter plausibility, expected instructional effectiveness, and real-world recommendation helpfulness. Our experiments based on a Java programming tutor show that proposed model significantly improves two popular multiple-skill knowledge tracing models on all these four aspects.

KEYWORDS

learner modeling; knowledge tracing; programming patterns; skill integration; Bayesian network

1 INTRODUCTION

Complex skill mastery requires not only the acquisition of individual basic component skills, but also practice in integrating such component skills with one another [1, 25]. Despite this recognized need, learner models in modern intelligent tutoring systems [2, 34, 43] have predominantly focused on teaching and assessing individual basic component skills (following a prerequisite-outcome ordering), yet haven't explicitly or systematically monitored the level of knowledge that is present in integrating basic component skills. For example, the most popular learner modeling approach, Bayesian knowledge tracing (BKT) [10], is based on decomposing domain

knowledge into individual basic component skills, and assuming that each basic component skill takes full responsibility for overall problem-solving performance. Even some more advanced learner models [9, 14, 26, 47] that address the responsibility assignment in a more sophisticated probabilistic method still decompose domain knowledge into individual basic component skills, and continue to ignore any possible integration or interactions among them. Defining and assessing skills without explicit and systematic specification of integration skills makes knowledge engineering and modeling easier (since the integration or interaction space can be much bigger), but it risks an early assertion of mastery by merely observing student success in basic component skill practices.

Recent research on algebra has provided empirical evidence to demonstrate that there is additional knowledge related to specific skill combinations; in other words, the knowledge about a set of skills is greater than the "sum" of the knowledge of individual skills [17], some skills must be integrated with other skills to produce behavior [25]. For example, students were found to be significantly worse at translating two-step algebra story problems into expressions (e.g., 800-40x) than they were at translating two closely matched one-step problems (with answers 800-y and 40x) [17]. This indicates that, at least in some domains, it is necessary to pay specific attention to skill integration in modeling student knowledge. Computer programming is arguably one of these domains. Research on computer science education and pedagogy has long argued that knowledge of a programming language can't be reduced to a sum of knowledge about different programming constructs, since there are many stable combinations or patterns (also known as schemas or plans) that must be taught and practiced [13, 41].

While the existence of integrating skills have been acknowledged in both cognitive science and teaching practices, there's almost no existing work that explores modeling integration skills in learner models. This involves changes in both parts of a learner model: its underlying *skill model* (specifying the skills in the domain, skills required by each problem and relationships among skills) and its *modeling approach* given a skill model (specifying the use of either a flat or a hierarchical structure in a Bayesian network). In this work, we introduce a novel integration-level approach to model learners' knowledge and provide fine-grained diagnosis: a Bayesian network based on a new kind of knowledge graph with progressive integration skills. We also introduce a novel multifaceted evaluation

UMAP'17, July 9–12, 2017, Bratislava, Slovakia
© 2017 ACM. 978-1-4503-4635-1/17/07...$15.00
DOI: http://dx.doi.org/10.1145/3079628.3079677

framework that includes assessments of performance prediction, parameter plausibility, expected instructional effectiveness, and real-world recommendation helpfulness. Following this framework, we perform an extensive evaluation and demonstrate that our model significantly improves upon two popular multiple-skill learner models in all four aspects. The remaining part of the paper starts with an extensive review, and then gives an introduction of the new modeling approach, the multifaceted evaluation framework, the results, and ends with the conclusion.

2 RELATED WORK

2.1 Knowledge Tracing for Multiple Skills

One major functionality of learner modeling is to maintain explicit knowledge estimations of domain skills over time. This process is called *knowledge tracing* [10, 11]. Such explicit knowledge estimations are critical for understanding learners' cognitive states and providing targeted remediation. In this work, we focus on learner models with explicit knowledge estimations on fine-grained skills with levels at which remediation can directly operate.

While many models have been constructed for single-skill knowledge tracing, multiple-skill knowledge tracing has long been a challenge. Each observed assessment unit (i.e., an observation, a step, an item, or a problem) involving multiple skills poses substantial challenges in assigning responsibility (credit or blame) to each individual skill for practical performance. Currently, there are two main streams of work that address this problem.

The first stream of work [14, 16, 26, 47] converts the many-to-many skill to item mapping into a one-to-many (or one-to-one) mapping during the training process, where a classic *Bayesian knowledge tracing* [10] paradigm can be applied[1]. Such models separately train each individual skill using a hidden Markov model which assumes that each skill is fully responsible for performance by duplicating the observations for each of the required skills (Figure 1a). This oversimplifies the responsibility assignment issue, but reduces modeling complexity. The parameters are the probability of initially knowing the skill (*init*), the probability of transferring from an unlearned to a learned state (*learn*), the probability of accidentally failing a known item (*slip*), and the probability of correctly answering an item by chance (*guess*). Variants on these models differ in how they conduct prediction and updating during the predicting phrase. One variant we consider in this paper is called *weakest knowledge tracing (WKT)*, which has been shown to have the best predictive performance on several datasets, as compared with other variants [14, 16, 47]. It takes the minimum of the predicted probability of success among involved skills as the final prediction. This model only updates the knowledge of the weakest skill when observing an incorrect response, and updates all skills otherwise. This serves as a low baseline for our later experiments.

The second stream of work [9, 31, 32] maintains the many-to-many skill-to-item mapping in both the training and predicting phrases (Figure 1b). Each individual skill is assigned responsibility according to the conditional probability table and the Bayesian rule. Here, we focus on the models that assume a conjunctive relationship among skills (i.e., success in an item requires knowing

all required skills) and that use noisy-AND gates for modeling the conjunctive relations. Noisy-AND gates were commonly used in many prior studies [6, 9, 44], due to their linear rather than exponential complexity in inference. We call such a model that uses item level noisy-AND gates with a flat structure among skills *conjunctive knowledge modeling (CKM)* and use it as a high baseline in this paper. These models closely relate to the popular psychometric model DINA [23], but they ultimately conduct dynamic knowledge estimation rather than static ability estimation. Each noisy-AND gate uses a *slip* parameter to capture the the probability of accidentally failing a known item, and a *guess* parameter to capture the probability of correctly answering an item by chance. In this avenue of work, some use a hierarchical structure among skills, yet focus on either the prerequisite relations among intrinsically different skills [6, 9, 24], or granularity relationships (including competency-based networks) [8, 9, 32, 33, 35], where higher level nodes denote more abstract, more general, aggregated skills at which level remediation doesn't directly operate. They are substantially different from the integration relationship that we model and the level of remediation that we target here. Also, most work doesn't model transition probabilities across time steps, due to the complexity imposed by the skill model in an arbitrary practice order.

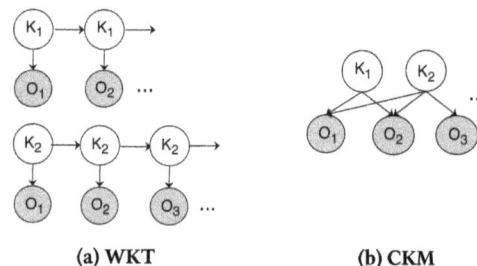

(a) WKT   (b) CKM

Figure 1: Main knowledge tracing models for multiple skills. O nodes represent binary observed student performance and K nodes represent binary latent skill knowledge levels.

2.2 Learner Model Evaluation

Evaluation methodology has been considered an important research topic in the field of user-adaptive systems. In the early years, the cumulative value of personalization was assessed in a user study by comparing performance achieved with a personalized system against performance achieved in a similar system that had personalization disabled [7]. A similar approach was used to compare two versions of personalization. More recently, it has been recognized that personalization is a result of several stacked processes, user or learner modeling. and the proponents of *layered evaluation* argued that holistic empirical evaluation should be complemented by approaches that independently assess each layer [5, 37].

Nowadays, a separate data-driven assessment of learner modeling has become popular in the field of adaptive educational systems, with predictive performance evaluation on held-out datasets [10] emerging as the gold standard. However, several researchers have recently expressed concerns about using prediction performance as the *only* approach. It has been shown that a highly predictive model can be useless for adaptive tutoring [15], and can have low parameter plausibility, as shown by our previous framework *Polygon* [20]. A recent *learner effort-outcomes paradigm (LEOPARD)* [15] offers a

---
[1]Note that recent work [16, 47] still conducts single-skill knowledge tracing on coarse-grained skill levels and treats multiple fined-grained skills (subskills) as features.

general framework for empirically evaluating learner models for adaptive tutoring. However, this framework is limited to single-skill practice learner models. Our evaluation framework presented below combines empirical evaluation with data-driven evaluation and extends both of our previous frameworks, LEOPARD and Polygon [15, 20], to the evaluation of complex skill practices.

2.3 Patterns in Programming Expertise

Experts in the area of psychology of programming have long argued that programming patterns form an important part of programming expertise [13, 41]. Most actively, all kinds of programming patterns, such as plans, techniques, templates, and "cliches", were used by researchers in the area of intelligent tutoring systems to support intelligent analysis of student programs [22, 30, 36, 46]. While such intelligent debuggers are able to both recognize and diagnose pattern errors, they do not maintain a model of student knowledge at the pattern level. Learner models on the level of patterns were first introduced by Brusilovsky [4], who used expert-suggested construct pairs as skills for problem sequencing; Weber [45] applied larger programming "episodes" as skills for adaptive recommendation of programming examples [46]. The more advanced episodic model has never been expanded or ported to another language, due to its complexity and high demand for knowledge engineering. In contrast, the simpler pair-based approach has been used in a few follow-up projects [27]. This paper continues to explore the simple pair-based representation, but applies modern probabilistic approach to conduct learner modeling, which also has the flexibility to incorporate more complex representations.

3 MODELING SKILL INTEGRATION

In this section, we introduce our two innovations for modeling skill integration: a new type of knowledge graph, and the Bayesian network built based on such a knowledge graph.

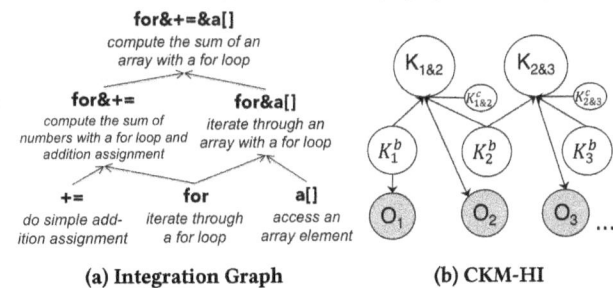

(a) Integration Graph   **(b) CKM-HI**

Figure 2: Integration graph and CKM-HI Bayesian network. O **nodes represent binary observed student performance and** K **nodes represent binary latent skill knowledge levels.**

3.1 Integration Graph

We propose an *integration graph* (Figure 2a) to represent the integration relationships among skills. The lowest level consists of basic component skills and the higher level consists of integration skills requiring integrating lower levels' skills. For example, in the Java programming domain in which we are working, experts identified an integration skill of "computing the sum of numbers with a for loop and addition assignment" based on more basic component skills, such as "doing simple addition assignment" and "iterating

through a for loop". Nodes and edges are correspondingly created in the graph. Simplified symbolic notations are used to label skills in the graph. For example, "for&+=" is used as the label for the integration skill. The labeling (coding) schema for the skill model, the notation of the skill nodes, and the depth of the graph can be designed according to the characteristics of the domain. In this work, we demonstrate one successful example of constructing and utilizing such a graph.

3.2 Learner Model Structure and Parameters

A Bayesian network is a natural way to use an integration graph that maintains its structure and each node's meaning. We propose a Bayesian network that we call *conjunctive knowledge modeling with hierarchical integration skills (CKM-HI)* based on an integration graph. Figure 2b shows the network structure of CKM-HI for modeling pair-based integration skills. Built based on CKM, CKM-HI also uses noisy-AND gates to model the relation between skills and items. This choice is suitable when each problem only has one solution that requires students know all of the underlying skills, and is necessary when each problem requires many skills (e.g., more than 3) to reduce computational complexity. This is the case for our dataset and many other (programming) tutoring systems. However, the core of CKM-HI is less about the probability distribution that we choose to model the skill to item relationship, but more about how we represent integration skills, the skill to skill and the skill to item relationships, which are explained as follows:

- Basic component skills and integration skills are represented by different nodes, so that the target of remediation can be clearly identified. Basic component skill nodes model the basic understanding and application of a component skill. For example, in Figure 2b, K_2^b represents the basic understanding and application of simple iteration through a for loop. Integration skill nodes represent the level of integrating component skills. For example, $K_{2\&3}$ represents the skill of integrating *for* and *a[]* for iterating through an array with a for loop. This is different from traditional WKT or CKM models, where these two kinds of skills can't be differentiated, and effectiveness of remediation could be reduced.
- Latent skills are organized in a hierarchical way. The lowest level consists of basic component skills, and the higher levels consist of integration skills requiring integrating lower-level skills. This hierarchical structure allows efficiency and accuracy in inference: once a student has mastered an integration skill, they should already have mastered its component skills. This avoids tedious assessment and the over-practicing of basic component skills.
- Integration skills are directly connected to items, and edges from basic component skills to items are removed if their integration skills are required. For example, O_2 requires the integration skill $K_{1\&2}$, so the edges from K_1^b to O_2, from K_2^b to O_2 are removed. In this way, remediation can directly operate at integration skill levels. This is different from granularity-based networks [8, 9, 32] including competency-based networks [33, 35] where higher level nodes represent aggregation (not integration) of lower level skills and aren't directly connected to items. As a result, remediation can't directly operate at their higher levels.

- Each integration skill node has its own parent node (e.g., $K^c_{2\&3}$ for $K_{2\&3}$), which denotes the level of cognitive load (or familiarity) that is required to conduct the integration. This means that the level of integration depends not only on the levels of basic component skills, but also on the cognitive load (or familiarity) in each specific integration. If we remove such nodes, the level of integration will be fully determined by the levels of basic component skills, which results in the definition of basic component skills encompassing integration. This increases the difficulty in diagnosing whether students should improve their basic component skills or their integration skills.
- Multinomial (here, binomial) distributions are used for integration skill nodes, where basic component skill nodes and cognitive load nodes are specified as parents to denote prerequisite relations. One can argue that noisy-AND gates could be used, yet multinomial distributions allow component skills to have different importance to integration, and have generated a better model than noisy-AND gates by our cross-validation experiments. However, for highly complex integration skills requiring many components, we can switch to noisy-AND gates for tractability.

To fully determine the network structure, we need to specify skill-to-item and skill-to-skill mappings. Two experts in Java programming performed the labeling following the same schema (with conflicts resolved), which was validated further in Section 5.1.2.

We learn all parameters from the data. We use an expectation maximization algorithm, since the network involves latent variables, and the standard junction-tree algorithm to conduct inference.

Admittedly, there are alternate ways to formulate the model; but in this work, we don't primarily aim to find the best model for modeling integration skills. Instead, we demonstrate the feasibility and value by using a reasonable way of modeling.

3.3 Performance Prediction and Dynamic Knowledge Update

After learning parameters from data (given the network structure), we apply the network for predicting problem performance and infer the knowledge level of each skill at each practice opportunity. For each student's first practice, the network uses the same prior probabilities (obtained by *init* parameters) for latent skill nodes (and cognitive load nodes) to predict their performance and update their levels of knowledge; after observing different students' practice sequences, the network starts to differentiate among students by maintaining different up-to-date knowledge estimates. In order to achieve this, CKM-HI follows the same dynamic BN roll-up mechanism as in [9]: it uses posterior knowledge probabilities conditioned on historical observations as the priors for the next time steps. Currently, CKM-HI doesn't model the transition probabilities of latent skills between time steps. Similar to [9, 32], we argue that the change in knowledge estimates is mainly determined by the new evidence (i.e., observed performance), since the learning gain from each practice would be ultimately translated into an observed performance that serves as the evidence for updating knowledge beliefs. Such a mechanism indeed can achieve good performance, as shown in the latter results section. We leave the incorporation

of learning dynamics, which is a non-trivial task for such a network with hierarchical structure among latent variables, for future studies.

4 MULTIFACETED EVALUATION

In this section, we introduce our multifaceted evaluation for learner models. There is growing concern of using performance prediction metrics as the only evaluation approach [15, 20]. Our multifaceted evaluation also examines the parameters and knowledge inference quality, under both data-driven and user study settings.

4.1 Performance Prediction

We report two popular prediction metrics used in evaluating learner (skill) models, root mean squared error (RMSE) and area under the receiver operating characteristic curve (AUC), based on a suggestion from a recent paper [39] that raised a concern in using only AUC for evaluation learner (skill) models[2].

4.2 Parameter Plausibility

Parameter plausibility has become an important aspect of examining learner models. It determines the accuracy and reliability of the latent knowledge inference. The foundational assumption behind knowledge-tracing learner models is that knowing the required skills generally leads to correct answers, and that not knowing the required skills generally leads to incorrect answers [3]. However, since the data usually contains noise (uncertainty), guess and slip parameters are introduced to tolerate exceptions where students still succeed, even if they are in an unlearned state, and where they fail, even if they are in a learned state. Such parameters should be relatively low; otherwise, they contradict our foundational assumptions and will generate inaccurate knowledge estimations [3, 38, 42]. One primary source of high guess or slip parameters is from an improper skill model. For example, if a skill model fails to identify several difficult skills of an item and students mostly reach a high knowledge level of the identified easier skills when facing this item, the learner model will use high slip parameters to explain the high ratio of incorrect performance that is observed in the data. Here, we compute the average value of guess or slip across skills or items for each model as the metrics that indicate parameter plausibility and prefer smaller values. These two metrics extend the parameter plausibility metrics proposed in our Polygon framework [20].

4.3 Expected Instructional Effectiveness

The ultimate goal of a learner model is to improve instructional effectiveness, which mainly consists of two aspects: 1) whether students can reach high knowledge levels for the targeted skills; and 2) how much effort students need to exert in order to reach the desired knowledge levels. The above-mentioned performance prediction and parameter plausibility metrics fail to give direct information on these two aspects. So, we propose a new evaluation dimension extending our recent *Learner Effort-Outcomes Paradigm (LEOPARD)* [15] from single skill to multiple-skill learner model evaluation. The details are explained as follows.

---

[2]When these two metrics result in a contradictory selection of models, we primarily focus on RMSE, according to [39].

Effort. This metric empirically quantifies the expected number of practices when the tutor stops instruction. It is computed by counting the number of practice attempts a student needs in order to reach a given mastery threshold on real data. This is similar to the original metric [15], but has one major difference, in that the basic component skill to item links are removed from the mapping when the integration skill is required, so that effort considered in integration skills won't be repeatedly counted for basic component skills (while effort solely for basic component skills is maintained). The following formulas explain the computation of *Effort* for mastering the set of skills Q on a dataset, given a mastery threshold R, based on computing effort for a single student u on a single skill q:

$$\text{Effort}(u, q) = \sum_{1 \le t \le |\mathbf{O}_{u,q}|} \prod_{1 \le t' \le t} \mathbf{I}(K_{u,q,t'} < R)$$

$$\text{Effort} = \frac{1}{|U|} \sum_{u \in U} \sum_{q \in Q} \text{Effort}(u, q) \qquad (1)$$

where t denotes the index of the observation sequence $\mathbf{O}_{u,q}$ of a student u on a skill q, $K_{u,q,t'}$ denotes the inferred knowledge at t^{th} observation, and $\mathbf{I}$ denotes an indicator function.

Score. This metric empirically quantifies the expected performance of students when the tutor stops instruction. It is computed by the actual ratio of correct performance on real data where the learner model asserts that a student reaches a given mastery threshold for all of the required skills of the current item. The original metric only applies when each item maps to a single skill by simply examining the performance sequence of each skill. which is not applicable to multiple-skill practices, since the responsibility of each skill for the performance is not clear. To address this, we jointly examine knowledge states for multiple skills. Following formula explains the computation of *Score* for mastering the set of skills Q on a dataset, given a mastery threshold of R:

$$\text{Score} = \frac{\sum_{1 \le t \le |\mathbf{O}|} \prod_{q \in Q_{O_t}} \mathbf{I}(K_{q,t} \ge R) \cdot \mathbf{I}(O_t = 1)}{\sum_{1 \le t \le |\mathbf{O}|} \prod_{q \in Q_{O_t}} \mathbf{I}(K_{q,t} \ge R)} \qquad (2)$$

where $\mathbf{O}$ denotes the overall observations, Q_{O_t} denotes the set of direct parent skills of the item corresponding to O_t, $K_{q,t}$ denotes the inferred knowledge level of a skill q at t^{th} observation.

Joint examination of Effort and Score across thresholds. Prior work examining expected effort has ignored examining expected performance [29]. Consider a learner model that tends to overestimate students' knowledge levels. Although the expected effort will be low, the expected performance will also be low, resulting in under-practicing. So we consider Effort and Score jointly in this work. Moreover, there are two important differences with the original LEOPARD framework: 1) different mastery thresholds are considered, since there is no ground truth of what mastery threshold should be used; and 2) we avoid imputation when mastery is not reached, since it could distort the original distribution, and focus on thresholds with sufficient data (i.e., with at least 20% of the complete data available to compute the metrics and at least 85% of skills with at least one student reaching mastery).

4.4 Real-World Recommendation Helpfulness

In addition to the data-driven evaluation, we also design a user study to examine the helpfulness of the remedial recommendations

that are generated by learner models. Admittedly, this is an indirect assessment of leaner models; yet, we argue that directly collecting users' feedback on learner models' knowledge inference involves non-trivial complication, and that the effectiveness of a learner model is ultimately reflected by remediation. The main task is to solve Java problems and rank recommended *subproblems* according their helpfulness for each participant in solving the original problem. A *subproblem* is an easier version of an original problem that primarily remediates one skill. Thus, a learner model's diagnosis can be "translated" into recommended subproblems. Subproblems are created systematically: first, skills in a problem are ordered by estimated difficulties (computed by the average success rate of problems requiring the current skill); then, for each skill, a subproblem is created by removing harder skills (if the remediated skill is the hardest, then the 2nd hardest skill will be removed). Since different skill models specify different skills for a problem, subproblems can be classified into those that address integration skills and those that don't. For two subproblems with the same basic component skills, we try to make sure the only difference is whether the basic component skills are integrated or just sequentially put together.

We compare recommendations generated from CKM-HI, CKM, WKT, and a *distractor*, which randomly picks an irrelevant subproblem. All learner models employ the same recommendation strategy: after a student makes an attempt, the learner model picks a subproblem that addresses the weakest skill and another that addresses the second weakest skill. We expect that recommendation strategies can have a non-trivial impact on learner models' effectiveness, so we examine two strategies: *MaxDiff* maximizes the difference of CKM-HI with baseline models by disallowing WKT and CKM to recommend subproblems that address integration skills, and *MinDiff* minimizes the difference of CKM-HI with baseline models by allowing WKT and CKM to have a 50% chance to pick subproblems that address integration skills if any basic component skill of the integration skill is identified to be remediated. We employ only the MaxDiff strategy in our user study and use the collected data to conduct simulation for the MinDiff strategy: whenever CKM or WKT picks a subproblem that addresses an integration skill, if its ranking is available from the same user on the same problem, then this ranking is assigned to the subproblem; otherwise, it will be assigned the best ranking. In doing so, we examine the upper and lower bounds of the difference among CKM-HI and the baselines.

Participants receive mixed, permutated recommendations from different models at the same time and are asked to give a non-repeated ranking to each subproblem. They are presented with the original problem and the selected subproblem side-by-side. They are asked (but not forced) to attempt subproblems before ranking, and can adjust rankings any time before attempting next problem. We design the study to focus on students with a basic understanding of component skills and on problems requiring integration, since CKM-HI is primarily designed for monitoring and remediating integration skills compared with its simpler counterparts. In fact, CKM-HI maintains knowledge inference accuracy for basic component skills and increases prediction accuracy for non-integration problems, since it avoids over-penalizing basic component skills. Our latter data-driven evaluation demonstrates CKM-HI's advantage on the overall dataset that includes all students and items.

```
public class Tester {
  public static void main(String[] args) {

    int[] array = {10, 15, 20, 25, 30, 35, 40, 45, 50, 55};
    int result = 0;
    int j = 0;

    while (j < 10) {
      result += array[j];
      j++;
    }

  }
}

What is the final value of result?
```

Figure 3: An example of QuizJET problem in *Arrays* topic.

Such a focused user study allows us to draw more powerful conclusions, given the limited number of participants. We choose seven problems from *Loops* and *Arrays* topics, each of which covers 1 to 5 integration skills, and recruit students who have some prior experience in Java. But since we can't fully guarantee participants' levels, we design a *pretrain* session with problems and examples testing and teaching basic component skills, and ask students to solve such problems before moving on to the next step. The study consists of four parts: 1) a background survey; 2) a pretrain session; 3) a pretest on all integration skills, where each problem targets one integration skill; and 4) the main task.

5 EXPERIMENTS

In this section, we report both data-driven and user study evaluations as we compare two popular multiple-skill knowledge tracing models WKT and CKM with our proposed model CKM-HI.

5.1 Data-Driven Evaluation

5.1.1 Dataset and Experimental Setup. We used a Java programming dataset collected through classroom studies between fall 2013 and fall 2015 at the University of Pittsburgh, from the system QuizJET [19]. Students are requested to give the output or the final value of a variable by comprehending a program (Figure 3). Only one answer is accepted. Each problem is generated by a template, and students can make multiple attempts, where each attempt corresponds to a new instantiation changing the values of some variables. For each problem, students need to apply multiple skills at the same time in order to succeed. The system (only) provides correctness (0/1) information for each attempt. Students decide whether to try a problem again or to move on to another problem. Problems are grouped by topics (e.g., *For Loops, ArrayList*). To reduce the complexity for analysis, we removed the two most complex topics (*Interface* and *Inheritance*), which resulted in 91 items. The final dataset contains 25,988 observations (including all attempts) from 347 students, with an average success rate of 67%. For all experiments, we conducted a 10-fold student stratified cross-validation; i.e., in each fold, we trained on 90% of students, and conducted prediction and inference for the remaining 10% of students. For training CKM and CKM-HI models, we compressed multiple attempts per item into a single attempt by computing the average success rate across attempts at the same item, since the network doesn't model the dynamics across attempts of the same item. Since students often fail at their first attempts and finally succeed in their last attempts (learning merely from correctness feedback), keeping only the first or last attempt will risk either overestimating or underestimating the difficulty of skills. For training WKT, we

kept the original multiple-attempt sequence, since WKT contains learning rate parameters. However, during the prediction phrase we kept all attempts in the test sets for all models, since all models perform dynamic knowledge updates and predictions at each time step, conditioned on historical performance.

For each metric, we conducted a two-sided paired t-test test (after confirming that normality wasn't violated) with a Bonferroni correction. We reported the common Cohen's d_{av} [28] for the effect size. We used the SMILE [12] toolkit to construct all the models. For each model, we initialized all root skill nodes' *init* parameters (the probability of initially knowing the skill) by the average success rate of problems that require this skill. We initialized cognitive load nodes $K^c_{i\&j}$ in CKM-HI in the same way. We initialized the *learn* parameter for WKT as 0.15, and all models' *guess* and *slip* parameters as 0.3. For each integration skill node $K_{i\&j}$ in CKM-HI, we initialized the CPT given the values of its parents K^b_i, K^b_j and $K^c_{i\&j}$ by setting { P(T|TTT)=0.99, P(T|TTF)=0.6, P(T|TFT)=0.6, P(T|TFF)=0.25, P(T|FTT)=0.6, P(T|FTF)=0.25, P(T|FFT)=0.4, P(T|FFF)=0.01 }.

5.1.2 Basic Component Skill to Item Mapping Validation. Individual basic component skill to item mapping provides a strong foundation for adding integration skills. In our Java programming tutor, one problem can easily require multiple skills. For example, the problem in Figure 3 requires the understanding and application of *WhileStatement*, *ArrayElement*, and *AddAssignment* (among others). We compared three sets of available mappings: 1) one from an automatic Java parser [18], which indexes an item with all concepts that appear in the code; 2) one from experts' dense labeling that considers only the important prerequisite and outcome concepts (i.e., those taught in the current topic), which is less dense than the previous one; and 3) one from experts' sparse labeling that considers only the important outcome concepts. We ran WKT with these three sets of skill models and compared the performance prediction metric RMSE through a 10-fold cross-validation. We found that the third mapping achieved significantly better prediction performance (p<.0001) with a large effect size (d_{av}>1) in each pairwise comparison. This skill model maps 4 basic component skills per item on average (ranging from 1 to 8) with a total of 72. This mapping was directly used in WKT and CKM. For integration skill to item mapping, we chose a sparse labeling from experts and didn't conduct further validation. One reason is due to the implementation (rather than theoretical) limitation of the toolkit being unable to run a more dense mapping of integration skills. Another reason, as we stated before, is that we primarily focus on demonstrating one successful way to model integration skills and leave finding the best skill model for future work. The final integration skill to item mapping indexes 2 integration skills per item on average (ranging from 1 to 5) with a total of 43. 47 (out of 91) items having at least one integration skill. This mapping was used to modify the chosen basic component skill to item mapping, and was used in CKM-HI.

5.1.3 Performance Prediction and Parameter Plausibility. Table 1 and Table 2 summarize the comparison of both performance prediction and parameter plausibility. We also report prediction on the first attempts of items, since they are usually important when conducting remediation. Both CKM-HI and CKM significantly beat WKT in all 6 metrics with a large effect size, with CKM-HI beating

Table 1: Comparison of performance prediction and parameter plausibility metrics, computed by averaging across 10 folds. The best result is denoted in bold.

Models	RMSE	AUC	RMSE (1st att.)	AUC (1st att.)	Guess	Slip
WKT	.4494	.6873	.4433	.7001	.4239	.2836
CKM	.4446	.7273	.4073	.7945	.3806	.2093
CKM-HI	**.4437**	**.7283**	**.4064**	**.7958**	**.3625**	**.1860**

Table 2: Statistical test p values and effect sizes for prediction performance and parameter plausibility comparison.

Models	RMSE	AUC	RMSE (1st att.)	AUC (1st att.)	Guess	Slip
CKM vs. WKT	*+	***+	***+	***+	***+	***+
CKM-HI vs. WKT	**+	***+	***+	***+	***+	***+
CKM-HI vs. CKM	**	*	***	*	***+	***+

* sig. at 0.05/3=0.017, ** sig. at 0.01/3=0.0033, *** sig. at 0.001/3=0.00033.
+ effect size ≥ 1 (large).

WKT with smaller p values and larger effect sizes. Further, CKM-HI also significantly outperforms CKM in all prediction metrics. Though it has a small effect size (d_{av}<.2), it is able to significantly outperform CKM in parameter plausibility with a large effect size. Clearly, we see an advantage in modeling integration skills over the two popular multiple-skill knowledge tracing models in both performance prediction and parameter plausibility. Admittedly, CKM-HI only achieves a small effect size prediction improvement over CKM; yet the advantage in parameter plausibility is non-trivial, which should significantly increase the accuracy of latent knowledge inference or diagnosis. Other evaluation aspects shown in latter sections will further reveal the advantage of CKM-HI over CKM. We hypothesize that this small effect size prediction gain can be due to CKM using less plausible parameters to fit the data, and that a larger prediction gain should be revealed if we impose parameter constraints. Due to the space limit, our experiments proving this hypothesis will be reported elsewhere in the future.

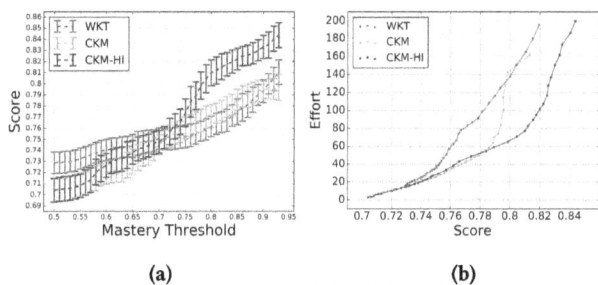

(a)   (b)

Figure 4: Comparison of CKM-HI, CKM and WKT on expected instructional effectiveness.

5.1.4 Expected Instructional Effectiveness. Figure 4a shows Scores plotted against mastery thresholds (with a 95% confidence interval across 10 folds). Figure 4b shows the combined Effort vs. Score graph with them connected by matching mastery thresholds. We consider a broad range of thresholds with enough data, as mentioned in Section 4.3: [0.5, 0.93]. Comparing CKM-HI with WKT on Scores, CKM-HI has worse Scores in low mastery thresholds, but much better Scores in high thresholds; when examining Effort and

Score jointly, CKM-HI requires much less Effort to reach the same Score across almost all thresholds. When comparing CKM-HI with CKM on Scores, CKM-HI has similar Scores in low mastery thresholds and much better Scores in high thresholds; when examining Effort and Score jointly, CKM-HI requires much less Effort to reach the same Score in most of the thresholds. These metrics clearly demonstrate that to reach the same expected performance, students who are guided by the CKM-HI model are expected to exert the least amount of effort, and that by using the same amount of effort, students guided by CKM-HI are expected to have higher performance, as compared with CKM and WKT. Surprisingly, although CKM significantly outperforms WKT in prediction, it requires similar Effort given same Scores in high thresholds.

5.2 User Study Evaluation

The main goal of our user study is to examine the real-world recommendation helpfulness of learner models. The user study was conducted with 20 students pursuing undergraduate or master's degrees in information science at the University of Pittsburgh. The study lasted for around 1.5 hours on average. All of the problems are of the same type as QuizJET. We deployed the same learner models that were constructed during data-driven evaluation, in order to make the comparison compatible. All participants reported that they had some prior experience with Java. The mean score for first and last attempts in pretraining (which tests on and teaches students about basic component skills) is 0.836 and 0.997. The mean score for first and last attempts in the pretest (where each problem tests students on one integration skill) is 0.893 and 0.907. The mean score for the first and last attempts in the main problems (which tests and teaches multiple integration skills at the same time) is 0.676 and 0.949. As the statistics show, participants generally know basic component skills, but still have some difficulty integrating them (particularly when multiple integration skills are required together). We report results by answering different research questions, which are shown as follows.

Does CKM-HI receive the highest ranking? We analyzed the ranking data in two common methods for both MaxDiff and MinDiff strategies: treating ranking as a continuous score or treating ranking as an ordinal score. For the first method, we first computed the aggregated score that a model receives from a student by averaging the scores across the 7 main problems (we found out that, on average, the relative ranking among models are persistent across the 7 problems, so computing an average shouldn't affect the conclusion). Since normality is violated and we have repeated measurements per participant, we conducted a two-sided Wilcoxon signed rank test and computed its effect size ($r=z/\sqrt{N}$) [40]. For the second method, we first kept only the recommendations where students gave the best rank, and then for each model for each student, we counted the number of times that a best-ranked recommendation was generated from the current model across the 7 main problems. Since normality is not violated in this case, we conducted a paired t-test and its effect size d_{av} [28]. Table 3 and Table 4 report the average values and statistical test results. We draw similar conclusions from two kinds of analysis for both strategies. CKM-HI beats both WKT and CKM significantly with a large effect size. Surprisingly, although CKM shows a significant prediction gain over WKT, its ranking

Table 3: Ranking result comparison averaging across participants (best results denoted in bold).

	Avg. rank		Avg. count	
	MaxDiff	MinDiff	MaxDiff	MinDiff
Distr.	4.30	4.30	0.4	0.4
WKT	3.27	2.99	0.95	3.2
CKM	3.36	3.02	0.85	3.3
CKM-HI	**2.11**	**2.11**	**5.6**	**5.6**

Table 4: Statistical test p values (with a Bonferroni correction) and effect sizes for ranking comparison.

	Avg. rank		Avg. count	
	MaxDiff	MinDiff	MaxDiff	MinDiff
WKT vs. Distr.	*+	**+		***+
CKM vs. Distr.	**+	**+		***+
CKM-HI vs. Distr.	**+	**+	***+	***+
CKM vs. WKT				
CKM-HI vs. WKT	**+	**+	***+	***+
CKM-HI vs. CKM	**+	*+	***+	**+

* sig. at 0.05/6=0.0083, ** sig. at 0.01/6=0.0017, *** sig. at 0.001/6=0.00017.
\+ effect size ≥ 0.5 (Wilcoxon signed rank test) and ≥ 1 (paired t-test).

is not significantly different from that of WKT. Considering all recommendations generated by each model (by the first continuous rank analysis), all learner models significantly outperform Distractor with a large effect size. Considering only recommendations received the best ranking (by the second count analysis), CKM-HI still significantly outperforms Distractor, but CKM and WKT can't maintain a similar significant effect under MaxDiff.

Does the higher ranking of CKM-HI come from recommending subproblems that address integration skills? We compared the average ranking of subproblems that address integration skills with those that only address basic component skills (after removing subproblems generated by Distractor). Under MinDiff, integration subproblems receive an average ranking of 1.9, as compared with 3.18 of the non-integration ones; under MaxDiff, integration subproblems receive an average ranking of 2.01, as compared with 3.28 of the non-integration ones. Both differences are significant by a two-sided Wilcoxon signed ranked test (since normality is violated) (p<.001) with large effect size (r>.5). We conclude that students indeed favor subproblems with integration skills during the remediation. Is CKM-HI more able to recommend such subproblems? We found out that among the recommended subproblems of a learner model, the percentile of those addressing integration skills are 84%, 13%, 10%, and 9% for CKM-HI, CKM, WKT, and Distractor under MinDiff, and 0% for CKM and WKT under MaxDiff (CKM-HI and Distractor remain the same). As a result, we conclude that the higher ranking of CKM-HI indeed comes from recommending subproblems that address integration skills.

Can we trust students' subjective rankings? Admittedly, it is a concern that the ranking data are subjective measurements. While we can't fully eliminate such noise, we tried to identify evidence from our collected data that could increase the trustability of these subjective rankings. First, we were able to demonstrate that all learner models receive significantly higher rankings than the Distractor, when considering all recommendations and the best ranked recommendations under MinDiff strategy. Second, we analyzed the

post-test questionnaire that asked about their ranking strategies (at most, two choices) and found that the highest two strategies aligned well with our ranking requirements; namely, they assigned a higher ranking to the subproblem that contains most of the concepts in the original problems, or that they used key concepts in a similar way to the original problem, rather than preferring a subproblem that contains more concepts. In future work, we plan to conduct a large-span and long-scale study to collect objective measurements.

6 CONCLUSION

In this paper, we advocate for the importance of modeling integration skills and have clearly demonstrated the feasibility and value of learner modeling for integration skills. Using a combination of analytical studies based on a Java programming dataset and a user study, we demonstrated that our proposed learner model, CKM-HI, offers significant improvements over two popular multiple-skill knowledge tracing models, WKT and CKM, over a range of aspects that are considered by our multifaceted evaluation framework: performance prediction accuracy, parameter plausibility, expected instructional effectiveness, and recommendation helpfulness. A combination of analytical and empirical approaches has enabled us to make some interesting observations about the limitations of performance prediction evaluation. By examining expected instructional effectiveness and recommendation helpfulness, we found out that a small (effect size) performance prediction gain can still lead to significant improvement in adaptive tutoring (CKM-HI vs. CKM); and surprisingly, a significant prediction gain can result in almost no improvement in adaptive tutoring (CKM vs. WKT).

Altogether, our paper brings three major contributions to the field of learner modeling and adaptive educational systems. First, we introduce a new type of knowledge graph that we call an integration graph, which shows how basic component skills progressively integrate and form new skills that are essential to describe domain expertise. Second, we create a novel integration-level learner model based on an integration graph, which outperforms traditional multiple-skill knowledge tracing models. Third, we introduce a multifaceted learner modeling evaluation framework over a range of aspects, including analytical evaluation and user-study evaluation. The evaluation component of this paper could be considered as an example of the application of this evaluation framework.

In future work, we plan to explore skill integration beyond the single context reported in this paper, while continuing to contribute to best practices in evaluating adaptive educational systems. In particular, we plan to explore automated methods for extracting integration skills that advance our preliminary approach [21].

ACKNOWLEDGMENTS

This research was supported by Andrew Mellon Predoctoral Fellowship from University of Pittsburgh. The learner model was constructed based on the SMILE Engine from BayesFusion, LLC (https://www.bayesfusion.com/). We also thank Rosta Farzan, Igor Labutov for giving valuable suggestions.

REFERENCES

[1] Susan A Ambrose, Michael W Bridges, Michele DiPietro, Marsha C Lovett, and Marie K Norman. 2010. *How learning works: Seven research-based principles for smart teaching.* John Wiley & Sons.

[2] John R Anderson, Albert T Corbett, Kenneth R Koedinger, and Ray Pelletier. 1995. Cognitive tutors: Lessons learned. *The Journal of the learning sciences* 4, 2 (1995), 167–207.

[3] Ryan Baker, Albert Corbett, and Vincent Aleven. 2008. More Accurate Student Modeling through Contextual Estimation of Slip and Guess Probabilities in Bayesian Knowledge Tracing. In *International Conference on Intelligent Tutoring Systems.* Springer, 406–415.

[4] Peter Brusilovsky. 1992. Intelligent Tutor, Environment and Manual for Introductory Programming. *Educational and Training Technology International* 29, 1 (1992), 26–34.

[5] Peter Brusilovsky, Charalampos Karagiannidis, and Demetrios Sampson. 2004. Layered evaluation of adaptive learning systems. *International Journal of Continuing Engineering Education and Lifelong Learning* 14, 4/5 (2004), 402 – 421.

[6] Cristina Carmona, Eva Millán, José-Luis Pérez-de-la Cruz, Mónica Trella, and Ricardo Conejo. 2005. Introducing prerequisite relations in a multi-layered Bayesian student model. In *International Conference on User Modeling.* Springer, 347–356.

[7] David Chin. 2001. Empirical Evaluations of User Models and User-Adapted Systems. *User Modeling and User-Adapted Interaction* 11, 1-2 (2001), 181–194.

[8] Jason Collins, Jim Greer, and Sherman Huang. 1996. Adaptive assessment using granularity hierarchies and Bayesian nets. In *Intelligent Tutoring Systems.* Springer, 569–577.

[9] Cristina Conati, Abigail Gertner, and Kurt Vanlehn. 2002. Using Bayesian Networks to Manage Uncertainty in Student Modeling. *User Modeling and User-Adapted Interaction* 12, 4 (2002), 371–417.

[10] Albert T Corbett and John R Anderson. 1995. Knowledge tracing: Modeling the acquisition of procedural knowledge. *User Modeling and User-Adapted Interaction* 4, 4 (1995), 253–278.

[11] Michel C Desmarais and Ryan S Baker. 2012. A review of recent advances in learner and skill modeling in intelligent learning environments. *User Modeling and User-Adapted Interaction* 22, 1-2 (2012), 9–38.

[12] Marek J Druzdzel. 1999. SMILE: Structural Modeling, Inference, and Learning Engine and GeNIe: a development environment for graphical decision-theoretic models. In *Proceedings of the Sixteenth National Conference on Artificial Intelligence (AAAI-99).* 902–903.

[13] D. J. Gilmore and T. R. G. Green. 1988. Programming plans and programming expertise. *The Quarterly Journal of Experimental Psychology Section A* 40, 3 (1988), 423–442.

[14] Yue Gong, Joseph E Beck, and Neil T Heffernan. 2010. Comparing knowledge tracing and performance factor analysis by using multiple model fitting procedures. In *Intelligent Tutoring Systems.* Springer, 35–44.

[15] José P González-Brenes and Yun Huang. 2015. Your model is predictive – but is it useful? theoretical and empirical considerations of a new paradigm for adaptive tutoring evaluation. In *Proc. 8th Intl. Conf. Educational Data Mining.* 187–194.

[16] José P González-Brenes, Yun Huang, and Peter Brusilovsky. 2014. General features in knowledge tracing: Applications to multiple subskills, temporal item response theory, and expert knowledge. In *Proc. 7th Int. Conf. Educational Data Mining.* 84–91.

[17] Neil T. Heffernan and Kenneth R. Koedinger. 1997. The composition effect in symbolizing: The role of symbol production vs. text comprehension. In *the Nineteenth Annual Conference of the Cognitive Science Society.* Lawrence Erlbaum Associates, 307–312.

[18] Roya Hosseini and Peter Brusilovsky. 2013. JavaParser: A Fine-Grained Concept Indexing Tool for Java Problems. In *The First Workshop on AI-supported Education for Computer Science (AIEDCS).*

[19] I-H Hsiao, Sergey Sosnovsky, and Peter Brusilovsky. 2010. Guiding students to the right questions: adaptive navigation support in an E-Learning system for Java programming. *Journal of Computer Assisted Learning* 26, 4 (2010), 270–283.

[20] Yun Huang, José P González-Brenes, Rohit Kumar, and Peter Brusilovsky. 2015. A framework for multifaceted evaluation of student models. In *Proc. 8th Int. Conf. Educational Data Mining.* 203–210.

[21] Yun Huang, Julio Guerra, and Peter Brusilovsky. 2016. Modeling skill combination patterns for deeper knowledge tracing. In *Proceedings of the 6th Workshop on Personalization Approaches in Learning Environments (PALE 2016).*

[22] W. Lewis Johnson and Elliot Soloway. 1985. PROUST: Knowledge-Based Program Understanding. *IEEE Transactions on Software Engineering* 11, 3 (1985), 267–275.

[23] Brian W Junker and Klaas Sijtsma. 2001. Cognitive assessment models with few assumptions, and connections with nonparametric item response theory. *Applied Psychological Measurement* 25, 3 (2001), 258–272.

[24] Tanja Käser, Severin Klingler, Alexander Gerhard Schwing, and Markus Gross. 2014. Beyond knowledge tracing: Modeling skill topologies with bayesian networks. In *International Conference on Intelligent Tutoring Systems.* Springer, 188–198.

[25] Kenneth R Koedinger, Albert T Corbett, and Charles Perfetti. 2012. The Knowledge-Learning-Instruction framework: Bridging the science-practice chasm to enhance robust student learning. *Cognitive science* 36, 5 (2012), 757–798.

[26] Kenneth R Koedinger, Philip I Pavlik Jr, John C Stamper, Tristan Nixon, and Steven Ritter. 2011. Avoiding Problem Selection Thrashing with Conjunctive Knowledge Tracing. In *Educational Data Mining.* 91–100.

[27] Amruth N. Kumar. A Scalable Solution for Adaptive Problem Sequencing and its Evaluation. In *4th International Conference on Adaptive Hypermedia and Adaptive Web-Based Systems (AH'2006).* Springer Verlag, 161–171.

[28] Daniël Lakens. 2013. Calculating and reporting effect sizes to facilitate cumulative science: a practical primer for t-tests and ANOVAs. *Frontiers in psychology* 4 (2013), 863.

[29] Jung In Lee and Emma Brunskill. 2012. The Impact on Individualizing Student Models on Necessary Practice Opportunities. In *Proceedings of the 5th International Conference on Educational Data Mining.* www.educationaldatamining.org, 118–125.

[30] Chee-Kit Looi. 1991. Automatic debugging of Prolog programs in a Prolog intelligent tutoring system. *Instructional Science* 20, 2 (1991), 215–263.

[31] Michael Mayo and Antonija Mitrovic. 2001. Optimising ITS behaviour with Bayesian networks and decision theory. *International Journal of Artificial Intelligence in Education* (2001), 124–153.

[32] Eva Millán and José Luis Pérez-De-La-Cruz. 2002. A Bayesian diagnostic algorithm for student modeling and its evaluation. *User Modeling and User-Adapted Interaction* 12, 2-3 (2002), 281–330.

[33] Robert J Mislevy and Drew H Gitomer. 1995. The role of probability-based inference in an intelligent tutoring system. *ETS Research Report Series* 1995, 2 (1995).

[34] Antonija Mitrovic, Michael Mayo, Pramuditha Suraweera, and Brent Martin. 2001. Constraint-based tutors: a success story. In *International Conference on Industrial, Engineering and Other Applications of Applied Intelligent Systems.* Springer, 931–940.

[35] Rafael Morales, Nicolas Van Labeke, and Paul Brna. 2006. Approximate modelling of the multi-dimensional learner. In *Intelligent Tutoring Systems.* Springer, 555–564.

[36] William R. Murray. 1985. Heuristic and formal methods in automatic program debugging. In *9-th International Joint Conference on Artificial Intelligence.* 15–19.

[37] Alexandros Paramythis and Stephan Weibelzahl. 2005. A Decomposition Model for the Layered Evaluation of Interactive Adaptive Systems. In *10th International User Modeling Conference,* Vol. 3538. Springer Verlag, 438–442.

[38] Zachary A Pardos and Neil T Heffernan. 2010. Navigating the parameter space of Bayesian Knowledge Tracing models: Visualizations of the convergence of the Expectation Maximization algorithm. *Educational Data Mining* 2010 (2010), 161–170.

[39] Radek Pelanek. 2015. Metrics for Evaluation of Student Models. *Journal of Educational Data Mining* 7, 2 (2015), 1–19.

[40] Robert Rosenthal, H Cooper, and LV Hedges. 1994. Parametric measures of effect size. *The handbook of research synthesis* (1994), 231–244.

[41] Elliot Soloway and Kate Ehrlich. 1984. Empirical Studies of Programming Knowledge. *IEEE Trans. Software Engineering* SE-10, 5 (1984), 595–609.

[42] Brett van De Sande. 2013. Properties of the bayesian knowledge tracing model. *JEDM-Journal of Educational Data Mining* 5, 2 (2013), 1–10.

[43] Kurt Vanlehn, Collin Lynch, Kay Schulze, Joel A Shapiro, Robert Shelby, Linwood Taylor, Don Treacy, Anders Weinstein, and Mary Wintersgill. 2005. The Andes physics tutoring system: Lessons learned. *International Journal of Artificial Intelligence in Education* 15, 3 (2005), 147–204.

[44] Kurt VanLehn, Zhendong Niu, Stephanie Siler, and Abigail S Gertner. 1998. Student modeling from conventional test data: A Bayesian approach without priors. In *International Conference on Intelligent Tutoring Systems.* Springer, 434–443.

[45] Gerhard Weber. 1996. Episodic learner modeling. *Cognitive Science* 20, 2 (1996), 195–236.

[46] Gerhard Weber. 1996. Individual selection of examples in an intelligent learning environment. *Journal of Artificial Intelligence in Education* 7, 1 (1996), 3–31.

[47] Yanbo Xu and Jack Mostow. 2012. Comparison of methods to trace multiple subskills: Is LR-DBN best?. In *Proc. 5th Intl. Conf. Educational Data Mining.* 41–48.

Out of the Fr-"Eye"-ing Pan

Towards Gaze-Based Models of Attention during Learning with Technology in the Classroom

Stephen Hutt[1], Caitlin Mills[2], Nigel Bosch[3], Kristina Krasich[1], James Brockmole[1], Sidney D'Mello[1]

[1]University of Notre Dame, [2]University of British Columbia, [3]University of Illinois at Urbana-Champaign

{shutt|sdmello}@nd.edu

ABSTRACT

Attention is critical to learning. Hence, advanced learning technologies should benefit from mechanisms to monitor and respond to learners' attentional states. We study the feasibility of integrating commercial off-the-shelf (COTS) eye trackers to monitor attention during interactions with a learning technology called GuruTutor. We tested our implementation on 135 students in a noisy computer-enabled high school classroom and were able to collect a median 95% valid eye gaze data in 85% of the sessions where gaze data was successfully recorded. Machine learning methods were employed to develop automated detectors of mind wandering (MW) – a phenomenon involving a shift in attention from task-related to task-unrelated thoughts that is negatively correlated with performance. Our student-independent, gaze-based models could detect MW with an accuracy (F_1 of MW = 0.59) significantly greater than chance (F_1 of MW = 0.24). Predicted rates of mind wandering were negatively related to posttest performance, providing evidence for the predictive validity of the detector. We discuss next steps towards developing gaze-based, attention-aware, learning technologies that can be deployed in noisy, real-world environments.

Author Keywords

eye-gaze; cyberlearning; intelligent tutoring systems; mind wandering; attention-aware learning

1 INTRODUCTION

Imagine you are tutoring a student in cell biology only to realize that the student has completely "zoned out." Although the plan is for the two of you to collaboratively explain osmosis, the student's attention has drifted to unrelated thoughts of lunch, the football game, or an upcoming vacation. You might try to momentarily reorient his or her attention by asking a probing question. However, if attentional focus continues to wane, you realize that you must adapt your instruction to better engage the student. You might re-engage attention by switching topics or even suggesting a break, thereby giving the student an opportunity to recharge. This

form of dynamic adaptivity was only possible because you had the ability to continually monitor your student's levels of attentional focus, to detect when their attention, and to adapt your instruction to address attentional lapses as they occurred.

The attention-awareness capabilities exhibited in the example are beyond the radar of current educational technologies that are largely unaware of users' attentional states. It is important that we address this gap because it is widely acknowledged that attention is crucial for effective learning. Cognitive processes such as prior knowledge activation, inference generation and comprehension all demand attentional resources [23, 31, 54]. Students who are unable to sustain attentional focus are more likely to engage in self-distracting and other unproductive behaviors [19], which leads to superficial understanding as opposed to deep comprehension.

Accordingly, our goal is to develop learning technologies that model a user's attentional state and can respond accordingly as a means to improve attentional focus and learning outcomes [16]. As an initial step in this direction, we focus on mind wandering (MW), the attentional shift from task-related processing towards internal task-unrelated thoughts [57]. In the context of learning, both lab and field studies have consistently reported MW rates in the 20%-50% range [39, 48, 49, 61, 62]. Although individual differences in trait-level MW have been shown to be positively correlated with creative problem solving and prospective planning [37], a recent meta-analysis of 88 independent samples indicated a negative correlation between MW and performance across a variety of tasks [44]. MW negatively impacts a learner's ability to attend to external events [50, 56], to encode information into memory [53], and to comprehend learning materials [18, 52, 56]. Hence, MW is generally found to be detrimental to learning outcomes.

MW is related to other forms of disengagement, such as boredom, behavioral disengagement, and off-task behaviors [2, 3, 32, 36, 65], it is inherently distinct because it involves internal thoughts rather than overt expressive behaviors. This raises two challenges. First, while other disengaged behaviors often involve detectable behavioral markers (e.g., yawns signaling boredom), MW is an internal state that can be difficult to distinguish from being on-task [57]. Secondly, because MW can occur outside of conscious awareness the onset and duration of MW remains an open question [58].

Despite these challenges, there has been some progress toward automatic detection of MW (discussed further in Related Works section). Eye tracking is an attractive technique for detecting attentional states like MW due to decades of scientific evidence in support of an *eye-mind link* that suggests a tight coupling between attentional states and eye movements [13, 27, 46]. Until recently, the cost of research-grade eye trackers has limited the applicability of eye tracking in real-world environments at scale. However the recent introduction of consumer off-the-shelf (COTS) eye trackers (retailing for \$100 to \$150) has ushered forth an exciting era by affording the application of decades of lab-based research on eye gaze, attention, and learning to real-world classrooms, thereby affording new discoveries about how students learn, and designing innovations to sustain attention during learning.

1.1 Novelty

There are three novel aspects to this work. First, it is currently unknown whether COTS eye trackers can be implemented with sufficient fidelity in noisy classroom settings so as to afford collection of actionable gaze data. We address this challenge by tracking gaze while high-school students learn biology, as part of their biology class, with GuruTutor (or Guru) [40, 41], an intelligent tutoring system (ITS) with conversational dialogues (see Figure 1). We show, for the first time, that it is feasible to use COTS eye trackers to collect valid data from entire classes of students in the real-world context of an uncontrolled classroom environment.

Second, we demonstrate that the gaze data collected is of sufficient fidelity to detect a critical form of attentional lapses, specifically MW. Previous work has shown that MW can be detected using eye tracking in Guru [28] (discussed further in Related Work section), but this was done using data collected in a very controlled lab environment. We investigate how detectors developed using similar supervised machine learning methods perform on data collected in a more noisy and complex environment.

Third, the previous study on gaze-based MW detection with Guru [28] used *global* gaze features. These features encode general eye movements (e.g., number of gaze fixations) and are independent of what is displayed on the screen. In the context of Guru, eye gaze on specific areas of interest might be of importance for MW detection due to the dynamically changing visual display (see Figure 1). Accordingly, we investigate whether there are added advantages to utilizing a new set of *locality* features that are sensitive to gaze on specific locations on the screen.

1.2 Related Work

The idea of attention-aware user interfaces was proposed almost a decade ago [51], including for education contexts [45]. Prior to this, [22] discussed the use of eye tracking to increase the bandwidth of information available to an ITS in an aptly titled paper "Broader Bandwidth in Student Modeling: What if ITS Were "Eye" TS?" Similarly, [1] followed up on some of these ideas by demonstrating how particular beneficial instructional strategies could only be launched via a real-time analysis of eye gaze. Most of the recent work on leveraging eye gaze to increase the bandwidth of learner models has been pioneered by Conati and colleagues [8, 11, 12, 29, 30, 38] .

Conati et al. [11] provide an excellent review of much of the existing work in this area. We can group the research into three categories: (1) offline-analyses of eye gaze to understand attentional processes, (2) modeling of attentional states, and (3) closed-loop systems that respond to attention in real-time. Offline-analysis of eye movements has enjoyed considerable attention in cognitive psychology, and educational psychology for several decades (e.g. [24, 26, 33, 38, 43]). However, online models of learner

attention are just beginning to emerge (e.g. [5–8, 12, 17, 30]). Closed-loop attention-aware systems are few and far between (for a more or less exhaustive list see [15, 22, 55, 64]).

MW detection is related to attentional state modeling as both entail identifying the focus of a user's attention. However, MW is inherently different from other forms of attention (i.e., fatigue, distractibility, object-of focus) because the eyes might be fixated on the appropriate external stimulus, but very little is being processed. To date, MW has rarely been considered as an aspect of a user's state that warrants detection and corrective action (but see recent work by [14, 42]). As such, automated approaches to detect MW in near real-time are in their infancy [17, 20].

Eye movements offer a promising methodology for automatically detecting MW due to well-known relationships between visual attention and the locus of eye gaze. For example, MW has been associated with longer fixation durations [47] as well as more blinking during reading [59]. Researchers have recently leveraged these relationships to build gaze-based MW detectors during reading [4, 6]. In these studies, MW was measured via pseudo-random thought probes that were interspersed during the reading process. Supervised classification models were successful in discriminating between "yes" and "no" responses to the probes using eye gaze features and were validated in a manner that generalized to new students.

Gaze-based MW detection has also been applied to more complex visual stimuli, such as film viewing [34]. In this study, participants viewed a 32.5-minute film and reported when they caught themselves MW. Supervised learning models were built using both global and locality gaze features (defined above). Locality features were superior in terms of predicting MW, ostensibly due to their sensitivity to the dynamic content being displayed on the screen.

Of particular relevance is a previous lab study on detecting MW during learning with Guru, the same ITS we explore here [28]. Students' eye gaze was tracked with a Tobii EyeX (another COTS eye tracker) as they completed a 30-40 minute learning session with Guru. Students reported MW by responding to pseudo-random thought probes throughout the session. A variety of supervised classification models were trained to detect MW from global gaze features alone, achieving person-independent accuracies that were substantially greater than chance.

All current work on gaze-based MW detection, such as the reading studies [4, 6], the film study [34] and ITS study [28] have been limited to using training data collected in the laboratory. Laboratory environments have the advantage of relatively consistent lighting and freedom from distractions from other students, cell phones, ambient sounds, and numerous other factors. In contrast, we consider the possibility of building MW detectors from eye-gaze data collected in the noisy real-world context of a computer-enabled classroom. In contrast to the lab, students in our study were subject to all the usual distractions of a high school classroom, which makes the data far noisier.

2 IMPLEMENTATION

Our implementation involves integrating eye tracking into an ITS called GuruTutor.

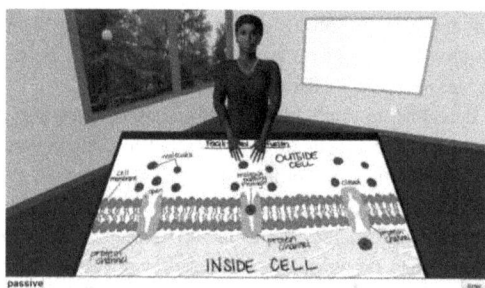

Figure 1. Screenshot of Guru in the CGB phase

2.1 Guru Tutor

GuruTutor (Guru) is an ITS designed to teach biology topics through collaborative conversations in natural language. It was modeled after interactions with expert human tutors and has been shown to be effective at promoting learning and retention at levels similar to human tutors [40].

Guru engages the student through natural language conversations, using an animated tutor agent that references a multimedia workspace (see Figure 1). The tutor communicates via synthesized speech and gestures, while students communicate by typing responses, which are analyzed using natural language processing techniques. Guru maintains a student model [60] throughout the session, which it uses to tailor instruction to individual students.

Guru teaches introductory biology topics (e.g., osmosis; protein function) in line with state curriculum standards in short sessions, typically lasting 15 to 40 minutes. Each topic involves interrelated concepts and facts. Guru begins with a basic introduction to motivate the topic, which is then followed by a five-phase session that develops students' understanding of the topic. The five phases are described below. **Common-Ground-Building (CGB) Instruction.** Biology lessons often involve specialized terminology that needs to be understood before it is possible to move on to deeper knowledge building activities. Therefore, Guru begins with a collaborative lecture phase that covers basic information and terminology relevant to the topic. **Intermittent Summaries (Summary).** Following CGB, students construct their own natural language summaries of the material covered in CGB. These summaries are automatically analyzed to determine which concepts require further tutoring in the remainder of the session. **Concept Maps.** For the target concepts, students complete skeleton concept maps, node-link structures that are automatically generated from text (see Figure 2). **Scaffolded Dialogue.** Next, students complete a scaffolded natural language dialogue in which Guru uses a Prompt $\rightarrow$ Feedback $\rightarrow$ Verification Question $\rightarrow$ Feedback $\rightarrow$ Elaboration cycle to cover target concepts. If a student shows difficulty mastering particular concepts, a second Concept Maps phase is initiated followed by an additional Scaffolded Dialogue phase. **Cloze Task.** The session concludes with a cloze task requiring students to complete an ideal summary of the topic by filling in missing information by retrieving it from memory

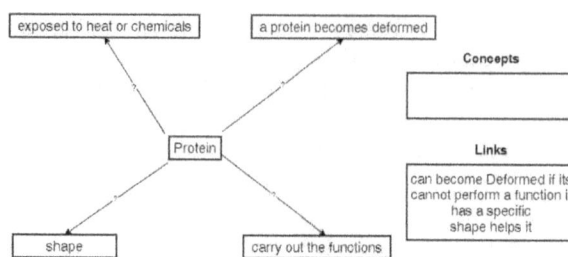

Figure 2. Example Concept Map

2.2 Integrating Eye Tracking in Guru

Our first task was to integrate eye tracking into Guru. In line with the goals of the project, we chose a COTS eye-tracker called the EyeTribe that retails for $99. The eye tracker was affixed to a laptop computer just below the screen.

Our goal was to facilitate eye tracker setup and calibration by the students themselves. This was accomplished via on-screen instructions that included a mixture of images, interactive tools, and text directions. The instructions first guided students on positioning using live feedback, followed by information on the calibration process itself. This is followed by a nine-point calibration process, where nine points appear on the screen in turn and students fixate on each until it disappears.

2.3 Iterative Testing & Refinement

We completed several testing and refinement cycles to improve the implementation to be as user friendly and autonomous as possible. Laboratory participants were compensated with research credit, while classroom participants were compensated with a $10 gift card. Students provided written assent while their parents provided written consent prior to participating in the study, which was approved by the University's Institutional Review Board and the principal of the school.

Lab Testing

The software was initially tested in the lab on individual students. Undergraduate students who had not used the software before were asked to follow the calibration instructions and complete a session on one biology topic with Guru. The setup process was observed and pain-points were noted. The students were then interviewed about their experience with the system. Insights gleaned from this testing were used to improve the clarity of the on-screen instructions and increase the level of feedback that users receive during the eye tracker calibration process.

Individual Testing in School – 9 Participants

Initial testing of the implementation was done in after-school sessions with high-school student volunteers. Students completed the eye tracking setup along with one Guru session. Each student was observed by a researcher, who noted incidents and recorded student questions. After the session, students were interviewed about the software, including how easy it was to use, how well they understood what they needed to do, and whether they understood why they were doing each step. This informed our development of the software and streamlined the on-screen instructions, providing additional help as needed.

Small Group Testing in School – 7 Participants

As a step towards testing with entire classes of students, we tested the implementation with a group of seven student volunteers after school. Students were given instructions as a group and then interviewed individually once they had completed the session. This allowed us to identify issues with scaling of the software that might arise when working with full classes of students. As a result, we further improved the instructions and addressed other technological challenges.

Classroom Pilot – 35 Participants

The final stage of the iterative development process was a classroom pilot using the specific classroom used for main data collection. We piloted with two class periods during students' regular biology classes. A key observation at this stage was the range of times it took students to complete a Guru session, which had not been as apparent in previous iterations. Students finished the session up to twenty minutes apart, which poses challenges as these students could be sources of distraction for others.

With respect to usability, the overall conclusion was that the students could independently complete the setup and calibration process via the on-screen instructions. In other words, they could use the Guru implementation with minimal guidance from the researchers and the resultant eye gaze was deemed sufficiently valid for larger-scale data collection. One final development was a seating position check and potential recalibration of the eye tracker halfway through the session, in case head position had changed considerably.

2.4 Main Data Collection in Classroom

Students were 9th and 10th graders enrolled in a Biology 1 class. We collected data from 135 students (41% male) over the course of two school days in students' regular biology classroom. Students were compensated with a $10 gift card for their participation in the study.

Students had biology class on alternating days, so the two days of data collection included different students. Each class period consisted of an introduction to the software, 30 minutes of completing a biology session using Guru, a short break, and another 30-minute Guru session on a different biology topic. The following topics were included in the study: Protein Function, Carbohydrate Function, Osmosis, Interphase, Facilitated Diffusion and Biochemical Catalysts, with students randomly assigned a topic (except that they could not get the same topic for both sessions). The classroom layout remained unchanged from the setup used for standard teaching, with the addition of two laptops per desk. The laptops were provided by the high school. Each laptop had an eye tracker affixed below the screen. Class sizes ranged from 14 to 30 students based on regular enrollment. Two researchers were present during data collection to answer procedural questions from students and address any hardware or software issues they encountered.

2.5 Eye Tracking Validity

The majority of students were able to use the software, including eye tracker calibration, without any intervention from the experimenters. However, running the software for a full day presented new challenges. Over the course of the two days, there was the potential to collect 270 sessions as each of the 135 students completed two sessions. The software was completely successful (students able to run through a Guru session and we collected gaze data with no issues) for 85% of the sessions. The following is a breakdown of the causes for the 15% missing sessions: (1) Hardware failure: some of the computers had incorrect drivers for the USB 3.0 ports, preventing the functionality of the eye tracker. (2) Background processes: several computers attempted to automatically update during the session, causing an increased load on the processor which caused the software to occasionally crash. (3) Calibration failure: students who failed calibration three times continued without eye tracking.

The eye tracker records a validity for each sample based on number of eyes tracked and the quality of the tracking. We considered a valid sample to include at least one eye tracked. Figure 3 shows a histogram of percent of valid gaze points per session. Of the 85% of sessions where eye tracking was collected, we observed a median validity rate of 95% per session (mean was 89%). We consider this promising given the difficulties presented by the relatively unconstrained classroom environment, where students were free to fidget, look around the room, and even occasionally laid their heads on the table as they interacted with Guru. If we enforce a stricter validity threshold of both eyes tracked, mean validity drops to 71%, median to 75%, still promising scores.

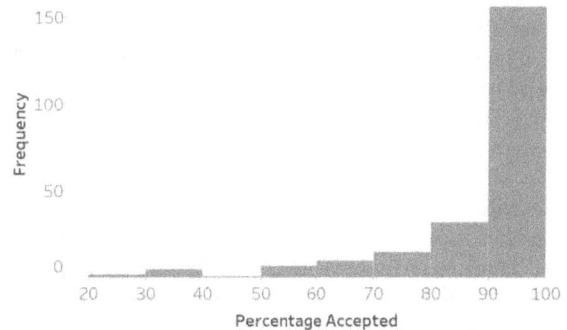

Figure 3. Histogram showing gaze validity rate per session where eye tracking was recorded

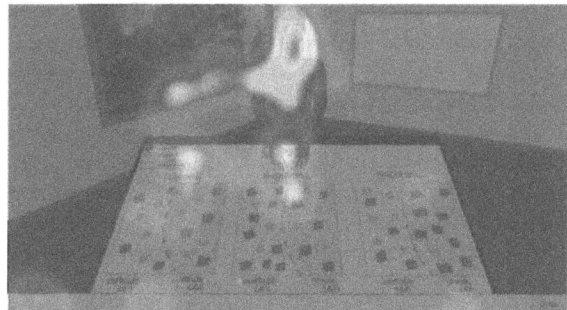

Figure 4. Heatmap overlay showing participants eye gaze in CCB phase. Red indicates high concentration of fixations, purple low concentration of fixations

Figure 4 shows an example heatmap from the CGB phase for one participant, illustrating gaze concentration. We note the largest concentration of gaze on the tutor's face and upper body, followed by the multimedia panel, and the response box (on the bottom). Visualizing several such heatmaps served as a good initial check for the quality of eye gaze. Our overall conclusion was that we were able to track eye gaze with a reasonable accuracy when small groups of students used a COTS eye trackers in a noisy real-world environment.

3 MIND WANDERING DETECTION

Our next step was to leverage the eye gaze data to build automated mind wandering (MW) detectors. We adopted a supervised learning approach, which required labeled data, collected using thought probes.

3.1 Thought Probes

Mind wandering was measured during learning with Guru using auditory thought probes, which is a standard approach in the literature [56]. MW was first defined to the participants. Instructions and MW reporting procedure were extensively tested and refined in the preliminary studies described above. Participants were required to demonstrate understanding of how to respond to the thought probes (via multiple choice questions and feedback) before proceeding.

Participants were probed at pseudo-random intervals with probes occurring every 90-120 seconds, based on previously observed MW rates in Guru [35]. The probes automatically paused the tutoring session. If the tutor was speaking at the time the probe was to be triggered, the probe was delayed until the tutor finished speaking. The probe consisted of an auditory beep along with an opaque overlay on screen, instructing the participant to press the "N" key if they were not mind wandering, "I" if they were intentionally (deliberately) mind wandering, or "U" if they were unintentionally (spontaneously) mind wandering. In this study, we do not differentiate between intentional and unintentional mind wandering, so both "I" and "U" responses were considered MW. Participants encountered an average of 12 probes over the course of each session with a mean MW rate of 28% (SD = 24%, Min = 0%, Max = 100%).

It is important to emphasize a few points about the method used to track MW. First, this method relies on self-reports because MW is an inherently conscious phenomenon, which requires self-awareness for reporting [58]. Second, self-reports of MW have been objectively linked to patterns in pupillometry [21], eye-gaze [47], and task performance [44], providing validity for this approach. However, at this time, there are no reliable neurophysiological or behavioral markers that can accurately substitute for the self-report methodology [58]. Indeed, this is the very reason we set out to build objective gaze-based MW detectors. The limits of thought probes are considered further in the Discussion section. Our use of thought-probes to measure MW is consistent with the state of the art in the psychological and neuroscience literatures [58].

3.2 Feature Engineering

We calculated features from 30-second windows (window size was based on previous work [4, 28]) preceding each auditory probe. We investigated two types of gaze features: global gaze (from previous work [28]) as well as a new set of locality features. Global gaze features focus on general gaze patterns and are independent of the content on the screen, whereas locality features encode where gaze is fixated. We also considered a set of context features to encode information from the session.

Global Gaze Features. Eye movements were measured by fixations (i.e., points in which gaze was maintained on the same location) and saccades (i.e., the movement of the eyes between fixations). We calculated fixations and saccades from the raw eye gaze data using the Open Gaze and Mouse Analyzer (OGAMA) [63]. We considered six general measures across the 30-second window (bolded in Table 1), from which we computed the number, mean, median, minimum, maximum, standard deviation, range, kurtosis, and skew of the distributions, yielding 54 features. We also included three other features (see Table 1), yielding a total of 57 global gaze features.

Table 1. Eye-gaze features. Bolded cell indicates that nine descriptives (e.g., mean) were used as features (see Text)

Feature	Description
Fixation Duration	Elapsed time in ms of fixation
Saccade Duration	Elapsed time in ms of saccade
Saccade Length	Distance of saccade in pixels
Saccade Angle Absolute	Angle in degrees between the x-axis and the saccade
Saccade Angle Relative	Angle of the saccade relative to previous gaze point.
Saccade Velocity	Saccade Length / Saccade Duration
Fixation Dispersion	Root mean square of the distances of each fixation to the average fixation position
Horizontal Saccade Proportion	Proportion of saccades with relative angles <= 30 degrees above or below the horizontal axis
Fixation Saccade Ratio	Ratio of fixation duration to saccade duration

Locality Gaze Features. In contrast to the global features, the locality features were based on locality of gaze. Specifically, a 10 × 8 grid was overlaid on the screen. Each cell represented a feature and was assigned a weight proportional to the number of gaze fixations on that corresponding location (see Figure 5). In addition to these 80 locality features, we included an additional "out of bounds" feature that encoded the proportion of fixations that were off the screen bounds.

Context Features. The gaze features were complemented by eight features that provide a snapshot of the student-tutor interaction. One feature was the assigned biology *topic*. A second encoded participants' *pretest* scores. The next three features represented participants' progress within Guru, such as the *current phase* of the session (e.g., cloze, concept map), the amount of elapsed *time into the session*, and the amount of elapsed *time into the current phase*. The last three features focused on participants' performance within Guru, measured as the proportion of *positive*, *neutral*, and *negative* feedback received.

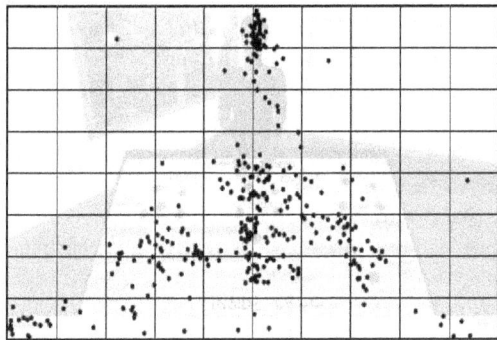

Figure 5. Example grid used for locality features, the count of fixations in each cell becomes a feature

3.3 Classification Models and Validation

We focused on Bayesian Networks because they yielded the best performance compared to several other standard classifiers on this task in our previous work [28]. We used the default implementation from the Weka data mining package [25].

In total, there were 2,720 probes during the Guru sessions. Of those, 386 were discarded due to insufficient eye gaze data (< 1 fixation) in the respective window to compute any of the global features, ostensibly due to students looking away from the screen, chatting with a neighbor, or closing their eyes. The remaining 2,334 instances were used across all feature sets to ensure a fair comparison. Features that could not be computed (e.g. distribution features when there is only one fixation) were treated by the models as missing data and values were imputed based on the training set.

We validated the models with a leave-several-participants-out cross-validation scheme. For each fold, instances from a random 66% of the participants were assigned to a training set and the instances of the remaining 33% participants were assigned to a test set. This process ensures that no instances of any individual participant could appear in both the training and test sets within a fold. This process was repeated for 15 folds and the results were accumulated before computing accuracy metrics.

Students reported MW in 23% of the 2,334 instances, giving a substantial data skew. Class imbalance poses a challenge as supervised learning methods tend to bias predications towards the majority class label. To compensate for this concern, we used the SMOTE algorithm [9] to create synthetic instances of the minority class by interpolating feature values between an instance and its randomly chosen nearest neighbors until the classes were equated. SMOTE was *only applied on the training sets*; the original class distributions were maintained in the testing sets in order to ensure validity of the results.

3.4 Results

The classification results are shown in Table 2. Because our intention is to detect instances of MW, we focus on the precision, recall, and F_1 score of the MW class as our key metric. This is a strict evaluation criterion as the base rate of MW is only 23% in our data. For comparison, a chance-level baseline was created by

randomly assigning the MW label to 23% of the instances and computing accuracy accordingly.

Table 2. MW detection results for school data

Feature Set	F_1 MW	Precision MW	Recall MW
Global	0.59	0.55	0.65
Locality	0.59	0.51	0.70
Context (Cntxt)	0.49	0.58	0.43
Global + Locality	0.46	0.51	0.41
Global + Context	0.53	0.51	0.53
Locality + Context	0.49	0.59	0.42
Global + Locality + Cntxt	0.44	0.53	0.38
Chance	*0.24*	*0.22*	*0.26*

The results indicated that: (1) all models substantially outperformed the chance-baseline; (2) both global and locality models had similar F_1 MW scores, but slightly different precision and recall scores; (3) the combined global + locality model had (surprisingly) lower performance than either feature set alone; and (4) adding context to the individual models did not result in any improvement; if anything it reduced classification accuracy.

Proportionalized confusion matrices for the gaze-based models are shown in Table 3. We note that the errors for global and locality models were skewed towards false positives (vs. misses), which would explain the higher recall with respect to the Global + Locality model, we saw a higher proportion of misses, which would explain its lower recall score.

Locality features relate to spatial location of gaze, however, each phase of Guru had different screen content (e.g., Figure 1 vs. Figure 2). To examine if this caused bias against locality features, we compared global vs. locality models for the Common Ground Building phase - the only phase with enough data to build phase-specific models. The number of available instances was reduced to 1,259 (from 2,334) and MW rate increased to 30%. Classification results are shown in Table 4, where we note no substantial differences compared to the phase-independent models shown in Table 2, assuaging concerns of bias.

Table 3. Confusion matrices for gaze-based models

Actual Global	Predicted MW	Not MW
MW	0.65 (hit)	0.35 (miss)
Not MW	0.52 (false pos.)	0.48 (correct rej.)
Locality	MW	Not MW
MW	0.70 (hit)	0.30 (miss)
Not MW	0.56 (false pos.)	0.44 (correct rej.)
Global + Locality	MW	Not MW
MW	0.41 (hit)	0.59 (miss)
Not MW	0.31 (false pos.)	0.69 (correct rej.)

To further explore the validity of our detector we investigated whether predicted MW was related to posttest performance in the same way reported MW was. Participant-level *reported* MW rate was negatively correlated with posttest score ($rho = -.189$ $p = .058$) while *predicted* MW was also negatively correlated with posttest for detectors built with both the Global ($rho = -.112$, $p = .269$) and Locality ($rho = -.177$, $p = .076$) feature sets.

Table 4. Models built for CGB phase

Feature Set	F_1 of MW	Precision of MW	Recall of MW
Global	0.59	0.55	0.64
Local	0.61	0.58	0.65
Global + Local	0.44	0.54	0.37

Feature Analysis

We compared the global gaze features across instances of MW versus not MW to characterize the differences in gaze during MW. Cohen's d, an effect size measure, was used to assess the direction and magnitude of the differences between the two classes [10]. For each class (MW and Not MW) the average for each feature across instances was computed. Cohen's d was computed by calculating the difference of each feature across MW and Not MW divided by the pooled standard deviation. Positive d values for a feature indicate higher values for instances of MW compared to instances of Not MW. Twenty (out of 57) of the effect sizes observed are consistent with small effects, using the convention that .2, .5, and .8 for small, medium, and large effects respectfully [10] the remaining effect sizes were less than .2 suggesting that no one feature dominated, but that a combination was needed for MW detection.

To establish which features contributed most to MW detection, the ten largest effect sizes were ranked in terms of their absolute Cohen's d. Fewer fixations ($d = -.41$) and saccades ($d = -.40$) (which are by definition highly correlated) were found for MW, and fixations were more dispersed ($d = .23$). Differences in median and mean saccade velocity ($d = -.33$, $d = -.32$ respectively), range of saccade angles ($d = -.26$), mean saccade duration ($d = .24$), maximum saccade angle ($d = -.24$), maximum and median saccade duration ($d = .23$, $d = .22$ respectively) suggest that saccades were slower, longer and covered a smaller range of angles during MW. These findings are consistent with previous work on eye gaze surrounding MW in reading, which also found number of fixations to be predictive [4], highlighting consistent differences in eye gaze features across learning tasks. These effects suggest that during MW, students focus on fewer points on the screen for a longer time. In addition, the effects for saccade duration and fixation dispersion suggest that these points are likely to be more spread around the screen rather than focusing in on information or visual stimulus such as diagrams.

4. GENERAL DISCUSSION

It is widely acknowledged that attention is necessary for learning [39]. An attention-aware learning technology [16, 42] that can monitor and react to a student's attentional state could assuage the cost of attentional failures (like MW), thereby improving learning. However, until now, the high cost of eye trackers (which are the most robust method to track visual attention) has relegated these

technologies to the confines of the lab. We addressed this issue in the current paper by studying the feasibility of using COTS eye trackers in a real world classroom environment.

4.1 Main Findings

We have shown that, although the classroom provides a noisier environment than the lab, it is still feasible to collect valid eye tracking data with COTS eye trackers. Further, to maintain ecological validity, students were relatively unconstrained and independent in our study. We did give initial guidance with respect to seating position for calibration, however students were free to fidget, move, and behave as they would in a classroom. Despite this, we were able to achieve a median gaze validity of 95%. This is for the students where the gaze was collected at all. We were unable to collect data for 15% of sessions, however, this was primarily for reasons beyond our control (e.g., hardware issues with school computers and auto update).

Validity, however, does not imply usefulness. To address this, we built person-independent MW detectors based on the gaze data collected in the classroom. Our main finding was that our models were moderately accurate at detecting MW in a person-independent fashion despite the numerous challenges involved, such as class imbalance, noisy gaze data, and unrestricted movements. Importantly, our MW F_1 score of .59 was higher than the previous score of .49, achieved in a lab study with the same learning environment [28], although the comparison should be taken with a modicum of caution since the two studies differed along multiple factors (e.g., student population, type of eye tracker). Nevertheless, these results are encouraging as a detector with similar accuracy was used to successfully trigger interventions that improved learning gains in the context of reading [14]. We also extended the previous work that only investigated global gaze features, by exploring locality features as well as a combination of the two. This did not yield any performance improvements over the global features alone. One possibility is that the global features are sufficient for this task. However, it is more likely that the locality features considered here were too simplistic and benefits may be gained by refining them (see Future Work). In analysis of features we observed consistent differences with previous work in eye gaze and MW [4], most notably that when MW, students are more likely to have fewer, more spread out fixations than when not MW.

4.2 Applications

The key application of this work is to develop an attention-aware version of Guru that detects and combats MW in real-time. Such a system has a number of paths to pursue to re-engage students when MW is detected. One immediate effect of MW is that a student fails to attend to a unit of information or event because they are consumed by internal, off-task thoughts. To combat this, one approach may be to simply repeat the missed information (e.g., "John, let me repeat that...") or to direct the user's attention to an area of the screen that may help them (e.g., "John, you might want to look at the image showing the enzyme breakdown..."). A more involved approach might be to ask the student a content question (e.g., "John, what happens to an enzyme when it is subjected to heat?") or ask the student to self-explain a concept. Additional measures might be needed if MW persists despite interventions. One option is to simply change to a new activity. Guru might even suggest changing topics or offering a choice for what students would prefer to do next. If all else fails, Guru might even suggest that the student take a break.

It is important to consider that the aforementioned interventions rely on MW detection, which is inherently imperfect. The detector may issue a false alarm, suggesting that a student is MW when they are not, or it could miss that a student is MW. In our view, MW detection does not need to be perfect as long as there is a modicum of accuracy. Imperfect detection can be addressed with a probabilistic approach, where the detector outputs a MW likelihood that is then used to determine whether an intervention is triggered (i.e., if the likelihood of MW is 70%, then there is a 70% chance of an intervention). The interventions should also be designed to "fail-soft" in that there are no harmful effects to learning if delivered incorrectly.

Beyond MW detection and response, COTS eye tracking in the classroom opens doors to several potential applications. One involves monitoring attentional states beyond MW (e.g., focused attention, alternating attention) so as to ensure that limited attentional resources are being optimally deployed [16]. Another application is alternate interaction methods that use eye-gaze as input, keeping learning novel and interesting. A further application is large-scale user testing of new learning technologies in the classroom. Student eye-gaze could also be used as a feedback tool to teachers, who can revise instruction/materials based on what captures students' attention.

4.3 Limitations

There were several limitations of this work. Our system was designed to include a low-cost eye tracker so that it may scale to classrooms. However, COTS eye trackers have a low sampling-rate, limiting their accuracy compared to research-grade eye trackers. Further, factors beyond our control, such as incorrect USB drivers on a school-owned computer, meant that for some of the sessions, no eye tracking was collected at all.

With regard to MW detection, we are limited by the features used in the supervised learning models. We used a small subset of gaze features and did not model any temporal gaze patterns. For example, if a participant had multiple fixations in one area, were these concentrated or distributed across time? In addition, we only considered a small number of contextual features.

At this time, locality features are not related directly to content and do not use Areas of Interest (AOI's). Guru's display is not fixed and changes throughout the tutorial phases. To further investigate locality features would require separate AOIs and corresponding models per phase. Because students spend different amounts of time in each phase, there were not enough instances to build phase-specific models.

A further limitation relates to the use of thought probes, which require users to be mindful of their MW and respond honestly. Although this method has been previously validated [21, 44, 47] there is no clear alternative to track a highly internal state like MW outside of potentially measuring brain activity in an fMRI scanner. One futuristic possibility is to combine self-reports and wearable electroencephalography (EEG) as a means of collecting

more accurate MW responses, but it is unclear if this can be done in the wild.

4.4 Future Work

The results discussed here invite several possibilities for improvement that we will address as future work. First, we will explore a more refined set of locality features for MW detection. Example locality features involve fixations on various parts of the display, such as the tutor agent, aspects of the multimedia panel, the response box, and so on. When images are present, we will analyze image-specific gaze fixations, such as proportion of fixations on images, number of components fixated on, and fixation durations on different components. Guru uses a slow-reveal animation, where image components appear as they referenced in the session. This affords computing of animation-based locality features that measure gaze latencies to different image components as they are revealed.

We also plan to integrate our detectors into Guru to detect MW in real-time. Here, the MW probes will be triggered based on the detector's real-time probabilistic assessment of MW instead of the pseudo-random probing. Alignment between students' reports and the detector's estimates will be used to evaluate the detector's real-time MW accuracy when applied to new students. The detectors will be refined based on the outcome of these studies. The refined detector will then be used to deliver interventions (as noted above), leading to an attention-aware version of Guru.

4.5 Conclusion

The recent introduction of COTS eye trackers has ushered in an exciting time for gaze-based technologies that assist learning in the classroom. We have shown that valid and actionable eye-gaze data can be collected in an unconstrained manner despite the noisy real-world classroom environment. Our findings suggest that it might finally be possible to apply decades of lab-based research on eye gaze, attention, and learning to classrooms, thereby affording new discoveries about how students learn while designing new interfaces to sustain attention during learning.

5. ACKNOWLEDGMENTS

This research was supported by the National Science Foundation (NSF) (DRL 1235958 and IIS 1523091). Any opinions, findings and conclusions, or recommendations expressed in this paper are those of the authors and do not necessarily reflect the views of the NSF.

Thanks to fellow lab members for their assistance in the data collection, to the students for their valuable feedback and to our teacher consultant (not named to protect student privacy) for welcoming us into their classroom.

REFERENCES

[1]   Anderson, J.R. 2002. Spanning seven orders of magnitude: A challenge for cognitive modeling. *Cognitive Science*. 26, 1 (2002), 85–112.

[2]   Arroyo, I. et al. 2007. Repairing disengagement with non-invasive interventions. *Proceedings of the 2007 Conference on Artificial Intelligence in Education: Building Technology Rich Learning Contexts That Work* (Amsterdam, The Netherlands, 2007), 195–202.

[3]   Baker, R.S.J. d. 2007. Modeling and understanding students' off-task behavior in intelligent tutoring systems. *Proceedings of the*

SIGCHI Conference on Human Factors in Computing Systems (New York, NY, USA, 2007), 1059–1068.

[4]   Bixler, R. and D'Mello, S. 2016. Automatic gaze-based user-independent detection of mind wandering during computerized reading. *User Modeling and User-Adapted Interaction*. 26, 1 (2016), 33–68.

[5]   Bixler, R. and D'Mello, S.K. 2015. Automatic gaze-based detection of mind wandering with metacognitive awareness. *User Modeling, Adaptation and Personalization* (Dublin, Ireland, 2015), 31–43.

[6]   Bixler, R. and D'Mello, S.K. 2014. Toward fully automated person-independent detection of mind wandering. *User Modeling, Adaptation, and Personalization* (Aalborg, Denmark, 2014), 37–48.

[7]   Blanchard, N. et al. 2014. Automated physiological-based detection of mind wandering during learning. *Intelligent Tutoring Systems* (Switzerland, 2014), 55–60.

[8]   Bondareva, D. et al. 2013. Inferring learning from gaze data during interaction with an environment to support self-regulated learning. *International Conference on Artificial Intelligence in Education* (Memphis, TN, USA, 2013), 229–238.

[9]   Chawla, N.V. et al. 2002. SMOTE: Synthetic minority over-sampling technique. *J. Artif. Int. Res.* 16, 1 (Jun. 2002), 321–357.

[10] Cohen, J. 2013. *Statistical power analysis for the behavioral sciences*. Taylor & Francis.

[11] Conati, C. et al. 2013. Eye-tracking for student modelling in intelligent tutoring systems. *Design recommendations for intelligent tutoring systems*. 1, (2013), 227–236.

[12] Conati, C. and Merten, C. 2007. Eye-tracking for user modeling in exploratory learning environments: An empirical evaluation. *Knowledge-Based Systems*. 20, 6 (2007), 557–574.

[13] Deubel, H. and Schneider, W.X. 1996. Saccade target selection and object recognition: Evidence for a common attentional mechanism. *Vision research*. 36, 12 (1996), 1827–1837.

[14] D'Mello, S.K. et al. 2016. Attending to attention: detecting and combating mind wandering during computerized reading. *Proceedings of the 2016 CHI Conference Extended Abstracts on Human Factors in Computing Systems* (2016), 1661–1669.

[15] D'Mello, S.K. et al. 2012. Gaze tutor: A gaze-reactive intelligent tutoring system. *Int. J. Hum.-Comput. Stud.* 70, 5 (May 2012), 377–398.

[16] D'Mello, S.K. 2016. Giving eyesight to the blind: towards attention-aware AIED. *International Journal of Artificial Intelligence in Education*. 26, 2 (2016), 645–659.

[17] Drummond, J. and Litman, D. 2010. In the zone: Towards detecting student zoning out using supervised machine learning. *Intelligent Tutoring Systems* (Pittsburgh, PA, USA, 2010), 306–308.

[18] Feng, S. et al. 2013. Mind wandering while reading easy and difficult texts. *Psychonomic Bulletin & Review*. 20, 3 (2013), 586–592.

[19] Forbes-Riley, K. and Litman, D. 2011. When does disengagement correlate with learning in spoken dialog computer tutoring? *Artificial Intelligence in Education* (Auckland, New Zealand, Jul. 2011), 81–89.

[20] Franklin, M.S. et al. 2011. Catching the mind in flight: using behavioral indices to detect mindless reading in real time. *Psychonomic Bulletin & Review*. 18, 5 (Oct. 2011), 992–997.

[21] Franklin, M.S. et al. 2013. Window to the wandering mind: pupillometry of spontaneous thought while reading. *The Quarterly Journal of Experimental Psychology*. 66, 12 (2013), 2289–2294.

[22] Gluck, K.A. et al. 2000. Broader bandwidth in student modeling: What if ITS were "Eye" TS? *International Conference on Intelligent Tutoring Systems* (2000), 504–513.

[23] Graesser, A.C. et al. 2007. Inference generation and cohesion in the construction of situation models: Some connections with computational linguistics. *Higher level language processes in the brain: Inference and comprehension processes*. (2007), 289–310.

[24] Graesser, A.C. et al. 2005. Question asking and eye tracking during cognitive disequilibrium: Comprehending illustrated texts on devices when the devices break down. *Memory & Cognition*. 33, 7 (2005), 1235–1247.

[25] Hall, M. et al. 2009. The WEKA data mining software: An update. *SIGKDD Explor. Newsl.* 11, 1 (Nov. 2009), 10–18.

[26] Hegarty, M. and Just, M.A. 1993. Constructing mental models of machines from text and diagrams. *Journal of Memory and Language*. 32, 6 (Dec. 1993), 717–742.

[27] Hoffman, J.E. and Subramaniam, B. 1995. The role of visual attention in saccadic eye movements. *Perception & psychophysics*. 57, 6 (1995), 787–795.

[28] Hutt, S. et al. 2016. The eyes have it: gaze-based detection of mind wandering during learning with an intelligent tutoring system. *The 9th International Conference on Educational Data Mining* (Raleigh, NC, USA, 2016), 86–93.

[29] Jaques, N. et al. 2014. Predicting affect from gaze data during interaction with an intelligent tutoring system. *Intelligent Tutoring Systems:*, (Honolulu, HI, USA, Jun. 2014), 29–38.

[30] Kardan, S. and Conati, C. 2012. Exploring gaze data for determining user learning with an interactive simulation. *User Modeling, Adaptation, and Personalization* (Montreal, Canada, Jul. 2012), 126–138.

[31] Linnenbrink, E.A. 2007. The role of affect in student learning: A multi-dimensional approach to considering the interaction of affect, motivation, and engagement. *Emotion in Education*. R. Pekrun, ed. Elsevier. 107–124.

[32] M. Cocea and S. Weibelzahl 2011. Disengagement detection in online learning: validation studies and perspectives. *IEEE Transactions on Learning Technologies*. 4, 2 (Jun. 2011), 114–124.

[33] Mathews, M. et al. 2012. Do your eyes give it away? Using eye tracking data to understand students' attitudes towards open student model representations. *Intelligent Tutoring Systems* (Chania, Crete, Greece, Jun. 2012), 422–427.

[34] Mills, C. et al. 2016. Automatic gaze-based detection of mind wandering during film viewing. *The 9th International Conference on Educational Data Mining*. (Raleigh, North Carolina, 2016).

[35] Mills, C. et al. 2015. Mind wandering during learning with an intelligent tutoring system. *Artificial Intelligence in Education* (Madrid, Spain, Jun. 2015), 267–276.

[36] Mills, C. et al. 2014. To quit or not to quit: predicting future behavioral disengagement from reading patterns. *Intelligent Tutoring Systems* (Honolulu, HI, USA, Jun. 2014), 19–28.

[37] Mooneyham, B.W. and Schooler, J.W. 2013. The costs and benefits of mind-wandering: a review. *Canadian Journal of Experimental Psychology*. 67, 1 (Mar. 2013), 11–18.

[38] Muir, M. and Conati, C. 2012. An analysis of attention to student-adaptive hints in an educational game. *International Conference on Intelligent Tutoring Systems* (Chania, Crete, 2012), 112–122.

[39] Olney, A.M. et al. 2015. Attention in educational contexts: The role of the learning task in guiding attention. *The Handbook of Attention*. J. Fawcett et al., eds. MIT Press.

[40] Olney, A.M. et al. 2012. Guru: A computer tutor that models expert human tutors. *Intelligent Tutoring Systems* (Chania, Crete, Greece, Jun. 2012), 256–261.

[41] Person, N.K. et al. 2012. Interactive concept maps and learning outcomes in Guru. *Florida Artificial Intelligence Research Society Conference* (Marco Island, FL, USA, May 2012), 456–461.

[42] Pham, P. and Wang, J. 2015. AttentiveLearner: improving mobile MOOC learning via implicit heart rate tracking. *Artificial Intelligence in Education* (Madrid, Spain, 2015), 367–376.

[43] Ponce, H.R. and Mayer, R.E. 2014. Qualitatively different cognitive processing during online reading primed by different study activities. *Computers in Human Behavior*. 30, (Jan. 2014), 121–130.

[44] Randall, J.G. et al. 2014. Mind-wandering, cognition, and performance: a theory-driven meta-analysis of attention regulation. *Psychological Bulletin*. 140, 6 (Nov. 2014), 1411–1431.

[45] Rapp, D.N. 2006. The value of attention aware systems in educational settings. *Computers in Human Behavior Special issue: Attention aware systems*. 22, 4 (Jul. 2006), 603–614.

[46] Rayner, K. 1998. Eye movements in reading and information processing: 20 years of research. *Psychological Bulletin*. 124, 3 (Nov. 1998), 372–422.

[47] Reichle, E.D. et al. 2010. Eye movements during mindless reading. *Psychol Sci.* 21, 9 (Sep. 2010), 1300–1310.

[48]   Risko, E.F. et al. 2013. Everyday attention: Mind wandering and computer use during lectures. *Computers & Education*. 68, (2013), 275–283.

[49]   Risko, E.F. et al. 2012. Everyday attention: Variation in mind wandering and memory in a lecture. *Applied Cognitive Psychology*. 26, 2 (2012), 234–242.

[50]   Robertson, I.H. et al. 1997. "Oops!": performance correlates of everyday attentional failures in traumatic brain injured and normal subjects. *Neuropsychologia*. 35, 6 (Jun. 1997), 747–758.

[51]   Roda, C. and Thomas, J. 2006. Attention aware systems: Theories, applications, and research agenda. *Computers in Human Behavior*. 22, 4 (2006), 557–587.

[52]   Schooler, J.W. et al. 2004. Zoning out while reading: Evidence for dissociations between experience and metaconsciousness. *Thinking and seeing: Visual metacognition in adults and children*. MIT Press. 203–226.

[53]   Seibert, P.S. and Ellis, H.C. 1991. Irrelevant thoughts, emotional mood states, and cognitive task performance. *Mem Cognit*. 19, 5 (Sep. 1991), 507–513.

[54]   Shernoff, D.J. et al. 2014. Student engagement in high school classrooms from the perspective of flow theory. *Applications of Flow in Human Development and Education: The Collected Works of Mihaly Csikszentmihalyi*. M. Csikszentmihalyi, ed. Springer Netherlands. 475–494.

[55]   Sibert, J.L. et al. 2000. The reading assistant: Eye gaze triggered auditory prompting for reading remediation. *Proceedings of the 13th Annual ACM Symposium on User Interface Software and Technology* (New York, NY, USA, 2000), 101–107.

[56]   Smallwood, J. et al. 2008. When attention matters: the curious incident of the wandering mind. *Memory & Cognition*. 36, 6 (Sep. 2008), 1144–1150.

[57]   Smallwood, J. and Schooler, J.W. 2006. The restless mind. *Psychological Bulletin*. 132, 6 (Nov. 2006), 946–958.

[58]   Smallwood, J. and Schooler, J.W. 2015. The science of mind wandering: Empirically navigating the stream of consciousness. *Annual Review of Psychology*. 66, (2015), 487–518.

[59]   Smilek, D. et al. 2010. Out of mind, out of sight: Eye blinking as indicator and embodiment of mind wandering. *Psychological Science*. (Apr. 2010).

[60]   Sottilare, R.A. et al. 2013. *Design recommendations for intelligent tutoring systems: Volume 1-learner modeling*. US Army Research Laboratory.

[61]   Szpunar, K.K. et al. 2013. Interpolated memory tests reduce mind wandering and improve learning of online lectures. *Proc. Natl. Acad. Sci. U.S.A.* 110, 16 (Apr. 2013), 6313–6317.

[62]   Szpunar, K.K. et al. 2013. Mind wandering and education: from the classroom to online learning. *Front Psychol*. 4, (2013), 495.

[63]   Vosskuhler, A. et al. 2008. OGAMA (Open Gaze and Mouse Analyzer): open-source software designed to analyze eye and mouse movements in slideshow study designs. *Behav Res Methods*. 40, 4 (Nov. 2008), 1150–1162.

[64]   Wang, H. et al. 2006. Empathic tutoring software agents using real-time eye tracking. *Proceedings of the 2006 Symposium on Eye Tracking Research &Amp; Applications* (New York, NY, USA, 2006), 73–78.

[65]   Wixon, M. et al. 2012. WTF? Detecting students who are conducting inquiry without thinking fastidiously. *User Modeling, Adaptation, and Personalization* (Montreal, Canada, Jul. 2012), 286–296.

Probabilistic Perspectives on Collecting Human Uncertainty in Predictive Data Mining*

Kevin Jasberg
Web Science Group
Heinrich-Heine-University Duesseldorf
Duesseldorf, Germany 45225
kevin.jasberg@uni-duesseldorf.de

Sergej Sizov
Web Science Group
Heinrich-Heine-University Duesseldorf
Duesseldorf, Germany 45225
sizov@hhu.de

ABSTRACT

In many areas of data mining, data is collected from human beings. In this contribution, we ask the question of how people actually respond to ordinal scales. The main problem observed is that users tend to be volatile in their choices, i.e. complex cognitions do not always lead to the same decisions, but to distributions of possible decision outputs. This human uncertainty may sometimes have quite an impact on common data mining approaches and thus, the question of effective modelling this so called human uncertainty emerges naturally.

Our contribution introduces two different approaches for modelling the human uncertainty of user responses. In doing so, we develop techniques in order to measure this uncertainty at the level of user inputs as well as the level of user cognition. With support of comprehensive user experiments and large-scale simulations, we systematically compare both methodologies along with their implications for personalisation approaches. Our findings demonstrate that significant amounts of users do submit something completely different (action) than they really have in mind (cognition). Moreover, we demonstrate that statistically sound evidence with respect to algorithm assessment becomes quite hard to realise, especially when explicit rankings shall be built.

CCS CONCEPTS

•**Information systems** →**Recommender systems;** Data mining; •**Human-centered computing** →**Design and evaluation methods;** *User models; User studies;*

KEYWORDS

Human Uncertainty; Measurement Uncertainty; Identifiability; Distinguishability, Distribution-Paradigm; User Noise

*Full dataset and evaluation routines available at https://jasbergk.wixsite.com/research

UMAP'17, July 9–12, 2017, Bratislava, Slovakia
© 2017 ACM. ISBN 978-1-4503-4635-1/17/07...$15.00.
DOI: http://dx.doi.org/10.1145/3079628.3079675

1 INTRODUCTION

A broad range of algorithms and approaches in data mining aim at modelling and predicting aspects of human behaviour. These efforts are motivated by many practically relevant applications, including various recommender systems, content personalisation, targeted advertising, along with many others. This involves implicit or explicit knowledge about user behaviour, either by observing user interactions or by asking users explicitly.

We take this as an opportunity to ask the question of how people actually proceed when making decisions (e.g. creating ratings or other forms of feedback) while interacting with information systems. For example, many users make their decisions with considerable uncertainty in many situations, i.e. they would not exactly reproduce their decisions when asked twice or multiple times. This **Human Uncertainty**, as we understand it in this contribution, appears to be a characteristic feature of the cognitive process of decision making which influences its outcome, making it circumstantial and temporally unstable; the outcome appears to be more or less fluctuating randomly when repeating a decision making. Consequently, we may assume that observed decisions are drawn from individual distributions. Moreover, and even more important, our knowledge about such distributions may be very limited, due to natural limitations of known measurement methodologies. One of these methodologies, which has already been used in recent research on data mining, is based on a frequentist approach and observes repeated user actions. Another approach, yet insufficiently discussed in this context, is based on a Bayesian approach and requires user perceptions. Both of these approaches have so far not been discussed sufficiently in the field of user modelling and personalisation. However, we will demonstrate that there are far-reaching implications of such considerations, especially for the statistical evidence of data mining results and the sometimes associated monetary decisions (e.g. when opting for the better recommender).

Motivating Example. As a motivating example, we consider the task of rating prediction (common to recommender systems), along with the **Root Mean Square Error** (RMSE) as a widely used metric for prediction quality. In a systematic experiment with real users (described in more detail in forthcoming sections), individuals rated certain movie trailers multiple times. Figure 1a shows that only 35% of all users show constant rating behaviour, whereas about 50% use two different answer categories and 15% of all users make use of three or more categories. Based on these observations, we compute the RMSE for three recommender systems (designed by definition of their predictors π) for each rating trial. Figure 1b depicts the RMSE outcomes and their frequency. It becomes apparent at once that

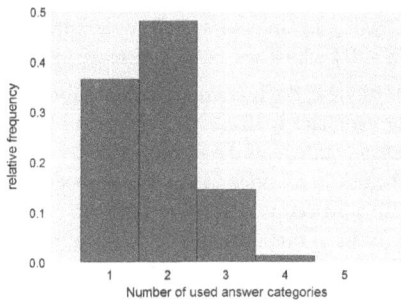

(a) Relative frequency of the amount of used answer categories

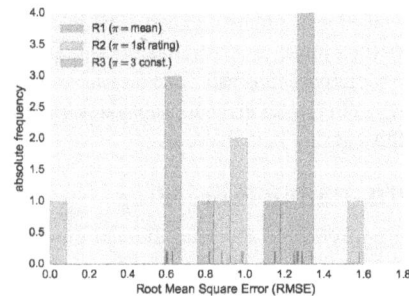

(b) Distribution of RMSE outcomes for each rating trial

Figure 1: Uncertain user ratings and impact on the RMSE

the RMSE itself yields a particular degree of uncertainty, emerged from uncertain user feedback. When ranking these recommender systems, Figure 1b allows for three possible results

$$(R1 \prec R2 \prec R3) \ \vee \ (R2 \prec R1 \prec R3) \ \vee \ (R1 \prec R3 \prec R2) \quad (1)$$

depending on the rating trial, where the relation $\prec$ denotes "better than". This problem is most obvious for recommender $R1$ as it could be both, the best or the worst recommender, although it operates for same users rating the same items. In addition, it may be possible that further repetitions of ratings would lead to even more ranking possibilities. This naturally implies to esteem the RMSE as a distribution rather than single scores. Consequently, the question changes from "Is $R1$ better than $R2$?" to "How likely is it that $R1$ is better than $R2$?". Changing this question can be considered as a paradigm shift, i.e. from **point-paradigm** to **distribution-paradigm**, providing the possibility to detect and to visualise many interesting but so far hidden effects within the field of user modelling, personalisation and adaptation.

The Problem. Grounded on real user experiments it can be shown that there is often a significant overlap in two metric's distributions when assessing competing data mining approaches. During our analyses, we often encountered ranking error probabilities of 33% or even more when evaluating by scores only. At this point, we must emphasise that this problem is not immanent to this novel paradigm, but has always been present implicitly in data records, provided that these are based on human behaviour. The distribution-paradigm

is just able to make some fundamental problems visible. On these findings, it becomes imperative to explore possible propagations of human uncertainty in order to maintain statistically sound and adequate methods of data mining. However, in addition to the analysis of human uncertainty itself, the question of information quality in terms of reliability and validity also plays a major role and must be considered as well. As we're going to show in forthcoming sections, one has to repeat a rating task on the same item for a several hundred times in order to quantify the human uncertainty with acceptable precision.

To restate our problems in short: We have to include human uncertainty in our decisions on algorithm assessment to exclude impacting errors, but with the most naive and simplest method to perform, we cannot gather enough information to quantify this uncertainty with necessary precision.

Research Questions. In this contribution, we introduce two diametrically opposed approaches of gathering uncertainty information. Due to the lack of sufficiently profound discussions in the literature of computer science that addresses human uncertainty, the compatibility of cognition and action, and the impact of these topics on commonly accepted techniques in data mining, we want to examine the relevance of this subjects in more detail. In this spirit, we will focus on the following research questions:

Research Question Q1: How do actual feedback responses differ from intended ones (in terms of probabilistic approaches)?

Research Question Q2: What implications become apparent by contrasting diverse uncertainty models (e.g. the impact on evaluation metrics like the RMSE)?

These questions are examined on the basis of user experiments that mimic the task of recommender systems. The indications and implications presented in this contribution are nevertheless not limited to this field but do apply for most of common data mining approaches that explicitly account for human feedback.

2 RELATED WORK

In this paper, we exemplify our approach using recommender systems [15] and focus specifically on the validity of human uncertainty measurements in rating scenarios.

The relevance of our contribution arises from the fact that the ubiquitous human uncertainty sometimes has a vast influence on the evaluation of different prediction algorithms. For this comparative assessment, different metrics are used to determine the prediction quality, such as the root mean squared error (RMSE), the mean absolute error (MAE), the mean average precision (MAP) and many others [1]. These and other quality-related quantities in recommender assessment (e.g. user satisfaction, precision/recall, etc.) are summarised in [9]. Although we exemplify the impact of measurement validity on the RMSE, the main results of this contribution can be easily adopted for alternative assessment metrics without substantial loss of generality, since they all share in common the need for uncertain human input.

The idea of uncertainty is not only related to predictive data mining but also to measuring sciences such as metrology. Recently, a paradigm shift was initiated on the basis of a so far incomplete theory of error [7]. In consequence, measured properties are currently modelled by probability density functions and quantities calculated therefrom are now assigned a distribution by means of a convolution of these densities. This model is described in [11]. A feasible framework for computing these convolutions via Monte-Carlo-simulation is given by [12]. We take this model as a basis for our own modelling of uncertainty for addressing similar issues in the field of computer science.

The complexity of human perception and cognition can be addressed by means of latent distributions. This idea is widely used in cognitive science and in statistical models for ordinal data. For example, so-called CUB models for ordinal data [10] assume the Gaussian as a latent response model underlying the observations. We adopt the idea of modelling user uncertainty by means of individual Gaussians following the argumentation in [10] for constructing our individual response models.

The impacts of human uncertainty for recommendation results have been frequently discussed in recent work from different perspectives. Observations presented in [3, 4] have shown that it can significantly influence results of recommender evaluation. The methodology applied there is based on repeating rating scenarios for same users-items-pairs and represents the current standard in latest research such as [2]. In this paper, the same methodology is explored and compared to a new Bayesian method, which we have derived from the latest research on cognitions of uncertainty in educational scenarios [8].

3 DATA MODELLING

3.1 The Re-Rating Proceeding

One way of deriving a user's rating-distribution is based on the **frequentist definition of probability**, i.e. the probability of an event to occur is equal to its relative frequency for infinite trials. Deduced from this definition we receive a probability density function (PDF) by simply asking users to re-rate the same item several times and computing Maximum-Likelihood-Parameters for a given data model. We will refer to this scenario as the **re-rating-proceeding**.

In mathematical terms: Let $U \subseteq \mathbb{N}$ be a finite set of Users and $I \subseteq \mathbb{N}$ a finite set of items to be rated. Let $S = \{1, 2, 3, 4, 5\}$ denote the set of possible ratings on the commonly used five-star ordinal scale, then the tensor $r_{u,i,t} \in S$ represents the tth rating from user $u \in U$ for item $i \in I$ where $t = 1, \ldots, N$. By forcing user u to rate the same item i multiple times, we obtain the sample

$$r_{u,i,\bullet} := \{r_{u,i,t} \mid t = 1, \ldots, N\} \tag{2}$$

representing t draws from the random variable $R_{u,i}$. The corresponding rating-distribution represented by the PDF $f_R : \hat{S} \to \mathbb{R}$ can be generated by performing the ML-algorithm for a chosen data model (e.g. Gaussians, CUB-Models, etc.), assuming a continuous scale $\hat{S}$ as well as a non-vanishing variance of $r_{u,i,\bullet}$. We then denote the standard deviation $\sigma_{u,i} := \sqrt{\mathrm{Var}(R_{u,i})}$ as the operationalised human uncertainty of user u on item i. For this uncertainty we have to regard two facts:

- A single user rates multiple items with unequal precision and thus produces a user-specific distribution with draws $\{\sigma_{u,i} \mid i \in I\}$ which we call the **user-specific noise** $\Sigma(u)$.

- A single item is rated by multiple users having unequal precision, emerging an item-specific distribution with draws $\{\sigma_{u,i} \mid u \in U\}$ which we call the **item-specific noise** $\Sigma(i)$.

From this point of view, the human uncertainty for a specific user and item can be seen as a realisation of the joint PDF of $\Sigma(u)$ and $\Sigma(i)$. The biggest advantage of the re-rating-proceeding is that the users can, on the one hand, stick to the usual procedure but repeat several times. This procedure therefore seems to be very feasible, although it might be assumed that repetitions of a certain rating task are limited. However, the data obtained is easy to process. The disadvantages arise when we leave the view of probability theory and take the view of statistics, for then we are not able to know the parameters accurately, since we only calculate them on samples rather than the population. As a result, the parameters itself are subject to a so-called measurement uncertainty. In other words, we cannot measure the human precision in sufficient quality, but only locate it within confidence intervals. This measurement uncertainty becomes an important factor since it propagates in every quantity derived from these rating-distributions.

3.2 The PDF-Rating Proceeding

An alternative approach of accessing human precision is based on the **Bayesian definition of probability**, i.e. the probability of an event to occur is the degree of one's personal confidence in this occurrence. Under this assumption, one can obtain a rating-distribution directly from requiring a user's personal confidence of the appropriateness for each possible rating that a scale provides. We will denote this procedure as the **pdf-rating-proceeding**.

In mathematical terms: Having a 5-Star-Scale $S = \{1, \ldots, 5\}$, a user associates to each possible rating $s \in S$ a degree of personal confidence about the appropriateness of s concerning the item to be rated. The personal confidence is entered by a second Scale $S_C = \{1, \ldots, 5\}$. Hence, a given rating

$$r_{u,i} = \{(1, n_1), (2, n_2), (3, n_3), (4, n_4), (5, n_5)\} \tag{3}$$

is given by a family of two-dimensional vectors in $S_L \times S_C$ where the values for ones personal belief are considered as specific weights for each of the associated ratings. In order to retrieve the rating-distribution, this rating is converted into its frequentist equivalent by use of the transformation

$$\tau : r_{u,i} \mapsto (\underbrace{1, \ldots, 1}_{n_1\text{-times}}, \underbrace{2, \ldots, 2}_{n_2\text{-times}}, \ldots, \underbrace{5, \ldots, 5}_{n_5\text{-times}}). \tag{4}$$

since the absolute histogram of this frequentist translation will exactly reproduce the data initially entered by the user. We then perform a ML-Estimation on $\tau(r_{u,i})$ to find the optimal parameters for a chosen data model. The great advantage of the pdf-rating is, that all necessary data can be obtained by one rating only which grants a better viability and saves valuable time for improving the system, i.e. the machine-learning-process speeds up significantly. The disadvantages might be that this new and yet unusual method is not immediately accepted by users.

3.3 Composed Quantities

The RMSE, as a metric for model-based prediction quality, is a suitable example to demonstrate the impact of human uncertainty as well as the limited precision of its measurement on composed quantities. **Composed Quantities**, in this contribution, are quantities that compute as a function of large amounts of uncertain arguments. So, a composed quantity becomes a random variable itself whose density function emerges as a convolution of the density functions of its arguments.

For further considerations, we assume all ratings to be normally distributed random variables $R_{u,i} \sim \mathcal{N}(\mu_{u,i}, \sigma_{u,i})$ (rationally, it exhibits maximum entropy along all distributions with finite mean/variance and support on $\mathbb{R}$). Accordingly, the RMSE

$$\text{RMSE} = \sqrt{\sum_{(u,i) \in \mathcal{U} \times \mathcal{I}} \frac{(\pi_{u,i} - R_{u,i})^2}{n}} \qquad (5)$$

materialises as a composition of continuous maps of random variables and thus becomes a random variable itself. Its distribution emerges as a convolution of $n \leq U \cdot I$ density functions and computations can be easily done via Monte-Carlo-Simulation [12].

In case of exactly known rating-distributions, we get a clear distribution for the RMSE. However, since each dataset represents only one sample rather than the entire population, point estimators are inappropriate here. Instead, confidence intervals have to be specified [14]. In that sense, we cannot simply determine a single rating-distribution for each user-item-pair, but have to compute a variety of distributions with the associated parameters drawn from corresponding confidence intervals. In consequence, even for large-scale computations, the resulting RMSE does not possess a stable density function. However, there exist borderline cases which reveal the maximum range in which we can expect results for the density function of the RMSE.

4 METHODOLOGY AND EXPERIMENTS

4.1 The Experiment

Our experiment is set up with Unipark's[1] survey engine whilst our participants were committed by the crowdsourcing platform Clickworker[2]. During the experiment, participants watched theatrical trailers of popular movies and television shows and provided ratings using the re-rating-proceeding and pdf-ratings-proceeding respectively[3]. The submitted ratings have been recorded for five out of ten fixed trailers so that the remaining trailers act as distractors triggering the misinformation effect, i.e. memory is becoming less accurate because of interference from post-event information.

4.2 Evaluation Methodology

Research Question Q1: Here, we examine the difference between actual and intended ratings as obtained by the re-rating and pdf-rating respectively. To this end, we compare the rating distributions as well as the distributions of the variances (userspecific and item-specific noise) resulting from the different measurement methods.

Equality of distributions: To compare the distributions induced by actions as well as cognitions, we consider point-estimation parameters and go on three factors: On the one hand, we compare the distribution type by means of a two-sample-KS-test. Even if

the equality of two PDFs has to be rejected, the available rating-distributions may nevertheless possess the same expectation or variance that could be assigned to a user within a recommender system for a future rating. Therefore we perform Welch's t-test to compare the expected values as well as Levene's test to investigate homoscedasticity. It will turn out that all item-specific-noise distributions retrieved from the PDF-rating-procedure share a conspicuous common feature: The equality of expectations throughout all items. This hypothesis is explored by Welch's t-test as well. All testing is performed with a significance level of $\alpha = 0.05$.

Validity of distributions: We will also focus on validity of the distributions, that is the precision with which the relevant parameters can be localised. For all rating-distributions this can be done easily by comparing the length of the parameters' confidence intervals, due to an explicitly given parametric data-model. For the Noise-Distributions we do not have these parametric data-models. Instead, a Monte-Carlo-Simulation is used in which we sample the variances from their confidence intervals. For every resulting noise-distribution we then compute the percentiles $q \in [0, 1]$, so that re-sampling will result into a distribution for each of this percentiles. In doing so, the standard deviation $\sigma(q)$ of q becomes a measure for the precision with which the noise-distribution can be obtained. Thus, we simply compare the quantiles' standard deviations when deduced from the re-rating and pdf-rating.

Research Question Q2. Here, we examine implications of human uncertainty and their visualisation by a given measurement method. For this purpose, we will focus on evaluation metrics and discuss the possible implications for the RMSE as an example. In particular, we will investigate the influence of measuring precision and the distinguishability of two RMSE-distributions. Due to the fact that it is quite difficult to specify a closed form for the RMSE's density function [6], we will perform a Monte-Carlo-Simulation as described in [12]. In our simulations, we observe six different recommender systems, designed by defining their predictors via

$$\pi_{(u,i)}^k := \begin{cases} \text{mean within all rating trials} & k = 1 \\ (k-1)^{\text{th}} \text{ rating} & k = 2, \dots, 6 \end{cases} \qquad (6)$$

where k denotes the k-th recommender system.

Equality of distributions: Since the MC-simulation is an artificial generation of draws, hypothesis testing can not be executed directly on this data set in order to validate whether both measurement methods produce the same RMSE or not. This is because a simple increase in the MC-trials can be used to significantly detect any effect, even if this is not possible from the underlying data set. For this reason, we freeze the parameters of the incoming variables to the corresponding point estimators and indirectly simulate the hypothesis tests. To this end, we reduce the number of MC-trials to the actual sample size of the collected data and carry out the hypothesis test on these reduced samples. However, we repeat this 10^6 times and consider the relative frequency h of the rejection of equality. If $h > \alpha - 1$ holds, a possible effect can be considered to be proven with significance level α.

Validity/Reliability of distributions: In case of the RMSE, validity is closely linked to reliability as the inaccurate location of the rating-distributions' parameters (validity) induces diverse

---

[1] http://www.unipark.com/de/
[2] https://www.clickworker.de/
[3] A full description can be found on https://jasbergk.wixsite.com/research

outcomes for any re-sampling (reliability). The validity in terms of precision is observed by sampling the percentile's distributions again and compare their standard deviations when sampled from the re-rating-proceeding as well as the pdf-rating-proceeding. The effect size of reliability will be demonstrated by considering borderline cases of the RMSE which reveal the maximum span in which we can expect results for its density function.

Distinguishability: Our analyses will reveal that two recommender systems $R1$ and $R2$ may not only have different PDFs $f_{R1}(x)$ and $f_{R2}(x)$ for the RMSE, but also do these PDFs overlap very often. Thus each ranking $R1 < R2$ is always subject to an error

$$P_\varepsilon := P(R1 > R2) = \int_{-\infty}^{\infty} f_{R2}(x)\big(1 - F_{R1}(x)\big)\,\mathrm{d}x \quad (7)$$

where $F_{R1}(x)$ denotes the cumulative distribution function of the RMSE-distribution of $R1$. In this context, we investigate how strongly one recommender must deviate from another, so that this can be significantly recognised by the RMSE, i.e. the probability of ranking error diminishes to less than five percent. To this end, we assume to have perfectly known rating-distributions and compute the RMSE for two recommender systems with adjustable prediction quality. Theoretically, the arithmetic mean $\bar{x}_{u,i}$ of ratings throughout all rating trials appears to be the optimal predictor, because this is the value which is obtained on average in the case of an infinite repetition and thus produces the smallest sum of squared deviations. Hence, we define the optimal recommender by setting $\pi_{u,i} := \bar{x}_{u,i}$. To this optimum we additionally create a copy which we distort by artificial noise generated from re-sampling its predictors $\pi_{new} \in [(1-p)\pi_{old} \,;\, (1+p)\pi_{old}]$. In this case, a noise fraction of p means that those new predictors deviate from the originals by $(100 \cdot p)\%$. The RMSE thereby receives a shift on the x-axis so that it's possible to calculate a declining error probability $P_\varepsilon(p)$ for a given ranking. In this process, we observe the amount of noise that is necessary to fulfil the distinguishability-condition $P_\varepsilon < 0.05$.

4.3 Results

Altogether 67 people from Germany, Austria and Switzerland participated in this experiment. This group can be parted into 57% females and 43% males whose ages range from 20 to 60 years whilst over 60% of our participants where aged between 20 and 40. This group also includes a good average of lower, medium and higher educational levels. The rating frequency habits range from rarely to often in uniform distribution. According to this data we can assume to have gathered a cross-sectional data, generally reflecting the German speaking population from these three countries.

Research Question Q1. The comparison of rating-distributions deduced from actions and cognitions in terms of the KS-test shows that descriptive deviations are not significant in 207 of 301 cases ($\approx$ 98%). The comparison of expectations by means of Welch's t-test reveals that these do not differ significantly from one another in 175 of 211 cases ($\approx$ 83%). Similarly, Levene's test shows that a deviation from homoscedacity was only significant in 175 of 211 cases ($\approx$ 82%). A more detailed breakdown by items is given in Table 1. Overall, the probabilistic ratings may indeed possess descriptive deviations, but all are within the range of random fluctuations. Unfortunately, any of the investigated distributions is ambiguous, since its parameters

	KS-Test		Welch's t-Test		Levene-Test	
	n. rejected	rejected	n. rejected	rejected	n. rejected	rejected
Item 1	59 (1.00)	0 (0.00)	52 (0.88)	7 (0.12)	52 (0.88)	7 (0.12)
Item 2	39 (0.98)	1 (0.02)	34 (0.85)	6 (0.15)	33 (0.82)	7 (0.17)
Item 3	31 (0.94)	2 (0.06)	23 (0.70)	10 (0.30)	26 (0.79)	7 (0.21)
Item 4	45 (1.00)	0 (0.00)	38 (0.84)	7 (0.16)	37 (0.82)	8 (0.18)
Item 5	33 (0.97)	1 (0.03)	28 (0.82)	6 (0.18)	26 (0.76)	8 (0.24)

Table 1: Hypothesis testing on the rating-distributions (absolute counts first, fractions in brackets). – The absolute count varies as the number of ratings with non-vanishing variance changes for each item.

	KS-Test		Welch's t-Test		Levene-Test	
	n. rejected	rejected	n. rejected	rejected	n. rejected	rejected
ISN	0 (0.00)	5 (1.00)	0 (0.00)	5 (1.00)	1 (0.20)	4 (0.80)
USN	0 (0.00)	67 (1.00)	33 (0.49)	34 (0.51)	55 (0.82)	12 (0.18)

Table 2: Hypothesis testing on the noise-distributions – absolute counts first, fractions in brackets

can only be located within confidence intervals. For the assessment of mean value precision, we consider this quantity for each rating distribution obtained from re-rating (μ_r) as well as pdf-rating (μ_p) together with the 95%-intervals and compare their length with aid of the auxiliary variable

$$\Delta_\mu := \ell(I_{95}(\mu_r)) - \ell(I_{95}(\mu_p)). \quad (8)$$

If $\Delta_\mu > 0$, then the length $\ell(I_{95}(\mu_r))$ of the re-rating-interval is greater than the length $\ell(I_{95}(\mu_p))$ of the pdf-rating-interval, i.e. the pdf-rating appears to be more precise in locating the mean value. The analysis of the standard deviation is done analogously. Figure 2 depicts the distribution of these length differences. It can be seen that the mass-ratio of improvements and deteriorations is very balanced. At the same time, it can be seen that the strength of these deteriorations are small in comparison to the strength of improvements. The expectations show that on the average, the pdf-rating will produce a slight increase of overall precision. However, this analysis is merely based on descriptive considerations so far. For both of the parameters μ and σ, hypothesis testing reveals that more than 80% of all correspondences do not differ significantly. This certainly does not mean that equality can be accepted in all these cases, but this is a possibility that can't be rejected. In Figure 2c, we gradually allow this possibility, beginning with the smallest differences. It turns out that the precision of the pdf-rating gains very quickly when the fraction of equalities for non-significant deviations increases.

A comparison of noise distributions leads to a contrary result (see Table 2). For the item-specific noise as well as the user-specific noise, the corresponding distributions can be regarded as significantly different with respect to the different measurement methods. These findings are substantiated by the approximation of underlying data-models. In any case, the item-specific noise (ISN) is following power-law-distributions when measured via re-rating and respectively following Gaussians when measured via pdf-rating. These highly significant deviations indicate that the perceived noise differs form the observable noise. The power-law-distribution would claim that many people are quite certain whereas larger uncertainty only manifests for a few people. This doesn't perfectly match the everyday experience and may emerge due to the limitations of the conventional rating instrument, i.e. customers are forced to choose

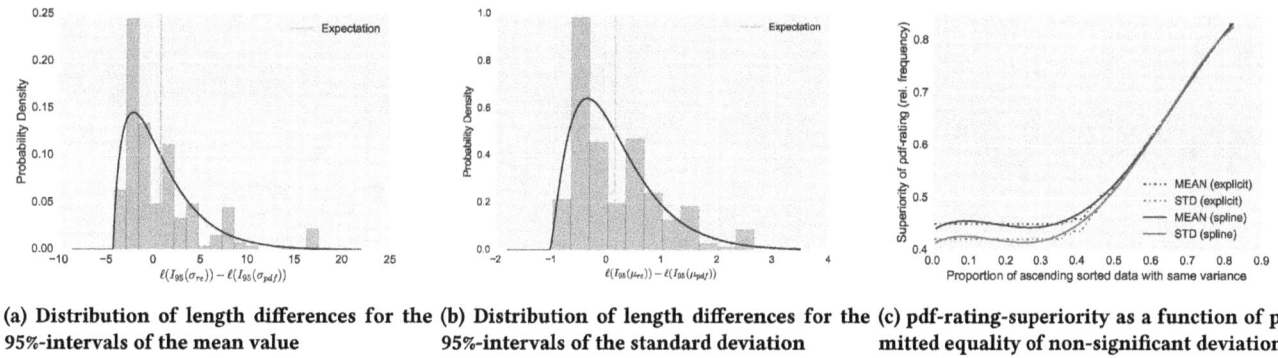

(a) Distribution of length differences for the 95%-intervals of the mean value

(b) Distribution of length differences for the 95%-intervals of the standard deviation

(c) pdf-rating-superiority as a function of permitted equality of non-significant deviations

Figure 2: Analysis of the rating-distributions' precision depending on the applied method of gathering uncertainty

precisely one discrete rating option. But unfortunately this "all or nothing" does not match human cognitions when making decisions. This interpretation is supported by the fact that an outstanding majority had chosen more than one answer category. Thus by forcing a user to rate on discrete scales, the user will always select the mode of his "inner distribution" or perhaps some value nearby, depending on external influences. In contrast, the Gaussian data-model indicates, that many people possess the more or less the same uncertainty and that deviations in both directions are equally likely whereas large deviations are less likely than small deviations. In our experiments we located this common uncertainty to be 1.3 stars. Welch's t-test indicates that only 10% of all ISN distributions possess a significantly different expectation when using the pdf-proceeding. This is a strong indication for a latent cognition that is present for the majority of observed users.

For our investigations of the validity in terms of measurement precision, we compute the percentile distributions for each corresponding ISN and USN by re-sampling. In doing so, the standard deviations of these percentile distributions naturally become a measure of noise precision. The auxiliary quantity $\delta_q := \sigma_r(q) - \sigma_p(q)$ is positive for $\sigma_p(q) < \sigma_r(q)$ indicating superiority of the pdf-rating. A counting proves the invariance of the precision under measurement methodologies for lower percentiles as well as the superiority of the pdf-rating for higher percentiles.

The exploration of the USN validity must be considered more carefully. When computing scatter plots for δ_q against q, there are three repetitive **archetypes** to be spotted, which are monotonic behaviour (**homogeneity**), at least two clusters (**clustered**), and high dispersion with no visible relationship (**irregularity**). Having these descriptions in mind, all scatter plots were independently assigned to a category by two analysts (inter-rater reliability $\varrho = 0.99$). The quantitative extent of these archetypes within our data records summarises as follows: 28% of all users can be considered homogeneous, 27% can be considered irregular and 45% of all users tend to be clustered. Representatives of these archetypes can be seen in Figure 3. Homogeneous users (3a) either show no significant effect (constant line) or a functional relationship, so that the uncertainty by action can be converted into uncertainty by cognition and vice versa. Cognition and action are closely linked for these users, i.e. they make their decisions very thoughtfully and possibly not based on feelings. For the cluster archetype it can be seen, that those users

allow for options in the pdf-rating which they would otherwise never have considered. Action and perception are not in harmony, i.e. these users probably use mainly their gut feeling for making decisions. The irregular archetype does not show any relationship between action and cognition. Probably, those users have not rated seriously and just clicked through the online survey.

Research Question Q2. Evaluation of the hypothesis testing indicates that the RMSE-distributions from both rating proceedings are fundamentally different for any of the simulated recommender systems. In particular, this is caused by a significant shift of the distributions' expectations, whereas the standard deviations does not differ significantly in any case. Accordingly, it can be concluded that the measurement uncertainty mainly affects the location-parameter of the RMSE and that its spread can thus only be impacted significantly by the human uncertainty. This σ-invariance under measurement proceeding is consistent with our findings from research question Q1, i.e. that the rating-distributions (containing the human uncertainty information) are more or less equivalent.

Nevertheless, the pdf-rating provides an information gain that might result into precision enhancement or reliability growth. When plotting the auxiliary variable δ_q against the sampled percentiles q of the RMSE-distributions, the pdf-rating outperforms the re-rating in any case. This precision even increases monotonically for higher percentiles. Thus, the pdf-rating is theoretically supposed to limit the number of possible outcomes for any re-sampling of the RMSE-distribution.

Figure 4 reveals the tremendous impact of both, human uncertainty and measurement uncertainty, on composed quantities. The ambiguity of the rating-distributions also lead to an ambiguity of the RMSE with a large range of possibilities. Whilst we can recognise a good resolution for a few RMSEs in the best case, this is virtually no longer possible for the worst case. The higher precision of the pdf-rating can also been observed here: Within the worst case, a density function is shifting to the right, so that the error probability decreases. Within the best case, the densities are moving closer to the expected distributions. Hence, the range of possible RMSEs is just a smaller subinterval of the range yielded by re-ratings. However, the fundamental problem can not be solved even with the pdf-rating, since very large overlaps are still possible. The obvious way of reducing the measurement uncertainty is to reduce the length of confidence intervals that scale with $1/\sqrt{N}$.

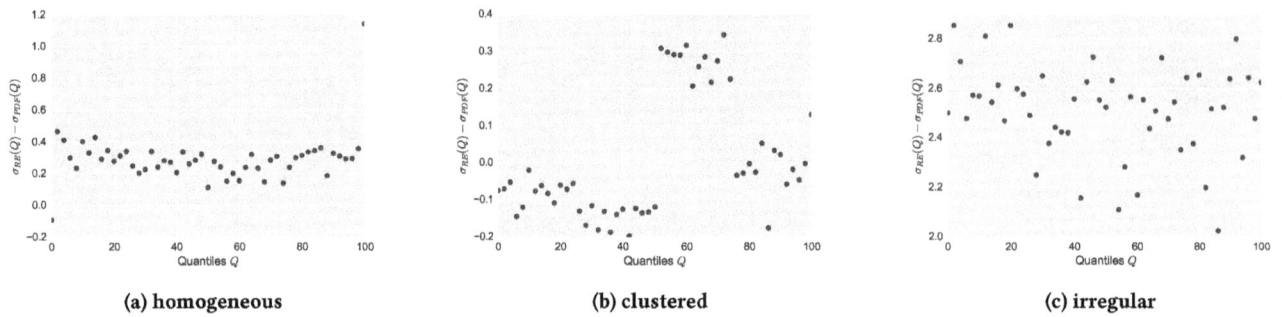

(a) homogeneous

(b) clustered

(c) irregular

Figure 3: Examples of user archetypes revealing ranges where cognition is more precise than action

Thus, the larger our sample, the smaller the intervals and the borderline cases of the RMSE will converge into a stationary state. By freezing the point estimators of all rating-distributions while artificially increasing the sample size, we may estimate the necessary amount of ratings to enforce convergence, so we can speak of the *true* RMSE of a recommender system. When opting for the intersection area of the minimum and maximum RMSE as a measure of this convergence, we may show the necessity of 1000-2000 ratings in order to gain intersections of more than 90%, i.e. the minimum and maximum RMSE become mostly equivalent. This means that every user in a real rating scenario would have to re-evaluate the same item at least 1000 times to locate the RMSE-distribution accurately. However, when using the pdf-rating proceeding, a particular user would yet still have to repeat the rating task at least 40 times.

So far we have only considered the effects of measurement uncertainty on a single RMSE-distribution. However, human uncertainty (associated to the width of the RMSE-distribution) leads to a much more fundamental problem, which is invariant under change of methods, namely the distinguishability of different recommender systems. This distinguishability is affected by the fact that two distributions may be overlapping. This implies a a non-vanishing probability that one system outperfoms another, although a ranking with respect to the expected value would indicate the opposite. Figure 5 shows the curve of the error probability for the ranking $X_{opt} < X_{noise}$ where X_{opt} is the optimal recommender and X_{noise} its noise-distorted copy, whose prediction quality is worse by design. We can see that the error probability for the re-rating drops below the 5% mark much earlier than the error probability for the pdf-rating. In line with common hypothesis tests, we define this 5% mark as the borderline of evidence. Thus, distinctions to the optimum can be considered to be significant only after passing this borderline. It is apparent that by means of the re-rating, smaller differences can be detected significantly in contrast to the pdf-rating.

5 DISCUSSION AND CONCLUSIONS

Discussion. Within our experiments, the normal distribution appears to be a good data model, for it is easy to handle, widely used in cognitive science for description of human properties and can not be rejected in more than 98% of our data records.

When it comes to a comparison of the re-rating against the pdf-rating, a careful analysis of the individual distribution parameters show that the respective differences are only significant for less than 20% of the data. Overall, the rating-distributions may have descriptive deviations, but all lie within the range of random fluctuations. Unfortunately, each distribution is not unique, since we

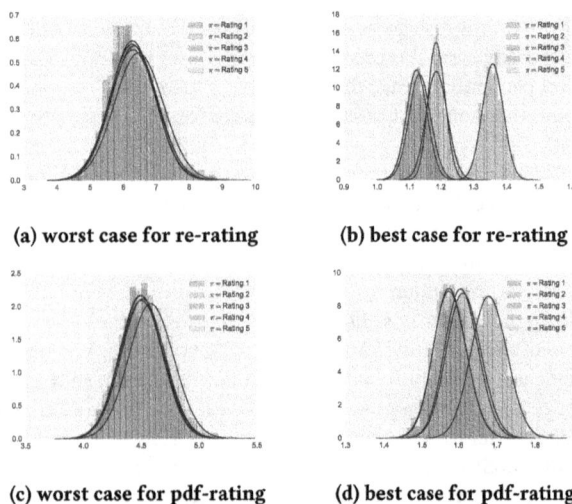

(a) worst case for re-rating

(b) best case for re-rating

(c) worst case for pdf-rating

(d) best case for pdf-rating

Figure 4: Borderline cases for the RSME of different recommender systems using re-rating and pdf-rating.

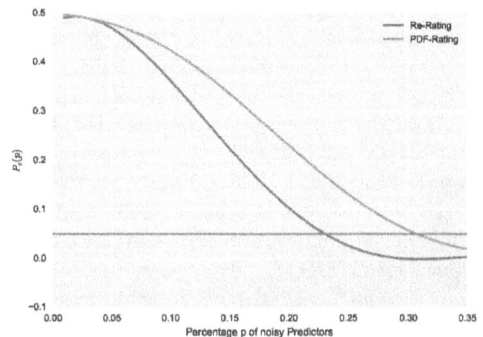

Figure 5: Error Probabilities for the ranking $X_{opt} < X_{noise}$ using the re-rating and pdf-rating

can only assign the parameters within confidence intervals due to a finite sample size (precision) and simulations on this basis would have to sample those parameters from their intervals (leading to reliability concerns). The comparison of confidence intervals shows that both measument approaches, model more precisely about half of the data set. The improvements of the pdf-rating for one half of this data is very large compared to the deterioration of the other half. So, on average a slight gain in overall precision occurs when using the pdf-rating. However, there are hardly any significant differences between the two methods for the rating-distributions.

The picture changes, when we consider the distributions of the variances. The actual ratings here lead to power-law-distributions, i.e. only a few people got a high extent of uncertainty while many people have very little uncertainty. This is contrary to our every-day experience and might be an artefact of the rating instrument in which users are forced to make a discrete decision and don't have the possibility to allow other options to a certain degree. On the other hand, the distributions obtained by the pdf-rating, are normally distributed and always possess the same expectation for the ISN. Accordingly, all users show a common uncertainty on average while each individual is scattering more or less. This essentially points to an immanent cognition, which has often been addressed specifically in our experimental setting. In case of reliability testing, the pdf-rating also leads to a higher precision, which increases sharply for higher percentiles. Overall, there is a strong deviation of the results of both measurement methods within the noise distributions. This indicates that the perceived uncertainty as an operationalisation for cognitive uncertainty is tremendously different from the uncertainty that is actually measurable through actions. This suggests that users are not able to tell us what is really going on in their minds by answering on commonly used scales.

Concerning the RMSE, both measurement approaches will lead to significant changes of the density location whereas the density spread retains. This invariance of spread under measurement approaches indicates, that the impact of human uncertainty on composed quantities can be addressed separately from the measurement method. But nevertheless, the measurement uncertainty leads to an ambiguity of the RMSE-distribution. The range of possibilities in our example range from a total overlapping (no distinguishing at all) to very good distinguishability. The superiority of the pdf-rating in terms of precision can be observed in the range of possible outcomes. This range is just a smaller subinterval of the range yielded from re-ratings. Anyway, the fundamental problem of identifying the true distribution remains unsolved, since there are still very large intersections in the worst case. This is because the precision is set up by a frequentist translation of the entered user confidence and thus we can only reach a maximum sample size of $N = 25$. Although this is five times larger than the underlying sample size of the re-rating-proceeding, it is still far from the barrier of $N = 1000$ for which the RMSE converges into a stationary state.

Our analysis of distinguishing between the RMSE of an optimal recommender and the those of a distorted copy reveals that by re-rating, lower differences can be detected significantly. In this case, the precision of the pdf-rating cannot impact this simulation because the expected distributions (stationary states) were assumed. However, both approaches have in common that the fundamental problem of distinctness still exists. This means that a recommender can only be distinguished from a supposedly better one to a certain limit, i.e. there is a natural barrier from which beyond there is only one equivalence class at good recommenders and rankings are no longer possible. This is the first statistically sound proof for the so far only as a theoretical quantity existing Magic Barrier [17].

It is striking that the approach which provides a location of the true state more accurately, will lead to significant distinctions only in the case of larger differences. On the other hand, the approach which detects significant distances for smaller deviations, does not allow the true RMSE to be located at all. However, both properties - (1) limiting the possibilities for the true state of two RMSEs and (2) distinguishing them - are important in real applications. Accordingly, none of the presented methods can solve both meshing problems simultaneously.

In the end, there is still the question of which specific measurement approach fits to a specific situation. It has been shown that the distinguishability problem of a composed quantity is invariant under the measuring method and the gain in precision only marginally limits the possible states of its density. Thus, the choice of a specific approach does not matter. Likewise, the rating-distributions retrieved from both methodologies do not differ significantly. Therefore, if analyses are carried out directly on the rating-distributions (e.g. when clustering in collaborative filtering is operated on the basis of density intersection as a measure for the similarity of two ratings), then the selection of a specific measurement method is also irrelevant. Blatant deviations do arise in the consideration of variances. Hence, if an explicit consideration of the uncertainty is in the focus of analysis (e.g. providing additional products, search results, etc. which the user might like), then the selection of adequate measuring method is crucial. Here, the actual choice for a particular approach depends on whether human actions or human decisions shall be used for the analysis.

Conclusion. What are the consequences for user modelling and predictive data mining in general? The essence of our contribution is the revelation of the following problems:

(1) People are not able to tell us what they really mean.
(2) Human uncertainty affects the evidence of data analysis.
(3) Human uncertainty can not be measured exactly.

At this point it must be said that these problems are not grounded in this new perspective presented here, but have always been present in data analysis. The approaches used in this contribution are just able to make these problems visible. Furthermore, these problems do not only occur in this special example, but have also been proven by us in other situations of user feedback before. These problems are therefore likely to affect any area of computer science where user feedback has to be worked on. In particular, the field of user modelling, personalisation and adaptation is strongly impacted. For this reason, it becomes crucial to examine the extent of impact of human uncertainty and measurement uncertainty in other situations within this field of research. It is also necessary to find proper solutions for these problems in order to keep our systems optimally adapted to human beings, i.e. not to a priori exclude appropriate possibilities and making decisions on the basis of perhaps inadequate statistical analyses. We will continue to address these issues in further research.

REFERENCES

[1] Xavier Amatriain (Ed.). 2012. *Workshop on Recommendation Utitlity Evaluation: Beyond RMSE September*. ACM, Dublin, Ireland.

[2] Xavier Amatriain and Josep Pujol. 2009. Rate It Again: Increasing Recommendation Accuracy by User Re-rating. In *Proceedings of the Third ACM Conference on Recommender Systems*. ACM, 173–180.

[3] Xavier Amatriain, Josep M. Pujol, and Nuria Oliver. 2009. I Like It... I Like It Not: Evaluating User Ratings Noise in Recommender Systems. In *17th International Conference on User Modeling, Adaptation, and Personalization: Formerly UM and AH (UMAP '09)*. 247–258.

[4] Joeran Beel, Marcel Genzmehr, Stefan Langer, Andreas Nürnberger, and Bela Gipp. 2013. A Comparative Analysis of Offline and Online Evaluations and Discussion of Research Paper Recommender System Evaluation. In *Proceedings of the International Workshop on Reproducibility and Replication in Recommender Systems Evaluation (RecSys '13)*. 7–14.

[5] Andy Buffler, Saalih Allie, and Fred Lubben. 2001. The development of first year physics students' ideas about measurement in terms of point and set paradigms. *International Journal of Science Education* 23, 11 (2001), 1137–1156.

[6] F Kenneth Chan. 2011. Miss Distance–Generalized Variance Non-Central Chi Distribution. In *AAS/AIAA Space Flight Mechanics Meeting*. 11–175.

[7] Michael Grabe. 2011. *Grundriss der Generalisierten Gauß'schen Fehlerrechnung*. Springer Berlin Heidelberg.

[8] Susanne Heinicke and Kevin Jasberg. 2015. Learning About Measurement Uncertainty in an Alternative Approach to Traditional Error Calculation. In *Electronic Proceedings of the ESERA 2015 Conference*, Vol. Part 1: Learning science: conceptual understanding. p. 265–270.

[9] Herlocker. 2004. Evaluating collaborative filtering recommender systems. *ACM Transactions on Information Systems* 22, 1 (2004), 5–53.

[10] Maria Iannario. 2014. Modelling Uncertainty and Overdispersion in Ordinal Data. *Communications in Statistics - Theory and Methods* 43 (2014), 771–786. Issue 14.

[11] JCGM. 2008. *Guide to the Expression of Uncertainty in Measurement*. Technical Report. BIPM.

[12] JCGM. 2008. *Supplement 1 to the GUM - Propagation of distributions using a Monte Carlo method*. Technical Report. BIPM.

[13] Tien et.al. Nguyen. 2013. Rating Support Interfaces to Improve User Experience and Recommender Accuracy. In *Proceedings of the 7th ACM Conference on Recommender Systems*. ACM, 149–156.

[14] Peck and Jay L. Devore. 2017. *Statistics: The Exploration and Analysis of Data*. Brooks / Cole.

[15] Francesco Ricci, Lior Rokach, and Bracha Shapira. 2015. *Recommender Systems Handbook*. Springer.

[16] Alan Said and Alejandro Bellogín. 2014. Comparative recommender system evaluation: benchmarking recommendation frameworks. In *Proceedings of the 8th ACM Conference on Recommender systems*. ACM, 129–136.

[17] Alan Said, Brijnesh Jain, Sascha Narr, and Till Plumbaum. 2012. Users and Noise: The Magic Barrier of Recommender Systems. In *User Modeling, Adaptation, and Personalization*. Vol. 7379. Springer Berlin / Heidelberg, 237–248.

[18] Alan Said and Domonkos Tikk. 2012. Recommender systems evaluation: A 3D benchmark. In *ACM RecSys 2012 workshop on Recommendation utility evaluation: beyond RMSE, Dublin, Ireland*. ACM, 21–23.

[19] Sergej Sizov. 2016. Assessment of Rating Prediction under Response Uncertainty. In *ACM Conference on Web Science*.

User Perception of Next-Track Music Recommendations

Iman Kamehkhosh
TU Dortmund, Germany
iman.kamehkhosh@tu-dortmund.de

Dietmar Jannach
TU Dortmund, Germany
dietmar.jannach@tu-dortmund.de

ABSTRACT

Many of today's music streaming websites and apps provide personalized next-track listening recommendations based on the user's current and past listening behavior. In the research literature, various algorithmic approaches to determine suitable next tracks can be found. However, almost all of them were evaluated in offline experiments using, for example, manually created playlists as a gold standard. In this work, we aim to check the external validity of insights that are obtained through such offline experiments on historical datasets. We conducted an online user study involving 277 subjects in which the participants evaluated the suitability of four different alternatives of continuing a given set of playlists. Our results indicate that manually created playlists can in fact represent a reasonable gold standard, an insight for which no evidence existed in the literature before. Furthermore, our work was able to confirm that considering playlist homogeneity aspects does not only lead to performance improvements in offline experiments – as indicated by past research – but also to a better quality perception by users. However, the observations also revealed that user studies of this type can be easily distorted by item familiarity biases, because the participants tend to evaluate continuation alternatives better when they know the track or the artist.

CCS CONCEPTS

•**Information systems** →**Recommender systems;** *Music retrieval;* •**Human-centered computing** →**User studies;**

KEYWORDS

Music Recommendation; Perceived Quality; User Study

1 INTRODUCTION

Many modern online music streaming services and mobile apps provide the functionality of generating virtually endless playlists of tracks based on the user's recent listening behavior. The problem of determining suitable playlist continuations has also been explored in the academic literature, and a variety of algorithmic approaches was proposed in the last two decades. To determine such *next-track music recommendations*, these algorithms rely on various types of information, including musical features, meta-data, social tags, or the user's current location and context [4, 5, 17, 31].

Similar to the general field of recommender systems, the evaluation of playlisting algorithms in academia is mainly accomplished through offline experimental designs [25]. A common approach to benchmark different algorithms is to use playlists created by music enthusiasts as a gold standard. Such "hand-crafted" playlists can be easily obtained from music platforms like last.fm in large quantities. A typical experimental procedure is then to hide individual tracks, e.g., the last track, from a given and assumedly well-designed playlist and let the algorithms predict the hidden tracks [3, 17, 24]. Using such a design, standard information retrieval (IR) measures like Recall or the Mean Reciprocal Rank can be applied. In addition, other quality factors can be assessed with quantitative metrics, e.g., the coherence of the recommended tracks with the given playlist in terms of their musical features [22].

So far, however, limited evidence exists that such computational quality measures are correlated with the actual quality perception of music listeners. One main question in that context is if the hand-crafted playlists are truly representative of the tastes of many users, i.e., if the hidden tracks are considered to be suitable continuations by users other than the creator of the playlist. If this is not the case, being able to predict the hidden track can be of limited value.

In other domains, like movie recommendations, different studies indicate that better performance of algorithms in offline experiments, e.g., in terms of prediction accuracy, does not necessarily translate into a better quality perception by the users or into a positive impact on business metrics. Likewise, it is not always fully clear in which cases users appreciate the recommendation of more diverse or novel items [9, 11, 14, 15].

With this work, we aim to assess to what extent the outcomes of offline experiments in the music domain correlate with the users' quality perception.[1] This question regarding the external validity of findings obtained through offline experiments on historical data has, to our knowledge, not been analyzed in the music recommendation literature to a large extent, even though the limitations of offline experiments are also well-known in the music information retrieval literature, see, e.g., [29].

In the remainder of this paper we first review different insights regarding the performance of different playlists algorithms that were obtained from offline experiments. Next, we describe the design of a user study in which the participants assessed the quality of possible playlist continuations generated by different algorithms. We then discuss the results in detail and in particular check the results for possible familiarity biases, i.e., if the participants considered a suggested continuation as a better match when they already knew the track. The work ends with a discussion of previous works and practical implications of our findings.

UMAP'17, July 9–12, 2017, Bratislava, Slovakia
© 2017 ACM. 978-1-4503-4635-1/17/07...$15.00
DOI: http://dx.doi.org/10.1145/3079628.3079668

---

[1]For a detailed discussion of the perceived quality of recommendations see [27].

2 OFFLINE ANALYSES: COMMON SETUPS AND PAST OBSERVATIONS

2.1 Common Offline Experiment Setups

In [4], different possible ways of evaluating automated playlist generation algorithms are reviewed. Since field tests (A/B tests) are rarely possible in academic environments and user studies in the music domain require significant efforts [29], most researchers resort to ex-post analyses and simulation experiments based on existing datasets.

Datasets. The datasets used in the literature are often collections of listening logs, e.g., of last.fm users [40], or collections of manually created playlists shared by music enthusiasts, e.g., [30]. Publicly shared playlists have the potential advantage that they are in many cases created with much care by music lovers, e.g., with respect to the included artists, track transitions, etc. [10]. Automatically recorded listening logs, in contrast, can be biased by an existing playlisting algorithm implemented on the site (e.g., an automated radio station). Also, they can contain situations where the user listened to an entire album, which means that the order of the tracks is not necessarily determined by considerations regarding, e.g., track transitions, but by other, not music-related factors. In our user study, we therefore rely on hand-crafted playlists as a gold standard for the evaluation.

Computational Metrics. Regarding the evaluation procedure and the computational metrics, one common approach in the recent literature is to split the available playlists into training and test sets, and to let different algorithms predict the last, held-out track of each playlist in the test set [4, 17, 33, 41].

Using this setup, typical information retrieval measures can be applied, including in particular Recall (hit rate), which in our case of only one held-out track is proportional to Precision. In addition, one can not only determine whether a playlister managed to predict the right track, but also if it was at least able to predict the correct artist, genre, or topic. Furthermore, one can measure the homogeneity of the recommended tracks, e.g., in terms of the tempo, and their coherence with the last tracks, e.g., in terms of the genre.

In this work, we will focus on the comparison of such IR measures with the users' quality perceptions. Other computational metrics for assessing playlist continuations were proposed in the literature, e.g., based on the average likelihood of tracks appearing together in playlists [29]. Such approaches are however less popular in the literature and have certain limitations as discussed in [4].

2.2 Insights from Offline Experiments

Some of the more recent works that relied on the described "hide-last-track" evaluation approach to benchmark playlisting algorithms include [4, 17, 21, 24] or [22].

In [4], a number of algorithms were compared using different datasets of publicly shared playlists. The set of algorithms included two different rule-mining approaches (association rules and sequential patterns), a k-nearest-neighbor approach, as well as two baseline strategies that recommend the most popular tracks of a selected set of artists. The first of these baselines simply recommends the greatest hits of the artists that appear in the user's most recent listening history. The second, in addition, recommends the most popular tracks of similar artists.

The two following main observations were made:

i) The k-nearest-neighbor (*kNN*) approach led to the best accuracy results across all datasets, when a small n was chosen when determining Recall@n. This situation corresponds to the problem of determining next-track recommendations. Using the nearest neighbors is also favorable in terms of the Recall compared to other, more complex techniques like Bayesian Personalized Ranking (BPR) [36], a comparably recent learning-to-rank method, which is optimized for implicit feedback recommendation scenarios.

ii) A newly proposed simple method called "Collocated Artists – Greatest Hits" (*CAGH*), which recommends the most popular tracks of artists that have often been listened to together in the recent past, however, also led to competitive results. When very long recommendation lists were considered, the method was even consistently better than the *kNN* method.

In other studies [17, 21, 22, 24], the following additional insights were obtained:

iii) Considering additional signals (e.g., musical features, track meta-data, or past listening sessions) in combination with the track co-occurrences captured by the *kNN* method can lead to further accuracy improvements. Incorporating such signals also helps to make the playlist continuations more homogeneous and coherent with the recently listened tracks.

iv) An evaluation using multiple metrics in parallel showed that the comparably simple *CAGH* method mentioned above is particularly competitive in predicting the topic (expressed through tags), genre, or artist of the next track to be played [21].

Given these observations, the goal of our research is to validate the suitability of the offline research setup in general and, more specifically, to test if there is a correspondence between the insights obtained from the offline studies and the subjective quality experience of the users. This leads us to the following research questions, which we aim to answer through a user study.

RQ-1: Are hand-crafted playlists suitable as a gold standard for the evaluation of playlisting algorithms? In other words, will people other than the playlist creator consider the hidden track as a suitable continuation?

RQ-2: Can the consideration of *additional signals*, e.g., musical features or meta-data into the recommendation process improve the perceived quality of the next-track recommendations? Do the observed effects depend on the specific underlying *theme* of a playlist?

RQ-3: How do approaches like *CAGH*, which focus on the most popular items of the artists and which achieve good results in offline experiments, fare in terms of the users' subjective quality perception? Would it be a "safe" strategy to use *CAGH* in practical applications?

RQ-4: Since item familiarity can be a confounding factor in recommender systems user studies that involve popularity-based baselines (like *CAGH*) [23], we ask: Do study participants consider recommendations as more suitable when they already know (and like) the tracks?

3 USER STUDY DESIGN

3.1 General Procedure for Participants

We created an online application for the purpose of our user study.[2] The participants of the study, which were recruited via different mailing lists, were guided by the application through multiple steps. In an initial step, the application displayed a welcome screen, on which the general purpose of music recommender systems was briefly explained. Then, the participants had to accomplish the following four tasks.

(1) First, the users had to listen to 30-second excerpts of a four-item playlist.[3] The user interface consisted of four vertically aligned audio controls to start and stop the playback of each track. No information about the artists or the tracks themselves was displayed.

(2) When the participants had listened to the tracks, they were asked five questions about the similarity of the songs of the playlist in different dimensions. The questions were related to the emotion, energy, theme, genre, and tempo of the tracks. Using 7-point Likert scale items, the participants could state their degree of agreement (from "not at all" to "completely") that "all songs have the same tempo", etc. The sequence of the questions was randomized across participants. When answering the questions, the participants could listen to the tracks again if they wanted to.[4]

(3) The participants were then presented with four alternative playlist continuations, which were displayed in randomized order across participants. Again, the participants could listen to excerpts of 30 seconds and then state on a 7-point Likert scale item to what extent they agree that the track suits the given playlist (from "not at all" to "perfectly"). In addition, they could indicate if they liked the song (yes, no, indifferent) and if they know the track's artist, the track itself, or both. Again, no information about the recommended tracks was displayed. A screen capture of this part of the application is shown in Figure 1. At all times, the participants could listen to all tracks of the playlist individually or listen to a 30-second summary of all tracks.

(4) In the last step, the participants were asked questions regarding their age group and their music experience. A 7-point Likert scale item ("I randomly listen to music" to "I am a professional") was used for the latter response item. The participants could finally leave some comments and then submit their answers.

The participants could repeat this trial consisting of four steps for up to five different playlists. We discuss the selection of the playlists next.

3.2 Selection of Playlists

We used five different playlists in the experiment, which we obtained from three different music platforms (*artofthemix.org, last.fm, 8tracks.com*).

In theory, every participant could have evaluated the possible continuations for all five playlists. In reality, however, most participants completed only one trial and in the end 300 trials were completed by 277 participants. The assignment of the trials was mainly based on a round-robin scheme across the participants to obtain an even number of samples for each playlist. The assignment of the playlist of the first trial was therefore a random one from the participant's perspective.

Since one of our goals was to assess if the choice of the most suitable next track is influenced by certain characteristics of the playlists, we selected the five playlists in a way that each one was very homogeneous in exactly one dimension. We determined the homogeneity of the tracks in the respective dimension by examining the musical features of the tracks as provided by *the.echonest.com*, by considering the social tags assigned by the users to the tracks on last.fm, by analyzing the tracks' lyrics, and by using artist meta-data and expert judgments. We used the following set of playlists.

(1) *Topic-playlist*: This playlist was organized by its creator around the topic *Christmas*. The tracks of the playlist are Christmas pop songs from the 1970s and 1980s.

(2) *Genre-playlist*: This playlist contained tracks of the genre "Soul". We retrieved the genre information of the track artists from *the.echonest.com*.

(3) *Mood-playlist*: The mood playlist contains *romantic* songs. We relied on a semi-automatic analysis of the song lyrics to validate the homogeneity of the playlist in this respect by comparing the TF-IDF (Term Frequency/Inverse Document Frequency) vectors of the tracks of the playlist.

(4) *Tempo-playlist*: The tracks of this playlist all have a similar tempo. The average tempo is 125 beats per minute (bpm) with a standard deviation of only 2 bpm.

(5) *Energy-playlist*: This playlist is homogeneous with respect to the *energy* value provided by the API of *the.echonest.com*. The energy value is based on various types of information, including the loudness of the track. The average energy value of the tracks was at 0.86 on a scale of 0 to 1, with a standard deviation of only 0.02.

When selecting the playlists, we tried our best to make sure that each playlist was homogeneous only in one dimension. We furthermore only selected playlists that contained at most one track per artist. Finally, we commonly avoided choosing playlists that a) contain generally very popular tracks and artists or b) were extreme, e.g., in terms of the tempo. We used the number of occurrences of artists and tracks in the datasets to determine their general popularity level. The detailed descriptions of all playlists can be found online.[5]

Overall, the selection of five playlists with varying characteristics shall help us to test the quality perception for a broader set of *types* of playlists. From the finally selected playlists, we retained only the first five tracks, of which the last one was hidden in the experiment.

3.3 Selection of Recommendation Techniques

In each trial, the study participants were presented with four alternative tracks to continue the given playlist. One of the options was the track that was chosen by the playlist creator, i.e., the hidden

---

[2]The survey can be accessed at https://ls13ap85.cs.tu-dortmund.de:8443/music-survey
[3]The previews were taken from the music service of Spotify. The excerpts were usually not the first 30 seconds of the tracks.
[4]Since these questions refer to the given playlist, we ask them immediately after the participants had listened to the tracks (and before presenting the recommendations) to avoid confusion.

[5]http://ls13-www.cs.tu-dortmund.de/homepage/umap2017-music/playlists.pdf

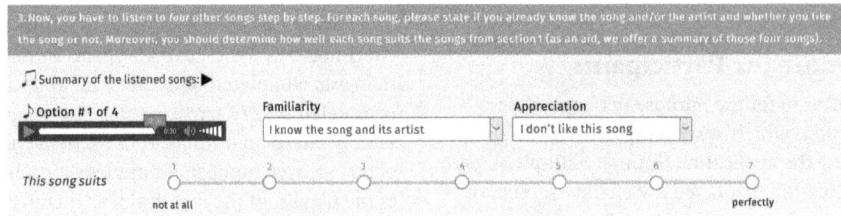

Figure 1: Evaluating one of four possible continuations.

track. The other three alternatives were automatically determined using playlisting algorithms from the literature and were presented in randomized order. To train the algorithms we used the dataset from which the playlist was originally taken.[6]

Selection Rationale. The following algorithms were included in the experiment. Technical details will be given below.

- *kNN:* A nearest-neighbor method used, e.g., in [4], which performs generally well in terms of the hit rate and which is used as a baseline in a number of research works.
- *CAGH:* A method that selects the greatest hits of certain artists, and which therefore recommends comparably popular items [3, 21]. Including this method helps us also to assess the effects of recommending popular tracks to some extent.
- *kNN+X:* A hybrid method that uses *kNN* as a baseline but considers additional (musical) features to improve the prediction accuracy and to increase the homogeneity of the playlists [24]. The inclusion of this method in the experiment helps us assess the value of considering additional features with respect to the users' quality perception.

Algorithm Details. The general task of next-track recommendation techniques is to determine the relevance of a *target track* t^* with respect to a given playlist beginning (listening history) h.

3.3.1 kNN. The used *kNN* method takes the playlist beginning h as an input and identifies other playlists in the training data that contain the same tracks. The main assumption is that if there are additional tracks in a similar past session (i.e., the "neighbors"), chances are good that these tracks suit the current listening history h, too.

Technically, given a listening history h, we first compute the binary cosine similarity of h and the other sessions from the training data. The similarity values are then sorted and a set N_h of nearest neighbor sessions of h is determined. The *kNN* score of a target track t^* is then computed as the sum of the similarity values of h and neighbor sessions $nbr \in N_h$ which contain t^* (Equation 1). Note that the indicator function $1_{nbr}(t^*)$ returns 1 if nbr contains t^* and 0 otherwise.

$$score_{kNN}(h, t^*) = \sum_{nbr \in N_h} sim_{cosine}(h, nbr) \cdot 1_{nbr}(t^*) \quad (1)$$

In our experiments, we set $k=300$ to determine the playlist continuations, a parameter that was used for the same datasets also in [24].

---

[6]The public playlist collections from *last.fm* and *artofthemix.org* that were used in the experiments can be found at http://ls13-www.cs.tu-dortmund.de/homepage/umap2017-music/datasets.zip.

3.3.2 CAGH. The *CAGH* method recommends the greatest hits of artists that either appear in the playlist beginning h or are similar to the artists in h. The similarity of two artists is estimated based on artist co-occurrences in the playlists. Technically, given a user's current listening history h, the *CAGH* algorithm computes the relevance score of a target track t^* by means of Equation 2 .

$$score_{CAGH}(h, t^*) = \sum_{b \in A_h} sim_{artist}(a_{t^*}, b) \cdot cnt(t^*) \quad (2)$$

A_h is the set of artists in current history, $cnt(t^*)$ is the number of occurrences of t^* in the training data, which corresponds to the most frequently occurring tracks of the respective artists in the dataset, and a_{t^*} is the artist of the target track. As a measure of similarity of two artists $sim_{artist}(a_{t^*}, b)$, we count how often two artists appear together in the sessions of the training set.

3.3.3 Hybrid: kNN+X. In our experiment, we use the scoring scheme proposed in [24] to combine the scores returned by the *kNN* method with a score that expresses the suitability of a candidate track in terms of a certain (musical) feature.

Given a scoring function of a feature $score_f$, the combined score is computed as

$$score_{hybrid}(h, t^*) = \alpha \cdot score_{kNN}(h, t^*) + (1 - \alpha) \cdot score_f(h, t^*) \quad (3)$$

where the weight factor α is used to balance the relative importance of the baseline and the feature scores. The following feature scoring functions were used:

- *Topic-Scorer:* We use the social tags assigned to the tracks to determine the topic of a playlist. As done in [24], we compute TF-IDF vectors for each track using the tags. The average cosine similarity of the TF-IDF vectors of the tracks of a playlist represents the homogeneity level in terms of the topic.

  The topic score $score_{topic}$ of a target track t^* with the TF-IDF vector $\vec{t^*}$, given a history h consisting of tracks $t_1, \ldots, t_n$ with the TF-IDF vectors $\vec{t_1}$ to $\vec{t_n}$ is computed as follows.

$$score_{topic}(h, t^*) = sim_{cosine}\left(\frac{\Sigma_{t_i \in h} \vec{t_i}}{|h|}, \vec{t^*} \right) \quad (4)$$

- *Genre-Scorer:* To determine the genre of a playlist, we use the genres of the artists of its tracks.[7] The same content-based approach as the one used above for topics can be used for the genres. The TF-IDF vectors for each track are computed using the genres of its artist. The average cosine

---

[7]Genre information about individual tracks was in most cases not available to us.

similarity of the TF-IDF vectors of the tracks of a playlist is then used to measure its homogeneity level in terms of the genre. Similar to the topic score, Equation 4 can be used for computing the genre score $score_{genre}$.

- *Mood-Scorer:* Similar to [18], we applied a mood classification method to determine the general mood of the tracks based on their lyrics. First, list of mood-related social tags was used to create an initial ground truth set for a selected number of moods. The lyrics of the ground truth tracks were then processed and TF-IDF vectors were generated. A Support Vector Machines (SVM) classifier was finally applied on the generated TF-IDF vectors to create a binary predictive model for each target mood. These models were then used to predict the mood of unlabeled tracks.

  As a result, each track is labeled with a set M_t of moods. Accordingly, we build a set M_h of moods for each playlist. Each mood in this set is weighted by the number of occurrences of that mood divided by the number of the tracks of the playlist (w_m). For a target track t^*, the mood score $score_{mood}$ is then computed as the sum of the weights of the common moods of the target track M_{t^*} and the given history M_h, i.e., $1_{M_h}(m) = 1$ if M_h contains the mood of the target track m and 0 otherwise.

$$score_{mood}(h, t^*) = \sum_{m \in M_{t^*}} w_m \cdot 1_{M_h}(m) \qquad (5)$$

- *Tempo and Energy-Scorer:* Musical features such as the tempo or the energy can be relevant factors when selecting tracks, e.g., for a workout or a party playlist. We correspondingly use the proposed scoring scheme in [24] for such numerical features based on the mean μ_h and standard deviation σ_h of the observed values in the given playlist (listening history). Given a history h and a feature value of a target track f_{t^*}, the value of the probability density function of a Gaussian distribution is used as a numerical feature score for tempo and energy.

$$score_{numfeature}(h, t^*) = \frac{1}{\sigma_h \sqrt{2\pi}} e^{-\frac{(f_{t^*} - \mu_h)^2}{2\sigma_h^2}} \qquad (6)$$

To compute the scores for our user study, we determined the weight (α) for the hybrid scorer by optimizing the hit rate on the training data as done in [24].[8]

4 RESULTS AND OBSERVATIONS

4.1 Participation Statistics

We recruited study participants by inviting students of university classes in Germany and Brazil, by sending emails to friends and colleagues, and by posting invitations on social network sites. 300 trials were completed by 277 subjects during a period of 8 weeks.[9] Each of the 5 playlists was evaluated 60 times. Most (83%) of the participants were aged between 20 and 40 and the majority of the participants was from Germany (43%) or Brazil (40%). On a scale

between 1 and 7, the median of the self-reported experience with music was 5, i.e., the participants were on average quite experienced or interested in music.

The average time for participants to complete one trial was at about 10 minutes. On average, they listened to about 22 seconds (of 30) of each track of the playlist and about 26 seconds of the recommended track. This indicates that the participants completed the survey carefully.

4.2 Study Outcomes

In the following, we will discuss the outcomes of the study with respect to the research questions from Section 2.2.

Determining a Ranking. The ultimate goal of many existing research papers is to determine a ranking of different algorithms, e.g., with respect to their accuracy. Since our goal is to determine the correspondence of offline results with the results obtained through the user study, we use a ranking-based approach to investigate the different research questions.

We use two different rank-aggregation strategies.[10]

(1) We report how often each recommendation technique was the *winner*, i.e., how often its recommendation was considered the most suitable alternative continuation. In each trial, an alternative was counted as the most suitable, if (a) it was rated higher than the other alternatives and (b) the *suitability* value assigned to it was greater than four. We set this threshold to avoid counting it as a "win" when a recommendation was actually not good, but merely better than other, even worse alternatives. In 10% of the cases, no clear winner could be determined based on these rules.

(2) We apply the Borda Count (BC) rank aggregation strategy to determine the *ranking of all four alternatives*. The responses provided by the participants are used as implicit ranking information. In the Borda Count computation scheme, the highest ranked alternative gets $n-1$ points, where n is the number of alternatives to be ranked. Each subsequent alternative gets one point less, so that the lowest-ranked alternative gets no points.

The result scores of the four different track continuation alternatives (i.e., the three ranking algorithms and the hidden track) are given in Table 1. To investigate to what extent familiarity aspects may affect the results, we report the results for two different configurations. In the "All Tracks" configuration, we consider the rankings of all trials (which fulfill the above-mentioned criteria). In the "Novel Tracks" configuration, we consider only trials where the participants indicated that they did not already know the most suitable track or its artist, which was the case in about 70% of all trials with a unique winner. To compute the Borda Count for novel tracks, we used a variant of the Borda Count from [12], which is designed for the aggregation of partial rankings (BC_{avg}).

4.2.1 RQ-1: Are hand-crafted playlists suitable for the evaluation of playlisting algorithms? In 41% of all trials with a unique winner, the participants selected the track as the most suitable continuation

---

[8]In the combinations of the *kNN* method with the topic and tempo scorers, α was set to 0.3 and in other combinations it was set to 0.7.

[9]We removed 9 additional participants from the study who did not listen to any track of the given playlist.

[10]The data collected in our study is ordinal, i.e., a ranking of the response levels is possible. However, we cannot assume equidistance between the response levels, which ranged from "(1) not suitable at all" to "(7) perfectly suitable". Using descriptive statistics like the mean and the standard deviation to aggregate the results would therefore be questionable from a methodological perspective.

Table 1: Ranking results.

Strategy	All Tracks		Novel Tracks	
	Ranked #1	BC	Ranked #1	BC_{avg}
Hidden Track	41%	645	43%	580
CAGH	46%	649	32%	403
kNN	25%	520	19%	477
kNN+X	30%	594	36%	631

that was originally picked by the creator of the given playlist. The difference between the score of the hidden track and the alternative computed by the *CAGH* method, which focuses on popular tracks that are often already known to the study participants, is not statistically significant.[11] The same ranking of the algorithms is obtained when the Borda Count is used.

When considering only trials in the evaluation where the participants did not know the track or its artist, the hidden track was significantly more often chosen as the most suitable option than the other alternatives; see the right-hand part of Table 1. The hidden track was also a good choice when using the Borda Count method; in this case, however, the *kNN+X* method significantly outperformed the other alternatives.

Overall, we see this as clear indicator that the manually created playlists used in the experiments are of good quality and that it can, in general, be meaningful to use such playlists as gold standard in offline experiments. Assuming that (many) publicly shared playlists are in fact created with care also means that these playlists can be used as a reliable source for detecting hidden patterns and relationships between tracks that can be exploited by next-track recommendation algorithms.

4.2.2 RQ-2: Can considering additional (musical) signals in the recommendation process improve the users' quality perception? To answer this question, we can compare the suitability assessments of the methods *kNN* and *kNN+X*. The latter method considers different additional signals in the recommendation process and outperforms the pure *kNN* method in offline experiments. Our results clearly show that considering different additional signals also leads to a statistically significant improvement in the quality (suitability) perception by the study participants. The *kNN+X* method was considered as more suitable than the *kNN* method in both configurations and on both measures, which indicates that the users in fact preferred track continuations that are coherent with the recently played tracks in different dimensions. When considering only novel track recommendations, the *kNN+X* method was actually the best performing one in terms of the Borda Count and the second best one in terms of the other measure (frequency of winning).

Coherence aspects were, however, not equally important for all tested signals. Additional analyses, which we do not report here for space reasons, showed that coherence in terms of the genre and the topic of the playlist was particularly important for the participants, i.e., in these cases, the *kNN+X* recommendation were generally ranked higher than those of the *kNN* method. An exception from this general pattern was observed for the *tempo*-oriented playlist, where the *kNN* and the *CAGH* method were on average ranked

higher than the *kNN+X* method. This was unexpected for two reasons. First, the tracks that were recommended by the *kNN* and the *CAGH* method was at about 75 bpm and far away from the average tempo of the given playlist, which was at 125 bpm. Second, 68% of the participants had in fact correctly identified the tempo as an underlying theme of the playlist according to the questionnaire (see Table 2). As a result, this indicates that in some cases homogeneity in terms of the tempo might be less important for users than other characteristics like artist homogeneity. The sometimes limited importance of the tempo was also observed in [20] based on an analysis of a larger pool of public playlists.[12]

4.2.3 RQ-3: How do popularity-based approaches like CAGH fare in terms of the subjective quality perception by users? The *CAGH* method not only leads to competitive results in offline experiments [21], its recommendations are also often considered to be very suitable by the participants of our study. This also indicates that using the hit rate *can be* one suitable proxy measure to evaluate different algorithms in offline experiments. However, when we only consider the participants' suitability assessments for tracks that are novel to them, the *CAGH* method does not perform as well as other approaches and even has the lowest performance across all possible alternatives with respect to the Borda Count.

Overall, according to our experiment, the popularity-biased *CAGH* can be considered as a "safe" strategy to determine generally suitable tracks in practice, particularly when it comes to cold start users. The capability of such a technique to help users discover new tracks or artists over time is, however, limited. In cases where item discovery is considered as a key value-adding feature, e.g., of an online streaming service, *CAGH* might therefore not be the best choice.

4.2.4 RQ-4: Do subjects consider recommendations as more suitable when they already know (and like) the tracks? With this research question, we aim to understand if the results of studies like ours can be biased by item familiarity effects, i.e., if the study participants tend to like a recommendation when they already know the track. Such an effect was observed in a user study in the movie domain in [23], where the simple recommendation of generally popular movies was the "winning" strategy.

The analyses in the previous sections indeed suggest that such effects can also exist in the music domain. There are measurable differences between the ranking of the alternatives when it comes to known or novel track recommendations. Specifically, the popularity-based *CAGH* method works particularly well when all trials are considered, but users found its recommendations often not appropriate when they did not know the track already. This means that the strong performance of the *CAGH* in our experiment in one configuration might be a light overestimation of the true performance of the method in practical settings.[13]

We analyze the differences between the algorithms in terms of the familiarity of users with their track recommendations in more depth in the following section.

---

[11]To test for statistical significance, we use the Mann-Whitney U test with $p < 0.05$.

[12]The relevance of different musical aspects can depend on the listening context. The inclusion of tracks in a playlist that all have a similar tempo might for example be desirable when listening to music while doing sports.

[13]The findings reported in [23] are based on a study on Mechanical Turk, and the motivation of the participants to provide reliable answers might be lower than in our experiment with volunteers that had no monetary incentive.

4.3 Analysis of Track Familiarity and Affinity

During the user study, when the participants assessed the suitability of a track as a possible continuation for the given playlist, they were asked to indicate if they already knew the recommended track or at least its artist. In addition, they could specify to what extent they *liked* the track, independent of its suitability for the given playlist. The results regarding the users' familiarity with the recommended alternatives are shown in Figure 2.

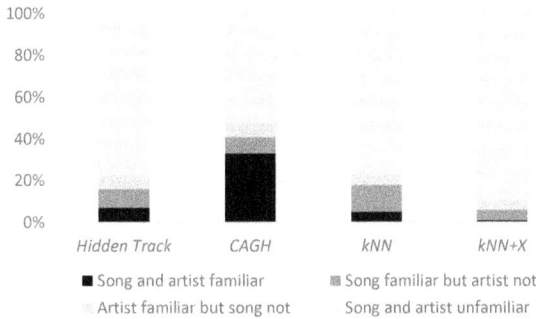

Figure 2: Familiarity level of alternative next-track recommendations in all trials.

The *CAGH* method by design recommends popular tracks, and it is not surprising that in almost half of the trials the subjects were already familiar with the tracks in some form. The hybrid *kNN+X* method, which focuses on coherence aspects, in contrast, recommended the largest amount of novel items. In about 90% of the trials, the recommended items were completely unknown to the study participants. However, this tendency of recommending novel tracks did not hurt the quality perception of users when compared with the plain *kNN* method (as shown in Table 1), maybe because the novel track recommendations were coherent with the recent listening history. A different effect was previously observed for the movie domain in [11], where novel item recommendations led to a lower quality perception.

Looking at the like/dislike statistics for the tracks themselves – we omit the detailed results for space reasons – we observed that the tracks that were recommended by the *CAGH* method were liked in about 60% of the cases. For all other alternatives, the percentage was much lower and at about 40% with no significant differences between the *kNN* and the *kNN+X* method. This indicates that the study participants distinguished if they generally liked a certain track or if they considered a track to be a suitable continuation for the given playlist. This is another indication that the study participants answered the questionnaire with care.

4.4 Perception of Playlist Characteristics

The results in Section 4.2 showed that the participants found playlist continuations more often suitable when they were coherent with the recently played tracks. The final question we analyze in this paper is to what extent the study participants actually *noticed* that there is an underlying design rationale for the different playlists and if they could identify the underlying theme.

During the experiment, we asked the users to answer to what extent they agree that the tracks of the given playlist had similar characteristics, e.g., in terms of the tempo or mood, see Section

Table 2: Frequencies of dominating characteristics as perceived by the participants.

True Theme	Topic	Genre	Mood	Tempo	Energy
Subjective Perception	Topic (95%)	Genre (55%)	Topic (40%)	Tempo (68%)	Genre (48%)

3. The main result of this analysis is shown in Table 2. The first row of the table shows the true underlying design rationale of the playlists. The second row shows the "winner" in terms of the users' perception. Looking, for example, at the column labeled with "Topic", we see that in 95% of the trials, the tracks of the playlist were indeed considered to be more similar to each other in terms of the topic than in any other dimension. Across all trials, the participants correctly identified the true theme of the playlist as a winner in almost two third of the cases.

In two cases, the participants, however, considered other themes as being more important than the true one. In the case of the *mood*-playlist, the participants more often found the tracks to be more similar in terms of the topic (40%) than in terms of the mood. About 30% of the users (not reported in the table) found the mood to be the dominating feature. Since the mood coherence of the playlist was identified by us based on the lyrics of the tracks, we believe that the fact that the participants could only listen to 30-second excerpts and probably did not focus on the lyrics contributed to this result. The *energy*-based playlist was the second one where we observed deviations. 48% of the participants rather felt that the tracks are connected by the genre than by the energy level (35%, not reported in the table). The reasons could be that some of the participants were less familiar with the term energy than with other concepts or that the energy level, as computed by *the.echonest.com*, does not always correlate well with the users' perception.

5 RESEARCH LIMITATIONS

Evaluating recommenders with user studies is challenging in different ways. In the music domain, the participants have to invest a considerable amount of time as they are required to listen to a number of tracks during the experiment. In our setup, we therefore limited the number of tracks in the given playlist to four and only provided 30-second previews of the tracks. Since we used excerpts that were selected and provided by a commercial service (Spotify), we are confident that the excerpts are representative of the tracks. Furthermore, all of the tracks in the experiment were not longer than usual pop songs and each track exhibited limited within-track variation of the tempo or harmonics.

Another challenge is that recommending mostly popular items might lead to a familiarity bias, i.e., the participants tend to rate items they already know highly [23] and dislike items they do not know, as was observed in [11] for the movie domain. In our experiment, we therefore selected playlists that did not contain too popular tracks and we did not reveal additional track or artist information. Furthermore, we explicitly asked the participants to indicate whether or not they knew the track already to quantify possible biases.

A more general limitation of laboratory studies is that when users feel being supervised or in a "simulation" mode, they might behave differently than when they are within one of their normal music listening environments. To alleviate this problem, we provided an online application to enable users to participate in the study when and where they wanted to.

Academic user studies in the music domain often have a limited size and in many cases only involve 10 to 20 participants in total [4]. Our study involved 277 participants and 300 trials, leading to 60 trials per condition. The majority of the study participants were university students in Germany and Brazil. While this population of digital natives might be representative of many users of today's digital music services, it still has to be shown to what extent the findings of the study generalize to other types of music listeners and to other types of musical genres.

Finally, our study was based on a specific collection of five tracks and we have to be aware that the choice of the playlists might have impacted the observed outcomes. To minimize this threat to validity, we have selected the playlists used in the experiments in a way that they (a) cover a broader range of music preferences, and (b) that they were assembled by their creators with different design rationales in mind. We, however, limited the number of playlists in the experiment to five in order to end up with a sufficient number of participants per playlist.

6 RELATED WORKS

Laboratory or online studies on music recommendation, and in particular on playlist generation, are comparably rare. The work by Barrington et al. [2] is one of the few exceptions. Similar to our work, they compare different music playlisting approaches in a user study. Their set of compared algorithms includes Apple's Genius collaborative filtering based system and, among others, a method based on artist similarity. As part of their experiment, they revealed the artist and track information in one condition and did not disclose this information in another. An interesting insight was that the Genius system was "overwhelmingly superior" when no information was displayed, whereas the artist-based method was perceived to produce slightly better recommendations in the other case. This effect is to some extent related to our observation regarding possible familiarity effects that can influence the users' evaluation of a recommendation. Overall, however, the main goal of the work by Barrington et al. was to compare content-based and collaborative filtering based methods. Our main goal, in contrast, was to validate the results obtained in offline experiments as was done for other recommendation domains in [8, 14, 19, 26] or [37].

A smaller number of user studies can be found in the literature that focus on specific aspects of different music recommendation scenarios. There are works that investigate, e.g., the role of track orders, track positions, and the problem of recommending *collections of items* [16]; works on the recommendation or selection of a suitable playlist for *groups of users* [34]; works on location-based contextualized music recommendation [5]; works that analyze the effect of visualizations and user control on the user experience [1]; and works that address the question of how different personality traits of users impact their perception of music [6, 13, 32]. In our study, we in contrast focused on a very general recommendation scenario and the comparison of offline algorithm performance and the subjective user experience.

Finding new performance measures that correlate with the subjective user experience was the goal of the recent work by Craw

et al. [7]. In their work, a new computational metric is proposed that balances listening events and explicit ratings to avoid that the recommendation of less popular items is "punished". They validated that their metric corresponds to the perceived quality assessment by music listeners through a user study involving 132 subjects. We see their work as complementary to ours, as we were not interested in defining new measures but in the assessment of the usefulness of commonly used IR measures.

Such IR measures, while often used in the literature, are not the only computational metrics that can be used to assess the quality of playlists. One can, for example, compute the diversity of a playlist (e.g., in terms of the genres), determine the coherence of the individual tracks in various dimensions, or analyze the smoothness of the transitions between two consecutive tracks. The main question when relying on such computational metrics, however, is if they are representative of the users' quality perception. One way to investigate this aspect is to analyze hand-crafted playlists in order to see if music enthusiasts follow certain (implicit) guidelines when they create playlists and, for example, select tracks for inclusion that are homogeneous in certain respects or not. Examples of works that investigated such patterns in playlists are [10, 20, 38] and [39]. The existence of such patterns indicates that certain quality characteristics, e.g., diversity, *can* in general be relevant when making playlist recommendations, but users might have different preferences regarding how diverse a playlist should be [39]. Furthermore, the relevance of certain aspects can depend on the contextual situation of the user. In our work, we therefore focused on traditional IR measures and consider the investigation of these other aspects as important areas for future work.

Overall, we see our work as one further contribution in the context of user-centered evaluation approaches for recommendation systems, which have gained increasing popularity in recent years and which led to the development of new evaluation frameworks [27, 35]. For the domain of Music Information Retrieval, Lee and Price [28] recently discussed the limitations of the current research practice in the field and stressed the importance of user-centered evaluation approaches. They also conducted a qualitative user study, where the goal was to better understand the various factors that can have an influence on the users' quality perception of (commercial) music services. The overall goal of their research is to develop a more comprehensive evaluation approach that considers a variety of relevant factors beside accuracy, including the user interface design or privacy and trust aspects.

7 CONCLUSIONS

In this work, we have investigated the quality perception of playlist continuation proposals generated by different next-track music recommendation techniques. Since several observations obtained in offline experiments could be reproduced in the user study, one main insight of the work is that hand-crafted playlists shared by music enthusiasts can indeed be a valuable basis for designing and evaluating recommendation algorithms. Furthermore, our work provided evidence that recent approaches that focus both on playlist coherence and prediction accuracy not only lead to better results in offline experiments, but also lead to an improved quality perception by users.

REFERENCES

[1] Ivana Andjelkovic, Denis Parra, and John O'Donovan. 2016. Moodplay: Interactive Mood-based Music Discovery and Recommendation. In *UMAP '16*. 275–279.

[2] Luke Barrington, Reid Oda, and Gert R. G. Lanckriet. 2009. Smarter than Genius? Human Evaluation of Music Recommender Systems. In *ISMIR '09*. 357–362.

[3] Geoffray Bonnin and Dietmar Jannach. 2013. Evaluating the Quality of Playlists Based on Hand-Crafted Samples. In *ISMIR '13*. 263–268.

[4] Geoffray Bonnin and Dietmar Jannach. 2014. Automated Generation of Music Playlists: Survey and Experiments. *ACM Computing Surveys* 47, 2 (2014), 26:1–26:35.

[5] Matthias Braunhofer, Marius Kaminskas, and Francesco Ricci. 2013. Location-aware Music Recommendation. *International Journal of Multimedia Information Retrieval* 2, 1 (2013), 31–44.

[6] Pei-I Chen, Jen-Yu Liu, , and Yi-Hsuan Yang. 2015. Personal Factors in Music Preference and Similarity: User Study on the Role of Personality Traits. In *CMMR '15*.

[7] Susan Craw, Ben Horsburgh, and Stewart Massie. Music Recommenders: User Evaluation Without Real Users?. In *IJCAI '15*. 1749–1755.

[8] Paolo Cremonesi, Franca Garzotto, Sara Negro, Alessandro Papadopoulos, and Roberto Turrin. 2011. Comparative Evaluation of Recommender System Quality. In *CHI EA'11*. 1927–1932.

[9] Paolo Cremonesi, Franca Garzotto, and Roberto Turrin. 2012. Investigating the Persuasion Potential of Recommender Systems from a Quality Perspective: An Empirical Study. *Transactions on Interactive Intelligent Systems* 2, 2 (2012), 11:1–11:41.

[10] Sally Jo. Cunningham, David. Bainbridge, and Annette. Falconer. 2006. 'More of an Art than a Science': Supporting the Creation of Playlists and Mixes. In *ISMIR '06*. 240–245.

[11] Michael D. Ekstrand, F. Maxwell Harper, Martijn C. Willemsen, and Joseph A. Konstan. 2014. User Perception of Differences in Recommender Algorithms. In *RecSys '14*. 161–168.

[12] Peter Emerson. 2013. The Original Borda Count and Partial Voting. *Social Choice and Welfare* 40, 2 (2013), 353–358.

[13] Bruce Ferwerda, Mark Graus, Andreu Vall, Marko Tkalčič, and Markus Schedl. 2016. The Influence of Users' Personality Traits on Satisfaction and Attractiveness of Diversified Recommendation Lists. In *EMPIRE '16 Workshop at RecSys '16*. 43–47.

[14] Florent Garcin, Boi Faltings, Olivier Donatsch, Ayar Alazzawi, Christophe Bruttin, and Amr Huber. 2014. Offline and Online Evaluation of News Recommender Systems at swissinfo.ch. In *RecSys '14*. 169–176.

[15] Carlos A. Gomez-Uribe and Neil Hunt. 2015. The Netflix Recommender System: Algorithms, Business Value, and Innovation. *ACM Transactions on Management Information Systems* 6, 4 (2015), 13:1–13:19.

[16] Derek L. Hansen and Jennifer Golbeck. 2009. Mixing It Up: Recommending Collections of Items. In *CHI '09*. 1217–1226.

[17] Negar Hariri, Bamshad Mobasher, and Robin Burke. 2012. Context-Aware Music Recommendation Based on Latent Topic Sequential Patterns. In *RecSys '12*. 131–138.

[18] Xiao Hu, J. Stephen Downie, and Andreas F. Ehmann. 2009. Lyric Text Mining in Music Mood Classification. In *ISMIR '09*. 411–416.

[19] Dietmar Jannach and Kolja Hegelich. 2009. A Case Study on the Effectiveness of Recommendations in the Mobile Internet. In *RecSys '09*. 205–208.

[20] Dietmar Jannach, Iman Kamehkhosh, and Geoffray Bonnin. 2014. Analyzing the Characteristics of Shared Playlists for Music Recommendation. In *RSWeb '14 Workhop at RecSys '14*.

[21] Dietmar Jannach, Iman Kamehkhosh, and Geoffray Bonnin. 2016. Biases in Automated Music Playlist Generation: A Comparison of Next-Track Recommending Techniques. In *UMAP '16*. 281–285.

[22] Dietmar Jannach, Iman Kamehkhosh, and Lukas Lerche. 2017. Leveraging Multi-Dimensional User Models for Personalized Next-Track Music Recommendation. In *SAC '17*.

[23] Dietmar Jannach, Lukas Lerche, and Michael Jugovac. 2015. Item familiarity as a possible confounding factor in user-centric recommender systems evaluation. *i-com Journal for Interactive Media* 14, 1 (2015), 29–40.

[24] Dietmar Jannach, Lukas Lerche, and Iman Kamehkhosh. 2015. Beyond "Hitting the Hits": Generating Coherent Music Playlist Continuations with the Right Tracks. In *RecSys '15*. 187–194.

[25] Dietmar Jannach, Markus Zanker, Mouzhi Ge, and Marian Gröning. 2012. Recommender Systems in Computer Science and Information Systems–A Landscape of Research. In *EC-Web '12*. 76–87.

[26] Evan Kirshenbaum, George Forman, and Michael Dugan. 2012. A Live Comparison of Methods for Personalized Article Recommendation at Forbes.com. In *ECML/PKDD '12*. 51–66.

[27] Bart P. Knijnenburg, Martijn C. Willemsen, Zeno Gantner, Hakan Soncu, and Chris Newell. 2012. Explaining the User Experience of Recommender Systems. *User Modeling and User-Adapted Interaction* 4-5 (2012), 441–504.

[28] Jin Ha Lee and Rachel Price. 2016. User experience with commercial music services: An empirical exploration. *Journal of the Association for Information Science and Technology* 67, 4 (2016), 800–811.

[29] Brian McFee and Gert R. G. Lanckriet. 2011. The Natural Language of Playlists. In *ISMIR '11*. 537–542.

[30] Brian McFee and Gert R. G. Lanckriet. 2012. Hypergraph Models of Playlist Dialects. In *ISMIR '12*. 343–348.

[31] Joshua L Moore, Shuo Chen, Thorsten Joachims, and Douglas Turnbull. 2012. Learning to Embed Songs and Tags for Playlist Prediction. In *ISMIR '12*. 349–354.

[32] Melissa Onori, Alessandro Micarelli, and Giuseppe Sansonetti. 2016. A Comparative Analysis of Personality-Based Music Recommender Systems. In *EMPIRE '16 Workshop at RecSys '16*. 55–59.

[33] John C. Platt, Christopher J. C. Burges, Steven Swenson, Christopher Weare, and Alice Zheng. 2001. Learning a Gaussian Process Prior for Automatically Generating Music Playlists. In *NIPS '11*. 1425–1432.

[34] George Popescu and Pearl Pu. 2012. What's the Best Music You Have?: Designing Music Recommendation for Group Enjoyment in Groupfun. In *CHI EA '12*. 1673–1678.

[35] Pearl Pu, Li Chen, and Rong Hu. 2011. A User-centric Evaluation Framework for Recommender Systems. In *RecSys '11*. 157–164.

[36] Steffen Rendle, Christoph Freudenthaler, Zeno Gantner, and Lars Schmidt-Thieme. 2009. BPR: Bayesian Personalized Ranking from Implicit Feedback. In *UAI '09*. 452–461.

[37] Marco Rossetti, Fabio Stella, and Markus Zanker. 2016. Contrasting Offline and Online Results when Evaluating Recommendation Algorithms. In *RecSys '16*. 31–34.

[38] Andy M. Sarroff and Michael Casey. 2012. Modeling and Predicting Song Adjacencies in Commercial Albums. In *SMC '12*.

[39] Malcolm Slaney and William White. 2006. Measuring Playlist Diversity for Recommendation Systems. In *AMCMM '06*. 77–82.

[40] Roberto Turrin, Massimo Quadrana, Andrea Condorelli, Roberto Pagano, and Paolo Cremonesi. 2015. 30Music Listening and Playlists Dataset. In *Poster Proceedings RecSys '15*.

[41] Linxing Xiao, Lie Lu, Frank Seide, and Jie Zhou. 2009. Learning a Music Similarity Measure on Automatic Annotations with Application to Playlist Generation. In *ICASSP '09*. 1885–1888.

"Personal Social Dashboard": A Tool for Measuring Your Social Engagement Effectiveness in the Enterprise

Shiri Kremer-Davidson, Inbal Ronen, Avi Kaplan, Maya Barnea
IBM Research - Haifa
Israel
{shiri, inbal, avika, mayab}@il.ibm.com

ABSTRACT

Social media platforms have become popular in many enterprises. Employees build their social eminence by effectively engaging on these platforms. Becoming socially eminent in the organization is a personal journey and many employees need guidance to succeed. In this paper, we describe a tool called Personal Social Dashboard deployed within our enterprise. The tool provides feedback to employees on how effectively they engage in the enterprise social network by maintaining a set of scores covering different aspects of one's social role, such as Activity, Network, Reaction, and Eminence. We provide a description of the tool with a subsequent study of its use within the company and effect on employees' behavior in the company's social network.

CCS CONCEPTS

• CCS → **Human-centered computing** → **Collaborative and social computing** → **Collaborative and social computing systems and tools**

KEYWORDS

Social media, enterprise, workplace, collaboration, social analytics, social engagement analytics, eminence, influence, social effectiveness

1 INTRODUCTION

Employee engagement has become a central theme for many HR organizations in the enterprise [21,22,24,31]. Engaged employees are more satisfied at work, and thus perform better [11, 18]. A Google study showed that companies fostering a culture of knowledge sharing and collaboration increase morale and job satisfaction, and thus attract talent and reduce retention [20]. One way of fostering engagement and collaboration within the

UMAP '17, July 09-12, 2017, Bratislava, Slovakia
© 2017 Association for Computing Machinery.
ACM ISBN 978-1-4503-4635-1/17/07...$15.00
http://dx.doi.org/10.1145/3079628.3079664

enterprise is through the usage of enterprise social media tools, such as Jive [14], IBM Connections [12], and Yammer [33]. Employees contribute and collaborate in these tools through authorship of content items such as micro-blogs, files, and wikis, and through engagement and feedback mechanisms such as liking, sharing, and commenting. According to a McKinsey report [25], incorporation of social technologies results in a 25% productivity increase. Through their contributions and interactions on those tools, employees become engaged and get an opportunity to build their voice within the organization and promote their eminence and influence.

A recent paper by the authors [17] defines the term *socially eminent* as being socially successful, well known, and respected in the social networking sphere. It discusses the motivation of being socially eminent in the enterprise and constructs a set of tips and recommendations for raising social eminence by engaging effectively. Becoming socially eminent is a personal journey that requires employees to become dedicated to the process, which includes being active and involved in enterprise social networks, create engaging content, and get others to follow them. Naturally, not all employees know how or are able to socialize in an effective manner without some guidance. Starting the journey and failing to succeed in gaining enough engagement can result in frustration, that might draw employees to reduce their social activity and stay away from using the social network. Thus, employees can highly benefit from ongoing feedback and guidance through a tool.

There are several tools measuring a person's influence through social media on the web, such as Klout [15], PeerIndex [27], and Kred [16]. These tools aggregate social cues from various social networks such as Facebook, Twitter, and LinkedIn to compute an influence score. Measuring employees' voice and eminence within the enterprise does not only provide feedback to the employees themselves on their personal effectiveness in the internal social network, but also supply the organization with a general insight into employees' social engagement and the breadth of social networking tools usage.

We developed and deployed a unique and novel tool called "Personal Social Dashboard" (PSD) within our company for measuring employees' engagement effectiveness within the enterprise social network. It provides feedback to employees by exposing a set of scores covering different aspects of their social engagement focusing not only on their own activities but also on the reactions they receive and the perception of others of them and their content. The scores are *Activity* (activity of an employee), *Network* (connectedness of an employee), *Reaction* (reaction to employee's content), and *Eminence* (interaction of others with the employee). The tool also includes an *Overall* score - an average of the aforementioned four - providing users with an overall perspective on their social role. Although the tool is available to all, it is not necessarily intended to be used by all employees. Out of many personas of social activity [6,9], the tool targets employees who are at least somewhat socially active and who are motivated to increase their eminence within the enterprise. Such employees are probably also more interested in monitoring their progress than others. The tool is less valuable for employees who are not socially active or are not interested or too shy to become more so. Regardless of their persona, the PSD provides feedback employees could not obtain before.

In this paper we study this novel tool through analysis of its use and effect on employee behavior within an enterprise social network. We are not aware of any other research of such an application in the context of the workplace. The paper studies the following research questions: how are the tool and its features used; who are the tool's users; do tool users seem more motivated to increase their social role within the company than others; how effective is the tool for raising its users' social engagement; and if it influences its users' social behavioral patterns.

The paper is organized as follows: the next section includes related work, followed by the PSD system description. We then define the research settings for the analysis along with results. The last sections provide discussion and conclusions.

2 RELATED WORK

Our system aims at calculating numerical scores summarizing different aspects of social behavior within the enterprise. There are several works trying to infer influence, reputation, and other indicators from social media e.g. [1,7,29,32]. For example, Jacovi et al. [13] characterize and infer reputation of users of social media within the enterprise. They also point out that reputation may assume different forms such as: trust, influence, expertise, and impact. Anger and Kittl [3] describe a grounded approach for measuring influence or as they call it – social network potential (SNP) – of individual Twitter users. To calculate the SNP score, their algorithm takes into account the number of followers, mentions, retweets, and other quantitative activity indicators of a user.   Hajian and White [10] propose a formal model for measuring influence in a social network, in which influence is measured over likes and comments posts receive. Similarly, our PSD system measures performance indicators in social media based on raw activity data such as likes, comments and content creations.

There are many available online web tools for tracking social media influence and engagement over public social networks such as Klout, PeerIndex, and Kred. These tools usually extract digital footprints from online social platforms, which users leave behind. The data gathered is then processed into a score measuring some aspect of personal social performance, such as influence. Similarly, to our system, these systems calculate several performance indicators, each summarizing a different social aspect, which may

also be integrated into a single overall score. Klout uses social media analytics to measure online social influence and provides a single score, which is calculated from data collected from 9 major social networks [28]. Three other score types supplement the Klout score: true reach, amplification, and network. PeerIndex provides social media analytics based on user-generated data collected from social media sites. It measures influence scores by considering activity, audience, and authority. Kred computes measures of influence and outreach.

The tools mentioned above provide social analytics for their users by accessing several public social networking platforms. Other tools perform social analytics within the enterprise social network, and are usually platform specific. These tools allow members of the enterprise to monitor their social status within the social network along with guidance on how they may improve it. Jive, for example, includes a "reputation" center, where users can view their current status points, which are calculated based on their social activity within a community. In Chatter [8], community managers can use a reputation measuring tool within their community and track its members' reputation level determined by point values members acquire when they engage socially. Yammer recently added social and reputation mechanics to its platform with the integration of Badgeville [4], which analyzes users' social activity and evaluates reputation. Yammer also collaborated with Klout to integrate the Klout score into its network. To the best of our knowledge, our paper is the first research on such a social scoring system within the enterprise. We are also not aware of a system supporting the four scoring aspects we defined.

An effective way of encouraging users to engage with a system is to augment it with some form of gamification e.g. [2,5,26,34] - the use of game-like strategies to enhance user engagement, such as competition, status recognition, challenges, and rewards. In the context of social scoring systems as the one presented here, the scores themselves provide some sort of gamification, giving users the incentive of improving their online social status.

3 SYSTEM DESCRIPTION

The PSD is an innovative tool based on a Big Data analytics system. It captures interactions from social applications and stores the data in a graph representation. It then performs a series of tunable analytics to generate for each employee a set of five scores and their evidence.

The tool is built to empower employees on their social journey and motivate them to increase their social engagement and eminence within the company. The detailed feedback includes a set of scores, which help them understand different aspects of their social role in the enterprise. For each score, employees can inspect their score history, as well as evidence of what contributed to their score and what they should consider improving. The PSD's focus is not only to motivate more content contribution, but also to encourage more engaged socializing, which can potentially draw a wider crowd to one's content, increase interactions, and widen one's community of followers.

3.1 Enterprise Social Graph

The PSD is built over an enterprise social graph. The graph contains vertices and edges capturing social activity traces from social or collaboration applications. Its abstract model allows incorporating traces of any social network. The enterprise graph includes a vertex for every entity in the enterprise social network, such as person, blog, wiki, microblog, file, etc. Each directed graph edge represents a social activity performed among the entities represented by its end vertices. For example, if employee "E1" liked a blog entry "A" that was created by employee "E2", it would be represented in the graph by vertices "E1", "E2", and "A", along with a "created" edge from "E2" to "A" and a "liked" edge from "E1" to "A", as illustrated in Figure 1. As the graph contains all activity traces within the enterprise social network, our analytics can extract a full view of all past employee activities as well as all reactions to their activities.

3.2 Scores

PSD scores are calculated over the social graph. The four base scores comprise *Activity*, *Reaction*, *Network*, and *Eminence*. The PSD includes also an *Overall* score, which is an average of the four base scores. Each base score focuses on a different aspect of employee engagement. Activity focuses on the social activities the user performs, thereby assigning higher priority to more engaging contributions. For example, a new content contribution, such as a new blog entry, is weighted higher than a "comment", and a "comment" is weighted higher than a "like" activity. The Reaction score focuses on the amount of reactions one's content received from others (such as comments, likes, follows, etc.). Only others' activity can contribute to an increase in this score. The focus of the Eminence score is to capture how others perceive a person within the company. It examines how many people are trying to interact or share information with the person, follow the person, etc. The Network score focuses on the size of the explicit network along with followers and followees.

All score computation algorithms take a very rich set of indicators along with corresponding weights as input. The indicators are counters accumulated over the enterprise graph for each user, such as number of comments the user placed on blog entries, number of likes the user's microblogs received, number of people who shared files with the user, number of people who mentioned the user, etc. Such indicators are extracted from all social applications within the enterprise graph, capturing different aspects of social activities. Each indicator algorithm identifies a set of vertices or edges of relevance and passes them through a date decay component. This component reduces the power of older items according to the time passed since they were created or updated. Activity decay is the strongest, then Reaction, and the

lowest is Eminence. This allows for Activity to focus on relatively new contributions, for Reaction to give a bit more time for others to react on the contributions, and for Eminence to be built over a longer period. A weight is assigned to each indicator based on its source application (e.g. blog, wiki) and the engagement required to perform the activity. The algorithms then use a normalized weighted sum to calculate the scores over the indicators and weights. Similar weighting strategies have been applied by others for social networking extraction [30]. Our algorithms were influenced by previous work on employee reputation [13, 23].

PSD scores range from 1 to 100. In order to motivate people to become more socially active in an effective manner, the score schema makes it easier to increase lower scores and more difficult to increase higher scores. Employees with an Overall score between 0 and 19 are hardly active in the social arena. Scores between 20 and 59 represent employees who are somewhat socially active and contribute occasionally. Scores between 60 and 79 represent employees who are more socially active but are probably not top socially eminent. The highest scores, 80-100, belong to more socially eminent employees who have a wider presence in the enterprise social arena.

It is important to note that we do not expect all employees to get or even strive to get a perfect score of 100. As an enterprise contains many employees with different job roles and different activity levels, some are required to be very active, whereas others are free to use it as they like. However, employees who want to be more active and enjoy the benefits of being socially engaged and eminent can use the PSD to help them understand what to do in order to improve and use the score as a reference point for subsequent score changes.

The PSD includes a machine generated content detection system which recognizes large amounts of content contributions from individual accounts in a short period, potentially aimed at raising one's score. Presumably, the minority of all machine-generated content is for the sake of score increase, but as the aim of the PSD is to motivate employees to contribute their own content, such machine-generated content is ignored.

3.3 PSD User Interface

The PSD is a web application deployed in our company's intranet. Only employees themselves have access to their scores and no one else can see them (including their managers).

The PSD user interface is composed of a set of web pages. The tool entry page is the "Home" page, depicted in Figure 2. Its middle part contains the user's name, organization, profile picture, the Overall score, and a graph capturing the score change history. The latter is important as it visually summarizes the user's progress in the last six months. The bottom part includes details on each of the four basic scores.

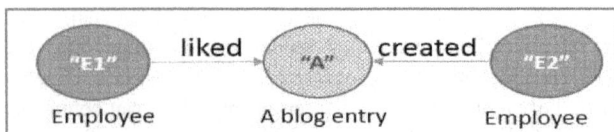

Figure 1. Sample Social Graph

Figure 2. PSD Home Page

Figure 3. PSD Reaction Evidence Page

Apart from the scores themselves, the average score of the employee's organizational unit and whole company are presented. This allows users to understand how they relate to others without exposing any scores.

The PSD includes four evidence pages, one per each basic score. An example of the Reaction evidence page is shown in Figure 3. Users can navigate through the pages by clicking on the specific scores on the Home page. Each evidence page's middle part is similar to the Home page part but focuses on a particular basic score. The bottom part includes a description of the score along with a set of aggregated indicators that were used by the algorithm. When pressing the title of each part, a relevant description of the indicator replaces the score description and provides more in-depth details on what is considered in the score. By using the evidence pages, employees can better understand what data the algorithms take into account and what engagement patterns the PSD is trying to motivate.

Due to technical issues, scores are currently computed and published only once a month. Thus, users are encouraged to reenter the tool on a monthly basis. The tool also exposes the date of the latest refresh of its scores. We raise this limitation in the Discussion section.

4 RESEARCH SETTING

We conducted an in-depth investigation of how employees use the PSD and whether it helps them socially engage more effectively.

4.1 IBM Connections

This research was performed over a dataset of an internal deployment of IBM Connections (Connections) within our company. Connections is an enterprise social networking platform including several collaboration applications. The Microblogging application enables writing microblogs on one's own or someone else's wall. Wikis enable co-editing of web pages. Forums allow discussions of topics and Blogs enable posting of blog posts. The Files application supports uploading and sharing files. Each

application enables commenting and liking of its entries as a means to engage over them. People can be directly addressed by using @mention in the text, which results in an email notification of the mentioned people. Connections enables inviting other employees into one's network. It also supports following people or content items. Employees are updated through their activity stream or via an email digest on all social activities within their network.

4.2 Quantitative Analysis Data

The analysis focused on the 7-months period (research period) following the release of the tool to all company employees (September 2015 – February 2016). It included the following main data sets: employee monthly PSD scores, log of all pages accessed by employees within the PSD application, and basic employee meta data such as their organization and manager. In order to examine the effect of the PSD on employee activity in Connections, we used the enterprise social graph, populated with all social activities performed within our enterprise in Connections since its deployment in 2007. The graph instance included ~40M vertices and ~212M edges. Among them were, for example, 873K blog entry vertices and 9.64M file vertices.

During the research period, 21,127 distinct company employees accessed the PSD at least once (out of 450K employees). Out of those, 83% were regular employees and 17% were managers. Most PSD users were from the Headquarters organization, followed by Services, Sales and Development. 184,829 page visits were logged during the research period.

As PSD scores were published on a monthly basis, we focused our analysis on the number of score periods during which users accessed the tool. Thus, if a user accessed the tool several times during the same monthly period, we counted this as one accessed score period.

4.3 User Survey

After the research period, we conducted a survey with PSD users who entered the tool during at least four score periods. We randomly selected 511 users with scores from all ranges and sent the survey via email with a link to a web form. We received 183 responses (36%) with a score distribution resembling the full set. The survey included a set of nine questions about the users' experience with the PSD. The questions inspected the usability of the scores, the tool's most valuable features and whether usage of the PSD changed the users' engagement in Connections in any way. Moreover, it included questions regarding whether the tool helped users become more socially eminent, reputable or in getting a voice and if so, whether this change would have happened without the tool and general thoughts about the tool. Most questions included responses on a Likert scale. All questions had an area for free-text comments.

5   RESULTS

The following section describes the results of our study. We define *PSD users* as employees who accessed the tool at least once during the research period and *Non-users* as employees who did not access the tool during that period. We consider only employees with an Overall score higher than 1, indicating they had been involved in at least some social activity. We examine score distributions of PSD users' vs. non-PSD users' to gain more insights into the populations. We than investigate whether PSD users increased their scores more than non-PSD users, whether part of this change can be attributed to the PSD and whether the PSD succeeded in motivating its users to socialize in a more engaging manner. We also report insights into tool usage.

5.1   Tool Features

In the survey, we asked participants to mark which features they found most valuable in the PSD. 80% specified the personal Overall score as most valuable followed by the average organization Overall score. This is probably because both scores combined provide an indication of one's relative position. Third was Activity score followed by the history graph, the other basic scores and the score detail pages. We speculate that the history graph was rated higher than the score detail pages as employees may be more interested in seeing if and to what level their efforts generated improvement over time than an indication on which particular score they needed to improve.

5.2   Users and Scores

The PSD tool computes scores for all employees independently of whether they ever accessed the tool. In this section's graphs, we use a single number to represent a score range. For example, score range 10 represents scores ranging from 1 to 10.

Due to some criticism on the meaningfulness or reliability of scores calculated by other social scoring measurement tools such as Klout, [19], we investigated whether survey participants found the PSD scores useful. Among the respondents, 69% found it "Useful", 25% "Slightly" and only 6% did not find it useful. We then investigated the Overall PSD score distribution at the beginning of the research period, focusing on the difference between PSD users and non-users, as captured in Figure 4. Indeed the score distributions were different. Most non-users have low scores and as scores increase, the number of employees rapidly

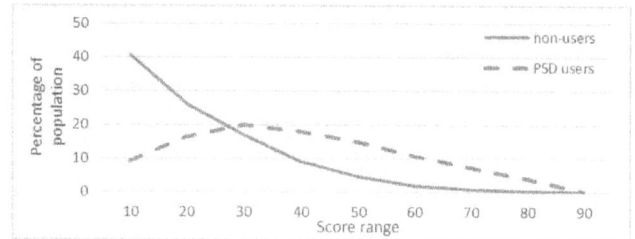

Figure 4. PSD score distribution across scores

decreases. The PSD users' score distribution peeks at 30 and decreases slowly. Although there are significantly fewer people with high scores, the figure confirms our intuition that the higher the score, the higher the probability that the employee is a PSD user. Apparently, the PSD attracts higher percentage of socially engaged employees than their portion in the company population.

We found that 58% of users accessed the tool during one score period only, 18% during two, 9% during three, and 14% during four score periods or more. Figure 5 shows the percentage of PSD users who accessed the PSD for two score periods or more per Overall score range. Interestingly, as the score increases, the tool is used more often.

When slicing the users by the company's organizations, employees from Corporate Headquarters accessed for the highest average number of score periods (2.16), followed by Systems (1.99) and Development (1.75). Services and Sales had a bit lower numbers and the Research organization had lowest (1.51). Thus, internal facing employees probably found it more important to socialize effectively inside the enterprise. Headquarters' lead may be attributed to the fact that this organization includes many people in leading roles who thus put more emphasis on being socially engaged.

We also looked at the difference between accesses of employees whose managers were PSD users vs. those whose managers were not. We found that employees of managers who accessed the tool during four periods or more, accessed it on average during 1.08 periods (compared to 0.08 in the general population). Thus, having managers who were PSD users raised the probability that their employees would enter the PSD as well. Possibly managers encouraged their employees to also use the tool.

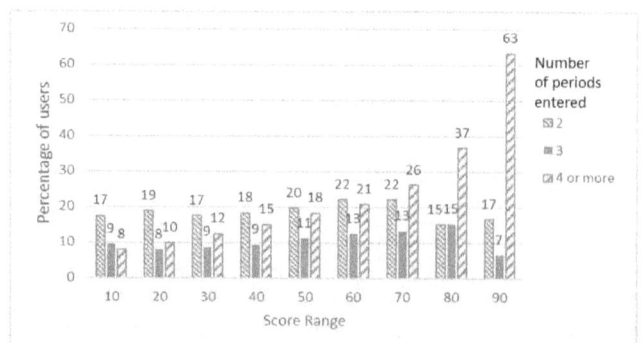

Figure 5. Percentage of users in Overall score range per number of accessed score periods

5.3   Score Change

In general, we expected employees who decided to use the PSD to be more motivated to increase their engagement within the enterprise than non-PSD users. To verify that there is indeed a stronger increase, we compared score change between PSD users' to non-users'. First, we conducted a set of one-tailed unpaired t-tests over the score difference between the beginning and the end of the investigated research period for all five scores and indeed found significant differences ($p<0.05$) for all. When examining the effects on each score level using one-tailed unpaired t-test, we also saw significant differences ($p<0.05$), apart from the 90-100 range. The percentage of employees who increased their score in each score level in the whole research period was between 0% to 38% for non-users, whereas for PSD users it was between 13% to 74%. Moreover, the average score change for both populations decreased as the score increased, as shown in Figure 6. This can be explained by the fact that the higher the score, the harder it is to raise it. Thus, in general, PSD users increased their score much more than non-PSD users, as expected.

We also examined the average score change in relation to the number of score periods the user accessed the PSD. Our hypothesis was that employees who accessed the tool during more periods were more interested in following their score change, and therefore were probably putting more effort into socializing in the social network. Figure 7 captures the average score increase in relation to number of score periods accessed. Employees who never accessed the PSD (period=0) had the lowest score increase. More frequent access periods increased the score more substantially. We expected the highest increase to be in Network and Activity scores as users can more easily influence those through their own social activity. Thus, we were surprised that Activity was third and not second. Eminence was second to increase. This is interesting as the user can hardly control this score directly. An explanation could be that employees' effort to add others to their network caused those to also follow and engage with them. Increasing the Reaction score is harder and as expected had the lowest increase.

5.4   Tool Impact on Social Effectiveness

To examine whether the PSD indeed assisted its users in being more socially active in an effective manner, we next narrowed our focus to employees who significantly increased their activity in a short time period and who would probably expect, as a result, to

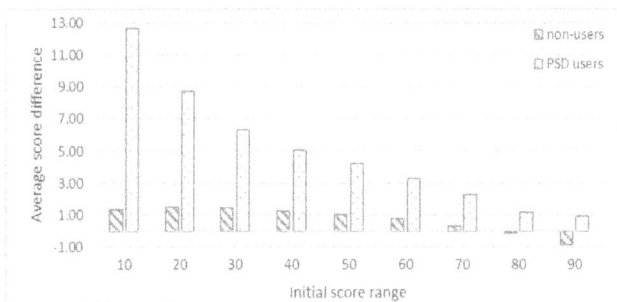

Figure 7. Average score increase by accessed score periods

gain back more engagement from others. We divided this set into PSD users and non-users and compared their activity effectiveness.

Thus, we first extracted employees in each score range under 80 who increased their Activity score by 5 points or more (more than half a score range) in the first three months. Higher scored employees socialize effectively and are thus not of interest to this analysis. We then categorized each of those users as "successful" if they also managed to raise their Eminence and Reaction scores by 5 points or more. This enabled focusing on employees who socialized more effectively as they managed to get higher levels of reaction to their contents and drew more employees to interact with them. We then divided the resulting sets into two groups: PSD users and non-users. Overall, we compared 1,930 PSD users to 29,440 non-users divided according to their initial score range. Figure 8 captures the results of this analysis indicating what percentage of employees, in each score range and for each user group, were classified as successful. On average, there was a 27% difference between the percentages of PSD users who were more successful during this period to non-users. Moreover, as score increased, higher percentages of PSD users were more successful, whereas for non-users it stayed the same. Thus, when focusing on sets of two similarly active (and probably motivated) populations which have both increased their activity in the time period, higher percentages of PSD-users were able to use their activity more efficiently across all score ranges. Thus, one can reason that the PSD indeed affected the socializing patterns of its users.

To further examine this, we asked participants whether they felt that using the PSD helped them become more socially eminent, reputable, or in getting a voice. 66% agreed, 20% were

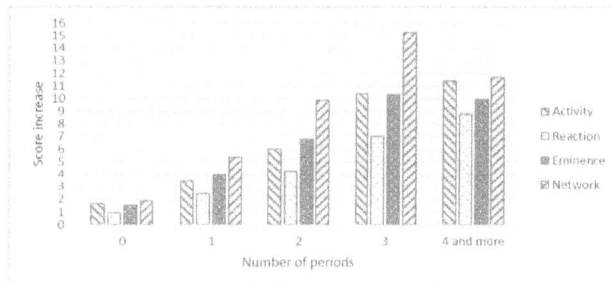

Figure 6. Average Overall score increase between first and last month of research period

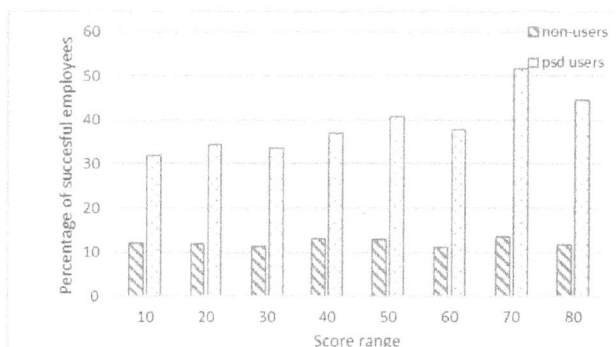

Figure 8. Percentage of successful users in each score range

undecided and 14% disagreed. One participant stated: "I am a competitive person and accustomed to metrics in my work. Having a score inspires me to improve and adopt what is new." Another commented: "Yes, the tool allowed me to see where I can be better. I may have a huge network but no one responds to my comments, but with the help of the tool, I can make a better choice of what to post." or "What you measure, is what you get. So the focus on that measurement is also changing my behavior to get better and e.g. use tags more (which was one of my "low scores")." Another participant was undecided: "It's like gamification - wanting to improve my score. In that respect, it helps to encourage Social, intrinsically. But it *is* only a measurement tool, it does not provide "help" to more socially eminent & reputable". There was also disagreement: "this tool is just a measure no driver".

In order to further understand the impact of the tool, we asked survey participants whether they believed the change would have happened without it. We found that 54% responded "no", 35% "yes", and 11% were "indecisive". Some of those who answered positively wrote: "Without the tool, I would not know if I am making progress in these attributes and what are the areas I can improve in. The description in each of the attributes are useful to direct actions in the areas to help enhance one's eminence." Another participant also stated: "Without the tool I have no way to measure my social participation or know what aspects of my social strategy are being more or less effective." An interesting comment was related to PSD effect on a team, which is collectively using it: "Due to PSD we could see the change happen quickly. Otherwise it would have taken a very long time for us to see the change. PSD has been one of the driving forces." Another participant commented: "I think the change would have happened without the tool because I do regularly assess what productivity tools I am using it to improve the way I work. However, I think the tool helps me to pinpoint where I might want to improve." Another stated: "My behavior is independent of the score."

To better qualify the effectiveness and benefits of the PSD and get an indication on its ROI, we asked participants how the PSD helped them or their team. We provided various options and an "other" option. In their responses, 68% marked that it "Increased social efficiency", 46% marked "Helped expertise sharing", 43% specified "Strengthened team collaboration", 12% indicated that it "Saved time", and 11% marked that it "Opened new business opportunities".

In the last question, we asked survey participants to specify their general opinion about the PSD. Some positive comments included "The PSD for us is a great way to leverage our social activities in our daily job, without the dashboard it would be hard to see how well we are doing. Also, it motivates oneself to be more active and to improve in any particular area." Another commented that "[the PSD is] a good tracker of individual social performance and a guide on which engagement parameter you need to improve to be socially connected." A negative comment was "nice stat but what does count in my area is competence and the tool is just counting activity and not quality." We will further refer to this last statement in the discussion section.

5.5 Tool Impact on Social Engagement

Changing behavioral patterns is not easy and takes time, but we set out to investigate whether the PSD effected its users' social engagement. Thus, we asked survey participants if the usage of the PSD changed their engagement. We found that 39% specified "Very much", 35% "Moderately", 14% "Slightly" and 12% stated "Not at all". Thus, 74% felt the PSD impacted their engagement. Many employees placed comments on this question reporting on the effect on their engagement patterns. Some specified that it made them analyze their current behavior and comprehend what they needed to modify in order to improve: "I am monthly checking my performance and adapting as I go. Example: I noticed that my reaction score was low so I started understanding why people were not picking up the messages I was sending on my profile. I started using the tag option and noticed reaction went up". Another specified: "It's a good indicator to see if what I'm working on is useful, interesting for others. This is helping me to focus more on some subjects and less on others". Others specified that it caused them to do more engaging activities: "it made me become more active in discussion and appreciate other ideas." or "Since we have the dashboard, I add comments and "likes" to the entries I previously just read". Only few specified that it had a negative impact on their engagement: "starting to make fake likes and not really useful comments, just to increase the score". The effect of such behavior is discussed in the next section.

6 DISCUSSION

The PSD was developed to help employees understand their role in the company's social network. Its purpose is to assist them in socializing more effectively and increasing their voice or eminence by providing important feedback not obtainable otherwise. We found that indeed the tool assisted its users to socialize in a more engaging manner and become more socially effective. Moreover, employees who embraced the PSD, on average increased their scores drastically. This was strengthened in the survey where participants stated that the change would not have happened without the tool. We plan to extend the PSD with personalized social activity recommendations based on employees' actual socializing patterns in order to further guide them in socializing more effectively.

One of the PSD's main limitation is its monthly score refresh. This may frustrate some users as they cannot get immediate feedback on their efforts. It may even lead to users abandoning it. Yet, eminence is not built in a short time and therefore inspecting its change over longer periods makes sense. We are working on removing this limitation in the near future. Another limitation is the fact that the PSD considers only the engagement and not the content of the activity. For example, the PSD does not distinguish between flattery comments to executives to more valuable comments or sentiment expressed in the text in its relevant score calculations. We hope to include such aspects in the future depending on accessibility of this data. Furthermore, we currently include four scores providing different aspects on one's social engagement. We are aware that other aspects may exist and plan to investigate and consider additional ones in the future.

In general, the PSD seemed to be less useful for hardly socially active employees. This is an expected result as such users have not found the need to be socially active and thus are probably not motivated to become more so. However, the nature of the score computation assists those who decide to start becoming more socially active to increase their score rapidly. Socially eminent employees also found value in the PSD, which provided them with evidence on their impact level. These socially eminent users help spread the word and motivate their followers to onboard. In general, not all employees are expected or should strive to achieve a score of 100. It depends on different factors such as job role, personality traits, etc. In the future, we plan to identify what score ranges and social behavioral patterns are expected in different job roles and customize the PSD accordingly.

The PSD scores' purpose is to motivate employees to socialize effectively. The scores should serve as a numerical indication of their status in their social journey. As one survey participant stated: "Without having a piece of measurement you are blind. I felt isolated prior to seeing my results and comparing my scores to my organization." But providing scores or rewards in response to an increase in social activity can motivate some employees to try to increase their scores through meaningless activity or spamming. The four-score approach along with the impact on the audience of one's activities makes it difficult to game the system over time. In the short term, users' Activity score may increase but soon their followers will notice the quantity increase and quality decrease which will stop them from reading and following the spammers. As a result, spammers' Reaction, Eminence, and Network scores will decrease. Such employees will eventually notice that there are no short cuts and that such activity results in decrease of their eminence.

Only employees themselves have access to their scores and even their managers cannot see them. This is crucial for protecting the privacy of employees and verifying that these scores cannot be used against them in any way. Interestingly, we see many employees sharing their scores through screen captures in the enterprise social network. Some employees mentioned they would like their managers to see their score improvement towards their yearly performance assessment. We are aware that peer pressure or manager request may pressure employees to expose scores (as well as any other private information). However, we trust the company to handle any identified privacy violations. Peer pressure or managers request can also cause employees to try to rapidly increase their score. We hope that in such cases employees will use the PSD's internal documentation (or any other sources of tips) to learn how to socialize effectively and will not start spamming.

In this paper, we mainly focused on how the PSD can help enterprise employees, but we did not explicitly discuss the enterprise's gain from such a tool. Survey participants indicated that the PSD helped their team in various scenarios. Research has shown that having a socially active and engaged workforce is beneficial to the company. As employee scores are logged over time, management could still perform analytics over aggregated scores and thus gain value without compromising on employee privacy. For example, companies could identify how their workforce is adopting social applications, where to spend their onboarding efforts, and whether these efforts are indeed effective, and more.

Although our research is limited to a single company using a single social networking system, we believe our findings are of importance and applicable to other researchers and developers who are working on other influence, reputation, or eminence measuring systems in the enterprise.

7 CONCLUSIONS

In this paper, we described a novel tool called Personal Social Dashboard and investigated its use and effect on employees' behavior in an enterprise social network.

The study provides several contributions. First, it describes the innovative PSD tool itself, which was developed over a Big Data analytics framework. Its social analytics system generates for each employee a set of five scores: Activity, Reaction, Eminence, Network, and Overall, helping employees understand different aspects of their social role in the enterprise, which they could not obtain otherwise. As a second contribution, the study revealed insights into such tool's users, highlighting the characteristics of its audience in the enterprise setting. Thirdly, we found evidence that the tool is indeed effective in raising its users' social engagement and effectiveness.

ACKNOWLEDGMENTS

We would like to thank Marie Wallace, Avinash Kohirkar, and Santosh S. Borse from IBM for their leadership role in making the Personal Social Dashboard a reality.

REFERENCES

[1]   Agarwal, N., Liu, H., Tang, L., and Yu, P. S. 2008. Identifying the Influential Bloggers in a Community. In *WSDM'08*, 207-218.

[2]   Andriotis, N. How Companies Use Gamification to Motivate Their Employees. Retrieved May 24, 2016 from http://www.efrontlearning.net/blog/2016/01/how-companies-use-gamification-to-motivate-their-employees.html

[3]   Anger, I. and Kittl, C. 2011. Measuring Influence on Twitter. In *I-KNOW'11*, 31.

[4]   Badgeville. https://badgeville.com/

[5]   Bista, S. K., Nepal, S., Colineau, N., and Paris, C. 2012. Using Gamification in an Online Community. In *CollaborateCom'12*, 611-618.

[6]   Brandtzaeg, P. B., and Heim, J. 2011. A Typology of Social Networking Sites Users. *IJWBC 7*, 1: 28-51.

[7]   Cha, M., Haddadi, H., Benevenuto, F., and Gummadi P. K. 2010. Measuring User Influence in Twitter: The Million Follower Fallacy. *ICWSM 10*, 10-17: 30.

[8]   Chatter. http://salesforce.com/eu/chatter/overview

[9]   Cohen, H. Social Media Personas: What You Need to Know. Retrieved May 25, 2016 from http://heidicohen.com/social-media-personas-what-you-need-to-know/

[10] Hajian, B., and White, T. 2011. Modelling Influence in a Social Network: Metrics and Evaluation. In *SocialCom'11*, 497-500.

[11] Harter, J. K., Schmidt, F. L., & Hayes, T. L. 2002. Business-unit-level relationship between employee satisfaction, employee engagement, and business outcomes: a meta-analysis. Journal of applied psychology 87, 2: 268.

[12] IBM Connections. http://www-03.ibm.com/software/products/en/conn

[13] Jacovi, M., Guy, I., Kremer-Davidson, S., Porat, S., and Aizenbud-Reshef, N. 2014. The Perception of Others: Inferring Reputation from Social Media in the Enterprise. In CSCW'14, 756-766.

[14] Jive. https://www.jivesoftware.com/

[15] Klout. https://klout.com/home

[16] Kred. http://home.kred/

[17] Kremer-Davidson, S., Ronen, I., Leiba, L., Kaplan, A. and Barnea, M., 2016, November. Raising your Eminence inside the Enterprise Social Network. In CSCW'16, 111-120.

[18] Kruse, K. 2012. Employee Engagement Research (Master List of 32 Findings). KEVIN KRUSE (Sep. 2012).

[19] Kumar, M. What's the Score? The Ultimate Guide to Social Scoring. Retrieved May 23, 2016 from http://www.slideshare.net/seomanish/whats-the-score-the-ultimate-guide-to-social-scoring

[20] Lafargue, V. Working better together. A study of collaboration and innovation in the workplace. Retrieved May 22, 2016 from https://apps.google.com/learn-more/working-better-together.html

[21] Lockwood, N.R. 2007. Leveraging Employee Engagement for Competitive Advantage. SHRM Research Quarterly 1: 1-12.

[22] MacLeod, D., Clarke, N. 2009. Engaging for Success: Enhancing Performance through Employee Engagement: A Report to Government. London: Department for Business, Innovation and Skills.

[23] Mark, g., Guy, I., Kremer-Davidson, S., and Jacovi, M. 2014. Most Liked, Fewest Friends: Pattern of Enterprise Social Media Use. In CSCW'14, 393-404.

[24] Markos, S., and Sridevi, M. S. 2010. Employee Engagement: The Key to Improving Performance. IJBM 5, 12: 89.

[25] McKinsey Global Institute. 2012. The Social Economy: Unlocking Value and Productivity Through Social Technologies.

[26] Neeli, B. K. 2012. A Method to Engage Employees Using Gamification in BPO Industry. In ICSEM'12.

[27] PeerIndex. https://www.brandwatch.com/peerindex-and-brandwatch/

[28] Rao, A., Spasojevic, N., Li, Z., and DSouza, T. 2015. Klout Score: Measuring Influence Across Multiple Social Networks. In IEEE BigData'15, 2282-2289.

[29] Resnick, P., Kuwabar, K., Zeckhauser, R., and Friedman, E. 2000. Reputation Systems. Communication of the ACM 43, 12: 45-48.

[30] Ronen, I., Shahar, E., UR, S., Uziel, E., Yogev, S., Zwerdling, N., and Ofek-Koifman, S. 2009. Social Networks and Discovery in the Enterprise (SaND). In SIGIR'09, 836-836.

[31] Saks, A. M. 2006. Antecedents and Consequences of Employee Engagement. In JMP 21, 7: 600-619.

[32] Tang, J., Sun, J., Wang, C., and Yang, Z. 2009. Social Influence Analysis in Large-Scale Networks. In SIGKDD'09, 807-816.

[33] Yammer. https://www.yammer.com/

[34] Zichermann, G., Cunningham, C. 2011. Gamification by Design: Implementing Game Mechanics in Web and Mobile Apps. O'Reilly Media, Inc

Adaptive City Characteristics: How Location Familiarity Changes What Is Regionally Descriptive

Vikas Kumar
University of Minnesota
Minneapolis, Minnesota, USA
vikas@cs.umn.edu

Saeideh Bakhshi
Facebook Inc.
Menlo Park, California, USA
saeideh@gatech.edu

Lyndon Kennedy
Futurewei Technologies, Inc.
Santa Clara, California, USA
lyndonk@acm.org

David A. Shamma
Centrum Wiskunde & Informatica
Amsterdam, The Netherlands
aymans@acm.org

ABSTRACT

Proliferation of GPS-enabled mobile devices has brought a plurality of location-aware applications leveraging the location characteristics in the shared content, like photos and check-ins. While these applications provide contextual and relevant information, they also assume geo-tagged contents to be representative of the geo-bounded characteristics of location. In this paper, however, we show that the characteristics geo-tagged contents capture about a location can vary based on the familiarity of user (sharing the content) with the location. Using a large dataset of geo-tagged photos, we learn descriptive spatial photo characteristics and user temporal-location-familiarity to highlight unique characteristics photos capture of location, which vary significantly if taken by locals versus tourists. We then propose a ranking-approach to find most representative photos for a given city. A user-based evaluation shows photos are more diverse and characteristic of location compared to other popular baselines while being representative of how locals and tourists would describe the city.

CCS CONCEPTS

• **Information systems → Geographic information systems;**
Multimedia and multimodal retrieval;

KEYWORDS

image content; retrieval; location-familiarity; tourists; locals

Figure 1: Distinct group of users in San Francisco. Spots of photos taken by locals are in blue and tourists spots are in red. Yellow trails might be either. Image ©①◎ Eric Fischer on Flickr: https://flic.kr/p/87P5qP.

1 INTRODUCTION

Location plays a critical role in personalizing and identifying relevant content for users in online services. Mobile services such as

The work was conducted while the authors were at Yahoo Labs.

Google Now, Yelp, and Foursquare have shown to elicit user experiences [24, 34] by leveraging the location. Other services, including online games [31] or shopping [18], have shown to provide better assistance while adapting to location. In the past decade, such location based services have grown further through geo-tagging and place-tagging. Users find it more easy now than ever to share contents tagged with location from their GPS-enabled mobile devices. This exponential growth of geo-tagged contents such as photos, check-ins etc provide valuable opportunity to study users' interaction patterns and their unique perceptions of surroundings.

Among many geo-tagged contents, online photo sharing popularized by systems like Instagram, Flickr, and Facebook, has made them an ubiquitous choice for users to learn and explore about a location. While browsing within limited screen-space on mobile

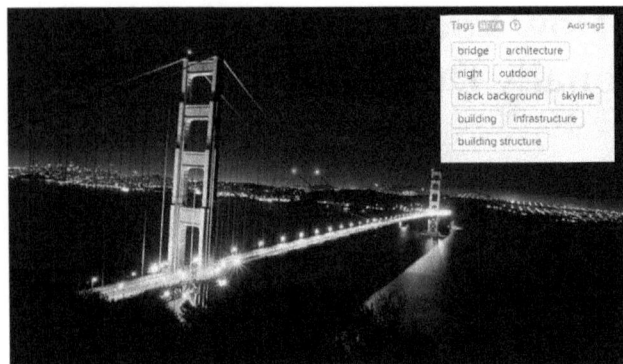

Figure 2: A sample photo of Golden Gate bridge in San Francisco and its *autotags* determined via computer vision.

devices, photos being more intuitive, illustrative, and far more succinct than words, allow users to peer into places that they would otherwise never see. They help choose travel destinations, influence decision making, planing, cognition as well as users' behavior at destinations [15]; as a result, it is critical for location-services to identify photos that capture diverse representation of location.

Geo-tagged photos have been studied extensively in the past decade [28]. They have been used in tag-aggregation research [3, 4, 19, 29], landmark detection [10, 20, 37], identifying representative icons or hero images for a city [5, 12]. In most of these applications, photos are judged by their social potential [1], content quality [5], or a combination of them [20] while assuming they capture *local* characteristics. However, in this paper, we question the very assumption of localness and provide a better understanding of how *well* photos capture the characteristics they represent of a location and if they vary based on who shares it. In other words, we analyze the effect location-familiarity of a user could have on photos they capture. For example, users who are less familiar with location, such as tourists, are likely to find popular landmarks or attractions to be more relevant to capture than locals. Similarly both locals and tourists are likely to be aware of popular landmarks in the city but some landmarks common among locals are likely to be unknown to most of the tourists. We show in this paper that geo-tagged contents result in different representations when users' familiarity with location is considered—challenging the assumption of *localness* in the geo-tagged content.

To learn the characteristics each photo captures about a location, we use computer-vision technique combined with information-theory method over a large-scale geo-tagged photos dataset publicly available from Flickr [32]. A set of descriptive spatial characteristics for each photos is determined, and the familiarity of the users sharing the photos are learned based on their temporal-spatial interactions. Two distinct categories of locals and tourists are identified, and results highlight how tourist with shorter engagement with location capture characteristics that differ significantly from those captured by locals. For example, in San Francisco, tourists tend to be interested in places of attraction such as monuments or bridges, whereas locals tend to find food or people more interesting to capture.

The characteristics learned from the model is then use to serve a common purpose similar to location-aware services, that is, retrieving representative photos of location. We devise a location-familiarity-based characteristic-score for each photo to re-rank photos of a city as seen by locals and tourists respectively. The re-ranked photos are then evaluated by human judges in an online survey where they assess the quality of photo sets compared to other popular baselines. The results from the survey (a) highlight the limitation of underlying assumptions of localness in traditional location-aware services, (b) emphasize the need to include users' familiarity with location, (c) show improved effectiveness from location-familiarity-based characteristic-score ranking for locals and tourists, and (d) demonstrate accuracy in identifying a diverse and accurate characteristics of locations while being representative of both locals and tourists respectively.

2 RELATED WORK

Online shared items with spatial footprints like geo-tagged photos, or check-ins, are shown to provide contextual meaningful content leading to more pleasant experiences in location-based services [24, 34, 35]. Such spatial limitations on items and users are shown to be be more efficient and accurate compared to traditional techniques [22, 23]; however, the location-based systems in their definition of *local-ness* of content overlook the affect of content owners' familiarity with location, that is, they consider the contents generated by locals and tourists to be equally representative of location.

While there exists several work in mining specific spatial characteristics from geo-tagged photos to learn about a location, such as, identification of landmarks [5], ranking characteristic photos for a landmark [20], characterizing preferences of international tourists [30], mining movement patterns [14], and identification of tourist hot spots [10]; there is rarely any focus on the distinction in these characteristics based on content owners' location-familiarity. It is important to note that if the purpose is to identify landmarks in a city then we already bias the analysis to places that are prevalent among tourists. In comparison, to identify distinct representations of a city to help users explore about unknown or novel destinations then systems are required to be adaptive to diverse crowds of the city i.e. locals and tourists. In a more recent work, Johnson et al. [17] in their analysis of localness of geo-tagged content suggest that only 70% of online shared contents represent what is local to the location and that this percentage decreases in more rural locations. In this work, we extend this result further by examining the content by learning descriptive characteristics to understand distinct representations users capture about the city based on their familiarity with the location.

The idea of distinct representations of a city is primarily motivated from existing literature in *geographical psychology*, also known as *psychogeography* [6]. It is a field that discusses the laws, methods, and inventive strategies for exploring an urban landscape. In its simplest form, it suggests that places in the same city can have different associations and effects on human emotions and behavior depending on their familiarity with location. For example, consumer psychology of tourism [21, 26] highlight differences in tourists' and locals' behavior depending on what a city has to offer. Tourists, in their short stay, are thus more likely to explore well known or famous attractions in the city while locals are likely to be interested in food, parks or other means of entertainments. For example, in San Francisco, tourists can be often seen at the ferry building, piers, or the Golden Gate bridge compared to locals who prefer to be at local restaurants, breweries, parks, stadiums etc. These differences are illustrated in maps of various cities in United States by Eric Fischer [8]. Figure 1 shows the areas of interest in San Francisco for locals and tourists by Fischer's metric; the map consists of points where a photo was taken with blue color representing a local user and red representing tourist.

Only a few recent studies measure the differences in users perception about a location [27, 36]. Using GPS traces they find specific routes of the city to be preferred by visitors, however, we expand the understanding of characteristics users capture in their photos with descriptive keyword for both locals and tourists. In this work, we thus aim to draw attention of existing location-based systems to reconsider the definition of localness of content while being representative to both locals and tourists respectively.

3 MODELING SPATIAL CHARACTERISTICS

Our first goal is to model descriptive spatial characteristics from geo-tagged photos. In this section, we start with an outline of the geo-tagged photos dataset available from Flickr. We then describe the computer vision technique along with information-theory metric we use to model the descriptive characteristics for each geo-tagged photo, to analyze the differences that users with different familiarity capture in the photos.

3.1 Dataset

We use the YFCC100M image dataset [32] consisting of 100 million publicly-available Creative Commons images from Flickr. The images have attributes such as the owner, acquisition timestamps, user-provided titles, descriptions, tags, and geo-tagging. For our analysis, we consider only the subset of geo-tagged images taken in United States. Further, we retrieved a multitude of social metrics from the Flickr API, such as the number of favorites, number of views and number of shares for each photo. For analysis, we only consider photos with at least 10 views and 10 favorites. We use these thresholds to consider photos shown to have potential for social engagement [1]. The resulting dataset consists of approximately 4.5 million images.

3.2 Descriptive Characteristics

To find the characteristics photos capture about a given location we leverage the visual content of each online shared geo-tagged photo using computer vision techniques. We learn meaningful descriptive characteristics from the photos in the form of keywords using a deep convolutional neural network that learns discriminative image representations, using large-scale collections of training examples pre-trained on the ImageNet dataset [7] provided by the Caffe framework [16]. The output of the last fully-connected layer (fc7) delivers a 4096-dimensional feature representation of each image. Using a linear support vector machine [33], the images are then classified along 1700 different ImageNet concepts. We refer to these automatically-detected keywords for the visual content as "characteristics" captured in the photo. A sample of the descriptive characteristics derived from a photo are shown in Figure 2.

In order to learn the spatial property of these characteristics and find the ones that *uniquely* identify with a location (a city), we model the keywords and locations into an information theory metric known as *conditional entropy*. The metric, defined as $H(X|Y)$, measures the certainty of variable X (bits of information) given the knowledge about variable Y. Smaller metric value implies higher certainty about variable X. We model set of characteristics C and the set of locations L as the random variables X and Y respectively; and formally define $h(c|l)$, see equation (1). This measures the certainty a characteristic (c) carries given the location (l).

$$h(c|l) = p(c, l) \times \log \frac{p(l)}{p(c, l)} : c \in C, l \in L. \tag{1}$$

In equation (1), $p(c)$ is the ratio of the number of photos with visual descriptor c to the total number of photos; and, $p(l)$ is the ratio of number of photos taken at the location l to the total number of photos. Finally, $p(c, l)$ is the joint probability of characteristic c and location l. A smaller entropy (higher certainty) implies a higher chance that the characteristic c is unique or highly certain given the location l. Likewise, higher entropy (less certainty) implies that the characteristic c is less likely or less certain to be representative of the location. For instance, the characteristic "outdoor", one of the most common visual descriptor in photos fails to uniquely identify with any given location having higher conditional entropy value. Whereas a tag like "latte" uniquely identifies with city of Seattle having a smaller conditional entropy value.

Note on Location: We evaluate the metrics with location referring to distinct cities in United States. The photo's location in form of latitude and longitude is converted to corresponding city using geocoding APIs[1]. Focusing on cities, instead of specific landmark or tourist spots allows us to understand the differences more accurately between the locals and tourists. It also allows to serve broadly for search retrieval purposes close to user queries exploring destinations that often starts at city level.

3.3 Location Familiarity: Locals Versus Tourists

To determine if users based on their familiarity capture unique photos of a location, we summarize photos into two distinct sets. The first set consists of all photos taken by locals (more familiar of the location) and the second set are photos taken by tourists (less familiar of the location).

The classification of users into locals or tourists is determined based on their temporal-spatial interaction patterns. The timestamps of photos taken in succession by user was leveraged to identify their temporal associations with each location. For a given location, we visualize the distribution of differences in timestamp of first and last photos taken by the user and segregate users into two sets with activity periods either to be (1) under 30 days, or (2) more than 30 days. Users with shorter activity at a location (city in our case) suggesting temporary presence are classified as *tourists*, and the latter group of users, suggesting longer presence, as *locals*. The choice of 30 days is also found to be consistent with the prior definitions used to identify locals [8, 11].

An individual is likely to be recognized as local in more than one location in the above classification. These locations can be the places where a user may have spent time during her childhood, or

---

[1]https://developer.yahoo.com/maps/rest/V1/geocode.html

Table 1: Top 5 tags unique for Seattle and San Francisco sorted by increased value of conditional entropy.

San Francisco		Seattle	
Locals	*Tourists*	*Locals*	*Tourists*
texture	urban	ocean	latte
graffiti	architecture	sunset	urban
people	skyline	sidewalk	architecture
monochrome	ferrybuilding	urban decay	skyline
portrait	bridge	biking	outdoor

college, or currently as a resident. Likewise, the same individual is likely to be a tourist in more than one location, where she may have shorter periods of interactions. A user do not identify as both a local and a tourist for the same location. Furthermore, we find percentage of locals and tourists are different for different cities. For instance, in San Francisco, the percentage of local users is 68%, while tourists constitute the remaining 32%. And, the percentage of local users decreases from larger urban cities to more rural cities with moderate population. In smaller cities, most users are identified as tourists due to lack of active periods of photography [17].

In this paper, we focus only on urban cities where we find fair representation of both locals and tourists from the dataset. For each location we segregate the photos taken by users into local and tourist sets. Using the conditional entropy metric, unique characteristics for each location is determined for both locals' and tourists' photos respectively. In Table 1, the top 5 descriptors for Seattle and San Francisco are shown with increasing metric value of conditional entropy (or decreasing certainty). The top descriptors in Seattle for locals are "ocean", "sunset" and "sidewalk" compared to those of tourists' "latte", "urban" and "architecture". A visual inspection of the photos from Seattle taken by locals are shown to include sunset and sunrise photos. We believe that this is due to time of a day when residents are involved in casual walk or jog along the lakeshores and parks. Whereas tourists' photos include shots of Pike Place Market, Starbuck's first cafe, the urban-architecture of Space Needle and Seattle skyline (popular tourist destination). Likewise, for San Francisco, photos taken by locals are found to consist of pictures of local pride parades, or the graffiti in Clarion Alley (a popular area known for street art), while photos taken by tourists, similar to those in Seattle, include urban settings and architecture influenced by the skyline, famous Golden Gate Bridge, and Bay Bridge—implying a clear evidence of varying characteristics that users capture in their photos based on how they associate with location.

3.4 A Comparison

There exist many approaches to learn unique spatial characteristics from geo-tagged photos. Kennedy et al. [20] used clustering to identify landmarks within a city, then TF-IDF to determine representative photos for the given landmark. Similarly, Chen et al. [5] in their work use both TF-IDF as well as conditional entropy in part to identify iconic places and a representative image icon from

geo-tagged photos within the city. Other approaches include characterizing preferences for tourists only [9, 30, 37], or discovering landmarks [13, 14, 25].

However, we emphasize and invite future work to reconsider the assumption of localness of the geo-tagged content. A proposition that a popular landmark in a city could indeed be well-known to both locals and tourists but there exist certain landmarks and characteristics that are likely only known to the true locals of the city. Our approach accounting for the location-familiarity of user in geo-tagged content show that inclusion of users' temporal patterns lead to different conclusions for the characteristics content represent about the location.

4 EVALUATION

Photos capture diverse representations of what cities are popularly known for and play an illustrative and intuitive role to allow other users to peer into different places within the city. They help users plan and choose their destinations[2] [15]. With such a critical role of photos in representation of city, we evaluate if the descriptive characteristics learned from photos are effective in identifying diverse representative photos of location. In this section, we describe a location-aware characteristics score to rank photos and explain evaluation setup including the assessment of quality of the photo sets compared to other popular baselines by human judges. We also evaluate how well these photos capture locals' and tourists' views of the city.

4.1 Location-Aware Characteristics Score

To identify and rank relevant photos, it is important to optimize for both content and perceived relevance of items [2]. Using the descriptive characteristics (c) derived from image content, and social engagement potential ($\#favorites$) as proxy for their relevance, we devise a characteristic-score $\mathrm{charScore}_g$, for each geo-tagged photo (g) at location (l) as:

$$\mathrm{charScore}_g = \frac{\log(\#\mathrm{faves}_g)}{\displaystyle\sum_{c \in \mathrm{chars}(g)} \frac{h(c|l)}{\mathrm{size}(\mathrm{chars}(g))}} \qquad (2)$$

The metric ranks photos with higher social engagement potential and unique characteristics of the location to the top. Higher social engagement, (more number of favorites[3]) implies higher relevance; and smaller the sum of conditional entropy implies higher the chances that candidate photo captures the representative characteristics of location. The score is calculated for each geo-tagged photo in the locals' and tourists' set respectively. Ranking photos in decreasing order of the score provide us the relevant, representative photos for the location, while unique to locals and tourists respectively.

---

[2]We find this to be evident in YFCC100M dataset too; The distribution of timestamps of user likes/favorites for photos at a location, and the distribution of timestamps of their uploads from the same location are compared. We find the first distribution to have statistically smaller ($p < 0.001$) mean than the later.

[3]We also investigated other social metric signals to rank photos such as number of views, number of shares etc. in characteristic score. However, in preliminary analysis by a group of 8–10 users, photos are found to be very similar to recommendations based on number of favorites. We choose to keep the social metric that is more available and intuitive across other domains.

Table 2: Age distribution of Survey Participants. Majority of our participants are in the age group of 30–40

Age Group	Total	Male	Own DSLR
0–20	8	62.5%	62.5%
20–30	97	70.0%	37.1%
30–40	106	67.0%	51.9%
40–50	30	60.0%	46.7%
50–60	20	50.0%	45.0%
Above 60	10	60.0%	40.0%

Table 3: Most survey participants are male with a higher percentage of participants sharing photos on Facebook. Flickr users tend to be more likely to own professional level cameras, like DSLRs.

Participants	Percent	Female	Own DSLR
Male	64.2%	—	51.0%
Female	35.8%	—	56.5%
Shares on Facebook	68.6%	38.7%	42.4%
Shares on Flickr	34.3%	29.1%	63.4%
Shares on Google Photos	17.7%	25.0%	41.7%

Table 4: A break down of the 271 survey participants.

City	Total	Local/Resident	Own DSLR
Boston	32	62.5%	34.3%
Los Angeles	39	51.2%	38.4%
Seattle	27	48.1%	25.9%
San Francisco	75	48.0%	61.3%
New York	47	42.6%	46.8%
Chicago	51	38.4%	41.1%

4.2 Survey Setup

To gather insights on quality of scoring the candidate photos and understand how well photos capture the diverse representation of a city, we design an online survey for a large-scale human-based evaluation. The participants are asked to choose a city from set of choices and assess four different unique set of photos for each city. The four sets are described below:

localR: Candidate set based only on photos taken by users identified as locals and sorted by the characteristic score.

touristR: Candidate set based only on photos taken by users identified as tourists and sorted by characteristic score.

geo-popularR: A baseline set that contains the most socially relevant photos of location, sorted by number of favorites.

popularR: A naive baseline set that contains photos irrespective of location, sorted by number of favorites.

We use top 20 photos in each set for evaluation. In our preliminary analysis, photos at top of the lists are found to be taken by expert users often with specific content like wedding, landscape, or portraits. The fan-following of these experts further resulted in unusual higher social engagement bias for these photos bringing in lack of *diversity* in the sets [38]. Although the quality and aesthetics

of these photos are un-questionable, the high correlation in their main theme made photos being more repetitive in candidate set. To address this issue, we, (a) filter out photos with similar characteristics in the set (determined using similarity between their characteristics-based feature vector), and (b) limit the number of photos to 2 per photographer in a given set. This helps achieve a diverse candidate photos set (see Figure 3(a) for an example set).

In the survey, participants answer a set of specific questions on a slider scale for each of four sets to assess the quality of retrieved photos. These questions primarily evaluate two qualities: (1) their diverse and characteristic representation of the city, and (2) whether they characterize what locals or tourists would think of the city. Correspondingly, as shown in Figure 3(b), each participant chooses a location (all within United States) and record her feedback for (a) "How characteristic are these photos of the location?", (b) "Rate the beauty or aesthetic quality of photos", and (c) "Do these photos represent the diversity of location?". Finally, whether photos are reflective of locals or tourists they answer: (d) "Do you think these photos characterize what locals think about the location?", and (e) "Do you think these photos characteristic what tourists think about the location?". As a final step, participants are asked to pick a set they think *best* represents the location. We keep the order of candidate photo sets randomized for every user, and a response is considered complete only when assessment for all four sets are recorded. In addition to quality assessment, we ask participants to provide their familiarity with location as a local or as a tourist; and, keywords that they think characterize the city in their own view.

5 RESULTS AND DISCUSSION

To participate in the survey, participants were invited via Amazon Mechanical Turks (limited to United States) and social media platforms such as Twitter, Facebook, and Google+. A total number of 271 participants completed the survey. Among those, 154 participants self-identify themselves as local to the cities they evaluate while 157 self-identify as tourists. The selection of cities were limited to six of the major locations in United States with balanced representation of both locals and tourists. Table 2 shows the age distribution of participants; and Table 3 shows gender, and platform these participants often use for photo sharing. Table 4 shows percentage of participants who self-identify as locals for each of six cities. There are no significant differences in our findings based on gender or age of participants.

5.1 User Keywords Versus Descriptive Characteristics

We evaluate the keywords users provided in survey describing the city in their own view. Locals are found to be more diverse in their description of cities compared to tourists. The 154 locals provided 217 unique keywords compared to only 159 keywords from the 157 tourists; that is 58% statistically more keywords per user. We also determine the most frequent occurring keywords (pre-processed with removal of stopwords and Porter stemming) for each city. The 20 most frequent keywords used by locals and tourists for San Francisco are illustrated in Figure 4. The high frequency of "food", "ocean" and "culture" among locals' descriptions compared to tourists' "architecture", "bridge" and "street" for San Francisco

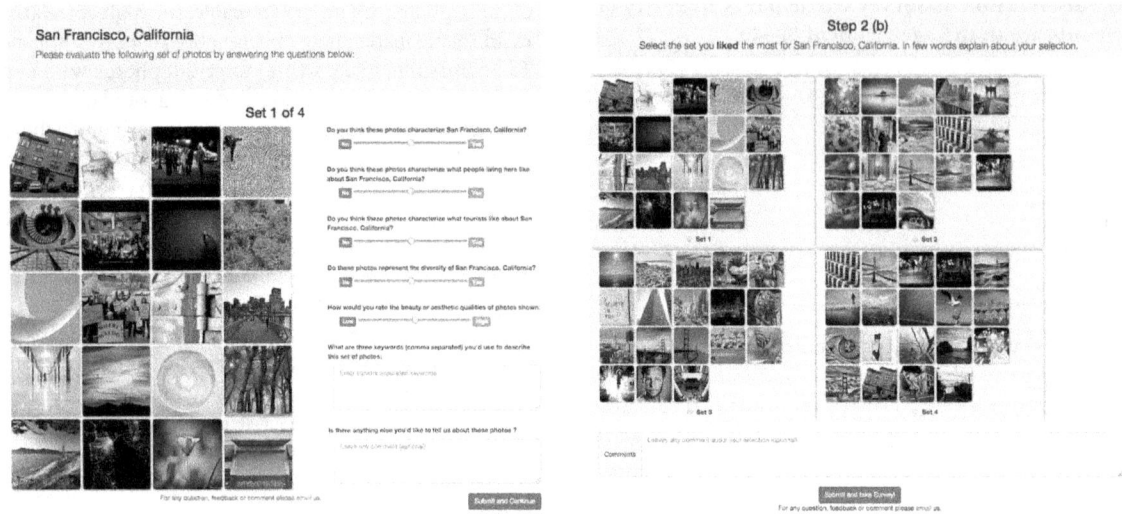

(a) Participant records their responses assessing each recommendation set on a slider scale.

(b) In final step of the survey, participants are asked to choose the set of photos that they prefer the most for given location.

Figure 3: Evaluation of Recommendation Sets by Participants

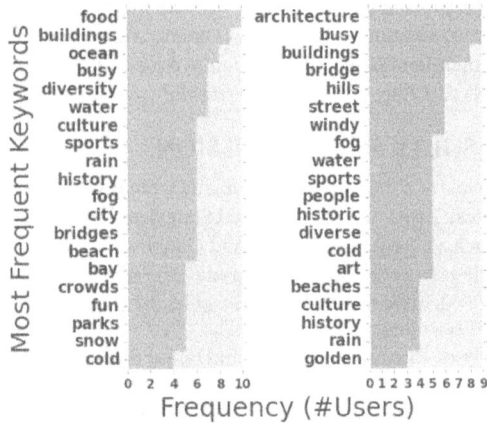

Figure 4: Most frequent keywords to describe a city by residents (left) and visitors (right).

emphasize the different ways users characterize the same city based on their familiarity—a result coherent to the descriptive spatial characteristics we learn about city from the geo-tagged photos. Similar distinctions are observed among other cities evaluated in the survey[4].

5.2 Photos Assessment

In this section, we evaluate the effectiveness of the characteristic score in ranking the diverse representative photos of a location. From the survey responses, participants are found to overall *prefer the candidate set based on tourists' photos*, with 52% selecting *touristR*, 23% *geo-popularR*, followed by 20% and 5% for *localR* and

---

[4]We do not discuss each city due to page limitations.

popularR respectively. The difference in percentages are found to be statistically significant from each other ($p < 0.01$) using a Chi-square proportion test. Nevertheless, we observe these percentages to be slightly different for each city. However, the order is same. The inter-rater agreement statistic or Cronbach's alpha is also found to be significant with value of 0.84.

Participants' response for each individual set is further examined to better understand their assessment for quality, diversity and how well they think photos capture the relevant meaningful characteristics of location. In Figure 5, the cumulative percentage of participants are shown for different scales of agreements (the continuous values of slider scale are converted to respective five segments similar to Likert scales). The percentages on the right reflect the percentage of participants who "Strongly Agree" or "Agree"; in the middle are the percentage of participants with *neutral* response; and in left are percentage of users who "Strongly Disagree" or "Disagree". The color shades represent each of the five Likert scales.

Result shows 86% of **participants strongly agree *touristR* being more characteristic of location** compared to only 70% agreement for *geo-popularR* and 65% for *localR*. The scores on characteristics, aesthetics, as well as diversity of photos from *touristR* are found to be higher and statistically significant to other sets using Kruskal-Wallis non-parametric test ($p < 0.001$). Furthermore, participants find *localR* photos to be more characteristic of what locals think about location (4th plot from top in Figure 5: 75% vs others) and *touristR* photos to be more characteristic of what tourists think about location (bottom of Figure 5: 80% versus others).

5.2.1 Discussion.
The overall higher preference for tourists set highlights the importance tourists play for these locations. In their short stay, these users are likely to capture destinations that are well-known and often better representative of what is popular within the city — an implicit design implication for location-based services. Services could become more accurate and efficient if only tourists

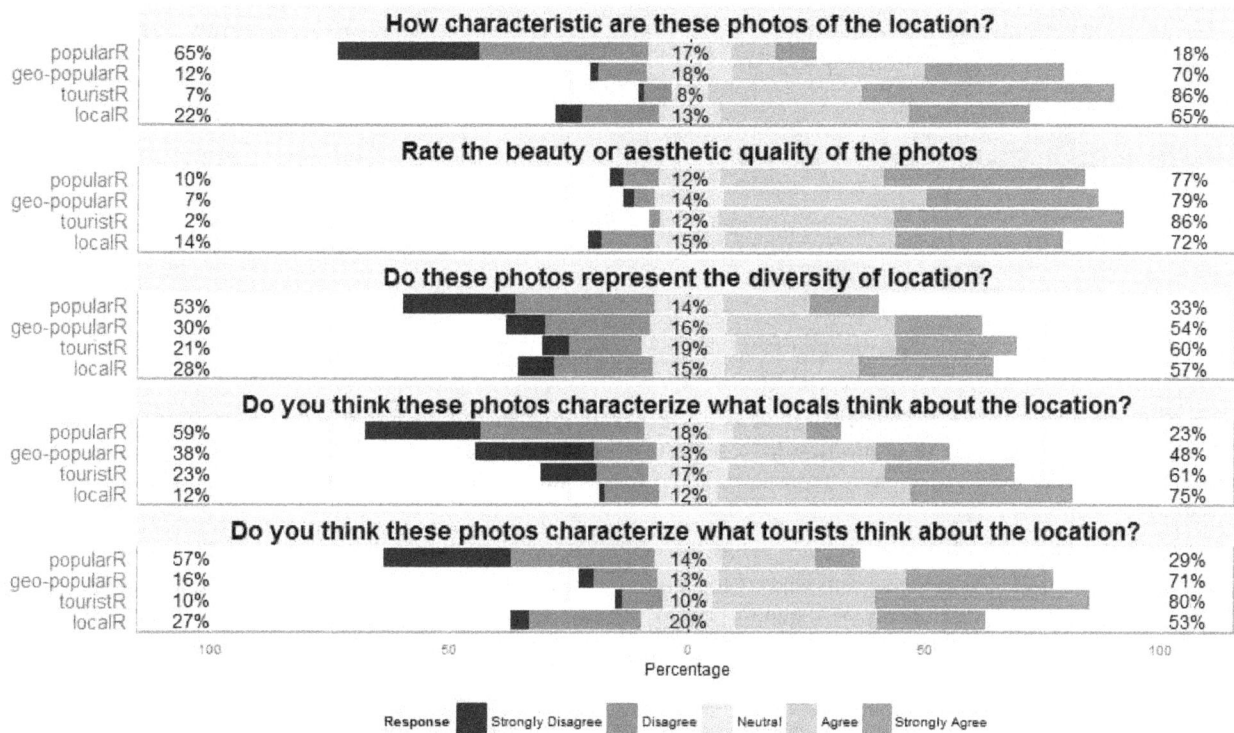

Figure 5: Cumulative Survey responses from recommendation assessment. Users unanimously agreed that *touristR* photos capture the best characteristics of location. However, users in the survey are shown to recognize the sets that characterize what locals and tourists think about location.

generated content is analyzed for content retrieval or ranking purposes instead of mining the whole dataset. One such scenario is seen in online systems when no pre-existing information available about the requesting user for any personalization, a phenomena also known as coldstart. In such scenario, we hypothesize that ranking items based on other similar users who in past were tourists at the location could be more effective. To understand this implication better, we investigate in next section if participants who identify as tourists have any significant difference in their opinion to the photo sets compare to those who identify as locals.

We draw two more conclusions from the results above: (1) the photos selected based on their visual content are able to capture representations of city that is more recognizable to users than the popular baselines; and, (2) their ability to distinguish the representations of city that matches with locals' and tourists' views respectively. These findings highlight the efficacy we achieve by adapting to the difference in preferences that exist between locals and tourists for a location.

5.3 Location Familiarity

We now analyze if the familiarity of participants with location affect their assessment of the photos. Among 154 participants, who self-identify as locals to the location, there is still larger percentage of users (44.8%) who prefer the *touristR*. Only 31.42% of these users prefer the local set i.e. *localR*. However, we notice a significant difference in percentage of participants, who self-identify as

tourists, in their preference for *localR* and *touristR*. There are only 9.7% of these participants who prefer the local set (*localR*) compared to 31.42% of the participants identified as locals. A major percentage of tourist participants prefer the *touristR* i.e. 60.3%. This difference in agreement between local and tourist participants underlines the **difference in perception among these users**. The awareness/familiarity of the participants who are locals are likely to recognize the characteristics in photos only known to locals than to the participants who are tourists. For example, trails, distinct coffee shops, unique restaurants, parks etc. We find the evidence of these differences in the feedback locals shared about the *localR* set:

So far, this set seems most "boston". Shows boston scenes (or scenes that could be from boston) around the year and in a variety of light and weather — Resident, Boston.

These feel more authentic and have a better NYC feel. Too many coffee cups, but we do love our coffee in NY. Definitely feels like a local took these — Resident, New York.

At least a few in this set that are clearly Los Angeles (e.g. union station) and blondes (hey, its LA), but still can't figure out how they relate at all to each other — Resident, Los Angeles.

Similar differences are observed in individual assessment of each candidate photo sets. As shown in Figure 6(a) and 6(b), higher percentage of participants who are locals (67%) find *localR* to be

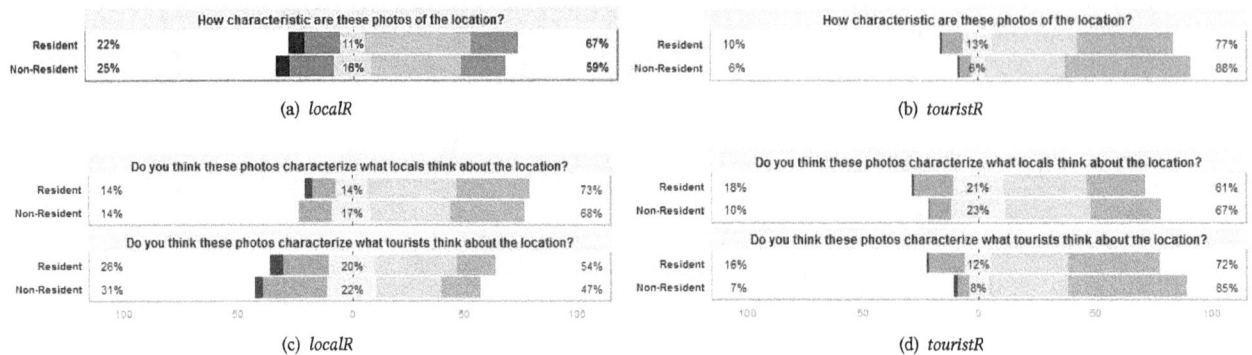

Figure 6: Difference in opinion of Locals (marked as Resident) Vs Tourists (marked as Non-Resident): (a) Locals find *localR* more characteristic/representative of location ($p < 0.05$), (b) Tourists find *touristR* more characteristic ($p < 0.01$), (c) Both locals and tourists find *localR* to be more representative of locals, and (d) Both locals and tourists find *touristR* to be more representative of tourists.

more characteristic of location than participants who are tourists (59%); while, higher percentage of tourists (88%) find *touristR* to be more characteristic of location than participants who are locals (77%)[5]. Moreover, the local participants find the local set (*localR*) to represent more of "what locals think about the location" than the tourist set (*touristR*)—73% vs 61%, while no difference observed in tourist participants response to the same question. However, both local and tourist participants agreed upon *touristR* to be highly characteristic of "what tourists would think about the location".

5.3.1 Discussion. In summary, participants reflect difference in their opinion for candidate set based on how familiar they are with location. The participants who are more familiar with location identify photos in local set more easily and find it delightful compared to tourists. On the other hand, participants who self-identify as tourists find tourist set highly representative of location compared to other baselines. This result highlight the accuracy of our metric in retrieving photos that uniquely representative of location while being adaptive to views of locals and tourists respectively. Result further underlines the importance of being adaptive to location-familiarity with geo-tagging as well as provide an alternative for problems such as cold-start in online location-based systems.

6   CONCLUSION AND FUTURE WORK

While location-based services in mobile social web provide multitudes of possibility to produce and consume information they also create an unique opportunity to better understand user interactions and their perceptions of surroundings. To our knowledge, this is the first work to not only emphasize that perceptions differ for individuals at a location but also be able to describe these perceptions with descriptive spatial characteristics. We demonstrate that geo-tagged content can vary based on how group of users perceive given their familiarity with location. We then devise a location-familiarity-aware characteristic-score that improves the effectiveness in retrieval of representative photos of location. Assessed by

---
[5]The differences found to be significant to each other using the non-parametric Wilcoxon rank sum test ($p < 0.05$)

human judges, the photos are shown to be diverse, representative,

and adaptive to characteristics familiar to locals and tourists respectively; an important result challenging the underlying assumption of *localness* in content for location-based services.

Nevertheless, there are some limitations to our approach that we would like to address in our future work. First, even though our approach is able to distinguish characteristics for large number of cities in the dataset, we only be able to discuss six cities for our evaluation. This is due to known limitations of time and effort involved in online human-based evaluations (a better approach would be to conduct an A/B test within large scale systems). The other limitation is that we did not consider context of users in our implementations such as time, year, or even season. Since a user could visit a city for different reasons and at different times of the year we believe contextual information could play more important role. For example, a tourist traveling for leisure compared to traveling for business may seek to explore different destinations in the city. Similarly, a tourist behavior could vary based on season of the year like snowy winters versus hot summers. We believe that adapting to such contexts could further help recognize and understand contextual characteristics captured in the content.

7   ACKNOWLEDGMENT

We thank Yahoo Flickr team for their support and feedback during this work, and our reviewers for their valuable feedback and suggestions on multiple aspects of this paper.

REFERENCES

[1] Saeideh Bakhshi, David A Shamma, Lyndon Kennedy, and Eric Gilbert. 2015. Why We Filter Our Photos and How It Impacts Engagement. In *Ninth International AAAI Conference on Web and Social Media*.
[2] Robin Burke. 2002. Hybrid recommender systems: Survey and experiments. *User modeling and user-adapted interaction* 12, 4 (2002), 331–370.
[3] Iván Cantador, Ioannis Konstas, and Joemon M Jose. 2011. Categorising social tags to improve folksonomy-based recommendations. *Web Semantics: Science, Services and Agents on the World Wide Web* 9, 1 (2011), 1–15.
[4] Iván Cantador, Martin Szomszor, Harith Alani, Miriam Fernández, and Pablo Castells. 2008. Enriching ontological user profiles with tagging history for multi-domain recommendations. (2008).
[5] Wei-Chao Chen, Agathe Battestini, Natasha Gelfand, and Vidya Setlur. 2009. Visual Summaries of Popular Landmarks from Community Photo Collections. In *Proceedings of the 17th ACM International Conference on Multimedia (MM*

'09). ACM, New York, NY, USA, 789–792. DOI : http://dx.doi.org/10.1145/1631272. 1631415

[6] Guy Debord. 1955. Introduction to a critique of urban geography. *Critical Geographies A Collection of Readings* (1955).

[7] J. Deng, W. Dong, R. Socher, L.-J. Li, K. Li, and L. Fei-Fei. 2009. ImageNet: A Large-Scale Hierarchical Image Database. In *Proceedings of the IEEE International Conference on Computer Vision and Pattern Recognition.*

[8] Eric Fischer. 2014. Locals and tourists. *A+ U-ARCHITECTURE AND URBANISM* 530 (2014), 30–33.

[9] Juan Carlos García-Palomares, Javier Gutiérrez, and Carmen Mínguez. 2015. Identification of tourist hot spots based on social networks: A comparative analysis of European metropolises using photo-sharing services and {GIS}. *Applied Geography* 63 (2015), 408 – 417. DOI : http://dx.doi.org/10.1016/j.apgeog.2015.08.002

[10] Juan Carlos GarcÃŋa-Palomares, Javier GutiÃŋrrez, and Carmen MÃŋnguez. 2015. Identification of tourist hot spots based on social networks: A comparative analysis of European metropolises using photo-sharing services and {GIS}. *Applied Geography* 63 (2015), 408 – 417. DOI : http://dx.doi.org/10.1016/j.apgeog.2015.08.002

[11] Fabien Girardin, Francesco Calabrese, Filippo Dal Fiore, Carlo Ratti, and Josep Blat. 2008. Digital footprinting: Uncovering tourists with user-generated content. *Pervasive Computing, IEEE* 7, 4 (2008), 36–43.

[12] Fabien Girardin, Andrea Vaccari, Re Gerber, and Assaf Biderman. 2009. Quantifying urban attractiveness from the distribution and density of digital footprints. *Journal of Spatial Data Infrastructure Research* (2009).

[13] Yingjie Hu, Song Gao, Krzysztof Janowicz, Bailang Yu, Wenwen Li, and Sathya Prasad. 2015. Extracting and understanding urban areas of interest using geo-tagged photos. *Computers, Environment and Urban Systems* 54 (2015), 240 – 254. DOI : http://dx.doi.org/10.1016/j.compenvurbsys.2015.09.001

[14] Piotr Jankowski, Natalia Andrienko, Gennady Andrienko, and Slava Kisilevich. 2010. Discovering Landmark Preferences and Movement Patterns from Photo Postings. *Transactions in GIS* 14, 6 (2010), 833–852. DOI : http://dx.doi.org/10.1111/j.1467-9671.2010.01235.x

[15] Olivia H Jenkins. 1999. Understanding and measuring tourist destination images. *The International Journal of Tourism Research* 1, 1 (1999), 1.

[16] Yangqing Jia, Evan Shelhamer, Jeff Donahue, Sergey Karayev, Jonathan Long, Ross Girshick, Sergio Guadarrama, and Trevor Darrell. 2014. Caffe: Convolutional Architecture for Fast Feature Embedding. *arXiv preprint arXiv:1408.5093* (2014).

[17] Isaac L Johnson, Subhasree Sengupta, Johannes Schöning, and Brent Hecht. 2016. The Geography and Importance of Localness in Geotagged Social Media. In *Proceedings of the 2016 CHI Conference on Human Factors in Computing Systems.* ACM, 515–526.

[18] Gerrit Kahl, Lübomira Spassova, Johannes Schöning, Sven Gehring, and Antonio Krüger. 2011. IRL SmartCart-a user-adaptive context-aware interface for shopping assistance. In *Proceedings of the 16th international conference on Intelligent user interfaces.* ACM, 359–362.

[19] Marius Kaminskas, Francesco Ricci, and Markus Schedl. 2013. Location-aware music recommendation using auto-tagging and hybrid matching. In *Proceedings of the 7th ACM conference on Recommender systems.* ACM, 17–24.

[20] Lyndon S. Kennedy and Mor Naaman. 2008. Generating Diverse and Representative Image Search Results for Landmarks. In *Proceedings of the 17th International Conference on World Wide Web (WWW '08).* ACM, New York, NY, USA, 297–306. DOI : http://dx.doi.org/10.1145/1367497.1367539

[21] Metin Kozak, Enrique Bigné, Ana González, and Luisa Andreu. 2004. Cross-cultural behaviour research in tourism: a case study on destination image. *Consumer psychology of tourism, hospitality and leisure* 3 (2004), 303–317.

[22] Vikas Kumar, Daniel Jarratt, Rahul Anand, Joseph A. Konstan, and Brent Hecht. 2015. "Where Far Can Be Close": Finding Distant Neighbors In Recommender

Systems. In *Proceedings of LocalRec Workshop in ACM conference on Recommender Systems.* 13–20. http://ceur-ws.org/Vol-1405/paper-03.pdf

[23] Justin J Levandoski, Mohamed Sarwat, Ahmed Eldawy, and Mohamed F Mokbel. 2012. Lars: A location-aware recommender system. In *Data Engineering (ICDE), 2012 IEEE 28th International Conference on.* IEEE, 450–461.

[24] Bin Liu, Yanjie Fu, Zijun Yao, and Hui Xiong. 2013. Learning geographical preferences for point-of-interest recommendation. In *Proceedings of the 19th ACM SIGKDD international conference on Knowledge discovery and data mining.* ACM, 1043–1051.

[25] Silvia Paldino, DÃ₃niel Kondor, Iva Bojic, Stanislav Sobolevsky, Marta C. GonzÃ₃lez, and Carlo Ratti. 2016. Uncovering Urban Temporal Patterns from Geo-Tagged Photography. *PLOS ONE* 11, 12 (12 2016), 1–14. DOI : http://dx.doi.org/10.1371/journal.pone.0165753

[26] RR Perdue, HJP Immermans, and M Uysal. 2004. *Consumer psychology of tourism, hospitality and leisure.* Vol. 3. CABI.

[27] Daniele Quercia, Rossano Schifanella, and Luca Maria Aiello. 2014. The shortest path to happiness: Recommending beautiful, quiet, and happy routes in the city. In *Proceedings of the 25th ACM conference on Hypertext and social media.* ACM, 116–125.

[28] Gillian Rose. 2008. Using photographs as illustrations in human geography. *Journal of Geography in Higher Education* 32, 1 (2008), 151–160.

[29] Pavel Serdyukov, Vanessa Murdock, and Roelof Van Zwol. 2009. Placing flickr photos on a map. In *Proceedings of the 32nd international ACM SIGIR conference on Research and development in information retrieval.* ACM, 484–491.

[30] Shiliang Su, Chen Wan, Yixuan Hu, and Zhongliang Cai. 2016. Characterizing geographical preferences of international tourists and the local influential factors in China using geo-tagged photos on social media. *Applied Geography* 73 (2016), 26 – 37. DOI : http://dx.doi.org/10.1016/j.apgeog.2016.06.001

[31] Ning Tan, Gaëtan Pruvost, Matthieu Courgeon, Céline Clavel, Yacine Bellik, and Jean-Claude Martin. 2011. A location-aware virtual character in a smart room: effects on performance, presence and adaptivity. In *Proceedings of the 16th international conference on Intelligent user interfaces.* ACM, 399–402.

[32] Bart Thomee, David A. Shamma, Gerald Friedland, Benjamin Elizalde, Karl Ni, Douglas Poland, Damian Borth, and Li-Jia Li. 2016. YFCC100M: The New Data in Multimedia Research. *Commun. ACM* 59, 2 (Jan. 2016), 64–73. DOI : http://dx.doi.org/10.1145/2812802

[33] Vladimir Vapnik. 1998. *Statistical Learning Theory.* Wiley, New York.

[34] Mao Ye, Peifeng Yin, and Wang-Chien Lee. 2010. Location recommendation for location-based social networks. In *Proceedings of the 18th SIGSPATIAL International Conference on Advances in Geographic Information Systems.* ACM, 458–461.

[35] Hongzhi Yin, Yizhou Sun, Bin Cui, Zhiting Hu, and Ling Chen. 2013. Lcars: a location-content-aware recommender system. In *Proceedings of the 19th ACM SIGKDD international conference on Knowledge discovery and data mining.* ACM, 221–229.

[36] Vincent W Zheng, Yu Zheng, Xing Xie, and Qiang Yang. 2010. Collaborative location and activity recommendations with gps history data. In *Proceedings of the 19th international conference on World wide web.* ACM, 1029–1038.

[37] Yan-Tao Zheng, Zheng-Jun Zha, and Tat-Seng Chua. 2012. Mining Travel Patterns from Geotagged Photos. *ACM Trans. Intell. Syst. Technol.* 3, 3, Article 56 (May 2012), 18 pages. DOI : http://dx.doi.org/10.1145/2168752.2168770

[38] Cai-Nicolas Ziegler, Sean M. McNee, Joseph A. Konstan, and Georg Lausen. 2005. Improving Recommendation Lists Through Topic Diversification. In *Proceedings of the 14th International Conference on World Wide Web (WWW '05).* ACM, New York, NY, USA, 22–32. DOI : http://dx.doi.org/10.1145/1060745.1060754

Investigating the Impact of Personality and Cognitive Efficiency on the Selection of Exercises for Learners

Juliet Okpo
University of Aberdeen
King's College
Aberdeen, UK AB24 3UE
r02jao15@abdn.ac.uk

Judith Masthoff
University of Aberdeen
King's College
Aberdeen, UK AB24 3UE
j.masthoff@abdn.ac.uk

Matt Dennis
University of Portsmouth
Lion Terrace
Portsmouth, UK PO1 3HE
matt.dennis@port.ac.uk

Nigel Beacham
University of Aberdeen
King's College
Aberdeen, United Kingdom AB24 3UE
n.beacham@abdn.ac.uk

Ana Ciocarlan
University of Aberdeen
King's College
Aberdeen, United Kingdom AB24 3UE
ana.ciocarlan@abdn.ac.uk

ABSTRACT

Adapting to learner characteristics is essential when selecting exercises for learners. This paper investigates how humans adapt next exercise selection to learner personality and invested mental effort to enable a future Intelligent Tutoring System to use these adaptations. Participants were presented with validated stories of a learner's personality at polarised levels, a validated story conveying the mental effort invested in carrying out a given task and an indication of a previous performance (just passing) at a simple arithmetic exercise. Participants were also shown a selection of validated exercises of varying difficulty levels and asked to select the exercise which they thought the learner should do next. We found that overall more difficult exercises were selected for learners who used little effort than for learners who used more effort. We found that although an exercise of slightly harder difficulty remains the most popular choice in the high and low self-esteem conditions, for low self-esteem, participants picked an exercise of lower or the same difficulty more often than in the high condition.

CCS CONCEPTS

•Human-centered computing → User models; •Applied computing → Computer-assisted instruction;

KEYWORDS

Exercise Selection, Adaptation, Personality, Mental effort, Performance, Cognitive Efficiency

1 INTRODUCTION

Capturing the effective behaviours of human tutors to create optimal learning tools has been a major motivation for work in Intelligent Tutoring Systems. Human tutors can effectively sense when a learner is challenged and provide individualized tutoring through careful considerations of the factors that affect the learning process of the learner. Tutoring is tailored to individual characteristics of the learner in order to improve learner performance. It is believed that an intelligent tutoring system can combine specific characteristics of a learner just like a human tutor and adapt teaching and learning to these characteristics for better learning outcomes. One major learner characteristic which is closely related to a learner is the learner's personality which is often overlooked in intelligent tutoring. Research in adaptive learning has considered aspects of the learners such as learner performance, learner mental effort, learning support and several other learner characteristics [10, 24]. In order for an Intelligent Tutoring System (ITS) to select the next exercise for learners, the selection process should be effective such that the relevant characteristics of the learner should be taken into consideration [2, 9, 10]. Very few works have used personality as a learner characteristic for adaptive task selection.

We believe that learner personality is worthy of investigation for adaptive exercise selection, as previous research has shown it to be important [7] in other areas of learning. In addition we will investigate cognitive efficiency (which is a balance between learner effort and performance, see below). In this paper, we will use a particular level of learner performance (just passing) and vary learner effort.

In this paper, we describe the construction and validation of a set of exercises with varying difficulties (Section 3), the validation of stories that express a learner's self-esteem (Section 4) and the construction of statements which describe the mental effort invested by learners (Section 5). We then use these in a user-as-wizard study which investigates the effect of learner personality and mental effort on task selection by participants playing the role of a teacher. The results will be used to inform the creation of an algorithm to allow a future intelligent tutoring system to consider learner personality and cognitive efficiency when selecting exercises for learners to complete.

2 RELATED WORK

There is considerable research on adapting learning content to different learner characteristics [9, 33]. In the area of task selection, the focus has been on the design of intelligent tutors that

UMAP '17, July 9–12, 2017, Bratislava, Slovakia
© 2017 ACM. 978-1-4503-4635-1/17/07...$15.00
DOI: http://dx.doi.org/10.1145/3079628.3079674

Table 1: Exercises Table. All exercises used 2 baskets.Six exercises were used of each type.

Type	No. of Balls	Ball Distribution	Basket total	Example exercise	Validated Difficulty
1	3	1 – 2	<10	(4)(9)(5)	1
2	4	1 – 3	<10	(3)(1)(5)(9)	2
3	4	2 – 2	<10	(6)(5)(3)(4)	2
4	4	2 – 2	≥10	(7)(5)(4)(6)	3
5	5	1 – 4	<10	(1)(1)(9)(2)(5)	3
6	5	2 – 3	<10	(6)(2)(3)(4)(3)	4
7	5	2 – 3	≥10	(2)(8)(6)(9)(3)	5

select learning tasks for the learner based on the learner's past performance, available learning support and recently, cognitive load (e.g. [1, 3, 4, 18, 30, 31]). [32] explores how the activities and principles in expert performance research can be used to design instructional formats based on cognitive load theory for skills mastery. In this work, they showed that learning tasks can be selected on the basis of an assessment of a learner's level of expertise.

Personality refers to an individual's whole psychological structure and this includes his or her temperament, character, intelligence, sentiments, attitudes, interests, beliefs, ambitions and ideals. A person's personality is shown by his/her disposition [16]. There have been several studies on adaptation to personality [7]. Self-esteem is defined as how favourably a person regards oneself [27]. For a learner to achieve better learning outcomes in a specific domain, they must believe in their abilities and this belief in the fact that they can produce a favourable outcome will in turn serve as motivation to learn. Self-esteem is seen as an important component of personality [20]. Self-esteem is one of the most widely studied personality concepts in psychology such that in 2001, 20,203 articles had self-esteem as a keyword which made self-esteem the most researched personality concept in comparison with concepts like neuroticism with 20,026 articles and locus of control with 13,428 articles [17]. Significant associations can be found between self-esteem and all personality traits such as openness, conscientiousness, extraversion, agreeableness and neuroticism [12]. For our study, it was decided that self-esteem was a good personality characteristic to investigate first.

Cognitive efficiency, the combination of invested mental effort and performance [5, 26], is also an important aspect of a learner's learning and learning outcomes in the context of assessment, so may need to be taken into account for exercise selection. Additionally, effective exercise selection may need to take learners' mental well-being into account, to keep them motivated. As research has shown that personality can predict and justify 32 to 56 percentages scores' variant of mental well-being [29, 34], this may provide another reason for taking personality into account.

Good estimation of difficulty level of exercises will allow good exercise sequencing [23] as well as better adaptation to the cognitive level of the learners. Previous research has investigated the estimation of difficulty level of exercises using different approaches. Quiz difficulty levels have been evaluated by [19] using similarity

measures. While the study investigates the estimation of difficulty of exercises in the learning domain, several other works on the estimation of the difficulty of exercises have been done in various domains using different estimation methods. A graph based strategy for difficulty level estimation for chemistry was used by [35]. Foteini et al presented a neuro-fuzzy approach for the estimation of exercises on search algorithms [13, 14]. In this method, specific characteristics of the exercises are taken as inputs to provide the difficulty of the exercises as output. Also in a report, the level of the difficulty of the exam was based on the item analysis approach where the difficulty of an item was understood as the proportion of persons who correctly answered a test item. This has to do with an inverse relationship such that the higher the proportion of those that answered the test item correctly, the lower the difficulty of the test item [11]. In this paper, we will not investigate how to automatically detect exercise difficulty, but validate exercise difficulty through human studies to allow us to use these validated difficulties in our main study.

3 EXERCISE DIFFICULTY VALIDATION

To investigate the effect of mental effort and personality on the difficulty of exercises, we first needed a set of exercises with validated difficulty levels for participants to select from. In this paper, we have used a simple addition exercise which asks learners to place differently weighted balls into a set number of baskets so that they weighed the same. For example, a learner might be given three balls: (2), (3) and (5) and asked to place them into two baskets. This is a very easy exercise as the heaviest ball is also the sum of the remaining two. Exercises can be made more challenging in many ways. For example, requiring more than one ball in both baskets: (2)(3) in one basket and (4)(1) in the other; increasing the basket total so that more balls are needed: (5)(4)(7)(9) in one and (3)(8)(2)(4)(6) in the other; and by increasing the number of baskets. With this in mind, we wanted to create a systematic way of increasing difficulty using these methods. To achieve this, we designed a validation study described in the next section.

Set 1 of 6

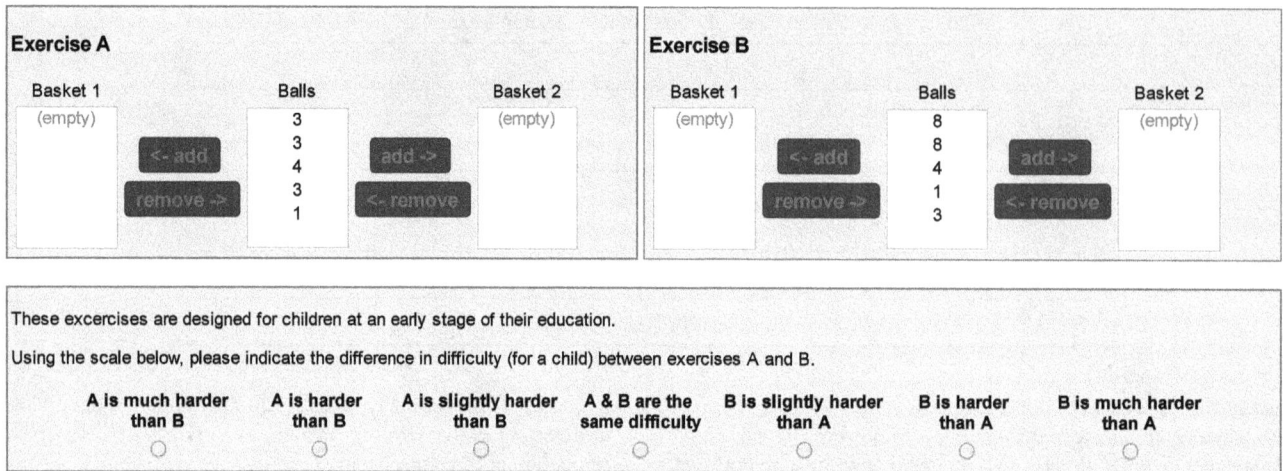

Figure 1: Interface for Difficulty Validation Study

Table 2: Results of Difficulty Validation

Study	Exercise Types	Num. Participants	Mean	Std. Dev	ztest
1	1 & 2	25	0.74	0.944	0.000
2	2 & 3	25	-0.13	0.808	0.978
3	3 & 4	25	0.20	0.993	0.006
4	4 & 5	25	-0.29	1.006	0.999
5	4 & 6	25	0.43	1.226	0.000
6	6 & 7	25	0.50	1.184	0.000

3.1 Study Design

Participants were recruited via Amazon's Mechanical Turk [22], a crowdsourcing tool. Participants required an acceptance rate of 90% to ensure good quality of responses and had to pass a Cloze test for English fluency to ensure they had enough literacy skills to understand the language used for the study. 155 participants took part in the study (74 females and 81 males).

Six pairs of two exercises with different estimated difficulty levels were shown to the participants. These exercises were generated using the rules described in Table 1. As previously discussed, we varied the complexity of the exercises by adjusting the number of balls required to be placed in each basket to solve the exercise, and by increasing the basket total.

We had six variants of the study in a between-subjects design, each investigating the difference in difficulty between two types of exercises. Each variant had twelve exercises (six of each type) for participants to solve, shown in pairs (one exercise of each type), where one exercise was expected to be easier than the other. Participants then rated which exercise they thought was easier on a scale as shown in Figure 1. Within each pair, the order was randomized so that the exercise we expected to be easier could appear on the left or right.

3.2 Results

To calculate a relative difficulty score between two exercises of different types, we transformed the scale shown in Figure 1 into numbers. If the exercise with the harder expected difficulty was deemed slightly harder this was scored as 1, harder as 2 and much harder as 3 (and corresponding negative scores for the reverse). If the exercises were deemed of the same difficulty a score of 0 was used. The score was averaged over the six comparisons of the two exercise types each participant did.

From our results in Table 2, the Z-test of the grand mean scores compared to 0 shows that exercise types 1 and 2 had a significant difference and therefore type 2 is more difficult than type 1. Exercise types 2 and 3 showed no significant difference. Exercise type 3 was then tested with exercise type 4 which gave a significant result showing that type 4 was more difficult than type 3 (or 2). Testing exercise type 4 against type 5 yielded no significant difference indicating that types 4 and 5 were of the same difficulty. We then tested exercise type 4 with type 6 and this returned a significant difference in difficulty with type 6 being more difficult than type 4 (or 5). Finally, exercise type 6 was tested with type 7 and the result showed a high significant difference proving that type 7 was more difficult than type 6. Consequently, we have been able to derive 5 levels of difficulty of exercises (see Table 2).

4 SELF-ESTEEM STORY VALIDATION

This section describes the creation and validation of stories which express learner self-esteem at polarized levels (high and low), following a similar approach to [6]

4.1 Story Development

To construct the stories, we used the well-established State Self-Esteem scale [15]. The SSES consists of 20 items that measure momentary fluctuations in self-esteem. For each story, we changed a selection of the questionnaire items into third person, inverting

Table 3: Mental Effort Statements Mapped to Effort Rating

| Description | Effort rating by participants (%) | | | | | | | | | | Average Rating |
	1 (none)	2	3	4	5	6	7	8	9	10 (max)	
no effort	95%		5%								1.10
minimal effort	24%	**52%**	14%	10%							2.10
little effort		24%	**71%**				5%				2.95
token effort		35%	10%	10%	15%	20%		5%		5%	4.25
some effort		5%	14%	52%		24%	5%				4.38
average effort				10%	71%	10%	10%				5.19
moderate effort				14%	**48%**	24%	10%			5%	5.52
quite a lot of effort		5%			10%	14%	33%	33%		5%	6.90
considerable effort					10%	24%	38%	14%	14%		7.00
substantial effort					10%	25%	30%	25%	10%		7.00
much effort			5%			14%	**52%**	24%	5%	0%	7.00
very much effort						10%	10%	48%	29%	5%	8.10
ultimate effort						10%	5%	0%	10%	76%	9.38
maximum effort						5%	5%		10%	81%	9.57
all possible effort							5%	5%	10%	**80%**	9.65

them where necessary. In trying to make the story real, we linked it with a character, a student called Nancy. The resulting stories are shown in Table 4.

4.2 Story Validation

40 participants saw one of the two stories in a between-subjects design (following a similar approach to [6]). Participants were crowd-sourced on Amazon's Mechanical Turk [22]. They were adults based in the US, had to pass an English fluency test and have an approval rating of 90%. To validate that the stories conveyed self-esteem at the desired level, participants were asked to rate the self-esteem of Nancy using the Rosenberg self-esteem questionnaire [28], which uses different terms to measure the same concept.

A between subjects T-test was performed on the self-esteem score between the high and low self-esteem stories, which was significant at $T(38) = 13.93$, $p < 0.001$. The mean self-esteem score

for high was 24.6 ± 3.68 SD and the mean for low was 8.0 ± 3.87 SD. The Rosenberg scale ranges from 0-30. Scores between 15 and 25 are within the normal range, while scores below 15 suggests low self-esteem [28]. The level of self-esteem for the low story is lower than the normal range. The level of self-esteem for the high story is at the top end of the normal range.

Given the large difference in the self-esteem levels between the two stories, we believe the stories are suitable for future studies to express high and low learner self-esteem.

5 MENTAL EFFORT STATEMENT VALIDATION

5.1 Statement Generation

Many statements can be used to describe the amount of mental effort that has been invested by a learner in carrying out a task. Unfortunately, we have not found a list that clearly defines varying levels of mental effort. To have a clear definition of invested mental effort, we wanted to map mental effort statements to numbers indicating the effort used, so that we could use a selection of statements in our studies. In a brain-storming session, three lecturers and a research student came up with 15 invested mental effort statements (see statements in Table 3).

5.2 Statement Validation

26 participants (staff and students of the University) completed the survey using an on-line survey tool (Survey Monkey) in about 5 minutes. The data from 21 participants were used (16 males, 4 females, 1 undisclosed). The other 5 participants were excluded due to the low quality of their responses (providing the same response for almost all statements, or not mapping 'no effort' to 1 as was indicated on the scale).

Table 4: Stories depicting High and Low Self Esteem

SE Level	Story
High	Nancy is a learner who is confident about her abilities. She is satisfied about the way she looks and feels good about herself. She thinks she is as smart as others and believes that others admire and respect her. She feels that she has a good understanding of things.
Low	Nancy is a learner who worries about the impression she makes and whether she is regarded as a success or a failure. She feels like she is not doing well and she believes she cannot understand the things she reads. Nancy thinks she is unattractive and is displeased with herself. She feels inferior to others.

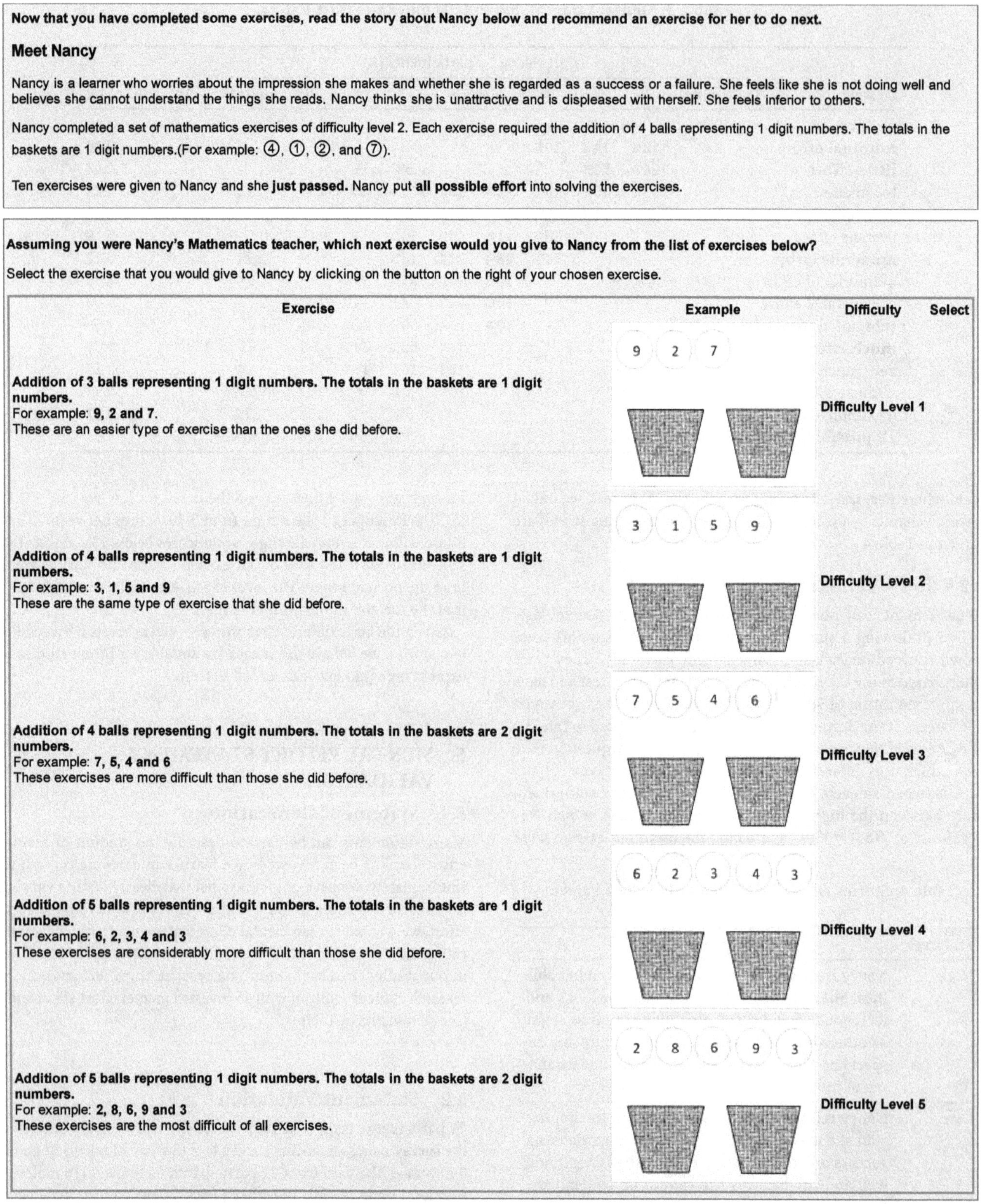

Now that you have completed some exercises, read the story about Nancy below and recommend an exercise for her to do next.

Meet Nancy

Nancy is a learner who worries about the impression she makes and whether she is regarded as a success or a failure. She feels like she is not doing well and believes she cannot understand the things she reads. Nancy thinks she is unattractive and is displeased with herself. She feels inferior to others.

Nancy completed a set of mathematics exercises of difficulty level 2. Each exercise required the addition of 4 balls representing 1 digit numbers. The totals in the baskets are 1 digit numbers.(For example: ④, ①, ②, and ⑦).

Ten exercises were given to Nancy and she **just passed.** Nancy put **all possible effort** into solving the exercises.

Assuming you were Nancy's Mathematics teacher, which next exercise would you give to Nancy from the list of exercises below?

Select the exercise that you would give to Nancy by clicking on the button on the right of your chosen exercise.

Exercise	Example	Difficulty	Select
Addition of 3 balls representing 1 digit numbers. The totals in the baskets are 1 digit numbers. For example: 9, 2 and 7. These are an easier type of exercise than the ones she did before.	9 2 7	Difficulty Level 1	
Addition of 4 balls representing 1 digit numbers. The totals in the baskets are 1 digit numbers. For example: 3, 1, 5 and 9 These are the same type of exercise that she did before.	3 1 5 9	Difficulty Level 2	
Addition of 4 balls representing 1 digit numbers. The totals in the baskets are 2 digit numbers. For example: 7, 5, 4 and 6 These exercises are more difficult than those she did before.	7 5 4 6	Difficulty Level 3	
Addition of 5 balls representing 1 digit numbers. The totals in the baskets are 1 digit numbers. For example: 6, 2, 3, 4 and 3 These exercises are considerably more difficult than those she did before.	6 2 3 4 3	Difficulty Level 4	
Addition of 5 balls representing 1 digit numbers. The totals in the baskets are 2 digit numbers. For example: 2, 8, 6, 9 and 3 These exercises are the most difficult of all exercises.	2 8 6 9 3	Difficulty Level 5	

Figure 2: Screenshot of the exercise selection stage of the study

Participants read the mental effort statements and mapped them to numbers from 1 to 10 with 1 representing no effort and 10 representing maximum effort. The order of the mental effort statements was randomized for each participant.

Table 3 shows the percentage of participants who mapped a statement to a particular number. Some statements (e.g. 'token effort') showed little agreement between participants, whilst others showed better agreement. We decided to use five statements (shown in bold) for the main study.

6 IMPACT OF PERSONALITY AND MENTAL EFFORT ON EXERCISE SELECTION

Using the set of exercises of validated difficulty levels and validated mental effort statements, we investigate what impact personality and mental effort have in selecting the next exercise for learners. In this study, we focus on learners who have 'just passed' as performance.

6.1 Methodology

We used the User-as-Wizard [21] methodology for our study where the role of the system is played by participants in selecting exercises for a learner to do next. This study builds on previous research investigating the impact of personality and performance in selecting the next exercise for learners [25] by including invested mental effort and using validated difficulty levels of exercises. Following the methodology used by [8], we use crowd-sourcing first to inspire the algorithm, and will validate results with teachers later, followed by investigating the actual impact on learners.

6.2 Participants

201 participants successfully completed the study (107 males, 94 females, 0 undisclosed; 26 aged 18 - 25, 114 aged 26 - 40, 59 aged 41 - 65, 1 aged 65 and 1 undisclosed; 27 were students, 9 were teachers and 165 other). The study was administered through crowd-sourcing on Amazon's Mechanical Turk (MTurk) [22]. To be eligible to be part of the study, participants had to pass an English Cloze test. Participants were also required to successfully complete 5 short exercises (of difficulty levels 1 to 5) similar to the ones that they could select for the learners to do next. In addition, participants had to have a 90% acceptance rate meaning that 90% of the work they do on MTurk is accepted by other requesters as being of good quality.

6.3 Materials

Validated stories conveyed the self-esteem of a fictional learner 'Nancy' (see Table 4). A sentence was added to indicate her past performance, and one of the validated mental effort statements was shown from the bold items in Table 3. The statements were selected to ensure a good spread of difficulties, and had good inter-rater agreement. However, we decided to exclude "no effort" and "maximum effort" as they were used in the explanation of the scale that participants saw in the validation experiment, and we excluded "average effort" as this could be affected by the learning domain. In addition, a set of exercises with validated difficulty levels (see Table 1) were presented to participants to select the one Nancy should do next.

6.4 Procedure

Participants began by completing five short exercises just like the ones that the learners would do so they gained an understanding of the different difficulty levels. The order of exercises presented to participants was from easiest to most difficult. In a between-subjects design, participants were then asked to select the exercise Nancy should do next given her self-esteem, past performance and invested mental effort, as shown in Figure 2. Participants were informed that it was their opinion that counted and as such there were no right or wrong answers.

6.5 Variables

The dependent variable for this study is the difficulty level of the exercise selected for Nancy to do next. Participants could choose between 5 difficulty levels (level 1 to 5). They were told that Nancy had done 10 exercises of difficulty level 2 before, and that she *just passed*. So, participants could select exercises of the same difficulty (level 2), or an easier difficulty (level 1) or of varying degrees of more difficulty (levels 3-5).

The independent variables used for this study are: learner self-esteem, high and low and their invested mental effort in solving the exercises (*minimal effort, little effort, moderate effort, much effort and all possible effort*).

6.6 Hypotheses

- **H1**: Overall, participants will select a more challenging exercise for High SE learners than for Low SE learners.
- **H2**: Overall, participants will select a more challenging exercise for learners with a lower mental effort than high mental effort
- **H3**: Participants will select a different difficulty level for the exercise depending on the combination of SE level and mental effort.

6.7 Results

Table 5 shows the results for each condition. We ran a 2-way ANOVA of the independent variables *self-esteem × effort* for *difficulty*. This was significant for both *effort* ($F(4, 200) = 4.12, p < 0.004$) and *self-esteem* ($F(1, 200) = 14.04, p < 0.001$), however, the interaction of *effort × self-esteem* was not significant.

Figure 3 shows the results overall for effort and self esteem. Looking at effort alone, it can be seen that a difficulty of 3 (*slightly harder than before*) is the most popular choice for all levels of effort. However, when effort is minimal or little, a higher percentage of participants recommend a higher level of difficulty than this (the majority choose a difficulty of 4 or 5). H2 is thus confirmed, participants did choose an exercise of higher difficulty for learners who required little effort to complete the exercise.

For self-esteem, Figure 3 shows that although an exercise of slightly harder difficulty (level 3) remains the most popular choice in both conditions, for low self-esteem, participants pick an exercise of lower or the same difficulty more often than in the high condition. Thus there is support for hypothesis H1.

With respect to hypothesis H3, we have evidence that both Self-Esteem and mental effort mattered to participants when selecting exercises overall, but as there is no interaction effect, we do not

Table 5: Exercise Selection Study Results

| | Selected difficulty level (% of participants) | | | | | | | | | |
| | 1 | | 2 | | 3 | | 4 | | 5 | |
Effort	High SE	Low SE	High SE	Low SE	High SE	Low SE	High SE	Low SE	High SE	Low SE
minimal effort	0	5	0	25	40	35	25	25	35	10
little effort	5	10	5	25	43	30	29	15	19	20
moderate effort	5	10	10	30	60	50	20	10	5	0
much effort	0	20	10	15	80	40	10	15	0	10
all possible effort	0	20	15	20	60	50	20	5	5	5

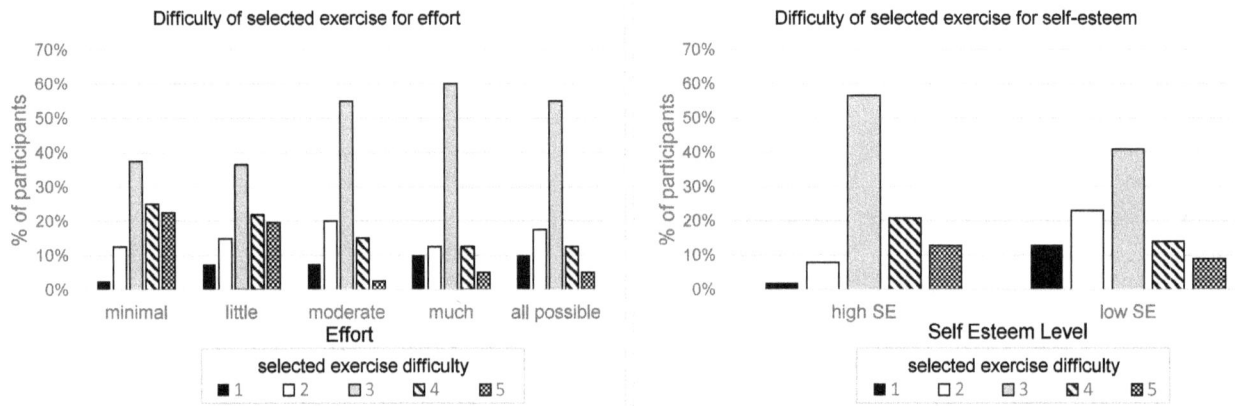

Figure 3: Chosen exercise difficulty for effort (left) and self-esteem (right).

have strong enough evidence to factor in both mental effort and self-esteem at the same time, meaning this is not well supported.

7 CONCLUSION AND FUTURE WORK

From this study we conclude that learner personality and mental effort are important considerations for exercise selection. We now have a set of exercises with validated difficulty levels, validated mental effort levels and validated personality trait stories. From our current findings, we now have an indication of how exercises can be selected to achieve better learning outcomes. We know that overall, according to our participants, more challenging exercises should be selected for those learners who completed the task with less effort. A further study is needed to investigate the actual effect on learners of doing so.

We also know that if learner self-esteem is low, participants selected an exercise of the same or easier difficulty more often. However, as there was no clear interaction effects discovered, further investigations are required to determine how best to proceed with a strategy for adaptation to both characteristics at the same time. A future study could investigate whether learners with low self-esteem who have 'just passed' really would prefer easier exercises than those with high self-esteem in a controlled setting.

In this paper, we only considered one learner performance (*just passed*). Obviously, learner performance will affect the difficulty of subsequent exercise selection, however it may be that mental effort and personality will trigger different adaptation strategies

for exercise selection at these performance levels. Future studies based on the methodology outlined in this paper will investigate this. Furthermore, we can investigate the effect of other personality traits using existing *Personality trait stories* to allow an ITS to adapt to other facets of learner personality. Based on previous research [7], we expect learner conscientiousness and neuroticism from the five-factor model to be relevant traits.

Due to the need for large amounts of data, this paper utilized crowd-sourcing to recruit participants. Any resulting adaptations require the input of experts in the learning domain for further refinement and to verify that the adaptations are appropriate. We can then incorporate these findings into an algorithm for an intelligent tutoring system to make use of these adaptations.

REFERENCES
[1] Gino Camp, Fred Paas, Remy Rikers, and Jeroen van Merrienboer. 2001. Dynamic problem selection in air traffic control training: A comparison between performance, mental effort and mental efficiency. *Comput Hum Behav* 17, 5 (2001), 575–595.
[2] Madeline M Carrig, Gregory G Kolden, and Timothy J Strauman. 2009. Using functional magnetic resonance imaging in psychotherapy research: A brief introduction to concepts, methods, and task selection. *Psychotherapy Research* 19, 4-5 (2009), 409–417.
[3] Gemma Corbalan, Liesbeth Kester, and Jeroen JG Van Merriënboer. 2006. Towards a personalized task selection model with shared instructional control. *Instructional Science* 34, 5 (2006), 399–422.
[4] Gemma Corbalan, Liesbeth Kester, and Jeroen JG van Merriënboer. 2008. Selecting learning tasks: Effects of adaptation and shared control on learning efficiency and task involvement. *CEP* 33, 4 (2008), 733–756.

[5] Lyn Corno and Mary Rohrkemper. 1985. The intrinsic motivation to learn in classrooms. *Research on motivation in education* 2 (1985), 53–90.

[6] Matt Dennis, Judith Masthoff, and Chris Mellish. 2012. The quest for validated personality trait stories. In *Proceedings of IUI 2012*. ACM, ACM, 273–276.

[7] Matt Dennis, Judith Masthoff, and Chris Mellish. 2015. Adapting Progress Feedback and Emotional Support to Learner Personality. *IJAIED* (2015), 1–55.

[8] Matt Dennis, Judith Masthoff, and Chris Mellish. 2016. Adapting progress feedback and emotional support to learner personality. *International Journal of Artificial Intelligence in Education* 26, 3 (2016), 877–931.

[9] Paula J Durlach and Jessica M Ray. 2011. *Designing adaptive instructional environments: Insights from empirical evidence*. Technical Report. DTIC Document.

[10] Paula J Durlach and Randall D Spain. 2014. *Framework for Instructional Technology: Methods of Implementing Adaptive Training and Education*. Technical Report. DTIC Document.

[11] Eduardo Backhoff Escudero, Norma Larrazolo Reyna, and Martín Rosas Morales. 2000. The level of difficulty and discrimination power of the Basic Knowledge and Skills Examination (EXHCOBA). *Revista Electrónica de Investigación Educativa* 2, 1 (2000), 2.

[12] LR Goldberg. 1980. Some ruminations about the structure of individual differences: Developing a common lexicon for the major characteristics of human personality. In *Invited paper, Convention of the Western Psychological Association, Honolulu, Hawaii*.

[13] Foteini Grivokostopoulou, Isidoros Perikos, and Ioannis Hatzilygeroudis. 2015. Estimating the Difficulty of Exercises on Search Algorithms Using a Neuro-fuzzy Approach. In *Tools with Artificial Intelligence (ICTAI), 2015 IEEE 27th International Conference on*. IEEE, 866–872.

[14] Foteini Grivokostopoulou, Isidoros Perikos, and Ioannis Hatzilygeroudis. 2017. Difficulty Estimation of Exercises on Tree-Based Search Algorithms Using Neuro-Fuzzy and Neuro-Symbolic Approaches. In *Advances in Combining Intelligent Methods*. Springer, 75–91.

[15] Todd F Heatherton and Janet Polivy. 1991. Development and validation of a scale for measuring state self-esteem. *Journal of Personality and Social psychology* 60, 6 (1991), 895.

[16] Anita Woolfolk Hoy. 2013. A reflection on the place of emotion in teaching and teacher education. *Advances in Research on Teaching* 18 (2013), 255–270.

[17] Timothy A Judge, Amir Erez, Joyce E Bono, and Carl J Thoresen. 2002. Are measures of self-esteem, neuroticism, locus of control, and generalized self-efficacy indicators of a common core construct? *Journal of personality and social psychology* 83, 3 (2002), 693.

[18] Danny Kostons, Tamara van Gog, and Fred Paas. 2010. Self-assessment and task selection in learner-controlled instruction: Differences between effective and ineffective learners. *Computers & Education* 54, 4 (2010), 932–940.

[19] Chenghua Lin, Dong Liu, Wei Pang, and Zhe Wang. 2015. Sherlock: A Semi-automatic Framework for Quiz Generation Using a Hybrid Semantic Similarity Measure. *Cognitive computation* 7, 6 (2015), 667–679.

[20] Abraham H Maslow. 1973. *On dominance, self-esteem, and self-actualization*. Maurice Bassett.

[21] Judith Masthoff. 2006. The user as wizard: A method for early involvement in the design and evaluation of adaptive systems. In *5th Workshop on User-centred Design and Adaptive Systems*. 460–469.

[22] MT. 2012. Amazon Mechanical Turk. http://www.mturk.com. (2012).

[23] Juliet Okpo. 2016. Adaptive exercise selection for an intelligent tutoring system. In *Proceedings of the 2016 Conference on User Modeling Adaptation and Personalization*. ACM, 313–316.

[24] Juliet Okpo, Matt Dennis, Judith Masthoff, Kirsten A Smith, and Nigel Beacham. 2016. Exploring Requirements for an Adaptive Exercise Selection System. In *Proceedings of the 6th Workshop on Personalization Approaches in Learning Environments (PALE 2016)*. 24th conference on User Modeling, Adaptation, and Personalization (UMAP 2016), CEUR workshop proceedings, this volume.

[25] Juliet Okpo, Matt Dennis, Kirsten Smith, Judith Masthoff, and Nigel Beacham. 2016. Adapting exercise selection to learner self-esteem and performance. In *Intelligent Tutoring Systems*. Springer, 517–518.

[26] Paul R Pintrich and Elisabeth V De Groot. 1990. Motivational and self-regulated learning components of classroom academic performance. *Journal of educational psychology* 82, 1 (1990), 33.

[27] Morris Rosenberg. 1986. *Conceiving the self*. RE Krieger.

[28] Morris Rosenberg, Carmi Schooler, Carrie Schoenbach, and Florence Rosenberg. 1995. Global self-esteem and specific self-esteem: Different concepts, different outcomes. *ASR* (1995), 141–156.

[29] Nabiollah Sadeghi, Zalina Mohd Kasim, Bee Hoon Tan, and Faiz Sathi Abdullah. 2012. Learning styles, personality types and reading comprehension performance. *English Language Teaching* 5, 4 (2012), 116.

[30] Ron JCM Salden, Fred Paas, and Jeroen JG Van Merriënboer. 2006. Personalised adaptive task selection in air traffic control: Effects on training efficiency and transfer. *Learning and Instruction* 16, 4 (2006), 350–362.

[31] Ana C Stephens, Eric J Knuth, Maria L Blanton, Isil Isler, Angela Murphy Gardiner, and Tim Marum. 2013. Equation structure and the meaning of the equal sign: The impact of task selection in eliciting elementary studentsfi understandings. *JMB 32*, 2 (2013), 173–182.

[32] Tamara Van Gog, K Anders Ericsson, Remy MJP Rikers, and Fred Paas. 2005. Instructional design for advanced learners: Establishing connections between the theoretical frameworks of cognitive load and deliberate practice. *Educational Technology Research and Development* 53, 3 (2005), 73–81.

[33] Tamara Van Gog, Liesbeth Kester, and Fred Paas. 2011. Effects of concurrent monitoring on cognitive load and performance as a function of task complexity. *Applied Cognitive Psychology* 25, 4 (2011), 584–587.

[34] M Vandad Sharifi, Ahmad Hajebi, and Reza Radgoodarzi. 2015. Twelve-month prevalence and correlates of psychiatric disorders in Iran: The Iranian Mental Health Survey, 2011. *Archives of Iranian medicine* 18, 2 (2015), 76.

[35] Gang Wu and Irene Cheng. 2007. An interactive 3D environment for computer based education. In *Multimedia and Expo, 2007 IEEE International Conference on*. IEEE, 1834–1837.

Imputing KCs with Representations of Problem Content and Context

Zachary A. Pardos
UC Berkeley
Berkeley, CA
USA
zp@berkeley.edu

Anant Dadu
IIT (BHU) Varanasi
Varanasi, UP
India
anant.dadu.cse14@iitbhu.ac.in

ABSTRACT

Cognitive task analysis is a laborious process made more onerous in educational platforms where many problems are user created and mostly left without identified knowledge components. Past approaches to this issue of untagged problems have centered around text mining to impute knowledge components (KC). In this work, we advance KC imputation research by modeling both the content (text) of a problem as well as the context (problems around it) using a novel application of skip-gram based representation learning applied to tens of thousands of student response sequences from the ASSISTments 2012 public dataset. We find that there is as much information in the contextual representation as the content representation, with the combination of sources of information leading to a 90% accuracy in predicting the missing skill from a KC model of 198. This work underscores the value of considering problems in context for the KC prediction task and has broad implications for its use with other modeling objectives such as KC model improvement.

KEYWORDS

Representation learning; skip-gram; KC prediction; skill tagging; bag-of-words; ASSISTments

1 INTRODUCTION

Crowdsourcing educational content [1] for tutoring systems and open educational resource sites allow teachers to tailor pedagogy to their students and become an integral part of the instructional design of material that shapes the platform. Crowdsourced content has, however, lacked the same meta-information, often in the form of "tags," that platform curated content has included. These tags help organize the contributed content to be searched for by other users. On the ASSISTments tutoring platform, these tags are comprised of 198 knowledge components (KC), or skill names, enumerated by the platform designers, and are integral in

UMAP '17, July 09-12, 2017, Bratislava, Slovakia
© 2017 Association for Computing Machinery.
ACM ISBN 978-1-4503-4635-1/17/07...$15.00
http://dx.doi.org/10.1145/3079628.3079689

generating reports for teachers, constructing mastery learning problem sets, and organizing content. In ASSISTments, where most content is now user contributed, continued surfacing of methods for imputing these tags is relevant to better integration of this content and propagation to other teachers.

The most straightforward approach to using existing tagged content to predict the tags of untagged content is to assume that regularities in the text of the content might be indicative of their appropriate tags. This intuition is most commonly applied in the form of learning a function between the word distribution of a document and its label. In this paper, we investigate problem context as a new source of information for skill tag prediction. The intuition is that the problem IDs encountered by the students to the left and right of the problem in question, could serve as an abstract signature of that problem's skill, which may generalize to other problems with a similar context. We explore the use of the skip-gram model for representing problems and their relationships to one another in Euclidian space learned from sequences of problem IDs, as encountered by students in ASSISTments.

2 BACKGROUND

Our task can be seen as beginning with a problem by skill association matrix, called a Q-matrix [4], where all the skill associations for a random subset of questions have been hidden. Prior work has used the text of problems to learn their skill labels using bag-of-words with an SVM [2], predicting the skill of the problem (out of 106) with 62% accuracy. Other work by [3] utilized the same technique and predicted the skill (out of 39) with a reported Kapa between .65 and .70. Other paradigms, like non-negative matrix factorization, have been applied towards learning the entire Q-matrix from scratch in testing scenarios where knowledge is not changing [5]. When multiple Q-matrix definitions are present, algorithms have been applied to permute them together to maximize performance prediction and thereby produce a hybrid single Q-matrix [6]. A recurrent neural network was used to learn pre-requisite relationships between skills in ASSISTments [7] by learn representations at the skill level and then querying the model to determine how responses to candidate pre-requisite skills relatively affected candidate post-requisite skill response predictions. This was a skill by skill matrix induction (or attribute to attribute as referred to in Psychometrics). All the methods mentioned apply various models to extract information from student responses. The method we introduce in this paper, explores the utility of context. A Bayesian Network model has recently been described [8] as capturing application context; however, the use of the word context in that work described the combining of skills with additional, more granular skills or difficulties associated with the problem and arranging these levels of latent nodes in a hierarchy of knowledge components [8]. Our use of the word context captures a more behavioral source of information.

We use a skip-gram model to form a continuous vector representation of each problem. The skip-gram model, and its Continuous Bag-of-Words (CBOW) counterparts, are the state of the art techniques used in computational linguistics, and more commonly known as word2vec [9], an optimized software package released by Google containing both models. These models are in many ways a simpler version of the earlier Neural Net Language Model (NNLM) [10] with the non-linear activations removed and a fixed context window instead of the Markov state of the NNLM. The major advantage of the proposed techniques is that it is very efficient in terms of computational complexity and since the representation is created from linear transformations, it is valid to manipulate with simple vector arithmetic. Skip-gram models are finding expanded use inside and outside of NLP, with applications to machine translation [11], computer vision [12], dependency parsing [13] [14], sentiment analysis [14], biological gene sequencing [15], exploring college course similarities [16], and recommendation systems [17]. Since, at their core, skip-grams were intended to represent words based on the many contexts they appear in and then reason about their relationships given their learned continuous embedding [18] [19]; they were an appropriate choice for our task of representing problems based on their problem contexts and reasoning about their relationships to one another and the skills they represent.

3 PLATFORM & DATA

ASSISTments is an online web platform used primarily for middle and high-school science and math problem solving. The knowledge component model used in the dataset we chose contained 198 unique skills covering mostly middle and high-school math. While it has been 10 years since the original design of its skill model [20], which contained 106 skills [20] (used in [2] [3]), the granularity of its present KC model is still set to match the granularity of the official platform curated questions it asks. Intelligent Tutoring Systems (ITS) like the Cognitive Tutor for Algebra prompts students to answer questions at the step level, which often corresponds to a highly granular knowledge component defined through the time intensive human process of initial cognitive task analysis followed by data-driven refinement. Due to this granular approach, knowledge component models in the Cognitive Tutor for Algebra exceed 2,000 unique knowledge

components. ASSISTments has taken a more pragmatic approach to pedagogical design, prompting students with broader level questions than Cognitive Tutors and then breaking those questions down into sub-parts in the form of scaffolding if answered incorrectly or if help is pre-emptively sought. The reasoning for this approach, in part, is to allow teachers to become a primary source of content contribution through a content authoring system which does not require the same level of familiarity with cognitive theory and programming needed for Cognitive Tutors. It is worthy to note that while CTAT (Cognitive Tutor Authoring Tools) have much improved in their usability, they are still not at the ease-of-use level as ASSISTments' authoring tools and teachers do not currently have any means, to our knowledge, of adding and sharing their content in Cognitive Tutors. Of the nearly 80,000 top level problems in ASSISTments (non-scaffolding), 71% have no skill associated with them. ASSISTments does not track students' cognitive mastery per skill, as the Cognitive Tutors do [21], so this skill tagging is not as critical to learning in ASSISTments; however, the lack of a skill tag makes the item more difficult to find among other teachers and also prevents responses to that item from being included in a skill level report available to teachers. The missing skill information for these items also adds considerable noise to the many knowledge tracing based approaches used by researchers in dozens of papers studying these data, since these missing KC items and the learning which occurred during interactions with them are often filtered out.

We conducted our analyses on the ASSISTments 2012-2013 school year dataset[1] and considered only the following five attributes:

- *user id*: student unique anonymous identifier
- *problem id*: unique ID of original problems/questions
- *skill name*: The single[2] skill associated with the problem
- *correctness on first attempt*: The correctness of response given by the student to the problem on his or her first attempt and without first asking for help.
- *base sequence id*: The problem set ID containing the problem associated with the student's response. While problems can belong to multiple problem sets, a particular response belongs to a problem answered within the context of a problem set. Problem sets are the level at which teachers assign work to students.

Table 1: ASSISTments 2012-2013 Dataset description before and after filtering out problems with no KC.

	original	after removing items with missing KCs
Responses	6,123,270	2,630,080
Problems	179,999	50,988
Users	46,674	28,834
Problem sets (base sequence IDs)	110,648	102,104

[1] https://sites.google.com/site/assistmentsdata/home/2012-13-school-data-with-affect
[2] ASSISTments' internal KC model allows for several skills to be tagged to the same problem; however, in this dataset, each problem is tagged to at most one skill. In personal communication with the ASSISTments Platform we learned that while the

majority of problems are internally tagged with only a single skill, the additional tags of the few multi-tagged problems have been removed in this dataset, leaving only the first skill tag in terms of its arbitrary alpha-numeric order.

Table 1 summarizes the dataset. The average number of unique problems and skills attempted by each user was 86.93 and 12.53, respectively[3]. We also incorporated the problem text of each of the problems in our pre-processed dataset to predict the KC tags associated with them to replicate [2] on this dataset. There were two versions of the problem text used, one with HTML markup stripped out and one with the markup left inside. We included the HTML version in analysis because the tags include image meta information which might be relevant to classification. Out of the 50,348 problems in our pre-processed dataset, 50,339 had problem text information made available by ASSISTments.

Our dataset consists of student responses to problems, however, the problems they engage with is restricted to those contained within problem sets assigned by their teacher. The interface allows them to jump around between existing assignments but it is more common for students to complete a problem set before moving on to the next.

4 METHODOLOGY

Our primary methodology treats the sequence of problem IDs encountered by each student as training instances for our representation learning models. All problem IDs in the dataset are used in the unsupervised representation learning phase. We cross-validate the optimization of the skip-gram parameters and the prediction of the skill labels by problem and base sequence ID by associating learned vector representations with skills using the training set of problems and attempting to predict the skill of the problem representations in the test set. We explore manipulations of the representation for classification using various levels of machine supervision.

4.1 Representation learning with skip-grams

A skip-gram is a simple three-layer neural network with one input layer, one hidden layer, and one output layer (Figure 1). The input is a one-hot representation of the problem ID (dummy variablized) with a one-hot output for each of the specified number of problems in context. The number of problems in context is two times the window size, which is a hyper parameter of the model. The objective of the model is to predict the problems in context given the input problem. Since multiple problems are being predicted, the loss function (categorical cross-entropy) is calculated for each problem in context. The second major hyper parameter is the size of the hidden layer, which ultimately is equivalent to the number of dimensions of the resultant continuous representation since it is the weights associated with the edges stemming from the one-hot position of the problem to all the nodes in the hidden layer that serve as the vector after training. In a skip-gram, the output vector of the hidden layer is: $\mathbf{h} = \mathbf{W}^T \mathbf{x}$

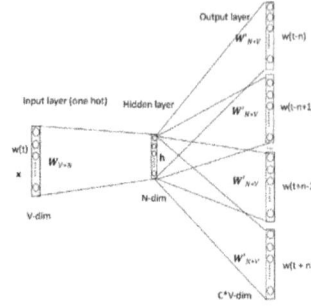

Figure 1. Skip-gram architecture

Where $\mathbf{x}$ is the one-hot input of a problem and $\mathbf{W}$ is the weight matrix of the connections from the one-hot to each of the nodes in the hidden layer. There is an output for each problem ID, the larger the value, the greater the chances of that problem being in context.

Each problem ID, i, is defined by: $z_i = \mathbf{W}_i'^T \mathbf{h}$

The final output is a softmax, which normalizes the outputs into probabilities: $\mathbf{y}^i = \dfrac{e^{z^i}}{\sum_{j \in Problems} e^{z^j}}$

With a loss being the sum of the categorical cross-entropy for every problem in the context window:

$$C = - \sum_{\substack{j \in Problems \\ in\ context}} \log \mathbf{y}^j$$

To train the model, we passed one sequence of problem IDs per student as the input. Each row has all the problems attempted by the student in chronological order. We used two different ways of tokenizing problems. First, we used problem IDs as inputs irrespective of the student's first attempt correctness on them. In the second version, we concatenate the correctness of the response with the problem ID which created two representations for each problem ID. This allowed us to explore if problem and correctness context was important for skill classification.

4.1.1 Distance based classification

After learning the vector representations of problems using the skip-gram model, we created a centroid (skill vector) to represent each skill by averaging together the problem IDs in the training set associated with that skill. For predicting the test set problem IDs, we look to see which skill vector each test set problem vector is closest to. We compare using closeness measures of both Euclidian and cosine distance.

We explored several different metrics to optimize in order to determine the best set of skip-gram hyper parameters:

1. Variance: In this approach, we tried to minimize the average variance across each dimension for each KC.

$$costfunction(x) = argmin\left(\frac{1}{kc}\sum_{i=1}^{i=kc}\frac{1}{d}\sum_{k=1}^{k=d} var(x_{ik})\right)$$

$$var(x_d) = \frac{1}{pc}\sum_{j=1}^{j=pc}\left\|x_{dj} - m_d\right\|^2$$

here x is calculated for different parameters of the skip-gram, kc is the total number of unique knowledge components in the data, d is the total number of dimensions and x_{ik} is the vector of kth dimension of problem vectors belonging to i^{th} knowledge

---

[3] Our analyses were conducted on a randomly chosen 80% user ids. The remaining 20% will be used for future studies

component, pc is the total number of problems, m_d is the mean of all the problem vectors for d^{th} dimension and x_{dj} is the value of the dth dimension for j^{th} problem vector.

2. Cosine Distance: Minimizing the angular distance of problem vectors of the same skill:

$$costfunction(x) = argmin\left(\frac{1}{kc}\sum_{i=1}^{i=kc} median_{j \in pc_i}\{cosinedistance(x_j, m_i)\}\right)$$

$$cosinedistance(\bar{a}, \bar{b}) = 1 - \frac{\bar{a}.\bar{b}}{\|\bar{a}\|\|\bar{b}\|}$$

3. Euclidean Distance: Minimizes the Euclidian distance between problem vectors of the same skill:

$$costfunction(x) = argmin\left(\frac{1}{kc}\sum_{i=1}^{i=kc} median_{j \in pc_i}\{euclideandistance(x_j, m_i)\}\right)$$

$$euclideandistance(\bar{a}, \bar{b}) = \|\bar{a} - \bar{b}\|$$

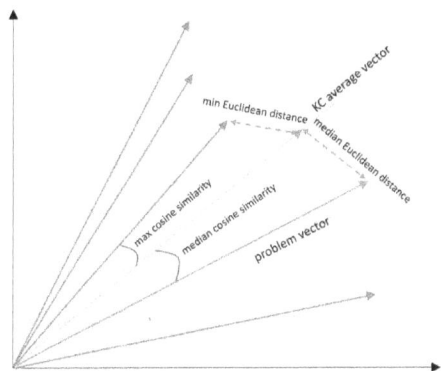

Figure 2: Geometric examples of three optimizations

Figure 2 shows the geometric meaning of our three distance based optimization approaches.

4.1.2 Supervised learning approaches

The distance based approaches were predicated on the assumption that problems of the same skill would cluster together naturally in the learned representation space. If they do not cluster together, the vector representation may nevertheless encode enough information to be classified in a supervised fashion. We use a neural network classifier for the supervised approach, which takes as input the vector representation and has the skill as the label. The neural net was a single hidden layer feed forward network with a 100 node hidden layer and used either a logistic or rectified linear unit function activation (relu). The relu function is defined by $f(x) = max(0, x)$. The logistic function is defined $f(x) = \frac{1}{1+e^{-x}}$. The loss function used is cross-entropy with a softmax layer as the output layer.

4.2 Bag-of-Words

In this approach, we applied bag-of-words to convert the problem text description to a vector the size of the vocabulary. The problem text was converted into sparse matrix such that each word behaves like a feature. The weights are given to each word for each sample using term frequency and inverse document

frequency. It is generally referred to as tf-idf transform. We treated word stemming (true/false) as a hyper parameter of the method. Stop word removal was not an effective filtration based on training set prototyping, so it was not employed in the experiments. Keeping or stripping the text of HTML tags was another hyper parameter. We tested two different classification algorithms for mapping from bag-of-words to label; neural networks and Naive Bayes. There were eight combinations of hyper parameters in total for the bag-of-words models.

4.3 Evaluation

In total, our experiments included two approaches (1) skip-grams and (2) bag-of-words. For skip-grams, hyper parameters (windows size & vector length) were searched using four different methods (a) vector variance minimization, (b) cosine angle minimization, (c) Euclidian distance minimization, and (d) validation set error minimization – this method created a 20% subset of the training set to serve as a validation set and chose the hyper parameters which optimized skill prediction accuracy on this validation set. Two prediction approaches were tried for predicting the skill of the problems in the test set: (1) neural network based classification of the vector to the skill and (2) distance based approach to vector/skill association. A 5-fold cross-validation (CV) was used throughput, with the entire evaluation process repeating within each CV phase. Two different CVs were tried, one where problem IDs were randomly placed in one of 5 CV bins, and the other where base sequence IDs (problem sets) and their problems were randomly placed into one of 5 CV bins. The reason for the base sequence ID CV was the suspicion that copies of the same problem (with different numbers filled in) may show up within a problem set labeled with a different problem ID. This is frequently done in ASSISTments "Skill Builder" problem sets which allow students to keep practicing problems until they answer N correct in a row (often 3 or 5 as set by the teacher). In this case, the bag-of-words classification would be made too easy since some problems with the exact same text would appear in the train and test. This also makes skip-gram classification easier since the prediction could simply use the skill of the problems immediately surrounding the problem. The base sequence ID CV split is meant as a more rigorous test of the generalization ability of the experiments. The evaluation procedure flow diagram can be seen in the Appendix Figure at the end of the paper.

5 EXPERIMENTS AND RESULTS

The results in this section report the cross-validated accuracy with which the algorithms' top prediction of skill matches the skill associated with the problem IDs in the test folds of the CV. The exact same CV assignments were used across all experiments. All bar charts in this section represent the average accuracy of experiments collapsed on the value represented by each bar. The companion table ebfore each chart gives the exact experimental parameters of the top 5 performing models.

5.1 Distance based approach

This approach evaluated how well the problem representations of the skip-gram would cluster together by skill and thereby be classifiable using skill vector averages. Accuracies ranged from ~15% to ~34% on average in predicting the correct skill of problems out of 198 possible skills. The base sequence ID CV proved to be much more difficult a task, as anticipated, than problem level CV. Using correctness (C) information in the tokenization helped marginally but the distance measure for choosing the nearest skill and the optimization types did not make a difference, as can be seen in Table 2 and Figure 3 (all problem based CV type).

Table 2: Top 5 experiments using distance

Rank	Optimization	Token	Acc
1	Cosine	Correctness	0.3395
2	Euclidian	Correctness	0.3348
3	Variance	Correctness	0.3335
4	Euclidian	no Correctness	0.3313
5	Cosine	no Correctness	0.3252

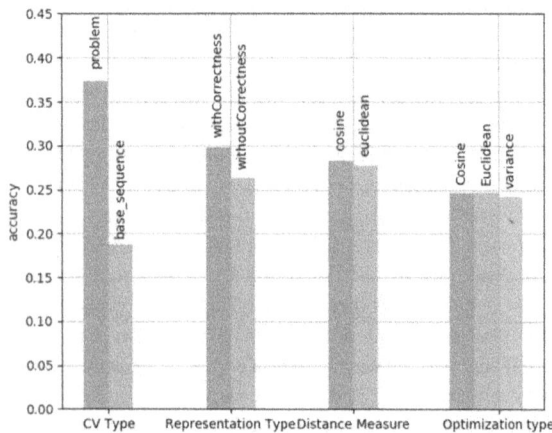

Figure 3: Avg. accuracies from distance experiments

5.2 Distance based (with validation set)

We tried another approach for hyper parameter searching to improve our model. In this approach, the training set was split into 20% sub-test set and 80% sub-train set and the entire prediction methodology was applied on the sub-test dataset as the test set. The parameters with minimum error were selected to build the actual model. Also note that within the validation optimization, we used the same type of prediction method that is set to be applied to the test set for the experiment. As can be seen in Table 3 and Figure 4, the accuracy increased by a significant margin to between ~25% to ~55% using a validation set to choose hyper parameters.

Table 3: Top 5 experiments using distance with validation

Rank	Distance	Token	CV	Acc
1	Euclidean	C	P	0.5597
2	Cosine	C	P	0.5490
3	Euclidean	noC	P	0.5000
4	Cosine	noC	P	0.4917
5	Euclidean	C	B	0.2941

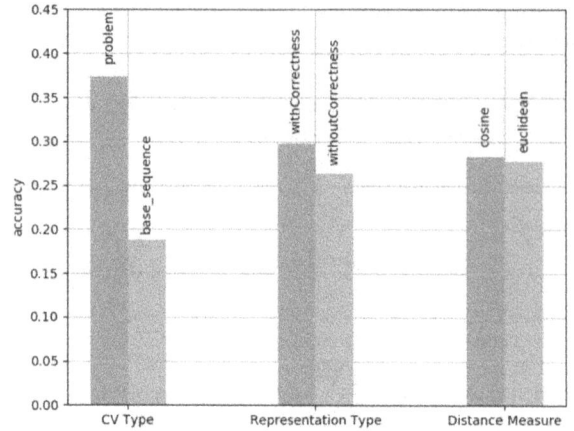

Figure 4: Avg. accuracies from distance experiments using a validation set to optimize hyper parameters

5.3 Supervised learning approach

In these experiments, instead of relying on the continuous vector representations of problems to cluster together by skill, the representations from the training sets are used as inputs to a neural network that learns to classify the skill of the vector representation. Experiments in this section significantly increase again, reaching a new height with individual experiment accuracies between ~50% and ~86%.

Table 4: Top 5 experiments using supervised classification

Rank	Optimization	Token	CV	Acc
1	Validation	noC	P	0.8643
2	Validation	C	P	0.8585
3	Variance	noC	P	0.8489
4	Variance	C	P	0.8418
5	Cosine	C	P	0.7086

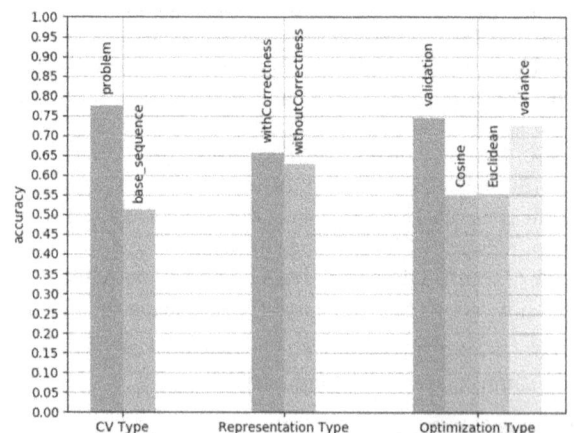

Figure 5: Avg. accuracies from supervised experiments

As seen in Table 4 and Figure 5, the best experiment used a validation set to optimize skip-gram hyper parameters, and in this experiment no correctness information (noC) was added to the problem token.

5.4   Summary and min-count parameter

The best supervised method (86%) beat the best distance based method (56%) by 30 percentage points. These were the accuracies of getting the skill correct on the first prediction but the accuracies improve somewhat if the correct skill can be within the top 5 or 10 predictions(recall @ 5 or 10), as shown in Figure 6. Also shown is the accuracy (y-axis) as the skip-gram parameter of min-count is varied (x-axis). Min-count specifies the minimum number of observations of a token for it to be included in the model. Skip-gram representations quickly lose their integrity when very low frequency words are included. It is therefore common practice to set a minimum count for each word. The tradeoff is that with a higher threshold, fewer words make it in. In the case of ASSISTments, a higher min count meant a higher number of problems wouldn't make it into the analysis. Figure 7 shows what percentage of the responses in the dataset are covered with various settings of min-count. When correctness is concatenated with the problem, min-count has an even more severe effect since a problem is only included in analysis if both the correct and incorrect response concatenated token appears with a frequency above min-count. We chose a min-count of 5 for all experiments in the previous results sections as it covers 99.02% of the data without using correctness and 86.63% with correctness, while keeping a reasonable minimum token frequency.

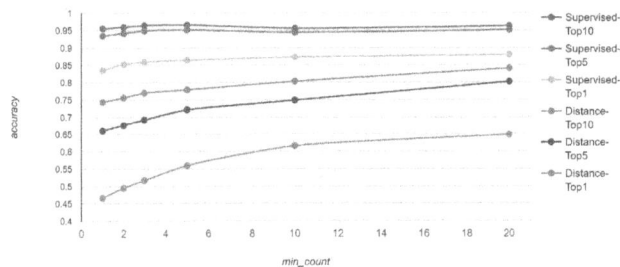

Figure 6: Accuracy variation by min-count for the best supervised learning and distance based models.

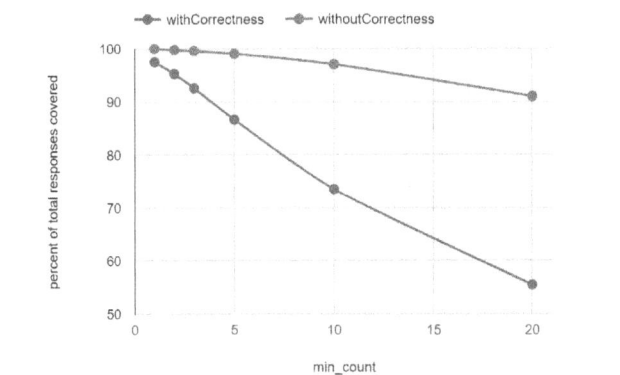

Figure 7: Percent of the dataset covered with various settings of min-count for with and without correctness

5.5   Bag-of-words results

The bag-of-words approach is the only method in this paper which uses the content of the problem (text) to make classifications of the problem's skill. Both a simple 100 node single

hidden layer feed-forward neural network (NN) and a Naïve Bayes model were evaluated. The models' accuracies ranged from ~50% to 88% as seen in Figure 8. Neural networks outperformed Naïve Bayes by 25 percent. As with the representation learning approach, problem level CV was easier to predict than base sequence level CV. While filtering out HTML was better on average in these experiments, the best performing models were the ones that kept this markup which often contained information about the problems' images.

Table 5: Top 5 experiments for bag-of-words. The CV type for all experiments was 'problem' level

Rank	Alg.	Stemming	Parsing	Acc
1	NN	No ST	HTML	0.8818
2	NN	ST	HTML	0.8810
3	NN	No ST	No HTML	0.8646
4	NN	ST	No HTML	0.8629
5	NB	No ST	No HTML	0.7502

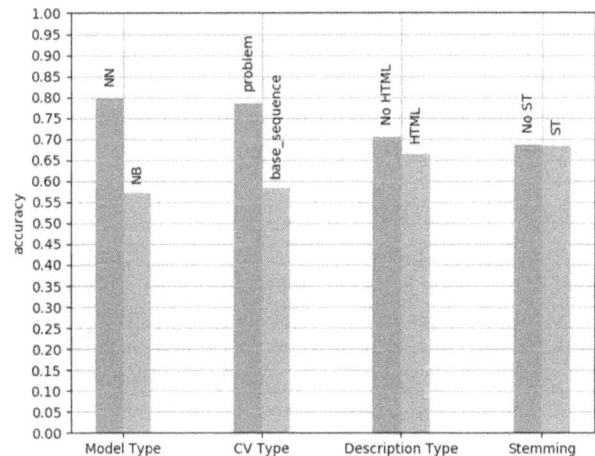

Figure 8: Avg. accuracies from bag-of-words experiments

5.6   Ensemble of content and context models

To improve overall prediction, we combined the two methods by taking the representation vectors from the best skip-gram model and concatenated them with the best bag-of-words vectors for each problem. We chose the best experiment parameters for both the CV types for all the different model approaches. We then trained the supervised neural net on the concatenation of the vectors to learn their skills from the training set problems. We summarize our results for kc tagging in Table 6. All the best models shown use the validation optimization type. The token type is with Correctness concatenation except for the combined and supervised model with the problem CV, which performed best without correctness information. For the bag-of-words model, no word stemming was used and HTML was kept as part of the BOW. When the content and context were combined, the accuracy increased by 2.12% to 90% for the CV split type of problem and a similar amount for the base sequence CV. The plot in Figure 9 shows the accuracies (recall @ N) for the different models.

Table 6: Top models from the four categories, including the ensemble (combined) category for both base sequence (B) and problem (P) level CV

Rank	Model	Acc (B)	Acc (P)
1	Combined	0.7322	0.9030
2	BOW	0.7260	0.8818
3	Supervised	0.6547	0.8643
4	Distance	0.2941	0.5597

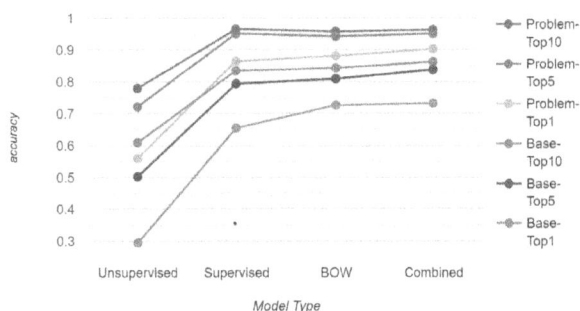

Figure 9: Avg. top N (recall @ N) accuracies for the best models + ensembles from all categories

6 CONCLUSION & DISCUSSION

In this paper, we explored the novel predictive value of problem sequence context for imputing the KC of a problem and compared it to the value of using the problem text to classify its KC. We found that the relevant information to the task in the problem context (86% accuracy) was on par with the information from the problem's text (88% accuracy) with the combination of the two producing results which were better still (90%). The skip-gram model clustered problems of the same skill moderately close to one another, allowing for 56% accuracy with a distance based approach; however, adding a non-linear classification step to classify the vector was needed to boost accuracy up to the bag-of-words level. The increase from 25% to 56% accuracy by using a validation set suggests that the skip-gram can overfit with respect to our task and that being mindful of its generalization on a hold-out is prudent. The best performing context models did *not* use correctness information, a relative surprise given the number of KC model refinement techniques that use correctness almost exclusively.

In the case of a newly added problem, the bag-of-words approach has the clear advantage of not needing any response or interaction data to be collected before making a classification. The skip-gram, on the other hand, would require at least 5 students to encounter the new problem and then encounter more problems afterwards to fill a windows size of N. This may occur fairly quickly, but is not guaranteed to. On the other hand, the contextual skip-gram approach generalizes to problems of any type, including problems with only video, images, or interactives that are not clearly amenable to the bag-of-words approach. What this work underscores is that sequence context has a role to play in KC modeling work, including the potential to learn how to improve KC models by analyzing learned problem representations.

Acknowledgements. We would like to thank Seth Adjei for his assistance with the ASSISTments problem text data and description of how the skill tags were created for the public 2012-2013 dataset.

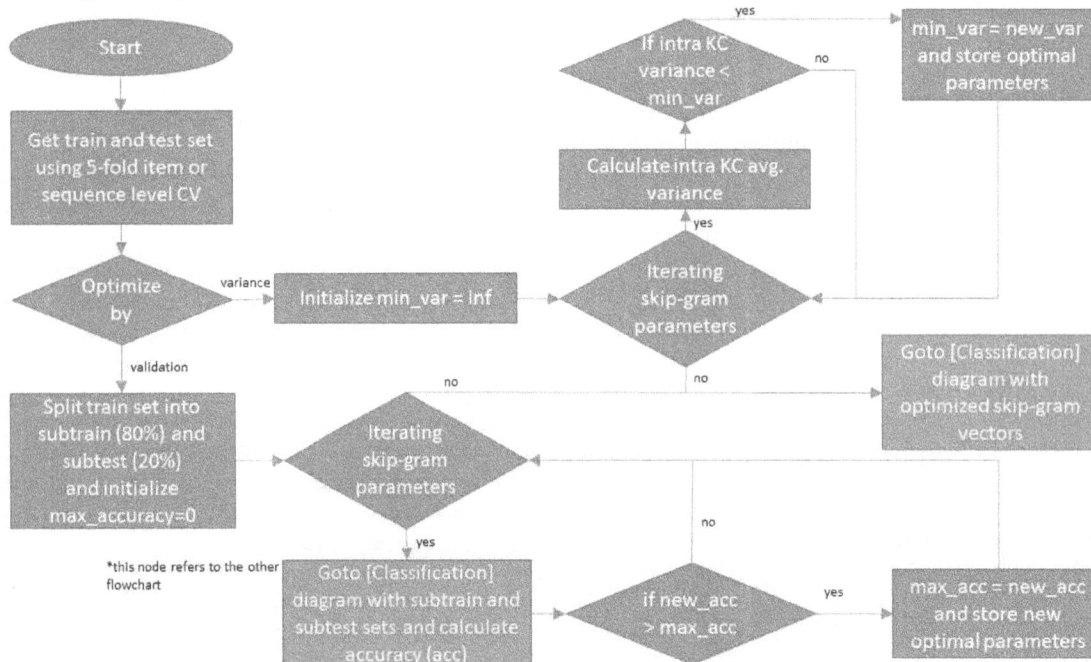

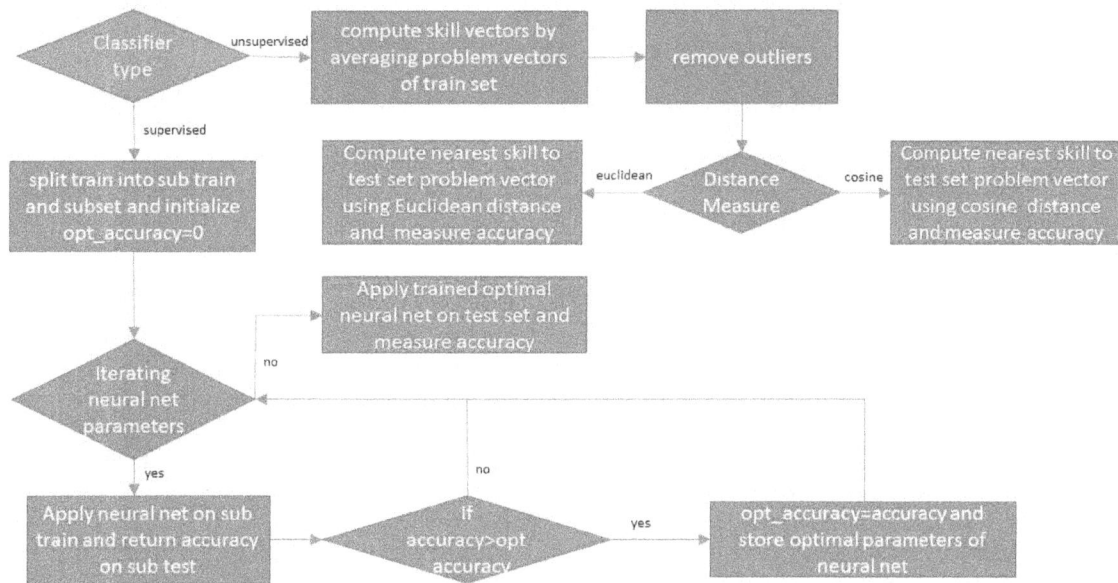

Appendix Figure. Flow diagrams documenting the evaluation process for all experiments in the study. The top diagram depicts the skip-gram hyper parameter search process while the bottom diagram depicts the process for KC classification.

7   REFERENCES

[1]   D. Porcello and S. Hsi, "Crowdsourcing and curating online education resources," *Science,* vol. 341, pp. 240--241, 2013.

[2]   M. Birenbaum, A. E. Kelly and K. K. Tatsuoka, "Diagnosing knowledge states in algebra using the rule-space model," *Journal for Research in Mathematics Education,* pp. 442--459, 1993.

[3]   M. KarlovčecMariheida, M. Córdova-Sánchez and Z. A. Pardos, "Knowledge Component Suggestion for Untagged Content in an Intelligent Tutoring System," in *International Conference on Intelligent Tutoring Systems,* pp. 195-200, 2012.

[4]   C. P. Rosé, P. Donmez, G. Gweon, A. Knight, B. Junker, W. W. Cohen, K. R. Koedinger and N. T. Heffernan, "Automatic and Semi-Automatic Skill Coding With a View Towards Supporting On-Line Assessment.," in *AIED,* pp. 571-578, 2005.

[5]   M. C. Desmarais, "Mapping question items to skills with non-negative matrix factorization," *ACM SIGKDD Explorations Newsletter,* vol. 13, no. 2, pp. 30-36, 2012.

[6]   H. Cen, K. Koedinger and B. Junker, "Learning factors analysis–a general method for cognitive model evaluation and improvement," in *International Conference on Intelligent Tutoring Systems,* pp. 164-175, 2006.

[7]   C. B. J. H. J. G. S. S. M. G. L. J. &. S.-D. J. Piech, "Deep knowledge tracing," in *Advances in Neural Information Processing Systems (pp. 505-513),* 2015.

[8]   Y. Huang, "Deeper knowledge tracing by modeling skill application context for better personalized learning," in *Proceedings of the 2016 Conference on User Modeling Adaptation and Personalization,* pp. 325-328, 2016.

[9]   T. Mikolov, K. Chen, G. Corrado and J. Dean, "Efficient estimation of word representations in vector space," *arXiv preprint arXiv:1301.3781,* 2013.

[10] Y. Bengio, R. Ducharme and P. Vincent, "A Neural probabilistic language model," *Journal of Machine Learning Research,* vol. 3, pp. 1137-1155, 2003.

[11] T. Mikolov, Q. V. Le and I. Sutskever, "Exploiting similarities among languages for machine translation," *arXiv preprint arXiv:1309.4168,* 2013.

[12] A. Frome, G. S. Corrado, J. Shlens, S. Bengio, J. Dean and T. Mikolov, "Devise: A deep visual-semantic embedding model," in *Advances in neural information processing systems,* pp. 2121-2129, 2013.

[13] M. Bansal, K. Gimpel and K. Livescu, "Tailoring Continuous Word Representations for Dependency Parsing," in *ACL (2),* 2014.

[14] D. Santos, C. Nogueira and M. Gatti, "Deep Convolutional Neural Networks for Sentiment Analysis of Short Texts," in *COLING,* 2014.

[15] E. Asgari and M. R. K. Mofrad, "Continuous Distributed Representation of Biological Sequences for Deep Proteomics and Genomics," *PloS One, 10(11), e0141287,* 2015.

[16] Z. A. Pardos and A. Nam, "The School of Information and its Relationship to Computer Science at UC Berkeley," in *Proceedings of the iConference,* Wuhan, China, 2017.

[17] O. Barkan and N. Koenigstein, "Item2vec: neural item embedding for collaborative filtering," in *Machine Learning for Signal Processing (MLSP), 2016 IEEE 26th International Workshop,* 2016.

[18] T. Mikolov, I. Sutskever, K. Chen, G. S. Corrado and J. Dean, "Distributed representations of words and phrases and their compositionality," in *Advances in neural information processing systems,* pp. 3111-3119, 2013.

[19] T. Mikolov, W.-t. Yih and G. Zweig, "Linguistic Regularities in Continuous Space Word Representations.," *HLT-NAACL,* vol. 13, pp. 746-751, 2013.

[20] L. Razzaq, N. Heffernan, M. Feng and Z. A. Pardos, *Journal of Technology, Instruction, Cognition, and Learning,* vol. 5, no. 3, pp. 289-304, 2007.

[21] A. T. Corbett and J. R. Anderson, "Knowledge tracing: Modeling the acquisition of procedural knowledge," *User Modeling and User-Adapted Interaction,* pp. 253-278, 1994.

Experimental Analysis of Mastery Learning Criteria

Radek Pelánek
Masaryk University
Brno, Czech Republic
pelanek@mail.muni.cz

Jiří Řihák
Masaryk University
Brno, Czech Republic
thran@mail.muni.cz

ABSTRACT

A common personalization approach in educational systems is mastery learning. A key step in this approach is a criterion that determines whether a learner has achieved mastery. We thoroughly analyze several mastery criteria for the basic case of a single well-specified knowledge component. For the analysis we use experiments with both simulated and real data. The results show that the choice of data sources used for mastery decision and setting of thresholds are more important than the choice of a learner modeling technique. We argue that a simple exponential moving average method is a suitable technique for mastery criterion and propose techniques for the choice of a mastery threshold.

KEYWORDS

mastery learning; learner modeling; Bayesian knowledge tracing; exponential moving average

1 INTRODUCTION

Mastery learning is an instructional strategy that requires learners to master a topic before moving to more advanced topics. A key aspect of mastery learning is a mastery criterion – a rule that determines whether a learner has achieved mastery. Mastery criteria have been studied already 40 years ago [6, 15, 24], but at that time typically only for static tests and small scale applications. Nowadays, mastery learning is used on large scale in dynamic, adaptive educational systems [11, 22].

A typical application of mastery criterion within a modern educational system is the following. A learner solves a problem or answers a question in the system. Data about learner performance are summarized by a model of learner knowledge or by some summary statistic. Mastery criterion takes this summary and produces a binary verdict: "mastered" or "not mastered". Based on this verdict, the system adapts its behavior: it either presents more problems from the same topic or moves the learner to another topic. The mastery criterion typically takes an external parameter (threshold), which specifies its strictness.

Mastery criterion gives a binary output. Most education systems use some kind of visualization (e.g., progress bars, skillometers, open learner models) that give learners a sense of progress towards the mastery goal. These visualizations are closely related to mastery criterion; in fact they can often be viewed as mastery criterion with different thresholds.

In this paper we thoroughly analyze the basic scenario for detecting mastery – we assume to have well-specified fine-grained knowledge components, i.e., sets of items related to same skill, such that these items can be treated as indistinguishable (potentially differentiated by simple parameters as difficulty or time intensity). We do not consider relation between knowledge components (e.g., prerequisites).

Simple mastery criteria are N correct in row [11, 13] or average success rate from last N attempts. More complex methods are based on models of learner knowledge and the use of mastery threshold policy. A model provides probabilistic prediction that the next answer will be correct and mastery is declared if the prediction is over a given threshold.

There exists an extensive research on learner modeling [5]. This research typically uses personalization through mastery learning as a motivation. However, evaluation of models is typically not done by evaluating the impact on mastery criterion, but instead using evaluation of predictive accuracy on historical data using metrics like RMSE or AUC [19]. Evaluation of mastery criterion is more difficult, particularly because mastery is a latent construct that cannot be directly measured.

Recent research studied impact of learner models on mastery decision. The ExpOps method [14, 23] gives an expected number of opportunities needed. This estimate is computed without using learner data, just based on assumptions of the used model, so the provided estimate may be misleading if the assumptions do not correspond to the behavior of real learners. Another proposal are effort and score metrics [10], which use historical data to estimate the effort needed to reach mastery and the performance after mastery.

Most of the research on mastery criterion was done in relation with the Bayesian knowledge tracing (BKT) model [4]; this model is also often used in practice with a standard mastery threshold 0.95. The role of this threshold was analyzed by Fancsali et al. [7, 8] by using simulated data (generated by the BKT model) to show the relation between the threshold and proportion of learners with premature mastery and over-practice. Simulated data were also used by Pardos and Yudelson [16] to study mean absolute deviation from the "true moment of learning". They focused on the analysis of a relation between predictive accuracy metrics and moment of learning detection. Baker et al. [2] also studied the moment of learning using the BKT model, but they focused on "hindsight analysis" with the use of the full sequence of learner attempts. The goal was to detect at which moment learning occurred using a rich set of features (e.g., response times, hint usage). Yudelson and Koedinger [26] used several large data sets to study differences in mastery decisions done by two variants of the BKT model and showed that the impact of replacing standard model with individualized can be substantial (as measured by time spent).

Recent research [12, 23] proposed general instructional policies applicable to any predictive model: predictive similarity [23] and predictive stability [12] policies. For evaluation authors used the above described techniques: ExpOps [23] and effort and score metrics [12]. These instructional policies focus on stopping not just in the case of mastery, but also for wheel-spinning learners who are unable to master a topic [3]. These works, however, pay little attention to the choice of thresholds.

In this work we analyze different mastery criteria using experiments with both simulated and real data. We compare mastery decisions by the standard BKT model and the basic N consecutive correct criterion. We analyze the decisions of the exponential moving average method under different situations. We also explore the impact of usage of response times in mastery criterion. We explore several techniques for the analysis, including comparison with ground truth (for simulated data) and novel effort-score graphs.

Based on results of these experiments we argue that it is sufficient to use simple methods for mastery criterion; specifically, the exponential moving average method is simple and sufficiently flexible to fit many applications. Rather than focusing on the choice and parameter fitting of learner models, it is more important to focus on tuning mastery thresholds and on the choice of data that are used to make the decision (e.g., whether to use of response times).

2 TECHNIQUES FOR DETECTING MASTERY

Our aim is not to introduce new mastery criteria, but to provide insight into behavior of already proposed criteria. In this section we describe previously used methods in a single setting.

2.1 Notation

We consider only the case of learning for a single knowledge component. We assume that for each learner we have a sequence of answers to items belonging to this knowledge component. Examples of knowledge components and items are "single digit multiplication" with items like "6 × 7" or "indefinite articles" with items like "a/an orange".

We use the following notation: k is the order of an attempt, θ_k is a skill estimate for the k-th attempt, $P_k \in [0, 1]$ is a predicted probability of correct answer at the k-th attempt, and c_k gives the observed correctness of the k-th attempt. As a basic case we consider only correctness of answer, i.e., dichotomous $c_k \in \{0, 1\}$. It is also possible to consider "partial credit" answers (e.g., based on the usage of hints or on the response time), i.e., real valued $c_k \in [0, 1]$. A typical mastery criterion is a "mastery threshold criterion" which uses a threshold T and declares mastery when the skill estimate (or alternatively the probability of correct answer) is larger than T.

Figure 1 provides specific illustration based on simulated data. Since these are simulated data, we know the ground truth (the black line; mastery achieved at the 8th attempt). The colored lines show estimates by several methods. Mastery decisions would depend

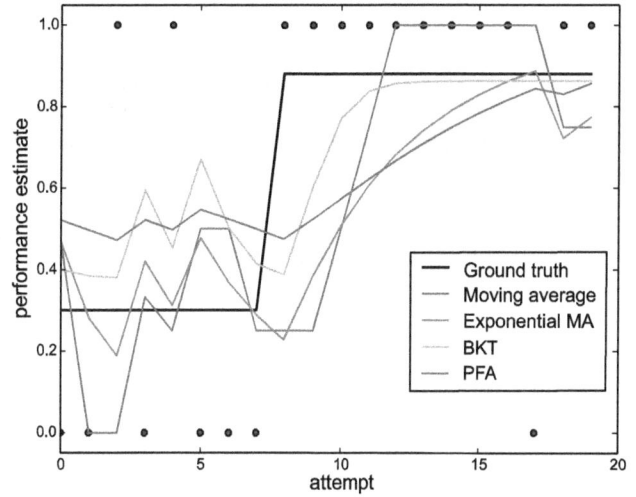

Figure 1: Illustrative comparison of performance estimation techniques for a sequence of answers of a a single simulated student (B2 from Table 1). The black line is the ground truth probability of correct answer and the dots are the simulated answers.

on particular thresholds, e.g., for a threshold $T = 0.9$ the moving average method would declare mastery at the 12th attempt.

2.2 Methods without Assumptions about Learning

Basic mastery criteria use only simple statistics about past answers without explicitly modeling the learning process.

2.2.1 Consecutive Correct. The simplest mastery criterion is "N consecutive correct answers" (NCC) (N-in-row, "streak"). With this method we simply count the number of consecutive correct answers and declare mastery once the count reaches the threshold N. As a progress bar we can simply use the current count. One of the disadvantages of this method is that any mistake (even if it is just a typo) means that the learner has to "start again from zero" and this can be demotivating. Nevertheless, this simple method is often practically used and can be successful [13].

2.2.2 Moving Average. Another simple statistics that can be used for mastery criterion is moving average. The basic average for a moving window of size n is $\theta_k = \frac{1}{n} \sum_{i=1}^{n} c_{k-i}$. In addition to n we now need a second parameter: a threshold T. Mastery is declared when $\theta_k \geq T$. One disadvantage of this approach is that it is not suitable for a progress bar. Consider a window of size $n = 6$ and a recent history of attempts 1, 1, 0, 1, 0 ($\theta_k = 0.6$). If the learner answers correctly, the recent history becomes 1, 0, 1, 0, 1 and the moving average remains the same ($\theta_{k+1} = 0.6$), i.e., the progress bar does not improve after the correct answers.

A natural extension, which circumvents this problem, is to use weighted average and give more weight to recent attempts, i.e., $\theta_k = \sum_{i=1}^{k} w_i \cdot c_{k-i} / \sum_{i=1}^{k} w_i$, where w_i is a decreasing function (this approach is equivalent to the "time decay" approach discussed in [18] and also closely related to [9]).

2.2.3 Exponential Moving Average. The moving average approach is often used specifically with exponential weights; this variant is called exponential moving average (EMA). This choice of weights often provides good performance [18] and it has the practical advantage of easy implementation, since it can be easily computed without the need to store and access the whole history of learners attempts.

If we choose the weights to be given by an exponential function $w_i = (1-\alpha)\alpha^{(i-1)}$, we can compute the exponential moving average θ_k after k steps as follows:

- initialization: $\theta_0 = 0$,
- update: $\theta_k = \alpha \cdot \theta_{k-1} + (1-\alpha) \cdot c_k$.

The mastery criterion remains $\theta_k \geq T$.

2.3 Methods based on Learner Models

A more sophisticated approach to detecting mastery is based on the usage of learner models. These models estimate learners knowledge and predict the probability that the next answer will be correct. These models are naturally used with the mastery threshold rule – mastery is declared once the estimate of knowledge is above a given threshold. Note that learner models can be used also with more complex instructional policies, e.g., predictive similarity [23] and predictive stability [12]. These policies deal not just with mastery, but also with wheel-spinning learners that are unable to master a topic. In this work, however, we consider only the basic mastery threshold policy.

2.3.1 Bayesian Knowledge Tracing. Bayesian knowledge tracing (BKT) [4] assumes a sudden change in knowledge. It is a hidden Markov model where skill is a binary latent variable (either learned or unlearned). The model has 4 parameters: P_i is the probability that the skill is initially learned, P_l is the probability of learning a skill in one step, P_s is the probability of incorrect answer when the skill is learned (slip), and P_g is the probability of correct answer when the skill is unlearned (guess). Note that BKT can also include forgetting; the described version corresponds to the variant of BKT that is most often used in research papers.

The estimated skill is updated using a Bayes rule based on the observed answers; the prediction of student response is then done based on the estimated skill. In the following we use θ_k and θ'_k to distinguish prior and posterior probability during the Bayesian update (θ_k is the prior probability that the skill is learned before the k-th attempt and θ'_k is the posterior probability that the skill is learned after we have taken the k-th answer into account):

$$\theta_1 = P_i$$
$$\theta'_k = \begin{cases} \frac{\theta_k(1-P_s)}{\theta_k(1-P_s)+(1-\theta_k)P_g} & \text{if } c_k = 1 \\ \frac{\theta_k P_s}{\theta_k P_s+(1-\theta_k)(1-P_g)} & \text{if } c_k = 0 \end{cases}$$
$$\theta_{k+1} = \theta'_k + (1-\theta'_k)P_l$$
$$P_k = P_g \cdot \theta_k + (1-P_s) \cdot (1-\theta_k)$$

Estimation of model parameters (the tuple P_i, P_l, P_s, P_g) can be done using several techniques (the expectation-maximization algorithm, stochastic gradient descent or exhaustive search).

2.3.2 Logistic Models. Another commonly used class of learner models are models based on logistic function, e.g., Rasch model, Performance factor analysis [17], or the Elo rating system [18]. These models utilize assumption of a continuous latent skill $\theta \in (-\infty, \infty)$ and for the relation between the skill and the probability of correct answer use the logistic function $\sigma(x) = \frac{1}{1+e^{-x}}$ (the function can be easily extended to capture guessing in multiple-choice questions).

A simple technique of this type is Performance factor analysis (PFA) [17]. The skill estimate is given by a linear combination of the initial skill and past successes and failures of a student: $P_k = \sigma(\beta + \gamma \cdot s_k + \delta \cdot f_k)$, where β is the initial skill, s_k and f_k are counts of previous successes and failures of the student during the first k attempts, γ and δ are parameters that determine the change of the skill associated with a correct and incorrect answer. Parameters β, γ, δ can be easily estimated using standard logistic regression.

3 ANALYSIS AND COMPARISON OF CRITERIA

Now we compare the described mastery criteria under several circumstances and discuss general methodological issues relevant to the evaluation of mastery criteria.

3.1 Data

For our analysis we use both real and simulated data, since each of them has advantages and disadvantages. Real data directly correspond to practical applications. However, the evaluation of mastery criteria is difficult, since mastery is a latent construct and we do not have objective data for its evaluation. With simulated data we know the ground truth and thus we can perform more thorough evaluation, but the results are restricted to simplified conditions and depend on the choice of simulation parameters.

3.1.1 Simulated Data. For generating simulated data we use both the BKT model and a logistic model. We have selected parametrizations of these models in such a way as to cover a wide range of different learning situations (e.g., high/low prior knowledge, slow/fast learning, high/low guessing). Table 1 provides description of simulation scenarios used in experiments. In all cases we generate 50 answers for each learner.

The BKT model is used in its basic form of the model. It can be used in a straightforward way to generate data and the ground truth mastery is clearly defined by the model. For the logistic model we consider a simple linear growth of the skill. More specifically, for the initial skill θ_0 we assume normally distributed skill $\theta_0 \sim N(\mu, \sigma^2)$ and we consider linear learning $\theta_k = \theta_0 + k \cdot \Delta$, where Δ is either a global parameter or individualized learning parameter. In the case of individualized Δ we assume a normal distribution of its values with a restriction $\Delta \geq 0$. As a ground truth mastery for this model we consider the moment when the simulated learner has 0.95 probability of answering correctly according to the ground truth parameters.

The source codes of all experiments with simulated data is available[1].

3.1.2 Real Data. We use real data from two educational systems. The first is a system for practice of Czech grammar and spelling

---

[1]https://github.com/adaptive-learning/umap2017-mastery

Table 1: Specification of models used for generating simulated data. "Bn" are BKT models, "Ln" are logistic models.

	Parameters			
B1	$P_i = 0.15$	$P_l = 0.35$	$P_s = 0.18$	$P_g = 0.25$
B2	$P_i = 0.25$	$P_l = 0.08$	$P_s = 0.12$	$P_g = 0.3$
B3	$P_i = 0.1$	$P_l = 0.2$	$P_s = 0.1$	$P_g = 0.15$
B4	$P_i = 0.1$	$P_l = 0.3$	$P_s = 0.4$	$P_g = 0.05$
B5	$P_i = 0.05$	$P_l = 0.1$	$P_s = 0.06$	$P_g = 0.2$
B6	$P_i = 0.1$	$P_l = 0.05$	$P_s = 0.1$	$P_g = 0.5$
L1	$\theta_0 \sim N(-1.0, 1.0)$	$\Delta = 0.4$		
L2	$\theta_0 \sim N(-0.4, 2.0)$	$\Delta = 0.1$		
L3	$\theta_0 \sim N(-2.0, 2.0)$	$\Delta = 0.15$		
L4	$\theta_0 \sim N(0.0, 0.7)$	$\Delta \sim N(0.15, 0.1)$		
L5	$\theta_0 \sim N(-2, 1.3)$	$\Delta \sim N(0.45, 0.15)$		
L6	$\theta_0 \sim N(-0.7, 1.5)$	$\Delta \sim N(0.6, 0.3)$		

(umimecesky.cz). The system implements mastery learning based on the exponential moving average method. The system visualizes progress using progress bar with highlighted thresholds (mastery levels) 0.5, 0.8, 0.95, and 0.98. The main mastery level (used for example for evaluation of homework within the system) is given by a threshold 0.95. The value of α depends on the type of exercise. For the analysis we use data from the basic grammar exercise with multiple-choice questions with two options (items of the type "a/an orange"). For this exercise the system uses $\alpha = 0.9$. The data set consist of over 40 000 answer sequences (each sequence is for a learner and particular knowledge component).

The second system is MatMat (matmat.cz) – an adaptive practice system for basic arithmetic with items of the type "6 × 7" with free-form answers. The system implements adaptive behavior even within a practice of a single knowledge component; items are chosen to be of an appropriate difficulty for a particular learner [21]. The data set was filtered to contain only learners with more than 10 answers. The used data set consist of 330 000 answers from more than 8 000 learners.

3.2 Evaluation Methods

With simulated data we have the advantage that we know the ground truth moment of learning. Clearly we want the moment when mastery is declared to be close to this ground truth, so the basic metric to optimize is mean absolute deviation between the ground truth mastery moment and detected mastery moment. This metric has been used in previous research [16]. However, in practical applications there is an asymmetry in errors in mastery decision. Typically, we are more concerned about under-practice (mastery declared prematurely) than about over-practice (lag in declared mastery). This aspect was also noted in previous work, e.g., [6] considers 'ratio of regret of type II to type I decision errors'. To take this asymmetry into account, we consider weighted mean absolute deviation (wMAD), where we put w times more weight to under-practice than to over-practice (we use $w = 5$ unless state otherwise).

Analysis of mastery criteria for real data is more difficult than for simulated data, because now we cannot analyze the decision

with respect to correct mastery decisions (these are unknown). One possible approach is to compare the degree of agreement between different methods. This analysis cannot tell us which method is better, but it shows whether the decision which one to use is actually important – if mastery decisions by two methods are very similar, we do not need to ponder which one is better and we can use the simpler one for implementation in a real system. To evaluate the agreement of two methods, we use Spearman's correlation coefficient over the mastery moment for individual learners (alternative methods are also possible, e.g., using Jaccard index over sets of learners in the mastery state).

Another approach is to measure effort (how long it takes to reach mastery) and score after mastery (probability of answering correctly after mastery was declared). This type of evaluation was used in previous research [10, 11]. These metrics have to be interpreted carefully due to attrition biases in data, particularly when the used system already uses some kind of mastery learning [20].

3.3 Comparison of BKT and NCC

As a first experiment we compare the mastery threshold criterion based on the commonly used BKT model and the simplest mastery criterion N consecutive correct. We compare these methods over simulated data generated by a BKT model. Moreover, to avoid the issue of parameter fitting, we simply use the optimal ground truth BKT parameters for detecting mastery, i.e., this is the optimal case for application of the BKT model.

To make mastery decision we need to choose thresholds: N for the NCC method and T for BKT. We optimize these parameters for each simulated scenario. Since we optimize a single parameter, we use a simple grid search.

The experiments were performed as follows. We choose BKT parameters. We generate sequences of 50 answers for 10 000 simulated learners. We use this training set to fit the thresholds by optimizing the wMAD metric using the grid search. Then we generate a new set of 10 000 learners and use this test set for evaluation – computation of the metric wMAD for both methods and also correlation of their mastery decisions.

Table 2 shows results of this experiment for different scenarios from Table 1. The optimized thresholds are between 0.9 and 0.97 for BKT and between 2 and 8 for NCC. With respect to wMAD, BKT is typically better, but the difference is not large. The correlation between mastery decisions is typically very high. From the perspective of a student, these results mean that mastery is declared by both methods at the same or very similar time. Larger difference between BKT and NCC occurs only in the case with a high slip and a low guess.

The summary of this experiment is that even in the best case scenario, where data perfectly correspond to model assumptions, BKT does not bring significant improvement over the basic mastery decision criterion.

3.4 Role of Response Times

In the next experiment we use real data from the MatMat system and explore the relative importance of the choice of a model and the choice of input data, specifically whether to use learners response times. In the case of basic arithmetic it makes sense to include

Table 2: Comparison of BKT and NCC mastery criteria over simulated data.

	Threshold		wMAD		
	NCC	BKT	NCC	BKT	Cor.
B1	2	0.92	2.56	2.42	0.88
B2	4	0.97	6.2	5.76	0.97
B3	2	0.95	2.81	2.48	0.92
B4	1	0.9	2.72	2.13	0.74
B5	4	0.97	3.77	3.62	0.99
B6	8	0.97	11.48	10.33	0.94

fluency (learners' speed) as a factor in the mastery decision. Does it matter whether we include response times? How much?

For the choice of a skill estimation model we consider the following two variants:

- The basic exponential moving average (EMA) method with $\alpha = 0.8$.
- A logistic learner model (denoted as M) described in detail in [21].

The basic difference between these two approaches is that the model takes into account difficulty of items, whereas the EMA approach completely ignores item information. The model thus can better deal with the adaptively collected data (learners are presented items of different difficulty).

For the choice of input data we consider also two variants:

- Only the basic correctness data, i.e., the response value is binary (0 or 1).
- Combination of correctness and response times (denoted as $+T$). The response value for wrong answers remains 0; the response value for correct answers is linearly decreasing for response times between 0 and 14 seconds; for longer times the response value is 0. The constant 14 is set as a double of the median response time, i.e., a correct answer with median response time has the response value 0.5.

We compare four models obtained as combinations along these two dimensions: EMA, EMA+T, M, M+T. We evaluate agreement between them to see which model aspects makes larger difference. To analyze mastery decision, it is necessary to choose mastery thresholds. However, the studied methods differ in the scales of their output values, e.g, EMA + T gives smaller values than EMA. It is therefore not easy to choose thresholds for a fair comparison. To avoid biasing the results by a choice of specific thresholds, we compare directly orderings of learners by different methods. For each learner we compute the final skill estimate and we evaluate agreement of methods by the Spearman correlation coefficient over these values.

Figure 2 shows correlations of the four studied methods for four knowledge components from the MatMat system. We see that the correlation between EMA and the model approach is typically higher than correlation between approaches with and without use of response time. Particularly the variants with timing information (EMA+T and M+T) are highly correlated. From this analysis we cannot say which approach is better, but we see that the impact of

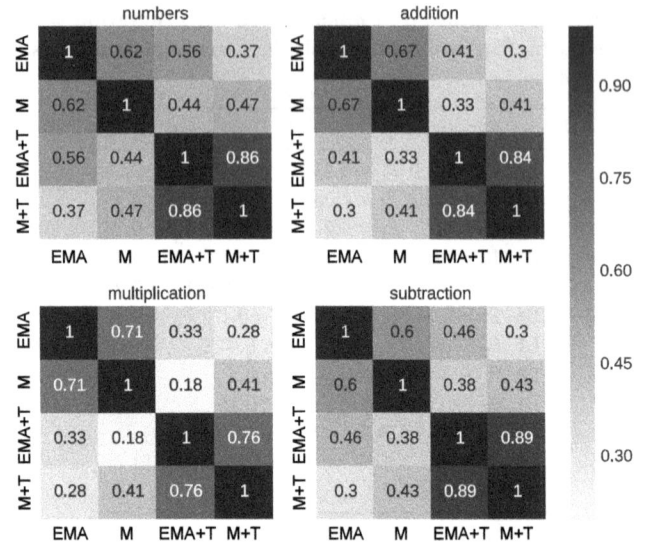

Figure 2: Spearman correlation between different learner skill estimation methods for different knowledge components (Matmat data).

using response times is larger than the impact of using a learner model.

3.5 Analysis of the EMA Method

The reported results and our experience from practical application within the system for Czech grammar suggest that EMA is a reasonable method for detecting mastery. Therefore, we analyze its behavior in more detail.

EMA as a mastery criterion has two parameters: the exponential decay parameter α and the threshold T. By tuning these two parameters we can obtain different behaviors. Both parameters have values in the interval $(0, 1)$. Increase in both of these parameters leads to an increase of the length of practice, for values approaching 1 the increase is very steep.

The basic nature of this increase is apparent when we analyze the number of consecutive correct answers that guarantee passing a threshold for a given α (a sufficient, but not necessary condition): $N \geq \log_{\alpha}(1 - T)$. For example for a threshold $T = 0.95$ we get the following relation between α and number of attempts N:

α	0.7	0.75	0.8	0.85	0.9	0.95
N	9	11	14	19	29	59

Note that EMA can also exactly emulate the N consecutive correct criterion, e.g., when we use $\alpha = 0.5$ and $T = 1 - 0.5^N$, getting N consecutive correct becomes both sufficient and necessary condition for passing the threshold.

We analyze EMA parameters for simulated data using the same methodology as in the experiment comparing BTK with NCC. In this case we use data generated by both BKT and logistic models, optimizing parameters and thresholds with respect to the wMAD metric. As a baseline for comparison we use the NCC method.

Table 3: Comparison of mastery criteria over simulated data: NCC, the EMA method with fixed $\alpha = 0.95$, and the full EMA method.

| sc | N | \multicolumn{3}{c}{Parameters} | | | NCC | \multicolumn{2}{c}{wMAD} | |
		α_{95}	α	T		EMA$_{95}$	EMA
B1	2	0.1	0.7	0.5	2.48	2.48	2.45
B2	4	0.5	0.75	0.75	6.45	6.23	6.07
B3	3	0.3	0.5	0.75	2.66	2.66	2.42
B4	1	0.1	0.2	0.8	2.82	3.47	2.31
B5	4	0.4	0.7	0.75	3.76	3.64	3.59
B6	7	0.7	0.75	0.92	11.04	10.45	10.41
L1	8	0.7	0.9	0.6	3.92	3.34	2.63
L2	17	0.85	0.9	0.9	9.02	8.44	7.64
L3	14	0.85	0.9	0.85	7.39	6.21	5.04
L4	15	0.85	0.8	0.98	10.28	10.7	10.3
L5	8	0.7	0.7	0.95	5.13	4.97	4.97
L6	8	0.7	0.6	0.98	6.67	7.12	6.87

Table 3 shows results. We see that EMA achieves slightly better performance than NCC, for BKT scenarios the difference is typically small, for scenarios corresponding to slow learning according to the logistic model assumptions the difference can be quite pronounced. The optimal EMA parameters vary depending on the scenario – both α and T.

When we fix the threshold $T = 0.95$ and vary only the parameter α, the quality of mastery decisions (as measured by the wMAD metric) is typically better than for the NCC method, but worse than when EMA is used with full flexibility.

To explore the impact of the choice of metric, we explored different values of the weight w, which specifies the relative importance of under-practice (premature mastery) to over-practice. The key factor influencing the optimal value of α is the learning scenario, but the choice of w also has nontrivial impact. For example in the L6 scenario, the optimal value of α (for fixed threshold 0.95) varies between 0.52 and 0.73 depending on the weight w.

3.6 Effort and Score Analysis

Our results suggests that the setting of thresholds is a key aspect of mastery detection. Therefore, we need methods that could be used to choose threshold values for practical systems – the wMAD metric used in previous experiments is applicable only to simulated data for which we know the ground truth. For this purpose we explore the idea of measuring effort and score [10–12] and propose a visualization using an effort-score graph.

We measure effort and score metrics as follows: effort is the average number of attempts needed to reach mastery; score is the average number of correct answers in k attempts that follow after reaching mastery (reported experiment uses $k = 5$, the results are not sensitive to this choice). Note that there may be learners that do not reach mastery or that do not have enough attempts after mastery was reach. Treatment of these issues (e.g., whether to use value imputation as in [10]) may influence results, particularly when comparing similar methods. For the presented analysis these issues are not fundamental.

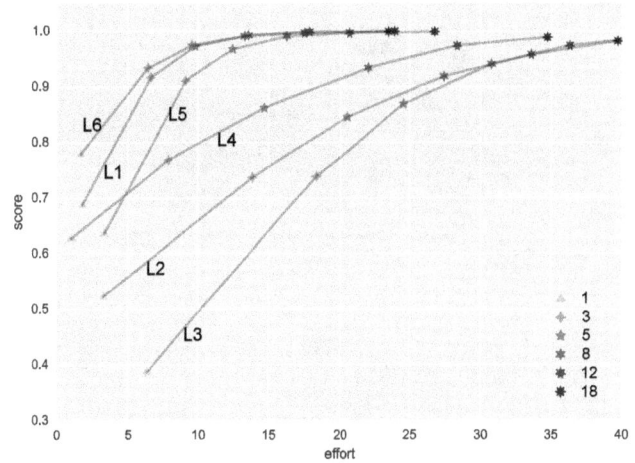

Figure 3: The effort-score graph for simulated data and the N consecutive correct method with variable N. The lines correspond to Ln scenarios from the Table 1.

To analyze the impact of the choice of threshold, we use effort-score graphs. Figure 3 shows this graph for the Ln subset of our simulated data and the basic NCC mastery criterion. The curve shows the trade-off between effort and score. By using higher mastery thresholds, the score of learners who achieved mastery improves, but at the cost of higher effort. A reasonable choice of threshold is the point at which the effort-score curve starts to level off, i.e., where additional effort does not bring improvement in performance. This is a heuristic approach, but note that it leads to similar conclusions about the choice of a threshold as experiments that utilize the ground truth (reported in Table 3).

The technique can thus be useful for setting of thresholds for real data. Figure 4 shows the effort-score graph for data from the Czech grammar and spelling system. In this case the results are provided for the EMA method with $\alpha = 0.9$ and different values of thresholds (this directly corresponds to the approach used in the actual implementation). Curves correspond to several knowledge components of varying difficulty. For easy knowledge components the score is high even for low thresholds; higher values of threshold only increase the effort, but by acceptable margin. For difficult knowledge components, the score levels off only after the threshold is over 0.95. The analysis thus suggests that the value 0.95 is a reasonable compromise.

4 DISCUSSION

We conclude with a discussion of implications of presented results. We also discuss wider context, simplifying assumptions of our experiments, and opportunities for future work.

4.1 What Matters in Mastery Criteria?

Our results suggest that there is not a fundamental difference between simple mastery criteria (consecutive correct, exponential moving average) and more complex methods based on the use of learner modeling techniques. The important decisions are what data to use for mastery decision and the choice of thresholds.

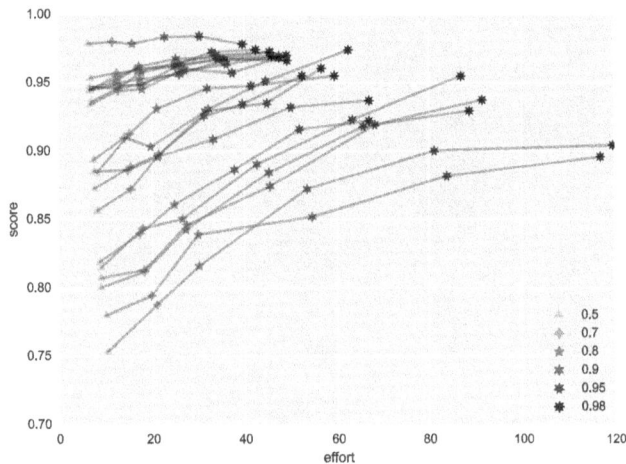

Figure 4: The effort-score graph for real data and the EMA method with $\alpha = 0.9$ and variable thresholds. The lines correspond to knowledge components of varying difficulty.

The choice of mastery thresholds involves the trade-off between the risk of premature mastery and over-practice. Even small changes in thresholds can have large impact on learners practice, so setting of this parameter should get significant attention in development of systems utilizing mastery learning. The choice of thresholds depends on a particular application, because applications differ in the relative costs of premature mastery and over-practice. General research thus cannot provide universal conclusions about the choice of threshold, but it can provide more detailed guidance for techniques that can help with the choice of thresholds. As a practical tool for this choice we propose effort-score graphs, which can be easily constructed from historical data. It would be useful to further elaborate other techniques described in previous work [7, 10].

4.2 Exponential Moving Average

Our results and previous work [18] suggest that the exponential moving average method provides a reasonable approach to detecting mastery. The method has two parameters: the exponential decay parameter α and the threshold T. Together these two parameters provide enough freedom so that the method can provide good mastery decision in different situations (e.g., different speeds of learning, levels of initial knowledge, presence of guessing).

The technique is very simple to implement and use for online decisions. The technique is also directly applicable for visualization of progress to learners (typically using some kind of progress bar). It has an intuitive behavior – an increase in estimated skill after a correct answer, a decrease after a wrong answer. Such behavior may seem trivial and straightforward, but it does not necessarily hold for alternative methods. For example simple moving average often stays the same after a correct answer and some learners models may even increase skill estimate after a wrong answer (because such behavior fits training data).

4.3 Role of Learner Models

Our results suggest that learner modeling techniques are not fundamental for detecting mastery. However, that does not mean that they are not useful. Learner models are very useful for obtaining insights using offline analysis of data. One of key assumptions of our analysis is that we have well-specified knowledge components. Learner modeling techniques are useful for discovery and refinement of knowledge components and their relations. However, once this offline analysis is done, it may be better to use simpler, more robust methods for online decisions. This argument is closely related to Baker's proposal for "stupid tutoring systems, intelligent humans" [1] – using analytics tools to inform humans and then implement relatively simple, but well-selected and well-tuned methods into computer systems.

4.4 Limitations and Future Work

Our analysis uses several simplifying assumptions. Lifting these assumptions provides interesting directions for future work.

We assume well-specified, isolated knowledge components of suitable granularity. In the case of strong relations among knowledge components, the difference between learner modeling techniques and simple techniques may be larger, since learner modeling techniques may utilize information from several knowledge components for mastery decision. An interesting issue is the interaction between level of granularity of knowledge components and the choice of mastery thresholds.

We do not consider wheel-spinning learners [3] who are unable to master a knowledge component and instead of continued practice would benefit from redirection to one of prerequisite knowledge components. This issue has been addressed by policies developed in previous work [12, 23]. These policies have been evaluated for learner modeling techniques; it may be interesting to explore their combination with exponential moving average.

We do not consider forgetting. This is particularly important issue in the case of factual knowledge (e.g., foreign language vocabulary), but even in the case of mathematics previous research have shown that the mastery speed is related to future performance [25]. Instead of treating mastery as a permanent state, it would be better to treat it as a temporary state that needs reassessment. An interesting direction is an integration of mastery criteria with research on spacing effects.

Finally, in the presented analysis we ignore potential biases present in real data, particularly attrition bias [20]. This can be potentially an important issue for the analysis of effort-score graphs. It would be useful to develop techniques for detecting and overcoming such biases in the effort-score analysis.

REFERENCES
[1] Ryan S Baker. 2016. Stupid Tutoring Systems, Intelligent Humans. *International Journal of Artificial Intelligence in Education* 26, 2 (2016), 600–614.
[2] Ryan SJD Baker, Adam B Goldstein, and Neil T Heffernan. 2011. Detecting learning moment-by-moment. *International Journal of Artificial Intelligence in Education* 21, 1-2 (2011), 5–25.
[3] Joseph E Beck and Yue Gong. 2013. Wheel-spinning: Students who fail to master a skill. In *Proc. of Artificial Intelligence in Education*. Springer, 431–440.
[4] Albert T Corbett and John R Anderson. 1994. Knowledge tracing: Modeling the acquisition of procedural knowledge. *User modeling and user-adapted interaction* 4, 4 (1994), 253–278.

[5] Michel C Desmarais and Ryan SJ Baker. 2012. A review of recent advances in learner and skill modeling in intelligent learning environments. *User Modeling and User-Adapted Interaction* 22, 1-2 (2012), 9–38.

[6] John A Emrick. 1971. An Evaluation Model for Mastery Testing. *Journal of Educational Measurement* 8, 4 (1971), 321–326.

[7] Stephen E Fancsali, Tristan Nixon, and Steven Ritter. 2013. Optimal and Worst-Case Performance of Mastery Learning Assessment with Bayesian Knowledge Tracing. In *Educational Data Mining*.

[8] Stephen E Fancsali, Tristan Nixon, Annalies Vuong, and Steven Ritter. 2013. Simulated Students, Mastery Learning, and Improved Learning Curves for Real-World Cognitive Tutors.. In *AIED Workshops*.

[9] April Galyardt and Ilya Goldin. 2015. Move your lamp post: Recent data reflects learner knowledge better than older data. *Journal of Educational Data Mining* 7, 2 (2015), 83–108.

[10] José P González-Brenes and Yun Huang. 2015. Your model is predictive - but is it useful? theoretical and empirical considerations of a new paradigm for adaptive tutoring evaluation. In *Proc. of Educational Data Mining*.

[11] David Hu. 2011. How Khan academy is using machine learning to assess student mastery. (2011). http://david-hu.com/2011/11/02/how-khan-academy-is-using-machine-learning-to-assess-student-mastery.html.

[12] Tanja Käser, Severin Klingler, and Markus Gross. 2016. When to Stop?: Towards Universal Instructional Policies. In *Proc. of Learning Analytics & Knowledge*. ACM, 289–298.

[13] Kim Kelly, Yan Wang, Tamisha Thompson, and Neil Heffernan. 2015. Defining Mastery: Knowledge Tracing Versus N-Consecutive Correct Responses. In *Proc. of Educational Data Mining*.

[14] Jung In Lee and Emma Brunskill. 2012. The Impact on Individualizing Student Models on Necessary Practice Opportunities. In *Proc. of Educational Data Mining*. 118–125.

[15] George B Macready and C Mitchell Dayton. 1977. The use of probabilistic models in the assessment of mastery. *Journal of Educational and Behavioral Statistics* 2,

2 (1977), 99–120.

[16] Zachary A Pardos and Michael V Yudelson. 2013. Towards Moment of Learning Accuracy. In *AIED 2013 Workshops Proceedings Volume 4*. 3.

[17] Philip I. Pavlik, Hao Cen, and Kenneth R. Koedinger. 2009. Performance Factors Analysis-A New Alternative to Knowledge Tracing.. In *Proc. of Artificial Intelligence in Education (AIED) (Frontiers in Artificial Intelligence and Applications)*, Vol. 200. IOS Press, 531–538.

[18] Radek Pelánek. 2014. Application of Time Decay Functions and Elo System in Student Modeling. In *Proc. of Educational Data Mining*. 21–27.

[19] Radek Pelánek. 2015. Metrics for Evaluation of Student Models. *Journal of Educational Data Mining* 7, 2 (2015).

[20] Radek Pelánek, Jiří Řihák, and Jan Papoušek. 2016. Impact of Data Collection on Interpretation and Evaluation of Student Model. In *Proc. of Learning Analytics & Knowledge*. ACM, 40–47.

[21] Jirí Rihák. 2015. Use of Time Information in Models behind Adaptive System for Building Fluency in Mathematics.. In *Proc. of Educational Data Mining*.

[22] Steve Ritter, Michael Yudelson, Stephen E Fancsali, and Susan R Berman. 2016. How Mastery Learning Works at Scale. In *Proc. of ACM Conference on Learning@Scale*. ACM, 71–79.

[23] Joseph Rollinson and Emma Brunskill. 2015. From Predictive Models to Instructional Policies. In *Proc. of Educational Data Mining*.

[24] George Semb. 1974. The Effects of Mastery Criteria and Assignment Length on College-Student Test Performance. *Journal of applied behavior analysis* 7, 1 (1974), 61–69.

[25] Xiaolu Xiong, Shoujing Li, and Joseph E Beck. 2013. Will You Get It Right Next Week: Predict Delayed Performance in Enhanced ITS Mastery Cycle.. In *FLAIRS Conference*.

[26] Michael V Yudelson and Kenneth R Koedinger. 2013. Estimating the benefits of student model improvements on a substantive scale. In *EDM 2013 Workshops Proceedings*.

Using Eye Gaze Data and Visual Activities to Infer Human Cognitive Styles: Method and Feasibility Studies

George E. Raptis
HCI Group, Dept. of Electrical and
Computer Engineering
University of Patras, Greece
raptisg@upnet.gr

Christina Katsini
HCI Group, Dept. of Electrical and
Computer Engineering
University of Patras, Greece
katsinic@upnet.gr

Marios Belk
Cognitive UX GmbH, Germany &
Dept. of Computer Science
University of Cyprus, Cyprus
belk@cognitiveux.de

Christos Fidas
Dept. of Cultural Heritage
Management and New Technologies
University of Patras, Greece
fidas@upatras.gr

George Samaras
Dept. of Computer Science
University of Cyprus, Cyprus
cssamara@cs.ucy.ac.cy

Nikolaos Avouris
HCI Group, Dept. of Electrical and
Computer Engineering
University of Patras, Greece
avouris@upatras.gr

ABSTRACT

Recent research provides evidence that individual differences in human cognitive styles affect user performance and experience in diverse application domains. However, state-of-the-art elicitation methods of cognitive styles require researchers to apply explicit, in-lab, and time-consuming "paper-and-pencil" techniques, rendering real-time integration of cognitive styles' elicitation impractical in interactive system design. Aiming to elaborate an implicit elicitation method of cognitive styles, this paper reports two feasibility studies based on an eye-tracking multifactorial model. In both studies, participants performed visual activities of varying characteristics, and the eye-tracking analysis revealed quantitative differences on visual behavior among individuals with different cognitive styles. Based on these differences, a series of classification experiments were conducted, and the results revealed that gaze-based implicit elicitation of cognitive styles in real-time is feasible, which could be used by interactive systems to adapt to the users' cognitive needs and preferences, to better assist them, and improve their performance and experience.

CCS CONCEPTS

• **Human-centered computing** → HCI theory, concepts and models • **Computing methodologies** → Machine learning approaches

KEYWORDS

Human Cognitive Styles; Eye-Tracking; Visual Search Tasks; Visual Decision-Making Tasks; User Study.

UMAP'17, July 9-12, 2017, Bratislava, Slovakia
© 2017 ACM. ISBN 978-1-4503-4635-1/17/07...$15.00.
DOI: http://dx.doi.org/10.1145/3079628.3079690.

1 INTRODUCTION

People develop different strategies when they seek, process, retrieve, and reconstruct information, as they are characterized by different cognitive attributes (*e.g.*, skills, abilities, styles) [1]. Recent research provides empirical evidence that individual differences, in such cognitive attributes, affect task performance and user experience across diverse application domains, such as e-learning [2], information visualization [3], security [4], e-shopping [5], web search [6], and video-gaming [7].

To understand and explain empirically the observed differences in mental representation and information processing, a number of researchers [8–11] have focused on high-level cognitive processes, known as *cognitive styles*. Cognitive styles refer to the preferred way an individual processes information, and they describe a person's typical mode of thinking, remembering, or problem solving [12]. The integration of cognitive styles as a human design factor would be beneficial for interactive system users, as they would experience real-time services and functionalities, tailored to their individual needs and preferences, through adaptation and personalization frameworks.

However, the barrier in such research endeavors is the explicit and non-real-time elicitation of the human cognitive styles. Nowadays, their elicitation is based on traditional in-lab (*e.g.*, "paper-and-pencil" [11, 13]) and time-consuming (*e.g.*, 15-20 mins [11, 13]) techniques, rendering real-time integration of cognitive styles' elicitation impractical in interactive system design.

To overcome this issue, implicit elicitation mechanisms could be used. These mechanisms provide information regarding user characteristics through intelligent and automatic modelling processes, while the user is interacting with the system. Such information is extracted transparently, without interrupting the users, while performing activities. Given that there is a strong correlation among human cognitive styles, activity, and visual behavior [14], and as visual scanning and processing are principal stages of performing visual activities, eye gaze data could reveal measurable differences and allow for inferring cognitive styles. Hence, eye-tracking mechanisms could be used to implicitly elicit cognitive styles in real-time, based on quantitative differences on visual behavior within certain types of visual activities.

The motivation underlying our work is moving toward an implicit and real-time elicitation framework of human cognitive styles, based on an *eye-tracking multifactorial model* of: *human cognition, visual behavior*, and *activity* factors (Fig. 1). Such a model could provide appropriate data for any interactive system to know, and adapt to the users' cognitive needs and preferences, to better assist them (*e.g.,* improve task performance and user experience), so they can benefit from adaptation interventions. Such a framework should rely both on ground-truth data derived from state-of-the-art, credible, and validated tools used traditionally for cognitive styles' elicitation, and on quantitatively measured differences on visual behavior within certain types of activities, evidenced on validated and credible studies.

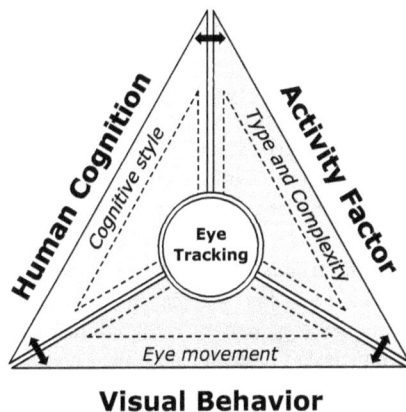

Figure 1: Eye-tracking multifactorial model for implicit elicitation of cognitive styles. It consists of three main factors: human cognition, visual behavior, and activity.

Aiming to create an eye-tracking multifactorial model to identify human cognitive styles implicitly and in real-time, and provide the classification results as a service to any information system, to dynamically adapt to its users' characteristics, the contribution of this paper is two-fold: i) analyze eye gaze data, aiming to reveal gaze behavior and patterns that are indicative of people with different cognitive styles, and ii) infer cognitive styles using such eye gaze data, while performing certain types of activities. Thus, this paper details the method used to model users' visual behavior, and reports two feasibility studies to justify the use of the eye-tracking multifactorial model to elicit human cognitive styles implicitly and in real time, using varying parameters of visual activity and eye gaze measures.

The reminder of the paper is structured as follows. First, we provide an overview of related research in implicit elicitation of human cognitive styles. Next, we present the interplay among the factors of the eye-tracking multifactorial model. This is followed by two studies that we performed to examine the feasibility of the proposed implicit elicitation process. We conclude the paper with a discussion on the main findings, limitations, and future steps.

2 RELATED WORK

Several studies [15–17] suggest an interplay effect among human cognitive styles and user visual behavior while performing certain types of activities. To the authors' knowledge, none of them has elaborated on an implicit and real-time elicitation framework of human cognitive styles based on eye gaze data, taking into consideration varying activity factors (*e.g.,* type, complexity).

Barrios et al. [18] developed AdELE, an adaptive framework of e-learning resources, which detects users' cognitive styles based on the holistic/analytic and verbal/imagery dimension [8] through eye-tracking. However, no sufficient evaluation regarding the user classification was provided. Moreover, AdELE does not consider the type and the characteristics of the activity (*e.g.,* difficulty, sequence), which influence the visual behavior [19, 20].

Nisiforou and Laghos [17] showed that individuals with different cognitive style, have different visual approaches in terms of low-level eye-tracking metrics (*e.g.,* number of fixations) when performing visual search tasks. However, the visual strategy (*e.g.,* scan-paths) the users followed was discussed only qualitatively, and despite the insights gained, such non-quantitative differences could not be used to elicit cognitive styles implicitly in in-real time scenarios. Moreover, they did not investigate other types of activity and varying activity factors (*e.g.,* complexity, sequence).

A number of studies have reported alternative methods to infer human cognitive styles, which are majorly limited to navigation schemes. Belk et al. [21] proposed a set of navigation metrics to reveal the holistic or analytic cognitive style of individuals, when performing a Web navigation task. Chen and Liu [22] proposed a method to identify users' cognitive styles by tracking their behavior with navigation tools. Wang et al., [23] proposed a method to identify cognitive styles from user-generated social media content. Chan et al. [24] tracked how users with different cognitive styles use mobile Web search tools in e-journals.

While the aforementioned research endeavors contribute towards the implicit elicitation of human cognitive styles, they are limited to the application domain (*e.g.,* e-learning, e-commerce). In addition, these approaches are unable to leverage principal stages of information processing (*e.g.,* visual scanning and visual processing) to accurately infer human cognitive styles in activities where interactions with means other than eye gaze are limited.

In contrast to high-level cognitive processes, a number of studies have reported on using eye gaze data to identify low-level cognitive attributes (*e.g.,* skills and abilities). Steichen et al. [20, 25] classified individuals according to their perceptual speed, verbal and visual working memory attributes when performing information visualization tasks; Yelizarov and Gamayunov [26] developed a mechanism to detect its users' cognitive overload and adapt the amount of displayed information accordingly.

Therefore, we argue that eye-tracking mechanisms could be used to implicitly classify the individuals based on their high level cognitive processes (*i.e.,* cognitive styles) in real-time while performing activities of varying characteristics (*e.g.,* type complexity). Nowadays, this is realistic, as the recent technological advances have enabled the development of affordable, robust and mainstream eye-tracking solutions.

3 MULTIFACTORIAL MODEL FOR IMPLICIT ELICITATION OF COGNITIVE FACTORS

In order to explore a visual scene, humans perform varying visual activities which incorporate information processing to some extent, depending on the nature of the visual activity, and thus they involve human cognition. These are the three main factors (*i.e.*, human cognition, activity, and visual behavior) which form the eye-tracking multifactorial model (Fig. 1) that we propose to infer human cognitive styles, and their interplay has a major impact on individuals' task performance and user experience [14]. The reminder of this section is concerned with the eye-tracking multifactorial model for the implicit elicitation of cognitive styles (*i.e.*, factors, eye-tracking, and implicit elicitation method).

3.1 Human Cognition Factor

The *human cognition* factor reflects on theories of individual differences in information processing, suggesting that individuals have preferred ways of seeking, representing, processing and retrieving information, depending on their individual cognitive skills and abilities, (*e.g.*, perceptual speed and memory load) [10, 27, 28]. Several researchers have focused on high-level cognitive processes to explain empirically such observed differences [1]. These processes are called *cognitive styles*, and a number of them have been developed and studied over the years [8, 10, 11, 28].

The human cognition factor of our multifactorial model is based on a fundamental and credible [29, 30] cognitive style theory: the *Field Dependence-Independence (FD-I)* [10]. FD-I classifies people as field-dependent (FD) or field-independent (FI). FDs tend to prefer a more holistic way when processing visual information, and have difficulties in identifying details in complex scenes [10]. On the other hand, FIs tend to prefer a more analytical information processing approach, pay attention to details, and easily separate simple structures from the surrounding visual context [10].

Several studies have provided empirical evidence that the differences among FD and FI individuals reflect on their task performance and user experience. Mewed et al. [5] have shown that FI consumers developed a more analytical information processing strategy on decision-making e-shopping tasks (*e.g.*, selecting a yogurt product). Raptis et al. [7] evidenced that FI gamers performed better, in terms of game assets collection, when playing a cultural heritage adventure game. Shinar et al. [31] evidenced that FD drivers were less adaptive and efficient in changing environments (*e.g.*, curve negotiating), where the perceptual load was drastically increased and the target area (*i.e.*, the road) changed iteratively within their visual field.

3.2 Visual Behavior Factor

The *visual behavior* factor reflects on visual perception (*i.e.*, the ability to identify, organize and interpret the surrounding environment by processing visually displayed information). Visual perceptual span varies in visual tasks, depending on diverse task sub-characteristics (*e.g.*, difficulty, sequence, and hierarchy level), and it is interrelated with eye movements [32]. The basic eye movements are saccades, fixations, smooth pursuits, compensatory eye movements, vergence, and optokinetic nystagmus [33].

Research has revealed that individuals with different cognitive style, differ in visual behavior. Shi et al. [34] showed that FD drivers produced less and slower fixations when driving; Zhuomin and Wanyi [35] revealed that FI users fixated on web advertisements for longer time periods during Web navigation; Wijnen and Groot [36] used scan-paths produced by participants' fixations to show that FI individuals develop a more analytical and systematic strategy to find hidden figures within complex ones; Huang and Byrne [37] used lateral eye movements (*i.e.*, left and right eye shifts) to evidence that holistic individuals tended to produce more left shifts when viewing an image, while analytic individuals tended to produce a majority of right shifts; Puig et al. [38] showed that FIs had stronger eye convergence than FDs; and that the angle of eye vergence was larger for the FIs compared to the vergence angle of the FDs on visual attention tasks. Hence, we argue that in our multifactorial model, the most suitable visual behavior factor depends on the visual activity characteristics.

3.3 Activity Factor

Activity characteristics, such as type (*e.g.*, visual exploration, visual search, pattern recognition) influence visual behavior of individuals with different cognitive styles [14]. Visual activities can be broken into smaller components (*i.e.*, visual tasks), which, according to Gidlöf et al. [39], can be broadly classified as *visual search tasks* and *visual decision-making tasks*. During visual search tasks, individuals look for specific information in a given information complex (*e.g.*, pattern recognition), while on visual decision-making tasks, individuals make choices among alternatives (*e.g.*, graphical password creation).

Raptis et al. [40] revealed that FI gamers developed more and longer fixations while visually searching for in-game assets when playing an adventure game. Mawad et al. [5] showed that FDs produced less and shorter fixations on visual decision-making tasks (*e.g.*, select a dairy product to buy). Nisiforou et al. [17] showed that FDs produced more saccades and fixations while searching for differences in shapes. Crosby and Peterson [41] evidenced that individuals with different cognitive styles differ in the way they visually search for information on sorted and unsorted lists, as they follow different visual scanning strategies (*i.e.*, different scan-paths).

Apart from type, tasks differ in other characteristics, such as difficulty, complexity, sequence, and hierarchy level, which affect the performance and the experience of individuals with different cognitive styles [3, 32]. Conklin et al. [42] showed that FDs had longer and more random eye movements during visual search tasks, as the complexity of the background scene increased. Nisiforou et al. [19] showed that the visual search strategies of FD and FI individuals were complexity-dependent on Web navigation. For webpages of low complexity the visual search strategies of FD and FI individuals were similar. However, the scan-paths of FD individuals appeared to be more disoriented and scattered on webpages of medium and high complexity, in contrast to FI individuals, who displayed more oriented and organized scan-paths.

3.4 Eye-tracking Layer

The aforementioned studies suggest that there are inter-dependencies among human cognition, visual behavior, and activity factors, which affect individuals' performance and user experience. To leverage on the interplay among these factors, eye gaze data are used. The eye-movement data is captured through eye-tracking tools, which serve as the connection layer among the factors, helping us understand the visual behavior and the strategy of individuals with different cognitive styles when performing activities of varying characteristics.

A number of eye-tracking data and measures of diverse complexity have been developed, such as fixations and saccades, fixation duration [33], trending scan-path analysis [43], and gaze transition and stationary entropies [44]. The selection of the most suitable eye-tracking metrics depends on the activity characteristics. To perform a credible eye-tracking analysis, specific areas of interest (AOIs) (*i.e.*, clustered sub-regions of the displayed stimulus in which the eye-tracking metrics are applied) must be defined appropriately [25].

Depending on the three factors of the multifactorial model, specific eye-tracking metrics and AOIs are defined, to proceed on the user modelling process and elicit human cognitive styles implicitly and in real-time.

3.5 Implicit Elicitation

The user modeling process for eliciting users' cognitive styles entails three main phases: *data collection*, *data processing,* and *classification.*

Data Collection

Collecting data of users is the initial step for implicit elicitation of cognitive styles. In our multifactorial model, the data refers to raw eye gaze data, which is captured through the eye-tracking layer. The raw eye gaze data varies, depending on the eye-tracking technology (*e.g.*, sampling frequency) used. The gaze data is assigned to each user profile, and provided to the next phase for data processing.

Data Processing

The data processing phase is two-fold: i) to decide which eye-tracking measure is the most suitable to perform the classification, and ii) to transform the data to the corresponding measure. The selection of the most suitable measures depends on the activity and the cognitive style characteristics. The transformation of the data entails both the form of the eye-tracking metrics set (*e.g.*, fixation duration, gaze entropies), and the definition of the AOIs in the displayed stimuli.

Classification

The final phase to elicit cognitive styles is the classification process. When the transformed eye-tracking measures are provided in our model, the corresponding individuals are classified based on their cognitive style. The classification is based on a valid data set, provided by credible studies, which is used to train our model to make predictions. Along with the classification process, the prediction certainty is estimated for each individual.

4 FEASIBILITY STUDIES

In order to examine the feasibility of the proposed implicit elicitation process, we conducted two studies, with individuals performing different types of visual activity based on Gidlöf et al. [39] (*i.e.*, a visual search and a visual decision-making activity), with FD-I being the independent cognitive style variable.

Both studies consist of two phases: *classification metrics extraction* and *classification experiment.* Phase A consists of an eye-tracking study aiming to reveal whether there are statistically significant differences in individuals' visual behavior while performing activities of specific type, and identify which these are. These differences reflect on specific eye-tracking measures and AOIs, which are intended to be used as classification parameters to train the learning model used for the classification experiment in Phase B. To perform the classification experiment in Phase B, we conducted a second eye-tracking study, following the same experimental design as in Phase A. Its purpose was to collect the gaze data from a new set of users (testing set), to evaluate the classification model. We used the WEKA [45] data mining toolkit for model learning and evaluation. The training and testing sets used (for both feasibility studies) were balanced.

In both studies, the participants' eye movements were recorded with Tobii Pro Glasses 2 wearable system, while performing each activity. Following common practice, we focused on where and when fixations occurred. Fixations were extracted using a customized velocity threshold identification (I-VT) algorithm [46], based on the I-VT algorithm provided by Tobii.

4.1 Study I – Visual Search Activity

The first feasibility study entails a visual search activity. FD-I measures the ability of individuals to identify simple details in complex visual scenes, and thus, it reflects on visual search, and specifically on pattern recognition [10]. The pattern recognition activity was based on a traditional "paper-and-pencil" FD-I elicitation tool: *Group Embedded Figures Test (GEFT)* [13, 47], as it is a ground-truth tool for FD-I classification. GEFT consists of 25 pattern recognition tasks of varying complexity (*i.e.*, very easy, easy, medium, difficult and very difficult [9, 48], based on the visual complexity of the pattern). For each task, the participants are asked to identify and outline a simple figure within a complex one. The test consists of two main sections, with each section lasting 5 minutes and consisting of 9 pattern recognition tasks. The number of simple figures correctly identified constitute the score (ranging from 0 to 18), which is used to classify the subject as FD or FI (*i.e.*, the higher the score, the more FI the subject is).

Phase A: Classification Metrics Extraction

Hypothesis. The following null hypothesis was formed: *H0_1*: there is no significant difference between FDs and FIs in terms of visual behavior throughout visual pattern recognition tasks of varying difficulty.

Study procedure. We recruited 67 participants (29 females), ranging in age between 20 and 47 (31.1 ± 6.4), who had to meet a set of minimum requirements (*i.e.*, have never taken the GEFT before, and have no vision problems). Each participant undertook GEFT, and their score ranged from 1 to 18 (11.4 ± 3.7).

Study analysis. The analysis of the gaze data focuses on the comparison of participants' visual search strategy in relation to their cognitive style and the difficulty level of each pattern recognition task. We focused on the visual search behavior of the extreme types of FDs and FIs, as personalization has significant impact on such users. According to the participants' GEFT scores, we had 9 extreme FDs (*i.e.*, individuals who scored lower than 6) and 12 extreme FIs (*i.e.*, individuals who scored higher than 15).

According to the FD-I theory, we expected that FDs and FIs would follow a different visual search strategy. FIs were expected to follow a more oriented and organized approach, while FDs a more disoriented one. An eye-tracking metric that quantifies such behavior is the *gaze transition entropy* proposed by Krejtz et al. [44]. In general, entropy measures the lack of order or predictability (*i.e.*, the higher the entropy, the more disordered a system is). Accordingly, the gaze transitions made through specific AOIs of a stimulus, and the stationary distribution of eye-movements over the stimulus, have an impact on visual search behavior. They are expressed through transition entropy H_t, and stationary entropy H_s. Lower values of H_t indicate more careful viewing of AOIs, while greater H_t values indicate more randomness and more frequent switching between AOIs. Lower values of H_s are obtained when fixations tend to be concentrated on certain AOIs, while greater H_s indicates that visual attention is distributed more equally among AOIs. Each complex form of the pattern recognition task was divided into three vertical AOIs (Fig. 2), as originally performed in Krejtz et al. [44].

For each entropy type, we performed a within-subjects 2x5 ANOVA, with cognitive style (FD and FI) and task difficulty (very easy; easy; medium; difficult and very difficult) as the independent variables, and H_t and H_s as the dependent variables. In both cases, the 2x5 ANOVA tests met all assumptions.

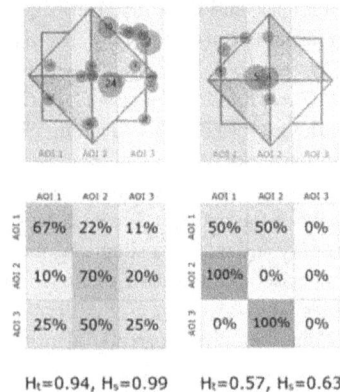

$H_t=0.94$, $H_s=0.99$ $H_t=0.57$, $H_s=0.63$

Figure 2: The scan-paths are transformed in transition matrixes, displaying the probability to perform a gaze transition across three vertical AOIs. The matrixes are then transformed in transition H_t and stationary H_s entropies.

Gaze transitions among AOIs. The results indicated that there was a statistically significant interaction effect between cognitive style and visual search task difficulty for transition entropy H_t ($F=6.212$, $p<.01$, *partial* $\eta^2=.430$). On very easy, easy and moderate tasks FIs had similar H_t values with FDs. However, as the complexity of the background figures increased, the H_t values

differed significantly, with FIs having lower levels of H_t than FDs in both cases ($t=2.141$, $df=18.014$, $p=.046$ for difficult tasks, and $t=2.221$, $df=18.815$, $p=.038$ for very difficult tasks). The higher H_t values of FDs indicate more randomness regarding their eye movements and a more exploratory character of their visual attention, rather than a systematic approach (Fig. 3).

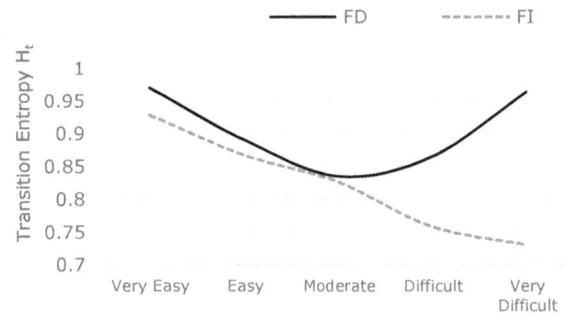

Figure 3: FI individuals produced more gaze transitions among AOIs (expressed in transition entropy H_t) than FDs. Their difference increases, as the task complexity increases

Distribution of visual attention on AOIs. The results indicated that there was a statistically significant interaction effect between cognitive style and visual search task difficulty for stationary entropy H_s ($F=3.406$, $p=.019$, *partial* $\eta^2=.292$). On very easy, easy and moderate tasks FIs had similar H_s values with FDs. However, as the complexity of the background figures increased, the H_s values differed significantly, with FIs having lower levels of H_s than FDs in both cases ($t=2.217$, $df=14.705$, $p=.043$ for difficult tasks, and $t=2.189$, $df=18.928$, $p=.041$ for very difficult tasks). Higher H_s values mean that subjects distribute their visual attention more equally among AOIs; lower ones show that their fixations are concentrated on certain AOIs (Fig. 4).

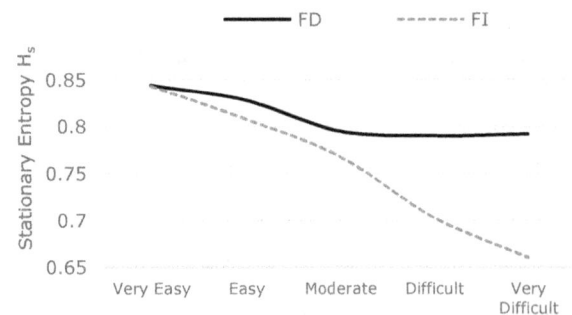

Figure 4: FD individuals distributed their attention more equally among AOIs (expressed in stationary entropy Hs) than FIs; the difference increases as the task complexity

Both findings indicate that individuals who have different cognitive styles, have also quantitatively different visual search approaches (in terms of transition and stationary entropies), when performing pattern recognition tasks of varying complexity. Their differences in visual search strategy are strongly correlated with the complexity factor of each task, which is highly correlated with participants' completion time and total score of GEFT [49].

Phase B: Classification Experiment

Training phase. The first step of the classification process is to build and test the training model. We formed the model training set, based on the extracted classification metrics of Phase A (*i.e.*, transition and stationary entropies). For model learning, we tried a number of different classifier types (Logistic Regression, Naïve Bayes, k-Nearest Neighbors, Classification and Regression Trees, and Support Vector Machines), with feature selection and 5-fold cross-validation for model evaluation (as we had a small dataset). Naïve Bayes (NB) performed best in terms of accuracy and, precision and recall (*i.e.*, F measure). NB classifier had accuracy of 80% (statistically significant difference from the other classifiers tested) and F measure of 72%. As a baseline of comparison, we used a classifier that always selects the most likely class (ZeroR).

The training model was based on the gaze entropies for both difficult and very difficult tasks, and thus the users should perform both tasks to collect the appropriate data. It is worth examining the training and testing performance of models based on each difficulty level. For the difficult task, k-Nearest Neighbor (kNN) classifier performed best (accuracy: 72%, and F measure: 71%); and for the very difficult task, NB classifier performed best (accuracy: 75%, and F measure: 72%).

Testing phase. To validate our classification scheme, we conducted a second eye-tracking study to collect gaze data and form the testing set. We recruited 21 individuals (9 females), aged between 25 and 41 (30.5 ± 4.2), who had to meet a set of minimum requirements (*i.e.*, had never taken GEFT before, and have no vision problems). All participants undertook GEFT, and their scores ranged between 4 and 18 (11.1 ± 3.9). Ten individuals were classified as FD, and eleven were classified as FI. Participants' eye-movements were recorded, and then analyzed in transition and stationary gaze entropies, forming the classification metric vector.

The task of the classifier is to infer whether a user belongs on either the FD or FI category for a given measure. Based on gaze entropies (both transition and stationary) and on difficulty levels (difficult and very difficult), NB classified correctly 81% of users (9/10 FDs and 8/11 FIs were correctly identified). The prediction certainty of NB classifier was 82.22% ± 16.67% for FDs, and 79.86% ± 19.88% for FIs. A notable point is that the false predictions were made on relatively low certainty rates (60.4% for the misclassified FD, and 50.6%, 61.3%, and 65.4% for the misclassified FIs).

As discussed, it is worth investigating whether we can achieve high accuracy scores, based only on one task difficulty level, to decrease the number of tasks required by the user to perform, and consequently the time needed, to infer the cognitive style. Based on gaze entropies for the difficult task only, kNN classified correctly the 67% of users (7/10 FDs and 7/11 FIs). Based on gaze entropies for the very difficult task, NB classified correctly the 76% of users (9/10 FDs and 7/11 FIs).

The NB classifier had high accuracy score (81%) when based on both task types (higher than the baseline classifier: 53%, as our sample was balanced). High accuracy was also achieved using only the very difficult task (76%), meaning that the cognitive style could be inferred measuring the gaze entropies only for one type of difficulty, and thus perform the classification in less time, which is vital in real-time applications.

4.2 Study II – Visual Decision-Making Activity

The second feasibility study entails a visual decision-making activity. Graphical user authentication (GUA) is a representative visual decision-making activity, as the users create their graphical passwords by visually scanning, processing, and deciding on the available options. For our study, a recognition-based GUA scheme was designed and developed, following guidelines of well-cited GUA schemes [50, 51]. The GUA scheme (Fig. 5) consisted of a grid of 120 unique images, and the users had to select five images in a specific order, to create their graphical password. Each image could only be selected once in a single password. The provided image policy was based on existing approaches and is typical in recognition-based GUAs [52, 53]. The graphical authentication activity consists of five sequential tasks (*i.e.*, selection of the first, second, third, fourth and fifth images).

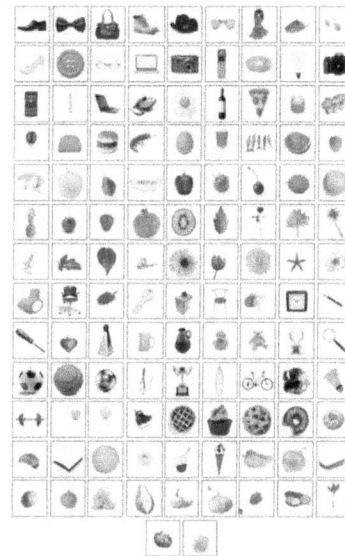

Figure 5: The GUA scheme consisted of 120 images (AOIs). Users had to select five images to create their passwords.

Phase A: Classification Metrics Extraction

Hypothesis. The following null hypothesis was formed: *H0₂*: there is no significant difference between FDs and FIs in terms of visual behavior throughout visual decision making tasks of specific sequence.

Study procedure. We recruited 51 individuals (16 females), aged between 18 and 40 (29.3 ± 5.8), who had to meet a set of minimum requirements (*i.e.*, have never taken GEFT before, have no vision problems, and have no experience with recognition-based GUA schemes). Each participant undertook the GEFT to be classified as FD or FI. Next, the participants used the designed GUA scheme to create a graphical key.

Study analysis. The analysis of the gaze data focuses on the comparison of participants' visual decision-making strategy in relation to their cognitive style and the sequence of each image selection task. Like in the visual search study, we focused on the extreme FDs and FIs. According to their GEFT scores (ranged between 4 and 17; 9.9 ± 3.1), we had 9 FDs and 11 FIs.

Several studies [7, 29, 54] indicate that FIs need more time to complete a visual decision-making task, as they tend to follow a more analytical approach. Such behavior reflects on low-level eye-tracking metrics, such as *fixation duration* and *number of fixations*. Hence, for each metric, we performed a within-subjects 2x5 ANOVA, with cognitive style (FD and FI) and task sequence (1st image selection; 2nd image selection; 3rd image selection; 4th image selection; 5th image selection) as the independent variables; and fixation duration and fixation count as the dependent variables. The AOIs of the study were the 120 grid images. In both cases, the 2x5 ANOVA tests met all assumptions.

Fixation duration per image selection. The results indicated that there is a statistically significant interaction effect between cognitive style and task sequence level on fixation duration (F=4.386, p=.003, *partial* η^2=.171). The fixation duration of FIs (54.30 ± 32.12 sec) was significantly longer than FDs' (19.78 ± 18.80 sec), from GUA load until the selection of the first image (F=29.664, p<.001, *partial* η^2=.259). No significant differences of fixation duration were revealed between FIs and FDs on selecting the second, third, fourth, and fifth image (Fig. 6).

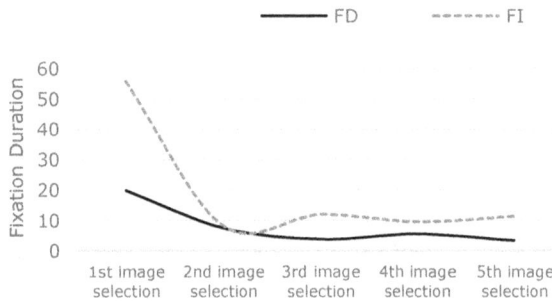

Figure 6: FIs had longer fixations than FDs, from the GUA load until the selection of the first image.

Fixation count per image selection. The results indicated that there is a statistically significant interaction effect between cognitive style and task sequence level on fixation count (F=4.172, p=.004, *partial* η^2=.156). The fixations made on the AOIs by FIs (76.01 ± 51.11) were significantly more than the ones made by FDs (24.89 ± 20.09), from GUA load until the selection of the first image (F=25.952, p<.001, *partial* η^2=.224). No significant differences of fixation count were observed between FIs and FDs on selecting the second, third, fourth, and fifth image (Fig. 7).

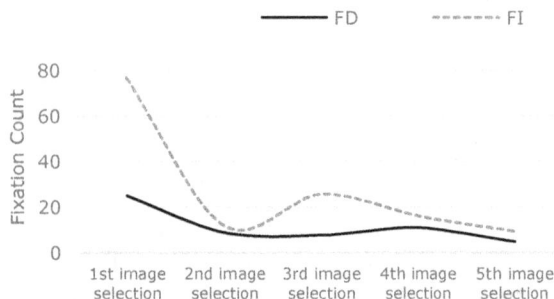

Figure 7: FIs produced more fixations than FDs, from the GUA load until the selection of the first image.

Both analyses show that FIs have significantly more and longer fixations than FDs for the selection of the first image. The difference of the two groups lies in the analytical nature of FIs, which in this case, is reflected on the larger number of images they visually scanned before deciding the first image, compared to the holistic nature of FDs, which is reflected on a more random selection of images, and thus a quicker first image selection.

Phase B: Classification Experiment

Training phase. The first step of the classification process is to build and test the training model. We formed the model training set, based on the extracted classification metrics of Phase A (*i.e.*, number and duration of fixations until the first image selection). For model learning, we tried a number of different classifier types (Logistic Regression, Naïve Bayes, k-Nearest Neighbors, Classification and Regression Trees, and Support Vector Machines), with feature selection and 5-fold cross-validation for model evaluation (as we had a small dataset). Naïve Bayes (NB) and Logistic Regression (LR) performed best in terms of accuracy and, precision and recall (*i.e.*, F measure). NB classifier had accuracy of 76.5% and F measure of 76%, while LR classifier had accuracy of 76.0% and F measure of 74%. As a baseline of comparison, we used a classifier that always selects the most likely class (ZeroR classifier).

Testing phase. To validate our classification scheme, we conducted a second eye-tracking study to collect gaze data and form the testing set. We recruited 20 individuals (9 females), aged between 25 and 38 (29.7 ± 4.1), who had to meet a set of minimum requirements (*i.e.*, have never taken GEFT before, have no vision problems, and have no experience with recognition-based GUA schemes). Each participant undertook the GEFT, to be classified as FD or FI, Their scores ranged from 3 to 18 (9.1 ± 3.4), and then, they used our GUA scheme to create a graphical key. Ten individuals were classified as FD and ten were classified as FI. Participants' eye-movements were recorded, and then analyzed in number and duration of fixations from page load until the first image selection. The fixation count and duration values for each individual form the classification metric vector, which then was used for the classification process.

The task of the classifier is to infer if a user belongs on either the FD or FI category for that measure. NB classified correctly 90% of users. All FDs were correctly identified, while 8/10 of FIs were correctly identified. The prediction certainty for FDs was 92.61% ± 1.96%, and for FIs it was 92.49% ± 8.49%. The false predictions had lower rates (75% and 81%). LR classified correctly 95% of users. All FDs were correctly identified, while 9/10 of FIs were correctly identified. The prediction certainty for FDs was 72.57% ± 6.38, and for FIs it was 80.59 ± 16.88. The false prediction had the lowest rate (56%).

Both classifiers (NB and LR) had high levels of accuracy, based on the extracted eye-tracking metrics, much higher than the baseline classifier (50%, as our sample was balanced). This level of accuracy was achieved by only using the data for the 1/5 (20%) of the total tasks required to create a graphical key. For this scope the elicitation is performed in less than one minute, and this could be an input to future adaptation and personalization schemes.

5 DISCUSSION

We proposed a method to infer human cognitive styles based on an eye-tracking multifactorial model. It consists of three main factors (human cognition, visual behavior, and activity), with an eye-tracking mechanism serving as the connection layer among them. The captured eye-tracking data is then used to classify individuals based on their cognitive style through an implicit elicitation process of three phases (data collection, data processing, and classification). As outlined in the introduction, the contribution of this work is two-fold: i) to investigate whether individuals of different cognitive styles have quantitatively measured differences in visual behavior and patterns (*e.g.*, number of fixations, gaze entropies, scan-paths) and ii) to infer cognitive styles using specific gaze measures, while performing activities of varying characteristics (*e.g.*, type, complexity, sequence),

To investigate the aforementioned questions, we conducted two feasibility studies, in which, individuals who were characterized as field-dependent or field-independent performed two visual activities of different type (*i.e.*, visual search and visual decision-making) and different characteristics (*i.e.*, complexity and sequence). Their eye movements were captured, processed, and transformed into specific eye-tracking measures, which were used to identify differences in the visual strategy the participants followed when performing each activity.

The eye-tracking analysis revealed that field-independent individuals followed a more organized and oriented visual search strategy when performing visual search tasks of increased difficulty, while field-dependent individuals followed a more disoriented approach. Their differences were quantitatively measured on transition and stationary gaze entropies. Based on these eye-tracking measures, we formed a training learning model on Naïve Bayes classifier (as it performed best). To test our model, we used the gaze entropy measures of a new dataset, and 81% of users were correctly identified, when considering both difficulty types; 67% when considering only the difficult tasks; and 76% when considering only the very difficult tasks.

When performing visual decision-making activities, field-independent individuals produced more and longer fixations on the first of the tasks required (sequence dependent activity). Based on both eye-tracking measures we formed a training learning model on Naïve Bayes and Logistic Regression classifiers (as they performed best). To test our model we used the fixation count and duration measures of a new dataset, and both classifiers performed well (90% accuracy rate for Naïve Bayes, and 95% accuracy rate for Logistic Regression).

In both cases, the classification scheme identified individuals correctly, based on their cognitive style, with high accuracy, and with low prediction certainty rates for misclassified individuals. Both classifiers were based on a small amount of collected eye gaze data to infer cognitive styles, and thus, the classification was completed in short-time. For example, in the visual decision-making sequence-dependent activity (Study I), the classification was based on only one of the five sequential tasks (20% of total tasks). Hence, the findings indicate that real-time elicitation is feasible.

In view of designing interactive systems that can adapt to individuals' preferred ways to visually process information, these findings provide important indicators as to which particular eye-tracking measures could be monitored for predicting and adapting to the various cognitive styles. Moreover, the findings indicate that such an implicit elicitation is feasible, and the model proposed can be used as a service for providing the classification results to information systems which support eye-gaze tracking, so the users can benefit from adaptation interventions.

Given that the recent technological advances have a major impact on the eye-tracking industry, the development and integration of affordable, robust, and mainstream eye-tracking solutions are expected to be widely applied to modern environments (*e.g.*, mixed reality) and assistive technology frameworks. In such frameworks, the eye movements play an important role, and thus, implicit elicitation through integrated eye-tracking tools, is realistic. Such an implicit elicitation mechanism could be complemented with varying eye gaze features, other interaction features, performance features, etc.

Regarding the generalizability of our method, the proposed model consists of dynamic and expandable layers (human cognition, visual behavior, activity), which form a knowledge base. The knowledge base is updated continuously with new validated data from credible studies, aiming to build more accurate learning models to improve implicit elicitation performance. In both studies the areas of interest were selected to be applicable to any corresponding visual activity type, thus contributing in the generalizability of our method. In particular, for the visual search activity, the overall task region was divided into three horizontal areas of same size, following Krejtz et al. [44] original approach. For the visual decision-making task, the areas of interest were the grid images.

The next step of this research is to conduct more feasibility studies, considering other cognitive styles, activity characteristics, and application domains, and increasing sample size, aiming to enhance the accuracy of the classification process, surpassing the limitations of the present studies. We envisage to develop an integrated implicit elicitation mechanism of cognitive styles to inform adaptive decisions in real-time based on eye-gaze data.

6 CONCLUSION

This paper revealed that individual differences in cognitive styles are quantitatively reflected on eye gaze data (gaze entropies, fixation duration and count) while users perform visual activities of varying type (*e.g.*, visual search, visual decision-making) and varying characteristics (*e.g.*, complexity, sequence). Moreover, this paper reported two classification experiments, which revealed that gaze data could drive the elaboration of an implicit elicitation process of human cognitive styles, with high accuracy level. Real-time and implicit elicitation of cognitive styles would open unprecedented opportunities for improving user experience and task performance through adaptation and personalization on a plethora of application and research domains, where literature has evidenced that individual differences, such as field dependence-independence, have a significant impact.

REFERENCES

[1] Maria Kozhevnikov 2007. Cognitive styles in the context of modern psychology: Toward an integrated framework of cognitive style. *Psychological Bulletin.* 133, 3 (2007), 464–481. DOI: http://dx.doi.org/10.1037/0033-2909.133.3.464.

[2] Nikos Tsianos, Panagiotis Germanakos, Zacharias Lekkas, Costas Mourlas, and George Samaras 2009. Eye-Tracking Users' Behavior in Relation to Cognitive Style within an E-learning Environment. *2009 Ninth IEEE International Conference on Advanced Learning Technologies* (Jul. 2009), 329–333. DOI: http://dx.doi.org/10.1109/ICALT.2009.110.

[3] Dereck Toker, Cristina Conati, Ben Steichen, and Giuseppe Carenini 2013. Individual user characteristics and information visualization: Connecting the dots through eye tracking. *Proceedings of the SIGCHI Conference on Human Factors in Computing Systems.* (2013), 295–304. DOI: http://dx.doi.org/10.1145/2470654.2470696.

[4] Marios Belk, Christos Fidas, Panagiotis Germanakos, and George Samaras 2015. Do human cognitive differences in information processing affect preference and performance of CAPTCHA? *International Journal of Human-Computer Studies.* 84, (2015), 1–18. DOI: http://dx.doi.org/10.1016/j.ijhcs.2015.07.002.

[5] Franco Mawad, Marcela Trías, Ana Giménez, Alejandro Maiche, and Gastón Ares 2015. Influence of cognitive style on information processing and selection of yogurt labels: Insights from an eye-tracking study. *Food Research International.* 74, (2015), 1–9. DOI: http://dx.doi.org/10.1016/j.foodres.2015.04.023.

[6] Khamsum Kinley, Dian Tjondronegoro, Helen Partridge, and Sylvia Edwards 2012. Human-computer interaction: the impact of users' cognitive styles on query reformulation behaviour during web searching. *Proceedings of the 24th Australian Computer-Human Interaction Conference on - OzCHI '12* (New York, New York, USA, 2012), 299–307. DOI: http://dx.doi.org/10.1145/2414536.2414586.

[7] George E. Raptis, Christos A. Fidas, and Nikolaos M. Avouris 2016. Do Field Dependence-Independence Differences of Game Players Affect Performance and Behaviour in Cultural Heritage Games? *Proceedings of the 2016 Annual Symposium on Computer-Human Interaction in Play - CHI PLAY '16* (New York, New York, USA, 2016), 38–43. DOI: http://dx.doi.org/10.1145/2967934.2968107.

[8] Richard Riding and Indra Cheema 1991. Cognitive Styles—an overview and integration. *Educational Psychology.* 11, 3-4 (Jan. 1991), 193–215. DOI: http://dx.doi.org/10.1080/0144341910110301.

[9] Herman A. Witkin 1950. Individual Differences in Ease of Perception of Embedded Figures. *Journal of Personality.* 19, 1 (Sep. 1950), 1–15. DOI: http://dx.doi.org/10.1111/j.1467-6494.1950.tb01084.x.

[10] Herman A. Witkin, Carol A. Moore, Donald R. Goodenough, and Patricia W. Cox 1975. Field-Dependent and Field-Independent Cognitive Styles and their Educational Implications. *ETS Research Bulletin Series.* 1975, 2 (Dec. 1975), 1–64. DOI: http://dx.doi.org/10.1002/j.2333-8504.1975.tb01065.x.

[11] Christopher W. Allinson and John Hayes 1996. The Cognitive Style Index: A Measure of Intuition-Analysis For Organizational Research. *Journal of Management Studies.* 33, 1 (Jan. 1996), 119–135. DOI: http://dx.doi.org/10.1111/j.1467-6486.1996.tb00801.x.

[12] Daniel Patanella et al. 2011. Cognitive Styles. *Encyclopedia of Child Behavior and Development.* Springer US. 382–383. DOI: http://dx.doi.org/10.1007/978-0-387-79061-9_611.

[13] Philip K. Oltman, Evelyn Raskin, and Herman A. Witkin 1971. *Group Embedded Figures Test.* Consulting Psychologists Press.

[14] George E. Raptis, Christos A. Fidas, and Nikolaos M. Avouris 2016. Using Eye Tracking to Identify Cognitive Differences: A Brief Literature Review. *20th Pan-Hellenic Conference in Informatics* (Patras, Greece, 2016). DOI: http://dx.doi.org/10.1145/3003733.3003762.

[15] Christian Gütl, Maja Pivec, Christian Trummer, Victor Manuel García-Barrios, Felix Mödritscher, Juergen Pripfl, and Martin Umgeher 2005. Adele (adaptive e-learning with eye-tracking): Theoretical background, system architecture and application scenarios. *European Journal of Open, Distance and E-Learning.* 8, 2 (2005).

[16] Efi A. Nisiforou and Andrew Laghos 2013. Do the eyes have it? Using eye tracking to assess students cognitive dimensions. *Educational Media International.* 50, 4 (Dec. 2013), 247–265. DOI: http://dx.doi.org/10.1080/09523987.2013.862363.

[17] Efi Nisiforou and Andrew Laghos 2016. Field Dependence–Independence and Eye Movement Patterns: Investigating Users' Differences Through an Eye Tracking Study. *Interacting with Computers.* 28, 4 (Jun. 2016), 407–420. DOI: http://dx.doi.org/10.1093/iwc/iwv015.

[18] Victor Manuel García Barrios, Christian Gütl, Alexandra M. Preis, Keith Andrews, Maja Pivec, Felix Mödritscher, and Christian Trummer 2004. AdELE: A Framework for Adaptive E-Learning through Eye Tracking. *Applied Sciences.* (2004).

[19] Efi A. Nisiforou, Eleni Michailidou, and Andrew Laghos 2014. Using Eye Tracking to Understand the Impact of Cognitive Abilities on Search Tasks. 46–57. DOI: http://dx.doi.org/10.1007/978-3-319-07509-9_5.

[20] Ben Steichen, Giuseppe Carenini, and Cristina Conati 2013. User-adaptive information visualization. *Proceedings of the 2013 international conference on Intelligent user interfaces - IUI '13* (New York, New York, USA, 2013), 317. DOI: http://dx.doi.org/10.1145/2449396.2449439.

[21] Marios Belk, Efi Papatheocharous, Panagiotis Germanakos, and George Samaras 2013. Modeling users on the World Wide Web based on cognitive factors, navigation behavior and clustering techniques. *Journal of Systems and Software.* 86, 12 (Dec. 2013), 2995–3012. DOI: http://dx.doi.org/10.1016/j.jss.2013.04.029.

[22] Sherry Y. Chen and Xiaohui Liu 2008. An Integrated Approach for Modeling Learning Patterns of Students in Web-Based Instruction. *ACM Transactions on Computer-Human Interaction.* 15, 1 (May 2008), 1–28. DOI: http://dx.doi.org/10.1145/1352782.1352783.

[23] Yi Wang, Jalal Mahmud, and Taikun Liu 2016. Understanding Cognitive Styles from User-Generated Social Media Content. *Proceedings of the Tenth International AAAI Conference on Web and Social Media (ICWSM 2016)* (Cologne, Germany, 2016).

[24] Chu-Han Chan, Chen-Wei Hsieh, and Sherry Y. Chen 2014. Cognitive styles and the use of electronic journals in a mobile context. *Journal of Documentation.* 70, 6 (2014), 997–1014. DOI: http://dx.doi.org/10.1108/JD-02-2014-0035.

[25] Ben Steichen, Michael M.a Wu, Dereck Toker, Cristina Conati, and Giuseppe Carenini 2014. Te,Te,Hi,Hi: Eye gaze sequence analysis for informing user-adaptive information visualizations. *Lecture Notes in Computer Science (including subseries Lecture Notes in Artificial Intelligence and Lecture Notes in Bioinformatics).* 8538, (2014), 183–194. DOI: http://dx.doi.org/10.1007/978-3-319-08786-3_16.

[26] Anatoly Yelizarov and Dennis Gamayunov 2014. Adaptive Visualization Interface That Manages User's Cognitive Load Based on Interaction Characteristics. *Proceedings of the 7th International Symposium on Visual Information Communication and Interaction - VINCI '14* (New York, New York, USA, 2014), 1–8. DOI: http://dx.doi.org/10.1145/2636240.2636844.

[27] Andreas Demetriou, George Spanoudis, Michael Shayer, Antigoni Mouyi, Smaragda Kazi, and Maria Platsidou 2013. Cycles in speed-working memory-G relations: Towards a developmental–differential theory of the mind. *Intelligence.* 41, 1 (Jan. 2013), 34–50. DOI: http://dx.doi.org/10.1016/j.intell.2012.10.010.

[28] Michael Kirton 1976. Adaptors and innovators: A description and measure. *Journal of Applied Psychology.* 61, 5 (1976), 622–629. DOI: http://dx.doi.org/10.1037/0021-9010.61.5.622.

[29] Charoula Angeli, Nicos Valanides, and Paul Kirschner 2009. Field dependence–independence and instructional-design effects on learners' performance with a computer-modeling tool. *Computers in Human Behavior.* 25, 6 (Nov. 2009), 1355–1366. DOI: http://dx.doi.org/10.1016/j.chb.2009.05.010.

[30] Dane M. Chapman and Judith G. Calhoun 2006. Validation of learning style measures: implications for medical education practice. *Medical Education.* 40, 6 (Jun. 2006), 576–583. DOI: http://dx.doi.org/10.1111/j.1365-2929.2006.02476.x.

[31] D. Shinar, E.D. McDowell, M.J. Rackoff, and T.H. Rockwell 1978. Field dependence and driver visual search behavior. *Human Factors.* 20, 5 (1978), 553–560.

[32] Peter Wittek, Ying-Hsang Liu, Sándor Darányi, Tom Gedeon, and Ik Soo Lim 2016. Risk and Ambiguity in Information Seeking: Eye Gaze Patterns Reveal Contextual Behavior in Dealing with Uncertainty. *Frontiers in Psychology.* 7, (Nov. 2016). DOI: http://dx.doi.org/10.3389/fpsyg.2016.01790.

[33] Andrew T. Duchowski 2007. *Eye tracking methodology: Theory and practice.* Springer London.

[34] Licheng Shi, Yuling Hu, and Jiali Wang 2016. Effects of cognitive styles on eye fixations: Evidence from drivers' eye movements. *International Journal of Psychology.* 51, 1153 (2016).

[35] Shi Zhuomin and Zheng Wanyi 2014. An Eye-tracking Study on the Differences Between Two Cognitive Styles of Individuals in Reading Advertising. *Journal of Marketing Science.* 10, 3 (2014), 128–145.

[36] James L.C. Wijnen and Cees J. Groot 1984. An eye movement analysis system (EMAS) for the identification of cognitive processes on figural tasks. *Behavior Research Methods, Instruments, & Computers.* 16, 3 (May 1984), 277–281. DOI: http://dx.doi.org/10.3758/BF03202402.

[37] Ming-Shiunn Huang and Brian Byrne 1978. Cognitive style and lateral eye movements. *British Journal of Psychology.* 69, 1 (1978), 85–90. DOI: http://dx.doi.org/10.1111/j.2044-8295.1978.tb01635.x.

[38] Maria Solé Puig, Laura Puigcerver, J. Antonio Aznar-Casanova, and Hans Supèr 2013. Difference in Visual Processing Assessed by Eye Vergence Movements. *PLoS ONE.* 8, 9 (Sep. 2013), e72041. DOI: http://dx.doi.org/10.1371/journal.pone.0072041.

[39] Kerstin Gidlöf, Annika Wallin, Richard Dewhurst, and Kenneth Holmqvist 2013. Using eye tracking to trace a cognitive process: Gaze behaviour during decision making in a natural environment. *Journal of Eye Movement Research.* 6, 1 (2013). DOI: http://dx.doi.org/10.16910/jemr.6.1.3.

[40] George E. Raptis, Christos A. Fidas, and Nikolaos M. Avouris 2016. Differences of Field Dependent/Independent Gamers on Cultural Heritage Playing: Preliminary Findings of an Eye-Tracking Study. 199–206. DOI: http://dx.doi.org/10.1007/978-3-319-48974-2_22.

[41] Martha E. Crosby and W. Wesley Peterson 1991. Using Eye Movements to Classify Search Strategies. *Proceedings of the Human Factors Society Annual Meeting.* 35, 20 (Sep. 1991), 1476–1480. DOI: http://dx.doi.org/10.1177/154193129103502012.

[42] Rodney C. Conklin, Walter Muir, and Frederick J. Boersma 1968. Field Dependency-Independency and Eye-Movement Patterns. *Perceptual and Motor Skills.* 26, 1 (Feb. 1968), 59–65. DOI: http://dx.doi.org/10.2466/pms.1968.26.1.59.

[43] Sukru Eraslan, Yeliz Yesilada, and Simon Harper 2016. Eye tracking scanpath analysis on web pages. *Proceedings of the Ninth Biennial ACM Symposium on Eye Tracking Research & Applications - ETRA '16* (New York, New York, USA, 2016), 103–110. DOI: http://dx.doi.org/10.1145/2857491.2857519.

[44] Krzysztof Krejtz, Andrew Duchowski, Tomasz Szmidt, Izabela Krejtz, Fernando González Perilli, Ana Pires, Anna Vilaro, and Natalia Villalobos 2015. Gaze Transition Entropy. *ACM Transactions on Applied Perception.* 13, 1 (Dec. 2015), 1–20. DOI: http://dx.doi.org/10.1145/2834121.

[45] Mark Hall, Eibe Frank, Geoffrey Holmes, Bernhard Pfahringer, Peter Reutemann, and Ian H. Witten 2009. The WEKA data mining software. *ACM SIGKDD Explorations Newsletter.* 11, 1 (Nov. 2009), 10. DOI: http://dx.doi.org/10.1145/1656274.1656278.

[46] Oleg V Komogortsev, Denise V Gobert, Sampath Jayarathna, Do Hyong Koh, and Sandeep M. Gowda 2010. Standardization of Automated Analyses of Oculomotor Fixation and Saccadic Behaviors. *IEEE Transactions on Biomedical Engineering.* 57, 11 (Nov. 2010), 2635–2645. DOI: http://dx.doi.org/10.1109/TBME.2010.2057429.

[47] Mohammad Khatib and Rasoul Mohammad Hosseinpur 2011. On the Validity of the Group Embedded Figure Test (GEFT). *Journal of Language Teaching and Research.* 2, 3 (May 2011). DOI: http://dx.doi.org/10.4304/jltr.2.3.640-648.

[48] Kurt Gottschaldt 1938. Gestalt factors and repetition. *A source book of Gestalt psychology.* Kegan Paul, Trench, Trubner & Company. 109–135. DOI: http://dx.doi.org/10.1037/11496-009.

[49] George E. Raptis, Christos A. Fidas, and Nikolaos M. Avouris 2017. On Implicit Elicitation of Cognitive Strategies using Gaze Transition Entropies in Pattern Recognition Tasks. *Proceedings of the 2017 CHI Conference Extended Abstracts on Human Factors in Computing Systems - CHI EA '17* (New York, New York, USA, 2017), 1993–2000. DOI: http://dx.doi.org/10.1145/3027063.3053106.

[50] Rachna Dhamija and Adrian Perrig 2000. Deja Vu-A User Study: Using Images for Authentication. *USENIX Security Symposium* (2000), 4.

[51] Martin Mihajlov and Borka Jerman-Blažič 2011. On designing usable and secure recognition-based graphical authentication mechanisms. *Interacting with Computers.* 23, 6 (Nov. 2011), 582–593. DOI: http://dx.doi.org/10.1016/j.intcom.2011.09.001.

[52] Robert Biddle, Sonia Chiasson, and P.C. Van Oorschot 2012. Graphical passwords. *ACM Computing Surveys.* 44, 4 (Aug. 2012), 1–41. DOI: http://dx.doi.org/10.1145/2333112.2333114.

[53] Yao Ma, Jinjuan Feng, Libby Kumin, and Jonathan Lazar 2013. Investigating User Behavior for Authentication Methods. *ACM Transactions on Accessible Computing.* 4, 4 (Jul. 2013), 1–27. DOI: http://dx.doi.org/10.1145/2493171.2493173.

[54] Christina Katsini, Christos Fidas, Marios Belk, Nikolaos Avouris, and George Samaras 2017. Influences of Users' Cognitive Strategies on Graphical Password Composition. *Proceedings of the 2017 CHI Conference Extended Abstracts on Human Factors in Computing Systems - CHI EA '17* (New York, New York, USA, 2017), 2698–2705. DOI: http://dx.doi.org/10.1145/3027063.3053217.

Group Recommendations by Learning Rating Behavior

Dimitris Sacharidis
TU Wien
E-Commerce Group
Austria
dimitris@ec.tuwien.ac.at

ABSTRACT

In many domains, it is often required to provide recommendations for groups, instead of individual users. Existing approaches try to compensate for the lack of group profiles, by either merging individual profiles, or treating users separately and then fusing the recommendations. Both paradigms thus fail to account for the different roles and behaviors people assume when making group decisions. In this work, we propose two novel group recommendation models that explicitly try to model the behavior of group members and distinguish it from that when they act alone. A detailed evaluation has shown that our models consistently provide significantly better recommendations. In addition, useful conclusions are drawn regarding the favorable settings of existing techniques.

KEYWORDS

Collaborative Filtering; Group Recommendation; Latent Factors

1 INTRODUCTION

Recommender systems are nowadays ubiquitous, providing recommendations in diverse domains, e.g., for movies/tv programs (Netflix), e-commerce (Amazon), music (Spotify), apps (Apple App Store and Google Play), books (Goodreads). Usually, the underlying mechanism for providing recommendations, follows the principles of collaborative filtering (CF), where the idea is to leverage the observed interests and ratings from other users [22]. More recently, and following their success at the Netflix prize, *latent factor models* have become the standard in materializing the CF idea [10, 11].

While traditional research on recommender systems has almost exclusively focused on providing recommendations to *single* users, there exist many cases, where the system needs to suggest items to *groups* of users [1, 4, 16–18, 25]. As examples, consider a group of friends seeking to go together on a vacation, or a family that decides on a movie to watch at home. Existing methods for group recommendations basically follow one of two paradigms. The first, hereafter termed PROF-AGG, is to explicitly construct a group profile by combining (aggregating) the profiles of individual members. In this way, the group can be treated as a *pseudo user*, and thus standard techniques can be employed to provide recommendations

for the group. The second paradigm, termed REC-AGG, is to first compute recommendations for each member separately, and then employ an aggregation strategy across them to compile the group recommendations. Inspired by social choice theory, numerous aggregation strategies for profiles and recommendations exist.

These two paradigms share some drawbacks. First, they assume certain decision dynamics within an group, i.e., the aggregation strategy, and often fix on this. Second, they treat group members the same as individual users, mostly assuming that the behavior and preferences of users in groups is identical to that when they decide alone. Of course, there are some notable exceptions that avoid these drawbacks. For instance the hybrid switching strategy of [3] (albeit between group, general, and individual recommendations) for the former, INTRIGUE [1] where not all members are treated equally, [21] that includes personality and social trust, and [7] that considers relationship strength for the latter. However these works rely on additional information about group members, which one cannot assume in a pure CF setting.

For groups that are relatively long-standing, it is reasonable to expect that sufficient information has been collected in order to build a group profile, eliminating the need for artificial profile aggregation. However, we note that in this case the recommender may suffer from cold-start problems. For instance, the system would not be able to assess *cold items* for which no or very few ratings by any group is available, even though this item may have been rated by individual users. Similarly, such a system cannot provide recommendations for *cold groups*, with no or little group profile, even though members of the groups may have individual profiles. An approach to counter these cold-start problems would be to employ PROF-AGG, which however defeats the purpose at it inherits its shortcomings.

In this work, we propose methods that address the aforementioned issues. We assume a pure collaborative filtering setting, where only a history of user-item ratings along with a few group-item ratings are available. This is a reasonable assumption, as past work has considered such sparse group profiles [8, 12], and a relevant challenge was set up [19]. The problem we address is how to best exploit the group and user profiles for group recommendations. We base our approach on the understanding that people assume different roles (e.g., leaders or followers) when in groups, or even across groups (e.g., in work and in family), and thus may exhibit substantially different behavior compared to them acting individually. Our proposed methods attempt to explicitly *learn the discrepancies between individual and group rating behavior*.

Our first model, termed RESIDUAL, presupposes that the group rating differs from the average member rating by a sum of *residuals* for each group member. For a particular user and a particular group, her residual rating captures the difference between her individual

UMAP '17, July 09-12, 2017, Bratislava, Slovakia
© 2017 Copyright held by the owner/author(s). Publication rights licensed to Association for Computing Machinery.
ACM ISBN 978-1-4503-4635-1/17/07...$15.00
http://dx.doi.org/10.1145/3079628.3079691

and group ratings averaged over all items in the group profile. As only very few of these residuals can actually be computed, due to the sparsity in the group profiles, we employ matrix factorization to predict the missing residuals. RESIDUAL can thus account for different rating behavior of users within groups and across groups. Our second model, termed TRIAD, presupposes that group ratings are computed as a weighted average of member ratings. Therefore, the weight of a particular user captures her behavior change as a group member. TRIAD learns the user behavior weights together with conventional latent factors by jointly examining user and group ratings. While both models assume that group ratings are generated by a linear combination of individual ratings, our evaluation shows that they perform well even when this may not be the case, e.g., in least-misery or dictatorship situations.

Evaluating group recommendations is a particularly complex task. Even when ground truth data is available, a rather rare sighting [5, 12, 24], measuring the satisfaction of user in group decisions remains an open research topic [15]. To handle the absence of real data, researchers typically resort to one of two approaches. In the first, the group rating of an item is synthesized to be the average (or some other aggregate) of individual ratings. Then, one can use standard evaluation metrics to quantify how far the predicted group ratings is from the synthesized. In the second approach, the predicted group recommendations are evaluated for each group member individually, and then averaged [2, 3]. As both approaches compute some average satisfaction, they tend to favor average aggregation strategies as remarked in [14].

More generally, presuming a particular group satisfaction metric (e.g., the average member satisfaction) naturally introduces bias. To combat this, we make a simple but significant contribution towards an unbiased evaluation of group recommenders under synthetic datasets. We construct multiple sets of synthetic group ratings assuming different group satisfaction criteria, and measure the performance of a group recommender at each. Then, a method consistently outperforming others under multiple criteria constitutes a stronger and less biased indication of its effectiveness.

We perform a detailed evaluation on real and synthetically generated group ratings under a broad range of group aggregation strategies. We compare existing methods and identify their favorable settings. More importantly, we evaluate our two proposed models and find that they are significantly more accurate than the standard methods in all settings and under multiple evaluation criteria.

The remainder of this paper is structured as follows. Section 2 defines the problem and establishes the necessary background describing existing group recommendation methods. Section 3 presents our two proposed models for group recommendations. Then, Section 4 presents a thorough experimental evaluation of existing work and ours. Finally, Section 5 concludes the paper.

2 PROBLEM DEFINITION AND BACKGROUND

In Section 2.1, we first formally define the group recommendation problem. Then, in Section 2.2 we briefly overview a simple latent factor model. In Section 2.3, we categorize existing work on group recommendations.

2.1 Problem Definition

We consider a set of users $\mathcal{U} = \{u_i\}$, a set of items $\mathcal{V} = \{v_j\}$, and a set of groups $\mathcal{G} = \{g_k\} \subseteq 2^{\mathcal{U}}$; we use the subscripts i, j, k to refer to an individual user, item, or group, respectively. Further, we assume we have a set $\mathcal{R}^{\mathcal{U}}$ of user-item ratings, and a set $\mathcal{R}^{\mathcal{G}}$ of group-item ratings. Then, the problem of recommending items to groups can be abstractly stated as follows.

Problem 1. [Collaborative Filtering Group Recommendation] Given $\mathcal{U}$, $\mathcal{V}$, $\mathcal{G}$ and ratings $\mathcal{R}^{\mathcal{U}}$, $\mathcal{R}^{\mathcal{G}}$, predict for each group $g_k \in \mathcal{G}$ the rating of each not previously consumed item.

Throughout this paper, we follow the notational convention that bold small letters, e.g., $\mathbf{x}$, indicate column vectors, and bold capital letters, e.g., $\mathbf{A}$, denote matrices.

2.2 Matrix Factorization for Recommendations

A family of very popular techniques for providing item recommendations is the latent factor models, also known as *matrix factorization* [10]. The basic idea is to view the user-item ratings as a sparse matrix, for which we wish to predict the values of its empty cells. This is achieved by computing a low-rank approximation of the rankings matrix.

Specifically, we assume that each user u_i is associated with an f-dimensional factor (column) vector $\mathbf{u}_i$, and similarly each item v_j with an f-dimensional factor vector $\mathbf{v}_j$. Then, the predicted rating of item v_j by user u_i is computed as the inner product of the corresponding factor vectors:

$$\hat{r}_{ij} = \mathbf{u}_i^T \mathbf{v}_j. \tag{1}$$

Under this model, the objective is then to compute the factor vectors of each user and item so that they provide accurate estimations of the known ratings without overfitting. Note that there are many ways to formulate this goal; here we consider the simplest approach which minimizes the regularized squared error on the set of ratings [10]:

$$\sum_{(u_i, v_j) \in \mathcal{R}^{\mathcal{U}}} (r_{ij} - \mathbf{u}_i^T \mathbf{v}_j)^2 - \lambda(\|\mathbf{U}\|_F^2 + \|\mathbf{V}\|_F^2),$$

where $\mathbf{U}$, $\mathbf{V}$ denote the $f \times |\mathcal{U}|$ user matrix and the $f \times |\mathcal{V}|$ item matrix, respectively, consisting of all user and item factor vectors, λ is a parameter controlling the extent of regularization, and $\|\mathbf{A}\|_F$ denotes the Frobenius norm of matrix $\mathbf{A}$ used for regularization.

To minimize the objective function and determine the factor vectors, one can apply standard techniques, e.g., Alternating Least Squares (ALS), or Stochastic Gradient Descent (SGD).

2.3 Group Recommender Systems

Literature on group recommenders is rich; we refer the reader to [9, 14] for a systematic treatment of this research area. In this work, we consider collaborative filtering techniques, focus on the task of recommending a single item to the group, and optimize primarily for the prediction error, i.e., the difference between the predicted and the actual group rating.

In the absence of group profiles, the recommender system needs to compensate. There are two basic paradigms in which an existing recommender for individual users can be extended to provide group recommendations. In PROF-AGG, also referred to as aggregated model [3] or group model [13], a group profile is created by aggregating the profiles of group members. In REC-AGG, recommendations for group members are compiled independently, and are then fused to create group recommendations. Essentially, in the CF case, both paradigms perform an aggregation of either actual or predicted ratings.

There are numerous aggregation strategies that one can employ in either paradigm. These are mostly inspired by social choice theory ideas; see [13] for an overview, and a study on how people select recommendations for a group so as to balance the preferences of the group members. Popular strategies include taking the average, the minimum a.k.a. least misery principle of not strongly displeasing any member, the maximum for satisfying the maximum pleasure among members, the product. For reference we mention the following: MusicFX [16] implements a least misery criterion in group modeling (PROF-min); POLYLENS [18] aggregates recommendations assuming least misery (REC-min); INTRIGUE [1] is an interesting hybrid that identifies sub-groups among groups (e.g., children, or disabled persons), creates a model for each sub-group (PROF-AGG), and then fuses the sub-group recommendations under a weighted scheme (REC-avg); Yu's TV recommender [25] constructs group profiles so as to minimize distance among individual profiles (PROF-AGG); the content-based TV recommender in [24] investigates the optimal aggregation strategy for group modeling (PROF-AGG).

A significant line of work concerns the evaluation of group recommenders. The seminal work of [15] studies what factors influence group satisfaction and how it differs from individual satisfaction. A comparison of PROF-AGG strategies can be found at [23]. Various CF-based rank aggregation techniques (e.g., [6]) for REC-AGG are examined in [2]. A comparison of both PROF-AGG and REC-AGG CF-based techniques in [3] concludes that group profile modeling is better than recommendation aggregation.

Other approaches for group recommendations have also appeared. Most notably, the information matching approach of [8], denoted as INF-MATCH, predicts the relevance (instead of the rating) of items to groups. Each user is assumed to give ratings according to a 2-Poisson mixture model, where one component describes the ratings for relevant items (those with rating above some threshold), and the other those for irrelevant or unrated items. Similarly, each item receives ratings according to another 2-Poisson mixture model. INF-MATCH predicts the relevance probability of an item to a user by taking into account the mixture models of all items and users. Then, to predict the relevance probability of an item to a group, INF-MATCH follows the Least Misery strategy, assigning to the group the minimum relevance probability among its members.

3 OUR GROUP RECOMMENDER MODELS

In this section, we present our contributions to the group recommendation problem. In Section 3.1, we describe RESIDUAL that tries to estimate the difference in the behavior of a user in a group and alone. In Section 3.2, we present TRIAD that learns the strength with which a user enforces her preferences in a group.

3.1 The Residual Model

The residual model, denoted as RESIDUAL, predicts the rating of an item v_j by group g_k as:

$$\hat{r}_{kj} = \frac{1}{|g_k|} \sum_{u_i \in g_k} (\hat{r}_{ij} + \hat{\xi}_{ik}), \qquad (2)$$

where $\hat{r}_{ij}$ is the predicted rating (according to some model) of item v_j by user u_i, and $\hat{\xi}_{ik}$ is the *predicted residual rating* of user u_i when in group g_k. The intuition, here is that the actual group rating r_{kj} differs from the average user rating by some (unknown, but estimated) group-specific user residual ξ_{ik}. Note that when $\hat{\xi} = 0$ for all users and groups, the RESIDUAL model essentially becomes the REC-avg technique described in Section 2.3.

In the following, we discuss how we compute the predicted residual ratings. Consider a user u_i being a member of group g_k, and let $\mathcal{V}_k$ denote the set of items group g_k has rated. Then, given ratings $\mathcal{R}^{\mathcal{G}}$, and a model for predicting user-item ratings, we define the *residual rating* ξ_{ik} of user u_i in group g_k as:

$$\xi_{ik} = \frac{1}{|\mathcal{V}_k|} \sum_{v_j \in \mathcal{V}_k} (r_{kj} - \hat{r}_{ij}). \qquad (3)$$

Now, consider the sparse $|\mathcal{U}| \times |\mathcal{G}|$ matrix Ξ, which has value ξ_{ik} computed as above when user $u_i \in g_k$, value $\xi_{ik} = 0$ when $u_i \notin g_k$, and unknown value elsewhere. We factorize the Ξ matrix into a $f_\xi \times |\mathcal{U}|$ matrix $\mathbf{P}$ and a $f_\xi \times |\mathcal{G}|$ matrix $\mathbf{Q}$, using a technique similar to that in Section 2.2, to obtain a rank f_ξ approximation. Then, the predicted residual rating of user u_i when in group g_k is:

$$\hat{\xi}_{ik} = \mathbf{p}_i^T \mathbf{q}_k,$$

where $\mathbf{p}_i$ is the factor vector in matrix $\mathbf{P}$ corresponding to user u_i, and $\mathbf{q}_k$ is the factor vector in matrix $\mathbf{Q}$ corresponding to group g_k.

To better understand the reasoning behind the RESIDUAL model, consider the following. Assume that we have a complete set of ratings for group g_k, i.e., all items have a group rating and thus $\mathcal{V}_k = \mathcal{V}$. Then, for each member u_i of g_k, its predicted residual rating is equal to its residual rating $\frac{1}{|\mathcal{V}|} \sum_{v_j \in \mathcal{V}} (r_{kj} - \hat{r}_{ij})$. Replacing this value into Equation 2 and expanding we obtain:

$$\hat{r}_{kj} = \frac{1}{|g_k|} \sum_{u_i \in g_k} \hat{r}_{ij} + \frac{1}{|\mathcal{V}|} \sum_{v_j \in \mathcal{V}} r_{kj} - \frac{1}{|g_k||\mathcal{V}|} \sum_{u_i \in g_k} \sum_{v_j \in \mathcal{V}} \hat{r}_{ij}.$$

Then computing the mean of $\hat{r}_{kj}$ over all items $v_j \in V$, we derive:

$$E_{v_j \in V}[\hat{r}_{kj}] = \frac{1}{|\mathcal{V}|} \sum_{v_j \in \mathcal{V}} r_{kj},$$

where $E_{v_j \in V}[]$ denotes expectation over items v_j taken uniformly at random from V. In other words, the mean predicted rating of group g_k is equal to the average actual rating that group g_k gives to items.

Learning. In our implementation of the RESIDUAL model, we use matrix factorization as the underlying model for predicting user-item ratings, which requires matrices $\mathbf{U}, \mathbf{V}$ as its parameters, as defined in Section 2.2. In addition, RESIDUAL requires two additional matrices $\mathbf{P}, \mathbf{Q}$ factorizing matrix Ξ of residual ratings as described.

First, we learn parameters $\mathbf{U}, \mathbf{V}$ from the set $\mathcal{R}^{\mathcal{U}}$ of user-item ratings using SGD, similar to [10]; details are omitted. Next, we compute the set of non-empty entries of matrix Ξ according to Equation 3. Finally, we learn $\mathbf{P}, \mathbf{Q}$ using SGD on the aforementioned set of Ξ entries; details are omitted.

3.2 The Triad Model

The triad model, denoted as TRIAD, predicts the rating of an item v_j by group g_k as:

$$\hat{r}_{kj} = \frac{1}{|g_k|} \sum_{u_i \in g_k} b_i \cdot \hat{r}_{ij}, \qquad (4)$$

where $\hat{r}_{ij}$ is the predicted rating of item v_j by user u_i, and b_i is the *group behavior* of user u_i. The intuition here is that each user has a global (unknown) behavior when she becomes a member of a group. Similar to RESIDUAL, setting $b_i = 1$ for all users, makes the TRIAD model identical to the REC-avg technique described in Section 2.3.

TRIAD uses matrix factorization to predict user-item ratings (Section 2.2). Therefore, it employs matrices $\mathbf{U}, \mathbf{V}$ and Equation 1 to predict $\hat{r}_{ij}$. In addition, the TRIAD model uses a third parameter — hence its name, the $|\mathcal{U}|$-dimensional group behavior vector $\mathbf{b}$, containing the group behavior of each user.

To rewrite Equation 4 using matrices, we introduce some additional notation. For any group g_k, let $\mathbf{g}_k$ denote its $|\mathcal{U}|$-dimensional *user membership vector*, where its i-th coordinate has value $\frac{1}{|g_k|}$ if user u_i is a member of g_k, and zero otherwise. Moreover, let symbol $\circ$ denote the element-wise (Hadamard) product for vectors: $(\mathbf{x} \circ \mathbf{y})_{[i]} = \mathbf{x}_{[i]} \mathbf{y}_{[i]}$. Then, Equation 4 is equivalent to:

$$\hat{r}_{kj} = (\mathbf{g}_k \circ \mathbf{b})^T \mathbf{U}^T \mathbf{v}_j. \qquad (5)$$

Observe that the $(\mathbf{g}_k \circ \mathbf{b})^T$ matrix essentially plays the role of the $\frac{1}{|g_k|} \sum_{u_i \in g_k} b_i$ part in Equation 4.

Learning. In what follows we describe how to learn the TRIAD parameters. Note that contrary to RESIDUAL, all model parameters are learned together in one phase, using the user-item *and* the group-item ratings.

We make the assumption that each observed user rating r_{ij} (resp. group rating r_{kj}) follows a Gaussian distribution with mean $\hat{r}_{ij}$ (resp. $\hat{r}_{kj}$) and variance σ^2.

Therefore, given rankings $\mathcal{R}^{\mathcal{U}}, \mathcal{R}^{\mathcal{G}}$, the likelihood of the TRIAD model is:

$$p(\mathcal{R}^{\mathcal{U}}, \mathcal{R}^{\mathcal{G}} | \mathbf{U}, \mathbf{V}, \mathbf{b}) = \prod_{(i,j) \in \mathcal{R}^{\mathcal{U}}} \mathcal{N}(r_{ij}; \hat{r}_{ij}, \sigma^2) \prod_{(k,j) \in \mathcal{R}^{\mathcal{G}}} \mathcal{N}(r_{kj}; \hat{r}_{kj}, \sigma^2)$$

where $\mathcal{N}(x; \mu, \sigma^2)$ is the probability density function of the Gaussian distribution with mean μ and variance σ^2.

We next assign spherical Gaussian priors [20] on the model parameters:

$$p(\mathbf{U} | \sigma_{\mathbf{U}}^2) = \prod_{u_i} \mathcal{N}(\mathbf{u}_i; 0, \sigma_{\mathbf{U}}^2 \mathbf{I})$$

$$p(\mathbf{V} | \sigma_{\mathbf{V}}^2) = \prod_{v_j} \mathcal{N}(\mathbf{v}_j; 0, \sigma_{\mathbf{V}}^2 \mathbf{I})$$

$$p(\mathbf{b} | \sigma_{\mathbf{b}}^2) = \prod_{u_i} \mathcal{N}(b_i; 0.5, \sigma_{\mathbf{b}}^2)$$

We seek to maximize the posterior:

$$p(\mathbf{U}, \mathbf{V}, \mathbf{b} | \mathcal{R}^{\mathcal{U}}, \mathcal{R}^{\mathcal{G}}, \sigma_\theta) \propto p(\mathcal{R}^{\mathcal{U}}, \mathcal{R}^{\mathcal{G}} | \mathbf{U}, \mathbf{V}, \mathbf{b}) p(\mathbf{U} | \sigma_{\mathbf{U}}^2) p(\mathbf{V} | \sigma_{\mathbf{V}}^2) p(\mathbf{b} | \sigma_{\mathbf{b}}^2)$$

where $\sigma_\theta^2 = \{\sigma^2, \sigma_{\mathbf{U}}^2, \sigma_{\mathbf{T}}^2, \sigma_{\mathbf{b}}^2\}$, or minimize correspondingly the negative log posterior, which is equivalent (after eliminating terms depending on σ_θ^2 and constants) to minimizing the following regularized error function:

$$E = \sum_{(i,j) \in \mathcal{R}^{\mathcal{U}}} \left(r_{ij} - \mathbf{u}_i^T \mathbf{v}_j \right)^2 + \sum_{(k,j) \in \mathcal{R}^{\mathcal{G}}} \left(r_{kj} - (\mathbf{g}_k \circ \mathbf{b})^T \mathbf{U}^T \mathbf{v}_j \right)^2 +$$
$$+ \lambda_{\mathbf{U}} \|\mathbf{U}\|_F^2 + \lambda_{\mathbf{V}} \|\mathbf{V}\|_F^2 + \lambda_{\mathbf{b}} \|\mathbf{b}'\|^2, \qquad (6)$$

where $\lambda_{\mathbf{U}} = \sigma_{\mathbf{U}}^2/\sigma^2$, $\lambda_{\mathbf{V}} = \sigma_{\mathbf{V}}^2/\sigma^2$, $\lambda_{\mathbf{b}} = \sigma_{\mathbf{b}}^2/\sigma^2$, and $\mathbf{b}' = \mathbf{b} - 0.5\mathbf{I}$.

To learn the parameters $\mathbf{U}, \mathbf{V}, \mathbf{b}$ of TRIAD from the sets of ratings $\mathcal{R}^{\mathcal{U}}, \mathcal{R}^{\mathcal{G}}$, we perform SGD as follows. We rewrite Equation 6 as:

$$E = \sum_{(i,j) \in \mathcal{R}^{\mathcal{U}}} E_{\mathcal{R}^{\mathcal{U}}} + \sum_{(k,j) \in \mathcal{R}^{\mathcal{G}}} E_{\mathcal{R}^{\mathcal{G}}},$$

where:

$$E_{\mathcal{R}^{\mathcal{U}}} = \left(r_{ij} - \mathbf{u}_i^T \mathbf{v}_j \right)^2 + \lambda_{\mathbf{U}}' \|\mathbf{U}\|_F^2 + \lambda_{\mathbf{V}}' \|\mathbf{V}\|_F^2$$

$$E_{\mathcal{R}^{\mathcal{G}}} = \left(r_{kj} - (\mathbf{g}_k \circ \mathbf{b})^T \mathbf{U}^T \mathbf{v}_j \right)^2 + \lambda_{\mathbf{U}}' \|\mathbf{U}\|_F^2 + \lambda_{\mathbf{V}}' \|\mathbf{V}\|_F^2 + \lambda_{\mathbf{b}}' \|\mathbf{b}'\|^2,$$

and $\lambda_{\mathbf{U}}' = \lambda_{\mathbf{U}}/(|\mathcal{R}^{\mathcal{U}}| + |\mathcal{R}^{\mathcal{G}}|)$, $\lambda_{\mathbf{V}}' = \lambda_{\mathbf{V}}/(|\mathcal{R}^{\mathcal{U}}| + |\mathcal{R}^{\mathcal{G}}|)$, $\lambda_{\mathbf{b}}' = \lambda_{\mathbf{b}}/|\mathcal{R}^{\mathcal{G}}|$.

Algorithm 1 presents the learning algorithm for TRIAD. Initially random values are chosen for the TRIAD parameters (Line 1). Then, the outer loop (Lines 2–15) is executed until convergence (or a maximum number of iterations is reached). In each iteration of the outer loop, all ratings from $\mathcal{R}^{\mathcal{U}}$ and $\mathcal{R}^{\mathcal{G}}$ are considered in the inner loop (Lines 3–14). On the other hand, in each iteration of the inner loop, a single rating is considered. This rating is chosen to be drawn from a set of ratings with probability proportional to the set's size. This is accomplished by flipping a coin with probability $|\mathcal{R}^{\mathcal{U}}|/(|\mathcal{R}^{\mathcal{U}}| + |\mathcal{R}^{\mathcal{G}}|)$ (random variable X sampled at Line 4). Once the set of ratings to draw from has been established, a rating is selected uniformly at random (Line 6 or 10). Then, the parameter values are updated in a gradient descent manner with learning rate η (Lines 7–9 or 11–13). An important thing to note is that a user rating r_{ij} updates vectors $\mathbf{u}_i$ and $\mathbf{v}_j$, whereas a group rating r_{kj} updates the user vectors of all g_k members (hence the matrix $\mathbf{U}$) and vectors $\mathbf{v}_j$ and $\mathbf{b}$.

To conclude the description of the learning algorithm, we need to compute the partial derivatives of $E_{\mathcal{R}^{\mathcal{U}}}$ and $E_{\mathcal{R}^{\mathcal{G}}}$ with respect to TRIAD parameters. Define the prediction error for user rating r_{ij} as $e_{ij} = r_{ij} - \mathbf{u}_i^T \mathbf{v}_j$. Then, the non-zero partial derivatives of $E_{\mathcal{R}^{\mathcal{U}}}$ are those with respect to all elements of vectors $\mathbf{u}_i$ and $\mathbf{v}_j$:

$$\frac{\partial E_{\mathcal{R}^{\mathcal{U}}}}{\partial \mathbf{u}_i} = -2e_{ij}\mathbf{v}_j + 2\lambda_{\mathbf{U}}'\mathbf{u}_i$$

$$\frac{\partial E_{\mathcal{R}^{\mathcal{U}}}}{\partial \mathbf{v}_j} = -2e_{ij}\mathbf{u}_i + 2\lambda_{\mathbf{V}}'\mathbf{v}_j.$$

Note that these derivatives are essentially identical to those used in the SGD for learning the standard matrix factorization model described in Section 2.2 (after setting $\lambda_{\mathbf{U}}' = \lambda_{\mathbf{V}}' = \lambda$).

Similarly, define the prediction error for group rating r_{kj} as $e_{kj} = r_{kj} - (\mathbf{g}_k \circ \mathbf{b})^T \mathbf{U}^T \mathbf{v}_j$. Then, the non-zero partial derivatives of $E_{\mathcal{R}^{\mathcal{G}}}$ are those with respect to elements of matrix $\mathbf{U}$ and vectors

Algorithm 1: TRIAD-Learn

Input: $\mathcal{R}^{\mathcal{U}}, \mathcal{R}^{\mathcal{G}}, \lambda'_U, \lambda'_V, \lambda'_b$
Output: U, V, b
Variables: X Bernoulli random variable with probability $|\mathcal{R}^{\mathcal{U}}|/(|\mathcal{R}^{\mathcal{U}}| + |\mathcal{R}^{\mathcal{G}}|)$

1 Initialize U, V, b at random according to their priors
2 **repeat**
3   **repeat**
4       $x \leftarrow$ sample of Bernoulli random variable X
5   **if** $x = 1$ **then**
6   Draw pair (i, j) from $\mathcal{R}^{\mathcal{U}}$
7          $\mathbf{u}_i \leftarrow \mathbf{u}_i - \eta \frac{\partial E_{\mathcal{R}^{\mathcal{U}}}}{\partial \mathbf{u}_i}$
8          $\mathbf{v}_j \leftarrow \mathbf{v}_j - \eta \frac{\partial E_{\mathcal{R}^{\mathcal{U}}}}{\partial \mathbf{v}_j}$
9   **else**
10   Draw pair (k, j) from $\mathcal{R}^{\mathcal{G}}$
11         $U \leftarrow U - \eta \frac{\partial E_{\mathcal{R}^{\mathcal{G}}}}{\partial U}$
12         $\mathbf{v}_j \leftarrow \mathbf{v}_j - \eta \frac{\partial E_{\mathcal{R}^{\mathcal{G}}}}{\partial \mathbf{v}_j}$
13         $\mathbf{b} \leftarrow \mathbf{b} - \eta \frac{\partial E_{\mathcal{R}^{\mathcal{G}}}}{\partial \mathbf{b}}$
14   **until** all ratings from $\mathcal{R}^{\mathcal{U}}, \mathcal{R}^{\mathcal{G}}$ are drawn
15 **until** convergence

$\mathbf{v}_j, \mathbf{b}$:

$$\frac{\partial E_{\mathcal{R}^{\mathcal{U}}}}{\partial U} = -2e_{kj}\mathbf{v}_j(\mathbf{g}_k \circ \mathbf{b})^T + 2\lambda'_U U$$

$$\frac{\partial E_{\mathcal{R}^{\mathcal{G}}}}{\partial \mathbf{v}_j} = -2e_{kj}(\mathbf{g}_k \circ \mathbf{b})^T U^T + 2\lambda'_V \mathbf{v}_j$$

$$\frac{\partial E_{\mathcal{R}^{\mathcal{G}}}}{\partial \mathbf{b}} = -2e_{kj}\mathbf{g}_k \circ U^T \mathbf{v}_j + 2\lambda'_b \mathbf{b}.$$

4 EXPERIMENTAL EVALUATION

In Section 4.1 we detail our experimental setting, describing the datasets and the evaluation metrics used. Then in Section 4.2 we present the results of our study.

4.1 Experimental Settings

4.1.1 Real Dataset. To evaluate our methods on a realistic setting, we use the data from the observational study of [5], henceforth denoted as REAL. Students from four universities were arranged into groups of 2–4 members. Each member was asked to individually rate on a 5-point scale the attractiveness of 11 popular European capitals as a touristic destination. Then, the groups convened and jointly agreed on their top-2 preferred destinations. Overall, there were 200 users partitioned across 60 groups.

For our purposes, we convert the ranking of destinations within each group into group rating scores using logarithmic discounting (e.g., as in the NDCG metric). Accordingly, the top ranking object receives the maximum score, while object at rank r receives the maximum score divided by $\log(1 + r)$. As only three ranks exist in our dataset, the top destination was rated with 5, the second with 3.15, and all the rest with 2.5. The resulting group ratings are split into training and test sets with a fixed ratio of 4:1.

4.1.2 Synthetic Datasets. We construct synthetic groups and group ratings based on the popular MovieLens 1M dataset[1]. It consists of $|\mathcal{U}| = 6,040$ users, $|\mathcal{V}| = 3,952$ items (movies), and

Table 1: Synthetic Group Ratings Parameters

Parameter	Symbol	Values	Default
group size	$|g_k|$	2 – 8	3
ratings per group	$|\mathcal{V}_k|$	50 – 200	100
training ratings to total	$|\mathcal{V}_k^t|/|\mathcal{V}_k|$	30% – 90%	80
relevance threshold	ρ	3	3

$|\mathcal{R}^{\mathcal{U}}| = 1,000,209$ user-item ratings on an integer scale of 1 to 5. We note that this dataset contains no groups or group-item ratings.

We synthetically construct groups, assigning users to groups uniformly at random. In each setting, all groups have the same number of members, denoted as $|g_k|$; we vary $|g_k|$ from 2 up to 8 users. In all settings, we keep the number of groups fixed to $|\mathcal{G}| = 50$, and the number of distinct users across all groups to 100.

Each group gives ratings to the same number of items $|\mathcal{V}_k|$, which are chosen uniformly at random among all items. In the experiments, we vary $|\mathcal{V}_k|$ from 50 up to 200. For the evaluation, we split the ratings into training and test sets, and we vary the ratio $|\mathcal{V}_k^t|/|\mathcal{V}_k|$ of training to total ratings from 30% up to 90%. Table 1 summarizes the parameters of our construction of group ratings.

The scores of the group ratings are assigned according to different strategies, resulting in 7 distinct datasets as detailed in the following.

AVERAGE. The rating a group g_k gives to an item v_j is equal to the average rating across the group members, i.e.,

$$r_{kj} = \frac{1}{|g_k|} \sum_{u_i \in g_k} r_{ij}.$$

This type captures the setting where all group members jointly and equally make a decision.

LEAST-MISERY. The rating of group g_k to item v_j is equal to the minimum rating among the group members, i.e.,

$$r_{kj} = \min_{u_i \in g_k} r_{ij}.$$

This models the case where the group behaves under a least-misery principle, so as not to displease any individual member.

DICTATOR. The rating of group g_k to item v_j is equal to the rating of one group member, chosen uniformly at random, i.e., $r_{kj} = r_{ij}$, where $i \sim unif[1, |g_k|]$. This type models the case where decisions in a group are governed by the desires of a single person, e.g., the boss of a company, the child in a family.

In the next four types, the rating of group g_k to item v_j is a weighted average rating across the group members. It is the definition of the weights that differs.

WEIGHTED-GLOBAL. Each user is assigned a uniformly random weight, and thus the group g_k rating to v_j is

$$r_{kj} = \frac{1}{\sum_i w_i} \sum_{u_i \in g_k} w_i r_{ij},$$

where $w_i \sim unif[0, 1]$. Note that the weight of a particular user *persists* across groups — hence the characterization global. This type assumes users have a consistent predefined behavior when in groups, e.g., always willing to compromise.

LEADER-GLOBAL. Each user u_i has a global weight either very small $w_i = 0.1$, or very large $w_i = 10$, where the latter is chosen with a probability $\frac{1}{|g_k|}$, so that in a group there is on average one

---

[1]http://grouplens.org/datasets/movielens/

person with strong opinion. This captures the case where users are either leaders ($w_i = 10$) or followers ($w_i = 0.1$) when in groups.

WEIGHTED-LOCAL. Each group member is assigned a uniformly random weight, and thus the group rating is

$$r_{kj} = \frac{1}{\sum_i w_{ik}} \sum_{u_i \in g_k} w_{ik} r_{ij},$$

where $w_{ik} \sim unif[0, 1]$. The difference with WEIGHTED-GLOBAL is that users may have different weights across groups, capturing thus the case where users exhibit group-specific behavior.

LEADER-LOCAL. Each member u_i of a group g_k has a weight either very small $w_{ik} = 0.1$, or very large $w_{ik} = 10$, where the latter is chosen with a probability $\frac{1}{|g_k|}$. Here, a user may exhibit different bipolar behavior across groups, e.g., follower among co-workers, leader among friends.

4.1.3 Methods. We evaluate our proposed group rating prediction models, RESIDUAL and TRIAD, against variants of PROF-AGG and REC-AGG using average (avg), minimum (min), maximum (max), and product (prd) aggregation strategies, and the INF-MATCH method described in Section 2.3.

The PROF-AGG, REC-AGG, and RESIDUAL methods require a module to predict user-item ratings. In our implementation, we have used the matrix factorization model described in Section 2.2. The model parameters (**U** and **V**) were learned using SGD, where the hyperparameters factor dimensionality ($f = 10$), regularization parameter ($\lambda = 0.005$), and learning rate of SGD ($\eta = 0.005$) were determined by cross validation. Moreover, the factorization of matrix Ξ in RESIDUAL was also determined by SGD ($f = 6$, $\lambda = 0.001$, $\eta = 0.025$). Similarly, parameters **U**, **V**, **b** of TRIAD were determined by SGD ($f = 10$, $\lambda'_U = \lambda'_V = \lambda'_b = 0.001$, $\eta = 0.005$). Finally, the Poisson-mixture parameters of INF-MATCH were determined by the Expectation Maximization algorithm as discussed in [8].

4.1.4 Evaluation Metrics. Our proposed methods, similar to other matrix factorization techniques, are designed to minimize the prediction error of the group ratings. Hence the two main evaluation metrics we employ are mean square error variants. Nonetheless, to obtain a more general picture of performance, we also consider two ranking metrics. We note that the reported values of these metrics are the averages across at least 9 different runs, each with different train/test data splits and random seeds for the SGD.

RMSE. The Root Mean Square Error is computed as:

$$\text{RMSE} = \sqrt{\frac{1}{|\mathcal{G}|} \sum_{g_k \in \mathcal{G}} \frac{1}{|\mathcal{V}_k^{ev}|} \sum_{v_j \in \mathcal{V}_k^{ev}} (r_{kj} - \hat{r}_{kj})^2},$$

where $\mathcal{V}_k^{ev}$ is the set of test (evaluation) items for group g_k. The metric captures the overall accuracy of the predicted group ratings; lower values are better.

M-RMSE. The maximum RMSE within a group is computed as:

$$\text{M-RMSE} = \max_{g_k \in \mathcal{G}} \sqrt{\frac{1}{|\mathcal{V}_k^{ev}|} \sum_{v_j \in \mathcal{V}_k^{ev}} (r_{kj} - \hat{r}_{kj})^2},$$

and indicates the worst-case accuracy across any group. Compared to RMSE, this metric better captures the robustness of the recommender system, as low values indicate that *all groups* will receive good recommendations.

The next two metrics measure the quality of the items' ranking induced by the predicted ratings. For group g_k, let $L_k = v_{j_{(1)}}, v_{j_{(2)}}, \ldots$ denote the list of test items in $\mathcal{V}_k^{ev}$ ranked decreasingly be their predicted group rating $\hat{r}_{kj_{(i)}}$.

NDCG@N. The Discounted Cumulative Gain (DCG) at rank N for group g_k is:

$$\text{DCG}_k@N = r_{kj_{(1)}} + \sum_{i=2}^{N} \frac{r_{kj_{(i)}}}{\log(i+1)}.$$

The Ideal Discounted Cumulative Gain (IDCG) is defined as the maximum possible DCG, achieved when the items are ranked decreasingly by ther actual group rating. The Normalized Discounted Cumulative Gain at rank N is then computed as the average ratio of DCG over IDCG across all groups:

$$\text{NDCG}@N = \frac{1}{|\mathcal{G}|} \sum_{g_k \in \mathcal{G}} \frac{\text{DCG}_k@N}{\text{IDCG}_k@N}.$$

NDCG takes values in the range $[0, 1]$, where higher values are better.

The last metric measures the quality of the ranking with respect to their relevance. For this reason, we must introduce a relevance criterion. Specifically, we treat a test set item as *relevant* when its actual group rating is greater than a threshold ρ. For group g_k, let $L_k^{rel} = v_{j_{[1]}}, v_{j_{[2]}}, \ldots$ denote the list of *relevant* test items in $\mathcal{V}_k^{ev}$ ranked decreasingly be their *actual* group rating $r_{kj_{[i]}}$. Note the distinction between the i-th ranked relevant item $v_{j_{[i]}}$ according to its actual rating and the i-th ranked item $v_{j_{(i)}}$ according to its predicted rating.

MAP. The Mean Average Precision is

$$\text{MAP} = \frac{1}{|\mathcal{G}|} \sum_{g_k \in \mathcal{G}} \frac{1}{|L_k^{rel}|} \sum_{i=1}^{|L_k^{rel}|} \frac{i}{rank_k(v_{j_{[i]}})},$$

where $rank_k(v_{j_{[i]}})$ is the rank of item $v_{j_{[i]}}$ in the list L_k (which is sorted according to predicted ratings). MAP takes values in the range $[0, 1]$, where higher values are better.

4.2 Results

4.2.1 Real Dataset. Table 2 presents the metric values for all methods. In the first two columns where prediction error is measured, lower values are better. In the last three columns showing ranking performance, higher values are better. In each column we mark the best obtained value in bold. Note that INF-MATCH produces only a ranked list of items and cannot predict ratings; thus we cannot compute its prediction error.

We should note that predicting the behavior of groups in REAL is a difficult task, as also observed in [5]. As a general conclusion, all metric values for all methods are considerably worse than their counterparts in the synthetically generated datasets. To some extent, this can be attributed to the fact that this is a small dataset involving few items that more or less are all equally preferable. Our methods in particular are hindered by two additional facts, that there are

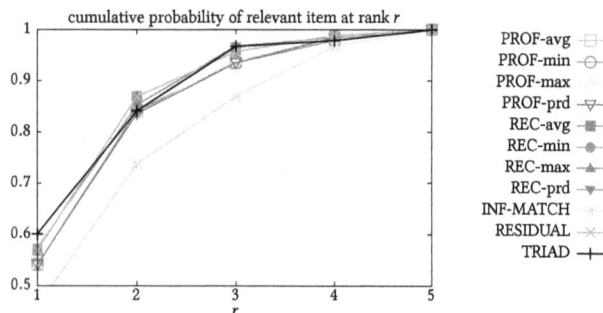

Figure 1: Chance of relevant item among first *r* results in REAL

Table 2: Metrics for REAL

	RMSE	M-RMSE	NDCG@3	NDCG@5	MAP
PROF-avg	1.041	**1.814**	0.785	0.676	0.218
PROF-min	0.919	2.170	0.772	0.682	0.209
PROF-max	1.766	2.518	0.788	0.682	0.218
PROF-prd	1.311	2.415	0.779	0.682	0.218
REC-avg	1.007	1.955	0.829	**0.791**	0.227
REC-min	0.974	1.894	0.829	**0.791**	0.227
REC-max	1.109	2.609	0.829	**0.791**	0.227
REC-prd	1.947	3.698	**0.844**	0.640	0.232
INF-MATCH	—	—	0.635	0.498	0.178
RESIDUAL	**0.822**	2.172	0.829	**0.791**	0.227
TRIAD	0.837	2.137	0.828	0.676	**0.241**

only few group ratings to learn from, and that users are not shared among groups.

Nonetheless, it is important to notice that our proposed methods achieve their goal of minimizing the prediction error of the group ratings, as they have by far the lowest RMSE values. Looking at the M-RMSE column, we note however that there is some variance in the prediction error across groups. In particular, there exist a few groups for which our method did not have the lowest prediction error. For these groups, it turns out that averaging their profiles (PROF-avg) was a better approach.

To assess ranking quality, we set the relevance threshold to 3, meaning that only the top-2 destinations chosen by the groups are considered relevant. We observe that our methods have a good performance but not always the best. TRIAD achieves the best MAP, while RESIDUAL has the second best NDCG at rank 3 and the best at rank 5. We also note that among the existing methods, aggregating the predictions (REC-AGG) was a better approach than aggregating profiles (PROF-AGG) with respect to ranking evaluation metrics.

As there is at most two relevant items in (the test subset of) REAL, we also investigated how far in the ranked list compiled by each recommender would we have to go in order to see the first relevant item. Figure 1 plots the cumulative probability of seeing the first relevant item at each rank. All methods returned a relevant item in their first 5 positions, and thus their cumulative probability at rank 5 is 1. With the exception of INF-MATCH, all methods exhibit similar performance. Note that TRIAD has the highest chance of returning a relevant item as the first result (60.1%). TRIAD has also the highest chance (tied with REC-prd) of returning a relevant item among the top-3 (96.7%), while RESIDUAL has the highest chance (tied with REC-{avg, min, max}) for returning a relevant item among the top-2 (86.9%) and among the top-4 (98.9%).

4.2.2 Synthetic Datasets. In the first round of experiments, we investigate the performance of all methods in the standard scenario, i.e., when all synthetic group ratings parameters are set to their default values (see Table 1). Tables 3 through 8 summarize the quality of the group recommendation for six of the synthetic datasets; AVERAGE is omitted due to lack of space.

We note that we have excluded the prd and max variants of the PROF-AGG and REC-AGG methods due to their poor performance (see Table 2 for REAL), especially in the prediction error metrics (RMSE and M-RMSE). Although their ranking quality was good, it was never better that the avg and min variants. For similar reasons, we have also excluded INF-MATCH; e.g., in one setting its MAP was at about 0.4, while all others were above 0.9.

Overall, we make the following important observations. First, in all strategies and under all metrics (except for two cases under MAP), our models are the best methods, often by far.

Second, regarding prediction error, RESIDUAL and TRIAD are much more accurate than existing methods, particularly so in the four weighted average datasets (WEIGHTED and LEADER variants). This is to be expected, since our methods are explicitly designed to learn the best way to linearly combine individual ratings. In almost all other settings, they are the two best methods. Even in their least favorable datasets (LEAST-MISERY and DICTATOR), where group ratings are not linear combinations of user ratings, they have a clear benefit over the second best. Note that TRIAD is always the best method under the RMSE metrics, and is thus the recommended approach when prediction error matters.

Third, with respect to the ranking metrics, RESIDUAL and TRIAD are still the best methods (except these two MAP cases) but by a smaller margin. This is to be expected, as they are explicitly designed to optimize for prediction error instead. Note that RESIDUAL in LEAST-MISERY is the best method under NDCG, and second best under MAP. Despite the solid performance of our methods, we see an opportunity in designing group recommenders explicitly targeting ranking quality.

Fourth, existing approaches cannot take advantage of the group rating history and have thus relatively poor performance, except in extreme cases that are tailor-made for them, namely AVERAGE for REC-avg, and LEAST-MISERY for REC-min. Overall the REC-AGG variants have significantly lower prediction error in all strategies considered, but among them REC-avg is the winner. This is a non-surprising observation that corroborates the fact that averaging works well in most cases [14]. On the other hand, with respect to ranking quality, the PROF-AGG variants perform marginally better in some strategies, and in two cases are even the best methods.

In the second round of experiments, we study the sensitivity of all methods as we vary the synthetic group ratings parameters. Figures 2 through 3 present the results of our study. It is clear that our models are robust and remain the best under all examined settings. On the other hand, the performance of existing approaches, and particularly of the PROF-AGG variants, varies significantly.

In the last round of experiments, we investigate the performance under a cold-start scenario. As before, we consider 50 groups populated with 100 distinct users. For 10 of these groups, we assign profiles under the WEIGHTED-GLOBAL scheme that have zero group ratings (extreme cold) up to 30 ratings (warm). We then ask the recommender to provide predictions for 100 items for these

Table 3: Metrics for LEAST-MISERY

	RMSE	M-RMSE	NDCG@5	NDCG@10	MAP
PROF-avg	1.762	2.803	0.974	0.974	**0.889**
PROF-min	1.763	2.792	0.973	0.973	0.887
REC-avg	0.469	1.053	0.968	0.970	0.871
REC-min	0.451	1.070	0.970	0.971	0.866
RESIDUAL	0.443	1.081	**0.975**	**0.974**	0.888
TRIAD	**0.389**	**1.016**	0.972	0.972	0.884

Table 4: Metrics for DICTATOR

	RMSE	M-RMSE	NDCG@5	NDCG@10	MAP
PROF-avg	1.103	1.964	0.782	0.532	0.941
PROF-min	1.087	2.009	0.782	0.514	0.936
REC-avg	0.499	1.122	0.780	0.531	0.934
REC-min	0.705	1.723	0.779	0.526	0.934
RESIDUAL	0.406	0.739	0.779	0.503	0.932
TRIAD	**0.347**	**0.726**	**0.789**	**0.547**	**0.941**

Table 5: Metrics for WEIGHTED-GLOBAL

	RMSE	M-RMSE	NDCG@5	NDCG@10	MAP
PROF-avg	1.157	2.167	0.976	0.98	0.913
PROF-min	1.152	2.205	0.975	0.979	0.911
REC-avg	0.378	0.6	0.975	0.979	0.914
REC-min	0.593	1.169	0.976	0.979	0.909
RESIDUAL	0.362	0.564	0.977	0.979	0.914
TRIAD	**0.319**	**0.478**	**0.979**	**0.982**	**0.923**

Table 6: Metrics for LEADER-GLOBAL

	RMSE	M-RMSE	NDCG@5	NDCG@10	MAP
PROF-avg	1.249	2.155	0.977	0.984	0.935
PROF-min	1.244	2.167	0.977	0.984	**0.942**
REC-avg	0.425	0.872	0.975	0.981	0.929
REC-min	0.636	1.373	0.975	0.982	0.931
RESIDUAL	0.381	0.674	0.977	0.984	0.939
TRIAD	**0.344**	**0.633**	**0.981**	**0.987**	0.94

Table 7: Metrics for WEIGHTED-LOCAL

	RMSE	M-RMSE	NDCG@5	NDCG@10	MAP
PROF-avg	1.129	2.119	0.974	0.977	0.9
PROF-min	1.122	2.147	0.974	0.977	0.896
REC-avg	0.404	0.714	0.97	0.974	0.897
REC-min	0.591	1.204	0.972	0.976	0.896
RESIDUAL	0.537	1.426	0.973	0.977	0.898
TRIAD	**0.341**	**0.614**	**0.975**	**0.978**	**0.904**

Table 8: Metrics for LEADER-LOCAL

	RMSE	M-RMSE	NDCG@5	NDCG@10	MAP
PROF-avg	0.946	1.908	0.973	0.977	0.877
PROF-min	0.941	1.91	0.972	0.976	0.878
REC-avg	0.416	0.902	0.974	0.978	0.892
REC-min	0.64	1.383	0.973	0.976	0.885
RESIDUAL	0.374	0.549	0.973	0.977	0.888
TRIAD	**0.331**	**0.480**	**0.977**	**0.980**	0.897

10 groups and measure the prediction error; results are shown in Figure 4. Note that the behavior of REC-avg is the same regardless of the size of the profiles; small variations are due to randomness. In the extreme case of empty group profiles, our methods exhibit significant prediction error. Clearly, REC-avg should be the method of choice for such situations. However, the important thing to notice is that as the group profiles increase in size, our methods, TRIAD particularly, are able to quickly reduce the prediction error. When only

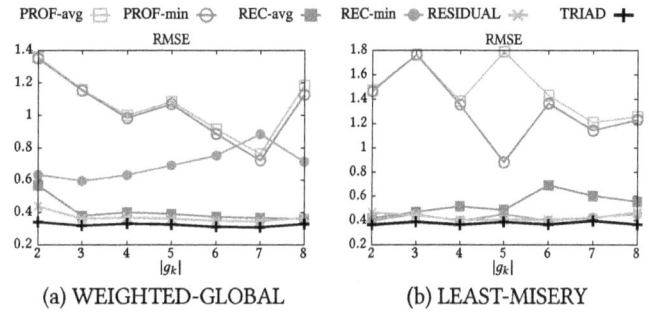

(a) WEIGHTED-GLOBAL   (b) LEAST-MISERY

Figure 2: RMSE vs number of users per group

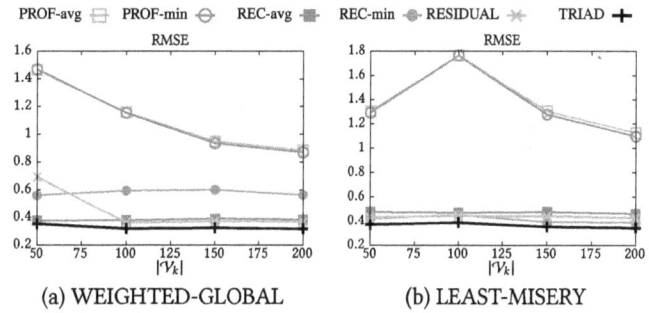

(a) WEIGHTED-GLOBAL   (b) LEAST-MISERY

Figure 3: RMSE vs number of ratings per group

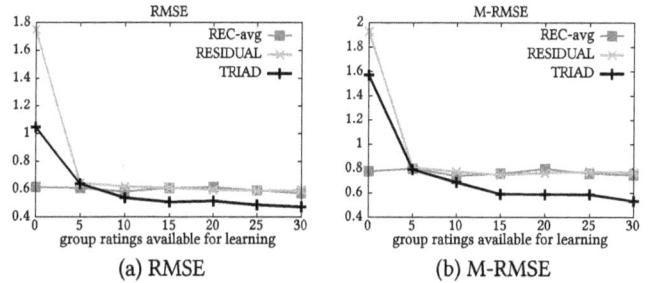

(a) RMSE   (b) M-RMSE

Figure 4: Prediction error for cold-start groups

5 group ratings are available, TRIAD achieves comparable RMSE to REC-avg, while it reduces the maximum RMSE across groups (M-RMSE). As the profile size increases, TRIAD further reduces the variance of RMSE among groups.

5 CONCLUSIONS

This work proposes two group recommenders that explicitly model the difference in the behavior of users when they are members of a group and individually. An experimental study with real and synthetic group ratings demonstrates the superiority of our proposed methodology according to all evaluation metrics studied. In particular, the TRIAD model, which explicitly learns the behavior of users in groups, is the best method in the large majority of the experiments. The RESIDUAL model is often the second best method, and in some settings under ranking evaluation metrics, is even the best. We also find that aggregating individual recommendations generally provides better recommendations for the group compared to when constructing an aggregate group profile.

ACKNOWLEDGMENTS

The author would like to thank Amra Delic for compiling the REAL dataset.

REFERENCES

[1] Liliana Ardissono, Anna Goy, Giovanna Petrone, Marino Segnan, and Pietro Torasso. 2003. Intrigue: Personalized Recommendation of Tourist Attractions for Desktop and Hand Held Devices. *Applied Artificial Intelligence* 17, 8-9 (2003), 687–714. https://doi.org/10.1080/713827254

[2] Linas Baltrunas, Tadas Makcinskas, and Francesco Ricci. 2010. Group recommendations with rank aggregation and collaborative filtering. In *RecSys*. 119–126. https://doi.org/10.1145/1864708.1864733

[3] Shlomo Berkovsky and Jill Freyne. 2010. Group-based recipe recommendations: analysis of data aggregation strategies. In *RecSys*. 111–118. https://doi.org/10.1145/1864708.1864732

[4] Andrew Crossen, Jay Budzik, and Kristian J. Hammond. 2002. Flytrap: intelligent group music recommendation. In *IUI*. 184–185. https://doi.org/10.1145/502716.502748

[5] Amra Delic, Julia Neidhardt, Thuy Ngoc Nguyen, Francesco Ricci, Laurens Rook, Hannes Werthner, and Markus Zanker. 2016. Observing Group Decision Making Processes. In *Proceedings of the 10th ACM Conference on Recommender Systems, Boston, MA, USA, September 15-19, 2016*. 147–150. https://doi.org/10.1145/2959100.2959168

[6] Cynthia Dwork, Ravi Kumar, Moni Naor, and D. Sivakumar. 2001. Rank aggregation methods for the Web. In *WWW*. 613–622. https://doi.org/10.1145/371920.372165

[7] Mike Gartrell, Xinyu Xing, Qin Lv, Aaron Beach, Richard Han, Shivakant Mishra, and Karim Seada. 2010. Enhancing group recommendation by incorporating social relationship interactions. In *Proceedings of the 2010 International ACM SIGGROUP Conference on Supporting Group Work, GROUP 2010, Sanibel Island, Florida, USA, November 6-10, 2010*, Wayne G. Lutters, Diane H. Sonnenwald, Tom Gross, and Madhu Reddy (Eds.). ACM, 97–106. https://doi.org/10.1145/1880071.1880087

[8] Jagadeesh Gorla, Neal Lathia, Stephen Robertson, and Jun Wang. 2013. Probabilistic group recommendation via information matching. In *WWW*. 495–504. http://dl.acm.org/citation.cfm?id=2488432

[9] Anthony Jameson and Barry Smyth. 2007. Recommendation to Groups. In *The Adaptive Web, Methods and Strategies of Web Personalization*, Peter Brusilovsky, Alfred Kobsa, and Wolfgang Nejdl (Eds.). Springer, 596–627.

[10] Yehuda Koren. 2008. Factorization meets the neighborhood: a multifaceted collaborative filtering model. In *SIGKDD*. 426–434. https://doi.org/10.1145/1401890.1401944

[11] Yehuda Koren, Robert Bell, and Chris Volinsky. 2009. Matrix Factorization Techniques for Recommender Systems. *IEEE Computer* 42, 8 (Aug. 2009), 30–37. https://doi.org/10.1109/MC.2009.263

[12] Qiuxia Lu, Diyi Yang, Tianqi Chen, Weinan Zhang, and Yong Yu. 2011. Informative household recommendation with feature-based matrix factorization. In *CAMRa*. ACM, 15–22.

[13] Judith Masthoff. 2004. Group Modeling: Selecting a Sequence of Television Items to Suit a Group of Viewers. *User Model. User-Adapt. Interact.* 14, 1 (2004), 37–85. https://doi.org/10.1023/B:USER.0000010138.79319.fd

[14] Judith Masthoff. 2015. Group Recommender Systems: Aggregation, Satisfaction and Group Attributes. In *Recommender Systems Handbook*. 743–776. https://doi.org/10.1007/978-1-4899-7637-6_22

[15] Judith Masthoff and Albert Gatt. 2006. In pursuit of satisfaction and the prevention of embarrassment: affective state in group recommender systems. *User Model. User-Adapt. Interact.* 16, 3-4 (2006), 281–319. https://doi.org/10.1007/s11257-006-9008-3

[16] Joseph F. McCarthy and Theodore D. Anagnost. 1998. MusicFX: An Arbiter of Group Preferences for Computer Supported Collaborative Workouts. In *Proceedings of the 1998 ACM Conference on Computer Supported Cooperative Work (CSCW '98)*. ACM, New York, NY, USA, 363–372. https://doi.org/10.1145/289444.289511

[17] Kevin McCarthy, Maria Salamó, Lorcan Coyle, Lorraine McGinty, Barry Smyth, and Paddy Nixon. 2006. CATS: A Synchronous Approach to Collaborative Group Recommendation. In *FLAIRS*. 86–91. http://www.aaai.org/Library/FLAIRS/2006/flairs06-015.php

[18] Mark O'Connor, Dan Cosley, Joseph A. Konstan, and John Riedl. 2001. PolyLens: A recommender system for groups of user. In *ECSCW*. 199–218.

[19] Alan Said, Shlomo Berkovsky, Ernesto William De Luca, and Jannis Hermanns. 2011. Challenge on context-aware movie recommendation: CAMRa2011. In *Proceedings of the 2011 ACM Conference on Recommender Systems, RecSys 2011, Chicago, IL, USA, October 23-27, 2011*, Bamshad Mobasher, Robin D. Burke, Dietmar Jannach, and Gediminas Adomavicius (Eds.). ACM, 385–386. https://doi.org/10.1145/2043932.2044015

[20] Ruslan Salakhutdinov and Andriy Mnih. 2007. Probabilistic Matrix Factorization. In *NIPS*. 1257–1264. http://papers.nips.cc/paper/3208-probabilistic-matrix-factorization

[21] Lara Quijano Sánchez, Juan A. Recio-García, Belén Díaz-Agudo, and Guillermo Jiménez-Díaz. 2013. Social factors in group recommender systems. *ACM TIST* 4, 1 (2013), 8:1–8:30. https://doi.org/10.1145/2414425.2414433

[22] Badrul M. Sarwar, George Karypis, Joseph A. Konstan, and John Riedl. 2001. Item-based collaborative filtering recommendation algorithms. In *WWW*. 285–295. https://doi.org/10.1145/371920.372071

[23] Christophe Senot, Dimitre Kostadinov, Makram Bouzid, Jérôme Picault, and Armen Aghasaryan. 2011. Evaluation of Group Profiling Strategies. In *IJCAI*. 2728–2733. http://ijcai.org/papers11/Papers/IJCAI11-454.pdf

[24] Christophe Senot, Dimitre Kostadinov, Makram Bouzid, Jérôme Picault, Armen Aghasaryan, and Cédric Bernier. 2010. Analysis of Strategies for Building Group Profiles. In *User Modeling, Adaptation, and Personalization, 18th International Conference, UMAP 2010, Big Island, HI, USA, June 20-24, 2010. Proceedings (Lecture Notes in Computer Science)*, Paul De Bra, Alfred Kobsa, and David N. Chin (Eds.), Vol. 6075. Springer, 40–51. https://doi.org/10.1007/978-3-642-13470-8_6

[25] Zhiwen Yu, Xingshe Zhou, Yanbin Hao, and Jianhua Gu. 2006. TV Program Recommendation for Multiple Viewers Based on user Profile Merging. *User Model. User-Adapt. Interact.* 16, 1 (2006), 63–82. https://doi.org/10.1007/s11257-006-9005-6

Let's Dance: How to Build a User Model for Dance Students Using Wearable Technology

Augusto Dias Pereira dos Santos
The University of Sydney
J12, NSW 2006, Australia
Augusto.Dias@sydney.edu.au

Kalina Yacef
The University of Sydney
J12, NSW 2006, Australia
Kalina.Yacef@sydney.edu.au

Roberto Martinez-Maldonado
University of Technology Sydney
Ultimo NSW 2007 Australia
Roberto.Martinez-Maldonado@uts.edu.au

ABSTRACT

Motor skill learning is an area where wearable technology and user modelling can be synergistically combined for providing support. In this paper, we explore how a simple accelerometer sensor can be used to capture motion data associated with critical aspects of learning in the context of social dancing. We developed a prototype mobile app that tracks students' motion data whilst they practise dance exercises. This paper describes a set of features, such as rhythm duration, consistency and body motion, which can be automatically tracked and included into a dance student model. These dancing features can be presented back to the students as feedback, in the form of i) summaries, ii) visualisations or iii) narratives. We illustrate the feasibility and potential of modelling these features through a study with beginner students taking dance classes during three weeks.

KEYWORDS

open learner model; automatic feedback; wearable devices; dance education; motor learning

ACM Reference format:

Augusto Dias Pereira dos Santos, Kalina Yacef, and Roberto Martinez-Maldonado. 2017. Let's Dance: How to Build a User Model for Dance Students Using Wearable Technology. In Proceedings of UMAP '17, Bratislava, Slovakia, July 09-12, 2017, 9 pages.
DOI: http://dx.doi.org/10.1145/3079628.3079673

1 INTRODUCTION

Research in personalised education technologies has largely focused on domains where people perform learning tasks by interacting with and through personal computers [3,23]. This way, models of students' behaviour can be commonly inferred from the student's logged interactions with the learning platform (mostly performed via keyboards, mice and, more recently, touches). These student models, which can be computed whilst the learning activity unfolds, can serve to create mechanisms that capture the student's state of learning and respond with personalised actions or feedback [19]. When it comes to learning motor skills such as dancing, the tasks, by nature, require the student to move and use the available space. As a result, clicks and keystrokes to model students' behaviour are not a sufficient or even appropriate source of data to create user models serving the needs of motor learning [14]. Santos [23] recently highlighted both the need and the potential of supporting motor learning through the combination of user modelling and machine learning with recent advances in wearable and mobile technologies.

A wide range of wearable and mobile devices are making its way into our daily lives, generating new challenges for embodied interaction design but also enabling new possibilities such as motion tracking [21]. Wearable devices can be attached to users' bodies to track data such as body movement, steps and heart rate [1]. Some microcontrollers found in wearable devices can also be found in mobiles (e.g. accelerometers and gyroscopes). As these devices become more affordable, there is potential for critical aspects of motor learning tasks to be easily tracked at a fine enough level of granularity and become part of user models [23].

Social dance education is one of the various motor learning activities that could benefit from these emerging technologies. Examples of social dance styles include ballroom, salsa, bachata, zouk, and forró. One common initial challenge for social dance students is to synchronise their moves to the rhythm of the music [2]. Students need to learn how to identify the underlying rhythm of the music, interpret its beat and synchronise their steps and body movements with it [2]. This process requires the development of a series of cognitive and motor skills that can only be mastered through structured and regular practice. Moreover, opportunities for practice with feedback are scarce, especially in large social dance classes which commonly have dozens of students. Social dance teachers may see hundreds of students per week, preventing them from giving individual feedback, and be aware of students' improvement [12].

In this paper, we explore how simple wearable technology can capture relevant motion data and extract key information needed to support social dance learning. This information could enable teachers and/or teaching systems to provide personalised feedback on students' performance and suggest actions for improvement. We developed a prototype mobile app (the Forró Trainer) that students can use to practice dancing exercises. The app tracks their motion automatically in the background. The paper describes important features that can be extracted from these data, such as rhythm and consistency, which can serve to build dancing student models. We report on a laboratory study (N=10) that evaluates how these modelled dancing features can be presented back to the students in the form of i) summaries, ii) visualisations or iii) narratives. In short, the contribution of this paper is a study that shows how a simple accelerometer sensor can be used to capture motion data and model critical features of learning in the context of social dancing.

The rest of the paper is structured as follows. Section 2 presents related work on motion modelling and describes common challenges in social dance learning. Section 3 describes our approach to model dancing features that can be presented back to the students as feedback. Section 4 presents technical details about how we operationalised our approach. Section 5 illustrates a feasibility study with beginner students taking dance classes during three weeks. Finally, we summarise our findings and describe opportunities for future work in Section 6.

2   BACKGROUND

2.1   Modelling Movement

Current advances in pervasive computing allow designing novel ways of supporting learning activities in-situ, where learning occurs [11]. For example, some research work has explored how accelerometers worn on different body parts can be used to effectively classify types of physical activity such as sitting, standing, walking on level ground, walking up and down, running, etc. [9,17]. In terms of motor learning, a recent review [23] describes the various strategies and activities that rely on data-intensive digital technologies to support learning in activities such as karate, table tennis, snowboarding, swimming, violin playing, handwriting, among others. For example, learning to play musical instruments has benefited from user modelling approaches. In one study, authors investigated how accelerometer data can be used to create mechanisms to help students learn how to play samba percussion instruments [18]. The data collected was presented back to the students, and compared with the expert model to promote awareness. Similarly, SYSSOMO [10] supports piano students in identifying hand coordination problems.

In the dance domain, researchers have used transducers, mounted on the students' shoes, to help students in learning rhythm while dancing [5]. Authors analysed and processed the data to trigger acoustic feedback to help students to follow the beat of the music. Students had a positive impression of the system, but authors identified that their system was not able to detect when students started their stepping sequence on the second or third beat of the music bar. Accelerometers have also been successfully used to model body movements, in the context of ballet dancing, comparing experts with non-expert students [11,26]. These studies investigated in which position of the body accelerometers can provide with insights about their posture and movement dynamics. Other attempts to enhance dance classes with technology include: using augmented feedback (tactile, video, sound) for learning dance choreographies [4]; combining motion capture, augmented reality, telepresence and electro-active polymer clothing to create an immersive dance experience

[24]; and, a game that teaches traditional Greek dance using multiple depth sensors [15]. Our approach differs from the related work described above by exploring how motion data can be associated with critical aspects of rhythm learning in the context of social dancing. Also we propose to use these data to inform the students regarding their learning process.

2.2   Social Dancing

Our study was conducted in the context of learning to dance Forró. In a regular Forró class, after a warm up, teachers commonly demonstrate how to perform a new exercise. The teacher usually counts from 1 to 4 to associate each movement to the beat of the music. Then, they ask students to perform the movements, providing some feedback as needed. This sequence can be repeated until the class finishes or the students master the new exercise. This is a common approach to a three-part class pattern: initiation, response and evaluation [6]. For many novice students, one of the main challenges is to learn rhythm-keeping skills. This means doing the dance moves in synchrony with the music beats, throughout the whole song. Some students experience difficulty recognising the music beats or coordinate their legs and body with the beats. These issues can be overcome with repeated practice to improve music listening and motor coordination [2]. Students currently rely on teacher guidance to evaluate their practice. However, since teachers usually oversee dozens of students at the same time, students commonly receive very limited feedback [12]. Furthermore, when students practice by themselves (e.g. at home), they usually do not get any feedback, which can also discourage them from practising. This suggests the need for providing automated feedback to students so they can practice as often as needed. Dance movements are often cyclical and repetitive, Motion data collected can serve as a basis for creating automated support systems [5]. If motion patterns are matched with relevant song information, it may be possible to generate feedback to support students' learning of rhythm-keeping.

3   APPROACH

We aim at harnessing the potential of increasingly available lightweight technology to provide a scalable solution for anyone having a smartphone. The following sub-sections describe the features that we chose to model because they are most important in dancing, and the ways we provide feedback to the students.

3.1   Modelling Dance Education Features

Learning about rhythm and acquiring skills to dance with the rhythm of the song involve several elements. In this study, we focus our attention on four features that have been identified in the literature as critical for rhythm learning. Table 1 summarises the features we propose.

3.1.1 Practice. Mastering motor learning skills is strongly correlated with repeated practice [13]. In dancing, a learner needs to practice not only to strengthen the body in preparation for the continued physical activity but also to develop coordination and other key physio-cognitive skills required for the dance style [7]. *How do we model* this *feature?* By logging the number of times a student practiced using the student's learning app.

3.1.2 Rhythm BPM. Students must understand rhythm in order to learn how to dance properly [2]. Keeping an accurate timing is crucial in dance. Good rhythmic skills imply to precisely synchronise body movements with the beat of the song, and maintain this synchrony throughout the whole song. To assess whether a student moves their body to the rhythm of song, the beats of the song can be compared with the timing of the student's body movements. *How do we model this feature?* Using the algorithm described in section 4.2, we calculate the average beats per minute (BPM) from student's motion data.

3.1.3 Rhythm Consistency. As mentioned above, students also need to maintain the correct BPM throughout the whole song, and across several practices. *How do we model this feature?* We calculate the coefficient of variation of the student's BPM across the full dancing exercise.

3.1.4 Body Motion. This feature refers to the extent to which a student is aware of whether their body movements are tuned to the music. When students are fully aware of how their body is moving and have control over this movement, they can properly communicate their movement and perform the dance effectively [7]. *How do we model this feature?* Decompose the student's movement raw acceleration data in each of the 3 axes (x, y, z) to extract acceleration patterns, rhythm and consistency.

3.2 Providing Visual and Narrative Feedback

After collecting data and inferring indicators that are important according to key literature, the next challenge is to define how to present these data in a way that makes sense to the users and can support reflection. In several learning contexts where some visual feedback is shown back to the students, the solutions commonly include showing data using bar charts, line graph, tables, pies, and text [25]. In some motor learning studies, the attempts to provide feedback have mostly followed similar approaches. For example, a line graph [18] was used to help percussion students to reflect on their performance. In a piano training system [10], visual cues and informative texts were presented as corrective cues. However, other non-visual ways to provide feedback have also been explored. For example, in dance, the use of audio cues have been used to make students follow the beats of the song [5]. In the context of martial arts, vibrotactile actuators have been suggested to make the learner "feel" the problems with their body movements [22]. Still, there is no

consensus on what the proper way to present information to teacher and students is. In this study, we choose to explore four different approaches to provide feedback to the students about the features listed in the previous section:

3.2.1 Summaries / Tables. Using this representation, we provide the student with an overview of different aspects of their performance. The summary contains averages and standard deviations of the features mentioned in Section 4.1, aggregated by different characteristics of each feature, for instance: exercise type, music type, axes of the body (e.g. see Tables 3, 4, 5 and 6).

3.2.2 Visualisations. We built simple charts presenting essentially the temporal aspects of the data: for example, the student's performance during one exercise, and how it evolved during the week (e.g. see Fig 3).

3.2.3 *Narratives.* We created narrative stories, similarly to the feedback a dance instructor would provide. For example: "We suggest you practice more often, both daily and weekly. It is important to recall the movements we do in class" (e.g. see Table 7). Ideally, these narratives would be automatically generated by configuring rules or more sophisticated [16].

3.2.4 Social Comparison. We provide students with ways to compare their progress towards their goal against other learners and against the teacher (gold standard). This is a common strategy in learning, called Open Social Modelling [8] that may benefit students.

4 APPARATUS & MODEL BUILDING

This section describes how we implemented our approach for motion capture, rhythm detection and provision of feedback.

4.1 Forró Trainer App

The Forró Trainer app provides exercises to improve rhythm keeping by practising several Forró dance movements. It includes songs with different levels of difficulty, so students can progressively improve their skills. We followed a co-design approach for developing the app features. This process included dance teachers (interviews), students (from ad-hoc usability tests), PhD UX/UI students, and industries best practices. These stakeholders contributed to the following design decisions: a) use a song as a reference to measure student's rhythm ability; b) provide multiple songs inside the app; c) use bread crumbs to help with the app navigation; d) have multiple exercises that evaluate different abilities; e) include instructions on how to do the exercises; and f) include a countdown before the song starts.

Table 1: **Features of the dance learner model**

Feature name	Description	How to model this features
Practice	How much and how often the student practiced	Logging the number of times a student practice using the student's learning app
Rhythm BPM	Rhythm of the student in a practice session	Calculating the average rhythm of the student, as detected by the algorithm (Section 4.2).
Rhythm Consistency	Consistency during the practice sessions	The coefficient of variation of the different rhythms detected in one exercise session
Body Motion	Description of the student's movements in the three dimension space	Decompose the raw acceleration data in each of the 3 axes (x, y, z) to extract acceleration patterns, rhythm and consistency.

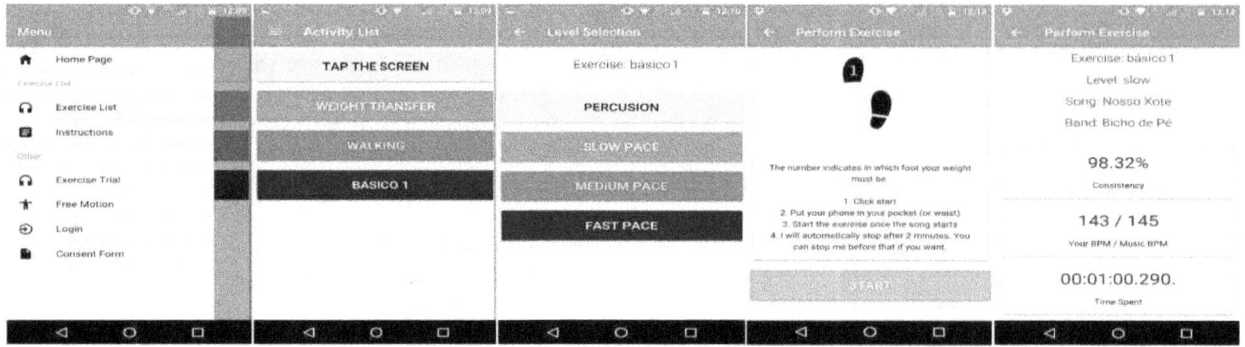

Figure 1: **Forró Trainer App. Screenshots, from left to right: menu, activity list, difficulty level list, instructions, and performance result for the last exercise.**

Fig 1 shows sample screenshots of the app. The first image shows a menu that contains the activity list and instructions. The menus in the second and third images allow the student to select the activity and the difficulty level of the songs (which can be slow paced, medium paced or fast paced). An exercise is therefore created by selecting an activity, a difficulty level and a song (not shown). Next, the app shows the instructions of the selected activity and the start button. After the exercise is finished, the student can see their performance results.

The main activity used for this study was *Básico 1*. This is the first exercise of Forró and includes many fundamental skills that are used in other Forró exercises. Forró songs have a quaternary tempo (1-4) to which the dancers need to synchronise their steps. In the Básico 1 activity, the student needs to perform a movement in an 8-beat pack: 1) move left foot forward, 2) change weight to right foot, 3) move left foot to the original position, 4) pause, 5) move right foot backward, 6) change weight to left foot, 7) move right foot to the original position, 8) pause. Then, the same sequence must be repeated over and over.

To use this app, students launch the exercise they wish to perform and place the smartphone in one of their pockets. As the music starts, they commence dancing. While the students do their movements, the accelerometer records their motion, in three dimensions, with a 100 Hz frequency. Regarding the mobile phone position on the body, tests in the lab demonstrated that using the mobile phone in any trousers/shorts' pocket produced the same accuracy as the hips and lower back. This makes the app easy to use, as students do not need additional equipment to attach the mobile phone to their body.

4.2 Sensor Data to Rhythm Analysis

In order to extract the motion data from the accelerometer sensors embedded in the students' smartphones, we created an algorithm which translates body movements to BPM (beats per minute) and compares this information with the song's BPM. Fig 2 presents an accelerometer data sample from a participant while performing a specific dance exercise (Básico 1). The red dots represent the peaks detected by our approach and are used to generate the student's BPM.

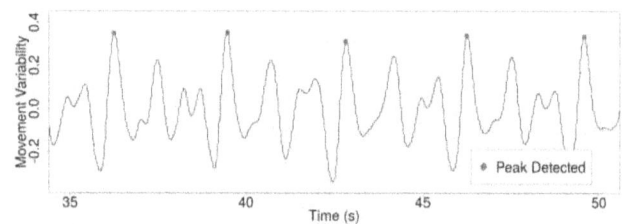

Figure 2: **Time series of motion data from a participant while performing a dance exercise. Red dots show peaks detected using our approach.**

We used the time between peaks (TBP) [9] to calculate the interval between movements with most variability in motion. The local maxima is, in practical terms, the movement that anticipates the first beat of an eight-beat cycle of the song, when the student is in the middle of the first step forward, where the acceleration is at its peak. The peaks are detected by local maxima in a 3 seconds range moving window. This range was chosen based on the expected TBP for Forró songs. For example, in a song with 142 BPM, the expected TBP for the student's movement is 3.38 seconds (the bellow formula, isolating $\overline{TBP}$). A 3 second range covers the detection of peaks in the different Forró songs' BPM. Using the average of TBP during a one-minute exercise sample (removing outliers), it is possible to calculate the student's BPM using formula (1).

$$Student's\ BPM = \left(60 \div \left(\overline{TBP} \div 1000\right)\right) \times 8 \quad (1)$$

1000 in the equation converts the values of $\overline{TBP}$ from milliseconds to seconds. $\overline{TBP}$ is calculated using the milliseconds timestamps collected from each reading, instead of using the number of readings that differ one peak from the other, to ensure more precision. The value 60 at the beginning of the formula is to convert from seconds to minutes while 8, in the end, converts from user steps to song beats (eight-beat cycle). Using this information, we can then calculate two metrics: a) how similar is the student's BPM and the song BPM; and b) consistency while doing the exercise, which is the coefficient of variation from the TBP values. In this study, a consistency measure with an average higher than 98% is considered very good. A score higher than 99% would be excellent". If it is lower than 90%, the student is out of the rhythm.

The *Student's BPM* is calculated for the three axes, in their original form and inverted form. This allows the algorithm to work regardless of the device orientation. The axis with the best consistency result is chosen as the correct axis and its result presented to the user. The comparison of body movement with the song's BPM is used to generate the dance student performance score. For instance, if a song has a 142 BPM tempo and the student's movements translate to a 135 BPM tempo, the student's movement is detected as slower than the song. The coefficient of variation of the student's rhythm along the duration of the exercise represents the student consistency, which is immediately presented to the student as a percentage.

4.3 Model Building

Activity data collected from the students while they use the app is used to define a dance learner model. Some of these data include: the number of times they did each exercise/song, when they did the exercises (date, time), the performance of each exercise (consistency, user BPM) and the acceleration of their movement (z, y, x) while doing the exercises.

4.4 Modelling and Data Representations

To display information about the four dance student model features, we selected four types of data representation. Table 2 summarises the combination between features and data representations. Although students could do other activities using the app, and we have access to other types of data, like the students actions on the app, in this study we based the learner model mostly on the Básico 1 activity.

4.4.1 Representation of Practice data.

Summary. This shows the number of times the student practised each exercise and the number of attempts done for each level. The student can also see the total number of times practised and the period (in days) when the practice occurred (see Table 3).

Visualisation. Two bar charts were presented, containing: 1) the frequency they practised each exercise by day, and 2) how many times they practice each level by day. Having distinct colours for each exercise and each level (e.g. see Fig 3-a).

Narrative. In all cases, feedback provided as a text narrative includes two pieces: a diagnosis narrative and actionable narrative (which suggests what the student can do to fix a problem). See an example narrative in Table 7, row 1.

Social Comparison. A summary table shows the number of times practised (as in Table 3) against other students.

4.4.2 Representation of Rhythm BPM data

Summary. By interweaving these two sources of information (the song's beat and the student's BPM) we can derive conclusions such as: the student is faster/slower than or follows the correct rhythm; how often the students is correct or wrong during a song, This table also organises the data by exercise and level, but presents the number of times the student was moving their body in time with the song, slower, or faster than the song (see Table 4).

Visualisation. This visualisation presents side by side two boxplot charts showing the comparison between the student's worst and best result (based on their rhythm and consistency performance) for the song 'Nosso Xote' while doing the Básico 1 activity. The boxplot summarises the data about the rhythm of the student during their attempt. Usually, their rhythm varies a lot in the worst case but not in the best case (e.g. see Fig 3-c).

Narrative. These narratives focus on the student's mistakes of performing slower/faster than the songs and suggesting exercises that can improve their listening skills regarding rhythm. See an example narrative in Table 7, row 2.

4.4.3 Representation of Rhythm Consistency data.

Summary. Consistency represents the overall variability of the student's rhythm during a 1-minute exercise. If the student maintains the same rhythm throughout the whole song, their score is close to 100%. The score decreases if the student does not maintain a regular consistency, losing the rhythm during the exercise. A score consistently below 90% means the student struggles following the rhythm. This summary contains the minimum, maximum, average and standard deviation consistency organised by exercise and by level (see Table 5).

Visualisation. Focusing on one specific song/exercise, student's progress is shown throughout different practices over time. A line chart shows all the attempts the students perform for the song 'Nosso Xote' (Bicho de Pé), slow level difficulty, activity Básico 1. The line chart contains coloured dots, order by the time of the attempt, representing if the student's attempt was correct (green), slower (blue) or faster (red) than the song (e.g. see Fig 3-b).

Table 2: **Representation of the dance learner model features**

| Model features and aspects | Ways to provide feedback (data representations) | | | |
	Summary	Visualisation	Narrative (text)	Social Comparison
Practice	Number of times practised	Visual chart with the number of times practised per day	Recommendations on what to focus the next practice	Comparing practice data with peers
Rhythm BPM	How many times the student was on the correct tempo	Boxplot chart comparing the BPM of the best and the worst practised exercise	Elaborate on the student's aptitude to follow the tempo	
Rhythm Consistency	Student's consistency per exercise type and level	Distribution of consistency over time for a specific exercise and song	Recommendations on how to improve	Comparing consistency data with their peers
Body Motion	Rhythm and acceleration data comparing worst x best practice	Two charts comparing how well the student followed the music and how s/he moved in the best and the worst practised exercise	Explain the data presented and give recommendations on how to improve	Comparing their movement chart with the teacher's

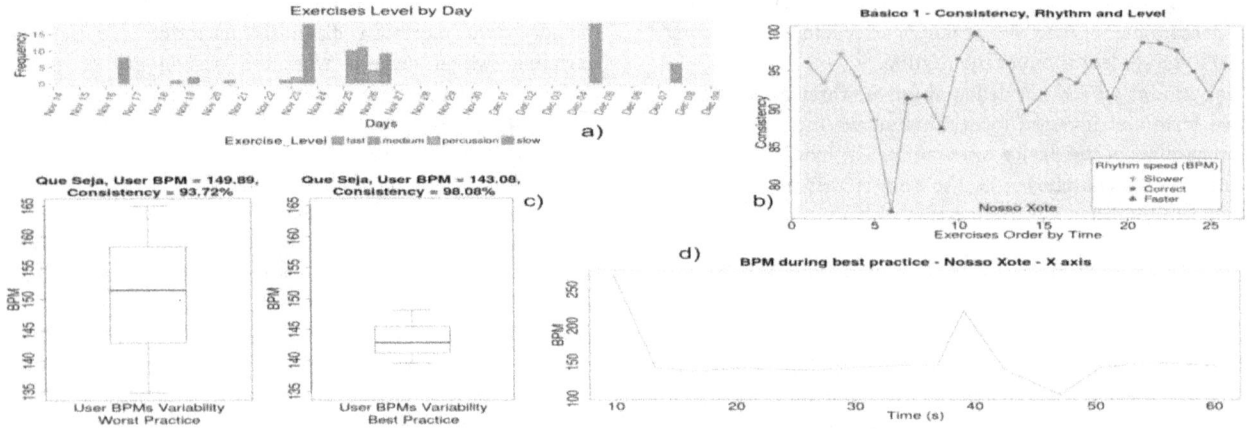

Figure 3: Sample of the visualisations used. a) practice by day (4.4.1), b) progress between attempts (4.4.2), c) comparison between two attempts (4.4.3), d) rhythm during one attempt (4.4.4).

Narrative. Students are given details (average, strong and weak points) about their consistency and are recommended an exercise based on their main weaknesses or strength detected in past exercises. See an example narrative in Table 7, row 3.

Social Comparison. A summary table compares the student with peers regarding their consistency during the activity Básico 1 (as in Table 5).

Table 3: Example of Practice – Summary

Time practised for each exercise		Time practised for each Level	
Tap	9	Percussion	4
Weight Transfer	10	Slow	21
Walking	1	Medium	4
Básico 1	21	Fast	12

Table 4: Example of Rhythm BPM – Summary

Rhythm Evaluation by Level in Básico 1				
Exercise	Total	Too Slow	Correct	Too Fast
Slow Paced	11	0	11	0
Medium Paced	2	0	2	0
Fast Paced	8	1	7	0

Table 5: Example of Rhythm Consistency – Summary

Consistency by Level in Básico 1					
Exercise Level	Total	Min (%)	Mean (%)	Max (%)	Standard Deviation (%)
Slow Paced	11	97.77	98.56	99.31	0.53
Medium Paced	2	98.59	98.59	98.60	0.00
Fast Paced	8	95.71	97.69	98.80	0.94

Table 6: Example of Body Motion – Summary

Movement Rhythm – Worst x Best – Nosso Xote (BPM ≈ ~142.5)					
Case	X axis (Lateral)		Y axis (Vertical)		Z axis (Depth)	
	BPM	Cns(%)*	BPM	Cns(%)*	BPM	Cns(%)*
Worst	135.26	72.69	142.83	98.13	142.82	98.17
Best	142.83	98.58	143.74	99.27	142.41	98.37

*Consistency

Table 7: Examples of Narrative Feedback

Practice - Diagnosis: you have an average of 2 practice sessions per day and had 12 days without practice. Most of your practice sessions were performed during class. Actionable Feedback: you could practice more often daily and weekly. It is important to recall the movements we do in class.

Rhythm BPM - Diagnosis: Dear student, you have no correct attempt while doing the Tap exercise. In all the 9 attempts you were slower than the song. Actionable Feedback: We suggest you practice more the Tap exercise until you can consistently achieve correct rhythm. The Tap exercise will help you developing your ability to listen properly to the rhythm of the song.

Rhythm Consistency - Diagnosis: Dear student, you have an average consistency of 98.56% on the Básico 1 activity. Your lowest consistency was 95.71% doing the Danielle song. Actionable Feedback: The result of your consistency score along your practice at the Básico 1 activity are really good. The lowest consistency score doesn't seem to be a problem since you recovered the score in following attempts.

Body Motion - Diagnosis: Dear student, your best attempt has higher speed when compared with you worst attempt. Actionable Feedback: A higher speed means that your movements were more defined and clear, it means you were more precise on the movement. You should aim to have more precision and confidence in your movement, your dance will be clear and your partner will better understand your movements

4.4.4 Representation of Body Motion data

Summary. This shows the student's movement in the three axes (x, y, z). One table presents the student's rhythm (BPM) and consistency for each axis in both practices (see Table 6). Expert body motion data indicated the same rhythm and high consistency (above 97%) in all axes. Another table shows the raw accelerometer data mean and standard deviation, also for the three axes and both cases. The standard deviation of experts is usually higher than in most student samples, highlighting the larger amplitude and higher confidence that experts have in using the space.

Visualisation. Two visualisations presented the comparison between worst and best attempts. The first consists of two line charts presenting the different rhythm the student had in their sessions. In a perfect scenario, with 100% consistency, the chart

Table 9: **5-likert scale result for the participant's interview. Average and standard deviation of each group of questions. Average colours ranging from red (min) to green (max), standard deviation ranging from green (min) to red (max).**

		Summary		Visualization		Narrative		Social Comparison	
		Avg	Std	Avg	Std	Avg	Std		
Practice	Clarity	4.333	0.784	4.111	0.751	4.519	0.802	4.593	0.572
	Usefulness	3.704	1.265	3.444	1.086	4.074	1.072	4.111	0.934
Rhythm BPM	Clarity	4.259	0.944	2.926	1.357	4.593	0.501		
	Usefulness	3.889	1.121	2.630	1.043	4.481	0.580		
Rhythm Consistency	Clarity	4.556	0.577	3.222	1.601	4.630	0.565	4.593	0.572
	Usefulness	4.222	1.013	3.148	1.562	4.593	0.636	4.111	0.934

will have a flat line, indicating that the student had the same rhythm throughout the whole song. In a weaker scenario, the student has fluctuations in the chart (e.g. see Fig 3-d). The second visualisation presented two waves (line charts) of the accelerometer data of one of the student's axes. In a good attempt, the chart will have a sinusoidal-like shape, with a regular period between peaks. In a weak case, the wave will present an irregular distance between peaks (e.g. see Fig 2).

Narrative. Following argument presented in the summary of this subsection, i.e. the student should have the same rhythm in all axes, a constant rhythm during the whole song and a higher standard deviation in the accelerometer data. See an example narrative in Table 7, row 4, suggesting how this standard can be achieved.

Social Comparison. The chart presents the same information as the second chart of section 4.4.4 (Fig 2), comparing with the teacher's data.

5 STUDY

The experiment was carried out in a lab. Ten students were recruited for this study and assigned the role of dance students. All of them were IT graduates or PhD students, 5 females and 5 males, 5 were already familiar with dancing Forró. From the 10 participants, 8 completed the 3-week course, one participant withdrew and another did not participate in the course but use the app to record their performance while doing the exercises. Nine of the participants participated in a final interview and gave feedback on the data representations using their own data. Participants were invited to take a weekly 30-minute personal

lesson on Forró over the course of 3 weeks. Participants used the Forró Trainer app during the lessons and at home. Each week, they were asked to practice a specific exercise 3 times before the lesson and 3 times after the lesson, to track their progress. After the lessons, each participant was asked to give feedback on the various data representations described in Section 4.4. The 15 aspects of Table 2 were evaluated, using a 5-likert scale questionnaire about the clarity and usefulness of each data representation. We used the same questionnaire that evaluated multimodal feedback for traditional education assessments [20].

5.1 Study results

A summary of the students' usage of the app and the data used to build the dance learner model is presented in Table 8. We can highlight some of the information of this table such as: Student 8 had a great improvement during the classes, most likely because s/he practised at home, with the second highest number of practices (columns 2-4). Student 5 was the most engaged using the app. All students achieved higher consistency in the exercise at least one time (see Max column). In columns 5-7, it is possible to identify students' patterns about being more times faster than slower (or the inverse) when having incorrect attempts. This last information is important since it was not easy for students to keep track of their common mistakes.

Table 9 depicts the quantitative results of the students' responses. We colour-coded the cells of the average columns from red (minimum average value) to dark green (maximum value) and the standard deviation cells the opposite, from dark green (minimum standard deviation value) to red (maximum

Table 8: **Summary of students' practices**

Student ID	# of Practices at Básico 1 activity			Rhythm at Básico 1			Consistency at Básico 1, song 'Nosso Xote'			
	Slow Paced	Medium Paced	Fast Paced	Too Slow	Correct	Too Fast	Min	Average	Std Dev	Max
Student 1	16	5	6	1	24	2	95.25	98.27	0.99	99.06
Student 2*	5	2	0	5	2	0	97.8	97.97	0.17	98.15
Student 3**	4	3	1	0	7	1	91.44	96.44	3.54	99.07
Student 4	8	6	3	2	14	1	98.32	98.54	0.16	98.8
Student 5	39	14	45	4	96	8	86.41	96.96	3.37	99.47
Student 6	11	2	8	1	20	0	97.95	98.55	0.44	99.06
Student 7	15	13	7	2	24	9	84.26	93.95	4.46	98.15
Student 8	43	11	10	21	27	16	76.5	93.76	4.69	99.93
Student 9	14	5	1	2	15	4	75.95	92.83	9.75	98.89
Student 10	12	7	3	4	17	1	93.86	97.78	1.76	98.86

Columns 2-4: Number of times practice in each level   5-7: Detail of wrong attempts when compare to the song   8-11: Statistics on the consistency score
*Did the exercises without attending to the classes   ** Withdrew from the study

value). Dark green average cells depict a higher value, in average, among all students and if matched with a dark green standard deviation cell, for the same line/column, it means that the average point has a low variance, demonstrating more relevance for the combination (avg & std). Based on the results showed on the table, we can observe that personalised text feedback was the most preferred data representation, with the highest point of clarity and usefulness, especially when presenting information about Rhythm Consistency and Rhythm BPM (Column 3, rows 2 & 3). Body Motion was the type information with more opportunity for improving data representation and further exploration since students could not understand the data (Row 4). The visualisation of Consistency and BPM also open an interesting opportunity since students could not understand the visualisations provided. Therefore, different visualisations could be better understood by the students (Column 2, rows 2 & 3). The summary and social comparison of Practice was clear but not useful. There is no need to explore further this information or other types of representation (Column 1, rows 1 & 5). The results with regards to the visualisations may be strongly influenced by the type of charts chosen to represent the information. We used simple and vastly used techniques like bar, line and boxplot charts. This may suggest that visualisations tailored for this particular information would increase the potential of this data to be useful for dance students.

During the interview, some students commented that they would like to see the visualisations together with the personalised text feedback, so they could learn how to interpret the visualisation and rely just on the visualisations after a while. This was put into words by one of the students as follows: *"I would like to put a chart or graph related to this feedback. Then, I [would be able] to learn about this feedback. I [would be able to] diagnose the chart after seeing this. After learning about the chart [together with the narrative feedback], I would be able to see the chart and know what it means"*. For the summary, they suggested to colour code the cells of the table so it highlights good/bad data. This was described by a student as follows: *"If [the tables] would have some kind of colours and visual clues, it would be good for me"*. The summary comparing students' performance was appreciated by good performing students and disliked by low-performing students, even though low-performing students reported being somehow motivated to improve. One of these students said: *"I really want to do more [exercises], so I can beat everyone else. I really want to work hard now"*, and other two low and high performing students added: *"It does not improve my confidence because everyone is better than me"* and *"This makes me feel really good, I didn't practice as much as other students but my average is quite high"*. In terms of body motion information, some students suggested using a drawing of a human body to present information about the xyz-axes for providing a clearer way to see the data. This was described by a student as follows: *"It would be good to explain in terms of your body, like forwards, backwards, left and right instead of xyz"* and *"If you want people to understand it, it would be better to have a diagram, xyz"*. Some students also would like to have a place to define their goals. *"If*

you have a kind of threshold for goal settings" and *"I can set different targets and different goals in the number of exercises"* Some other minor suggestions were made, that will be used to improve the app, the student open learner model and the open learner model to be provided to the teacher.

The study presented in this paper shows that it is possible to extract simple yet useful features using wearable technology, such as practice, rhythm and consistency, and that others can be extracted but need to be better communicated, such as body motion. The results are limited by the environment in which it was executed. In a live scenario, with students from a dance school, the feedback needs to be better tailored to the specific case and the students' motivation.

6 CONCLUDING REMARKS

In this paper, we presented a first step towards supporting dance learning with personalised technology. Our results point out the potential of harnessing massively adopted wearable technology for assisting social dance students by capturing precise and useful information about their rhythm. We presented a student modelling approach and presented information about critical aspects of rhythm and dancing skills to students for promoting awareness and reflection. This work can serve as a foundation to further explore how motor learning students can benefit from different types of feedback. There are still many challenges ahead regarding the data representation and how to exploit it for more insightful and actionable feedback. This work should be seen as an initial attempt to pave the way by building an important part of the structure and features of the dance learner model.

ACKNOWLEDGMENTS

This work was partially supported by CNPq (Conselho Nacional de Desenvolvimento Científico e Tecnológico - Brazil) under Grant No.: 207539/2014-6, and UFRGS (Universidade Federal do Rio Grande do Sul). Thanks, Henrique Dias Pereira dos Santos for his contributions with the concept and development of the Forró Trainer app.

REFERENCES

[1] Woodrow Barfield, 2015. *Fundamentals of wearable computers and augmented reality.* CRC Press.

[2] Paulette Côté-Laurence, 2000. The role of rhythm in ballet training. *Research in Dance Education 1,* 2, 173-191.

[3] Michel C. Desmarais and Ryan S. J. d. Baker, 2012. A review of recent advances in learner and skill modeling in intelligent learning environments. *User Modeling and User-Adapted Interaction 22,* 1, 9-38.

[4] Dieter Drobny and Jan Borchers, 2010. Learning basic dance choreographies with different augmented feedback modalities. In *CHI'10 Extended Abstracts on Human Factors in Computing Systems* ACM, 3793-3798.

[5] Dieter Drobny, Malte Weiss, and Jan Borchers, 2009. Saltate!: a sensor-based system to support dance beginners. In *CHI'09 Extended Abstracts on Human Factors in Computing Systems* ACM, 3943-3948.

[6] Laura L Flippin, 2013. Salsa Remixed: Learning Language, Culture, and Identity in the Classroom. *Working Papers in Educational Linguistics (WPEL) 28,* 2, 5.

[7] Jill Green, 2002. Somatic knowledge: The body as content and methodology in dance education. *Journal of Dance Education 2,* 4, 114-118.

[8] Julio Guerra, 2016. Open Social Learner Models for Self-Regulated Learning and Learning Motivation. In *Proceedings of the 2016 Conference on User Modeling Adaptation and Personalization* ACM, 329-332.

[9] Piyush Gupta and Tim Dallas, 2014. Feature selection and activity recognition system using a single triaxial accelerometer. *IEEE Transactions on Biomedical Engineering 61*, 6, 1780-1786.

[10] Aristotelis Hadjakos, Erwin Aitenbichler, and Max Mühlhäuser, 2008. Syssomo: A pedagogical tool for analyzing movement variants between different pianists.

[11] Christopher W Hinton-Lewis, Elle McDonough, Gene M Moyle, and David V Thiel, 2016. An Assessment of Postural Sway in Ballet Dancers During First Position, Relevé and Sauté with Accelerometers. *Procedia Engineering 147*, 127-132.

[12] Lu-Ho Hsia, Iwen Huang, and Gwo-Jen Hwang, 2016. Effects of different online peer-feedback approaches on students' performance skills, motivation and self-efficacy in a dance course. *Computers & Education 96*(5//), 55-71.

[13] Avi Karni, Gundela Meyer, Christine Rey-Hipolito, Peter Jezzard, Michelle M. Adams, Robert Turner, and Leslie G. Ungerleider, 1998. The acquisition of skilled motor performance: Fast and slow experience-driven changes in primary motor cortex. *Proceedings of the National Academy of Sciences 95*, 3 (February 3, 1998), 861-868.

[14] David Kirsh, 2013. Embodied cognition and the magical future of interaction design. *ACM Trans. Comput.-Hum. Interact. 20*, 1, 1-30.

[15] Alexandros Kitsikidis, Kosmas Dimitropoulos, Deniz Uğurca, Can Bayçay, Erdal Yilmaz, Filareti Tsalakanidou, Stella Douka, and Nikos Grammalidis, 2015. A Game-like Application for Dance Learning Using a Natural Human Computer Interface. In *International Conference on Universal Access in Human-Computer Interaction* Springer, 472-482.

[16] Cole Nussbaumer Knaflic, 2015. *Storytelling with data: a data visualization guide for business professionals*. John Wiley & Sons.

[17] Jennifer R Kwapisz, Gary M Weiss, and Samuel A Moore, 2011. Activity recognition using cell phone accelerometers. *ACM SigKDD Explorations Newsletter 12*, 2, 74-82.

[18] Kohei Matsumura, Tomoyuki Yamamoto, and Tsutomu Fujinami, 2011. The role of body movement in learning to play the shaker to a samba rhythm: An exploratory study. *Research Studies in Music Education 33*, 1 (June 1, 2011), 31-45.

[19] Gordon McCalla, Julita Vassileva, Jim Greer, and Susan Bull, 2000. Active Learner Modelling, 53-62.

[20] Michael Phillips, Michael Henderson, and Tracii Ryan, 2016. Multimodal feedback is not always clearer, more useful or satisfying. In *Show Me The Learning. Proceedings ASCILITE 2016*, S. BARKER, S. DAWSON, A. PARDO and C. COLVIN Eds., Adelaide, 512-522.

[21] Leyland Pitt, Jan Kietzmann, Karen Robson, Kirk Plangger, Emily Treen, Jeannette Paschen, and David Hannah, 2017. Understanding the Opportunities and Challenges of Wearable Technology. In *Creating Marketing Magic and Innovative Future Marketing Trends* Springer, 139-141.

[22] Olga C Santos, 2017. Toward Personalized Vibrotactile Support When Learning Motor Skills. *Algorithms 10*, 1, 15.

[23] Olga C. Santos, 2016. Training the Body: The Potential of AIED to Support Personalized Motor Skills Learning. *International Journal of Artificial Intelligence in Education 26*, 2, 730-755.

[24] Vidhu V Saxena, Tommy Feldt, and Mohit Goel, 2014. Augmented Telepresence as a Tool for Immersive Simulated Dancing in Experience and Learning. In *Proceedings of the India HCI 2014 Conference on Human Computer Interaction* ACM, 86.

[25] B. Schwendimann, M. Rodriguez-Triana, A. Vozniuk, L. Prieto, M. Boroujeni, A. Holzer, D. Gillet, and P. Dillenbourg, 2016. Perceiving learning at a glance: A systematic literature review of learning dashboard research. *IEEE Transactions on Learning Technologies PP*, 99, 1-1.

[26] David V Thiel, Julian Quandt, Sarah JL Carter, and Gene Moyle, 2014. Accelerometer based performance assessment of basic routines in classical ballet. *Procedia Engineering 72*, 14-19.

Enhancing Student Models in Game-based Learning with Facial Expression Recognition

Robert Sawyer
Department of Computer Science
North Carolina State University
rssawyer@ncsu.edu

Andy Smith
Department of Computer Science
North Carolina State University
pmsmith4@ncsu.edu

Jonathan Rowe
Department of Computer Science
North Carolina State University
jprowe@ncsu.edu

Roger Azevedo
Department of Psychology
North Carolina State University
razeved@ncsu.edu

James Lester
Department of Computer Science
North Carolina State University
lester@ncsu.edu

ABSTRACT

Recent years have seen a growing recognition of the role that affect plays in learning. Because game-based learning environments elicit a wide range of student affective states, affect-enhanced student modeling for game-based learning holds considerable promise. This paper introduces an affect-enhanced student modeling framework that leverages facial expression tracking for game-based learning. The affect-enhanced student modeling framework was used to generate predictive models of student learning and student engagement for students who interacted with CRYSTAL ISLAND, a game-based learning environment for microbiology education. Findings from the study reveal that the affect-enhanced student models significantly outperform baseline predictive student models that utilize the same gameplay traces but do not use facial expression tracking. The study also found that models based on individual facial action coding units are more effective than composite emotion models. The findings suggest that introducing facial expression tracking can improve the accuracy of student models, both for predicting student learning gains and also for predicting student engagement.

KEYWORDS

Student Modeling, Affect, Game-based Learning

1 INTRODUCTION

Affect plays a central role in learning [3, 8, 9, 48]. Positive emotions, such as curiosity and joy, can lead students to engage more deeply in learning, while emotions such as boredom and frustration can lead students to resort to unproductive behaviors including hint abuse and gaming the system, or even to completely disengage [37, 48]. Students exhibit a range of emotions when interacting with adaptive learning environments [13]. Building on recent advances in our understanding of affect, which stem from both manually coded protocols [15, 35] and automated techniques [7, 10, 36], affect-enhanced student models that track and dynamically respond to affect on a moment-by-moment basis offer significant potential for enhancing adaptive learning environments.

While student modeling has long been a goal of the user modeling community [19, 33], student modeling work to date has focused primarily on cognitive aspects of learning [1]. Recent student modeling work has begun to consider how to augment student models with affect [12], as well as to tailor support based on students' affective states, such as confusion, frustration, and boredom [14, 17]. Models of affect have also been used to predict students' reactions to virtual agents [25, 29] and better understand student motivation and off-task behavior [40].

Game-based learning has been studied in a broad range of subject matters and student populations [11, 20, 42, 49]. Because game-based learning environments are designed to provide students with engaging learning experiences, they offer a rich "laboratory" for investigating affect-enhanced student models. This paper reports on an investigation of affect-enhanced student modeling for game-based learning. Specifically, using a game-based learning environment for microbiology education, CRYSTAL ISLAND [38], we compare two approaches to student modeling: an affect-enhanced student model that uses facial expression tracking in addition to gameplay data, and a baseline student model that uses only gameplay data. We compare the accuracy of the models for predicting both student learning (measured with normalized learning gain) and student presence (a facet of engagement measured with participant perception of transportation into a virtual environment through a standard self-report instrument [4]). In addition, we compare two competing approaches to affect recognition—composite emotion models and models based on individual facial action coding units—to explore how different types of facial expression tracking can support affect-enhanced student modeling.

UMAP '17, July 09-12, 2017, Bratislava, Slovakia
© 2017 Association for Computing Machinery.
ACM ISBN 978-1-4503-4635-1/17/07...$15.00
http://dx.doi.org/10.1145/3079628.3079686

2 RELATED WORK

Learning and affect are inextricably linked. It has been found, for example, that positively valenced emotions tend to support student learning [37]. Confusion has been shown to be beneficial to learning in certain contexts [16], yet students experiencing anxiety or anger tend to be less efficient learners [37]. Student affect correlates with problem-solving performance [39] and is predictive of user interactions with virtual agents [25]. Recognizing the potential for affect to inform student modeling in learning environments, recent work with automated affect detectors has found that integrating detectors into Bayesian knowledge tracing models can improve predictive accuracy of student performance [12].

Although there are many open questions about which emotions or sets of emotions offer the greatest potential for adaptive learning environments, as well as which sets of multimodal data streams can best support adaptivity in learning environments, facial expression tracking has emerged as a promising means for inferring learning-centric emotions [10, 28]. Arroyo et al. [2] used facial expressions in combination with other sensors to trigger interventions, which appeared to increase on-task behavior and reduce hint-abuse. Bosch et al. [7] created models that accurately predict student affect with facial action units in a classroom setting that generalized across multiple days and multiple classrooms. Grafsgaard et al. [24] found an additive relationship between facial expressions, dialogue acts, and task performance in a tutoring system, and more recent work in this line of investigation found that male and female students exhibit significant differences in facial expressions [43]. Collectively, this work suggests that facial expressions provide a window into affect and learning that can be utilized by student models to support adaptive learning environments.

Upon detecting student affective states, adaptive learning environments can deliver a broad range of possible supports for student learning and emotion regulation. For example, D'Mello et al. [14, 17] devised a modified version of AutoTutor that delivered affect-sensitive dialogue moves, facial displays of emotion, and synthesized speech patterns in response to student affect. Results indicated that the affect-sensitive interventions had a positive impact on student learning among low prior knowledge students, but a neutral or even harmful impact on student learning in other conditions. DeFalco et al. [18] found that self-efficacy-oriented feedback messages, which were delivered in response to detected learner frustration, helped to enhance student learning in a simulation-based training environment for military combat medics. However, the feedback messages were not found to mitigate occurrences of frustration itself during training.

Although student modeling has been investigated for decades in the intelligent tutoring systems community [44], only recently has student modeling research turned to game-based learning. Baker et al. [6] analyzed game-trace logs in the Virtual Performance Assessments system to create assessment models of students' ability to design controlled experiments and apply inquiry skills. Using evidence-centered design, Bayesian network-based stealth assessments of student knowledge have been explored in both the Physics Playground and a modified version of the popular game, Plants vs. Zombies [26, 41], and other work in this vein has explored deep learning-based models of stealth assessment for game-based learning [31]. Student goal recognition has also been investigated in game-based learning, with approaches spanning Bayesian networks [34], Markov logic networks [5], and long short-term memory networks [32]. The affect-enhanced student modeling approach presented here extends earlier work in student modeling for game-based learning to exploit facial expression data to improve student models' predictive accuracy.

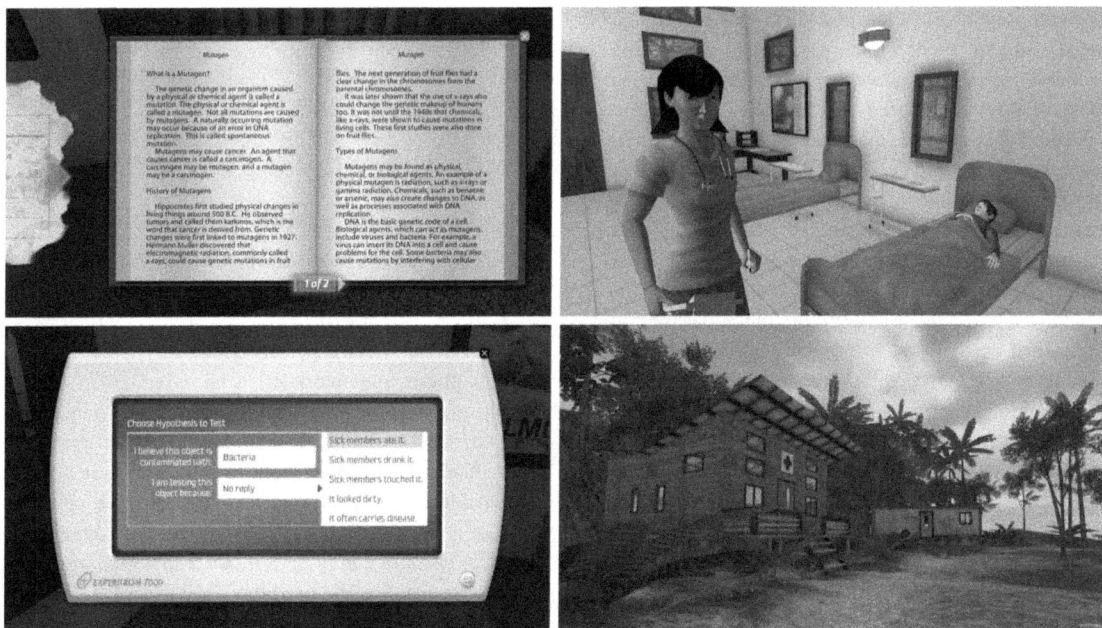

Figure 1. Screenshots from CRYSTAL ISLAND illustrating a virtual textbook, non-player characters, the virtual scanner, and game environment.

3 CRYSTAL ISLAND

We explore affect-enhanced student modeling in a study conducted with an intelligent game-based learning environment for science problem solving in microbiology, CRYSTAL ISLAND [38]. Intelligent game-based learning environments integrate the personalized learning supports of intelligent tutoring systems [27, 45] with the engaging interactions afforded by game technologies. In CRYSTAL ISLAND, students take on the role of a medical field agent tasked with investigating an epidemic on a remote island research station. The student must discover the source and identity of the disease as well as recommend a treatment plan to aid the infected members of the island's research team.

In CRYSTAL ISLAND, students engage in a range of problem-solving actions to gather information, test hypotheses, and diagnose a solution. Examples of student activities in the game include exploring the island environment, conversing with non-player characters, running tests on potentially contaminated items in a virtual laboratory, and completing an in-game diagnosis worksheet to report findings and solve the mystery. The open-world game environment features several buildings, including an infirmary, dining hall, laboratory, and various residences where the student can gather information by talking to characters. Relevant microbiology concepts about viruses, bacteria, immunization, and how diseases spread are found in virtual books and articles scattered throughout the buildings of the island. Students use knowledge gained from both the informational texts and dialogue with non-player characters to diagnose the illness and solve the mystery. Students successfully complete the game by submitting a worksheet to the camp nurse with the correct diagnosis, identified transmission object, and treatment solution.

4 METHODS AND DATA

To investigate the potential contributions of affect to student modeling, we compare two approaches. First, we created an affect-enhanced student model that uses facial expression tracking in combination with gameplay. As students played CRYSTAL ISLAND, video was captured of their facial expressions. We created predictive student models that used both the facial expression data stream and the gameplay data stream to predict students' learning and students' sense of presence, a core component of engagement. We then created a baseline student model that also predicts students' learning and presence but only uses the gameplay data stream. We compare the performance of these two models and explore the impact of two approaches to facial recognition tracking for affect-enhanced student modeling: (1) composite emotion models and (2) models based on individual facial action coding units.

4.1 Participants and Experimental Setup

The study involved 37 college age students that interacted with the CRYSTAL ISLAND game-based learning environment in a lab setting. Four students were removed due to partial or missing data, resulting in 33 students (M = 19.9 years old, SD = 1.30), of

which 17 (51.5%) were female. All remaining students played the game to completion, and time spent playing the game ranged from 26.4 to 105.1 minutes (M = 63.7, SD = 18.4). Prior to interacting with the game, students completed a 20-question multiple-choice test assessing their conceptual and application-based understanding of microbiology. At conclusion of gameplay, students completed a Presence Questionnaire [46] and again completed the same microbiology assessment.

4.2 Survey Measures

In order to assess student learning, we examined students' performance on the microbiology content test administered before and after students' interactions with CRYSTAL ISLAND. Using the difference between the pre-test score (Pre-Test) and post-test score (Post-Test), Normalized Learning Gain was calculated for each student participating in the study. Normalized Learning Gain is the difference between Post-Test and Pre-Test, standardized by the total amount of improvement or decline possible from the Pre-Test. Students achieved positive Normalized Learning Gain on average (M = 0.226, SD = 0.315), with 25 of the 33 (75.8%) students achieving positive Normalized Learning Gain (Post-Test greater than Pre-Test).

$$\text{Normalized Learning Gain} = \begin{cases} \dfrac{\text{Post} - \text{Pre}}{1 - \text{Pre}} & \text{Post} > \text{Pre} \\[2mm] \dfrac{\text{Post} - \text{Pre}}{\text{Pre}} & \text{Post} \leq \text{Pre} \end{cases}$$

We use presence as a proxy for engagement in the game environment. In order to assess student presence, the Presence Questionnaire was used to measure players' self-reported perceptions of *presence* [47], which refers to a participant's perception of transportation into a virtual environment. The questionnaire contains a series of 30 questions that students answer on a 7-point scale to characterize their in-game experience with a virtual environment. The questionnaire consists of several subscales for measuring presence, such as involvement, sensory fidelity, adaptation/immersion, and interface quality. To measure presence, we summed the numeric responses to all 30 questions to obtain a presence score for each student, which ranged from 116 to 209 (M = 155, SD = 23.4).

4.3 Facial Expression Recognition

Facial expression features were extracted automatically through a video-based facial expression tracking system, iMotions.[1] The iMotions system extracts facial features that correspond to the Facial Action Coding System (FACS) [21, 22]. It uses an objective three-phase framework of facial detection from image input, feature detection (i.e., locating position of facial landmarks), and feature classification to report an evidence score representing the likelihood of a particular affective measure being present. A separate classifier is used for each affective measure, ranging from low-level facial expression features such as Action Units (AUs) to more complex, composite affective measures, such as *Surprise* and *Joy*. We used the facial expression tracking system to monitor students during gameplay to provide real-time

---

[1] The iMotions software was previously commercially available as FACET and the research-focused toolbox CERT [30].

evidence scores for 20 AUs and 9 composite affective measures. The 9 composite affective measures include *Anger, Surprise, Frustration, Joy, Confusion, Fear, Disgust, Sadness,* and *Contempt.* Table 1 displays the relationships between composite affective measures and AUs as defined by iMotions.

Table 1. Breakdown of Composites by contributing AU.

Composite Measure	Contributing AUs
Joy	6 + 12
Sadness	1 + 4 + 15
Surprise	1 + 2 + 5 + 26
Fear	2 + 4 + 5 + 7 + 20 + 26
Anger	4 + 5 + 7 + 23
Disgust	9 + 15 + 16
Contempt	12 + 14

Predictive models require higher-level features than are provided by the evidence scores. We performed feature engineering to transform the evidence scores to a representation that could be effectively used by the student models. We used a method with relative thresholding by amplitude and summed over durations to minimize the effect of micro expressions. First, the evidence scores were standardized for each student by subtracting the mean evidence and dividing by the standard deviation evidence over their entire episode. While iMotions calibrates the evidence scores over the first few observations, it does not account for the potential variability of evidence for students. Thus, dividing by the standard deviation of a student's evidence score over the episode accounts for potential variability in expressiveness of individuals. Events were added to the affect log for the duration that the standardized evidence scores rose above a threshold of one. These events represent moments when evidence scores rose one standard deviation above the mean evidence score for a particular student. The duration of these events in each affective measure (i.e., the 20 AUs and 9 Composites) is summed over the gameplay episode of a student. The final feature used in student modeling is this sum (i.e., the duration of the evidence score was above one standard deviation above the mean evidence score) divided by the total time the student spent playing the game. These affective features thus represent the proportion of gameplay duration that the respective affective evidence score was one standard deviation above the mean evidence score for a particular student.

4.3 Gameplay Behavior Logging

Gameplay interactions with CRYSTAL ISLAND were recorded in a granular timestamped game log for each student. From these game interaction logs, several measures were calculated to summarize student behavior in the game-based learning environment. The actions recorded include how students gather information (e.g., reading books and articles, speaking with non-player characters), select and organize information (e.g., editing the diagnosis worksheet), and test their hypotheses (e.g., scanning objects, submitting the worksheet as the final solution). The

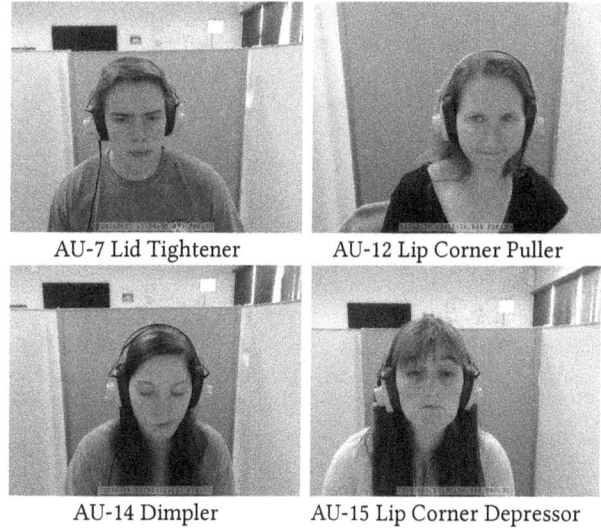

AU-7 Lid Tightener — AU-12 Lip Corner Puller

AU-14 Dimpler — AU-15 Lip Corner Depressor

Figure 2. Examples of AUs used.

measures used as features in predictive modeling include both the number of actions performed and the duration of actions with varying lengths. The set of actions reported includes conversations with non-player characters (*ConversationCount* and *ConversationDuration*), items scanned in the virtual laboratory (*ScannerCount*), books and articles read (*BooksReadCount* and *ReadingDuration*), edits to the diagnosis worksheet (*WorksheetCount* and *WorksheetDuration*), and the number of times the worksheet was submitted for final evaluation (*SubmitCount*). These measures were also standardized by the total time the student spent playing the game to represent rate-per-minute for counts and proportion of time spent performing each of the actions over a given duration (Table 2). The units for counts are shown in counts-per-minute, while the units for durations are in seconds-per-minute, representing a proportion out of 60.

Table 2. Mean and standard deviations of gameplay behaviors.

Gameplay Behaviors	Mean (per minute)	Standard Deviation
ConversationCount	0.797	0.216
BooksReadCount	0.352	0.119
WorksheetCount	0.352	0.159
SubmitCount	0.029	0.017
ScannerCount	0.389	0.223
ConversationDuration	7.900	2.070
ReadingDuration	24.100	5.280
WorksheetDuration	5.150	1.970

5 RESULTS

We used three different subsets of the full feature set in order to compare predictive student models of Normalized Learning Gain and Presence. The first feature subset (Gameplay) consisted of only the 8 gameplay features (actions and durations of select actions) to represent a baseline model without affect information. The second feature subset consisted of the gameplay actions and the 9 different composite affective features (Gameplay+Composites). The third feature subset consisted of the gameplay actions with the 20 different AU affective features (Gameplay+AUs). The composite features and AUs are treated separately due to multicollinearity issues stemming from the fact that composites are combinations of the AUs. The AUs provide a more granular measure while the composites provide a higher level, more interpretable measure of affect. We compare the performance of each feature subset predicting Normalized Learning Gain and Presence for a total of 6 models (3 feature subsets x 2 response variables), with 2 being baseline models using only gameplay features, and the other 4 being affect-enhanced models of student learning and presence.

Variables for a linear model were chosen using a forward stepwise linear regression where features were selected from their respective subset to optimize leave-one-out cross-validation (LOOCV) R^2. The reported models are the result of using the selected features in an ordinary least squares linear regression model.

5.1 Baseline Models

Baseline predictive models for Normalized Learning Gain and Presence were created using the stepwise feature selection process using the subset of 8 gameplay features. In addition to standard linear regression measures, (coefficients, standard error of coefficients, standardized coefficients and t-statistic for significance of feature), the leave-one-out cross validation R^2 is reported as the measure of the accuracy of the model.

The highest performing Normalized Learning Gain model using gameplay features for leave-one-out cross validation R^2 is shown in Table 1. This linear model uses two gameplay features to predict Normalized Learning Gain: *ScannerCount* and *ReadingDuration*. The model achieves a leave-one-out cross validation R^2 of 0.268. The negative coefficient of *ScannerCount* indicates that the more often students scan items in the virtual laboratory, the lower Normalized Learning Gain they achieve. Conversely, the longer students read, the higher their Normalized Learning Gain, an intuitive result since much of the microbiology assessment focuses on content found in the game-based learning environment's virtual books and articles.

Table 3. Resulting linear model predicting Normalized Learning Gain using gameplay features.

Baseline Model for Normalized Learning Gain			
	B	SE B	β	p-value
Scanner Count	-0.318	0.242	-0.224	0.198
Reading Duration	0.0279	0.0102	0.466	0.010*
Leave-One Out CV R^2 = 0.268			

Note: ** - p < 0.01, * - p < 0.05

The optimal Presence model using gameplay features under leave-one-out cross validation R^2 yields *ConversationCount* and *WorksheetCount* as the only two gameplay features used to predict Presence. This model achieves a leave-one-out cross

validation R^2 of 0.147. The negative coefficients for each of the features selected suggests that more conversations with non-player characters and more edits of the worksheet lead to lower Presence outcomes. The LOOCV R^2 for the Presence model is lower than the Gameplay model for Normalized Learning Gain, revealing that predictions for Presence using only gameplay features are worse relative to the total sum of squares for Presence than similar predictions using only gameplay features for Normalized Learning Gain. This indicates that Presence is more challenging to predict from Gameplay features than Normalized Learning Gain.

Table 4. Resulting linear model for predicting Presence from gameplay features.

Baseline Model for Presence			
	B	SE B	β	p-value
Conversation Count	-31.9	17.5	-0.294	0.078
Worksheet Count	-52.6	23.6	-0.359	0.034*
Leave-One Out CV R^2 = 0.147			

Note: ** - p < 0.01, * - p < 0.05

5.2 Affect-Enhanced Composite Models

Next, we explored the potential of affect-enhanced predictive models for Normalized Learning Gain and Presence by introducing the 9 composite affective measures with the previous 8 gameplay features denoted Affect-Enhanced Composite models. From this set of 17 features, we performed the same forward stepwise feature selection technique optimizing for LOOCV R^2 and report the resulting models.

Table 5. Resulting linear model for predicting Normalized Learning Gain from gameplay and composite-affect features.

Affect-Enhanced Composite Model for Normalized Learning Gain			
	B	SE B	β	p-value
Scanner Count	-0.369	0.237	-0.261	0.130
Reading Duration	0.0212	0.0106	0.364	0.049*
Surprise	-0.0183	0.0112	-0.246	0.111
Leave-One Out CV R^2 = 0.324			

Note: ** - p < 0.01, * - p < 0.05

The optimal Affect-Enhanced Composite model for predicting Normalized Learning Gain uses three features and achieves a LOOCV R^2 of 0.324. Of the three features selected from a potential 17, two are gameplay features (*ScannerCount* and *ReadingDuration*), and one is a Composite feature (*Surprise*). It is important to note that these two gameplay features are the same for the Baseline model for Normalized Learning Gain, indicating that adding *Surprise* to that model improves the predictive accuracy for Normalized Learning Gain from an LOOCV R^2 of 0.268 to 0.324. The coefficients of the two gameplay features are also similar to those of the Baseline model, indicating that the incorporation of *Surprise* improves the former model without making drastic changes to the former model parameter estimates. The negative coefficient of *Surprise* suggests that, holding other variables constant, more surprise leads to reduced Normalized Learning Gain.

Table 6. Resulting linear model for predicting Presence from gameplay and composite-affect features.

Affect-Enhanced Composite Model for Presence				
	B	SE B	β	p-value
Conversation Count	-39.3	16.4	-0.362	0.024*
Worksheet Count	-64.0	21.6	-0.437	0.006**
Disgust	-4.56	1.95	-0.369	0.027*
Confusion	-2.20	1.29	-0.325	0.099
Sadness	3.44	1.20	0.560	0.008**
Leave-One Out CV R^2 = 0.245				

Note: ** - p < 0.01, * - p < 0.05

The optimal Affect-Enhanced Composite model for Presence achieves a LOOCV R^2 of 0.245, improving on the Baseline LOOCV R^2 of 0.147. This model uses five features, with the same two gameplay features (*ConversationCount* and *WorksheetCount*) as the Baseline model and three features from the set of Composite measures (*Disgust, Confusion,* and *Sadness*). The negative coefficients of *Disgust* and *Confusion* indicate that students experiencing more duration with elevated standardized evidence score for these composite emotions exhibited lower Presence. Conversely, students with a higher proportion of expressed *Sadness* reported higher Presence. This Affect-Enhanced Composite model also indicates an additive effect in the sense that the same gameplay features were maintained, but the predictive accuracy is improved by incorporating several Composite features.

5.3 Affect-Enhanced AU Models

While the Affect-Enhanced Composite models improve upon the Baseline models, the Action Units (AUs) measured by iMotions provide low-level feature evidence scores that offer a more granular level of facial expression features than the Composite measures. Creating predictive models from this more granular measure of affect may produce a more accurate affect-enhanced model at the cost of interpretability since the AUs constitute a lower-level facial expression feature than the Composite measures. There are 20 AUs measured by iMotions, yielding a total feature set of 28 when including the gameplay features that can potentially be used in modeling students' normalized learning gain and presence.

Using the forward stepwise feature selection optimizing LOOCV R^2 for predicting Normalized Learning Gain from the feature set of 20 AUs and 8 Gameplay features generates a model with six features and a LOOCV R^2 of 0.475. The two gameplay

features selected (*ScannerCount* and *ReadingDuration*) are the same as the Affect-Enhanced Composite model and Baseline model for Normalized Learning Gain. The other four features were AUs, including *AU1 Inner Brow Raiser, AU14 Dimpler, AU15 Lip Corner Depressor,* and *AU43 Eyes Closed.* Because the *Sadness* measure is partially composed of *AU1 Inner Brow Raiser* (as indicated by Table 1), the inclusion of *AU1 Inner Brow Raiser* shows the similarity between the affect-enhanced models because *Sadness* was included in the Composite-Affect Normalized Learning Gain model. The coefficients for both Gameplay features remain similar to both the Affect-Enhanced Composite Normalized Learning Gain model and the Baseline Normalized Learning Gain model. The addition of the AUs into this linear model provides a greater LOOCV R^2 than either the baseline Normalized Learning Gain model or Affect-Enhanced Composite Normalized Learning Gain model. Thus, the Affect-Enhanced AU Normalized Learning Gain model exemplifies the additive value of more granular affective measures in the predictive models for Normalized Learning Gain, compared to the Affect-Enhanced Composite Normalized Learning Gain model.

Table 7. Resulting linear model from predicting Normalized Learning Gain.

Affect-Enhanced AU Model for Normalized Learning Gain				
	B	SE B	β	p-value
Scanner Count	-0.294	0.203	-0.207	0.159
Reading Duration	0.0353	0.0087	0.590	< 0.001**
AU1	-0.0290	0.0085	-0.413	0.002**
AU14	-0.0548	0.0157	-0.534	0.002**
AU15	0.0470	0.0186	0.390	0.018*
AU43	-0.0340	0.0163	-0.265	0.048*
Leave-One Out CV R^2 = 0.475				

Note: ** - p < 0.01, * - p < 0.05

An Affect-Enhanced AU Presence model was created using the feature set of 20 AUs and 8 gameplay features and the same feature selection techniques as the previous models. This resulted in five selected features, the same two gameplay features from the previous Presence models (*ConversationCount* and *WorksheetCount*) along with three AUs. The included AUs were *AU7 Lid Tightener, AU12 Lip Corner Puller,* and *AU28 Lip Suck.* While the gameplay features are the same as the Affect-Enhanced Composite and Baseline Presence models, none of the AUs included in the Affect-Enhanced AU Presence model contribute to the composite features included in the Affect-Enhanced Composite model. The Affect-Enhanced AU Presence model results in an increased LOOCV R^2 over both the Affect-Enhanced Composite model and Baseline model. Since this model preserves similar coefficients for the same features used in the Baseline Presence model, it appears the AUs improve the predictive accuracy of the Baseline in terms of LOOCV R^2.

Table 8. Resulting linear model from predicting Presence from gameplay and AU-affect features.

Affect-Enhanced AU Model for Presence			
	B	**SE B**	**β**	**p-value**
Conversation Count	-26.5	15.9	-0.244	0.107
Worksheet Count	-58.3	21.5	-0.398	0.011*
AU7	-4.89	1.58	-0.581	0.005**
AU12	3.88	1.61	0.440	0.023*
AU28	-2.01	0.822	-0.367	0.022*
Leave-One Out CV R^2 = 0.296			

Note: ** - $p < 0.01$, * - $p < 0.05$

The predictive accuracy of the three families of student models is shown in Figure 3. The results show that including facial expression features improved the predictive power of the models for both learning gains and presence. Similarly, models utilizing action unit features achieved higher predictive accuracy than models using the composite emotion labels. This superior performance was achieved for both learning gains and presence. While the models of learning gains outperform their counterparts for presence for each model structure, the Affect-Enhanced Composite Presence model shows a larger increase from the Baseline than the Affect-Enhanced Composite Normalized Learning Gain model, while the Affect-Enhanced AU Normalized Learning Gain model shows a larger increase from utilizing AU features than the Presence model.

The Affect-Enhanced models use the same gameplay features as the Baseline models, with the addition of several affective features. Thus, the Baseline models are nested within the Affect-Enhanced models, with the Affect-Enhanced models acting as "full models" and the Baselines as "reduced models." Since the Baseline models are nested within their respective Affect-Enhanced Composite and Affect-Enhanced AU models, an F-test provides a measure of the contributions of the additional features included in the full models over the reduced models. Results from this test show that the Affect-Enhanced Composite Normalized Learning Gain model's addition of one additional feature (*Surprise*) does not show significant improvement over the Baseline Normalized Learning Gain model ($F(1,29)$ = 2.70, p = 0.11). The Affect-Enhanced AU Normalized Learning Gain model's addition of four features shows significant improvement over the Baseline Normalized Learning Gain model ($F(4, 26)$ = 5.12, p = 0.004) in terms of reduction in residual sum of squares.

For the Presence models, results indicate that both the Affect-Enhanced Composite ($F(3, 27)$ = 3.37, p = 0.033) and Affect-Enhanced AU ($F(3, 27)$ = 3.95, p = 0.019) Presence models' incorporation of three affective features show significant improvement over the Baseline Presence model in terms of reduction in sum of squared errors.

6 DISCUSSION

The results of the study suggest that affect-enhanced student models can improve upon predictive accuracy compared to models based exclusively on student behavior in the learning environment. By augmenting gameplay data with facial expression data, affect-enhanced student models significantly outperformed models using only gameplay features. Additionally, the models using the more granular action unit data significantly outperformed models using the composite emotions. These results highlight the importance of decisions about the granularity of affect data representation.

Across multiple feature sets, predictive models for Normalized Learning Gain outperformed models for Presence, as measured by leave-one-out cross validation R^2. In all of the Normalized Learning Gain models, *ReadingDuration* is included with high significance. The virtual books and articles contain information relevant to questions presented in the microbiology assessment, making it a strong candidate for predicting the learning gain assessed by the microbiology test. For both learning gains and presence, the models utilizing the more granular AUs achieved significantly higher predictive accuracy than those utilizing composite emotions. This could be due to a

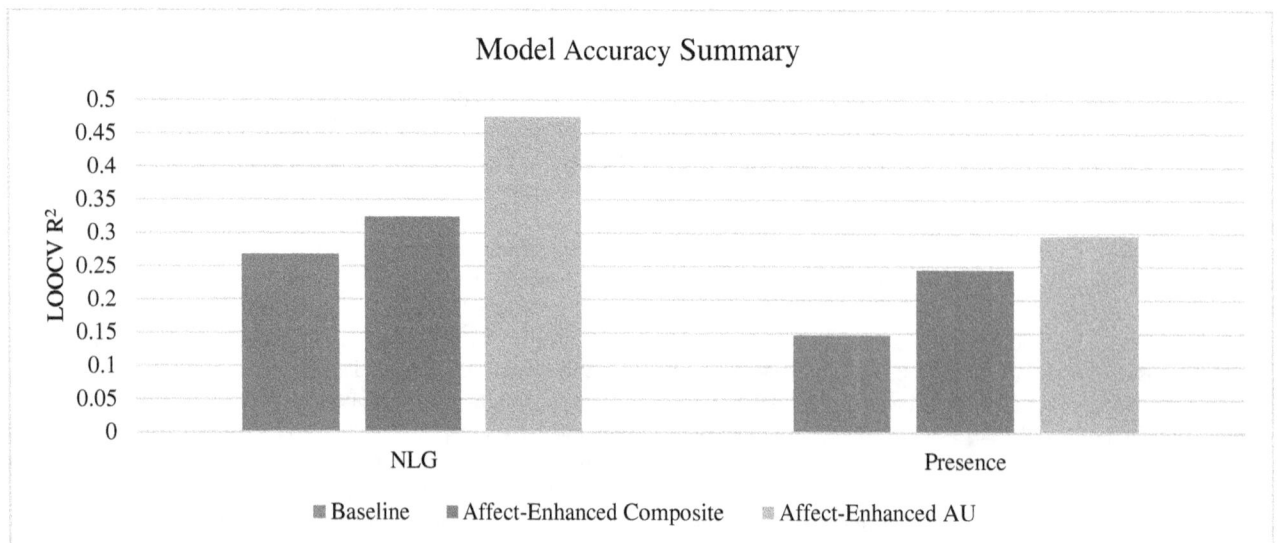

Figure 3. Summary of leave-one-out cross validation R^2 for Baseline and Affect-Enhanced

variety of factors. First, the automatic tagging of AUs may be more accurate, which is plausible as action units represent more concretely represented phenomena than the composite emotions. In addition, the facial expression tracking framework underlying the emotion recognition system was trained on a library of posed faces, which are potentially more expressive than emotions that appear in a learning context. It could also be the case that important information is being captured by AUs that is not captured by the composite emotion labels. For example, an AU may be conveying a subtle expression of an emotion not captured by the composite labeling. It is also possible that the AUs are representing a contextually-specific response not captured by the composite labels, such as signaling increased cognitive load.

Analysis of the specific emotions present in the composite models show that less *Surprise* is more predictive of learning gains. The result highlights the need to further investigate where in the gameplay activity the periods of *Surprise* tend to occur. Similarly, for presence measures, the model shows less *Disgust* and less *Contempt* and increased *Sadness* to be predictive of presence. While the relationship for *Disgust* and *Contempt* align with what one would expect for increased presence, increased *Sadness* does not appear to align, though could potentially be related to students' empathy for the sick patients in the mystery or emotional investment in solving the mystery.

Many of the AUs found to be significant in this work have previously been found as commonly occurring AUs that have predictive significance for tutoring outcomes [23]. The presence of *AU14 Dimpler* being negatively associated with learning is a result also found in a study of affect in tutoring [24], which found *AU14 Dimpler* to be an indicator of lower engagement and higher frustration. *AU1 Inner Brow Raiser* is associated with surprise, which was the only emotion present in the composite model, further strengthening the need to further investigate which game events are triggering the reaction. For the presence models, *AU7 Lid Tightener* and *AU28 Lip Suck* were negatively associated with presence. These AUs have been associated with increased mental effort, which may negatively impact student perceptions of "transportation" into the virtual environment.

While AUs may produce better models, using them sacrifices some of the interpretability found in the composite models. For example, one can imagine designing an adaptive intervention to induce *confusion*, or perhaps reduce *frustration*, but it is not as clear what the design implications would be for inducing or decreasing a specific AU. While some AUs can be related to composite emotions, others may be more difficult to categorize or require additional information to contextualize. On the other hand, composite emotions may not always be more interpretable, as shown by the features in the presence model. The trade-off between predictive ability and interpretability is one that requires further investigation, and may depend on the types of adaptivity that a game-based learning environment is designed to provide. One approach to improving interpretability would be to investigate how these models differ as students move through a game. While the data presented here was accumulated through complete playthroughs of a game, examining how facial expressions evolve as students transition between affective states throughout different phases of the gameplay session may help identify specific game events or

contexts that produce the most desirable reactions. For example, expressions of frustration may be distributed evenly through the session, or they may be triggered by specific events. A more granular analysis of the data may help identify such scenarios, allowing for targeted and effective supports to be incorporated into the game-based learning environment.

7 CONCLUSION

Affect is integral to learning and problem solving in adaptive learning environments. Creating affect-enhanced student models has the potential to provide the foundation for the next generation of adaptive learning environments that are more effective and more engaging. Because game-based learning environments are specifically designed for the dual goals of increasing learning effectiveness and increasing student engagement, the prospect of introducing affect-enhanced student models into game-based learning environments may be a particularly fruitful line of investigation. Creating affect-enhanced student models that leverage facial expression analysis could potentially yield student models that can more accurately predict student learning and engagement and, ultimately, contribute to improved student experiences through more informed adaptation.

In this work we have investigated affect-enhanced student models with a game-based learning environment. Baseline models using gameplay features were created to predict normalized learning gain and presence using a forward stepwise feature selection methodology. Two sets of affect-enhanced student models, one based on composite emotion models and one based on action units, were created. Both affect-enhanced student models augmented gameplay data with these features sets. Results show that the affect-enhanced student models improve upon the predictive accuracy of baseline models. The additional features incorporated in the affect-enhanced models were also found to significantly contribute to predictive accuracy, suggesting that the affective features provide additive value. The action-unit-based affect-enhanced models performed better than the composite-based affect-enhanced models, achieving predictive accuracy improvements for both student learning (as measured by normalized learning gain) and student engagement (as measured by presence). In future work, it will be important to investigate the integration of affect-enhanced student models into runtime game-based learning environments. Explorations of run-time integration should include early prediction modeling and game-based adaptation that uses the affect-enhanced student models to guide both cognitive and affective scaffolding and to understand their impact on learning processes and outcomes.

Acknowledgements

We thank our collaborators in the Center of Educational Informatics and the SMART Lab at North Carolina State University. This study was supported by funding from the Social Sciences and Humanities Research Council of Canada. Any opinions, findings, and conclusions or recommendations expressed in this material are those of the author(s) and do not necessarily reflect the views of the Social Sciences and Humanities Research Council of Canada.

REFERENCES

[1]   Aleven, V., Mclaughlin, E., Glenn, R. and Koedinger, K. 2016. Instruction Based on Adaptive Learning Technologies. *Handbook of Research on Learning and Instruction.* R. Mayer and P. Alexander, eds. Routledge, London, UK.

[2]   Arroyo, I., Ferguson, K., Johns, J., Dragon, T., Mehranian, H., Fisher, D., Barto, A., Mahadevan, S. and Woolf, B. 2007. Repairing Disengagement with Non-Invasive Interventions. In *Proceedings of the 13th International Conference on Artificial Intelligence in Education.* Los Angeles, CA, 195–202.

[3]   Azevedo, R. and Aleven, V. eds. 2013. *International Handbook of Metacognition and Learning Technologies.* Springer New York.

[4]   Azevedo, R., Taub, M., Mudrick, N.V., Martin, S.A. and Grafsgaard, J. 2017. Using Multi-Channel Trace Data to Infer and Foster Self-Regulated Learning Between Humans and Advanced Learning Technologies. *Handbook of self-regulation of learning and performance.* D.H. Schunk and J.A. Greene, eds. Routledge, London, UK.

[5]   Baikadi, A., Rowe, J., Mott, B. and Lester, J. 2014. Generalizability of Goal Recognition Models in Narrative-Centered Learning Environments. In *Proceedings of the 22nd Conference on User Modeling, Adaptation, and Personalization.* Springer, Aalborg, Denmark, 278–289.

[6]   Baker, R. and Clarke-Midura, J. 2013. Predicting Successful Inquiry Learning in a Virtual Performance Assessment for Science. In *Proceedings of the 21st International Conference on User Modeling, Adaptation and Personalization.* Springer, Rome, Italy, 203–214.

[7]   Bosch, N., D'Mello, S., Ocumpaugh, J., Baker, R. and Shute, V. 2016. Using Video to Automatically Detect Learner Affect in Computer-Enabled Classrooms. *ACM Transactions on Interactive Intelligent Systems,* 6 (2), 17:1-26.

[8]   Calvo, R. and D'Mello, S. 2011. *New Perspectives on Affect and Learning Technologies.* Springer. New York, New York, USA.

[9]   Calvo, R., D'Mello, S., Gratch, J. and Kappas, A. 2015. *The Oxford Handbook of Affective Computing.* Oxford University Press. New York, New York, USA.

[10]   Calvo, R. and Mello, S. 2010. Affect Detection: An Interdisciplinary Review of Models, Methods, and Their Applications. *IEEE Transactions on affective computing,* 1 (1), 18–37.

[11]   Clark, D., Tanner-Smith, E. and Killingsworth, S. 2016. Digital Games, Design, and Learning: A Systematic Review and Meta-Analysis. *Review of Educational Research,* 86 (1), 79–122.

[12]   Corrigan, S., Barkley, T. and Pardos, Z. 2015. Dynamic Approaches to Modeling Student Affect and Its Changing Role in Learning and Performance. In *Proceedings of the 23rd International Conference on User Modeling, Adaptation and Personalization.* Springer, Dublin, Ireland, 92–103.

[13]   D'Mello, S. 2013. A Selective Meta-Analysis on the Relative Incidence of Discrete Affective States during Learning with Technology. *Journal of Educational Psychology,* 105 (4), 1082–1099.

[14]   D'Mello, S. and Graesser, A. 2012. AutoTutor and Affective AutoTutor: Learning by Talking with Cognitively and Emotionally Intelligent Computers that Talk Back? *ACM Transactions on Interactive Intelligent Systems,* 15 (212), 434–442.

[15]   D'Mello, S. and Graesser, A. 2014. Confusion and Its Dynamics during Device Comprehension with Breakdown Scenarios. *Acta Psychologica,* 151, 106–116.

[16]   D'Mello, S., Lehman, B., Pekrun, R. and Graesser, A. 2014. Confusion can be Beneficial for Learning. *Learning and Instruction,* 29, 153–170.

[17]   D'Mello, S., Lehman, B., Sullins, J., Daigle, R., Combs, R., Vogt, K., Perkins, L. and Graesser, A. 2010. A Time for Emoting: When Affect-Sensitivity Is and Isn't Effective at Promoting Deep Learning. In *Proceedings of the International Conference on Intelligent Tutoring Systems.* Springer, Pittsburgh, PA, 245–254.

[18]   Defalco, J., Georgoulas-Sherry, V., Paquette, L., Baker, R., Rowe, J., Mott, B. and Lester, J. 2016. Motivational Feedback Messages as Interventions to Frustration in GIFT. In *Proceedings of the Fourth GIFT User Symposium(GIFTSym4).* Princeton, NJ, *25-35.*

[19]   Desmarais, M. and Baker, R. 2011. A Review of Recent Advances in Learner and Skill Modeling in Intelligent Learning Environments. *User Modeling and User-Adapted Interaction,* 22 (1–2), 9–38.

[20]   Easterday, M., Aleven, V., Scheines, R. and Carver, S. 2016. Using Tutors to Improve Educational Games: A Cognitive Game for Policy Argument. *Journal of the Learning Sciences,* 26 (2), 226–276.

[21]   Ekman, P. and Friesen, W. 1977. *Facial Action Coding System.*

[22]   Ekman, P. and Rosenberg, E. 1997. *What the Face Reveals: Basic and Applied Studies of Spontaneous Expression Using the Facial Action Coding System (FACS).* Oxford University Press. New York, New York, USA.

[23]   Grafsgaard, J., Wiggins, J., Boyer, K., Wiebe, E. and Lester, J. 2013. Automatically Recognizing Facial Expression: Predicting Engagement and Frustration. In *Proceedings of the 6th International Conference on Educational Data Mining.* Memphis, TN, 43-50.

[24]   Grafsgaard, J., Wiggins, J., Vail, A., Boyer, K., Wiebe, E. and Lester, J. 2014. The Additive Value of Multimodal Features for Predicting Engagement, Frustration, and Learning during Tutoring. In *Proceedings of the 16th International Conference on Multimodal Interaction (ICMI '14).* Istanbul, Turkey, 42–49.

[25]   Harley, J., Carter, C., Papaionnou, N., Bouchet, F., Landis, R., Azevedo, R. and Karabachian, L. 2016. Examining the Predictive Relationship between Personality and Emotion Traits and Students Agent-Directed Emotions: Towards Emotionally-Adaptive Agent-Based Learning Environments. *User Modelling and User-Adapted Interaction,* 26 (2–3) 177–219.

[26]   Kim, Y., Almond, R. and Shute, V. 2016. Applying Evidence-Centered Design for the Development of Game-Based Assessments in Physics Playground. *International Journal of Testing,* 16 (2), 142–163.

[27]   Koedinger, K. and Aleven, V. 2016. An Interview Reflection on "Intelligent Tutoring Goes to School in the Big City." *International Journal of Artificial Intelligence in Education,* 26 (1), 13–24.

[28]   De la Torre, F. and Cohn, J. 2011. *Facial Expression Analysis.* Springer London.

[29]   Lallé, S., Mudrick, N., Taub, M., Grafsgaard, J., Conati, C. and Azevedo, R. 2016. Impact of Individual Differences on Affective Reactions to Pedagogical Agents Scaffolding Related Work on Students' Reactions to Pedagogical Agents. In *Proceedings of International Conference on Intelligent Virtual Agents.* Springer, Los Angeles, CA, 269-282.

[30]   Littlewort, G., Whitehill, J., Wu, T., Fasel, I., Frank, M., Movellan, J. and Bartlett, M. 2011. The Computer Expression Recognition Toolbox (CERT). In *Proceedings of the 11th International Conference on Automatic Face & Gesture Recognition and Workshops.* IEEE, Santa Barbara, CA, 298–305.

[31]   Min, W., Frankosky, M., Mott, B., Rowe, J., Wiebe, E., Boyer, K. and Lester, J. 2015. DeepStealth: Leveraging Deep Learning Models for Stealth Assessment in Game-Based Learning Environments. In *Proceedings of the Seventeenth International Conference on Artificial Intelligence in Education.* Springer, Madrid, Spain, 277–286.

[32] Min, W., Mott, B., Rowe, J., Liu, B. and Lester, J. 2016. Player Goal Recognition in Open-World Digital Games with Long Short-Term Memory Networks. *International Joint Conference on Artificial Intelligence.* AAAI Press, Burlingame, CA, 197-203.

[33] Mitrovic, A. 2012. Fifteen Years of Constraint-Based Tutors: What We Have Achieved and Where We Are Going. *User Modeling and User-Adapted Interaction,* 22 (1–2) 39–72.

[34] Mott, B., Lee, S. and Lester, J. 2006. Probabilistic Goal Recognition in Interactive Narrative Environments. In *Proceedings of the Twenty-First National Conference on Artificial Intelligence.* AAAI Press, Boston, MA, 187–192.

[35] Ocumpaugh, J., Baker, R. and Rodrigo, M. 2015. Baker Rodrigo Ocumpaugh Monitoring Protocol (BROMP) 2.0 Technical and Training Manual.

[36] Paquette, L., Rowe, J., Baker, R., Mott, B., Lester, J., DeFalco, J., Brawner, K., Sottilare, R. and Georgoulas, V. 2015. Sensor-Free or Sensor-Full: A Comparison of Data Modalities in Multi-Channel Affect Detection. *Proceedings of the 8th International Conference on Educational Data Mining.* Madrid, Spain, 93–100.

[37] Pekrun, R. 2011. Emotions as Drivers of Learning and Cognitive Development. *New Perspectives on Affect and Learning Technologies.* R.A. Calvo and S.K. D'Mello, eds. Springer. 23–39.

[38] Rowe, J., Shores, L., Mott, B. and Lester, J. 2011. Integrating Learning, Problem Solving, and Engagement in Narrative-Centered Learning Environments. *International Journal of Artificial Intelligence in Education,* 21 (1-2), 115–133.

[39] Sabourin, J. and Lester, J. 2014. Affect and Engagement in Game-Based Learning Environments. *IEEE Transactions on Affective Computing,* 5 (1), 45–56.

[40] Sabourin, J., Rowe, J., Mott, B. and Lester, J. 2013. Considering Alternate Futures to Classify Off-Task Behavior as Emotion Self-Regulation: A Supervised Learning Approach. *Journal of Educational Data Mining,* 5 (1), 9–38.

[41] Shute, V., Wang, L., Greiff, S., Zhao, W. and Moore, G. 2016. Measuring Problem Solving Skills via Stealth Assessment in an Engaging Video Game. *Computers in Human Behavior,* 63, 106–117.

[42] Taub, M., Mudrick, N. V., Azevedo, R., Millar, G.C., Rowe, J. and Lester, J. 2017. Using Multi-Channel Data with Multi-Level Modeling to Assess In-Game Performance during Gameplay with Crystal Island. *Computers in Human Behavior,* DOI:https://doi.org/10.1016/j.chb.2017.01.038.

[43] Vail, A.K., Grafsgaard, J.F., Boyer, K.E., Wiebe, E.N. and Lester, J.C. 2016. Gender Differences in Facial Expressions of Affect During Learning. In *Proceedings of the 24th Conference on User Modeling, Adaptation and Personalization (UMAP 2016).* ACM, Halifax, Canada, 65–73.

[44] VanLehn, K. 2006. The Behavior of Tutoring Systems. *International Journal of Artificial Intelligence in Education,* 16 (3), 227–265.

[45] VanLehn, K. 2011. The Relative Effectiveness of Human Tutoring, Intelligent Tutoring Systems, and Other Tutoring Systems. *Educational Psychologist,* 46 (4), 197–221.

[46] Witmer, B., Jerome, C. and Singer, M. 2005. The Factor Structure of the Presence Questionnaire. *Presence: Teleoperators and Virtual Environments,* 14 (3), 298–312.

[47] Witmer, B. and Singer, M. 1998. Measuring Presence in Virtual Environments: A Presence Questionnaire. *Presence: Teleoperators Virtual Environments,* 7 (3), 225–240.

[48] Woolf, B., Burleson, W., Arroyo, I., Dragon, T., Cooper, D. and Picard, R. 2009. Affect-Aware Tutors: Recognising and Responding to Student Affect. *International Journal of Learning Technology,* 4 (3-4), 129–164.

[49] Wouters, P., van Nimwegen, C., van Oostendorp, H. and van der Spek, E. 2013. A Meta-Analysis of the Cognitive and Motivational Effects of Serious Games. *Journal of Educational Psychology,* 105 (2), 249–265.

A Deep Architecture for Content-based Recommendations Exploiting Recurrent Neural Networks

Alessandro Suglia
Department of Computer Science
University of Bari Aldo Moro
alessandro.suglia@gmail.com

Claudio Greco
Department of Computer Science
University of Bari Aldo Moro
claudiogaetanogreco@gmail.com

Cataldo Musto
Department of Computer Science
University of Bari Aldo Moro
cataldo.musto@uniba.it

Marco de Gemmis
Department of Computer Science
University of Bari Aldo Moro
marco.degemmis@uniba.it

Pasquale Lops
Department of Computer Science
University of Bari Aldo Moro
pasquale.lops@uniba.it

Giovanni Semeraro
Department of Computer Science
University of Bari Aldo Moro
giovanni.semeraro@uniba.it

ABSTRACT

In this paper we investigate the effectiveness of Recurrent Neural Networks (RNNs) in a top-N content-based recommendation scenario. Specifically, we propose a *deep* architecture which adopts Long Short Term Memory (LSTM) networks to jointly learn two embeddings representing the items to be recommended as well as the preferences of the user. Next, given such a representation, a logistic regression layer calculates the relevance score of each item for a specific user and we returns the top-N items as recommendations.

In the experimental session we evaluated the effectiveness of our approach against several baselines: first, we compared it to other *shallow* models based on neural networks (as Word2Vec and Doc2Vec), next we evaluated it against state-of-the-art algorithms for collaborative filtering. In both cases, our methodology obtains a significant improvement over all the baselines, thus giving evidence of the effectiveness of deep learning techniques in content-based recommendation scenarios and paving the way for several future research directions.

CCS CONCEPTS

• **Information systems** → **Recommender systems**; • **Computing methodologies** → **Neural networks**;

KEYWORDS

Recommender Systems, Deep Learning, Recurrent Neural Networks, Content Representation

ACM Reference format:
Alessandro Suglia, Claudio Greco, Cataldo Musto, Marco de Gemmis, Pasquale Lops, and Giovanni Semeraro. 2017. A Deep Architecture for Content-based Recommendations Exploiting Recurrent Neural Networks. In *Proceedings of UMAP '17, Bratislava, Slovakia, July 09-12, 2017,* 10 pages.
DOI: http://dx.doi.org/10.1145/3079628.3079684

1 INTRODUCTION

According to *Barry Schwartz*, people deal with the so-called *paradox of choice* [49]. This means that we can't psychologically and physiologically make an informed choice in scenarios where we face several alternatives and we have to discern among all the available options. Nowadays, in the *Big Data era*, this issue is much more felt. Given the plethora of different information sources today available, it is difficult to effectively find what we are looking for, thus an intelligent system which knows exactly what we like and what we want may be very useful to speed-up daily jobs and improve human activities. Systems able to deal with the *information overload problem* are called "recommender systems" [42]. They have the effect of guiding the user in a personalized way to interesting or useful objects in a large space of possible options. As reported in [8], recommender system techniques can be divided in different classes by exploiting several representations of users and items to generate recommendations.

Among the available paradigms, the recent exponential growth of textual data, made available through open knowledge sources as Wikipedia or Freebase[1], gave new lymph to the research in the area of Content-based Recommender Systems (CBRS) [29]. Indeed, such systems need *textual content* since they rely on the descriptions of the items to provide users with recommendations. This process is typically carried out by matching the features describing the items a user liked, which are stored in her *profile*, with those describing the items currently available the user did not rate yet.

It immediately follows that the effectiveness of content-based recommendation strategies tremendously depend on the way the items as well as the preferences of the target user are modeled [13], since a poor representation certainly loses a lot of relevant information and leads the algorithm to generate poor recommendations. It is not by chance that most of the research effort in the area of CBRS has been carried out to introduce *semantics-aware representations* [14], as those based on the use of ontologies [9, 30] or distributional semantics [35, 37], and to evaluate richer sets of features, as those available in Linked Open Data cloud [15, 32, 34].

At the same time, deep learning [28] architectures gained more and more attention, since they obtained outstanding performance in a broad range of machine learning-related scenarios, ranging from classical tasks as machine translation [2] and speech recognition

---

[1]http://www.freebase.com

[21] to very *visionary* ones, as learning a textual description of a given image[2] or beating human players in challenging games like *Go* [50].

Several work tried to exploit such architectures also to model *textual content*: the most popular attempt towards this direction is certainly Word2Vec (W2V) [31], which adopts a *shallow* deep model consisting of a two-layers neural network to learn dense vector-space representations of words, called *word embeddings*. Moreover, other models as Recurrent Neural Networks (RNNs) [43] and Long-Short Term Memory Networks (LSTMs) [24] have been recently investigated as well, and results [21, 53] showed that deep learning architectures tend to overcome the performance of state of the art algorithms.

As a consequence, in this article we follow this research direction and we investigate the effectiveness of techniques based on *deep learning* to represent textual content in a content-based recommendation scenario. To this end, we introduce a novel architecture, *Ask Me Any Rating (AMAR)*, which jointly learns a user and an item embedding. The former is used to model the user preferences and the latter exploits LSTMs to learn the item embedding from the item description. The resulting representations are used to feed a logistic regression layer to calculate the relevance of a certain item for the target user.

Even if the use of LSTMs in machine learning tasks can't be considered as *new*, up to our knowledge this is the first attempt evaluating the use of such architectures for *content-based recommendations*. This work significantly extends the preliminary results presented in [33] by providing more details on the components of the architecture and by carrying out a more solid and extensive experimental evaluation, which now includes different datasets, more combination of parameters, and more challenging baselines.

To sum up, in this paper we provide the following contributions:

- We propose a novel architecture based on deep neural networks to provide users with content-based recommendations;
- We evaluate the impact of LSTMs to represent textual data in a content-based recommendation scenario;
- We validate our methodology by comparing it to several baselines against two state of the art datasets;

The rest of the article is organized as follows. In Section 2 we give an overview of the literature in the area of Deep Learning and CBRS. Next, the methodology we propose is depicted in Section 3: first, we provide some basics of RNNs, then we describe the modules constituting our deep architecture. Finally, the findings emerging from the experimental evaluation and the conclusions of this work are given in Section 4 and 5, respectively.

2 RELATED WORK

The adoption of deep learning techniques in the area of Recommender Systems is a recent research trend. The first article investigating the effectiveness of such models is due to Salakhutdinov et al. [45], who proposed the use of Restricted Boltzmann Machines to model user-item interactions and to provide collaborative recommendations.

However, despite its novelty, many deep learning architectures have been already investigated in literature: as an example, Wang et al. [57] used Stacked Denoising Autoencoders [56] to jointly learn collaborative and content-based features which are then incorporated in a standard collaborative filtering model. The same technique has been also adopted by Strub et al. [52]. Differently, the use of Convolutional Neural Network (CNNs) is proposed in [55], where the authors introduce a latent factor model for music recommendation whose features are learned by using CNNs. In this case, experiments showed a significant improvement with respect to the classical representation based on *bag of words*. A neural network model which combines wide and deep neural networks is presented in [10]. In particular they try to jointly learn a wide linear model which leverage co-occurences of hand-crafted features by cross-products transformation and a deep neural network in order to achieve both *memorization* and *generalization*, which are really useful properties for effective recommender systems. Differently from our approach it considers only contextual features associated to the user and does not learn a specific user embedding which can be able to capture latent relationships between user preferences. Another relevant attempt in the area of music recommendation based on deep learning is due to Wang et al. [58], who used deep belief networks to learn features from audio content and provide users with personalized recommendations. Finally, Zhang et al. [61] propose a deep learning architecture to perform collaborative filtering exploiting distributed representations.

All these contributions showed that models based on deep learning often overcome state-of-the-art algorithms. However, it did not emerge an architecture which overall performed the best, since each deep learning architecture has its own peculiarities and advantages. Clearly, a detailed overview of such models is out of the scope of this article: we suggest to refer to [5] for an extensive analysis.

The first distinguishing aspect of this article lies in the fact that none of the already proposed approaches exploit deep learning techniques to provide *pure* content-based recommendations. The most similar attempts towards this direction are due to Ozsoy et al. [39] and to Musto et al. [36], who recently proposed the use of Word2Vec [31] to learn word embeddings representing items and user profiles. Their experiments showed that CBRS based on word embeddings can obtain results comparable to those obtained by other content-based approaches and by algorithms for collaborative filtering based on matrix factorization. However, this technique can't be labeled as a as *real* deep learning approach since it relies on a two-layers neural network, while typically deep architectures should include four levels, at least.

In this article we investigate the effectiveness of Recurrent Neural Networks (RNNs) to model textual content for CBRS. The use of such models has been recently evaluated by Hidasi et al. [23], who proposed a novel approach for *session-based recommendations* based on RNNs. In this approach the authors adapt classic RNNs by introducing a novel ranking loss function and obtained a significant improvement over state of the art algorithms. As proved by the authors, such architectures can be useful to model *sequences of data* of arbitrary length, as the interactions occurring in a session. Similarly, we exploited this insight to model the content feeding a CBRS, as the *plot* of a movie, as a *sequence of terms*. This choice is due to the

---

[2]http://googleresearch.blogspot.it/2014/11/a-picture-is-worth-thousand-coherent.html

fact that the effectiveness of RNNs in natural-language related tasks has been already proved by several contributions [21, 51, 59], where they got results at least comparable to those obtained by other deep learning models as CNNs [62]. The effectiveness of RNNs for recommendation tasks is also proved by Florez et al. [17]. In this work ratings are predicted by exploiting a latent representation learnt from item descriptions by a RNN. Finally, another approach applied to item modeling is described in [18], in which CNNs have been applied to web pages and used to recommend interesting pages related to the one read by the user.

The use of LSTMs to model textual content in CBRS is the second distinguishing aspect of this work: the only similar contribution is due to Almahairi et al. [1], who used LSTMs to model textual content (textual *reviews*, in that case) to feed a collaborative recommendation algorithm. Another interesting work which tries to learn item representation directly from raw text description is presented in [3], which applies a bidirectional *Gated Recurrent Unit (GRU)* network to encode item description and an embedding for each tag associated to the item. This approach is really similar to the one we propose, but differently from our work here the authors decide to use a custom cross entropy function which is a linear combination of two different loss functions which try to optimize both the item representation and the tag representation for a given item.

3 METHODOLOGY

In this section we provide a comprehensive description of our approach based on deep learning: first, we introduce some basic concepts about RNNs and LSTMs, next we depict the architecture of our model.

3.1 Basics of RNNs and LSTMs

In the past years, deep learning has offered to scientists computational models organized in *multiple processing layers* able to learn from data using a general learning algorithm called *back-propagation* [28, 48]. Typically, these approaches combine different modules, each of which transforms the input representation to a representation which becomes progressively more abstract. By combining an adequate number of transformation layers and by using back-propagation to indicate how the network's parameters should change to improve their performance on the current task, these architectures are able to learn very complex functions and to discover intricate structures directly from the training data. As previously shown, these methods have dramatically improved the state of the art in several fields in a plenty of different machine learning tasks transforming the way by which common problems are tackled.

In this article, we focused on RNNs [43]. They are considered the main model able to manage *sequential data of arbitrary length*. It is a class of artificial neural networks in which the connections between the units allow the presence of *cycles*. Figure 1 describes the computational graph of a generic RNN, in its *compact* version and in its *unfolded* version in which the loop is represented as a series of repeated trasformations which involves the same parameters. Many recurrent neural networks in fact can be described with the

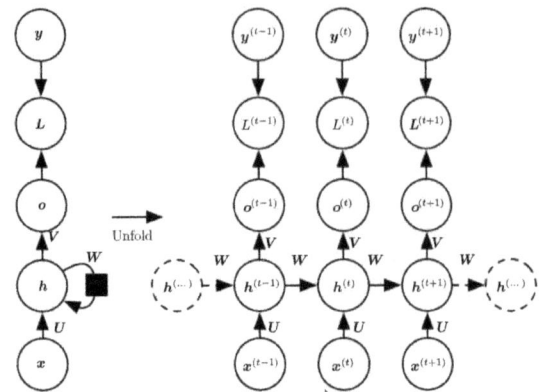

Figure 1: An example of a generic RNN: on the left the compact form of the computational graph is depicted, on the right there is its unfolded version computed in order to apply the *Backpropagation through time* algorithm (image adapted from [20]).

following equation:

$$h^{(t)} = f(h^{(t-1)}, x^{(t)}, \theta)$$

where $h^{(t)}$ represents the state of the RNN at the timestep t which is the results of the application of a generic transformation f applied considering the previous state of the RNN $h^{(t-1)}$, the current input $x^{(t)}$ and the network parameters θ which are shared through each timestep $t = 1, 2, \ldots, T$. As a consequence, this class of networks can carry out the training process by taking into consideration the information coming from earlier states, as well. However, due to gradient computation applied to the same shared parameters θ, the RNNs suffer of the well-known problem of the *vanishing/exploding gradient* [6]. Indeed, especially when long-term dependencies have to be learned, the back-propagation algorithm can make the parameters too small (or too huge), thus making impossible to learn complex functions. As a consequence, LSTMs [24] emerged to solve such a problem. They are a specialization of RNNs which use cells with a more complex structure that allows the neural network to make more elaborate computations and interpretations. Several variants of the original architecture originally introduced in [24] have been proposed in literature [22]. However, in this work we exploited the most widely used one, presented in [19].

As previously shown, beyond solving the vanishing/exploding gradient problem, this structure well-performed in several tasks where short and long-term dependencies have to be learnt. In the following, we will show how LSTMs have been used to learn an embedding for the textual content describing the items recommended by a CBRS.

3.2 Architecture

The architecture we propose is partially inspired by the model based on LSTMs recently proposed in a Question Answering (QA) scenario [60]. Our choice is based on a simple insight: as in QA, given a question, an answer is provided on the ground of the available facts, CBRS can provide suggestions on the ground of the *description* of the available items given a *profile* of the user. Accordingly, we

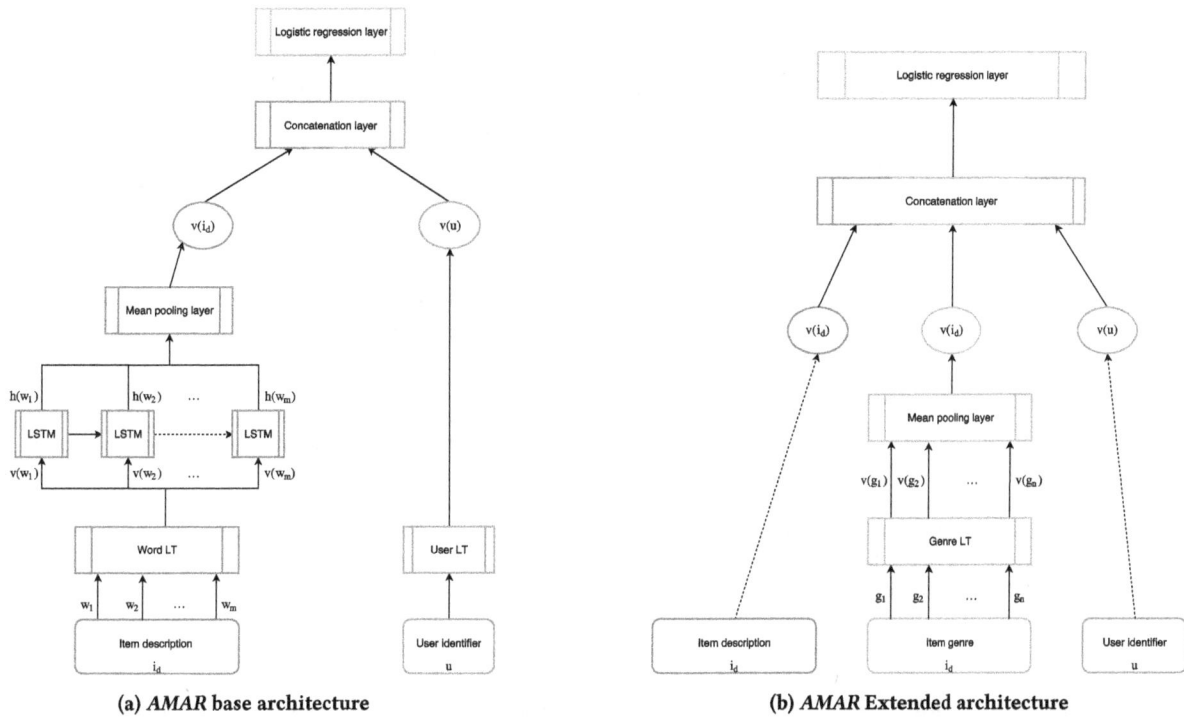

(a) *AMAR* base architecture

(b) *AMAR* Extended architecture

Figure 2: Two instances of the AMAR recommender system framework: both the figures depict the forward pass of the neural network which represents how the input data are processed through each layer obtaining a representation which is used to estimate the probability of a like for the given item

decided to exploit the *analogy* between question and user profile (and, clearly, between answers and recommendations) to design the following architecture, named *Ask Me Any Rating (AMAR)*.

AMAR Base. The proposed architecture implements a content-based recommender system able to predict a score $s(u, i)$ which defines the probability that a user u would *like* a specific item i. In a nutshell, our approach is based on two different modules which jointly learn continuous vector representations for each user $u \in U$ and for each item $i \in I$ that are used to feed a classifier which generates the preference estimation.

Generally speaking, our architecture (see Figure 2a) consists of the following layers:

- **Lookup table layer:** extracts from a specific weight matrix the vector representation associated to a given user (or item, respectively);
- **LSTM module:** an RNN network with LSTM units;
- **Mean pooling layer:** calculates the mean of the input vectors;
- **Concatenation layer:** concatenates the input vectors;
- **Logistic regression layer:** exploits logistic regression to calculate the relevance of the item for a certain user.

An important component of our architecture is the *lookup table layer* which generates dense representations of its input. Given a set of elements A, each of them can be represented as a d-dimensional vector contained in a $W \in \mathbb{R}^{|A| \times d}$ embedding matrix. Let $e_j \in \mathbb{R}^{|A|}$, which is all zeros except for the j-th index in which there is the

value 1. For each $a \in A$ we assign an index j, $1 \le j \le |A|$. We define the *embedding* of a generic element a as the vector representation $v(e_j)$ given by $e_j^\top W$. Intuitively, $v(e_j)$ can be intended as the j-row of the related embedding matrix.

Formally, given a set of items I and a set of users U, our architecture learns a d_i-dimensional embedding for each $i \in I$ and a d_u-dimensional embedding for each $u \in U$. This process is carried out according to the workflow presented in Figure 2a.

Each user u is given in input to a *user lookup table (User LT)* which generates a d_u-dimensional *user embedding* $v(u)$ considering a weight matrix W_u. Each word $w_1, w_2, \dots, w_m$ of the item description i_d associated to the item i is given in input to a *word lookup table (Word LT)* which generates a d_w-dimensional embedding $v(w_j)$ for each word w_j, $1 \le j \le m$ considering a weight matrix W_w. Clearly, at the first step of the learning process the weight matrixes W_u and W_w are initialized according to a predefined probability distribution.

Next, these word representations $v(w_k)$ are sequentially passed through an *LSTM network* with s hidden units which generates for each of them a s-dimensional latent representation $h(w_j)$ using an LSTM cell. The motivation behind the adoption of LSTM is twofold: first, as stated in the Introduction, several work already showed that LSTM can overcome shallow models (see [21, 51, 54]). Moreover, we chose to adopt LSTM since such networks are very effective when sequences of input have to be modeled. Given that the textual description of the items can be easily viewed as a sequence of terms, it was straightforward for us to investigate the adoption of LSTMs in a content-based recommendation scenario. Once the latent representation are computed by the LSTM network, the *item embedding* $v(i)$ is obtained by a *mean pooling layer* which averages the latent representations $h(w_k)$ for all the words in the textual description of the item.

The resulting representations $v(u)$ and $v(i)$ are then concatenated through a *concatenation layer*. The resulting (d_u+d_i)-dimensional feature vector is given as input to a *logistic regression layer* which finally predicts the score $s(u,i)$. Formally, these operations can be expressed by the following expression:

$$y = \text{sigmoid}(W_{ih}[v(i_u), v(i_d)] + b_{ih})$$

where $W_{ih} \in \mathbb{R}^{(d_u+d_d) \times 1}$ is a weight matrix, $b_{ih} \in \mathbb{R}$ is a bias term and the square brackets denote the concatenation operation between two vectors. The *logistic regression layer* is able to learn in its parameters W_{ih} and b_{ih} relevant relationships between the user and the rated items useful for the preference estimation $s(u,i)$.

In order to perform the *top-N* recommendation task, the recommender system should generate a list of suggestions ordered by the item relevance with regard to the user profile. The presented architecture provides recommendations for a given user u by sorting items in decreasing order according to the score $s(u,i)$ for each item i.

AMAR Extended. As previously stated, a relevant research line in the area of CBRS is to investigate the effectiveness of features different from those extracted from the simple textual description of the items. Accordingly, we provided AMAR with a very *modular* and *extensible* architecture, in order to make the model able to learn a representation of the items $i \in I$ by also exploiting features different from the textual description.

This architecture, called *AMAR Extended*, extends the previous one by adding a module able to process supplementary features associated to each item. The *AMAR* Extended architecture proposed in this work associates a list of genres $g_1, g_2, \ldots, g_n$ to each item, as shown in figure 2b. Each genre is passed in input to a *genre lookup table (Genre LT)* which generates a d_g-dimensional embedding $v(g_k)$ for each genre g_k, $1 \leq k \leq n$ considering a weight matrix W_g. Next, a *mean pooling layer* averages the resulting representations $v(g_k)$ by giving a *genres embedding* $v(i_g)$ which is concatenated to the user and item embeddings to evaluate the recommendation score.

Clearly, in this preliminary attempt we chose to extend the architecture by only modeling information about the *genre* of the items, since we can assume that such an information is available for all the domains, but different set of features (as the *cast* of a movie or the *author* of a book) can be easily introduced without modifying the logic which inspired the architecture.

4 EXPERIMENTAL EVALUATION

In the experimental session we evaluated the effectiveness of the above described deep architecture against several baselines, in the task of *top-N recommendation* leveraging binary user feedback. First, we compared it to other models based on (shallow) neural

networks *(Experiment 1)*, next we evaluated it against state-of-the-art techniques such as algorithms for matrix factorization, user-user and item-item collaborative filtering *(Experiment 2)*.

4.1 Experimental Design

Datasets: Experiments were carried out against two state-of-the-art datasets, as Movielens 1M (ML1M)[3] and DBbook. The first is a a widespread dataset for movie recommendations, while the latter focuses on book recommendations and is exploited in the *ESWC 2014 Linked-Open Data-enabled Recommender Systems challenge*[4]. Some statistics about the datasets are provided in Table 1.

A quick analysis of the table shows two datasets very different from each other. ML1M is larger than DBbook, but it is less sparse so it is more suitable for collaborative filtering-based algorithms. On the other side, DBbook is sparser and unbalanced towards negative preferences (only 45.85% of positive ratings), and this makes the recommendation task very challenging.

Protocol: Experiments were performed by adopting different protocols for the chosen datasets. As regards ML1M, we first applied a *binarization procedure* to convert the original dataset preferences expressed on a 5-point Likert scale, to 0 or 1. In particular, we considered as *positive* preferences only those ratings equal to 4 or 5, as *negative* all the others. After having applied the above-mentioned binarization procedure, we carried out a *k*-fold cross-validation by splitting the original dataset in five different folds. For each fold, we maintained the ratio between positive and negative ratings per user. On the other side, the single training/test split which was used in the ESWC 2014 Challenge is exploited for DBbook. Similarly, no processing was needed for the ratings since they were already available as *binarized*.

The effectiveness of our algorithm is evaluated by calculating the F1-Measure of the recommendation list [42]. In order to make our experiments reproducible, all the metrics are calculated by using the *RiVal toolkit* [44] following the *TestRatings* strategy [4]. The final F1@K measure for each algorithm is computed averaging the F1@K measure obtained on each fold. Statistical significance is assessed by exploiting *Mann-Whitney U* test (*P-value*=0.05), chosen after running the *Shapiro-Wilk* test[5], which revealed the non-normal distribution of the data. *P-values* are calculated by using the *RiVal toolkit*, as well.

Items Representation: To feed our content-based deep architecture, we collected *textual descriptions* of the items. Specifically, we used a ML1M mapping[16] to provide each movie with textual features. For each item, we used the mapping to obtain the *Wikipedia* page from which are extracted the first two sections or the abstract of the entity using the property *abstract* of the *DBpedia ontology*[6]. If a reference for a given item is not present in the used mapping[7], the IMDb synopsis was used otherwise the concatenation of the user reviews. On the other side, for DBbook we collect the *plots* of the books. In this case, data were made available during the ESWC 2014 Challenge. In both cases, textual descriptions were processed by removing stop words and performing tokenization.

---

[3]http://grouplens.org/datasets/movielens/
[4]http://challenges.2014.eswc-conferences.org/index.php/RecSys
[5]http://en.wikipedia.org/wiki/Shapiro-Wilk_test
[6]http://dbpedia.org/ontology/
[7]Some URIs are incorrect in the original mapping and for this reason not resolvable.

	ML1M	DBbook
Users	6,040	6,181
Items	3,301	6,733
Ratings	1,000,209	72,372
Sparsity	94.98%	99.83%
Positive Ratings	57.22%	45.85%
Avg. ratings/user $\pm \sigma$	157.11±182.93	11.70±5.85
Median/mode per user	90/23	11/5
Avg. ratings/item $\pm \sigma$	293.98±393.88	10.74±27.14
Median/mode per item	147/1	4/1

Table 1: Description of the datasets.

To feed AMAR Extended, we also collected information about the *genres* of both movies and books. In the first case, we provided each movie with the genres already available in ML1M data. As regards DBbook, we queried DBpedia and we used as genres the objects associated to the property literaryGenre or genre of the DBpedia ontology. If none of them were present, we used the objects associated to the property dcterms:subject.

Baselines: in order to confirm the effectiveness of our approach, we compared it with several state-of-the-art techniques, as *collaborative filtering, traditional content-based recommender system* and *embedding-based recommender systems*. A brief description of each algorithm follows:

Popularity a non-personalized technique which recommends most-popular items to users. Specifically, the algorithm suggest the items with the highest ratio of positive ratings over the total number of ratings.

U2U k-nearest neighbor user-based collaborative filtering [41], where the preference estimation is computed according to the preference expressed by users similar to the one to whom the suggestions will be generated.

I2I k-nearest neighbor item-based collaborative filtering [47], uses similarities between the rating patterns of items to estimate the preference of a given user for a given item.

BPRMF a matrix factorization model for item recommendation based on *Bayesian Personalized Ranking optimization criterion (BPR-Opt)* [40].

WRMF a weighted matrix factorization algorithm based on the *Alternating Least Squares (ALS)* learning method [25].

BPRSlim *Sparse Linear Methods (SLIM)* for item recommendation using *BPR-Opt* [38].

TF-IDF *Vector Space Model (VSM)* with *TF-IDF* weighting scheme [46] is used to represent each item description. The user representation is the centroid of the items rated positively by the user. The preference estimation score is computed as the cosine similarity between the item representation and the user representation.

Word2Vec (W2V) additional baselines are proposed using W2V representation learn from both the item descriptions using different W2V training strategies (*SG* and *CBOW*) and pre-trained word embeddings such as *Word2vec Google News*[8] (*W2V-PRE*). The recommendation score is generated

using the *cosine similarity* between the item represented by averaging word embeddings of its description and the user profile represented by averaging positively rated item representations, by following the recommendation pipeline proposed by Musto et al. in [36].

GloVe Exploited the pre-trained *GloVe Wikipedia 2014 + Gigaword 5*[9] word embeddings to generate recommendations according to the same procedure used for *W2V*.

Doc2Vec (D2V), also known as *Paragraph Vector* [27], is another embedding-based algorithm. In particular, item representations are learnt from the item descriptions corpus and they are used to generate the user profile, averaging those that are positively rated by a given user. The recommendation score is computed as in the previous case, using the generated item description and user representation.

As regards the implementation details, *collaborative filtering* and *Popularity* baselines are available in MyMediaLite[10] and Scikit-learn[11], while approaches based on word embeddings are implemented by using the code available in the *Gensim* library for W2V[12] and D2V[13].

Overview of the Parameters: AMAR and AMAR Extended are trained by using RMSProp as optimizer. The parameter α is set to 0.9 and learning rate is set to 0.001. Models are trained for 25 epochs, by setting batch sizes to 1536 for ML1M and to 512 for DBbook, respectively. As cost function we choose the *binary cross entropy*[14], which is typically used for classification tasks since it tries to minimize the errors in the classification. Due to the computational costs requested by the models, the dimension of the learned embeddings d_w and d_u are fixed to 10. For the *LSTM module* we fixed s to 10.

As regards the CBRS based on W2V and D2V, we learn embeddings of dimension 300 and 500 by using the *Skip-Gram (SG)* and the *Continuous Bag-of-Words (CBOW)* methodologies for the former, and the *Distributed Memory Model (DM)* and the *Distributed Bag-of-Words (DBOW)* methodologies for the latter. Word embeddings are learnt by using the textual description of the items as corpus. Descriptions are gathered as previously described.

---

[8]https://code.google.com/archive/p/word2vec/

[9]http://nlp.stanford.edu/projects/glove/
[10]http://www.mymedialite.net/documentation/item_prediction.html
[11]http://scikit-learn.org/
[12]https://radimrehurek.com/gensim/models/word2vec.html
[13]https://radimrehurek.com/gensim/models/doc2vec.html
[14]https://en.wikipedia.org/wiki/Cross_entropy

	ML1M	
	F1@5	**F1@10**
W2V-SG-300	0.490	0.580
W2V-SG-500	0.485	0.580
W2V-CBOW-300	0.490	0.581
W2V-CBOW-500	0.487	0.579
W2V-PRE	*0.500*	*0.587*
GloVe	0.485	0.575
D2V-SG-300	0.479	0.571
D2V-SG-500	0.481	0.574
D2V-DBOW-300	0.482	0.574
D2V-DBOW-500	0.481	0.573
AMAR	0.555	0.641
AMAR+	**0.558**	**0.644**

Table 2: Results of Experiment 1 on ML1M data. The best-performing baseline is reported in italics while the overall best configuration is highlighted in bold.

	DBbook	
	F1@5	**F1@10**
W2V-SG-300	0.541	0.645
W2V-SG-500	0.542	0.645
W2V-CBOW-300	0.539	0.645
W2V-CBOW-500	0.540	0.645
W2V-PRE	0.548	*0.655*
GloVe	*0.552*	*0.655*
D2V-DM-300	0.540	0.652
D2V-DM-500	0.537	0.653
D2V-DBOW-300	0.54	0.654
D2V-DBOW-500	0.54	0.654
AMAR	0.564	0.662
AMAR+	**0.565**	**0.662**

Table 3: Results of Experiment 1 on DBbook data. The best-performing baseline is reported in italics while the overall best configuration is highlighted in bold

On the other side, I2I and U2U are evaluated by setting the neighborhood size to 30, 50 and 80, while the matrix factorization algorithms are run by learning 10, 30 and 50 latent factors.

Source code: The source code of our content-based recommendation algorithm based on deep learning has been published on GitHub[15]. The recommendation framework is implemented using *Torch7* [12] exploiting the *NVIDIA CUDA* libraries bindings to run the code on a Titan X GPU. The *LSTM network* architecture used in this work is based on the *SeqLSTM* module implemented in the *rnn package*[16].

4.2 Discussion of the results

Results of *Experiment 1* on ML1M and DBbook data are provided in Table 2 and 3, respectively. Each line reports the name of the configuration and its parameters, as the size of the embedding and the training methodology. The configuration based on pre-trained word vectors is reported as W2V-PRE, while AMAR Extended is reported as AMAR+ for the sake of brevity.

Results clearly show that AMAR and AMAR+ are able to significantly outperform all the baselines based on word embeddings on both the datasets. The improvement is particularly huge on ML1M (+6% over the best-performing baseline), but the gap is statistically significant on DBbook as well. As regards the baselines, neither the size of the vectors nor the training methodology significantly affects the results, since the gaps are never statistically significant. Moreover, it is worth to note that the best configuration is that based on pre-trained word embeddings. This means that the quality of learnt embeddings strictly depends on the amount (and on the quality) of the data that feed the learning algorithm. Indeed, in this case the embeddings pre-trained by Google and those pre-trained using *GloVe* beat those trained on the textual content gathered from the dataset, even if those embeddings are based on *exogenous knowledge* which is wider and not strictly related to a specific recommendation domain.

However, regardless this interesting finding, this first experiment showed the usefulness of exploiting *more complex* deep architectures for content-based recommendation tasks, since results showed that the introduction of LSTMs and the development of a deep architecture as AMAR can lead to more effective recommendations. This is an expected behavior, since neural networks are able to learn models from huge number of ratings and to extract relevant features from item descriptions.

Furthermore, as previously stated, both RNNs and LSTMs are particularly useful to model sequences of data as the *textual description* of the items, thus it is not surprising that a better representation of textual content can lead to a better accuracy of the recommendation algorithm. Indeed, the embedding-based baselines are not able to fill the gap due to their ineffectiveness to represent items and users by a simple mean of pre-trained word embeddings. In addition, in this particular setting we are interested in modeling the whole sequence of terms which describes the item rather than each single word given a window of contextual terms (as Word2Vec does).

Moreover, it is worth to note that these results are obtained with a very *light* optimization of the parameters of the models. It is likely that by introducing regularization techniques, tuning hyperparameters and using early stopping procedures better performances may be obtained. Indeed, given the difficulty of *RNNs* to converge to satisfying minima, more epochs are typically required to obtain better results.

Next, the insight of extending the original architecture by introducing extra features as the *genre* lead to promising results. Indeed, we obtained an improvement (even if *not significant*) on both datasets. This supports the idea that more (and diverse) *semi-structured* features describing the items to be recommended can further improve the accuracy of the suggestions. Clearly, further analysis are needed to assess which extra features are worth to be used and how they do affect the overall results, but these preliminary results pave the way to several developments of our architecture which will be investigated in the future.

---

[15]https://github.com/nlp-deepcbrs/amar
[16]https://github.com/Element-Research/rnn#rnn.SeqLSTM

	ML1M	
	F1@5	**F1@10**
Popularity	0.425	0.525
I2I-30	0.432	0.527
I2I-50	0.431	0.528
I2I-80	0.430	0.527
U2U-30	0.427	0.525
U2U-50	0.425	0.524
U2U-80	0.424	0.523
BPRMF-10	0.424	0.522
BPRMF-30	0.425	0.524
BPRMF-50	0.424	0.524
WRMF-10	0.419	0.520
WRMF-30	0.423	0.522
WRMF-50	0.425	0.525
BPRSlim	*0.446*	*0.548*
AMAR	0.555	0.641
AMAR+	**0.558**	**0.644**

Table 4: Results of Experiment 2 on ML1M data. The best-performing baseline is reported in italics while the overall best configuration is highlighted in bold.

	DBbook	
	F1@5	**F1@10**
Popularity	0.532	*0.645*
TF-IDF	0.532	*0.645*
I2I-30	*0.536*	0.64
I2I-50	0.534	0.64
I2I-80	0.531	0.64
U2U-30	0.536	0.639
U2U-50	0.528	0.636
U2U-80	0.522	0.634
BPRMF-10	0.507	0.631
BPRMF-30	0.508	0.631
BPRMF-50	0.507	0.631
WRMF-10	0.514	0.632
WRMF-30	0.518	0.635
WRMF-50	0.519	0.636
BPRSlim	0.511	0.632
AMAR	0.564	0.662
AMAR+	**0.565**	**0.662**

Table 5: Results of Experiment 2 on DBbook data. The best-performing baseline is reported in italics while the overall best configuration is highlighted in bold.

Next, in *Experiment 2* we compare our content-based approach to other baselines in the area of recommender systems. Results reported in Table 4 and 5 show that both AMAR and AMAR+ can significantly outperform all the state-of-the-art algorithms we consider. The improvement is even larger than that observed in Experiment 1, since the average gap between AMAR and the best-performing baseline is between 10 and 13% on ML1M and around 3% on DBbook.

These results further prove the effectiveness of our strategy, since also widespread and well-performing techniques based on matrix factorization are outperformed by AMAR and AMAR+. Another interesting finding of Experiment 2 is that our deep architecture is the only configuration able to overcome the simple popularity-based baseline on DBbook. As previously stated, this dataset is very challenging since it is very sparse and many users have just a few positive ratings, thus it is very difficult to model users' preferences in a classic recommendation task. These characteristics of the dataset lead to poor performance all the other algorithms we take into account, except our deep architecture which is able to significantly overcome it. This interesting outcome further validates the results obtained by our framework and confirms the effectiveness of deep architectures for content-based recommendation tasks.

5 CONCLUSIONS AND FUTURE WORK

In this article we present AMAR, a modular and extensible architecture exploiting deep neural networks to provide users with content-based recommendations.

The model is based on LSTM networks, a particular class of RNNs particularly able to deal with sequences of data of arbitrary length, as the content describing the items to be recommended. Specifically, we develop an approach which jointly learns two embeddings representing both the items to be recommended as well as the preferences of the users. Given such representations, recommendations are provided by exploiting a logistic regression layer which calculates the likelihood that a user will like a certain item. In the experimental evaluation we compare our approach to several baselines, and results show that our deep architecture is able to significantly overcome both algorithms based on (shallow) neural networks as W2V and D2V as well as widespread and well-performing techniques for collaborative filtering and matrix factorization.

We plan to extend the proposed work along three different directions: optimization, architecture and additional features. Regarding optimization, training could be improved by applying early stopping and regularization techniques, by using different weight initialization schemes and by designing a proper cost function for the *top-N recommendation*. An additional improvement could be obtained by doing hyperparameter optimization. From the architectural perspective, different neural network architectures could be used to generate item representations to better extract relevant features from item descriptions. Another improvement could be obtained by adding more dense layers to the *concatenation layer* for capturing more complex relations between features to lead to a better classification. Furthermore, we will also investigate the adoption of other kind of neural network architectures to model the *textual features*, such as *Convolutional Neural Networks (CNNs)* which show their effectiveness in a broad range of natural language-related tasks [7, 26] and RNNs equipped with Gated Recurrent Units (GRUs) [11], which have a simpler structure than *LSTMs* but show comparable results. Preliminary results investigating the integration of further semi-structured features as the *genre* of the items to be recommended lead to little improvements in the overall accuracy of the system, thus encouraging us to design different variants of AMAR+ modeling additional information coming from important data silos such as Linked Open Data or Web and social media.

REFERENCES

[1] A. Almahairi, K. Kastner, K. Cho, and A. C. Courville. 2015. Learning Distributed Representations from Reviews for Collaborative Filtering. In *Proceedings of the 9th ACM Conference on Recommender Systems, RecSys 2015, Vienna, Austria, September 16-20, 2015*. 147–154.

[2] Dzmitry Bahdanau, Kyunghyun Cho, and Yoshua Bengio. 2014. Neural machine translation by jointly learning to align and translate. *arXiv preprint arXiv:1409.0473* (2014).

[3] Trapit Bansal, David Belanger, and Andrew McCallum. 2016. Ask the GRU: Multi-task Learning for Deep Text Recommendations. In *Proceedings of the 10th ACM Conference on Recommender Systems (RecSys '16)*. ACM, New York, NY, USA, 107–114.

[4] Alejandro Bellogin, Pablo Castells, and Ivan Cantador. 2011. Precision-oriented evaluation of recommender systems: an algorithmic comparison. In *Proceedings of the fifth ACM conference on Recommender systems*. ACM, 333–336.

[5] Y. Bengio. 2009. Learning deep architectures for AI. *Foundations and trends® in Machine Learning* 2, 1 (2009), 1–127.

[6] Y. Bengio, P. Simard, and P. Frasconi. 1994. Learning long-term dependencies with gradient descent is difficult. *Neural Networks, IEEE Transactions on* 5, 2 (1994), 157–166.

[7] Phil Blunsom, Edward Grefenstette, and Nal Kalchbrenner. 2014. A Convolutional Neural Network for Modelling Sentences. In *Proceedings of the 52nd Annual Meeting of the Association for Computational Linguistics*. ACL, 655–665.

[8] Robin Burke. 2002. Hybrid recommender systems: Survey and experiments. *User modeling and user-adapted interaction* 12, 4 (2002), 331–370.

[9] Iván Cantador, Alejandro Bellogín, and Pablo Castells. 2008. Ontology-based personalised and context-aware recommendations of news items. In *Proceedings of the 2008 IEEE/WIC/ACM International Conference on Web Intelligence and Intelligent Agent Technology-Volume 01*. IEEE Computer Society, 562–565.

[10] Heng-Tze Cheng, Levent Koc, Jeremiah Harmsen, Tal Shaked, Tushar Chandra, Hrishi Aradhye, Glen Anderson, Greg Corrado, Wei Chai, Mustafa Ispir, and others. 2016. Wide & Deep Learning for Recommender Systems. *arXiv preprint arXiv:1606.07792* (2016).

[11] K. Cho, B. Van Merriënboer, C. Gulcehre, D. Bahdanau, F. Bougares, H. Schwenk, and Y. Bengio. 2014. Learning phrase representations using RNN encoder-decoder for statistical machine translation. *arXiv preprint arXiv:1406.1078* (2014).

[12] Ronan Collobert, Koray Kavukcuoglu, and Clément Farabet. 2011. Torch7: A matlab-like environment for machine learning. In *BigLearn, NIPS Workshop*.

[13] Marco De Gemmis, Leo Iaquinta, Pasquale Lops, Cataldo Musto, Fedelucio Narducci, and Giovanni Semeraro. 2010. Learning preference models in recommender systems. In *Preference Learning*. Springer, 387–407.

[14] Marco de Gemmis, Pasquale Lops, Cataldo Musto, Fedelucio Narducci, and Giovanni Semeraro. 2015. Semantics-Aware Content-Based Recommender Systems. In *Recommender Systems Handbook*. Springer, 119–159.

[15] Tommaso Di Noia, Roberto Mirizzi, Vito Claudio Ostuni, and Davide Romito. 2012. Exploiting the web of data in model-based recommender systems. In *Proceedings of the sixth ACM conference on Recommender systems*. ACM, 253–256.

[16] Tommaso Di Noia, Roberto Mirizzi, Vito Claudio Ostuni, Davide Romito, and Markus Zanker. 2012. Linked open data to support content-based recommender systems. In *Proceedings of the 8th International Conference on Semantic Systems*. ACM, 1–8.

[17] Omar U Florez. 2014. Deep Learning of Semantic Word Representations to Implement a Content-Based Recommender for the RecSys ChallengeâĂŹ14. In *Semantic Web Evaluation Challenge*. Springer, 199–204.

[18] Jianfeng Gao, Patrick Pantel, Michael Gamon, Xiaodong He, and Li Deng. 2014. Modeling Interestingness with Deep Neural Networks. In *Proceedings of the 2014 Conference on Empirical Methods in Natural Language Processing, EMNLP 2014, October 25-29, 2014, Doha, Qatar, A meeting of SIGDAT, a Special Interest Group of the ACL*. 2–13.

[19] F. A Gers, J. Schmidhuber, and F. Cummins. 2000. Learning to forget: Continual prediction with LSTM. *Neural computation* 12, 10 (2000), 2451–2471.

[20] Ian Goodfellow, Yoshua Bengio, and Aaron Courville. 2016. *Deep Learning*. MIT Press. http://www.deeplearningbook.org.

[21] A. Graves, A. Mohamed, and G. Hinton. 2013. Speech recognition with deep recurrent neural networks. In *Acoustics, Speech and Signal Processing (ICASSP), 2013 IEEE International Conference on*. IEEE, 6645–6649.

[22] Klaus Greff, Rupesh Kumar Srivastava, Jan Koutník, Bas R Steunebrink, and Jürgen Schmidhuber. 2015. LSTM: A search space odyssey. *arXiv preprint arXiv:1503.04069* (2015).

[23] Balázs Hidasi, Alexandros Karatzoglou, Linas Baltrunas, and Domonkos Tikk. 2015. Session-based Recommendations with Recurrent Neural Networks. *arXiv preprint arXiv:1511.06939* (2015).

[24] Sepp Hochreiter and Jürgen Schmidhuber. 1997. Long short-term memory. *Neural computation* 9, 8 (1997), 1735–1780.

[25] Yifan Hu, Yehuda Koren, and Chris Volinsky. 2008. Collaborative filtering for implicit feedback datasets. In *Data Mining, 2008. ICDM'08. Eighth IEEE International Conference on*. Ieee, 263–272.

[26] Yoon Kim. 2014. Convolutional neural networks for sentence classification. *arXiv preprint arXiv:1408.5882* (2014).

[27] Quoc V Le and Tomas Mikolov. 2014. Distributed representations of sentences and documents. *arXiv preprint arXiv:1405.4053* (2014).

[28] Yann LeCun, Yoshua Bengio, and Geoffrey Hinton. 2015. Deep learning. *Nature* 521, 7553 (2015), 436–444.

[29] Pasquale Lops, Marco De Gemmis, and Giovanni Semeraro. 2011. Content-based recommender systems: State of the art and trends. In *Recommender systems handbook*. Springer, 73–105.

[30] Stuart E Middleton, David De Roure, and Nigel R Shadbolt. 2009. Ontology-based recommender systems. In *Handbook on ontologies*. Springer, 779–796.

[31] Tomas Mikolov, Kai Chen, Greg Corrado, and Jeffrey Dean. 2013. Efficient estimation of word representations in vector space. *arXiv preprint arXiv:1301.3781* (2013).

[32] Cataldo Musto, Pierpaolo Basile, Pasquale Lops, Marco de Gemmis, and Giovanni Semeraro. 2017. Introducing linked open data in graph-based recommender systems. *Information Processing & Management* 53, 2 (2017), 405–435.

[33] Cataldo Musto, Claudio Greco, Alessandro Suglia, and Giovanni Semeraro. 2016. Ask Me Any Rating: A Content-based Recommender System based on Recurrent Neural Networks. (2016).

[34] Cataldo Musto, Pasquale Lops, Pierpaolo Basile, Marco de Gemmis, and Giovanni Semeraro. 2016. Semantics-aware graph-based recommender systems exploiting linked open data. In *Proceedings of the 2016 Conference on User Modeling Adaptation and Personalization*. ACM, 229–237.

[35] Cataldo Musto, Fedelucio Narducci, Pasquale Lops, Giovanni Semeraro, Marco De Gemmis, Mauro Barbieri, Jan Korst, Verus Pronk, and Ramon Clout. 2012. Enhanced semantic tv-show representation for personalized electronic program guides. In *International Conference on User Modeling, Adaptation, and Personalization*. Springer Berlin Heidelberg, 188–199.

[36] C. Musto, G. Semeraro, M. de Gemmis, and P. Lops. 2016. Learning Word Embeddings from Wikipedia for Content-Based Recommender Systems. In *Advances in Information Retrieval*. Springer, 729–734.

[37] Cataldo Musto, Giovanni Semeraro, Pasquale Lops, and Marco de Gemmis. 2014. Combining distributional semantics and entity linking for context-aware content-based recommendation. In *User Modeling, Adaptation, and Personalization*. Springer, 381–392.

[38] Xia Ning and George Karypis. 2011. Slim: Sparse linear methods for top-n recommender systems. In *Data Mining (ICDM), 2011 IEEE 11th International Conference on*. IEEE, 497–506.

[39] Makbule Gulcin Ozsoy. 2016. From Word Embeddings to Item Recommendation. *arXiv preprint arXiv:1601.01356* (2016).

[40] Steffen Rendle, Christoph Freudenthaler, Zeno Gantner, and Lars Schmidt-Thieme. 2009. BPR: Bayesian personalized ranking from implicit feedback. In *Proceedings of the twenty-fifth conference on uncertainty in artificial intelligence*. AUAI Press, 452–461.

[41] Paul Resnick, Neophytos Iacovou, Mitesh Suchak, Peter Bergstrom, and John Riedl. 1994. GroupLens: an open architecture for collaborative filtering of netnews. In *Proceedings of the 1994 ACM conference on Computer supported cooperative work*. ACM, 175–186.

[42] Francesco Ricci, Lior Rokach, and Bracha Shapira. 2015. Recommender systems: introduction and challenges. In *Recommender Systems Handbook*. Springer, 1–34.

[43] D Rumelhart, G Hinton, and R Williams. 1986. Learning representations by back-propagating errors. Lett. Nat., 323: 533-536. (1986).

[44] Alan Said and Alejandro Bellogín. 2014. Rival: a toolkit to foster reproducibility in recommender system evaluation. In *Proceedings of the 8th ACM Conference on Recommender systems*. ACM, 371–372.

[45] R. Salakhutdinov, A. Mnih, and G. Hinton. 2007. Restricted Boltzmann machines for collaborative filtering. In *Proceedings of the 24th international conference on Machine learning*. ACM, 791–798.

[46] Gerard Salton and Christopher Buckley. 1988. Term-weighting approaches in automatic text retrieval. *Information processing & management* 24, 5 (1988), 513–523.

[47] Badrul Sarwar, George Karypis, Joseph Konstan, and John Riedl. 2001. Item-based collaborative filtering recommendation algorithms. In *Proceedings of the 10th international conference on World Wide Web*. ACM, 285–295.

[48] Jürgen Schmidhuber. 2015. Deep learning in neural networks: An overview. *Neural Networks* 61 (2015), 85–117.

[49] Barry Schwartz. 2004. *The paradox of choice: Why more is less*. HarperCollins.

[50] David Silver, Aja Huang, Chris J Maddison, Arthur Guez, Laurent Sifre, George Van Den Driessche, Julian Schrittwieser, Ioannis Antonoglou, Veda Panneershelvam, Marc Lanctot, and others. 2016. Mastering the game of Go with deep neural networks and tree search. *Nature* 529, 7587 (2016), 484–489.

[51] Richard Socher, Christopher D Manning, and Andrew Y Ng. 2010. Learning continuous phrase representations and syntactic parsing with recursive neural networks. In *Proceedings of the NIPS-2010 Deep Learning and Unsupervised Feature Learning Workshop*. 1–9.

[52] F. Strub and J. Mary. 2015. Collaborative Filtering with Stacked Denoising AutoEncoders and Sparse Inputs. In *NIPS Workshop on Machine Learning for eCommerce*.

[53] Ilya Sutskever, Oriol Vinyals, and Quoc V Le. 2014. Sequence to sequence learning with neural networks. In *Advances in neural information processing systems*. 3104–3112.

[54] K. S. Tai, R. Socher, and C. D. Manning. 2015. Improved semantic representations from tree-structured long short-term memory networks. *arXiv preprint arXiv:1503.00075* (2015).

[55] Aaron Van den Oord, Sander Dieleman, and Benjamin Schrauwen. 2013. Deep content-based music recommendation. In *Advances in Neural Information Processing Systems*. 2643–2651.

[56] P. Vincent, H. Larochelle, I. Lajoie, Y. Bengio, and P. Manzagol. 2010. Stacked denoising autoencoders: Learning useful representations in a deep network with a local denoising criterion. *The Journal of Machine Learning Research* 11 (2010), 3371–3408.

[57] Hao Wang, Naiyan Wang, and Dit-Yan Yeung. 2015. Collaborative deep learning for recommender systems. In *Proceedings of the 21th ACM SIGKDD International Conference on Knowledge Discovery and Data Mining*. ACM, 1235–1244.

[58] X. Wang and Y. Wang. 2014. Improving content-based and hybrid music recommendation using deep learning. In *Proceedings of the ACM International Conference on Multimedia*. ACM, 627–636.

[59] T.-H. Wen, A. Heidel, H. Lee, Y. Tsao, and L.-S. Lee. 2013. Recurrent neural network based language model personalization by social network crowdsourcing.. In *INTERSPEECH*. 2703–2707.

[60] J. Weston, A. Bordes, S. Chopra, and T. Mikolov. 2015. Towards AI-complete question answering: A set of prerequisite toy tasks. *arXiv preprint arXiv:1502.05698* (2015).

[61] J. Zhang, H. Cai, T. Huang, and H. Xue. 2015. A Distributional Representation Model For Collaborative Filtering. *CoRR* abs/1502.04163 (2015). http://arxiv.org/abs/1502.04163

[62] X. Zhang, J. Zhao, and Y. LeCun. 2015. Character-level convolutional networks for text classification. In *Advances in Neural Information Processing Systems*. 649–657.

Measuring Student Behaviour Dynamics in a Large Interactive Classroom Setting

Vasileios Triglianos⋆, Sambit Praharaj†, Cesare Pautasso⋆, Alessandro Bozzon†, Claudia Hauff†

⋆University of Lugano, Faculty of Informatics, Lugano, Switzerland
{name.surname}@usi.ch
†Delft University of Technology, Web Information Systems, Delft, the Netherlands
s. praharaj@student.tudelft.nl
{a.bozzon,c.hauff}@tudelft.nl

ABSTRACT

Digital devices (most often laptops and smartphones), though desired tools by students in a higher education classroom, have in the past been shown to serve more as distractors than supporters of learning. One of the reasons is the often undirected nature of the devices' usage. With our work we aim to turn students' digital devices into teaching and communication tools by seamlessly interleaving lecture material and complex questions in the students' browser through ASQ, a Web application for broadcasting and tracking interactive presentations. ASQ's fine-grained logging abilities allow us to track second by second to what extent students are engaging with ASQ which in turn enables insights into student behaviour dynamics. This setup enables us to conduct "in situ" experiments. Based on the logs collected in a longitudinal study over a ten week period across 14 lectures with more than 300 students, we investigate (i) to what extent ASQ can be reliably employed to assess attention and learning in the classroom, and (ii) whether different in-class question spacing strategies impact student learning and engagement.

1 INTRODUCTION

In post-secondary classroom-based learning, teaching units of forty-five or ninety minute units are common. Past studies have shown that students' attention rates during such sessions vary significantly with regular episodes of inattention [4, 10, 14, 18]. A second complicating factor in the modern classroom is the distraction that modern technology — such as personal laptops, smartphones and tablets — affords to students [6, 8, 17, 21], a factor that has been shown to decrease several metrics associated with student learning including retention, attention and exam grades.

One potential solution to this issue is to ban laptops completely from the classroom or at least create "laptop-free zones" within large classroom areas [1]. Such a drastic measure though is not realistic to transfer to all higher education classrooms. Instead of

resisting this new wave of classroom technologies, we aim to gain a deeper understanding into how it fits into students' learning habits.

In this work we report on a *case study* in a large higher education classroom that attempts to tackle student inattention and distractions through modern technology in tandem. One proactive approach to reducing inattention during such classes is active learning [5] — students not only passively listen to the lecturer, but also actively participate in the learning process. In order to facilitate active learning components in a classroom with hundreds of students, we adapted and deployed ASQ [19], an open-source Web-mediated teaching tool that incorporates interactive teaching elements (by offering a variety of practice questions) and keeps detailed logs of students' ASQ-related Web browser activities. We selected a 10-week undergraduate course (*Web and Database Technology*) for more than 300 Computer Science students as our target due to the diverse range of possible question types (from multiple-choice, text-based to programming and database queries) and conducted a longitudinal study of ASQ's usage.

Encouraging positive use of digital technologies in the classroom is not new. Previous work addressed the effect of personal response systems (colloquially known as "clickers") on student attention and engagement [7, 11]. Other studies have explored the impact of laptops in the classroom for note-taking [17, 21] or undirected use [8]. While providing insights on the relationship between digital technologies and students behaviour, many prior works suffer from one main technical limitation: they assume the students' devices to be complementary to, and not integrated with, the lecture experience. In our work, we take the next step and turn the students' devices from potential distractors into a teaching and communication tool by *seamlessly* interleaving lecture material and *complex* questions such as programming questions in each student's browser.

Previous work is also largely affected by a methodological limitation: experiments took place in a controlled setting, where the students' identities were known, and they were explicitly assigned to experimental conditions that could have harmed their learning experience.

These issues of privacy and fairness are not compatible with the requirements of a real-world course, where students must be guaranteed equal treatment, and privacy must be preserved.

These requirements were at the center of our use case, and defined our experimental methodology: participation was optional, students' identity concealed, and the learning set-up equal for all participants. Intuitively, changing the experimental conditions

UMAP'17, July 9–12, 2017, Bratislava, Slovakia
© 2017 ACM. 978-1-4503-4635-1/17/07...$15.00
DOI: http://dx.doi.org/10.1145/3079628.3079671

might make our experiments not comparable with previous work. To this end, we first focused on the following research question:

RQ1 *To what extent can a Web-based, privacy-preserving teaching tool be reliably used to assess the attention and learning outcomes of students?*

To answer this question, we analyse the ASQ user logs collected throughout our target course, and compare the obtained results with the findings collected from a systematic analysis of the literature. For instance, it is well-known that the activity of answering practice questions is benefiting students by increasing their engagement in the classroom [16]. Confirming these results, provides evidence of the suitability of ASQ as a platform for longitudinal "in-situ" experiments, thus enabling the investigation of additional research questions.

Next to exploring the impact of ASQ on several student behaviour metrics, we also investigated one dimension of practice questions that so far has not received a lot of attention: their spacing in time as they are interleaved with slides during the entire class duration.

RQ2 *Does the practice question strategy — questions are deployed uniformly across the entire lecture or with bursts of several questions at the same time — have any impact on student engagement and student learning?*

The remainder of the paper is organized as follows: §2 discusses related work; §3 introduces the ASQ platform, while §4 describes the experimental setting; §5 discusses the findings of our analysis and §6 summarizes the main lessons learned.

2 BACKGROUND

In this section we will first describe the impact of laptops and other digital devices (such as personal response systems) on the higher education classroom experience and then move on to discuss studies of question spacing in classrooms.

2.1 Digital technology in the classroom

Wood et al. [21] examined the impact of multi-tasking in lectures in particular through digital means: 145 undergraduate students took three classes of 20 minutes, each followed by a 15-item multiple choice quiz. Students were randomly assigned to one of seven experimental conditions. The learning performance (the percentage of correctly answered quiz questions) was found to be significantly and negatively impacted by multi-tasking (also confirmed in [15]), in particular when it involves highly-engaging social networks such as Facebook.

Closer to our own experimental setup, in one of the seven conditions the participants were free to use or not use their laptops (i.e. no multi-tasking was forced on them); it was found that those students opting not to use digital technologies achieved a higher learning performance than those that did. A similarly designed study and result was reported in [17], where not only the participants' multi-tasking was investigated but also the impact it had on participants in direct view of the multi-tasker — the distraction to the non-multi-tasking peers was significant and they in turn reached lower test scores than non-distracted peers. A much larger study by Aguilar-Roca et al. [1] across 800 students and 15 lectures did not find detrimental effects to students in the proximity of laptop users as measured in exam grades. As [17, 21], Fried [6]

relied on an undergraduate psychology student class to reach the same conclusion through weekly self-reports and the students' test performance. In [8] a binary setup was employed: students were either allowed to use their laptop in class for any activity of their choice or disallowed to use their laptop at all. Students in the "open laptop" condition were found to remember less of the lecture content than students in the "closed laptop" condition. Finally, Ravizza et al. [13] performed the most natural experiment by routing students' Internet traffic in class through a proxy that logged all online activities during class time which was subsequently classified as either class-related or class-unrelated. They found (not surprisingly given past research) that class-unrelated Internet usage (e.g. the use of social networks or emailing) was common among students that chose to use their laptop in class and was negatively related to class performance. More surprisingly, class-related Internet usage did not benefit students, their class performance (usually measured through an after-lecture quiz or final course grades) did not increase over students that did not use their laptops in class.

Despite the varying experimental setups (cf. Table 1), the multitude of studies converge on the same conclusion: the use of digital devices in the classroom is not advantageous for students' learning performance due to students' multi-tasking behaviour and the available distractions. Nevertheless, students themselves perceive technology in the classroom as mostly useful instead of distracting [3, 9]. Since the complete ban of technology in the classroom is often not feasible (though less radical ideas such as laptop-free zones within a large classroom have shown promise [1]), we aim in our work to take advantage of technology to establish an additional communication channel between students and lecturers.

Previously, the use of personal response systems[1] ("clickers") has been explored as one potential positive use case for interactive technologies (besides laptops) in large classrooms. Mayer et. al al [11] found students engaged in in-class multiple-choice question answering through clickers to have higher learning gains than students engaged through the same questions without clickers. Notably, this latter group did also not fare any better than the control group of students who did not receive those in-class questions. Gauci et. al [7] made clicker usage in their classroom voluntary and found students who participated in answering in-class questions this way (in contrast to [11] it was not possible to answer questions without a clicker) to achieve higher exam results than those who did not. Importantly, low-performing students (those with low marks in a prerequisite course) were found to benefit more than mid- and high-achieving students. These results show that a guided and restricted usage of technology can benefit students' learning.

2.2 In-class questions

It is a well-established fact that active learning, in all its various forms, is effective in increasing students' learning performance compared to the traditional lecture setup where students are passive recipients of information [12]. In large classes, active learning is most often associated with questions that allow immediate automated feedback, such as multiple-choice questions or (relevant in our use case) programming questions evaluated through unit

---

[1]Such personal response systems can either be dedicated pieces of hardware or software installed on mobile phones and laptops.

testing. Recently, Weinstein et al. [20] explored the benefit of quiz spacing in the classroom: in a within-subject design (45 students) two spacing strategies — interspersed and at-the-end — were compared with each other. Similarly to our own study, the questions (five per lecture) in the interspersed condition followed directly the slides containing the necessary information, while in the at-the-end condition all questions were placed at the end of the lecture. The achieved quiz scores in the interspersed condition were found to be significantly higher than in the at-the-end condition. This difference in learning performance though vanished when the students were tested one last time nearly three weeks after the last lecture.

To summarize, previous works (often conducted in simulated classrooms with assigned conditions) have shown that undirected use of digital devices in the classroom leads to distractions and ultimately degrades the students' learning performance. At the same time, the directed use of technology has shown promise. With respect to in-class quizzes, there is little doubt in the literature that interactive classes improve students' learning performance, however, there is very little work discussing and exploring the benefits of question spacing. Our work adds additional knowledge to this issue and explores to what extent a platform such as ASQ can enable students laptop to function as directed devices in the classroom.

3 OVERVIEW OF THE ASQ PLATFORM

ASQ [19] is a Web-based tool that allows lecturers to deliver interactive lectures directly on students' Web browsers. ASQ has been designed and developed to increase the lecturer's awareness of the level of understanding in the classroom, and to turn student devices from potential distractors to a novel communication channel. Lecturers control the progression of slides from their own device, and changes to the current slide are automatically propagated to all connected student browsers.

In ASQ lecture slides are encoded in HTML5. Slides might contain interactive exercises of various types, including – but not limited to: multiple-choice, multiple answers, open questions, text highlight, SQL queries, and Javascript functions. Figures 1–2 show two examples of question types: *SQL*, which comprises a text editor for the writing of SQL queries performed on an in-browser database instance, and a results pane to visualise the query results; and *text highlighting*, where students are asked to highlight the type (synchronous and asynchronous) of Javascript methods.

The answers submitted by students are available to the lecturer for review and discussion in real-time.

3.1 Capturing students' interactions

Figure 3 provides a high-level overview of ASQ's distributed event collection and analysis architecture. The student's version of the presentation slides is a Web application which establishes a low latency bi-directional communication with the application server via the WebSockets protocol. Student interactions with the client-side Web application generate *events* that are captured in the Web browser, emitted to the server and stored in the event log database. ASQ does not require students to log in, and events are captured as soon as the browser connects to a running ASQ presentation session. Closing the browser tab that renders the ASQ presentation will

disconnect the student. Each student is given a unique identification token for each presentation session and active connection. The token expires when the browser session expires, i.e. when the Web browser that established the initial connection to ASQ closes. This allows us to associate students with the events they generate, while preserving students' privacy across multiple lectures.

ASQ tracks different types of events (Table 2) that are generated by the browser during a presentation session; occurrences of such events are immediately sent to the ASQ server. Examples of events include: (i) connecting to the ASQ presentation; (ii) submitting an answer to a question; (iii) switching to another browser tab, or to another application, which may make the ASQ window invisible.

Figure 4 provides an example of the sequence of events emitted by three students during the first 15 minutes of a lecture. The first student has a low level of engagement as he immediately hides the ASQ window and then disconnects after 3 minutes without answering any questions. The second student shows a high level of engagement with the slides (which are never hidden after the initial connection) and also submits one answer to a question. The third student presents several context switches where ASQ is repeatedly hidden and shortly thereafter becomes visible again. This behavior continues also after the student submits an answer.

4 METHODOLOGY & USE CASE

In order to answer our research questions, we first need to define engagement metrics based on the events emitted by each student's browser (§4.1). In §4.2 we then introduce the question spacing strategies we explored in our use case, followed by a brief description of our annotation of question difficulty in §4.3. Finally, in §4.4 we introduce our target undergraduate course in more detail.

4.1 Modeling slide and question engagement

For each student, events are aggregated in order to compute *slide* and *question* engagement metrics. The former refers to engagement during the non-interactive parts of the presentation session, i.e. the content slides presented by the lecturer. The latter refers to engagement during the interactive (question-containing) slides of the session. We consider a student engaged with the slides if they are visible to the student in his or her browser. Conversely, we consider a student not to be engaged if the lecture slides are not visible to him or her (e.g. due to activities such as browsing the Web, emailing and so on).

We use the `tabvisible` and `tabhidden` events to detect whether the ASQ Web browser tab of the student is visible or not as well as the `answersubmit` event to detect if a student has submitted an answer to a question. We assume that a session s (full lecture from the time a presentation starts and ends in ASQ) of length $T(s)$ starts at second 1 and ends at second $T(s)$. For every student v, for every second t of session s we create an indicator variable $visible(v, s, t)$ which is 1 if the ASQ tab is visible and 0 otherwise. The mean slide engagement $MSE(v, s)$ of a student across s is the number of seconds the ASQ tab is visible, normalised by the session length:

$$MSE(v, s) = \frac{1}{T(s)} \sum_{t=1}^{T(s)} visible(v, s, t) \qquad (1)$$

Table 1: Related work overview: column 2 reports the number of lectures and the length of each lecture (in minutes). Column "Simulated" indicates whether the experiment was conducted in a simulated classroom (✓) or a natural classroom (✗) setting. Students' behaviours can be determined as follows: assigned condition (behaviour determined by experimental condition assigned), self-reports (students report on their behaviour/distraction), human observers (observers sit behind students and observe them) or online activity logging (through a proxy server or ASQ in our work). The "Learning performance measurement" reports how students were evaluated on their learning performance.

	#Lectures (time)	#Students	Simulated	#Exp. conditions	Logging type(s)	Learning performance measurement	Class	Incentive
[21]	3 (20 minutes)	145	✓	7: Facebook – Texting – Natural Technology Use – Word Processing – pen and paper – MSN – email	Assigned condition	15 multiple-choice (MC) questions immediately after the lecture	Research methods, Statistics	$15 or course credit
[17]	1 (45 minutes)	44	✓	2: Multitasking – Non-multitasking	Assigned condition	20 MC questions immediately after the lecture	Introductory Psychology	Course credit
[6]	20 (75 minutes)	137	✗	2: Open laptop – Closed laptop	Weekly self-reports	4 exams and 10 homework assignments	General Psychology	None
[8]	1 (N/A)	44	✗	2: Open laptop – Closed laptop	Assigned condition and voluntary online activity logging	20 MC and open questions immediately after the lecture	Communications	None
[15]	1 (60 minutes)	64	✓	2: Open laptop – Closed laptop	Assigned condition	10 MC questions immediately after the lecture	N/A	$15 or course credit
[13]	15 (100 minutes)	84	✗	3: Class-related Internet usage – Nonacademic Internet usage – No Internet usage	Online activity logging	Final exam	Introductory Psychology	Course credit
[7]	36 (50 minutes)	175	✗	2: Personal response system (PRS) usage – No PRS	PRS logging	Midterm, final exam	Psychology: Control of Body Function	None
[1]	13 (50 minutes)	800	✗	2: Zoned laptop use – Uncontrolled laptop use	Assigned condition	Final exam	Bio 93: DNA to Organisms	None
Our work	14 (90 minutes)	89-319	✗	2: High engagement with ASQ – Low engagement with ASQ	ASQ activity logging	123 questions (MC, highlight, fill-in-the-blank) interspersed in lectures	Web & Database Technology	None

Figure 1: SQL question in ASQ.

Figure 2: Text-highlighting question

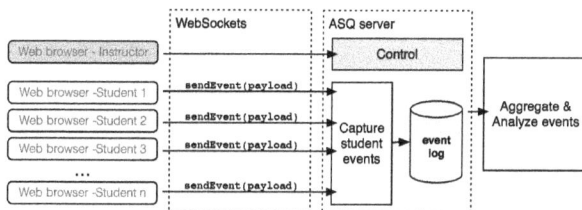

Figure 3: ASQ's architecture.

A student v's question engagement is exclusively defined over the interactive (question) slides in s; it is the fraction of questions

$q \in Q(s)$ (with $Q(s)$ being the set of all questions in session s) that v submitted an answer for:

$$\text{MQE}(v, s) = \frac{1}{|Q(s)|} \sum_{q \in Q(s)} submitted(v, q) \qquad (2)$$

Here, $submitted(v, q)$ is 1 if v submitted an answer to q and 0 otherwise.

4.2 In-class question strategies

As noted in §2 there is little research (apart from [20]) exploring the advantages or disadvantages of certain question spacing strategies in the classroom. To fill this gap and inspired by [20] the course

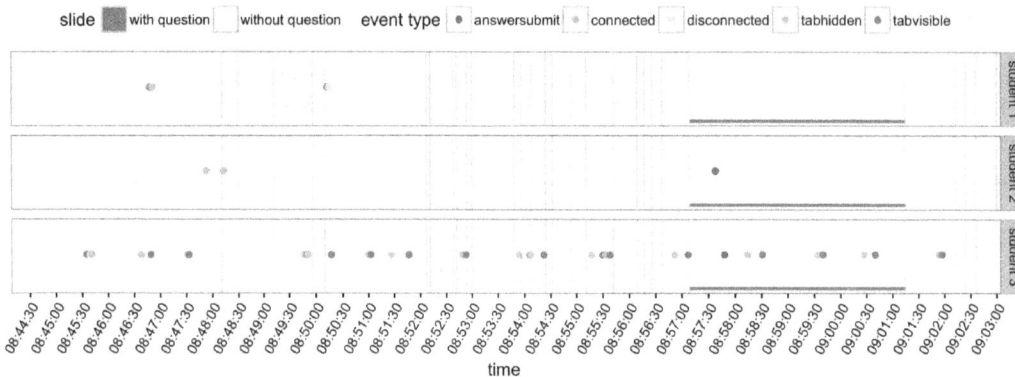

Figure 4: Sequence of events for three example viewers during the first 15 minutes of Lecture 2, *HTML*. Each vertical line represents a slide change — there are 29 slides shown in total, one of which is a question slide.

Table 2: Events monitored by ASQ relevant for this paper.

Event Name	Description
tabhidden	0 pixels from the browser tab that displays the ASQ web app becomes visible on the user's screen.
tabvisible	At least 1 pixel from the browser tab that displays the ASQ web app becomes visible on the user's screen.
answersubmit	A student submits an answer for an ASQ question (an exercise can have multiple questions).
connected	A student connects to the ASQ server.
disconnected	A student disconnects from the ASQ server.

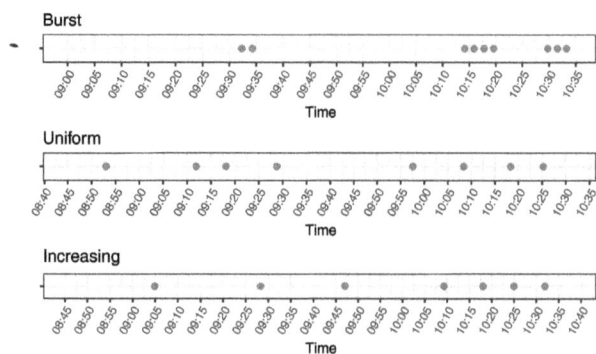

Figure 5: A temporal view of question strategies - each dot represents a question.

instructors initially designed the set of questions in each lecture according to one of the following three question strategies (with the strategies being randomly assigned to each lecture):

Burst (b): questions appear in bursts, each burst contains at least two questions; bursts can be randomly spread across a 90 minute lecture.

Uniform (u) questions are distributed uniformly in time across a 90 minute lecture;

Increasing (i) questions are placed with increasing frequency towards the end of each 45 minute period (two such periods exist per lecture with a 15 minute break in-between).

Figure 5 shows three example lectures (i.e. Cookies & session, SQL continued, Database introduction) and their question distribution across time.

After both class instructors had trialed all three question strategies in the first six lectures, it was decided to drop the increasing questions strategy from further consideration as it turned out to be very challenging to align the lecture material with this strategy. Subsequently, in the remaining 8 lectures only the burst and uniform question strategies were implemented.

4.3 Question difficulty

In our analysis, we also consider the difficulty of the questions posed to the students. All questions were created by the instructors of the course and manually annotated in accordance with the revised Bloom's taxonomy [2] — questions on the *remembering* and *understanding* level were considered to be *easy* and questions on the *applying* level were considered to be *difficult*. None of the questions belonged to higher Bloom levels.

4.4 Course overview

The data for this study was collected during the 2016/17 edition of a first year Bachelor course teaching Web technology and database concepts to Computer Science students at the Delft University of Technology. The course took place between November 14, 2016 and January 20, 2017. Table 3 presents the topic overview of the 14 lectures[2]; each lecture lasted 90 minutes, after 45 minutes a fifteen minute break occurred. The course topics were split across two instructors (I_1 and I_2), the in-class question strategy was randomly assigned. Overall, six lectures implemented the bursts

---

[2]In total, the course contained 15 lectures; one had to be excluded from our analysis due to a faulty logging mechanism.

question strategy and six lectures implemented the uniform question strategy, equally distributed across both instructors. Every lecture contained between seven and 13 question of various types: multiple-choice, multiple-answer, highlighting, SQL-query creation and fill-in-the-blank questions; in all but one lecture (CSS) the easy exercises outnumbered the difficult ones.

5 RESULTS

In this section we report on the analysis of the usage logs created by ASQ during the 10 weeks and 14 logged lectures of the course. First, in §5.1 we analyse the *slide* and *question* engagement of students across lectures, and compare the findings with previous work to assess the suitability of ASQ as a privacy-preserving platform for "in-situ" experiments. In §5.2 we study whether question strategies affect students' engagement with the lecture material.

5.1 RQ1: ASQ as an experimental platform

Table 3 reports the course attendance statistics, and data about the percentage of students using ASQ to visualise slides and to interact with questions. In each lecture, the students were counted by one of the authors ten minutes after the official start of the lecture.

Engagement across lectures. Over the course of the class, student attendance dropped from initially 319 to approximately 100 students — an attendance drop also seen in comparable courses at the same institution.

The usage of ASQ also fluctuated: while in the first three lectures more than 90% of the students used ASQ at least for some time during the lecture, novelty wore off and in later lectures the usage varied with between 65% and 80% of students connected to ASQ. Of those students that used ASQ, between 63% and 85% answered at least one question, while at most 27% of students submitted answers to all of a lecture's questions; in three lectures (all on database topics) fewer than 3% of students were such all-answer-submitting students. Across the 14 lectures we only observe 4 lectures (Conceptual design, CSS, HTML and HTTP) where at least half of the ASQ connected students submitted answers to more than half of the posed questions. These results are lower than expected, but not completely surprising. Not all students are equally compelled to experience lectures through their own devices (some students prefer pen and paper when being given the choice [1]), and their preference could vary according to topic. Also, questions varied in complexity; for topics like *SQL* (where SQL queries needed to be produced by students during the lecture), answering all questions was objectively harder than for lectures with mostly multiple-choice or multiple-answer questions. These results show that ASQ has been well-received by the course's students, and that a significant number of such students has been actively engaged with the lecture material and with questions.

Engagement within lectures. The fine-grained logging abilities of ASQ allow us to also investigate the students' engagement with ASQ beyond submitting responses to questions. Let us consider the students' *slide* and *question* engagement, as defined in §4.1.

The distribution of students engaged with slides for each lecture is plotted in Figure 6. Focusing on the first lecture (HTTP), we observe that half of the students are engaged with the slides

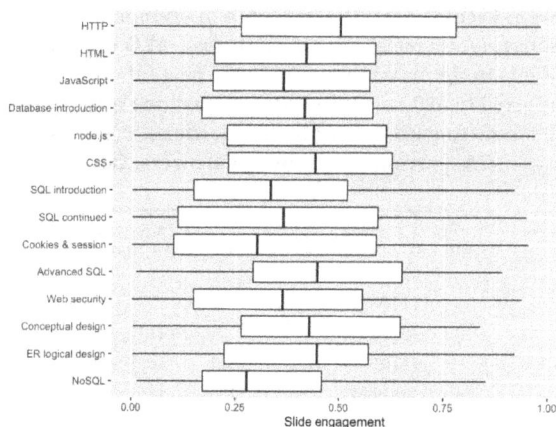

Figure 6: Distribution of slide engagement (computed per student) across all lectures. A value of 1 (0) indicates that ASQ was always (never) visible during class time.

between 25% and 76% of the lecture time. In subsequent lectures, the slide engagement drops, reaching its lowest median w.r.t. the median slide engagement in the final lecture (NoSQL) where half the students using ASQ have the non-question slides visible or in focus less than 30% of the time. Again, we confirm prior works, e.g. [8], that have shown learners to be distracted by the availability of digital devices (laptops in particular). Even though ASQ offers a directed, continuous and structured laptop use during the course of a lecture, students are still distracted (which we infer from the fact that the ASQ window is hidden most of the time).

For each lecture, we compute the Spearman rank correlation coefficient between students' question and slide engagement percentages. A correlation close to 1.0 would indicate that students with high slide engagement are also interacting with almost all questions. Table 3 shows the results of this analysis in the $\rho(S, Q)$ column. In the first lecture we observe a correlation of $\rho_{HTTP} = 0.72$ which indicates a strong relationship between slide and question engagement. In later lectures this relationship decreases in strength, reaching its lowest point in the final lecture with $\rho_{NoSQL} = 0.39$. This trend could be explained by the increasing complexity of the addressed topics, that might have discouraged students from participating in some or all of the question activities.

In contrast to previous studies, e.g. [6, 8, 21], we cannot compare our ASQ-using student population to the non-using population, as we only measure learning performance through questions posed within ASQ. Due to our privacy-aware setup, students attending lectures did not login to ASQ, nor did they provide their university IDs. As all question activities are formative assessments and students do not identify themselves when connecting to ASQ it is unclear why so many chose to not *attempt* to answer some of these questions. The lack of identification prohibits us to use the final exam score (as done in previous works) as learning performance measurement.

Although we *cannot* gather insights about students that chose to not consume lecture material through ASQ, we observed clear trends for students that did use the platform: slide and question engagement are strongly and positively correlated. We find this

Table 3: Lecture overview, reported in temporal order of delivery. Legenda. INS: instructor ($I1$ or $I2$). QS: the question strategy (b=burst, i=increasing and u=uniform). #EQ and #HQ: number of easy and hard questions in the slides. #STU: number of students in the classroom. %ASQ: the percentage of students in the classroom connected to ASQ. %SQ: the percentage of students connected to ASQ and answering at least one question (≥ 1 question submitted). %AQ: percentage of students connected to ASQ and submitting an answer to all questions. $\rho(S, Q)$: Spearman rank order correlation between *slide* and *question* engagement scores. %CA: percentage of correct answers. Correlations significant at the $p < 0.01$ level are marked with a †.

Lecture	INS	QS	#EQ	#HQ	#STU	%ASQ	%SQ	%AQ	$\rho(S, Q)$	%CA
HTTP	I1	b	6	4	319	99.7%	74.5%	26.1%	0.72†	62.16
HTML	I1	u	4	4	238	94.5%	79.1%	27.6%	0.58†	47.75
JavaScript	I1	i	5	5	192	91.1%	81.1%	8.0%	0.69†	48.14
Database introduction	I2	i	6	1	204	83.8%	78.9%	10.5%	0.60†	49.66
node.js	I1	b	5	3	208	64.9%	74.1%	15.6%	0.66†	65.53
CSS	I1	u	2	5	163	82.8%	79.3%	21.5%	0.72†	64.88
SQL introduction	I2	b	4	5	196	75.0%	79.6%	8.2%	0.57†	52.05
SQL continued	I2	u	6	2	157	87.9%	76.8%	2.9%	0.44†	54.41
Cookies & session	I1	b	5	4	133	97.0%	78.3%	11.6%	0.51†	49.76
Advanced SQL	I2	u	7	3	89	87.6%	62.8%	0.0%	0.64†	65.52
Web security	I1	u	4	4	151	70.9%	74.8%	14.0%	0.50†	48.46
Conceptual design	I2	b	11	2	83	65.1%	83.3%	13.0%	0.42†	60.26
ER logical design	I2	u	4	4	125	68.0%	84.7%	2.4%	0.40†	54.49
NoSQL	I2	b	8	0	89	76.4%	69.1%	11.8%	0.39†	61.61

Table 4: Overview of correlations between *slide* and *question* engagement, computed separately for each instructor, each question strategy and the four combinations of instructor and strategy. N is the number of items to correlate. %CA is the percentage of correct answers. Correlations significant at the $p < 0.01$ level are marked with a †

Condition	N	$\rho(S, Q)$	%CA
Question strat. *uniform*	768	0.50†	51.92
Question strat. *bursts*	851	0.61†	59.65
Instructor $I1$	1224	0.63†	55.47
Instructor $I2$	741	0.45†	55.02
$I1$ +*uniform*	467	0.58†	50.25
$I1$ + *bursts*	582	0.67†	60.85
$I2$ + *uniform*	301	0.39†	55.58
$I2$ + *bursts*	269	0.47†	56.75

alignment of results an indication of the suitability of a platform like ASQ for teaching and experimental purposes.

5.2 RQ2: Impact of question strategies

Are questions strategies influencing the engagement levels of the students? To address **RQ2**, we analyse slide and question engagement for lectures adopting *uniform* and *burst* question strategies. The results are reported in Table 4 (rows 2-3).

The correlation between slide and question engagement scores is higher for the *burst* than the *uniform* condition. This means that in the *uniform* condition with one question on the topic of the previous 5-10 slides, students are more likely to engage with the question than in the *burst* condition where at least some of the questions are likely to be about material more than 10 slides in the past. Drilling down further, we also consider in the analysis the

role that the instructors, with their individual lecture style (and question styles) as well as addressed topics, might have played on the engagement level of students. Table 4 (rows 3-8) show that instructors clearly played a role. Despite the absolute differences in correlations, we observe that for both instructors the *burst* strategy leads to a higher correlation between slide and question engagement than the *uniform* strategy.

6 LESSONS LEARNED

This section summarises what the authors learned from the usage of ASQ in the classroom. The fourth and fifth authors are the instructors and designers of the *Web and Database Technology* course.

On the effectiveness of online questions to reduce distractions. The results presented in the previous sections are mixed: while initially many students adopt ASQ, over the course of the class the adoption rate decreases. Although ASQ offers a directed use of a digital device to follow and engage with a large classroom lecture, a significant fraction of students are engaged elsewhere through browser activities (as also indicated in prior works). A qualitative inspection of the collected statistics show that the engagement of students with ASQ varies across lectures, and also within the same lecture. Take for instance the graphs in Figure 7–9; they show for each lecture second the number of students connected to ASQ (those are all students with ASQ either visible or hidden) and the number of students having ASQ visible on their screen. Javascript (Figure 9) is an example of lecture where it is possible to observe a growing engagement trend, both before and after the lecture's break, that is correlated with the progression of questions. During the CSS lecture (Figure 8), questions provided only local increases in the number of engaged students, with no observable trend. Finally, lecture HTTP shows how the effect of questions changes during the

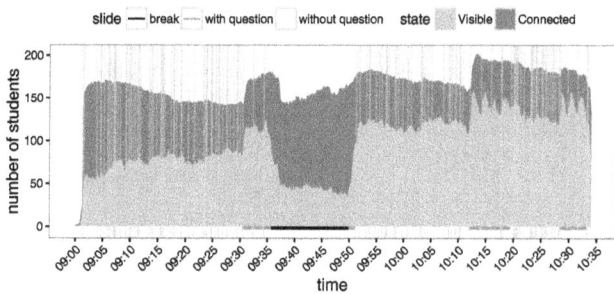

Figure 7: Temporal evolution of connected and slide engaged students during the *HTTP* lecture. Evidence of distracted behaviour in the second half of the lecture.

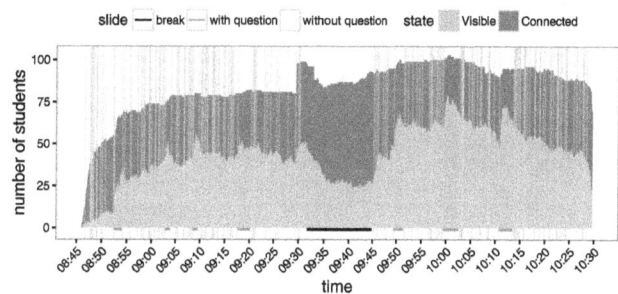

Figure 8: Temporal evolution of connected and slide engaged students during the *CSS* lecture. No clear slide engagement trend can be observed.

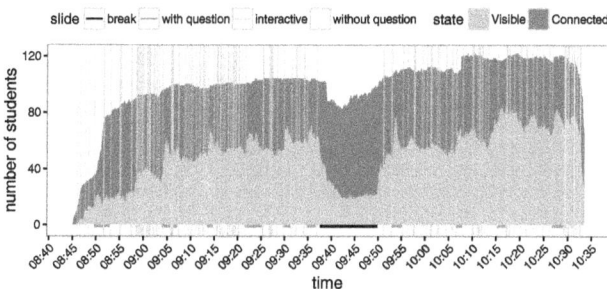

Figure 9: Temporal evolution of connected and slide engaged students during the *Javascript* lecture. Evidence of increasing slide engagement trend. Three interactive non-question slides are marked in green.

lecture. Before the break, the burst of questions helped in increasing students' engagement. After the break, each peak due to a new question is immediately followed by a sudden drop, which indicates that students were prone to distract themselves after answering the question.

Interactive slides beyond questions. In the JavaScript lecture (Figure 9), apart from the question slides a small number of additional slides contained interactive features to showcase JavaScript's abilities in the browser (such as a typing game and a text selection tool). However, when we explore whether those slides led to additional engagement (i.e. bringing students back from the other activities) we do not find this to be the case — for very few connected students the ASQ status changes from invisible to visible. This result is not supporting one of the authors' assumptions that more attractive/engaging ASQ slides lead to more direct student engagement.

Lecturer experience. The design of lecture material for a system like ASQ can be challenging for the instructor. In addition to obvious technical complexities (such as the creation of slides in HTML5), the design of a lecture experience enhanced with several, pertinent, and rich questions is not trivial. While this is an intrinsic difficulty in the design of lectures, we felt the problem to be exacerbated by the need for pre-defined question strategies, which sometimes

"forced" the redistribution of content to account for the temporal allocation of questions.

7 CONCLUSIONS

Large student cohorts are becoming more common in post-secondary education. Bachelor-level courses are lectured in large classrooms that can easily include hundreds of students. Under such conditions, students are easily distracted — especially through the ubiquitous availability of digital devices.

To gain a better understanding on the *positive* role that technology can play in large higher-education classrooms, in this work we reported on a case study where a Web-based, privacy-preserving teaching tool (ASQ) has been put into use to support lectures with interactive teaching elements.

We conducted a longitudinal study over 10 weeks of lectures, operating under strict *privacy* and *fairness* requirements, both obvious ethical concerns in real-world courses. We analysed the resulting usage logs, and established the suitability of ASQ as platform for "in-situ" privacy-preserving research in education. We investigated how different practice question strategies affected students' engagement with lecture material. We show that question strategies can be of influence, but also observe the important role played by lecturers and lecture topics.

These results provide plenty of inspiration for future work. ASQ will allow us to easily perform new use cases in other education settings (e.g. different courses, or education level). We plan to investigate (i) how different instructors influence student learning and student engagement and what are the causes for the observed differences, (ii) how more complex question types (e.g. to implement an entire program) can be broken down and incorporated into the lecture, and (iii) how the real-time insights we have about students' engagement can be reflected back to them in the live classroom to raise awareness and self-reflection.

Acknowledgements. This research was partially supported by the Extension School of the Delft University of Technology.

REFERENCES

[1] Nancy M Aguilar-Roca, Adrienne E Williams, and Diane K O'Dowd. 2012. The impact of laptop-free zones on student performance and attitudes in large lectures. *Computers & Education* 59, 4 (2012), 1300–1308.

[2] Lorin W Anderson, David R Krathwohl, and Benjamin Samuel Bloom. 2001. *A taxonomy for learning, teaching, and assessing: A revision of Bloom's taxonomy of educational objectives*. Allyn & Bacon.

[3] William M Baker, Edward J Lusk, and Karyn L Neuhauser. 2012. On the use of cell phones and other electronic devices in the classroom: Evidence from a survey of faculty and students. *Journal of Education for Business* 87, 5 (2012), 275–289.

[4] Diane M Bunce, Elizabeth A Flens, and Kelly Y Neiles. 2010. How long can students pay attention in class? A study of student attention decline using clickers. *Journal of Chemical Education* 87, 12 (2010), 1438–1443.

[5] Scott Freeman, Sarah L Eddy, Miles McDonough, Michelle K Smith, Nnadozie Okoroafor, Hannah Jordt, and Mary Pat Wenderoth. 2014. Active learning increases student performance in science, engineering, and mathematics. *Proceedings of the National Academy of Sciences* 111, 23 (2014), 8410–8415.

[6] Carrie B Fried. 2008. In-class laptop use and its effects on student learning. *Computers & Education* 50, 3 (2008), 906–914.

[7] Sally A Gauci, Arianne M Dantas, David A Williams, and Robert E Kemm. 2009. Promoting student-centered active learning in lectures with a personal response system. *Advances in Physiology Education* 33, 1 (2009), 60–71.

[8] Helene Hembrooke and Geri Gay. 2003. The laptop and the lecture: The effects of multitasking in learning environments. *Journal of computing in higher education* 15, 1 (2003), 46–64.

[9] Robin H Kay and Sharon Lauricella. 2011. Exploring the benefits and challenges of using laptop computers in higher education classrooms: A formative analysis. *Canadian Journal of Learning and Technology/La revue canadienne de lʼapprentissage et de la technologie* 37, 1 (2011).

[10] Sophie I Lindquist and John P McLean. 2011. Daydreaming and its correlates in an educational environment. *Learning and Individual Differences* 21, 2 (2011), 158–167.

[11] Richard E Mayer, Andrew Stull, Krista DeLeeuw, Kevin Almeroth, Bruce Bimber, Dorothy Chun, Monica Bulger, Julie Campbell, Allan Knight, and Hangjin Zhang. 2009. Clickers in college classrooms: Fostering learning with questioning methods in large lecture classes. *Contemporary educational psychology* 34, 1 (2009), 51–57.

[12] Michael Prince. 2004. Does active learning work? A review of the research. *Journal of engineering education* 93, 3 (2004), 223–231.

[13] Susan M Ravizza, Mitchell G Uitvlugt, and Kimberly M Fenn. 2016. Logged In and Zoned Out: How Laptop Internet Use Relates to Classroom Learning. *Psychological Science* (2016), 0956797616677314.

[14] Evan F Risko, Nicola Anderson, Amara Sarwal, Megan Engelhardt, and Alan Kingstone. 2012. Everyday attention: variation in mind wandering and memory in a lecture. *Applied Cognitive Psychology* 26, 2 (2012), 234–242.

[15] Evan F Risko, Dawn Buchanan, Srdan Medimorec, and Alan Kingstone. 2013. Everyday attention: Mind wandering and computer use during lectures. *Computers & Education* 68 (2013), 275–283.

[16] Henry L Roediger and Andrew C Butler. 2011. The critical role of retrieval practice in long-term retention. *Trends in cognitive sciences* 15, 1 (2011), 20–27.

[17] Faria Sana, Tina Weston, and Nicholas J Cepeda. 2013. Laptop multitasking hinders classroom learning for both users and nearby peers. *Computers & Education* 62 (2013), 24–31.

[18] John Stuart and RJD Rutherford. 1978. Medical student concentration during lectures. *The lancet* 312, 8088 (1978), 514–516.

[19] Vasileios Triglianos and Cesare Pautasso. 2013. ASQ: Interactive Web Presentations for Hybrid MOOCs. In *Proc. of WWW*. 209–210. DOI:http://dx.doi.org/10.1145/2487788.2487894

[20] Yana Weinstein, Ludmila D Nunes, and Jeffrey D Karpicke. 2016. On the placement of practice questions during study. *Journal of Experimental Psychology: Applied* 22, 1 (2016), 72.

[21] Eileen Wood, Lucia Zivcakova, Petrice Gentile, Karin Archer, Domenica De Pasquale, and Amanda Nosko. 2012. Examining the impact of off-task multitasking with technology on real-time classroom learning. *Computers & Education* 58, 1 (2012), 365–374.

Inferring Contextual Preferences Using Deep Auto-Encoding

Moshe Unger, Bracha Shapira, Lior Rokach and Ariel Bar

Ben-Gurion University of the Negev and Telekom Innovation Laboratories at
BGU

P.O. Box 84105, Beer-Sheva, Israel

mosheun@post.bgu.ac.il, {bshapira, liorrk, arielba}@bgu.ac.il

ABSTRACT

Context-aware systems enable the sensing and analysis of user context in order to provide personalized services. Our study is part of growing research efforts examining how high-dimensional data collected from mobile devices can be utilized to infer users' dynamic preferences. We present a novel method for inferring contextual user preferences by using an unsupervised deep learning technique applied to mobile sensor data. We train an auto-encoder for each user preference with contextual data that based on past user interaction with the system. Given new contextual sensor data from a user, the patterns discovered from each auto-encoder are used to predict the most likely preference in the given context. This can greatly enhance a variety of services, such as mobile online advertising and context-aware recommender systems. We demonstrate our contribution with a point of interest (POI) recommender system in which we label contextual preferences based on the interaction of users with categories of items. Empirical results utilizing a real world dataset of mobile users show a significant improvement (16% to 73% improvement) in classification accuracy compared with state of the art classification methods. [1]

CCS CONCEPTS

• **Information Systems** → Data Mining; • **Computing Methodologies** → Neural Networks

KEYWORDS

User Profiling; Deep Learning; Auto-encoder; Context; Mobile

1 INTRODUCTION

Context-aware computing is defined as software that adapts according to its location of use, the collection of nearby people and objects, as well as changes to those objects over time [25].

The emergence and penetration of smart mobile devices has given rise to the development of context-aware systems that utilize sensors to collect available data about users in order to improve services [21]. As a consequence, predicting the preferences of mobile users is important to a range of stakeholders, because of its ability to improve service performance, enhance mobile user experience, increase financial profit for advertisers, and more.

Analyzing user behavior and interests has attracted a considerable amount of research attention in the past few years [23,14]. Traditionally, preference modeling focuses on learning a strong set of beliefs and interests about users that are true in general, but not specifically for a certain circumstance [5,15]. However, a user's profile and interests may change over time and depend on contextual situations [14]. For example, by mining a mobile user's sensor data, the system may be able to determine the context of the user (e.g., a mobile user in the context of "eating in fast food restaurants" or "busy and not available for any further interaction with the mobile phone"); such information could help advertisers deliver targeted personalized advertisements, based on the user's dynamic and changing context.

Most of the research conducted in the area of context-aware computing has considered limited contextual factors (e.g., location or time) for modeling user's context [29,12,24]. In the methods suggested, users have to input their preferences manually in order to receive the personalized services. Moreover, this research did not provide the personalized services based on extracting the users' preferences automatically. These methods are further limited by the deficiency of their information and unable to provide new users with personalized services. We aim to address these limitations, and in this research we show how to automatically infer contextual user preferences by utilizing high-dimensional sensor data from the user's mobile phone. We suggest automatically labeling contextual user interactions from a recommender system (RS) which suggests relevant points of interest (POIs) to the user.

Performing an embedding task using deep learning on unlabeled data can greatly improve supervised learning [10]. Because predicting context based on a large set of circumstances is a complex task [21], we suggest using unsupervised deep learning representation to model user preferences; this technique can greatly reduce the dimensionality and noise of the feature space and reveal relationships between the features. We assume that each user preference is affected differently by specific contextual conditions; thus, we propose training a deep auto-encoding model for each category of items (e.g., food, nightlife spots) that have been rated by users, as shown in Figure 1 and further detailed in section 4.1. Each model is trained by sensor data and represents implicit contextual situations related to each genre. We show that these models are distinct enough to distinguish between different contextual preferences of users. Given new raw sensor data, we find the best model that share the same sensor patterns, in order to predict the category of an item that reflects the user's context. The categories may be defined according to the level of granularity required by the target system's functionality and the available information about the categories. We also show how to reduce the number of trained networks by suggesting a similarity measure between the learned deep auto-encoders models.

We evaluated our proposed method on real world data that was collected via an Android mobile application, where users provided positive feedback regarding POIs that were recommended to them. We conducted an extensive user study with 90 users over a period of four weeks. We showed that our approach achieved significantly better results than existing state of the art classification algorithms.

The major contributions of this paper include the following: first, we suggest a novel approach for modeling users' dynamic interests utilizing high-dimensional sensor data from the users' mobile phones (e.g., Wi-Fi networks, accelerometers, light, microphones, etc.). Based on the sensor data, we are able to better understand the user's rich contextual feature space. We apply an unsupervised deep learning technique that extracts the most important contextual features and discovers significant correlations between them. By applying an unsupervised method for modeling contextual user preferences, we demonstrate how supervised learning can be enhanced by jointly learns an embedding task using unlabeled sensor data.

Our second contribution relates to the new user problem; we show how the application of deep learning and unsupervised learning of contextual interests can be used to address this problem. Third, we show how to utilize the deep architecture of contextual feature space by suggesting a similarity measure between contextual interests in order to produce more robust models.

The rest of this paper is structured as follows: section 2 presents related work, and section 3 describes the methods of modeling unsupervised context and inferring contextual user preferences. Section 4 presents the setup of the field experiments and discusses the evaluation of the collected data. In section 5 we discuss the results, and finally in section 6 we conclude and outline our plans for future research.

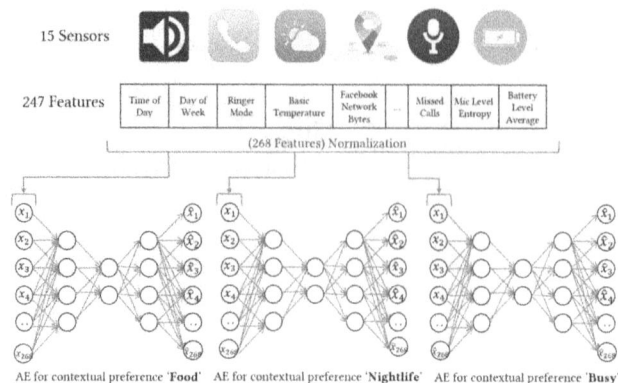

AE for contextual preference 'Food'   AE for contextual preference 'Nightlife'   AE for contextual preference 'Busy'

Figure 1: Model Illustration

2 RELATED WORK

In this section, we provide background and survey related work. We first focus on the area of implicit learning of contextual user preferences and its use in multiple domains, such as recommender systems. Then, we discuss related work of predicting user preferences with machine learning techniques.

By understanding a user's preferences with regard to products and services, more relevant advertisements can be provided, customer loyalty can be built, and customer retention and sales increased [6]. Context plays an important role in determining the relevance of a service provided by an application to the user's needs and interests. Context-aware systems [21,22] capture a broad range of contextual attributes (such as the user's current position, activity, and surrounding environment), in order to identify the user's context, and what services might interest the user. Although this area of research has been studied by many researchers [8,23], there is just a small amount of research which utilizes implicit learning of contextual interactions in order to infer contextual preferences for context-aware applications and services.

Analyzing user interests regarding products and services can be laborious and computationally demanding in dynamic systems like eBay which handles a vast amount of products that change constantly. This endeavor becomes more challenging when the application does not permit the employment of systems that might interfere with the user experience, or direct interaction with the user. However, it is possible to utilize the user's contextual preferences when they interact with the system. For instance, a user's interests can be connected to the items he/she has rated in recommender systems [23]. Thus, we focus on discovering contextual patterns when similar genres or categories of items are consumed or rated by users in recommender systems.

Defining context that is relevant to an application service, as well as identifying the primary contexts in which people use the service, is a complex task. Therefore, most researchers focus on explicit context [1,29,26] which is significantly more comprehensible to human experts and users alike. However, explicit context has several shortcomings considering privacy, data availability, and usability perspectives. For example, using explicit context such as weather conditions for a recommendation service may raise privacy issues [12], since the exact context of the user in known to the service. Moreover, determining explicit context is a resource-demanding task since it requires input from users, knowledge from a domain expert, or collecting labeled contextual information. On the other hand, establishing context-aware services based on knowledge of context in an implicit manner may address these weaknesses. Implicit context can be derived from basic user interaction with the system. In addition, contextual factors can be obtained automatically by applying unsupervised learning techniques on available raw data (e.g., mobile sensors) [28].

Predicting user context can be formulated as human activity recognition (HAR) or classification [8], where HAR is based on the physical model, such as walking and smoking [27], and classification relies on machine learning techniques, which use a large amount of data to train a supervised model for specific activities. An emerging area of machine learning that has generated significant attention is deep learning, which can improve inference accuracy and robustness in noisy complex environments, especially when sensor data is limited (either by feature or sampling rates) [2,13]. In deep learning models, features are learned in a supervised or unsupervised manner. Although some research [24, 9] has achieved over 95% accuracy for activity classification using a supervised deep learning model, this approach is limited in practical use for the following reasons. First, the predefined activities were chosen based on the domain used and only a few sensors were chosen for the prediction task; more accurate context prediction could be achieved by utilizing different contexts from multiple sources and considering the correlations between them [11]. Second, human activities are very diverse and often unpredictable, which makes it quite difficult to model or label all possible activities in one single deep network.

Our approach identifies and uses ratings acquired by users in similar contextual situations. In our approach, user's current preferences are modeled in an unsupervised manner, which is able to distinguish different circumstances under which users interact with various categories of items. These preferences are learned automatically from various mobile sensors that provide environmental information such as weather, location, and time. In addition, since we aim to reduce the dimensionality and noise of the feature space, we apply an unsupervised deep learning technique to embed the user's contextual preference. The latent representation from the deep layers can reflect relationships between the environmental sensors that will contribute to the discovery of other behavioral situations that share the same contextual user preferences.

3   METHOD

Our method infers the contextual preferences of users in terms of both the users' availability for receiving proactive notifications (e.g., advertisements, recommendations, etc.) and their preferred contextual preferences. This is based on our assumption that when relevant training data exists, deep learning can be used to infer any user preference from sensor data. The method consists of two phases, as presented in Figure

2: The first is the training phase in which we apply auto-encoding on contextual (sensor) data collected from users' interactions within a recommender system. We build several deep neural networks for different splits of the data according to the granularity levels of categories (Figure 2a and Algorithm 1). The second phase is the prediction phase, where we use current (new) contextual data recorded from the users' mobile phone. We utilize the learned deep models to reconstruct the input data in each contextual model and select the network that best fits the data with minimal error. The current preference of the user can be predicted based on the contextual model selected (Figure 2b and Algorithm 2).

3.1   Phase 1 – Training Auto-Encoders Using Contextual Interactions

Context is often determined based on correlated sensor data which typically reflects the environmental situation of the user [8]. We perform auto-encoding on the sensor data (e.g., Wi-Fi networks, accelerometers, light, etc.) collected from users' mobile devices in order to discover related contextual situations under which users interact with the system. In the recommender system domain, users give explicit or implicit feedback about items which are often grouped by categories. Thus, when a user provides contextual feedback about a specific item, it is reasonable to imply that the user is interested in the item's category given his/her current context. Since we assume that there are different circumstances under which users interact with the system, we split the users' interactions into k known categories of items that are present within the data and train k auto-encoders. This phase results in a set of trained networks, each representing the contextual patterns of the user that can be applied to his/her preferred category in a given context.

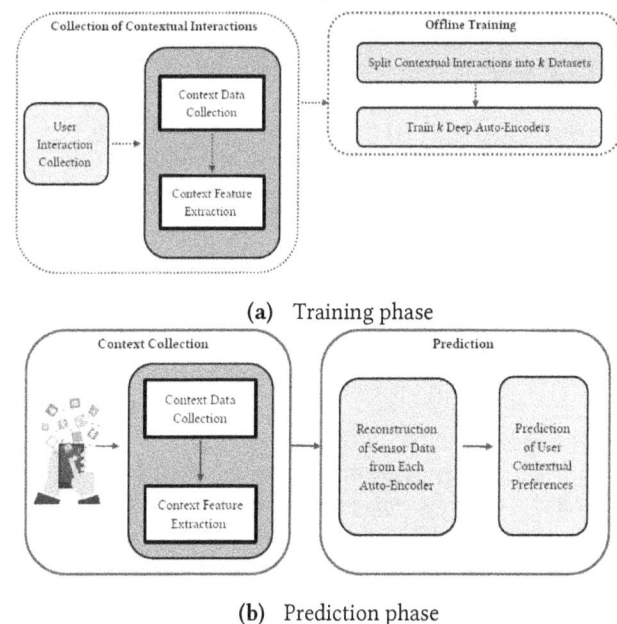

(a)   Training phase

(b)   Prediction phase

Figure 2: Method Overview

The auto-encoding is performed by an unsupervised learning algorithm that applies backpropagation which is aimed at setting the value of the targets so they are equal to the value of the inputs [20]. In the training phase, the auto-encoder tries to learn the function $h_{W,b}(x) = \hat{x} \approx x$, where W and b are the weights of the network's edges. The major advantage of auto-encoders is their ability to implicitly learn certain underlying characteristics of the input data. By putting constraints on the neural network, we can discover an interesting data structure, which is composed of a limited number of hidden units in each layer that force the network to learn a compressed representation of the context input.

Algorithm 1: Training Auto-Encoders Using Contextual Interactions

Input: S - contextual interactions, l - number of hidden units in each layer, f - activation function, k - number of contextual preferences
Output: W_k - weight matrix for each contextual preference k
1 Divide S to S_k datasets by k contextual preferences;
2 **for** *each* k **do**
3    $S'_k \leftarrow$ Normalize all samples in S_k;
4    $AE_k \leftarrow$ Train an auto-encoder (l, f) on S'_k;
5    $W_k \leftarrow$ Retrieve weight matrix from AE_k;
6 **return** W_k

Algorithm 1 provides a detailed description of the training phase. Specifically, it describes how to model and train contextual interaction data using auto-encoders in order to represent contextual patterns. The input for the algorithm is a training set $S = \{s_1, s_2, \ldots, s_n\}$ of user' interactions. Each sample s_i is r-dimensional, containing $r - 1$ context features which were extracted from the raw sensor data collected from mobile devices, as well as the item's category which has been rated positively by the user. l is a vector which specifies the number of hidden units in each layer; k is the number of contextual user categories, and f is the activation function for the neural network. We used the sigmoid activation function for this task due to its nonlinear nature. The k contextual preferences include the genres of items and a special category that represents the user's availability to receive recommendations. The algorithm learns the contextual patterns that characterize each of the categories.

The output of the algorithm is a set of weights W_k that were learned in each auto-encoder AE_k under a specific contextual preference k. The algorithm starts by splitting the dataset S into k datasets (line 1), based on the contextual preferences that have been positively rated by the user. Then we normalize each dataset S_k (line 3); the normalization includes the conversion of nominal values to a set of binary indicators and normalization of all numeric variables to {0...1}. The result is a modified dataset S'_k which is r'-dimensional. Next, an auto-encoder (AE_k) is trained on the normalized training set of genre k (line 4). The neural network is designed to include l_i hidden units in each layer and activate function f. After the auto-encoder is trained, for each network k and layer i we retrieve the matrix W_{k_i}, which contains the learned weights between the layers. Finally, we retrieve the matrix W_k which contains the set of weights for each network AE_k.

3.2 Phase 2 – Predicting User Preferences Using Contextual Data

The process of predicting user preference from a new contextual sensorial sample t is described in Algorithm 2. For example, we would like to predict if the user is available for recommendation or which genre of POI will be most preferred by the user in the current context. To accomplish this, we must select the neural network (AE_k) that is able to reconstruct the input values of sample t with minimal error. In order to do so, we normalize the new record (line 1) and calculate res_k for each k, which is the reconstructed output from each AE_k (line 3). Then, we calculate the Euclidian distance between the normalized input t' and the output res_k (line 4). In order to predict the contextual preference of the user, we select the network that has the least reconstruction error (RE) and return the preference that this network represents.

Algorithm 2: Classifying Contextual Preference from a New Contextual Sample

Input: k - number of contextual preferences, t - new contextual sample, f - activation function, W_k - weight matrix for each k
Output: $preference$ - classified contextual preference of user
1 $t' \leftarrow$ normalize t;
2 **for** *each* k **do**
3    $res_k \leftarrow$ activate f on each element in $t'W_k$;
4    $RE(res_k, t') \Leftarrow \sum_{i=1}^{r'} (res_{k_i} - t'_i)^2$;
5 $preference \leftarrow \min_k (RE(res_k, t'))$;
6 **return** $preference$

---

4 EVALUATION

4.1 Field Experiment and Data Collection

Our research focuses on applying an unsupervised method for modeling user context from mobile device data, in order to infer contextual user preferences. Specifically, we aim to infer availability for receiving recommendations ("busy") and preferred categories of items ("food," "nightlife spot"). We evaluated our method on data that was collected from mobile device sensors; the data derived from a field experiment in which users interacted with a recommender system (RS) that provided recommendations of POIs (obtained from the Foursquare[2] API) and received users' feedback about the provided recommendations. Our proposed method is aimed at modeling the implicit context for which the POIs are relevant and uses past contextual interactions of users in order to predict the preferred POI category. In order to obtain data for the evaluation of the algorithm, we developed an Android application which monitors the user's location and recommends popular POIs nearby.

90 students between the ages of 20 and 45 (53 male and 37 female) from two academic institutions participated in the experiment which took place for a month long period. We selected POIs from Foursquare that covered the cities in which participants lived and studied. The selected POIs were categorized as "food" or "nightlife spots" and had received at least 10 check-ins by Foursquare users.

---

[2] https://developer.foursquare.com/

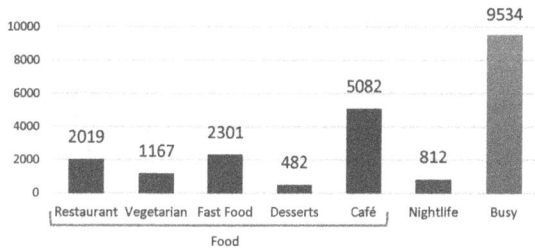

Figure 3: Users' Positive Interactions Based on Item Categories

"Food" POIs contained more specific lower level categories such as "café," "desserts," "fast food," "vegetarian," and "restaurants."

Every 30 minutes the application pops up a dialog box accompanied by a notification sound that asks whether the user is available for recommendations. If the user selects the "not now" option, we assume that the user's context is "busy." If the user responds positively, the application presents three recommendations for the user to rate using the following rating options: like, dislike, and check-in. "Like" means that the user finds the recommended POI suitable for his/her current context; dislike indicates negative feedback. The "check-in" feedback enabled the users to signal that they were currently at the recommended POI. The user's response, i.e., pressing "not now" or rating a POI, was immediately sent to the server with the sampled sensor's data that was collected for 10 seconds. The application was designed to avoid repeating the same recommendations in consecutive recommendations.

The application used a popularity-based RS algorithm. When the user confirms that he/she is available for recommendation, the RS gathers all of the POIs that are at most 500 meters away from the user's current location. The RS calculates the popularity index for each of the POIs, which is the number of "like" and "check-in" actions it received, relative to the other POIs. Then the algorithm randomly selects three POIs, when the probability of selecting a certain POI is proportional to its popularity index. Figure 3 presents the amount of feedbacks obtained from users for each category. Overall, the system collected 21,397 instances of user feedback during the four weeks of the experiment.

In order to acquire data from a variety of sensors we used Android APIs and the Funf [19]. As presented in Table 1, we collected data from various types of sensors which include environmental information, user activity, mobile state, and user behavioral data. In particular, we collected raw data from the following sensors: accelerometer, Wi-Fi, battery, light, orientation, magnetic field, gravity, audio level, and location. Additional information was derived as well, such as the sampling timestamp, day of the week, time of day, weather conditions, activity recognition, screen-log, call-log, and traffic statistics of certain applications installed on the user's mobile device (i.e., Facebook, WhatsApp, Waze, Chrome, and Moovit). In order to derive the weather conditions, we used a publicly available forecast API [3] which maps GPS coordinates to weather

---

[3] https://developer.forecast.io/

information. Raw data collected by the sensors and the additional information listed above were aggregated, analyzed, and engineered to generate 247 features, as shown in Figure 4. These features define the user's context. Due to limited space, we will only provide limited examples of the feature engineering process.

Accelerometer, magnetic field, orientation, and gravity are sensors that produce raw data in the form of a 3D axis and sample nearly 100 records per second for each axis. We calculated the average, median, standard deviation, correlation, minimum and maximum values, range, first and third quarters, RMS, and entropy for each axis. From the timestamp, we calculated the part of the week (midweek, weekend) and time of day (dawn, morning, afternoon, night). We also added information regarding the device's screen mode. To do so, we constantly sampled the timestamps in which the user turned on and off his/her mobile device's screen and the action that was made (i.e., "screen turned on" and "screen turned off"). We extracted three features regarding the screen log which indicate the percent of time the screen was on: during the last 20 minutes, the last 10 minutes, and the past minute.

Table 1: Collected Sensor Data

Contextual Conditions	Contextual Factors
Environmental Data	Date and Time
	Weather
	Light
	Microphone
User Activity Data	Accelerometer
	Orientation
	Magnetic field
	Gravity
	Location (GPS)
Mobile State Data	Screen Log
	Battery
	Ringer mode
User Behavioral Data	Human interaction with phone (call log, SMS log)
	Running applications
	Network traffic

4.2 Evaluation Setup

We trained a series of classification models in order to predict users' contextual preferences from sensor data. We split the data by the record's timestamp using 80% for training and the remaining 20% for testing. The time-based splitting considered the data collected in the last week of the experiment as the test set, while the first three weeks were considered as the training set. The time-based splitting represents real-life scenarios, whereas prediction models are trained based on historical data in order to predict future samples. We compared our suggested auto-encoder model with several well-known classification models, including: Artificial Neural Network (ANN), C4.5 Decision Tree (C4.5), Random Forest (RF), and Support Vector

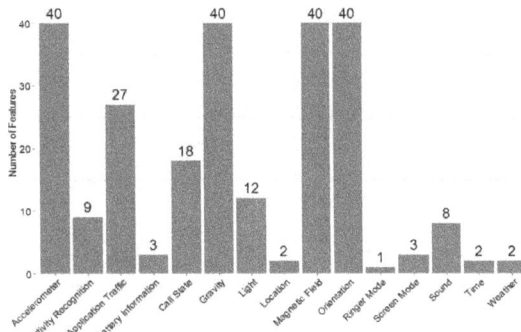

Figure 4: Extracted Features for Each User Interaction

Machine (SVM), using WEKA's implementation. For the decision trees, we applied C4.5 with minimum instances of 5, 10 and 20. We report the best results achieved with minimum instances of 20. For the SVM, we applied the radial basis function (RBF) kernel method. We applied Random Forest with an ensemble size of 10 trees. In order to train neural network we transformed nominal values of features to binary values, which resulted in 268 features. For the ANN, we trained a single network which contained four hidden layers, with (268, 120, 40, 3) hidden units in each layer respectively (e.g., 120 hidden units in the second layer). After a calibration process, we configured the learning rate to 0.3 and trained the network with 500 epochs. We trained all auto-encoders with five layers, with (268, 120, 40, 120, 268) hidden units in each layer respectively (e.g., 40 hidden units in the deepest layer). In order to avoid overfitting, we trained each auto-encoder with a maximum of 50 epochs.

We observed that the dataset had a certain level of imbalance, i.e., some items' categories were less popular than the others and could be considered as minority class labels (see Figure 3). In order to improve the accuracy of the traditional classification models, we applied SMOTE [4] on the dataset, as a preprocessing step before training the classifiers. The SMOTE procedure was applied on the minority class "nightlife" and was configured with a neighborhood size of five instances and a sampling ratio of 100%, resulting in 1,956 instances of "nightlife" contextual feedback. We used the accuracy, false positive (FP), and area under curve (AUC) [2,7] as our prediction accuracy measures.

5 RESULTS

5.1 Inference of Contextual Preferences

We aimed to train a model that would be able to classify a test set of contextual preferences at different granularity levels. Specifically, we first distinguished between three different contexts representing high level categories: food, nightlife spot, and busy. Second, we distinguished between more detailed contextual categories including: restaurant, vegetarian, fast food, desserts, café, nightlife spot, and busy, based on Foursquare categories. Training a prediction model in order to estimate more refined context categories can enable the model to determine more focused interests. For example, if a context inference model can refine the "like food" context to more

detailed contexts, such as "like desserts" or "like vegetarian food," a recommender system can suggest additional relevant contextual recommendations.

We applied several prediction models on the test data using 268 features. Table 2 presents results for the three high level categories. As observed, our model outperforms all of the tested classification algorithms by at least 45% in terms of accuracy and by 23% in terms of AUC. Auto-encoding produced better results than all classifiers since it can better handle high dimensional, noisy and complex sensor data. We can also observe that the auto-encoding outperforms ANN by at least 30% in terms of AUC. This can be explained by the fact that in the auto-encoding we trained three separate networks, while in the ANN a single network is trained. Although both models of ANN and auto-encoding have good characteristics of feature learning, sharing the weights between the different contextual preferences in one single network has led to poor results. Thus, separating the data between the networks obtained better results and implies that the models are diverse enough to capture unique patterns for each contextual preference.

Table 2: Prediction of Three High Level Preferences

Prediction Model	Accuracy	FP	AUC
Auto-Encoding	**0.971**	**0.025**	**0.927**
ANN	0.643	0.317	0.714
C4.5	0.668	0.298	0.751
Random Forest	0.657	0.3	0.739
SVM	0.658	0.312	0.673

High-dimensional data often contains many redundant features. Both theoretical analysis and empirical evidence [16] show that along with irrelevant features, redundant features affect the accuracy of learning algorithms and thus should be eliminated. In order to improve the prediction accuracy of the compared classification algorithms, we performed correlation feature selection (CFS) using WEKA's implementation on the training set, resulting in the selection of the 14 best features. We then applied the classification models on the test data using those features. For auto-encoding, we used (14, 4, 14) hidden units in each layer and for ANN we used (14, 7, 3) hidden units in each layer. Results are shown in Table 3. We can observe that applying CFS improved the AUC of all of the compared prediction models, however, this improvement is negligible. Auto-encoding produced better results than all classifiers, but the accuracy was reduced by 22% compared to the analysis with high level categories. This phenomenon can be explained by the fact that the auto-encoder can better represent high-dimensional data and correlations between features using all available features.

In order to further highlight the impact of high-dimensional data on the results accuracy, we examined how different amounts of sensors affected the inference accuracy, as shown in Figure 5. We performed a series of feature selection and ranking analyses using the info gain measure and ranked the sensors according to their features. For example, the first ranked

Table 3: Prediction of Preferences Applying Feature Selection

Prediction Model	Accuracy	FP	AUC
Auto-Encoding	**0.792**	**0.145**	**0.875**
ANN	0.630	0.347	0.695
C4.5	0.682	0.281	0.774
Random Forest	0.657	0.295	0.77
SVM	0.594	0.374	0.610

Table 4: Prediction of Seven Detailed Preferences

Prediction Model	Accuracy	FP	AUC
Auto-Encoding	**0.884**	**0.035**	**0.918**
ANN	0.475	0.278	0.674
C4.5	0.51	0.289	0.71
Random Forest	0.484	0.347	0.685
SVM	0.5	0.318	0.617

features, latitude and longitude, represented the GPS which was the most significant sensor for the prediction of three high level categories. After ranking all sensors by their ranked features, we performed the classification task and classified the three categories, according to different settings that included different numbers of sensors: for the first setting (three on the x-axis), we chose the top three ranked sensors: GPS (location), weather, and time. The second setting (five on the x-axis) included five sensors: GPS (location), weather, time, call state, and ringer mode. The third setting included eight sensors: five sensors from the previous setting, plus orientation, accelerometer, and gravity. The final setting included nine sensors: the eight sensors from the last setting and the application traffic sensor. The settings included 7, 29, 149, and 176 features respectively.

Figure 5 shows that applying auto-encoding improved the AUC when considering five or more sensors. This phenomenon supports previous results (as presented in Table 2 and 3) that showed that auto-encoding can better represent high-dimensional data and correlations between features. However, compared to the analysis of three high level categories the use of auto-encoding in this setting improved the accuracy by 7%. This can be explained by the fact that reducing noisy and complex sensor data can improve classification results. Hence, performing sensitivity analysis to determine the optimal number of sensors for the classification task can be very effective for improving the classification results. Table 4 presents results for the detailed categorical contexts. We distinguished between seven different contextual categories including: restaurant, vegetarian, fast food, desserts, café, nightlife spot, and busy, based on Foursquare categories. We applied the same supervised learning algorithms, using the time-based splitting method. For auto-encoding, we trained seven neural networks with the same setting used for predicting the three high level contexts.

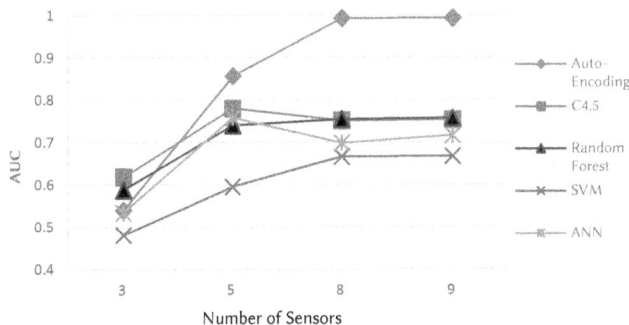

Figure 5: Prediction Results of Three High Level Preferences for Different Numbers of Sensors

As can be observed, the prediction of a detailed categorical preference is a challenging task; state of the art classifiers obtained worse results and accuracy was reduced by at least 30%. This may be because the detailed items' categories are conceptually more similar to each other, compared to three high level categories. In this setting, auto-encoding proved to be the best classifier with a relatively small decrease in the prediction accuracy of 9.8% (compared to results obtained in the prediction of high level categories). Similar results were observed when we applied CFS with the aim of classifying seven items' categories. To summarize, at different granularity levels auto-encoding proved to be the best prediction method, with accuracy that ranged from 0.88 to 0.97.

5.2 Contexts' Similarities

Measuring similarities between the contextual preferences of users can be very effective at improving the quality of recommendations [21]. A common approach for this task is to aggregate ratings from a number of similar context segments. While most studies [17,18] center on the task of calculating similarities between categorical or explicit contexts, we focus on implicit context information. Specifically, we aim to detect similarities between pairs of contextual preferences of users, by comparing their trained networks respectively.

In order to do so, we first measure the average reconstruction error of each contextual user interaction from the test set on each trained auto-encoder. The reconstruction error is calculated by the Euclidian distance between each contextual user interaction in the test set (i.e., a vector of 268 sensor features) with its reconstructed output from the auto-encoder, as explained in Algorithm 2, line 4. As presented in Equation 1, $RE_{c_i \to c_j}$ denotes the average reconstruction error of each user interaction associated with contextual preference c_i (e.g., food), when applying it on the model AE_j (e.g., model of nightlife spots). Then, in order to compute the similarity between the two contextual preferences in a symmetric way, we consider the different number of instances from each contextual preference in the test set, as presented in Equation 2. W_{c_i} denotes the weight of the samples in the training set with contextual preference i.

$$Sim(c_i, c_j) = \frac{RE_{c_i \to c_i}}{RE_{c_i \to c_j}} \tag{1}$$

$$WeightedSim(c_i, c_j) = \frac{W_{c_i} \cdot Sim(c_i, c_j) + W_{c_j} \cdot Sim(c_j, c_i)}{W_{c_i} + W_{c_j}} \tag{2}$$

Table 5 summarizes the similarities between the contextual preferences: food, busy, and nightlife spots. 'Food' and 'busy' have the highest similarity (0.62), which implies that, on average,

Table 5: Context Similarity Matrix

Contextual Preference	Busy	Food	Nightlife
Busy	1	0.62	0.53
Food		1	0.51
Nightlife			1

the auto-encoder model for 'food' reconstructs samples with 38% greater accuracy than the auto-encoder model for 'busy'. As the table indicates, the models have major differences between them. This implies that when applying user interactions associated with specific contextual preferences on another auto-encoder model, the reconstruction error is high (between 38% and 49%). Therefore, we can conclude that each of the models managed to learn the different contextual patterns that are reflected in the network weights. This findings support our results from previous experiments (compared to ANN), which showed that weights on the networks cannot be shared, due to learning unique contextual patterns from each trained network.

We further analyzed the data in an effort to detect similarities between contextual preferences of users that rated only food items. Table 6 shows the similarities between the different food categories. This analysis reveals interesting patterns between the models; for example, when users like 'fast food' POIs they also might like 'vegetarian' POIs, as their similarity is 85%. In addition, we can observe that café had the most unique contextual patterns, since it has the lowest similarity to other food categories.

Table 6: Food Similarity Matrix

Food Category	Café	Desserts	Fast Food	Restaurant	Vegetarian
Café	1	0.47	0.58	0.6	0.58
Desserts		1	0.63	0.69	0.76
Fast Food			1	0.78	0.85
Restaurant				1	0.75
Vegetarian					1

5.3 New User Problem

The evaluations described so far contained records of all of the participants in both the training and test sets. Real-life context inference solutions might require handling new users whose records are not yet included in the training set. We examined the feasibility of predicting three high level contextual preferences for users new to the system (new users for which the system was lacking training data). Additional analysis was performed to simulate this scenario. We split the data according to the user's perspective in a "leave one out" fashion, i.e., the test set contained records of a single user, while the training set contained the rest of users' records. Accuracy results of this analysis are shown in Figure 6.

The accuracy results of the compared prediction models were much lower, while the AUC with auto-encoding obtained higher results.

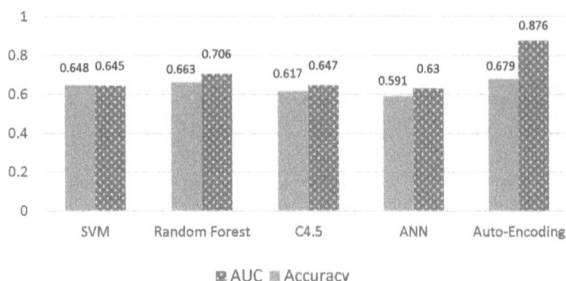

Figure 6: Prediction of Three High Level Preferences for New Users

These results indicate that auto-encoding can improve the inference accuracy, even for new users. However, in order to further improve the inference accuracy, the models still require some sensor records from the user in order to produce satisfactory accuracy results.

6 CONCLUSION

In this paper we presented a novel approach for inferring contextual user preferences by applying auto-encoding on sensor data. Our solution relies on the identification and usage of positive feedback acquired in contextual situations. We demonstrate our contribution utilizing a point of interest (POI) recommender system in which we label contextual interests of users according to their implicit interactions with items' categories. In order to collect rich contextual data, we conducted an extensive field study over a period of four weeks with a group of ninety users. The experimental results show that we were successfully able to predict preferred items' categories at different granularity levels. In all settings, the auto-encoding approach was superior to the traditional state of the art classification methods in terms of accuracy, FP, and AUC. The results indicate that the proposed auto-encoder is the most effective method tested for modeling contextual patterns when dealing with high-dimensional sensor data. We showed that our approach can handle the cold start problem with an improvement of 24% in the AUC, compared to other classification models. We also introduced a similarity measure in order to estimate how the similarity between two different contextual conditions influences users' rating behavior.

During the experiments we observed that it is possible to train an accurate prediction model with a relatively small number of sensors. In addition, training a separate model for each user preference can capture unique patterns that improve classification accuracy.

In future work we plan to investigate the impact of negative interaction feedback on the prediction accuracy. We aim to generalize the proposed approach to numeric ratings and investigate interactions between groups of users and groups of contextual preferences. In addition, we plan to apply factorization machines on the deep models in order to identify new contextual situations.

REFERENCES

[1] Baltrunas, Linas, and Francesco Ricci. "Experimental evaluation of context-dependent collaborative filtering using item splitting." User Modeling and User-Adapted Interaction 24.1-2 (2014): 7-34.

[2] Bishop, Christopher M. "Pattern Recognition." Machine Learning (2006)

[3] Bobadilla, Jesús, et al. "Recommender systems survey." Knowledge-Based Systems 46 (2013): 109-132.

[4] Chawla, N. V., Bowyer, K. W., Hall, L. O., & Kegelmeyer, W. P. (2002). SMOTE: synthetic minority over-sampling technique. Journal of artificial intelligence research, 321-357.

[5] Chen, Enhong, et al. "Discerning individual interests and shared interests for social user profiling." World Wide Web (2016): 1-19.

[6] Chen, Peng-Ting, and Hsin-Pei Hsieh. "Personalized mobile advertising: Its key attributes, trends, and social impact." Technological Forecasting and Social Change 79.3 (2012): 543-557.

[7] Hand, David J., and Robert J. Till. "A simple generalisation of the area under the ROC curve for multiple class classification problems." Machine learning 45.2 (2001): 171-186.

[8] Hoseini-Tabatabaei, Seyed Amir, Alexander Gluhak, and Rahim Tafazolli. "A survey on smartphone-based systems for opportunistic user context recognition." ACM Computing Surveys (CSUR) 45.3 (2013)

[9] Jiang, Wenchao, and Zhaozheng Yin. "Human activity recognition using wearable sensors by deep convolutional neural networks." Proceedings of the 23rd ACM international conference on Multimedia. ACM, 2015.

[10] Kingma, Diederik P., et al. "Semi-supervised learning with deep generative models." Advances in Neural Information Processing Systems. 2014.

[11] König, Immanuel, Bernd Niklas Klein, and Klaus David. "On the stability of context prediction." Proceedings of the 2013 ACM conference on Pervasive and ubiquitous computing adjunct publication. ACM, 2013.

[12] Lane, Nicholas D., et al. "A survey of mobile phone sensing." Communications Magazine, IEEE 48.9 (2010): 140-150.

[13] Lane, Nicholas D., and Petko Georgiev. "Can deep learning revolutionize mobile sensing?." Proceedings of the 16th International Workshop on Mobile Computing Systems and Applications. ACM, 2015.

[14] Lee, Wei-Po. "Deploying personalized mobile services in an agent-based environment." Expert Systems with Applications 32.4 (2007): 1194-1207.

[15] Li, Rui, et al. "Towards social user profiling: unified and discriminative influence model for inferring home locations." Proceedings of the 18th ACM SIGKDD international conference on Knowledge discovery and data mining. ACM, 2012.

[16] Liu, Liwei, et al. "Using context similarity for service recommendation."Semantic Computing (ICSC), 2010 IEEE Fourth International Conference on. IEEE, 2010.

[17] Liu, Liwei, Nikolay Mehandjiev, and Dong-Ling Xu. "Context similarity metric for multidimensional service recommendation." International Journal of Electronic Commerce 18.1 (2013): 73-104.

[18] Liu, Huiqing, Jinyan Li, and Limsoon Wong. "A comparative study on feature selection and classification methods using gene expression profiles and proteomic patterns." Genome informatics 13 (2002): 51-60.

[19] Nadav Aharony, et al. "Social fMRI: Investigating and shaping social mechanisms in the real world." Pervasive and Mobile Computing 7.6 (2011): 643-659.

[20] Ng, Andrew. "Sparse autoencoder."CS294A Lecture notes (2011): 72.

[21] Perera, Charith, et al. "Context aware computing for the internet of things: A survey." IEEE Communications Surveys & Tutorials 16.1 (2014): 414-454.

[22] Prekop, Paul, and Mark Burnett. "Activities, context and ubiquitous computing." Computer Communications 26.11 (2003): 1168-1176.

[23] Qian, Xueming, et al. "Personalized recommendation combining user interest and social circle." IEEE transactions on knowledge and data engineering 26.7 (2014): 1763-1777.

[24] Ronao, Charissa Ann, and Sung-Bae Cho. "Human activity recognition with smartphone sensors using deep learning neural networks." Expert Systems with Applications 59 (2016): 235-244.

[25] Schilit and Theimer D. Billsus, C.A. Brunk, C. Evans, B. Gladish, and M. Pazzani. "Adaptive Interfaces for Ubiquitous Web Access". Comm. ACM, vol. 45, no. 5, pp. 34-38, 2002.

[26] Sun, Fei, et al. "What We Use to Predict a Mobile-Phone Users' Status in Campus?." Computational Science and Engineering (CSE), 2013 IEEE 16th International Conference on. IEEE, 2013.

[27] Unger, Moshe, et al. "Contexto: lessons learned from mobile context inference." Proceedings of the 2014 ACM International Joint Conference on Pervasive and Ubiquitous Computing: Adjunct Publication. ACM, 2014.

[28] Unger, Moshe, et al. "Towards latent context-aware recommendation systems."Knowledge-Based Systems 104 (2016): 165-178.

[29] Zheng, Yong, Bamshad Mobasher, and Robin Burke. "User-Oriented Context Suggestion." Proceedings of the 2016 Conference on User Modeling Adaptation and Personalization. ACM, 2016.

Weighted Random Walk Sampling for Multi-Relational Recommendation

Fatemeh Vahedian, Robin Burke & Bamshad Mobasher
Center for Web Intelligence, DePaul University
243 S Wabash ave
Chicago, Illinois 60604
(fvahedia,rburke,mobasher)@cs.depaul.edu

ABSTRACT

In the information overloaded web, personalized recommender systems are essential tools to help users find most relevant information. The most heavily-used recommendation frameworks assume user interactions that are characterized by a single relation. However, for many tasks, such as recommendation in social networks, user-item interactions must be modeled as a complex network of multiple relations, not only a single relation. Recently research on multi-relational factorization and hybrid recommender models has shown that using extended meta-paths to capture additional information about both users and items in the network can enhance the accuracy of recommendations in such networks. Most of this work is focused on unweighted heterogeneous networks, and to apply these techniques, weighted relations must be simplified into binary ones. However, information associated with weighted edges, such as user ratings, which may be crucial for recommendation, are lost in such binarization. In this paper, we explore a random walk sampling method in which the frequency of edge sampling is a function of edge weight, and apply this generate extended meta-paths in weighted heterogeneous networks. With this sampling technique, we demonstrate improved performance on multiple data sets both in terms of recommendation accuracy and model generation efficiency.

CCS CONCEPTS

•**Information systems** → **Social recommendation; Personalization;** *Collaborative filtering; Social networks;* Social tagging;

KEYWORDS

Weighted meta-path generation, Multi-relational recommender system, Heterogeneous information network

ACM Reference format:
Fatemeh Vahedian, Robin Burke & Bamshad Mobasher. 2017. Weighted Random Walk Sampling for Multi-Relational Recommendation. In *Proceedings of UMAP'17, July 09-12, 2017, Bratislava, Slovakia, , 8 pages.*
DOI: http://dx.doi.org/10.1145/3079628.3079685

1 INTRODUCTION

Recommender systems based on complex heterogeneous networks have been studied extensively in recent years. A heterogeneous information network (HIN) is defined as a network with multiple types of nodes [9] (for example, user, groups, pages and photos) and multiple types of edges (for example, a "friendship" relation between users, "follow" relation between user and pages and a "like" relation between a user and a post). Such networks are a natural way to express the multiplicity of connections between types of information in social media applications: for example, users, employers, interest groups, educational institutions, job postings, posts, and comments are different entities in the LinkedIn social network, connected by a variety of relations. The complexity of heterogeneous networks poses two challenges for recommender systems: (1) the problem of integrating a wide variety of data effectively into a recommendation framework, and (2) the problem of responding to many potential recommendation tasks, because of the wide variety of items present.

The main intuition in work with heterogeneous information networks is that nodes with meaningful semantics can be found by following certain typed paths on a heterogeneous network [17]. In other words, in a heterogeneous information network, two nodes can be connected via different types of paths. Due to the multiplicity of node and edge types in heterogeneous networks, these paths may contain different node types and link types in different orders and they can have various lengths. For example, the relation between LinkedIn users u and v might be friend of a friend, friend of co-worker, or friend of a fellow alumnus to name just a few of the possible two-step paths. In heterogeneous network terminology, these different relations composed of sequences of edge types are known as *meta-paths*. *Meta-path expansion* is the process that begins at a starting node and follows all possible paths that conform to the meta-path to yield a set of destination nodes.

Recent research on multi-relational recommendation in heterogeneous networks has shown that extended meta-paths (those that connect beyond the immediate neighbors of users and target items) are effective in generating relations on which to base recommendations. This benefit has been demonstrated with several different recommendation algorithms including multi-relational matrix factorization [14, 15], weighted hybrid of low-dimensional components [3, 4, 12, 13] and non-negative matrix factorization [17, 18].

However, these models all assume a uniform preference associated with all relations in the network. In many networks, however, there are weighted edges that provide important information: for example, if users provide explicit rating values, these encode useful information about preferences, and it is best not to ignore them.

For example, Figure 1 represents a fraction of movie dataset in which user provides rating value for each movie in range of $1-5$. In this figure user "Bob" rated movie "Whiplash" 2 which indicates that this user did not like the movie. A meta-path expansion following *user – movie – genre – movie* usually takes this edge and adds all "Drama" movies to the list of "Bob" preferences ignoring the rating value. However, the reason that "Bob" rated this movie 2 may be that he does not enjoy the "Drama" genre. Therefore, following a meta-path $Bob \rightarrow Whiplash \rightarrow Drama \rightarrow *$ can be a poor user preference projection for this user. On the other hand, "Alice" rated movie "Xmen" 5, which represents the highest interest in that movie. Therefore, a meta-path following $Alice \rightarrow Xmen \rightarrow "IanMcKellen" \rightarrow *$ can be a stronger representation of user preferences based on an actor of movies.

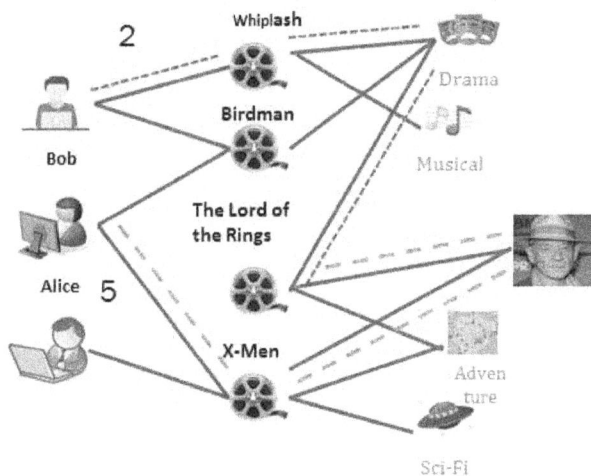

Figure 1: Example of weighted network in movie dataset

What we see from this example is that the recommender system should give greater preference to paths containing highly-weighted edges over paths containing low-weighted edges. The only previous work on weighted heterogeneous networks breaks each meta-path into various similar rated paths [10] then combines all of them together. This method multiplies the problem of meta-path generation (typically the most computationally-expensive step in model generation). This model uses weighted meta-paths only for the calculation of user-user similarities: thus, it works only with meta-paths that start from a user node and end with another user node. The technique cannot be generalized for other type of meta-paths, starting from an arbitrary node type and ending to another node type.

In our prior work [16], we introduced a random walk sampling method for heterogeneous weighted graphs in which meta-paths are generated using exponential sampling that prefers highly-rated edges, and build a recommendation model from the resulting collection of paths. In this paper, we provide a more detailed explanation of the weighted random walk sampling algorithm and provide experimental results for three real world datasets. We show improvements in both accuracy and efficiency of using weighted

meta-path sampling and compare the accuracy of this method with three graph-based recommendation algorithms.

2 RANDOM WALK SAMPLING

Christoffel et al. [5] introduced a random walk sampling algorithms to calculate the transition probability in a random walk model to rank items and generate recommendation model. This model works from an unweighted bipartite graph which represents the binary relations among user and items. Building on this approach, we propose a method for generating meta-paths in a heterogeneous network using biased random walk sampling. This method has the advantage of creating greater efficiency in meta-path generation and allowing for sensitivity to user ratings.

The goal of meta-path generation is to create a relation based on paths through the network. For example, the extended *user – movie – actor – movie – user* meta-path enables the system to start with a given user and find other users that have watched movies containing actors in common with the user's movies. The semantics of this operation of meta-path expansion is that the end result is a set of destination nodes (in this case, users) weighted by how many of the expanded meta-paths reach that node.

A random-walk version of this process chooses edges from the next relation in the meta-path randomly instead of following all possible paths. This is more efficient than generating all paths and the number of samples can be chosen to be large enough to provide a good estimate of what a full expansion would provide [5]. In this work, we look specifically at networks involving a single "rating" edge from user to item. In other words, the first connection from a user is assumed to be to an item and is assumed to have a weight that represents the user rating with higher rated items being more preferred. This construction is common in recommendation contexts where users' quantitative preferences can be gathered. The proposed algorithm is not limited to a single weighted edge and can be extended for any number of weighted edges.

Algorithm 1 Random walk meta-path generation

Require: $l \leftarrow [u]$ // Initialize path with starting node: user
Require: $m \leftarrow$ metapath // Queue of edge types
   function GENERATE(l,m)
      if $m \neq \{\}$ **then**
         $me \leftarrow$ POP(m); // Next edge type
         $n \leftarrow l[1]$ //Current node
         $E \leftarrow$ GETEDGES(n, me) // Get edges of type me
         if $me =$ user-item **then**
             $\langle n, j, v \rangle \leftarrow$ WSAMPLE(E) //weighted
         else
             $\langle n, j, v \rangle \leftarrow$ USAMPLE(E) //uniform
         PUSH(j, l); //Add node j to path
         MPGENERATE(l,m)
      else
         return l

Random walk meta-path expansion uses the process shown in Algorithm 1. The function *Generate* takes as input a single user as the start node and a meta-path and returns a single random walk starting from the user node and guided by the meta-path.

The *USample* function implements uniform sampling of the edge set: an edge is chosen at random from the edges available at the current node. The *WSample* function also selects a random edge from the edge set. However, the probability of choosing an edge is proportional to e^w, where w is the edge weight.

Exponential sampling: the *WSample* is defined to guide the random walker to prefer the highly weighted edges through the random walk process. We use the well established exponential sampling and select the edge with the probability proportional to e^w. The exponential sampling guaranties our goal which is to select the highly weighted edge through meta-path generation. In this way, the random walker more likely moves to the edge that user rated higher which can capture user preferences more significantly.

For example, in a movie dataset, consider the goal of generating expansions of the meta-path $user - movie - actor - movie$, for user u. The algorithm would proceed as follows:

(1) The random walker starts from u. Is the next edge weighted? Yes, $user - movie$ is a weighted edge, and there are three such edges e_1 (weight 5), e_2, (weight 1), and e_3 (weight 3).

(2) Function *WSample* returns a weighted edge $user - movie$ in the way that the probability of selecting that edge is proportional to e^w, where w is the edge weight. In our example, e_1 would be chosen with probability 87%, e_3 with probability 12%, and e_2 with probability 1%.

(3) Random walker moves from u to a movie m based on selected edge in step 2.

(4) Random walker is at the movie m. The next edge type in the meta-path is $movie - genre$. The algorithm checks if the next edge is weighted or not.

(5) The next edge $movie - genre$ is not weighted. Therefore, function *USample* returns a random edge from movie m and genres that m belongs to.

(6) Random walker moves to genre g based on selected edge in step 4.

(7) Considering target meta-path, next edge is $movie - genre$. The $movie - genre$ an unweighted edge, therefore function *USample* is again used, returning a random edge that leads to a movie m'.

(8) Random walker moves to movie m'.

Although all the meta-paths generated in this paper started from a user node and an initial weighted edge, this algorithm is sufficiently flexible to handle meta-paths where the weighted edge appears at any point in the path. For example, if an unweighted social relation of the user was available in the movie dataset, such as $user - friend$, a meta-path $user - friend - movie - actor - movie$ can be generated following this algorithm. The application of the algorithm to paths with multiple weighted edges is something we hope to explore in future work.

3 MODEL GENERATION

We are interested in recommendation models that make use of multiple relations simultaneously. For the work reported here, we build our recommendation models using multi-relational matrix factorization (DMF) [6, 15], and incorporate relations built from the extended meta-paths described above. In multi-relational matrix factorization, one *target* relation is predicted and the remaining

auxiliary relations are used as side information. For example, if the task is to recommend movies to users, the user-movie relation is the target relation and the other links between nodes such as movie-genre and movie-actor are auxiliary. We have shown that in our previous works that incorporating extended relations based on meta-paths improves the accuracy of recommender systems based on multi-relational matrix factorization [14, 15].

For the experiments described below, we compare factorized models built using our prior unweighted breadth-first meta-path expansion with those built using the sampling-based algorithm described above. In each case, we use two- and three-step meta-paths originating from the user node. We have developed in our prior work a meta-path pruning technique based on normalized information gain [13, 15]. Pruning removes the meta-paths that contribute little to recommendation accuracy, improving both performance and training time.

4 EXPERIMENTS AND EVALUATION

For each dataset, the target relation was randomly partitioned into 80% training and 20% test data. Relations were generated from the training data starting with the direct relations used in the basic DMF model and adding two-step and three-step meta-paths starting from the first entity of the target relation.

We built multi-relational factorization models for each collection of relations using the implementations of DMF made available by the authors of [6]. [1] This implementation is self-contained and requires no external parameter setting other choosing an optimization criterion. We chose Bayesian Personalized Ranking as the optimization criterion (BPR-opt), as described in [6]. For all recommendation models, we evaluated recall and precision on recommendation lists of length one through ten.

4.1 Datasets

In our experiments, we used three real world datasets in different areas. Below is a detailed explanation of these datasets.

Yelp. This dataset[2] contains user ratings of different businesses. The node types in this network are user, business, location, category, and check-in. We performed P-core filtering as described in [7] to remove users and businesses with fewer than 5 ratings. The network schema of this network can be found in Figure 2 (b) showing the node types and relations among them. The generated meta-paths for this network are: $user - biz - category$, $user - biz - checkIn$, $user - biz - location$, $user - biz - category - biz$, $user - biz - chekIn - biz$ and $user - biz - location - biz$.

Table 1 shows detailed statistics of the number of nodes and relations in this dataset as well as number of relations in each generated meta-path (Mp).

Book Crossing. Book Crossing [3] contains user rating of books. Using ISBN as a key, we gathered additional book information from the GoodReads book site[4] including genre, tags (called "book shelves" in GoodReads) and authors. As in the Yelp case, a 5-core of the network was extracted so that each user and each book had

---

[1] http://ismll.de/catsmf/mrFac.tar.gz
[2] https://www.yelp.com/dataset-challenge
[3] http://www2.informatik.uni-freiburg.de/ cziegler/BX/
[4] https://www.goodreads.com/

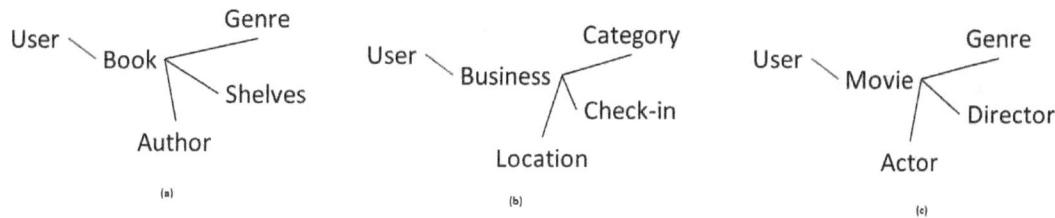

Figure 2: Network Schema: (a) Book Crossing, (b) Yelp, (c) MovieLens

Table 1: Yelp dataset- Number of node types and relations

Node	#	Edge	#	Mp	#
user	11,937	ub	216,000	ubc	234,498
business	6,884	bc	20,409	ubh	1,113,600
category	443	bh	74,426	ubl	84,534
checkIn	165	bl	6,750	ubcb	37,993,942
location	160			ubhb	28,470,410
				ublb	10,796,490

Table 3: MovieLens dataset: Number of node types and relations

Node	#	Edge	#	Mp	#
user	2,113	um	855,597	umg	36,538
movie	10,197	mg	20,809	umd	450,973
genre	20	md	10,155	uma	7,434,030
director	4,060	ma	231,742	umgm	11,845,899
actor	95,319			umdm	2,747,252
				umam	7,245,378

a least 5 ratings. As Figure 2 (a) shows, there are 5 nodes in this network: user, books, genres, shelves and authors. In this network, the $user - book$ edge is weighted in the range of 1-10. Meta-paths $user - book - genre$, $user - book - shelve$, $user - book - author$, $user - book - genre - book$, $user - book - shelve - book$, $user - book - author - book$ were generated based on random walk sampling. See Table 2 for details regarding number of entities, relations and generated meta-paths.

Table 2: Book Crossing dataset: Number of node type and relations

Node	#	Edge	#	Mp	#
user	7,026	ub	118,701	ubg	245,135
book	9,432	bg	64,584	ubs	4,499,328
genre	1,689	bs	1,803,222	uba	82,627
shelve	65,379	ba	11,599	ubgb	31,011,825
author	4,073			ubsb	37,738,430
				ubab	1,090,022

MovieLens. This dataset is an extension of well-known Movie-Lens 1M dataset[5]. We linked the movies of MovieLens dataset with their corresponding web pages at Internet Movie Database (IMDb) and Rotten Tomatoes movie review systems. In this dataset, the weighted edge represents the user rating values for each movie. The nodes in this this network are shown in Figure 2 (c). The generated meta-paths is this network were: $user - movie - genre$, $user - movie - actor$, $user - movie - director$, $user - movie - genre - movie$, $user - movie - actor - movie$ and $user - movie - director - movie$. Details about the nodes and relations appear in Table 2.

4.2 Comparison Algorithms

In order to compare the accuracy of our recommender model to graph based recommendation algorithms, we use random walk based algorithms which are also considered state of the art model in graph-based recommendation settings.

- P_α^3 [5] The nodes in a bipartite graph are ranked based on transition probabilities after short random walks between users and items. P^3 perform random walks of fixed length 3 starting from a target user vertex. This model raises the transition probabilities to the power of a fitted parameter α, which has been shown to improve accuracy.
- RP_β^3 The popularity-based re-ranking model which is proposed [5] to compensate for the influence of popular items in the recommendation list.
- HL A node ranking algorithm to increases both recommendation accuracy and diversity [5]. This model is a weighted linear aggregation of scores from two algorithms which are HeatS [20] a heat diffusion across the bipartite user-item graph and ProbS [20], which is an item ranking method similar to P_α^3.

For the three models: P_α^3, RP_β^3 and HL we used the provided code by authors [6] to run the random walk based model experiments. We also used the parameter tuning suggested in [5] to find the best value of α, β and λ for each dataset.

In addition to these graph-oriented recommendation algorithms, we used the original DMF model restricted to only the direct network relations, to demonstrate the benefit of adding extended paths. Finally, we also used another multi-relational factorization model, CATSMF, using direct links of the network [6]. The CATSMF

---

[5]http://grouplens.org/datasets/movielens/1m/

[6]Java port: github.com/jcnewell/MyMediaLiteJava

model [6] was introduced to improve the efficiency of the DMF model by limiting the parameters needed for the auxiliary relations by coupling them together.

5 RESULTS AND DISCUSSION

For each dataset, we used five-fold cross validation, computing recall and precision for each user in each fold using recommendation lists of length 1 through 10. We also calculated the normalized information gain for each meta-path generated. In the figures below, the labels DMF and CATSMF are used for the original (direct relation) factorization model, DMF-2 is the label for the extended meta-path model with two-step paths, and DMF-3 is used for the extended meta-path model with both two- and three-step paths. DMF-IG is a variant of DMF-3 where the paths with low information gain have been pruned.

5.1 MovieLens

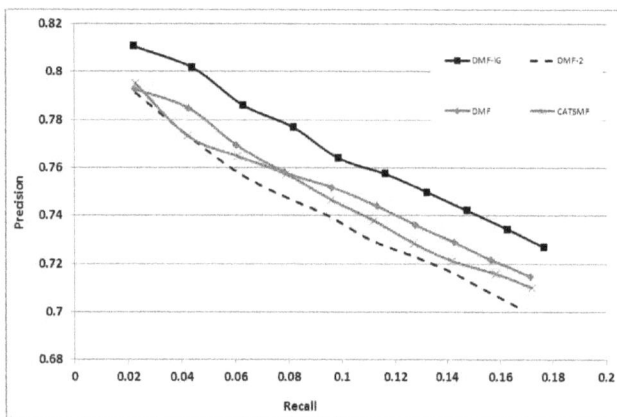

Figure 3: MovieLens dataset: Recall vs. precision for DMF models

Figure 3 compares the different DMF variants, showing recall and precision curves for movie recommendation lists of length one through ten. Interestingly, DMF-2 has lower accuracy than the model using only the direct relations. Figure 4 suggests a possible reason for this: the very low information gain for the genre relation, which is not surprising since there are a relatively small number of very common genre categories for movies, and knowing that a user likes one comedy, for example, is not very predictive about other comedies. On the other hand, DMF-IG, in which the less informative *user − movie − genre* and *user − movie − genre − movie* relations are removed, offers superior accuracy across the different list sizes.

We separated out the random-walk recommenders into Figure 5 because of scale differences. As the figure shows, these algorithms have considerably worse recall/precision performance than their multi-relational counterparts.

5.2 Book Crossing

The precision and recall curve for Book recommendation in Book Crossing dataset is shown in Figure 7 for all seven algorithms. The

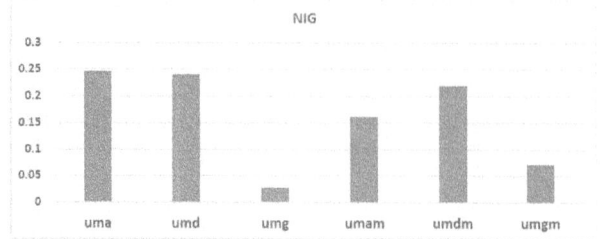

Figure 4: Normalized Information gain value for MovieLens dataset

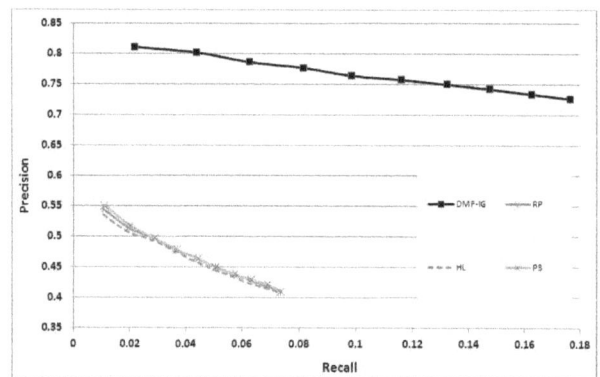

Figure 5: MovieLens dataset: Recall vs. precision: DMF-IG vs. random-walk based recommenders

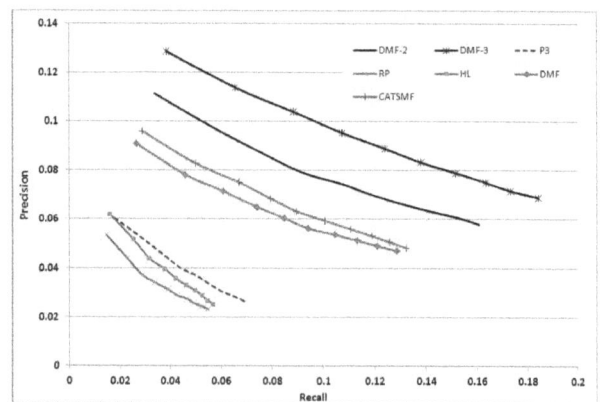

Figure 6: Recall vs. precision for Book Crossing dataset

black lines show our proposed methods, red curves represent the baseline multi-rleational matrix factorization and blue line show graph based recommendation algorithms. In the Book Crossing dataset, adding random walk based meta-paths significantly enhances the accuracy of recommendation model and the DMF-2 and DMF-3 outperform all the baseline methods. No pruned model was generated for this dataset because all of the meta-paths had good information values.

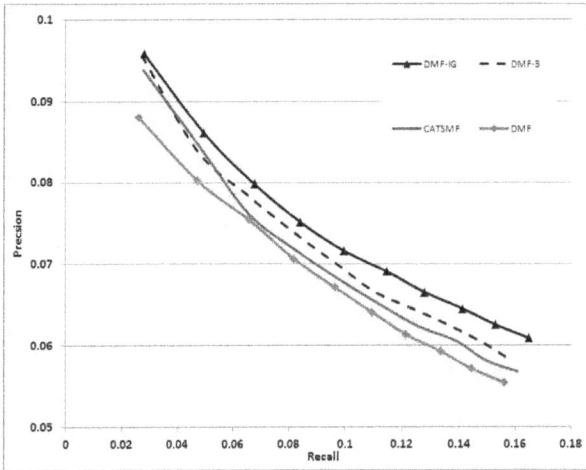

Figure 7: Recall vs. precision for Yelp dataset

5.3 Yelp

Figure 7 depicts precision and recall results for business recommendation in Yelp network. The normalized information gain value of generated meta-paths in Yelp dataset is shown in Figure 9. As Figure 9 shows the meta-path $user - biz - checkIn$ and $user - biz - chekIn - biz$ are the less informative paths in this network therefore, those paths were removed from the model to create DMF-IG. In Yelp datset, adding all two steps and three steps meta-paths as side information to DMF model (DMF-3) enhances the accuracy of recommendation slightly while DMF-IG shows significant improvement over both DMF and CATSMF.

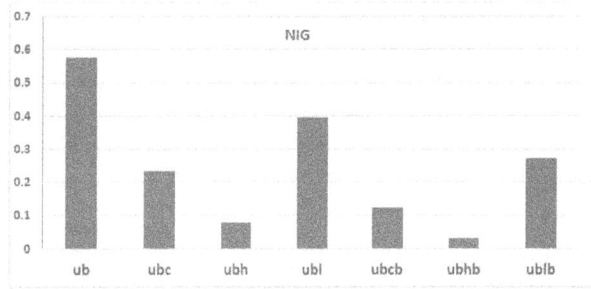

Figure 8: Recall vs. precision for Yelp dataset

As with the MovieLens experiment, due to scale, we have a separate figure for the random-walk based recommenders. These algorithms show very low accuracy compared to the multi-relational alternatives.

In order to evaluate the ability of our model to predict highly-rated items, we performed another experiment using the Yelp

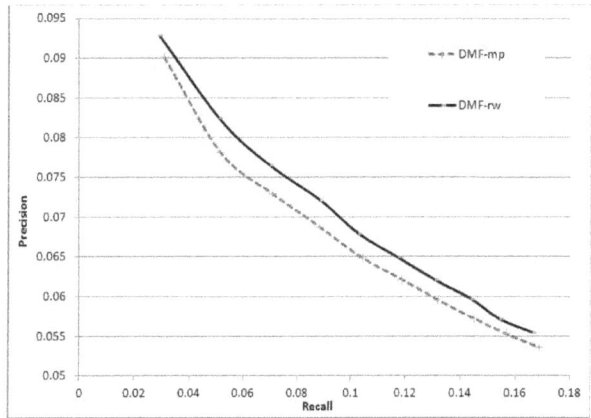

Figure 9: Normalized Information gain value for yelp dataset

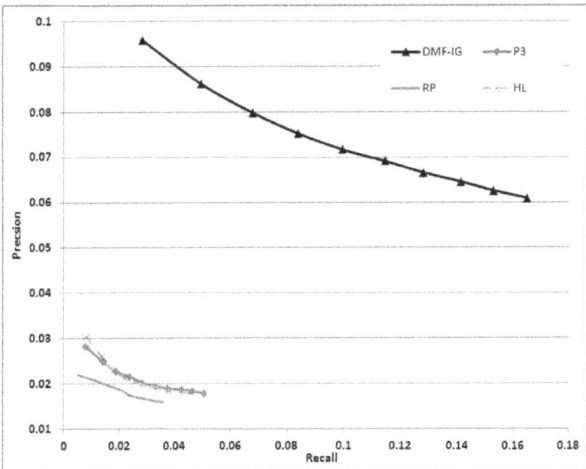

Figure 10: Recall vs. precision for Yelp dataset

dataset including just those results for items that are highly-rated by the user. The resulting metrics are referred to as US-recall and US-precision in [2]. We used a threshold of 3 and only counted recall and precision "hits" for items with ratings above this amount. Figure 10 compares recommendations generated using an unweighted relation generation technique (DMF-mp) with the algorithm described in this paper for weighted sampling (DMF-rw).

5.4 Efficiency

As might be expected, random walk sampling for meta-path generation is much faster than generating the full meta-path relations. We quantify these differences in this section. All the meta-path generation experiments were executed on a Windows 7 workstation equipped with an Intel Core i7 3.40GHz processor and 16GB RAM. The meta-path generation code was implemented in Java.

Figure 11 shows the time required to generate the 6 different types of meta-paths for the Book Crossing dataset using the random walk based method and the complete breadth-first method. Mp-Rw represents the execution for random walk model and MP-Pc denotes the full expansion of each meta-path. In Book Crossing dataset generating 4 of meta-paths through genre and shelve nodes by random walk sampling is much faster than original way and takes less than 5% of the time required by the baseline technique (MP-Pc).

The difference is not notable for the meta-paths through author node, which requires about the same amount of time for both methods. The reason for this difference is that many of the books in the dataset only have a single author. The branching factor for the *book — author* meta-path step is therefore low and the random walk and bread-first methods generate comparable numbers of paths.

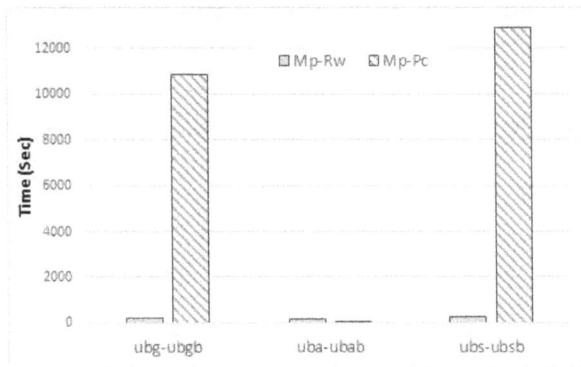

Figure 11: Book Crossing: Meta-path generation execution time

A similar efficiency gain is found in the MovieLens dataset. On our test machine, the random walk method takes less than 5% of the time required by the baseline technique to generate *user — movie — actor* and *user — movie — actor — movie* meta-paths. The execution time is shown in Figure 12. In this dataset, generating the meta-paths going through director of movies require similar time for both approaches. Similar to authors in Book Crossing, in MovieLens, the *movie — director* edge is for the most part an one-to-one edge while the *movie — actor* edge might show 50 actors associated with one movie. Since meta-path generation is a major portion of the overall learning time for this system, the random sampling technique would be strongly preferred even if its accuracy were not better.

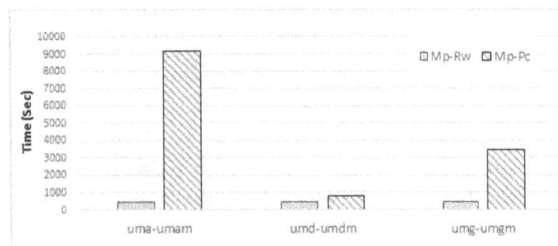

Figure 12: MovieLens dataset: Meta-path generation execution time

6 RELATED WORK

Multi-relational recommender systems for heterogeneous networks have been studied extensively in recent years, Yu et .al proposed a method [17, 19] to combine user feedback with different types of entity relationships in a collaborative filtering way. This study take advantage of diffused observed user implicit feedback along

different meta-paths to generate possible recommendation model. The prediction model is obtained by applying matrix factorization techniques on the diffused user preferences to calculate latent representations for users and items accordingly. These latent features are combined in a weighted way to define a global recommendation model. Furthermore, this model generates a different entity recommendation models for different user clusters to distinguish user interests using *Bayesian Ranking* optimization. These models use the non-negative matrix factorization approach to construct recommendation [17, 19]. The latent features for factorization models requires a user-item projection of user preferences. As a result, these models only use the meta-paths which start from user type node and end at an item type node, such as *user — movie — * — movie*. The advantage of our model over this work is that we can extend both item and user profiles following meta-paths and we propose a metric to measure the effectiveness of those meta-paths.

Shi et.al [10] proposed *SemRec* model, which uses weighted meta path to consider attribute values on links in information networks. SemRec uses a path based similarity to find the similar users of a active user under a given meta-path. The rating score of the target user u on an item i is obtained according to the rating scores of the similar users on the item rating intensity. Based on rating prediction model, several prediction score can be made for a pair u, i. This model also constructs the final hybrid recommendation model as a weighted score to integrate generated meta-paths.

In addition to network-oriented techniques, a separate thread of research has developed in multi-relational matrix factorization to make predictions for highly correlated data. Singh and Gordon [11] proposed collective matrix factorization, as a model of pairwise relation data. This model factors each relation matrix with a generalized linear link function in which the factors of different models are tied together if an entity type is involved in more than one relation.

Coupled matrix factorization and tensor factorization can extend the multi-relational model to deal with higher arity relations as shown in [1]. Recent work attempts to integrate the network-based and factorization-based strains of research, using multi-relational factorization but with relations composed from network paths.

A context-dependent matrix factorization model, *HETEROMF*, proposed in [8] that considers a general latent factor for every entity type in addition to context-dependent latent factors for every context in which the entities participate. This model learns a general latent factor for every entity and transfer matrices for every context, to convert the general latent factors into a context-dependent latent factor.

7 CONCLUSION

In the complex social networks, it is essential to make use of all the information that is available about users and items to enhance the accuracy of personalized recommender systems. Expanding extended meta-paths to generate user and item profiles is an effective way to capture additional information in a heterogeneous network. Where meta-path includes edges that represent user ratings, it makes sense to incorporate these rating values to more precisely represent user preferences.

In this paper we explored a weighted sampling method to generate meta-paths in weighted heterogeneous networks as the basis for multi-relational recommendation models. We showed the results for three real world datasets and found that weighted sampling can be an effective basis for recommendation generation, especially when combined with information-gain-based relation pruning. Local graph methods, including other random-walk-based algorithms, were not as effective as those incorporating extended relations. We found that random sampling of edges improved recommendation accuracy while greatly reducing the computational requirements of model generation.

In our future work, we will be exploring other multi-relational algorithms and hybrid models using weighted sampling and extend the application of weighted sampling to other types of weighted edges including the problem of combining weights when meta-path generation involves multiple weighted edges.

ACKNOWLEDGMENTS

This work was supported in part by the National Science Foundation under Grant No. IIS-1423368 (Multi-dimensional Recommendation in Complex Heterogeneous Networks).

REFERENCES

[1] Evrim Acar, Tamara G. Kolda, and Daniel M. Dunlavy. 2011. All-at-once Optimization for Coupled Matrix and Tensor Factorizations. *CoRR* abs/1105.3422 (2011). http://arxiv.org/abs/1105.3422

[2] Nicola Barbieri, Giuseppe Manco, Riccardo Ortale, and Ettore Ritacco. 2012. Balancing prediction and recommendation accuracy: hierarchical latent factors for preference data. In *Proceedings of the 2012 SIAM International Conference on Data Mining*. SIAM, SIAM, 1035–1046.

[3] Robin Burke and Fatemeh Vahedian. 2013. Social Web Recommendation using Metapaths. In *RSWeb@RecSys*.

[4] Robin D. Burke, Fatemeh Vahedian, and Bamshad Mobasher. 2014. Hybrid Recommendation in Heterogeneous Networks. In *UMAP 2014*. 49–60. DOI: http://dx.doi.org/10.1007/978-3-319-08786-3_5

[5] Fabian Christoffel, Bibek Paudel, Chris Newell, and Abraham Bernstein. 2015. Blockbusters and Wallflowers: Accurate, Diverse, and Scalable Recommendations with Random Walks. In *Proceedings of the 9th ACM Conference on Recommender Systems (RecSys '15)*. ACM, New York, NY, USA, 163–170. DOI: http://dx.doi.org/10.1145/2792838.2800180

[6] Lucas Rego Drumond, Ernesto Diaz-Aviles, Lars Schmidt-Thieme, and Wolfgang Nejdl. 2014. Optimizing Multi-Relational Factorization Models for Multiple Target Relations. In *CIKM 2014*. ACM, New York, NY, USA, 191–200. DOI: http://dx.doi.org/10.1145/2661829.2662052

[7] Jonathan Gemmell, Thomas Schimoler, Bamshad Mobasher, and Robin Burke. 2012. Resource Recommendation in Social Annotation Systems: A Linear-weighted Hybrid Approach. *J. Comput. Syst. Sci.* 78, 4 (July 2012), 1160–1174. DOI: http://dx.doi.org/10.1016/j.jcss.2011.10.006

[8] Mohsen Jamali and Laks Lakshmanan. 2013. HeteroMF: recommendation in heterogeneous information networks using context dependent factor models. In *Proceedings of the 22nd international conference on World Wide Web*. ACM, 643–654.

[9] Chuan Shi, Yitong Li, Jiawei Zhang, Yizhou Sun, and Philip S Yu. 2015. A survey of heterogeneous information network analysis. *arXiv preprint arXiv:1511.04854* (2015).

[10] Chuan Shi, Zhiqiang Zhang, Ping Luo, Philip S. Yu, Yading Yue, and Bin Wu. 2015. Semantic Path Based Personalized Recommendation on Weighted Heterogeneous Information Networks. In *Proceedings of the 24th ACM International on Conference on Information and Knowledge Management (CIKM '15)*. ACM, New York, NY, USA, 453–462. DOI: http://dx.doi.org/10.1145/2806416.2806528

[11] Ajit P. Singh and Geoffrey J. Gordon. 2008. Relational Learning via Collective Matrix Factorization. In *Proceedings of the 14th ACM SIGKDD International Conference on Knowledge Discovery and Data Mining (KDD '08)*. ACM, New York, NY, USA, 650–658. DOI: http://dx.doi.org/10.1145/1401890.1401969

[12] Fatemeh Vahedian. 2014. Weighted hybrid recommendation for heterogeneous networks. In *RecSys '14*. 429–432. DOI: http://dx.doi.org/10.1145/2645710.2653366

[13] Fatemeh Vahedian and Robin D. Burke. 2014. Predicting Component Utilities for Linear-Weighted Hybrid Recommendation. In *RSWeb 2014*. http://ceur-ws.org/Vol-1271/Paper7.pdf

[14] Fatemeh Vahedian, Robin D. Burke, and Bamshad Mobasher. 2015. Network-Based Extension of Multi-Relational Factorization Models. In *Poster Proceedings of the 9th ACM Conference on Recommender Systems, RecSys 2015, Vienna, Austria, September 16, 2015*. http://ceur-ws.org/Vol-1441/recsys2015_poster14.pdf

[15] Fatemeh Vahedian, Robin D. Burke, and Bamshad Mobasher. 2016. Meta-Path Selection for Extended Multi-Relational Matrix Factorization. In *Proceedings of the Twenty-Ninth International Florida Artificial Intelligence Research Society Conference, FLAIRS 2016, Key Largo, Florida, May 16-18, 2016*. 566–571. http://www.aaai.org/ocs/index.php/FLAIRS/FLAIRS16/paper/view/12859

[16] Fatemeh Vahedian, Robin D. Burke, and Bamshad Mobasher. 2016. Weighted Random Walks for Meta-Path Expansion in Heterogeneous Networks. In *Poster Proceedings of the 9th ACM Conference on Recommender Systems, RecSys 2015*. ACM. http://ceur-ws.org/Vol-1688/paper-11.pdf

[17] Xiao Yu, Xiang Ren, Yizhou Sun, Quanquan Gu, Bradley Sturt, Urvashi Khandelwal, Brandon Norick, and Jiawei Han. 2014. Personalized Entity Recommendation: A Heterogeneous Information Network Approach. In *Proceedings of the 7th ACM Conference on Web Search and Data Mining*. ACM, 283–292.

[18] Xiao Yu, Xiang Ren, Yizhou Sun, Bradley Sturt, Urvashi Khandelwal, Quanquan Gu, Brandon Norick, and Jiawei Han. 2013. Recommendation in Heterogeneous Information Networks with Implicit User Feedback. In *Proceedings of the 7th ACM Conference on Recommender Systems (RecSys '13)*. ACM, New York, NY, USA, 347–350. DOI: http://dx.doi.org/10.1145/2507157.2507230

[19] Xiao Yu, Xiang Ren, Yizhou Sun, Bradley Sturt, Urvashi Khandelwal, Quanquan Gu, Brandon Norick, and Jiawei Han. 2013. Recommendation in Heterogeneous Information Networks with Implicit User Feedback. In *Proceedings of the 7th ACM Conference on Recommender Systems (RecSys '13)*. ACM, New York, NY, USA, 347–350. DOI: http://dx.doi.org/10.1145/2507157.2507230

[20] T. Zhou, Z. Kuscsik, J.G. Liu, M. Medo, J.R. Wakeling, and Y.C. Zhang. 2010. Solving the apparent diversity-accuracy dilemma of recommender systems. *Proceedings of the National Academy of Sciences* 107, 10 (2010), 4511–4515.

Inferring Students' Sense of Community from Their Communication Behavior in Online Courses

Wen Wu
Department of Computer Science
Hong Kong Baptist University
Hong Kong, China
cswenwu@comp.hkbu.edu.hk

Li Chen
Department of Computer Science
Hong Kong Baptist University
Hong Kong, China
lichen@comp.hkbu.edu.hk

Qingchang Yang
Adaptive Learning Center
Hong Kong Baptist University
Hong Kong, China
yqc@teamcrushsport.com

ABSTRACT

Sense of community is regarded as the reflection of students' feelings of connectedness with community members and commonality of learning expectations and goals. In online courses, sense of community has been proven to influence students' learning engagement and academic performance. Low sense of community is also one of the reasons for drop out. However, existing studies mainly acquire students' sense of community via questionnaires, which demand user efforts and have difficulty in obtaining real-time feeling during students' learning process. In addition, although communication is helpful to enhance students' sense of community, little work has empirically compared the impact of different online communication tools. In this paper, we are motivated to derive students' sense of community from their communication behavior in online courses. Concretely, we first identify a set of features that are significantly correlated with students' sense of community, which not only include their activities carried out in both synchronous and asynchronous online learning environment, but also their linguistic content in conversational texts. We then develop inference model to unify these features for determining students' sense of community, and find that LASSO performs the best in terms of inference accuracy.

CCS CONCEPTS

•Human-centered computing → User studies; •Applied computing → Collaborative learning;

KEYWORDS

Online learning; sense of community; prediction; synchronous/ asynchronous communication

1 INTRODUCTION

In recent years, online learning, which is defined as the process of using Internet to acquire knowledge, access learning materials, and interact with others [1], has become popular.

UMAP '17, July 9-12, 2017, Bratislava, Slovakia
© 2017 ACM. 978-1-4503-4635-1/17/07...$15.00
DOI: http://dx.doi.org/10.1145/3079628.3079678

According to the data collected by Class Central, by 2016, around 58 million students worldwide have taken at least one course, and the total number of courses has grown to 6,850.

In learning environment, sense of community is one of the popularly used metrics to measure students' feeling that they connect to community members in a course-based context and the feeling that the community helps them to acquire knowledge and meet learning goals [18]. In physical classroom, sense of community is shown to be related to students' learning perception and actual performance [9, 30]. In online courses, it also plays an important role. Specifically, students with high sense of community tend to be active in online learning, feel satisfied with academic programs, become interested in the studied course, and be motivated to accumulate course knowledge [11, 19, 34, 35], whereas those with low sense of community easily feel anxious or isolated [30], which is one of the reasons for drop out [20]. Therefore, knowing students' sense of community has the potential to provide them with more personalized learning supports so as to improve their learning effectiveness and potentially alleviate the high dropout issue.

However, the issue of how to obtain students' sense of community in online courses has not been well solved. The existing studies mainly rely on questionnaires to explicitly acquire students' sense of community (such as 20-item Rovai's Classroom Community Scale [18]), which not only demand high user efforts, but also have difficulty in obtaining students' real-time sense of community during their learning process. Another limitation is that although communication has been proven to be effective in improving students' social interaction and their feeling of connectedness in online courses [5, 8, 25], little work has empirically compared students' usage of different communication tools (such as chat room, discussion forum, note-taking facility) and explored what communication tools may be more helpful to enhance students' sense of community. Therefore, we have aimed to answer the following two research questions:

RQ1: *How do various communication tools affect students' sense of community in online courses?*

RQ2: *To what extent can sense of community be inferred from students' online communication behavior?*

In order to address the two questions, we conduct our experiment with 489 college students in an online learning system called "eBanshu" (www.ebanshu.com), which provides both synchronous and asynchronous online communication tools. Concretely, the synchronous communication tools include *chat room* for students to exchange messages in real time, *hand-up facility* for students to ask questions to instructors in the online class, *note-taking* and *note-sharing facility* that allow students to take notes and share their written notes with others. The asynchronous tools include *discussion forum* where students can ask and/or answer other students' questions, *material-sharing facility* for students to share their learning materials with others, and *assignment submission facility* for students to submit assignments to instructors.

We have first performed a correlation analysis to study the relationship between students' behavior in using communication tools and their sense of community. Particularly, the behavioral features not only include students' in-class and after-class activities (such as the numbers of messages posted in chat room and discussion forum respectively), but also qualitative linguistic characteristics embedded in textual contents. Based on the results, a total of 15 features are found significantly correlated with students' sense of community. Among them, there are 6 activity features (e.g., number of using hand-up facility), 5 content features (e.g., number of social process words in each chat message), 2 personal properties (i.e., pre-course interest and pre-course knowledge) and 2 environmental features (i.e., numbers of instructors' and classmates' activities in each lesson). We have then built inference model based on these features to predict students' sense of community. We have concretely tested six popular regression models and found LASSO shows the best accuracy.

In the following, we first introduce related work (Section 2). We then give the details of our experimental setup (Section 3) and results analysis (Section 4). We finally discuss the implications and draw a conclusion (Section 5 and 6).

2 RELATED WORK

2.1 Sense of Community

The most widely accepted definition of sense of community was proposed by McMillan and Chavis [10] in 1986 based on [21, 28]. Their definition is "a feeling that members have of belonging, a feeling that members matter to one another and to the group, and a shared faith that members' needs will be met through their commitment to be together".

In the education domain, Rovai [18] defined classroom community (i.e., a community of learners) as "a feeling that members have of belonging, a feeling that members matter to one another and to the group, that they have duties and obligations to peers and to the school, and that they possess shared expectations that members' educational needs will be met through their commitment to shared goals". It consists of two components: *Connectedness* - feeling of connectedness with community members; *Learning* - commonality of learning expectations and goals. Specifically, *Connectedness* is the feeling of belonging and acceptance of bonding relationships. *Learning* is the feeling that knowledge and meaning are actively constructed within the community, that the community enhances the acquisition of knowledge and understanding, and that members' learning needs are satisfied.

2.2 Sense of Community and Learning

The sense of community within the physical classroom was shown important, because it is significantly correlated with students' classroom attitudes, perception of learning, and actual academic performance [9]. If students fail to feel the sense of community, they are likely to be anxious, defensive and not willing to take the risks involved in learning [30].

Recently, the importance of sense of community on online learning has been explored. It was shown in [19, 27, 34, 35] that online learners who have stronger sense of community tend to perceive greater cognitive learning, have higher satisfaction with their academic programs, accumulate more knowledge and achieve better academic performance. It was also found that sense of community could affect the retention rate, which may alleviate the dropout issue [11, 32, 35, 37].

In terms of how to build sense of community in the online environment, computer-mediated communication tools have been shown useful [5, 8, 25]. For instance, Sveningsson [25] observed that students' sense of community is closely related to their usage of web chat, whereas Dawson [5] found that the online forum discussion could facilitate the development of a strong community. However, the limitation is that little work has empirically compared different communication tools in terms of their effect on enhancing students' sense of community in online courses.

2.3 Measurement of Sense of Community

Rovai's Classroom Community Scale [18] is used to measure students' sense of community in virtual classrooms. It consists of 20 statements (each statement is rated on a 5-point Likert scale from 1 "strongly disagree" to 5 "strongly agree"), among which 10 statements are related to *Connectedness* (e.g., *"I feel connected to others in this course"*), and 10 are related to *Learning* (e.g., *"I think that this course results in only modest learning"*).

However, using questionnaires to acquire students' sense of community unavoidably demands user efforts. In order to solve the problem, Shea [23] used students' demographic information and teaching presence (i.e., process of design, facilitation, and direction of cognitive and social processes) to predict their sense of community. But the limitation of his method is that the sense of community cannot be obtained in real time during their learning process. In addition, little work has in depth studied the role of students' online communication behavior in predicting their sense of community.

We are thus interested in not only exploring what communication tools can be more helpful to enhance students' sense of community, but also investigating how to infer students' real-time sense of community from their communication behavior in online courses.

3 EXPERIMENTAL SETUP

3.1 Materials and Participants

In order to answer our research questions (see Section 1), we conducted an experiment on eBanshu online learning system, which was released in 2013 and has been used by more than

20 universities in China with over 33,000 students who have enrolled on 100 courses so far. In this website, instructors can use video cameras and digitizers (for writing notes) to give real-time lectures. In the online class, students can communicate with instructors and peers through a text chat room, ask or answer questions by using the hand-up facility, and take notes and share them (see Figure 1). After class, they can leave messages in a course-based discussion forum, share learning materials, and submit assignments. These communication tools are provided for students to freely use, not counted in their final assessment.

From March to June 2015, a total of 1,559 students, from Hebei Normal University in China enrolled in 16 elective courses in 3 different subject types: liberal arts (including 9 courses, e.g., "Comparative Literature"), science (6 courses, e.g., "Discrete Mathematics"), and engineering (1 course, "Microcomputer Principles and Interface Description"). Each student enrolled in one course, and the average number of enrollments per course is 97.3 (min=50, max=209, st.d.=42.2). Each course lasted for 12 weeks, with 2 lessons given every week (each lesson took 1 hour). At the end, students received credit if they passed the assignments and examinations. We sent survey invitation to all of the 1,559 students before they attended class, of whom 508 students accepted. After filtering out incomplete and invalid answers that they gave to the survey questions, we finally got 489 students' data (with 408 females). Their ages range from 20 to 25 and the students are from 11 different majors (e.g., English, Physics, Mathematics, Pedagogy).

3.2 Procedure and Measurement

3.2.1 User survey. In the questionnaire asked before they took course, we included some questions about the student's personal properties, such as **age, gender, pre-course interest** (*"Before learning, my interest in the course is (): from 1 'very low' to 5 'very high'"*) and **pre-course knowledge** (*"Before learning, I have obtained () of the needed knowledge: from 1 'none' to 5 'all'"*). Besides, some course-related factors are also included [15, 17]: **subject type of each course** (i.e., liberal art, science, or engineering), **course structure** (the number of sections in each course), and **assessment structure** (the number of assignments).

When students finished the course, we asked them to fill in a post-course questionnaire in order to acquire their **sense of community**. We assessed the student's sense of community with Rovai's 20-statement Classroom Community Scale (as introduced in Section 2.3), which reaches satisfactory convergent and discriminant validity [18]. In addition to its original classification (*Connectedness* and *Learning* two sub-scales [18]), we proposed a new classification in order to assess students' perception of *Interaction with Instructor (InterInstructor, for short)* and *Interaction with Other Students (InterStudent)*. Specifically, *InterInstructor* is assessed by 10 items selected from the Classroom Community Scale (e.g., *"I feel that I am encouraged to ask questions"*) and 1 new item (*"I feel I can actively interact with my instructor during the online course"*); and *InterStudent* is also assessed by 11

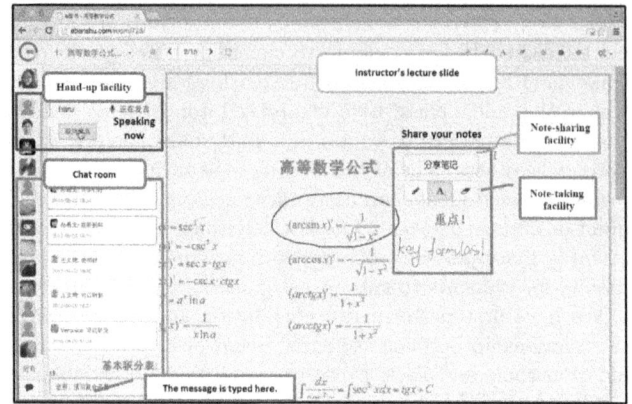

Figure 1: Snapshot of the synchronous instruction interface in eBanshu (www.ebanshu.com).

Table 1: List of students' online behavioral features

Activity features	In-class activities#	Frequency of using hand-up facility
		Number of messages posted in chat room
		Frequency of taking notes
		Frequency of sharing notes
		Class attendance rate
	After-class activities	Frequency of sharing learning materials
		Number of messages posted in discussion forum
		Assignment submission rate
Content features+	Message length	Number of words per sentence
	Psychological presence	Number of social process words per message
		Number of affective process words per message
		Number of cognitive process words per message
	Task engagement	Number of fully-engaged sentences
		Number of somewhat-engaged sentences
		Number of disengaged sentences

Each in-class activity (except class attendance rate) is measured in terms of both average number per lesson and total number during the whole course.

+ Content features are extracted from students' messages posted in chat room and discussion forum.

statements, including the other 10 items in the Classroom Community Scale (e.g., *"I feel that students in this course care about each other"*) and 1 new item (*"I feel I can actively interact with other students during the online course"*).

3.2.2 Objective online learning behavior. eBanshu system automatically recorded students' learning behavior in a log file, which includes not only the activities they carried out in class and after class, but also their text messages posted in chat room and discussion forum.

From the log file, we extracted two types of features: activity features and content features (see Table 1). The activity features are further divided into two categories: **in-class activity features** that include students' attendance rates, frequency of using hand-up facility, number of messages posted in chat room, number of notes taken in class, and frequency of sharing notes; **after-class activity features** that include students' assignment submission rates, frequency of sharing learning materials, and number of messages posted in discussion forum.

The content features include **sentence length, psychological presence**, and **task engagement** of messages students posted in chat room and discussion forum. To be

Table 2: Measurement of message content's psychological presence and task engagement level (the coding process for psychological presence is referred to [14])

Psychological presence		
	Coding	
Social presence	Occurrence of social process words in CLIWC# sub-categories: *social* (e.g., "talk"), *friend* (e.g., "buddy"), *family* (e.g., "daughter"), and *human* (e.g., "adult").	
	Occurrence of affective process words in CLIWC sub-categories: *affect* (e.g., "happy"), *positive emotion* (e.g., "nice"), *negative emotion* (e.g., "hurt"), *anger* (e.g., "hate"), *anxiety* (e.g., "worried"), and *sadness* (e.g., "sad").	
Cognitive presence	Occurrence of cognitive process words in CLIWC sub-categories: *insight* (e.g., "think"), *causation* (e.g., "because"), *discrepancy* (e.g. "should"), *tentative* (e.g., "perhaps"), *certainty* (e.g., "always"), *inhibition* (e.g., "constrain"), and *inclusive* (e.g., "include").	
Task engagement		
Fully-engaged	Occurrence of words/phrases that are closely related to learning (e.g., "assignment", "exam").	
Somewhat-engaged	Occurrence of words/phrases that are somewhat related to learning (e.g., "ask for leave", "technical support").	
Disengaged	Occurrence of words/phrases that are unrelated to learning (e.g., greeting words like "hello", modal particle words like "wow").	

CLIWC is short for "Chinese Linguistic Inquiry and Word Count" dictionary.

Table 3: Students' sense of community, personal properties, and course-related features

Sense of community	Overall	Mean=3.51 (st.d.=0.56)
	Connectedness	Mean=3.59 (st.d.=0.52)
	Learning	Mean=3.43 (st.d.=0.71)
	InterInstructor	Mean=3.52 (st.d.=0.66)
	InterStudent	Mean=3.50 (st.d.=0.54)
Personal properties	Age	20-25
	Gender	Female: 409 (83.6%); Male: 80 (17.4%)
	Pre-course interest	Mean=3.77 (st.d.=0.79)
	Pre-course knowledge	Mean=2.44 (st.d.=0.69)
Course-related features	Course structure	Mean=17.17 (st.d.=15.44)
	Assessment structure	Mean=6.00 (st.d.=9.77)

specific, sentence length is taken as a manifest indicator of students' sustained interaction [22]. Psychological presence evaluates whether students' online communication content can foster collaborative and meaningful learning, which is defined in two categories [13]: *social presence* (the degree of awareness of others in an interaction) and *cognitive presence* (the extent of both reflection and discourse in the construction of meaningful outputs). To encode the psychological presence of each message, we adopted a popularly used text analysis tool, Chinese Linguistic Inquiry and Word Count (CLIWC) dictionary [14]. If a word (in a message) belongs to "social process" or "affective process" (see the coding in Table 2), it is taken as the indicator of *social presence* [13]. Otherwise, if the word is coded as "cognitive process", it is classified as *cognitive presence* [13]. As for task engagement, it measures whether the posted message is related to the course content [4]. Each message sentence's task engagement level was manually determined by counting the occurrences of learning-related word/phrase. If the sentence contains word/phrase like "assignment" or "exam", it is classified as "fully-engaged". If it contains word/phrase such as "ask for leave" or "technical support", it is classified as "somewhat-engaged". Otherwise, if the sentence contains word/phrase that is not relevant to the learning task (such as "hello" or "wow"), it is classified as "disengaged". The definition of each engagement level is given in Table 2.

Table 4: The results of Kolmogorov-Smirnov (K-S) and Shapiro-Wilk (S-W) test on sense of community overall scale and sub-scales

	K-S			S-W		
	Stat.	df	sig.	Stat.	df	sig.
SC_Overall	0.071	489	0.000	0.990	489	0.002
SC_Connectedness	0.089	489	0.000	0.968	489	0.000
SC_Learning	0.110	489	0.000	0.956	489	0.000
SC_InterInstructor	0.097	489	0.000	0.983	489	0.000
SC_InterStudent	0.102	489	0.000	0.964	489	0.000

4 RESULTS AND ANALYSIS

4.1 Data Overview

We are interested in verifying whether students' behavior in using different communication tools is correlated with their sense of community. Before reporting the correlation results, we first describe our collected data. In terms of our participants' sense of community (see Table 3), the reliability test of our used Rovai's Classroom Community Scale shows that its internal consistency coefficient (Cronbach's alpha) is 0.888, and the coefficients of the sub-scales *Connectedness*, *Learning*, *InterInstructor*, and *InterStudent* are 0.724, 0.811, 0.747, and 0.803 respectively. These values are all above 0.70, suggesting that the corresponding statements have satisfactory internal validity [12]. From Table 3, we see that the mean value of the *Overall* scale of sense of community (with 20 statements) is 3.51 out of 5 (st.d.=0.56). Regarding the sub-scales, the mean values of *Connectedness* (with 10 statements), *Learning* (with 10 statements), *InterInstructor* (with 11 statements), and *InterStudent* (with 11 statements) are 3.59 (st.d.=0.52), 3.43 (st.d.=0.71), 3.52 (st.d.=0.66), and 3.50 (st.d.=0.54) respectively. Besides, in order to choose the appropriate correlation measurement, we check the normality of sense of community scales using the Kolmogorov-Smirnov (K-S) and Shapiro-Wilk (S-W) tests. According to the results (see Table 4), both *Overall* scale and four sub-scales are not normally distributed at the 0.05 significant level (*Sig.*<0.05). In addition, it can be seen in Table 3 that most of students were interested in the enrolled courses (pre-course interest: mean=3.77, st.d.=0.79) and had few prior course knowledge (mean=2.44, st.d.= 0.69). As for course structure and assessment structure, they are respectively 17.17 (the average number of sections across all courses) and 6 (the average number of assignments).

The results of analyzing students' activities and message contents are given in Table 5. The average course attendance rate is 99.2%, indicating that the students took the majority of online lessons. Moreover, during the whole course, 98.8% of students posted at least one message in chat room and 59.7% had experience of using the hand-up facility. Additionally, although over half of students (57.1%) took at least one note in the online class, only 18.0% shared their written notes with others for at least one time. After class, the average assignment submission rate is 78.7%. Besides, 77.3% of the students shared their learning materials at least once. Relatively, the percentage of students who used discussion forum is lower, with 37.7%. On the other hand, the average numbers of activities among all students in using these

Table 5: Statistical results of analyzing students' activities and message contents

Behavioral features	Results	
Activity features	# (%) of st-udents who carried out the activity	# of activi-ties per stu-dent during whole course
# of using hand-up facility	292 (59.7%)	Mean=1.4
# of chat messages	483 (98.8%)	Mean=57.3
# of taking notes	279 (57.1%)	Mean=7.3
# of sharing notes	88 (18.0%)	Mean=0.97
Average course attendance rate: 99.2%		
# of material sharing	378 (77.3%)	Mean=2.8
# of forum messages	184 (37.7%)	Mean=0.7
Average assignment submission rate: 78.7%		

Content features	Chat room	discussion forum
# of words per sentence	Mean=3.60	Mean=4.41
# of social process words per message	Mean=0.46	Mean=1.47
# of affective process words per message	Mean=0.19	Mean=1.14
# of cognitive process words per message	Mean=0.81	Mean=4.47
% of fully-engaged sentences	16.5%	46.3%
% of somewhat-engaged sentences	23.5%	28.0%
% of disengaged sentences	60.0%	25.7%

Table 6: The results of Kolmogorov-Smirnov (K-S) and Shapiro-Wilk (S-W) test on students' online activities

	K-S			S-W		
	Stat.	df	sig.	Stat.	df	sig.
# of using hand-up facility	0.307	489	0.000	0.589	489	0.000
# of chat messages	0.213	489	0.000	0.660	489	0.000
# of taking notes	0.384	489	0.000	0.284	489	0.000
# of sharing notes	0.415	489	0.000	0.249	489	0.000
Average course attendance rate	0.134	489	0.000	0.907	489	0.000
# of material sharing	0.185	489	0.000	0.830	489	0.000
# of forum messages	0.325	489	0.000	0.571	489	0.000
Average assignment submission rate	0.233	489	0.000	0.750	489	0.000

tools show that the frequency of posting messages in chat room is largely higher than those of others, with mean 57.3, vs. average 7.3 times of taking notes, 2.8 times of sharing materials, 1.4 times of using hand-up facility, 0.97 times of sharing notes, and 0.7 messages posted in discussion forum.

Therefore, the above results demonstrate that in online class, our studied students were more active in communicating with others synchronously through chat room, followed by asking question to instructors directly through the hand-up facility. After class, they more frequently shared learning materials, but the frequency of posting content in discussion forum was relatively low. Table 6 shows the results of K-S and S-W test, indicating that all of the activity features are not normally distributed ($Sig. < 0.05$).

As for message content (see Table 5), the average sentence length of messages in chat room is significantly shorter than that in discussion forum (3.60 vs. 4.41, $p < 0.05$ via two-tailed paired t-test), which indicates that students like to write shorter sentence during synchronous communication. In addition, although the quantity of messages posted in discussion forum is lower than that in chat room, the quality seems better. Specifically, in discussion forum, students used more social process words (mean=1.47 vs. 0.46 in chat room messages, $p > 0.05$), affective process words (1.14 vs. 0.19, $p > 0.05$), and cognitive process words (4.47 vs. 0.81, $p < 0.05$), which indicates they prefer to show their psychological presence using the asynchronous communication tool. Another phenomenon is that both types of messages (in discussion forum and chat room) include more cognitive

process words than social and affective process words, implying that through sustained communication, students are more inclined to construct meaning (i.e., exerting cognitive presence) than to enhance interaction (i.e., exerting social presence). In terms of the message's task engagement level, we find discussion forum contains a high proportion of learning-related messages (46.3% fully-engaged and 28.0% somewhat-engaged messages, vs. 25.7% disengaged). In comparison, in chat room, students posted more disengaged messages (60%) than fully-engaged messages (16.5%) and somewhat-engaged messages (23.5%).

4.2 Correlation Analysis

Because of the abnormal distribution of sense of community scores and activity features (see Tables 4 and 6), we use the Spearman correlation coefficient [36] to measure the relationship between students' communication behavior and their feeling of community. The results are given in Table 7.

4.2.1 Activity features and sense of community. It can be seen that there are significant correlations between students' activities in using communication tools and their sense of community. As for students' in-class activities, the number of messages students posted in chat room is significantly positively correlated with their sense of community w.r.t. both *Overall* scale and four sub-scales *Connectedness, Learning, Interaction with Instructor (InterInstructor)*, and *Interaction with Other Students (InterStudent)*. In addition, students' usage of hand-up facility has a significantly positive correlation with their sense of community in terms of *Learning* and *InterInstructor* sub-scales, indicating if students use hand-up facility more frequently, they are more likely to feel that the community can not only enhance their acquisition of knowledge and understanding (i.e., *Learning*), but also promote the interaction with their instructors (i.e., *InterInstructor*).

Regarding the after-class activities, it shows that when the number of learning materials students shared increases, their perception of *Learning* community also increases. In addition, students' assignment submission rate is significantly positively correlated with their sense of community w.r.t. *Learning* and *InterInstructor* sub-scales.

Thus, our results indicate that the usage of both synchronous online communication tools (like chat room and hand-up facility) and asynchronous communication tools (such as material sharing and assignment submission facilities) may enhance students' sense of community. In turn, strong sense of community may lead to students' increasing use of these communication tools. However, we fail to find significant correlations between students' behavior of taking notes, sharing notes, and posting messages in discussion forum, and their sense of community.

4.2.2 Content features and sense of community. In terms of messages' textual content, five features extracted from conversational texts of chat room show significant correlation with students' sense of community. More specifically, students who use larger number of social process words, affective process words, or cognitive process words in chat messages

Table 7: Correlations between implicit features and students' sense of community (*$p < 0.05$ and **$p < 0.01$)

			Sense of community				
			Overall	Connectedness	Learning	InterInstructor	InterStudent
Activity features							
In-class activities		Average # of using hand-up facility per lesson	0.084	0.057	0.101*	0.106*	0.070
		Total # of using hand-up facility	0.087	0.062	0.102*	0.108*	0.073
		Average # of chat messages per lesson	0.169**	0.133**	0.171**	0.176**	0.138**
		Total # of chat messages	0.168**	0.134**	0.168**	0.175**	0.136**
		Average # of taking notes per lesson	0.041	0.019	0.048	0.054	0.023
		Total # of taking notes	0.041	0.018	0.047	0.054	0.022
		Average # of sharing notes per lesson	0.011	0.021	0.005	0.010	0.014
		Total # of sharing notes	0.012	0.020	0.004	0.011	0.014
		Average course attendance rate	0.045	0.042	0.052	0.048	0.036
After-class activities		Total # of sharing materials	0.074	0.080	0.098*	0.080	0.046
		Total # of forum messages	-0.017	-0.022	-0.008	-0.007	-0.033
		Average assignment submission rate	0.088	0.080	0.097*	0.124**	0.062
Content features							
Message length	Chat room	# of words per sentence	0.043	0.010	0.084	0.065	0.028
	Discussion forum	# of words per sentence	-0.018	-0.030	-0.012	-0.015	-0.032
Psychological presence	Chat room	# of social process words	0.177**	0.141**	0.182**	0.188**	0.149**
		# of affective process words	0.175**	0.140**	0.187**	0.189**	0.143**
		# of cognitive process words	0.174**	0.123**	0.195**	0.187**	0.144**
	Discussion forum	# of social process words	0.017	-0.02	0.042	0.034	-0.010
		# of affective process words	0.037	0.027	0.037	0.033	0.035
		# of cognitive process words	-0.012	-0.025	-0.003	-0.004	-0.028
Task engagement	Chat room	# of fully-engaged sentences	0.136**	0.092*	0.154**	0.153**	0.099*
		# of somewhat-engaged sentences	0.162**	0.117**	0.184**	0.170**	0.144**
		# of disengaged sentences	0.081	0.079	0.064	0.072	0.081
	Discussion forum	# of fully-engaged sentences	-0.045	-0.055	-0.011	-0.026	-0.054
		# of somewhat-engaged sentences	0.036	0.033	0.036	0.021	0.047
		# of disengaged sentences	-0.012	0.003	-0.031	0.002	-0.037
Miscellaneous features							
Personal properties		Gender	0.039	-0.006	0.072	0.055	0.022
		Age	-0.066	-0.088	-0.039	-0.038	-0.079
		Pre-course interest	0.162**	0.209**	0.118**	0.157**	0.153**
		Pre-course knowledge	0.102*	0.076	0.131**	0.106*	0.085
Course-related features		Course structure	-0.023	-0.024	-0.021	-0.016	-0.038
		Assessment structure	0.010	0.011	0.006	0.008	0.016
Environmental features+		Instructors' aggregated activities	0.101*	0.089*	0.108*	0.118**	0.084
		classmates' aggregated activities	0.057	0.090*	0.052	0.028	0.062

+ Number of aggregated activities per lesson refers to the total number of activities carried out in each lesson. Specifically, for instructors, the activities include posting messages in chat room, taking notes, and sharing notes. While for students, the activities include using hand-up facility, posting messages in chat room, taking notes, and sharing notes.

are inclined to perceive stronger sense of community in terms of both *Overall* scale and four sub-scales, which implies the positive relationship between students' psychological presence and sense of community.

In addition, we observe that the numbers of chat messages which contain content fully or somewhat relevant to learning tasks are significantly correlated with students' sense of community (w.r.t. all of the scales) in a positive way. That is, when students post more fully-engaged or somewhat-engaged sentences in chat room, they are likely to perceive stronger sense of community.

However, there exists no significant correlation between the content features extracted from forum messages and students' sense of community in our study.

4.2.3 Miscellaneous features and sense of community. In addition to behavioral features, we find that some personal properties and environmental features are also associated with students' sense of community. Particularly, students who are more interested in the studied course (i.e., pre-course interest) or gain richer knowledge before class (i.e., pre-course knowledge) tend to show stronger sense of community, especially in terms of *Overall* scale and two sub-scales *Learning* and *InterInstructor*. The findings are basically consistent with Brown's observation [2] that students who are familiar with the online course tend to feel strong sense of community, because those who with less prior knowledge normally require more interaction with and support from online instructors.

Moreover, it shows that students' sense of community is related to their instructors' and classmates' behavior in synchronous online class. To be specific, the average number of instructors' aggregated in-class activities is significantly positively correlated with students' sense of community in terms of *Overall* scale and three sub-scales *Connectedness*, *Learning*, and *InterInstructor*, and the average number of classmates' aggregated in-class activities significantly correlates with students' feeling that they belong and connect to the online classroom community (i.e., *Connectedness* sub-scale).

However, our data reveal that students' age, gender, and course-related features (i.e., course structure and assessment structure) fail to show significant correlation with their sense of community ($p > 0.05$). Additionally, using analysis of variance (ANOVA), we notice that the mean differences of sense of community (w.r.t. both *Overall* scale and four sub-scales) across three subject types (i.e., liberal arts, science, and engineering) are not significant ($p > 0.05$).

In summary, 15 (out of totally 34) features are empirically proven to have significant correlation with students' sense of community values. Among them, there are more behavioral features (11 = 6 activity features + 5 content features) relative to miscellaneous features (4 = 2 personal properties + 2 environmental features). Particularly, students' activities carried out in class exhibit stronger correlation than their after-class activities. Regarding content features, the text

Table 8: RMSE results of testing regression models (Note: the models that significantly outperform the baseline are identified in bold, $p < 0.05$ via two-tailed paired t-test; and the value inside the parenthesis indicates the improvement percentage against the baseline approach)

	Baseline	LASSO	PR	Rule	GP	SVR	RBF
SC_Overall	0.1510	**0.1311* (13.2%)**	**0.1338* (11.4%)**	0.1479 (2.0%)	0.1456 (3.6%)	0.1471 (2.6%)	0.1428 (5.43%)
SC_Connectedness	0.1308	**0.1102* (15.8%)**	**0.1117* (14.6%)**	**0.1178* (9.9%)**	**0.1167* (10.8%)**	**0.1183* (13.4%)**	**0.1131* (13.5%)**
SC_Learning	0.1621	**0.1479* (8.8%)**	**0.1501* (7.4%)**	0.1593 (1.7%)	0.1557 (3.9%)	0.1560 (3.8%)	0.1567 (3.3%)
SC_InterInstructor	0.1570	**0.1403* (10.6%)**	**0.1416* (9.8%)**	**0.1421* (9.5%)**	**0.1441* (8.2%)**	0.1477 (5.9%)	0.1470 (6.4%)
SC_InterStudent	0.1412	**0.1219* (13.7%)**	**0.1228* (13.0%)**	**0.1258* (10.9%)**	**0.1262* (10.6%)**	**0.1286* (8.9%)**	**0.1237* (12.4%)**

contents of messages posted in chat room are more strongly correlated with sense of community, in comparison with contents extracted from forum messages.

4.3 Sense of Community Prediction

For the next step, we are interested in inferring the students' sense of community based on the 15 significant features identified in the previous section.

4.3.1 Inference model. Formally, a standard form of regression model can be represented as $y = f(x) + \epsilon$, where x denotes an input vector (in our case, it contains the identified features such as the number of posted chat messages, the number of social process words per message, etc.), y denotes a scalar output (in our case, it gives the predicted sense of community score), and ϵ is the additive noise. Our purpose is then to estimate the regression function $f(\cdot)$. In our experiment, we tested six popularly used regression models [7, 23, 33] for inferring students' sense of community: 3 linear methods including *Least Absolute Shrinkage and Selection Operator (LASSO)*, *Pace Regression (PR)*, and *M5 Rules (Rule)*, and 3 non-linear methods including *Gaussian Process (GP)*, *Support Vector Regression (SVR)*, and *Radial Basis Function Network (RBF)*.

Specifically, *LASSO* [26] is a shrinkage and selection method for linear regression to solve the following optimization puzzle: $\min_{\beta_0, \beta} \left(\frac{1}{2N} \sum_{i=1}^{N} (y_i - \beta_0 - x_i^T \beta)^2 + \lambda \sum_{j=1}^{p} |\beta_j| \right)$, where N is the number of observations, y_i is the response at observation i, and x_i is a vector of p values at observation i. The parameters β_0 and β are the scalar and p-vector *LASSO* coefficients respectively. λ is the nonnegative weight given to the regularization term (the $L1$ norm). As for the regularization in *LASSO*, it is a powerful mathematical tool for reducing over-fitting, as it adds a penalty term to the objective function and controls the model complexity using that penalty term. *Pace Regression* [29] is a typical form of linear regression analysis, which improves on classical ordinary least squares regression by evaluating the effect of each variable. It is applicable when some of the input features are mutually dependent. *M5 Rules* [6] also assumes a linear distribution of the input features, but it is grounded on the separate-and-conquer strategy to build a decision tree. The advantage of *M5 Rules* is that it costs less calculation and can deal with the datasets with missing values.

As for non-linear models, *Gaussian Process* [16] defines a probabilistic regression based on Bayesian theory and statistical learning theory: $f(x) \sim gp(\mu(x), k(x, x'))$, where $\mu(x)$ stands for the mean function and $k(x, x')$ is the covariance function, which can handle datasets with small number of

samples and/or many input features. As for the *Support Vector Regression* algorithm [24], the main idea is to minimize error and individualize the hyperplane which maximizes the margin. It maps the data into a high dimensional feature space via a nonlinear mapping and transforms the optimization problem into dual convex quadratic programs, which can get global optimum solution more efficiently. *Radial Basis Function Network* [3] is an artificial neural network having advantages of easy design, good generalization, and strong tolerance to input noise. It mainly uses radial basis functions as activation functions and the output of the network is a linear combination of radial basis functions of the inputs and neuron parameters.

4.3.2 Procedure. We randomly selected 80% of 489 students who participated in our user survey to train each model and tested it on the remaining 20% students. To avoid any biases, we performed 10-fold cross validation, and measured the accuracy via the metric *Root Mean Square Error (RMSE)*, which is a commonly used measure of the difference between predicted value and ground truth (the lower, the better) [31]. All significance tests were done using two-tailed paired t-test at the $p < 0.05$ level. Formally, we define a student's sense of community as a 5-dimension vector $sc_u = (sc_u^1, sc_u^2, ..., sc_u^5)^T$, where sc_u^1 represents the *Overall* scale and sc_u^2 to sc_u^5 respectively represent the four sub-scales *Connectedness*, *Learning*, *InterInstructor*, and *InterStudent*. The means and standard deviations of the five dimensions at the normalized 0-1 scale are: *Overall* (mean=0.53, st.d.=0.15), *Connectedness* (mean=0.57, st.d.=0.13), *Learning* (mean=0.49, st.d.=0.16), *InterInstructor* (mean=0.56, st.d.=0.16), and *InterStudent* (mean=0.53, st.d.=0.14).

4.3.3 Prediction results. The results are shown in Table 8. We observe that the six regression models all achieve significant improvements against the baseline that simply uses the average value of training data as the predicted score for all of the testing samples ($p < 0.05$), among which the linear methods *LASSO* and *Pace Regression* perform better than non-linear methods. *LASSO* is further better than *Pace Regression* in terms of all the five dimensions (average RMSE value: 0.1303 vs. 0.1320). It is probably because LASSO has the ability to deal with the over-fitting problem that may occur in our dataset (more features and fewer samples). In contrast, some methods like *SVR* and *RBF Network* fail to reach satisfying prediction accuracy, which may be due to the linear characteristics of our data that do not fit their non-linear assumption.

In addition to the RMSE values, we also report the improvement percentage ($= \frac{|RMSE_{testmodel} - RMSE_{Baseline}|}{RMSE_{Baseline}}$) that each model achieves against the baseline. It shows that the improvement percentage returned by LASSO w.r.t. the *Overall* scale is 13.2%. As for the four sub-scales of sense of community, *Connectedness* is the easiest one inferred by LASSO (15.8% accuracy increase relative to the baseline), followed by *InterStudent* (13.7%), *InterInstructor* (10.6%), and *Learning* (8.8%), implying that our identified features are more effective at reflecting students' feeling of connectedness with community members.

5 DISCUSSION

5.1 Major Findings

In our work, we not only reveal the correlation between students' communication behavior in online courses and their sense of community, but also build regression model for inferring students' sense of community based on their behavior.

First of all, we find both students' activities (6 features) and message contents (5 features) are significantly correlated with their sense of community. In synchronous class, we observe that students' sense of community increases as their usage of chat room or hand-up facility rises. This may be because the immediate and direct interaction can make students feel more connected to the community and achieve their learning goals. In turn, feeling stronger sense of community may encourage students to behave more actively in using these communication tools. After class, we find that students' usage of material-sharing and assignment-submission facilities are significantly correlated with their sense of community in terms of the *Learning* sub-scale. As for content features, the psychological presence and task engagement level of the messages posted in chat room show significant correlation with students' sense of community. In addition, students' pre-course interest, pre-course knowledge, and the average numbers of instructors' and classmates' aggregated in-class activities are also significantly postively correlated with students' sense of community. However, we fail to observe any significant findings regarding students' behavior in discussion forum, which is probably because the delayed communication may make students feel less motivated to interact.

Motivated by the correlation results, we further developed inference model to identify students' sense of community based on these significant features. Concretely, we tested six machine learning algorithms including *LASSO, Pace Regression, M5 Rules, Gaussian Process, Supported Vector Regression*, and *Radial Basis Function Network*. Our results demonstrate that all of the models significantly outperform the baseline, and *LASSO* performs the best. The possible reason is that *LASSO* is capable of alleviating the over-fitting issue, and the linear relationship between input and output as defined in this model may better fit the characteristic of our data. Another observation is that *Connectedness* and *InterStudent* sub-scales are easier to be predicted relative to *InterInstructor* and *Learning* sub-scales, probably because students' feeling of connectedness with community members and their perception of interaction with learning peers can be better reflected by the significant features.

5.2 Implications

Therefore, we believe that our results are suggestive for researchers to better understand the relationship between students' usage of different communication tools and their sense of community in online courses, as well as for practitioners to improve existing online learning systems. For instance, more synchronous tools such as chat room and hand-up facility may be incorporated into current products, so as to enhance students' connectedness and interaction with community members. In addition, instructors could increase their initiatives in using these communication tools in synchronous class, as their in-class behavior is positively correlated with students' sense of community. Instructors could also assign more homework due to the positive relationship between sense of community and assignment submission.

Furthermore, the ability to infer a student's sense of community from her/his online communication behavior could be potentially helpful to address the dropout issues in current online courses. As instructors would be able to know their students' sense of community in real time, once the value degrades below an acceptable threshold, they may offer pertinent and timely supports to their students. For instance, when it shows students perceive lower sense of community in terms of *Learning* and *InterInstructor* sub-scales, instructors could ask more questions in class so as to encourage students to answer by using hand-up facility, while for those who feel lower sense of community regarding *Connectedness* and *InterStudent* sub-scales, more chat sessions could be organized for narrowing the distance between learning peers.

6 CONCLUSION AND FUTURE WORK

Although students' sense of community plays an essential role in online learning, how to acquire it in real time remains a big concern. Our study suggests that it is feasible to infer students' sense of community from their communication behavior in online courses. To be specific, we first identified a set of features which are significantly correlated to sense of community, not only including students' activities carried out in both synchronous and asynchronous environments, but also their linguistic content in conversational texts. We then compared six regression models in terms of their ability of unifying these features into automatically predicting students' sense of community, among which *LASSO* shows the best performance.

Our work has several future directions. Firstly, we plan to validate our findings on more students with diverse backgrounds (e.g., age, nationality, ethnic background). Secondly, we will try to further improve our prediction model by considering more features, such as the semantic content of message texts. We will also perform qualitative interviews to in depth understand students' thoughts.

ACKNOWLEDGMENTS

We thank all participants who took part in our user survey. We also thank Hong Kong Research Grants Council (RGC) for sponsoring the research work (under project RGC/HKBU12200415).

REFERENCES

[1] Mohamed Ally. 2004. Foundations of educational theory for online learning. *Theory and Practice of Online Learning* 2 (2004), 15–44.

[2] Ruth E Brown. 2001. The process of community-building in distance learning classes. *Journal of Asynchronous Learning Networks* 5, 2 (2001), 18–35.

[3] Sheng Chen, Colin FN Cowan, and Peter M Grant. 1991. Orthogonal least squares learning algorithm for radial basis function networks. *IEEE Transactions on Neural Networks* 2, 2 (1991), 302–309.

[4] Sue-Jen Chen and Edward J Caropreso. 2004. Influence of personality on online discussion. *Journal of Interactive Online Learning* 3, 2 (2004), 1–17.

[5] Shane Dawson. 2006. Online forum discussion interactions as an indicator of student community. *Australasian Journal of Educational Technology* 22, 4 (2006), 495–510.

[6] Geoffrey Holmes, Mark Hall, and Eibe Frank. 1999. Generating rule sets from model trees. In *Australasian Joint Conference on Artificial Intelligence (AI 1999)*. Springer, 1–12.

[7] François Mairesse, Marilyn A Walker, Matthias R Mehl, and Roger K Moore. 2007. Using linguistic cues for the automatic recognition of personality in conversation and text. *Journal of Artificial Intelligence Research* (2007), 457–500.

[8] Joanne M McInnerney and Tim S Roberts. 2004. Online learning: Social interaction and the creation of a sense of community. *Educational Technology & Society* 7, 3 (2004), 73–81.

[9] John Paul McKinney, Kathleen G McKinney, Renae Franiuk, and John Schweitzer. 2006. The college classroom as a community: Impact on student attitudes and learning. *College Teaching* 54, 3 (2006), 281–284.

[10] David W McMillan and David M Chavis. 1986. Sense of community: A definition and theory. *Journal of Community Psychology* 14, 1 (1986), 6–23.

[11] Robert L Moore. 2014. Importance of developing community in distance education courses. *TechTrends* 58, 2 (2014), 20–24.

[12] Jum C Nunnally, Ira H Bernstein, and Jos MF ten Berge. 1967. *Psychometric Theory*. Vol. 226. JSTOR.

[13] Murat Oztok, Daniel Zingaro, Clare Brett, and Jim Hewitt. 2013. Exploring asynchronous and synchronous tool use in online courses. *Computers & Education* 60, 1 (2013), 87–94.

[14] James W Pennebaker, Ryan L Boyd, Kayla Jordan, and Kate Blackburn. 2015. The development and psychometric properties of LIWC2015. *UT Faculty/Researcher Works* (2015).

[15] Krystal Phirangee, Carrie Demmans Epp, and Jim Hewitt. 2016. Exploring the relationships between facilitation methods, students' sense of community, and their online behaviors. *Online Learning Consortium* (2016).

[16] Carl Edward Rasmussen. 2006. Gaussian processes for machine learning. *Citeseer* (2006).

[17] Ido Roll, Leah P Macfadyen, and Debra Sandilands. 2015. Evaluating the Relationship Between Course Structure, Learner Activity, and Perceived Value of Online Courses. In *Proceedings of the 2nd ACM Conference on Learning@ Scale (L@S 2015)*. ACM, 385–388.

[18] Alfred P Rovai. 2002. Development of an instrument to measure classroom community. *The Internet and Higher Education* 5, 3 (2002), 197–211.

[19] Alfred P Rovai. 2002. Sense of community, perceived cognitive learning, and persistence in asynchronous learning networks. *The Internet and Higher Education* 5, 4 (2002), 319–332.

[20] Alfred P Rovai and Hope Jordan. 2004. Blended learning and sense of community: A comparative analysis with traditional and fully online graduate courses. *The International Review of Research in Open and Distributed Learning* 5, 2 (2004).

[21] Seymour B Sarason. 1974. *The psychological sense of community: Prospects for a community psychology*. Jossey-Bass.

[22] Sarah Schrire. 2006. Knowledge building in asynchronous discussion groups: Going beyond quantitative analysis. *Computers & Education* 46, 1 (2006), 49–70.

[23] Peter Shea. 2006. A study of students' sense of learning community in online environments. *Journal of Asynchronous Learning Networks* 10, 1 (2006), 35–44.

[24] Alex J Smola and Bernhard Schölkopf. 2004. A tutorial on support vector regression. *Statistics and Computing* 14, 3 (2004), 199–222.

[25] Malin Sveningsson. 2001. *Creating a sense of community: Experiences from a Swedish web chat*. Ph.D. Dissertation. Linköpings universitet.

[26] Robert Tibshirani. 1996. Regression shrinkage and selection via the lasso. *Journal of the Royal Statistical Society. Series B (Methodological)* (1996), 267–288.

[27] Jesus Trespalacios and Ross Perkins. 2016. Sense of Community, Perceived Learning, and Achievement Relationships in an Online Graduate Course. *Turkish Online Journal of Distance Education* (2016).

[28] Donald G Unger and Abraham Wandersman. 1985. The importance of neighbors: The social, cognitive, and affective components of neighboring. *American Journal of Community Psychology* 13, 2 (1985), 139–169.

[29] Yong Wang. 2000. *A new approach to fitting linear models in high dimensional spaces*. Ph.D. Dissertation. The University of Waikato.

[30] Rupert Wegerif. 1998. The social dimension of asynchronous learning networks. *Journal of Asynchronous Learning Networks* 2, 1 (1998), 34–49.

[31] Cort J Willmott, Steven G Ackleson, Robert E Davis, Johannes J Feddema, Katherine M Klink, David R Legates, James O'donnell, and Clinton M Rowe. 1985. Statistics for the evaluation and comparison of models. *American Geophysical Union* (1985).

[32] Robert H Woods Jr. 2002. How much communication is enough in online courses?–exploring the relationship between frequency of instructor-initiated personal email and learners' perceptions of and participation in online learning. *International Journal of Instructional Media* 29, 4 (2002), 377.

[33] Wen Wu and Li Chen. 2015. Implicit acquisition of user personality for augmenting movie recommendations. In *International Conference on User Modeling, Adaptation, and Personalization (UMAP 2015)*. Springer, 302–314.

[34] Wen Wu, Li Chen, and Qingchang Yang. 2016. Students' Personality and Chat Room Behavior in Synchronous Online Learning. In *Proceedings of ACM Conference on User Modeling, Adaptation and Personalization (UMAP 2016), Late-Breaking Results*. ACM.

[35] J Yuan and C Kim. 2014. Guidelines for facilitating the development of learning communities in online courses. *Journal of Computer Assisted Learning* 30, 3 (2014), 220–232.

[36] Jerrold H Zar. 1972. Significance testing of the Spearman rank correlation coefficient. *J. Amer. Statist. Assoc.* 67, 339 (1972), 578–580.

[37] Saijing Zheng, Mary Beth Rosson, Patrick C Shih, and John M Carroll. 2015. Understanding student motivation, behaviors and perceptions in MOOCs. In *Proceedings of ACM Conference on Computer Supported Cooperative Work & Social Computing (CSCW 2015)*. ACM, 1882–1895.

Towards a Long Term Model of Virtual Reality Exergame Exertion

Soojeong Yoo
University of Sydney
Sydney, NSW 2006
syoo6624@uni.sydney.edu.au

Tristan Heywood
University of Sydney
Sydney, NSW 2006
they2559@uni.sydney.edu.au

Lie Ming Tang
University of Sydney
Sydney, NSW 2006
liemingtang@gmail.com

Bob Kummerfeld
University of Sydney
Sydney, NSW 2006
bob.kummerfeld@sydney.edu.au

Judy Kay
University of Sydney
Sydney, NSW 2006
judy.kay@sydney.edu.au

ABSTRACT

Virtual reality (VR) exergames have the potential to be a fun way to get exercise. People have different preferences and responses when it comes to both exercising and playing games, meaning that there are potential benefits from creating a user model for exergaming. This could support various forms of personalization, such as game recommenders, and personalization within a game. We define a VR exergame user model, VRex, that represents a user's exertion as well as their goals and preferences for exercise and for games. We illustrate the use of VRex to represent 18 users who played 4 games, based on data about their actual and perceived exertion and their satisfaction with each game. This demonstrates the diversity of the user models, in terms of the user model's components. This is the first work to explore the design of user models for virtual reality exergames and has the potential to serve as a foundation for game personalization, recommenders and open model interfaces.

KEYWORDS

User Modeling, Exergames, Virtual Reality Games

1 INTRODUCTION

For many people, achieving the recommended levels of physical activity is a significant challenge. This is a problem, as a lack of exercise poses serious health risks [11]. Fortunately, as little as 10 minutes of exercise can be very beneficial [15]. Virtual reality games offer a promising way of motivating people to exercise, by making exercise fun. Exergames, which are games designed explicitly to give people exercise, have been shown to make exercise more enjoyable and to improve physical fitness [12]. Our work explores how to gain these benefits from virtual reality (VR) games. This is because VR games can provide good levels of exercise, while also being highly enjoyable. [31].

UMAP'17, July 9–12, 2017, Bratislava, Slovakia
© 2017 ACM. ISBN 978-1-4503-4635-1/17/07...$15.00.
DOI: http://dx.doi.org/10.1145/3079628.3079679

VR is an important platform for exergaming because of its ability to provide immersive and engaging experiences. We expect that the more fun and compelling an exergame is, the less the player is aware of the exercise they are doing. Additionally, some VR platforms such as the HTC Vive are particularly well suited for exergaming due to their ability to provide 'room scale' experiences. Many VR games on the Vive require the player to engage their whole body and move around the room as they play. This full body movement means a game can give significant exertion, even when it was not explicitly designed to give the player exercise. The availability and fast dropping cost of emerging VR hardware such as the HTC Vive has the potential to allow the general public access to the benefits of VR exergaming.

While VR exergames are effective in providing motivation, they do not currently take account of information about the user, such as their fitness level or goals and preferences. Just this information would be used by a fitness advisor who creates a workout plan. This means that current VR exergames do not offer a workout personalized for the user. This can limit their exercise outcomes [17]. Additionally, without tailored exercises, individuals risk over-exertion, and significant health risks [11].

Personalization offers a way to overcome such problems. Both personalized game recommendation and within-game personalization could make VR games more effective in providing good exercise while being enjoyable. Such personalization needs a user model that represents key aspects of the user, such as their game and exercise preferences, fitness and exercise goals. The emerging availability of consumer devices for sensing heart-rate (HR) make it possible to model exertion [19] within game play.

In this paper, we present the design for a user model for virtual reality exergames, the VRex (VR exergaming) model. This is intended to serve three main roles which we characterize in terms of key questions a system should be able to answer.

(1) *Recommending VR games on exertion and game preferences*:
  - Which games will give me a good cardio workout?
  - Which will work particular muscle groups eg arms?
  - Which will give me a good game experience?
(2) *In-game personalization*: Personalize a particular game by taking account of the individual's goals and previous playthroughs of this game.
  - How hard is the user working compared with their target?

- Should the game change to make the user exercise harder, use different muscles, or reduce the intensity?
- Should the game provide the user with feedback on their exertion, and if so, how should this be timed and presented in order to avoid it being ignored or causing distraction from the VR game?

(3) *Exertion and activity OLM*: Create open learner models (OLMs), that enable an individual to gain insights into their long term physical activity, based on the integration of data from multiple games and other sources, such as depth-sensing cameras, smartphones, smart-watches and worn activity trackers.

- How much does a particular VR game contribute to my long term fitness goals?
- How much does my VR gaming session contribute to my overall exercise?

2 BACKGROUND

This section reviews work on VR exergames and personalized exergames followed by work on measuring exertion.

2.1 Virtual reality exergames

Despite the considerable work published on exergames, little has focused on exercising in VR. Much work on VR exergames used exercycle machines [2, 25], with a VR HMD. Players cycled to travel around the virtual environment. This was enough fun to motivate sedentary users to exercise, with the immersive game distracting the user from the exercise, making it more fun. However, its use is restricted to special VR-enhanced cycles.

By contrast, inexpensive Google Cardboard smartphone HMD can be used for VR exergaming [30]. In this work, an app tracked the user's physical steps using the smartphone's accelerometer as they ran on the spot in the physical world to move in the virtual world. The paper reports a study in which participants found the game was fun and engaging, as well as good exercise. Notably, some participants suggested that the game would be more engaging if the exercise and game world were tailored for them, such as making the game easier for novice players. This is in line with work on tailoring real-time physical activity coaching systems [21]. The recent release of consumer VR hardware points to a emerging possibility for widely available VR exergaming.

2.2 Personalised exergames

Previous work on VR exergames has also found the need for personalization to deliver appropriate levels of exercise to individuals and making the game progressively more challenging to keep people engaged [9]. Work by Sinclair et al. [26] recommended taking account of both how attractive the user found the game and the player's physiological state, balancing the game challenge and exercise intensity. Other work by Hardy et al. [10] used a similar model but this also took account of the user's calendar to adjust the exercise intensity.

2.3 Measuring Exertion

Measuring the intensity of the exercise people experience in VR exergames is at the core of our user model. This section reviews

background informing the design of models for perceived and actual exertion, as well as fitness. There are many ways to measure exertion, physical activity and fitness [5, 27] and there are important guidelines for the recommended levels of activity for good health [11, 24]. The gold standard for measuring both exertion and physical fitness is VO^2max [8, 20, 28]. However, this requires the user to wear an oxygen mask. This is a problem for VR games where the user is wearing a HMD and engaging in an exergame. However, this level of accuracy is also unnecessary; consumer devices that measure heart-rate give a quite useful measure that we now describe.

Actual Exertion. There is a correlation between a person's heart-rate as a percentage of their maximum heart-rate, and the intensity of the exercise they are engaged in [14]. As a result government guidelines label exercise that produces a heart-rate between 50% and 70% of the individual's maximum as moderate exercise. Vigorous exercise raises the individual's hear- rate beyond this [6]. The recommended amount of exercise is then stated in terms of minutes of moderate or vigorous exercise. A simple but widely used estimate of maximum heart-rate uses the formula 220 - user's age [18]. Using this, and measuring heart-rate in each minute, provides an estimate of how many minutes of moderate and vigorous exercise a person has done.

Perceived Exertion. This is commonly measured with the Borg measure of perceived exertion, based on a questionnaire completed after exercise [4]. Table 1 shows the mapping of Borg scores to heart-rate [3].

Intensity	Max HR (%)	Borg score (RPE)
No exertion	20 - 39	6 - 7
Very light	40 - 59	8 - 10
Light	60 - 69	11 - 12
Moderate	70 - 79	13 - 14
Heavy	80 - 89	15 - 16
Very Heavy	90 - 99	17 - 18
Maximum	100	19 - 20

Table 1: Mapping exercise intensity, heart-rate, Borg intensity and heart-rate

Measures of Fitness. Resting heart-rate tends to be inversely related to physical fitness and low values are associated with lower mortality [13]. It is also relatively easy to measure, either by taking manual measurement or with smart watches and fitness devices. This makes resting heart-rate one useful indicator of fitness over the long term. Another fitness measure is *heart-rate recovery*, how quickly a person's heart-rate returns to their rest heart-rate following intense exercise. A faster recovery rate is associated with increased fitness [23]. There are protocols for measuring it, such as the change from the peak heart-rate after set exercise, to that measured 2 minutes later [7]. It is possible to get an estimate of this, by measuring the heart-rate decrease over 2 minutes after playing of an exergame.

Public health recommendations. These are based on meta-analyses of many studies and they provide guidance on desirable levels of exercise [11, 24]. At their simplest, they recommend 30 minutes of moderate activity most days, or half that time for intense activity.

3 VREX MODEL

As a starting point to designing a user model for exertion in VR games, we identified the competency questions for the user model. There are three classes of these, each related to the very different roles the user model could play. We listed them in the introduction and we return to them in the discussion section. While our broad goals need to involve both exertion and game preferences, this paper restricts the focus to the former. For the latter, it will be important to link the VRex model with models of game preferences, such as Orji et al's [22]. In addition, it will be useful to link to work modeling user's goals [1].

Table 2 shows an overview of the VRex user model. The first column is the type ID for each category, for example the Game Model has four data types, each with their respective ID (G1-4). Next is the name of the model component and the third column is its description. The table shows the 3 parts of the model: Game Model describes each game; Long term exertion and fitness model; and Game Session Model. Components within these link to each other.

The data defined in the "Game Model" is related to the game itself. G1 provides a unique game ID and G2 provides the human-readable name of the game, to present in a user interface. G3 describes the parts of the body exercised in the game. G4 is linked to score, as it can give us a clearer picture about whether the player is having difficulties with the game and how many retries or attempts the player made.

The next block of the model represents long term exertion and fitness, representing the various measures described in the last section and we describe below how it is fits with the part of the model for each game session.

Finally, the "Game Session" model represents a single game session, the user's enjoyment and actual exertion measures. The game summary models four aspects. Game ID (S1) is the game's unique identifier, which is used to link with the Game Model. Game score (S2) is a tuple for player achievements, such as a score and number of deaths. S3 and S4 track when the game started and ended. For example, is a player has a low score(S2) and a long playtime (S4 − S3), this may indicate the game is too difficult.

Since it is important to track user's responses to games, the Game Session Model records a player's enjoyment score (A1) and feeling of immersion within the virtual world (A2). Perceived exertion (A3) and DOMS (A4) track the user's assessed level of exertion to be interpreted along with the actual exertion in the "Actual Exertion Measure" part of the model.

Actual exertion represents how hard the player worked, based on their heart-rate before starting the game (E1), the 10-second heart-rate peak (E2), the 2 minute recovery rate (E3), the player's maximum heart-rate (E4), how many minutes the player exercised at moderate intensity activity (E5), and at vigorous intensity activity (E6). These parts of the model can then be used to determine the exertion in one session. This contributes to and can be compared against the long term exertion and fitness model to find out whether the player is meeting or exceeding their target and whether an easier or harder game should be recommended.

4 STUDY DESIGN

We designed a study to populate the VRex user models. This was done by capturing and analyzing data from people as they played a series of VR games. We transformed each participant's data into the relevant components of the VRex model components. Then we analysed the user model components from each game to gain insights into the variability of these between users since this points to the importance of personalization across our three user modelling goals: game recommendation, within-game personalization and long term OLMs.

Our lab-study involved 18 participants, each playing four VR games (Fruit Ninja, Holopoint, Hot Squat and *Portal Stories: VR*) from Steam[1] using the HTC Vive[2] head mounted display (HMD). The game order was varied so that three people used each of the 6 possible game orderings of the first three games. *Portal Stories: VR* was always the last session as we used this game as a baseline game since it involves limited exertion.

Study Setup. The interactive space was approximately 3 x 3 meters, of a dedicated VR lab. The equipment was: 1 x HTC Vive HMD; 2 x HTC Vive Base Stations; 2 x Controllers; 1 x Desktop PC running Windows 8.1 with Intel Core i7 3.4 GHz, 16 GB RAM, and Nvidia Geforce GTX 960 graphic card; 1 x Speaker System; 1 x Microsoft Kinect version 2 (for video recording); and 1 x Heart-rate Chest Strap. Two Lighthouse sensors, tracking the user's position in the physical space, were mounted on tripods and placed on opposite corners of the room where they were approximately 2 metres from the floor. Users wore a Polar T34 heart-rate chest strap monitor for the whole study period, including preliminary paper work and all 4 game sessions and the break times between them.

We recorded video through a Microsoft Kinect and audio through the HTC Vive HMD itself. The video was later used for analysis.

Data Collection. The heart beats detected by the Polar T34 chest strap were transmitted to a Moteino LoRa (Arduino Uno compatible) located on the participants body. The Moteino was powered by the spare USB port on the Vive and it sent the received heart beat data to a near by computer. We needed to process this raw data to account for noise, which involved both missing and extraneous data. This was based on a filtering and sliding window smoothing.

This part of the data collection was critical for the measure of actual exertion, E1-6 in VRex. We recorded the start and end time for each game (S3 and S4 in VRex). The recordings of the actual game play were then analysed to determine the scores achieved by participants (S2 in VRex).

Selection of the Virtual Reality Games. We chose the four VR games, as shown in Figure 1, from the Steam online store for the HTC Vive so that they would involve a range of types and levels of physical activity. Table 3 summarises the parts of the body (G3 in VRex) each game involves. The table indicates the predicted level of exertion by the number of ticks. Broadly, Fruit Ninja involves just arms, Hot Squat, the large leg and gluteal muscles needed to squat and Holopoint has a mix. The fourth game, *Portal Stories: VR*, was our baseline low exertion condition; it is a puzzle game, requiring little movement. We now describe each game.

---

[1]http://store.steampowered.com
[2]https://www.vive.com

ID	Model Component Name	Description (illustrative examples)
	Game Model	
G1	ID	Unique game Identifier (eg. FN001v2017.1)
G2	Name	Game name for use in interfaces, may not be unique (eg. Fruit Ninja)
G3	Body parts	Tuple represents parts of body exercised and how much (eg. [arm:high, glutes:moderate])
G4	Scoring	Tuple representing format of scores from a session (eg [number:score, number:deaths])
	Long term exertion and fitness model	
Fit1	VO2max	User's VO^2Max fitness measure (eg 50)
Fit2	rest-HR	Rest heart-rate (eg 60)
Fit3	2-min-recovery	Heart-rate drop in 2-min recovery protocol (eg 40)
Fit4	Top Heart-rate	User's maximum heart-rate
PG1	Daily moderate activity target	Target for moderate+ activity in minutes per day (eg 30)
PG2	Daily vigorous activity target	Target for vigorous activity in minutes per day (eg 15)
WGA1	Actual moderate activity	moderate+ activity in minutes each day (eg 40, 21, 55)
WGA1	Actual vigorous activity	vigorous activity in minutes each day (eg 20, 0, 0)
	Game Session Model	
	Game Summary – data source is the game	
S1	Game ID	Identifier for game, used to link to game model
S2	Score	Tuple for game score in this session, depends on game (eg score:7; deaths:3)
S3	Session Start	Time actual game play started (date and time)
S4	Session End	Time actual game play ended (date and time)
	User Preferences, perceived exertion, DOMS – data source is user answers	
A1	Game Preference	Enjoyment (1 - 7 scale)
A2	Immersion Preference	Responsive, compelling, and proficient (1 - 7 scale)
A3	Perceived exertion	This is determined through the Borg measure
A4	DOMS	Tuple for perceived delayed-onset-muscle-soreness score (timestamp, score 1 - 7, body part)
	Actual Exertion Measures – data comes from Heart-rate sensor when worn	
E1	HR-before	Estimated minimum heart-rate in period before game start
E2	HR-peak	Peak 10-second HR level
E3	HR-2-min-Recovery	From worn heart-rate sensor data, after game end
E4	Player's max heart-rate	Gained by removing the player's age from 220
E5	Moderate activity time	Time in minutes of moderate intensity activity (50+%)
E6	Vigorous activity time	Time in minutes of vigorous intensity activity (70+%) where this is a subset of E5

Table 2: VRex user model. Top block is the game model. Next is the user's long term exertion and fitness model. Remainder is the model for a single session of a VR game.

Game	Arms	Legs	Steps
Fruit Ninja	✓✓✓		
Hot Squat		✓✓✓	
Holopoint	✓✓	✓✓	✓✓
Portal Stories: VR	✓		

Table 3: Physical movement. ✓ = Light use; ✓✓ = Moderate use; ✓✓✓ = Heavy use.

Hot Squat. The player stands still while a series of barriers move towards them. Players must squat in order to duck under the barriers and must stand up again between barriers. As the game progresses, the barriers move faster and the distance between them decreases, forcing the player to squat faster.

Holopoint. The player holds a virtual bow in one hand while the other hand draws arrows from behind the player's head. Enemies appear all around the player, making it necessary to continuously turn around to check for enemies behind. The enemies must be shot with the bow and arrow and upon being hit will launch a projectile at the player, which the player must either side-step or duck under to avoid being hit and killed.

Fruit Ninja VR. The player holds a virtual samurai sword in each hand. Fruit flies into the air in front of the player, who must slice as much fruit as possible in one minute; this is repeated for 10 minutes.

Portal Stories: VR. This is a puzzle game where the player moves through different rooms, each with their own puzzle. In one hand, the player holds a virtual device which allows them to teleport to any horizontal surface in their line of sight. In the other they hold a device which acts as a 'tractor beam', allowing the player to pull certain objects towards them.

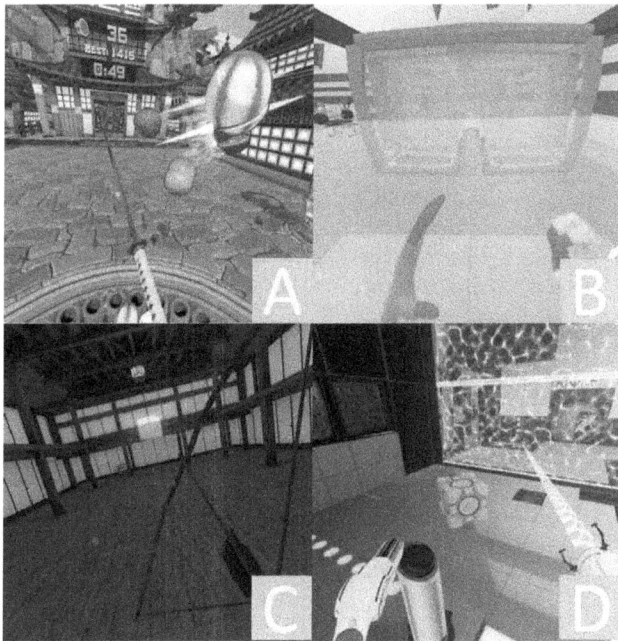

Figure 1: Screenshots of games: (A) Fruit Ninja, (B) Hot Squat, (C) Holopoint and (D) Portal Stories:VR

Study Procedure

We sent an email invitation to University mailing lists to recruit potential participants. They completed a screening questionnaire. We excluded participants with medical conditions and those susceptible to motion sickness. The day before each participant's study session, we informed them to avoid eating a heavy meal or drinking an hour before the study and to wear shoes that were comfortable to exercise in.

Sessions. Each session ran up to one and a half hours. At the beginning of the study (ethics approval ID 2016/089), we asked participants to wear a chest strap heart-rate monitor (Polar T34) while they completed consent forms. Participants then did the standard Vive tutorial for 6.5 minutes. This introduced how to interact with controllers and how to move safely in the play area inside the virtual environment. Right after the tutorial, participants played their first game. This was varied across participants so that 3 of the 18 participants played one of the 6 possible ordering sequences of the three games chosen for exertion (Fruit Ninja, Holopoint and Hot Squat). We advised participants that we would stop them after 10 minutes in each game. However, we emphasised that they should stop whenever they wished, for whatever reason (which could have included feeling tired or bored). *Portal Stories: VR* was always the last game. Since it does not require much exertion, we could use this to compare the heart-rate measures across the participants both for this game as well as the games involving more exertion.

Post-study. The day after their session, participants were contacted and asked whether they were feeling any effects of the exercise, such as soreness in specific muscle groups. ($\checkmark$ = light, $\checkmark\checkmark$ = moderate, $\checkmark\checkmark\checkmark$ = hard). This provided the data for A4 in VRex.

Eliciting user preferences and perceived exertion

Typically, it is recommended to take short breaks of at least two minutes between bouts of exercise, to increase exercise output and performance, with the actual time depending on the individual [16]. In our study, after each game we asked the participants to take a break of at least 2 minutes, with a maximum of 10 minutes. During this time, participants filled out the Borg questionnaire [11, 17] for perceived exertion, A3 in VRex. They also answered the Presence questionnaire [29] as a measure of immersion, A2 in VRex. At the end of the last session, we asked for a rating of enjoyment for each game (likert scale, 1 to 7, 1 very boring and 7 high enjoyment) for A1 in VRex and we asked them to explain their score.

In addition, while participants took each break, they continued to wear the chest heart-rate monitor, which monitored their heart-rate. This enabled us to determine the 2 minute-recovery, E3 in VRex.

5 RESULTS

The study enabled us to collect the data needed to populate the VRex model for a game session, for each of the 4 games. Since this game session model has 14 components, we provide an overview of selected components to illustrate the variability of these parts of the model across our participants and the ways we could use them. We then illustrate the VRex Game Session Model, for one game, Holopoint and two participants.

Table 4 summarises participants' background information. Our 18 participants were 18 to 36 (mean 26). Three (P1, 5 and 8) indicated they exercised regularly. (The VRex long term model could represent this in Fit1 - Fit3). Participants were also asked about prior experience with VR gaming, as this could affect the results. For example, experienced players may reach higher and more difficult levels, possibly increasing exercise intensity. Equally, they may play more efficiently, with less exertion. Long term data from many users will reveal the actual impact of game experience on exertion levels. Only P7, 8 and 12 had prior experience with VR gaming. The table shows each participant's maximum heart-rate, calculated as 220 minus age [18].

	Participant ID																	
	1	2	3	4	5	6	7	8	9	10	11	12	13	14	15	16	17	18
Age	26	21	22	18	36	23	24	34	24	31	27	26	26	35	25	34	24	26
Exercise	$\checkmark$				$\checkmark$			$\checkmark$										
VR games							$\checkmark$	$\checkmark$				$\checkmark$						
MAX HR	194	199	198	202	184	197	196	186	196	189	193	194	194	185	195	186	196	194

Table 4: Participant background information.

Table 5 summarises the user model component values of each game in a heat map for moderate and vigorous minutes of activity and rating of perceived exertion (RPE). We would expect the Borg perceived exertion to match the minutes of vigorous activity. In addition, we include the score or level achieved in the games, but only score for Fruit Ninja as it only had one level.

The table caption explains the mapping of colors to minutes and Borg RPE (which are based on Table 1). The table shows that only a few participants perceived Fruit Ninja as highly exerting and most did not actually have >=8 of the 10 minutes in vigorous or even moderate exercise. Most participants rated Hot Squats higher for perceived exertion than they did the other games. Despite this, however, participants usually had the most minutes of moderate exercise when playing Holopoint. This is in line with the fact that participants found the muscle fatigue of the squats made them stop before their heart-rate became high. A set of models like this could drive a recommender.

ID	1	2	3	4	5	6	7	8	9	10	11	12	13	14	15	16	17	18
							Fruit Ninja											
Score	788	1415	1380	723	855	801	998	1180	851	744	1180	1413	871	603	1262	892	1213	941
Moderate	0:00	11:15	10:20	10:01	10:12	10:33	10:03	9:21	9:40	9:53	12:01	10:22	9:46	9:49	9:37	10:08	1:56	10:18
Vigorous	0:00	6:40	0:00	0:00	0:00	9:53	7:46	0:00	0:00	3:04	4:41	0:00	2:45	0:00	6:11	0:00	0:00	0:19
RPE	7	6	11	8	12	9	6	12	13	14	14	13	8	11	9	12	13	13
							Hot Squat											
Level	3	3	3	3	3	3	3	3	3	3	3	3	3	3	3	3	3	3
Moderate	3:33	7:37	9:43	8:54	7:34	10:05	2:45	7:45	9:54	4:49	5:39	3:03	10:03	6:09	6:00	4:21	9:06	10:15
Vigorous	0:00	6:31	5:03	0:57	0:00	8:59	1:18	0:00	8:28	1:16	2:46	0:00	7:08	1:27	4:31	0:29	2:17	6:39
RPE	14	15	18	12	13	17	20	15	18	16	18	19	17	17	16	18	17	16
							Holopoint											
Level	3	4	7	5	5	5	6	11	6	4	3	11	5	2	5	5	4	9
Moderate	5:30	11:15	10:27	9:52	10:50	11:41	10:13	9:24	8:42	9:57	10:16	9:42	10:12	9:51	9:55	7:42	10:01	10:25
Vigorous	0:00	7:40	0:00	2:06	1:08	8:07	7:46	1:56	0:19	6:43	5:42	0:58	0:48	1:56	7:51	0:00	3:55	8:19
RPE	8	13	12	8	14	9	10	14	14	12	17	16	13	13	11	14	15	15
							Portal Stories : VR											
Level	5	9	6	5	5	6	4	8	9	7	6	6	8	7	4	6	4	6
Moderate	0:00	10:37	8:33	8:03	0:00	9:07	10:10	0:00	9:58	10:19	9:50	0:00	10:01	10:11	11:14	0:00	0:00	11:13
Vigorous	0:00	0:00	0:00	0:00	0:00	0:00	0:00	0:00	0:00	0:00	0:00	0:00	0:00	0:00	0:00	0:00	0:00	0:00
RPE	6	6	11	6	7	6	6	6	9	6	7	7	6	8	6	6	8	6

Table 5: Participant game scores and heat mapped minutes of moderate and vigorous exercise (white: 0-1, light-blue: 2-7; dark-blue: 8-10). Borg RPE (white: <9; light-blue: 9-12; dark-blue: >=13

We now consider the key actual exertion components of the VRex model, E5 and E6, which represent the minutes of moderate and vigorous activity and the perceived exertion A3. Figure 2 shows these for Holopoint. We chose this because participants achieved considerable levels of activity in this game and they also seemed to enjoy it, reflected both in the scores and that we had to stop them. The x-axis shows the participants, sorted by the amount of vigorous activity measured (E6). The left axis shows the number of minutes of moderate (first blue bar in each set) and vigorous (red, third bar) exercise. So, for example, three participants (P1, 3 and 16) never reached the threshold for vigorous activity, at 70% of their maximum heart rate. At the other end of the scale, the last 5 participants (P2, 7, 15, 6 and 18) had over 7 vigorous activity minutes out of the 10 for the game, indicating considerable exertion, about half the daily recommended dose. The three participants who reported doing regular exercise, P1, 5 and 8 are all in the first half of the graph (at ranks 1, 7 and 8).

The right axis labels shows Borg RPE with individual scores in the green bar (in the middle of the moderate and vigorous minutes). It is important to gain understanding of the accuracy of this score since it would be valuable to know whether it is a good measure for people to provide for a recommender. If it correlates well with the proportion of game time in moderate or vigorous activity, it would be valuable. Equally, if the correlation is less strong, it may

be important to have actual exertion measures. We might have expected the Borg RPE to rise across the graph, along with minutes of vigorous activity, however this does not seem to be the case. Qualitatively, these results have some interesting cases. The lowest scores are for P1 and the left and P4 in the middle of the graph. The next lowest scoring group appear as 3 of the rightmost 4 participants. So the Borg RPE does not appear to reflect minutes of vigorous activity for individuals.

Overall, the heart-rate consistently correlated for the three active games, Fruit Ninja, Hot Squat and Holopoint but it was consistently lower for *Portal Stories: VR.*

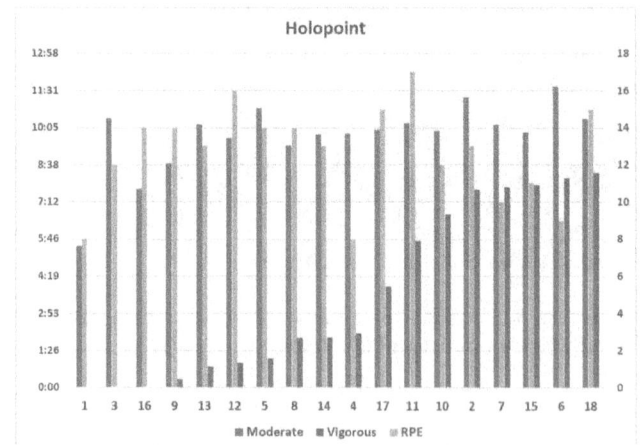

Figure 2: All 18 participants minutes of moderate+ (50+% of max minutes) and vigorous (70+% of max minutes) activity, and Borg perceived exertion (RPE) in Holopoint

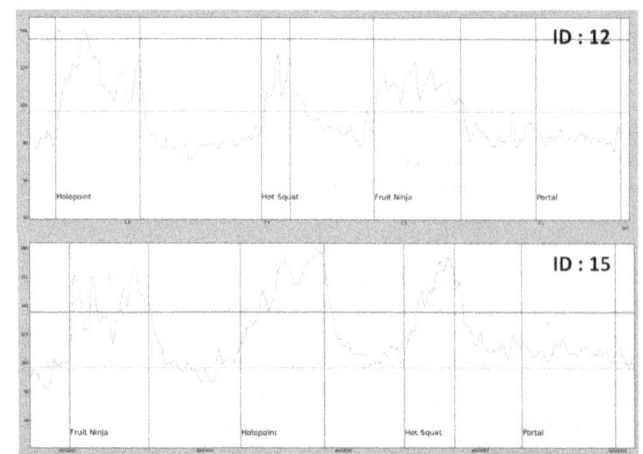

Figure 3: Moderate and Vigorous intensity exercise for P12 and 15, red horizontal line = vigorous and yellow line = moderate

Now we show examples of the heart-rate over the full 4 games and the breaks between them. Figure 3 shows this for two participants with very different profiles. These participants played the games in different orders. Participant 12 (top) had just a short time of vigorous activity, in Holopoint, and in most of the time in the active games, they reached moderate (50%) intensity. (This was not the case for the final *Portal stories: VR*). Participant 15, has a very different profile, with considerable vigorous activity time for all three games (Fruit Ninja, Holopoint, and Hot squat) and moderate for Portal stories: VR.

Table 6 illustrates the VRex Game Session Model Holopoint for the case of these two participants, P12 (left) and 15. We chose these participants as their ages are similar (26 and 25 respectively) so our calculations give a similar maximum heart-rate.

ID	Model Component	Participant 12	Participant 15
	Game summary		
S1	Game ID	Holopoint (12)	Holopoint (15)
S2	Score	Max wave:11, deaths:3	Max wave:5, deaths:5
S3	Session Start	20:34:20, 14/12/2016	15:57:00, 27/01/2017
S4	Session End	20:44:35, 14/12/2016	16:07:05, 27/01/2017
	User preferences		
A1	Game Preference	5	7
A2	Immersion Preference	6, 7, 7	7, 7, 7
A3	Perceived Exertion	13	11
A4	DOMS	Legs (✓)	Legs (✓✓✓)
	Actual exertion		
E1	HR-before	75 BPM	79 BPM
E2	HR-peak	143 BPM	183 BPM
E3	HR-2 min recovery	117 BPM	146 BPM
E4	Player's max HR	194 BPM	195 BPM
E5	Moderate activity time	9:42	9:55
E6	Vigorous activity time	0:58	7:51

Table 6: VRex model for P12 (left) and P15 (right)

For the "Game Summary" components of the Game Model, P12 appears to be a better player, as the S1 component shows they reached wave 11 with 3 deaths while participant 15 reached only wave 5 with 5 deaths. S3 and S4 shows similar session lengths, due to the 10 minute limit on games in our study design. Despite P12's high game performance, they rated the game as 5 for enjoyment (A1) and 6 for immersion, with compelling and proficient scores being maximum (A2). P15 rated A1 and A2 with maximum scores. In terms of perceived exertion (A3), P12 gave a moderate intensity rating of 13, while P15 rated it 11, which means that it was light intensity. The A4 measure here is clearly confounded by the fact that all players played 4 games; including it for all games reflects collecting a single score.

Now we consider the E1-6 measures. It turns out that both had similar initial heart-rate (E1) and their similar age gives them a

similar max level (E4). However, all the measures suggest that P12 is fitter than P15: P15's peak actual heart-rate was 183 (E2), far higher than P12's at 143; 2-minute recovery (E3) for P15 level was 146, while P12 was 117. In addition, while both players had at least moderate activity for most of the game (E5), P15 had almost 8 minutes at a vigorous level.

In light of this model, a recommender might offer different games to P12 and 15. For example, P12 might prefer a game that is more immersive, has more difficult gameplay than Holopoint, and provides more exertion. P15, on the other hand, seems to like Holopoint very much, even though they are not skilled at it. Longer term data may be needed, from subsequent sessions (if any) to assess whether such players will keep playing Holopoint.

6 DISCUSSION

We now assess the VRex model in terms of its design goals. We do this in terms of the questions posed in the introduction, explaining how our study indicates that the VRex model addresses them. In our work, we have demonstrated how to build the models, based on data from the user, the game itself and a heart-rate monitor. In the future, we envisage that these could be automatically captured and delivered to a long term user model. This could be done by suitable augmentation of the hardware and game software. Since the HMD can utilise head-phones to deliver the audio, these could be altered to capture in-ear pulse measures, as in the Bragi-dash[3], which uses oximeter sensors. The game software could send information about game performance, such as the player's score, how many retries, or the time it took to complete a level. Even the elicited measures, such as the Borg rating, could be incorporated in the game. After the game, we could also elicit this and the post-game DOMS measure using message-based queries with tools like Telegram[4] or Slack chat-bot[5].

Recommending VR games for their exertion as well as game preferences.

A collaborative recommender for VR games would require people to release parts of their VRex session model. Our rich and detailed models could support content-based recommenders that could explain their recommendations in terms of the components of the model. Our results suggest that the Borg measures may be of limited use if actual exertion is what is important to people. We return to the questions.

- Which games will give me a good cardio workout? Recommendations should draw on the exertion levels combined with game play time and overall game rating since length of play as well as exertion level are both important.
- Which will work particular muscle groups eg arms? Games could be described in terms of the muscle groups involved and the VRex model could combine this with the elicited DOMS rating to advise users about the games that can help them build muscles they want to target.
- Which will give me a good game experience? This requires the elicited measures. Suitable game design could make

³ https://www.bragi.com/thedash/
⁴ https://www.telegram.org
⁵ https://www.slack.com

it easy to report these at the end of the game (or even at major stages, such as going to a new level).

In-game personalization

There are potential benefits from using the VRex model to drive personalization that answers our questions:

- How hard is the user working right now, compared with their own goal targets (and medical knowledge and advice)?
- Should the game be changed now to make the user work harder, use different muscles, or cut back, and even stop?
- Should the game provide the user with feedback on their exertion, and if so, how to time this and present it to avoid it being ignored or causing distraction from the VR game?

To make games adaptive the VRex model needs to be available in a long term model that different games can access. In addition, it is important that the player can keep track of their progress on the fly so they can determine whether they should push themselves harder. However, the information needs to be presented in a way that suits their preferences. For example, if a player prefers a game that is not very realistic, which can be determined by their game and immersion preference, then it may be acceptable to display information within their view in the form of a HUD. Another aspect to consider is if the player is performing vigorous activity, it may be difficult to gain their attention; it may be better to use visual indicators over text, such as slowly fading in a red tint, indicating they are close to over-exertion.

Exertion and activity OLM

Over the long term, the VRex model can help us answer questions such as: how much does a particular VR game contribute to my long term fitness goals; how much does my VR gaming session contribute to my overall exercise. Figure 4 illustrates this potential

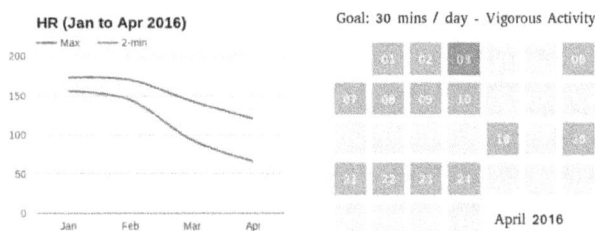

Figure 4: Mockup of long-term views of the VRex model. Left is max and 2-min HR from playing Holopoint over 4 months. Right is a calendar where green indicates meeting their target 30 minutes of vigorous activity.

in a mockup of parts of a hypothetical user's VRrex long term model (left) from Jan to Apr 2016 and meeting their target for vigorous activity minutes (right) in Apr 2016. This hypothetical user had 2 goals: improve HR and to achieve 30 minutes of vigorous activity per day. In this example, the left figure shows that the user's max HR dropped over the 4 months and the 2-min HR has dropped

even more. This suggests that the user not working as hard but is recovering faster after each game. The right figure shows a calendar view, with green for 14 days the model recorded data indicating they met their target of 30 minutes of vigorous activity a day, during the month of April in 2016. This allows users to see when and how often they reach their goal over time.

7 CONCLUSIONS

This work was motivated by the potential for VR games to be both fun and good exercise. Our particular goal is to harness data as people play VR games so that we can build a user model which could serve three main roles: recommending games; personalising the game and exercise experience; and enabling people to track their exercise within VR games. We have described how we designed the VRex model to meet these goals. We then presented a user study which was designed to capture the data to build the game session part of VRex models. Our results demonstrate the richness of the models and the very different game and exercise experiences of our participants. This points to the need for personalization that accounts for both people's fitness and how much they like games. The current work was limited to game play in a single block of somewhat over 1 hour. This is a promising foundation for future work that explores long term user modelling.

ACKNOWLEDGMENTS

Special thanks to the School of Psychology at the University of Sydney and Australian Department of Defense for lending us the HTC Vive.

REFERENCES

[1] Debjanee Barua, Judy Kay, Bob Kummerfeld, and Cécile Paris. 2014. Modelling long term goals. In *International Conference on User Modeling, Adaptation, and Personalization*. Springer, 1–12.
[2] John Bolton, Denis Lirette, Mike Lambert, and Ben Unsworth. 2014. PaperDude : A Virtual Reality Cycling Exergame. *CHI '14 Extended Abstracts on Human Factors in Computing Systems* (2014), 475–478. DOI:http://dx.doi.org/10.1145/2559206.2574827
[3] Gunnar Borg. 1982. Psychophysical bases of perceived exertion. (1982).
[4] Gunnar Borg. 1998. Borg ffis perceived exertion and pain scales. *Human Kinetics* July 1998 (1998), 104 vii.
[5] Carl J Caspersen, Kenneth E Powell, and Gregory M Christenson. 1985. Physical activity, exercise, and physical fitness: definitions and distinctions for health-related research. *Public health reports* 100, 2 (1985), 126.
[6] BetterHealth Channel. 2017. Exercise Intensity. (2017). https://www.betterhealth.vic.gov.au/health/healthyliving/exercise-intensity
[7] Christopher R Cole, JoAnne M Foody, Eugene H Blackstone, and Michael S Lauer. 2000. Heart rate recovery after submaximal exercise testing as a predictor of mortality in a cardiovascularly healthy cohort. *Annals of internal medicine* 132, 7 (2000), 552–555.
[8] Gaston Godin, RJ Shephard, and others. 1985. A simple method to assess exercise behavior in the community. *Can J Appl Sport Sci* 10, 3 (1985), 141–146.
[9] Kristoffer Hagen. 2016. Gameplay as Exercise Designing an Engaging Multiplayer Biking Exergame. (2016), 1872–1878.
[10] Sandro Hardy, Stefan Göbel, Michael Gutjahr, Josef Wiemeyer, and Ralf Steinmetz. 2011. Adaptation Model for Indoor Exergames. September (2011), 1–13.
[11] William L. Haskell, I. Min Lee, Russell R. Pate, Kenneth E. Powell, Steven N. Blair, Barry A. Franklin, Caroline A. Macera, Gregory W. Heath, Paul D. Thompson, and Adrian Bauman. 2007. Physical activity and public health: Updated recommendation for adults from the American College of Sports Medicine and the American Heart Association. *Circulation* 116, 9 (2007), 1081–1093. DOI:http://dx.doi.org/10.1161/CIRCULATIONAHA.107.185649
[12] Han-Chung Huang, May-Kuen Wong, Ju Lu, Wei-Fan Huang, and Ching-I Teng. 2017. Can using exergames improve physical fitness? A 12-week randomized controlled trial. *Computers in Human Behavior* 70 (2017), 310–316. DOI:http://dx.doi.org/10.1016/j.chb.2016.12.086

[13] Magnus Thorsten Jensen, Poul Suadicani, Hans Ole Hein, and Finn Gyntelberg. 2013. Elevated resting heart rate, physical fitness and all-cause mortality: a 16-year follow-up in the Copenhagen Male Study. *Heart* 99, 12 (2013), 882–887.

[14] Juha Karvonen and Timo Vuorimaa. 1988. Heart Rate and Exercise Intensity During Sports Activities. *Sports Medicine* 5, 5 (1988), 303–311. DOI:http://dx.doi.org/10.2165/00007256-198805050-00002

[15] Matthew J. Klein and Christina S. Simmers. 2009. Exergaming: virtual inspiration, real perspiration. *Young Consumers: Insight and Ideas for Responsible Marketers* 10, 1 (2009), 35–45. DOI:http://dx.doi.org/10.1108/17473610910940774

[16] Stephanie Lee. 2016. How Long You Should Rest Between Sets for the Biggest Training Benefits. (2016). http://vitals.lifehacker.com/how-long-you-should-rest-between-sets-for-the-biggest-t-1782785683

[17] Steven R. McClaran. 2003. The effectiveness of personal training on changing attitudes towards physical activity. *Journal of Sports Science and Medicine* 2, 1 (2003), 10–14. DOI:http://dx.doi.org/10.1097/00005768-200105001-01188

[18] A Mesquita, M Trabulo, M Mendes, JF Viana, and R Seabra-Gomes. 1996. The maximum heart rate in the exercise test: the 220-age formula or Sheffield's table? *Revista portuguesa de cardiologia: orgao oficial da Sociedade Portuguesa de Cardiologia= Portuguese journal of cardiology: an official journal of the Portuguese Society of Cardiology* 15, 2 (1996), 139–44.

[19] B. M. Nes, I. Janszky, U. Wisløff, A. Støylen, and T. Karlsen. 2013. Age-predicted maximal heart rate in healthy subjects: The HUNT Fitness Study. *Scandinavian Journal of Medicine and Science in Sports* 23, 6 (2013), 697–704. DOI:http://dx.doi.org/10.1111/j.1600-0838.2012.01445.x

[20] J Adam Noah, David K Spierer, Atsumichi Tachibana, and Shaw Bronner. 2011. Vigorous energy expenditure with a dance exer-game. *J Exerc Physiol Online* 14, 4 (2011), 13–28.

[21] Harm op den Akker, Valerie M Jones, and Hermie J Hermens. 2014. Tailoring real-time physical activity coaching systems: a literature survey and model. *User modeling and user-adapted interaction* 24, 5 (2014), 351–392.

[22] Rita Orji, Julita Vassileva, and Regan L Mandryk. 2014. Modeling the efficacy of persuasive strategies for different gamer types in serious games for health. *User Modeling and User-Adapted Interaction* 24, 5 (2014), 453–498.

[23] Sergej M Ostojic, Marko D Stojanovic, and Julio Calleja-Gonzalez. 2011. Ultra short-term heart rate recovery after maximal exercise: relations to aerobic power in sportsmen. *Chin J Physiol* 54, 2 (2011), 105–110.

[24] Russell R Pate, Michael Pratt, Steven N Blair, William L Haskell, Caroline A Macera, Claude Bouchard, David Buchner, Walter Ettinger, Gregory W Heath, Abby C King, and others. 1995. Physical activity and public health: a recommendation from the Centers for Disease Control and Prevention and the American College of Sports Medicine. *Jama* 273, 5 (1995), 402–407.

[25] Lindsay Alexander Shaw, Burkhard Claus Wunsche, Christof Lutteroth, Stefan Marks, Jude Buckley, and Paul Corballis. 2015. Development and Evaluation of an Exercycle Game Using Immersive Technologies. *8th Australasian Workshop on Health Informatics and Knowledge Management (HIKM 2015)* January (2015), 27–30.

[26] Jeff Sinclair, Philip Hingston, and Martin Masek. 2007. Considerations for the design of exergames. In *Proceedings of the 5th international conference on Computer graphics and interactive techniques in Australia and Southeast Asia*. ACM, 289–295.

[27] Scott J Strath, Leonard A Kaminsky, Barbara E Ainsworth, Ulf Ekelund, Patty S Freedson, Rebecca A Gary, Caroline R Richardson, Derek T Smith, Ann M Swartz, and others. 2013. Guide to the assessment of physical activity: clinical and research applications. *Circulation* 128, 20 (2013), 2259–2279.

[28] Alasdair G. Thin and Nicola Poole. 2010. *Dance-Based ExerGaming: User Experience Design Implications for Maximizing Health Benefits Based on Exercise Intensity and Perceived Enjoyment.* Springer Berlin Heidelberg, Berlin, Heidelberg, 189–199. DOI:http://dx.doi.org/10.1007/978-3-642-14484-4_16

[29] Bob G Witmer and Michael J Singer. 1998. Measuring Presence in Virtual Environments: A Presence Questionnaire. *Presence: Teleoper. Virtual Environ.* 7, 3 (1998), 225–240. DOI:http://dx.doi.org/10.1162/105474698565686

[30] Soojeong Yoo. 2016. VRun : Running-in-place virtual reality exergame. (2016), 1–5. DOI:http://dx.doi.org/10.1145/3010915.3010987

[31] Soojeong Yoo, Christopher Ackad, Tristan Heywood, and Judy Kay. 2017. Evaluating the Actual and Perceived Exertion Provided by Virtual Reality Games. In *Proceedings of the 2017 CHI Conference Extended Abstracts on Human Factors in Computing Systems*. ACM, 3050–3057.

Get to the Bottom: Causal Analysis for User Modeling

Shi Zong
The Ohio State University
Columbus, OH, USA
zong.56@osu.edu

Branislav Kveton
Adobe Research
San Jose, CA, USA
kveton@adobe.com

Shlomo Berkovsky
CSIRO
Eveleigh, NSW, Australia
Shlomo.Berkovsky@csiro.au

Azin Ashkan*
Google Inc.
Mountain View, CA, USA
azin@google.com

Zheng Wen
Adobe Research
San Jose, CA, USA
zwen@adobe.com

ABSTRACT

Weather affects our mood and behavior, and through them, many aspects of our life. When it is sunny, people become happier and smile, but when it rains, some get depressed. Despite this evidence and the abundance of weather data, weather has mostly been overlooked in the machine learning and data science research. This work shows how causal analysis can be applied to discover the effects of weather on TV watching patterns and how it can be applied for user modeling. We make several contributions. First, we show that some weather attributes, e.g., pressure and precipitation, cause significant changes in TV watching patterns. Second, we compare the results obtained for different levels of user granularity and different types of users. This showcases that causal analysis can be a valuable tool in user modeling. To the best of our knowledge, this is the first large-scale causal study of the impact of weather on TV watching patterns.

KEYWORDS

Weather; Causal Analysis; User Modeling

1 INTRODUCTION

Weather affects our mood and, thus, human behavior. One of the pronounced examples is the *seasonal affective disorder* – prolonged lack of sunlight that can potentially depress people [21]. Although indirectly, weather affects various aspects of our lives, including our work and study, purchasing behavior, and more. For example, Hirshleifer [8] and Saunders [26] found that stock returns on cloudy days are lower than on sunny days. Similarly, Murray *et al.* [19] and Parsons [20] discovered strong effects of sunlight on consumer expenditure. Social research also linked weather conditions to crime [7] and even to suicide rates [3].

In this work, we extend our early work [29] and set out to thoroughly examine the effects of weather on the TV watching activity.

---

*Work done while at Technicolor Research.

UMAP'17, July 9–12, 2017, Bratislava, Slovakia
© 2017 ACM. 978-1-4503-4635-1/17/07...$15.00
DOI: http://dx.doi.org/10.1145/3079628.3079688

It is reasonable to assume that the overall TV watching levels are weather dependent, e.g., people watch more TV when it rains, and this has been partially shown by Barnett *et al.* [4] and Roe and Vandebosch [23]. However, our main goal is to further assess the effect of weather on the TV watching patterns. That is, we are rather interested to explore whether people watch *different genres* of programs in different weather conditions.

We posit that this knowledge can have several important implications. First, marketers may be willing to adjust the content and ratio of the advertisements to the target audience to whom they will be exposed [10]. Second, the technical configuration of the communication network, e.g., replica placement on content-delivery network servers, may be tuned to facilitate a more efficient content delivery [9]. Third, TV content and video-on-demand service providers may benefit from this knowledge and adapt their recommendations accordingly [28].

Several prior works incorporated weather into personalized systems [1, 2, 5]. We would like to stress three limitations of these works. First, the weather was treated as an auxiliary *contextual* dimension rather than a parameter that directly impacts user behavior. Second, relatively simple correlation-based methods were applied to discover the impact of weather on user behavior. Third, prior works used only small-scale datasets collected exclusively for research purposes. In fact, the largest weather-related dataset, previously used in personalization research, contains fewer than 5k ratings [5]. We believe that it is pivotal to thoroughly examine the factors affecting user behavior, as these are likely to improve the quality of the personalization. We also believe that causal analysis and large-scale data are the necessary tools for such an examination; these may uncover hidden biases in real-world problems.

To this end, we advocate in this work the use of causal analysis for modeling the impact of weather on observable TV watching behavior. To the best of our knowledge, this is the first work to apply causal analysis to a nation-scale dataset containing more than *10M watching events* of more than *0.6M users*. We propose and apply an efficient technique for learning the causal dependencies between weather conditions and the users' TV watching behavior patterns. We also discuss about the motivation for applying causal analysis. Hence, the main contribution of our work lies in demonstrating and validating the application of causal analysis for the purposes of modeling dependencies in user behavior.

2 MATCHING FOR CAUSALITY

The problem of estimating causal effects from observational data, such as changes due to weather conditions, is central to many disciplines [18, 22, 27]. It can be formalized as follows. Let $\{1, \ldots, n\}$ be a set of n units i, such as individuals. Let $T_i \in \{0, 1\}$ indicate the treatment of unit i. That is, $T_i = 0$ if unit i is *control* and $T_i = 1$ if the unit is *treated*. Then unit i has two *potential outcomes*, $Y_i(1)$ if the unit is treated and $Y_i(0)$ otherwise. The unit-level causal effect of the treatment is the difference in potential outcomes

$$\tau_i = Y_i(1) - Y_i(0),$$

and the *average treatment effect on treated (ATT)* is

$$\mathbb{E}_{i:T_i=1}[\tau_i] = \mathbb{E}_{i:T_i=1}[Y_i(1)] - \mathbb{E}_{i:T_i=1}[Y_i(0)],$$

where $\mathbb{E}_{i:T_i=1}[Y_i(1)]$ is the expected outcome of treatment on treated units and $\mathbb{E}_{i:T_i=1}[Y_i(0)]$ is the expected outcome of not being treated on treated units. Note that $\mathbb{E}_{i:T_i=1}[\tau_i]$ cannot be directly computed, because $Y_i(0)$ is unobserved in treated units $\{i : T_i = 1\}$.

Since the assignment to treatment and control groups is usually not random, the expected outcome of not being treated on control units, $\mathbb{E}_{i:T_i=0}[Y_i(0)]$, is a poor estimate of the expected outcome of not being treated on treated units, $\mathbb{E}_{i:T_i=1}[Y_i(0)]$. The key challenge in causal analysis is to eliminate the resulting imbalance between the distributions of treated and control units. A popular approach of balancing the two distributions is the *nearest-neighbor matching (NNM)* [6, 13, 16, 24]. In this work, we match each treated unit to its nearest control unit based on its covariates, and then the response of the matched unit serves as a *counterfactual* for the treated unit. In particular, the ATT is estimated as

$$\text{ATT} \approx \frac{1}{n_T} \sum_{i:T_i=1} \left(Y_i(1) - Y_{\pi(i)}(0) \right), \qquad (1)$$

where $n_T = \sum_{i=1}^{n} T_i$ is the number of treated units, $Y_i(1)$ is the observed response of treated unit i, and $Y_{\pi(i)}(0)$ is the observed response of the *matched* control unit $\pi(i)$. The *covariate* of unit i, which is essentially a d-dimensional feature vector $\mathbf{x}_i \in \mathbb{R}^d$, should be chosen such that the potential outcomes of unit i are statistically independent of T_i given $\mathbf{x}_i$. In this case, the estimate in Eq. (1) resembles that of a randomized experiment.

3 CAUSAL EFFECTS OF WEATHER ON TV CONTENT

In this section, we discuss how to apply the NNM framework from Section 2 to analyze the causal effects of weather on TV watching. We illustrate the methodology with an example query "*does high temperature cause watching more drama?*". In Section 3.1, we introduce the notions of treatment, control, and potential outcomes. We justify our choice of covariates in Section 3.2 and explain our NNM method in Section 3.3.

3.1 Treatment, Control, and Outcomes

Our *units* (events of interest) are TV watching events i; and we are interested in estimating the causal effect of weather on these events. The *treatment* T_i is an indicator of the treatment weather at event i, such as that the temperature is high. We denote the *potential outcomes* at event i under control and treatment by $Y_i(0)$ and $Y_i(1)$,

respectively. The potential outcomes are indicators of the watched content under control and treatment. For instance, in our example query, the treatment and potential outcomes are

$$T_i = \mathbb{1}\{\text{temperature is high at event } i\},$$

$$Y_i(0) = \mathbb{1}\{\text{drama watched at event } i \text{ if the temperature is low}\},$$

$$Y_i(1) = \mathbb{1}\{\text{drama watched at event } i \text{ if the temperature is high}\}.$$

We discuss how to determine high and low temperatures in Section 5.1.

We measure the *effect* of treatments by the ATT in Eq. (1). In our domain, the ATT is the expected increase in the frequency of watching some content due to the treatment weather, such as the expected increase in the frequency of watching drama due to high temperature. If the ATT is significantly above zero, we claim that high temperature *increases* the frequency of watching drama. If the ATT is significantly below zero, we claim that high temperature *decreases* the frequency of watching drama. Finally, if the ATT is near zero, we claim that high temperature has *no effect* on watching drama. We provide a detailed discussion about how to measure the significance of effects in Section 5.2.

3.2 Covariates and Ignorability

A key step in causal analysis is to break the dependence between potential outcomes and treatments, in order to mimic a randomized experiment. This can be done under the assumption of *unconfoundness* or *ignorability* [22, 25]. The ignorability assumption says that the potential outcomes are statistically independent of the treatment given the covariates. In particular,

$$(Y_i(0), Y_i(1)) \perp T_i \mid \mathbf{x}_i$$

for any TV watching event i, where $\mathbf{x}_i \in \mathbb{R}^d$ are the covariates of event i. In this paper, the covariates are the profile of the user at event i, the location of event i, and the time of event i. The profile is the distribution over watched TV genres of the user (see Section 5.1), which clearly affects $(Y_i(0), Y_i(1))$. The time affects the availability of content. For instance, as shown in Fig. 1, the frequency of watching TV genres can change dramatically over time. Finally, both the time and location are good predictors of the weather, which is the treatment.

Our ignorability assumption says that what the user would have watched under different weather conditions at event i, $(Y_i(0), Y_i(1))$, depends on the profile of the user at event i, the location of event i, and the time of event i; but does not depend on treatment T_i. For example, the fact that the temperature is high should not correlate with what the user would have watched under high and low temperatures. The ignorability assumption is hard to validate in practice [25], but we believe that our choice of covariates renders it reasonable in our setting. Properly chosen covariates reduce, if not entirely eliminate, the dependence between potential outcomes and the treatment. Then the observed effect is likely due to the causation through the treatment.

We illustrate our ignorability assumption on an example. Consider a family where the parents like to watch drama. When the temperature is high, the children play outside and the parents watch drama. When the temperature is low, the children are at home and the whole family watches family movies. In this case, the potential

---

Algorithm 1 Large-scale matching of treatment and control events using random partitioning.

1: // Random partitioning
2: Partition covariates $\{x_i\}_{i=1}^n$ into k random clusters $\{C_\ell\}_{\ell=1}^k$ such that $n/k \leq |C_\ell| \leq n/k + 1$ for all $\ell \in [k]$
3:
4: // Matching
5: **for all** $\ell = 1, \ldots, k$ **do**
6:     **while** $|C_\ell \cap \{i : T_i = 1\}| > 0$ **do**
7:         Choose a random treated event i from
8:             $C_\ell \cap \{i : T_i = 1\}$
9:         Find the nearest control event j to event i in
10:            $C_\ell \cap \{i : T_i = 0\}$
11:        Match the events i and j, $\pi(i) \leftarrow j$
12:        Remove the events from $C_\ell, C_\ell \leftarrow C_\ell \setminus \{i, j\}$
13:    **end while**
14: **end for**

---

outcomes are determined solely by the profile of the family. In particular, they are determined independently of whether event i is treated or not, implying that the family subconsciously decides on what to watch when the temperature is high or low before either of these happens. Th erefore, the potential outcomes are statistically independent of the instance of the weather at event i and our ignorability assumption holds.

3.3 Efficient Matching via Clustering

The number of TV watching events can be large, on the order of millions. Naive implementations of NNM from Section 2 are impractical in this setting because their running time is $O(n^2)$. In our work, we propose a computationally-efficient variant of NNM based on the idea of *quantization* [11].

Our algorithm for NNM is presented in Algorithm 1. Th e algorithm has two main stages. First, we randomly partition all covariates into k clusters $\{C_\ell\}_{\ell=1}^k$. Second, we match randomly chosen treated events in each cluster C_ℓ to their nearest control events in that cluster, until no treated events are left. We choose treated events randomly to avoid biases in the matching due to a particular order. Th e clusters are also chosen randomly. When the number of events n is large and the number of clusters is reasonably small, we expect the distribution of the covariates in each cluster to closely resemble that of $\{x_i\}_{i=1}^n$, and therefore NNM on the clusters should be similar to that on $\{x_i\}_{i=1}^n$.

Our matching algorithm is surprisingly simple, effective, and its computational cost is only $O\left(k(n/k)^2\right) = O\left(n^2/k\right)$. Th e number of clusters k can be used to trade off the computational complexity of NNM for its quality. When k is chosen appropriately, such as $k = \sqrt{n}$, the computation cost is $O\left(n^{3/2}\right)$. In our experiments, $n \approx 10^7$ and we choose $k = 200$. Th is allows us to fi nd nearest neighbors for millions of treated events in less than an hour, on a computer with 16 GB main memory and 2.5 GHz Intel Core i7 processor. We experimented with other values of k and our causal findings are not sensitive to the choice of k, only the computational cost of the matching is. We investigate the quality of the proposed algorithm in Section 5.

4 DATASET

In this work, we used a dataset gathered by a leading Australian national TV broadcaster. Th e broadcaster offers two services: live broadcast, and a catch-up TV service available through a Web-based portal, which allows users to watch on-demand any program that they may have missed. We obtained the complete Australia-wide portal logs for a period of 26 weeks, from February to September, 2012. Th e original dataset includes more than 21.4M viewing events of about 1.3M unique users, who collectively watched more than 11k unique programs. We randomly choose 50% of these users and conduct all experiments on this set of users.

Each viewing event is represented by the user's IP address, viewing date (with no time stamp), and program ID. We use the IP addresses of the users as their unique identifiers, since little user information is available[1]. In addition to the program ID, program meta-data contains its title, duration, publication date, and a single genre tag from 14 genres (see Table 1). Th ese genre tags are labeled by the broadcaster. No information about the watched portion of the program is available. A more detailed description of the dataset can be found in Xu *et al.* [28].

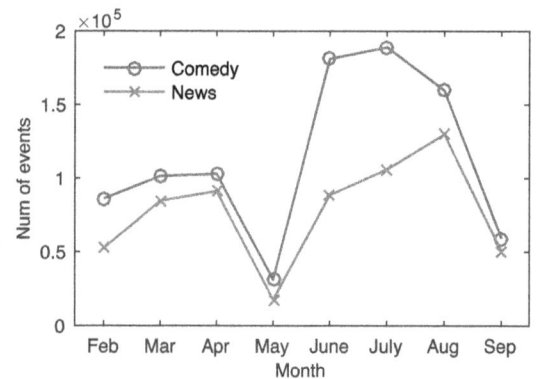

Figure 1: Number of events for *Comedy* and *News* over months in our dataset.

Table 1 shows the distribution of viewing events across TV genres. Not surprisingly, some genres are more popular than others. We also observe in Fig. 1 that the relative frequency of TV genres changes over time[2]. In April, the number of watched *Comedies* is almost the same as that of *News*. In June, the number of *Comedies* is twice as high as that of *News*. Th ese imbalances provide us with an opportunity to analyze what factors lead to the changes of users' watching behavior.

To collect the required weather data, we used the IP2Location[3] API to convert the IP addresses into the geographic locations of the users: longitude, latitude, city, and state. Given the locations and the dates of the viewing events, we used the WorldWeatherOnline[4] API to obtain the weather logs for the dates of the events.

---

[1] Such identifiers may be noisy, as multiple users (e.g., household members) may share the same IP and one user (e.g., at home and at work) may have multiple IPs. However, these are real data gathered by the broadcaster.
[2] The drop in May is due to a technical problem that caused some data loss.
[3] http://www.ip2location.com
[4] http://www.worldweatheronline.com

Weather conditions in Australia change quite dramatically across different geographic locations.Th e weather inland is hotter and drier than along the coast.Th e northern regions that are closer to the equator are warmer than the southern ones. To get a better idea of how the weather in Australia looks like, we anecdotally map weather conditions in Australia to other locations all over the world. We observe that the weather in the inner part of Australia is comparable to Sahara and Sonora deserts.Th e weather in the regions near the coast is similar to Southern California, San Francisco Bay Area, and Florida in the United States. We describe weather conditions by *weather attributes*.Th e weather attributes are eight numerical features extracted from weather logs that characterize different aspects of weather, such as *Temperature*, *Pressure*, and *Humidity* (see Table 1).

5 CAUSAL MODELING OF WEATHER EFFECT

Causal analysis is important for user modeling, as it can help determine factors that drive changes in user behavior. Liang *et al.* [17] showed that the idea of causal analysis can be used to model user exposure in recommender systems. In this section, we estimate the effect of weather on users' TV watching behavior by conducting causal analysis of weather attributes from Section 4. In Section 5.1, we describe our experimental setup. In Section 5.2, we analyze the average causal effects on the data of the whole of Australia. In Section 5.3, we conduct causal analysis at the level of individual users; and in Section 5.4, we conduct causal analysis on two groups of users. Finally, in Section 5.5, we showcase the necessity for causal inference.

5.1 Experimental Setup

We define one treatment variable for each weather attribute in Table 1.Th erefore, we have 8 weather-attribute treatments. In each attribute, we treat the events in the tail of the distribution of that attribute. Specifically, if the tail of the distribution is on the low (high) end of the range, we consider the 20% of the events with the lowest (highest) values of the attribute as the treatment group and the rest as the control group (see Fig. 2). We denote these high-value and low-value treatment groups by "H" and "L", respectively.The position of the tail is estimated automatically from the skewness of the distribution. We list all treatments in Table 1.

The events in the tail of the distribution are extreme by definition, and therefore they are a natural candidate for being chosen as treatments. We choose the 20% cutoffs separately for each month, as the boundaries of the "high" and "low" weather attribute values change over time, e.g., summer vs. winter temperature.Th e 20% cutoff is chosen such that the number of treated events is reasonably large. We experimented with cutoffs of 15% and 25%, and the results were similar to those of the chosen 20% cutoff.

We define a pair of potential outcomes $(Y_i(0), Y_i(1))$ for each TV genre in Table 1.Th erefore, we estimate 14 effects. In this setting, the ATT in Eq. (1) is the expected change in the frequency of watching a given TV genre due to being treated. For example, consider the effect of *high temperature* weather on watching *Dramas* that was discussed in Section 3.1. Note that we estimate the effect on TV program genres, rather than on individual TV programs, as many programs may not have enough treated events to allow

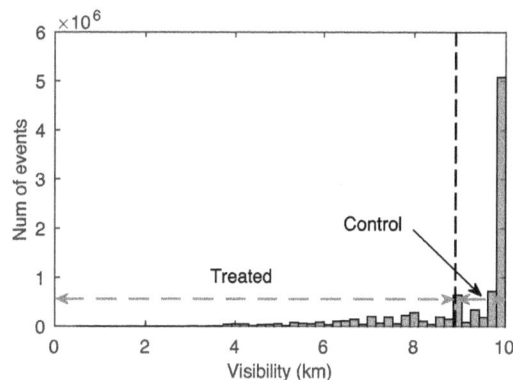

Figure 2:Th e treatment and control groups for weather attribute *Visibility*.Th e treated events are 20% of all events with lowest visibility.Th e control events are the remaining 80% of all events.

accurate causal analysis.Th erefore, we experiment with a higher genre-level of content granularity.

Finally, as discussed in Section 3.2, the covariates of a watching event i are the profile of the user at i, the time of i, and the location of i. In this paper, the user profile is a vector of the frequency of watching TV genres.Th is profile is a 14-dimensional vector $(m_{u,1}/m_u, \ldots, m_{u,14}/m_u)$, where $m_{u,y}$ is the number of events where user u watches genre y and $m_u = \sum_{i=1}^{14} m_{u,i}$ is the total number of events of u. Such a profile naturally captures high-level preferences of the user[5].

5.2 Causal Analysis on the Population of Whole Australia

In ourfi rst experiment, we conduct causal analysis on the whole population of Australia.Th at is, for every treatment j and genre y in Table 1, we match all treated events to control events by Algorithm 1 and then estimate the ATT in Eq. (1). We denote the resulting ATT by $\text{ATT}_{j,y}$ and refer to it as the *empirical effect of treatment j on genre y*.

Note that $\text{ATT}_{j,y}$ is random, because the matching π computed by Algorithm 1 is random.Th us, we need to be careful when we evaluate the estimated effect. Consider the following example. Suppose that only one event is treated, where the user does not watch drama; and that this event is randomly matched to another event, where the user watches drama.Th en it may seem that the treatment leads to watching no drama. While this may be true, it is unlikely because this effect is estimated from only one matched pair of treated and control events. Below we propose a variant of $\text{ATT}_{j,y}$ that allows us to eliminate statistically insignificant effects.

---

[5]We also experimented with another type of a user profile, which was estimated using SVD from the watched TV programs.Th is profile is inspired by the low-dimensional representation of latent user profiles in matrix factorization [14]. We observe similar patterns to those in this paper, and therefore do not report them.

Category	Frequency	Category	Frequency
Drama	19.51%	Pre-school	19.31%
Children	17.01%	Comedy	11.37%
Docs	10.61%	Lifestyle	8.06%
Panel	5.95%	News	4.10%
Arts	2.69%	Education	0.58%
Kids	0.50%	Sport	0.24%
Indigenous	0.05%	Shop	0.02%

TV genres.

Weather attribute	Treated
Temperature	High
Feels-like temperature	High
Wind speed	High
Cloud cover	High
Pressure	Low
Humidity	Low
Visibility	Low
Precipitation	High

Weather attributes and their treated values.

Table 1: TV genres and weather attributes as described in Section 4.

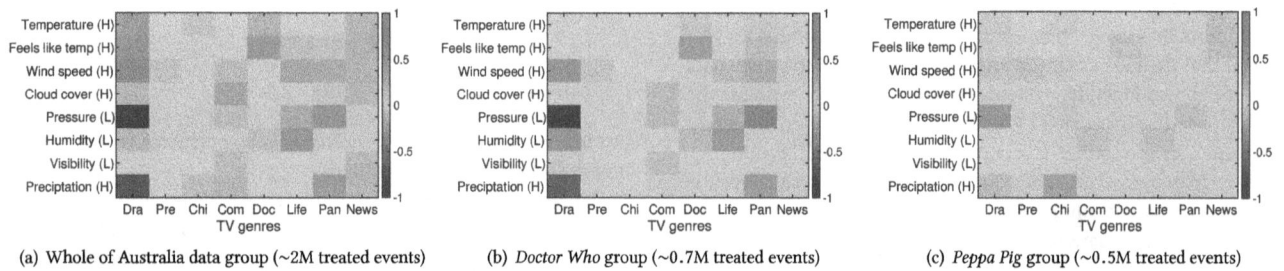

(a) Whole of Australia data group (~2M treated events)   (b) *Doctor Who* group (~0.7M treated events)   (c) *Peppa Pig* group (~0.5M treated events)

Figure 3: High-probability effects $\widetilde{\text{ATT}}_{j,y}$ in 8 most popular genres due to 8 weather-attribute treatments for: (a) whole of Australia, (b) users who watched *Doctor Who*, and (c) users who watched *Peppa Pig*. Th e effects are multiplied by 100 and can be interpreted as changes in the percentage of watching TV genres. "H" and "L" denote high and low value treatments in Table 1.

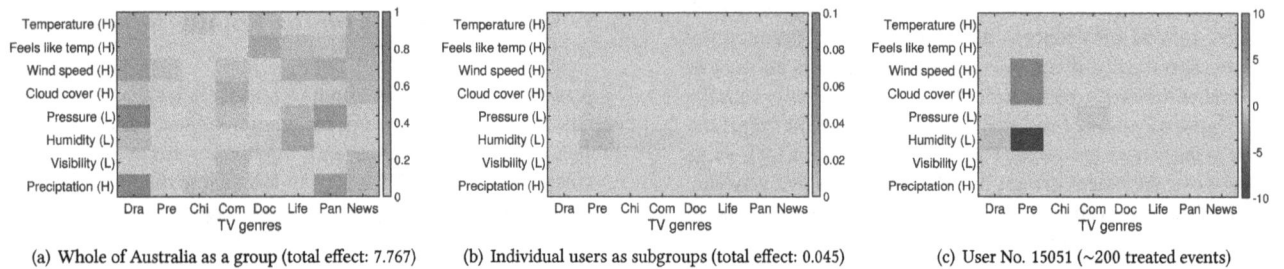

(a) Whole of Australia as a group (total effect: 7.767)   (b) Individual users as subgroups (total effect: 0.045)   (c) User No. 15051 (~200 treated events)

Figure 4: (a, b) Effects in context G, $\widetilde{\text{ATT}}_{j,y}^{G}$, when G is the whole population of Australia and individual users, respectively. (c) High-probability effects $\widetilde{\text{ATT}}_{j,y}$ for user No. 15051. Th e effects are multiplied by 100 and can be interpreted as changes in the percentage of watching TV genres.

To eliminate statistically insignificant effects, we propose *high-probability effect of treatment j on genre y*,

$$\widetilde{\text{ATT}}_{j,y} = \begin{cases} \max\{\text{ATT}_{j,y} - c \cdot \text{se}_{j,y}, 0\}, & \text{ATT}_{j,y} > 0; \\ \min\{\text{ATT}_{j,y} + c \cdot \text{se}_{j,y}, 0\}, & \text{ATT}_{j,y} < 0, \end{cases} \quad (2)$$

where $\text{se}_{j,y}$ is the standard error in the estimate of $\text{ATT}_{j,y}$, and $c > 0$ is a tunable parameter that controls the degree of confidence. This metric can be justified as follows. If the estimated effect is

positive, $\text{ATT}_{j,y} > 0$, and significant in the sense that it is larger than c times the standard error, then this effect should be reported as $\widetilde{\text{ATT}}_{j,y} > 0$. Similarly, if the estimated effect is negative, $\text{ATT}_{j,y} < 0$, and significant in the sense that it is smaller than c times the standard error, then this effect should be reported as $\widetilde{\text{ATT}}_{j,y} < 0$. In all other case, $\widetilde{\text{ATT}}_{j,y} = 0$ and the effect is not significant.

In our experiment, we choose $c = 4$. From the central limit theorem, $\text{ATT}_{j,y}$ is close to normally distributed when the number

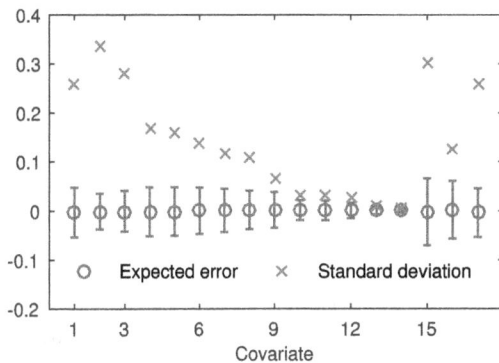

Figure 5: Comparison of the expected errors in matching in each covariate and the standard deviation of that covariate.

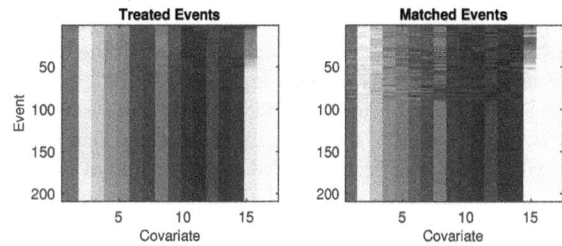

Figure 6: Treated covariates of user No. 15051 with the covariates of their matched events.

of treated events is large, at least 30 [15]. In this case, $\text{ATT}_{j,y} - 4 \cdot se_{j,y}$ can be viewed as a high-probability lower bound on the true effect if this effect is positive, and $\text{ATT}_{j,y} + 4 \cdot se_{j,y}$ can be viewed as a high-probability upper bound on the true effect if this effect is negative. These upper and lower bounds hold with probability of at least $1 - 10^{-4}$. When the number of treated events is small, less than 30, we set $\widetilde{\text{ATT}}_{j,y} = 0$. In this case, it is unreliable to substitute the unknown standard deviation of $\text{ATT}_{j,y}$ with its empirical estimate $se_{j,y}$ and guarantees cannot be provided in general [15], unless we make strong assumptions on the distribution of $Y_i(1) - Y_{\pi(i)}(0)$ in Eq. (1).

We report $\widetilde{\text{ATT}}_{j,y}$ for all treatments j and genres y in Fig. 3(a). Note that at this granularity level, there are around 2M treated events for each weather attribute. We observe some insightful trends. For example, there is around 1% decrease in watching *Dramas* when the pressure is low and precipitation is high. A reason for this may be that rainy days tend to make people sad and they prefer not to watch dramas, which are unlikely to cheer them up. Although a 1% decrease may seem small, considering the fact that *Dramas* account for about 20% of all watching events, this is about a 5% relative decrease in this genre. This decrease observed on rainy days comes at the account of the more entertaining *Panel* programs, which increase by about 0.6%. Considering that *Panel* only account for 6% of the watching events, their relative increase is as high as 10%. We were not able to validate these intuitive explanations. Nevertheless, they suggest that our weather attributes may be indicative of complex human behavior patterns, which would be difficult to uncover otherwise.

All matching methods should be followed by an assessment of their quality (Section 2). In Fig. 5, we report the quality of our matching in each covariate. In particular, we report the expected error in matching in each covariate and compare it to the standard deviation of that covariate. We observe two trends. First, all expected errors are close to 0, which means that we do not introduce systematic biases in any covariate. Second, standard deviations of all errors are consistently smaller than that of the corresponding covariate. This shows that we match accurately in all covariates. Hence, our estimated effects are likely to be causal.

5.3 Causal Analysis on Individual Users

One of the goals of user modeling is to inform personalization. In this subsection, we partition our dataset into individual users and conduct causal analysis of these users. From the technical point of view, the causal analysis of a single user is no different from that in Section 5.2. The only difference is that the set of treated events in the estimate of ATT in Eq. (1) includes only the events of that user. We denote the resulting high-probability effect in Eq. (2) by $\widetilde{\text{ATT}}_{j,y}^k$ and refer to it as the *high-probability effect of treatment j on genre y of user k*.

We note that several users in our dataset have very significant and different effects from that in Fig. 3(a), which reports high-probability effects for whole of Australia. In Fig. 4(c), we report the high-probability effects on an individual with more than 2,000 watching events. Even for this user, there are only around 200 treated events for each weather attribute. Unfortunately, most users in our dataset have much less watching events than 2,000. The number of users with more than 2,000 events is only 41, among 578,308 users. If the user does not have enough treated events, the high-probability effect in Eq. (2) is likely to be zero, based on the discussion in Section 5.2. In Fig. 3(a), we do not observe significant effects for *Pre-school* genre when weather changes. However, in Fig. 4(c), high cloud cover, high wind speed, and low humidity all have large affects on the user's preference towards *Pre-school* TV programs. This indicates that conducting causal analysis on individual users can help reveal more complicated TV watching patterns.

As the counterfactuals are unobserved, there is no ground truth for causal analysis in general. To validate our causal findings, we need to validate the quality of matching on this user. In Fig. 6, we visualize the covariates of treated events from this user along with the covariates of matched events. In each plot, each column represents a covariate (Section 3.2), which is the profile of the user, the time of the event, and the location of the event. Each row represents an event. A quick visual inspection reveals that the plots look similar. The correlation coefficient between the entries of these two plots is 0.998, which indicates that they are almost identical. This shows that our matching can balance systematic biases between treated and control groups well, even on an individual user level.

To determine which level of granularity is most appropriate for user modeling, we have to summarize the effects on all users, similarly to Fig. 4(a). However, we cannot simply sum up the effects on individual users, as they may cancel each other. Consider the following example. The whole population of users consists of two users with the same number of events. For user 1, the treatment increases the probability of watching *Drama* by 10%. For user 2, the treatment decreases the probability of watching *Drama* by 10%. On average, the effect of the treatment on watching *Drama* is zero. However, when the effect is viewed in the context of individual users, the treatment appears to be effective. Below we propose a metric that reflects this intuition.

Let $G = \{G_k\}_{k=1}^K$ be a partitioning of all events into K groups G_k, such as that each user is assigned to a single group. Let $\widehat{\text{ATT}}_{j,y}^k$ be the *high-probability effect of treatment j on genre y in group k*. Then we define the gain of conditioning on groups in G as

$$\widehat{\text{ATT}}_{j,y}^G = \sum_{k=1}^K \frac{|G_k \cap \{i : T_i = 1\}|}{\sum_{\ell=1}^K |G_\ell \cap \{i : T_i = 1\}|} \left| \widehat{\text{ATT}}_{j,y}^k \right|, \qquad (3)$$

and refer to it as the *effect of treatment j on genre y in context G*. This is a convex combination of the absolute high-probability effects in each group, weighted proportionally to the number of treated events in each group. The larger the number of treated events in the group, the higher the confidence on the corresponding ATT, and the higher the contribution of this group to $\widehat{\text{ATT}}_{j,y}^G$.

We also define *total effect in context G* as

$$\widehat{\text{ATT}}^G = \sum_j \sum_y \widehat{\text{ATT}}_{j,y}^G, \qquad (4)$$

which summarizes the significance of all effects, for every pair of the treatment and outcomes, given G. This is a strong indicator of how good the granularity of context G is for causal effects.

In Fig. 4(a), we report $\widehat{\text{ATT}}_{j,y}^G$ when G is a single group, all the users in the dataset. Note that these are simply absolute effects from Fig. 3(a). In Fig. 4(b), we report $\widehat{\text{ATT}}_{j,y}^G$ when each group in G is an individual user. For many genres in Fig. 4(a), the effects are significant, for instance for *Drama*, *Panel* and *News*. Differences between these two plots also reveal some trends. We observe that if we further consider smaller subgroups, such as individual users, then there are nearly no causal effects on average. The reason is that we do not have sufficient data for most users if considered individually. In our dataset, most users have less than 200 watching events, which means they have even less treated events. When the number of watching events is limited, we observe large ATTs but they also come with large standard errors. Therefore, most high-probability effects in Eq. (2) are zero, and so is their convex combination in Eq. (3).

We conclude by making the following remarks. On one hand, we can observe significant effects when the groups are sufficiently large, such as the data of the whole of Australia. Although we have higher confidence in our estimated effects on these large groups, they only show overall trends for a large population, which can hardly be valuable for user-level personalization. On the other hand, if we have enough treated events for an individual user, we can observe even stronger effects. However, most of our users do not have that many watching events. Thus, there is a tradeoff between the size of the subgroups and the confidence of our estimators. In the following subsection, we show that there are other levels of granularity of context that allow us to estimate significant effects.

5.4 Causal Analysis on a Group of Users

In this subsection, we choose the most popular TV programs and conduct causal analysis of groups of people with different watching preferences. In our dataset, *Doctor Who* is the most popular TV program in *Drama* and *Peppa Pig* is the most popular in *Pre-school*. We use these two programs as the grouping criteria and build up two groups by selecting users who watched *Doctor Who* and *Peppa Pig* at least once, respectively. There are 85,252 users in the *Doctor Who* group and 25,731 users in the *Peppa Pig* group. Only 3,606 users watched both programs, so that the sets of users in these two groups are substantially different.

We repeat the causal analysis of Section 5.2 and Section 5.3 in these two groups. The obtained results in terms of the high-probability effect $\widehat{\text{ATT}}_{j,y}$ in Eq. (2) for all treatments j and genres y are summarized in Fig. 3(b) and Fig. 3(c). Note that for each weather attribute, we have around 0.7M and 0.5M treated events in these two groups, respectively. Fig. 3 reveals some insightful trends. First, the three groups of users (i.e., the whole population in Australia, users who watched *Doctor Who*, and users who watched *Peppa Pig*) show different TV watching patterns. For example, we observe significant decrease for *Drama* when temperature is high in Fig. 3(a) but do not observe them in Fig. 3(b) and Fig. 3(c). However, there are also some consistent results observed across these groups. For example, we observe significant decrease in *Drama* when pressure is low and precipitation is high. As another example, there is no significant effect on *Pre-school* programs when weather attributes change. These findings confirm our claims in Section 5.2 and Section 5.3 that weather attributes may be indicative of patterns in user TV watching behavior, which can be revealed through causal analyses. Second, we observe more significant effects when grouping users rather than treating them individually. Comparing Fig. 3(b) to Fig. 4(b) validates our claim that a sufficient number of treated events is needed to estimate significant effects.

Fig. 3 and Fig. 4 also provide insights on how to model user behavior. As discussed in Section 5.3, it is a challenge to balance the group size and the confidence of the estimators. In our work, we observe that we do not obtain significant effects for most of the individual users, as the watching records of a single user are limited. At the same time, the results obtained from the whole population cannot inform user-level personalization. In this subsection, we demonstrate that one way to benefit from the two worlds is to group users with similar watching preferences in order to model their TV watching patterns.

5.5 Why Causal Analysis?

In earlier sections, we showed that causal inference is a useful tool for user modeling. In this subsection, we show the necessity for causal analysis. Causal analysis and matching on covariates can correct systematic biases in data. We illustrate this by comparing two matching methods. The first method matches treated events based on covariates (see Section 3). The second method matches treated events randomly.

Let us consider the following example. We randomly choose 20% of events from the city of Brisbane as treated events and use the ATT in Eq. (1) to estimate causal effects. Note that the treatment is random, and therefore the true effects are zero. First, we choose

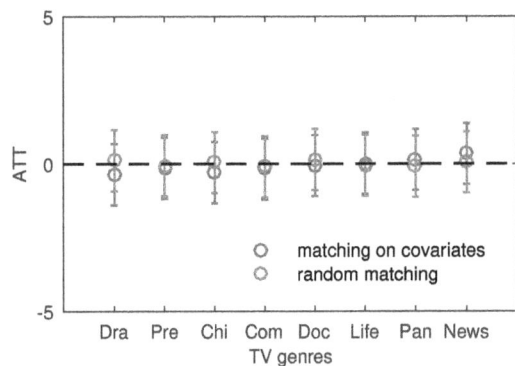

(a) Both treated and control events are from Brisbane. The confidence radii are the same as in Eq. (2). The effects are multiplied by 100 and can be interpreted as changes in the percentage of watching TV genres.

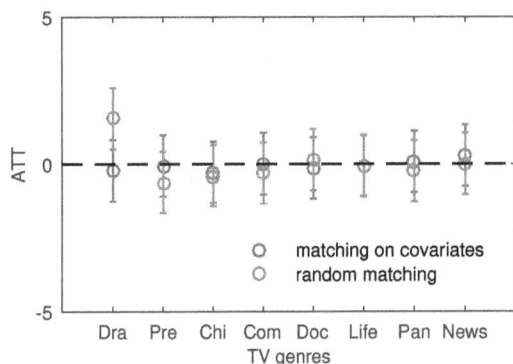

(b) Treated events are from Brisbane and control events are from the whole Australia. The confidence radii are the same as in Eq. (2). The effects are multiplied by 100 and can be interpreted as changes in the percentage of watching TV genres.

Figure 7: Comparisons of two matching methods.

control events from Brisbane and report the ATT in Fig. 7(a). We observe that both matching methods predict near-zero causal effects, which is correct. The reason is that the distributions of covariates, conditioned on the treatment and control, are the same. This shows that if the treated and control events are balanced, both matching methods work well.

Now we choose control events from the whole Australia and repeat the above experiment. Fig. 7(b) shows our results. We observe that random matching predicts higher absolute values of the ATT than matching on covariates. For instance, it estimates more than 1% increase in *Drama* and this is statistically significant. We know that this is incorrect because the true effects are zero. The reason is that random matching matches treatment events from Brisbane to control events from the whole Australia. Since the covariates in Australia are distributed differently from those in Brisbane, we get biases. Thus, the statistically significant increase in watching *Drama* is due to the fact that people in Australia watch less *Drama* on average (19.51%) than in Brisbane (20.89%). The distributions of covariates, conditioned on the treatment and control, are typically different in practice, because treatments are not assigned randomly, but rather conditionally randomly. We claim that our proposed

method can correctly balance this imbalance, and therefore it should be preferred in practice for user modeling tasks.

6 CONCLUSIONS

In this paper, we study whether and how weather affects users' TV watching behavior. We conducted causal analyses using nation-scale Australian dataset and discovered interpretable causal relationships between weather conditions and users' watching behavior. We repeated the causal analysis at the granularity of individual users, but in most cases individual data turned out to be insufficient for obtaining reliable results. This has driven further sensitivity analyses of our approach that discovered substantial differences across subgroups of users. To the best of our knowledge, this is the first causal analysis of a large-scale dataset looking at the interplay between weather and TV watching.

Our work also raises several questions. First, in our work, our treatment variable was binary; we set hard thresholds for the "high" and "low" groups of each attribute. However, there exist works dealing with continuous treatment [12] and we posit that our dataset is rich enough for weather attributes to uncover more accurate watching patterns if these methods were used. Second, we only focused on the causal analysis and its sensitivity and did not evaluate how the learned weather dependencies can be exploited. We strongly believe these weather attributes can be incorporated into more sophisticated weather-aware recommender systems [1], and improve the quality of the generated recommendations.

It is also worth noting that the work was done in a domain-agnostic way and did not involve any meteorologists. Certain weather attributes, such as temperature and feels-like temperature or humidity and precipitation, are clearly correlated. We believe that some domain knowledge of these correlations could help us to identify the set of most influential attributes and dramatically improve our results. We also leave this work for the future.

REFERENCES

[1] G. Adomavicius and A. Tuzhilin. Context-aware recommender systems. In *Recommender Systems Handbook*, pages 191–226. 2015.
[2] L. Baltrunas, B. Ludwig, S. Peer, and F. Ricci. Context relevance assessment and exploitation in mobile recommender systems. *Personal Ubiquitous Comput.*, 16(5):507–526, June 2012.
[3] A. Barker, K. Hawton, J. Fagg, and C. Jennison. Seasonal and weather factors in parasuicide. *The British Journal of Psychiatry*, 165(3):375–380, 1994.
[4] G. A. Barnett, H.-J. Chang, E. L. Fink, and W. D. Richards. Seasonality in television viewing a mathematical model of cultural processes. *Communication Research*, 18(6):755–772, 1991.
[5] M. Braunhofer and F. Ricci. *Contextual Information Elicitation in Travel Recommender Systems*, pages 579–592. Springer International Publishing, Cham, 2016.
[6] M. Caliendo and S. Kopeinig. Some practical guidance for the implementation of propensity score matching. *Journal of Economic Surveys*, 22(1):31–72, 2008.
[7] E. G. Cohn. Weather and crime. *British Journal of Criminology*, 30(1):51–64, 1990.
[8] T. S. David Hirshleifer. Good day sunshine: Stock returns and the weather. *The Journal of Finance*, 58(3):1009–1032, 2003.
[9] S. Dernbach, N. Taft, J. Kurose, U. Weinsberg, C. Diot, and A. Ashkan. Cache content-selection policies for streaming video services. In *35th Annual IEEE International Conference on Computer Communications, INFOCOM 2016, San Francisco, CA, USA, April 10-14, 2016*, pages 1–9, 2016.
[10] A. Farahat and M. C. Bailey. How effective is targeted advertising? In *Proceedings of the 21st International Conference on World Wide Web*, pages 111–120. ACM, 2012.
[11] R. M. Gray and D. L. Neuhoff. Quantization. *IEEE Trans. Inform. Theory*, 44(6):2325–29, 1998.
[12] K. Hirano and G. W. Imbens. The propensity score with continuous treatments. In *Applied Bayesian Modeling and Causal Inference from Incomplete-data Perspectives*.

Wiley, 2004.

[13] G. King and R. Nielsen. Why propensity scores should not be used for matching. Working paper, 2016.

[14] Y. Koren and R. M. Bell. Advances in collaborativefi ltering. In *Recommender Systems Handbook*, pages 77–118. 2015.

[15] E. L. Lehmann and J. P. Romano. *Testing statistical hypotheses*. Springer Texts in Statistics. Springer, New York, third edition, 2005.

[16] S. Li, N. Vlassis, J. Kawale, and Y. Fu. Matching via dimensionality reduction for estimation of treatment effects in digital marketing campaigns. In *Proceedings of the 25th International Joint Conference on Artificial Intelligence*, 2016.

[17] D. Liang, L. Charlin, J. McInerney, and D. M. Blei. Modeling user exposure in recommendation. In *Proceedings of the 25th International Conference on World Wide Web*, WWW '16, pages 951–961, Republic and Canton of Geneva, Switzerland, 2016. International World Wide Web Conferences Steering Committee.

[18] S. L. Morgan and C. Winship. *Counterfactuals and Causal Inference: Methods and Principles for Social Research*. Cambridge University Press, 2014.

[19] K. B. Murray, F. Di Muro, A. Finn, and P. P. Leszczyc.Th e effect of weather on consumer spending. *Journal of Retailing and Consumer Services*, 17(6):512–520, 2010.

[20] A. G. Parsons.Th e association between daily weather and daily shopping patterns. *Australasian Marketing Journal (AMJ)*, 9(2):78–84, 2001.

[21] T. Partonen and J. Lönnqvist. Seasonal affective disorder. *The Lancet*, 352(9137):1369–1374, 1998.

[22] J. Pearl. *Causality*. Cambridge University Press, 2009.

[23] K. Roe and H. Vandebosch. Weather to view or not:Th at is the question. *European Journal of Communication*, 11(2):201–216, 1996.

[24] D. B. Rubin. Matching to remove bias in observational studies. *Biometrics*, pages 159–183, 1973.

[25] D. B. Rubin. Estimating causal effects of treatments in randomized and nonrandomized studies. *Journal of Educational Psychology*, 66(5):688–701, 1974.

[26] E. M. Saunders. Stock prices and wall street weather. *The American Economic Review*, 83(5):1337–1345, 1993.

[27] P. Spirtes, C. N. Glymour, and R. Scheines. *Causation, Prediction, and Search*. MIT press, 2000.

[28] M. Xu, S. Berkovsky, S. Ardon, S. Triukose, A. Mahanti, and I. Koprinska. Catch-up TV recommendations: show old favourites andfi nd new ones. In *ACM Conference on Recommender Systems*, pages 285–294, 2013.

[29] S. Zong, B. Kveton, S. Berkovsky, A. Ashkan, N. Vlassis, and Z. Wen. Does weather matter?: Causal analysis of TV logs. In *Proceedings of the 26th International Conference on World Wide Web Companion, Perth, Australia, April 3-7, 2017*, pages 883–884, 2017.

Interactive Prior Elicitation of Feature Similarities for Small Sample Size Prediction

Homayun Afrabandpey
Helsinki Institute for Information Technology HIIT, Dept. of Computer Science, Aalto University
homayun.afrabandpey@aalto.fi

Tomi Peltola
Helsinki Institute for Information Technology HIIT, Dept. of Computer Science, Aalto University
tomi.peltola@aalto.fi

Samuel Kaski
Helsinki Institute for Information Technology HIIT, Dept. of Computer Science, Aalto University
samuel.kaski@aalto.fi

ABSTRACT

Regression under the "small n, large p" condition, of small sample size n and large number of features p in the learning data set, is a recurring setting in which learning from data is difficult. With prior knowledge about relationships of the features, p can effectively be reduced, but explicating such prior knowledge is difficult for experts. In this paper we introduce a new method for eliciting expert prior knowledge about the similarity of the roles of features in the prediction task. The key idea is to use an interactive multidimensional-scaling (MDS) type scatterplot display of the features to elicit the similarity relationships, and then use the elicited relationships in the prior distribution of prediction parameters. Specifically, for learning to predict a target variable with Bayesian linear regression, the feature relationships are used to construct a Gaussian prior with a full covariance matrix for the regression coefficients. Evaluation of our method in experiments with simulated and real users on text data confirm that prior elicitation of feature similarities improves prediction accuracy. Furthermore, elicitation with an interactive scatterplot display outperforms straightforward elicitation where the users choose feature pairs from a feature list.

CCS CONCEPTS

• **Computing methodologies** → **Machine learning**; • **Human - centered computing** → **Human computer interaction (HCI)**;

KEYWORDS

Interaction; prior elicitation; regression; small n large p; visualization

1 INTRODUCTION

Regression analysis becomes difficult when the sample size is substantially smaller than the number of features. "Small n, large p" refers to the generic class of such problems which arise in different fields of applied statistics such as personalized medicine [4, 17] and text data analysis [7, 15]. The problem poses several challenges to standard statistical methods [12] and demands new concepts and models to cope with the challenges. An important challenge is

UMAP'17, July 9–12, 2017, Bratislava, Slovakia
© 2017 ACM. 978-1-4503-4635-1/17/07...$15.00
DOI: http://dx.doi.org/10.1145/3079628.3079698

that prediction by fitting regression models using traditional techniques is an ill-posed task in "small n, large p" and is unlikely to be accurate and reliable. Regularization methods [18, 21] have been proposed to cope with this challenge; however, the improvement they can give is limited. Additionally, modelling could use prior information, i.e. information available about the problem prior to observing the learning data. Prior information is often available only as the experience and knowledge of experts. Prior elicitation is the process of quantifying and extracting user's prior knowledge. The extracted knowledge can be used to improve an underlying model. The two main questions in the process are how to quantify the prior knowledge, and how to plug-in the extracted prior knowledge to the model.

Garthwaite et al. [8] proposed a method of defining the full prior distribution for a generalized linear model by quantifying experts' opinions on different statistics such as the median, lower and upper quantiles. Interactive Principal Component Analysis (iPCA) [11] supports data analysis of multivariate data sets through modification of the model parameters by the user. The drawback of these types of prior elicitation is that they assume users are experts in the underlying model and not just domain-experts. To solve this problem, observation-level interaction has been proposed where the focus is on interaction between the user and the data rather than model parameters [3, 6]. Using the extracted knowledge from the interaction, the parameters of the underlying model are tuned to reflect the user's knowledge. In recent work, Daee et al. [5] proposed a method of eliciting user's knowledge on the relevance and/or weight values of single features to improve the predictions in a sparse linear regression problem. Similarly, Micallef et al. [13] proposed an interactive visualization to extract user's knowledge on the relevance of individual features for a prediction task.

In this paper, we present a novel approach on interactive prior elicitation of pairwise similarities of features in "small n, large p" prediction task. The proposed approach uses an interactive MDS-type scatterplot of the features to let users give feedback on their pairwise similarities, in the sense of how similarly they would affect the predictions. Based on this input, the system learns a new similarity metric for the features and redraws the scatterplot. Finally, the learned metric is used to define a prior distribution for the prediction parameters. The proposed approach shields users from the technicalities of the underlying model. The contributions of this paper can be summarized as:

- User's prior knowledge is quantified as the prior covariance of the regression coefficients in a Bayesian linear regression model. Using this interpretation, our system lets the user manipulate the prior distribution of the model parameter indirectly by his feedback, without having to understand modelling details.

- Feedback is collected on pairwise similarities of the features rather than the data, parameters or single features. This type of feedback is complementary to all earlier approaches.
- The prior is elicited with an MDS-type of interactive visualization that has earlier been used for visualizing similarities of data items.

Our simulation results and preliminary user study demonstrate that when collecting pairwise similarity knowledge using the proposed interactive intelligent interface, users are able to provide more informative feedback, and the performance of the underlying model increases in prediction tasks.

2 OVERVIEW

To motivate our algorithm and for the purpose of clarity, we illustrate our basic idea with a simple use case. We used the sentiment data set [2] which contains text reviews and the corresponding rating values (taken from www.amazon.com) of four product categories. Each review is represented using a vector of keywords that appear in at least 100 reviews within the same category. We focus on the *kitchen appliances* category where there are 5149 reviews, each represented by a feature vector of size 824 [10]. The task is to learn a model that linearly relates the keywords (which here are features) to the ratings (outputs) to predict the ratings from the textual content of the reviews. This is a supervised learning task where we have a training set of inputs $X \in \mathbb{R}^{5149 \times 824}$ and outputs $y \in \mathbb{R}^{5149 \times 1}$. To simulate the "small n, large p" paradigm, we randomly select 100 reviews and their corresponding ratings as the training set.

A linear regression model for this task can be defined using a parameter vector $\beta = (\beta_1, \beta_2, ..., \beta_{824}) \in \mathbb{R}^{824 \times 1}$. Mathematically, the model is

$$y = X\beta + \epsilon \tag{1}$$

where $\epsilon \sim \mathcal{N}(0, \sigma_{noise}^2 I)$ is the residual noise. Equation 1 induces a Gaussian likelihood as $y|\beta, \sigma_{noise}^2 \sim \mathcal{N}(X\beta, \sigma_{noise}^2 I)$. The goal is to learn the posterior distribution of β given the training data.

Inferring the posterior of the parameters in the Bayesian setting requires a prior distribution. In data sets with large sample sizes, the choice of the prior distribution will have a minor effect on the posterior inferences; however, since we assumed a "small n, large p" data set, the role of the prior distribution becomes more important. Setting prior distributions is a difficult task and requires knowledge on both the domain and the model parameters. In this paper, we introduce a method for helping in this task, by learning and refining a good prior distribution for the prediction parameters using feedback given by a user. User's knowledge is assumed to be about the pairwise similarities of the keywords with regard to the role they have in the prediction task. In other words, we mean that keywords have a similar effect on the rating values (the values of the regression coefficients are similar). As an example, keywords "**good**" and "**excellent**" have a similar role in the prediction since both of them convey information that the user will give a high rating to the product, while keywords "**bad**" and "**good**" are dissimilar.

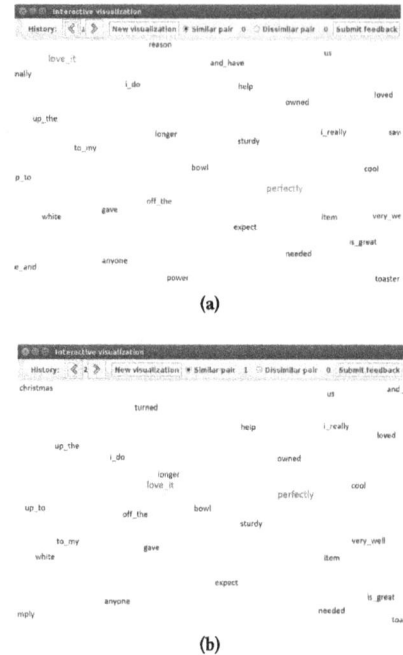

(a)

(b)

Figure 1: The scatterplot (a) before submitting feedback, and (b) after submitting feedback and requesting a new visualization. The scatterplots are zoomed in suitably to better show the keywords

Figure 1 illustrates an example interaction between the user and our system. Keywords (features) are visualized to the user on the scatter plot, where she can zoom in/out by scrolling down/up the mouse. The user investigates the distances among keywords and decides whether two keywords should be closer to each other (similar) or farther away from each other (dissimilar) based on her prior knowledge. As an example, the user concluded that according to her prior knowledge, the distances between keywords "**love_it**" and "**perfectly**" should be less than what is shown in the scatterplot. She selects these keywords by clicking on them (their color will change to green as shown in Figure 1a), selecting similar/dissimilar box in the menu bar and clicking on the submit button. Then the user can ask for a new visualization (**New Visualization** button in Figure 1) to see the effect of her feedback on the distances between keywords (Figure 1b), or she can continue giving more feedback according to current distances. As shown in Figure 1b, the one feedback given by the user modifies the distances between keywords, however it was not informative enough to make distances perfect. This will iterate until the user is satisfied with the visualization. The knowledge extracted from the user is used to build a proper covariance matrix for the prior distribution of the prediction parameter β. Finally, using the obtained prior, we compute the posterior of the prediction parameters.

3 INTERACTIVE PRIOR ELICITATION OF PAIRWISE SIMILARITIES

We reformulate the Interactive Neighbor Retrieval Visualizer [14] to a method for prior elicitation on features. To visualize the features for the user, we use the original data space as the representation for the features in the high-dimensional space. More precisely, we define $f_i = [x_{1i}, \ldots, x_{ni}]^T$ as the original representation of the ith feature, where x_{ni} is the ith element of the nth sample. With this definition, we have D features, each of which is an n-dimensional vector. We define $\{g_i\}_{i=1}^D$ as the corresponding low-dimensional projections of $\{f_i\}_{i=1}^D$, to be learned from user feedback.

At each iteration t, we define the similarity matrix of the features in the high-dimensional space as

$$P^t = \left[p_{j|i}^t = \frac{\exp(-\parallel f_i - f_j \parallel_{A^t}^2 / \sigma_i^2)}{\sum_{k \neq i} \exp(-\parallel f_i - f_j \parallel_{A^t}^2 / \sigma_i^2)} \right]_{i,j=1}^D, \quad (2)$$

where A^t is the unknown similarity metric between the features, $\parallel f_i - f_j \parallel_A^2 = (f_i - f_j)^T A (f_i - f_j)$ and σ_i^2 is a scaling parameter. The unknown similarity metric A^t encodes the user feedback and is learned iteratively by interaction with the user. The metric is initialized to unit matrix.

To find the location of the points in the visualization space at iteration t, an analogous matrix is defined for the low-dimensional projections:

$$Q^t = \left[q_{j|i}^t = \frac{\exp(-\parallel g_i^t - g_j^t \parallel^2 / \sigma_i^2)}{\sum_{k \neq i} \exp(-\parallel g_i^t - g_k^t \parallel^2 / \sigma_i^2)} \right]_{i,j=1}^D. \quad (3)$$

Finally, the locations of the points in the low-dimensional space are obtained by optimizing the following expected cost function [14]:

$$\mathbb{E}[C] = \mathbb{E}_{A|F}[\lambda \mathbb{E}_i[KL(P_i, Q_i)] + (1 - \lambda)\mathbb{E}_i[KL(Q_i, P_i)]], \quad (4)$$

where $\mathbb{E}_{A|F}$ denotes the expectation over the posterior distribution of the learned metric given the feedbacks F, and $\mathbb{E}_i$ is expectation over the training set points. Since the high-dimensional distributions P_i are functions of the unknown metric A, the cost function is represented as the expectation over the possible metrics. The parameter $\lambda \in [0, 1]$ controls the relative importance of recall and precision of the display [19]. The final similarity metric A^{final}, learned in the last iteration of user interaction, is used to define a prior distribution for the regression weights according to equations 5 and 6:

$$C = \left[c_{ij} = \exp(-\frac{\parallel f_i - f_j \parallel_{A^{final}}^2}{2\sigma^2}) \right]_{i,j=1}^D, \quad (5)$$

$$\beta \sim \mathcal{N}(0, \sigma_{noise}^2 \tau^2 C), \quad (6)$$

where σ and τ are scalar scale parameters. In our implementation, the value of σ is set by cross-validation.

By defining this prior distribution for the regression coefficients, and gamma prior distributions on τ^{-2} and σ_{noise}^{-2}, the posterior distribution is analytically intractable, but can be efficiently approximated using Variational Bayes (e.g., [1, Chapter 10]). This gives a Gaussian posterior approximation for β. Pseudocode of the proposed method is presented in Algorithm 1.

4 SIMULATION EXPERIMENT

We conducted a simulated study on the data set introduced in Section 2 with two scenarios where a simulated user (i) gives all feedbacks at once, and (ii) gives feedback sequentially. As baselines, we used Bayesian linear regression with unit prior covariance and

---

Algorithm 1: Interactive Prior Elicitation Pseudocode

1: Set $A^0 = I$ and $t = 0$.
2: **while** user gives more feedback **do**
    b. Optimize the cost function 4 using the metric A^t and find the position of the features in the low-dimensional space, $[g_i^t]_{i=1}^D$, at iteration t.
    c. Ask the user to give feedback about the similarity of the role of the features.
    d. Set $t = t + 1$.
    e. Learn the new metric A^t using the method introduced in [20] and the user feedback.
3: Compute the matrix C using A^{final} (Eq. 5) and define a prior distribution for the weights as $\beta \sim \mathcal{N}(0, \sigma_{noise}^2 \tau^2 C)$.
4: Compute the posterior of the weights and use that to predict output for a new sample.

Bayesian linear regression with the prior covariance used in the first round of our method ("Without Feedback" in the following, since the prior is obtained by setting $A = I$ and without using feedback). We used a set of 3149 randomly selected reviews with their corresponding ratings to construct the simulated user. This is done by using the mean of the posterior distribution of the regression coefficient vector of a Bayesian linear regression model trained on the randomly selected data. The simulated user assumes two similarity clusters: (i) features with the highest 30 regression coefficients and (ii) features with the lowest 30 regression coefficients. Features in these two clusters are dissimilar to each other. Since there are enough samples (3149) compared to the dimensionality of the data (824), the posterior mean of the regression coefficient is a good representative of the true values of the feature weights and consequently the similarity of the role of the features in the prediction task.

The remaining samples are randomly partitioned into training and test sets. The results reported in this section are averaged over 10 simulated user construction iterations and 50 random training data selection. Figure 2a shows simulation results for the first scenario, in which the proposed method is evaluated with an increasing number of randomly selected training samples, from 50 to 500. Figure 2b shows the changes of Mean Squared Errors (MSE) on the test data with 100 randomly selected training samples when the simulated user gives feedback sequentially in 60 rounds; round 0 works without feedback. The simulated user gives 10 similarity feedback and 10 dissimilarity feedback in each round.

From Figure 2, it can be concluded that assuming pairwise similarity/dissimilarity knowledge from the user, the proposed method improves the predictions by extracting prior knowledge.

5 USER STUDY

We conducted a user study on 10 university students to empirically evaluate our two hypotheses that (i) collecting prior knowledge on the pairwise similarity of the features improves predictions, and (ii) the interactive interface helps users to give better feedback and consequently improves the predictions more. To evaluate the first hypothesis, we consider the same baselines used in the previous section. To evaluate the second hypothesis, we implemented two versions of our system, both with the same underlying model, but

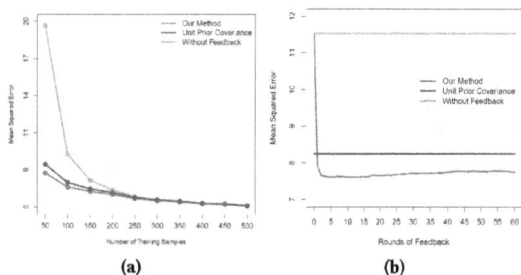

Figure 2: Simulation results for (a) batch feedback, (b) sequential feedback.

with different interfaces: the proposed interactive interface and a simple non-interactive list visualization of the features. In the list visualization, the order of the features is random and fixed during the whole experiment for a user. The user goes through the list and selects the pairs which are similar or dissimilar according to her prior knowledge and gives feedback on them. As far as we know, there are no earlier methods for the same task.

We designed a between-subject study, where each participant performed two prior elicitation tasks with different interfaces and different data collections: the sentiment data set introduced in Section 2 and the reviews from the Yelp data set challenge (www.yelp.com/dataset_challenge). Users were asked to give feedback on pairwise similarity/dissimilarity of the words in the role they have in the prediction. For the Yelp data, we used a subset with 4086 reviews. In both data sets, we set a threshold on the tf-idf values (see [16]) of the words to choose 300 words. To simulate a "small n, large p" training data, we randomly selected five subsets of each data set with 100 samples, and used the rests for test. Therefore, the training set for each task contains 100 samples and 300 features. Each of the selected five subsets (from each data set) was used once for the interactive interface and once for the non-interactive interface with different users. Users interact with each interface for 20 rounds and give 5 feedbacks (similarity/dissimilarity) per round. The study was balanced with respect to the combination of the type of interface, task and order. After both tasks, a short semi-structured interview was conducted with each participant.

Figures 3a and 3b show MSEs on test data as a function of the number of feedback iterations for the two data sets. According to the figures, extracted prior knowledge improves the mean squared errors of the predictions compared to both baselines. The difference between the MSE values obtained by the interactive interface and the non-interactive interface shows the amount of improvement made to the predictions using the interface. To test the statistical significance of the improvements, we used the procedure introduced in [13]. The distance between the average curves in the last round (round 20 in Figure 3) is used as the test statistics. By assuming that there is no difference between the results obtained by the interactive interface and other methods, we compute the distribution of the test statistics by performing 10^5 permutations of the labels (interactive interface, non-interactive interface, etc.). Finally, the proportion of the permutations with higher values of test statistics compared to the test statistics using true labels, is used as p-value of the significance test. Based on this test, the improvements made by our

interactive interface against the "Unit Prior Covariance" ($p = 0.048$ for the sentiment and $p = 0.016$ for the YELP data set) and the "Without Feedback" ($p = 0.0$ for the sentiment and $p = 0.0$ for the YELP data set) baselines in both data sets are statistically significant, while for against the non-interactive interface, the improvements are not statistically significant ($p = 0.73$ for the sentiment and $p = 0.56$ for the YELP data set) which might be due to the small number of users.

It should be noted that since only a small portion of the words are meaningfully related to the rate prediction task, i.e. most of the words are verbs (am, is, etc.) or subjects (I, he, etc.) which are difficult for the user to give feedback, users gave their best feedback in the first couple of rounds which causes prior elicitation to best improve the prediction errors in the first half of the rounds. But, in the second half, prediction errors either improve slowly because of the repetitive feedbacks given by the user, or even sometimes drop since some users gave feedback on irrelevant words. In the

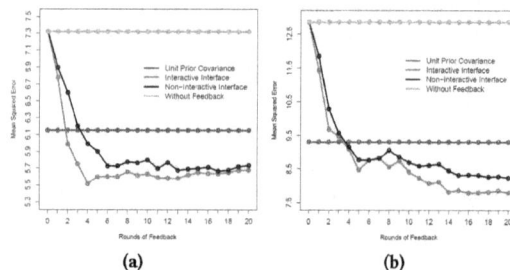

Figure 3: Changes of prediction MSE by increasing number of feedbacks for (a) the subset of the sentiment data set and (b) the subset of the Yelp data set.

interview, 8 out of 10 users reported that the intelligent interface helped them to accomplish the task. However, 5 users stated that they preferred the simple interface over the intelligent one. This is not surprising since people often prefer simpler systems over more complex ones [9] even if the complex system benefits them in accomplishing the required task.

6 DISCUSSION AND CONCLUSION

In this paper, we presented a new method and a prototype implementation of an interactive prior elicitation system which elicits an expert's prior knowledge on feature similarities to improve prediction accuracy. The system involves an intelligent user interface which helps the user in the interaction. We believe that this is an important step toward more efficient interactive prior elicitation methods. The main novelties are the type of feedback assumed from the user and the interpretation of the extracted knowledge as prior covariance for the parameter of the linear regression model.

In the current implementation, we pruned the number of features to avoid overwhelming the user; however, for the general case of a large number of features, we are working on an active learning version of the method to prioritize the feature pairs and allow scaling up to a much larger number of features.

7 ACKNOWLEDGMENTS

This work has been supported by the Academy of Finland (Finnish Center of Excellence in Computational Inference Research COIN; grants 294238 and 292334). We acknowledge the computational resources provided by the Aalto Science-IT project.

REFERENCES

[1] Bishop, C. M. *Pattern Recognition and Machine Learning*. Springer, 2006.
[2] Blitzer, J., Dredze, M., and Pereira, F. Biographies, bollywood, boom-boxes and blenders: Domain adaptation for sentiment classification. In *ACL*, vol. 7 (2007), 440–447.
[3] Brown, E. T., Liu, J., Brodley, C. E., and Chang, R. Dis-function: Learning distance functions interactively. In *Proceedings of the IEEE Conference on Visual Analytics Science and Technology (VAST)* (2012), 83–92.
[4] Costello, J. C., Heiser, L. M., Georgii, E., Gönen, M., Menden, M. P., Wang, N. J., Bansal, M., Hintsanen, P., Khan, S. A., Mpindi, J.-P., et al. A community effort to assess and improve drug sensitivity prediction algorithms. *Nature Biotechnology 32*, 12 (2014), 1202–1212.
[5] Daee, P., Peltola, T., Soare, M., and Kaski, S. Knowledge elicitation via sequential probabilistic inference for high-dimensional prediction. *arXiv preprint arXiv:1612.03328* (2016).
[6] Endert, A., Han, C., Maiti, D., House, L., and North, C. Observation-level interaction with statistical models for visual analytics. In *Proceedings of the IEEE Conference on Visual Analytics Science and Technology (VAST)* (2011), 121–130.
[7] Forman, G. An extensive empirical study of feature selection metrics for text classification. *Journal of Machine Learning Research 3* (2003), 1289–1305.
[8] Garthwaite, P. H., Al-Awadhi, S. A., Elfadaly, F. G., and Jenkinson, D. J. Prior distribution elicitation for generalized linear and piecewise-linear models. *Journal of Applied Statistics 40*, 1 (2013), 59–75.
[9] Hearst, M. *Search user interfaces*. Cambridge University Press, 2009.
[10] Hernández-Lobato, J. M., Hernández-Lobato, D., and Suárez, A. Expectation propagation in linear regression models with spike-and-slab priors. *Machine Learning 99*, 3 (2015), 437–487.
[11] Jeong, D. H., Ziemkiewicz, C., Fisher, B., Ribarsky, W., and Chang, R. iPCA: An interactive system for PCA-based visual analytics. In *Computer Graphics Forum*, vol. 28, Wiley Online Library (2009), 767–774.
[12] Johnstone, I. M., and Titterington, D. M. Statistical challenges of high-dimensional data. *Philosophical Transactions of the Royal Society of London A: Mathematical, Physical and Engineering Sciences 367*, 1906 (2009), 4237–4253.
[13] Micallef, L., Sundin, I., Marttinen, P., Ammad-ud din, M., Peltola, T., Soare, M., Jacucci, G., and Kaski, S. Interactive elicitation of knowledge on feature relevance improves predictions in small data sets. In *Proceedings of the 22Nd International Conference on Intelligent User Interfaces*, IUI '17, ACM (2017), 547–552.
[14] Peltonen, J., Sandholm, M., and Kaski, S. Information retrieval perspective to interactive data visualization. *EuroVis-Short Papers* (2013), 49–53.
[15] Qu, L., Ifrim, G., and Weikum, G. The bag-of-opinions method for review rating prediction from sparse text patterns. In *Proceedings of the 23rd International Conference on Computational Linguistics*, Association for Computational Linguistics (2010), 913–921.
[16] Sparck Jones, K. A statistical interpretation of term specificity and its application in retrieval. *Journal of documentation 28*, 1 (1972), 11–21.
[17] Tian, L., Alizadeh, A. A., Gentles, A. J., and Tibshirani, R. A simple method for estimating interactions between a treatment and a large number of covariates. *Journal of the American Statistical Association 109*, 508 (2014), 1517–1532.
[18] Tibshirani, R. Regression shrinkage and selection via the lasso. *Journal of the Royal Statistical Society. Series B (Methodological)* (1996), 267–288.
[19] Venna, J., Peltonen, J., Nybo, K., Aidos, H., and Kaski, S. Information retrieval perspective to nonlinear dimensionality reduction for data visualization. *Journal of Machine Learning Research 11* (2010), 451–490.
[20] Yang, L., Jin, R., and Sukthankar, R. Bayesian active distance metric learning. In *Proceedings of the Twenty-Third Conference on Uncertainty in Artificial Intelligence*, AUAI Press (2007), 442–449.
[21] Zou, H., and Hastie, T. Regularization and variable selection via the elastic net. *Journal of the Royal Statistical Society: Series B (Statistical Methodology) 67*, 2 (2005), 301–320.

An Analysis on Time- and Session-aware Diversification in Recommender Systems

Vito W. Anelli, Vito Bellini, Tommaso Di Noia,
Wanda La Bruna, Paolo Tomeo, Eugenio Di Sciascio*
Polytechnic University of Bari
Via E. Orabona, 4
Bari, Italy
{vitowalter.anelli,vito.bellini,tommaso.dinoia,wanda.labruna,paolo.tomeo,eugenio.disciascio}@poliba.it

ABSTRACT

In modern recommender systems, diversity has been widely acknowledged as an important factor to improve user experience and, more recently, intent-aware approaches to diversification have been proposed to provide the user with a list of recommendations covering different aspects of her behavior. In this paper, we propose and analyze the performances of two diversification methods taking into account temporal aspects of the user profile: in the first one we adopt a temporal decay function to emphasize the importance of more recent items in the user profile while in the second one we perform an evaluation based on the identification and analysis of temporal sessions. The two proposed methods have been implemented as temporal variants of the well-known xQuAD framework. In both cases, experimental results on Netflix 100M show an improvement in terms of accuracy-diversity balance .

1 INTRODUCTION

Recommender systems are designed to meet the users' needs suggesting relevant items in a personalized fashion. As recommendations are usually presented in form of list or group, the user experience strongly depends on the overall quality of such recommendations and, the diversity among them has been identified as one of the most important quality factor [6, 13]. Generally, accuracy and diversity are considered as contrasting properties, due to the demonstrated trade-off between them in offline evaluation [6]. In spite of that, a recent user's behaviour study proved that diversity in recommendations has an important positive impact on user satisfaction [8]. Moreover, in [15] the authors show that by taking into account the users propensity towards diversity, it is possible to foster the recommendation diversity without affecting accuracy or even slightly improve it. The diversity issue has been originally addressed in the Information Retrieval field. As user queries are often ambiguous and their intent is not clear, proposing a set of answers covering different intents may increase the

*Authors are listed in alphabetical order.

probability that users find at least one relevant document [7, 17]. The concept of intent-aware diversification has then been applied to the Recommender Systems field [21] and extensively studied thus producing new algorithms and evaluation metrics [18, 20, 22]. Here, user intents as defined in Information Retrieval have been mapped to user interests with reference to item characteristics.

Very often, in the design of the model behind a recommendation engine, the user profile is considered as a static snapshot without taking into proper account its temporal dimension. Actually, the importance of analyzing temporal aspect for user modeling has been proved to affect the final recommendation results [9–11].

Based on the above observations, in this paper we investigate the effect on the trade-off between accuracy and diversity of a recommendation list when dealing with temporal aspects of the user profile. The intuition behind our idea is that temporal dynamics might allow to better understand the user interests with respect to the items characteristics and then provide a more accurate intent-aware diversification. Therefore, this work presents two intent-based modeling methods that exploit the time dimension in a user profile. The first one analyses the frequency of interaction between the users and the items features using a temporal decay function in order to emphasize *persistence* and *recency* of an intent. The other method is based of a new session analysis technique of user ratings for intent modeling. Considering that a session is usually defined as a set of consecutive ratings with a very small gap of time among them (e.g. less than one hour in music [10]), we provided a wide definition of session tailored for movie ratings. In particular, such method is designed to highlight *importance*, *persistence* and *recency* of an intent among user sessions. We experimentally evaluated such methods with the large scale movie dataset published in the context of Netflix Prize Context [4]. The experimental results demonstrated that the analysis of temporal aspects in the user profile leads to better accuracy-diversity balance and intent-aware diversity compared to the original xQuAD. As an additional benefit, the aggregate diversity results improved too thus demonstrating to produce more personalized recommendations.

To the best of our knowledge, this is the first attempt in the investigation of how temporal dynamics affect diversity in recommendations.

2 RELATED WORK

A list of recommendations can be diversified in an implicit or explicit manner [3]. While the implicit diversification is used to increase the average distance between pairs of items in the recommendation list, the explicit method diversifies the recommendations trying to cover the user interests represented via categories or other descriptive information of the items. Therefore, the explicit diversification is known as Intent-Aware since it considers the likeness of user intents in information retrieval and user interests in recommender systems [21]. Explicit Query Aspect Diversification (xQuAD) is one of the most well-known intent-aware framework originally proposed for query results diversification [17] and then adapted to the recommendation [20] field. In a nutshell, xQuAD aims at maximizing the coverage of the inferred interests while minimizing their redundancy in a recommendation list.

The importance of taking into account the temporal dynamics in recommender systems has been recently pointed out in different works for diverse recommendation domains. A method to model user sessions in music domain was proposed in [10]. It considers as session each set of consecutive ratings without an extended time gap between them. Considering that there are various psychological phenomena that lead to a set of ratings to be grouped into a single session, such method captures these effects by means of user session biases. [11] presented a collaborative filtering algorithm able to model time drifting of user preferences and the results on the Netflix dataset indicated the importance of unveiling temporal effects in order to produce more accurate recommendations. A more recent method proposed to take advantage of temporal information in user behavior is called Time-based Markov Embedding [9], used to find the best next-song recommendation via Latent Markov Embedding.

In this work we aim at exploring the exploitation of temporal dynamics in user intents to provide a better intent-aware diversification.

3 INTENT-AWARE DIVERSIFICATION FOR RECOMMENDATIONS

Typically, a recommender system produces a list of personalized recommendations for each user. According to [1], a re-ranking of such list can be applied to improve its diversity, without modifying the recommendation process. However, finding the most diverse results is a NP-hard problem and hence several heuristics have been proposed [12]. Most previous diversification approaches are based on a greedy selection strategy [2, 5, 17]. Such strategy selects the next most relevant item only if that item is diverse with respect to the items already selected [12]. Algorithm 1 describes the

---

Data: The original list R, $N \leq n$
Result: The re-ranked list S

1   S = $\langle \rangle$;
2   **while** $|S| < N$ **do**
3     $i^* = \underset{i \in R \setminus S}{\operatorname{argmax}} f_{obj}(i, S, u)$;
4   S = S $\circ$ i^*;
5   R = R $\setminus \{i^*\}$
6   **end**
7   **return** S.

Algorithm 1: The greedy strategy.

---

working scheme of a greedy selection method. For the purpose of this work, we consider xQuAD, one of the most well-known intent-aware greedy heuristics. It maximizes the coverage of the inferred

interests while minimizing their redundancy. xQuAD was proposed for search diversification in information retrieval by Santos et al. [17], as a probabilistic framework to explicitly model an ambiguous query as a set of sub-queries that are supposed to cover the potential aspects of the initial query. More recently, it has been adapted for recommendation diversification by Vargas and Castells [20], replacing query and relative aspects with user and items features, respectively. The expression of the xQuAD objective function is

$$f_{obj}(i, S, u) = \lambda \cdot r^*(u, i) + (1 - \lambda) \cdot div(i, \overline{S}, u) \quad (1)$$

with $\overline{S}$ representing the set of the items belonging to R not already in S and $div(i, \overline{S}, u)$ defined as

$$div(i, \overline{S}, u) = \sum_f p(i|f, u) \cdot p(f|u) \cdot \prod_{j \in S}(1 - p(j|f, u)) \quad (2)$$

In Equation (2) $p(i|f, u)$ represents the likelihood of item i being chosen given the feature f and is computed as a binary function that returns 1 if the item contains f, 0 otherwise; $p(f|u)$ represents the interest of user u in the feature f and is usually computed as the relative frequency of the feature f on the items rated by user u. In other words, xQuAD fosters the idea of promoting items that are simultaneously highly related to at least one of the features of interest for the user and slightly related to the features of the items already recommended. In particular, this work focuses on the intent modeling in the xQuAD framework, namely the aforementioned $p(f|u)$ component in Equation (2).

4 INTENT MODELING WITH TEMPORAL DYNAMICS

In this section, we propose two methods to exploit temporal analysis for intent modeling in diversification that we call **session-based** and **time-based intent modeling**. Both relies on the intuition that user intent can change during the interaction with the system and the simple computation of features frequency in the user profile may not represent the current user interests.

4.1 Time-Based Intent Modeling

In order to valorize *persistence* and *recency* of an intent, we propose to analyze the frequency of interaction between the user u and the feature f and to weight each interaction by a temporal decay function. More formally, the following formula computes the interest of the user u with respect to the feature f:

$$p(f|u) = \frac{\sum_{i \in R(u)} cov(f, i) disc(u, i)}{\sum_{i \in R(u)} disc(u, i)} \quad (3)$$

where $R(u)$ indicates the set of rating provided by the user u; $cov(f, i)$ is a binary function returning 1 if the item i is associated with the feature f, 0 otherwise; $disc(i, u)$ is a temporal decay function returning lower values for older ratings, and higher values for the most recent ones. Inspired by [11], as decay function we adopted the following exponential function

$$disc(u, i) = e^{-\beta \cdot |t_{u,last} - t_{u,i}|} \quad (4)$$

where $t_{u,last}$ indicates the timestamp of the last rating of the user u and $t_{u,i}$ the timestamp when user u rated i; $\beta > 0$ controls the decay rate.

In our experimental setting we adopted the Netflix dataset which contains ratings from October 1998 until October 2005. This information affects the choose of β because a too big value of beta could make the initial ratings not valuable at all. We decided to consider all the ratings valuable with a very smooth curve and a minimum value of 10^{-6}. Hence β value was set to 1/200 obtaining $2,831 * 10^{-6}$ for the farest rating over time.

4.2 Session-Based Intent Modeling

User sessions definition. Session analysis is quite common in music domain, since users are used to listen to many songs in sequence. There a session is represented by a set of consecutive ratings with a small gap of time between them [10]. Conversely, sessions are not easy to find in movie domain, since users typically watch a small number of movies in brief timeslots and the temporal gap among visions or ratings could be large (sometimes several days or even months). In our setting, in order to identify user sessions we propose an EM clustering used to train two univariate Gaussian Mixture Models (with equivariance and variable variance). The number of clusters has been evaluated based on the Bayesian Information Criterion considering the fitted models with a number of clusters from 1 up to 300. In order to remove outliers from each session s, for each computed cluster we do not consider ratings falling outside the interval $[\mu_s - \sigma_s, \mu_s + \sigma_s]$, with μ_s and σ_s being respectively the mean and the standard deviation of ratings distribution for the session s.

Intent modeling. Once user sessions are determined, they can be used to analyze the user activities taking into account the temporal dynamics. In this work we present an approach to model the users intents over time, by considering three key properties: *importance*, *persistence* and *recency* of an intent among the user sessions. The first property indicates the importance of an intent in each session computed as the percentage of items covering that intent. The second property considers how many sessions the intent is important for, therefore it sums the importance of the intent for each sessions. Finally, the third property focuses on the intent freshness, penalizing old sessions with a temporal decay function.

More formally, the following formula computes the interest of the user u with respect to the feature f:

$$p(f|u) = \frac{\sum_{s \in S(u)} \frac{\sum_{i \in I(s)} cov(f,i)}{|F(s)|} disc(s,u)}{\sum_{s \in S(u)} disc(s,u)} \qquad (5)$$

where $S(u)$ indicates sessions computed for the user u; $I(s)$ is the set of items in s; $cov(f,i)$ is a binary function returning 1 if the item i is associated with the feature f, 0 otherwise; $F(s)$ represents the set of features associated with all the items in s; $disc(s)$ is the temporal decay function adapted to handle the sessions instead of the items, considering a session as an item in Equation (4) where the session date is that of the last rated item in such session. As for the previous case, β value was set to 1/200.

5 EXPERIMENTAL SETTING

Dataset. In order to verify our research questions and evaluate our proposal, we used the popular movie datasets derived from the Netflix Prize Context [4]. Netflix dataset contains over 100 million ratings provided by ˜480,000 users on ˜17,000 movies. Such

ratings were collected between 1998 and 2005 and associated with the relative date. However, such dataset contains noise added on purpose for reasons of privacy, as explained in the Netflix Prize Rules*: "some of the rating data for some customers in the training and qualifying sets have been deliberately perturbed in one or more of the following ways: deleting ratings; inserting alternative ratings and dates; and modifying rating dates". Indeed, we found that some users rated an exaggerated number of movies in some days: 30% of all the users have rated at least 61 movies in the most *prolific* day. Therefore, in order to train the session-based user model on a clean subset of the dataset, we selected a sample of users removing the outliers by means of the following steps: (i) we discarded the users with less than 20 ratings as at this stage of our study we are not interested in evaluating the cold users behavior; (ii) we ordered the users in decreasing order of the maximum number of daily interactions and discarded the top 30%; (iii) we ordered the users in decreasing order of the average number of daily interactions and discarded the top 30%. The dataset used for training the models contains 233,452 users, 18,104,476 rating and 17,763 movies. We built training and test sets by employing a 80%-20% holdout temporal split for each user.

Recommendation algorithms. We evaluated our approaches w.r.t. the xQuAD baseline via a re-ranking of the BPRMF [16] and BPRSLIM [14] algorithms resulting recommendations. We trained both models using the MyMediaLite† implementation upon the dataset described in Section 5 to produce for each user a Top-300 recommendations list (**R** in Algorithm 1, used to compute $r^*(u,i)$ in Equation (1)), and then we re-ranked those lists using xQuAD. The resulting recommendations lists are the baselines we compare against. xQuAD uses side information to lead to diversified recommendations. In this work the diversification is based on the movie genre feature. In Netflix dataset this information is not explicitly provided. In order to extract the genre information, we mapped each movie with the corresponding Freebase resource by means of its title and year of release and we then selected the corresponding genres. Overall, the number of distinct genres extracted is 266.

In our evaluation, the time-based and session-based intent modelings proposed in Section 4 are used as alternatives to the pure frequency based intent modeling in the original xQuAD. These two variations of xQuAD, are denoted as: TB_xQuAD, SB_xQuAD, where *TB* stands for time-based and *SB* for session-based. The resulting evaluated algorithms are then:

- BPRMF + xQuAD (baseline)
- BPRMF + Time-based xQuAD variant (TB_xQuAD)
- BPRMF + Session-based xQuAD variant (SB_xQuAD)
- BPRSLIM + xQuAD (baseline)
- BPRSLIM + Time-based xQuAD variant (TB_xQuAD)
- BPRSLIM + Session-based xQuAD variant (SB_xQuAD)

Metrics. In order to evaluate *accuracy*, we measured nDCG. As for *individual diversity*, namely the degree of dissimilarity among all items in the list provided to a user, was measured by ERR-IA as it has been shown [19] to be the metric targeted by xQuAD, while for *aggregate diversity* we computed the Catalog Coverage (percentage of items recommended at least to one user). An evaluation on the

---

*http://netflixprize.com/rules.html
†http://www.mymedialite.net

(a) Results for BPRMF

(b) Results for BPRSLIM

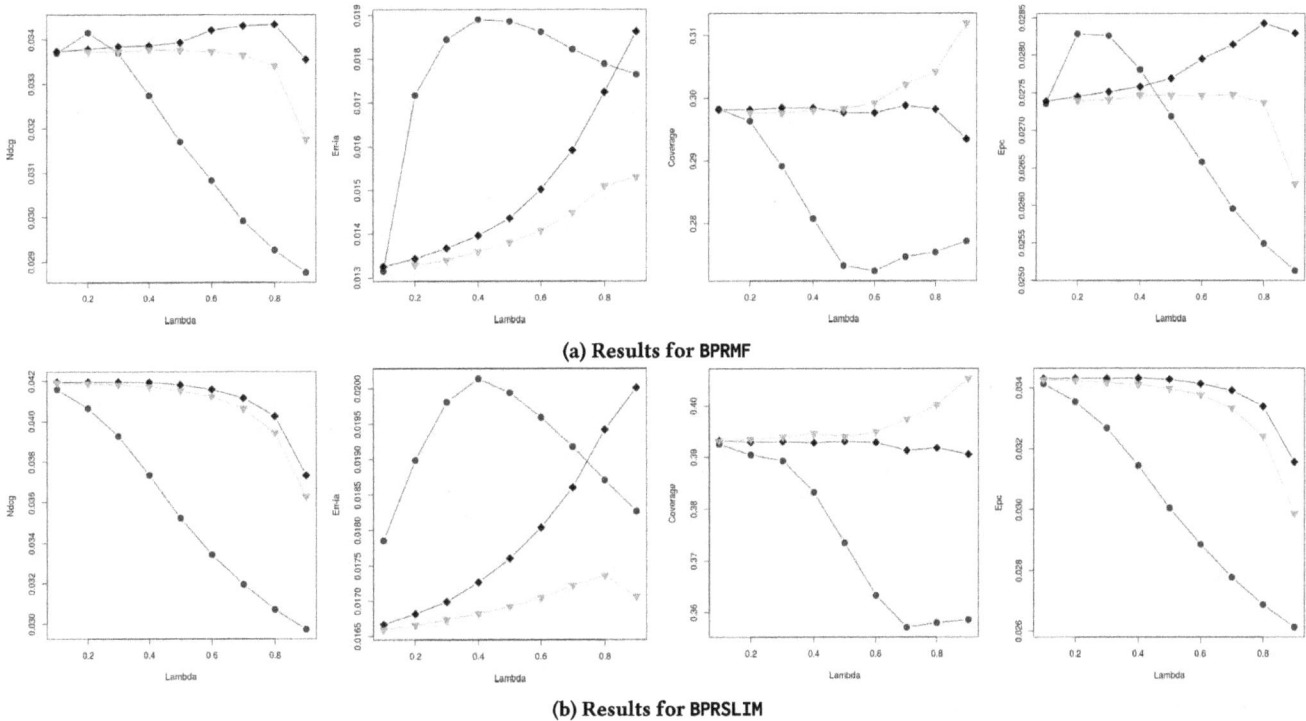

Figure 1: Curves obtained by varying λ from 0.1 to 0.9 (step 0.1), using BPRMF and BPRSLIM as recommendation algorithm. From left to right we plot the values of nDCG, ERR-IA, Catalog Coverage and EPC. The blue line represents values for the base xQuAD evaluation while the black and yellow lines represent respectively values for the time-based and session-based version of xQuAD

novelty of computed results has been done through EPC (Expected Popularity Complement) [19]. For all the aforementioned metrics we used the implementation provided by RankSys framework‡ on the Top-10 recommendation list.

Results Discussion. Charts in Figure 1a and Figure 1b show the curves for nDCG, ERR-IA, Catalog Coverage and EPC, for both BPRMF and BPRSLIM variants. Very interestingly both the time- and session-based version of xQuAD improves results in terms of accuracy, aggregate diversity as well as of novelty independently of the recommendation algorithm adopted. Generally, the time-based variant of xQuAD performs better than the session-based one but for Catalog Coverage where we have better results for the session-based implementation of xQuAD. It is worth noticing that the base version of xQuAD outperforms its time-based variants up to a certain value of λ for both BPRMF and BPRSLIM. For the former this value lies between 0.8 and 0.9 while for the latter between 0.7 and 0.8. Hence, in case we are interested in higher values of diversity, time may play an important role. This observation is also strengthen by the higher values we obtain in terms of precision, catalog coverage and novelty. In Table 1 we see that with $\lambda = 0.8$ we obtain the best result in terms of trade-off among the various metrics we measured in our experiments.

Algorithm	Ndcg@10	ERR IA@10	Coverage@10	EPC@10
BPRMF+XQUAD	0.029264	**0.01789**	0.27540	0.02549
BPRMF_SB_XQuAD	0.03340	0.01510	**0.30417**	0.02737
BPRMF_TB_XQuAD	**0.03433**	0.01724	0.29820	**0.02843**
BPRSLIM+XQUAD	0.03072	0.01870	0.35799	0.02686
BPRSLIM_SB_XQuAD	0.03943	0.01736	**0.40021**	0.03240
BPRSLIM_TB_XQuAD	**0.04026**	**0.01942**	0.39183	**0.03339**

Table 1: Comparative results in terms of accuracy, individual diversity and aggregate diversity with $\lambda = 0.8$

6 CONCLUSIONS AND FUTURE WORK

In this paper we investigate the role of temporal information while modeling a user profile in computing diversified recommendations. We propose two different time-dependent user modelings which take into account also the user rating history. One of the two proposed methods bases on a new session analysis technique by considering those periods where the user interacted in a more constant way with the system. Experimental results demonstrated that considering temporal dynamics leads to better accuracy-diversity balance and better intent-aware diversification. The results we obtained in this preliminary investigation are quite promising and we are currently extending our experimental evaluation to different datasets in diverse domains as well as to other metrics in order to measure the quality of the recommendations not just in terms of accuracy when time is taken into account.

REFERENCES

[1] Gediminas Adomavicius and YoungOk Kwon. 2012. Improving Aggregate Recommendation Diversity Using Ranking-Based Techniques. *IEEE Transactions on Knowledge and Data Engineering* 24, 5 (May 2012), 896–911. DOI: http://dx.doi.org/10.1109/TKDE.2011.15

‡https://github.com/RankSys/RankSys

[2] Azin Ashkan, Branislav Kveton, Shlomo Berkovsky, and Zheng Wen. 2015. Optimal Greedy Diversity for Recommendation.. In *IJCAI*, Qiang Yang and Michael Wooldridge (Eds.). AAAI Press, 1742–1748.

[3] Fabiano Belém, Rodrygo Santos, Jussara Almeida, and Marcos Gonçalves. 2013. Topic Diversity in Tag Recommendation. In *Proceedings of the 7th ACM Conference on Recommender Systems (RecSys '13)*. ACM, New York, NY, USA, 141–148. DOI: http://dx.doi.org/10.1145/2507157.2507184

[4] James Bennett, Stan Lanning, and Netflix Netflix. 2007. The Netflix Prize. In *In KDD Cup and Workshop in conjunction with KDD*.

[5] Jaime Carbonell and Jade Goldstein. 1998. The Use of MMR, Diversity-based Reranking for Reordering Documents and Producing Summaries. In *Proceedings of the 21st Annual International ACM SIGIR Conference on Research and Development in Information Retrieval (SIGIR '98)*.

[6] Pablo Castells, Neil J. Hurley, and Saul Vargas. 2015. *Novelty and Diversity in Recommender Systems*. Springer US, Boston, MA, 881–918. DOI: http://dx.doi.org/10.1007/978-1-4899-7637-6_26

[7] Olivier Chapelle, Shihao Ji, Ciya Liao, Emre Velipasaoglu, Larry Lai, and Su-Lin Wu. 2011. Intent-based Diversification of Web Search Results: Metrics and Algorithms. *Inf. Retr.* 14, 6 (Dec. 2011), 572–592. DOI: http://dx.doi.org/10.1007/s10791-011-9167-7

[8] Michael D. Ekstrand, F. Maxwell Harper, Martijn C. Willemsen, and Joseph A. Konstan. 2014. User Perception of Differences in Recommender Algorithms. In *Proceedings of the 8th ACM Conference on Recommender Systems (RecSys '14)*. ACM, New York, NY, USA, 161–168. DOI: http://dx.doi.org/10.1145/2645710.2645737

[9] Ke Ji, Runyuan Sun, Wenhao Shu, and Xiang Li. 2015. Next-song Recommendation with Temporal Dynamics. *Know.-Based Syst.* 88, C (Nov. 2015), 134–143. DOI: http://dx.doi.org/10.1016/j.knosys.2015.07.039

[10] Noam Koenigstein, Gideon Dror, and Yehuda Koren. 2011. Yahoo! Music Recommendation: Modeling Music Ratings with Temporal Dynamics and Item Taxonomy. In *Proceedings of the Fifth ACM Conference on Recommender Systems (RecSys '11)*. ACM, New York, NY, USA, 165–172. DOI: http://dx.doi.org/10.1145/2043932.2043964

[11] Yehuda Koren. 2009. Collaborative Filtering with Temporal Dynamics. In *Proceedings of the 15th ACM SIGKDD International Conference on Knowledge Discovery and Data Mining (KDD '09)*. ACM, New York, NY, USA, 447–456. DOI: http://dx.doi.org/10.1145/1557019.1557072

[12] Onur Küçüktunç, Erik Saule, Kamer Kaya, and Ümit V. Çatalyürek. 2014. Diversifying Citation Recommendations. *ACM Transactions on Intelligent Systems and Technology* 5, 4, Article 55 (Dec. 2014), 21 pages. DOI: http://dx.doi.org/10.1145/2668106

[13] Sean M. McNee, John Riedl, and Joseph A. Konstan. 2006. Being Accurate is Not Enough: How Accuracy Metrics Have Hurt Recommender Systems. In *CHI '06 Extended Abstracts on Human Factors in Computing Systems (CHI EA '06)*. 1097–1101.

[14] Xia Ning and George Karypis. 2011. Slim: Sparse linear methods for top-n recommender systems. In *Data Mining (ICDM), 2011 IEEE 11th International Conference on*. IEEE, 497–506.

[15] Tommaso Di Noia, Jessica Rosati, Paolo Tomeo, and Eugenio Di Sciascio. 2017. Adaptive multi-attribute diversity for recommender systems. *Inf. Sci.* 382-383 (2017), 234–253.

[16] Steffen Rendle, Christoph Freudenthaler, Zeno Gantner, and Lars Schmidt-Thieme. 2009. BPR: Bayesian personalized ranking from implicit feedback. In *Proceedings of the twenty-fifth conference on uncertainty in artificial intelligence*. AUAI Press, 452–461.

[17] R.L.T. Santos, C. Macdonald, and I. Ounis. 2010. Exploiting Query Reformulations for Web Search Result Diversification. In *WWW '10*. 881–890.

[18] Saúl Vargas, F. Maxwell Harper, Martijn C. Willemsen, and Pablo Castells. 2014. Coverage, Redundancy and Size-awareness in Genre Diversity for Recommender Systems. In *Proceedings of the 8th ACM Conference on Recommender Systems (RecSys '14)*. 209–216.

[19] Saúl Vargas and Pablo Castells. 2011. Rank and Relevance in Novelty and Diversity Metrics for Recommender Systems. In *Proceedings of the Fifth ACM Conference on Recommender Systems (RecSys '11)*. 109–116.

[20] S. Vargas and P. Castells. 2013. Exploiting the Diversity of User Preferences for Recommendation. In *OAIR '13*. 129–136.

[21] Saul Vargas, Pablo Castells, and David Vallet. 2011. Intent-oriented Diversity in Recommender Systems. In *Proceedings of the 34th International ACM SIGIR Conference on Research and Development in Information Retrieval (SIGIR '11)*. ACM, New York, NY, USA, 1211–1212. DOI: http://dx.doi.org/10.1145/2009916.2010124

[22] Jacek Wasilewski and Neil Hurley. 2016. Intent-Aware Diversification Using a Constrained PLSA. In *Proceedings of the 10th ACM Conference on Recommender Systems (RecSys '16)*. ACM, New York, NY, USA, 39–42. DOI: http://dx.doi.org/10.1145/2959100.2959177

Deriving Item Features Relevance from Past User Interactions

Leonardo Cella
leonardo.cella@mail.polimi.it
Politecnico di Milano

Stefano Cereda
stefano1.cereda@mail.polimi.it
Politecnico di Milano

Massimo Quadrana
massimo.quadrana@polimi.it
Politecnico di Milano

Paolo Cremonesi
paolo.cremonesi@polimi.it
Politecnico di Milano

ABSTRACT

Item-based recommender systems suggest products based on the similarities between items computed either from past user preferences (collaborative filtering) or from item content features (content-based filtering). Collaborative filtering has been proven to outperform content-based filtering in a variety of scenarios. However, in item cold-start, collaborative filtering cannot be used directly since past user interactions are not available for the newly added items. Hence, content-based filtering is usually the only viable option left.

In this paper we propose a novel feature-based machine learning model that addresses the item cold-start problem by jointly exploiting item content features and past user preferences. The model learns the relevance of each content feature from the collaborative item similarity, hence allowing to embed collaborative knowledge into a purely content-based algorithm. In our experiments, the proposed approach outperforms classical content-based filtering on an enriched version of the Netflix dataset, showing that collaborative knowledge can be effectively embedded into content-based approaches and exploited in item cold-start recommendation.

1 INTRODUCTION

Item-based algorithms are widespread methods for recommending relevant items to users [4]. Because predictions rely on the computation of similarities between pairs of items, they have good runtime performance and their recommendations are easy to explain. Collaborative Filtering (CF) similarities usually leads to good predictive accuracy, especially if trained with regard to suitable optimization objective functions [3]. The downside of CF algorithms is that similarities are only available for items with a – possibly large – number of ratings. Thus for entirely new items – i.e., ones that have no ratings – CF methods are not capable of computing recommendations. Moreover, CF are biased toward popular *Blockbuster* items, thus reducing the chances of novel recommendations. This happens because algorithms are trained (e.g., tuned) to achieve the best performance in terms of available ratings. This creates the rich-get-richer effect for popular items, which results in reducing the coverage of recommendations.

The new-item problem can be solved by using Content-Based Filtering methods (CBF). CBF requires that items are represented via a set of features – or attributes – that capture their intrinsic characteristics. The quality of CBF is severely limited by three factors [7]:

- quality is linked to the availability of a number of significant, well-structured, editorial-generated attributes (such as genres, actors, directors in the movie domain); however, many recommender systems base their recommendations on unstructured, user-generated attributes (i.e., tags, reviews) most of which are noisy or scarcely relevant;
- recommendations to each user do not use the ratings of other users, therefore ignoring potentially useful collaborative information;
- recommended items are similar to previously rated items, thus reducing diversity of recommendations.

Because of these limitations, a significant challenge to address with CBF is feature weighting, i.e., how to identify how much a feature is important in defining the perceived similarity between items.

Feature weighting can be viewed as an extension of the feature selection problem, where the goal is to provide an evaluation measure used to score and filter the different features. The choice of evaluation distinguishes between the three main categories of feature weighting algorithms: filters, embedded methods and wrappers [2].

Filter methods produce a feature set which is not tuned to a specific type of rating predictive model. Filter methods use a proxy measure instead of the error rate to score a feature subset. Common filters in recommender systems are based on TF-IDF weighting schemes [6].

Embedded methods perform feature weighting as part of the rating model construction process. Examples in recommender systems are Factorization Machines [10], UFSM [1] and SSLIM [8].

Wrapper methods use a pre-trained CF predictive model to score features, with a two-step approach. A CF algorithm is used to produce a model (step 1) and the wrapper methodology consists in using the CF model to assess the relative usefulness of features (step 2).

The main contributions of this work is a general, simple and straightforward wrapper method to make content-based algorithms ratings-aware by plugging learnable attribute weights onto them. The core principle is that if a feature co-occurs frequently only within similarly co-rated items, then that feature is a good candidate to be included as a relevant feature in defining the similarity between items.

UMAP'17, July 09-12, 2017, Bratislava, Slovakia
© 2017 ACM. 978-1-4503-4635-1/17/07...$15.00
DOI: http://dx.doi.org/10.1145/3079628.3079695

We conducted two experimental evaluations of the proposed method using the Netflix dataset enriched with attributes from IMDB. The experiment results show that the proposed model outperforms state-of-art CBF in both the warm-start and new-item scenarios.

2 RELATED WORKS

Some attempts have been done to reduce the quality gap between CF and CBF. Past works operate along two directions: filtering and embedded methods.

Filtering methods have underpinnings in information theory and information retrieval [6] and evaluate features without involving any learning algorithm. Filtering methods weight features with the goal of maximizing the information gain (e.g., TF-IDF or entropy-based weighting) and mitigating synonymy (e.g., LSA). As an example, the work in [9] adopts a TF-IDF approach in which users are considered as *documents* and the TF-IDF component is normalized across all users. The main drawback of filtering methods is that they do not take into account the ratings of users, therefore ignoring if the feature-based similarity between items is aligned with the user perception of similarity.

Embedded methods incorporate feature weighting as part of the rating learning process, and use the objective function of the learning process to guide searching for relevant features. Examples in recommender systems are SSLIM [8], UFSM [1] and Factorization Machines [10]. SSLIM adopts a Sparse Linear method with Side information for learning a sparse similarity matrix that is used for computing top-N recommendations [8]. The training incorporate both ratings from users and features about items. The main drawback of this approach is that the similarity is computed directly, without computing feature weights, and therefore cannot be used for new items. User-Specific Feature-based Similarity Models (UFSM) learn a personalized linear combination of similarity functions known as global similarity functions for cold-start top-N item recommendations. UFSM can be considered as a special case of Factorization Machines [1]. The main drawback of embedded methods is the coupling between the collaborative and content components of the model. When used on datasets with unstructured user-generated features (e.g., tags) the noise from the features propagate to the collaborative part, affecting the overall quality of the model. For this reason, when used in the new item scenario, predictive accuracy is only marginally improved with respect to content based techniques.

3 LEAST SQUARES FEATURE WEIGHING

As in any recommender system, we consider the problem of recommending items from a set I to users in the set U, and item features are picked from a set F. $\mathbf{R}^{|U| \times |I|}$ is the feedback matrix (either explicit or implicit). $\mathbf{A}^{|I| \times |F|}$ is the binary item feature matrix, in which $a_{if} = 1$ iff item i has feature f. In a generic item similarity model, given a item similarity matrix $S^{|I| \times |I|}$, the predicted relevance $\hat{r}_{ui}$ of item i for user u is computed as

$$\hat{r}_{ui} = \sum_{j \in N_k(i)} r_{uj} s_{ij} \tag{1}$$

where $N_k(i)$ is the set of k nearest neighbors of item i according to the similarity model. In top-N recommendation, the N items with the largest predicted relevance are recommended to the user. Notice that this approach allows to estimate the predicted rating for any item i as long as the similarities between i and any other item $j \in I$ can be computed, new items included.

Feature weighing. In its simplest formulation, feature weighing consists in computing the array of weights $\mathbf{w} \in \mathbb{R}^{|F|}$ such that each entry $w_f \in \mathbf{w}$ reflects the importance of the feature $f \in F$ for the given task. In other words, if two features f and f' have weights $w_f > w_{f'}$, then feature f is more relevant than f' for the task. We define the weighted similarity s_{ij} between items i and j as

$$s_{ij}^{(w)} = \sum_{f \in F} w_f a_{if} a_{jf} = \langle \mathbf{w}, \mathbf{a}_i \odot \mathbf{a}_j \rangle \tag{2}$$

where $\mathbf{a}_i, \mathbf{a}_j \in \{0, 1\}^{|F|}$ are the feature vectors of items i and j respectively and $\odot$ is the element-wise product.

In the case of binary attribute matrices, a typical feature weighting scheme is TF-IDF that weights the features in F proportionally to their specificity.

The proposed approach. In this work, we propose a solution based on least squares (LSQ) optimization to automatic feature weighing. Automatic feature weighing aims at inferring the weights in $\mathbf{w}$ from a collaborative model. Given the item-to-item weight matrix $S^{(CF)} \in \mathbb{R}^{|I| \times |I|}$ computed with collaborative filtering, the optimal weight vector $\mathbf{w}^*$ can be determined by solving the following LSQ problem:

$$\underset{\mathbf{w}^*}{\operatorname{argmin}} \, ||S^{(CF)} - S^{(w)}||_F^2 \tag{3}$$

where $S^{(w)} \in \mathbb{R}^{|I| \times |I|}$ is the pairwise weighted similarity matrix computed with (2). This LSQ formulation allows to compute the optimal weight vector $\mathbf{w}^*$ capable to reconstruct the CF similarity matrix by means of simple weighted CBF similarity with minimal error. Since our goal is to learn a set of feature weights so that CBF similarities mimic as close as possible CF ones, there is no need to add a regularization term, thus greatly simplifying the optimization. In the case of the simple linear weighing scheme of (2), the problem boils down to the following simple linear regression

$$\underset{\mathbf{w}^*}{\operatorname{argmin}} \sum_{i \in I} \sum_{j \in I \setminus \{i\}} \left(s_{ij}^{(CF)} - \langle \mathbf{w}, \mathbf{a}_i \odot \mathbf{a}_j \rangle \right)^2 \tag{4}$$

which can be efficiently solved analytically. We call our approach LFW (Least-squares Feature Weighing).

When a new item is added to the catalog, we use $\mathbf{w}^*$ to compute its weighted similarity w.r.t. the previously existing items. Then, it can be recommended to users by using Equation 1. We conjecture that our model is capable to weight features in accordance to their *collaborative relevance*. If this conjecture holds, the learned weighting scheme should outperform traditional, fully content-based weighting schemes (like TF-IDF) in the new item scenario without exhibiting a severe degradation of performance in standard (warm-start) scenario.

It is worth noting that the collaborative similarity matrix $S^{(CF)}$ can be obtained with any CF algorithm. In our experiments, we used SLIM since it has been extensively proven to achieve state-of-the-art performance in many CF tasks [11].

4 EVALUATION

We performed experiments to confirm that our approach (a) is capable to produce useful recommendations in an item cold-start scenario without (b) incurring into severe degradation of performance in warm-start scenarios.

Dataset. For our experiments, we used a version of the Netflix dataset enriched with structured and unstructured attributes extracted from IMDB. This dataset has 250k users, 6.5k movies and 8.8M ratings in 1-5 scale. The rating data is enriched with 4699 binary attributes representing various kinds of meta-information on movies such as director, actor, genres and user-generated tags.

Evaluation procedure. To investigate the new-item scenario, we performed a 70/30 random hold-out split over items. To investigate the item warm-start scenario, we instead split over users with the same proportions. The final partitioning of the dataset is show in Figure 1. The sub-matrix A was used to train SLIM first, and then to fit SLIM similarities with our LFW model. The hyper-parameters of SLIM were tuned on a separate validation set extracted from A before fitting LFW. The neighborhood size k was tuned on a second validations set extracted from B by using ROC-AUC. The models fit on A were used to generate recommendations both in the new-item and in the warm-start scenario.

Sub-matrices B and C were used exclusively in evaluation. In the new-item scenario, the ratings in A were used as user-profile to score the items in C, the ground truth. In the warm-start scenario, we held-out 30% of the positive ratings (> 3) of every user as ground truth and used the remaining ratings as user profiles. In both scenarios, the ground truth is composed only by items with rating > 3. We used accuracy metrics (Precision, Recall, MRR, MAP and NDCG) to evaluate the ranking recommendation quality. We also evaluate the Coverage and Diversity in recommendation by using the definitions in [5]. Notice that, since the user profiles and ground truth differ in the two scenarios analyzed, their results are not directly comparable.

Baselines. We used simple unweighted cosine similarity (Cosine) and TF-IDF-weighted cosine similarity (CosineIDF) as CBF baselines to evaluate the performance of LFW in both scenarios [1]. SLIM was used as additional CF baseline in the warm-start scenario.

Figure 1: Dataset partitioning with dimensions.

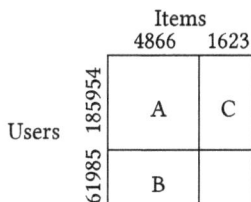

Discussion. Let us discuss the new-item scenario first, since it is the main focus of our work. In Table 1, we report the accuracy metrics for different recommendation list sizes N. LFW consistently outperforms all the baselines in all metrics at any value of N. We want to highlight that LFW differs from the other CBF baselines solely in the feature weighing scheme. Therefore, the improvement in performance must be due to a better feature weighing discovered by our approach.

In Table 2, we report the results for the item warm-start scenario. For space reasons, we report only the values for $N = 5$. As expected, the CF approach based on SLIM has the best predictive accuracy in the warm-start scenario. Interestingly, LFW still outperforms both Cosine and Cosine TF-IDF baselines by a even large margin with respect to the new item scenario. In summary, LFW cannot compete with SLIM in warm-start scenarios, also due to its CBF nature. Still, its degradation in performance is much less evident than the other CBF baselines.

Table 1: Performance evaluation for the new-item scenario.

Algorithm	n	Precision	Recall	MRR	MAP	NCDG
LFW	5	**0.1323**	**0.0825**	**0.2551**	**0.1062**	**0.0940**
	25	**0.0858**	**0.2406**	**0.2795**	**0.0915**	**0.1715**
	50	**0.0654**	**0.3459**	**0.2822**	**0.0950**	**0.2097**
Cosine	5	0.0938	0.0502	0.1984	0.0748	0.0622
	25	0.0624	0.1473	0.2189	0.0573	0.1127
	50	0.0485	0.2231	0.2218	0.0582	0.1411
CosineIDF	5	0.0950	0.0533	0.2068	0.0752	0.0654
	25	0.0658	0.1564	0.2280	0.0605	0.1192
	50	0.0510	0.2348	0.2309	0.0621	0.1486

Table 2: Performance evaluation for the warm-start scenario.

Algorithm	N	Precision	Recall	MRR	MAP	NCDG
SLIM	5	**0.1383**	**0.1497**	**0.2819**	**0.1342**	**0.1453**
LFW	5	<u>0.0640</u>	<u>0.0577</u>	<u>0.1438</u>	<u>0.0744</u>	<u>0.0597</u>
Cosine	5	0.0334	0.0277	0.0826	0.0270	0.0302
CosineIDF	5	0.0337	0.0258	0.0855	0.0276	0.0296

Table 3: Evaluation of coverage and diversity.

Algorithm	new-item		warm-start	
	Coverage	Diversity	Coverage	Diversity
SLIM	-	-	0.1683	**4.0585**
LFW	<u>0.8897</u>	**5.3628**	<u>0.4891</u>	<u>2.1289</u>
Cosine	0.9236	4.1529	**0.5723**	1.1519
CosineIDF	**0.9495**	4.2061	0.5684	1.1517

---

[1]We experimented also with other similarity metrics (e.g. Pearson), but those were consistently outperformed by these baselines, so we do not report them here.

In Table 3, we report the evaluation of coverage and diversity for the top-5 recommendations in both scenarios. In the warm-start scenario, "traditional" CBF algorithms have greater coverage than CF, whereas CF has greater diversity in the warm-start scenario. nterestingly, LFW seems to "take the best" from both worlds, achieving CBF-level coverage and CF-level diversity in both scenarios.

5 QUALITATIVE ANALYSIS

The good performances in both scenarios suggest that the weight vector w^* is capable of highlighting the importance of the various features in terms of the user-perceived similarity. In order to understand this concept better, we provide a qualitative analysis on how features are weighted differently by two methods, namely Cosine TF-IDF and our method LFW.

In Table 4, we report the highest and lowest weighted features by LFW. For example, Jay Roach is the director of both "Meet the Parents" and "Meet the Fockers", and of the Austin Powers series. All these movies are comedy and target roughly the same audience, hence they are good candidates of being recommended by a CF algorithm despite having very different casts. Lois Maxwell has acted as Miss Moneypenny – James Bond's secretary – in the first 14 Bond movies. Hence, she represents another important cluster of movies. Interestingly, Lois Maxwell has higher importance than the various directors or main characters of Bond movies, since they changed frequently among them. On the other hand, the feature "snakebite" hardly identifies similar movies (for example, it is shared by completely different movies like "Kill Bill: Vol. 2" and "Siddharta"). Analogously, the feature "giant spider" is shared by two masterpieces ("The Lord of the Rings" and "Harry Potter") and a collection of 12 minor unrelated movies.

Table 4: Features relevance learned by LFW.

Most relevant features	Least relevant features
Molly Ringwald	snakebite
Jay Roach	John Ashton
Lois Maxwell	Ally Sheedy
motorcycle accident	giant spider
Jayne Eastwood	stable

Table 5 shows that TF-IDF, by weighing features proportionally to their rarity, can hardly capture any interesting relationship from the actual movie consumption. Surprisingly, features representing genres (such as comedy and thriller) have low weights.

To shed a light on this, in Table 6 we report the features that differ the most between LFW and TF-IDF. The weights vectors of both methods were first normalized in [0, 1] before computing their difference feature-wise. It is interesting to see that LFW raises the relevance of genres w.r.t. TF-IDF, which are definitely an important set of features that receive a really low TF-IDF weight. Conversely, the relevance of very rare countries of origin in our dataset (e.g. Brazil and Romania) is strongly decreased. For example, we have only 2 Brazilian movies with just 20 ratings in common in our dataset.

Table 5: Features relevance according to TF-IDF.

Most relevant features	Least relevant features
knowledge	drama
Iran	comedy
Bulgaria	film independent
China	thriller
Argentina	romance

Table 6: Feature importance LFW vs TF-IDF.

LFW >TF-IDF	LFW < TF-IDF
USA	Brazil
drama	Romania
Molly Ringwald	Peru
comedy	Philippines
film independent	George P. Cosmatos

6 CONCLUSION AND FUTURE WORK

In this paper, we propose a feature-based linear regression framework for personalized recommendation. We presented a novel approach to compute item feature scores that defines their relevance according to expressed user preferences. In contrast to traditional recommender systems, our approach solves both the item and the user cold start issues. Moreover, it has a linear temporal complexity with respect to item features, and thus it is lighter than the state of the art competitor models. Future directions include the development of personalized feature weighing tools and the extensive evaluation of this approaches with different datasets and CF algorithms.

REFERENCES

[1] Asmaa Elbadrawy and George Karypis. 2015. User-Specific Feature-Based Similarity Models for Top-n Recommendation of New Items. *ACM Trans. Intell. Syst. Technol.* 6, 3, Article 33 (April 2015), 20 pages. DOI : http://dx.doi.org/10.1145/2700495

[2] Isabelle Guyon and André Elisseeff. 2003. An Introduction to Variable and Feature Selection. *J. Mach. Learn. Res.* 3 (March 2003), 1157–1182. http://dl.acm.org/citation.cfm?id=944919.944968

[3] Domonkos Tikk Istvn Pilszy. 2009. Recommending new movies: even a few ratings are more valuable than metadata. *RecSys 09 Proceedings of the third ACM conference on Recommender systems* (2009), 93 – 100. DOI : http://dx.doi.org/10.1145/1639714.1639731

[4] Jon Herlocker Shilad Sen J. Ben Schafer, Dan Frankowski. 2007. Collaborative Filtering Recommender Systems. *Lecture Notes in Computer Science (LNCS)* 4321 (2007), 291, 324. DOI : http://dx.doi.org/10.1007/978-3-540-72079-9_9

[5] Marius Kaminskas and Derek Bridge. 2016. Diversity, Serendipity, Novelty, and Coverage: A Survey and Empirical Analysis of Beyond-Accuracy Objectives in Recommender Systems. *ACM Trans. Interact. Intell. Syst.* 7, 1, Article 2 (Dec. 2016), 42 pages. DOI : http://dx.doi.org/10.1145/2926720

[6] Pasquale Lops, Marco De Gemmis, and Giovanni Semeraro. 2011. Content-based recommender systems: State of the art and trends. In *Recommender systems handbook.* Springer, 73–105.

[7] Dunja Mladenic. July 1999. Text-Learning and Related Intelligent Agents: A Survey. *IEEE Intelligent Systems* 14 (July 1999), 44–54. DOI : http://dx.doi.org/10.1109/5254.784084

[8] Xia Ning and George Karypis. 2012. Sparse Linear Methods with Side Information for Top-N Recommendations. In *Proceedings of the 21st International Conference on World Wide Web (WWW '12 Companion)*. ACM, New York, NY, USA, 581–582. DOI : http://dx.doi.org/10.1145/2187980.2188137

[9] Yannis Manolopoulos Panagiotis Symeonidis, Alexandros Nanopoulos. 2007. Feature-Weighted User Model for Recommender Systems. *UM 07 Proceedings of the 11th international conference on User Modeling* (2007), 97 – 106. DOI :

http://dx.doi.org/10.1007/978-3-540-73078-1_13

[10] Steffen Rendle. 2012. Factorization Machines with libFM. *ACM Trans. Intell. Syst. Technol.* 3, 3, Article 57 (May 2012), 22 pages. DOI : http://dx.doi.org/10.1145/

2168752.2168771

[11] George Karypis Xia Ning. 2011. SLIM: Sparse Linear Methods for Top-N Recommender Systems. IEEE. DOI : http://dx.doi.org/10.1109/ICDM.2011.134

A Clustering Approach for Personalizing Diversity in Collaborative Recommender Systems

Farzad Eskandanian
Center for Web Intelligence
DePaul University, Chicago
feskanda@depaul.edu

Bamshad Mobasher
Center for Web Intelligence
DePaul University, Chicago
mobasher@cs.depaul.edu

Robin Burke
Center for Web Intelligence
DePaul University, Chicago
rburke@cs.depaul.edu

ABSTRACT

Much of the focus of recommender systems research has been on the accurate prediction of users' ratings for unseen items. Recent work has suggested that objectives such as diversity and novelty in recommendations are also important factors in the effectiveness of a recommender system. However, methods that attempt to increase diversity of recommendation lists for all users without considering each user's preference or tolerance for diversity may lead to monotony for some users and to poor recommendations for others. Our goal in this research is to evaluate the hypothesis that users' propensity towards diversity varies greatly and that the diversity of recommendation lists should be consistent with the level of user interest in diverse recommendations. We propose a pre-filtering clustering approach to group users with similar levels of tolerance for diversity. Our contributions are twofold. First, we propose a method for personalizing diversity by performing collaborative filtering independently on different segments of users based on the degree of diversity in their profiles. Secondly, we investigate the accuracy-diversity tradeoffs using the proposed method across different user segments. As part of this evaluation we propose new metrics, adapted from information retrieval, that help us measure the effectiveness of our approach in personalizing diversity. Our experimental evaluation is based on two different datasets: MovieLens movie ratings, and Yelp restaurant reviews.

KEYWORDS

Recommender Systems; Diversity; Personalization; Collaborative Filtering;

ACM Reference format:
Farzad Eskandanian, Bamshad Mobasher, and Robin Burke. 2017. A Clustering Approach for Personalizing Diversity in Collaborative Recommender Systems. In *Proceedings of UMAP'17, July 09-12, 2017, Bratislava, Slovakia,*, 5 pages.
DOI: http://dx.doi.org/10.1145/3079628.3079699

1 INTRODUCTION

Recommender systems help users find useful items by tailoring recommendations to the users' tastes and preferences. From the

beginning, much of the attention in recommender systems research has been devoted to generating accurate recommendations. But, focusing only on accuracy as an objective may prevent recommender systems from taking the risk of recommending items that are different from those seen by user in the past. This, in turn may lead to monotony in users' interactions with the system. Indeed, recommending too many similar or redundant items are well-known drawbacks of many of the traditional recommendation algorithms. In recent years other criteria beyond accuracy, such as diversity and novelty of recommendations, have been studied as important factors affecting the effectiveness of recommendation for users [10, 17, 18]. In particular, "diversity" is a list-wise property that may add another dimension of quality and utility to the recommendation lists generated for a user by the system. In our context, diversity refers to the distribution of categories, genres, or topical areas with a recommended list of items

Many of the approaches studied so far to incorporate the notion of diversity in recommendation have focused on increasing the diversity of recommendation lists for all users while maintaining accuracy. Early work in information retrieval, for instance, has involved re-ranking the search results in a way that would increase the topic diversity of the top results. One such approach involves a re-ranking algorithm called Maximal Marginal Relevance (MMR) [2]. *Marginal relevance* is defined as a linear combination of relevance (to the query) and dissimilarity of retrieved documents in the search results. The core ideas behind this re-ranking approach have been extended to the area of intent-aware diversification [1, 15]. Other approaches have tried to incorporate the notion of diversity into the learning to rank process [7, 16].

However, many of these methods generally assume that the user's preference or tolerance for diversity is constant across all users. This assumption, however, may not be appropriate in many situations. As an example consider the domain of movie recommendations (e.g., Netflix). One can imagine two extreme cases: one user, with very narrow movie interests, likes to receive as recommendations only science fiction movies made within the last 10 years; another user has a much broader taste in movies and would prefer a more diverse set of movies from many genres in her recommendation list. Obviously, any attempt to increase the diversity of recommendations in a uniform way for all users will result in poor recommendations for the first user. For this reason it is important to adapt the diversity of recommendations to users based on their degree of tolerance and propensity for diversity. In other words, recommender systems need not only personalize the recommendation lists based on users' preferences or tastes, but also personalize the degree of diversity in the recommendation lists.

Personalizing diversity has been discussed in some recent work. For example, one study [4] has considered a content-based approach to modeling users' interests and attempting to diversify recommendations based on the content information on items (such as item features). Another work [13] has addressed the need to increase the coverage of user propensity toward diversity and at the same time, reducing redundancy for diversity. Both of these solutions are based on a post-processing approach that accounts to a greedy re-ranking of the recommendation results.

Our goal is not only to develop recommendation algorithms that personalize the results based on past preferences, but also tailor the degree of diversity in the recommendation lists to users' tolerance for diversity. To this end, we are proposing a pre-filtering approach to personalize diversity by automatically segmenting the users based on their preferences on the predefined categories (topics, genres, etc.) associated with items. We perform this clustering using a novel approach that takes into account similarities among users based on the distribution of categories in their user profiles, and this resulting in segments of users with the same degree of interest or propensity for diversity. We then employ a user-based collaborative filtering approach to compare the recommendations in the general population (without diversity-based segmentation) with those obtained for each segment separately.

Our experimental evaluation performed on two different data sets, shows that the proposed clustering approach is effective in tailoring the diversity of recommendation lists to user's propensity for diversity.

2 MEASURING DIVERSITY

There are two primary frameworks for measuring diversity in recommender systems. The first framework is based on the pairwise similarity of items in a list called Intra-List Similarity (ILS) [18]. The other framework is called intent-aware diversification [1, 12] and has been mostly used in the Information Retrieval. The goal of intent-aware diversification is that in case of ambiguous queries the system should try to cover as many aspects or subtopics associated with the query as possible in order to increase the likelihood that the aspect corresponding to user's real intent is covered by search results.

Ideally, a diversification method should have two characteristics. First, it should diminish the amount of redundancy in the recommendation list. Secondly, it should cover all of the aspects that are interesting to user in order to personalize the level of diversity. From this perspective, our definition of diversity is similar to [13]. Both of these properties require category information for items. Fortunately, in many domains such information is usually available (e.g., genres in movies, cuisine type in restaurants, or topic categories of news stories). One goal of this research is to develop a diversity metric that can effectively capture both of the aforementioned characteristics, thus providing a uniform measure of the personalization of diversity in recommendation lists. We discuss our proposed metric, adapted from information retrieval, in Section 4.3

Assuming that a set of categories C already exists, the information about item categories can be used to model and measure the interest of user in each of those categories. Usually, the interaction

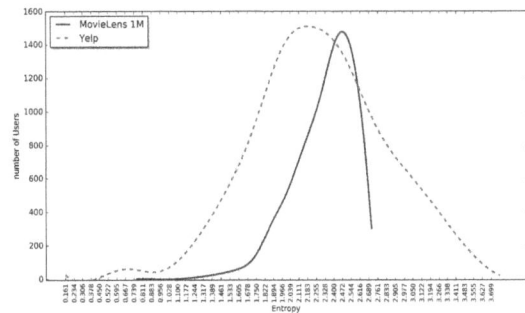

Figure 1: Entropy Distribution of user profiles.

of user u with the system is captured by the ratings $r(u, i)$ assigned to each of items $i \in I_u$, where I_u is the user profile (the collection of user's ratings on items in the set of all items I). Furthermore, we assume that each item in I belongs to one or more categories in C. Using ratings in user profile I_u, we can define the likelihood of the interest of user u in category c_k by:

$$P(c_k|u) = \frac{\sum_{i \in I_u} r(u, i)P(i \in c_k)}{\sum_{c_j \in C} \sum_{i \in I_u} r(u, i)P(i \in c_j)} \quad (1)$$

The likelihood of user being interested in a category c depends on the ratings of user on the items which belong to this category. Also the probability that each item belongs to this category $P(i \in c)$ is used as a coefficient to the ratings. A similar approach is used in [1, 14]. If we compute these values for every category in C, we get a representation of a user's profile as a distribution over categories.

To measure the degree of tolerance for diversity for a user u we use the Shannon entropy:

$$\mathcal{H}(u) = -\sum_{c \in C} P(c|u) \, log_2(P(c|u)) \quad (2)$$

High entropy in a categorical distribution of user profile represents high interest of user in diversity. Figure 1 shows the distribution of entropy values across the MovieLens and Yelp restaurant user profiles. The high variance of interest in diversity can be seen specially in the Yelp dataset. Our goal in this work is to develop an automated approach for segmenting users based on this diversity variance, so that users with with the same propensity for diversity are grouped together. We would then use standard collaborative recommendation algorithm on each segment separately. In an earlier work we showed that based on such segmentation the diversity level of users will be preserved in the recommendations [5]. But, the previous approach was based on manual segmentation of user profiles and the the metric used for diversity was Inter-List Distance (ILD) which does not capture user's preferences over genres, but only the spread of categories in the user's profile.

3 CLUSTERING USER PROFILES

We propose a clustering approach to automatically segment users who share the same level of diversity in their user profiles.

To segment the users based on their degree of preference in diversity we use K-Medoids clustering. K-Medoids is a partition-based clustering that uses the pair-wise distance of data points

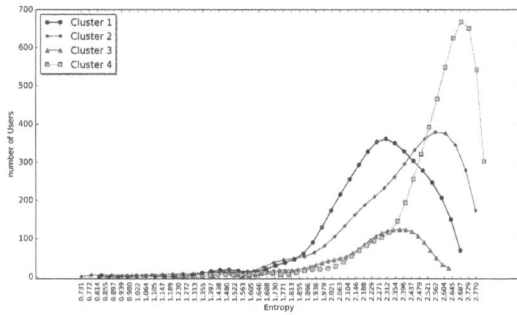

Figure 2: User clusters in MovieLens

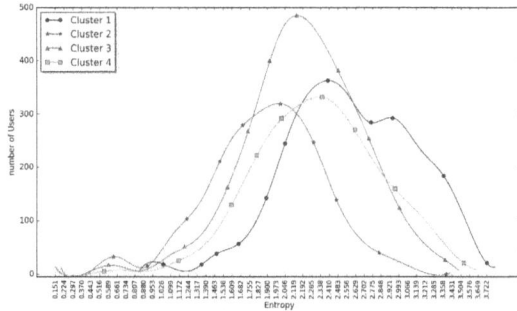

Figure 3: User clusters in Yelp.

like K-Means but instead of computing the mean centroids to minimize the within-cluster sum of distances it uses the data points themselves as centroids. To use K-Medoids we need to specify an appropriate distance metric that can measure distance between two distributions. KL-divergence is a measure of difference between two distributions but it does not satisfy two properties of a distance metric, symmetry and triangle inequality. For our purposes, symmetry is a critical property. A similar and smoother measure called Jensen-Shannon divergence [8, 9] that is symmetric but still does not hold the triangle inequality can be used safely, since K-Medoids clustering does not exploit the latter property.

Therefore, in order to define the distributional similarities between categorical distributions of user profiles, we use Jensen-Shannon divergence. The distance between two users u, v is defined by:

$$D_{\mathcal{JS}}(u,v) = \frac{1}{2}\left[D_{\mathcal{KL}}(u \parallel avg_{u,v}) + D_{\mathcal{KL}}(v \parallel avg_{u,v})\right] \quad (3)$$

Where:

$$D_{\mathcal{KL}}(u \parallel v) = \sum_{c \in C} P(c|u)\, log\frac{P(c|u)}{P(c|v)} \quad (4)$$

$$avg_{u,v}(c) = \frac{1}{2}(P(c|u) + P(c|v)) \quad (5)$$

4   EVALUATION

In this section, we discuss about our experiments design and our evaluation results.

	Size	Entropy	Method	NDCG	NDCG_IA	α-NDCG
Cluster 3	714	2.252	Div-Clust	0.203	**0.189**	**0.683**
			Standard	**0.232**	0.182	0.616
Cluster 1	1604	2.264	Div-Clust	0.285	**0.261**	**0.802**
			Standard	**0.292**	0.255	0.791
Cluster 2	1580	2.377	Div-Clust	0.227	**0.186**	**0.714**
			Standard	**0.229**	0.163	0.625
Cluster 4	2142	2.567	Div-Clust	0.195	0.137	**0.680**
			Standard	**0.231**	**0.158**	0.664

Table 1: MovieLens results for $\alpha = 0.6$.

	Method	α=0.1	α=0.3	α=0.6	α=0.9
Cluster 3	Div-Clust	**0.5631**	**0.6608**	**0.6826**	**0.6686**
	Standard	0.5062	0.5864	0.6159	0.6178
Cluster 1	Div-Clust	**0.7698**	**0.8014**	**0.8021**	**0.7887**
	Standard	0.7469	0.7901	0.7917	0.7806
Cluster 2	Div-Clust	**0.6098**	**0.6959**	**0.7143**	**0.7034**
	Standard	0.5358	0.6089	0.6251	0.6173
Cluster 4	Div-Clust	0.5885	0.6631	**0.6798**	**0.6721**
	Standard	**0.6204**	**0.6662**	0.6642	0.6478

Table 2: MovieLens results for α-NDCG with different α values.

	Size	Entropy	Method	NDCG	NDCG_IA	α-NDCG
Cluster 2	1592	1.884	Div-Clust	0.0066	0.2133	**0.3648**
			Standard	**0.0101**	**0.2659**	0.3628
Cluster 3	2329	2.201	Div-Clust	0.0231	**0.2513**	**0.5725**
			Standard	**0.0233**	0.2471	0.4753
Cluster 4	1765	2.323	Div-Clust	**0.0173**	**0.2068**	**0.5371**
			Standard	0.0143	0.1899	0.4609
Cluster 1	2336	2.602	Div-Clust	**0.0298**	**0.1831**	**0.6835**
			Standard	0.0266	0.1351	0.5168

Table 3: Yelp results for $\alpha = 0.3$.

	Method	α=0.1	α=0.3	α=0.6	α=0.9
Cluster 2	Div-Clust	**0.3052**	**0.3648**	0.4035	0.4222
	Standard	0.2973	0.3628	**0.4084**	**0.4286**
Cluster 3	Div-Clust	**0.4937**	**0.5725**	**0.5959**	**0.6016**
	Standard	0.3801	0.4753	0.5262	0.5432
Cluster 4	Div-Clust	**0.4519**	**0.5371**	**0.5777**	**0.5906**
	Standard	0.3833	0.4609	0.4942	0.5037
Cluster 1	Div-Clust	**0.5981**	**0.6835**	**0.7162**	**0.7236**
	Standard	0.4191	0.5168	0.5624	0.5738

Table 4: Yelp results for α-NDCG with different α values.

4.1   Dataset

MovieLens 1M [6] is a widely known dataset in literature. It contains about 1 million ratings from 6,040 users and 3,706 movies. There are a total of 18 binary indicated movie genres available in this dataset. The second dataset is Yelp restaurants reviews that contains 8,022 users and 5,199 businesses based on 104,576 ratings. For this dataset we have only focused on categories of restaurants (cuisine type) which number around 120. All of the ratings for both data sets are in the range of 1 to 5.

4.2   Experimental Setup

For each dataset, 80% of the ratings is used for training sets and the remaining 20% is used for testing sets. The standard collaborative recommender used in our experiments is user-based kNN (*Standard*) [11] as a baseline method. Also, we use the same recommender system for each segment separately, after clustering users (*Div-Clust*) to compare the results both in terms of accuracy and diversity. The recommendation list size in all of our experiments is fixed at 20 and the number of neighbors is fixed to 25.

4.3 Metrics

In order to evaluate the result, we use three measures of rankings. First, the standard *NDCG* metric is used to measure only the accuracy of recommendation list in terms of user's preferences on recommended items. The second, metric is *NDCG_IA* [1]; an elegant metric that measures the accuracy of results for each category based on $P(c|u)$. This metric captures the degree of personalization of diversity in the recommendation list based on the user's past tolerance for diversity. But, it also captures relevance of the results in terms of test items ranked in each category for each user. Given $P(c|u)$, For each category preference of user, we treat any item that does not belong to this category as irrelevant and compute its category-dependent rank at cutoff k as $NDCG(u, k|c)$. Therefore, *NDCG_IA* is defined as follows:

$$NDCG\_IA(u, k) = \sum_c P(c|u)NDCG(u, k|c)$$

The third metric α-*NDCG* is used only for the purpose of measuring personalization in diversity, but not relevance of the results. α-*NDCG* was originally introduced in the context of information retrieval [3] to measure both relevance and redundancy in terms of information nuggets (topics) associated with search results.

Our work heavily relies on categorical distribution of user profiles to measure the degree to which diversity is personalized for each user. To use this metric for our purposes, we need to adapt it to the recommender systems context. In our context, α is a factor to penalize the redundancy of items in a rank list. We define the *gain vector* of α-*NDCG* as follows:

$$G[k] = \sum_{c \in C} P(i_k \in c)P(c|u)(1 - \alpha)^{r_{c,k-1}}$$

Where $r_{c,0} = 0$ and

$$r_{c,k-1} = \sum_{j=1}^{k-1} P(i_j \in c),$$

Essentially, this represents the number of items ranked up to position $k - 1$ that is known to contain category c according to $P(i \in c)$. Note that large values of α diminish the influence of personalization factor $P(c|u)$ and thus α-*NDCG* is only a measure of diversity based on categories.

4.4 Results and Discussions

In this section we discuss the results of performing collaborative filtering with and without the proposed segmentation approach.

After modeling user profile distributions based on categories in each of two datasets, we plotted the entropy distribution of users in each cluster to determine the effectiveness of clustering in capturing different levels of interest in diversity. In Figures 2 and 3, we can see various peaks for each cluster that show the density of users

at different entropy values. The clusters in all of our results, are ordered based on the mean entropy values of each cluster.

The results of our experiments are shown in Tables 1 and 3 for MovieLens and Yelp datasets, respectively. In all of the tables, clusters are ordered based on the average entropy of user profiles in them. In Table 1, the results for *NDCG* does not show any significant changes for clusters 1 and 2. For the other two cluster we see a little drop in accuracy. In terms of *NDCG_IA* the results of all the clusters except cluster 4 is higher in *Div-Cluster*. This indicates that, overall, the clusters result in a fairly accurate representation of user interests across various categories. The reason for the anomalous behavior of cluster 4 is that, as indicated in Figure 2, this cluster has the highest average entropy among all other clusters. This means that there is a high degree of uncertainty about the interest of users in diversity in that cluster. In this situation, personalization based on preference distributions is ineffective.

In terms of α-*NDCG* we get improvements for all of the segments indicating that the segmentation is effective in personalizing diversity. In Table 2 we show the results of various α values to see trade-off behavior between redundancy of content and personalization of diversity. When $\alpha = 0.1$ the penalty for redundancy will be very small. Larger α values result in a higher degree of personalization based on the distribution of categories. We see this effect on cluster 4 when we look at Table 2. In this table the results of this cluster for *Div-Clust* is lower than *Standard* when α is small. As α increases the results get reversed. This shows that for this cluster redundancy in recommendations is higher for *Standard* and personalization of categories is not strong enough to increase the value of α-*NDCG* in *Div-Clust*.

The same methodology was used to evaluate the results of the Yelp dataset. These results are depicted in Tables 3 and 4. Except for cluster 2, We see better results in terms of both *NDCG_IA* and α-*NDCG* for this dataset. Even for some clusters we see higher *NDCG*. The main reason for this behavior is larger variance in the entropy distribution that we see in Figure 1 compared to MovieLens. Most probably the results of cluster 2 is due to noise in that cluster since we get low accuracy even for *Standard* recommender.

5 CONCLUSIONS

In this work, we have proposed a new approach for personalizing diversity by clustering the users based on their tolerance for diversity. In contrast to most of the work in this area that uses a greedy re-ranking approach for diversification, we use a pre-filtering approach that can be integrated into any collaborative recommender system. The adapted α-*NDCG* metric shows the effectiveness of our method.

REFERENCES

[1] Rakesh Agrawal, Sreenivas Gollapudi, Alan Halverson, and Samuel Ieong. 2009. Diversifying search results. In *Proceedings of the second ACM international conference on web search and data mining*. ACM, 5–14.

[2] Jaime Carbonell and Jade Goldstein. 1998. The use of MMR, diversity-based reranking for reordering documents and producing summaries. In *Proceedings of the 21st annual international ACM SIGIR conference on Research and development in information retrieval*. ACM, 335–336.

[3] Charles LA Clarke, Maheedhar Kolla, Gordon V Cormack, Olga Vechtomova, Azin Ashkan, Stefan Büttcher, and Ian MacKinnon. 2008. Novelty and diversity in information retrieval evaluation. In *Proceedings of the 31st annual international ACM SIGIR conference on Research and development in information retrieval*. ACM, 659–666.

[4] Tommaso Di Noia, Vito Claudio Ostuni, Jessica Rosati, Paolo Tomeo, and Eugenio Di Sciascio. 2014. An analysis of users' propensity toward diversity in recommendations. In *Proceedings of the 8th ACM Conference on Recommender Systems*. ACM, 285–288.

[5] Farzad Eskandanian, Bamshad Mobasher, and Robin D. Burke. 2016. User Segmentation for Controlling Recommendation Diversity. In *Proceedings of the Poster Track of the 10th ACM Conference on Recommender Systems (RecSys 2016), Boston, USA, September 17, 2016*. http://ceur-ws.org/Vol-1688/paper-24.pdf

[6] F Maxwell Harper and Joseph A Konstan. 2016. The movielens datasets: History and context. *ACM Transactions on Interactive Intelligent Systems (TiiS)* 5, 4 (2016), 19.

[7] Neil J Hurley. 2013. Personalised ranking with diversity. In *Proceedings of the 7th ACM Conference on Recommender Systems*. ACM, 379–382.

[8] Lillian Lee. 1999. Measures of distributional similarity. In *Proceedings of the 37th annual meeting of the Association for Computational Linguistics on Computational Linguistics*. Association for Computational Linguistics, 25–32.

[9] Jianhua Lin. 1991. Divergence measures based on the Shannon entropy. *IEEE Transactions on Information theory* 37, 1 (1991), 145–151.

[10] Sean M McNee, John Riedl, and Joseph A Konstan. 2006. Being accurate is not enough: how accuracy metrics have hurt recommender systems. In *CHI'06 extended abstracts on Human factors in computing systems*. ACM, 1097–1101.

[11] Xia Ning, Christian Desrosiers, and George Karypis. 2015. A comprehensive survey of neighborhood-based recommendation methods. In *Recommender systems handbook*. Springer, 37–76.

[12] Rodrygo LT Santos, Craig Macdonald, and Iadh Ounis. 2010. Exploiting query reformulations for web search result diversification. In *Proceedings of the 19th international conference on World wide web*. ACM, 881–890.

[13] Saúl Vargas, Linas Baltrunas, Alexandros Karatzoglou, and Pablo Castells. 2014. Coverage, redundancy and size-awareness in genre diversity for recommender systems. In *Proceedings of the 8th ACM Conference on Recommender systems*. ACM, 209–216.

[14] Saúl Vargas and Pablo Castells. 2013. Exploiting the diversity of user preferences for recommendation. In *Proceedings of the 10th Conference on Open Research Areas in Information Retrieval*. LE CENTRE DE HAUTES ETUDES INTERNATIONALES D'INFORMATIQUE DOCUMENTAIRE, 129–136.

[15] Saul Vargas, Pablo Castells, and David Vallet. 2011. Intent-oriented diversity in recommender systems. In *Proceedings of the 34th international ACM SIGIR conference on Research and development in Information Retrieval*. ACM, 1211–1212.

[16] Jacek Wasilewski and Neil Hurley. 2016. Incorporating Diversity in a Learning to Rank Recommender System.. In *FLAIRS Conference*. 572–578.

[17] Mi Zhang and Neil Hurley. 2008. Avoiding monotony: improving the diversity of recommendation lists. In *Proceedings of the 2008 ACM conference on Recommender systems*. ACM, 123–130.

[18] Cai-Nicolas Ziegler, Sean M McNee, Joseph A Konstan, and Georg Lausen. 2005. Improving recommendation lists through topic diversification. In *Proceedings of the 14th international conference on World Wide Web*. ACM, 22–32.

Personality Traits and Music Genres: What Do People Prefer to Listen To?

Bruce Ferwerda
Department of Computational
Perception
Johannes Kepler University
Altenberger Strasse 69
4040, Linz, Austria
bruce.ferwerda@jku.at

Marko Tkalcic
Faculty of Computer Science
Free University of Bozen-Bolzano
Piazza Domenicani 3
I-39100, Bozen-Bolzano, Italy
marko.tkalcic@unibz.it

Markus Schedl
Department of Computational
Perception
Johannes Kepler University
Altenberger Strasse 69
4040, Linz, Austria
markus.schedl@jku.at

ABSTRACT

Personality-based personalized systems are increasingly gaining interest as personality traits has been shown to be a stable construct within humans. In order to provide a personality-based experience to the user, users' behavior, preferences, and needs in relation to their personality need to be investigated. Although for a technological mediated environment the search for these relationships is often new territory, there are findings from personality research of the real world that can be used in personalized systems. However, for these findings to be implementable, we need to investigate whether they hold in a technologically mediated environment. In this study we assess prior work on personality-based music genre preferences from traditional personality research. We analyzed a dataset consisting of music listening histories and personality scores of 1415 Last.fm users. Our results show agreements with prior work, but also important differences that can help to inform personalized systems.

CCS CONCEPTS

•**Human-centered computing** → User models; User studies;
•**Information systems** → *Recommender systems;*

KEYWORDS

Music, Personality, Recommender Systems, User Modeling

ACM Reference format:
Bruce Ferwerda, Marko Tkalcic, and Markus Schedl. 2017. Personality Traits and Music Genres: What Do People Prefer to Listen To?. In *Proceedings of UMAP '17, July 9-12, 2017, Bratislava, Slovakia, , 4 pages.*
DOI: http://dx.doi.org/10.1145/3079628.3079693

1 INTRODUCTION

Personality traits are increasingly being incorporated in systems to provide a personalized experience to the user. Personality has shown to be a stable construct and is often used as a general user

model to relate behavior, preferences, and needs to [16]. Relating behavior, preferences, and needs to such a general model allows for implementation across platforms [1]: it can be inferred from one platform and implemented into the other. The advantage of personality traits being applicable across platforms is that questionnaires can be omitted (by inferring personality from a different platform) and situations where data is scarce (e.g., cold-start problem [24]) can be overcome.

There is a growing body of research investigating and exploring the relationship between personality traits of users and technologically mediated behavior, preferences, and needs (e.g., health [15, 22], education [2, 18], movies [3], music [7–9, 23]). However, extensive personality research has been done already on real world (social) interactions that may apply to a technological setting as well. Since technologies are becoming increasingly ubiquitous and pervasive, the possibilities that users have reach much further than in real world situations. It is for these real world findings that we need to verify whether they still apply in a technological setting before able to implement them for personalization.

In this work we assess one of these personality related findings of real world interactions. We look at prior work of Rentfrow & Gosling [20] in which they investigated whether personality is related to preferences for specific music genres. To investigate the relationship between personality and music genre preferences, we used a subset of the myPersonality dataset. Next to users' personality scores, this subset consist of the listening history of Last.fm (an online music streaming service) [1] users. By analyzing the listening histories of 1415 users in relation to their personality, we found agreements with prior work of Rentfrow & Gosling, but also important differences. Our insights may help to inform personalized music systems. For example, music recommender systems can improve their cold-start recommendations by knowing which music genres to recommend to their users.

2 RELATED WORK

Currently, there are two different personality related research directions focusing on: 1) personality-based personalization, (e.g., health [22], education [2, 18], movies [3], music [7–9, 23]) and 2) implicit personality acquisition from user-generated content (e.g., Facebook [11, 14], Twitter [19], Instagram [10, 12], and fusing information [21]). Since traditional personality research is done in real world settings, both of the aforementioned research directions often explore new territory: personality relationships in a technological

[1] http://www.last.fm/

context. For example, in the area of personality-based personalization Ferwerda et al. [13] looked at differences in how users browse for music (i.e., browsing music by genre, activity, or mood) in an online music streaming service. Others investigated personality-based diversity preferences in recommender systems (e.g., [3, 6]): Chen, Wu, & He [3] investigated diversity preferences in movie recommendations. In the area of implicit personality acquisition research mainly focuses on user-generated content of users' social media accounts. Quercia et al. [19] found that how users behave on Twitter consist of cues to predict their personality. Similarly, Golbeck, Robles, & Turner [14] were able to develop a personality predictor based on the characteristics of a user's Facebook account.

There are also results from traditional personality research that can inform design of personalized technologies. For example, research in education has shown that there are differences in learning that can be related to the personality of the individual (see [5] for an overview). Although the right personalized technology still needs to be investigated, the results from the real world can inform to which personality traits to pay attention to. Other findings are seemingly more directly transferable to a technological setting. Rentfrow & Gosling [20] found that personality traits are related to music genre preferences. By testing preferences within predefined sets of 20 music pieces, they asked their participants to rate the preference for each of the songs (0 - 20 scale: no preference - strong preference). Although their findings may look like they are directly implementable for personalization, current online music systems (e.g., online music streaming services) provide their users with an almost unlimited amount of content that is directly at their disposal. Not only provide this convenience for the user, it also allows them to easily explore content outside of their initial interest. Hence, users may be prone to try out different content more than they in real life would do and even their preference may change more often or becomes more versatile. Therefore, it is important to assess whether results from the real world still apply in a fast growing technological environment.

In this work we explore a dataset of an online music streaming service consisting of the total listening history of their users. We use this dataset to investigate whether music genre relationships exists with the personality of the listener, and whether the found relationships are in line with findings of Rentfrow & Gosling [20].

3 METHOD

In order to investigate the relationship between personality and music genre preferences in an online music streaming service, we made use of the myPersonality dataset. [2] The dataset originates from a popular Facebook application ("myPersonality") that is able to record psychological and Facebook profiles of users that used the application to take psychometric (e.g., personality, attitudes, skills) tests. The dataset contains over 6 million test results, with over 4 million Facebook profiles. Users' personality in the myPersonality application was assessed using the Big Five Inventory to measure the constructs of the five factor model: openness to experience, conscientiousness, extraversion, agreeableness, and neuroticism.

We only used the subset of the myPersonality dataset that contains the music listening history of Last.fm users (i.e., play-count

of artists that a user listened to). The subset consists of users' complete listening histories (i.e., from the moment they started to use Last.fm) until April 27 (2012). We complemented the dataset by adding the listening events of each user until December 18 (2016) by using the Last.fm API. [3] A total of 2312 Last.fm users with ~40 million listening events from 101 countries are represented in the subset.

Through the Last.fm API, we crawled additional information about the artists by using the "Artist.getTopTags" endpoint. This endpoint provided us with all the tags that users assigned to an artist, such as instruments ("guitar"), epochs ("80s"), places ("Chicago"), languages ("Swedish"), and personal opinions ("seen live" or "my favorite"). Tags that encode genre or style information were filtered for each artist. The filtered tags were then indexed by a dictionary of 18 genre names retrieved from Allmusic. [4] For each user, the artists that were listened to were aggregated by the indexed genre with their play-count. The genre play-count for each user was then normalized to represent a range of $r\epsilon[0,1]$, this in order to be able to compare users with differences in the total amount of listening events.

4 ANALYSIS

For the analysis we filtered out users with zero play-counts (users who registered, but did not make use of Last.fm) and people listening to less than five different artists. This left us with a total of 1415 users (~20 million listening events) of 83 countries in our final dataset for analysis.

Spearman's correlation was computed between personality traits and the genre play-count to assess the relationship of personality and genre preferences. Alpha levels were adjusted using the Bonferroni correction to limit the chance on a Type I error. The reported significant results adhere to alpha levels of $p < .001$.

5 RESULTS

The results show significant correlations between personality traits and genre preferences (see Table 1). Below the results related to each personality trait. A positive correlation indicates that participants scoring high in the personality trait show a higher tendency to listen to such music genre, while a negative correlation indicates the opposite effect.

Openness to Experience
Those users scoring high on the openness to experience trait show most correlations with different music genres. They show correlations with new age ($r = .101$), classical ($r = .136$), blues ($r = .120$), country ($r = .106$), world ($r = .134$), folk ($r = .214$), jazz ($r = .139$), and alternative ($r = .115$) music. This indicates that open users tend to listen to a wide variety of music genres.

Conscientiousness
Conscientious users only show a correlation with folk ($r = -.115$) and alternative ($r = -.104$) music. However, the correlation coefficient indicates a negative correlation meaning that conscientious music listeners tend to listen less to folk and alternative music.

---

[2] http://mypersonality.org/

[3] http://www.last.fm/api
[4] http://www.allmusic.com

	O	C	E	A	N
R&B	-.002	.026	**.103**	.021	-.012
Rap	-.019	-.017	**.129**	.008	-.049
Electronic	.077	-.029	.034	-.033	-.002
Rock	-.055	-.016	-.072	-.017	.057
New Age	**.101**	.008	-.067	-.019	-.031
Classical	**.136**	-.037	-.064	-.032	.000
Reggae	.017	-.042	.061	.009	-.041
Blues	**.120**	-.011	.023	-.011	-.044
Country	**.106**	-.049	-.002	**.104**	-.012
World	**.134**	-.021	-.006	-.028	-.020
Folk	**.214**	**-.115**	-.044	**.104**	.002
Easy Listening	.041	.010	.018	-.027	-.012
Jazz	**.139**	-.007	.042	.031	-.061
Vocal (a cappella)	**.120**	-.020	.006	-.021	.006
Punk	.002	-.061	-.020	.001	.030
Alternative	**.115**	**-.104**	-.031	.060	**.101**
Pop	-.034	.035	.056	.056	-.030
Heavy Metal	-.031	-.023	-.076	-.069	-.001

Table 1: Spearman's correlation between music genres and personality traits: (O)penness to experience, (C)onscientiousness, (E)xtraversion, (A)greeableness, and (N)euroticism. Significant correlations after Bonferroni correction are shown in boldface (*p* <.001).

Extraversion
Extraverts are positively correlated with: r&b (*r* =.103) and rap (*r* =.129) music. The results show that extraverts seem to listen more to r&b and rap music compared to other genres.

Agreeableness
Agreeable users show to be positively correlated with country (*r* =.104) and folk (*r* =.104) music, meaning that they on average tend to listen more to these music genres.

Neuroticism
Neurotic users show a positive correlation with alternative (*r* =.101) music, meaning that they listening on average more to alternative music than to the other genres.

6 DISCUSSION

Our results show significant correlations between personality traits of users and the music genres that they prefer to listen to. The goal of this study was to see whether the results of prior work [20] in a real world context would also be valid when analyzing online listening behavior. In order to make a comparison, the results of the work of Rentfrow & Gosling are shown in Table 2. They analyzed the music pieces that they presented to their participants on its music attributes, and divided the music genres into four categories: reflective & complex, intense & rebellious, upbeat & conventional, and energetic & rhythmic (see Table 3 for a mapping with the music genres). Instead of preselecting music pieces for participants to rate, we analyzed historical behavior of online music listeners. Hence, our data consists of so many music pieces that we were not able to

	O	C	E	A	N
Reflective & Complex	**.41**	-.06	-.02	.03	.04
Intense & Rebellious	**.15**	-.03	**.08**	.01	-.01
Upbeat & Conventional	-.08	**.18**	**.15**	**.24**	-.04
Energetic & Rhythmic	.04	-.03	**.19**	**.09**	-.01

Table 2: Correlations between music attributes and personality traits of prior work of Rentfrow & Gosling [20]: (O)penness to experience, (C)onscientiousness, (E)xtraversion, (A)greeableness, and (N)euroticism. Significant correlations are shown in boldface.

Reflective & Complex	Classical	Jazz	Blues	Folk
Intense & Rebellious	Alternative	Rock	Heavy Metal	
Upbeat & Conventional	Country	Pop	Religious	Sound Tracks
Energetic & Rhythmic	Rap & Hip-Hop	Soul & Funk	Electronica & Dance	

Table 3: Mapping of music attributes and genres of the work of Rentfrow & Gosling [20].

make such genre mapping based on the music attributes. We refer to both Table 2 and Table 3 for comparisons with prior work on the correlations and the genre mapping respectively.

For the openness to experience personality trait, we found agreements with prior work of Rentfrow & Gosling [20]. For example, they found that open people prefer to listen to reflective & complex genres (e.g., classical, blues, jazz, and folk music) as well as to intense and rebellious music (e.g., rock, alternative). However, our results also show additional correlations with other music genres. Our results show that those who score high on the openness to experience trait have a more divers genre listening behavior than found by prior work. The preferences for such a diverse range of music genres may be explained by the traditional nature of this personality trait. Open people have been shown to have a preference for variety in general [4], which may also be applied to music genre preferences.

Rentfrow & Gosling [20] showed that conscientious people have a preference for upbeat & conventional music (e.g., country, pop, religious, and sound track music), whereas our results show a negative correlation for alternative and folk music. However, in line with our results, the replication of the Rentfrow & Gosling study by Langmeyer, Guglhör-Rudan, & Tarnai [17] found the conscientiousness personality trait to be negatively correlated with intense & rebellious music (e.g., alternative music).

In line with prior works [17, 20], our results show that extraverts have a preference for r&b and rap music, which can be mapped to the energetic & rhythmic music (e.g., rap, hip-hop, and soul music) attribute.

Also the agreeableness personality trait shows agreements with prior work. Our results show that agreeable users tend to listen more to country and folk music. Rentfrow & Gosling [20] showed that their results indicate that agreeable people especially have a preference for upbeat & conventional music, such as country, pop, and religious music.

Lastly, we found a correlation with those scoring high on neuroticsm and a preference for the alternative music genre. Although Rentfrow & Gosling [20] did not find any relationship with the neuroticism trait in their work, the replication study of Langmeyer, Guglhör-Rudan, & Tarnai [17] did. They found that neuroticism correlates with intense & rebellious (e.g., alternative, rock, and heavy metal music).

7 CONCLUSION & LIMITATIONS

In this work we investigated the relationship between music genres and personality traits by analyzing online music listening behavior of Last.fm users. Besides investigating this relationship, we foremost wanted to see whether there are agreements with the results of Rentfrow & Gosling [20] of music genre preferences in a real world context. By analyzing a large scale dataset of Last.fm music listening histories, we were able to find distinct relationships between personality traits and music genres, but also agreements with prior findings of Rentfrow & Gosling (and the replication study of Langmeyer, Guglhör-Rudan, & Tarnai [17]).

Although we found support for all our findings, it is difficult to make direct comparisons with the results of prior work [17, 20]. One problem that we were facing is that they clustered their results into categories of music attributes (see Table 2 and Table 3). Although a mapping to music genres is provided (Table 3), it is not possible for us to see to what extent correlations exist between personality traits and music genres. We could only identify whether the music genre correlations that we found exist in the music attributes mapping. Prior work was able to make music attributes inferences by preselecting music pieces for their participants. In contrast, We analyzed a dataset consisting of ~20 million listening events, making it impossible to assess the pieces on their music attributes.

By not clustering the analyzed music genres on its music attributes, we are able to provide more fine-grained correlations between music genres preferences and personality traits. This may be especially useful for personality-based personalized systems. Although music genres may be the same on an attribute level, they may have a complete different impact on the user. Hence, music genre differentiation is important to have for personalized systems.

Our work contributes to the personality-based work for personalized systems. We provide with our work insights on whether and how music personality-based results from the real world transfers to a technological context. By analyzing a large scale dataset we are also able to provide insights based on a more realistic scenario.

8 ACKNOWLEDGMENTS

Supported by the Austrian Science Fund (FWF): P25655. We would also like to thank Michal Kosinski and David Stillwell of the myPersonality project for sharing the data with us.

REFERENCES

[1] Iván Cantador, Ignacio Fernández-Tobías, and Alejandro Bellogín. 2013. Relating personality types with user preferences in multiple entertainment domains. In *CEUR Workshop Proceedings*. Shlomo Berkovsky.

[2] Guanliang Chen, Dan Davis, Claudia Hauff, and Geert-Jan Houben. 2016. On the impact of personality in massive open online learning. In *Proceedings of the 2016 conference on user modeling adaptation and personalization*. ACM, 121–130.

[3] Li Chen, Wen Wu, and Liang He. 2013. How personality influences users' needs for recommendation diversity?. In *CHI'13 Extended Abstracts on Human Factors in Computing Systems*. ACM, 829–834.

[4] Paul T Costa and Robert R MacCrae. 1992. *Revised NEO personality inventory (NEO PI-R) and NEO five-factor inventory (NEO-FFI): Professional manual*. Psychological Assessment Resources, Incorporated.

[5] Boele De Raad and Henri C Schouwenburg. 1996. Personality in learning and education: A review. *European Journal of personality* 10, 5 (1996), 303–336.

[6] Bruce Ferwerda, Mark Graus, Andreu Vall, Marko Tkalcic, and Markus Schedl. 2016. The influence of users' personality traits on satisfaction and attractiveness of diversified recommendation lists. In *4 th Workshop on Emotions and Personality in Personalized Systems (EMPIRE) 2016*. 43.

[7] Bruce Ferwerda and Markus Schedl. 2014. Enhancing Music Recommender Systems with Personality Information and Emotional States: A Proposal.. In *UMAP Workshops*.

[8] Bruce Ferwerda and Markus Schedl. 2016. Personality-Based User Modeling for Music Recommender Systems. In *Joint European Conference on Machine Learning and Knowledge Discovery in Databases*. Springer, 254–257.

[9] Bruce Ferwerda, Markus Schedl, and Marko Tkalcic. 2015. Personality & Emotional States: Understanding Users' Music Listening Needs.. In *UMAP Workshops*.

[10] Bruce Ferwerda, Markus Schedl, and Marko Tkalcic. 2015. Predicting personality traits with instagram pictures. In *Proceedings of the 3rd Workshop on Emotions and Personality in Personalized Systems 2015*. ACM, 7–10.

[11] Bruce Ferwerda, Markus Schedl, and Marko Tkalcic. 2016. Personality traits and the relationship with (non-) disclosure behavior on facebook. In *Proceedings of the 25th International Conference Companion on World Wide Web*. International World Wide Web Conferences Steering Committee, 565–568.

[12] Bruce Ferwerda, Markus Schedl, and Marko Tkalcic. 2016. Using instagram picture features to predict usersfi personality. In *International Conference on Multimedia Modeling*. Springer, 850–861.

[13] Bruce Ferwerda, Emily Yang, Markus Schedl, and Marko Tkalcic. 2015. Personality traits predict music taxonomy preferences. In *Proceedings of the 33rd Annual ACM Conference Extended Abstracts on Human Factors in Computing Systems*. ACM, 2241–2246.

[14] Jennifer Golbeck, Cristina Robles, and Karen Turner. 2011. Predicting personality with social media. In *CHI'11 extended abstracts on human factors in computing systems*. ACM, 253–262.

[15] Sajanee Halko and Julie A Kientz. 2010. Personality and persuasive technology: an exploratory study on health-promoting mobile applications. In *International Conference on Persuasive Technology*. Springer, 150–161.

[16] Oliver P John and Sanjay Srivastava. 1999. The Big Five trait taxonomy: History, measurement, and theoretical perspectives. *Handbook of personality: Theory and research* 2, 1999 (1999), 102–138.

[17] Alexandra Langmeyer, Angelika Guglhör-Rudan, and Christian Tarnai. 2012. What do music preferences reveal about personality? *Journal of Individual Differences* (2012).

[18] Michael J Lee and Bruce Ferwerda. 2017. Personalizing online educational tools. In *Proceedings of the 2017 ACM Workshop on Theory-Informed User Modeling for Tailoring and Personalizing Interfaces*. ACM, 27–30.

[19] Daniele Quercia, Michal Kosinski, David Stillwell, and Jon Crowcroft. 2011. Our Twitter profiles, our selves: Predicting personality with Twitter. In *Proceedings of the International Conference on Social Computing (SocialCom)*. IEEE, 180–185.

[20] Peter J Rentfrow and Samuel D Gosling. 2003. The do re mi's of everyday life: the structure and personality correlates of music preferences. *Journal of personality and social psychology* 84, 6 (2003), 1236.

[21] Marcin Skowron, Marko Tkalčič, Bruce Ferwerda, and Markus Schedl. 2016. Fusing social media cues: personality prediction from twitter and instagram. In *Proceedings of the 25th international conference companion on world wide web*. International World Wide Web Conferences Steering Committee, 107–108.

[22] Kirsten A Smith, Matt Dennis, and Judith Masthoff. 2016. Personalizing reminders to personality for melanoma self-checking. In *Proceedings of the 2016 Conference on User Modeling Adaptation and Personalization*. ACM, 85–93.

[23] Marko Tkalčič, Bruce Ferwerda, David Hauger, and Markus Schedl. 2015. Personality correlates for digital concert program notes. In *International Conference on User Modeling, Adaptation, and Personalization*. Springer, 364–369.

[24] Marko Tkalcic, Matevz Kunaver, Andrej Košir, and Jurij Tasic. 2011. Addressing the new user problem with a personality based user similarity measure. In *Proceedings of the 1st International Workshop on Decision Making and Recommendation Acceptance Issues in Recommender Systems*. Citeseer, 106.

Improving Cold Start Recommendation by Mapping Feature-Based Preferences to Item Comparisons

Saikishore Kalloori
Free University of Bozen - Bolzano
Piazza Domenicani 3, I - 39100
ksaikishore@unibz.it

Francesco Ricci
Free University of Bozen - Bolzano
Piazza Domenicani 3, I - 39100
fricci@unibz.it

ABSTRACT

Many Recommender Systems (RSs) rely on user preference data in the form of ratings or likes for items. Previous research has shown that item comparisons can also be effectively used to model user preferences and build RS. However, users often express their preferences by referring to specific features of the items. For instance, a user may like Italian movies more than Indian ones or like action-thriller movies. In this paper, we map such preferences over features to comparisons between items. For instance, when a user's favorite feature is 'action', we then assume that 'action' movies are preferred to some of the movies that are not 'action'. In this work we effectively incorporate these feature based comparisons in a RS and show that such preferences can be effectively combined along with other item comparisons. Moreover, we also study the usefulness of the available features.

CCS CONCEPTS

•Information systems → Recommender systems; Personalization;

KEYWORDS

Comparisons; Collaborative Filtering; User Modeling; Cold-Start

1 INTRODUCTION

Recommender systems (RSs) exploit user's preferences for items in the form of explicit or implicit feedback and identify novel items estimated to be interesting and relevant for the target user [14]. For example, Collaborative Filtering (CF) [14] relies on a user-item rating matrix and generates recommendations by leveraging rating-based similarities between users or items. However, ratings have few disadvantages. For instance, if most of the user rated items are 5 stars, then it is difficult to understand which items the user likes the most among them. In our previous research, in order to address these problems, we have shown that, instead of using ratings, item comparisons, such as, item A is preferred to item B, can be effectively used to compute recommendation [6].

But, there are many situations where also preferences over features may be a natural way for the user to signal what types of items she likes. For instance, a user may like an item because of its specific features, e.g., the actors of the movie, and express her preferences by commenting such features. In fact, recently, some authors have tried to exploit these type of preferences. In [9] the authors proposed a recommendation model that combines both item related preferences (item likes) with feature-based preferences (feature likes) in order to generate recommendations. Besides, Content Based approaches, even though are built by collecting ratings for items, they explicitly refer to features of the items in the generated user model, and in Utility based approaches [1] the relative importance of the item features is used to generate recommendations.

In this paper we also try to model and use user preferences expressed over features. To achieve this goal, we have extended a recommendation model based on item comparisons and studied how preferences over features could be encoded as comparisons between items. Modeling user preferences over features in the form of pairwise item comparisons has not been explored in RSs so far.

In order to encode feature preferences into comparisons between items we define a rule to selectively identify the best set of item comparisons that effectively express the given feature preferences. For instance, when a user's favorite feature is 'action' then we form pairwise comparisons between items which have the 'action' feature and some of the items that are not 'action'. It is worth noting that a naive approach would generates a quadratic number of comparisons (as function of the items that have or not a target feature). But not all these comparisons may be necessary. Hence, we have explored an alternative solution and designed a procedure for deriving a reduced number of item comparisons: we consider only the item comparisons that refer to items that were already mentioned in other item comparisons explicitly made by users, hence focusing on a denser set of comparisons.

Our results demonstrate that there is a benefit in using item comparisons derived from feature preferences especially in severe cold-start situation; and using both types of item comparisons, our recommendation model improves cold start recommendation for new users when compared to a model that is based only on item comparisons. We evaluated the performance of the proposed model against (a) Bayesian Personalized Ranking (BPR), (b) Most popular items (popularity), and (c) Content Based Filtering, which uses only feature preferences. Our recommendation model has better recommendation performance against the compared algorithms, especially in severe cold-start situation. We also show that feature selection may improve the recommendation quality in the non cold-start phase.

UMAP'17, July 9–12, 2017, Bratislava, Slovakia

© 2017 Copyright held by the owner/author(s). Publication rights licensed to ACM.
978-1-4503-4635-1/17/07...$15.00
DOI: http://dx.doi.org/10.1145/3079628.3079696

The paper is structured as follows. In the next section we discuss related work. Next we will describe how to generate item comparisons and the underlying recommendation technology. This is followed by the description of the conducted experiments and the obtained results. Finally, we mention some limitations that will be addressed in future work.

2 RELATED WORK

Collaborative Filtering is a popular recommendation technique and several improvements of the basic model have been proposed to improve the model performance by taking advantage of additional information associated with items [7], e.g., implicit preferences, content and user features [5], temporal dynamics, contextual conditions [3] and personality information [4]. It has also shown that incorporating feature information can increase the performance of top-N recommender systems [11]. Few authors have proposed to use features while explaining their recommendation to users [18]. In this work, we exploit explicit feature preferences as additional information. Differently from the above methods, we model them in the form of item comparisons and we use them in a recommender that is based on such comparisons.

Modeling user preferences in the form of comparisons has shown great success. For instance, Bayesian personalized ranking (BPR) is a popular ranking algorithms that was applied to implicit data. Several researchers have tried to use additional information, such as, the number of item views [8, 12], to improve its performance. In [2] it was shown that by using item comparisons, in a number almost equal to that of ratings, one can produce even better recommendations.

Popular decision making techniques, such as, Analytic Hierarchy Processing (AHP) [16] or Conjoint Analysis [17], use comparison between product features to understand users interest. AHP is a popular multi-criteria decision making technique where the feature importance weights are acquired by asking the user to perform pairwise comparisons between product features. While, Conjoint Analysis is a technique often used in marketing research that uses comparisons in order to derive user interests on items. It is often used to measure, analyze and predict how users are likely to respond to new features of the existing products or new products being developed. In our work, we use such feature preferences to derive comparisons between items.

3 DERIVING ITEM COMPARISONS

Let U be the set of users and I be the set of items. We also denote with I^n the set of items which are liked by at least n users. In fact, we assume to have a data set that contains (positive-only) user preferences on items and on features of items. Using this data set, we will construct, for each user, a profile containing item comparisons that represent the user preferences over features and another profile that includes the item comparisons derived from the preferences expressed over items.

Mapping Feature Preferences to Item Comparisons: Let F_u be the set of features that the user u likes. We define the set of implicitly liked items I_u^{k+} as:

$$I_u^{k+} = \{i \in I^n : i \text{ has at least } k \text{ features in } F_u\} \quad (1)$$

The threshold k is the number of liked features that an item must possess in order to assume that the item is liked. Using I_u^{k+} we can now generate a set of item comparisons $ICF(u)$ derived from user u feature preferences:

$$ICF(u) = \{(u,i,j)|i \in I_u^{k+} \wedge j \in I^n \setminus I_u^{k+}\} \quad (2)$$

where (u,i,j) means that user u prefers item i to item j. In our experiments we will show that different values of k and n will give rise to different item comparisons and consequently different performances of the RS.

Mapping Item Preferences to Item Comparisons: We now derive item comparisons using item preferences in a similar way as in [13]. For each user we assume that an item i is preferred to item j if the user liked the item i and not liked the item j. We define I_u^+ as the set of items that a user u has expressed her explicit preference, i.e., the set of items that the user liked. Using I_u^+ we can generate another set of item comparisons $ICI(u)$, generated by using the user u item preferences:

$$ICI(u) = \{(u,i,j)|i \in I_u^+ \wedge j \in I^n \setminus I_u^+\} \quad (3)$$

We note that in Equation 2 and 3, we have used I^n instead of I to generate item comparisons. If we had instead considered the sets $I \setminus I_u^+$ and $I \setminus I_u^{k+}$, we would have generated a much larger number of item comparisons. In fact, we want to identify a small set of (important) item comparisons, as, not all the possibly true item comparisons are important for our goal, which is, to train a model that will predict missing item comparisons. We consider important comparisons those among items that were already mentioned in other item comparisons explicitly made by the users. We concentrate on these because in collaborative filtering, which is also our target prediction model, an item rating or a comparison can be predicted only when it belongs to the profile of some users.

As we mentioned above, after obtaining the item comparisons in $ICF(u)$ and $ICI(u)$, by using equation 2 and 3, we take the union of them. However, in this way, one can generate conflicts, that is, one may derive that i is preferred to j and the opposite judgement from the item preferences. In such cases, we simple ignore the item comparison obtained from the feature preferences, hence giving more importance to the item preferences.

4 RECOMMENDATION TECHNIQUES

In this section we present the comparison prediction and item ranking algorithms. When comparisons are used as source of preference information, the core problem for the RS is to predict unknown comparisons and aggregate them to produce personalized rankings of the items. We denote with r_{uij} the true comparison given by the user u to the pair (i,j) and r_{uij}^* the predicted one. The prediction formula for unknown comparisons is:

$$r_{uij}^* = \frac{1}{|U_{ij}|} \sum_{v \in U_{ij}} sim(u,v) * r_{vij} \quad (4)$$

Where U_{ij} is the set of users that have compared the items i and j, and $sim(u,v)$ is the similarity score between user u and v. In our previous research we proposed two user-to-user similarity metrics for nearest neighbor (NN) approaches for item comparison prediction [6]: (i) Goodman and Kruskal's gamma (GK) and (ii) Expected Discounted Rank Correlation (EDRC). In this paper we still use

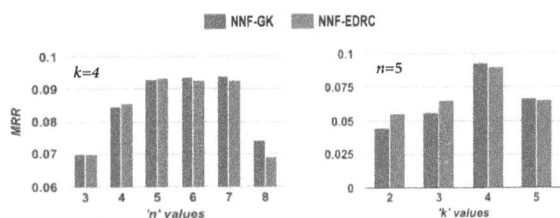

Figure 1: MRR results for different 'k' and 'n' values

them. We denote with NN-GK and NN-EDRC the nearest neighbour prediction algorithms that use these two similarity metrics. After having predicted the missing item comparison we aggregate them to compute a personalized item score v_{ui} by averaging the r^*_{uij} predictions, as done by [2, 6]:

$$v_{ui} = \frac{\sum_{j \in I \setminus \{i\}} r^*_{uij}}{|I|} \qquad (5)$$

For each user u the items are then ranked by descending values of the v_{ui} scores.

5 EXPERIMENTAL EVALUATION

5.1 Data Set

In order to test our hypothesis we needed a dataset containing both item and feature preferences. The only publicly available data set with such preferences, which we could identify, is the PoliMovie dataset [10]. For each user in the dataset, there are preferences expressed explicitly for movies and for their features, in the form of likes. The dataset contains a total of 420 users and 1962 movies. Movies are described by features such as genre, cast, direction and year. There are 3794 distinct features. A total of 4208 item preferences and 5551 feature preference are in the dataset. Each user has given at least 4 item preferences and 6 feature preferences and on an average a user expressed 10 item and 13 feature preferences.

5.2 Evaluation Procedure

We address the following research question: can the item comparisons generated using item and feature preferences be beneficially combined to produce good recommendation? Moreover, we want to understand which features are more useful for improving the recommendation performance.

In order to address the first research question, we built the models NNF-GK and NNF-EDRC, which are NN models with GK or EDRC user-to-user similarity metrics. They are trained with all the item comparisons generated from feature preferences (i.e., the sets $ICF(u)$ for all users) and an increasing number of item comparisons generated by incrementally converting one item preference for each user, into the corresponding item comparisons. This means, given an item preference of the user u for item i we generate the item comparisons in the set $ICI(u)$ (where in Eq. 3 i is fixed) and we add them to the training set of the model. We also built the NN-GK and NN-EDRC models that use only the item comparisons generated from incrementally considering the item preferences. Hence, we use the letter 'F' to denote a model that also use feature preferences.

In order to investigate the second research question, we built several versions of the NNF-GK and NNF-EDRC models trained

with all the available item preferences, but only with the item comparisons derived from one single type of feature preferences; for instance, only preferences over the genre of the movies, and we compared their performance.

In the training and test split of the data, as we mentioned above, the feature preferences were either all considered in the training (in the NNF-GK and NNF-EDRC models) or not (in the NN-GK and NN-EDRC models), after having converted them into item comparisons. Instead, we split the item preferences in the dataset into training (70%), and converted them into item comparisons, and the remaining (30%) was considered as test item preferences to predict. This split was randomly produced three times, and the experimental results are averages of three runs.

For each test user we calculated her personalized ranked list using Equation 5 and tested its quality by using three widely-adopted ranking metrics:

MRR: Mean Reciprocal Rank averages, for each user, the rank position in the recommended list R_u, of the test item appearing in the highest position. We note that we have positive only feedback so all the test items are considered as relevant.

Recall: Recall is defined as the ratio of the number of test items retrieved over the total number of items in the test set.

MAP: Mean Average Precision is the average of precision values at the rank positions where items present in test set occur. This is further averaged over all test users to give the final precision value.

In Section 3, we have introduced two parameters: k is the minimum number of features that an item must possess in order to be considered as a liked item; and n is the minimum number of users that have to like an item in order to use this item in the item comparisons generated by both item and feature preferences. We have searched for the optimal values of these parameters, for the models that uses only the feature preferences, by trying different combinations of these parameters. We evaluated the model performance (on the test set) using all the considered metrics, but we show here only the MRR results. Similar results were obtained for the other metrics. We found that for $k = 4$ and $n = 5, 6, 7$ the system obtains the best results. Figure 1 shows the impact of n and k on the system performance, for the fixed, best, value of the other meta-parameter. For different values of k and n, different sets of item comparisons, and consequently different RS performance, are obtained. Smaller values of k and n produce larger sets of comparisons, but less indicative of the user preferences; the opposite holds for large values of k and n. For instance, when $k = 4$, for $n = 3, 4, 5, 6, 7, 8$, for each user, on an average, 3674, 1876, 685, 389, 162, and 127 comparisons are generated respectively. In the rest of our experiments, we used $k = 4$ and $n = 5$.

5.3 Baseline Methods

We have compared the proposed approach to three baseline algorithms.

POP is the non-personalised method that ranks items in terms of their popularity (the number of likes from all the users).

CBF is a pure content-based method that ignores item preferences and ranks items based on how well their features match the user's feature preferences; it uses the Jaccard similarity of the set of features liked by a user and the set of item features.

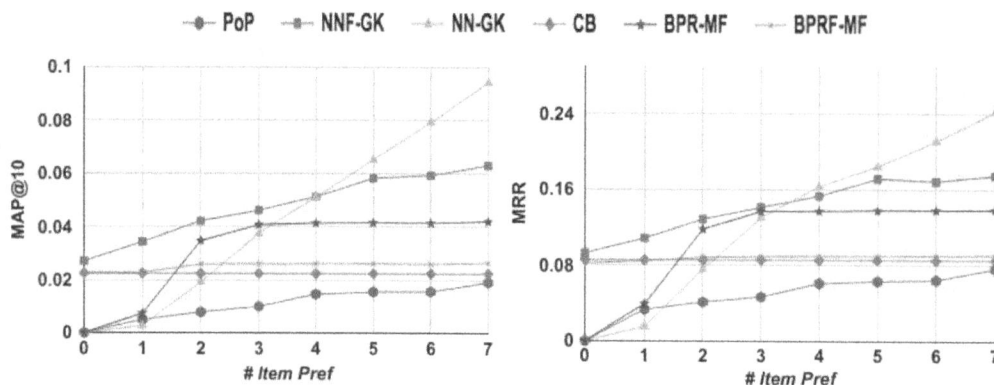

Figure 2: Ranking performance of the considered models. 'F' in the model acronyms signals that the model uses also item comparisons derived from feature preferences.

BPR(F)-MF is Bayesian Personalized Ranking with Matrix Factorization [13]. BPR-MF uses only item preferences while BPRF-MF uses also the item comparisons generated from feature preferences.

5.4 Results Evaluation

Figure 2 shows the recommendation performance of the tested models. We note that the item comparisons generated from feature preferences are beneficial in the cold start phase: when zero or only a few (i.e., up to 3) item preferences for each user are considered. We obtained similar results for Recall@10, hence we do not show these results. We also show only the performance of our NN model when the GK similarity measure is used. Very similar results are obtained for NN-EDRC. Also BPRF-MF, in cold-start situation, can benefit from the item comparisons derived from feature preferences, but the performance of this model does not improve much if more item preferences are used.

However, we also observe that as the number of item preferences increases, the contribution brought by the item comparisons generated from feature preferences diminishes. Above a certain number of item preferences (e.g., 4 for NN-GK and 1 for BPR-MF), the feature preferences are not helpful anymore. Hence, in conclusion, according to this experiment, feature preferences can be useful only when the RS has access to a small number of item preferences.

In a second experiment, we analyzed the contribution brought by different types of feature preferences. Since the previous experimental results showed that the impact of feature preferences decreases after a certain number of item preferences are used, we wanted to understand if a careful selection of the type of used feature preferences can make them more useful, even in the non cold start phase. In order to test this, we built several models using: a) the item comparisons obtained from all the item preferences (in the training), and b) all the item comparisons generated from a single type of feature preferences.

Table 1 shows that the recommendation performance using the preferences over the 'cast' of the movie can even give a boost to the model performance (higher values of the considered metrics). Other feature preferences are not that useful. Thus, feature preferences can also be useful when more item preferences are available, but a feature selection procedure is in order.

Table 1: Recommendation performance for NNF-GK using different type of feature preferences.

Model	MAP@10	MRR	Recall@10
NN-GK + Cast prefs	0.120	0.2999	0.187
NN-GK + Country prefs	0.102	0.258	0.158
NN-GK + Year prefs	0.102	0.264	0.160
NN-GK	0.102	0.265	0.156
NN-GK + Genre prefs	0.0197	0.0728	0.0509

6 CONCLUSION AND FUTURE WORK

In this work, we have incorporated feature based preferences in a RS that is using item comparisons to model the user and we have shown that such preferences can help to improve the system performance, especially in the cold start phase. We also ranked the features according to their contribution to the system performance. This has shown that even in the non cold start phase a selective use of certain feature preferences can improve the performance of a recommender trained on the item based preferences.

We note that in our approach, in order to use feature preferences, we first identify the items that a user may like because of their features (Equation 1) and then we generate item comparisons (Equation 2) for training the model. In the future, we will try to directly combine these items with those that are explicitly liked by the user and then derive item comparisons in a single step.

Moreover, in our experiments, we added incrementally the item comparisons generated from one item preference without following a particular order. However, one may also want to observe the effect of alternative active learning item preference selection strategies [15].

One final observation is related to a limitation of the present work. Namely, we found the optimal values of the meta-parameters k and n using a single model that is based on feature preferences only. We will make a deeper analysis and optimize the meta-parameters for each specific tested model. Moreover, we plan to conduct online experiments to understand when/where different types of preferences are useful. We aim at identifying important situation where eliciting feature preferences is especially useful, e.g., for better explaining the generated recommendations.

REFERENCES

[1] H. Blanco and F. Ricci. Inferring user utility for query revision recommendation. In *Proceedings of the 28th Annual ACM Symposium on Applied Computing*, pages 245–252. ACM, 2013.

[2] L. Blédaité and F. Ricci. Pairwise preferences elicitation and exploitation for conversational collaborative filtering. In *Proc. Hypertext & Social Media '15*, pages 231–236, 2015.

[3] M. Braunhofer and F. Ricci. Contextual information elicitation in travel recommender systems. In *Information and Communication Technologies in Tourism 2016*, pages 579–592. Springer, 2016.

[4] I. Fernández-Tobías, M. Braunhofer, M. Elahi, F. Ricci, and I. Cantador. Alleviating the new user problem in collaborative filtering by exploiting personality information. *User Modeling and User-Adapted Interaction*, 26(2-3):221–255, 2016.

[5] Z. Gantner, L. Drumond, C. Freudenthaler, S. Rendle, and L. Schmidt-Thieme. Learning attribute-to-feature mappings for cold-start recommendations. In *Data Mining (ICDM), 2010 IEEE 10th International Conference on*, pages 176–185. IEEE, 2010.

[6] S. Kalloori, F. Ricci, and M. Tkalcic. Pairwise preferences based matrix factorization and nearest neighbor recommendation techniques. In *Proc. RecSys 2016*, pages 143–146. ACM, 2016.

[7] Y. Koren and R. Bell. Advances in collaborative filtering. In *Recommender systems handbook*, pages 77–118. Springer, 2015.

[8] L. Lerche and D. Jannach. Using graded implicit feedback for bayesian personalized ranking. In *Proceedings of the 8th ACM Conference on Recommender systems*, pages 353–356. ACM, 2014.

[9] M. Nasery, M. Braunhofer, and F. Ricci. Recommendations with optimal combination of feature-based and item-based preferences. In *Proceedings of the 2016 Conference on User Modeling Adaptation and Personalization*, pages 269–273. ACM, 2016.

[10] M. Nasery, M. Elahi, and P. Cremonesi. Polimovie: a feature-based dataset for recommender systems. In *ACM RecSys 2015 CrowdRec Workshop*, 2015.

[11] X. Ning and G. Karypis. Sparse linear methods with side information for top-n recommendations. In *Proceedings of the sixth ACM conference on Recommender systems*, pages 155–162. ACM, 2012.

[12] S. Rendle and C. Freudenthaler. Improving pairwise learning for item recommendation from implicit feedback. In *Proceedings of the 7th ACM international conference on Web search and data mining*, pages 273–282. ACM, 2014.

[13] S. Rendle, C. Freudenthaler, Z. Gantner, and L. Schmidt-Thieme. Bpr: Bayesian personalized ranking from implicit feedback. In *Proceedings of the twenty-fifth conference on uncertainty in artificial intelligence*, pages 452–461. AUAI Press, 2009.

[14] F. Ricci, L. Rokach, and B. Shapira. Recommender systems: Introduction and challenges. In *Recommender Systems Handbook*. Springer, 2015.

[15] N. Rubens, M. Elahi, M. Sugiyama, and D. Kaplan. Active learning in recommender systems. In *Recommender systems handbook*, pages 809–846. Springer, 2015.

[16] T. L. Saaty. Decision making with the analytic hierarchy process. *International journal of services sciences*, 1(1):83–98, 2008.

[17] M. Scholz. From consumer preferences towards buying decisions-conjoint analysis as preference measuring method in product recommender systems. *BLED 2008 Proceedings*, page 28, 2008.

[18] N. Tintarev and J. Masthoff. Effective explanations of recommendations: user-centered design. In *Proceedings of the 2007 ACM conference on Recommender systems*, pages 153–156. ACM, 2007.

The Force Within: Recommendations Via Gravitational Attraction Between Items

Vikas Kumar
University of Minnesota
Minneapolis, Minnesota, USA
vikas@cs.umn.edu

Lyndon Kennedy
Futurewei Technologies, Inc.
Santa Clara, California, USA
lyndonk@acm.org

Saeideh Bakhshi
Facebook Inc.
Menlo Park, California, USA
saeideh@gatech.edu

David A. Shamma
Centrum Wiskunde & Informatica
Amsterdam, The Netherlands
aymans@acm.org

ABSTRACT

Recommendation systems rely on various definitions of similarities. These definitions while having numerous design factors in different domains help identify and recommend relevant content. For example, similarity between users, or items, are measured based on, but not limited to, explicit feedback such as ratings, thumbs up; or/and implicit feedback such as clicks, views etc; or/and based on composition of item such as tags, metadata etc. In this paper, we explore a similarity model while very intuitive to find similar items using a very common natural law of attraction between bodies, that is gravitational law. We show how the two attributes, relative mass and distance between the bodies, of gravitation law can be interpreted for an effective personalized recommendations; in both spatial and non-spatial domains. Finally, we illustrate the use of distance and mass in a non-spatial domain and we exhibit the accuracy in recommendations against popular baselines.

CCS CONCEPTS

• **Information systems** → **Collaborative filtering**; **Similarity measures**; **Recommender systems**; *Personalization*;

KEYWORDS

Recommender Systems; Newtons's Gravitational Law; Similarity; MovieLens.

1 INTRODUCTION

With numerous independent online content providers, such as Facebook, Netflix, Spotify, and Amazon, people are often faced with a problem of needle in haystack. In such large information spaces they often rely on some help to find relevant content. Personalized recommendation systems among other alternatives play a crucial

This research was conducted while the authors were at Yahoo Labs and Flickr.

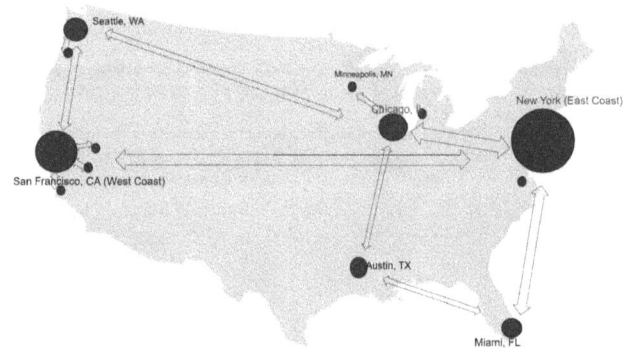

Figure 1: San Francisco is more similar to New York and Chicago (other bigger cities); and, places like Berkeley or New Jersey (read: moons) are more attracted to their nearby bigger cities San Francisco and New York respectively.

role in making such web services more usable and engaging for their users by identifying more meaningful and relevant contents, directly impacting the success and revenue of such businesses [2].

In most of the recommendation systems, the underlying model rely on similarities either in preferences of users or in items to find relevant and meaningful content [3, 13, 15]. For example, Amazon provides recommendation of items *similar* to recently browsed/bought, or based on alike users who have bought similar items. Furthermore, studies show descriptive similarities allow recommendations to be more transparent to users with potential of explanations [7]. For example, Pandora[1], a music recommendation site, provides a short explanation note on similarity in tonality, rhythm or use of chorus with user past preferences to explain why a song is chosen for the station.

There exist various models that further explore multiple dimensions of similarity, for example, location-similarity of users [11], content [17] or even latent factors [10]. However, recommendation systems literature rarely considered a model based on the natural law of attraction. In this paper, we take a step back on complexity of algorithms and define what we believe resonates with one of the most natural way of determining similarity between items—a

---

[1]http://www.pandora.com

method that provides recommendations using similarity defined by Newton's universal law of gravitation.

The gravitational law measures affinity between two items based on their relative mass and distance between them. It suggests that a bigger or massive body have more influence than smaller bodies; and that, this influence reduces as bodies move farther apart from each other. For example, a smaller body like a moon to a planet even though being closer have lesser influence on the planet than other massive bigger bodies like its parent star or another giant planet. However, with respect to moon, it has the biggest influence from its massive mother planet. It is this relation between the bodies with respect to their mass and distance that allow to explore a natural form of similarity model between items in the space of recommendation systems. Intuitively, it is not hard to find nature of similar effects in recommendation systems. For instance, the rating similarity or influence between massively popular movies like *The Godfather* and *The Shawshank Redemption* is high, though very different in storyline, as they are rated by *most* of the users rather than just *alike* users. At the same time, *The Godfather*, a mafia movie, influence many other not-so-popular mafia movies like *Mean Streets*[2]. Likewise, in spatial-domain such as location-based restaurant recommendations one can easily see why San Francisco (SF), a large metropolitan and distinct urban-economy lifestyle very similar to New York (NYC) are more influential to each other than their neighboring cities. On the other hand, the relatively smaller cities like Berkeley (near SF) and New Jersey (near NYC) are primarily influenced by their neighboring bigger cities SF and NYC respectively than each other as illustrated in Figure 1 (analogous to influence we observe between moons and planets versus planets to planets).

In this paper, we model similarity between items in recommendation systems using gravitational model and compare against traditional definitions. We explore how two main features of this model, relative mass and distance, are open for interpretations and can be defined in various ways. For example, mass can be measured based on, but not limited to, ratings, cast, size, popularity, box-office collection, page-rank etc. Whereas, distance between items can be measured in one or more information spaces such as, but not limited to, geodesic distance for spatial items such as restaurants and POIs; and semantic distance for non-spatial items such as music, movies, and text. Finally, we conclude with results from one of the non-spatial domain of movie recommendations and discuss the ease of explain-ability of the model.

2 SIMILARITY MODELS

There exist multiple methods in recommendation literature to define similarity between two items, commonly referred to as neighbor based approach. For example, cosine-similarity calculates the similarity between items based on dot product of two vectors, each can be representing user ratings, or views/clicks etc. Likewise, there exists other common methods such as Jaccard, Pearsons as well as Log-likelihood for defining similarity [12] between items. Furthermore, similarity models can be a combination across multiple dimensions of similarity to calculate a more comprehensive value, such as, a linear combination of similarity between explicit feedback

---

[2]The similarities are as observed on MovieLens platform.

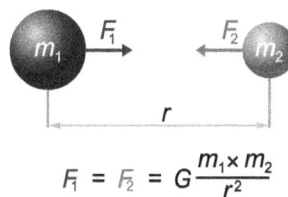

$$F_1 = F_2 = G \frac{m_1 \times m_2}{r^2}$$

Figure 2: Newton's Law of Universal Gravitation. ⓒⓘⓞ Dennis Nilsson, Wikipedia

(user rating vectors), implicit feedback (views/clicks) or content (tags), as shown in Equation 1, where co-efficients α, β, γ can be learned using regression techniques [8].

$$
\begin{aligned}
\text{similarity}(i, j) = & \alpha \times \text{rating}_{\text{sim}}(i, j) \\
& + \beta \times \text{views}_{\text{sim}}(i, j) \\
& + \gamma \times \text{tags}_{\text{sim}}(i, j)
\end{aligned}
\tag{1}
$$

More recent models calculate similarity among items based on latent factors, a model common with matrix factorization techniques [10]. There exists other sophisticated techniques such as tensor factorization [9] and restricted Boltzmann machines [14], capable to learn similarities from latent correlations between items to optimize for accurate recommendations [1]. However, though accurate they add more complexity to the understanding of similarity limiting the power of explainable recommendations. We believe that a method that resonates with the most natural way of defining affinity is like recognizing missing side of same coin.

3 GRAVITATIONAL MODEL

Newton, around three centuries ago, defined one of the most common law of physics between two bodies known as gravitational law of attraction. The law defines a force of attraction (F) between two bodies proportional to the product of their masses (m_1 and m_2) and inversely proportional to the square of distance (r) between their centers as illustrated in Figure 2.

Likewise, we postulate that a similar model could help us describe the affinity between items that exist in the information space of online systems. An advantage of such model lies in open interpretation of relative effect size and distance. Leveraging multiple definitions implicitly favors the model to be adaptable in diverse information spaces. For example, the *mass* of an item can be represented in both simple scalar or vector forms. The basic requirement can be that it reflects the relative size (or importance), such as popularity of item, with respect to other items. For instance, in music recommendation, mass of an artist can be based on number of ratings, number of views or number of plays etc. A vector mass of the artists can also be modeled as a representation of item size over multiple dimensions. For example, artist represented with popularity in specific genres of music, or preference with specific cluster of users[4]. It can also be combination of heterogeneous parameters such as brand value, number of followers, number of recent popular releases etc.

Similar to mass, relative *distance* can also be represented in a scalar or vector form. For spatial items, such as restaurants, POIs,

etc, the geodesic distance provide an easy alternative. However, for non-spatial items, it can be challenging. One alternative is based on semantic dissimilarity measured using the content or composition of items. The available metadata for items, or user provided tags can play an important role in defining the semantic distance. We discuss the tag-based semantic distance in our experiment. As an alternative, we believe Wikipedia with its global reach on various topics can determine the semantic relatedness [6] for various types of items in online information space. Atlasify[3], an open source project using Wikibrain API[4], is an example on how semantic relatedness can help determine the distance between items with no spatial footprint.

4 EXPERIMENT

To study if the gravitational model is effective, we setup an offline experiment using MovieLens 10M ratings dataset. The dataset is publicly available from MovieLens platform[5]. It consists of 10 million ratings and 100,000 tags for 10,000 movies by 72,000 users.

4.1 Model

We use the popularity of movies, measured by log of number of ratings, as value for relative size or mass of the movie. That is, more the number of ratings, more popular the movie is and thus higher is the mass of the movie. The log is used to minimize the effect of movies like *Toy Story* and *The Matrix* which are like black holes due to their massive popularity compared to other items in the system.

For distance, movies being non-spatial items we use semantic dis-similarities. Using tag applications we calculate the similarity in user perceived composition of movies using cosine. Each movie is represented as vector, of equal length, with series of relevance value as determined by tag genome [16] for each tag-movie pair. Higher the similarity between movies in this semantic space, lesser is the distance between them. Finally, using the Newton's model, we combine the mass and distance to determine the gravitational similarity[6] between two movies, m_i and m_j, as shown in Equation 2 as $g_{\text{sim}}(m_i, m_j)$:

$$g_{\text{sim}}(m_i, m_j) = \frac{\text{mass}(m_i) \times \text{mass}(m_j)}{[\text{distance}(m_i, m_j)]^2} \quad (2)$$

where:
$$\text{mass}(m_i) = \log(\text{num\_ratings}_{m_i})$$
$$\text{distance}(m_i, m_j) = (1 - \text{tag}_{\text{sim}}(m_i, m_j))$$

4.2 Personalized Recommendations

To generate personalized recommendation for each user, traditional item-item collaborative filtering technique is used where instead of the usual cosine similarity between items, we use the gravitational similarity in the equation to predict user (u) ratings for an unknown movie (m) where Nb(m) is the Neighbors of m.

$$\text{pred}(u, m) = \frac{\sum_{i \in \text{Nb}(m)} g_{\text{sim}}(i, m) \times rating(i, u)}{\sum_{i \in \text{Nb}(m)} g_{\text{sim}}(i, m)} \quad (3)$$

For top-N recommendations we select the N most highly rated predictions from the list of each user. Finally, we compare the prediction and recommendation accuracy of our model against traditional techniques, discussed in next section.

4.3 Metrics

For prediction accuracy, we use 90% of the 10 million ratings for learning similarities and use rest 10% for test. As a metric, the traditional RMSE is used to determine accuracy of the predictions. We compare our results against other well known collaborative filtering techniques i.e., ItemItem, UserUser, and Matrix Factorization. For recommendation accuracy, we determine Precision, Recall and Mean Average Precision for each test user in the dataset. The test data is created by randomly sampling 10% of users. We hide 20% of their ratings and use rest 80% for training purpose. A recommendation is considered relevant if we find user has rated the movie 4 stars or higher in 20% of hidden ratings. Final metrics are average of observed values over all test users. Similar to prediction accuracy, we again compare the results with other baselines.

5 RESULTS

The results for both prediction and recommendation metrics are shown in Table 1. Lower RMSE for Gravity model at 0.92 compared to traditional collaborative filtering techniques i.e. ItemItem and UserUser, is a significant result[7]. Performing better than traditional CF techniques highlights the effectiveness of this similarity model in predicting ratings. Nevertheless, we find matrix factorization still a hard algorithm to beat in predictions and stands out with best RMSE of 0.91.

But, as known, RMSE numbers do not really paint the right picture of accurate recommendations [2]. Real users rarely notice difference in predicted ratings of a movie from 4.5 to 5.0 while, such minuscule differences play a huge role on overall RMSE. TopN recommendations in such cases provide a better alternative. Related recommendation metrics Precision, Recall and MAP thus help measure how well a set of recommendation is relevant for users, and Gravitational model stands out against all the other techniques. We observe statistically significant ($p < 0.001$) and much higher level of accuracy on each of the metric of Precision (0.08), Recall (0.28) and MAP (0.275).

We believe the significant improvement is in part due to the bias of gravitational model to popular items. A popular movie in general is highly likely to be rated by users. This popularity bias, though questionable, and probably a concern with ideal recommendations, we believe capture a very important implicit bias of users. A recent work by Harper et al. [5] confirms this implicit bias in users choice for recommendations on same MovieLens platform. They show users to choose recommendations that provide more popular items over recommendations with less popular ones.

We also study two more metrics, shown in Table 1, namely diversity and spread. With implicit bias towards popular items, we would expect the recommendations to be less diverse. We find this to be true for Gravitational model compared to other techniques but not worse than UserUser. However, with better spread, i.e. how

---

[3]http://www.atlasify.com/about.html
[4]https://shilad.github.io/wikibrain/
[5]http://grouplens.org/datasets/movielens
[6]The similarity values are normalized between 0.0 and 1.0 post the calculation.

[7]The difference in predicted ratings are found to be statistically significant with p-value<0.001 in Kruskal-Wallis test.

Table 1: RMSE and TopN results in MovieLens 10M dataset, best performance marked as (*). Gravitational based model does significantly well on recommendation metrics (than prediction metrics) for top 20 recommendations with comparable diversity and spread.

Metrics	ItemItem	UserUser	MatrixF	Gravity
RMSE	1.030	1.060	0.910*	0.920
Precision@20	0.001	0.019	0.010	0.080*
Recall@20	0.001	0.060	0.040	0.280*
MAP@20	0.024	0.088	0.046	0.275*
Intra-list Diversity@20	0.960	0.022	0.315	0.024
Spread@20	0.310	0.100	0.120	0.140

many distinct items does recommendation able to cover while recommending for users reflect that our preliminary model of gravitational similarity to be an effective algorithm for recommendations.

6 CONCLUSION

To our knowledge, this is the first work to consider and discuss the gravity and effective definition of Newton's law of attraction in recommendation systems. We propose and show the how using gravitational model in design of similarity result in efficient recommendations. We also discuss how With possible alternate interpretations of effective size and distance, the expression of gravitational model can be adapted for various recommendation domains.

Nevertheless, we also recognize certain limitations to this work that we can address in future. In our current approach, we do not consider or measure the nature of new items that model can recommend, which can potentially impact the design of recommendation. We believe that an online experiment with actual users would clearly benefit our model to further understand the role of gravity in recommendations. We also aim to study the model in various other domains like news, music, restaurants as we believe that these domains will exhibit the implicit popularity bias, an important factor observe in the gravitational model.

We further believe that there is a valuable byproduct of the gravitational model in online information spaces; that is, Visualization. With the items modeled by their intuitive size and distance between them, cluster of items could be visualized for navigational purposes in the same way as we navigate through solar systems in a galaxy (ex: Figure 1). One can choose or navigate through stars (most influential item of the cluster) and find similar planets (other influential items in cluster) and their moons (least influential but highly similar) to further explore categories, or other nearby influential star.

REFERENCES

[1] Amir Albadvi and Mohammad Shahbazi. 2009. A hybrid recommendation technique based on product category attributes. *Expert Systems with Applications* 36, 9 (2009), 11480–11488.

[2] Xavier Amatriain. 2016. Past, Present, and Future of Recommender Systems: An Industry Perspective. In *Proceedings of the 21st International Conference on Intelligent User Interfaces*. ACM, 1–1.

[3] Robin Burke. 2002. Hybrid recommender systems: Survey and experiments. *User modeling and user-adapted interaction* 12, 4 (2002), 331–370.

[4] Evangelia Christakopoulou and George Karypis. 2016. Local Item-Item Models For Top-N Recommendation. In *Proceedings of the 10th ACM Conference on Recommender Systems (RecSys '16)*. ACM, New York, NY, USA, 67–74. DOI: http://dx.doi.org/10.1145/2959100.2959185

[5] F. Maxwell Harper, Funing Xu, Harmanpreet Kaur, Kyle Condiff, Shuo Chang, and Loren Terveen. 2015. Putting Users in Control of Their Recommendations. In *Proceedings of the 9th ACM Conference on Recommender Systems (RecSys '15)*. ACM, New York, NY, USA, 3–10. DOI: http://dx.doi.org/10.1145/2792838.2800179

[6] Brent Hecht, Samuel H Carton, Mahmood Quaderi, Johannes Schöning, Martin Raubal, Darren Gergle, and Doug Downey. 2012. Explanatory semantic relatedness and explicit spatialization for exploratory search. In *Proceedings of the 35th international ACM SIGIR conference on Research and development in information retrieval*. ACM, 415–424.

[7] Jonathan L Herlocker, Joseph A Konstan, and John Riedl. 2000. Explaining collaborative filtering recommendations. In *Proceedings of the 2000 ACM conference on Computer supported cooperative work*. ACM, 241–250.

[8] LEE Jung-Hyun. 2004. User preference mining through hybrid collaborative filtering and content-based filtering in recommendation system. *IEICE TRANSACTIONS on Information and Systems* 87, 12 (2004), 2781–2790.

[9] Alexandros Karatzoglou, Xavier Amatriain, Linas Baltrunas, and Nuria Oliver. 2010. Multiverse recommendation: n-dimensional tensor factorization for context-aware collaborative filtering. In *Proceedings of the fourth ACM conference on Recommender systems*. ACM, 79–86.

[10] Yehuda Koren, Robert Bell, and Chris Volinsky. 2009. Matrix factorization techniques for recommender systems. *Computer* 8 (2009), 30–37.

[11] Justin J Levandoski, Mohamed Sarwat, Ahmed Eldawy, and Mohamed F Mokbel. 2012. Lars: A location-aware recommender system. In *Data Engineering (ICDE), 2012 IEEE 28th International Conference on*. IEEE, 450–461.

[12] Sean Owen, Robin Anil, Ted Dunning, and Ellen Friedman. 2011. *Mahout in action*. Manning Shelter Island.

[13] Paul Resnick, Neophytos Iacovou, Mitesh Suchak, Peter Bergstrom, and John Riedl. 1994. GroupLens: an open architecture for collaborative filtering of netnews. In *Proceedings of the 1994 ACM conference on Computer supported cooperative work*. ACM, 175–186.

[14] Ruslan Salakhutdinov, Andriy Mnih, and Geoffrey Hinton. 2007. Restricted Boltzmann machines for collaborative filtering. In *Proceedings of the 24th international conference on Machine learning*. ACM, 791–798.

[15] Badrul Sarwar, George Karypis, Joseph Konstan, and John Riedl. 2001. Item-based collaborative filtering recommendation algorithms. In *Proceedings of the 10th international conference on World Wide Web*. ACM, 285–295.

[16] Jesse Vig, Shilad Sen, and John Riedl. 2012. The tag genome: Encoding community knowledge to support novel interaction. *ACM Transactions on Interactive Intelligent Systems (TiiS)* 2, 3 (2012), 13.

[17] Valentina Zanardi and Licia Capra. 2008. Social ranking: uncovering relevant content using tag-based recommender systems. In *Proceedings of the 2008 ACM conference on Recommender systems*. ACM, 51–58.

Encoding Users as More Than the Sum of Their Parts

Recurrent Neural Networks and Word Embedding for People-to-people Recommendation

Antoine Lefebvre-Brossard
Polytechnique Montreal
antoine.lefebvre-brossard@polymtl.
ca

Alexandre Spaeth
e-180.com and Polytechnique
Montreal
alexandre.spaeth@polymtl.ca

Michel C. Desmarais
Polytechnique Montreal
michel.desmarais@polymtl.ca

ABSTRACT

Neural networks and word embeddings are powerful tools to capture latent factors. These tools can provide effective measures of similarities between users or items in the context of sparse data. We propose a novel approach that relies on neural networks and word embeddings to the problem of matching a learner looking for mentoring, and a tutor that is willing to provide this mentoring. Tutors and learners can issue multiple offers/requests on different topics. The approach matches over the whole array of topics specified by learners and tutors. Its performance for tutor-learner matching is compared with the state of the art. It yields similar results in terms of precision, but improves the recall.

KEYWORDS

Social recommender systems, User modeling for rec-ommendation, People recommendation, Content-based recommender

CCS CONCEPTS

• **Human-centered computing** → **Collaborative filtering**
; • **Computing methodologies** → *Neural networks*;

1 INTRODUCTION

In recent years, neural networks have become dominant in multiple domains such as computer vision, reasoning and natural language processing, to name only a few (see for eg. [2, 10, 11]). They have also started to be used in recommender systems where they obtain similar gains [4, 6, 15–17].

Our work explores the use of neural networks in people-to-people recommendation in a tutor-learner context (for eg. [13]). In this context, a learner expresses the wish to meet someone with a sought expertise to learn a specific topic, and the tutor expresses the will to engage in tutoring on such topic. Typically, the matching of tutor-learner pair can involve free and/or structured text/tags describing the topic to learn/teach, and involve collaborative filtering type of data in the form of implicit votes deducted from different types of contacts the users can engage with. The context is therefore well suited to content boosted collaborative filtering and, to our knowledge, deep learning approaches in this domain are only emerging [3, 5, 14, 16, 17]. But the interest is rapidly gaining

speed as shown by a recent workshop on the topic of Deep learning for recommender systems [1].

We propose a framework based on word encodings and Recurrent Neural Networks to address the typical issue of sparsity with textual descriptions. In addition, we expand from the perspective of matching a learner request to a tutor offer by taking into account the general profiles of the two in the matching process, namely their history of past expertise requests and offers. The assumption behind is that interest in topics tend to cluster, and taking advantage of that information can enhance the quality of the matches.

We evaluate the performance of the framework as a content based recommendation framework, as well as its performance when it is combined with collaborative filtering. The performance is similar to the state of the art in terms of precision, but it improves over the latent semantic analysis (LSA) baselines on recall.

2 APPLICATION CONTEXT AND DATA

The tutor-learner matching task is studied in [13] with data from the commercial site e-180.com. We use an updated version of this data set.

In this site, a user can post different offers to teach one-on-one a topic he or she is well acquainted with, and a learner can post requests to learn about a topic. Users can browse and search for offers and for requests, view the associated user profile, initiate message exchanges through the site, and ultimately arrange a contact in person.

This data creates a typical implicit vote matrix where users are items. And it also contains content data, namely the offer/requests posts, and tags. The tags are chosen by the user to describe expertise, but auto-completed to make sure that tags are correctly spelled.

Figure 1 shows the distribution of the number of contacts of all types, per user and on a $\log_{10}$ basis.

The tutoring offers and learning requests posted by users will be referred to as an *expertise* for the rest of this paper. Each expertise has a description in either French, English or both, and tags associated to it. General statistics about the data can be seen in Table 1.

Contact data	
Active users	17 592
Views	163 657
Messages	50 204
Meetings	24 090
Total	237 951
Users with an expertise	
French	2908
English	6077
Bilingual	331
Total	8654
Number of expertises	
French	7770
English	9643
Bilingual	664
Total	16 749
Mean number of words per expertise	
French	14.834
English	20.044
Unique tags	12 141
Mean tags per expertise	4.704

Table 1: General statistics on the data

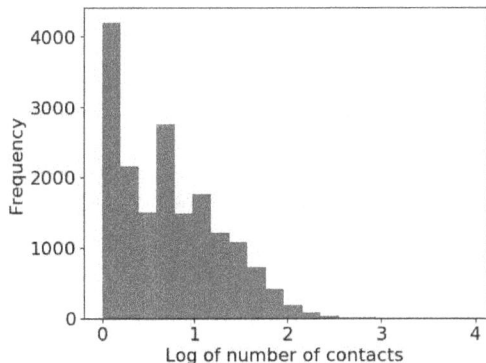

Figure 1: Distribution of the number of contacts (view, message or meeting) per user.

3 MODEL

The proposed model addresses the problem of integrating two sources of content data, expertises (offer and request descriptions) and tags. Descriptions are free texts and we can take advantage of their syntactic structures, or at least of each word's context. Recurrent Neural Networks (RNN) are appropriate tools for that purpose. However and akin to vector space models, they face the issue of sparse data incurred by the small number of words in a description in relation to the large vocabulary. To address this issue, words are embedded as vectors of a small number of latent dimensions. Then, an RNN takes the sequence of words in a description to output a vector representing a "deep" representation of this description. This approach bear similarities to [3] who used word embeddings and RNN to recommend scientific papers.

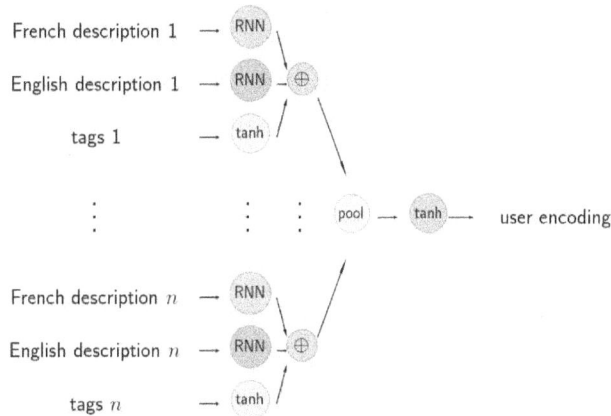

Figure 2: Full model of the user encoding where ⊕ is a concatenation and circles of the same colour share parameters if there is any parameter to share

A general view of the model can be seen in Fig. 2. Each user is encoded in a single vector created by encoding the French and English descriptions. The tags are encoded separately and combined to the description vectors.

The concatenation of tag and description vectors into a single vector represents the globality of this user's expertise offer and requests.

Details of the model are provided below.

3.1 Description Encoding

Because users present their interests in French, English or both, two RNNs [7] were used to encode the descriptions, an example of which was given in Fig. 3. For the same reason, different word embedding matrices were used for the two languages. Because most descriptions are fairly short, and in order to reduce the number of parameters, we adopted the simplest form of RNN. For a description of length T, at each step t, the embedding of the word is given by x_t and the hidden state by h_t. The final output of the RNN is given by $\hat{y}_T$. Formally, we have:

$$
\begin{aligned}
h_t &= \tanh\left(W^{(D)}x_t + U^{(D)}h_{t-1} + b^{(D)}\right) \\
\hat{y}_T &= h_T \\
h_0 &= 0
\end{aligned}
\tag{1}
$$

where $W^{(D)} \in \mathbb{R}^{n_{\text{hid}} \times n_{\text{emb}}}$, $U^{(D)} \in \mathbb{R}^{n_{\text{hid}} \times n_{\text{hid}}}$ and $b^{(D)} \in \mathbb{R}^{n_{\text{hid}}}$. The dimensions given by $n.$ are hyperparameters to select. The hyperbolic tangent function (tanh) is commonly used in neural networks to transform real values in the $[-1, 1]$ range.

3.2 Tag Encoding

Because the tags have no syntactic structure, tags corresponding to both languages can be encoded together in a single sparse vector. Furthermore, contrary to text, there is not enough training data to

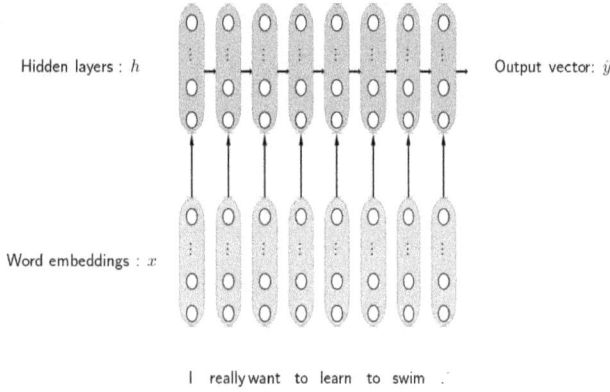

Figure 3: Encoding of user interests using a recurrent neural net (RNN) represented by the hidden layer.

train tag embeddings and we use a simple bag-of-word approach to create a sparse vector, where each element is the number of times the tag has appeared in the expertise. This vector is then reduced using a linear combination of this vector followed by a tanh activation function. Here we have x the sparse bag-of-words vector and $\hat{y}$ the output of this function.

$$\hat{y} = \tanh\left(W^{(T)}x + b^{(T)}\right) \tag{2}$$

where $W^{(T)} \in \mathbb{R}^{2n_{\text{hid}} \times n_{\text{tag}}}$ and $b^{(T)} \in \mathbb{R}^{2n_{\text{hid}}}$. It is to be noticed that the hyperparameter n_{hid} is the same as the one defined in the text encoding section. Because the number of tags is defined by the data, n_{tag} depends on the data and is not a hyperparameter.

3.3 Interest combination

To combine the expertise encodings of each user, two different pooling methods were tested, (1) averaging each dimension over the interests or (2) taking the max of each dimension. These will be referred to as mean-pooling and max-pooling.

For each given user's expertises, both description vectors and the tag vector are concatenated to a vector of size $4n_{\text{hid}}$. The pooling is then made over all of the user's expertises. Another linear combination followed by a softmax activation function reduces this user encoding to a vector of size n_{hid}.

3.4 Recommendation

Similarities between two users can the be obtained by cosine similarity using

$$s_{i,j} = \frac{u_i^T u_j}{||u_i|| \, ||u_j||} \tag{3}$$

where u_i, u_j are the encodings of users i and j. Users can then be recommended on the basis of this similarity.

4 TRAINING

To train the model, we took advantage of the implicit data in the form of profile views, conversations and meetings. Each pair of user having had a contact in at least one of these respects is treated as a datapoint. These pairs are then randomly grouped in batches of size b. Let $U \in \mathbb{R}^{b \times n_{\text{hid}}}$ be the batch containing the first members of the pairs, encoded by the model and $V \in \mathbb{R}^{b \times n_{\text{hid}}}$ be the batch containing the second members. Furthermore, let $c \in \mathbb{R}^b$ be the contact weights. This contact weight is 0 by default and the following values are added, akin to [13]:

+1   if either one or both have seen the other's profile
+2   if there was an exchange of message between the two
+4   if there was a meeting between the two

The loss function J is given by

$$
\begin{aligned}
J = &\frac{1}{b} \sum_{i=1}^{b} \sum_{j=1}^{n_{\text{hid}}} c_i \left(U_{ij} - V_{ij}\right)^2 - \\
&\alpha \left(\frac{1}{b} \sum_{i=1}^{b} \sum_{j=1}^{n_{\text{hid}}} \left(U_{ij} - \bar{v}_j\right)^2 + \frac{1}{b} \sum_{i=1}^{b} \sum_{j=1}^{n_{\text{hid}}} \left(V_{ij} - \bar{u}_j\right)^2 \right) \\
\bar{u} = &\frac{1}{b} \sum_{i=1}^{b} U_{i,\cdot} \\
\bar{v} = &\frac{1}{b} \sum_{i=1}^{b} V_{i,\cdot}
\end{aligned}
\tag{4}
$$

with α a hyperparameter. Recall that b is the size of the groupings. The second term of the loss has a regularizing effect without which the optimum is to have equal vector encoding no matter what. In practice, we found that setting it to 0.5 works well.

The model used batches of size 8 and hidden dimension $n_{\text{hid}} = 50$. It was trained using gradient descent and the Adam optimizer [9].

5 EXPERIMENTS

To test the different models, the training was done on data from 2012 to 2015 and then tested on data from January 1st 2016 to June 1st 2016. Since the comparison was made on the expertise encoding, only users with at least one expertise were used.

A recommendation is considered good if the user was met or messaged, given that the profile had been viewed. Because a user doesn't need to click on a user's profile to send a message or set up a meeting, but can directly click an offer or request, some conversations and meetings have no profile view associated to them. Because the information is still seen when sending a message or setting up a meeting, we assumed there was always a profile view associated to a conversation or meeting.

Let

$$
\begin{aligned}
v_{i,j} &= \begin{cases} 1 & \text{if } view_{i,j} \lor message_{i,j} \lor meeting_{i,j} \\ 0 & \text{else} \end{cases} \\
c_{i,j} &= \begin{cases} 1 & \text{if } message_{i,j} \lor meeting_{i,j} \\ 0 & \text{else} \end{cases} \\
r_{i,j} &= j\text{th recommended user to user } i
\end{aligned}
\tag{5}
$$

	@1	@5	@10	@50	@100
Content-based alone					
Neural max	0.094	**0.203**	**0.235**	0.194	0.174
Neural mean	0.085	0.201	0.229	**0.196**	**0.175**
LSA max	**0.099**	0.190	0.207	0.176	0.159
LSA mean	0.097	0.185	0.212	0.176	0.159
CF (baseline)	*0.093*	*0.207*	*0.236*	*0.195*	*0.175*
Content-based + collaborative filtering (CF)					
Neural max + CF	0.109	0.222	0.256	0.233	0.209
Neural mean + CF	**0.111**	0.221	0.263	**0.244**	**0.218**
LSA max + CF	0.104	**0.234**	0.259	0.235	0.210
LSA mean + CF	0.100	0.229	**0.264**	0.238	0.215

Table 2: F1 of the various models. Best F1 in bold at reach retreived subset size, from 1 to 100.

We then have as precision and recall metrics

$$precision = \frac{\sum_{i=1}^{U} \sum_{j=1}^{R} c_{i,r_{i,j}}}{\sum_{i=1}^{U} \sum_{j=1}^{R} v_{i,r_{i,j}}}$$

$$recall = \frac{\sum_{i=1}^{U} \sum_{j=1}^{R} c_{i,r_{i,j}}}{\sum_{i=1}^{U} \sum_{j=1}^{U} c_{i,j}}$$

(6)

We also took advantage of the availability of word embeddings available online and trained on much larger datasets to limit the number of parameters we had to train ourselves. The English embeddings were taken from [12] and the French ones from [8].

The benchmark we compared ourselves to is the approach used in [13] which uses a TF-IDF over the bag-of-words of the descriptions followed by dimensionality reduction with SVD (LSA). To determine the similarity between users, either an average of the cosine similarities between their expertises was taken, or their maximum.

Following [13], we combined the model using both types of pooling and the LSA methods used as benchmark to a collaborative filtering approach. A matrix was created from values obtained in the training and was reduced using SVD. A new similarity was obtained between users by taking the cosine similarity between the rows of this reduced matrix. Recommendations were then based on the sum of this similarity and the ones obtained from the previous models.

6 RESULTS

The results are shown in Figure 4 and Table 2.

In the top figure, the content-based alone condition, descriptions and tags were used to create recommendations, whereas in the bottom figure both content and collaborative data was used.

The general trend we observe is that the proposed approach performance is slightly better than [13] in terms of F1, but it differs in terms of precision and recall. The content-based condition shows that the proposed approach has lower precision, but better recall than the bag-of-words with dimension reduction through SVD. The performance of the Neural max approach almost mimics the collaborative filtering approach alone.

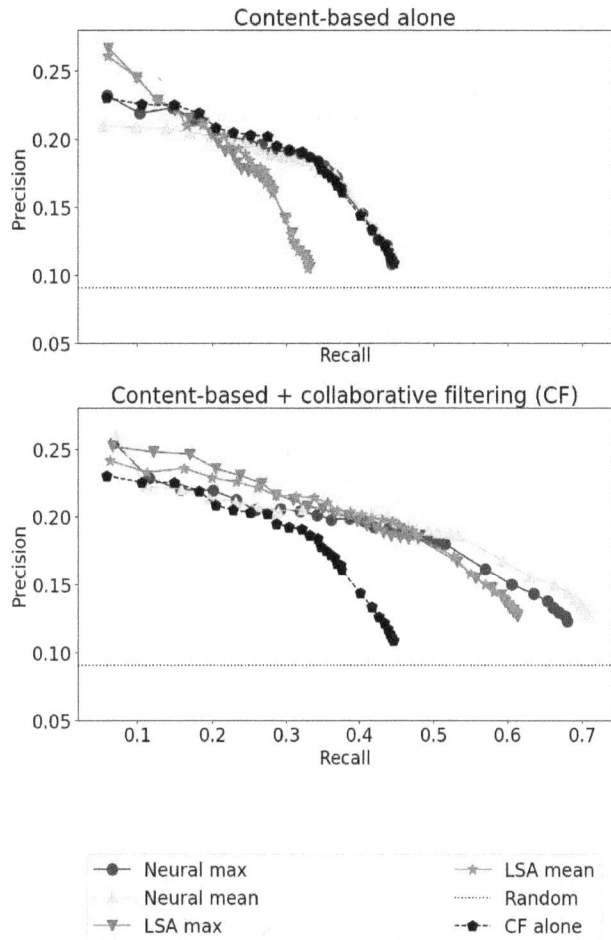

Figure 4: Precision-Recall curves of models and benchmarks

The combination of collaborative filtering with each of the two approaches shows a relatively similar performance. Both precision and recall are improved by taking advantage of collaborative filtering, and we observe a slight decrease in precision, and an increase in recall for the proposed approach compared to the bag-of-words+LSA approach.

7 CONCLUSION

This work introduces a new approach for the recommendation of users in a tutor-learner setting. By using a neural network to encode all of a user's expertises (offers to teach or requests to learn), a better recall rate is achieved than traditional LSA methods, at the expense of a slight decrease in precision. However, once the collaborative data is combined to the content-based approach, we find the performance of the approach comparable to the original bag-of-words and LSA approach.

Future work will try to determine if the lower precision at smaller recall rates is caused by the model or is a product of the sparsity of the data by testing the recommendations on users directly and not on historical data.

REFERENCES

[1] 2016. *DLRS 2016: Proceedings of the 1st Workshop on Deep Learning for Recommender Systems*. ACM, New York, NY, USA.

[2] Dzmitry Bahdanau, Kyunghyun Cho, and Yoshua Bengio. 2014. Neural machine translation by jointly learning to align and translate. *arXiv preprint arXiv:1409.0473* (2014).

[3] Trapit Bansal, David Belanger, and Andrew McCallum. 2016. Ask the GRU: Multi-task Learning for Deep Text Recommendations. In *Proceedings of the 10th ACM Conference on Recommender Systems*. ACM, 107–114.

[4] Oren Barkan, Noam Koenigstein, and Eylon Yogev. 2016. The Deep Journey from Content to Collaborative Filtering. *arXiv preprint arXiv:1611.00384* (2016).

[5] Heng-Tze Cheng, Levent Koc, Jeremiah Harmsen, Tal Shaked, Tushar Chandra, Hrishi Aradhye, Glen Anderson, Greg Corrado, Wei Chai, Mustafa Ispir, and others. 2016. Wide & deep learning for recommender systems. In *Proceedings of the 1st Workshop on Deep Learning for Recommender Systems*. ACM, 7–10.

[6] Robin Devooght and Hugues Bersini. 2016. Collaborative filtering with recurrent neural networks. *arXiv preprint arXiv:1608.07400* (2016).

[7] Jeffrey L Elman. 1991. Distributed representations, simple recurrent networks, and grammatical structure. *Machine learning* 7, 2-3 (1991), 195–225.

[8] Jean-Philippe Fauconnier. Jean-Philippe Fauconnier, year = 2016, url = http://fauconnier.github.io, urldate = 2017-02-23. (????).

[9] Diederik Kingma and Jimmy Ba. 2014. Adam: A method for stochastic optimization. *arXiv preprint arXiv:1412.6980* (2014).

[10] Alex Krizhevsky, Ilya Sutskever, and Geoffrey E Hinton. 2012. Imagenet classification with deep convolutional neural networks. In *Advances in neural information processing systems*. 1097–1105.

[11] Ankit Kumar, Ozan Irsoy, Jonathan Su, James Bradbury, Robert English, Brian Pierce, Peter Ondruska, Ishaan Gulrajani, and Richard Socher. 2015. Ask me anything: Dynamic memory networks for natural language processing. *CoRR*, abs/1506.07285 (2015).

[12] Jeffrey Pennington, Richard Socher, and Christopher D Manning. 2014. Glove: Global Vectors for Word Representation.. In *EMNLP*, Vol. 14. 1532–1543.

[13] Alexandre Spaeth and Michel C Desmarais. 2013. Combining collaborative filtering and text similarity for expert profile recommendations in social websites. In *International Conference on User Modeling, Adaptation, and Personalization*. Springer, 178–189.

[14] Aaron Van den Oord, Sander Dieleman, and Benjamin Schrauwen. 2013. Deep content-based music recommendation. In *Advances in neural information processing systems*. 2643–2651.

[15] Hao Wang, Naiyan Wang, and Dit-Yan Yeung. 2015. Collaborative deep learning for recommender systems. In *Proceedings of the 21th ACM SIGKDD International Conference on Knowledge Discovery and Data Mining*. ACM, 1235–1244.

[16] Zhongqing Wang and Yue Zhang. 2017. Opinion Recommendation using Neural Memory Model. *arXiv preprint arXiv:1702.01517* (2017).

[17] Lei Zheng, Vahid Noroozi, and Philip S Yu. 2017. Joint Deep Modeling of Users and Items Using Reviews for Recommendation. In *Proceedings of the Tenth ACM International Conference on Web Search and Data Mining*. ACM, 425–434.

Multilingual Search User Behaviors – Exploring Multilingual Querying and Result Selection Through Crowdsourcing

Ryan Lowe, Ben Steichen
Santa Clara University
500 El Camino Real
Santa Clara, California
{rjlowe,bsteichen}@scu.edu

ABSTRACT

The unprecedented increase in online search user diversity across the globe has led to new challenges for search engine providers. In particular, among these challenges is the need to better support individuals who are proficient in multiple languages. To investigate this particular user characteristic, this paper presents an analysis of multilingual search user behaviors through a series of large-scale studies using crowdsourcing. Results show that multilingual users make significant use of each of their languages when searching, and that there are significant differences in behaviors between querying and result selection. In addition, results show that language use strongly depends on a number of task factors and individual user characteristics. These results are discussed in terms of building novel adaptive multilingual search solutions that better support and adapt to users who have multiple language abilities.

KEYWORDS

Multilingual Search; Multilingual User Characteristics; User Study; Personalized Search; Crowd-Sourcing;

ACM Reference format:

H.5.m. [Information interfaces and presentation (e.g.,HCI)]: Miscellaneous; H.3.3 [Information Search and Retrieval]: Search process;

1 INTRODUCTION

Web information access systems increasingly need to cater for a wide variety of users from across the globe. This growing user diversification leads to a number of new challenges, particularly in terms of having to support a wide variety of user languages. A common solution to supporting different user languages is the process of "localization", whereby systems are adapted to different markets through the use of translation and cultural adaptation. This process typically yields a set of "unilingual" systems, each dedicated to a single market and target language.

However, one aspect that has typically been ignored by this process is the fact that many people across the globe are actually proficient in multiple languages. For instance, on average 94.6% of secondary education pupils in the European Union learn English in general programs, and 64.7% learn two or more languages[1]. Likewise, this trend is evident throughout the world, and it is estimated that there are many more people who know English as a second language than there are native speakers[2].

The abovementioned "unilingual" view of localization is hence greatly inadequate, as it typically does not support the growing multilingual user abilities or preferences of online users. Likewise, while there have been significant advances regarding the handling, retrieval, and automatic translation of multilingual information in the research area of Multilingual Information Access (MIA)[1], there has been a distinct lack of human-centered MIA research in terms of search user multilingualism.

By contrast, this paper presents a large-scale analysis of multilingual search users, in order to better understand these users' behaviors and preferences, as well as to inform the design and development of much more tailored and truly multilingual information access solutions. This paper extends prior survey results through behavioral studies regarding query language choices, as well as search result language preferences. Specifically, we aim to answer the following research questions:

- **RQ1**. Which of their language(s) do multilingual users generally use when querying and choosing search results?
- **RQ2**. What is the effect of language proficiency?
- **RQ3**. What are the effects of task type and domain?

Through an analysis of results from three user studies with over 2000 participants, the paper shows that multilingual search users tend to often use each of their different languages, and that their behavior depends on language proficiency, task type, and task domain. The results overall provide evidence regarding the benefits of better supporting multiple language abilities, and help towards designing adaptive search systems that support and adapt to multilingual users and their contexts.

UMAP '17, July 09-12, 2017, Bratislava, Slovakia
© 2017 Association for Computing Machinery.
ACM ISBN 978-1-4503-4635-1/17/07...$15.00
http://dx.doi.org/10.1145/3079628.3079702

---

[1] epp.eurostat.ec.europa.eu/statistics_explained/index.php/foreign_language_learning_statistics
[2] www.britishcouncil.org/learning-research-english-next.pdf

2 RELATED WORK

In the field of multilingual search, the majority of research has been concerned with the notions of Cross-language Information Retrieval (CLIR) and Multilingual Information Access (MLIA) [1]. This work typically investigates ways to (1) enhance query translation/disambiguation through Machine Translation [2], (2) enhance retrieval algorithms [1], or (3) enhance search interface aspects [3][4][5]. However, there has been comparably less research devoted to studying multilingual users. Likewise, the user characteristic of language proficiency has received relatively little attention in the User Modeling and Adaptation community.

By contrast, this paper specifically focuses on the characteristics, behaviors, and preferences of multilingual search users. Most similar to our work, there have been a few survey-, interview-, and focus group-based studies to investigate multilingual searching and browsing. For example, a survey in [6] explored monolingual and multilingual user behaviors in the digital libraries domain. Survey respondents indicated that they typically use multiple languages when searching in digital libraries, and that their language skills and field of knowledge in different academic fields have an impact on their search language choices. Likewise, the survey in [7] asked multilingual users to describe the degree to which they generally browse and search the web in multiple languages. The results from this survey suggested that language proficiency and type of content sought may play a role in language selections. Additionally, several interview and focus group studies [8][9] have provided some qualitative feedback regarding the unique challenges that multilingual users face when using multiple languages online, especially in terms of query formulation and reformulation in secondary languages (e.g. if a user's second language writing ability is limited).

In contrast to these attitudinal surveys, interviews, and focus group studies, our paper provides the first large-scale user studies that explicitly elicit user querying and search result selection behaviors from multilingual users. The results from our analyses thereby extend the above work through large-scale quantitative behavioral analyses. Additionally, our paper shows the extent to which task- and user-related attributes play a role in language selections, enabling recommendations towards building systems that support and adapt to users with multiple language skills.

3 EXPERIMENTAL SETUP

In order to answer the aforementioned research questions, we conducted a set of studies using the Crowdflower [3] crowdsourcing platform. In particular, three separate studies were set up to elicit user behaviors regarding query formulation (Studies 1 and 2) and search result choice (Study 3).

---

[3] www.crowdflower.com

3.1 Study 1

The first study focused on user query construction behaviors. Upon starting the study, participants were first asked to indicate the languages in which they had "some" proficiency (out of a choice of 7 languages), as well as their level of proficiency in each (on a scale of 1-5). A set of 10 search topic descriptions was then presented to the participant sequentially (i.e. one at a time). The description of a topic was displayed in each of the user's indicated languages (with the order of topic description languages being counterbalanced), and the participant was prompted to simply enter a query that they would use to search for information on this topic. Participants were instructed to type in the language that they would typically use for queries on this type of topic.

3.2 Study 2

Study 2 similarly focused on query elicitation behaviors, with participants again being presented with topics in each of their indicated languages. However, instead of providing a free text input field to type a search query, Study 2 offered a dropdown list of possible queries, and participants were asked to choose one preferred query from this list. The drop-down list contained one query per user language (with language orders again being counterbalanced). Once a query was selected, users were prompted to indicate the reasons as to why they had picked this query (using a set of checkbox options and a free text input field).

3.3 Study 3

In contrast to Study 1 and Study 2, which focused on query behavior, Study 3 focused on result list preferences. Similar to the above studies, participants were first asked to indicate their languages and proficiencies, and were then presented with a sequence of 10 search topic descriptions (with descriptions again being displayed in each of the user's indicated languages). In this study, however, a pair of search result lists was presented for each topic, with each list containing results in a different language, e.g. if a user had indicated proficiency in German and English, a German result list and an English result list with 10 results each would be displayed side-by-side (due to space limitations, only two lists were displayed, in participants' strongest languages). Participants were then prompted to indicate their preference, i.e. indicate which result list best satisfied the search topic for them. List ordering was counterbalanced to avoid any positioning bias. Also, participants were again presented with a list of checkboxes to indicate their reasons for this particular selection.

3.4 Participant Recruitment and Payment

Participants were recruited through the Crowdflower crowdsourcing platform, which allowed the pooling of eligible participants from multiple individual recruitment channels, and, crucially, from a large geographical range. To ensure response quality, only Tier 3 (the highest level) Crowdflower users were allowed to partake in the studies. As an additional quality control measure, the order in which checkbox options were presented was randomized (to detect participants always checking a box in the same position), and an additional security checkbox would appear after every 4th question that would request that the user check the security checkbox each time it appeared. If the security checkbox was not checked, we could assume the participant was spamming. We then manually verified and filtered through responses and discarded any responses that failed the verification checkbox or showed a clear pattern of selection bias. While we acknowledge that it is unlikely that we were able to completely eliminate the noise in our studies due to the nature of crowdsourced data, we believe our quality control measures were sufficient to ensure the accuracy of our data. Each participant was paid 20 cents for a set of 10 topics, with an average completion time of 4 minutes.

3.5 Topics, Translations, & Analysis

To provide an unbiased and diverse set of topics and query choices, a total of 100 topic descriptions and titles were sourced from CLEF [4] (2006-2011) and TREC [5] (2012-2014) campaigns. These topics were manually classified into 3 task type categories (fact finding, information gathering, doing) based on the classifications described in [10], as well as mapped to 10 task domains (Health, Science, Society, World Politics, Business, Entertainment, Sports, Nature, Home & Family, and Shopping). These tasks represent general Web search tasks, and are hence not biased towards eliciting multilingual search behaviours.

All topic descriptions and titles were manually translated to support a total of seven languages (English, French, German, Spanish, Italian, Chinese Simplified, Chinese Traditional).

Search result lists (for Study 3) were generated using the Bing Search API [6]. For the analysis of Study 1, the languages of free-text queries of participants were inferred using Google Translate [7].

Each of the language frequency results reported for RQ1, RQ2, and RQ3 in the next section were tested for statistical significance using Chi square tests, and found to be statistically significant at an alpha level of 0.05.

4 RESULTS

A total of 2170 participants took part in the studies, of which responses were retained from 1670 after filtering out invalid entries using the quality controls described above. 552 participants took part in task 1, 648 in task 2, and 479 in task 3.

4.1 Participant Demographics

Participants from a total of 54 different countries took part in the studies. As per the study requirements, all participants were proficient in a minimum of 2 out of the 7 supported languages.

In addition, 201 participants indicated that they were proficient in 3 languages, and 24 participants in 4 languages.

In terms of participants' first language (i.e. their most proficient language - L1 hereafter), the most common languages were Spanish (32.3%), English (27.8%), Italian (20.4%), German (8.7%), French (6.8%), Chinese Traditional (2.85%), and Chinese Simplified (1.01%) For L2 (i.e. their second most proficient language), the vast majority spoke English (54.8%), followed by French (17.3%), German (10.2%), Spanish (8.3%), Italian (7.1%), Chinese Simplified (1.3%), and Chinese Traditional (1.0%).

4.2 General Language Use (RQ1)

As posed in the first research question (RQ1), our studies aimed to investigate the degree to which multilingual users tend to choose different languages for search querying and result selections, particularly in terms of using either their first language (L1) or their secondary languages (L2/L3/etc.). Results from Study 1 showed that participants tended to use their primary languages significantly more than their secondary languages to write queries (use of L1 78.84% of the time, versus only 21.16% for L2/L3/L4). In Study 2, when choosing between pre-written queries, participants used their secondary languages to a higher degree, with L1 being used 68.15% of the time, versus 31.85% for L2/L3/L4. For Study 3, i.e. when choosing between search result lists, participants preferred their secondary languages even more significantly, with a use of 61.49% for L1 versus 38.51% for L2.

As shown in Figure 1, a more detailed breakdown of the results revealed significant differences between individual languages. In particular, participants with English as L1 (i.e. native English speakers) generally tended not to use their L2 when querying or selecting search result lists. By contrast, when English was not their primary language (i.e. non-English L1), participants used their L2 much more across all 3 studies.

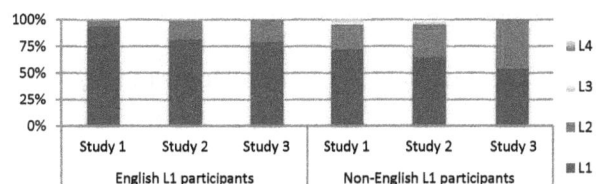

Figure 1: Languages used by participants who indicated English as their first language (referred to as English L1 participants) compared to non-English L1 participants

The results regarding participants' reasons for choosing particular languages revealed significant differences depending on what language had been chosen, i.e. depending on whether participants had chosen a query/result list in either their L1 or their L2. Most prominently, the breakdown of responses by non-English L1 participants showed that by far the most significant subjective reason for choosing L1 was their higher proficiency (further analysed below), as well as the perceived local relevance of the topic (see Figure 2). By contrast, L2 (which was English for most non-English L1 participants) was generally regarded as providing more trustworthy results, a more international

---

[4] Conference and Labs of the Evaluation Forum - www.clef-initiative.eu/
[5] Text REtrieval Conference - http://trec.nist.gov
[6] datamarket.azure.com/dataset/bing/search
[7] translate.google.com

perspective, higher general result relevance, as well as an increased relevance of results to the particular topic domain (further analysed below).

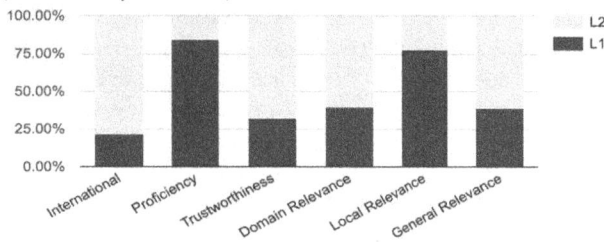

Figure 2: Reasons given by non-English L1 participants for preferring a result list in L1 or L2 (Study 3)

4.3 Effect of Language Proficiency (RQ2)

To further investigate the impact of language proficiency on language choices, we analyzed the relationship between participants' secondary language proficiency (as indicated by participants at the start of each study) and the frequency with which secondary languages were chosen for queries/result lists. Results showed again a significant difference between Studies 1, 2, and 3. In particular, for Study 1, a secondary language was rarely used for constructing queries when the participant had a low proficiency in this secondary language (less than 20% if the proficiency was 2 or lower). By contrast, for Study 2 and Study 3, participants tended to choose queries and result lists in their secondary languages much more frequently (over 35% even when the proficiency was as low as 2 out of 5 – see Figure 3)

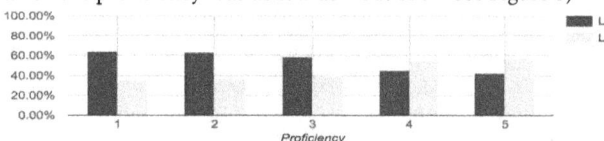

Figure 3: Effect of language proficiency on result list language preferences for non-English L1 participants (Study 3 results)

4.4 Effects of Task Type and Domain (RQ3)

In order to further investigate the effect of different topics, we analyzed language choices with respect to the pre-classified task type and domain associated with each search topic.

Results indicated that there was a significant effect of task type on user language choices, for both querying (Studies 1 and 2) and result list selections (Study 3). In particular, participants preferred to use their secondary language for search topics that were classified as Fact-Finding (47.86% L1 use compared to 52.14% L2 use), whereas they preferred using their primary language for topics of type Information Gathering (52.55% L1 use compared to 47.45% L2 use) and Doing (59.80% L1 use compared to 40.20% L2 use). Similarly, there was an effect in terms of topic domain, showing, for example, that participants used their secondary language much more for Entertainment, Science, or World Politics topics, whereas they tended to choose their L1 for topics related to Home & Family or Health (see Figure 4).

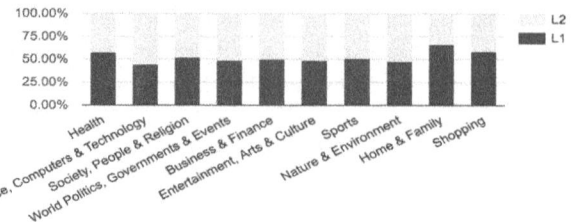

Figure 4: Language choice depending on topic domain for non-English L1 users (Study 3 results)

5 SUMMARY & DISCUSSION

The goal of the studies presented in this paper was to investigate what languages multilingual users generally use for online searching (RQ1), as well as how this use is influenced by user proficiency level (RQ2) and task type and domain (RQ3).

With respect to **RQ1**, study results showed that multilingual search users often tend to construct queries in their primary language (Study 1). Yet, participants often preferred search result lists in their secondary language (Study 3) when presented with this choice. Similarly, when given the choice between pre-written queries in different languages, users often select queries in their secondary language (Study 2) to search for information. These observations confirm that the current "unilingual" view of localized services does not reflect or support multilingual user behaviors and preferences.

Our additional analyses showed that these general findings may be explained by a significant effect of users' proficiency levels in their secondary languages (**RQ2**). Specifically, we observed a great disparity between the use of less proficient secondary languages when compared to that of higher proficiency languages. In addition, results showed that a user's indicated language proficiency played a much more exaggerated role when participants were tasked to write their own search queries compared to selecting from a list of queries. Similarly, since the data showed that multilingual users often prefer search result lists in their secondary language, the inhibiting factor for multilingual search mainly appears to stem from the query construction itself.

The data hence provides strong evidence that there is an opportunity for system designers to enhance information access for multilingual users by providing query elicitation features for secondary languages. Based on the findings from Study 2, an example feature could take the form of *multilingual query suggestions*, similar to current query suggestion techniques already provided in current Web search engines (e.g. "Related searches" features). Likewise, given that users often prefer secondary language results when presented with the choice, search systems could *adaptively retrieve and integrate multilingual search results* into result lists, through a combination of automatic query translation and result retrieval. Such a feature could take a similar form to the way current search engine result pages integrate information from various verticals (e.g. news, images, etc.), in line with the idea of aggregated search [11].

Lastly, results from the studies highlighted the fact that multilingual users gravitate more towards their secondary languages for particular task types and topic domains (**RQ3**). These results further indicate that there is a possibility to provide adaptive multilingual search support. For example, similar to research in aggregated search [12], multilingual search systems could provide adaptive support through retrieving and integrating multilingual results depending on the task type or domain. Such a feature could be further adapted by *retrieving and presenting personalized multilingual results* depending on each individual user's preferences.

6 CONCLUSION

In conclusion, the large-scale studies presented in this paper extend prior attitudinal studies, by showing that users who are proficient in multiple languages make significant use of each of their different languages for searching. In addition, the studies have revealed specific behavioral data regarding user querying and result list selection, showing for example that, when provided with choices in each of their languages, users can make much greater use of their secondary languages. In order to better support multilingual users, this paper has suggested several dedicated multilingual search engine features, including multilingual query suggestion, as well as adaptive multilingual result integration.

REFERENCES

[1] Peters, C., Braschler, M., and Clough, P. Multilingual Information Retrieval: From Research To Practice, chapt. 4, Springer Science & Business Media, (2012).

[2] Magdy, W., Jones, G.J.F.: An efficient method for using machine translation technologies in cross-language patent search. In: Proceedings of the 20th ACM Int. Conf. on Information and Knowledge Management. pp. 1925–1928 (2011)

[3] Steichen, B., Freund, L. Supporting the Modern Polyglot - A Comparison of Multilingual Search Interfaces. Proceedings of the ACM CHI Conference on Human Factors in Computing Systems (CHI 2015), pp. 3483-3492

[4] Petrelli, D., Levin, S., Beaulieu, M., and Sanderson, M. Which user interaction for cross-language information retrieval? Design issues and reflections. J. Assoc. Inf. Sci. Technol., 57, 5 (2006), 709–722.

[5] Amato, G., Cigarrán, J., Gonzalo, J., Peters, C., Savino, P.: MultiMatch – Multilingual/Multimedia Access to Cultural Heritage. Research and Advanced Technology for Digital Libraries, pp. 505–508 (2007)

[6] Clough, P., Eleta, I.: Investigating Language Skills and Field of Knowledge on Multilingual Information Access in Digital Libraries. International Journal of Digital Library Systems (IJDLS) 1, 89–103 (2010)

[7] Steichen, B., Ghorab, M.R., Lawless, S., O'Connor, A., and Wade, V. Towards Personalized Multilingual Information Access - Exploring the Browsing and Search Behavior of Multilingual Users. Proc. of int. conf. on User Modeling, Adaptation, and Personalization, (2014), 435-446.

[8] Anne Aula , Melanie Kellar, Multilingual search strategies, CHI '09 Extended Abstracts on Human Factors in Computing Systems. (2009)

[9] Chu, P., Komlodi, A., and Rózsa, G. Online search in english as a non-native language. In Proceedings of the 78th ASIS&T Annual Meeting: Information Science with Impact: Research in and for the Community (ASIST '15). American Society for Information Science, Silver Springs, MD, USA, , Article 40. (2015)

[10] Freund, L. A cross-domain analysis of task and genre effects on perceptions of usefulness. Inf. Process. Manage. 49, 5, 1108-1121. (2013)

[11] Sushmita, S., Joho, H., Lalmas, M., and Villa, R. Factors Affecting Click-through Behavior in Aggregated Search Interfaces. Proc. of 19th Int. Conf. on Inf. and Knowledge Management, (2010), 519–528.

[12] McCreadie, R., Macdonald, C., and Ounis, I. News vertical search: when and what to display to users. In Proceedings of the 36th international ACM SIGIR conference on Research and development in information retrieval (SIGIR '13). 253-262. (2013)

Modelling Embodied Mobility Teamwork Strategies in a Simulation-Based Healthcare Classroom

Roberto Martinez-Maldonado
Connected Intelligence Centre,
University of Technology Sydney,
Australia
Roberto.Martinez-Maldonado@uts.edu.au

Mykola Pechenizkiy
Department of Computer Science,
Eindhoven University of Technology,
the Netherlands
m.pechenizkiy@tue.nl

Simon Buckingham-Shum
Connected Intelligence Centre,
University of Technology Sydney,
Australia
Simon.BuckinghamShum@uts.edu.au

Tamara Power
Faculty of Health, University of
Technology Sydney, Australia
Tamara.Power@uts.edu.au

Carolyn Hayes
Faculty of Health, University of
Technology Sydney, Australia
Carolyn.Hayes@uts.edu.au

Carmen Axisa
Faculty of Health, University of
Technology Sydney, Australia
Carolyn.Hayes@uts.edu.au

ABSTRACT

In many situations, it remains critical for team members to develop strategies to effectively use the space and tools available to complete demanding tasks. However, despite the availability of sensors and analytics for instrumenting physical space, relatively little progress has been made in modelling the embodied dimensions of co-located teamwork. This paper explores an in-the-wild pilot study through which we explore a methodology to model embodied mobility teamwork strategies in the context of healthcare education. We developed the means for tracking, clustering and processing student-nurses' mobility data around a patient manikin. We illustrate the feasibility of our approach by discussing ways to make sense of these data to uncover meaningful trends, and the inherent challenges of applying physical space analytics in authentic settings.

KEYWORDS

Teamwork; Collaboration; Simulation-based Learning; Physical Analytics; Computer Vision; Proximity Data; Group Modelling

ACM Reference format:

Roberto Martinez-Maldonado, Mykola Pechenizkiy, Simon Buckingham-Shum, Tamara Power, Carolyn Hayes and Carmen Axisa. 2017. In *Proceedings of ACM User Modelling, Adaptation and Personalization conference, Bratislava, Slovakia, July 2017 (UMAP'17)*, 5 pages. DOI: 10.1145/3079628.3079697

1 INTRODUCTION AND RELATED WORK

Learning to collaborate, in general, and developing professional team practices, in particular, are skills that often require coaching [25]. Whether in education or professional contexts,

teamwork has the potential to help people develop critical thinking, reduce workload, and generate creative solutions [8]. Although the internet has promoted spatially distributed teamwork, co-present teamwork remains entrenched in our society, particularly in practice-based professions. Face-to-face (f2f) teamwork enables levels of collaboration not easily achievable in online group work [22]. In short, learning to work effectively in teams f2f, is a critical skill for our times, but often requires practice, awareness of group dynamics, and reflection. Providing quality feedback for such team processes can be challenging [29]. Many team-based situations (such as the one illustrated in Fig. 1) require members to interact with an ecology of objects and devices [32]; to develop strategies to optimise the use of the physical space [7]; or even to learn in ways that cannot be mediated by traditional user interfaces as they involve psychomotor skills [27]. Some evidence suggests that the spatial arrangements and dynamics can strongly shape the interactive processes and the ways people tackle their tasks [14; 15; 16]. This is particularly important in classrooms because teachers and students perform embodied actions [9] and establish various proximity arrangements [12] that can influence students'

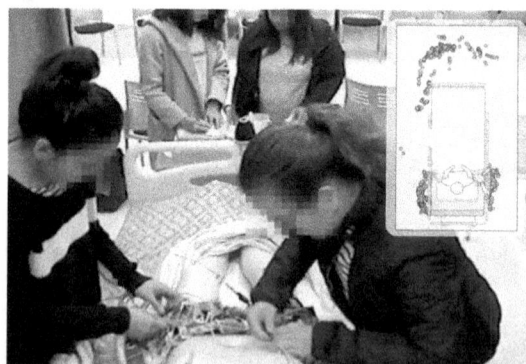

Figure 1. Four students tracked using a depth sensor while working at a healthcare simulation bed. Right: one minute of mobility data presented as an indoor map

engagement and learning. However, although understanding the mobility and proximity aspects of teamwork seems important, to date, little attention has been paid to conceiving ways to model and generate understanding of embodied mobility strategies.

A wide range of modelling and analytics efforts have explored how to generate understanding of *online* group processes to provide adapted team support (see reviews in [5; 11; 17; 28], with a few exceptions such as the ones outlined in [19]). Multimodal analytics solutions have partly focused on some physical aspects of student's learning by integrating data from multiple (often, but not always, physical) dimensions of student's activity [3]. For example, some studies have looked at analysing speech, gestures, handwriting, physical movements, facial expressions, gaze, and neuro-physiological signals which can all be critical aspects in co-present teamwork. Yet most of the advances in this area have been conducted under controlled laboratory conditions [4]. Thus, much work is still needed to find ways in which these approaches can solve challenges in realistic, mainstream scenarios.

Educational research literature has identified the importance of mobility and proximity primarily for teaching and classroom management (see a review in [21]). For instance, some authors have identified teaching proximity zones that can shape student's engagement [12] and embodied strategies that teachers can enact to orchestrate a classroom [9]. Similar embodied actions have been identified as important, but underexplored, for the case of patient engagement in healthcare education [6].

The body of work outlined above suggests both the need for and potential of developing modelling techniques to explore how physical aspects (such as mobility and proximity) can play a role in shaping epistemic elements of group work. The contribution of this paper is a pilot study through which we explore a methodology for modelling embodied mobility strategies of students practicing teamwork and professional skills in the classroom. We operationalise this in the context of nursing education where manikins are commonly used to represent patients in healthcare simulations (to be described in Section 2). We developed the means for tracking, clustering and processing students' mobility and proximity data around a patient manikin (Section 3) and demonstrate the feasibility of our methodology by suggesting ways in which these data may be associated with higher order mobility strategies enacted by teams in authentic classroom sessions (Section 4). Finally, we consider the potential and limitations of our approach for modelling teams' mobility, the inherent challenges of applying physical space analytics in-the-wild and avenues for future work (Section 5).

2 CONTEXT OF THE STUDY

Teamwork in simulation scenarios is a popular training technique in high risk industries such as aviation, energy and healthcare [2]. Healthcare simulations are commonly run as team-based learning experiences aimed at allowing healthcare students to engage in scenarios that mimic reality. The use of manikins as patients is increasingly common in nursing education worldwide [13]. This facilitates the practice of essential skills and avoids putting patients at risk [26]. Arguably, these simulations offer benefits for the development of teamwork, critical thinking, deterioration management and clinical skills [1]. The level of reality achieved during the simulations can result in students experiencing productive emotional and educational challenges [30].

This study was run in authentic laboratories where nursing classes are commonly conducted as scenarios involving simulated patients with acute or chronic conditions. The study focused on the 3-hour weekly classes conducted in Week 3 of a final-year subject in the Bachelor of Nursing at the University of Technology Sydney in 2016. In total, 580 students attended these classes with 20-27 students in each. The classrooms are equipped with 5 manikins in bed spaces (see Fig. 1). The manikins generate some physiological data and can be programmed to improve or deteriorate over time. In our pilot study, we focused on 5 randomly selected laboratory classes. Only the activity occurring in two of the available five beds was recorded in each class to allow students to opt out from the study. Thus, a total of 10 teams of varied sizes (56 students in teams, from 4 to 8 members each) and 4 teachers were involved in the study. The actual simulation task ran for 1-1.5 hours. In this time, students had to assess the condition of the patient, interact with him, assess chest pain symptoms, administrate medication, manage an adverse drug reaction and conduct an electrocardiogram analysis. Each student was asked to play one of 4 possible roles: a Team leader, the Patient, Nurses, and an Observer.

3 METHODOLOGY AND APPARATUS

In the following subsections we describe our methodology, which includes a mobility tracking solution, data modelling (with segmentation and visualisation examples) and means for making sense of the data in terms of emerging team strategies.

3.1 Mobility Data Tracking

Although some manikins have basic automated logging capabilities, often it is not possible to log the complete range of students' actions due to technology restraints and data accessibility limitations of the current equipment present in several universities. Moreover, these logs do not provide evidence about the ways nurses use the space around the patient and the proximity to the patient. To overcome this limitation, and achieve our goal of tracking student's mobility and proximity data, we positioned a depth sensor on the top of the bedhead. We used a modified version of a user skeletal tracking algorithm to record the raw coordinates of each team member. Depth cameras provide, for every pixel, a depth value that, along with the camera intrinsic features (image width w and height h in pixels, and focal angle f), can be processed to convert 3D depth positioning data points $p = (p_x, p_y, p_z)$ into 2D indoor mapping location points $l = (l_x, l_y)$ using the following formulas, assuming the camera is horizontally aligned: $l_x = p_x \sin \frac{f(\frac{w}{2} - p_x)}{w}$ and $l_y = p_x \cos \frac{f(\frac{w}{2} - p_x)}{w}$.

3.2 Mobility Data Clustering and Visualisation

Indoor localisation sensors are becoming increasingly available as they are a fundamental need in pervasive, context-aware settings [33]. Although other technologies can be used to capture mobility data (besides our depth-based solution), the ultimate goal is to be able to measure team members space usage and dynamics. Indoor analytics are readily available as adaptations of

Geographical Information Systems (GIS) functions: heatmap visualisation, dynamic simulation, and clustering can be applied to understand space usage patterns [10; 20]. Recent work suggests a range of possible applications of such analytics in healthcare settings [31]. The result of mapping our teamwork mobility data is similar to an indoor localisation student map around the patient manikin (e.g. Fig. 1, top-right). These raw data can be further processed and visualised as heatmaps or clusters of activity (e.g. Fig. 2, right).

3.3 Mobility Data Segmentation

Temporality is a key dimension to understand progression and gaining insights into team processes, as opposed to just inspecting final outcomes. One technique for automatically analysing collaborative learning processes consists in segmenting chronological data into segments of equal or different sizes (e.g. [24]). This has proven promising in serving as a proxy to model group processes, even though some details of the collaboration are aggregated [18]. The goal is to enable pattern recognition in low level actions where the order and timing of events matter. In our case, we achieve this segmentation by dividing student's activity into n segments in order to allow the comparison of teams by stages in the simulation. Fig. 3 shows examples of series of heatmaps generated (using an open source GIS application[1]) by dividing the student's activity in equally-sized quintiles. The number of segments (n) can be arbitrarily defined (e.g. a small n would facilitate human's sensemaking while a larger n could serve for automatic analysis purposes). Similarly, the size of the segments can be fixed (as in our case) or variable (e.g. splitting the data according to meaningful sub-tasks or events).

3.4 Sensemaking for Modelling Team Strategies

In order to generate understanding from raw mobility data, additional steps, besides segmentation and data visualisation, should be performed to facilitate sensemaking. Although there are different ways to explain the data by using contextual information, in our case, we illustrate three possible ways to contextualise the data. Firstly, inspired by work on classroom proximity zones [12], we identified the potential meaning that the space around the clinical beds had during the simulations. Fig. 2 (left) shows three zones. Zone A corresponds to the area closest to the patient, from where the nurses can easily talk to the patient and perform clinical procedures. Zone B corresponds to the end of the bed, where nurses usually gather to perform a shift handover and/or real time note taking which commonly includes reading and taking notes about assessment, action, response and recommendations for the next shift. Zone C corresponds to the space around the clinical bed which is commonly used by nurses that are enacting the role of observers. Nurses also need to walk to other rooms adjacent to the classroom to collect clinical equipment and medications.

Secondly, we propose to identify the clusters of mobility data corresponding to the areas where more physical activity was recorded to highlight what spaces were used the most by nurses at a given time (see Fig. 2, right). To facilitate the interpretation, we have circled the clusters with a different coloured contour according to the Zones where these clusters appeared. Thirdly, we suggest a way to encode the mobility data divided into segments by using an alphabet. The alphabet used in this case consists of itemising the mobility data for each proximity zone and segment as p^z, where p is the proximity zone (A, B or C in our study) and z is the number of clusters found in that zone. In our pilot study, we chose to identify the number of clusters z as 1 (not shown), 2 or * (more than two). For instance, the three clusters in proximity zone A in Fig. 2 (right) would be translated into one item A^* and the ones in zone C as C^2. This type of coding has been useful to automatically identify sequences of events that may differentiate high from low performing groups [23]. Given the small number of observed teams in our study (10), we illustrate how this coding can facilitate association of raw data with embodied team strategies.

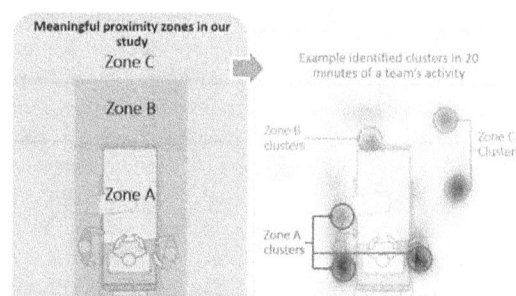

Figure 2. Left: proximity zones to a patient manikin. Right: heat- map of 20 min. of activity of a group with areas of intense activity

4 RESULTS

From Mobility Data to Embodied Strategies. We applied the methodology outlined in the previous section to the data we collected from the 10 beds of our study. We report on some of the brief comments that teachers gave about each group overall performance immediately after each class and those provided by two subject matter experts who looked at the series of heatmaps generated to facilitate the sensemaking of the mobility models.

Fig. 3 shows exemplars of three distinct types of strategies followed by the teams[3]. Two teams followed the Strategy 1 (example in Row 1), with teams commencing the simulation exclusively in zone B, (the space where nurses commonly work on the documentation about the patient and perform the shift handover, Row 1, Q1), to then approach the patient with the purpose of attending to him/her for the rest of the session while working across all the other zones (e.g. multiple clusters in zones A, B and C in Q2-4). A teacher referred to this strategy (of apparent initial inaction) as follows: "*some groups seemed to be slow before engaging with the patient*"; and added: "*this was good [if] they do a proper assessment of the patient before performing*

---

[1] Scripts for open-source QGIS (qgis.org), mobility tracking code, and raw mobility data for all the teams can be found in utscic.edu.au/healthsimlak-resources/

actions". A second strategy was exposed by other two teams (example in Row 2) where most of the mobility data was recorded very close to the patient's area (a majority of clusters in zone A for Row 2, Q1-4). A possible explanation was hinted by one of the teachers at the end if the class, as follow: "*sometimes it is nice that students [attend to the patient] from the beginning, but it [may also] indicate that they do not know the procedures [or] they [did] not read the information about the case*". A third strategy was observed in four of the teams that showed activity in zones A and B constantly and consistently through the whole simulation (e.g. see Q1-Q5 in Row 3). This may suggest that the team split in two, working close to the patient from the beginning to accomplish all the subtasks while also performing administrative tasks in zone B. The other two teams in our study showed a combination of the strategies identified above. In one of those cases, mobility data was missing for 1 quintile because of the teacher asked that group to do a special subtask elsewhere in the classroom. This got reflected in the mobility modelling. Additionally, some teams finished before other teams. This is reflected in the mobility models as it can be seen in Row 1 (Q5).

Encoding mobility data into discrete items: The last column of Fig. 3 shows how the clusters of mobility data can be encoded into discrete items. We can see that the resulting sequences of states can facilitate the interpretation of the data using a shorter format. For example, Strategy 1 can be characterised as a process that starts in the state with mobility data only in zone B of proximity (B^2 in Row 1). Strategy 2 can be characterised as a process mostly containing items A, near the patient zone, and Strategy 3 as a combination of items A and B in all the sequence.

In regards of reactions to the resulting mobility modelling, two teachers that commonly run healthcare simulations, said that they see potential in making visible this aspect of teamwork that would otherwise remain hidden. One explained that "*[the models] may help to actually see if students positioned themselves correctly [and] to find patterns of student's activity*". They also questioned the kind of claims that can be made based on these data. One teacher said that "*it would be interesting to know what people were saying or doing in specific places*". The other added that "*the models need to be complemented by the tutor to make sense of it*" and "*for some tasks people need to be in specific locations but for others they don't*".

5 CONCLUSIONS & DISCUSSION

We have presented a methodology to sense and model embodied mobility teamwork strategies in the context of healthcare simulation. We described the means for sensing, processing, visualising and processing student-nurses' mobility data that can be useful for modelling embodied strategies around a patient manikin. Our exemplars illustrate the methodology's potential by distilling at least three distinct, meaningful strategies (as judged by two subject matter experts) followed by the teams of our in-the-wild pilot study. Classroom settings can be

messy and are intrinsically unpredictable. For example, in our studies the four teachers allowed different lengths of time for the actual simulations and provided varied support and guidance. Thus, students' strategies could be greatly shaped by the classroom conditions. Similarly, teams were integrated in quite different ways. Teams were commonly formed by 4-5 students (e.g. as the ones modelled in Figure 3) but in one class, groups had up to 8 team members. These and other physical conditions can impose limitations and challenges for mobility tracking. In summary, visualising mobility data as indoor maps may be useful for generating understanding about embodied strategies or to aid teachers and learners in post-hoc reflection. We also proposed an approach for encoding these data into discrete sequences of states. In a larger dataset and/or with a different segmentation approach, it would be possible to itemise the mobility dataset to then mine frequent sequential patterns associated with teams' performance or outcomes.

The long term vision is for personalised and group-customised feedback to teams Whilst we have made progress in modelling mobility data in a way that is meaningful to domain specialists, the full analytics workflow must be automated in order to provide *timely feedback* to students and teachers. We aim that the methodology presented in this paper could serve as a basis for more complex approaches to enhance sensemaking of students' embodied strategies by mapping *trajectories of particular people* in the learning space. Future work could, for instance, explore the use of alternative tracking techniques of indoor localisation. We also aim to *integrate other logged information* such as behavioural and physiological data. In order to develop *user and group competency models*, larger datasets are required to validate the robustness and significance of the patterns. Finally, we need to extend the students and teachers involvement in a more *participatory design process*, to elicit insights and feedback on the resulting models. Ultimately, this work is not about higher fidelity surveillance of students, but about *empowering them with timely, actionable feedback* that builds their metacognition for teamwork. In conclusion, we propose that this paper helps to characterise, and contribute to, a substantive new stream opening up in user modelling and adaptive interaction, which will extend the field into the modelling of physical space and embodied activity in order to

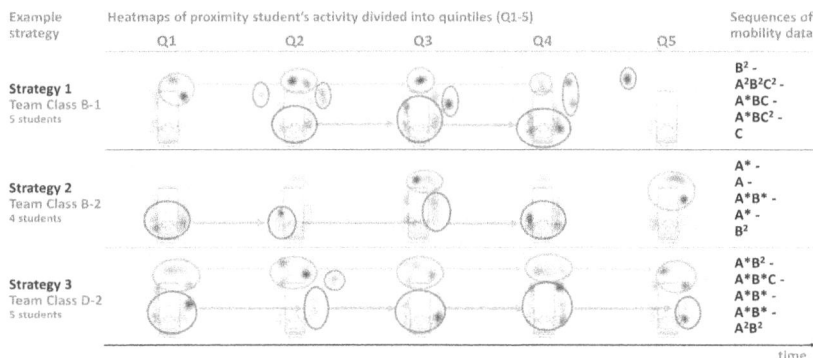

Figure 3. Heatmaps of nurses' activity divided in quintiles (Q1-5). Ovals indicate clusters of activity near (blue) far (orange) and further (green) from the manikin patient. Arrows indicate continuity of these clusters across time

support the many forms of authentic learning that go beyond personal computing, and online collaboration.

REFERENCES

[1] Al-Ghareeb, A. Z., and Cooper, S. J. 2016. Barriers and enablers to the use of high-fidelity patient simulation manikins in nurse education: an integrative review. *Nurse education today*, 36, 281-286.

[2] Beaubien, J., and Baker, D. 2004. The use of simulation for training teamwork skills in health care: how low can you go? *Quality & safety in health care*, 13, Suppl 1, i51-i56. DOI=10.1136/qshc.2004.009845

[3] Blikstein, P. 2013. Multimodal learning analytics. In Proceedings of the *Proceedings of the Third International Conference on Learning Analytics and Knowledge* (Leuven, Belgium, 2460316: ACM, 102-106. DOI=10.1145/2460296.2460316

[4] Blikstein, P., and Worsley, M. 2016. Multimodal Learning Analytics and Education Data Mining: using computational technologies to measure complex learning tasks. *Journal of Learning Analytics*, 3, 2, 220-238.

[5] Desmarais, M. C., and Baker, R. S. J. d. 2012. A review of recent advances in learner and skill modeling in intelligent learning environments. *User Modeling and User-Adapted Interaction*, 22, 1, 9-38. DOI=10.1007/s11257-011-9106-8

[6] Elsey, C., Challinor, A., and Monrouxe, L. V. 2016. Patients embodied and as-a-body within bedside teaching encounters: a video ethnographic study. *Advances in Health Sciences Education*(2016//), 1-24. DOI=10.1007/s10459-016-9688-3

[7] Goodyear, P., and Carvalho, L. 2014. Framing the analysis of learning network architectures. In L. Carvalho & P. Goodyear, Eds., *The architecture of productive learning networks*. Routledge, New York, NY, 48-70.

[8] Hilliges, O., Terrenghi, L., Boring, S., Kim, D., Richter, H., and Butz, A. 2007. Designing for collaborative creative problem solving. In Proceedings of the *Proceedings of the 6th ACM SIGCHI conference on Creativity \& cognition* (Washington, DC, USA, 1254980: ACM, 137-146. DOI=http://doi.acm.org/10.1145/1254960.1254980

[9] Ibrahim-Didi, K., Hackling, M. W., Ramseger, J., and Sherriff, B. 2017. Embodied Strategies in the Teaching and Learning of Science. In M. W. Hackling, J. Ramseger & H.-L. S. Chen, Eds., *Quality Teaching in Primary Science Education: Cross-cultural Perspectives*. Springer International Publishing, Cham, 181-221. DOI=10.1007/978-3-319-44383-6_8

[10] Jayarajah, K., Sen, R., Lee, Y., Nayak, S., Misra, A., and Balan, R. 2014. Group analytics and insights for public spaces. In Proceedings of the *Proceedings of the 12th ACM Conference on Embedded Network Sensor Systems* (Memphis, Tennessee, 2668375: ACM, 318-319. DOI=10.1145/2668332.2668375

[11] Jeong, H., and Hmelo-Silver, C. E. 2010. An Overview of CSCL Methodologies. In Proceedings of the *9th International Conference of the Learning Sciences (ICLS 2010)* (Chicago, USA, 29 Jun - 2 Jul 2010). ISLS, 920-921.

[12] Jones, F. H., Jones, P., and Jones, J. L. 2007. *Fred Jones tools for teaching: Discipline, instruction, motivation*: fredjones. com.

[13] Kardong-Edgren, S., Willhaus, J., Bennett, D., and Hayden, J. 2012. Results of the National Council of State Boards of Nursing National Simulation Survey: Part II. *Clinical Simulation in Nursing*, 8, 4 (4//), e117-e123. DOI=http://dx.doi.org/10.1016/j.ecns.2012.01.003

[14] Kendon, A. 1990. Spatial organization in social encounters: The F-formation system. *Conducting interaction: Patterns of behavior in focused encounters*, 209-238.

[15] Kirsh, D. 1995. The intelligent use of space. *Artificial Intelligence*, 73, 1-2, 31-68.

[16] Kirsh, D. 2013. Embodied cognition and the magical future of interaction design. *ACM Trans. Comput.-Hum. Interact.*, 20, 1, 1-30. DOI=10.1145/2442106.2442109

[17] Kumar, R., and Kim, J. 2014. Special Issue on Intelligent Support for Learning in Groups. *International Journal of Artificial Intelligence in Education*, 24, 1 (2014//), 1-7. DOI=10.1007/s40593-013-0013-5

[18] Martinez-Maldonado, R., Kay, J., Wallace, J., and Yacef, K. 2011. Modelling symmetry of activity as an indicator of collocated group collaboration. In Proceedings of the *International Conference on User Modeling, Adaptation and Personalization (UMAP 2011)*, 196-204.

[19] Martinez-Maldonado, R., Schneider, B., Charleer, S., Shum, S. B., Klerkx, J., and Duval, E. 2016. Interactive surfaces and learning analytics: data, orchestration aspects, pedagogical uses and challenges. In Proceedings of the *Proceedings of the Sixth International Conference on Learning Analytics & Knowledge* (Edinburgh, United Kingdom, 2883873: ACM, 124-133. DOI=10.1145/2883851.2883873

[20] Nandakumar, R., Rallapalli, S., Chintalapudi, K., Padmanabhan, V. N., Qiu, L., Ganesan, A., . . . Goenka, A. (2013). *Physical analytics: A new frontier for (indoor) location research*. Redmond, WA, USA.

[21] O'Neill, S. C., and Stephenson, J. 2014. Evidence-based classroom and behaviour management content in Australian pre-service primary teachers' coursework: Wherefore art thou? *Australian Journal of Teacher Education (Online)*, 39, 4, 1.

[22] Olson, J. S., Teasley, S., Covi, L., and Olson, G. 2002. The (currently) unique advantages of collocated work. In P. J. Hinds & S. Kiesler, Eds., *Distributed work: New research on working across distance using technology* MIT Press, Cambridge, MA, 113-136.

[23] Perera, D., Kay, J., Koprinska, I., Yacef, K., and Zaiane, O. 2009. Clustering and Sequential Pattern Mining of Online Collaborative Learning Data. *IEEE Transactions on Knowledge and Data Engineering* 21, 6, 759-772.

[24] Rosé, C., Wang, Y.-C., Cui, Y., Arguello, J., Stegmann, K., Weinberger, A., and Fischer, F. 2008. Analyzing collaborative learning processes automatically: Exploiting the advances of computational linguistics in computer-supported collaborative learning. *International Journal of Computer-Supported Collaborative Learning*, 3, 3, 237-271. DOI=10.1007/s11412-007-9034-0

[25] Salas, E., Sims, D. E., and Burke, S. 2005. Is there a "Big Five" in Teamwork? . *Small Group Research*, 36, 5, 1-46. DOI=10.1177/1046496405277134

[26] Sánchez-Ledesma, M. J., Juanes, J. A., Sáncho, C., Alonso-Sardón, M., and Gonçalves, J. 2016. Acquisition of Competencies by Medical Students in Neurological Emergency Simulation Environments Using High Fidelity Patient Simulators. *Journal of Medical Systems*, 40, 6 (2016//), 139. DOI=10.1007/s10916-016-0496-3

[27] Santos, O. C. 2016. Training the Body: The Potential of AIED to Support Personalized Motor Skills Learning. *International Journal of Artificial Intelligence in Education*, 26, 2, 730-755. DOI=10.1007/s40593-016-0103-2

[28] Schmidt, K., and Bannon, L. 2013. Constructing CSCW: The First Quarter Century. *Computer Supported Cooperative Work (CSCW)*, 22, 4-6 (August 2013), 345-372. DOI=10.1007/s10606-013-9193-7

[29] Tchounikine, P., Rummel, N., and McLaren, B. M. 2010. Computer Supported Collaborative Learning and Intelligent Tutoring Systems. In R. Nkambou, J. Bourdeau & R. Mizoguchi, Eds., *Advances in Intelligent Tutoring Systems*. Springer Berlin Heidelberg, Berlin, Heidelberg, 447-463. DOI=10.1007/978-3-642-14363-2_22

[30] Tripathy, S., Miller, K. H., Berkenbosch, J. W., McKinley, T. F., Boland, K. A., Brown, S. A., and Calhoun, A. W. 2016. When the mannequin dies, creation and exploration of a theoretical framework using a mixed methods approach. *Simulation in Healthcare*, 11, 3, 149-156.

[31] Van Haute, T., De Poorter, E., Crombez, P., Lemic, F., Handziski, V., Wirström, N., . . . Moerman, I. 2016. Performance analysis of multiple Indoor Positioning Systems in a healthcare environment. *International Journal of Health Geographics*, 15, 1, 7. DOI=10.1186/s12942-016-0034-z

[32] Vasiliou, C., Ioannou, A., and Zaphiris, P. 2014. Understanding collaborative learning activities in an information ecology: A distributed cognition account. *Computers in Human Behavior*, 41(12//), 544-553. DOI=http://dx.doi.org/10.1016/j.chb.2014.09.057

[33] Yassin, A., Nasser, Y., Awad, M., Al-Dubai, A., Liu, R., Yuen, C., and Raulefs, R. 2016. Recent Advances in Indoor Localization: A Survey on Theoretical Approaches and Applications. *IEEE Communications Surveys & Tutorials*.

Providing Control and Transparency in a Social Recommender System for Academic Conferences

Chun-Hua Tsai
University of Pittsburgh
135 N Bellefield Ave
Pittsburgh, PA 15260
cht77@pitt.edu

Peter Brusilovsky
University of Pittsburgh
135 N Bellefield Ave
Pittsburgh, PA 15260
peterb@pitt.edu

ABSTRACT

A social recommender system aims to provide useful suggestion to the user and prevent social overload problem. Most of the research efforts are spent on push high relevant item on top of the ranked list, using a weight ensemble approach. However, we argue the "learned" static fusion is not enough to specific contexts. In this paper, we develop a series visual recommendation components and control panel for the user to interact with the recommendation result of an academic conference. The system offers a better recommendation transparency and user-driven fusion through recommended sources. The experiment result shows the user did fuse the different recommended sources and exploration patterns among tasks. The post-study survey is positively associated with the system and explanation function effectiveness. This finding shed light on the future research of design a recommender system with human intervention and the interface beyond the static ranked list.

KEYWORDS

Social Recommendation; Explanation; Transparency; User Control

1 INTRODUCTION

The ranked list is the most distinct and visible feature of information retrieval and recommender systems. A lot of research efforts have been spent to push relevant items as high as possible on this list, while several measures have been created to assess the effectiveness of such ranking systems. However, what could be done if a particular context offers more then one important aspect of relevance, with each aspect requiring a different ranking? For example, in a personalized information retrieval system, search results could be ranked by their relevance to the query or their similarity to the user profile [1]. In a social system for academic conferences [6], recommended attendees could be ranked by their social distance, the similarity of their past publications, or the similarity of their interests, as reflected by shared bookmarks. The current way to resolve this problem in the field of recommender systems is to use

ensembling; namely, a weighted combination of two or more ranking approaches. Optimal weights for such an ensemble could be found using some ensemble training method, such as Breiman's stacked regression [5], and then used to fuse the sources within each context.

The problem with the "learned" static fusion is that in different situations, a user might prefer a particular aspect of relevance or a specific combination, and as a result, an average "best" fusion will never be adequate. For example, when searching for unknown but like-minded conference attendees, a user could obtain the best results by fusing an inverted social distance ranking with a regular interest similarity. Research on retrieval and recommender system interfaces suggest resolving this problem by engaging the user in selecting the best approach or fusion of approaches. Several projects in both fields demonstrated that users could learn and efficiently use these selection and fusion interfaces to obtain superior results [1, 12, 16].

Our paper expands the current work on user-controlled multi-aspect recommendations in two directions. First, in contrast to earlier work focused on item recommendations, we want to explore controllable recommendations of *people* as social and academic contacts. Second, we want to concentrate on an unexplored aspect of this research: explanation and transparency. The need to offer better transparency and explanations of recommendations is now generally recognized in the field [20]. However, this explanation becomes especially important for interfaces with a user-driven fusion of recommended sources. To combine individual sources in a meaningful way, users need to have a solid understanding of why a recommended person has been ranked high or low, according to a particular aspect of relevance, as well as in the integrated ranked list.

In this paper, we present RelExplorer [1], a system for recommending and exploring co-attendees at an academic conference. The system uses three separate recommender engines that suggest the most relevant attendees in respect to social distance, the relevance of their past work, and the similarity of current interests. RelExplorer allows users to fuse rankings produced by these recommendation sources according to the current need, explore the obtained unified ranking, and receive an extensive explanation of ranking results. To assess the value of the user-driven fusion and the overall explanation functionality of RelExplorer, we conducted a user study at two international conferences. In the following sections, we present the design of RelExplorer, introduce our studies, and review the obtained results.

UMAP'17, July 9-12, 2017, Bratislava, Slovakia
© 2017 Copyright held by the owner/author(s). Publication rights licensed to ACM.
978-1-4503-4635-1/17/07...$15.00
DOI: http://dx.doi.org/10.1145/3079628.3079701

---

[1]System Demo: http://halley.exp.sis.pitt.edu/cn3/portalindex.php

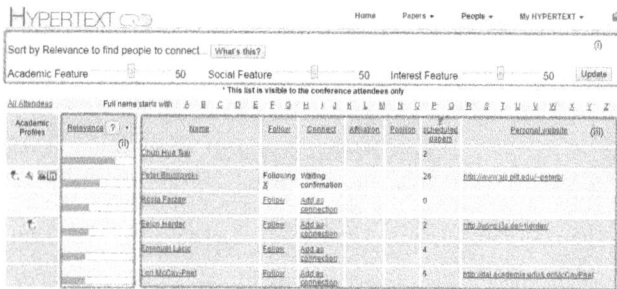

Figure 1: A screenshot of the RelExplorer system: (i) A control panel of three feature sliders. (ii) A ranking list of the personalized relevance score. (iii) The user profile information and social media functions from the Conference Navigator 3 System [6].

2 RELATED WORK

While early research on recommender systems mostly focused on ranking and prediction, it has been recently recognized that users will easily distrust even a perfect ranking if it lacks interpretability. To increase the overall level of user acceptance, [3, 16] have proposed the use of interactive recommendation interfaces with transparency and controllability in place of a static ranked list. Also, visualization techniques were explored to improve the comprehension of the recommendation result [8, 10]. Recent studies indicate the effectiveness of intelligent interfaces that support transparency, exploration, and controllability in various contexts, such as recommending conference talks [23], expert finding [9], people matching [7, 15, 17], and collaboration [2].

3 RELEXPLORER

3.1 System Design

Figure 1 shows a screenshot of the front-end view of the RelExplorer system. The view consists of three parts. 1) A control panel with three sliders that controls the fusion of three elementary recommender engines or *features*. The user can adjust the slider from 0-100 for Academic, Social, and Interest features, based on their current needs. The weight of each contributing engine in the fusion is determined by the selected weight, e.g. setting three features equally at 50 means that each component is weighted as 33.3%. 2) A set of bars show a fused relevance score, which is calculated as a linear combination of Academic, Social, and Interest features with selected weights. These features are discussed in more detail in section 3.2. 3) A basic user profile that includes name, affiliation and (for authors) titles of papers presented at the conference. Each name in the list is a link to the profile page that shows more personal information, along with visualized explanations of component rankings (see section 3.3 for details).

RelExplorer is embedded in the Conference Navigator System (CN3), a social support system for academic conferences [6]. The system has been used to support 37 conferences at the time of writing this paper. CN3 has 6,500 users, 6,398 articles, 11,939 authors, 28,590 bookmarks, and 1,336 social connections. To solve the cold start issue that occurs when users have no bookmarks

or social connections [21], we used the Aminer dataset [18]. This dataset includes 2,092,356 papers, 1,712,433 authors and 4,258,615 co-authorship. By combining the CN3 historical data and Aminer database, RelExplorer can produce necessary recommendations for CN3 users.

3.2 Recommendation Components

The RelExplorer uses three separate recommender engines that suggest co-attendees to meet on the basis of: 1) The similarity of past publications (Academic feature); 2) Social network distance (Social feature); and 3) Similarity of interests (Interest feature).

Academic Feature: The academic feature is determined by publication similarity between two attendees using cosine similarity [13, 22]. The function is defined as: $Sim_{Academic}(x, y) = (x \cdot y)/\|x\|\|y\|$, where x and y are word vectors for user x and y. For all attendees, we build documents assembled from titles and abstracts of their publications. We applied TF-IDF to create the document vector with a word frequency upper bound 0.5 and lower bound 0.01 to eliminate both common and rarely used words. We consider unigrams and bigrams to cover academic terms.

Social Feature: The social feature is calculated by collaborative network distance and neighbor similarity in the CN3 system and Aminer dataset. The goal is to generate the ranking of "most connected scholar" for the user. The function is defined as: $Sim_{Social}(x, y) = (1 - \theta)(p) + (\theta)(cn)$, where p is the shortest path between user x and y; cn is the number of common neighbors of user x and y; and θ is the weighting ratio between two methods. We adopted the Depth-first search (DFS) method to calculate shortest path p [19] and common neighborhood (CN) [14] for neighbor overlapping similarity. The formula cn is $\Gamma(x) \cap \Gamma(y)$, where $\Gamma()$ indicates the neighbors of a given user x and y in two-hop degrees.

Interest Feature: The interest feature is determined by the data of co-bookmarked papers and co-connection authors in the CN3 system. The goal of this feature is recommending the attendees of a conference who share similar interest. The function is defined as $Sim_{Interest}(x, y) = (b_x) \cap (b_y) + (c_x) \cap (c_y)$, where b_x, b_y represent the paper bookmarking of user x and y; c_x, c_y represents the friend connection of user x and y.

3.3 Explanation Components

RelExplorer provides four explanation components to justify and explain ratings produced by recommendation components.

SocialViz: Social similarity is explained using topology-based visualization that lets users understand the connection of any conference attendees (Figure 2a). This tool uses the interactive force layout project of D3.js [4] to show the shortest path to connect two users generated with the DFS method.

SocialBubble: This component (Figure 2b), uses an interactive bubble menu from d3.js [4] to show the common coauthorship neighborhood between two users. The middle circle shows an author who has the highest coauthor overlapping rate. The system will pick randomly if there is no single one-degree coauthor between the two users.

Publications: The attendees of the conference are usually scholars with a list of publications. This list is a useful way to become quickly familiar with a user of interest. To show user publications within

(a) SocialViz

(b) SocialBubble

Daqing He

About

School of Computer and Information Science, The Robert Gordon University, St. Andrew Street, Aberdeen AB25 1HG, Scotland, UK; University of Maryland, College Park, MD (University of Pittsburgh University)

Search research experiences: Search tactic, real-based information retrievable, personalized search session query expansion, User search collaborative exploration, Web search collaborative search

(c) Publications

(d) Text Analyzer

3. Modeling Skill Combination Patterns for Deeper Knowledge Tracing
Year: 2016
Venue: UMAP2016

4. Student Modeling Applications, Recent Developments & Toolkits [SMART tutorial]
Year: 2015
Venue: AIED_EDM2015

Abstract: The educational data mining community is starting to fulfill the promise of using data to improve education. The advancement of the field requires the community to be aware of existing tools and results from student modeling. But with a myriad of student modeling techniques and toolkits available, it is easy to be overwhelmed. In this tutorial we will cover popular and promising toolkits – and the theory behind them. We will demystify the acronym soup in the educational data mining field (BKT, IRT, 1PL, etc). We will help practitioners and researchers alike to get up to speed on student modeling using the latest technology. We are fortunate enough that the toolkits will be presented by the authors who developed them.

Text Filter: Only Me Only Target User Hybrid

19%

Text Similarity

This function helps you to explore your text in common (academic publications) with target user... You can find your text similarity in the right hand side indicator. The word cloud below highlights your commonly used terms. You can customize and compare the text difference by three sources - Only me, Only target User and Hybrid text.

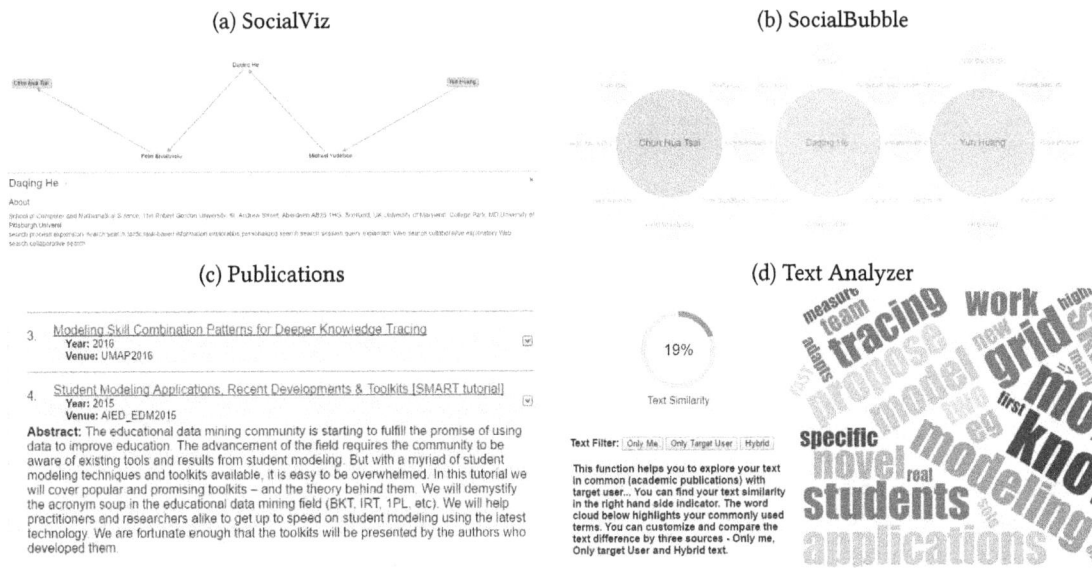

Figure 2: (*a*)*SocialViz* : a topology-based visualization based on an academic collaboration network. The green node represents the origin/target scholar and the yellow node is the path between them. This figure shows a reasonable path that goes through three scientists. (*b*)*SocialBubble* : the blue bubble and green bubble represent the origin and target user, respectively. The middle orange bubble is the co-author who has the highest number of co-authored paper with both the origin and the target scholar. The minor bubble represents coauthors of participating scholars. This tool helps to determine any indirect relationships between the origin and target users. (*c*)*Publications* : a global view of the publication list of the target scholar generated from both the conference data and the external Aminer dataset. (*d*)*TextAnalyzer* : this tool helps to understand the level of content similarity between the publications of the origin and target scholars. A document similarity percentage bar and word cloud are provided. The word cloud can be customized to individual/hybrid mode to compare the difference between the words.

and beyond the current conference, we use historic CN3 data [6] and the Aminer dataset [18]. This publication tool (Figure 2c) shows the publication list of a user with highlighted papers that appears in the same conference series as the current conference.

TextAnalyzer: This tool visualizes text similarity between two attendees (Figure 2d). It is shown as a percentage of the text similarity between two users and a word cloud [4] to explore and compare the most popular words in their publications.

4 USER STUDY

To assess the value of user-driven fusion and explanation functionality of RelExplorer, we conducted a user study at two international conferences: ACM Hypertext (HT) 2016 and ACM Conference on User Modeling, Adaptation and Personalization (UMAP) 2016, both held in Halifax, Canada. There were 65 attendees at HT and 115 attendees at UMAP. All attendees at both conferences received a CN3 account by email before the event date. Conference participants and authors were encouraged to use the system before the meeting began through an official email from the conference organizers.

4.1 Setup

For the user study, which was a controlled experiment at the conference venue, we recruited 16 attendees (5 female and 11 male) from both conferences; twelve were from HT and four were from UMAP. Half of them were aged 20 to 29 and the other half were aged 30 to

39. Among participants, there were 12 Ph.D. students, two master's students, and two junior faculty members. At the beginning of the study, we asked the participants to report their relevant experience using a five-point scale. On average, most of the participants had high confidence in using recommender systems (average 3.81 with a standard deviation of 1.04). Their background knowledge about recommender systems was relatively high (average 4.37 with a standard deviation of 0.61). Following that, we asked the participants to complete three simple training tasks and two search testing tasks. These tasks are described below. User actions performed in CN3 while completing the tasks were logged and timed.

Training: 1) Set up a recommendation factor weighting, based on your preferences, by using the control panel on top of the author page; 2) Sort the authors by relevance from high to low; 3) Click the top ranking author and review the information at different tabs.

Testing: *Task 1: Find Known Attendees* (a) Find two conference attendees you already know; (b) decide whether you need to follow each of them or connect to them in the system; (c) examine information about these participants to find out how these two people can help to establish new connections at this conference. *Task 2: Explore Unknown Attendees* (a) Find two conference attendees who you don't yet know in person but whom you are interested to meet and talk with; (b) decide whether you need to follow each of them or connect to them in the system; (c) examine information about these attendees to find out who could introduce you to them, or how you could introduce yourself to attract interest.

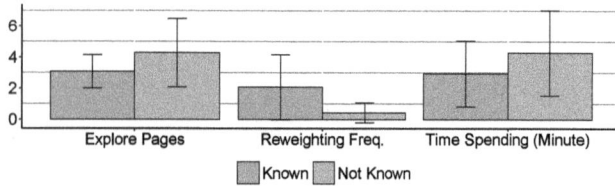

Figure 3: Experiment Measurement: a comparison of test value, included explore pages, re-weighting frequency and time spending between tasks.

4.2 Log Analysis

The log analysis (Figure 3) focused on comparing the number of explored user pages, the frequency of feature re-weighing in the attendee list, and the amount of time spent. We applied the Wilcoxon signed rank test with continuity correction to test the difference between tasks.

Re-weighting Frequency At average, the users applied 1.25 feature re-weighing (SD=1.73) while solving two user-finding tasks. This provides some evidence that weighing was useful in the context of given tasks. There was a significant effect for re-weighting frequency (p=0.008) between tasks. The user tends to change the control panel more frequently during the first task.

Explored Pages The test result indicates that finding and exploring known people requires fewer clicks (M=3.07, SD=1.07) than finding and exploring unknown people (M=4.28, SD=2.19). The difference approached the borderline of significance (p=0.06).

Time Spent It takes less time to finish the finding known-people task (M=2.93, SD=2.12) than to finish the finding unknown-people task (M=4.27, SD=2.75). The difference shows a trend toward significance (p=0.09). The tester engages with the system longer when exploring the new connections. This data correlates with the number of explored pages. When these findings are taken together, it hints that finding known and unknown people are reasonably different tasks that might need different types of interface support.

4.3 Questionnaire

We asked all study participants to fill in a questionnaire after the experiment. The questionnaire assessed their experience using a five-point Likert scale. Table 1 summarizes user perceptions about system and explanation effectiveness. According to the survey, the feedback of system usability (M=3.93, SD=0.85), satisfaction (M=3.93, SD=0.68), and reuse prospects (M=4.12, SD=0.80) is relatively high. The quality of people recommendation (M=3.87, SD=0.8) and information variety (M=4, SD=0.51) of the system also received positive feedback. The participants indicated that RelExplorer provided sufficient (M=4, SD=0.63) and easily understand (M=4, SD=0.73) explanations for the user to explore the people of interest at the conference.

Questions 11-14 show feedback on specific visualization components. The Publication List and Text Analyzer are positively assessed (M=3.81, SD=0.98) by the participants. SocialViz received the highest score (M=4. 25, SD=0. 57), which means that a topology-style display was useful to explore the social relations. Meanwhile, the SocialBubble received the lowest score (M=3.68, SD=0.94), which

Table 1: Post-Study Questionnaire Survey

Question	Score
Q1: I become familiar with the system very quickly.	4.00 (0.89)
Q2: The information provided in different tabs on a person's page was sufficient for me to find interested people.	3.93 (0.85)
Q3: I will frequently use this system in future conference.	4.12 (0.80)
Q4: I like the people recommendation result by the system.	3.87 (0.80)
Q5: The recommended result contained a lot of variety (of the control panel) for me to explore.	4.00 (0.51)
Q6: I have fun when I am using the system.	3.81 (0.91)
Q7: I have to invest a lot of effort to obtain a useful result from the system.	2.43 (0.96)
Q8: The system has no real benefit for me.	1.87 (1.08)
Q9: The information provided for the explanation was sufficient for me to explore the interested people.	4.00 (0.63)
Q10: I found the explanation is easy to understand.	4.00 (0.73)
Q11: ScholarViz Tab helps me to understand the people recommendation result.	4.25 (0.57)
Q12: ScholarBubble Tab helps me to understand the people recommendation result.	3.68 (0.94)
Q13: Publication List Tab helps me to understand the people recommendation result.	3.81 (0.98)
Q14: Text Analyzer Tab helps me to understand the people recommendation result.	3.81 (0.98)

indicates that this visualization was less useful in understanding the recommendation results.

5 DISCUSSION

In this paper, we presented a user-controlled social recommender system for exploring social contacts at academic conferences, which included several explanation components. The system offers a user-driven fusion of three recommender engines and a better level of transparency into the recommendation process. We conducted a user study to assess the value of user-driven fusion and explanation functionality. The experiment results show that attendees explored a range of different fusion settings when solving realistic attendee-exploration tasks. We also observed that more pages were explored and more time was spent when exploring the new social contacts. However, it is likely that when finding known attendees, participants rely on name search rather than on recommendation and explanations alone. The post-study survey shows positive feedback for system components and explanation effectiveness. The user feedback provides evidence that the system is useful for the user to explore the social contacts at a conference venue. Also, there is evidence that the explanation components helped the users to correctly interpret the recommendation results. In particular, the topology-style explanation received higher scores than both the text- and network-based explanations.

This study provided some evidence that the "best" fusion of recommended sources varies among users and tasks. It calls for a human-in-a-loop recommender system that combines user collaboration in helping and arranging information for solving a particular task [11]. However, in these systems, users need to have a good understanding of the recommended results and their component relevance aspects. It brings the challenges of designing an interface with transparency, explanation, and controls of the recommender system for user interaction. In future works, we plan to develop an interface that goes beyond the ranked list, and that will support diversity exploration and interaction among multiple aspects of relevance.

REFERENCES

[1] Jae-wook Ahn, Peter Brusilovsky, Daqing He, Jonathan Grady, and Qi Li. 2008. Personalized Web Exploration with Task Models. In *the 17th international conference on World Wide Web, WWW '08*. ACM, 1–10.

[2] Nesserine Benchettara, Rushed Kanawati, and Céline Rouveirol. 2010. A supervised machine learning link prediction approach for academic collaboration recommendation. In *Proceedings of the fourth ACM conference on Recommender systems*. ACM, 253–256.

[3] Svetlin Bostandjiev, John O'Donovan, and Tobias Höllerer. 2012. TasteWeights: a visual interactive hybrid recommender system. In *Proceedings of the sixth ACM conference on Recommender systems*. ACM, 35–42.

[4] Mike Bostock. 2016. D3. js-Data-Driven Documents (2016). *URL: https://d3js. org* (2016).

[5] Leo Breiman. 1996. Stacked Regressions. *Machine Learning* 24, 1 (July 1996), 49–64. DOI: http://dx.doi.org/10.1023/a:1018046112532

[6] Peter Brusilovsky, Jung Sun Oh, Claudia López, Denis Parra, and Wei Jeng. 2016. Linking information and people in a social system for academic conferences. *New Review of Hypermedia and Multimedia* (2016), 1–31.

[7] Jilin Chen, Werner Geyer, Casey Dugan, Michael Muller, and Ido Guy. 2009. Make new friends, but keep the old: recommending people on social networking sites. In *Proceedings of the SIGCHI Conference on Human Factors in Computing Systems*. ACM, 201–210.

[8] Niklas Elmqvist and Jean-Daniel Fekete. 2010. Hierarchical aggregation for information visualization: Overview, techniques, and design guidelines. *IEEE Transactions on Visualization and Computer Graphics* 16, 3 (2010), 439–454.

[9] Shuguang Han, Daqing He, Jiepu Jiang, and Zhen Yue. 2013. Supporting exploratory people search: a study of factor transparency and user control. In *Proceedings of the 22nd ACM international conference on Information & Knowledge Management*. ACM, 449–458.

[10] Chen He, Denis Parra, and Katrien Verbert. 2016. Interactive recommender systems: a survey of the state of the art and future research challenges and opportunities. *Expert Systems with Applications* 56 (2016), 9–27.

[11] Andreas Holzinger. 2016. Interactive machine learning for health informatics: when do we need the human-in-the-loop? *Brain Informatics* 3, 2 (2016), 119–131.

[12] Bart P. Knijnenburg, Svetlin Bostandjiev, John O'Donovan, and Alfred Kobsa. 2012. Inspectability and Control in Social Recommenders. In *6th ACM Conference on Recommender System*. 43–50. http://dl.acm.org/citation.cfm?id=2365966

[13] Christopher D Manning, Prabhakar Raghavan, and Hinrich Schütze. 2008. *Introduction to information retrieval*. Vol. 1. Cambridge university press Cambridge.

[14] Mark EJ Newman. 2001. Clustering and preferential attachment in growing networks. *Physical Review E* 64, 2 (2001), 025102.

[15] John O'Donovan, Barry Smyth, Brynjar Gretarsson, Svetlin Bostandjiev, and Tobias Höllerer. 2008. PeerChooser: visual interactive recommendation. In *Proceedings of the SIGCHI Conference on Human Factors in Computing Systems*. ACM, 1085–1088.

[16] Denis Parra and Peter Brusilovsky. 2015. User-controllable personalization: A case study with SetFusion. *International Journal of Human-Computer Studies* 78 (2015), 43–67.

[17] Luiz Pizzato, Tomasz Rej, Joshua Akehurst, Irena Koprinska, Kalina Yacef, and Judy Kay. 2013. Recommending people to people: the nature of reciprocal recommenders with a case study in online dating. *User Modeling and User-Adapted Interaction* 23, 5 (2013), 447–488.

[18] Jie Tang, Jing Zhang, Limin Yao, Juanzi Li, Li Zhang, and Zhong Su. 2008. Arnetminer: extraction and mining of academic social networks. In *Proceedings of the 14th ACM SIGKDD international conference on Knowledge discovery and data mining*. ACM, 990–998.

[19] Robert Tarjan. 1972. Depth-first search and linear graph algorithms. *SIAM journal on computing* 1, 2 (1972), 146–160.

[20] Nava Tintarev and Judith Masthoff. 2012. Evaluating the effectiveness of explanations for recommender systems. *User Modeling and User-Adapted Interaction* 22, 4-5 (1 Oct. 2012), 399–439. DOI: http://dx.doi.org/10.1007/s11257-011-9117-5

[21] Chun-Hua Tsai and Peter Brusilovsky. 2016. A personalized people recommender system using global search approach. *IConference 2016 Proceedings* (2016).

[22] Chun-Hua Tsai and Yu-Ru Lin. 2016. Tracing and Predicting Collaboration for Junior Scholars. In *Proceedings of the 25th International Conference Companion on World Wide Web*. International World Wide Web Conferences Steering Committee, 375–380.

[23] Katrien Verbert, Denis Parra, Peter Brusilovsky, and Erik Duval. 2013. Visualizing recommendations to support exploration, transparency and controllability. In *Proceedings of the 2013 international conference on Intelligent user interfaces*. ACM, 351–362.

Towards Improving E-commerce Users Experience Using Personalization & Persuasive Technology

Ifeoma Adaji

University of Saskatchewan, Saskatoon, Canada
ifeoma.adaji@usask.ca

ABSTRACT

With the increase in the number of e-commerce companies over the last decade, there is stiffer competition for e-businesses to win and retain customers. Companies have to give clients reasons to shop with them and become return customers. The use of personalization strategies and persuasive technology have been identified as means through which e-businesses can engage their clients and give them a unique shopping experience. To contribute to ongoing research in personalization and persuasive technology in e-commerce, my thesis proposes a framework that can create a personalized shopping experience for clients using the consumers' personality and shopping type. This paper presents the results of the first stage of my research which is a user study carried out on 324 e-commerce shoppers to identify the persuasive strategies and its implementation in an e-commerce site, Amazon, and to evaluate the persuasiveness of these strategies to consumers. The result of this thesis can contribute to ongoing research in development of personalization and persuasive strategies that work in e-commerce especially for new companies.

KEYWORDS

Personalization, persuasive technology, e-commerce

1 INTRODUCTION

With the increase in the number of e-businesses, competition for clients has become stiffer. Customers are constantly seeking for e-vendors that can provide shopping experiences that are tailored to their needs and relevant to who they are[18]. Research shows that in e-commerce, personalization is an effective means of increasing a customer's lifetime value and customer loyalty [14], hence is an effective strategy in making new customers and maintaining existing ones. Personalization is a means by which businesses can build customer loyalty by uniquely addressing each customer's needs within a given context [7].

It is the process of adapting products and services to meet customers' needs based on existing information about their previous activities in a given context [11]. Personalization is important in e-commerce because it has been shown to improve customers' lifetime value and customer retention [18]. There have been several attempts at personalization in e-commerce such as the use of recommender systems [16], personalization using shopping types of customers [15] and personality types of consumers [6]. However, these personalization strategies are not usually mapped to the persuasive strategies that works best with them. To bridge this gap, my research aims to build a framework that maps personalization strategies to the persuasive strategies that work best for them. Personalization will be achieved using personality and shopping types of the consumers.

2 RELATED WORK

2.1 Personalization Using Personality Types

The online oxford dictionary[1] defines personality as "the combination of characteristics or qualities that form an individual's distinctive character". These characteristics include values, attitudes, personal memories, social relationships, habits and skills [3]. There are various models that classify people based on their personality, with people in each group having a high tendency to behave in a particular way under certain situations. However, in my research, I will be using the Big Five Model [8] because it has been used extensively in consumer studies [9]. The Big Five model (also referred to as the Five-Factor Model) describes a person's personality using five dimensions: openness to experience, conscientiousness, extraversion, agreeableness and neuroticism [8]. People with extraversion traits are talkative, energetic and assertive while those with agreeableness trait are cooperative, good-natures and can be trusted. Conscientiousness trait describes people that are dependable, responsible and orderly, while neuroticism characterizes people that are calm and are not easily upset. People with personality trait, openness to experience, are known to be imaginative, independent-minded and intellectual.

Huang and Yang [9] investigated the relationship between personality traits and online shopping motivations using the Big

UMAP'17, July 9-12, 2017, Bratislava, Slovakia
© 2017 ACM. ISBN 978-1-4503-4635-1/17/07...$15.00.
DOI: http://dx.doi.org/10.1145/3079628.3079707

---

[1] http://www.oxforddictionaries.com/us/definition/american_english/personality

Five model. They mapped the Big Five model to online shopping motivations: adventure, idea, sociality, lack of sociality and convenience. According to their findings, consumers who are open to experience are likely to shop online for the adventure and possible ideas. On the other hand, the conscientious customers patronize online vendors because of convenience, while extraverted people are motivated to shop online due to social factors. The neurotic users are more persuaded to shop online by the need to not socialize. Despite the findings of the authors, they did not suggest persuasive strategies that can be implemented for each personality type.

2.2 Personalization Using Shopper Types

In e-commerce, there is currently no well-known standard of classifying shoppers. Identifying and understanding the various shopper types is important because it helps companies effectively tailor products and services to the various segments of customers [15]. Rohm and Swaminathan [15] identified shopper types based on the motivations of shoppers namely: 1) Shopping convenience. 2) Information seeking. 3) Immediate Possession. 4) Social interaction. 5) The retail shopping experience. 6) Variety seeking. Despite these classification of shoppers, the authors also did not suggest influence strategies that can persuade each shopping type to shop with an e-vendor.

2.3 Persuasive Technology

Persuasive technology is the use of interactive technology to change people's attitude and behavior without coercion or deception [12]. There are several principles used in implementing persuasive technology and these have been classified by various authors based on their functional role. One such framework is the Persuasive Systems Design (PSD) framework [12]. PSD is a systematic framework for designing and evaluating persuasive systems. It describes in detail the content, software functionality and design principles that are required in the development and evaluation of persuasive systems. It consists of 28 principles that are categorized into four groups based on the task they aim to accomplish: primary task support, dialogue support, system credibility support, social support. Primary task support principles support a system's user in achieving their primary objective or goal. Dialogue support principles support computer-human dialogue which provide feedback to users, with the aim of moving users towards their target behavior. System credibility support principles persuade users through the design of a system. Social support principles influence users by leveraging social influence. For a list of the principles and a detailed explanation of them, please see the [12].

3 RESEARCH METHOD

In order to achieve personalization using personality and shopper types and to further map the personalization methods to persuasive strategies, I plan to carry out my research in 3 main stages.

Stage 1: Identifying and evaluating e-commerce persuasive strategies.

The goal of this stage of my research is to identify and evaluate what persuasive strategies are being used by a successful e-commerce company. After reviewing the top e-commerce companies, I decided to use Amazon as a case study. I reviewed Amazon (using the PSD framework) in order to identify what persuasive strategies were used and how they were implemented [1]. I then carried out a study using 324 Amazon customers in order to evaluate the persuasiveness of these identified strategies. The result of this study is presented in section 4.

Stage 2: Evaluating personalization strategies using personality and shopper types

This stage of my research entails me identifying the behaviour of consumers based on their demographics data, their personality and shopping type and identifying what influence strategies will bring about the desired behaviour change for these consumers. My research is currently at this stage.

Stage 3: Implementing and evaluating an e-commerce prototype using findings from stage 2

At this stage, using the findings from stage 2, I will develop an e-commerce platform that will take advantage of customers' personality and shopping type in order to create a more personalized experience for them online. The system will be evaluated by real e-commerce users.

4 CURRENT PROGRESS AND RESULT

In order to determine the susceptibility of e-commerce users to the various persuasive strategies of a typical e-commerce platform, we initially evaluated Amazon as a persuasive system using the PSD framework [1]. To understand how persuasive these strategies are to actual Amazon shoppers, we carried out a study using 324 Amazon customers [2]. We then developed and tested a global research model and several sub-models using partial least-squares structural equation modelling (PLS-SEM) analysis based on the various demographics of the shoppers.

The following section describes the results from the global model and the sub-models based on demographics.

4.1 Global Model

We conducted a study of 324 Amazon shoppers to determine the persuasiveness of the influence strategies implemented by Amazon. The study investigated the factors that affect the perceived effectiveness, credibility and continuance intention for use of Amazon shoppers. We developed and tested a research model and carried out path modelling using partial least-squares structural equation modelling (PLS-SEM). We determined that our model met the minimum reliability and validity thresholds as suggested by [17]. We also calculated the path significance, total effect and effect sizes of the constructs. The result of our path modelling is shown in figure 1.

As shown in figure 1, the perceived review credibility, perceived product credibility and dialogue support explain almost 70% of the variance in the perceived credibility of Amazon. This shows the importance of reviews in an e-commerce platform, hence, e-businesses should incorporate product reviews on their websites. This result is in line with other studies that suggest that the reviews found on an e-commerce platform have an effect on the trust a customer has on the e-business. This trust further effects the purchase intention of the consumer [13], [5]. Our results also show that although perceived review credibility and perceived product credibility significantly influence perceived system credibility and are strong predictors of perceived system credibility (with almost 70% variance), perceived system credibility does not significantly influence continuance intention of shoppers in Amazon.

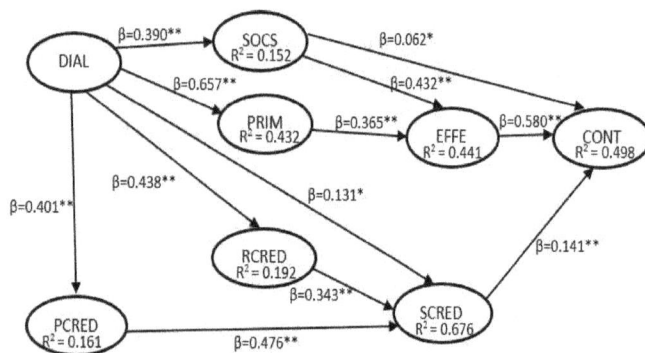

Figure 1: Global **model with results of PLS-SEM analysis.** * = <0.05, ** = < 0.01, *** = < 0.001 and **** = < 0.0001. DIAL = Dialogue support, SOCS = Social support, PRIM = Primary task support, EFFE = Perceived effectiveness, CONT'= Continuance intention, PCRED = Perceived product credibility, RCRED = Perceived review credibility, SCRED = Perceived system credibility

This could be because Amazon is a popular and well-known e-commerce company, therefore, consumers will continuously shop on Amazon despite their perceived credibility (or otherwise) of the system. This might not be the same with a new e-business. Another significant finding was that social support and primary task support can explain about 44% of the variance in perceived effectiveness of the system, which, in addition to perceived system credibility and social support can further predict half of the variance in continuance intention of consumers to shop with Amazon in the future. Of the three factors that predict continuance intention, perceived effectiveness was the most significant at β=0.580. This finding suggests that that the effectiveness of an e-business affects the customers' future possibility of sticking with an e-business. This is in line with the findings of [4] that suggests that continued patronage of customers is affected by the effectiveness of the e-business. Our results further suggest that although dialogue support significantly influences perceived product credibility and

perceived review credibility, it does not influence perceived system credibility. This indicates that the feedback (in the form of reviews and questions) shoppers receive and the ability to interact with other shoppers on Amazon does not influence their perceived credibility of the system. This is not in line with the conclusions of [10].

4.2 Personalization based on Reviews and Use Duration

We also explored the effect of the persuasive strategies on users based on 1) if the customers often review or rate products after purchase and 2) how long the consumers have been clients of Amazon. For the classification of users based on if they review or rate products, we developed two models, one for the Amazon consumers that often rate or review products and the other for the customers who never review or rate products after making a purchase. In table 1, we present the result of the multi group analysis that was carried out between the two models, in particular, we show the path coefficients between the constructs and the significance of these path coefficients for paths with significant results. The result shows that consumers who review/rate products and those who do not differ significantly with respect to the influence strategies. One interesting finding is that perceived review credibility significantly influenced the perceived system credibility of the customers who often take time out to review and rate products. This could be because this group of customers assume that other customers provide credible reviews because they also provide credible reviews, hence the system itself should be credible.

Table 1: Path coefficients and significance of the models for reviews and non-reviewers

PATH	Reviewers/ Raters	Non Reviewers/ Raters	Btw Group sig
DIAL->SOCS	0.504	0.166	<0.001
EFFE->CONT	0.638	0.380	<0.001
PCRED->SCRED	0.300	0.643	<0.01
RCRED->SCRED	0.482	0.080	<0.001
SCRED->CONT	0.090	0.300	<0.05
SOCS->CONT	0.038	0.260	<0.05

The second method of classifying consumers was based on how long they have been customers of Amazon. Based on this criteria, we grouped users in two, one group consisting of those that have used Amazon for five years or less and those that have used Amazon for more than five years. We used five years as a cut off based on the average time participants claim they have been customers of Amazon. We developed two models based on these groups and carried out multi-group analysis. In table 2, we present the result of the multi group analysis that was carried out between the two models for paths with significant results. Our result shows that the influence of dialogue support on perceived credibility was significantly higher for the new customers compared to existing customers. In addition, the effectiveness of the system influences existing customers to use it compared to new customers who were more influenced by social support to continue using the system. These results suggest that a one-size-fits all approach may not be effective in e-commerce as consumers differ in their susceptibility to the various influence strategies.

Table 2: Path coefficients and significance of the models for new and existing customers

PATH	New Customers	Existing Customers	Btw Group sig
DIAL->PCRED	0.558	0.375	<0.05
DIAL->RCRED	0.548	0.357	<0.05
EFFE->CONT	0.444	0.665	<0.001
RCRED->SCRED	0.225	0.419	<0.001
SOCS->CONT	0.194	-0.013	<0.05

5 CONCLUSION AND FUTURE WORK

Because of the increase in e-businesses, online companies have to put strategies in place to stay ahead of their competitors. The use of persuasive strategies have been shown to influence consumers in e-commerce. However, in order for these strategies to be effective, they have to be personalized. My research explores various personalization strategies that can lead to the desired behavior change in e-commerce consumers.

I am currently working on a new study that aims to identify the effect of persuasive strategies on users based on 1) their online personality 2) shopping behaviour/shopper type and 3) need for brand uniqueness. Consumers' personality and their shopping choices have been explored in e-commerce [6], [3], however, the persuasive strategy that influences the various personality traits has not been explored. Personalization of users based on their shopping behaviour has also received attention in e-commerce [15]. To contribute to this research area, I intend to map persuasive strategies to the shopping behaviors or consumers in order to improve the personalization strategy of the e-commerce platform.

ACKNOWLEDGEMENTS

The author would like to acknowledge her supervisor, Dr. Julita Vassileva, for all her assistance and support.

REFERENCES

1. I Adaji and J Vassileva. 2016. Evaluating Personalization and Persuasion in E-Commerce. *Proceedings of the International Workshop on Personalization in Persuasive Technology (PPT'16)*. Retrieved October 6, 2016 from http://ceur-ws.org/Vol-1582/8Adaji.pdf

2. Ifeoma Adaji and Julita Vassileva. 2017. Perceived Effectiveness, Credibility and Continuance Intention in E-commerce. A Study of Amazon. In *Proceedings of 12th International Conference on Persuasive Technology*.

3. Reza Barkhi and Linda Wallace. 2007. The impact of personality type on purchasing decisions in virtual stores. *Information Technology and Management* 8, 4: 313–330. https://doi.org/10.1007/s10799-007-0021-y

4. Anol Bhattacherjee. 2001. An empirical analysis of the antecedents of electronic commerce service continuance. *Decision Support Systems* 32, 2: 201–214. https://doi.org/10.1016/S0167-9236(01)00111-7

5. Judith A Chevalier and Dina Mayzlin. 2006. The Effect of Word of Mouth on Sales: Online Book Reviews. *Journal of Marketing Research* 43, 3: 345–354. https://doi.org/10.1509/jmkr.43.3.345

6. D Cunningham and L Thach. 2008. Innovative e-commerce site design: a conceptual model to match consumer MBTI dimensions to website design. *Journal of Internet*. Retrieved August 25, 2016 from http://www.tandfonline.com/doi/abs/10.1300/J179v06n03_01

7. M Eirinaki, M Vazirgiannis, and I Varlamis. 2003. SEWeP: using site semantics and a taxonomy to enhance the Web personalization process. *Proceedings of the ninth ACM*. Retrieved July 28, 2016 from http://dl.acm.org/citation.cfm?id=956765

8. Lewis R. Goldberg. 1990. An alternative description of personality: the big-five factor structure. *Journal of personality and social psychology* 59, 6: 1216. Retrieved August 22, 2016 from http://psycnet.apa.org/psycinfo/1991-09869-001

9. JH Huang and YC Yang. 2010. The relationship between personality traits and online shopping motivations. *Social Behavior and Personality: an*. Retrieved August 22, 2016 from http://www.ingentaconnect.com/content/sbp/sbp/2010/00000038/00000005/art00011

10. Tuomas Lehto and Harri Oinas-Kukkonen. 2015. Explaining and predicting perceived effectiveness and use continuance intention of a behaviour change support system for weight loss. *Behaviour & Information Technology* 34, 2: 176–189. https://doi.org/10.1080/0144929X.2013.866162

11. YW Li, TP Liang, and KK Wei. 2013. How Can Personalized Online Services Affect Customer Loyalty: The Relationship Building Perspective. *Service Science and Innovation (*. Retrieved July 28, 2016 from http://ieeexplore.ieee.org/xpls/abs_all.jsp?arnumber=6599367

12. Harri Oinas-Kukkonen and Marja Harjumaa. 2008. A systematic framework for designing and evaluating persuasive systems. In *Persuasive technology*. Springer, 164–176.

13. Do-Hyung Park, Jumin Lee, and Ingoo Han. 2007. The Effect of On-Line Consumer Reviews on Consumer Purchasing Intention: The Moderating Role of Involvement. *International Journal of Electronic Commerce* 11, 4: 125–148. https://doi.org/10.2753/JEC1086-4415110405

14. Doug Riecken. 2000. Introduction: personalized views of personalization. *Communications of the ACM* 43, 8: 26–28. https://doi.org/10.1145/345124.345133

15. Andrew J Rohm and Vanitha Swaminathan. 2004. A typology of online shoppers based on shopping motivations. *Journal of Business Research* 57, 7: 748–757. https://doi.org/10.1016/S0148-2963(02)00351-X

16. J. Ben Schafer, Joseph Konstan, and John Riedi. 1999. Recommender systems in e-commerce. In *Proceedings of the 1st ACM conference on Electronic commerce - EC '99*, 158–166. https://doi.org/10.1145/336992.337035

17. KKK Wong. 2013. Partial least squares structural equation modeling (PLS-SEM) techniques using SmartPLS. *Marketing Bulletin* 24, Technocal note 1. Retrieved November 19, 2016 from http://www.academia.edu/download/43189928/Smartpls.pdf

18. 2011. *How to win online: Advanced personalization in e-commerce; An Oracle white paper*.

Analyzing the Impact of Social Connections on Rating Behavior in Social Recommender Systems

Carine Pierrette Mukamakuza*
TU Wien
E-Commerce Group
Austria
carine@ec.tuwien.ac.at

ABSTRACT

Social recommenders provide recommendations taking also into account the social connections among their users. We attempt to formalize and investigate the degree of impact that social connections have to the rating behavior of users, by studying publicly available datasets. Our research will provide a better understanding of specific aspects of social connections that are important when making recommendations, and thus contribute towards more effective social recommenders.

KEYWORDS

Social Recommender Systems; Collaborative Filtering; Social Network Analysis

1 INTRODUCTION

With the information explosion, users come across difficulties while making choice for consuming items like movies, books, etc. In such cases, recommender systems may help users get satisfaction on the choice they make, by filtering through items and guiding them with recommendations. On the other hand, social networks are an indispensable tool in our daily life affecting directly and indirectly individual decisions and choices.

The idea of *Social Recommender Systems* is to incorporate the social context when making recommendations. The rationale is as follows. For a particular target item, the behavior of a target user depends on her individual preferences, but also on interpersonal influence from her social connections. Influential people may strongly affect the behavior of a person. The network structure thus is very important trying to understand the effect of the social network.

An example of a social recommender is shown in Figure 1, which depicts the rating behavior of users, denoted as u_i, on items, denoted as i_j, on the left, and the social connections among users on the right. The former is captured by the rating matrix R, where a

*Supervisors: Hannes Werthner, Dimitris Sacharidis

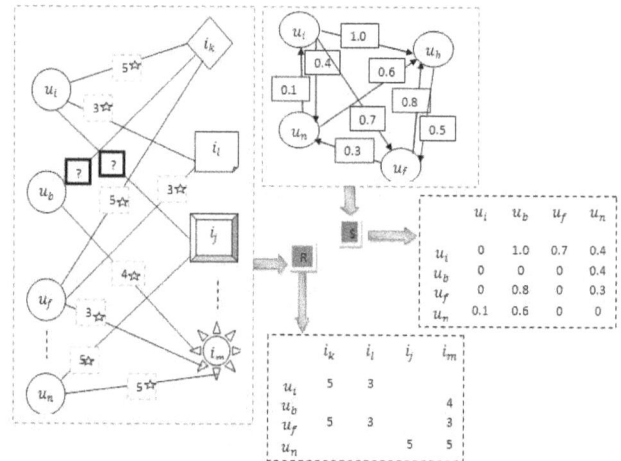

Figure 1: An example of user-item rating behavior and user-user social connections

non empty entry R_{ij} corresponds to the rating given by user u_i on item i_j. The latter is conveyed by the social adjacency matrix S, where entries portray the friendship strength between users. Social recommenders draw upon information from both matrices to predict ratings, under the assumption that a users behavior is influenced by her social connections.

Social recommendations is an active research area in the past few years but relatively young. Existing approaches suffer from certain weaknesses, and often make explicit assumptions about the impact of social ties that they never validate. They also fail to take into account the structure (local and global) of the social network and how much an impact it has on the rating behavior. This thesis will address this shortcoming, by systematically studying and quantifying this impact at different network levels. The ultimate goal is to design more effective social recommenders driven by traces of rating behavior in existing systems.

The remainder of this paper is structured as follows. Section 2 establishes the necessary background and overviews existing work. Section 3 introduces the research problem of the thesis, while Section 4 defines the methodology. Then, Section 5 presents preliminary results, and Section 6 concludes with the expected outcome.

2 RELATED WORK

Collaborative Filtering. Recommender Systems (RS) suggest items to the target user for consumption. The most commonly used method for making recommendations is Collaborative Filtering (CF). In CF approaches (Memory based and Model based), users and items with similar rating patterns are taken into account [2] to produce a recommendation for the target user.

The basic entity in CF is the user rating matrix, composed of a set of items $I = i_1, ...i_n$ and a set of users $U = u_1, ...u_m$. The ratings matrix $R = [R_{u,i}]n \times m$ contains the ratings given by users to items, where n represents the number of items and m number of users. CF exclusively uses the ratings in R to make recommendations.

Memory based methods for CF are divided into two categories. User-based techniques make the assumption that users had similar tastes in the past they are most likely to have the same tastes in the future, i.e., user preferences then to remain constant and stable over the time. Then to predict ratings of a target user, they utilize the ratings to the target item by a set of the users whose similarity level is closer to the target user, the neighborhood. On the other hand, item-based methods uses the target user's profile to compute the target item's similarity to other items rated by the target user.

Model based methods make predictions by learning parameters describing how ratings are generated. The most famous is the Matrix Factorization (MF) technique [6]. MF computes a low-rank approximation of the sparse rating matrix R [8] by multiplication of l-rank factors [9]. The rating matrix R is decomposed in two matrices: U User-aspect matrix and V Item-aspect matrix, with l representing the number latent factors/features. A rating r_{ij} is predicted by a dot product of vector U_i and item V_j: $R_{ij} \approx U_i^T V_j$, where $U \in R^{l \times m}$ and $V \in R^{l \times n}$ with $l < min(m, n)$.

The learning process tries to minimize an objective function that includes the sum of squared prediction errors and two regularization terms to alleviate overfitting.

Social Recommender Systems. In this work, we focus on CF-like techniques for making recommendations exploiting also social connections; for a more generic overview of this research area we refer to [1]. SRS operate similar to CF-based systems but differ in that they make recommendations taking into account the social connections between users. That is, SRS make use of the rating matrix R and the social adjacency matrix S. In the following, we review the most important related work.

In Trust-aware Recommender systems (TaRS) [7], the idea is to treat the social neighborhood of the target user in a manner similar to the rating neighborhood in user-based CF. In particular, the average rating of users in the social neighborhood is used to predict the target user's rating. They find that the best prediction accuracy is produced by considering only the direct friends; as the social distance away from the target user increases the model's performance becomes poorer. The coverage, which determines how many predictions the model is able to make, increases with the social distance from the target user. A hybrid with the user-based CF could not improve on both metrics.

SoRec [5] extends the basic MF model to incorporate the social network. The social adjacency matrix S is factorized into a user-specific matrix U and a factor-specific matrix F, where matrix U is also part of the factorization of the rating matrix. The latent feature vectors of users are then learnt based on both the rating and social network matrices. Social trust ensemble [4] builds on the hybrid

idea of [7], and defines a linear combination of basic MF predictions with social network predictions. The basic idea in Social Regularization [6] is to use the basic MF formula for predicting ratings, but force the learned user feature vectors to be similar between friends. This is achieved by introducing additional regularization terms in the objective function.

In the community-based models of [3], the idea of social regularization is taken one step further. A target user can belong to different communities and they should be regularized differently. If the target user has one community from which she is more interested in than another, that community should be weighed higher. The distance between the target user's feature vector and his/her interested communities is minimized by the MFC^+ model, while in the same community the distance between the target user's feature vector and those of other members of the community is minimized by the MFC model.

3 RESEARCH PROBLEM

The thesis investigates whether there exists a relationship between social connections and rating behavior. For this purpose, we study publicly available datasets, which are commonly used in the literature, containing both user-item ratings and user-user connections. We employ collaborative filtering techniques to associate users based on their behavior, and network analysis methods to associate users based on their connections, and examine whether correlations exist at different levels. In particular, we consider three levels: individual users, user-to-user, and groups/communities and pose the following research questions that seek correlations between social connections and rating behavior.

RQ0: What are the characteristics of social recommender systems datasets? The idea is to obtain basic statistics and insights of the general description of the dataset, in order to guide our research decisions made later on.

RQ1: Is the number of ratings by users related to their network centrality? The first question concerns the first level (individual users), and asks whether power users are also popular. The power of a user is simply the number of their ratings, while popularity is captured by various centrality metrics.

RQ2: Is the ratings similarity between users related to their friendship strength? The second question concerns the second level (user to user). The similarity of users based on ratings is determined as in CF, while friendship strength is directly estimated by the social distance between users.

RQ3: Do central users in the SN have a stronger influence in ratings? This is also about the second level. Users are classified into two categories based on their network centrality values: high (H), and low (L) centrality users. Then pairs of friends are divided into H-H, H-L, and L-L categories. We investigate whether the similarity of ratings is significantly higher in one of these categories.

RQ4: Do neighbourhood ratings of users imply strong social connections? This is about the third level (groups/communities). If we consider the rating neighborhood of a user in a CF manner, do we see strong social connections among these users? One way to answer this is to compute for every user the similarity of ratings in her neighborhood, and the average social distance among the neighbors. Then look across all users if a correlation between the ratings similarity and the average social distance exists.

RQ5: Do social communities imply similar ratings? This question is also on the third level. Suppose we have a way to identify communities in the social network and also quantify their strength. Then we can compute the ratings similarity of each community. Does the community strength correlate with ratings similarity?

4 METHODOLOGICAL APPROACH

In general, our study will use techniques from Social Network Analysis (centrality, community detection), Recommender Systems (Collaborative Filtering, Matrix Factorization), and Statistics (significance tests, correlation measures). Figure 2 presents a summary of the approaches that will be used in our research, and depict what is known and what our contributions will be.

In RQ1, we will primarily use network analysis, and particularly the node centrality to extract important users. For example, the degree centrality implies that a user is more important when the number of her friends grow; out-degree indicates the potential to influence many others, while in-degree shows prestige.

In RQ2, we will use CF techniques to compute similarity between users from the rating matrix, and network analysis to compute friendship strength between users in the Network. We then evaluate how friendship strength relates with the similarity results. For RQ3, we will use again node centrality to assess the importance of users, and classify them into categories. We then check whether ratings are more similar for pairs of users of certain categories.

The fourth question constructs groups using the neighborhood idea of CF methods. Then it uses social network concepts to compute the social distance in the neighborhood. RQ5 is based on social communities. CESNA and BIGCLAM are possible community detection methods. CESNA considers both structure and node attributes, while BIGCLAM only considers the structure of the social network. The next step will be to compute the ratings similarity of the each community from the rating matrix by using CF method and finally use correlation computation to compare both results.

In all questions, we quantify correlation between social connections and the rating behavior in different ways. For example, we can partition users based on a quantity of one aspect (e.g., social connections) and examine how another quantity of the other aspect (e.g., rating behavior) varies across partitions. Another way is to rank users (or pairs of users, or groups/communities) based on two quantities, one for each aspect, and then compare the rankings using standard techniques (e.g., Pearson, Spearman, Kendall Tao).

5 PRELIMINARY RESULTS

We have so far investigated the first two research questions.

RQ0. We discuss results on Filmtrust, a trust-based social site in which users can rate and review movies. The FilmTrust dataset was crawled from a movie sharing and rating website.[1] The dataset has two sub-datasets in it, a social network in addition to the user-item ratings. The social network among users is based on the trust between users, which makes it a directed network (trustee, trustor). Users can specify other users as trusted with a certain level of trust

[1] http://trust.mindswap.org/FilmTrust

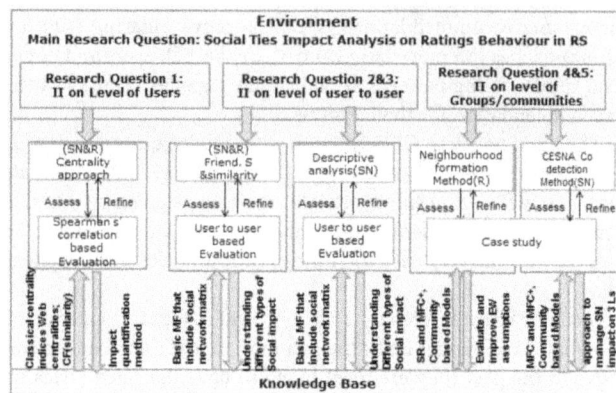

Figure 2: Methodological Approach

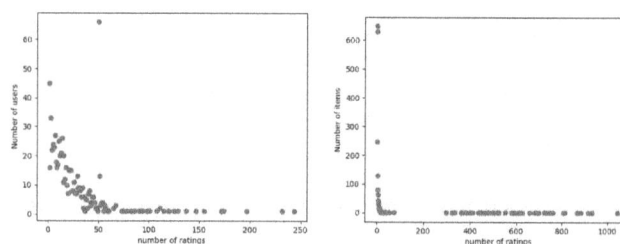

(a) Among users   (b) Among items

Figure 3: Distribution of NumOfRatings

from 1 to 10, but due to the sharing policy these trust values are not available. We can only access the network among users with trust value 1 if there is a connection and 0 otherwise.

Filmtrust contains 1508 users, 2071 items, 35497 ratings, and 1853 connections among users. Social cold users are 635 and social cold items are 133. The mean number of ratings per user is 23.5 with the minimum and the maximum being 1 and 244 respectively. The mean number of ratings per item is 17 with the minimum and the maximum 1 and 1044. Figure 3 draws the full distribution of the number of ratings. The ratings scale is from 0.5 to 4 with step 0.5. The mean rating score over all ratings is 3.0.

Regarding the social network, the mean in-degree is 2.3, with min and max of 1 and 59. The mean out-degree is 2.4, with the min and max of 0 and 59. Further analysis was conducted to determine types of users in the network and we found out that the network has 133 users who are "Talkers", where users out-degree is greater than in-degree number. We also found that 145 users are "Listeners", where users in-degree is greater than out-degree number. The last group with 85 users are "Communicators", having the same number of in-degree and out-degree.

RQ1. We consider various node centrality measures, including (In/Out-)Degree centrality to extract users popularity and visibility, Closeness centrality to get the idea of the information flow in the network, Betweenness centrality to distinguish bridge-users who are indispensable in the network, and PageRank in order to measure the importance of each user in the network.

To assess the relationship between centrality and number of ratings, we divide the users into three partitions according to their

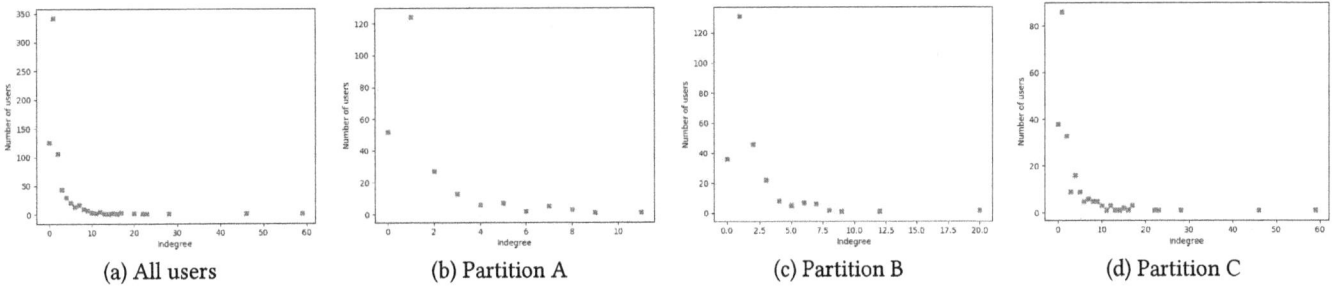

(a) All users   (b) Partition A   (c) Partition B   (d) Partition C

Figure 4: Distribution of In-Degree centrality among partitions on NumOfRatings

Table 1: ANOVA for partitions on NumOfRatings

	DF	Sum. Sq.	Mean Sq.	F value	Pr (>F)
partition	2	688	343.8	22.26	3.91×10^{-10}
Residuals	798	12323	15.4		

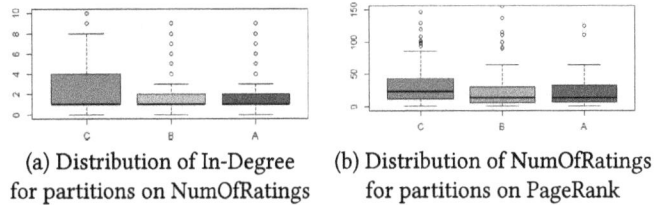

(a) Distribution of In-Degree for partitions on NumOfRatings   (b) Distribution of NumOfRatings for partitions on PageRank

Figure 5: The impact of NumOfRatings to Centrality

Table 2: Tukey HSD test for partitions on NumOfRatings

Pair	Diff. of Means	95% CI	p-value
B - A	0.401	[−0.398, 1.199]	0.46
C - B	1.734	[0.935, 2.533]	1.3×10^{-6}
C - A	2.135	[1.336, 2.933]	≈ 0

Table 3: ANOVA for partitions on PageRank

	DF	Sum. Sq.	Mean Sq.	F value	Pr (>F)
partition	2	17266	8633	12.73	3.91×10^{-10}
Residuals	801	543138	678		

Table 4: Tukey HSD test for partitions on PageRank

Pair	Diff. of Means	95% CI	p-value
A - B	-0.239	[−5.521, 5.043]	0.99
C - B	9.948	[4.666, 15.230]	3.3×10^{-5}
C - A	9.709	[4.427, 14.991]	5.3×10^{-5}

number of ratings. We determine the lower, middle, and upper terciles (3-quantiles) based on number of ratings, and divide according to them. Partitions are thus balanced, with each containing roughly 1/3 of all users. Partition A contains "cold" users having fewer than 11 ratings, B contains those with 11 or more ratings but fewer than 30, while C contains power users. The distribution of the In-Degree centrality for all users is shown in Figure 4(a), while that for the three partitions is in Figures 4(b)–(d). Note that a large plurality of users have only 1 incoming connection. We also observe that Partitions A and B roughly contain users with similar In-Degrees, e.g., mostly up to 10, while C contains more well connected users, i.e., with more than 20 incoming connections. A summary of the distribution is shown by the box plot of Figure 5(a), where the y-axis shows the In-Degree only up to 10 for increased readability.

To support these observations we perform ANOVA analysis to examine whether there is significant differences in the mean In-Degree of the partitions. The result is shown in Table 1, where an F value of 22.26 provides significant evidence against the hypothesis that the means are equal (p-value in the order of 10^{-10}). Following this result, we use the Tukey HSD test to compare pairs of partitions to locate where there is significance difference in their means. The difference of means and the corresponding 95% confidence interval for each pair are shown in Table 2. As suspected partitions A and B have mostly similar mean In-Degrees and no significant difference is observed. However, there is a significant difference when we compare B with C, and of course A with C. This implies that power users tend to receive more incoming connections that the other users, and thus answers RQ1 positively.

We also repeat the experimental setup on partitions created based on centrality values, and particularly on PageRank. As before three partitions were created based on terciles, and investigate the mean number of ratings per partition; see Figure 5(b). ANOVA shows there is significant evidence against all means being equal; see Table 3. The Tukey HSD test then shows significant differences for pairs B, C and A, C; see Table 4. This implies that highly central users tend to also be power users.

6 EXPECTED OUTCOME AND IMPACT

The main outcome of the thesis is the formulation and statistical analysis of the impact that social connections have in rating behavior. Can we predict how users rate items, and to what extent, purely by observing their position in the social network, and vice versa?

An additional contribution is the theoretical evaluation of the assumptions made by state of the art social recommenders, and whether they hold in various domains. Ultimately, we would have a better understanding of what aspects of social connections exactly affect rating behavior. This will bring us initial ideas towards a more realistic model for social recommendations, based on observed and quantifiable types of social influence.

REFERENCES

[1] Ido Guy. 2015. Social Recommender Systems. In *Recommender Systems Handbook*, Francesco Ricci, Lior Rokach, and Bracha Shapira (Eds.). Springer, 511–543. https://doi.org/10.1007/978-1-4899-7637-6_15

[2] Rong Jin, Joyce Y. Chai, and Luo Si. 2004. An automatic weighting scheme for collaborative filtering. In *SIGIR*. 337–344. https://doi.org/10.1145/1008992.1009051

[3] Hui Li, Dingming Wu, Wenbin Tang, and Nikos Mamoulis. 2015. Overlapping Community Regularization for Rating Prediction in Social Recommender Systems. In *RecSys*. 27–34. https://doi.org/10.1145/2792838.2800171

[4] Hao Ma, Irwin King, and Michael R. Lyu. 2009. Learning to recommend with social trust ensemble. In *SIGIR*. 203–210. https://doi.org/10.1145/1571941.1571978

[5] Hao Ma, Haixuan Yang, Michael R. Lyu, and Irwin King. 2008. SoRec: social recommendation using probabilistic matrix factorization. In *CIKM*. 931–940. https://doi.org/10.1145/1458082.1458205

[6] Hao Ma, Dengyong Zhou, Chao Liu, Michael R. Lyu, and Irwin King. 2011. Recommender systems with social regularization. In *WSDM*. 287–296. https://doi.org/10.1145/1935826.1935877

[7] Paolo Massa and Paolo Avesani. 2007. Trust-aware recommender systems. In *RecSys*. 17–24. https://doi.org/10.1145/1297231.1297235

[8] Jason D. M. Rennie and Nathan Srebro. 2005. Fast maximum margin matrix factorization for collaborative prediction. In *ICML*. 713–719. https://doi.org/10.1145/1102351.1102441

[9] Ruslan Salakhutdinov and Andriy Mnih. 2007. Probabilistic Matrix Factorization. In *NIPS*. 1257–1264. http://papers.nips.cc/paper/3208-probabilistic-matrix-factorization

Personalized Research Paper Recommendation using Deep Learning

Hebatallah A. Mohamed Hassan
Roma Tre University
Department of Engineering
Via della Vasca Navale 79
Rome, Italy 00146
hebatallah.mohamed@uniroma3.it

ABSTRACT

With the increasing number of scientific publications, research paper recommendation has become increasingly important for scientists. Most researchers rely on keyword-based search or following citations in other papers, in order to find relevant research articles. And usually they spend a lot of time without getting satisfactory results. This study aims to propose a personalized research paper recommendation system, that facilitate this task by recommending papers based on users' explicit and implicit feedback. The users will be allowed to explicitly specify the papers of interest. In addition, user activities (e.g., viewing abstracts or full-texts) will be analyzed in order to enhance users' profiles. Most of the current research paper recommendation and information retrieval systems use the classical bag-of-words methods, which don't consider the context of the words and the semantic similarity between the articles. This study will use Recurrent Neural Networks (RNNs) to discover continuous and latent semantic features of the papers, in order to improve the recommendation quality. The proposed approach utilizes PubMed so far, since it is frequently used by physicians and scientists, but it can easily incorporate other datasets in the future.

KEYWORDS

Recommender systems; personalization; deep learning; recurrent neural networks

1 INTRODUCTION

Recommender System (RS) for research articles is a very important application that helps researchers keeping track of their field of study. Moreover, it can aid the scientists (e.g., physicians) as a decision support tool. One way by which researchers find articles is following citations in other articles that they are interested in, but this limits them to specific citation communities, and it is biased towards heavily cited papers. Another method of finding articles is keyword-based search, which is a powerful approach, but it is also limited as it can be difficult to form queries to search with. This has opened the door to using recommendation methods as a way to help researchers finding interesting articles. Most of the current RSs are available for commercial applications, such as news, movies and music applications. On the contrary, few projects address scientific literature recommendation.

The existing RSs approaches can be classified into three types: content-based filtering, collaborative filtering and hybrid approaches. Content-based filtering uses the content of items which are highly rated by a user in order to find her preferences [17]. On the other hand, collaborative filtering utilizes the similarity between user's preferences and other similar users' preferences in order to recommend new items [7]. Hybrid RSs use a combination of content-based and collaborative filtering techniques [5]. Most of the current research paper recommendation systems are based on the bag-of-words model, that represents the number of times each word occurs in a document. The context of the words and the semantic similarity between words are not considered during the extraction and representation of the document features.

Recent advances in artificial neural networks (ANNs) have shown that continuous word vectors can be learned as a probability distribution over the words of a document. Deep learning architectures are basically ANNs of multiple non-linear layers. A key benefit of deep learning is the analysis and learning of massive amounts of unsupervised data, making it a valuable tool for big data analytics where raw data is largely unstructured. Using deep learning techniques to extract meaningful data representations makes it possible to obtain a semantic and relational understanding of the data from such high-dimensional textual data.

We intend to use deep learning techniques for recommending relevant research papers in PubMed[1] database, based on the semantic content of the papers that match user's preferences. User profiles will be built based on some basic information that a user may provide, such as the papers she is interested in, to be selected as input from a graphical user interface. Moreover, the profiles will be improved using user interaction information that can be extracted from users' logs.

The first part of this paper briefly presents the research goals, some of the research literature related to the existing approaches of designing research paper RSs. The other parts introduce the proposed system architecture, the technologies that we will use, and the evaluation methods. The paper is concluded by presenting the current research progress.

UMAP'17, July 9–12, 2017, Bratislava, Slovakia
© 2017 ACM. 978-1-4503-4635-1/17/07...$15.00
DOI: http://dx.doi.org/10.1145/3079628.3079708

---

[1]https://www.ncbi.nlm.nih.gov/pubmed

2 RESEARCH GOALS

This main research goals can be summarized as follows:

- To propose a novel personalized research paper recommendation approach that learns and utilizes the semantic representation of papers' titles and abstracts for matching users' interests.
- To study the effect of using deep neural networks, in particular word2vec[2] and long short-term memory (LSTM) techniques in extracting the semantic representation of the scientific papers' titles and abstracts for the recommendation task.
- To propose a comprehensive user modeling framework that combines user explicit and implicit feedback by allowing users to specify their preferred papers and by analyzing users behaviors.

3 RELATED WORK

There have been some attempts to develop recommendation systems for scientific literature. Citation databases such as CiteSeerX[3] apply citation analysis in order to identify papers that are similar to an input paper. Scholarly search engines such as Google Scholar[4] focus on classic text mining and citation counts. The research of [20] has also presented a recommendation system based on citations.

Other work was done based on articles content; many different types of continuous representations techniques such as Latent Dirichlet Allocation (LDA) [19] and Latent Semantic Analysis (LSA) [1, 9] have been used to describe the content of a document as a probability distribution of latent variables known as topics. The assumption behind those methods is that words that are related to each other will often appear in the same documents. The system illustrated in [1] used TF-IDF and LSA methods to discover groups of words that are equivalent in their meaning.

The authors of [19] presented a topic-based recommendation system that combines traditional collaborative filtering with topic modeling based on LDA model. Nascimento et al. [16] provided another example of a content-based RS for scientific articles recommendation. Their proposed solution utilized the n-grams models to generate queries from a particular article that is presented by the user, and then submit the generated queries on publicly available web sources of scientific papers. Their method used the titles and abstracts of the articles, and the similarity of the papers was calculated through the cosine similarity method.

In [21], the authors presented PURE, a content-based recommendation system that works on documents' titles and abstracts of the PubMed dataset. It automatically captures user preferences by using her response to the presented papers. Furthermore, PURE uses the well-known TF-IDF method and learns probabilistic model for computing relevant documents based on selected documents added by the user.

Docear [3] is an academic literature suite to search, organize, and create research articles. Its recommender system uses content-based methods to recommend articles. It builds a user model using the mind maps created by the user, and match it with Docear Digital Library. The authors claimed to have achieved good results based on the number of clicks gained, through around thirty thousand tested recommendation results.

Some authors suggested using collaborative filtering and ratings [6]. Ratings can be generated by considering citations as ratings. They can also be implicitly inferred by monitoring user's actions such as downloading or bookmarking a paper. The system proposed in [6], called Scienstein, combines different methods for providing literature recommendation. Scienstein integrated the traditional keyword-based search with citation analysis, author analysis, source analysis, implicit and explicit ratings. Instead of entering just keywords for searching documents, a user may provide entire documents as an input, include reference lists, and provides implicit and explicit ratings in order to improve the recommendation process.

In [10] a personalized academic research paper RS is presented. It recommends articles relevant to the research field of the users, supposing that researchers like their own articles. Based on this assumption papers similar to the ones previously written by users are recommended as relevant to them. This system uses a web crawler to retrieve research papers from IEEE Xplore[5] and ACM digital library[6]. It measures text similarity using bag-of-words and KNN methods to determine the similarity between two research papers and uses collaborative filtering methods to recommend the items.

Finally, the research of [14] proposed a novel method for integrating structural and contextual information to build a context specific network for generating recommendations for similar PubMed articles.

Some of the used methods have drawbacks, which limit their ability to deliver recommendations. For example, in the citation-based approaches, not all research papers are cited and hence cannot be recommended. Also, reference lists can contain irrelevant citations just because the author believes that well-known papers should be cited, or in order to promote other publications although they are irrelevant for the citing paper [6]. In addition, text-based RSs cannot identify related papers if different terms are used. Moreover, the basic topic modeling methods which are based on the traditional bag-of-words techniques, have the disadvantage that topics are probability distributions over a collection of words that represent a document, it does not consider the semantic relations between words. Thus, it may result in redundant topics that contain different words, but with the same meaning. In addition, these techniques don't take the context of the words into consideration.

Collaborative filtering in the research paper recommender systems domain would be ineffective as there is a huge number of papers compared with the number of users, and only few users rated the same papers. In domains such as movie recommendations, there are few items and many users such as in MovieLens[7] recommender system, and most movies have been watched and rated by at least some users [2]. Therefore, like-minded users can be found and recommendations can be given effectively.

The use of deep neural networks for Natural Language Processing (NLP) has recently received much attention; it provides high

---

[2]https://code.google.com/archive/p/word2vec/
[3]http://citeseerx.ist.psu.edu/index
[4]https://scholar.google.it/

[5]http://ieeexplore.ieee.org/Xplore/home.jsp
[6]http://dl.acm.org/
[7]https://grouplens.org/datasets/movielens/

quality semantic word representations. These models are usually trained on large amounts of data. In the last few years, deep neural network models have been applied to tasks ranging from machine translation to question answering, but not much attention is paid to the RSs area. For instance, in [15] and [12], the authors showed that LSTM can be used to build a language model and assess semantic similarity between sentences. To the best of our knowledge, there have been no work done before for recommending scientific articles based on LSTM.

4 RESEARCH METHODOLOGY

4.1 Data Collection

PubMed is one of the largest public databases in biological and medical sciences. It contains more than 26 million citations for biomedical literature from MEDLINE[8], life science journals, and online books. Each paper in MEDLINE is indexed using a controlled vocabulary, called Medical Subject Headings (MeSH), which is used to describe the main topics discussed. The set of MeSH terms is manually assigned by biomedical experts who scan each article.

We will use BioPython [4] library to crawl the PubMed database through PubMed Central (PMC) APIs[9], and download titles and abstracts of sample papers. Then, we will concatenate the title and abstract for each paper.

We will use only the titles and abstracts of the papers to calculate the similarity between the papers and recommend similar articles since they will be always publicly available. In addition, fetching and analyzing the full text of every paper would significantly slow down the process.

4.2 Language Modeling

Recurrent Neural Networks (RNNs) are deep models that are widely used when dealing with sequential data, unlike the traditional neural networks which assume that all inputs and outputs are independent of each other. RNNs have shown great promise in image and video captioning, time series prediction, NLP, text and music generation and much more tasks [11]. LSTM networks are a type of RNNs [8], that allows the model to learn longer-term dependencies than a traditional RNN.

Word2vec is one of state-of-the-art word embedding techniques, published by Google in 2013 [13], that learns distributed representations for words. It converts text into a numerical form that deep nets can understand. The idea of the word vectors is to represent a word by a dense vector in a semantic space, and other vectors close by should be semantically similar. Other deep recurrent neural network architectures had been previously proposed for learning word representations, but the major problem with those methods was the long time required to train the models. Word2vec learns quickly compared to other models. In general, parallelization is used to speed up the training process, so that larger models can be trained in a reasonable amount of time.

We will create a language model using the word2vec and LSTM techniques, in order to be used for measuring the relatedness of the scientific publications. Word2vec will be used for computing individual word representation for all the words from the collected

papers. We intend to use gensim Python package [18] for this purpose. Then, we will train a LSTM model using the vectors of words resulted from the word2vec step, in order to learn the semantic content of the research papers. This model will be used for the purpose of document embedding. In other words, the LSTM model will be utilized for representing an article according to the semantic representation of its words.

4.3 User Profile Creation

In order to recommend papers to users, we will model users' interests in user profiles. These profiles will represent users' tastes and opinions about papers. Such profiles could contain both long-term and short-term interests, gathered explicitly or implicitly.

One of the explicit feedback forms is to ask the user to explicitly specify papers which are relevant to her (which are satisfying information need). Implicit feedback is to collect data about user's preferences based on observations of the user's behavior from the transactions log like viewing abstracts or full-text articles.

In our study, we will build user profiles from users' explicit and implicit short-term interests; user can explicitly add or delete the preferred articles as an input to the recommender system, from which the title and abstract will be extracted and the semantic vectors will be calculated. In addition, we will infer users' interests based on viewing abstracts and clicking links to full-text articles while querying the PubMed Central in the same query session. We will assign high weights to the vectors that characterize the topics which the user is interested in, based on the user's actions; for instance, viewing abstract only should be weighted lower than viewing the whole paper.

4.4 Recommendation of papers

Using the constructed user profile and the feature vectors of the set of the candidate papers to recommend, the system will compute the cosine similarities between the papers in the user profile and the ones in the corpus, considering the weights that take into account the user feedback. Highly relevant papers will be ranked first for presentation. Therefore, the correctness of an item in the ranking list should be weighted by its position in the ranking. Figure 1 shows the high level architecture of the proposed method.

4.5 Evaluation Methods

We will compare the results from our recommendation engine with PubMed MeSH-based baseline. Similar to the PubMed recommender system proposed in [14], we will use MeSH-based paper similarities as the gold standard to evaluate the different methods. In the MeSH-based paper similarities, the quality of predictions for each paper is defined based on its distance compared to similar predictions from MeSH scores.

In addition to the described offline evaluation, we intend to conduct user studies in order to evaluate our proposed method. The participants will be asked to read and indicate how the recommended papers are relevant to their research.

5 CURRENT PROGRESS

The thesis is now in the initial phase. We are currently studying the different recommendation methodologies, deep learning techniques,

---

[8]https://www.nlm.nih.gov/bsd/pmresources.html
[9]https://www.ncbi.nlm.nih.gov/home/develop/api.shtml

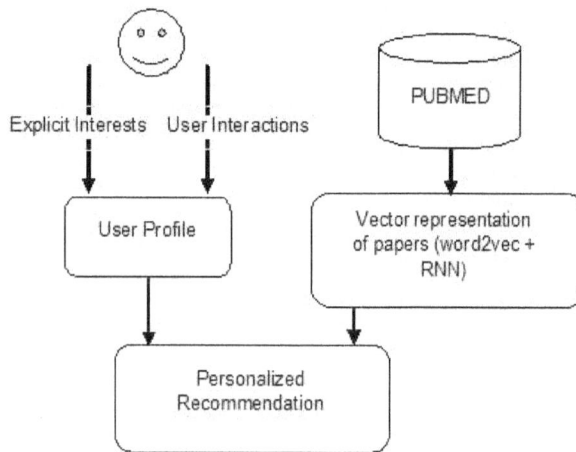

Figure 1: The proposed method

and reviewing the literature of the research paper recommender systems. The next steps will be the implementation of the proposed approach and the evaluation of its performance in comparison with other approaches in the literature.

ACKNOWLEDGMENTS

I would like to thank my advisors, Dr. Giuseppe Sansonetti for his comments that helped to improve this manuscript, Prof. Alessandro Micarelli and Dr. Fabio Gasparetti for their support and feedback in this research.

REFERENCES

[1] Titipat Achakulvisut, Daniel E Acuna, Tulakan Ruangrong, and Konrad Kording. 2016. Science Concierge: A fast content-based recommendation system for scientific publications. *PloS one* 11, 7 (2016), e0158423.

[2] Joeran Beel, Bela Gipp, Stefan Langer, and Corinna Breitinger. 2016. Research-paper recommender systems: a literature survey. *International Journal on Digital Libraries* 17, 4 (2016), 305-338.

[3] Joeran Beel, Stefan Langer, Marcel Genzmehr, and Andreas Nürnberger. 2013. Introducing Docear's research paper recommender system. In *Proceedings of the 13th ACM/IEEE-CS joint conference on Digital libraries*. ACM, 459-460.

[4] Peter JA Cock, Tiago Antao, Jeffrey T Chang, Brad A Chapman, Cymon J Cox, Andrew Dalke, Iddo Friedberg, Thomas Hamelryck, Frank Kauff, Bartek Wilczynski, and others. 2009. Biopython: freely available Python tools for computational molecular biology and bioinformatics. *Bioinformatics* 25, 11 (2009), 1422-1423.

[5] Luis M De Campos, Juan M Fernández-Luna, Juan F Huete, and Miguel A Rueda-Morales. 2010. Combining content-based and collaborative recommendations: A hybrid approach based on Bayesian networks. *International Journal of Approximate Reasoning* 51, 7 (2010), 785-799.

[6] Bela Gipp, Jöran Beel, and Christian Hentschel. 2009. Scienstein: A research paper recommender system. In *Proceedings of the international conference on emerging trends in computing (iceticâĂŽ09)*. 309-315.

[7] Jonathan L Herlocker, Joseph A Konstan, Loren G Terveen, and John T Riedl. 2004. Evaluating collaborative filtering recommender systems. *ACM Transactions on Information Systems (TOIS)* 22, 1 (2004), 5-53.

[8] Sepp Hochreiter and Jürgen Schmidhuber. 1997. Long short-term memory. *Neural computation* 9, 8 (1997), 1735-1780.

[9] Thomas K Landauer and Susan T Dumais. 1997. A solution to Plato's problem: The latent semantic analysis theory of acquisition, induction, and representation of knowledge. *Psychological review* 104, 2 (1997), 211.

[10] Joonseok Lee, Kisung Lee, and Jennifer G Kim. 2013. Personalized academic research paper recommendation system. *arXiv preprint arXiv:1304.5457* (2013).

[11] Zachary C Lipton, John Berkowitz, and Charles Elkan. 2015. A critical review of recurrent neural networks for sequence learning. *arXiv preprint arXiv:1506.00019* (2015).

[12] Tomas Mikolov, Martin Karafiát, Lukas Burget, Jan Cernockỳ, and Sanjeev Khudanpur. 2010. Recurrent neural network based language model.. In *Interspeech*, Vol. 2. 3.

[13] Tomas Mikolov, Ilya Sutskever, Kai Chen, Greg S Corrado, and Jeff Dean. 2013. Distributed representations of words and phrases and their compositionality. In *Advances in neural information processing systems*. 3111-3119.

[14] Shahin Mohammadi, Sudhir Kylasa, Giorgos Kollias, and Ananth Grama. 2016. Context-Specific Recommendation System for Predicting Similar PubMed Articles. In *Data Mining Workshops (ICDMW), 2016 IEEE 16th International Conference on*. IEEE, 1007-1014.

[15] Jonas Mueller and Aditya Thyagarajan. 2016. Siamese Recurrent Architectures for Learning Sentence Similarity.. In *AAAI*. 2786-2792.

[16] Cristiano Nascimento, Alberto HF Laender, Altigran S da Silva, and Marcos André Gonçalves. 2011. A source independent framework for research paper recommendation. In *Proceedings of the 11th annual international ACM/IEEE joint conference on Digital libraries*. ACM, 297-306.

[17] Michael J Pazzani and Daniel Billsus. 2007. Content-based recommendation systems. In *The adaptive web*. Springer, 325-341.

[18] Radim Rehurek and Petr Sojka. 2010. Software framework for topic modelling with large corpora. In *In Proceedings of the LREC 2010 Workshop on New Challenges for NLP Frameworks*. Citeseer.

[19] Chong Wang and David M Blei. 2011. Collaborative topic modeling for recommending scientific articles. In *Proceedings of the 17th ACM SIGKDD international conference on Knowledge discovery and data mining*. ACM, 448-456.

[20] Ian Wesley-Smith and Jevin D West. 2016. Babel: A Platform for Facilitating Research in Scholarly Article Discovery. In *Proceedings of the 25th International Conference Companion on World Wide Web*. International World Wide Web Conferences Steering Committee, 389-394.

[21] Takashi Yoneya and Hiroshi Mamitsuka. 2007. PURE: a PubMed article recommendation system based on content-based filtering. *Genome informatics* 18 (2007), 267-276.

Conversational Group Recommender Systems

Thuy Ngoc Nguyen*
Free University of Bozen-Bolzano
Piazza Domenicani 3
Bolzano, Italy
ngoc.nguyen@unibz.it

ABSTRACT

Recommending to a group of users is multifaceted as people naturally adapt to other members, and it may turn out that what they choose in a group does not fully match individual interests. Besides, it has been shown that the recommendation needs of groups go beyond the aggregation of individual preferences. In practice, it is much more difficult to predict group choices because users take into account the others' reactions and different users react to the group in different ways. Thus, in this research, we aim at exploiting an interactive and conversational approach to facilitate the group decision making process where the complex trade-off between the satisfaction of an individual and the group as a whole typically occurs and needs to be resolved. To attain this goal, we investigate approaches that can access a group situation and autonomously learn an adaptive interaction in a specific condition of the group.

KEYWORDS

Group recommender systems; Group decision processes; Human-computer interaction; User experience; Preference elicitation.

ACM Reference format:
Thuy Ngoc Nguyen. 2017. Conversational Group Recommender Systems. In *Proceedings of UMAP '17, Bratislava, Slovakia, July 09-12, 2017,* 4 pages.
https://doi.org/http://dx.doi.org/10.1145/3079628.3079704

1 INTRODUCTION

Recommender systems (RSs) are tools designed to alleviate information overload by suggesting items that are estimated to fit users' needs and preferences [22]. In many realistic scenarios, the recommended items are consumed by groups of users rather than by individuals [13]. For example, a group of friends or a family may be looking for a restaurant or an attraction site, to go together. The research on group recommender systems (GRSs) is studying methods for supporting a group of users in making decisions when considering a set of alternatives.

---

*This PhD thesis along with the results presented in this paper are made under the supervision of Francesco Ricci, Free University of Bozen-Bolzano.

Overall, whereas a substantial amount of research in the field of GRSs has focused on group recommendation algorithms, only little research has addressed the role of human-computer interaction in these systems. In particular, most of the previous research has assumed that based on the individual preferences alone, the system can predict a group choice or make good group recommendations. Their primary focus therefore is how to aggregate group members' preferences and identify the "best" items for a group. Conversely, in this research we assume that the knowledge of individual preferences prior to a group discussion does not suffice, and the system must track the group discussion in order to support the group decision making process. This assumption is clearly supported by the fact that there is no clear winner among several preference aggregation techniques that have been proposed in the literature [18], which implies that the group choice depends on the group discussion and not only on the pre-discussion individual preferences. In fact, social scientists studying group dynamics have also stressed the importance of the full decision process adopted by a group in determining the quality of the output decision [10], or in [24], the authors have shown that the degree to which preferences and information are shared within groups, is a key element to understand the group decision making process.

In the context of GRSs, still little attention has been devoted to understanding how the process of making choices in groups can be supported [7]. More concretely, the dynamics of group decision making has been so far under-examined, i.e., users' behavior in the context of a group is overlooked, and the observation of changes in users' preferences during the group decision making process is disregarded. Aside from that, the literature on user experience of RSs has also claimed that although RSs adapt their recommendations to user preferences, they typically do not adapt their interface to support the different decision-making strategies [14]. Driven by these observations, the objective of this research is to support decision making in groups by exploiting the interaction between users and a GRS. This consists of investigating mechanisms that predict a situation where group members are likely to experience in a context of a group, and then provide the most effective supporting actions according to that predicted situation.

2 PROBLEM STATEMENT AND HYPOTHESES

2.1 Situation assessment

Most GRSs developed so far apply a "one-size-fits-all" approach for all group settings, while with each setting, users are likely to react differently. In fact, there are several different kinds of social response to group pressures [10]. For example, group members may be consistent with their personal standards, or show conformity to the group opinion, or alternatively to react negatively to the group setting. Motivated by this finding, we conjecture that in different group situations, users' decision-making strategies tend to vary. Thus, it is essential to assess the group situation based on information observed from group settings such as how long a group session lasts and how much users interact with each other. More concretely, we need to deal with the issues: what individual and group features can be detected to assess the group situation and consequently optimize the system support.

2.2 Modeling users' preferences

One of the major challenges for GRSs is to optimally exploit the individual long-term preferences and those induced by the group dynamics called session-based preferences. The session-based preferences that are uncovered in a group discussion could be either consistent or not with the long-term interests that are acquired by the system before the group discussion. Thus, our hypothesis is that the preferences of users should be continuously acquired by observing the evolving behavior of users in the group session, and flexibly integrated with the long-term ones based on a specific situation of the group. Each individual preference model needs to be updated continuously according to the iterative revision of users' preferences during the discussion, and finally aggregated to generate a group preference model.

2.3 Group negotiation support

In most GRSs, users are given group recommendations, and based on these recommendations, they need to negotiate what to do. However, with interactive systems, the challenge is no longer simply recommending items but also guiding and helping users to make informed choices during the negotiation process. We hypothesize that the proactive adaptation of the interaction plays an important role in a group decision support system. In particular, based on the estimated group situation, the system can automatically adapt diverse types of actions, e.g., giving group recommendations, acquiring more information or suggesting a final choice, to support the process of making group decisions.

3 STATE OF THE ART

3.1 Preference aggregation techniques

Two general approaches have been proposed to generate group recommendations: i) *profile aggregation* - aggregate user profiles to create a single profile of the group to which conventional recommendation techniques can be applied, and ii) *recommendation aggregation* - generate individual recommendations for each group member and then combine them to construct a single set of recommendations for the group [13]. The combination of the two approaches, called hybrid switching, has also been exploited in [3]. These approaches have been compared, for instance, in the food recommendation domain [3] or in movie recommendation scenarios [5]. Overall, the choice of which approach is to be used may rely on the domain characteristics, the available data and the precise task. An example of the *profile aggregation* approach is given by *Let's Browse* [15], where an agent assists a group of people in browsing the website by suggesting new material likely to be of common interest. The *recommendation aggregation* method is employed in *Polylens* [21], a system that suggests movies to small

groups of people with similar interests. In general, how to optimally aggregate either preferences or ratings or recommendations, is a well-researched topic. In [18], the author gave an overview of different aggregation strategies to reach group decisions. Additionally, the performance of different rank aggregation strategies for generating group recommendations from individual recommendations was investigated by using simulated data of user groups [2].

No matter how the users' preferences are aggregated, most of these approaches have assumed that the personal preferences are adequate to generate group recommendations. In contrast, we believe that the preferences of users are better represented by the combination of both the individual's long-term interests and the session-based preferences.

3.2 Interactive group recommender systems

When it comes to the role of the user-system interaction, research on GRSs has attempted to design interfaces and techniques to support the full decision making process, including the entire preference elicitation and recommendation phases.

The first example is *Intrigue* [1], a tool that assists tour guides in designing tours for heterogeneous tourist groups (e.g., families with children and elderly) by providing recommendations and an interactive agenda. *Travel Decision Forum* [12] allows users to interact with embodied conversational agents representing group members, to define a set of shared preferences, which are discussed and modified by the members themselves. In *Collaborative Advisory Travel System* [19], the concept of critiquing-based RSs is applied, where users can provide feedback in terms of critiques on specific features while the "recommend - review - revise" cycle is repeated until the desired item is found. Also in this direction, *Where2eat* is a mobile app for restaurant recommendation that implements "interactive multi-party critiquing", an extension of the critiquing concept to a computer-mediated conversation between two individuals [11]. *Choicla* [23], a group decision support environment that allows the flexible definition of decision functionality in a domain-free setting. Similarly to critiquing, in *Choicla*, group members are asked to provide evaluations for different item features which are typically specified by a creator, a person who defines a decision task and configures the decision making process. *Hootle+* [17], a GRS that mainly supports the preference elicitation and negotiation process by enabling group members to accept or reject the proposed features and adjust their significance.

While these interactive GRSs mainly support users with recommendations, we speculate that to best support the group decision making process, the system needs to evaluate a group situation based on users' interaction and then automatically and continuously adapt its actions to the estimated condition.

3.3 Evaluation methods

User studies are usually carried out to evaluate the usability of a GRS and the perceived user satisfaction with the recommendations [3, 11, 17, 23]. Offline evaluation studies are limited by the lack of datasets that capture the preferences of users in real group contexts. For this reason, researchers have used data from standard datasets such as MovieLens[1] to test their group recommendation

---

[1]https://grouplens.org/datasets/movielens/

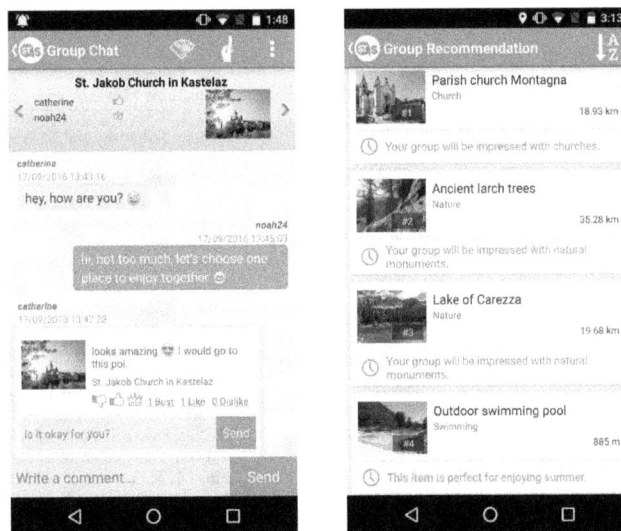

Figure 1: Screenshots of STSGroup, from left to right: (a) Group chat and (b) Group recommendations.

algorithms [2]. Besides, simulation approaches have been used to test conversational RSs [4, 16]. For example, user-system sessions, in which a user incrementally modifies a query to finally select or add a product, were simulated to perform evaluations [16].

In our research, we have developed a chat-based GRS, called STSGroup, which will be introduced later on. With the system, we can collect chat logs that are composed of messages and actions exchanged in real group contexts, and use them to discover possible changes in users' preferences. Moreover, we have designed a procedure that simulates the high degree of interactivity of users with STSGroup under different group situations in order to analyze the performance of the group recommendation model implemented in the system.

4 OVERVIEW OF THE RESEARCH PROGRESS

4.1 Group decision making study

In a first study we explored how people make decisions, and in particular on travel destinations, in a teamwork setting [8, 9]. The study was conducted within a cooperation research project of eleven universities worldwide. Since the study was based on the observations of real user behaviors, it was considered a starting point to understand what group and user features are important for explaining group dynamics and group choices.

The study included three phases: pre-study questionnaire, group meeting/discussion, and post-study questionnaire. The results of this observational study has indicated that group preferences are constructed during the process and stressed that research in GRSs should put more focus on the decision making process taking place in groups rather than on solving group recommendation problems in a mechanical way [9]. This conclusion was supported by the fact that more than two-thirds of the participants, whose the group decision was not in accordance with their most preferred destination, were still satisfied with the collective choice, besides common aggregation strategies in GRSs were hardly able to predict the outcome of the group decision making process.

4.2 Group recommendation model

Interactive GRSs based on critiquing-based techniques suffer from a general drawback: they require users to identify the features that they like or dislike, which can impose a significant cognitive burden on them, especially when the number of features is large [14]. They can also move the discussion on features of the items rather than on the items themselves. Thus, we have proposed a model that acquires users' preferences at the item level, in the form of user's evaluations of the items proposed in a group discussion, and then, based on these evaluations, it automatically determines the item's feature importance weights [20]. The technique, which we adopted to infer the user utility function from constraints on the same utility function by observing what the user likes and dislikes, was introduced in [25], and was applied to conversational RSs for individuals [4]. The individual utility functions consider both individual long-term and session-based preferences, which are aggregated to compute a group utility function that is used to generate group recommendations.

This model was implemented in a GRS to provide a real-time recommendation functionality based on observing a series of user-system interactions. The perceived quality of the group recommendations was evaluated by a user study, and the obtained results showed that the proposed model is able to enhance the perceived group recommendation quality [20].

4.3 Simulating group discussions

While the user study was important to understand whether the proposed recommendation model and GUI are effective and well accepted by users, it was insufficient to thoroughly evaluate its performance, which must be examined under the different conditions that users are likely to experience in a group setting. Thus, we have taken a step further by designing a simulation process to analyze the efficacy of the proposed preference and recommendation model. We studied the effect of alternative settings of the parameter that is used to balance the preference knowledge elicited before and during the group interaction in three user situations. We have considered three kinds of social impacts on users' behavior: (a) *independence* - the group has no effect on the user preferences, (b) *conversion* - the group setting nudges group members to be more similar to each other, and (c) *anti-conformity* - the group setting causes group members to react negatively. In particular, we simulated items that users propose to their group together with their evaluations for other members' proposals in the three situations. It is noteworthy that the proposed items and users' evaluations were simulated differently according to each situation.

We hypothesize that the optimal combination between long-term and session-specific preferences could vary according to specific conditions. We measure the quality of the top-N recommended items for a group, calculate the similarity between the top recommended item and the assumed group choice, and monitor how the utility of the top recommendation changes when the amount of elicited preferences grows. The offline experiments on simulated data have illustrated that the proposed model is able to correctly capture the changes in user preferences and shows some fundamental properties of long-term and session-based preference fusion in group recommendations.

4.4 User interface design

STSGroup (South Tyrol Suggests for Group) is a mobile app that we developed in order to support the process of making decision in groups [20]. It extends the STS app [6], a context-aware places of interest (POIs) recommender originally devoted to individuals. STSGroup targets the discussion stage, where group members' preferences can be elicited and shaped. Particularly, it facilitates the decision making process by allowing group members to join a group chat environment where they can express opinions through text messages and evaluations (see Figure 1a). Based on their actions, the system supports various tasks that the users are likely to undertake during the decision making process, such as comparing options or asking for recommendations (see Figure 1b).

The results of a user study showed that the usability of our system is better than the benchmark and the majority of users found it easy to understand and use.

5 FUTURE WORK

In order to address the first research question (Sec. 2.1), we will investigate techniques for learning individual and group features while observing the users' behavior in various group sessions. Based on the observation and learned characteristics, we will predict the situation of a group. Regarding the second goal (Sec. 2.2), we plan to test and refine the proposed preference revision and aggregation model in group recommendations with more diverse simulation conditions, such as the presence of a dominant member in a group, and with other datasets. For the last research question (Sec. 2.3), we plan to make our current system proactive by adapting the interaction to the specific condition of the group. We also intend to carry out a user study to observe the effects of this adaptivity on user experiences in a group decision making process.

REFERENCES

[1] Liliana Ardissono, Anna Goy, Giovanna Petrone, Marino Segnan, and Pietro Torasso. 2003. Intrigue: personalized recommendation of tourist attractions for desktop and hand held devices. *Applied Artificial Intelligence* 17(8-9) (2003), 687–714.

[2] Linas Baltrunas, Tadas Makcinskas, and Francesco Ricci. 2010. Group recommendations with rank aggregation and collaborative filtering. In *Proceedings of the 4th ACM conference on Recommender systems*. 119–126.

[3] Shlomo Berkovsky and Jill Freyne. 2010. Group-based recipe recommendations: analysis of data aggreagation strategies. In *Proceedings of the 4th ACM conference on Recommender systems*. 111–118.

[4] Henry Blanco and Francesco Ricci. 2013. Inferring user utility for query revision recommendation. In *Proceedings of the 28th ACM Symposium on Applied Computing*. 245–252.

[5] Ludovico Boratto and Salvatore Carta. 2015. The rating prediction task in a group recommender system that automatically detects groups: architectures, algorithms, and performance evaluation. *Journal of Intelligent Information Systems* 45(2) (2015), 221–245.

[6] Matthias Braunhofer, Mehdi Elahi, Francesco Ricci, and Thomas Schievenin. 2013. Context-aware points of interest suggestion with dynamic weather data management. In *Information and communication technologies in tourism 2014*. 87–100.

[7] Li Chen, Marco de Gemmis, Alexander Felfernig, Pasquale Lops, Francesco Ricci, and Giovanni Semeraro. 2013. Human decision making and recommender systems. *ACM Transactions on Interactive Intelligent Systems* 3(3) (2013), 17.

[8] Amra Delic, Julia Neidhardt, Thuy Ngoc Nguyen, and Francesco Ricci. 2016. Research methods for group recommender systems. In *Proceedings of RecTour*.

[9] Amra Delic, Julia Neidhardt, Thuy Ngoc Nguyen, Francesco Ricci, Laurens Rook, Hannes Werthner, and Markus Zanker. 2016. Observing Group Decision Making Processes. In *Proceedings of the 10th ACM Conference on Recommender Systems*. 147–150.

[10] Donelson R. Forsyth. 2014. *Group Dynamics* (6th ed.). Wadsworth Cengage Learning.

[11] Francesca Guzzi, Francesco Ricci, and Robin Burke. 2011. Interactive multi-party critiquing for group recommendation. In *Proceedings of the 5th ACM Conference on Recommender systems*. 265–268.

[12] Anthony Jameson. 2004. More than the sum of its members: challenges for group recommender systems. In *Proceedings of the working conference on Advanced visual interfaces*. 48–54.

[13] Anthony Jameson and Barry Smyth. 2007. Recommendation to Groups. *The Adaptive Web, LNCS* 4321 (2007), 596–627.

[14] Bart P. Knijnenburg, Niels JM Reijmer, and Martijn C. Willemsen. 2011. Each to his own: how different users call for different interaction methods in recommender systems. In *Proceedings of the 5th ACM conference on Recommender systems*. 141–148.

[15] Henry Lieberman, Neil Van Dyke, and Adriana Vivacqua. 1999. Let's browse: a collaborative browsing agent. *Knowledge-Based Systems* 12(8) (1999), 427–431.

[16] Tariq Mahmood and Francesco Ricci. 2007. Learning and adaptivity in interactive recommender systems. In *Proceedings of the 9th international conference on Electronic commerce*. 75–84.

[17] Jesus Omar Alvarez Marquez and Jurgen Ziegler. 2016. Hootle+: A Group Recommender System Supporting Preference Negotiation. In *CYTED-RITOS International Workshop on Groupware*. 151–166.

[18] Judith Masthoff. 2015. Group recommender systems: aggregation, satisfaction and group attributes. In *Recommender Systems Handbook* (2nd ed.), F. Ricci, L. Rokach, and B. Shapira (Eds.). Springer, 743–776.

[19] Kevin McCarthy, Lorraine McGinty, Barry Smyth, and Maria Salamo. 2006. The needs of the many: a case-based group recommender system. In *European Conference on Case-Based Reasoning*. 196–210.

[20] Thuy Ngoc Nguyen and Francesco Ricci. 2017. Dynamic Elicitation of User Preferences in a Chat-Based Group Recommender System. In *Proceedings of the 32nd ACM Symposium on Applied Computing*.

[21] Mark O'connor, Dan Cosley, Joseph A. Konstan, and John Riedl. 2001. PolyLens: a recommender system for groups of users. In *Proceeding of the 7th conference on European Conference on Computer Supported Cooperative Work*. 199 – 218.

[22] Francesco Ricci, Lior Rokach, and Bracha Shapira. 2015. Recommender systems: introduction and challenges. In *Recommender Systems Handbook* (2nd ed.). Springer US, 1–34.

[23] Martin Stettinger, Alexander Felfernig, Gerhard Leitner, Stefan Reiterer, and Michael Jeran. 2015. Counteracting serial position effects in the CHOICLA group decision support environment. In *Proceedings of the 20th International Conference on Intelligent User Interfaces*. 148–157.

[24] R. Scott Tindale and Tatsuya Kameda. 2000. Social sharedness as a unifying theme for information processing in groups. *Group Processes and Intergroup Relations* 3(2) (2000), 123–140.

[25] Walid Trabelsi, Nic Wilson, Derek Bridge, and Francesco Ricci. 2010. Comparing approaches to preference dominance for conversational recommenders. In *Proceedings of the 22nd IEEE International Conference on Tools with Artificial Intelligence*. 113–120.

Smart Technology for Supporting Dance Education

Augusto Dias Pereira dos Santos
Building J12, The University of Sydney
NSW 2006, Australia
Augusto.Dias@sydney.edu.au

ABSTRACT

My PhD project sits in the design space that investigates how smart technology can support dance education. My aim is to design, implement and evaluate a conceptual and technological solution that captures students' movement using wearable devices and help dance teachers and students enhance their awareness and promote reflection regarding dance skills acquisition using automated personalised feedback (charts, tables, text, etc.). I will explore how to acquire movement data that can represent key aspects of social dance learning, and how to use these data to support of students and teachers. For this, I created a mobile app that records students' movement while they are practicing dance exercises and creates a dance learner model. The learner model's features are exposed through the Open Learner Model to students and their teachers in order to support reflection and increase awareness. With the proposed work I expect to generate a deeper understanding of the aspects of the dance learner model which can be used to promote personalization and adaptation, and positively impact dance learning.

KEYWORDS

open learner model; automatic feedback; wearable devices; dance education; motor learning

1 INTRODUCTION

Research in personalised education technologies has largely focused on domains where people perform learning tasks by interacting with and through personal computers [3,18]. Traditionally, students interact with devices like computers and tablets using mouse, keyboard and touch interactions. This way the systems can infer the behaviour of students while using learning platforms. The student models that can be derived from clickstreams can provide hints about student's learning. This can serve to adapt the system to support students by performing automated personalised actions and providing feedback [16]. By contrast, motor learning scenarios, such as learning to dance, to practice sports or using manual tools, require other ways of

recording students' learning and progress. Students need to learn movements and use the space in specific forms, depending on the activity, in which clicks and keystrokes would not be enough to generate a meaningful learner model [9]. With the advances in wearable and mobile technologies, there is a potential opportunity to support motor learning, especially when combined with machine learning, personalisation and adaptive systems. This gap of technology support for motor learning was highlighted by Santos [18] in a recent work.

Social dance education is one of the various motor learning activities that could benefit from the emergence of new multimodal, wearable and tracking technologies. As in any learning scenarios, there are many challenges that could be addressed using technology, which could support teaching and learning dance. In a dance class, teachers may have to manage dozens of students at the same time. As a result, the feedback provided to the students is limited and often incomplete [8]. User modelling and wearables technology, together, could be applied to diminishing this problem, enhancing the teachers' awareness about the students, using students' learning and progress data, and also alleviating the teacher providing initial feedback for students automatically.

Learning to dance involves many psychomotor and cognitive challenges. Two of the most important challenges for novice dance learners are the ability to listen and interpret the song (musical skills) and being able to consciously move each part of their bodies, according to the teachers' instructions (motor skills) [2]. These two challenges come together for the students when they need to move their body according to the songs' rhythm. Some students may struggle to acquire musical skills, while others may have difficulties with motor skills. These issues can be overcome with repeated practice to improve music listening and motor coordination [2]. However, when students practice at home, they do not get any feedback regarding their performance, which can frustrate them and deter them from practising. User modelling approaches can be helpful to identify and model students' dancing problems, guide them to tailored exercises, provide automated feedback and enable them to practice without the presence of a teacher. Teachers can also have benefits, accessing the data that is exposed through the Open Learner Model (OLM), and reflect one how to improve or change their intervention in the classroom. The OLM here, consist in different ways of representing the user model, such as summaries, visualisations, dashboard, etc.

In this work, I plan to explore how data science and wearable technology can capture the students learning process in the context of social dance education, and which information is needed to support teaching and learning social dance with user modelling and automated personalised feedback. For this, I develop a system that students can use to practice dancing exercises while tracking their movement in the background. I will investigate different aspects of dancing that can be detected using wearable technology, explore different ways of exploiting this information to support students' learning and investigating different forms of presenting the data collected back to teachers and students using visualisations and other data representations. In short, the contribution of my work is to study how technology can be used to capture data from dance students, model relevant features of dance learning and exploit these data to increase students' and teachers' awareness, using automated feedback and the OLM.

2 RELATED WORK

Support for motor learning. Emerging sensing technologies are allowing researchers to investigate learning in the physical spaces [14,18]. In one study, authors placed accelerometer in the wrists and waist of students to understand the learning process of playing a samba percussion instrument [15]. They used the data collected from students' movement as a form of feedback to promote students' awareness. Students that visualised their movement compared with the instructor learn better than students that receive just a performance evaluation. In the same field of learning musical instruments, a system was created to help piano students diagnose hand coordination problems [6]. Using accelerometers attached to hands, wrists and arms of the students, the system translates the data into textual feedback and visual cues, comparing teacher's and student's performance. The system is able to provide valuable feedback, but the visualisations were difficult to be understood by musicians.

Sports practice is another field that is adopting technology to enhance learning. Researchers have explored activities like snowboard training [20], squats [17] and biceps curl exercise [11] and have used wearable devices such as accelerometers, bend and pressure sensors. Although I have identified theses several attempts to enhance motor learning scenarios through data modelling, there is a somewhat distinguishable agreement that we still are far away from understanding the most effective mechanisms for providing feedback for these physical activities.

Technology to enhance dance education. In the dance domain, researchers have used similar approaches to model and support learning. In one study, authors used a transducer, attached to the student's shoes, to help students in learning rhythm while dancing [5]. The sensors' data were automatically analysed. The system then triggered acoustic feedback to inform students if they were dancing out of the rhythm. Students liked this system, but this was only able to identify mistakes that happened on the first beat of a bar (strong beat). My approach is able to overcome this problem, detecting mistakes in any part of the song. Similarly, in the context of ballet dancing, researchers used accelerometers to model ballet postures and exercises to then compare experts and non-experts participants [7,21]. They placed many accelerometers in participants' bodies in order to

evaluate how motion metrics measured in different parts of the body correlate with the performance in different types of exercises and postures. This approach illustrates the promising outcomes that user modelling and motion sensors can generate to enhance motor learning spaces.

Other attempts to enhance dance classes with technology include: using of augmented feedback (tactile, video, sound) for learning dance choreographies [4]; combining motion capture, augmented reality, telepresence and electro-active polymer clothing to create an immersive dance experience [19]; and, a game that teaches traditional Greek dance using multiple depth sensors [10]. My approach goes beyond previous studies by aiming to create a solution that is unobtrusive, cheap and allow massive adoption using smartphones. I intend to elicit, from social dance experts what a dance learner model should contain in order to pinpoint the critical aspects of social dance learning. Then, I will explore the best ways to provide actionable feedback that can enhance awareness and provoke reflection for dance learners and their teachers.

Technologies to enhance teaching. One of the focus of my research is to provide information (summaries, visualisations, dashboard, etc.) to enhance teachers' awareness and increase their ability to help students. For example, Maldonado et al. [13] create a visualisation that shows to the teacher, in real-time, information about students during a collaborative activity. Similarly, a study [12] develop a tutoring system that enables teachers to track students' progress and identify learning stages and common problems in groups of students. These approaches demonstrate that data can be used not only to enhance students learning but also to increase teacher's capability of supporting students. I intend to use the OLM to expose the students' information and enhance teachers' interventions and pedagogy.

3 PROPOSED RESEARCH

I propose to design, implement and evaluate a conceptual and technological solution that has two main parts: 1) captures students' movement and body motion using wearable devices and 2) exploit these data to help dance teachers and students in enhancing their awareness and reflection regarding rhythm skill acquisition using automated personalised feedback and the data exposed by the OLM. My work seeks to answer the following research questions:

- Which information is important to be in the dance learner model that can help in increasing students and teachers awareness regarding rhythm skill acquisition?
- How can the information identified in the above research question be captured and extracted from student's movements using wearable devices?
- How to create an ecosystem that can provide automated personalised feedback to increase awareness and enhance the dialogue between teachers and students in dance education?
- What type of automated feedback is most useful in the context of personalised dance learning?

3.1 Dance Learning Ecosystem

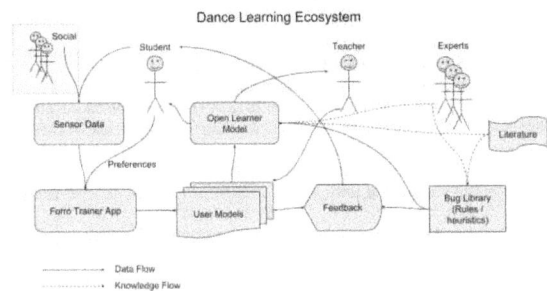

Figure 1: Components of Dance Learning Ecosystem.

I propose to address these questions through an approach that I have named the Dance Learning Ecosystem, which includes the dance learner, his/her peers, the teacher and technology in the feedback loop. The focus of the dance learning ecosystem is primarily to create an environment that can enhance the dialogue between students and the teacher. The main point of this dialogue is understanding what is expected from the students to learn and how they can achieve their goals by their own means. This strategy is based on the concepts of Self-Regulated Learning and sustainable feedback [1].

As shown in Fig. 1 there are three human roles in this ecosystem: **the student**, who use the system to generate data about their performance; **the teacher**, who uses the data collected to enhance their interventions; **the experts**, who feed the system with knowledge. Potentially the social aspect (**student's peers**), defined by the social interactions among students between themselves inside the classroom, also can be integrated into this ecosystem. This last aspect is not in the scope of this work.

In the technology side, the components present in this ecosystem are: **the mobile app**, Forró Trainer, which uses accelerometer and gyroscope to record students' movements and provide an interface to guide the students into different exercises and provide the appropriate feedback, using the Open Learner Model (OLM); **a web interface**, that displays the students' data (OLM) to the teacher; **the dance learner model**, which contains the students' data that are used to guide the student and display **the feedback** (charts, tables, text, etc.) based also on **the bug library** (list of common dancing mistakes), where the rules and actions of the system are stored. The teacher can also contribute to the user model generating expert samples to be compared with the students.

An example of how the movement data looks like is shown in Fig. 2. In this sample, the student is performing the correct movement and synchronised with the song (see blue peaks/valleys and beat number 1). In the middle of the sample, the student made a mistake (red line). After the mistake, the student recovers to the correct movement, but in the wrong beat of the song (orange peaks/valleys and beat number 3). I aim to perform this type of analysis automatically to generate formative and actionable feedback to support students in learning how to

dance. Teachers could use this information to plan different activities or understand which students need more attention.

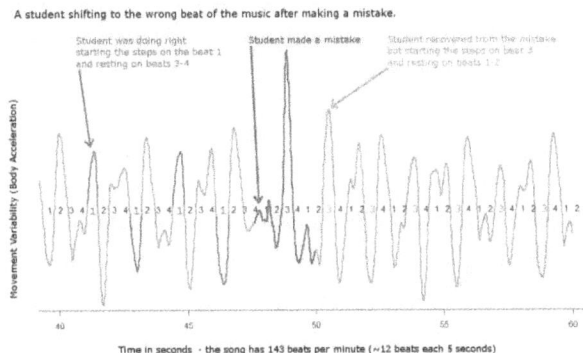

Figure 2: Sample of student movement data. Blue, correct movement; Red, a mistake; Orange, student in the wrong beat.

3.2 Methodology

In this thesis, I am focusing on rhythm learning, identified in the literature and by teachers as one of the most important aspects of dance learning [2].

The **first phase** of this research was to understand the role of rhythm learning in dance education, how dance teachers typically help their students learn it in large and small classes, what common problems they encounter and the feedback strategies they deploy. This was done through interviews with teachers. The **second phase** was to build and evaluate the accuracy of a rhythm detection algorithm. This was carried out by video-recording participants, with an auxiliary camera, while they were using the mobile app in their pocket and comparing the app result with experts.

In the **third phase**, combining the teacher interviews' outcome and the rhythm detection algorithm, I developed a mobile app that provides exercises to the students for practising individually, initially with a very basic feedback approach. I ran a lab study with 10 students, testing the app usability and collecting data in order to investigate different ways of presenting the information to the participant. Students then evaluate the different data representations. This phase also started gathering the elements of the dance learner model, choosing which features (from the data) are relevant to be stored in the model.

The **fourth phase** will be dedicated to shaping up the app to build the system I envisage, with an open learner model and data-driven feedback. I will create a bug library that generates specific feedback using rules triggered by the student's current performance data and the information stored in the dance learner model. The feedback rules are to deliver diagnosis and actionable feedback to improve the learning process. The bug library will be evaluated with teachers regarding its clarity, usefulness and correctness. Using focus groups with teachers, advanced and beginner students, this phase will use a co-design approach to improving the Open Learner Model, with narrative, storytelling and visualisations. The purpose of the OLM is to support reflection and awareness of students and teachers.

In the **fifth phase**, I will deploy, using a crossover study design, the improved and redesigned version of the app (from the fourth phase outcomes) in one dance school, focusing on evaluating the impact from the students' perspective. I plan to investigate if the app, the feedback rules and the OLM promote more awareness and reflection opportunities than with no app support. The outcomes of this phase will also be used to improve the app.

The **sixth phase** focuses evaluating the impact from the teachers' perspective. I plan to deploy the app and the ecosystem in several dance schools or studios. I plan to compare current teachers' method for assisting and remember students' profiles and difficulties. Currently, teachers use paper, tablets, video or just memory to keep track of their students. Does the app increase teachers' ability to track their students as well as teachers awareness?

A **seventh phase** will run in parallel with the phase 4-6. It focuses on the data, investigating how to design a recommender system that can adapt the app exercises based on the user, providing a tailored learning approach. This phase will be continuously used to improve the app, the feedback rules and the OLM.

3.3 Contributions

I expect to achieve the following contributions in this work:

- The methodology for evaluating how technology can support teacher and students of motor learning fields.
- The Ecosystem for enhancing awareness and reflection in Dance Education
- Algorithm to detect rhythm in dance students, using wearable devices
- Dance Learner Model and Open Learner Model
- Bug Library: Feedback Rules and Actions.

4 PROGRESS

So far I have concluded phases 1, 2 and 3. I interviewed 13 Forró dance teachers from different countries to understand their needs and how they see the role of rhythm in dance education. Teachers all agree that rhythm is important but have different methodologies to share this knowledge. In terms of feedback, the students' motivation is an important factor in choosing the proper strategy for providing feedback. For that reason, I plan to include students' preferences as part of the dance learner model.

The algorithm accuracy was compared with experts and I achieve better results in cases where the experts agree. In cases where the experts do not have unanimous decisions, the algorithm performs worst.

During the lab study in phase 3, we found that the app was easy to use and the data represented back to the students were very simple and we demonstrated that some students were able to reflect on their performance, especially regarding the number of times they practice.

REFERENCES

[1] David Carless, Diane Salter, Min Yang, and Joy Lam, 2011. Developing sustainable feedback practices. *Studies in Higher Education 36*, 4 (2011/06/01), 395-407.

[2] Paulette Côté-Laurence, 2000. The role of rhythm in ballet training. *Research in Dance Education 1*, 2, 173-191.

[3] Michel C Desmarais and Ryan S Baker, 2012. A review of recent advances in learner and skill modeling in intelligent learning environments. *User Modeling and User-Adapted Interaction 22*, 1-2, 9-38.

[4] Dieter Drobny and Jan Borchers, 2010. Learning basic dance choreographies with different augmented feedback modalities. In *CHI'10 Extended Abstracts on Human Factors in Computing Systems* ACM, 3793-3798.

[5] Dieter Drobny, Malte Weiss, and Jan Borchers, 2009. Saltate!: a sensor-based system to support dance beginners. In *CHI'09 Extended Abstracts on Human Factors in Computing Systems* ACM, 3943-3948.

[6] Aristotelis Hadjakos, Erwin Aitenbichler, and Max Mühlhäuser, 2008. Syssomo: A pedagogical tool for analyzing movement variants between different pianists.

[7] Christopher W Hinton-Lewis, Elle McDonough, Gene M Moyle, and David V Thiel, 2016. An Assessment of Postural Sway in Ballet Dancers During First Position, Relevé and Sauté with Accelerometers. *Procedia Engineering 147*, 127-132.

[8] Lu-Ho Hsia, Iwen Huang, and Gwo-Jen Hwang, 2016. Effects of different online peer-feedback approaches on students' performance skills, motivation and self-efficacy in a dance course. *Computers & Education 96*(5//), 55-71.

[9] David Kirsh, 2013. Embodied cognition and the magical future of interaction design. *ACM Trans. Comput.-Hum. Interact. 20*, 1, 1-30.

[10] Alexandros Kitsikidis, Kosmas Dimitropoulos, Deniz Uğurca, Can Bayçay, Erdal Yilmaz, Filareti Tsalakanidou, Stella Douka, and Nikos Grammalidis, 2015. A Game-like Application for Dance Learning Using a Natural Human Computer Interface. In *International Conference on Universal Access in Human-Computer Interaction* Springer, 472-482.

[11] Yousef Kowsar, Masud Moshtaghi, Eduardo Velloso, Lars Kulik, and Christopher Leckie, 2016. Detecting unseen anomalies in weight training exercises. In *Proceedings of the 28th Australian Conference on Computer-Human Interaction* ACM, 517-526.

[12] Leanna Lesta and Kalina Yacef, 2002. An Intelligent Teaching Assistant System for Logic. In *Intelligent Tutoring Systems: 6th International Conference, ITS 2002 Biarritz, France and San Sebastian, Spain, June 2–7, 2002 Proceedings*, S.A. CERRI, G. GOUARDÈRES and F. PARAGUAÇU Eds. Springer Berlin Heidelberg, Berlin, Heidelberg, 421-431.

[13] Roberto Martinez Maldonado, Judy Kay, Kalina Yacef, and Beat Schwendimann, 2012. An interactive teacher's dashboard for monitoring groups in a multi-tabletop learning environment. In *International Conference on Intelligent Tutoring Systems* Springer, 482-492.

[14] Roberto Martinez-Maldonado, Davinia Hernandez-Leo, Abelardo Pardo, and Hiroaki Ogata, 2017. Cross-LAK: learning analytics across physical and digital spaces. In *Proceedings of the 7th International Conference on Learning Analytics & Knowledge*.

[15] Kohei Matsumura, Tomoyuki Yamamoto, and Tsutomu Fujinami, 2011. The role of body movement in learning to play the shaker to a samba rhythm: An exploratory study. *Research Studies in Music Education 33*, 1 (June 1, 2011), 31-45.

[16] Gordon McCalla, Julita Vassileva, Jim Greer, and Susan Bull, 2000. Active Learner Modelling, 53-62.

[17] Kim Oakes, Katie A. Siek, and Haley MacLeod, 2015. MuscleMemory: identifying the scope of wearable technology in high intensity exercise communities. In *Proceedings of the Proceedings of the 9th International Conference on Pervasive Computing Technologies for Healthcare* (Istanbul, Turkey2015), ICST (Institute for Computer Sciences, Social-Informatics and Telecommunications Engineering), 2826193, 193-200.

[18] Olga C. Santos, 2016. Training the Body: The Potential of AIED to Support Personalized Motor Skills Learning. *International Journal of Artificial Intelligence in Education 26*, 2, 730-755.

[19] Vidhu V Saxena, Tommy Feldt, and Mohit Goel, 2014. Augmented Telepresence as a Tool for Immersive Simulated Dancing in Experience and Learning. In *Proceedings of the India HCI 2014 Conference on Human Computer Interaction* ACM, 86.

[20] Daniel Spelmezan and Jan Borchers, 2008. Real-time snowboard training system. In *CHI'08 Extended Abstracts on Human Factors in Computing Systems* ACM, 3327-3332.

[21] David V Thiel, Julian Quandt, Sarah JL Carter, and Gene Moyle, 2014. Accelerometer based performance assessment of basic routines in classical ballet. *Procedia Engineering 72*, 14-19.

4

Harnessing Virtual Reality Exergames and Physical Fitness Sensing to Create a Personalised Game and Dashboard

Soojeong Yoo
University of Sydney
Sydney, NSW 2006
syoo6624@uni.sydney.edu.au

ABSTRACT

Exercise is important for health and well-being. However, for many people, it can be hard to find the time or motivation to get the recommended amount of exercise. It has recently become apparent that virtual reality exergames, have the potential to address this problem, by helping people stay motivated to exercise. This research explores how to harness the motivating power of virtual reality exergames to support long-term physical activity. We do this by creating an infrastructure that captures data from virtual reality games, with physical data captured by sensors, then using this to provide a personal dashboard of in-game exertion and measures of fitness.

KEYWORDS

User Modeling; Exergames; Virtual Reality

1 INTRODUCTION

Motivating people to exercise is challenging even though it has health benefits. For example, exercise, even for 10 minutes, can have valuable cognitive benefits, temporarily increasing concentration [14]. Exercise also has a key role in reducing risks of cardio-vascular disease and some cancers[23]. However, according to the US National Heart, Lung and Blood institute [17], factors such as lifestyle, lack of nearby safe recreational facilities, health conditions, and age contribute to lack of activity.

Virtual Reality (VR) exergaming is a promising way to motivate people to become more active and help overcome sedentary lifestyles [14]. VR exergames provide immersive virtual worlds that could potentially distract distract players from the exercise and make it more fun [2, 21]. In particular, a study by Yoo el al. [26] demonstrated that playing VR games can provide a good level of exertion. However, without tailored exercise, players risk over-exerting themselves, which could cause significant health problems [9]. Personalisation could be a way to overcome such problems, as both game recommendation and within-game personalisation could make VR games more effective in delivering exercise while being enjoyable. This type of personalisation requires a user model that represents key aspects of the player, such as their game and exercise preferences, fitness, and exercise goals. Viewing long-term progress would also be useful as it has shown to motivate people towards reaching their set exercise goals.

This research builds upon the previous work on VR exergames, by harnessing the data from the multiple exergames a player may play over time. We will create an infrastructure that combines this with sensor data such as steps taken, heart rate and muscles activated. All this user data will be stored in a personally controlled long term user model [1] based on both game activity and the corresponding exertion level. This user model can play two particularly important roles. First, we will use it to drive a long term exercise and fitness dashboard that can give users a new form of feedback on their long term progress, and be part of long term reflection and self-monitoring and goal-setting for exercise. The second role is to drive personalisation of a VR game, to ensure the right level of challenge for the user's current goals. This research aims to make three main contributions.

- The first is the infrastructure for building a personally controlled user model of exercise and exertion, based on multiple games and sensors.
- The second is the design and evaluation of a dashboard which enables a user to explore that data in a form that shows their long term progress in terms of fitness and exertion, and how this relates to multiple VR exergames played.
- The third is the use of the same data for in-game feedback.

2 PRIOR WORK

This section reviews key types of exergames and their evaluations, drawing on both commercial systems and research studies, with a focus on the nature of the data relevant to a long-term user model for physical activity. We also explore previous work on personalised exergames and contrast how our research extends and differs from that. Finally, we discuss exertion and how previous work on exergames has measured it and the implications for a long-term user model for physical activity in VR.

2.1 Non-VR exergames

Although the exergames described in this section are not fully-immersive, there is still much that can be learned from them. The Nintendo Wii gaming console has been very popular for sport games in particular, utilising accessories such as the Wiimote and the balance board. Much of the research on the Nintendo Wii's fitness applications has focused on the elderly[16, 18]. The balance board accessory in particular has been an effective tool for helping the elderly regain or improve their balance, thus preventing falls from occurring [5]. This is useful tool for clinicians as it can aid in

UMAP '17, July 09-12, 2017, Bratislava, Slovakia
© 2017 ACM. ISBN 978-1-4503-4635-1/17/07...$15.00.
DOI: http://dx.doi.org/10.1145/3079628.3079710

improving dynamic balance and balance confidence in the elderly. Similarly the Microsoft Kinect, with its depth sensing camera for the PC, Xbox 360 & One, can track a user's whole body and detect certain gestures. It features a number of fitness games utilising the sensor[10].

The Kinect has also been demonstrated as a viable method to track and help improve skills of dancers. Research by Chan et al. [3] concluded that using a HMD would have been a better choice for their dance training system as the screen was not always in line-of-sight as some dance moves performed involved spinning around. Another Kinect-based system found not only to promote physical activity but also promising psychological results. The study tested their system called Astrojumper [6] with autistic and non-autistic children to motivate them to exercise. Their system was setup with three large rear-projected displays partially surrounding the user. The game is set in space, with the aim to dodge incoming virtual objects by jumping, ducking and swerving.

Games do not necessarily need to be designed for exercise to be considered as exergames, provided the input controllers can be modified to accept external sensors, such as using the Kinect to control a character in the World of Warcraft online game [19], which is traditionally played using a keyboard and mouse. Another example [4] utilised a Kinect and tracked the user's movement while they were playing the game, gradually making the screen darker if the player did not physically move around enough.

2.2 VR exergames

Exergaming is a term that is defined as a combination of video games and physical interaction instead of sedentary interaction. External devices can be used to feed input into a game. In one game, players ride through a virtual world using an Oculus Rift [21]. Interaction was achieved using a combination of an exercise bike that the player could physically pedal to traverse through the virtual world and a Kinect to detect motion, such as leaning and ducking to avoid obstacles. The results of the study indicated that the game significantly increased the participant's enjoyment and motivation compared to traditional desktop VR. Recently, work by Tuveri et al [25] utilised an exercycle and an Oculus Rift where they used gamification aspects such as trophies to motivate players. Another exercycle game [7] provided players with a multiplayer tank game, where players needed to capture the other team's flag, while avoiding being shot by enemy players.

Some exergames do not need to use large and expensive equipment. Research by Tregillus and Folmer [24] demonstrated that sensing steps using an accelerometer brings the cost down for VR experiences while enabling it to also be portable. Another study by Yoo and Kay [27] has explored VR exergame made for the Google Cardboard testing a prototype with running-in-place detected by a smartphone accelerometer.

2.3 Personalised exergames

Previous work on VR exergames has also found the need for personalization to deliver appropriate exercises to individuals and making the game progressively more challenging to keep people engaged [7]. Work by Sinclair et al. [22] proposed taking account of both

how attractive the user found the game and the player's physiological state, balancing the game challenge and exercise intensity. Other work by Hardy et al. [8] used a similar model but it also took the user's calendar into account to adjust the intensity of the exercise.

2.4 Personalisation and Dashboard

User modelling provides the foundation knowledge about a particular user to personalise the results [13]. This method has is used by major websites such as Google, Facebook and Amazon to recommend advertisements, search results, and products to their users.

Personalisation methods such as user modelling are also used in video games and could be applied to virtual reality experiences, particularly exergames. Recent work personalised an infinite Mario game's level in segments based on the player's performance and in-game behaviour [12]. However, in the case of exergames, an individual's characteristics or properties could also be used, such as their age, gender, height, weight, and heart rate. Work by Kang [11] proposed a model for personalisation that uses the information from the human body to prescribe appropriate exercises, which users can perform while wearing a HMD. Other work also by Shaw [20], implemented a virtual reality exergame with the Oculus Rift and an exercycle. It was personalised based on heart rate, where the virtual trainer would slow down if the exercise became too intense or if the player slowed down. The virtual trainer would send motivating messages to the player during the exercise to encourage them to work harder.

In our work, a user model is a set of beliefs about a user [15] and this is based on a store of personal data from multiple sources, including heart rate sensor to determine a user's heart rate zone, step counter, and muscles activated through smart clothing. The heart rate of the user will be determined from a chest strap that transmit live heart rate data.

2.5 Measuring exertion

Measuring the intensity of an exercise experience in VR exergames allows us to determine the health benefits it may provide. Typically, exertion can be measured in two ways, through actual exertion or perceived exertion. Actual exertion is usually measured by someone's heart-rate through chest, wrist, or ear heart-rate monitors. Perceived exertion is measured through a Borg questionnaire after the exercise, where people mark on a scale answers to questions related to how they feel. The Borg questionnaire can later be mapped to actual heart-rate, where we can contrast the two together, as it could be the case that someone had a high heart-rate during their exercise, indicating high exertion, but their perception is much less.

3 GAP AND RESEARCH QUESTIONS

Although much work has been conducted in the area of exergaming, there is little work on VR exergames and how the experiences can be adapted based on health data. In this research I propose that VR exergames are harnessed for modelling long-term physical activity preferences and recommendations for workouts based on data gained through physical activity sensors. The plan is to then use such a model in multiple games and visualise them in a fitness

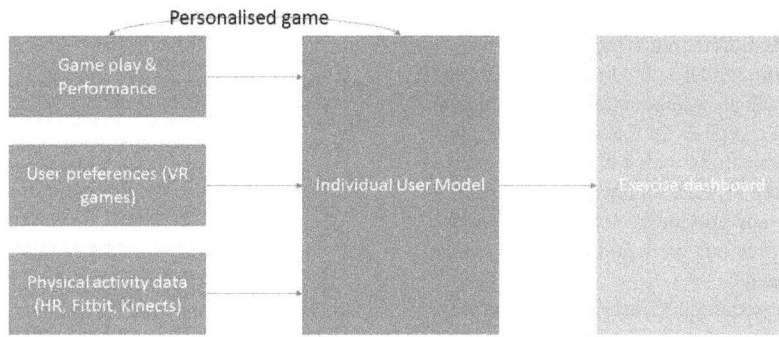

Figure 1: Personalised exercise architecture for long-term physical activity in VR games

dashboard where people can keep track of their progress over the long-term. In addition to creating a user model, I will also explore adding personalisation aspects within a VR exergame and test its effectiveness.

Therefore, to guide this research I ask the following questions:

(1) How can we create an infrastructure that enables a person harness data about their activity in multiple VR exergames and physiological and activity sensors?

(2) How can a dashboard be designed to show long-term progress of multiple VR games and other activities?

(3) How can the user model (health data and user progress used for the dashboard) be harnessed to personalise the VR exergame.

4 APPROACH AND PLAN

In this thesis, I will answer the previously defined research questions through different studies, shown in table 1. The table has four columns: the first describes the type of study and the year it is conducted and the second contains the name of the paper or activity. The last three columns are technology, literature review, and study. These are used to describe the type of activity, where the cells of these columns contain a tick if the activity is of that particular type.

My research started with an initial foundation study where I reviewed apps that were available at the time for Google Cardboard, categorised by their interaction method. There were five different interaction methods found: magnetic switch, instant gaze, dwelling gaze, tilt, and external controller[28]. This was published as a workshop paper in Spacial User Interaction (SUI) 2015.

In the following year, I started evaluating VR exergames, starting with one that I designed and developed called "VRun" for the Google Cardboard. I evaluated its effectiveness at providing exercise by running a lab study where participants were asked to test the prototype in three different display modes[27]. The main findings were that the VR exergame was preferred and that the game made people tired, showing potential at providing exercise. This work was published in OzCHI 2016 as a short paper.

In another study I evaluated the exertion provided by four HTC Vive exergames. I measured the actual and perceived exertion and found that exergames provide a significant amount of exertion and

Type / Time	Activity	Technology	Literature review	Study
Foundation studies (2015)	Controller-less Interaction Methods for Google Cardboard – (SUI'15)	✓		✓
	Review existing VR games that promote exercise		✓	
VR exergame studies (2016)	VRun: Running in place virtual reality exergame - (OZCHI'16)	✓		✓
	Evaluating the Actual and Perceived Exertion Provided by Virtual Reality Games – accepted as a LBW paper (CHI'17)		✓	✓
	Development VR running game using Google Cardboard and run a study	✓		
	Study existing VR exergames using HTC Vive and Heart-rate sensor		✓	
Long-term studies (2017)	Towards a long-term model of virtual reality exergame exertion – submitted as a long paper (UMAP'17)	✓		✓
	Complete prototype for in game personalisation.	✓		
	Systematic meta review for VR exergames		✓	
	Run a 6 weeks study where participants test the 4 game			✓

Table 1: Research timeline, each year top columns with darker color is paper publication

that their perceived exertion was less, possibly due the the immersiveness of VR and enjoyment of playing the games distracting them from the exercise[26]. This work was accepted as a work-in-progress paper at CHI 2017. I also used the data collected from the previous study to define a long-term user model and personalised exercise architecture (Figure 1) which was discussed and presented in a long paper accepted to UMAP 2017. One of the main findings was that people have different preferences and responses when it comes to both exercising and playing games, meaning that there are potential benefits from creating a user model for exergaming.

This could support various forms of personalisation, such as game recommenders, and personalisation within a game.

Future work will test the user model defined in the UMAP 2017 paper, where VR exergames will be recommended to participants based on their long-term data and goals. In this work we are planning to run 6 weeks (long-term) study with 4 different VR games where participants come to play VR games a few times a week and we will filled their data into our previously defined user-model. This work will extend upon previous work and will allow me to answer research questions 1 and 2.

In addition, I will build a personalised VR exergame for the HTC Vive. The game is personalised based on live health data, changing elements of the virtual world and the game's difficulty to match the skill and health of the player. So far, we managed to put the live heart rate data in the game scene. This work will be used to answer research question 3 as it focuses on personalisation within a game that I am designing and developing.

Finally, I also planning to explore more detailed literature review on VR exergames and find out what kind of methods and measurement people have been using.

ACKNOWLEDGMENTS

I would like to thank my supervisor, Judy Kay, for her guidance on this research.

REFERENCES

[1] Mark Assad, David J Carmichael, Judy Kay, and Bob Kummerfeld. 2007. PersonisAD: Distributed, Active, Scrutable Model Framework for Context-Aware Services. *Pervasive Computing* 4480 (2007), 55–72. DOI:http://dx.doi.org/10.1007/978-3-540-72037-9{_}4

[2] John Bolton, Mike Lambert, Denis Lirette, and Ben Unsworth. 2014. PaperDude: a virtual reality cycling exergame. In *CHI'14 Extended Abstracts on Human Factors in Computing Systems*. ACM, 475–478.

[3] J C P Chan, H Leung, J K T Tang, and T Komura. 2011. A Virtual Reality Dance Training System Using Motion Capture Technology. *IEEE Transactions on Learning Technologies* 4, 2 (2011), 187–195. DOI:http://dx.doi.org/10.1109/TLT.2010.27

[4] Anjana Chatta, Tyler Hurst, Gayani Samaraweera, Rongkai Guo, and John Quarles. Get off the Couch : An Approach to Utilize Sedentary Commercial Games as Exergames. (????), 47–56.

[5] Gustavo Duque, Derek Boersma, Griselda Loza-diaz, Sanobar Hassan, and Hamlet Suarez. 2013. Effects of balance training using a virtual-reality system in older fallers. (2013), 257–263.

[6] Samantha L Finkelstein, Andrea Nickel, and Evan A Suma. Astrojumper : Designing a Virtual Reality Exergame to Motivate Children with Autism to Exercise. (????).

[7] Kristoffer Hagen, Konstantinos Chorianopoulos, Alf Inge Wang, Letizia Jaccheri, and Stian Weie. 2016. Gameplay as Exercise. In *Proceedings of the 2016 CHI Conference Extended Abstracts on Human Factors in Computing Systems*. ACM, 1872–1878.

[8] Sandro Hardy, Stefan Göbel, Michael Gutjahr, Josef Wiemeyer, and Ralf Steinmetz. 2012. Adaptation model for indoor exergames. *Int J Comput Sci Sport* 11, 1 (2012), 73–85.

[9] William L Haskell, I-Min Lee, Russell R Pate, Kenneth E Powell, Steven N Blair, Barry A Franklin, Caroline A Macera, Gregory W Heath, Paul D Thompson, and Adrian Bauman. 2007. Physical activity and public health. Updated recommendation for adults from the American College of Sports Medicine and the American Heart Association. *Circulation* (2007).

[10] Maged N Kamel Boulos. 2012. Xbox 360 Kinect exergames for health. *Games for Health: Research, Development, and Clinical Applications* 1, 5 (2012), 326–330.

[11] Sun Young Kang, Kyung OcK Yi, Seung Ae Kang, and Ae Hyun Lee. 2016. Personalized Exercise Prescription Utilizing Virtual Fitness. In *Information Science and Applications (ICISA) 2016*. Springer, 1453–1458.

[12] Stephen Karpinskyj, Fabio Zambetta, and Lawrence Cavedon. 2014. Video game personalisation techniques: A comprehensive survey. *Entertainment Computing* 5, 4 (2014), 211–218.

[13] Judy Kay and Bob Kummerfeld. 2012. Creating personalized systems that people can scrutinize and control. *ACM Transactions on Interactive Intelligent Systems* 2, 4 (2012), 1–42. DOI:http://dx.doi.org/10.1145/2395123.2395129

[14] Matthew J. Klein and Christina S. Simmers. 2009. Exergaming: virtual inspiration, real perspiration. *Young Consumers: Insight and Ideas for Responsible Marketers* 10, 1 (2009), 35–45. DOI:http://dx.doi.org/10.1108/17473610910940774

[15] Alfred Kobsa. 2007. Generic user modeling systems. In *The adaptive web*. Springer, 136–154.

[16] Yocheved Laufer, Gali Dar, and Einat Kodesh. 2014. Does a Wii-based exercise program enhance balance control of independently functioning older adults? A systematic review. *Clinical Interventions in Aging* 9 (2014), 1803–1813. DOI:http://dx.doi.org/10.2147/CIA.S69673

[17] NIH. 2017. National Institute of Health. (2017). https://www.nhlbi.nih.gov/health/health-topics/topics/obe/causes

[18] Jungseo Park, Daehee Lee, and Sangyong Lee. 2014. Effect of virtual reality exercise using the nintendo wii fit on muscle activities of the trunk and lower extremities of normal adults. *Journal of physical therapy science* 26, 2 (2014), 271–273.

[19] Albert Skip Rizzo, Belinda Lange, Evan A Suma, and Mark Bolas. 2011. Virtual reality and interactive digital game technology: new tools to address obesity and diabetes. *Journal of diabetes science and technology* 5, 2 (2011), 256–264.

[20] LA Shaw, R Tourrel, BC Wunsche, and C Lutteroth. 2016. Design of a virtual trainer for exergaming. *Proceedings of the* (2016). DOI:http://dx.doi.org/10.1145/2843043.2843384

[21] Lindsay Alexander Shaw. 2014. *Development and evaluation of an exercycle game using immersive technologies*. Ph.D. Dissertation. The University of Auckland New Zealand.

[22] Jeff Sinclair, Philip Hingston, and Martin Masek. 2007. Considerations for the design of exergames. In *Proceedings of the 5th international conference on Computer graphics and interactive techniques in Australia and Southeast Asia*. ACM, 289–295.

[23] Paul D Thompson, David Buchner, Ileana L Piña, Gary J Balady, Mark A Williams, Bess H Marcus, Kathy Berra, Steven N Blair, Fernando Costa, Barry Franklin, Gerald F Fletcher, Neil F Gordon, Russell R Pate, Beatriz L Rodriguez, Antronette K Yancey, and Nanette K Wenger. 2003. Exercise and Physical Activity in the Prevention and Treatment of Atherosclerotic Cardiovascular Disease. (2003), 3109–3116. DOI:http://dx.doi.org/10.1161/01.CIR.0000075572.40158.77

[24] Sam Tregillus and Eelke Folmer. 2016. Vr-step: Walking-in-place using inertial sensing for hands free navigation in mobile vr environments. In *Proceedings of the 2016 CHI Conference on Human Factors in Computing Systems*. ACM, 1250–1255.

[25] Elena Tuveri, Luca Macis, Fabio Sorrentino, Lucio Davide Spano, and Riccardo Scateni. 2016. Fitmersive Games: Fitness Gamification through Immersive VR. In *Proceedings of the International Working Conference on Advanced Visual Interfaces*. ACM, 212–215.

[26] Soojeong Yoo, Christopher Ackad, Tristan Heywood, and Judy Kay. 2017. Evaluating the Actual and Perceived Exertion Provided by Virtual Reality Games. In *Proceedings of the 2017 CHI Conference Extended Abstracts on Human Factors in Computing Systems*. ACM, 3050–3057.

[27] Soojeong Yoo and Judy Kay. 2016. VRun: running-in-place virtual reality exergame. In *Proceedings of the 28th Australian Conference on Computer-Human Interaction*. ACM, 562–566.

[28] Soojeong Yoo and Callum Parker. 2015. Controller-less interaction methods for Google cardboard. In *Proceedings of the 3rd ACM Symposium on Spatial User Interaction*. ACM, 127–127.

Modelling User Behaviour based on Process

Mengdie Zhuang
University of Sheffield
Management School
Sheffield, UK
mzhuang1@sheffield.ac.uk

ABSTRACT

Search is designed primarily for human use, but we still lack efficient user models to evaluate search systems from the user's perspective. The purpose of this research is to identify user behaviour patterns during the search process, and develop a user model to illustrate the relationships between search behaviour and user perception, in order to predict user engagement in a cost-effective manner by using only behaviour data. To achieve this, we will use three datasets collected from previous studies containing both behavioural data from system log files and perception data. Ultimately, this research will yield a cost-efficient predictive model of user engagement that could be used to more effectively evaluate search systems.

1 INTRODUCTION

Searching for information in a myriad of systems and databases online is one of the most frequently executed task in daily and work life. A challenge that has challenged the research and professional communities for decades is how to evaluate an information retrieval (IR) system with the ultimate goal of optimising search services for users. Traditionally, search has been evaluated by system effectiveness(e.g., precision and recall). But that is only part of the story. Search is not only a single click, or just one result page; it is a dynamic, on-going process that usually consists of multiple interactions between the systems and the user. Currently, judging only from system effectiveness, we do not know whether the end-user uses or regards the highly ranked documents in the way that systems 'think' they are useful, and whether the user perceives the search experience was a positive one [26].

Instead of just system effectiveness, some studies have assessed user engagement, which is the quality of user experience of search, using two types of measures: user perception and user behaviour. However, neither of these two provide a comprehensive picture of search: user behaviour lacks the rationale behind certain actions, while collecting user perception data is time- and effort-consuming. I speculate that behaviour may indicate perception, and thus we should be able to gain a greater understanding of user engagement during search by examining both behaviour and perception measures. Therefore, in this project, I propose to identify user

behaviour patterns during the search process; discover the relationships between perception and behaviour; develop a user model to illustrate these relationships; and build a predictive model of user engagement based on the user model using relatively cost-effective behaviour measure. Ultimately, this research will augment the development of a cost-efficient predictive model of user engagement that would benefit both users and search service developers.

2 BACKGROUND AND RELATED WORK

2.1 Experience and Engagement

The third wave of HCI [5] shifted focus from technology for work to user experience (UX). Along with progress in searching algorithms, research interests in the IR field began to formulate user models that capture the pragmatism and pleasantries of UX. User Engagement (UE) is one method of assessing the quality of UX in search [21]. The definition of UE varies with different emphases such as being an enjoyable feeling [16], a dimension of usability that "encourages interaction" [23], system's ability to capture user's attention and interest [11], or simply a feeling of control from user [5] or of playfulness [27]. Attfield et al. [3] summarised that UE focuses on the positive aspects of UX, and concluded that UE connects the user and resources on an emotional, cognitive, and behavioural level. Indeed, UE is composed of both user's perception of the experience as well as behaviour during interaction with a system. A hallmark of a good system in this era of myriad choices is the ability to captivate users, for users to invest time, effort and emotion [17]. In this project, we adapted the definition by O'Brien and Toms [19] that UE is "characterised by challenge, aesthetic and sensory appeal, feedback, novelty, interactivity, perceived control and time, awareness, motivation, and interest and affect." Typically, two types of measures were used to assess UE: user perception and user behaviour. We assume that both types of measures are indicative of performance, opinion and outcomes of the search process.

2.2 User Perception Measures

A key characteristic of perception is its subjective nature, that is, each user may perceive differently of the same system. The dependence of perception (e.g., individual experience [6] and search tasks [8]) had been examined extensively. Although the various and vast influential factors mean that user perception is ultimately a somewhat abstract measure, perception is still a crucial element of UX that attracts research attention. Regardless of whether objective measures like search behaviour indicate a positive experience (e.g., dwell time and satisfaction [13]), they may be associated with more than one scenario or driven by different rationales, which could even be the opposite (e.g., dwell time and frustration [22]).

UMAP'17, July 9–12, 2017, Bratislava, Slovakia
© 2017 ACM. 978-1-4503-4635-1/17/07...$15.00
DOI: http://dx.doi.org/10.1145/3079628.3079705

Thus, objective measures alone do not provide a holistic picture of search, while measuring user perception provide more insights. Examples of perception measures include two UE questionnaires, Engagement and Influences on Engagement Questionnaires [27] and User Engagement Scale (UES) [20], that had been validated in various environments. [27]'s questionnaire was specially designed for multimedia systems, while the UES [20] had been tested in multiple system types.

Traditionally, most perception measures were collected using observations and self-reported methods, such as interviews and questionnaires, and thus require user responses to a set of questions or items. Directly and dynamically measuring perception requires constant and numerous efforts from researchers and the users, which are both laborious and time consuming [12, 15]. In addition, designing user perception experiments and analysing perception data requires substantial background knowledge from the researchers to account for various influential factors mentioned above. Therefore, dynamically assessing user perception has not yet been conducted fully and extensively. Moreover, due to the data collection cost, user perception measures are acquired in relatively small samples in terms of all search users, and more effort on assessing the reliability of individual perception measures across search context was suggested [12].

2.3 User Behaviour Measures

How a user interacts with a search system is measured typically by a set of low-level objective user actions (e.g., search queries [14], cursor movements [2], and dwell time [13]). Search behaviour had been studied to predict likelihood of specific outcomes of search (e.g., query reformulation [22] and satisfaction [13]). In general, the advantage of behaviour measures is that they avoid drawbacks caused by subjective measures (e.g., communication bias). Also, with potential to capture large amounts of data over time, they are also ideal for mathematical modeling, and can enhance the application of resulted models. With regards to UE, eye movements had been studied extensively (e.g., [7]). However, due to the required participant efforts (e.g., physical attendance), associated studies have the limitation of sample scale. Cursor movement is a proxy of eye movement, and related engagement studies were mainly performed in on-line news domain (e.g., [2]). However, the generalisation of cursor pattern will benefit from more in-lab studies. Lehmann et al. [17] examined UE using behaviour measures extracted from log files across 80 websites, and categorised these behaviour measures into three dimensions: Popularity, Activity and Loyalty. This study found that these three dimensions were not necessarily positively correlated, and the engagement model based on search behaviour may vary for different websites.

Still, several challenges remain, with a major one being that behaviour measures are only descriptive, rather than interpretive. That is to say, they require researchers' background knowledge for further interpretations. That is also why behaviour measures are often used as additional measures to enhance the conclusions, rather than as stand-alone measurements [9]. Also, users engage with websites in different ways, and different types of websites have various engagement models [17] rather than in a uniformed manner. Thus, a fixed set of behaviour measure may not be applicable across

all search contexts. Therefore, discussion and interpretation of data based on the search context is necessary, and more studies covering the variety of search environments are needed to augment the understanding of assessing engagement based on behaviour. To date, there is yet a precise engagement model based on behaviour.

2.4 Measures integrating perception and behaviour

For a robust evaluation of search, both types of measures are required. In fact, researchers have already started working towards this. [24] started exploring integrating behaviour with perception into one measure. But due to the effort (e.g., constant user feedback) required, this is atypical and rarely used. Other attempts were mainly applied in the satisfaction aspect (e.g., [1]), but stopped at the correlation stage without further attempts to propose new models. Moreover, Arapakis et al. [2] simplified perception measures of UE into three questions rather than a tested scale. Therefore, an integrated measure for assessing UE is still missing.

2.5 Summary and Research Questions

Measures based on either user perception or behaviour have certain drawbacks, challenges, and trade-offs. Thus, neither is optimal for measuring UE. User perception measures can provide insights. Such in-depth information cannot be replaced by looking only at behaviour measures. However, due to dependence on context and individual experience, substantial time and effort are required in designing user perception experiments, and collecting the data. On the other hand, behaviour measures have the potential to capture scalable data over time, hence efficiently provide quantitative data for mathematical modeling. As objective data, behaviour measures also avoid subjectivity issues. Nonetheless, using behaviour measures requires substantial background knowledge and insights from researchers to formulate hypotheses and provide interpretations. Both measures are valuable for assessing engagement, and ideally we can reduce the evaluation costs by collecting only one of these types of data.

I hypothesise that user behaviour is an indicator of user perception, and that user engagement in the search process draws insights from both behaviour and perception measures. Therefore, in this research, I aim to examine both types of measures; identify behaviour patterns during the search with respect to perception; develop a user model to illustrate the relationships between search behaviour and user perception, and ultimately create a cost-effective predictive model for user engagement. The following research questions form the basis of this research:

(1) What behaviour measures inform perceptions representing user engagement? And to what extent?
(2) How variable are the search behaviours resulted from RQ1 among users?
(3) What are the patterns of user behaviour that can be inferred from these differences resulted from RQ2?
(4) Can we reasonably predict user engagement based on patterns of behaviour resulted from RQ3?
(5) How do the methods resulted from RQ4 compare to other predictive methods?

3 PROGRESS TO DATE

3.1 Methodology

In the current literature, studies have revolved around one question: what is the ideal measure of engagement? Based on the definition we adapted from [19], it would be beneficial if a measure contains multiple attributes, thereby reflecting the multidimensionality of engagement. Also, an ideal measure should exhibit consistency for validity and reliability tests in similar search contexts. However, as identified in [17], different websites have different engagement models, and therefore it is not necessary for a scale to remain unchanged across all search environments. In the light of behaviour measures, the ideal measure should be cost-efficient in order to capture scalable data, as it is essential for mathematical modeling. Therefore, the perception measure I propose to use is the UES [20], which contained six dimensions: Aesthetic Appeal; Felt Involvement; Focused Attention; Novelty; Perceived Usability; and Endurability. Although differences (e.g. Facebook [4], Gaming [28]) had emerged, its dimensions remained consistent amongst IR systems. These strengths outweigh the drawbacks such as that it is a relatively new measure that could be enriched by studies on various search contexts. For behaviour measures, I chose to use the ones that can be extracted from log files, which provide the possibility of scalable data.

The three datasets (N=157, 354, 377) used in this study were collected in previous interactive IR studies, consisting of both UES data and log files. The first dataset was collected using the wikiSearch system [25] with designated tasks, while the second dataset was collected in the CLEF 2013 Cultural Heritage Track with non-purposeful task [10]. The third dataset is the CLEF 2015-2016 Interactive Social Book Search Track with both non-purposeful tasks and designated tasks. These differences of IR systems and search tasks allow for replications and investigation under different contexts, which will contribute to our understanding of generalisability of models. I will approach the problem using the following procedure:

(1) Derive a set of behaviour measures from literature.
(2) Score these behaviour measures using feature selection methods w.r.t. each UES dimensions.
(3) Apply sequence models onto the top-ranked behaviour measures to model users.
(4) Build the predictive model using the likelihood of the user model produced in previous step, and compare the results with other common classifiers.
(5) Compare the validity of results between the datasets.

Compared with related work looking at both types of measures, I aim at building a predictive model of UE rather than just identifying the correlation(e.g., [1]). Additionally, I propose to take the UES questionnaire [20] as a reference to shape the predictive accuracy of model based on behaviour measures, rather than emphasising the link between user-perceived engagement and behaviour. Also, the UES contains six dimensions, and thus fits the multi-dimensionality of engagement as defined in literature. Furthermore, works done in UE focused on search page component (e.g.,[2]), rather than the search process. Therefore instead, I propose to tackle this from a process perspective using sequence models, which can provide

an overall evaluation of search, and aid the understanding of how engagement builds up over time.

3.2 Preliminary Results

Preliminary studies show that selected behaviour measures were associated with UES [29]. Also, we found that the distribution of five defined search behaviour, adapted from Marchionini's information seeking process model [18], changed significantly in different stages of the search [30]. These two preliminary studies further suggest that user behaviour can be used as an indicator of user engagement, and there are certain behavioural patterns across search process.

3.2.1 Relationship between user perception and user behaviour [29]. To assess whether a relationship exists between user behaviour and user perception of IR systems, we used behaviour measures calculated from log files, and results from the UES to represent user perception. The data used was dataset 2 described above. Our results showed that two sub-scales of the UES, the aesthetics and usability perceptions, appear un-influenced by participants' interactions with the system. However, some behaviour(e.g, the total time on task, the number of pages added into bookbag.) was associated with the sub-scales attention, involvement and novelty. The emerging relationship between selected behaviour measures and the UES demonstrates that we may be able to isolate more behaviour measures that are indicative of user perception from log files. In addition, our research tested the structure UES scale, and like the wikiSearch results [21], we found four factors rather than six separate dimensions. This may be because both implementations were in IR systems, and not the focused task of a shopper [20]. We need also to revisit the UES so that the result consistently outputs distinctively reliable and valid factors that represent human perception. We also produced a set of information-seeking user archetypes (i.e., explorers, followers, and berry-pickers) defined by their behavioural features, which may be useful in guiding behaviour pattern recognition.

3.2.2 Dynamic behavioural changes in different stages of search process [30]. The key objective of this work was to test whether the distribution of search behaviour changes during different stages of the search process, and also whether it is appropriate to apply sequence model. Search behaviour were generated from log files and interpreted as 9 types based on Marchionini's information seeking process model [18]. Our results show that six defined behaviours: user-submitted query, system-suggested query, forward to items, evaluate relevant items, reflect, and answer, appear to change according to the stage of the search process. In 96.4% of the cases, participants continued to search after achieving the system success point. However, three defined behaviours, backward to items, backward to pages, and forward to e, appeared to be unaffected by time. This finding indicates the existence of certain search behaviour patterns over time.

4 FURTHER RESEARCH

The remainder of this project will revolve around 1) testing the generalisability of the two models by applying them in various search contexts; and 2) looking into the influence of individual differences on the models by taking personalisation into account.

5 CONTRIBUTIONS AND IMPACT

The ultimate products of this research are a user model to illustrate the relationship between search behaviour and user perception, and a cost-effective predictive model of user engagement based on the user model using only behaviour measures during search process. Together, these will help to gain deeper insights into the rationale behind search behaviour, and relationships between behaviour and perception. Ultimately, the predictive model will reduce the cost of evaluating search, by contributing a new user-centric evaluation measure that assess search dynamically.

REFERENCES
[1] Azzah Al-Maskari and Mark Sanderson. 2010. A review of factors influencing user satisfaction in information retrieval. *JASIST* 61, 5 (2010), 859–868.

[2] Ioannis Arapakis, Xiao Bai, and B Barla Cambazoglu. 2016. Predicting User Engagement with Direct Displays Using Mouse Cursor Information. In *Proc. SIGIR'16.* ACM, 103–112.

[3] Simon Attfield, Gabriella Kazai, Mounia Lalmas, and Benjamin Piwowarski. 2011. Towards a science of user engagement (position paper). In *WSDM Workshop on User Modelling for Web Applications.*

[4] Firdaus Banhawi and Nazlena Mohamad Ali. 2011. Measuring user engagement attributes in social networking application. In *Proc. STAIR'11.* IEEE, 297–301.

[5] Susanne Bødker. 2006. When second wave HCI meets third wave challenges. In *Proc. NordiCHI'06.* ACM, 1–8.

[6] C. L. Borgman. 1989. All users of information retrieval systems are not created equal: an exploration into individual differences. *Inf. Process. Manage.* 25, 3 (1989), 237–251.

[7] Georg Buscher, Susan T Dumais, and Edward Cutrell. 2010. The good, the bad, and the random: an eye-tracking study of ad quality in web search. In *Proc. SIGIR'10.* ACM, 42–49.

[8] Katriina Byström and Kalervo Järvelin. 1995. Task complexity affects information seeking and use. *Inf. Process. Manage.* 31, 2 (1995), 191–213.

[9] John P Charlton and Ian DW Danforth. 2010. Validating the distinction between computer addiction and engagement: online game playing and personality. *Behaviour & Information Technology* 29, 6 (2010), 601–613.

[10] Mark Michael Hall, Robert Villa, Sophie A. Rutter, Daniel Bell, Paul Clough, and Elaine G. Toms. 2013. Sheffield submission to the chic interactive task: Exploring digital cultural heritage. In *Proc. CLEF'13 Working Note.*

[11] Richard David Jacques. 1996. *The nature of engagement and its role in hypermedia evaluation and design.* Ph.D. Dissertation. South Bank University.

[12] Diane Kelly. 2009. Methods for evaluating interactive information retrieval systems with users. *Foundations and Trends in Information Retrieval* 3, 1—2 (2009), 1–224.

[13] Youngho Kim, Ahmed Hassan, Ryen W White, and Imed Zitouni. 2014. Modeling dwell time to predict click-level satisfaction. In *Proc. SIGIR'14.* ACM, 193–202.

[14] Alexander Kotov, Paul N Bennett, Ryen W White, Susan T Dumais, and Jaime Teevan. 2011. Modeling and analysis of cross-session search tasks. In *Proc. SIGIR'11.* ACM, 5–14.

[15] Mounia Lalmas, Heather O'Brien, and Elad Yom-Tov. 2014. Measuring user engagement. *Synthesis Lectures on Information Concepts, Retrieval, and Services* 6, 4 (2014), 1–132.

[16] Brenda Laurel. 1991. *Computers As Theatre.* Addison-Wesley Longman Publishing Co., Inc., Boston, MA, USA.

[17] Janette Lehmann, Mounia Lalmas, Elad Yom-Tov, and Georges Dupret. 2012. Models of User Engagement. In *Proc. UMAP'12.* Springer-Verlag, Berlin, Heidelberg, 164–175.

[18] Gary Marchionini. 1995. *Information seeking in electronic environments.* Cambridge University Press. 224 pages.

[19] Heather L. O'Brien and Elaine G. Toms. 2008. What is user engagement? A conceptual framework for defining user engagement with technology. *JASIST* 59, 6 (2008), 938–955.

[20] Heather L. O'Brien and Elaine G. Toms. 2010. The development and evaluation of a survey to measure user engagement. *JASIST* 61, 1 (2010), 50–69.

[21] Heather L. O'Brien and Elaine G. Toms. 2013. Examining the generalizability of the User Engagement Scale (UES) in exploratory search. *Inf. Process. Manage.* 49, 5 (2013), 1092–1107.

[22] Daan Odijk, Ryen W White, Ahmed Hassan Awadallah, and Susan T Dumais. 2015. Struggling and success in web search. In *Proc. CIKM'15.* ACM, 1551–1560.

[23] Whitney Quesenbery. 2003. *The five dimensions of usability.* Vol. 20. Lawrence Erlbaum Associates Mahwah, NJ.

[24] J. Tague. 1987. Informativeness as an ordinal utility function for information retrieval. *SIGIR Forum* 21, 3-4 (1987), 10–17.

[25] Elaine G Toms, Robert Villa, and Lori McCay-Peet. 2013. How is a search system used in work task completion? *Journal of information science* 39, 1 (2013), 15–25.

[26] Andrew Turpin and Falk Scholer. 2006. User Performance Versus Precision Measures for Simple Search Tasks. In *Proc. SIGIR'06.* ACM, 11–18.

[27] Jane Webster and Hayes Ho. 1997. Audience engagement in multimedia presentations. *ACM SIGMIS Database* 28, 2 (1997), 63–77.

[28] Eric N Wiebe, Allison Lamb, Megan Hardy, and David Sharek. 2014. Measuring engagement in video game-based environments. *Computers in Human Behavior* 32 (2014), 123–132.

[29] Mengdie Zhuang, Elaine G Toms, and Gianluca Demartini. 2016. *The Relationship Between User Perception and User Behaviour in Interactive Information Retrieval Evaluation.* Springer, 293–305.

[30] Mengdie Zhuang, Elaine G Toms, and Gianluca Demartini. 2016. Search behaviour before and after search success. In *In: Workshop on Search as Learning (SAL 2016) at SIGIR 2016.*

Recommender Systems as Multistakeholder Environments

Himan Abdollahpouri
DePaul University
Chicago, IL, USA
habdolla@depaul.edu

Robin Burke
DePaul University
Chicago, IL, USA
rburke@cs.depaul.edu

Bamshad Mobasher
DePaul University
Chicago, IL, USA
mobasher@depaul.edu

ABSTRACT

Recommender systems are typically evaluated on their ability to provide items that satisfy the needs and interests of the end user. However, in many real world applications, users are not the only stakeholders involved. There may be a variety of individuals or organizations that benefit in different ways from the delivery of recommendations. In this paper, we re-define the recommender system as a multistakeholder environment in which different stakeholders are served by delivering recommendations, and we suggest a utility-based approach to evaluating recommendations in such an environment that is capable of distinguishing among the distributions of utility delivered to different stakeholders.

1 INTRODUCTION

One of the key characteristics of recommender systems is an emphasis on personalization. Recommender systems are evaluated on their ability to provide items that satisfy the needs and interests of the end user, often extrapolated from known ratings or other indicators of interest. Researchers have also examined a variety of metrics (such as accuracy, diversity, novelty and so on) that can be used to measure aspects of the suitability of recommendation results to the target user. However, the end user as the receiver of recommendations is, for the most part, the only consideration for a successful algorithm.

Such focus is entirely appropriate. Users would not make use of recommender systems if they believed such systems were not providing items that matched their interests. Still, it is also clear that, in many recommendation domains, the user for whom recommendations are generated is not the only stakeholder in the recommendation outcome. A number of pertinent examples can be given. Reciprocal recommendation is the term applied to a situation in which a recommendation must be acceptable to both parties in a transaction. For example, in on-line dating, both parties must be interested in order for a match to be successful [8]. Other reciprocal recommendation domains including job seeking, peer-to-peer "sharing economy" recommendation (such as AirBnB, Uber and others), and on-line advertising [6].

It is also important to note that in many e-commerce retail settings, recommendation is viewed as a form of marketing and, as such, the economic considerations of the retailer will also enter

into the recommendation function. When recommender systems are evaluated "in the wild", metrics such as engagement, shopping cart size, or other variables more indicative of customer lifetime value are more likely to be used than traditional metrics from recommender systems research. In addition, a business may wish to highlight products that are more profitable or that are currently on sale, for example. Commercial recommender systems often use separate "business rules" functionality to integrate such items into the personalized recommendations generated through conventional means. Integrating the retailer as a stakeholder allows such considerations to be factored into the recommendation process.

We believe that, far from being special "edge cases", these examples illustrate a more general point about recommendation, namely, that recommender systems serve multiple goals and that a purely user-centered approach does not allow all such goals to enter into the design and evaluation of recommendation algorithms where appropriate. We believe that the scope of recommender system design and evaluation should be broadened to include the perspectives and utilities of multiple stakeholders.

In microeconomics, a similar shift occurred in the early part of the 21st century with the development of the theory of multisided platforms [4, 10]. Prior to that time, the traditional business model focused on a firm's ability to produce products and deliver them to customers at a price that could ensure profitability. This model was inadequate to explain Internet businesses such as search engines, that were giving their products away. Once multisided platform theory was developed, it enabled economists to look back at types of businesses that had existed for many years, such as credit card companies, shopping malls and stock exchanges, and recognize them as examples of multisided platforms as well [5].

The key property of a multisided platform is that it exists to reduce market frictions that may prevent parties from exchanging with each other if left unsupported. A shopping mall, for example, concentrates both retailers and shoppers so that shoppers only have to go to one destination and retailers can benefit from the foot traffic of their neighbors. Today's web economy hosts a profusion of multisided platforms, including such diverse examples as the advertising features of Google's search engine, which brings together searchers and advertisers; OKCupid, which brings together singles looking for dates; Etsy, which brings together shoppers and small-scale artisans; and Kiva.org, which brings together charitably-minded individuals with third-world entrepreneurs in need of capital.

Different recommendation scenarios can be distinguished by differing configurations of interests among the stakeholders. We divide the stakeholders of a given recommender system into three categories: consumers C, providers P, and platform or system S. The consumers are those who receive the recommendations. They are the individuals whose choice or search problems bring them to the platform, and who expect recommendations to satisfy those needs. The providers are those entities that supply or otherwise stand behind the recommended objects, and gain from the consumer's choice. The final category is the platform itself, which has created the recommender system in order to match consumers with providers and has some means of gaining benefit from successfully doing so.

Approaches to multistakeholder recommendation include recommendation hybrids [9], multiobjective optimization [1], and multi-agent architectures [15]. A diversity of techniques is needed because of the wide variety of utility configurations that may be encountered. In some settings, it is sufficient to optimize for aggregate utility across providers; in others, a balanced distribution over providers must be maintained. In some cases, system utility is purely a function of the utilities of the other stakeholders; in others, the system derives additional utility from certain matches and not from others. A multistakeholder model provides a framework in which such considerations can be explicitly represented as utilities and accounted for in evaluation.

2 RELATED WORK

There is a large body of recent work in recommender systems on incorporating diversity, novelty and other metrics into recommendation generation and evaluation. See, for example, [12, 13, 17]. This line of research has developed a number of techniques such as re-ranking and multi-objective optimization that can be use to integrate stakeholder concerns.

The concept of multiple stakeholders in recommender systems is suggested in a number of prior research works [2]. As discussed above, researchers on reciprocal recommendation have looked at bilateral considerations to ensure that a recommendation is acceptable to both parties in the transaction [14].

A more explicit utility-theoretic approach is taken by [11] in which a user's job seeking propensity is combined with their fit for a job description in ranking recruitment candidates in LinkedIn. This paper found that the combined utility yielded higher engagement rates than similarity alone.

There is a substantial literature in real-time targeted advertising in which advertisers' expected revenue and / or available budget are incorporated into the decision to deliver personalized advertising to a user. See [16] for an example.

3 CONCLUSION

There is increasing dissatisfaction with one-dimensional, accuracy-oriented evaluation of recommender systems [7]. In addition, real-world recommendation applications frequently require sensitivity to business needs and context. We claim that in order to create effective recommender systems in multisided platforms, it is necessary to explicitly represent the different stakeholders in the recommendation process and formalize their utilities. As discussed in [3], this approach is sufficiently general that a wide variety of recommendation scenarios can be represented including reciprocal recommendation, budget management, and others.

A utility-oriented approach allows us to represent such concerns explicitly and make clear modeling assumptions about the relative benefits of different aspects of recommendation outcomes. A multistakeholder approach highlights the multiple actors involved in

a given recommender system configuration and allows the concerns of each to be represented and accounted for in evaluation and design.

ACKNOWLEDGMENTS

This work is supported in part by the National Science Foundation under grant IIS-1423368.

REFERENCES

[1] Deepak Agarwal, Bee-Chung Chen, Pradheep Elango, and Xuanhui Wang. 2011. Click Shaping to Optimize Multiple Objectives. In *Proceedings of the 17th ACM SIGKDD International Conference on Knowledge Discovery and Data Mining (KDD '11)*. ACM, New York, NY, USA, 132–140.

[2] Robin Burke and Himan Abdollahpouri. 2016. Educational Recommendation with Multiple Stakeholders. In *Web Intelligence Workshops (WIW), IEEE/WIC/ACM International Conference on*. IEEE, 62–63.

[3] Robin D. Burke, Himan Abdollahpouri, Bamshad Mobasher, and Trinadh Gupta. 2016. Towards Multi-Stakeholder Utility Evaluation of Recommender Systems. In *Late-breaking Results, Posters, Demos, Doctoral Consortium and Workshops Proceedings of the 24th ACM Conference on User Modeling, Adaptation and Personalisation (UMAP 2016), Halifax, Canada, July 13-16, 2016*. http://ceur-ws.org/Vol-1618/SOAP_paper2.pdf

[4] David Evans, Richard Schmalensee, Michael Noel, Howard Chang, and Daniel Garcia-Swartz. 2011. *Platform economics: Essays on multi-sided businesses*. Competition Policy International.

[5] David S. Evans and Richard Schmalensee. 2016. *Matchmakers: The New Economics of Multisided Platforms*. Harvard Business Review Press.

[6] Ganesh Iyer, David Soberman, and J Miguel Villas-Boas. 2005. The targeting of advertising. *Marketing Science* 24, 3 (2005), 461–476.

[7] Dietmar Jannach and Gediminas Adomavicius. 2016. Recommendations with a Purpose. In *Proceedings of the 10th ACM Conference on Recommender Systems*. ACM, 7–10.

[8] Luiz Pizzato, Tomek Rej, Thomas Chung, Irena Koprinska, and Judy Kay. 2010. RECON: a reciprocal recommender for online dating. In *Proceedings of the fourth ACM conference on Recommender systems*. ACM, 207–214.

[9] Marco Tulio Ribeiro, Nivio Ziviani, Edleno Silva De Moura, Itamar Hata, Anisio Lacerda, and Adriano Veloso. 2015. Multiobjective pareto-efficient approaches for recommender systems. *ACM Transactions on Intelligent Systems and Technology (TIST)* 5, 4 (2015), 53.

[10] Jean-Charles Rochet and Jean Tirole. 2003. Platform competition in two-sided markets. *Journal of the European Economic Association* 1, 4 (2003), 990–1029.

[11] Mario Rodriguez, Christian Posse, and Ethan Zhang. 2012. Multiple objective optimization in recommender systems. In *Proceedings of the sixth ACM conference on Recommender systems*. ACM, 11–18.

[12] Barry Smyth and Paul McClave. 2001. Similarity vs. diversity. In *Case-Based Reasoning Research and Development*. Springer, 347–361.

[13] Saúl Vargas and Pablo Castells. 2011. Rank and relevance in novelty and diversity metrics for recommender systems. In *Proceedings of the fifth ACM conference on Recommender systems*. ACM, 109–116.

[14] Peng Xia, Benyuan Liu, Yizhou Sun, and Cindy Chen. 2015. Reciprocal Recommendation System for Online Dating. In *Proceedings of the 2015 IEEE/ACM International Conference on Advances in Social Networks Analysis and Mining 2015*. ACM, 234–241.

[15] Shuai Yuan, Ahmad Zainal Abidin, Marc Sloan, and Jun Wang. 2012. Internet Advertising: An Interplay among Advertisers, Online Publishers, Ad Exchanges and Web Users. *arXiv preprint arXiv:1206.1754* (2012).

[16] Weinan Zhang, Shuai Yuan, and Jun Wang. 2014. Optimal real-time bidding for display advertising. In *Proceedings of the 20th ACM SIGKDD international conference on Knowledge discovery and data mining*. ACM, 1077–1086.

[17] Cai-Nicolas Ziegler, Sean M McNee, Joseph A Konstan, and Georg Lausen. 2005. Improving recommendation lists through topic diversification. In *Proceedings of the 14th international conference on World Wide Web*. ACM, 22–32.

Towards Understanding Users' Motivation in a Q&A Social Network Using Social Influence and the Moderation by Culture

Ifeoma Adaji
University of Saskatchewan
Saskatoon, Saskatchewan, Canada
ifeoma.adaji@usask.ca

Julita Vassileva
University of Saskatchewan
Saskatoon, Saskatchewan, Canada
julita.vassileva@usask.ca

ABSTRACT

Active participation of users in Q&A social networks like Stack Overflow is key to the sustenance of the network. One way to encourage participation is to allow collaboration or cooperation between users in order to improve question and answer posts, and allow users to learn from one another. In order to implement strategies that encourage cooperation, it is important to understand what influences the users in the network to cooperate. In this extended abstract, we investigate the social support principles that influence cooperation in Stack Overflow. Using a sample size of 282 Stack Overflow users, we develop and test a global research model using partial least squares structural equation modelling (PLS-SEM). We further investigate any possible differences in the effect of these strategies between cultures, by testing two cultural subgroups; collectivist and individualist cultures. Our results show that social learning significantly influences cooperation in Stack Overflow at the global level. However, at the cultural subgroup level, recognition influences cooperation among collectivists, while social facilitation influences individualists to cooperate. These findings suggest possible design guidelines in the development of successful personalized Q&A social networking sites that encourage participation through cooperation.

KEYWORDS

Social influence, Culture, Persuasive strategies, Social network

1 INTRODUCTION

Question and answer social networks like Stack Overflow thrive when users post quality answers [2]. Collaboration between users has been shown to produce high quality answers [1]. Since high quality answer posts results in an active Q&A network [2], it is important to identify what influences users to cooperate, in order to implement strategies that could influence collaboration among other users, that can keep the network active.

In this extended abstract, we aim to understand what social support influence strategies motivate users in Stack Overflow to cooperate and further explore any differences in the effect of these influence strategies based on the culture of the users.

UMAP '17, July 09-12, 2017, Bratislava, Slovakia
© 2017 Copyright is held by the owner/author(s).
ACM ISBN 978-1-4503-4635-1/17/07. http://dx.doi.org/10.1145/3079628.3079647

This study was carried out using Stack Overflow because it currently has over four million registered users[1], thus, making participant recruitment possible.

Using a sample size of 282 Stack Overflow users and the social support influence strategies of the Persuasive Systems Design (PSD) framework [6] (which include *social facilitation*, *social comparison*, *normative influence*, *social learning*, *cooperation*, *competition* and *recognition*), we developed and tested a global research model using partial least squares structural equation modelling (PLS-SEM). To explore any possible differences that exist between cultures, we identified two cultural subgroups; collectivist and individualist cultures, and carried out multi-group analysis between them.

The result of our analysis shows that social learning significantly influences cooperation in Stack Overflow at the global level. At the cultural subgroup level, recognition influences cooperation in collectivists' culture, while social facilitation influences individualists to cooperate. These findings suggest possible design guidelines in the development of successful personalized Q&A social networking sites that encourage participation through cooperation.

2 METHODOLOGY, ANALYSIS & RESULTS

2.1 Evaluation of Global Measurements

We developed a hypothetical path model using the social support influence principles of the PSD framework [6] in order to investigate what influences users in Stack Overflow to cooperate. Our research model is made up of eight constructs (*social learning, social comparison, normative influence, social facilitation, cooperation, competition, recognition* and *perceived persuasiveness*) which were adopted from previously tested and validated scales of Stibe and Oinas-Kukkonen [8]. Each construct measured three items on a five-point Likert scale (1 = strongly disagree, 5 = strongly agree).

Participants were recruited through Amazon's Mechanical Turk (AMT). AMT has become an accepted means of soliciting users' responses [5]. The responses of 282 participants were accepted. Participation was voluntary and the study was approved by the ethics board of the University of Saskatchewan. Asians represented our collectivist culture subgroup while North

---

[1] https://data.stackexchange.com/StackOverflow/revision/325050/420211/count-of-all-users-all-questions-and-all-answers

Americans represented our collectivist culture subgroup. This is in line with previous studies on culture [7].

2.2 Evaluation of Global Measurements

As recommended by Wong [9], we confirmed the reliability and validity of the constructs used in our model. Indicator reliability of was established as all indicators had reliability values greater than 0.4 [4]. The composite reliability values for all latent variables were higher than the preferred threshold of 0.7 [9], hence high levels of internal consistency reliability were established among all latent variables. Convergent validity was confirmed as all of the average variance extracted AVE values were greater than the acceptable threshold of 0.5 [9]. The square roots of AVE was greater than the other correlation variables, hence discriminant validity was well established.

2.3 Global Model and Sub-Group Analysis

We carried out Partial Least Squares Structural Equation Modelling (PLS-SEM) using SmartPLS. The results of our path modelling, in particular the path coefficient (β value) between constructs and the significance or otherwise of these path coefficients in the global model is shown in figure 1. To determine the effect of the social support influence principles on culture, we split the data into two subgroups; one for the North American participants (the individualists) and the other for the Asian participants (the collectivists). This classification of cultures is in line with the research of Hofstede [3]. We then carried out multi-group analysis between the two subgroups to determine if there were any significant differences in the effect of the influence principles between these groups. The result of this is also presented in figure1.

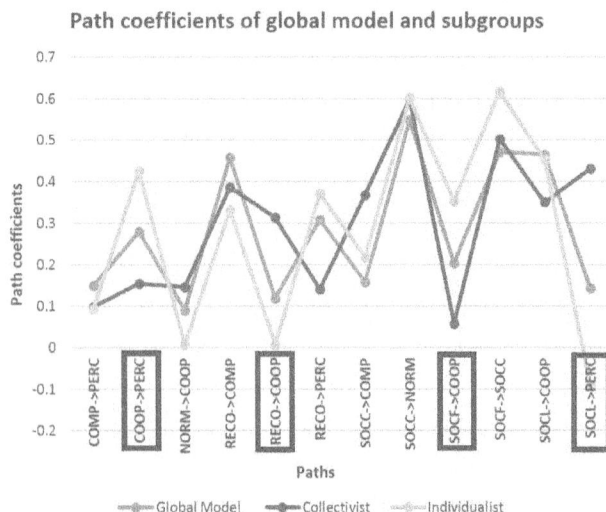

Figure 1. Path coefficients of the global model and subgroups. Rectangles in red show paths with significant differences between the subgroups. SOCL=Social learning, SOCC= Social comparison, NORM=Normative influence, SOCF= Social facilitation, COOP=Cooperation, COMP=Competition, RECO=Recognition, PERC=Perceived persuasiveness

In the global model, Social learning has the strongest effect on cooperation compared to social facilitation, normative influence and recognition. This suggests that social learning is a strong predictor of cooperation. The result of the multi group analysis between individualist and collectivist subgroups shows four significant differences between the two cultures. While recognition influences collectivists to cooperate with others in the system, social facilitation influences individualists to cooperate.

This result suggests that Stack Overflow users are influenced differently. Hence, a one-size-fits-all approach to implementing strategies that influence users to cooperate might not bring about the desired behavior change in the network.

3 CONCLUSION

Because collaboration among users has been shown to result in better quality posts in Q&A social networks, we explored what strategies influence collaboration between users in such a network. Using the result of a survey of 282 Stack Overflow users, we developed a structural model using PLS-SEM in order to identify what social support strategies influence users to cooperate in the network. We further split the data into two subgroups based on collectivist and individualist cultures to determine if the effect of the social influence principles differed based on culture. Our results suggest that social learning significantly influences cooperation in Stack Overflow at the global level compared to other strategies. However, at the cultural subgroup level, recognition influences cooperation among collectivists, while social facilitation influences individualists to cooperate. The preliminary result presented here suggest possible guidelines for designing personalized Q&A social networks that encourage cooperation among users.

REFERENCES

1. Ifeoma Adaji and Julita Vassileva. 2016. Modelling User Collaboration in Social Networks Using Edits and Comments. In *Proceedings of the 2016 Conference on User Modeling Adaptation and Personalization - UMAP '16*, 111–114. https://doi.org/10.1145/2930238.2930289
2. Gideon Dror, Dan Pelleg, Oleg Rokhlenko, and Idan Szpektor. 2012. Churn prediction in new users of Yahoo! answers. In *Proceedings of the 21st International Conference on World Wide Web*, 829–834.
3. GH Hofstede and G Hofstede. 2001. *Culture's consequences: Comparing values, behaviors, institutions and organizations across nations.* Retrieved February 26, 2017 from https://books.google.ca/books?hl=en&lr=&id=w6z18LJ_1VsC&oi=fnd&pg=PR15&dq=Hofstede&ots=x6hBzaJug4&sig=IcHNbUGyeLgIrVvvXy1oyDbaDRc
4. J Hulland. 1999. Use of partial least squares (PLS) in strategic management research: A review of four recent studies. *Strategic management journal.*
5. W Mason and S Suri. 2012. Conducting behavioral research on Amazon's Mechanical Turk. *Behavior research methods.*
6. Harri Oinas-Kukkonen and Marja Harjumaa. 2008. A systematic framework for designing and evaluating persuasive systems. In *Persuasive technology.* Springer, 164–176.
7. R Orji. 2016. The Impact of Cultural Differences on the Persuasiveness of Influence Strategies. *Adjunt proceedings of the 11th iternational conference on Persuasive Technology*: 38–41.
8. A Stibe and H Oinas-Kukkonen. 2014. Using social influence for motivating customers to generate and share feedback. *International Conference on Persuasive.*
9. KKK Wong. 2013. Partial least squares structural equation modeling (PLS-SEM) techniques using SmartPLS. *Marketing Bulletin* 24, Technical note 1.

Harvesting Entity-relation Social Networks from the Web: Potential and Challenges

Saeed Amal
University of Haifa
samal@campus.haifa.ac.il

Tsvi Kuflik
University of Haifa
tsvikak@is.haifa.ac.il

Einat Minkov
University of Haifa
einatm@is.haifa.ac.il

ABSTRACT

We describe a graph-based entity profiling system (GBEP) that extracts information about persons of interest from the Web and uses this information to construct a joint social graph. GBEP then employs graph-based measures to assess inter-personal relatedness, performing *social recommendation*. Importantly, GBEP provides detailed explanations for its suggestions in the form of relational connecting paths. Initial positive results were obtained for recommending related conference participants to each other using a joint social graph constructed for this purpose.

CCS CONCEPTS

• **Information systems** → **Collaborative and social computing systems and tools**; • **Computing methodologies** → *Information extraction*;

KEYWORDS

Graph-based Recommendation; Information Extraction

1 INTRODUCTION

Relational information about an entity of interest can be represented as an entity-relation graph. For example, a graph representing *Albert Einstein* would include links to nodes denoting entities or concepts such as 'University of Zurich', or 'Quantum Theory'. While relevant information about personas like Einstein is available in structured form from public resources like Wikipedia, for most persons, their profiles must be constructed from raw Web data. We apply information extraction techniques to automatically construct an *entity profile* in response to a query that specifies a *person* name. Importantly, multiple personal profiles can be readily unified into a joint graph, comprising a heterogeneous entity-relation social network. It is then possible to address complex queries such as: "Who are the *persons* most related to *person p*?", or, "*how* are the persons represented by nodes *p* and *q* related?"

Our prototype of GBEP automatically extracts relational information about persons of interest from on their homepages. We

then unify the graphs of multiple personal profiles to form a social network, in which similarity assessments and recommendation can take place. We report preliminary results of *social recommendation* using GBEP: ranking the participants of the IUI'15 conference by their relatedness to each other. Such application may promote the generation of new social and professional ties.

Previously, Adamic and Adar [1] extracted personal profiles from the Web, however their focus was on social community exploration, while we are interested in social recommendation. Accordingly, we place emphasis on presenting detailed supporting evidence to the user in the form of labeled and weighted relational connecting paths. Another recent related research pursues social recommendation in academic conferences [2], but they only consider direct co-authorship as indicator of social affinity. Our targeted social similarity suggestions are more extensive in that they involve diverse entities as well as indirect relations. Initial feedbacks suggest using GBEP is engaging and surprising.

2 GRAPH-BASED ENTITY PROFILING

Personal profile construction. Given a person name *t* and her homepage, we build a graph profile G_t which displays her connections with related typed entities E_t, which we identify from the semi-structured homepage. Entity mentions are often available in structured form being tagged with hyperlinks. In order to increase coverage, we also apply the Stanford named entity tagger [1] to identify *person*, *location* and *organization* entity name mentions that appear within the unstructured text. The target person *t* and the related named entities E_t are represented as typed nodes in G_t,[2] having a direct edge link from *t* to each related entity $e \in E_t$ (i.e., the personal graph is star-shaped.) Ideally, the graph edges should be assigned a semantic *relation type*, $r(t, e)$, that succinctly describes the identified inter-entity association. In our case study, we consider high-level relation types that characterise scholars, including *education* (i.e., *studied-at(t,e)*), *employment*, and *publications*. We assign the edge types automatically based on the local context that surrounds the entity mention (five tokens before and after the mention) and its content string. The results of 10-fold cross validation of a Naive Bayes classifier trained using a set of labeled examples and bag-of-word features measured 0.87 and 0.82 in precision and recall, respectively.

Connecting people. Personal profiles were constructed in this fashion for the participants of the Intelligent User Interfaces conference in 2015. Overall, 594 personal profiles were generated for participants for whom a homepage was identified. The individual

UMAP'17, July 09-12, 2017, Bratislava, Slovakia
© 2017 Copyright held by the owner/author(s).
ACM ISBN 978-1-4503-4635-1/17/07.
https://doi.org/http://dx.doi.org/10.1145/3079628.3079656

---

[1] http://nlp.stanford.edu/software/CRF-NER.shtml
[2] We leave disambiguation and unification to future work.

Source Entity	Target Entity	Total Weight
John Smith	Michael Jones	0.002

1 0.001: **John Smith-->Uppsala University-->Michael Jones**

Source Webpage: " *Uppsala University*" (Employment/)
Target Webpage: "Berdin visiting masters , *Uppsala University*" (Employment /Education)

2 0.000: **John Smith-->HCI-->Michael Jones**

Source Webpage: " *HCI*" (Publications /Employment /)
Target Webpage: "is *HCI*" (Employment /Education)

Figure 1: Presentation of the supporting paths for a computed inter-person relatedness score.

graphs were unified into a compact yet sparse joint social graph consisting of 70K edges and 23K nodes.

In this study, we wish to highlight to each participant a list of related conference attendants. It is likely that some of the predicted connections correspond to existing acquaintances, yet it is desired to bring to one's attention potential new acquaintances, and the respective social contexts. This task corresponds to the query: "who are the person nodes most related to p, and *why?*". We believe that the graph-based suggestions must be explained, so as to engage users and obtain their trust. Formally, this task involves ranking *person* nodes in the graph by their graph-based similarity to the node representing the focus person t. We apply the Personalized PageRank measure, conducting a two-step random walk process, to address this query [4]. The relatedness score of node p with respect to t equals the summation of the weights of the individual paths that connect them. Essentially, nodes that connect over a larger number of paths, as well as shorter paths, are assigned higher relatedness scores.

Recommendation systems typically only provide with numeric scores. In contrast, we provide the user with explanations for the suggestions made, namely the set of paths over which the entities connect in the graph, having a *path* denote a sequence of labeled *entities* and *relations*. Figure 1 displays the connecting paths between two (weakly linked) IUI participants whom we name here 'John Smith', and 'Michael Jones'. The figure shows the computed similarity score, along with two paths that account for their interpersonal relatedness. The first path connects the two persons via the entity 'Uppsala University' over a relation labeled as *employment* (for 'John Smith'), and *education* as well as *employment* for 'Michael Jones'. In addition to the predicted relation types, available lexical context is presented ('..visiting masters..'). This path seems interesting and non-trivial, as only a minority of researchers attended or visited Uppsala University. This fact may therefore ignite interest and motivate a conversation. The second path connects the two persons over the concept 'HCI'. This path is less interesting, as most of the conference participants are involved in HCI research. Indeed, the weight of this path is low (nearly zero); since a large number of *person* nodes link to the node denoting 'HCI', its contribution to the similarity score is low [4].

3 EVALUATION: SOCIAL RECOMMENDATION

We requested two dozens of IUI'15 participants to experience with the system over the Web, and provide us with feedback in free form. Following is a summary of their feedbacks.

Ranking quality. Some of the feedbacks pertained to the perceived correctness of the rankings. While one of the respondents commented that "the selected persons are adequate and the weight of the link as well", others noted cases in which persons who they knew well and collaborated with were ranked below people with whom they were less familiar with. Detailed feedbacks also pointed out some disambiguation issues, e.g., multiple mentions of the name "Huang" refer to different people, as well as errors in our third-part named entity tagger. These errors can be alleviated by improving named entity recognition. Learning from user feedback may also help promote informative paths. Nevertheless, we find the feedbacks to be encouraging; for example, one user defined 70% of the rankings as relevant and interesting. Although our main focus in not on optimizing the rankings by familiarity, we find that GBEP should be tuned and measured with respect to this requirement in the future to meet users expectations.

Surprise. Our goal is to rather point out new or unknown interesting ties, so as to encourage the user to make new contacts, or to 'break the ice' when being introduced to or meeting yet-unknown persons in a social setup such as a scientific conference. Connecting entities may suggest topics for conversation and encourage the exploration of mutual background. Several feedbacks indeed used the word 'surprised', e.g., "I was surprised to see A. at the top but when I checked out their research profile it makes some sense."

Clarity. Supposedly, detailing the relational paths that connect the user to a related person is more intuitive and convincing compared with mere numerical scores. Indeed, the comments cited so far indicate that the users took advantage of the system as intended, exploring the connecting paths that associate them to the suggested persons. The feedbacks indicate that this presentations increases users' engagement, e.g., consider the following positive comment collected in our survey: "I certainly found it an interesting activity to go through the list for 10 minutes and check out the home pages of some of these people for which I was unfamiliar (or in some cases had forgotten)".

In summary, we described a prototype for generating personal profiles that uses information extraction techniques to automatically process Web data into structured entities and relations information. We performed social recommendation using a graph that included the profiles of a scientific conference attendants. Initial feedbacks indicate that the suggested rankings, as well as the graph-based relational explanations generated, are sensible, surprising at times, and engaging. In the future, we would like to improve and personalize the random walk scheme using path-based learning techniques based on users' feedback[3, 4], and explore additional applications of this framework.

REFERENCES

[1] Lada A Adamic and Eytan Adar. 2003. Friends and neighbors on the Web. *Social Networks* 25, 3 (2003).
[2] Peter Brusilovsky, , Jung Sun Oh, Claudia López, Denis Parra, and Wei Jeng. 2017. Linking information and people in a social system for academic conferences. *New Review Of Hypermedia And Multimedia* (2017).
[3] Ni Lao, Einat Minkov, and William W. Cohen. 2016. Learning Relational Features with Backward Random Walks. In *Proceedings of the Annual Meeting of the Association for Computational Linguistics (ACL)*.
[4] Einat Minkov and William W Cohen. 2010. Improving graph-walk-based similarity with reranking: Case studies for personal information management. *ACM Transactions on Information Systems (TOIS)* 29, 1 (2010), 4.

2

Enhancing Collaborative Filtering with Friendship Information

Liliana Ardissono, Maurizio Ferrero, Giovanna Petrone, Marino Segnan

Dipartimento di Informatica, Università di Torino

Corso Svizzera 185

Torino, Italy 10149

[liliana.ardissono,giovanna.petrone,marino.segnan]@unito.it,maurizio.ferrero@edu.unito.it

ABSTRACT

We test the impact of integrating a measure of *common friendship* in collaborative filtering, in order to capture the intuition that socially interconnected groups of people tend to have similar tastes. An experiment on the Yelp dataset shows that using preference information derived from the commonalities of interests in networks of friends achieves higher accuracy than item-to-item collaborative filtering.

CCS CONCEPTS

•**Information systems** → **Recommender systems**; •**Human-centered computing** → **Collaborative Filtering**; **Social recommendation**;

KEYWORDS

Recommender systems; homophily and social networks

1 INTRODUCTION

Several models have been proposed to integrate explicit and implicit social information in collaborative recommenders; e.g., [2, 6]. We are interested in analyzing the impact of "group-based" friendship relations, which social science has associated to user similarity through the homophily phenomenon, according to which "similarity breeds connection" [7]. As homophily has been observed in several types of social networks, including digital ones [1], it is worth studying its relevance to collaborative recommender systems, which employ rating and/or tagging similarity for item suggestion.

Our research questions are: *"RQ1: Can the performance of a collaborative filtering recommender be improved by taking into account common friendship relations in groups of people? RQ2: How does this type of information influence performance if taken alone, or in combination with other sources of data about the user, such as rating behavior?"* In order to answer these questions, we compared the performance of collaborative filtering recommenders based on user ratings, community membership, group-based friendship relations, product selection, and combinations of these types of information. We tested the recommenders on a subset of the Yelp dataset [8] providing data about friends relations and item ratings on restaurants. The experiment showed that the integration of social and rating information outperforms the other algorithms,

even though, as observed in previous works, there is a trade-off between recommendation accuracy and coverage.

2 INTEGRATING SOCIAL INFORMATION IN COLLABORATIVE FILTERING

2.1 Dataset

The Yelp dataset [8] provides information about friendship relations and user ratings on various types of businesses. We selected the data about restaurants, considering only the users who rated at least 20 items. This restricted dataset (henceforth, "Yelp-Restaurants(20)") includes 8914 users, 23210 items and 419013 ratings. Its user-rating matrix has sparsity = 0.9979. An analysis of the structure of the social network underlying the dataset shows that: (i) The cumulative distribution of the number of ratings in the observed population follows the Power Law, with most users having rated few items. (ii) The cumulative distribution of the number of friends per user follows the Power Law, with most users having few or no friends. (iii) There is a positive correlation between the number of ratings provided by users and the number of friends they have: the most "isolated" users rated few items.

2.2 Recommendation Algorithms

We describe the Collaborative Filtering (CF) algorithms that we tested on the Yelp-Restaurants(20) dataset. All the algorithms are based on the K-nearest neighbors approach with K = 10. In the description we adopt the following notation: u is the user for whom the predictions are computed and v is another user; i is the item for which u's rating is estimated and j is another item; $\hat{r}_{ui}$ is the estimate of u's rating of i; $\overline{r}_i$ ($\overline{r}_j$) is the average rating received by item i (j); $\overline{r}_u$ ($\overline{r}_v$) is the average rating given to items by user u (v).
Item-to-item CF.

This algorithm assumes that u's preference for i can be inferred from the ratings (s)he gave to items j that the other users rated similarly to i; $\hat{r}_{ui}$ is computed as follows:

$$\hat{r}_{ui} = \overline{r}_i + \frac{\sum_{j \in N_u(i)} \sigma(i,j)(r_{uj} - \overline{r}_j)}{\sum_{j \in N_u(i)} |\sigma(i,j)|} \quad (1)$$

where: $N_u(i)$ is the set of neighbor items of i that have been rated by u; $\sigma(i,j)$ is the Pearson Similarity between i and j tuned with significance weighting; see [3]. $\sigma(i,j)$ is used to identify i's neighbors[1] and to weight their contributions to $\hat{r}_{ui}$.
Community-based user-to-user (U2U) CF.

This algorithm uses the ratings provided by u's neighbors from her/his community to estimate u's ones. As an aggregation factor for the formation of communities we considered direct friendship

UMAP '17, July 09-12, 2017, Bratislava, Slovakia

© 2017 Copyright held by the owner/author(s). ACM ISBN 978-1-4503-4635-1/17/07.
DOI: http://dx.doi.org/10.1145/3079628.3079629

---

[1]In order to select very similar items, only those for which $\sigma(i,j) \geq 0.5$ are considered as candidate neighbors of i.

relations *and* the number of common friends among users. Given u's community of friends, $\hat{r}_{ui}$ is computed as follows:

$$\hat{r}_{ui} = \bar{r}_u + \frac{\sum_{v \in N_i(u)} \sigma(u,v)(r_{vi} - \bar{r}_v)}{\sum_{v \in N_i(u)} |\sigma(u,v)|} \qquad (2)$$

where: $N_i(u)$ is the set of neighbors of u (according to $\sigma(u,v)$) who rated i. Moreover, $\sigma(u,v)$ is the modified Jaccard Similarity ($JS'(u,v)$) between u and v, computed by taking the number of common friends, and direct friendship relations, into account:

$$\sigma(u,v) = JS'(u,v) = \frac{|Friends_u \cap Friends_v| + 1}{|Friends_u \cup Friends_v|} \qquad (3)$$

$JS'(u,v)$ captures the concept of direct and mutual friendship in user groups: when u and v have no common friends, $JS'(u,v)$ returns a positive value so that they are not excluded from the set of candidates for preference estimation. However, it returns higher values for people socially connected at the group level.

Tag-based U2U CF.

The idea is that, as tags describe item types, rating an item j provides evidence of interest in other items having tags in common with j; e.g., see [4]. Moreover, the number of ratings given by the user to items tagged as t provides evidence about her/his degree of interest in t. Therefore, u's interests can be described as a vector X_u specifying the number of occurrences (frequencies) of the tags associated to the items (s)he rated: $X_u = < freq_{t1}, \ldots, freq_{tn} >$. Preferences are estimated user-to-user, by means of Equation 2. However, user similarity (denoted as $\sigma_T(u,v)$) is based on the common tags occurring in u and v's vectors. Specifically, $N_i(u)$ is the set of neighbors v of u who rated i, with $\sigma_T(u,v) \geq 0.5$ to select very similar neighbors. Moreover, $\sigma_T(u,v)$ is the cosine similarity between X_u and X_v, modified by means of significance weighting to consider the number of common tags in the two vectors:

$$\sigma_T(u,v) = \frac{\min(|T_{uv}|, \gamma)}{\gamma} cosineSimilarity(X_u, X_v) \qquad (4)$$

T_{uv} is the number of tags occurring in both X_u and X_v, and γ is threshold set to optimize the accuracy (F1) of the algorithm via regression testing.

Community+Tag-based U2U CF. We consider the joint contribution of community and tag-based similarities to generate predictions, assuming that they corroborate each other. Here, $\hat{r}_{ui}$ is computed using Equation 2, applied to users belonging to u's friends community. However, the similarity between users is the sum of the modified Jaccard Similarity (Equation 3) and the Tag-based one (Equation 4), normalized in $[0,1]$: $\sigma(u,v) = \frac{JS'(u,v) + \sigma_T(u,v)}{2}$

Friends-based U2U CF.

Given the principle that similarity breeds connection, and the results reported in [1], this algorithm exploits a selection of u's neighbors from her/his direct friends, considering the number of common friends among them, to predict u's preferences. Here, $\hat{r}_{ui}$ is computed using Equation 2, where $\sigma(u,v) = JS'(u,v)$ is the modified Jaccard Similarity between u and v; see Equation 3.

FilteredFriends-based U2U CF.

This algorithm exploits both friendship and rating behavior to estimate preferences, using these factors to select u's neighbors. We defined a hybrid user-to-user recommender that works as follows: firstly, it selects a set of candidate neighbors of u based on the rating

similarity on the items having at least one tag in common with i. Then, it sorts the set of candidates by friendship similarity, using the modified Jaccard Similarity in the network of u's direct friends, and it selects the best K neighbors on the basis of $JS'(u,v)$. We considered two similarity thresholds for the selection of neighbors to investigate the impact of social proximity and connection on prediction capabilities: $JS'(u,v) \geq 0$ and $JS'(u,v) \geq 0.1$. Then, it computes $\hat{r}_{ui}$ using Equation 2, where $\sigma(u,v)$ is $JS'(u,v)$.

3 EXPERIMENTAL RESULTS

We tested the performance of the previous algorithms on the Yelp-Restaurants(20) dataset by applying 5-fold cross-validation, after having randomly distributed users on folders. For each user, we used 80% of the ratings as learning set and 20% as test set. We evaluated the recommenders on their best 10 predictions. The evaluation produced the following results:

1) The Community-based U2U CF recommender obtains poor accuracy values, confirming that communities fail to provide specific information about user preferences [5].

2) Friends-based U2U CF ($JS'(u,v) \geq 0$) obtains poor accuracy values. However, by restricting neighbors to direct friends who have several common friends ($JS'(u,v) \geq 0.1$), it achieves the third-best accuracy results.

3) The combination of friendship and rating-based similarity is the most promising approach regarding accuracy. FilteredFriends U2U CF ($JS'(u,v) \geq 0.1$) outperforms all the other algorithms by restricting the pool of candidate neighbors to common friendship. However, it has limited user coverage (41%).

4 CONCLUSIONS

We compared the performance of different Collaborative Filtering recommenders to evaluate the usefulness of integrating social information with data about rating behavior. We discovered that the accuracy of predictions can improve by restricting the set of neighbor users to those belonging to the network of highly interconnected friends whose interests are similar to the user's ones. This work was funded by the University of Torino in the "Ricerca Locale" support program.

REFERENCES

[1] L.M. Aiello, A. Barrat, R. Schifanella, C. Cattuto, B. Markines, and F. Menczer. 2012. Friendship prediction and homophily in social media. *ACM Transactions on the Web (TWEB)* 6, 2 (2012), art. 9.

[2] A. Bellogín, I. Cantador, and P. Castells. 2010. A Study of Heterogeneity in Recommendations for a Social Music Service. In *Proceedings of the 1st International Workshop on Information Heterogeneity and Fusion in Recommender Systems*. ACM, New York, NY, USA, 1–8.

[3] C. Desrosiers and G. Karypis. 2011. A Comprehensive Survey of Neighborhood-based Recommendation Methods. In *Recommender systems handbook*, F. Ricci, L. Rokach, B. Shapira, and P.B. Kantor (Eds.). Springer, 107–144.

[4] J. Gemmel, T. Schimoler, B. Mobasher, and R. Burke. 2012. Resource recommendation in social annotation systems: a linear-weighted hybrid approach. *Journal of computer and system sciences* 78 (2012), 1160–1174.

[5] X. Xu H. Bisgin, N. Agarwal. 2010. Investigating Homophily in Online Social Networks. In *Proc. of Web Intelligence and Intelligent Agent Technology (WI-IAT)*. Toronto, Ontario, Canada, 533–536.

[6] X. Liu and K. Aberer. 2013. SoCo: A Social Network Aided Context-aware Recommender System. In *Proceedings of the 22Nd International Conference on World Wide Web*. ACM, New York, NY, USA, 781–802.

[7] M. McPherson, L. Smith-Lovin, and J. Cook. 2001. Birds of a feather: homophily in social networks. *Annual review of sociology* 27 (2001), 415–444.

[8] Yelp. Yelp Dataset Challenge. https://www.yelp.com/dataset_challenge.

Combining Supervised and Unsupervised Learning to Discover Emotional Classes

Miguel Arevalillo-Herráez
Universitat de València
Departament d'Informàtica
Avda. de la Universidad s/n
46100. Burjassot. Valencia, Spain
miguel.arevalillo@uv.es

Aladdin Ayesh
De Montfort University
School of Computer Science and Informatics
The Gateway
Leicester, UK LE1 9BH
aayesh@dmu.ac.uk

Olga C. Santos
Computer Science School, UNED
aDeNu Research Group. Artificial Intelligence Dept.
Calle Juan del Rosal, 16
28040. Madrid, Spain
ocsantos@dia.uned.es

Pablo Arnau-González
University of the West of Scotland
School of Engineering and Computing
Paisley, Lanark, Scotland PA1 2BE
Pablo.ArnauGonzalez@uws.ac.uk

ABSTRACT

Most previous work in emotion recognition has fixed the available classes in advance, and attempted to classify samples into one of these classes using a supervised learning approach. In this paper, we present preliminary work on combining supervised and unsupervised learning to discover potential latent classes which were not initially considered. To illustrate the potential of this hybrid approach, we have used a Self-Organizing Map (SOM) to organize a large number of Electroencephalogram (EEG) signals from subjects watching videos, according to their internal structure. Results suggest that a more useful labelling scheme could be produced by analysing the resulting topology in relation to user reported valence levels (i.e., pleasantness) for each signal, refining the original set of target classes.

KEYWORDS

class discovery; EEG; affective computing; user modelling; cluster analysis; personalization

ACM Reference format:
Miguel Arevalillo-Herráez, Aladdin Ayesh, Olga C. Santos, and Pablo Arnau-González. 2017. Combining Supervised and Unsupervised Learning to Discover Emotional Classes. In *Proceedings of UMAP '17, July 9-12, 2017, Bratislava, Slovakia, ,* 2 pages.
DOI: http://dx.doi.org/10.1145/3079628.3079630

1 INTRODUCTION

Over the last two decades, affective computing has stood out as a leading topic of research in the area of human computer interaction (HCI) [5], and advances have been applied in a wide range of application areas, such as e.g. information security [11], marketing [13],

education [17, 18]. One major challenge in this field is affect detection, which focuses on identifying emotions and other affective phenomena on the user. In general, most research works have focused on producing a supervised classification scheme based on a combination of features. These features can be of a very diverse nature, and come from one or several sources of information [14], from facial expressions [12] to physiological signals [7].

In this common setting, emotional labels are fixed in advance and constrain the analysis of the data within the specified classes. These labels generally consist of a binary value based on the presence or absence of a particular emotion, or relate to the dimensions of emotional models such as the bipolar space of valence (i.e., pleasure) and arousal [16]. In this paper, we follow on some previous work on frameworks to represent and identify emotions [2, 3] and propose a more dynamic and flexible framework to define labels (classes). We also make use of some initial labels that were set according to some particular emotional model, either following a categorical (e.g., happy, sad, bored) or a dimensional scheme (e.g., valence, arousal). However, these are only considered as tentative and are improved by studying implicit relations between the label and the topological structure of the data.

2 METHOD

The analysis carried out in this paper has used the EEG data contained in DEAP [9], a standard repository obtained during a laboratory study. In between other data, DEAP contains EEG signals of 32 people, which were recorded while watching 40 one-minute videos. It also contains self-reported valence levels [16] in the range from 1 to 9, obtained by using Self Assessment Manikins (SAM) [4]. As in other research works, e.g. [1, 9], these levels were converted into a nominal scale (negative/positive) by placing a threshold in the middle.

As a first step, we used a Self Organizing Map [10](SOM) to visually explore the internal structure of the EEG signals contained in DEAP [9], in terms of natural groupings. To this end, we used the same features as reported in DEAP. These are the logarithms of the spectral power in the θ, α, slow α, β and γ frequency bands for each of the 32 electrodes, along with the difference between the spectral power of the 14 symmetrical pairs of electrodes on the right and left hemisphere, in the α, β, θ and γ frequency bands.

Then the structure of the output was analysed, to check whether a meaningful relation between the clusters and the participant's self-reported labels could be found. This was done by computing the density of samples from each class in each SOM node, to identify inherent neighbourhood-based relations between the structure produced by the SOM and the valence label provided in the dataset. Results for a 3×3 SOM are shown in Figure 1. Nodes with more positive than negative samples are shown in green. Others are shown in orange, with a black dot at the center to clearly distinguish them in black and white printing. The intensity of the color is directly proportional to the proportion of samples in the majority class. The single-node green disconnected cluster at the top left-hand side of the SOM suggests that that samples in this node may have some particularities that make them different from others included in the other green cluster in the map. This result indicates that the positive class (green) could potentially be split into two classes, to better represent peculiarities of two different EEG signal structures with regard to the valence level of the emotion; and outline the potential of this methodology for class discovery and refinement.

Density from each class

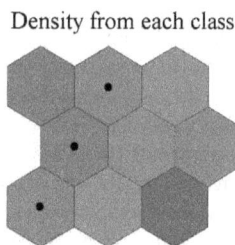

Figure 1: Proportion of samples from each class in each node of a 3×3 SOM.

3 CONCLUSIONS

In this work, we have investigated the combination of supervised and unsupervised learning methods to discover emotional classes; and we have illustrated the proposed method by using the EEG signals and valence labels contained in the public data set DEAP [9]. Still, there are issues that impose important constraints on the applicability of the proposed methodology and deserve further investigation. First, the structural similarity between the samples may be due or influenced by other factors which are not related to the label. In our case, EEG signals from the same subject may be structurally more similar than signals from different participants, whether or not they have been associated with a positive or a negative label. Second, the use of an unsupervised method implies that the meaning of the discovered classes is not automatically defined, and requires a further analysis to be determined. If several labels are simultaneously available for each sample, they may be

automatically combined to produce a more meaningful classification. However, the actual meaning of the resulting classes may still require human intervention. Third, most common difficulties in typical classification settings [15] still remain. For example, the optimum SOM size needs to be experimentally assessed, as it happens with the parameters associated with other related methods e.g. clustering [8] and vector quantization [6].

Acknowledgments. This work has been partly supported by the Spanish Ministry of Economy and Competitiveness through project BIG-AFF (TIN2014-59641-C{1,2}-1-P)

REFERENCES

[1] Pablo Arnau-González, Miguel Arevalillo-Herráez, and Naeem Ramzan. 2017. Fusing highly dimensional energy and connectivity features to identify affective states from EEG signals. *Neurocomputing* 244, 28 (2017), 81–89.

[2] A. Ayesh, M. Arevalillo-Herráez, and F. J. Ferri. 2014. Cognitive reasoning and inferences through psychologically based personalised modelling of emotions using associative classifiers. In *2014 IEEE 13th International Conference on Cognitive Informatics and Cognitive Computing.* 67–72.

[3] Aladdin Ayesh, Miguel Arevalillo-Herráez, and Francesc J. Ferri. 2016. Towards Psychologically based Personalised Modelling of Emotions Using Associative Classifiers. *International Journal of Cognitive Informatics and Natural Intelligence* 10, 2 (April 2016), 52–64.

[4] Margaret M Bradley and Peter J Lang. 1994. Measuring emotion: the self-assessment manikin and the semantic differential. *Journal of behavior therapy and experimental psychiatry* 25, 1 (1994), 49–59.

[5] Rafael A Calvo and Sidney D'Mello. 2010. Affect detection: An interdisciplinary review of models, methods, and their applications. *IEEE Transactions on Affective Computing* 1, 1 (2010), 18–37.

[6] Robert Gray. 1984. Vector quantization. *IEEE Assp Magazine* 1, 2 (1984), 4–29.

[7] S. Jerritta, M. Murugappan, R. Nagarajan, and K. Wan. 2011. Physiological signals based human emotion Recognition: a review. In *2011 IEEE 7th International Colloquium on Signal Processing and its Applications.* 410–415.

[8] Leonard Kaufman and Peter J Rousseeuw. 2009. *Finding groups in data: an introduction to cluster analysis.* Vol. 344. John Wiley & Sons.

[9] S. Koelstra, C. Muhl, M. Soleymani, Jong-Seok Lee, A. Yazdani, T. Ebrahimi, T. Pun, A. Nijholt, and I. Patras. 2012. DEAP: A Database for Emotion Analysis Using Physiological Signals. *IEEE Transactions on Affective Computing* 3, 1 (Jan 2012), 18–31.

[10] Teuvo Kohonen. 1998. The self-organizing map. *Neurocomputing* 21, 1 (1998), 1–6.

[11] Bin Mai, Thomas Parsons, Victor Prybutok, and Kamesh Namuduri. 2017. *Neuroscience Foundations for Human Decision Making in Information Security: A General Framework and Experiment Design.* Springer International Publishing, Cham, 91–98.

[12] Bishwas Mishra, Steven L Fernandes, K Abhishek, Aishwarya Alva, Chaithra Shetty, Chandan V Ajila, Dhanush Shetty, Harshitha Rao, and Priyanka Shetty. 2015. Facial expression recognition using feature based techniques and model based techniques: a survey. In *Electronics and Communication Systems (ICECS), 2015 2nd International Conference on.* IEEE, 589–594.

[13] Andres Navarro, Catherine Delevoye, and David Oyarzun. 2016. *Emotional Platform for Marketing Research.* Springer International Publishing, Cham, 491–501.

[14] Soujanya Poria, Erik Cambria, Rajiv Bajpai, and Amir Hussain. 2017. A review of affective computing: From unimodal analysis to multimodal fusion. *Information Fusion* 37 (2017), 98–125.

[15] Matthias Reif, Faisal Shafait, Markus Goldstein, Thomas Breuel, and Andreas Dengel. 2014. Automatic classifier selection for non-experts. *Pattern Analysis and Applications* 17, 1 (2014), 83–96.

[16] James A. Russell. 1979. Affective Space is Bipolar. *Journal of Personality and Social Psychology* (1979).

[17] Sergio Salmeron-Majadas, Miguel Arevalillo-Herráez, Olga C Santos, Mar Saneiro, Raúl Cabestrero, Pilar Quirós, David Arnau, and Jesus G Boticario. 2015. Filtering of spontaneous and low intensity emotions in educational contexts. In *International Conference on Artificial Intelligence in Education.* Springer, 429–438.

[18] Chih-Hung Wu, Yueh-Min Huang, and Jan-Pan Hwang. 2015. Review of affective computing in education/learning: Trends and challenges. *British Journal of Educational Technology* (2015).

The Adaptation of an Individual's Satisfaction to Group Context: the Role of Ties Strength and Conflicts

Francesco Barile
Department of Mathematics and
Applications
University of Naples Federico II
Naples, Italy
francesco.barile@unina.it

Judith Masthoff
Computing Science Department
University of Aberdeen
Aberdeen, UK
j.masthoff@abdn.ac.uk

Silvia Rossi
Department of Electrical Engineering
and Information Technology
University of Naples Federico II
Naples, Italy
silvia.rossi@unina.it

ABSTRACT

Recent studies on recommender systems raise attention to the importance of context, intended both as the external environment and even as the user's internal state, such as, for example, the mood in which the users are going to perform the recommended activities. This is a key factor also in the group recommendation domain, where the context is characterized by the presence of other people with whom the activities must be performed. In this case, social influences and relationships between users come into play, and the individual satisfaction that each user will obtain could change in relation to those social characteristics. In this work, we start an experimental analysis on how ties' strength and possible conflicts in a relationship can influence the opinion shift, with the aim to derive a model that can be used to adapt individual utilities to the "Group Context" before aggregating them into the group's ones.

KEYWORDS

Group Recommendation; Social Influence; Context-aware recommendation; Opinion Shift

1 INTRODUCTION

Recommendation Systems (RS) generally use very simplistic models, ignoring the fact that the interactions between the users and the system are made in a particular context (e.g., the external environment, or the user's internal state, such as, for example, the mood), while recent studies evidenced the importance of the context in which the recommended items have to be enjoyed [1]. As for individual RS, also in Groups Recommendation Systems (GRS), the context is a key factor that must be considered in the recommendation process. Studies on GRS that consider contextual aspects, usually try to determine factors that can be used as weights in the process of aggregation of individual satisfactions estimated by an individual RS [8, 9], or to determine the best strategies to apply for the specific group on the basis of the characteristics of the relationship between group's members [6]. Even if the individual recommendations are computed by an individual RS that is *Context-Aware*, such a system can barely consider the contextual information related

to the group of people with whom the individual must perform the recommended activities. Hence, GRS should assume that the individual's satisfactions computed for a single person might be adapted to the new *Group Context*. This is characterized by the presence of other people and their satisfaction influences those of the other individuals, in a phenomenon known as *Emotional Contagion* [4, 7].

To model the changing in the user's satisfaction depending on the Group Context, it is crucial to identify the factors characterizing this phenomenon. Starting from studies on opinion shifting and on positive and negative influence [10], we decided to focus the attention on the characteristics of bi-directional ties between group's members, and, in particular, on the *ties strength* [5], and on the *status of the mutual relationships*, by considering the possibility of having a conflicting situation or a peaceful and friendly status. To analyze the impact of these two factors on opinion shifting, in this work, we present an experimental analysis, based on a user study, where participants were required to fill in a simple questionnaire performed online.

2 A USER STUDY

At the start of the study, an English test was taken by each participant, and only those who passed the test have been included. We implemented the experiment as an online questionnaire on Amazon Mechanical Turk [1]. Then, after an explanation of the experiment, we present a view containing two evaluations for the same eight activities. We asked the participants to imagine that the first set of evaluations was made by them in the past, and that the second was made by a person with whom they have a relationship with particular characteristics. In particular, we asked for different ties strength, distinguishing between *weak*, *intermediate* and *strong* ties [5]. Regarding the status of the relationships, we consider the possibility of having a conflicting situation or a peaceful and friendly status, according to [10]. Finally, we ask the participants to rate their current preferences for the proposed activities, knowing their old preferences and the preferences of the other person and assuming that they may need to do one or more of these activities with the other person.

Each participant was asked to perform the test three times, answering for only 3 different configurations out of the 9 possible combinations, keeping the tie strength the same but varying the conflict. This choice is made to guarantee that the test occupies only few minutes, since, as suggested in [3], questionnaires that

[1] https://www.mturk.com/mturk/

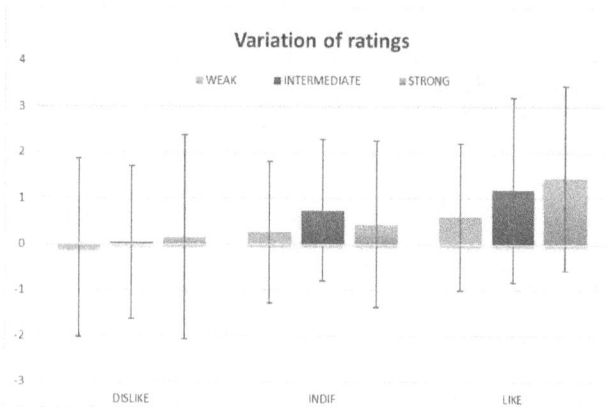

Figure 1: Average values for the ratings variation

take more than a few minutes to complete may produce a loss of concentration in participants. Hence, the designed questionnaire has been designed to require only 5 minutes to be completed. We recruit 60 participants, obtaining 180 answers. Since each answer contains 8 evaluations, we collected more than 1,400 evaluations. The participants were paid $ 0.50 for the participation in the test.

3 RESULTS ANALYSIS

Starting from the answers provided to the questionnaires, we evaluate the opinion shift by computing the variation between the new evaluations for the activities given by the participants in the test and the old evaluations, which had been shown to them at the start of the study. We consider as a positive shift a change towards the rating of the second person, while a negative shift is in the opposite case (e.g., the rating variation value will have the negative sign).

Figure 1 shows the general trends, illustrating the average values and standard deviations of the rating variations, grouped with respect to the different parameters that we impose into the experiment. The difference is statistically significant ($ANOVA$, $p < 0.001$).

As we can see, there is a general positive shifting in the case of good relationships, i.e. when the participant likes the other person, and, as we expected, this shifting increases when the strength of the ties became stronger. This behavior is in line with respect to many results present in the literature. We can, also, notice that for indifferent people there is still a positive shifting, and so an influence on the rating variations, even if the amplitude is lower than in the previous case. Moreover, notice that the combination of indifferent and intermediate is the one with the unexpected behavior, since it is the one with the highest result in the group suggesting a sort of "social conformance behavior" that has to be further explored. The last evidence is that for disliked people; the average variations are very small and, for weak ties, there is a small negative influence.

4 CONCLUSION

Context-aware recommender systems (CARS) is a relative recent field, addressing the problem of how to adapt recommendations to the specific contextual situation of the user, since users' preferences

may vary in relation to it, to generate more relevant recommendations [1, 11]. Since context is a key factor in the recommendation process, it must be considered also in Groups Recommendation Systems (GRS); in this case, GRS should assume that the individual preferences, estimated through individual RS, might be adapted to the new *Group Context*, characterized by the presence of other people, since their satisfaction can be influenced by the other individual ones [2, 4, 7].

Starting from these considerations, in this paper an experimental analysis is presented, based on a user study, in order to evaluate the impact of the *tie strength* and of the *status of the mutual relationships* on opinion shifting. The long-term objective is to derive a model to describe how the user's satisfaction changes in relation to the Group Context in which activities must be performed. Results show that, in general, positive shift increases according to the strength of the relationship, with more marked variations for friendly and peaceful relationships, even if negative shift can occur for conflicting relationship. Results also suggest that these two factors cannot be sufficient to describe a general model that applies to specific cases, but the analysis must be deepened considering other possibilities.

REFERENCES

[1] Gediminas Adomavicius and Alexander Tuzhilin. 2015. Context-aware recommender systems. In *Recommender systems handbook*. Springer, 191–226.
[2] Sigal G Barsade. 2002. The ripple effect: Emotional contagion and its influence on group behavior. *Administrative Science Quarterly* 47, 4 (2002), 644–675.
[3] Robin IM Dunbar and Matt Spoors. 1995. Social networks, support cliques, and kinship. *Human Nature* 6, 3 (1995), 273–290.
[4] Hillary Anger Elfenbein. 2014. The many faces of emotional contagion: An affective process theory of affective linkage. *Organizational Psychology Review* 4, 4 (2014), 326–362.
[5] Mark S Granovetter. 1973. The strength of weak ties. *American Journal of sociology* 78, 6 (May 1973), 1360–1380.
[6] Judith Masthoff. 2015. Group recommender systems: Aggregation, satisfaction and group attributes. In *Recommender Systems Handbook*. Springer, 743–776.
[7] Judith Masthoff and Albert Gatt. 2006. In pursuit of satisfaction and the prevention of embarrassment: affective state in group recommender systems. *User Modeling and User-Adapted Interaction* 16, 3-4 (2006), 281–319.
[8] Silvia Rossi, Francesco Barile, Antonio Caso, and Alessandra Rossi. 2015. Pre-trip Ratings and Social Networks User Behaviors for Recommendations in Touristic Web Portals. In *International Conference on Web Information Systems and Technologies*. Springer, 297–317.
[9] Silvia Rossi, Antonio Caso, and Francesco Barile. 2015. Combining users and items rankings for group decision support. In *Trends in Practical Applications of Agents, Multi-Agent Systems and Sustainability*. Springer, 151–158.
[10] Károly Takács, Andreas Flache, and Michael Mäs. 2014. Is there negative social influence? Disentangling effects of dissimilarity and disliking on opinion shifts. (2014).
[11] Yong Zheng, Bamshad Mobasher, and Robin Burke. 2015. Similarity-based context-aware recommendation. In *International Conference on Web Information Systems Engineering*. Springer, 431–447.

The Influence of City Size on Dietary Choices and Food Recommendation

Hao Cheng
Leibniz Universität Hannover
Hannover, Germany
cheng@ikg.uni-hannover.de

Markus Rokicki
L3S Research Center
Hannover, Germany
rokicki@l3s.de

Eelco Herder
L3S Research Center
Hannover, Germany
herder@l3s.de

ABSTRACT

Contextual features have been leveraged by recommender systems in many different domains. Traditional contextual features – such as location and time – have successfully been combined with collaborative filtering or content-based features. However, it is likely that there are other – domain-specific – features that may have even more impact. In this paper, we focus on the influence of city size on food preferences. Apart from location and time, our results show that city size can significantly boost the performance of food recommendation.

KEYWORDS

Online food; city size differences; food recommendation

1 INTRODUCTION

Location-related features are well-explored in recommender systems, including context-aware food or restaurant recommenders. However, in past studies, locational features were mostly extracted on the level of countries, states, or cities [1, 6, 12, 13]. In this paper, we focus on a relatively unexplored feature: the impact of *city size* on food recommendation. Researchers have found that socio-economic characteristics are largely shaped by city population size [2]. In addition, [9] shows differences in Asian cities with different sizes in the process of urbanization, diet change, and transformation of food supply chains.

In this paper, we first analyze food preferences in relation to city size in the large German online food community kochbar.de[1]. We then use city size for building a context-aware recommender system (CARS) and compare its impact on recommendation performance to several common spatio-temporal contexts. Compared with non-context–aware recommender systems, city size turned out to outperform other contexts with an improvement 48% using a matrix factorization model for item prediction.

2 RELATED WORK

There are many analyses of geographical differences in eating preferences. Ahn et al. built flavor networks to uncover the ingredient

[1]http://www.kochbar.de

This work was partially funded by the German Federal Ministry of Education and Research (BMBF) under project GlycoRec (16SV7172).

preferences of cuisines worldwide [1]. Howell et al. analyzed taste preferences for different countries [6]. Wagner et al. used server logs to reveal ingredient preferences in German-speaking countries [12]. West et al. analyzed web usage logs to discover nutrient patterns of American states [13].

Food recommender systems try to match recipes to user profiles. Freyne and Berkovsky [4] used two hybrid recommendation strategies, recipe-based and ingredient-based. Elahi et al. built a food recommendation application to interact with the user's long-term and short-term preferences [3]. Research on context-aware recommender systems [5] showed that including context features leads to more robust recommender systems. In this paper, we explore the impact of city size on food recommendation.

3 METHODOLOGY

Our study is based on a large-scale crawl from Kochbar.de [7]. It consists of over 400 thousand recipes published between 2008 and 2014, with more than 7 million ratings. As the ratings are overwhelmingly positive – 99% are 5-star ratings – similar as in [11], we treat the presence of ratings as positive feedback.

We have analyzed and selected two temporal and two locational features for the recommender models. *Day-of-the-week* (weekday and weekend) and *season* are derived from the upload time stamp of the recipes. The *inner border* (north-east, north-west, and south) context conditions are generated by mapping the cooks' location data to wikipedia data[2]. *City size* is derived by finding the closest city based on Geonames[3] location data and using Geonames city population data to group cities into five city sizes: metropolis ($>= 1m$), big-city $[500k, 1m)$, medium-city $[100k, 500k)$, small-city $[50k, 100k)$, and town $[15k, 50k)$.

For the recommendation task, we employ two baseline recommenders: the unpersonalized most-popular item recommender (MP) and Bayesian Personalized Ranking (BPR), a state-of-the-art matrix factorization model for item ranking [10]. These baseline algorithms are compared with corresponding *context-aware* recommenders, which are created by filtering users and items according to the relevant context factor. These algorithms are denoted as MP(ui) and BPR(ui). Then, the recommenders only recommend items that are in the same condition to the users. For instance, cosmopolitan users would receive recommendations for cosmopolitan recipes, based on ratings of other cosmopolitan users. We use random partitioning of the user-item matrix to monitor the bias caused by the algorithms with partitioning. The performances of the recommenders are evaluated in terms of mean average precision (MAP).

[2]https://en.wikipedia.org/wiki/Inner_German_border
[3]http://www.geonames.org

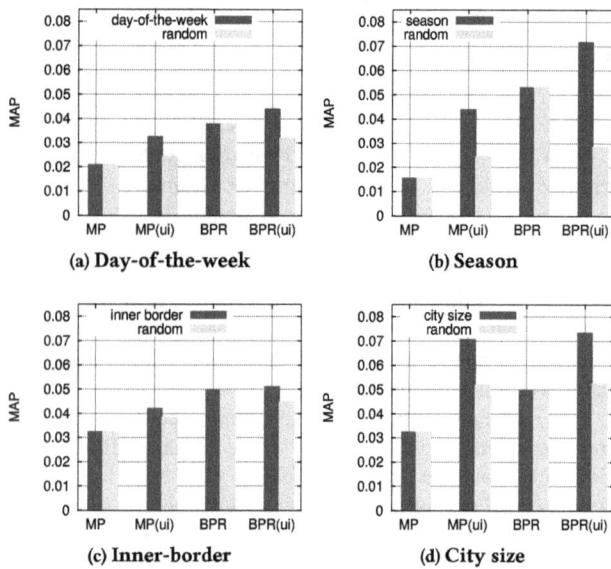

(a) Day-of-the-week

(b) Season

(c) Inner-border

(d) City size

Figure 1: Evaluation of Food Recommender Systems.

4 RESULTS

Data Analysis. We start with a brief overview on observed differences. Main dishes in metropolises ($M = 12.6$), big cities ($M = 12.5$), and small cities ($M = 12.3$) contain more ingredients than in medium-cities ($M = 11.52$, e.g. metropolitan vs. medium-city: $W = 11288000$, $p \ll .001$, $r = .15$). Metropolis and big city recipes contain categories like Orient, Turkey and Indonesia, whereas location categories for towns include local East-Frisian, Swabian and Thuringian cuisine, as well as some nearby countries like Denmark and Switzerland. As expected, spices are more frequently used in big cities ($M = 94.3\%$) and metropolises ($M = 93.4\%$) than in medium (91.3%) cities as well ($N = 45497$, $\chi^2 = 35$, $df = 4$, $p \ll .001$). Red meat is more eaten in big cities ($M = 38.4\%$) than in cosmopolitan ($M = 34.7\%$) and medium ($M = 36.4\%$) cities ($N = 45497$, $\chi^2 = 20.34$, $df = 4$, $p < .001$). In summary, metropolitan main dishes are more complicated and exotic than medium-city main dishes; in towns, people typically cook more traditional.

Recommendation Experiment. To analyze the impact of city size on CARS we compare its performance with other commonly used contexts. As the user-recipe matrix is very sparse and the ratings are overwhelmingly positive, the recommendation task is item ranking. We compare each context-based recommender with the baseline recommender with the data randomly partitioned using the same number of pseudo-conditions. When a CARS outperforms both its baseline and the random partitioning recommender, it can be concluded that the corresponding contextual feature improves the recommendation performance. This is the case for each of the contexts, as can be seen in Figure 1.

A direct comparison of recommendation performance for different contexts is not valid. Instead, we compare performance improvements of context-aware recommenders to their respective non-context-aware models using the different contextual features.

Profound improvements are shown in MP(ui) for the contexts season (184%) and city size (118%), and smaller, but significant improvements for day-of-the-week (56%) and inner border contexts (30%). The improvements for BPR(ui) are not as large as for MP(ui), but still remarkable for the contexts city size (48%), season (35%), and day-of-the-week (17%). However, the improvement found for the inner border context is fairly small (3%). The city size aware recommender BPR(ui) (MAP = 0.073) gives the best performance compared with the baseline recommender BPR (MAP = 0.05).

5 CONCLUSIONS

In this paper, we have shown that food preferences depend on the size of city that people are living in. Among others, in Germany, people in cosmopolitan cities eat more foreign food; people in smaller cities and towns eat more traditionally. Using city size has a positive impact on context-aware recipe recommendation – we observed a 48% increase in MAP compared to the baseline.

It is known that there are differences across city sizes in other areas as well, including civic involvement and economic performance [8]. Knowledge on the impact of city size can be effectively translated into measures to reinforce or counteract such effects. Therefore, it is likely that city size has an impact on context-based recommendations in general.

REFERENCES

[1] Yong-Yeol Ahn, Sebastian E Ahnert, James P Bagrow, and Albert-László Barabási. 2011. Flavor network and the principles of food pairing. *Scientific reports* 1 (2011).

[2] Luís MA Bettencourt, José Lobo, Dirk Helbing, Christian Kühnert, and Geoffrey B West. 2007. Growth, innovation, scaling, and the pace of life in cities. *Proceedings of the national academy of sciences* 104, 17 (2007), 7301–7306.

[3] Mehdi Elahi, Mouzhi Ge, Francesco Ricci, Shlomo Berkovsky, and Massimo David. 2015. Interaction Design in a Mobile Food Recommender System. In *Proceedings of the Joint Workshop on Interfaces and Human Decision Making for Recommender Systems, IntRS*. 49–52.

[4] Jill Freyne and Shlomo Berkovsky. 2010. Recommending food: Reasoning on recipes and ingredients. In *International Conference on User Modeling, Adaptation, and Personalization*. Springer, 381–386.

[5] Jonathan L Herlocker and Joseph A Konstan. 2001. Content-independent task-focused recommendation. *IEEE Internet Computing* 5, 6 (2001), 40–47.

[6] Patrick D Howell, Layla D Martin, Hesamoddin Salehian, Chul Lee, Kyler M Eastman, and Joohyun Kim. 2016. Analyzing Taste Preferences From Crowdsourced Food Entries. In *Proceedings of the 6th International Conference on Digital Health Conference*. ACM, 131–140.

[7] Tomasz Kusmierczyk, Christoph Trattner, and Kjetil Nørvåg. 2015. Temporality in online food recipe consumption and production. In *Proceedings of the 24th International Conference on World Wide Web Companion*. International World Wide Web Conferences Steering Committee, 55–56.

[8] Michael Parkinson, Richard Meegan, and Jay Karecha. 2015. City size and economic performance: Is bigger better, small more beautiful or middling marvellous? *European Planning Studies* 23, 6 (2015), 1054–1068.

[9] Thomas Reardon, David Tschirley, Michael Dolislager, Jason Snyder, Chaoran Hu, and Stephanie White. 2014. Urbanization, diet change, and transformation of food supply chains in Asia. *Michigan: Global Center for Food Systems Innovation* (2014).

[10] Steffen Rendle, Christoph Freudenthaler, Zeno Gantner, and Lars Schmidt-Thieme. 2009. BPR: Bayesian personalized ranking from implicit feedback. In *Proceedings of the twenty-fifth conference on uncertainty in artificial intelligence*. AUAI Press, 452–461.

[11] Markus Rokicki, Eelco Herder, Tomasz Kuśmierczyk, and Christoph Trattner. 2016. Plate and prejudice: gender differences in online cooking. In *Proceedings of the 2016 Conference on User Modeling Adaptation and Personalization*. ACM, 207–215.

[12] Claudia Wagner, Philipp Singer, and Markus Strohmaier. 2014. The nature and evolution of online food preferences. *EPJ Data Science* 3, 1 (2014), 1.

[13] Robert West, Ryen W White, and Eric Horvitz. 2013. From cookies to cooks: Insights on dietary patterns via analysis of web usage logs. In *Proceedings of the 22nd international conference on World Wide Web*. ACM, 1399–1410.

Behavioral Patterns Mining for Online Time Personalization

Tomas Chovanak
Slovak University of Technology in
Bratislava, Faculty of Informatics and
Information Technologies
Ilkovicova 2, 842 16 Slovakia
xchovanak@stuba.sk

Ondrej Kassak
Slovak University of Technology in
Bratislava, Faculty of Informatics and
Information Technologies
Ilkovicova 2, 842 16 Slovakia
ondrej.kassak@stuba.sk

Maria Bielikova
Slovak University of Technology in
Bratislava, Faculty of Informatics and
Information Technologies
Ilkovicova 2, 842 16 Slovakia
maria.bielikova@stuba.sk

ABSTRACT

Behavioral patterns represent repeating sequences or sets of actions, which website users often perform together. Such patterns can be used to identify user preferences, recommend interesting content to him, etc. For dynamic sites with fast changing content (e.g., news, social networks) we need to recognize such patterns in an online time. In this paper, we introduce a novel method for recognizing behavioral patterns in an online time over a data stream. Main contribution is a combination of global patterns with patterns specific for groups of similar users. We evaluated the method using a personalized recommendation task over datasets from news and e-learning domains and show that the combination of common global and specific group patterns reaches higher recommendation precision than its components used individually.

CCS CONCEPTS

• Information Systems → World Wide Web → Web mining • Computing methodologies → Machine learning → Learning paradigms → Supervised learning

KEYWORDS

Web Site Adaptation, Behavioral Patterns, Frequent Itemsets, Clustering, Data Stream, Personalized Recommendation

1 INTRODUCTION AND RELATED WORK

Nowadays there can be seen an increasing trend of dynamic sites, where the pages and thus also patterns remain actual only shortly. For this reason, it is needed to be able to identify behavioral patterns quickly and to react to frequent changes. The actual patterns can be used for improvement of user experience and satisfaction with the website in online time. It is possible to recommend to the user an interesting content, preload pages he is probably going to visit, predict session exit intent [4], etc.

The quality of behavioral patterns is proportional to similarity of users they are recognized from.

UMAP '17, July 09-12, 2017, Bratislava, Slovakia
© 2017 Copyright is held by the owner/author(s).
ACM ISBN 978-1-4503-4635-1/17/07.
DOI: http://dx.doi.org/10.1145/3079628.3079631

For this reason, it is suitable to cluster users based on their behavioral characteristics. We believe that usage of global patterns in combination with patterns specific for certain user groups, leads to higher quality results in tasks, where patterns are used (e.g., recommendation).

There exist various approaches concerning knowledge discovery from web usage data in form of behavioral patterns. They may be modelled as partitions of user navigation graph [3], association rules [5, 9], Markov models [6], symbols [7] or clusters of similar user sessions [5]. These patterns are typically applied for recommendation of interesting content to users [3, 9] or predicting users' behavior [5, 6]. A common disadvantage of these approaches is that they identify patterns offline, in accurate but computationally expensive way. Therefore, the patterns can become quickly outdated thus their usability for short-term tasks is highly limited.

To be able to recognize behavioral patterns in dynamically changing domains, it is important to use a simple representation, which is not computationally extensive and thus usable in data streams. An example of such representation is frequent closed itemsets [10], which is considered as compact, not redundant and effective representation, less complex than frequent sequences or association rules. Itemset is closed if there is no superset with the same support (number of occurrences in data) and it is frequent if its' support is greater than minimal support threshold.

Several approaches were proposed for frequent closed itemsets mining. *IncMine* [8] is fast and memory effective algorithm from data stream, which is important for dynamic sites processing. Unlike other approaches it performs patterns updates in small batches and approximates mining over a sliding window containing only most recent elements. Therefore, it can respond well to conceptual changes in data stream. It is also computationally more effective than exact frequent itemset mining algorithms because it considers only itemsets from limited history.

3 BEHAVIORAL PATTERNS MINING

We have proposed a method for behavioral patterns mining in online time from the user activity within the website. The method combines global patterns, identified from behavior of all website users, with group patterns identified for specific groups of similar users. In overall, our method comprises of two main steps performed simultaneously over data stream:

1. User clustering based on similarity of their behavior.
2. Global and group behavioral patterns mining.

Process of behavioral patterns mining is designed to be usable in an online time. As the sessions, represented as a set of performed actions (webpage visits, product purchases, etc.), come in a continuous stream, we process them by a single pass.

The users are clustered based on their previous behavior (frequencies of performed actions), stored in their user models. The user models are updated continuously after each session (set of related actions), so the method works always with up to date data and it is able to quickly react even to sudden and frequent changes. As a data stream of user sessions could be potentially infinite, we need to prevent possible memory overload. We represent user's behavior as frequency spectrum of his recent actions. User actions are stored in a queue with limited capacity to prevent high memory consumption. Our method clusters users in regular time intervals. For each user model, we trace its last usage time. Period required to mark the user model as old (to be deleted) is determined by method input parameter.

To be able to identify the groups of similar users continuously over time, we adopted approach enabling stream clustering. Chosen *CluStream* algorithm [1] (with k-means macroclustering) offers fast microclustering in online time with effective macroclustering step computing final clusters on demand.

Finally, the session becomes an input for *IncMine* algorithm modified to mine global as well as group behavioral patterns represented as frequent closed itemsets. It performs pattern mining simultaneously for each user group and for all users together. The behavioral patterns are identified and selected individually for every user by combination of global patterns and group (similar users from the same cluster) patterns.

4 EVALUATION AND CONCLUSIONS

We evaluated proposed method on recommendation task. Each user session was divided into train part used for behavioral patterns mining and test part used for evaluation of recommended pages to visit. Recommendations are generated as the most probable next user actions based on mined patterns.

We used two datasets from domains with different characteristics. First dataset comes from e-learning (ELS) site (24k sessions, 870 users, 2k pages) [2], second belongs to news site (NS) (334k sessions, 199k users, 85 page categories). We compare results of our method to two baseline approaches. First baseline uses for recommendation global behavioral patterns only mined with *IncMine* algorithm. Second uses group behavioral patterns only mined the same way as individual part of our method.

Recommendation results were compared by *precision* metric. We performed statistical unpaired t-test to compare *precision* of baseline methods. For both datasets our method reached significant increase of *precision* when compared to both baselines

(1.7% and 21.4% in ELS, 0.9% and 41.4% in NS). In addition to overall *precision*, we observed recommendation precision inside each user group during the stream processing. Proposed method reached for both datasets the highest precision, which shows that it is suitable to combine global and group patterns.

In addition, we compared proposed method with additional data stream algorithms for frequent itemsets mining (*CloStream* mining exact frequent closed itemsets and *EstDec+* mining maximal frequent itemsets) and data stream clustering alghoritm (ClusTree). Our combination of *IncMine* and *CluStream* performed in experiments the best.

Experiments show that for dynamic domain it is suitable to work with recent patterns only and to combine global and group patterns. Our method outperformed compared algorithms in all measurements. We also observed that additional computational cost caused by mining group behavioral patterns is constant, parallelizable and thus well maintainable in production environment.

Acknowledgement

This work was partially supported by grants APVV-15-0508 and VG 1/0646/15.

REFERENCES

[1] Aggarwal, C. C., et al. 2003. A framework for clustering evolving data streams. In: *Proceedings of the 29th international conference on Very large data bases - Volume 29*. VLDB Endowment, pp. 81-92.

[2] Bielikova, M. et al. 2014. ALEF: from application to platform for adaptive collaborative learning. *Recommender Systems for Technology Enhanced Learning.* Springer New York. pp. 195-225.

[3] Jalali, M., Mustapha, N., Nasir Sulaiman, M. and Mamat, A. 2010. WebPUM: A Web-based recommendation system to predict user future movements. *Expert Systems With Applications*, 37, 6201–6212.

[4] Kassak, O., Kompan, M., Bielikova, M. 2016. Student Behavior in a Web-Based Educational System: Exit Intent Prediction. Int. Scientific Journal Engineering Applications of Artificial Intelligence. Vol. 51, 136-149.

[5] Liraki, Z., Harounabadi, A., Mirabedini, J. 2015. Predicting the Users' Navigation Patterns in Web, using Weighted Association Rules and Users' Navigation Information. *Int. J. of Computer Applications*, vol. 110, no. 12.

[6] Makker, S., Rathy, R. K. 2011. Web Server Performance Optimization using Prediction Prefetching Engine. *Int. Journal of Computer Applications* (0975–8887), vol. 23, no. 9.

[7] Sevcech J., Bielikova M. 2017. Repeating Patterns as Symbols for Long Time Series Representation. *J. of Systems and Software.* vol. 127, 179-194.

[8] Quadrana, M., Bifet, A., Gavalda, R. 2015. An efficient closed frequent itemset miner for the MOA stream mining system. *AI Communications*, vol. 28, no. 1, pp. 143-158.

[9] Tyagi, S., Bharadwaj, K. K. 2012. Enhanced new user recommendations based on quantitative association rule mining. *Procedia Computer Science*, vol. 10, pp. 102-109.

[10] Zaki, Mohammed J., and Ching-Jui Hsiao. 1999. CHARM: An efficient algorithm for closed association rule mining. *Tech. Rep. 99*, (1999) vol. 10.

Modeling the Dynamics of Online News Reading Interests

Elena Viorica Epure
CRI, Panthéon-Sorbonne
Paris, France
Elena.Epure@malix.univ-paris1.fr

Benjamin Kille
DAI-Lab, TU Berlin
Berlin, Germany
benjamin.kille@dai-labor.de

Jon Espen Ingvaldsen
IDI, NTNU
Trondheim, Norway
jonespi@idi.ntnu.no

Rebecca Deneckere
CRI, Panthéon-Sorbonne
Paris, France
Rebecca.Deneckere@univ-paris1.fr

Camille Salinesi
CRI, Panthéon-Sorbonne
Paris, France
Camille.Salinesi@univ-paris1.fr

Sahin Albayrak
DAI-Lab, TU Berlin
Berlin, Germany
sahin.albayrak@dai-labor.de

ABSTRACT

Online news readers exhibit a very dynamic behavior. News publishers have been investigating ways to predict such changes in order to adjust their recommendation strategies and better engage the readers. Existing research focuses on analyzing the evolution of reading interests associated with news categories. Compared to these, we study also how relations among news interests change in time. Observations over a 10-month period on a German news publisher indicate that overall, the relations amid news categories change, but stable periods spanning months are also found. The reasons of these changes and how news publishers could integrate this knowledge in their solutions are subject to further investigation.

KEYWORDS

news reading dynamics; temporal analysis; news reading interests

1 INTRODUCTION

Publishers employ recommender systems to target online content and engage readers. They track reading interests to continuously infer strategies to match readers and content. Further, as events emerge, journalists add news articles to publishers' repertoires. This creates a highly dynamic environment where future interactions cannot be reliably predicted. In this work, we analyze whether relations among news categories exhibit regularities as they evolve. Such regularities, though they exist, would represent valuable information which publishers could exploit as competitive advantage. We reduce the complex problem to two rather simple questions: Which news category will users follow up reading articles of a given category? Will these transitioning patterns remain stable over time? This lets us devise a probabilistic approach to model the evolution of reading behavior. Our contribution is novel as it explicitly considers transitions amid categories.

2 RELATED WORK

In the news domain, online readers rarely express their reading interests explicitly. Nonetheless, recommender systems often rely

on such knowledge. In absence of this kind of information, publishers infer interests for news categories. In some cases, news category taxonomies are created in advance. Then, representative categories are selected for each article and included in the article's meta-data [3, 5]. In other cases, news categories are automatically identified from the article's content as either granular vocabularies [1] or broad news topics such as tourism or local news [6, 7].

Various works have analyzed the evolution of readers' interests from logs [6, 7] to improve news recommenders. Liu *et al.* [7] analyzed the Google News service. For each reader, the monthly average number of clicks per category was calculated. Then, the differences between the click distribution of the last assessed month and each of the previous months were plotted. They found that affinity to categories changed over time. Further, Li *et al.* [6] segmented the click history of news readers in consecutive time-frames from which they extracted the long- and short-term interests. The news interests of consecutive time-frames were compared through the KL-divergence score for each reader and the crowd average score plotted. Their evaluation indicates that short-term interests fluctuate, whereas, the long-term ones remained relatively stable.

Compared to these works, we drive the creation of news recommenders by assessing the progress of relations amid news interests. Specifically, we build on the analysis of Esiyok *et al.* [4] and we focus specifically on the temporal stability of category transitions.

3 EXPERIMENTS

Let $\mathcal{R} = \{r_m\}_{m=1}^{M}$, $\mathcal{A} = \{a_n\}_{n=1}^{N}$ refer to a news publisher's sets of readers and articles. The publisher observes the reading activity over time. Let $e = (e_r, e_a, e_t)$ define a reading event where each variable refers to reader, article, and time. For each reader, the publisher determines a sequence of events: $\Theta_r = \{e^{(k)} : e_r = r\}_{k=1}^{K}$ such that $e_t^{(k)} < e_t^{(k+1)}, \forall k \in K$. Let C refer to the set of news categories ($|C| = V$) and $c(e_a)$ to the category assigned to the event's article. The sequence of events associated with a specific reader r can be then transformed into a sequence of categories $C_u = (c(e_a^{(1)}), c(e_a^{(2)}), \ldots, c(e_a^{(K)}))$. If we consider C_u generated by a discrete first-order Markov Chain over news categories then the transition probabilities are represented by the matrix:

$$S = \begin{bmatrix} p_{11} & \cdots & p_{1V} \\ \vdots & \ddots & \vdots \\ p_{V1} & \cdots & p_{VV} \end{bmatrix} \quad p_{vw} \geq 0, \sum_{c_w \in C} p_{vw} = 1, \quad \forall v, c_v \in C.$$

We obtain p_{vw} as we divide the number of transitions from c_v to c_w by the number of transitions from c_v to any category.

Consequently, we can infer the evolution of reading behavior by observing the stationarity of S. Let t refer to an individual month, and T to the entire period. Let S_t refer to the transition matrix based on observations in $t \in T$. Let S_T refer to the transition matrix based on all observations. We apply a difference test based on the χ^2 statistic comparing each S_t with S_T [2]. If the test yields non-stationarity for the entire period then the computed values per month are plotted for getting insights into possible similar sub-periods. Then the test is applied again for those.

The evaluation uses event logs from January–October, 2015, from a German news publisher with 3 million weekly visits on average. Editors manually assign categories to articles. Events pass through a pre-processing pipeline: determining session reference, sorting chronologically, and splitting in reading episodes. Splitting connects events if they occurred within 1 min to 60 min apart (average of 20 min per reading is reported[1]). Finally, we computed each S_t and the S_T. If articles of successive events had multiple categories assigned, each element of the Cartesian product of categories counts as a transition. The χ^2 test is sensitive to even minor variations which we expect given the large data set. We multiplied the frequencies by a factor of 10^{-3} to counteract the sensitivity.

The results show that the reading behavior for the entire period is not stable ($Q = 5994.6$, df $= 889$, $p = 0$). However, stationary sub-periods were identified: January–Mars ($Q = 301.65$, $p = 0.038$, df $= 260$); April–July ($Q = 6.56$, $p > 0.99$, df $= 48$); September–October ($Q = 14.95$, $p > 0.99$, df $= 55$), and August is a singularity. Figure 1 illustrates transition probabilities for three news categories over the 10-month period. Point sizes reflect the probability. For instance, we observe that transitions remain mostly stable over the period April–July 2015. This yields for all three categories visible through the horizontally aligned points. At the same time, we observe times when transitions change significantly. Comparing the period January–March with April–July, we find hardly any similarity.

We conclude that there are rather stable periods whose connections exhibit irregular breaks in transition probabilities. As a result, preceding months appear to be an adequate basis to define strategies predicting future reading behaviors unless the reading patterns change drastically. We contemplate that various factors could cause such abrupt changes. These may include readers' changing interests due to seasons, publishers adjusting their websites, and breaking news events with long-term effects. Recognizing these fluctuations early on represents a major challenge publishers will have to address in the future. The ability to adjust quickly to major changes could become a decisive competitive advantage for publishers.

4 CONCLUSION AND PERSPECTIVES

Reading interests change over time. Still, we observed close to stationary transition probabilities for periods stretching multiple months. This indicates that publishers can exploit reading behavior to improve targeting content to readers and increasing activity on their platforms. We expect other factors to affect how well the system matches readers and contents. We observed breaks in reading behavior on multiple occasions. Anticipating these inconsistencies

---

[1]http://contentmarketinginstitute.com/2016/01/visitors-read-article/

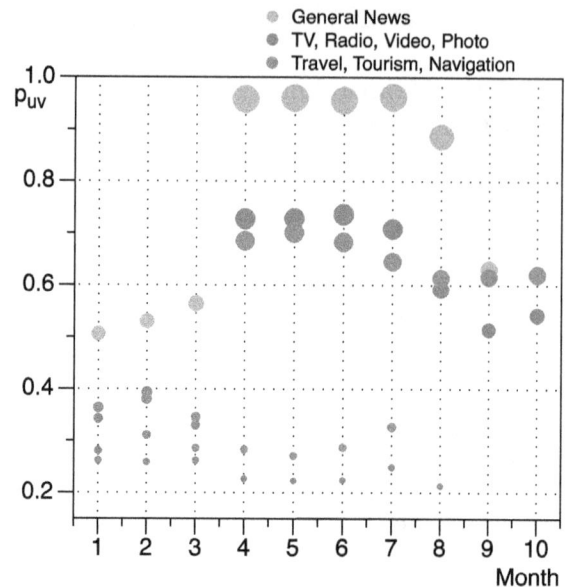

Figure 1: Transition probabilities per month from *General news* (orange), *Travel, Tourism, Navigation* (blue), *TV, Radio, Video, Photo* (violet) to the other categories between January and October 2015. Probabilities > 0.2 are displayed only.

creates another issues publishers will have to address. Further analysis is necessary to develop a broader understanding for the degree to which the categories determine reading behavior.

REFERENCES

[1] Amr Ahmed, Choon Hui Teo, S.V.N. Vishwanathan, and Alex Smola. 2012. Fair and Balanced: Learning to Present News Stories. In *Proceedings of the Fifth ACM International Conference on Web Search and Data Mining*. ACM, New York, NY, USA, 333–342. DOI : https://doi.org/10.1145/2124295.2124337

[2] F. Bickenbach and E. Bode. 2003. Evaluating the Markov Property in Studies of Economic Convergence. *International Regional Science Review* 26, 3 (2003), 363–392. DOI : https://doi.org/10.1177/0160017603253789

[3] E. V. Epure, J. E. Ingvaldsen, R. Deneckere, and C. Salinesi. 2016. Process mining for recommender strategies support in news media. In *Proceedings of the 10th International Conference on Research Challenges in Information Science*. 1–12. DOI : https://doi.org/10.1109/RCIS.2016.7549356

[4] Cagdas Esiyok, Benjamin Kille, Brijnesh-Johannes Jain, Frank Hopfgartner, and Sahin Albayrak. 2014. Users' Reading Habits in Online News Portals. In *Proceedings of the 5th Information Interaction in Context Symposium*. ACM, New York, NY, USA, 263–266. DOI : https://doi.org/10.1145/2637002.2637038

[5] Lihong Li, Wei Chu, John Langford, and Robert E. Schapire. 2010. A Contextual-bandit Approach to Personalized News Article Recommendation. In *Proceedings of the 19th International Conference on World Wide Web*. ACM, New York, NY, USA, 661–670. DOI : https://doi.org/10.1145/1772690.1772758

[6] Lei Li, Li Zheng, Fan Yang, and Tao Li. 2014. Modeling and Broadening Temporal User Interest in Personalized News Recommendation. *Expert Systems with Applications* 41, 7 (2014), 3168–3177.

[7] Jiahui Liu, Peter Dolan, and Elin Rønby Pedersen. 2010. Personalized News Recommendation Based on Click Behavior. In *Proceedings of the International Conference on Intelligent User Interfaces*. 31–40.

User Verification on Mobile Devices Using Sequences of Touch Gestures*

Liron Ben Kimon
Dept. of Software and Information Systems Engineering
Ben-Gurion University of the Negev
Beer Sheva, Israel
benkimol@post.bgu.ac.il

Yisroel Mirsky
Dept. of Software and Information Systems Engineering
Ben-Gurion University of the Negev
Beer Sheva, Israel
yisroel@post.bgu.ac.il

Lior Rokach
Dept. of Software and Information Systems Engineering
Ben-Gurion University of the Negev
Beer Sheva, Israel
liorrk@bgu.ac.il

Bracha Shapira
Dept. of Software and Information system engineering
Ben-Gurion University of the Negev
Beer Sheva, Israel
bshapira@bgu.ac.il

ABSTRACT

Smartphones have become ubiquitous in our daily lives; they are used for a wide range of tasks and store increasing amounts of personal data. To minimize risk and prevent misuse of this data by unauthorized users, access must be restricted to verified users. Current classification-based methods for gesture-based user verification only consider single gestures, and not sequences. In this paper, we present a method which utilizes information from sequences of touchscreen gestures, and the context in which the gestures were made. To evaluate our approach, we built an application which records all the necessary data from the device (touch and contextual sensors which do not consume significant battery life), and installed it on several Galaxy S4 smartphones. The smartphones were given to 20 volunteers to use as their personal phones for two-weeks. Using XGBoost on the collected data, we were able to classify between a legitimate user and the population of illegitimate users (imposters) with an average equal error rate (EER) of 4.78% and an average area under the curve (AUC) of 98.15%. Our method demonstrates that by considering sequences of gestures, as opposed to individual gestures, the accuracy of the verification process improves significantly.

---

†The full version of the author's guide is available as acmart.pdf document
¹It is a datatype.

CCS CONCEPTS

• **Security and privacy**→**Systems security**→Operating systems security→ Mobile platform security • **Human-centered computing**→ **Ubiquitous and mobile computing**→ **Ubiquitous and mobile devices**→Smartphones • **Security and privacy**→**Security services**→Authentication→**Biometrics.**

KEYWORDS

Continuous user verification; mobile; security; touchscreen gestures; sequence recognition; context; behavioral models; XGBoost;

1 INTRODUCTION

In order to assure that only the owner of the smartphone accesses personal data it is important to establish a reliable means of providing continuous user verification. The following are the necessary steps for continuous user verification: (1) continuously identify the user, (2) detect when the user is not an authorized user (i.e., the device is not under control of the owner); and finally (3) lock the device and notify the owner when unauthorized usage has been detected.

Previous studies considered single gestures when training their machine learning algorithm. However, intuitively, a sequence of gestures may capture a user's behavior and intent better than a single gesture. In order to perform a task while interacting with their phones users are required to perform a sequence of gestures that relate to the task. For example, consider the context of messaging; the user typically swipes down and taps on a message in the inbox. This sequence, along with features such as the speed, motion and location of the user touch activities on the screen, may better represent the user's behavior than any single gesture (taken out of context). With this understanding, we propose a novel technique for capturing the user's personal behavior. Specifically, we utilize a combination of strong features to learn a model. The features

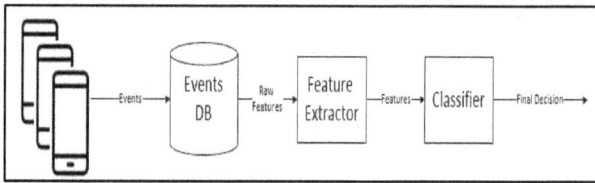

Figure 1. The user verification process

relate to the following two categories: Gesture Trace Features and Contextual Features.

The main contribution of our method is that unlike in other works, we utilized the information in the sequence of the last few gestures made by the user (instead of classifying a single gesture). The intuition is that when a user interacts with his/her smartphone, a set specific gestures are made in a certain way. Moreover, fewer false positives are made when the legitimate user touches the screen in a way unseen before. In our research we examined real users and their natural behavior without any usage constraints and achieved accurate results in real life scenarios.

To the best of our knowledge, there are no other works which consider gesture traces for each instance during the feature extraction process. We demonstrate that gesture trace features in combination with the explicit contextual features can greatly improve the accuracy of continuous verification.

2 SUGGESTED APPROACH

In this paper, we propose a novel verification method which continuously verifies users on mobile devices by monitoring and analyzing touchscreen gestures. To describe the approach, we provide the following definitions: (1) **Gesture** - The interaction a user makes on the device screen, starting from the moment the finger touches the screen, until the finger has been lifted. (2) **Gesture Trace** - The gestures that have been made prior to the current gesture (within a predetermined time). (3) **Context of a Gesture** - The state of the device (soft sensing) and the state of the user (hard sensing), while the gesture was made.

Whenever a gesture is made, and the raw sensor data has been collected, feature extraction is performed to create three feature vectors: (1) features describing the current gesture, (2) features describing the current context, and (3) features describing the gesture history. The final feature vector presented to the machine learning classifier M, is the concatenation of the last T feature vectors that capture the last sequence of gestures made.

A binary classification model M is trained where class '0' is the authorized user, and class '1' is a collection of other unauthorized users. The machine learning model needs to be robust and efficient to execute. Therefore, we opted a decision tree ensemble as our classifier - XGBoost (extreme gradient boosting). A detailed description of these steps is provided in the sections that follow (the process is illustrated in Figure 1).

Table 1. Average EER and AUC results for known and unknown attacks.

	EER	AUC
Known Attacks	4.78%	98.15%
Unknown Attacks	6.82%	96.25%

3 EXPERIMENTS AND RESULTS

In order to collect the data, we developed an application that extracts all of the necessary raw features from the mobile device (touch and contextual data). The application was responsible for detecting the touch events that were produced by the device, and their context (both hard and soft sensing). The application was installed on rooted Galaxy S4 smartphones given to 20 volunteers (2 weeks each). The volunteers used the phone as their own personal phone for this duration.

In order to evaluate the accuracy of the classification we simulated two types of attackers (thieves): (1) **Known attackers** – thieves who try to steal a smartphone for the second time or more. The thief and his/her behavior are known to the model. (2) **Unknown attackers** – thieves who try to steal a smartphone for the first time. The model does not know the thief and his/her behavior.

For both scenarios the average EER obtained when considering a sequence size of one instance, i.e., no sequence at all, was much higher than the EER when concatenating group of instances (The optimum sequence size is between 5 and 35).

For known attacks, an EER of 8.04% was achieved without gesture trace features, as opposed to an EER of 6.16% with gesture trace features. We performed a second experiment that focused on unknown attackers. With a sequence size of five sequences and a group of 15 instances when calculating the prediction, we were able to achieve an average EER of 4.78% and an average AUC of 98.15% for known attacks and an average EER of 6.82% and an average AUC of 95.55% for unknown attacks (The results are shown in Table 1).

We found that the optimum trace length T is 35 (but a trace of 5 gesture is still practical, the difference isn't significant). From our data collection experiment, we observed that a user performs 35 gestures in 13.8 seconds on average, with standard deviation of 25 seconds. From our trials it can be assumed that an uninformed attacker will perform at least 35 gestures to achieve his/her goal. This is because the attacker does not know the layout and the location of every application and file. We found that it takes only a few micro seconds to perform the classification task. Therefore, the attacker should be detected before the attack is complete.

Note, that by adjusting the classifier's threshold, the user can adjust the trade-off between the level of security (accuracy) and number of false positives to the user's preference.

4 Conclusion

In this work we propose a user verification method which utilizes the information from gained from observing a sequence of touch gestures. The method is power efficient, accurate, and practical -thus maintaining the usability of the device.

User Modeling for the Internet of Things

Bob Kummerfeld
University of Sydney
Sydney, NSW 2006
orcid.org/0000-0002-6046-6393
Bob.Kummerfeld@Sydney.edu.au

Judy Kay
University of Sydney
Sydney, NSW 2006
orcid.org/0000-0001-6728-2768
Judy.Kay@Sydney.edu.au

1 INTRODUCTION

The Internet-of-Things (IoT) consists of a large number of interconnected, low cost devices and the framework for managing them. While this provides the means for rich and ubiquitous personalized interaction, a key gap is the lack of support for user modeling to harness and manage personal data gathered from IoT. Our work fills this gap by creating the IoTum user modeling framework for Internet-of-Things applications. Our design goals were to make it *easy for IoT application developers* to use, tackling the difficulty of building ubicomp systems [1]. At the same time, we aimed to achieve *light-weight, flexible, powerful, reactive user modeling* that is *accountable, transparent and scrutable* [6].

Applications interact with IoTum via three primitives, *tell* to add evidence to a user model, *ask* to retrieve interpreted evidenced from the model and *listen* which establishes a monitoring process which can trigger the application. The first two of these have been part of many previous user modelling frameworks, including Personis [5, 7], the server by Kobsa and Fink [8], CUMULATE [2] and infobead [3]. However, IoTum is the first user modelling framework we are aware of that supports the last of these, the *listen*, which is key to making effective use of the many existing and emerging low cost sensors of IoT. Another important aspect is that IoTum maintains *provenance* information in the user model, to support accountability, scrutability and explanations [4]. There are also mechanisms to define the user model and do introspection on existing models. To demonstrate that it meets its design goals, we describe its use to build a nutrition chatbot.

The design of IoTum was based on four design goals:
DG1: It can support flexible user modeling for IoT applications.
DG2: It is quick and easy for an IoT application developer to integrate user modeling into their applications, to readily make use of new devices and to provide new ways to use these devices and their user modeling data.
DG3: It is light-weight enough to fit within IoT hardware constraints, where this may require the user modeling to operate on low power computers, such as RaspberryPi, and easily connect with devices and sensors.
DG4: It is easy-to-install and configure.

Our key contributions are the design of the IoTum framework, the first user modeling framework specifically designed to integrate with the rich eco-system of the Internet of Things and the demonstration of its effectiveness for building IoT applications.

2 ARCHITECTURE AND IMPLEMENTATION

The architecture of IoTum is based on the accretion/resolution approach of the Personis [6] system: information gathered about a user (evidence) is time stamped and added ("tell") to the relevant model attribute ("accretion"). When a value of an attribute is required ("ask"), the available evidence for the attribute is "resolved" by the application. Different applications may have different resolver functions for the same model attribute. The communication with the user model in IoTum is not the traditional client/server but instead a publish/subscribe approach. In IoTum, the "ask" operation consists of publishing an "ask" request to a topic consisting of the attribute and resolver name. In response, the application subscribes to the attribute name and IoTum publishes the resolved value for that topic. Unlike the previous client/server approaches, IoTum also allows applications to subscribe to a topic in "listen" mode. This ensures that applications will be notified when any "tell" or "ask" operation is performed.

IoTum is implemented using the pub/sub protocol MQTT and the Influxdb time-series database, with our demonstration application implemented using the node-red[1] graphical data-flow system.

3 EXAMPLE APPLICATION

We illustrate the power and ease of use of IoTum with a chat-bot app we created to help people to log their vegetable consumption. From the user perspective, the chat-bot runs each day at a specified time and asks the user how many serves of vegetables they ate that day (as in Figure 2). The answer is stored in the model using the "tell". We also created a calendar visualisation (Figure 3), presenting values resolved to produce the colours indicating consumption. From the implementor's perspective, this is quick to build, by drawing on available IoT tools and using IoTum to provide user modeling.

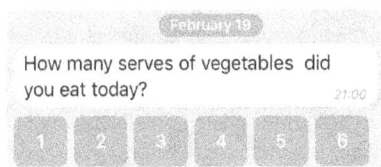

Figure 2: Chatbot that runs each evening, so user can log their vegetable intake for that day.

[1]http://mqtt.org, https://www.influxdata.com, https://nodered.org

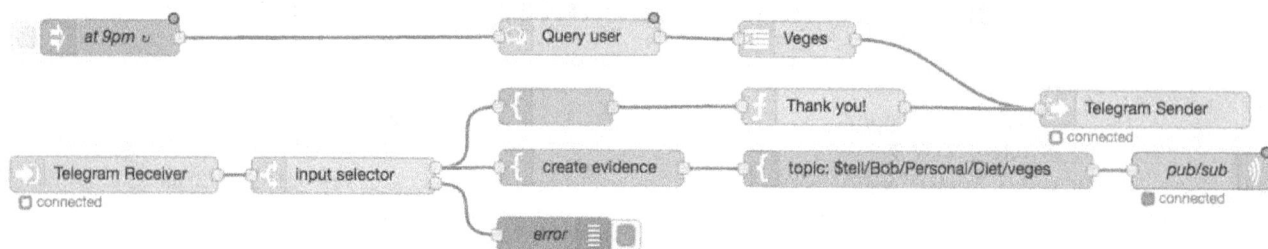

Figure 1: Node-RED application developer interface for the nutrition chatbot. The top 4-node flow drives the daily query to the user. The remainder handles the results returned by the chatbot. The three nodes, *create evidence*, *topic: ...* and *pub/sub*, send the result to IoTum

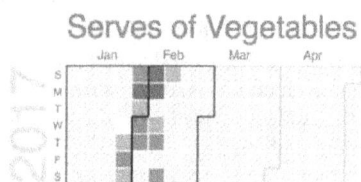

Figure 3: Vegetable Serves chatbot calendar visualization

This application uses the Telegram chat service. Figure 1 shows the full implementation of the chatbot using Node-red and the IoTum server. The full application is just 12 "nodes" and the use modelling is added with just the three on the lower flow, taking the user value provided, creating a piece of evidence in the appropriate format, doing the "tell" and publishing it. The calendar visualisation of the user model data was implemented in another 11 nodes. Essentially, the IoT developer can use IoTum to add user modelling to their toolkit.

4 DISCUSSION AND CONCLUSION

We briefly describe how IoTum meets its design goals.

DG1: flexible user modeling for IoT applications. IoTum is built using common tools for building IoT applications and has a full accretion/resolution user modeling system.

DG2: It is quick and easy for an IoT app developer to integrate user modeling into their applications. Node-red provides a wide range of tools used in IoT applications, including MQTT pub/sub services. The addition of the IoTum server allows easy integration of access to accretion/resolution user modeling.

DG3: It is light-weight enough to fit within IoT hardware constraints. All of the tools used in IoTum run on low power systems and are accessible from very low power systems such as microcontrollers (eg Arduino class machines).

DG4: It is easy-to-install and configure. IoTum tools are very easy to install and configuration is trivial.

Our goal was to bring user modeling to the world of IoT. To do this, we designed IoTum in the spirit of IoT software components, readily combined and light-weight. Our chatbot and associated calendar app illustrate how IoTum can be readily used to acquire user modeling information from the user using a simple chatbot

interface and how the IoT developer can access the user model, as in the calendar. Future work will need to evaluate IoTum in the context of applications that provide personalised IoT-based services; we will need to demonstrate that the approach is robust and effective for the hardware constraints and we will need to evaluate the scrutability and provenance with interfaces for users to scrutinise their user models. Our work contributes the first user modeling framework for IoT.

The full version of this paper is available at [9].

REFERENCES

[1] Gregory D. Abowd. 2012. What next, ubicomp?: celebrating an intellectual disappearing act. In *Proceedings of the 2012 ACM Conference on Ubiquitous Computing (UbiComp '12)*. ACM, New York, NY, USA, 31–40. DOI: http://dx.doi.org/10.1145/2370216.2370222
[2] Peter Brusilovsky, Sergey Sosnovsky, and Olena Shcherbinina. 2005. User modeling in a distributed e-learning architecture. In *International Conference on User Modeling*. Springer, 387–391.
[3] Eyal Dim, Tsvi Kuflik, and Iris Reinhartz-Berger. 2015. When user modeling intersects software engineering: the info-bead user modeling approach. *User Modeling and User-Adapted Interaction* 25, 3 (2015), 189–229.
[4] Alan Fekete, Judy Kay, Michael Franklin, Debjanee Barua, and Bob Kummerfeld. 2015. Managing information for personal goals (vision). In *Data Engineering Workshops (ICDEW), 2015 31st IEEE International Conference on*. IEEE, 30–33.
[5] J. Kay. 1995. The um toolkit for cooperative user modelling. *User Modeling and User-Adapted Interaction* 4, 3 (1995), 149–196.
[6] Judy Kay and Bob Kummerfeld. 2012. Creating personalized systems that people can scrutinize and control: Drivers, principles and experience. *ACM Transactions on Interactive Intelligent Systems (TiiS)* 2, 4 (2012), 24.
[7] Judy Kay, Bob Kummerfeld, and Piers Lauder. 2002. Personis: a server for user models. In *International Conference on Adaptive Hypermedia and Adaptive Web-Based Systems*. Springer, 203–212.
[8] Alfred Kobsa and Josef Fink. 2006. An LDAP-based user modeling server and its evaluation. *User Modeling and User-Adapted Interaction* 16, 2 (2006), 129–169.
[9] Bob Kummerfeld and Judy Kay. 2017. User Modeling for the Internet of Things. (2017). https://goo.gl/n90GDT

Impact of Individual Differences on User Experience with a Real-World Visualization Interface for Public Engagement

Sébastien Lallé
Department of Computer Science,
University of British Columbia,
Vancouver, Canada
lalles@cs.ubc.ca

Cristina Conati
Department of Computer Science,
University of British Columbia,
Vancouver, Canada
conati@cs.ubc.ca

Giuseppe Carenini
Department of Computer Science,
University of British Columbia,
Vancouver, Canada
carenini@cs.ubc.ca

CCS CONCEPTS

• **Human-centered computing** → **Human computer interaction (HCI)** → Empirical studies in HCI

KEYWORDS

User-adaptive visualization, Eye tracking, Public engagement

INTRODUCTION

There is increasing evidence that the effectiveness of Information Visualization (Infovis) is affected by the user needs and abilities. For instance, cognitive abilities (e.g., perceptual speed, working memory) [e.g., 1–4] have been shown to impact users' performance and satisfaction with a given visualization. These findings suggest that it can be valuable to develop visualization systems that can provide personalized support targeting specific user characteristics. Furthermore, recent research [e.g., 3,5] has shown that eye tracking data can be leveraged to identify the elements of a visualization for which specific user differences hinder user experience or performance, thus providing concrete information on which specific personalized support could be helpful for different users (e.g., users with low perceptual speed may benefit from help in processing legends [1]). Though these findings are encouraging toward the design of user-adaptive or customized visualizations, they are generally related to either fictional tasks or research prototypes. So, it is unclear if existing results on the value of user-adaptive visualizations can transfer to real-world settings.

In this work, we collaborated with a company to investigate whether and how current results can transfer to MetroQuest (MQ, *metroquest.com*), a commercial visualization-based framework. MQ aims at engaging the public in actual urban planning decisions that are often framed as preferential choices, i.e., selecting the most preferred solution out of a set of possible scenarios.

To this end, MQ interfaces typically include visualizations to help users comparing scenarios based on a variety of decision factors. Designing these visualizations is challenging due to the large diversity of their users.

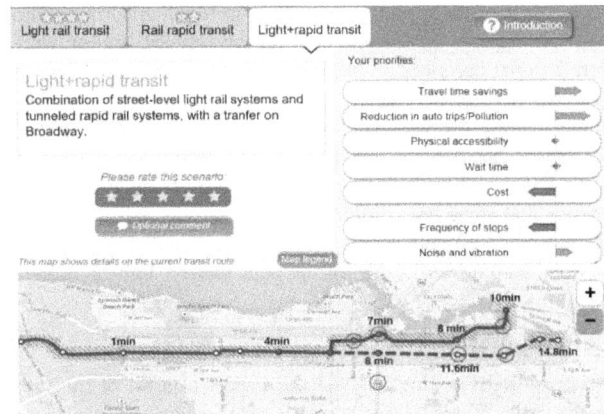

Fig. 1. Detail of the MetroQuest interface used in the study, available at *ubc.metroquest.com*

For instance, while complex visualizations conveying rich information would satisfy some users, they may overwhelm others. The challenge is exacerbated by the fact that MQ is typically used as a *walk-up-and-use* system (e.g., in public kiosks) that, in order to avoid attrition, must be self-explanatory and engaging to one-time uses. Although MQ results from years of iterative design of many walk-up-and-use commercial applications, MQ designers feel that ease-of-use and appeal of their interfaces would benefit from being able to quickly recognize the needs and abilities of their one-time users, and from providing personalized support accordingly. The two key visualizations that appear in most interfaces developed by MQ for urban planning decisions are a *map* and a *deviation chart*. Fig. 1 shows the sample MQ interface that we study in this paper. To investigate the feasibility of designing user-adaptive MQ interfaces using those two visualizations, we explore two research questions:

RQ1: Do user differences impact user experience (user satisfaction and decision quality) with our sample MQ interface?

RQ2: Do user differences impact the use of the map and the deviation chart in terms of gaze behavior?

To answer these questions, we conducted a user study in a laboratory setting in which 166 participants were asked to explore and rate according to their preferences three real transit scenarios in their own city (a preferential choice) using our MQ interface. In practice, users can view and compare the three scenarios with MQ by switching among the three tabs (one per scenario, as shown at the top of Fig. 1). In each tab a map and a deviation chart show how the current scenario would impact the City's public transit system.

Table 1. Impact of user differences on (1) user experience and (2) gaze data while processing MQ visualizations.

User Differences	(1) User experience with MetroQuest	(2) Gaze behavior while processing the visualizations
a) Visual Working Memory (WM)	• *Visualization preference* (high visual WM users preferred the charts over the maps)	• *Fixation rate* (lower visual WM users had lower fixation rate over the visualizations)
b) Spatial Memory	• *Chart usefulness* (lower spatial memory users found the chart less useful)	• *Visual comparison of scenarios* (users with lower spatial memory, perceptual speed, visual scanning and visualization literacy compared less the visualizations across scenarios)
c) Perceptual Speed; Visual Scanning; Visualization literacy	*No effect found.*	

Our results indicate that some user differences do impact user experience and gaze behavior with MQ, thus augmenting previous findings on the potential value of adaptation to user differences in Infovis. Most of these previous findings were obtained in studies where participants interacted with lab prototypes, and/or were given fictional tasks [e.g., 1–4]. Although our study was also run in a lab to collect gaze data, we focused on a widely commercialized framework, designed a realistic task of public engagement based on a real project, and recruited participants among the real target population. Thus, our findings provides evidence that some user differences may warrant personalization in commercial MQ applications to support preferential choice. This is a first step towards evaluating personalized Infovis in real settings.

MAIN FINDINGS FOR RQ1

To address RQ1, we investigated the impact of a set of the user characteristics (Table 2, first column) on self-reported measures of user experience with MQ. Results are summarized in the first column of Table 1, and described next.

Spatial memory (*storage capacity of the spatial arrangement of objects*). We found that users with low spatial memory considered the chart significantly less useful than users with high spatial memory, possibly because they can retain and manipulate less easily the spatial information encoded in the chart (e.g., the size and arrangement of the arrows).

Visual WM (*storage capacity of shapes and colors of visual objects*). We found that users with high levels of visual WM preferred the deviation chart over the map, whereas there is almost no difference for users with low levels of visual WM. The visual information in the chart is encoded in the size and color of the arrows, thus the fact that high visual WM users preferred the chart is consistent with the definition of visual WM.

These results on RQ1 provide insights on which user differences may warrant adaptive support in MQ, and how this support could be designed. For example, users with *low spatial memory*, who found the deviation chart less useful than their counterparts, may benefit from adaptations that increase the chart perceived usefulness (e.g., by showing less factors in the chart to ease its processing). It could also be interesting to explore an adaptation enabling low spatial memory users to not have the chart at all, as for these users, having two visualizations may not be ideal.

MAIN FINDINGS FOR RQ2

To address RQ2, we investigated the impact of our user characteristics on eye tracking metrics that capture users' gaze behavior over the map and the deviation chart. Results are summarized in the last column of Table 1, and described next.

Spatial memory (*defined before*), **visual scanning** (*capacity to actively find relevant information in our surroundings*), **perceptual**

speed (*speed when performing simple perceptual comparisons*), and **visualization literacy** (*ability to use standard visualizations*). We found that users with low levels of these four abilities compared both the maps and the charts less extensively across transit scenarios than their counterparts. This finding suggests that users with low levels of these abilities are at a disadvantage at comparing the visualizations, plausibly because they can retain less visual information (low spatial memory), scan the visualizations less quickly (low perceptual speed and visual scanning), or use standard visualizations less proficiently (low literacy). Since making such comparisons is crucial to understand the differences between scenarios, users with low levels of these abilities may benefit from personalized support to compare the visualizations.

Visual WM. We found that low visual WM users had a lower fixation rate over the map and the chart than their counterpart.

The fact that the five user differences listed in Table 2 impact gaze behavior in a way that is detectable by an eye tracker provides encouraging evidence that these user differences could be predicted in real-time using gaze data, so that adaptation could be triggered based on these differences. For example, the real-time detection of low spatial memory users, who found the chart less useful, could be used to provide these users with adaptation supporting the use of the chart, as previously suggested for RQ1.

CONCLUSION

We presented a user study to investigate the relationship between user differences and user experience in commercial MQ applications that rely on visualizations for supporting public engagement. We found that several user differences do impact user experience with MQ and gaze behavior while processing the MQ visualizations. These findings are an additional step toward understanding the impact of user differences on visualization processing and the need for personalization in real settings.

REFERENCES

1. C. Conati, G. Carenini, D. Toker, and S. Lallé. 2015. Towards User-Adaptive Information Visualization. In *Proc. of the 29th AAAI Conf. on Artificial Intelligence*. AAAI, Austin, TX, USA, 4100–4106.

2. V. Kellen, S. Chan, and X. Fang. 2007. Facilitating Conditional Probability Problems with Visuals. In *Proc. of the Int. Conf. on Human-Computer Interaction*. Springer, Beijing, China, 63–71.

3. K. Ooms, P. De Maeyer, and V. Fack. 2014. Study of the attentive behavior of novice and expert map users using eye tracking. *Cartography and Geographic Information Science* 41, 1: 37–54.

4. A. Ottley, E. M. Peck, L. T. Harrison, et al. 2016. Improving Bayesian Reasoning: The Effects of Phrasing, Visualization, and Spatial Ability. *IEEE Transactions on Visualization and Computer Graphics* 22, 1: 529–538.

5. B. Steichen, C. Conati, and G. Carenini. 2014. Inferring Visualization Task Properties, User Performance, and User Cognitive Abilities from Eye Gaze Data. *ACM Transactions on Interactive Intelligent Systems* 4, 2: Article 11.

Are Item Attributes a Good Alternative to Context Elicitation in Recommender Systems?

Amaury L'Huillier
LORIA - University of Lorraine
Campus Scientifique, B.P. 239
Vandoeuvre, France 54506
amaury.lhuillier@loria.fr

Sylvain Castagnos
LORIA - University of Lorraine
Campus Scientifique, B.P. 239
Vandoeuvre, France 54506
sylvain.castagnos@loria.fr

Anne Boyer
LORIA - University of Lorraine
Campus Scientifique, B.P. 239
Vandoeuvre, France 54506
anne.boyer@loria.fr

ABSTRACT

Context-aware recommendation became a major topic of interest within the recommender systems community as the context is crucial to provide the right items at the right moment. Many studies aim at developing complex models to include contextual factors in the recommendation process. Despite a real improvement on the recommendations quality, such contextual factors face users' privacy and data collection issues. We support the idea that context could be expressed in term of item attributes rather than contextual factors. To investigate that hypothesis, we designed an online experiment where 174 users were asked to describe the context in which they would listen the proposed songs for which we collected 12 musical attributes. We make available all the material collected during this study for research purposes and non-commercial use.

KEYWORDS

Context-Aware Recommender System; Context Elicitation; User Study

1 INTRODUCTION

Since it has been demonstrated that recommendations quality is not only about precision relatively to users preferences, current recommendation algorithms aim at integrating human factors in the recommendation process. Among them, context which is used to provide the right recommendations at the right moment is one of the most studied factors and its benefits no longer have to be demonstrated [1]. For example, context is crucial to recommende the right genre of music to a user in harmony with his activity or mood, or to recommend exhibits in a museum according to user's timeframe and people accompanying him.

Traditional Context-Aware Recommender Systems (CARS) collect and exploit information about the user situation (individuality, activity, location, time, and relations). Such information can be collected in several ways, by using sensors of the devices (GPS, temperature, light,...) or by cross-checking information gathered from other sources (e.g. inferring the weather from the geolocalization) [1]. A system can also directly question users about their context [1]. Once contextual factors are defined, several methods are used to exploit them as matrix factorization [2], tensors [5] or graph-based approaches [7]. Despite unquestionable benefits in term of recommendation quality, such approaches face many issues. First, collecting such information is intrusive, some researches have demonstrated that collecting personal data becomes less and less desirable [4] and could lead to mistrust [6]. Second, context is known to be a very dynamic dimension and changes of one contextual factors can lead to a completely different context. Such models then require a non-stop tracking to detect any change of contextual dimension in order to adapt their recommendations and this point supports the previous discussed limitation. Third, required pieces of information are sometimes partially or non observable by the system due to technical or privacy preservation issues (as an example, users may have blocked the geolocalization on their smartphone making them obsolete).

For all these reasons, we proposed in 2015 a new definition of context based on the sol basis of consumed item attributes [3]. Our model was based on attributes diversity evolution over time and was used to isolate sequences of consultations sharing similar attributes called Implicit Context. Thus, context was no more defined by user situation description but according to item attributes values and their evolutions. Rather than finding items consumed in similar context to provide recommendations, our model could be used to extract the dimensions (attributes) that characterize the current implicit context. Adapting recommendations to these implicit context could be a new way to provide contextualized recommendations. However, no existing relations between the set of features discribing an item and explicit context characteristics were shown.

With the study proposed in this paper, we intend to provide a real dataset to investigate the potential links between context features and item attributes. More specifficaly, we wonder how users associate items with explicit contexts in an online music service. We used a musical dataset in our study as listening contexts are numerous, can easily be made explicit, and finding item attributes does not constitute an obstacle. Such study could also fit e-learning, museum or e-commerce scenarii.

2 EXPERIMENT SETUP

For the purpose of our experiment, we created an online survey[2] to collect users' point of view as regards the context in which they would listen to tracks. These latter were selected on the basis of their preferred genres. Our goal was not to find the most suitable

UMAP '17, July 09-12, 2017, Bratislava, Slovakia
© 2017 Copyright held by the owner/author(s). 978-1-4503-4635-1/17/07.
DOI: http://dx.doi.org/10.1145/3079628.3079651

---

[1]https://www.spotify.com/, https://play.google.com/music/
[2]http://movit.tv/

tracks for each user but to find a way to collect information on how users assign context dimensions to tracks.

2.1 MATERIALS

Users were recruited using mailing lists and the average duration to complete the study was about twenty five minutes. The track dataset used contains 360 tracks randomly selected from a Last.fm [3] dataset collected from 28 June 2005 to 18 December 2014. We choose to randomly select tracks in a large dataset (more that 170,000 tracks) to avoid bias due to popularity. 30 tracks were selected for each of the following genre: rock, pop, rap, country, punk, jazz, hip-hop, classical, folk, metal, electronic, blues. The only selection criteria were to have only one track per artist for all the selected tracks and to ensure that every attributes could be retrieved through the Spotify API[4]. We then gathered 12 attributes for each track (10 attributes tracks, and 2 for artists).

- TRACK ATTRIBUTES: acousticness, danceability, duration, energy, instrumentalness, liveness, loudness, speechiness, tempo, valence;
- ARTIST ATTRIBUTES: genre, popularity.

In the first part of the survey, users were asked to give some demographic information (age, gender, socio-professional category) and some information about their listening habits (preferred genre, favorite place to listen to music, listening time per day, how they chose their music). The second part of the survey consisted in presenting 15 tracks to each user according to their prefered genres and ask them to assign adapted contexts to these tracks (see Table 1).

Table 1: Context dimensions and conditions collected

Context dimensions	Context conditions
Activity	relaxing, cleaning-up, cooking, driving, partying, reading, exercising, thinking, traveling, waking up, walking, working
Day	morning, day, evening, night
Energy	quiet, normal, energetic
Environment	personal, professional
Place	indoors, outdoors
Season	spring, summer, fall, winter
Social	alone, family, friends, couple
Weather	sunny, rainy, snowy, cloudy
Week	week, week-end

2.2 RESULTS

In order to reduce bias due to non conscientious responses, we decided to discard users who did not finished the study and obtained a final dataset of 172 users. By discarding records for tracks which were disliked (it is meaningless to ask users to specify the context for a track they will not listen to), we got a dataset of 1,507 tracks annotated (see Figure 1 for repartition).

[3] http://www.last.fm/fr/api
[4] https://developer.spotify.com/web-api/

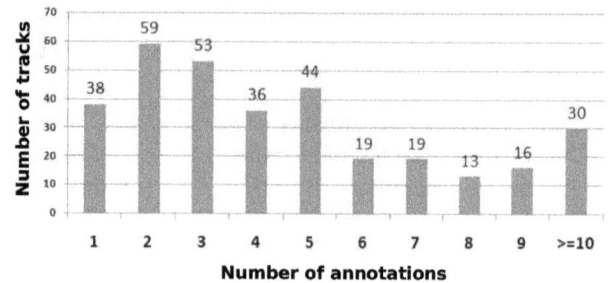

Figure 1: Number of times tracks were annotated

3 CONCLUSION

Implicit context appears to be a promising alternative to explicit context as it could be used to define user context while preserving his privacy and prevent data acquisition issues. In order to do so, overlaps between implicit and explicit context have to be highlighted and the data collected throught this study can be used to achieve this goal. We provide all the material collected during this study to encourage the research communtity to investigate relations between item attributes and explicit contexts.

Link to the data: **https://github.com/teamKiwi/umap2017**

This project has received funding from the European Union's Horizon 2020 research and innovation programme under grant agreement No 693150.

REFERENCES

[1] Gediminas Adomavicius and Alexander Tuzhilin. 2011. Context–aware Recommender Systems. *Recommender Systems Handbook* (2011), 217–253. https://doi.org/10.1007/978--0--387--85820--3_7
[2] Linas Baltrunas, Bernd Ludwig, and Francesco Ricci. 2011. Matrix Factorization Techniques for Context Aware Recommendation. In *Proceedings of the Fifth ACM Conference on Recommender Systems (RecSys '11)*. ACM, New York, NY, USA, 301–304. https://doi.org/10.1145/2043932.2043988
[3] Sylvain Castagnos, Amaury L 'huillier, and Anne Boyer. 2015. Toward a Robust Diversity-Based Model to Detect Changes of Context. In *27th IEEE International Conference on Tools with Artificial Intelligence (ICTAI 2015)*. Vietri sul Mare, Italy. https://doi.org/10.1109/ICTAI.2015.84
[4] Lorrie Faith Cranor. 2005. Hey, That's Personal! In *User Modeling 2005*, Liliana Ardissono, Paul Bruna, and Antonija Mitrovic (Eds.). Lecture Notes in Computer Science, Vol. 3538. Springer Berlin Heidelberg, 4–4. https://doi.org/10.1007/11527886_2
[5] Balázs Hidasi and Domonkos Tikk. 2012. *Fast ALS-Based Tensor Factorization for Context-Aware Recommendation from Implicit Feedback*. Springer Berlin Heidelberg, Berlin, Heidelberg, 67–82. https://doi.org/10.1007/978-3-642-33486-3_5
[6] Bart P. Knijnenburg and Alfred Kobsa. 2013. Making Decisions About Privacy: Information Disclosure in Context-Aware Recommender Systems. *ACM Trans. Interact. Intell. Syst.* 3, 3, Article 20 (Oct. 2013), 23 pages. https://doi.org/10.1145/2499670
[7] Hao Wu, Kun Yue, Xiaoxin Liu, Yijian Pei, and Bo Li. 2015. Context-Aware Recommendation via Graph-Based Contextual Modeling and Postfiltering. *International Journal of Distributed Sensor Networks* 11, 8 (2015), 613612.

Item Contents Good, User Tags Better: Empirical Evaluation of a Food Recommender System

David Massimo
Free University of Bozen-Bolzano
Bozen-Bolzano, Italy
david.massimo@stud-inf.unibz.it

Mehdi Elahi
Free University of Bozen-Bolzano
Bozen-Bolzano, Italy
meelahi@unibz.it

Mouzhi Ge
Faculty of Informatics, Masaryk University
Brno, Czech Republic
mouzhi.ge@muni.cz

Francesco Ricci
Free University of Bozen-Bolzano
Bozen-Bolzano, Italy
fricci@unibz.it

ABSTRACT

Traditional food recommender systems exploit items' ratings and descriptions in order to generate relevant recommendations for the users. While this data is important, it might not entirely capture the true users' preferences. In this paper, we analyse the performance of a food recommender that allows users to enter their preferences in the form of both ratings and tags, which are then used by a Matrix Factorization (MF) rating prediction model. The performed offline and online experiments have clarified the importance of user tags in comparison to content features. While item content contributes more to the quality of the prediction accuracy, user tags yields better ranking quality. Even more importantly, a live user study has revealed that a system variant, which leverages user tags in the prediction model and in the interface, achieves a significantly better user evaluation in terms of perceived effectiveness, choice satisfaction and choice difficulty.

1 INTRODUCTION

A variety of food recommender systems have been recently developed and evaluated [2, 6, 7]. However, they mostly implement the traditional content-based approach, which leverages the item descriptions (e.g., food categories and ingredients) that a user preferred in the past, in order to generate relevant and new recommendations for her. While content-based solutions could obtain a satisfactory level of recommendation quality, we conjecture that they might not fully model the users' specific preferences and tastes.

More novel recommendation algorithms have integrated tag data into matrix factorization, as additional features of the items. For instance, in [1] the authors proposed a modified version of the SVD++ matrix-factorization model that makes use of tagging information and achieves a substantial improvement of the recommender system performance. Along with this novel line of research, in [4] we have presented a food RS that leverages tags in the predictive model and in the human/computer interaction.

UMAP'17, July 9–12, 2017, Bratislava, Slovakia
© 2017 Copyright held by the owner/author(s). ACM ISBN 978-1-4503-4635-1/17/07.
DOI: http://dx.doi.org/10.1145/3079628.3079640

In this paper, we present the result of the offline and online experiments conducted on the system described in [4] in order to better understand the role that tags in preference elicitation and recommendation. The conducted offline experiments show that while item content features contribute more to the quality of the rating prediction accuracy of the system, tags are more useful for obtaining higher quality ranking. Moreover, the online evaluation shows that a system variant that uses tags in the prediction model and in the human/computer interaction achieves a better performance in terms of user perceived recommendation quality, choice satisfaction and choice difficulty.

2 SYSTEM PROTOTYPE

The proposed recommendation model is implemented in an Android-based app. The humam-computer interaction has been designed to support a user who would like to cook at home.

The user-system interaction process begins with the initial sign-up, where the user enters her age and gender. Then, she goes through the preferences elicitation steps, where she is first requested to enter her general preferences by specifying the recipes she eats or cooks at home. Afterward, in a second step, a list of selected recipes are presented to the user for rating. The user is also requested to "explain" the core motivation for an assigned rating, by optionally adding to a rated recipe some tags. In the supported interaction, the system gives two tagging possibilities to the user: (a) marking any ingredient as a tag, (b) adding other free tags that she deems as relevant to the recipe. At recommendation time the user is asked to provide session-based preferences, i.e., the ingredient (e.g., tuna fish) that she is willing to cook.

The full set of the previously entered ratings and tags are used to train the model described in [4] and the generated recommendations are post-filtered to suit the session-based preferences of the user. The system presents, one by one, recipe recommendations to the user and requests her to make a choice. Once the choice is made, the system presents the cooking instructions of the chosen recipe.

We have developed and evaluated various recommendation algorithms [4]. All of them implement rating-based MF (Matrix Factorization) models, extended to use different sources of data:

- **MF Content** extends MF by using item content features;
- **MF UTag** extends MF by using user tags;

- **MF UTag Content** extends MF by using both item content features and user tags.

3 EVALUATIONS AND RESULTS

The used recipe dataset has been obtained from *Total Wellbeing Diet* [3] and from authoritative online cook communities: *Food52* and *All recipes*. It contains 234 recipe items, each one described by features, such as, cooking instructions, ingredient list, dish categories they belong to. These recipes were rated and tagged by users who tried the system in several occasions.

We have collected 392 ratings and 394 tags (out of 120 unique tags) provided by 43 users, who participated in our experiment. The rating sparsity of the dataset is 96%. On average, the users rated 9.11 recipes. The number of item content features per rating (i.e., 9.14) is almost an order of magnitude larger than the number of user tags per rating (i.e., approximately 1).

In an offline experiment, for every user, a train set is created by considering 80% of her ratings as well as the entire set of the ratings of the other users. The remaining 20% of the ratings of that particular user are included in the test set. This process is iterated over the entire collection of users and the performance metrics, which are computed for every user, are then averaged. The results show that:

- **MF content** has MAE=0.814 (Mean Absolute Error), which is the best rating accuracy prediction and it is the second best in ranking accuracy, MRR=0.469 (Mean Reciprocal Rank);
- **MF UTag Content** is the second best in terms of rating accuracy prediction (MAE=0.866), but it is the best in terms of ranking accuracy (MRR=0.501);
- **MF UTag** has MAE=0.979, i.e., the worst rating accuracy prediction, but it is still better than plain MF (MAE=0.972), and has the worst ranking accuracy prediction (MRR=0.463), but again, still better than MF (MRR=0.416).

In a live user experiment, 31 participants were randomly assigned to two groups, each evaluating different version of the full Android mobile app recommender system. A first system version, which we call T, allows users to express preferences in the form of ratings and tags, while a second version, named as R, allows preferences' expression only in terms of ratings. These two versions generate recommendations by using the first and the second best performing models (according to the offline results). Indeed, the model used by T is MF UTag Content, which uses ratings, user tags and item content. The model used by system R, on the other hand, is MF Content, which uses user ratings and item content. The number of participants in the first group (T) was 12, whereas in the second group (R) was 19.

Each subject went through the whole user-system interaction process and then answered to a questionnaire, designed and validated by Knijnenburg [5], to measure: (1) perceived system effectiveness, (2) choice satisfaction and (3) choice difficulty. User's responses for the questions were averaged and the differences in performance where compared for statistical significance by using the Mann-Whitney test.

Significant differences between the two systems (p-value<0.05) have been observed for the following statements, among all those included in the questionnaire:

- *I make better choices with system* (perceived effectiveness);
- *I like the items I've chosen* (choice satisfaction);
- *I changed my mind several times before making a decision* (choice difficulty).

The first two statements are positively formulated (the higher the better), while the third statement is negatively formulated (the lower the better). The average responses of the participants to these statements, for system T are 3.7, 4.4, and 2.0, which are significantly better than the average responses of the system R users, with values 3.1, 3.7, and 2.4. Hence, the users believe that the system T shows recommendations that are more useful and more helpful in supporting them to make better choices, in comparison to the recommendations shown by system R. Moreover, the users liked more the recommended items presented by the system T than those listed by R. Finally, users evaluated the system T superior to the system R in enabling them to a make quick decisions without changing their minds several times.

4 CONCLUSION AND FUTURE WORKS

In this paper, we have investigated the role of tags in improving the quality of a food recommender system, in terms of rating prediction accuracy, ranking quality, perceived system effectiveness, and choice satisfaction and difficulty. The performed experiments show the advantages and the disadvantages of using tags in food recommendation.

In a future work, we would like to replicate the designed experimental study on a larger dataset, with a lower level of sparsity and more tag assignments. We believe that more tag assignments can allow to better understand the effects of tags. Further studies should also be carried out in order to study the temporal evolution of tagging patterns and user satisfaction over time.

REFERENCES

[1] Manuel Enrich, Matthias Braunhofer, and Francesco Ricci. 2013. Cold-Start Management with Cross-Domain Collaborative Filtering and Tags. In *Proceedings of the 13th International Conference on E-Commerce and Web Technologies*. Springer, 101–112.

[2] Jill Freyne and Shlomo Berkovsky. 2010. Intelligent food planning: personalized recipe recommendation. In *Proceedings of the 15th International Conference on Intelligent User Interfaces*. ACM, 321–324.

[3] Jill Freyne and Shlomo Berkovsky. 2013. Evaluating recommender systems for supportive technologies. In *User Modeling and Adaptation for Daily Routines*. Springer, 195–217.

[4] Mouzhi Ge, Mehdi Elahi, Ignacio Fernaández-Tobías, Francesco Ricci, and David Massimo. 2015. Using Tags and Latent Factors in a Food Recommender System. In *Proceedings of the 5th International Conference on Digital Health 2015 (DH '15)*. ACM, New York, NY, USA, 105–112. http://doi.acm.org/10.1145/2750511.2750528

[5] Bart P Knijnenburg, Martijn C Willemsen, Zeno Gantner, Hakan Soncu, and Chris Newell. 2012. Explaining the user experience of recommender systems. *User Modeling and User-Adapted Interaction* 22, 4-5 (2012), 441–504.

[6] Tomasz Kusmierczyk, Christoph Trattner, and Kjetil Nørvåg. 2015. Temporality in online food recipe consumption and production. In *Proceedings of the 24th International Conference on World Wide Web*. ACM, 55–56.

[7] Michele Trevisiol, Luca Chiarandini, and Ricardo Baeza-Yates. 2014. Buon appetito: recommending personalized menus. In *Proceedings of the 25th ACM conference on Hypertext and social media*. ACM, 327–329.

A Hybrid Recommendation Framework Exploiting Linked Open Data and Graph-based Features

Cataldo Musto
Dept. of Computer Science - University of Bari
cataldo.musto@uniba.it

Giovanni Semeraro
Dept. of Computer Science - University of Bari
giovanni.semeraro@uniba.it

Marco de Gemmis
Dept. of Computer Science - University of Bari
marco.degemmis@uniba.it

Pasquale Lops
Dept. of Computer Science - University of Bari
pasquale.lops@uniba.it

ABSTRACT

In this article we propose a *hybrid recommendation framework* based on classification algorithms as Random Forests and Naive Bayes. We fed the framework with several heterogeneous groups of features, and we investigate to what extent features gathered from the Linked Open Data (LOD) cloud (as the *genre* of a movie or the *writer* of a book)) as well as *graph-based features* calculated on the ground of the *tripartite* representation connecting users, items and properties in the LOD cloud impact on the overall accuracy of the recommendations. In the experimental session we evaluate the effectiveness of our framework on varying of different groups of features, an results show that both LOD-based and graph-based features positively affect the overall performance of the algorithm, especially in *highly sparse* recommendation scenarios.

CCS CONCEPTS

• **Information systems** → **Recommender systems**; *Web data description languages*; • **Computing methodologies** → *Supervised learning by classification*;

1 BACKGROUND AND METHODOLOGY

The huge availability of semantics-aware machine-readable data available in the so-called LOD cloud attracted researchers and practitioners in the area of recommender systems (RSs), willing to investigate how such information can be exploited to improve the effectiveness of existing algorithms or to tackle several problems RSs typically suffer from, as the well-known issue of *limited content analysis* [2].

In this article we investigated the impact of such *exogenous knowledge* on the performance of a *hybrid* recommendation framework based on classification techniques as Random Forests and Naive Bayes. In this work we followed the hybridization strategy which is typically referred to as *feature combination* [1], that is to say, we represented the items by means of different heterogeneous groups of features and we used this representation to feed the classifiers

with training examples. Such a model is then exploited to classify new and unseen items as *relevant* or not relevant for the *target user*.

We defined five different sets of features: three basic groups and two modeling the information gathered from the LOD cloud. In the first group fall **Popularity-based features**, encoding basic information about the items, such as the *number of ratings* received by the item and the *ratio* between positive ratings and the overall number of ratings; **Collaborative features**, modeling the information encoded in the *user-item matrix* which is typically exploited in collaborative filtering (CF) algorithms and **Content-based features**, representing the information extracted from textual descriptions of the items. Next, we introduced two groups of **LOD-based features**: *basic structured features*, as the *genre* of a *movie* or the author of a book, and **graph-based features** calculated on the ground of the graph-based representation obtained by connecting the users to the items they liked and, in turn, the items to the properties gathered from DBPEDIA. To gather LOD-based features we defined a subset of relevant properties by exploiting the outcomes of our previous research [3, 4] and we used SPARQL to extract such data. Finally, in our item representation we encoded five graph-based features, as *Degree Centrality, Average Neighbor Degree, PageRank* score, *Node Redundancy* and *Cluster Coefficient*.

2 EXPERIMENTAL EVALUATION

In the experimental evaluation we aimed to investigate how *LOD-based features* and *graph-based features* impact on the overall performance of the recommendations. Experiments were carried out on two datasets, i.e. MovieLens 1M[1], and DBBOOK[2]. As classification algorithms we used the implementations of *Random Forest* and *Naive Bayes* made available in the Weka Toolkit[3].

Popularity features were extracted by processing original data and by counting the ratings received by each item. As regards *collaborative features* we used a binary representation to encode positive and negative ratings. Next, to generate *content-based features* we processed the description of the items by using the Apache Lucene[4] library for tokenization, language detection and stop-words removal by exploiting the Snowball library[5] for stemming. Next, each item was mapped to a DBpedia entry in order to gather the features from the LOD cloud. In our setting, 3,300 MovieLens 1M

[1] http://grouplens.org/datasets/movielens/1m/
[2] http://challenges.2014.eswc-conferences.org/index.php/RecSys
[3] http://www.cs.waikato.ac.nz/ml/weka/
[4] https://lucene.apache.org/
[5] http://snowball.tartarus.org/

Table 1: Impact of LOD-based Features on MovieLens data.

F1@5	RF		NB	
	No-LOD	LOD	No-LOD	LOD
Popular (P)	0.5338	0.5312	0.5458	0.5320
Collaborative (C)	0.5618	0.5609	0.5486	0.5450
Content-based (T)	0.4913	**0.4943**	0.4913	**0.4932**
P+C	0.5635	**0.5642 (*)**	0.5483	0.5451
P+T	0.5051	**0.5079**	0.4965	**0.4974**
C+T	0.5187	**0.5188**	0.5180	0.5169
P+C+T	0.5246	0.5246	0.5189	0.5174

Table 2: Impact of LOD-based Features on DBbook data.

F1@5	RF		NB	
	No-LOD	LOD	No-LOD	LOD
Popular (P)	0.5610	**0.5659 (*)**	0.5576	**0.5577**
Collaborative (C)	0.5421	**0.5560**	0.5610	0.5564
Content-based (T)	0.5532	**0.5551**	0.5465	**0.5494**
P+C	0.5627	**0.5630**	0.5615	0.5580
P+T	0.5567	**0.5569**	0.5467	**0.5497**
C+T	0.5549	**0.5553**	0.5464	**0.5491**
P+C+T	0.5583	0.5560	0.5468	**0.5497**

Table 3: Impact of Graph-based Features.

	MovieLens		DBbook	
	RF	NB	RF	NB
Baseline	0.5635	0.5486	0.5627	0.5615
Baseline+Trip.	0.5621	0.5483	0.5607	0.5542
Baseline+LOD	0.5642	0.5451	0.5659	0.5580
Baseline+LOD+Trip.	**0.5678(*)**	**0.5481**	**0.5667(*)**	**0.5589**

baseline the best-performing configuration emerged from the previous tables and we extended the representation by introducing *tripartite* features. By considering MovieLens dataset, a positive impact only emerged when *graph-based* features are merged with *LOD-based* ones. Indeed, both RF and NB are able to improve F1@5 with a statistically significant improvement when *tripartite graph-based features* are exploited. This means that the topological information coming from the injection of the features gathered from the LOD cloud can improve the performance of our framework. Overall, the best configuration for ML data is that based on both *LOD-based* and *tripartite graph-based* features which uses RF. Similar outcomes emerge if we take into account the results on DBbook data. Also in this case, when *LOD-based* features are included in the representation, graph-based features produce a significant increase of F1@5.

To sum up, several interesting outcomes emerge from these experiments: first, RF was the classification algorithm able to take the best out of our hybrid data representation. Another interesting outcome is the connection between the *sparsity* of the dataset and the choice of the features to be included in the model. When the dataset is not sparse, *collaborative* features along with non-personalized *popularity-based* emerge as the most informative ones. On the other side, when data are sparse, collaborative features need to be replaced or coupled with different information sources. These results further confirmed the outcomes behind this research, since they clearly showed that the injection of exogenous data points gathered from the LOD cloud (in the form of both *semantics-aware content-based features* and *topological tripartite* ones) can significantly improve the predictive accuracy of our recommendation framework, leading to an interesting improvement over the baselines.

REFERENCES

[1] R. Burke. 2002. Hybrid recommender systems: Survey and experiments. *UMUAI* 12, 4 (2002), 331–370.
[2] M. de Gemmis, P. Lops, C. Musto, F. Narducci, and G. Semeraro. 2015. Semantics-Aware Content-Based Recommender Systems. In *Recommender Systems Handbook*, Francesco Ricci, Lior Rokach, and Bracha Shapira (Eds.). Springer, 119–159.
[3] C. Musto, P. Basile, P. Lops, M. de Gemmis, and G. Semeraro. 2017. Introducing linked open data in graph-based recommender systems. *Information Processing & Management* 53, 2 (2017), 405–435.
[4] C. Musto, P. Lops, P. Basile, M. de Gemmis, and G. Semeraro. 2016. Semantics-aware Graph-based Recommender Systems Exploiting Linked Open Data. In *UMAP 2016*. 229–237. DOI : http://dx.doi.org/10.1145/2930238.2930249

entries and 6,600 items (98.02%) from DBbook (85% of the items) were successfully mapped. Finally, *graph-based features* were calculated by exploiting the Jung framework[6], a Java library to manage graph-based data. The performance of each configuration of our recommendation framework was evaluated in terms of *F1@5*. Metrics were calculated through the Rival toolkit[7] in order to ensure the reproducibility of the results. Statistical significance was assessed by exploiting Wilcoxon test.

Discussion of the Results. By analyzing the behavior of LOD features on MovieLens data (Table 1), it emerges that the only configuration that benefits of such injection is the one exploiting *content-based features*. This can be probably due to the low sparsity of the dataset, which makes superfluous most of the features except *collaborative* ones. However, even if these experimental settings showed that the adoption of LOD features has to be carefully evaluated, the overall best configuration (highlighted with (*)) actually *includes LOD features*, since the configuration merging popular, collaborative and LOD features obtained the higher F1@5. A similar pattern was noted on DBbook, since RF is the algorithm which takes the best from the LOD-based features. An interesting outcome emerging from this experiment is that when data are sparse, as for DBbook, *LOD-based* data points represent a good alternative also to *collaborative* features. Indeed, in this experiment *Popular+LOD* obtained the best overall F1@5. This means that, when the rating patterns are noisy, LOD features can be used to enrich the representation with new and relevant information.

Next, we evaluated the impact of graph-based features on our recommendation framework. For each dataset we considered as

---

[6]http://jung.sourceforge.net/
[7]http://rival.recommenders.net/

Combining Long-term and Discussion-generated Preferences in Group Recommendations

Thuy Ngoc Nguyen
Free University of Bozen-Bolzano
Piazza Domenicani 3
Bolzano, Italy
ngoc.nguyen@unibz.it

Francesco Ricci
Free University of Bozen-Bolzano
Piazza Domenicani 3
Bolzano, Italy
fricci@unibz.it

ABSTRACT

In this abstract we discuss how long-term and discussion-generated preferences can be appropriately combined in supporting group decision making. We measure the quality of a group recommendation model by varying the importance given to these two types of preferences in different group scenarios, where the group setting may impact on user's behavior. The results of a simulation experiment illustrate that when users' preferences are not influenced by the group, the preference aggregation model should weigh more the long-term preferences. In contrast, when discussion-generated preferences tend either to align with each other or to diverge due to the group setting, it is beneficial to take into account more the discussion-generated preferences, which help to capture the newly arising interests of the users.

CCS CONCEPTS

• **Information systems → Recommender systems**;

KEYWORDS

Recommender Systems; Group Recommendations; Conversational Systems; Preference Elicitation.

ACM Reference format:
Thuy Ngoc Nguyen and Francesco Ricci. 2017. Combining Long-term and Discussion-generated Preferences in Group Recommendations. In *Proceedings of UMAP '17, Bratislava, Slovakia, July 09-12, 2017*, 2 pages.
https://doi.org/http://dx.doi.org/10.1145/3079628.3079645

1 INTRODUCTION

Group Recommender Systems (GRSs) are tools that aim at supporting groups of users in making decisions when considering a set of alternatives [4, 5].

While a considerable amount of research on GRSs has focussed on algorithmic solutions for computing high quality group recommendations on the base of the individuals' preferences, the dynamic aspect of group decision making has been so far explored much less. In fact, researchers in social sciences have pinpointed that the recommendation needs of groups go beyond the bare identification of items that fit the aggregation of individual preferences [5]. In a

recent observational study on group decision processes the authors has further shown that group preferences are constructed during the group decision making process [2]. For these reasons, it is necessary to analyse and model the interactions between users and the system, in order to collect preferences emerging in the group discussion and help the group members in reaching a consensus.

In a previous work, we attempted to exploit the user interactions with the system by introducing a group recommendation model that is based not only on individual long-term preferences but also session-based preferences, i.e., the discussion-generated preferences that can be inferred from users' feedback on the considered options, during the group session. The proposed model was implemented in a GRS that provides a chat environment in which a variety of decision support and recommendation functions are integrated [6]. Even though the results obtained from a controlled live user study showed that the proposed system has a very good usability and perceived recommendation quality, the user study itself was inadequate to fully assess the system performance, which requires to be examined in different situations where users are likely to go through in a group setting.

Motivated by this challenge, in the study reported in this abstract, we have designed a generic simulation process to analyze the appropriateness and the efficacy of the proposed recommender while using three different preference combination schemes: when the importance of the long-term and session-based preferences is equal; when a much stronger importance is given to the long-term preferences; and when greater importance is given to the session-specific preferences. These approaches were assessed in three different group dynamics scenarios, which are inspired by the three typical kinds of social impacts on users' behavior [3]: (a) *independence* - the group has no effect on the user preferences; (b) *conversion* - the group setting nudges group members to be more similar to each other; and (c) *anti-conformity* - the group setting pushes the group members to be more divergent. We hypothesize that the more the users disclose their preferences, the better the group recommendations become. Thus, we measure the quality of group recommendations when the amount of elicited preferences grows.

The results of our study show that the proposed model can correctly capture the changes in user preferences, and as more feedback is acquired in the simulated group session, the efficacy of the model raises. Our results show that: in the scenarios (a), a GRS requires less discussion-generated preferences while in the scenario (b) and (c) it must cater for the session-based preferences to faster identify the preferences of the group.

Table 1: The rank position of the group choice in the recommended ranking list - random groups of 5 users.

t	Independence			Conversion			Anti-conformity		
	$\sigma = 0.1$	$\sigma = 0.5$	$\sigma = 0.9$	$\sigma = 0.1$	$\sigma = 0.5$	$\sigma = 0.9$	$\sigma = 0.1$	$\sigma = 0.5$	$\sigma = 0.9$
1	5.3	3.5	1.3	4.6	2.4	1.6	11	10.8	12
2	4.8	3	1.3	4.5	2.3	1.5	10.3	10.5	11.7
3	3.9	2.6	1	4.3	1.6	1.4	8.3	10.4	11
4	3.2	2.5	1	3.3	1.2	1.4	8.2	10.2	10.2
5	2.7	2.4	1	2.5	1.1	1.3	8.2	9.6	9.8
6	2.5	2.3	1	2.2	1	1.3	7.7	8.8	9.7
7	2.4	1.6	1	1.6	1	1.2	7.1	8.7	9.2
8	2.3	1.5	1	1.5	1	1.1	6.3	8.5	9.1
9	2.2	1.3	1	1.1	1	1	6.1	8.4	8.8
10	2	1.3	1	1	1	1	5.7	8.1	8.5

2 GROUP RECOMMENDATION MODEL

We call $w^{(u)}$ and $w_G^{(u)}$, the utility vector that represents the preferences of user u expressed before and during a discussion of group G, respectively. Utility functions are defined by these vectors and are linear in the features of the items. The vector $w^{(u)}$ is learned by using pre group discussion item ratings and a content-based approach [6]. Next, the system searches for the utility vectors of the group members $w_G^{(u)}$ ($u \in G$) that satisfy the constraints in $\phi_G^{(u)}$, on the session-based user preferences, and maximize the cosine similarity of these vectors with the vector $w^{(G)}$, which is the aggregated utility vector of the group. Here, $\phi_G^{(u)}$ is the set of constraints on the preferences of the user u inferred from her evaluations of the items discussed in the group discussion [1, 7]. For instance if a user liked an item we assume that the utility of this item for her is larger than the utility of an item that she did not like. The resulting optimization problem is formulated as follows:

$$w_G^{(u)} = \arg\max \cos(w_G^{(u)}, w^{(G)}) \text{ s.t. } w_G^{(u)} \text{ sat. } \phi_G^{(u)} \qquad (1)$$

Each user utility vector $w^{(u)}$ is continuously updated by a linear combination of the long term and short term utility vectors (which changes as new session-based preferences are revealed):

$$w^{(u)} = \sigma w^{(u)} + (1 - \sigma) w_G^{(u)}, \sigma \in [0, 1] \qquad (2)$$

The final recommended items are generated by using the group model that aggregates the group's members preference models; in our case, we use the *Average* aggregation function.

3 EXPERIMENTS AND RESULTS

We generated groups randomly to simulate heterogeneous groups. Next, we simulated items that the users propose to their group and their evaluations (e.g., liked or disliked) for the proposed items, in the following three scenarios: *independence, conversion* and *anti-conformity*. Item proposals and evaluations are simulated by assuming that the users have, while interacting in a group, new utility functions that depend on the scenario. For instance in the conversion scenario the utility functions of the group members are more similar than they were before the discussion. In each scenario, we investigated the effect of the parameter σ (see Eq. 2) on the recommendation quality when the number of proposed items t grows, i.e., when the number of elicited preference constraints increases. We have studied the following cases: $\sigma = 0.1, 0.5$, and 0.9. Note that

when larger values of σ are used the recommender weighs more the long-term preferences of the users.

In the *independence* scenario, Table 1 shows that the rank of the group choice in the recommendation list is approaching the top as more items are evaluated (t grows). As expected, the system learns better and better the users' preferences. Moreover, when $\sigma = 0.9$, the recommender can immediately rank the group choice in the top position even with a small number of evaluated items. When $\sigma = 0.5$ and 0.1 the recommender needs more user feedback to rediscover the unchanged user preferences from the group discussion.

In the *conversion* scenario, since the users have more similar preferences, the ranking position of the group choice, when $\sigma = 0.5$ and 0.1, is higher than when the same values are used in the *independence* scenario, but this does not hold for $\sigma = 0.9$. In particular, when $\sigma = 0.9$, the recommender requires the evaluations of at least 5 proposed items from each group member to position the group choice at rank 1.3, while in the first scenario only one discussed item was needed to achieve that rank position.

In the *anti-conformity* scenario i.e., when the group members express preferences that are more diverse, it is harder for the learning process to rank the group choice in the top position. In fact, in this case for all the considered values of σ, the group choice goes below the top 10 (when $t = 1$). In contrast to the first two scenarios, we notice that in this case a smaller value of σ is more effective.

REFERENCES

[1] Henry Blanco and Francesco Ricci. 2013. Inferring user utility for query revision recommendation. In *Proceedings of the 28th ACM Symposium on Applied Computing*. 245–252.

[2] Amra Delic, Julia Neidhardt, Thuy Ngoc Nguyen, Francesco Ricci, Laurens Rook, Hannes Werthner, and Markus Zanker. 2016. Observing Group Decision Making Processes. In *Proceedings of the 10th ACM Conference on Recommender Systems*. 147–150.

[3] Donelson R. Forsyth. 2014. *Group Dynamics* (6th ed.). Wadsworth Cengage Learning.

[4] Anthony Jameson and Barry Smyth. 2007. Recommendation to Groups. *The Adaptive Web*, LNCS 4321 (2007), 596–627.

[5] Judith Masthoff. 2015. Group recommender systems: aggregation, satisfaction and group attributes. In *Recommender Systems Handbook* (2nd ed.), F. Ricci, L. Rokach, and B. Shapira (Eds.). Springer, 743–776.

[6] Thuy Ngoc Nguyen and Francesco Ricci. 2017. Dynamic Elicitation of User Preferences in a Chat-Based Group Recommender System. In *Proceedings of the 32nd ACM Symposium on Applied Computing*.

[7] Walid Trabelsi, Nic Wilson, Derek Bridge, and Francesco Ricci. 2010. Comparing approaches to preference dominance for conversational recommenders. In *Proceedings of the 22nd IEEE International Conference on Tools with Artificial Intelligence*. 113–120.

Evaluation of Learners' Adjustment of Question Difficulty in Adaptive Practice of Facts

Jan Papoušek
Masaryk University
Brno, Czech Republic
jan.papousek@mail.muni.cz

Radek Pelánek
Masaryk University
Brno, Czech Republic
pelanek@mail.muni.cz

ABSTRACT

Personalized educational systems are able to provide learners questions of specified difficulty. Since learners differ, the appropriate level of difficulty may vary and it may be impossible to find an universal setting. We implemented a version of an adaptive educational system for geography practice that allows learners to adjust difficulty of questions. We evaluated this feature using a randomized control experiment. The overall results show only a small effect of the adjustment. A more detailed analysis, however, shows that for some groups of learners the effect can be important, although not necessarily advantageous. The collected data from the experiment provide insight into how to tune question difficulty automatically.

1 INTRODUCTION

User modeling allows us to develop personalized learning environments that make learning experience tailored towards individual learners. Using learner modeling techniques [2] we can estimate probability that a learner can answer a question or solve a problem. Based on these predictions we can automatically choose items of appropriate difficulty [9]. But what is an appropriate level of difficulty? This is typically a parameter that is specified externally by developers of a learning system. The choice of this parameter has been addressed in previous research, but without clear results [4, 5, 8].

A natural idea is to allow learners to manipulate the difficulty of questions. In addition to better tailored system behaviour, previous research suggests that a sense of control (or even perception of control, rather than the actual objective level of control) can increase engagement [6]. On the other hand, research on self-regulated study [1] shows that people are prone to mismanaging their own learning. A recent research explored self-adaptation of difficulty in math practice [3]. The authors did not find any impact of the availability of difficulty setting on learning, engagement, or students' self-belief. The study, however, has several limitations, e.g., the setting of an error rate interacted with gamification aspects of the user interface and the used sample size was small (48 students in each condition). We present a similar experiment, but for a different type of knowledge (learning geography facts) and using a large scale experiment with thousands of users and millions of answers.

2 EXPERIMENT

We use a system for an adaptive practice of geographical facts, e.g., names and locations of countries or cities. The system is available online at outlinemaps.org. Learners can use the system with different 'contexts' (combinations of a map and a type of place, e.g., European states) . The system collects data about the correctness of answers and based on the collected data it estimates the current knowledge of a particular learner and personalizes the provided practice [9]. A key parameter in the adaptive algorithm is "target difficulty", which sets the average error rate of learners that the system is aiming at.

In our experiment we let some learners modify the parameter based on their preferences. The practice within the system is presented in groups of 10 questions; after each series of 10 questions the systems shows a summary feedback to learners. At this moment we have inserted a new dialog box with a question "How difficult would you like the questions to be?" with 5 choices: "much harder", "harder", "same", "easier", "much easier". We call answers to these questions "ratings" (not "settings", because in a placebo condition they do not have any impact on the algorithm).

We have performed a standard randomized control trial with three experimental conditions: 1) *normal* – a control group, a standard version of the system without the dialog box; 2) *placebo* – the dialog is shown, but does not have any impact on the behaviour of the adaptive algorithm; 3) *adjustment* – the dialog is shown and the answer changes the target error rate (+20%, +10%, 0%, -10%, -20%).

In all cases the initial setting of the target error rate parameter is 35% (the value is based on results of the previous experiment [8]). The experiment was performed from October 2016 to January 2017 and we have collected roughly 8 200 000 answers from 85 000 learners. To make our research reproducible we make the analyzed data set available[1].

3 RESULTS

At first, we analyze ratings provided by users. Mostly, we have only one rating from a particular learner per context. Majority of learners do not provide any rating at all. Since the ratings are provided after finishing a practice set, we assume the main factor determining a learner's rating is an error rate achieved during the recent practice set, therefore we divide all ratings to buckets based on the error rate. Figure 1 shows the relation between ratings and the recent error rate (based on the last 10 questions).

The basic relation is intuitive – successful learners want more difficult questions, unsuccessful learners want easier questions. The "appropriate" ratings have the shape of inverted-U curve with the

---

[1]http://data.outlinemaps.org/2016-ab-user-difficulty-adjustment.zip

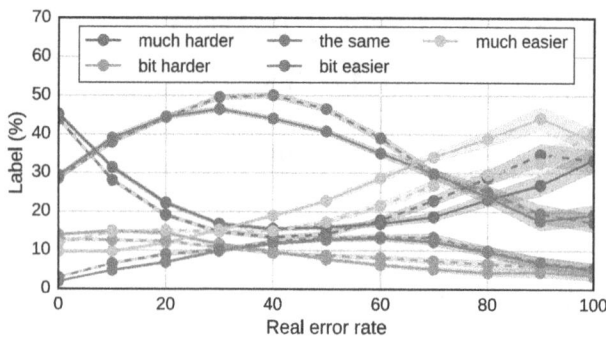

Figure 1: Learners' ratings with respect to the error rate achieved during the recent practice set. Solid lines stand for placebo condition, dashed lines stand for adjustment condition. The shaded areas shows 95% confidence intervals.

maximum at the error rate around 35%. This result is in agreement with our previous experiments that showed that target error rate 35% is suitable [8].

For high error rates the results are intriguing. As could be expected the ratio of "bit harder" ratings is very small. Unexpectedly, highly unsuccessful learners often provide "more difficult" rating. Although the number of highly unsuccessful learners is relatively small, this trend is statistically significant and consistent for both placebo and adjustment conditions. We interpret this trend as presence of a systematic "irony" in responses of a subgroup of users and we hypothesize that this behaviour is connected to disengagement with the system. This result should serve as a caution – preferences expressed by learners may reflect not just their true preferences with respect to the concerned question, but may also incorporate other aspects of their (affective) state.

The data also show a relation between ratings and context difficulty. The percentage of "much harder" ratings increases with decreasing context difficulty (e.g., European states are easier than African cities, at least for users of the used system). This observation indicates that our algorithm for adaptive practice is not adaptive enough and there is room for improvement – the algorithm could take into account the difficulty of a particular context.

The main point of the experiment is to find whether the dynamic adjustment leads to higher engagement and learning. As a measure of engagement we use a survival rate – the ratio of learners who answer at least 100 questions. To compare learning among conditions, we utilize "reference questions" – for each context separately every tenth question is selected randomly without any influence of the adaptive algorithm and we use data from these questions to construct learning curves. For more detailed discussion of the used evaluation approach see [7].

On the global level, we do not see any large differences among conditions (100 question survival rates are: normal 29.1%, placebo 27.5%, adjustment 28.3%). As expected, the engagement for the placebo condition is worse than for the control group. The dialog box asking for learners' ratings has negative impact on learners' engagement. For the adjustment condition the negative effect of the

dialog is partially compensated by the benefits of the difficulty adjustment. However, the benefits of the difficulty adjustment are not sufficient to overweight the disadvantage of the additional dialog box. For learning we also do not have any significant differences in overall learning rates. Since many learners do not provide any ratings at all, it is not much surprising – most learners in placebo and adjustment conditions keep the original target error rate and thus their practice is the same as for the control group.

However, a more detailed analysis shows that for specific cases there are some trends. When we consider 30% easiest contexts (e.g., Europe states), the learning is actually worse for the adjustment condition. It is probably caused by learners' tendency to set lower difficulty even on easy contexts (e.g., by externally motivated learners from schools). Another more detailed analysis disaggregates the overall results with respect to learners – specifically based on their preference for easy or difficult questions. The results are interesting particularly for the group of learners who prefer easy questions – for this group the adjustment hampers the speed of learning, but increases engagement. The adjustment is clearly beneficial only for the group of learners who prefer difficult questions – for them it improves the speed of learning without any significant impact on engagement.

Overall, however, our experiment suggests that instead of giving learners control over the difficulty setting, we should rather develop better methods for automatic adjustment of target difficulty.

REFERENCES

[1] Robert A Bjork, John Dunlosky, and Nate Kornell. 2013. Self-regulated learning: Beliefs, techniques, and illusions. *Annual Review of Psychology* 64 (2013), 417–444.

[2] Michel C Desmarais and Ryan SJ Baker. 2012. A review of recent advances in learner and skill modeling in intelligent learning environments. *User Modeling and User-Adapted Interaction* 22, 1-2 (2012), 9–38.

[3] Brenda RJ Jansen, Abe D Hofman, Alexander Savi, Ingmar Visser, and Han LJ van der Maas. 2016. Self-adapting the success rate when practicing math. *Learning and Individual Differences* 51 (2016), 1–10.

[4] Brenda RJ Jansen, Jolien Louwerse, Marthe Straatemeier, Sanne HG Van der Ven, Sharon Klinkenberg, and Han LJ Van der Maas. 2013. The influence of experiencing success in math on math anxiety, perceived math competence, and math performance. *Learning and Individual Differences* 24 (2013), 190–197.

[5] Derek Lomas, Kishan Patel, Jodi L Forlizzi, and Kenneth R Koedinger. 2013. Optimizing challenge in an educational game using large-scale design experiments. In *Proceedings of the SIGCHI Conference on Human Factors in Computing Systems.* ACM, 89–98.

[6] Thomas W Malone and Mark R Lepper. 1987. Making learning fun: A taxonomy of intrinsic motivations for learning. *Aptitude, learning, and instruction* 3, 1987 (1987), 223–253.

[7] Jan Papoušek, Vít Stanislav, and Radek Pelánek. 2016. Evaluation of an Adaptive Practice System for Learning Geography Facts. In *Proc. of Learning Analytics & Knowledge.* ACM, 40–47.

[8] Jan Papoušek, Vít Stanislav, and Radek Pelánek. 2016. Impact of Question Difficulty on Engagement and Learning. In *Proc. of Intelligent Tutoring Systems (LNCS),* Alessandro Micarelli, John C. Stamper, and Kitty Panourgia (Eds.), Vol. 9684. Springer.

[9] Radek Pelánek, Jan Papoušek, Jiří Řihák, Vít Stanislav, and Juraj Nižnan. 2017. Elo-based learner modeling for the adaptive practice of facts. *User Modeling and User-Adapted Interaction* 27, 1 (2017), 89–118.

An Evaluation of Learning-to-Rank Methods for Lurking Behavior Analysis

Diego Perna
DIMES, University of Calabria
d.perna@dimes.unical.it

Andrea Tagarelli
DIMES, University of Calabria
andrea.tagarelli@unical.it

ABSTRACT

Computational approaches to lurking behavior analysis in online social networks (OSNs) have been developed in the last few years. However, the complexity of the problem hints at the opportunity of learning from past lurking experiences as well as of using a variety of behavioral features, including any available information on the activity and interaction of lurkers and active users in an OSN. In this paper, we leverage this opportunity in a principled way, by proposing a machine-learning framework which, once trained on lurking/non-lurking examples from multiple OSNs, allows us to predict the ranking of unseen lurking behaviors, ultimately enabling the prioritization of user engagement tasks.

CCS CONCEPTS

•**Information systems** →**Learning to rank;** *Social recommendation; Social networks;*

KEYWORDS

lurking; learning-to-rank; behavior analysis; user engagement

1 INTRODUCTION

Lurking in an online social network (OSN) refers to hte behavior exhibited by registered members who do not significantly take an active and tangible role in the interaction with other members [11]. Lurkers are used to gain benefit from information produced by other users, although their presence is legitimated [6], expected or even welcome [2, 10]. More importantly, lurkers might hold potential *social capital*, because they acquire knowledge from the OSN. Therefore, it might be desirable to make lurkers' social capital available to other users through mechanisms of *engagement* [3, 4, 8].

Computational analysis of lurking behaviors has been recently tackled from different perspectives, mainly following unsupervised learning paradigms (e.g., [5, 14]).[1] Nevertheless, to further improve our understanding of a behavioral analysis problem that is inherently dynamic as well as sensitive to many aspects relating to an OSN, several challenges remain open and need to be investigated.

---

[1]Note also that the 2015 edition of the UMAP conference hosted the first tutorial on lurking behavior analysis; see http://umap2015.com/tutorial.html

In this paper we aim to capitalize on the *learning-to-rank* (LTR) theory [7] by developing a principled machine-learning based ranking framework for the analysis of lurking behaviors. LTR adopts a supervised approach to learning from past user experiences, which in our setting might be annotated according to the degree of lurking behavior shown by users. LTR training is accomplished according to a set of features which, being possibly of different types, would capture different aspects that might be potentially useful predictors of lurking behaviors. By learning from different, properly engineered features, LTR can be a robust approach in cases where it would be difficult to gather sufficient and significant evidences of the lurking status from the graph of user relationships. In addition, by inheriting robustness to outliers of some machine learning methods, LTR models can be useful to handle inconsistent or fake lurking behaviors.

In this work, we propose the first LTR framework to analyze lurkers in OSNs. By exploiting state-of-the-art LTR methods, we develop a *learning-to-lurker-rank* methodology whose key aspects are: (i) the use of the *unsupervised LurkerRank* (LR) method [12, 13] to derive binary or graded relevance labels, and (ii) a feature engineering phase that accounts for *relational, media-based, activity rate,* and *platform-specific* information on the commitment and interaction of users from different OSNs.[2]

2 METHODOLOGY

Datasets. We built our evaluation data from 23 user relation networks and media databases gathered from Twitter (5), Instagram (9), Flickr (5), FriendFeed, GooglePlus, StackOverflow, and GitHub. (Details on the evaluation data are available as online supplementary material.)

Training data. LTR training data consists of triplets ⟨*query, object, relevance label*⟩. In our setting, each query corresponds to one of the 23 network datasets, each object corresponds to a user's feature vector, and the relevance label denotes one or several grades of lurking, so that the higher grade a user has, the more lurker the user is. More specifically, we used LR to produce lurking scores upon which we derived the relevance labels: users at *top-p%* ranked and *bottom-q%* ranked portions of a LurkerRank solution were labeled as relevant (i.e., lurkers) and non-relevant (i.e., not-lurkers), respectively. We also considered graded relevance by a finer-grain segmentation of the selected sublist of lurkers.

Feature engineering. We extracted and organized the features into four categories. *Relational* features correspond to local topology properties of a node (i.e., user) in a graph, which are defined according to the three principles at the basis of the *topology-driven lurking model* described in [12, 13]. *Media based* features describe a user's actions performed or received in relation to the media in

---

[2]Supplementary material can be found at: http://people.dimes.unical.it/andreatagarelli/ltlr/

Table 1: LTR performance on test data

method	measure	Relational features		All features	
		Binary	Graded	Binary	Graded
AdaRank	P@10	.539	.174	.617	.348
AdaRank	P@100	.513	.168	.610	.350
AdaRank	P@1000	.981	.246	.796	.671
AdaRank	MAP	.686	.581	.618	.611
AdaRank	nDCG@10	.538	.405	.610	.304
AdaRank	nDCG@100	.515	.917	.608	.286
AdaRank	nDCG@1000	.513	.188	.623	.235
Coor.Asc.	P@10	1.00	.996	1.00	.935
Coor.Asc.	P@100	1.00	1.00	1.00	1.00
Coor.Asc.	P@1000	.990	.636	.989	.687
Coor.Asc.	MAP	1.00	1.00	1.00	1.00
Coor.Asc.	nDCG@10	1.00	.984	1.00	1.00
Coor.Asc.	nDCG@100	1.00	.920	1.00	1.00
Coor.Asc.	nDCG@1000	1.00	.851	1.00	1.00
LamdaMART	P@10	1.00	1.00	1.00	1.00
LamdaMART	P@100	1.00	1.00	1.00	1.00
LamdaMART	P@1000	.990	.636	.993	.745
LamdaMART	MAP	1.00	1.00	1.00	1.00
LamdaMART	nDCG@10	1.00	.741	1.00	1.00
LamdaMART	nDCG@100	1.00	1.00	1.00	1.00
LamdaMART	nDCG@1000	1.00	1.00	1.00	1.00
RankNet	P@10	.991	.952	1.00	1.00
RankNet	P@100	.858	.888	1.00	1.00
RankNet	P@1000	.712	.707	.966	.966
RankNet	MAP	.710	.387	1.00	.404
RankNet	nDCG@10	.994	.572	1.00	.612
RankNet	nDCG@100	.887	.463	1.00	.495
RankNet	nDCG@1000	.739	.399	.980	.417

the OSN (e.g., posts, images). These are divided into *latent* actions (e.g., views/clicks), *least-effort* actions (e.g., likes, favorites, mentions), and *most-effort* actions (e.g., comments, replies). *Activity rate* features aim to capture temporal aspects of the user's activity, in terms of frequency and latency [14]. Moreover, we include further *platform-specific* indicators of the degree of a user's commitment and engagement. (Details on feature engineering are available as online supplementary material.)

Framework setting. We resorted to four state-of-the-art LTR methods: *RankNet* [1], *Coordinate Ascent* [9], *AdaRank* [16], and *LambdaMART* [15]. We used the Java implementations of *RankLib* under the *The Lemur Project*, with default settings.[3] We trained and tested through 5-cross-validation each of the LTR methods using *MAP*, *P@k*, and *nDCG@k* criteria, with $k \in \{10, 100, 1000\}$, both for optimization (except for RankNet) and evaluation.

For each of the datasets, we devised two cases depending on the type of relevance label: in the first one, dubbed Binary, we considered *binary* relevance, i.e., lurking and not-lurking users, while in the second, dubbed Graded, we considered *m* grades of relevance of lurking. We will present results based on the setting of Binary corresponding to top-5% and bottom-5% users by LR as relevant and not-relevant, respectively, and the setting of Graded with $m = 3$ corresponding to top-5% (relevance 3), second 5% (relevance 2), third to fifth 5% (relevance 1) as relevant and bottom-25% as not-relevant. Moreover, we evaluated the effect of using either *relational features* only or *all features* for the training data.

3 RESULTS

Table 1 reports on performance of LTR methods on test data, for varying measures and settings. We observe that, among the LTR

methods, LambaMART and Coordinate Ascent achieve the best results. This is substantially in line with the current literature, as the two methods have shown to outperform others in several application scenarios. The representative pairwise approach, RankNet, can also perform well, although it needs to train data with all features to behave comparably to the two aforementioned listwise methods, for the binary relevance case. By contrast, the other listwise method, AdaRank, performs quite poorly in most cases.

Empirical evidence indicates that LTR can be effective in ranking lurkers with the Binary scenario, but also with the more difficult testbed Graded. More precisely, some LTR methods are able to well predict the ranking of lurkers trained according to the (graded or not) relevance labels originally provided by LR. While best-performing LambdaMART and Coordinate Ascent can optimally predict the correct rank on test data even with relational features only, a general trend is that a combination with media-based and activity rate features should be used to improve the ranking performance. Moreover, there is a partial evidence that the ranking performance tends to improve when all features are used.

Conclusion. In this work, we propose the first LTR framework to analyze lurkers in OSNs. Overall, our learning-to-lurker-rank framework turns out to be a promising tool for predicting the lurking behaviors, which can be useful to trigger engagement strategies for such users.

REFERENCES

[1] C. J. C. Burges, T. Shaked, E. Renshaw, A. Lazier, M. Deeds, N. Hamilton, and G. N. Hullender. 2005. Learning to rank using gradient descent. In *Proc. Int. Conf. on Machine Learning (ICML)*. 89–96.

[2] N. Edelmann. 2013. Reviewing the definitions of "lurkers" and some implications for online research. *Cyberpsychology, Behavior, and Social Networking* 16, 9 (2013), 645–649.

[3] R. Farzan and P. Brusilovsky. 2011. Encouraging user participation in a course recommender system: An impact on user behavior. *Computers in Human Behavior* 27, 1 (2011), 276–284.

[4] J. Imlawi and D. G. Gregg. 2014. Engagement in Online Social Networks: The Impact of Self-Disclosure and Humor. *Int. J. Hum. Comput. Interaction* 30, 2 (2014), 106–125.

[5] R. Interdonato and A. Tagarelli. 2016. To trust or not to trust lurkers?: Evaluation of lurking and trustworthiness in ranking problems. In *Proc. Int. Conf. and School on Advances in Network Science (NetSci-X) (LNCS)*, Vol. 9564. 43–56.

[6] J. Lave and E. Wenger. 1991. *Situated Learning: Legitimate Peripheral Participation.* Cambridge University Press.

[7] Tie-Yan Liu. 2011. *Learning to Rank for Information Retrieval.* Springer.

[8] F. D. Malliaros and M. Vazirgiannis. 2013. To stay or not to stay: modeling engagement dynamics in social graphs. In *Proc. ACM Conf. on Information and Knowledge Management (CIKM)*. 469–478.

[9] D. Metzler and W. B. Croft. 2007. Linear feature-based models for information retrieval. *Inf. Retr.* 10, 3 (2007), 257–274.

[10] Z. Pan, Y. Lu, and S. Gupta. 2014. How heterogeneous community engage newcomers? The effect of community diversity on newcomers' perception of inclusion: An empirical study in social media service. *Computers in Human Behavior* 39 (2014), 100–111.

[11] N. Sun, P. P.-L. Rau, and L. Ma. 2014. Understanding lurkers in online communities: a literature review. *Computers in Human Behavior* 38 (2014), 110–117.

[12] A. Tagarelli and R. Interdonato. 2013. "Who's out there?": Identifying and Ranking Lurkers in Social Networks. In *Proc. Int. Conf. on Advances in Social Networks Analysis and Mining (ASONAM)*. 215–222.

[13] A. Tagarelli and R. Interdonato. 2014. Lurking in social networks: topology-based analysis and ranking methods. *Social Netw. Analys. Mining* 4, 230 (2014), 27.

[14] A. Tagarelli and R. Interdonato. 2015. Time-aware Analysis and Ranking of Lurkers in Social Networks. *Social Netw. Analys. Mining* 5, 1 (2015), 23.

[15] Q. Wu, C. J. C. Burges, K. M. Svore, and J. Gao. 2010. Adapting boosting for information retrieval measures. *Inf. Retr.* 13, 3 (2010), 254–270.

[16] J. Xu and H. Li. 2007. AdaRank: a boosting algorithm for information retrieval. In *Proc. ACM SIGIR Conf. on Research and Development in Information Retrieval (SIGIR)*. 391–398.

---

[3] http://www.lemurproject.org

Learning Inclination to Empathy from Social Media Footprints

Marco Polignano
marco.polignano@uniba.it
University of Bari (Italy)

Pierpaolo Basile
pierpaolo.basile@uniba.it
University of Bari (Italy),

Gaetano Rossiello
gaetano.rossiello@uniba.it
University of Bari (Italy)

Marco de Gemmis
marco.degemmis@uniba.it
University of Bari (Italy)

Giovanni Semeraro
giovanni.semeraro@uniba.it
University of Bari (Italy)

ABSTRACT

In recent years we are witnessing a growing spread of social media footprints, as the consequence of the wide use of applications such as Facebook, Twitter or LinkedIn, which allow people to share content that might provide information about personal preferences and aptitudes. Among the traits that can be inferred, empathy is the ability to feel and share another person's emotions and we consider it as a relevant aspect for the profiling and recommendation tasks. We propose a method that predicts its level for the user by exploiting her social media data and using linear regression algorithms. The results show which are the most relevant correlations among the different groups of user's features and the empathy level predicted.

CCS CONCEPTS

•**Information systems** →**Personalization**; Social networks;
•**Computing methodologies** →**Natural language processing**;

KEYWORDS

Social medium footprint, Empathy, Machine Learning

1 BACKGROUND AND MOTIVATIONS

The massive spread of social media over mobile devices has significantly changed the way people communicate today. The interaction with social media allows a person's to feed her digital identity with preferences, interests, aptitudes. That information, usually known as social media footprints, is available on the web and can be exploited by others to discover that person's tendencies, styles of life, and also affective and psychological traits [2, 4]. For this reason, we want to investigate whether (and how) it is possible to predict the empathy inclination of a user. According to Hogan [3], empathy can be correlated with social self-confidence, even-temperedness, sensitivity and nonconformity. Therefore, a subject who shows high empathy is a very emotional and sensitivity person because not only she is inclined to understand others' emotions, but she is also able to feel some strong emotions for them. We believe that personalization systems working in some specific domains, such as movie or music recommendation, would benefit from the knowledge of this affective aspect of the user.

UMAP '17, July 9–12, 2017, Bratislava, Slovakia
© 2017 Copyright held by the owner/author(s). ACM ISBN 978-1-4503-4635-1/17/07.
DOI: http://dx.doi.org/10.1145/3079628.3079639

2 EMPATHY INCLINATION PREDICTION MODEL

The proposed model is based on the idea that several aspects of the user life might contribute to infer user inclination to empathy. We exploit several kinds of features, as sketched in Fig.1, to predict an empathy score by different linear regression models.

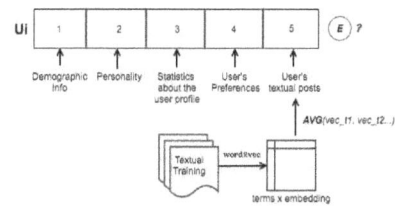

Figure 1: Empathy prediction model

Each user U_i is represented as the concatenation of five features vectors. Each vector captures a particular aspect of the user profile. User's preferences are obtained by analyzing her likes grouped by topics over social media and they include likes over pages, artists, movies and many other topics of interest. The representation used is the SVD for the representation through relevant combinations of *concepts* and LDA for a combination of *descriptive topics*. Textual content (posts) shared by the user, in order to understand her writing style and the semantics behind the words. The text is analyzed by a pipeline performing basic NLP operations, as well as operations for annotating emoticon and for removing character repetitions longer than two inside words. In order to capture the semantics behind the words, we use the word2vec algorithm [6] over all the textual posts in the collection for learning 200-dimension vectors, by considering only words that occur at least 10 times and 10 epochs of learning. In order to better characterize the textual content written by each user, we divide the whole vocabulary of word2vec vectors into clusters, which should represent topics of discussion. For this purpose, we run the k-Means algorithm over the word embeddings matrix containing all the word vectors from the vocabulary.

3 EXPERIMENTAL SESSION

The aim of the experiment is to predict the user's empathy by exploiting information explicitly available on her Facebook profile, as well as implicit information that can be inferred, as explained in Sec. 2. Moreover, we want to identify which groups of features are more important for obtaining an accurate prediction. More

Table 1: Relevant results of empathy level prediction

Approach	c	All Features		Filtered Features	
		MAE	RMSE	MAE	RMSE
SMO_{poly}	1	12.7137	19.1565	*5.714*	*7.8407*
SMO_{rbf}	2	5.9543	8.2432	*5.6673*	7.8631
SMO_{rbf}	8	6.539	8.7748	5.686	*7.8236*
Lr	-	22.7929	34.4679	5.7854	7.7269
Sr	-	6.1045	8.233	6.1045	8.233

precisely, we formulated the following research questions: **RQ1.** Is it possible to predict empathy from digital footprints?; **RQ2.** What are the most important features for an accurate prediction?

The dataset used in the experiment, proposed by Kosinski [5], contains information about 4 millions of Facebook users. Data are collected using the *"myPersonality"* Facebook application. We removed those users who have not terminated the questionnaire or who were not linkable to other data (Demographic, BIG5, Activity, Status), after this step, the dataset is composed by 903 users, 178, 766 status updates. The range of the empathy value is 0-80. We exploit three different regression algorithms: 1) *Linear Regression (Lr)* [7], 2) *Simple Regression (Sr)* [1], 3) different configurations of kernel of the *SVM Regression with SMO algorithm (SMO)* [8]. For the *SMO* we used the polynomial kernel (SMO_{poly}) and the Radial Basis Function (RBF) kernel (SMO_{rbf}), by varying the c parameter from 1 to 8. We propose two simple baselines in order to compare the proposed approach with alternative options. The former always predicts the most frequent value in the dataset *(Majority, Value Predicted= 8, MAE= 7.4784, RMSE= 10.8258)*, while the latter computes the empathy score as the simple average of EQS observed in the dataset *(Avg EQS, Value Predicted= 13.9169, MAE= 6.8457, RMSE= 9.0757)*. As for the evaluation metrics, we adopted the Root Mean Square Error (RMSE) and the Mean Absolute Error (MAE).The evaluation protocol was 10 folds cross validation.

4 DISCUSSION OF RESULTS

We execute a first experiment by running *Lr, Sr*, and *SMO* by using all the features of the dataset. We compared the results in Tab. 1 with our baselines observing that using *SMO* with a polynomial kernel is not a good choice, having a large number of features. On the contrary, *SMO* with an *RBF* kernel is able to overcome both the baselines by setting $c = 1$ ($MAE = 5.9101, RMSE = 8.2341$). These results allow us to answer positively to **RQ1**. Interesting results are obtained by *Sr*. MAE and RMSE are better than the baselines, despite this algorithm creates a regression function considering only the feature with higher variance in the dataset. Due to these findings, we decided to perform feature selection. We exploit the correlation-based feature subset selection for finding the set of "most informative" features for the prediction task. The selected features are those with high correlation with the prediction class and low correlation among them. We obtained a set of 37 features. The best result in term of MAE (5.6673) is obtained by the SMO_{rbf}, with $c = 2$. This configuration does not provide the best RMSE (7.8236) that it is achieved by SMO_{rbf} with $c = 8$. For the SMO_{poly} configuration, the best result for both MAE and RMSE is obtained with $c = 1$ (5.714, 7.8407). Analyzing the features emerged after the

selection process, we observed that for an accurate prediction we have to consider the user's *religion* (Nonreligious/Atheist), *country* (AG, EG, KW, HN, AR, SR), *relationship_status* (Separated), *personality* (extroversion, agreeableness) and some relevant word2vec clusters: *cluster_1*: game, team, soccer, battle, race, fans, bowling; *cluster_13*: dear, cheers, goody, extraordinaire, excitedly; *cluster_21*: personality, motivation, destiny, ability, vision; *cluster_24*: facebook, phone, message, internet, video. These correlations can be used as hints for user profiling and *partially* provide an answer for **RQ2**, therefore we decided to perform an ablation analysis for further investigation. We selected the best configuration SMO_{rbf} with $c = 1$ and we removed one set of features at a time. By removing groups of features such as *demographic, activity, LDA*, we observed a slight change of MAE and RMSE. On the contrary, by removing the set of features about *personality*, a significant increase of both MAE (9.6308) and RMSE (9.0815) is observed. This provides a more specific answer for **RQ2**: **personality traits** are the key for effective empathy prediction.

5 CONCLUSION

In this paper, we investigated the problem of mining social media footprints to infer the user's inclination toward empathy. The main outcome of the experiments are: feature selection reduces the noise in the training data and increases the accuracy of prediction; a strong correlation is observed among empathy and personality traits. As a future work, we plan to include the findings described in this preliminary study as part of the user profile.

6 ACKNOWLEDGEMENT

This research has received funding from the European Union's Horizon 2020 research and innovation programme under the Marie Sklodowska-Curie grant agreement N. 691071.

REFERENCES

[1] Allen L Edwards. 1976. An introduction to linear regression and correlation. (1976).

[2] Eric Gilbert and Karrie Karahalios. 2009. Predicting tie strength with social media. In *Proceedings of the SIGCHI conference on human factors in computing systems*. ACM, 211–220.

[3] Robert Hogan. 1969. Development of an empathy scale. *Journal of consulting and clinical psychology* 33, 3 (1969), 307.

[4] Lauren A Jelenchick, Jens C Eickhoff, and Megan A Moreno. 2013. "Facebook depression?" Social networking site use and depression in older adolescents. *Journal of Adolescent Health* 52, 1 (2013), 128–130.

[5] Michal Kosinski, Sandra C Matz, Samuel D Gosling, Vesselin Popov, and David Stillwell. 2015. Facebook as a research tool for the social sciences: Opportunities, challenges, ethical considerations, and practical guidelines. *American Psychologist* 70, 6 (2015), 543.

[6] Tomas Mikolov, Kai Chen, Greg Corrado, and Jeffrey Dean. 2013. Efficient estimation of word representations in vector space. *arXiv preprint arXiv:1301.3781* (2013).

[7] John Neter, Michael H Kutner, Christopher J Nachtsheim, and William Wasserman. 1996. *Applied linear statistical models*. Vol. 4. Irwin Chicago.

[8] John Platt. 1998. Sequential minimal optimization: A fast algorithm for training support vector machines. (1998).

Using System Dynamics to Model Student Performance in an Intelligent Tutoring System

María T. Sanz, David Arnau
Universitat de València
Department de Didàctica de la
Matemàtica
Avda. Tarongers, 4
Valencia, Spain 46022
m.teresa.sanz@uv.es
david.arnau@uv.es

José A. González-Calero
Universidad de Castilla-La Mancha
Departamento de Matemáticas
Plaza de la Universidad, 3
Albacete, Spain 02071
jose.gonzalezcalero@uclm.es

Miguel Arevalillo-Herráez
Universitat de València
Departament d'Informàtica
Avda. de la Universidad s/n
Burjassot, Valencia, Spain 46100
miguel.arevalillo@uv.es

ABSTRACT

One basic adaptation function of an Intelligent Tutoring System (ITS) consists of selecting the most appropriate next task to be offered to the learner. This decision can be based on estimates, such as the expected performance of the student, or the probability that the student successfully solves each particular task. However, the computation of these values is intrinsically difficult, as they may depend on other complex latent variables that also need to be estimated from observable quantities, e.g. the current student's ability. In this work, we have used system dynamics to model learning and predict the student's performance in a given exercise, in an existing ITS that was developed to teach students solve arithmetic-algebraic word problems. The high correlation between the predicted and real scores outlines the potential of this type of modeling as a prediction tool to support the decision about the next task that should be offered to the learner.

KEYWORDS

user modeling; instructional modeling; system dynamics; learning curve

ACM Reference format:
María T. Sanz, David Arnau, José A. González-Calero, and Miguel Arevalillo-Herráez. 2017. Using System Dynamics to model student performance in an Intelligent Tutoring System. In *Proceedings of UMAP '17, July 9-12, 2017, Bratislava, Slovakia*, , 2 pages.
DOI: http://dx.doi.org/10.1145/3079628.3079635

1 INTRODUCTION

A key adaptation function of Intelligent Tutoring Systems (ITS) consists of selecting the teaching sequence that best suit a particular learner, by taking the learner's needs and preferences into account. Such a function usually requires a subject-dependent assessment of the difficulty of a task, combining information related to the task with a student model that contains information about the learner's current abilities. In this work, we have used an existing ITS that was

specifically built for the learning of arithmetical and algebraic word problem solving (HBPS) [1–3], and applied system dynamics [5] to model the learning process. The resulting model is able to predict the student's performance in a given task with reasonable accuracy, and can hence be used to decide what activity to offer next. The high correlation between the real and the predicted learner's performance on previously unseen problems ($r = 0.65$) supports the utility of this unexplored type of modeling in this context.

2 PROPOSED METHOD

Our dynamic model is based on the intrinsic relationships illustrated in Figure 1 between the learner's performance at solving a given task, the learner's competence in arithmetic problem solving and the difficulty of the activity. This model assumes that the learner's performance can be predicted by using the problem difficulty and the learner's current ability. In addition, the relative learner's performance on the last problem is also an indicator of his/her competence in arithmetic problem solving. Hence, it can be used to modify the student's current ability, closing the loop in Figure 1.

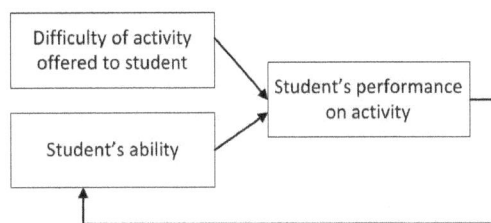

Figure 1: Conceptual diagram showing the influence between variables

In some way, this model matches the behavior of a human tutor. After observing a student solving an exercise, a human tutor internally builds a mental model of the learner's ability. This model is then used to suggest the next exercise that best matches the student's current level of competence, based on how well the subject has coped with the last few problems attempted and considering the difficulty of the problems that are available.

3 MODEL CONSTRUCTION AND VALIDATION

3.1 Data collection

A collection of 26 arithmetic word problems was prepared and solved by 64 students that belong to three natural groups from the fourth grade (9-10 years old) by using the ITS described in [1]. While they solved the problems, we logged a number of variables, including the number of attempts that each student made to solve each problem step.

3.2 Model construction

The data collected was divided into training and validation data. Logged data for the first 16 problems was used for training, using the table-based method proposed in [4] to fit the functions that relate the influences between the variables depicted in Figure 1. Then, the information gathered while the students solved the last 10 problems was employed to validate the resulting model.

The student's performance at each problem was computed as a score based on the number of attempts that the student made at each step. For example, if a student solved a two-step word problem by making 5 attempts in the first step and 2 in the second, his/her performance was computed as $\frac{1/5+1/2}{2} = 0.35$. When a student did not complete an exercise, the computation was similar but the denominator was the total number of steps that were required in the solution path that the student was following. The difficulty of a problem was estimated from the complexity of the conceptual schemes [7] that are needed to solve it, according to previous studies that empirically relate each conceptual scheme to the probability that the student reaches a correct solution e.g. [6, 7].

3.3 Model validation

The plot in Figure 2 presents a comparison between the predicted and real scores obtained for the 10 problems that were used for validation purposes, to test whether the fitted functions generalize to previously unseen data. The correlation obtained is $r = 0.65$. When this same correlation is measured on the first 16 problems (the training data), a correlation of $r = 0.71$ is obtained. These results indicate that the model generalizes well and allows for a reliable prediction of the problem score.

4 CONCLUSIONS

In this work, we have presented an initial attempt to apply system dynamics to produce a learning model for arithmetic word problem solving. The resulting model allows us to predict the student's performance at solving a particular word problem with a reasonable accuracy. This prediction is based on the complexity of the problem's mathematical structure and the student's competence in arithmetic problem solving. The validation of the model confirms its potential to help the system suggest an adequate next task that maximizes learning gains. Despite that this work has been developed in a mathematical context, the model proposed is sufficiently general to be applied in other domains.

Future extensions of the current work include the definition of more reliable estimates that better approximate the main variables considered in our model, i.e., difficulty of a given word problem and

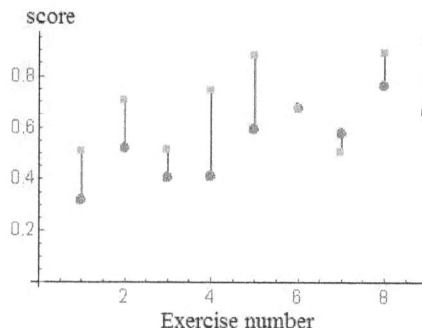

Figure 2: Predicted (blue circles) and real (yellow squares) scores, in the last (previously unseen) 10 exercises used for validation.

the learner's current ability and performance on the last exercise. Another already planned extension consist of considering other variables that have a known influence on the learning process but have not been considered in this work, such as the user's affective state [8]. In addition, a comparison between the output of the model and the predictions made by human tutors would allow for a better assessment of the results reported.

ACKNOWLEDGEMENTS

This work has been partly supported through different projects by the Spanish Ministry of Economy and Competitiveness (TIN2014-5964-C2-1-P), the Spanish Ministry of Education (EDU2015-69731-R (MINECO/FEDER)) and the Conselleria d'Educació, Investigació, Cultura i Esport (GV2016-118, GVPROMETEO2016-143).

REFERENCES

[1] Miguel Arevalillo-Herráez, David Arnau, and Luis Marco-Giménez. 2013. Domain-specific knowledge representation and inference engine for an intelligent tutoring system. *Knowledge-Based Systems* 49 (9 2013), 97–105.

[2] David Arnau, Miguel Arevalillo-Herráez, and José Antonio González-Calero. 2014. Emulating Human Supervision in an Intelligent Tutoring System for Arithmetical Problem Solving. *IEEE Transactions on Learning Technologies* 7, 2 (April 2014), 155–164.

[3] David Arnau, Miguel Arevalillo-Herráez, Luis Puig, and José Antonio González-Calero. 2013. Fundamentals of the design and the operation of an intelligent tutoring system for the learning of the arithmetical and algebraic way of solving word problems. *Computers & Education* 63 (2013), 119 – 130.

[4] Antonio Caselles. 2008. *Modelización y simulación de sistemas complejos*. Universitat de València, Valencia, Spain.

[5] Jay W. Forrester. 1961. *Industrial Dynamics*. MIT Press, Cambridge, England.

[6] Pere Ivars and Ceneida Fernández. 2016. Problemas de estructura multiplicativa: Evolución de niveles de éxito y estrategias en estudiantes de 6 a 12 años. *Educación Matemática* 28, 1 (2016), 9–38.

[7] Mary . S. Riley, James. G. Greeno, and Joan. L. Heller. 1983. Development of Children's Problem-Solving Ability in Arithmetic. In *The development of mathematical thinking*, H. P. Ginsburg (Ed.). Academic Press, New York, 153–196.

[8] Sergio Salmeron-Majadas, Miguel Arevalillo-Herráez, Olga C. Santos, Mar Saneiro, Raúl Cabestrero, Pilar Quirós, David Arnau, and Jesus Boticario. 2015. Filtering of Spontaneous and Low Intensity Emotions in Educational Contexts. In *Artificial Intelligence in Education - 17th International Conference, AIED 2015, Madrid, Spain, June 22-26, 2015. Proceedings*. 429–438.